TAFSĪR TADABBUR AL-QUR'AN

(A Reflective Commentary of the Qur'an)

BRITISH LIBRARY CATALOGUING IN PUBLICATION DATA

A catalogue record for this book is available from the British Library

ISBN: 978 -1-78991-163-3 (pbk)

First Edition

PUBLISHED BY

The World Federation of Khoja Shia Ithna-Asheri Muslim Communities

Registered Charity in the UK No. 282303

The World Federation is an NGO in Special Consultative Status with the Economic and Social Council (ECOSOC) of the United Nations

Islamic Centre, Wood Lane, Stanmore, Middlesex,

United Kingdom, HA7 4LQ

www.world-federation.org

Cover design and typesetting by: ZH Designs

THE WORLD

FEDERATION

OF KSIMC

TAFSĪR TADABBUR AL-QURʾAN

(A Reflective Commentary of the Qurʾan)

VOLUME 1/30
30th Juzʾ
Surahs 78 - 114

by

A team of scholars under the supervision of
Shaykh Mohammad Saeed Bahmanpour
and Shaykh Dr Tahir Ridha Jaffer

THE WORLD FEDERATION OF KSIMC

CONTENTS

FOREWORD

When Adam (a) was relegated to the earthly life and God accepted his repentance, He gave him and his progeny a comforting promise: 'Should any guidance come to you from Me, those who follow My guidance shall have no fear, nor shall they grieve' (Q2:38). Since that time, the guidance has come to the children of Adam uninterruptedly through God's Messengers and Scriptures. Undoubtedly, the Qur'an is the most brilliant among those guidelines of God. It sealed the revelation forever, became the most outstanding source of light for humanity, and represented the fulfilment of the promise of God to the children of Adam (a).

As children of Adam (a), we have been blessed by the fulfilment of the promise, yet after receiving the Book, we have the responsibility of reading and understanding it. It is reported from Imam al-Sadiq (a) that, "The Qur'an is the trust of God (given) to His creation; therefore it is expected from every Muslim to look at this trust and to recite (a minimum of) 50 verses of it every day."[1] And it is not mere recitation which is expected, but understanding and reflection as well. As Imam Ali (a) has stated, "Beware! There is no benefit in a recitation in which there is no deliberation."[2]

The present book has been compiled skilfully and with a deep knowledge of the Qur'an. It helps us to understand the Qur'an better and makes it easy to reflect on its verses. Anyone familiar with tafsir literature would immediately realize the novel and innovative method used in this work which makes the interpretation of the Qur'an accessible to a wide range of readers. It not only provides a lucid exposition of the verses of the Qur'an, but delves into discussions on vocabulary, etymology, grammar and syntax of the verses in such a simple and comprehensible way that readers with no knowledge of Arabic and no background in Qur'anic studies will find it easy to understand.

Yet there is something more to this work which is missing in almost all other *tafsīr* literature. Under the heading 'Reflective Learning', it tries to

---

[1] *Kāfī*, 2/609.

[2] *Kāfī*, 1/36.

find out the connection of every verse to our daily life and our personal experience. It is reported from Imam al-Husayn (a) that, "The Book of God is based on four things: expression, allusion, subtleties, and realities. The expression is for the common people, the allusion is for the elite, the subtleties are for the friends of God, and the realities are for the prophets."[3] *Tafsīr* literature is to do with the interpretation of the expression of the Qur'an. However, the 'reflective learning' in this work tries to open a door for the reader to the underlying allusions in every verse in the most contemporary and understandable manner.

Thus, to all those who are willing to understand the interpretation of the expressions of the Qur'an, and yet are eager to go beyond that and are enthusiastic to get some allusions from the Qur'an for their everyday life, reading this work will be extremely helpful.

Mohammad Saeed Bahmanpour
Tehran, Dec 2022

[3] *Jāmiʿ al-Akhbār*, 1/41.

PRESIDENT'S MESSAGE

كِتَابٌ أَنْزَلْنَاهُ إِلَيْكَ مُبَارَكٌ لِيَدَّبَّرُوا آيَاتِهِ وَلِيَتَذَكَّرَ أُولُوا الْأَلْبَابِ

(This is) a Scripture that We have revealed unto you, full of blessing, that they may ponder its revelations, and that men of understanding may reflect (38:29)

The Qur'an continuously urges its readers to reflect upon its message. The World Federation as part of its publication and propagation of faith has endeavored over the years to support projects and initiatives that promote reflecting on the verses of the Holy Qur'an.

In 1993, the Islamic Education Board (IEB) of The World Federation published its first ever Qur'anic reflective book targeted at madrasah students, under the title '*Subḥānallāh – The wonders of creation in the Holy Qur'an*'. The objective then was to produce a concise book which would portray those parts of the Holy Qur'an, which deal with the wonders of creation and human experience.

In 2004, IEB published another book titled: "*Noble Qur'an' - 40 Ahadith*", as part of a series of booklets of 40 *Ahadith* on different subjects. The *Ahadith* that were selected from various sources were short and simple, and therefore easy to understand and memorise. They were focused on the merits and importance of various matters such as reading, reflecting, and respecting, that have been mentioned in the Holy Qur'an.

In 2005, IEB published the English version of the '*Introduction to the Science of Tafsīr of the Qur'an*' by Ayatullah Ja'far Subhani, translated by Shaykh Saleem Bhimji.

In 2010, the first major thematic exegesis of the Holy Qur'an '*Message of the Qur'an*' Volume 1 compiled by a group of Muslim scholars under the guidance of Ayatullah Al-Uzma Shaykh Nasir Makarim Shirazi was published by The World Federation in English translated by Shaykh Saleem Bhimji and edited by Abbas Jaffer. This work introduced a new style of exegesis of the Noble Qur'an to the English-speaking world. By taking a thematic approach to the study of the Verses of the Qur'an the author was able to unlock the sublime teachings of the Qur'an in a lucid and easy to understand manner.

In 2013, The World Federation took the reflective practices on the Holy Qur'an to the madrasah classroom by publishing the Tarbiyah Curriculum Framework for Madrasah Education through its Madrasah Center of Excellence (MCE), where the entire curriculum was based on a Qur'anic worldview as expounded by the Ahlul Bayt (a). There was a recognition that madaris whilst dwelling in recitation, *tajwīd*, and limited reflections missed the fundamental point of applying a Qur'anic reflective approach in our lives. Thus, the entire curriculum that has more than 600 lessons begins each lesson with a verse of the Holy Qur'an and how this applies to the lesson in consideration, be it *fiqh*, history, *akhlāq*, or *aqā'īd*.

By the Grace of Allah (swt), in 2021, The World Federation Islamic Education Department is once again blessed with the opportunity to facilitate a new Qur'anic publication, titled: "*Tafsīr Tadabbur al-Qur'an*" ('A Reflective Commentary of the Qur'an') by a team of scholars under the supervision of Shaykh Mohammad Saeed Bahmanpour and Shaykh Dr Tahir Ridha Jaffer. As alluded to in the foreword to this book, there is something more to this *tafsīr*, which is missing in other *tafsīr* literature. Under the heading 'Reflective Learning', it tries to explore the connection of every verse to our daily life and personal experience. It is this distinguishing practical dimension of the *tafsīr* at hand that readers with no knowledge of Arabic, nor any background in Qur'anic studies - will find easy to understand.

The World Federation is grateful to the co-authors and all those who have supported in the publication of this first volume, with the hope and prayers that future volumes will continue to add to the further reflective learnings from the rest of the chapters of the Holy Qur'an, Inshallāh.

Safder Jaffer
President
The World Federation of KSIMC
17th January 2023

PUBLISHER'S FOREWORD

In the Name of Allah, the Most Compassionate, the Most Merciful

ذَٰلِكَ الْكِتَابُ لَا رَيْبَ فِيهِ هُدًى لِلْمُتَّقِينَ

This is the Book, there is no doubt in it, a guidance to the God-wary. (Q2:2)

The Holy Qur'an is an unprecedented Divine Book, revealed by the Almighty unto the Holy Prophet (s) both in one go – in keeping with the norm of previous Divine scriptures which were revealed in this manner[1] – and in a gradual mode over the span of the twenty three years of the mission of the Holy Prophet (s).

In order to fathom its true reality, a wise person would start with the Holy Qur'an itself to see how it defines itself. In the second verse of the second chapter, Allah explains that it is a lofty and guarded scripture, which has no statement in it that would raise doubts. Its goal is to guide those whose hearts are open to guidance and those who observe all the aspects of its message, both on the inner and exterior planes.

The above insights are amongst many that are going to be shared in the framework of this blessed *tafsīr* project. Under the supervision of Sh Mohammad Saeed Bahmanpour, along with the collaborative expert feedback from Sh Dr Tahir Ridha Jaffer, our authors have adopted a methodology of compiling a *tafsīr* which combines some of the profound and insightful content of several contemporary Qur'anic commentaries by eminent authorities in the field.

In the context of illustrating the progressive developmental effect of the Holy Qur'an that Allah (SWT) alludes to[2] - the authors have uniquely explained how this Divine Book informs, warns and awakens mankind through advice (*maw'iẓah*) and prescribing cures (*shifā'*) for maladies of

---

[1] Q3:3 He has sent down upon you, [O Muhammad], the Book in truth, confirming what was before it. And He revealed the Torah and the Gospel.

[2] Q10:57 O mankind!. There has indeed come to you advice from your Lord, and a healing for what [disease] is in the breasts, and a guidance and a mercy for the believers.

the heart and mind (such as ignorance, arrogance, and spiritual vices), thereby guiding humanity to what is righteous and felicitous in both private and public life. This is a manifestation of the concept of guidance (*hudā*), through which one qualifies to receive a special Divine Reward and Mercy (*raḥmah*).

Indeed, reflection upon the pearls which are the meanings of the Holy Qur'an and acting upon them is the path to the greatest Divine Blessings that are much higher than any worldly, transient and material acquisitions,[3] whereby the Most Exalted (praise be to Him) elevates one's spirit to the higher lofty realms of eternal realities.

When approached, the Islamic Education Department was delighted to accept the offer of collaboration by the authors, and is extremely honoured to facilitate this very needed project for the English-speaking community, which will address many contemporary issues and be a resource for understanding the deep meanings of the verses of the Holy Qur'an compiled from the works of scholars who are specialists in Qur'anic exegesis.

This resource will be indispensable for those who do not speak Arabic and Persian, but have a thirst for knowledge, especially those who lecture and teach.

We pray for Allah to bless these noble efforts of our scholars, and to reward them with the good of both worlds.

For any enquiries or comments, kindly write to: islamiceducation@world-federation.org.

Islamic Education Department
The World Federation of KSIMC
17th January 2023 - 23rd Jamadi al-Thani 1444 AH.

[3] Q10:58 Say, 'In Allah's grace and His mercy - let them rejoice in that! It is better than what they amass.'

TADABBUR AL-QUR'AN

INTRODUCTION

The Qur'an is the last and most comprehensive revelation of God to man-kind. It was the declared miracle of Prophet Muhammad (s) to his nation. It came at the end of a long series of communications that God had revealed to different Prophets (a) in the course of human history. The Qur'an not only confirms what was contained in previous scriptures but is an authority and guardian (*muhaymin*) over them all (Q5:48).

The Qur'an is a living connection between God and His creation. It is a book of guidance and wisdom in the form of laws, admonitions, histories, parables, and rational argument. About this great bounty and blessing to mankind, Q10:57 states:

يَا أَيُّهَا النَّاسُ قَدْ جَاءَتْكُمْ مَوْعِظَةٌ مِنْ رَبِّكُمْ
وَشِفَاءٌ لِمَا فِي الصُّدُورِ وَهُدًى وَرَحْمَةٌ لِلْمُؤْمِنِينَ

O mankind! There has indeed come to you advice from your Lord,
and a healing for what [disease] is in the breasts,
and a guidance and a mercy for the believers.

It is no wonder that a tradition from Imam al-Sajjad (a) states: If I was alone in the world, I would not be lonely as long as the Qur'an was by my side.[1]

ABOUT THIS COMPILATION

This compilation draws on the work of several exegetes and exegeses, with an emphasis on the interpretation offered by the followers of the school of the Ahl al-Bayt (a). It is an attempt to present a simple *tafsīr* of the Qur'an and encourage interactive reading and reflection on God's word.

Many reports state that the Imams of the Ahl al-Bayt (a) would read the Qur'an in an interactive manner, for instance: When Imam al-Ridha (a)

[1] Kulaynī, *al-Kāfī*, 2/602.

would finish reciting Surat al-Ikhlās, he would say three times, "Thus is Allah, our Lord." When he would recite a verse that stated, *'O you who believe'*, he would say silently, "Labbayk, my Lord!" And when he would finish Surat al-Kāfirūn, he would say, "My Lord is Allah, and my religion is Islam."[2]

Furthermore, in the chapter that is named after the Prophet (s) himself, God invites us to ponder over the Qur'an to demonstrate that our hearts are open and receptive to His message. Q47:24 states:

أَفَلَا يَتَدَبَّرُونَ الْقُرْآنَ أَمْ عَلَىٰ قُلُوبٍ أَقْفَالُهَا

Do they not reflect on the Qur'an, or are there locks on the hearts?

It is in obedience to this call from God that we have called our humble attempt at a reflective *tafsīr*, *Tadabbur al-Qur'an* (Reflection on the Qur'an).

A NOTE ON *TADABBUR* (REFLECTION)

There is a vast difference between *tadabbur* and *tafsīr*. *Tafsīr* is to do with revealing the meaning of a verse. This was the task of the Prophet (s) and his righteous successors (a), and was thereafter undertaken by specialist scholars. On the other hand, *tadabbur* means reflection and pondering about the message of a verse. It involves internalizing the import of the verse, taking admonition, and making changes thereafter. *Tadabbur* is a divine injunction for all.

THE FORMAT OF THE WORK

1. Each chapter begins with the text and its translation, followed by a brief introduction, a background of its revelation, the suggested link to the previous chapter, and the merits of its recitation as mentioned in the traditions. Of course, these merits are only deserved by the one who reads the chapter with sincerity and applies its message in his life.
2. Thereafter, the *tafsīr* of a verse or set of verses is presented, with a brief explanation of the relevant vocabulary. At the end of each portion of *tafsīr*, we have provided a brief summary of the verses under consideration, and a suggestion for reflective learning. The reader may choose other aspects of the verse for reflection as well.

---

[2] Ṣadūq, *'Uyūn Akhbār* 2/44.

We have only made suggestions about action points occasionally because these are different for everybody. However, there is no doubt that *tadabbur* should be followed by action and change.

3. Throughout the *tafsīr*, we have attempted to show the connection of the verses under review with other verses of the Qur'an, to demonstrate the cohesiveness of its message.
4. Relevant traditions and supplications from the Prophet (s) and his household (a) have been mentioned, which add to the understanding of many verses.
5. The Arabic text of all the traditions quotation has been included in the footnotes for those who may be interested. Of course, evaluating the soundness of *hadith* is a discipline in itself, and for this reason we have provided full references of the traditions we have used.
6. We began with the *tafsīr* of the 30th *juz'* of the Qur'an for two reasons: i) The surahs of that section are well known and commonly recited in the daily prayers, ii) traditionally, the exegesis of these surahs tend to be very brief.

By God's permission, this volume will be a forerunner to the *tafsīr* of the entire Qur'an.

ACKNOWLEDGEMENTS

First and foremost, the compilers of this *tafsīr* acknowledge that this work is a result of God's mercy and grace, without which we would not have completed this volume. We ask for His continual guidance in the course of this project.

We are indebted to Sh Mohammed Saeed Bahmanpour and Sh Tahir Ridha Jaffer for their diligent review and valuable suggestions. They have always been at hand to offer guidance in a field in which they have great experience and knowledge.

We are also grateful to the World Federation of KSIMC for publishing the work.

We hope that readers will benefit from this compilation, and thereby together we can hasten the reappearance of our Imam (af).

'Our Lord, accept [this] from us. Indeed, You are all-Hearing, all-Knowing.'

London, Dec 2022

SURAT AL-NABA'
THE NEWS (78)

PART 1: VERSES 1 - 20

TEXT AND TRANSLATION

سُورَةُ النَّبَإِ

بِسْمِ اللهِ الرَّحْمٰنِ الرَّحِيمِ

عَمَّ يَتَسَاءَلُونَ ﴿١﴾ عَنِ النَّبَإِ الْعَظِيمِ ﴿٢﴾ الَّذِي هُمْ فِيهِ مُخْتَلِفُونَ ﴿٣﴾ كَلَّا سَيَعْلَمُونَ
﴿٤﴾ ثُمَّ كَلَّا سَيَعْلَمُونَ ﴿٥﴾ أَلَمْ نَجْعَلِ الْأَرْضَ مِهَادًا ﴿٦﴾ وَالْجِبَالَ أَوْتَادًا ﴿٧﴾
وَخَلَقْنَاكُمْ أَزْوَاجًا ﴿٨﴾ وَجَعَلْنَا نَوْمَكُمْ سُبَاتًا ﴿٩﴾ وَجَعَلْنَا اللَّيْلَ لِبَاسًا ﴿١٠﴾
وَجَعَلْنَا النَّهَارَ مَعَاشًا ﴿١١﴾ وَبَنَيْنَا فَوْقَكُمْ سَبْعًا شِدَادًا ﴿١٢﴾ وَجَعَلْنَا سِرَاجًا
وَهَّاجًا ﴿١٣﴾ وَأَنْزَلْنَا مِنَ الْمُعْصِرَاتِ مَاءً ثَجَّاجًا ﴿١٤﴾ لِنُخْرِجَ بِهِ حَبًّا وَنَبَاتًا
﴿١٥﴾ وَجَنَّاتٍ أَلْفَافًا ﴿١٦﴾ إِنَّ يَوْمَ الْفَصْلِ كَانَ مِيقَاتًا ﴿١٧﴾ يَوْمَ يُنْفَخُ فِي
الصُّورِ فَتَأْتُونَ أَفْوَاجًا ﴿١٨﴾ وَفُتِحَتِ السَّمَاءُ فَكَانَتْ أَبْوَابًا ﴿١٩﴾ وَسُيِّرَتِ الْجِبَالُ
فَكَانَتْ سَرَابًا ﴿٢٠﴾

In the name of God, the Beneficent, the Merciful.

About what do they ask one another? [1] *About the great news,* [2] *that over which they are in disagreement.* [3] *Not at all! They shall soon come to know.* [4] *Again, not at all! They shall soon come to know.* [5] *Have We not made the earth a cradling expanse?* [6] *And the mountains as pegs [therein]?* [7] *And We created you in pairs.* [8] *And We made your sleep for rest.* [9] *And We made the night a cloak.* [10] *And We made the day for seeking livelihood.* [11] *And We constructed above you seven strong [heavens].* [12] *And We made [therein] a shining lamp.* [13] *And We send down from the clouds water pouring forth abundantly,* [14] *that We may bring forth thereby grain and vegetation,* [15] *and gardens of dense growth.* [16] *Indeed, the Day of separation [and final Judgement] is an appointed time.* [17] *The Day on which the trumpet shall be blown, and you shall come forth in multitudes.* [18] *And the heaven shall be opened so that it shall have [multiple] gateways.* [19] *And the mountains shall be set in motion so that they become [like] a mirage.* [20]

INTRODUCTION

This is the first chapter in the last section (*juz'*) of the Qur'an. Its name comes from the second verse, which mentions a great and important news, about which people asked one another. The chapter is also called *ʿAmma* (about what), *Tasā'ul* (asking one another) and *Muʿṣirāt* (rain-clouds), all words and terms used in the chapter itself.[1]

Surat al-Naba' (78) was the 80th chapter to be revealed. It has forty verses and was revealed in Makka, after Surat al-Maʿārij (70).[2]

The themes of the five adjoining chapters, al-Qiyāmah (75), al-Insān (76), al-Mursalāt (77), al-Naba' (78) and al-Nāziʿāt (79) resemble one another, and all describe aspects of the Hereafter.

Surat al-Naba' begins with a question and ends with a warning. After mentioning the great event (the Day of Judgement) that people were talking to each other about, it speaks of the manifestations of God's power in the heavens and the earth, and of the bounties bestowed on man so he can prepare in this life for the Hereafter for which he was created. These serve as proofs that God, the Creator, can easily bring this world to an end and usher in a new phase of existence. From this preamble, the events that will herald the advent of the Day of Judgement are mentioned. Hell and Paradise are described in detail.

Finally, a stern warning is issued to mankind of the accountability and punishment that awaits the disbelievers on that Day.

LINK TO THE PREVIOUS CHAPTER

The previous chapter, Surat al-Mursalāt, ends with a mention of the Day of Judgement, and a warning to those who would deny it. Surat al-Naba' continues the theme, remarking on the scepticism of the disbelievers about that Day, and providing details of the events that would lead up to it.

---

1 Ṭabrasī, *al-Bayān*, 10/637.

2 Maʿrifat, *'Ulūm-i Qur'ānī*, p. 90.

Surat al-Mursalāt mentions the Day of Separation (*yawm al-faṣl*) and then highlights the enormity of that Day by asking, *'And what will make you know what the Day of Separation is?'* It does not go into further detail except to state that it will be a time of great regret for those who denied the truth and the Day of Resurrection. In Surat al-Naba', *yawm al-faṣl* is mentioned again, and this time the Day is identified as the Last Day, whose time had always been appointed. It is the Day when the Trumpet will be sounded, and creation will come forth and assemble in groups.

Finally, both chapters speak of the fate of two groups on the Day of Separation: the deniers (*mukadhdhibūn*) and the God-wary (*muttaqūn*). In fact, Surat al-Mursalāt repeats the phrase *'Woe on that Day to the deniers'* ten times. Surat al-Naba' provides further details of what will happen to these two groups.

MERITS OF RECITATION

- A tradition from the Prophet (s) states: On the Day of Judgement, God shall quench the thirst of the one who recites this surah with a cool drink.[3]
- A tradition from Imam al-Sadiq (a) states: Whoever recites Surat al-Naba' every day will be called to the sacred house of God (for *haj* or *ʿumrah*) within that year, God-willing.[4]

  Indeed, this is a good habit for people who yearn to visit the Kaʿbah.

EXEGESIS

VERSES 1 - 5

عَمَّ يَتَسَاءَلُونَ ﴿١﴾ عَنِ النَّبَإِ الْعَظِيمِ ﴿٢﴾ الَّذِي هُمْ فِيهِ مُخْتَلِفُونَ ﴿٣﴾ كَلَّا سَيَعْلَمُونَ ﴿٤﴾ ثُمَّ كَلَّا سَيَعْلَمُونَ ﴿٥﴾

About what do they ask one another? [1] *About the great news,* [2] *that over which they are in disagreement.* [3] *Not at all! They shall soon come to know.* [4] *Again, not at all! They shall soon come to know.* [5]

---

3 Nūrī, *Mustadrak al-Wasā'il*, 4/355.

عَنِ الرَّسُولِ (صَلَّى اللهُ عَلَيْهِ وَآلِهِ) – مَنْ قَرَأَ سُورَةَ «عَمَّ يَتَسَاءَلُونَ» سَقَاهُ اللهُ بَرْدَ الشَّرَابِ يَوْمَ الْقِيَامَةِ.

4 Baḥrānī, *al-Burhān*, 5/563.

عَنِ الصَّادِقِ (عَلَيْهِ السَّلَامُ) – وَمَنْ قَرَأَ «عَمَّ يَتَسَاءَلُونَ» لَمْ يَخْرُجْ سَنَتَهُ إِذَا كَانَ يُدْمِنُهَا فِي كُلِّ يَوْمٍ حَتَّى يَزُورَ بَيْتَ اللهِ الْحَرَامِ، إِنْ شَاءَ اللهُ.

1-5.1 The chapter begins with commenting in wonder about why such a thing was being questioned or talked about in the first place.[5] This is meant to intrigue the addressee.[6]

[*ʿAmma* (عَمَّ, about what)] is truncated from *ʿan mā.*

[*Yatasāʾalūn* (يَتَسَاءَلُونَ, they ask one another)] is a reference to the fact that the disbelievers constantly questioned and discussed a particular issue with the Prophet (s), with the Muslims, and mostly, amongst themselves.

1-5.2 Asking questions to seek knowledge has been encouraged in the Qurʾan. Q16:43 states:

فَاسْأَلُوا أَهْلَ الذِّكْرِ إِنْ كُنْتُمْ لَا تَعْلَمُونَ

... So ask those whom We granted inspiration if you do not know.

However, sometimes questions are asked with the intent to ridicule. The tone of the verse suggests that the polytheists were querying something obvious,[7] or doing so out of mockery rather than for seeking the truth.

1-5.3 The question asked by God is immediately answered by Him in the second verse. They are asking each other about the great news (*al-nabaʾ al-ʿaẓīm*).

[*al-Nabaʾ* (النَّبَإِ, the news)] is a term used to signify the transmission of important and beneficial news.[8] From it is derived the term *Nabī* which means a Prophet (a) who brings news of the unseen, like the Hereafter, to the people.

Nabaʾ is different from *khabar,* which also means news. *Khabar* is the report of actions and events,[9] while *nabaʾ* denotes news that requires action.

In this verse, the adjective *ʿaẓīm* (great) is for further emphasis.[10]

1-5.4 As is made clear from the rest of the chapter, this great news was the news of the Hereafter, a world that awaited after death,

---

[5] Shīrāzī, *Namūneh,* 26/5.

[6] Qarāʾatī, *Nūr,* 10/359.

[7] Ṭabāṭabāʾī, *al-Mīzān,* 20/159

[8] Rāghib, *al-Mufradāt.*

[9] Ṭabāṭabāʾī, *al-Mīzān,* 18/366.

[10] Shīrāzī, *Namūneh,* 26/6.

and a Day when the dead would be resurrected to account for their actions and receive their just recompense. This is a recurring theme in the Makkan surahs, and about which the disbelievers spoke to each other incredulously and mockingly.[11]

Some exegetes have stated that the great news refers to the revelation of the Qur'an, or to the Prophet (s) himself, or to the fundamentals of faith. However, the context of the chapter suggests that it is referring to the events of the Hereafter.[12]

1-5.5 There are many reports that speak of the *ta'wīl* (interpretation) of the term *al-naba' al-ʿaẓīm* as a reference to the *wilāyah* (guardianship) of Ali b. Abi Talib (a), about which there was a dispute amongst the people. Two reports are cited below as examples:

1. *Shīʿa* source: A tradition from Imam al-Sadiq (a) states: *Al-naba' al-ʿaẓīm* refers to the *wilāyah* [of Ali (a)].[13]
2. *Sunni* source: A tradition from the Prophet (s) states: It refers to the *wilāyah* of Ali (a) which they will be questioned about in their graves. Not a single dead person, in the east or the west, on land or at sea, will remain except that [the angels] Munkar and Nakīr will ask him about the authority of the Commander of the Faithful. They will be asked, "Who is you Lord? What is your religion? Who is your Prophet? And who is your Imam?"[14]

The exegesis (*tafsīr*) of the great news being the Day of Judgement does not exclude other interpretations and applications (*ta'wīl*) of its meaning at later times as long as they are narrated by the Prophet (s) or the Imams (a). Indeed, there are many hidden layers of meaning to each verse.[15]

The merits of Imam Ali (a) and his prominent role on the Day of Judgement are many. As examples we will quote only three:

i) A tradition from the Prophet (s) states: The first person from this nation who will arrive at the side of its Prophet (s) on the

---

[11] Ṭabrasī, *al-Bayān*, 10/639.

[12] Shīrāzī, *Namūneh*, 26/6.

[13] Kulaynī, *al-Kāfī*, 1/207.

عَنِ الصَّادِقِ (عَلَيْهِ السَّلَامُ) - قَالَ النَّبَأُ الْعَظِيمُ الْوِلَايَةُ.

[14] Shīrāzī, *Namūneh*, 26/7, referring to the following tradition:

عَنِ الرَّسُولِ (صَلَّى اللهُ عَلَيْهِ وَآلِهِ) - وِلَايَةُ عَلِيٍّ يُتَسَاءَلُونَ عَنْهَا فِي قُبُورِهِمْ، فَلَا يَبْقَى مَيِّتٌ فِي شَرْقٍ وَلَا غَرْبٍ، وَلَا فِي بَرٍّ وَلَا فِي بَحْرٍ إِلَّا وَمُنْكَرٌ وَنَكِيرٌ يَسْأَلَانِهِ عَنْ وِلَايَةِ أَمِيرِ الْمُؤْمِنِينَ بَعْدَ الْمَوْتِ، يَقُولَانِ لِلْمَيِّتِ: مَنْ رَبُّكَ؟ وَمَا دِينُكَ؟ وَمَنْ نَبِيُّكَ؟ وَمَنْ إِمَامُكَ؟

[15] Ibid.

Day of Judgement will be the one who accepted Islam first, [and that is] Ali b. Abi Talib (a).[16]

ii) Another tradition from the Prophet (s) states: ...I will be given the Standard of Praise (*Liwāʾ al-Ḥamd*) and I will give it to Ali to bear, and I shall seek his assistance in attending to the intercession of the sinners...[17]

iii) A tradition from Imam Ali (a) states: I am God's standard for Paradise and Hell; no one enters them except by my criterion.[18]

1-5.6 *'That over which they are in disagreement.'*: This disagreement could have been between the polytheists themselves, or between them and the Prophet (s), or between them and the Muslims. Some polytheists were inclined to believe in a sort of life after death while others were doubtful.[19] Q27:66 states:

بَلِ ٱدَّارَكَ عِلْمُهُمْ فِي الْآخِرَةِ بَلْ هُمْ فِي شَكٍّ مِنْهَا بَلْ هُمْ مِنْهَا عَمُونَ

Nay, they have no knowledge of the Hereafter. Nay, they are in doubt about it. Nay, they are quite blind to it!

Some polytheists accepted that the soul might persist after death, but they were openly sceptical about the idea of a bodily resurrection. Some went as far as insulting the Prophet (s) for informing them of it. Q34:7,8 state:

وَقَالَ الَّذِينَ كَفَرُوا هَلْ نَدُلُّكُمْ عَلَىٰ رَجُلٍ يُنَبِّئُكُمْ إِذَا مُزِّقْتُمْ كُلَّ مُمَزَّقٍ
إِنَّكُمْ لَفِي خَلْقٍ جَدِيدٍ ﴿٧﴾ أَفْتَرَىٰ عَلَى اللَّهِ كَذِبًا أَمْ بِهِ جِنَّةٌ

But those who disbelieve say: Shall we point out to you a man who will tell you that when you are completely disintegrated [in the earth], you will then be created anew? He has invented a lie about God or there is madness in him...

---

16 Majlisī, *Biḥār*, 39/220.

عَنِ الرَّسُولِ (صَلَّى اللهُ عَلَيْهِ وَآلِهِ) – أَوَّلُ هٰذِهِ الْأُمَّةِ وُرُودًا عَلَى نَبِيِّهَا يَوْمَ الْقِيَامَةِ أَوَّلُهُمْ إِسْلَامًا، عَلِيُّ ابْنُ أَبِي طَالِبٍ عَلَيْهِ السَّلَامُ.

17 Ṣadūq, *al-Khiṣāl*, 2/415.

عَنِ الرَّسُولِ (صَلَّى اللهُ عَلَيْهِ وَآلِهِ) – فَإِنِّي أُعْطَى لِوَاءَ الْحَمْدِ فَأُعْطِيهِ يَحْمِلُهُ، وَأَتَّكِئُ عَلَيْهِ عِنْدَ قِيَامِ الشَّفَاعَةِ.

18 Kulaynī, *al-Kāfī*, 1/197.

عَنْ أَمِيرِ الْمُؤْمِنِينَ (عَلَيْهِ السَّلَامُ) – أَنَا قَسِيمُ اللهِ بَيْنَ الْجَنَّةِ وَالنَّارِ، لَا يَدْخُلُهَا دَاخِلٌ إِلَّا عَلَى حَدِّ قَسْمِي.

19 Ṭabrasī, *al-Bayān*, 10/639.

1-5.7 *'Not at all! They shall soon come to know. Again, not at all! They shall soon come to know.'*: These two verses make it clear that God was warning those who denied the Day of Judgement that there was no point in their vain talk and the reality was not as they assumed; in fact, they would come to know the magnitude of their error as soon as they left this world behind.

1-5.8 The use of *sa* (سَ) indicates that they would know in the near future. Indeed, the Hereafter is near, and compared to it, the life of this world will be less than the blink of an eye.[20]

1-5.9 Some exegetes have said that the repetition of the verses is for emphasis, while others believe that the first mention is the realization gained at death, while the second refers to the realization gained on the Day of Judgement.[21]

Q39:56 mentions the intense regret of the disbelievers and wrongdoers at that time:

يَا حَسْرَتَىٰ عَلَىٰ مَا فَرَّطْتُ فِي جَنْبِ اللَّهِ وَإِنْ كُنْتُ لَمِنَ السَّاخِرِينَ

... Woe to me for what I neglected in regard to God,
and that I was amongst the mockers!

They would vainly plead to return to the world to put things right. Q42:44 states:

وَتَرَى الظَّالِمِينَ لَمَّا رَأَوُا الْعَذَابَ يَقُولُونَ هَلْ إِلَىٰ مَرَدٍّ مِنْ سَبِيلٍ

...And you will see the wrongdoers (al-ẓālimīn) *when they behold the punishment, saying, "Is there any way to return [to the former world]?"*

SUMMARY OF THE VERSE

In these verses, God summarizes the mockery of the polytheists about the Day of Judgement and their disagreement with the Prophet (s), the Muslims, and each other, about its advent. Thereafter, He warns them that it would not be long before they would come to realize the truth of it.

---

20 Shīrāzī, *Namūneh*, 26/8.

21 Ibid, 26/9.

REFLECTIVE LEARNING

The polytheists were asking questions, not to learn the truth, but already having made up their minds about the matter.

Let me reflect on my attitude when I question matters. Is it with an open mind and with an intention of gaining clarity, or is it to seek validation for something that I have already decided about?

VERSES 6 - 16

أَلَمْ نَجْعَلِ الْأَرْضَ مِهَادًا ﴿٦﴾ وَالْجِبَالَ أَوْتَادًا ﴿٧﴾ وَخَلَقْنَاكُمْ أَزْوَاجًا ﴿٨﴾ وَجَعَلْنَا
نَوْمَكُمْ سُبَاتًا ﴿٩﴾ وَجَعَلْنَا اللَّيْلَ لِبَاسًا ﴿١٠﴾ وَجَعَلْنَا النَّهَارَ مَعَاشًا ﴿١١﴾ وَبَنَيْنَا
فَوْقَكُمْ سَبْعًا شِدَادًا ﴿١٢﴾ وَجَعَلْنَا سِرَاجًا وَهَّاجًا ﴿١٣﴾ وَأَنْزَلْنَا مِنَ الْمُعْصِرَاتِ
مَاءً ثَجَّاجًا ﴿١٤﴾ لِنُخْرِجَ بِهِ حَبًّا وَنَبَاتًا ﴿١٥﴾ وَجَنَّاتٍ أَلْفَافًا ﴿١٦﴾

Have We not made the earth a cradling expanse? [6] *And the mountains as pegs [therein]?* [7] *And We created you in pairs.* [8] *And We made your sleep for rest.* [9] *And We made the night a cloak.* [10] *And We made the day for seeking livelihood.* [11] *And We constructed above you seven strong [heavens].* [12] *And We made [therein] a shining lamp.* [13] *And We send down from the clouds water pouring forth abundantly,* [14] *that We may bring forth thereby grain and vegetation,* [15] *and gardens of dense growth.* [16]

6-16.1 Now a series of questions, mentioning twelve signs of God, is asked of those who are in doubt that He will bring about a Day of Judgement. In the next eleven verses, the disbelievers are asked to consider examples of how God's power is already manifest in the creation all around them. These signs are designed with purpose and effectiveness in order to allow human beings to live comfortably in this phase of their journey.

The signs are meant to convince mankind that if God could create such a sophisticated system for their survival, He can certainly do it again in the world to come.

6-16.2 *'Have We not made the earth a cradling expanse?'*: The disbelievers are asked to consider the expansive earth, which provides for them everything they need.

[*Alam Najʿal* (أَلَمْ نَجْعَل, have We not made?)]. This phrase governs every subsequent mention of God's great signs in the next verses. It points out that it is God who has placed these blessings at the disposal of mankind;[22] therefore, He will remove them when He chooses to bring the world to an end.

We have discussed God's use of the pronoun 'We' instead of 'I' in the *tafsīr* of Surat al-Kawthar (108).

[*Mihād* (مِهَاد, cradle)] is derived from *mahd*, meaning a rocking cradle or a place of rest.[23] It also refers to a place that is prepared and organized.[24] Indeed, the earth provides everything man needs to live. Its soft crust makes it suitable for habitation and most places on it allow human beings and other creatures to build their homes, harvest its land and seas, extract its minerals, and lay the dead to rest.

6-16.3 *'And mountains as pegs [therein]?'*: [*Awtād* (أَوْتَاد, pegs)] (sing. *watad*) means pegs or stakes. Modern science has recognized that the mountains extend underground by 10-15 times their apparent height, thereby 'pegging' and stabilizing the earth's tectonic plates. They secure its surface against the inner pressure caused by its central molten core, and the outer pressure resulting from the moon's gravitational pull. Their strong presence reduces the shaking of the earth, protects and cradles human settlements, and regulates weather patterns.

Amongst the scientific miracles of the Qur'an is its mention of this marvellous design many centuries before man discovered it.

In the opening sermon of *Nahj al-Balāghah*, Imam Ali (a) makes a reference to this by stating: "And He pegged the shaking earth with rocky mountains."[25]

6-16.4 *'And We created you in pairs.'*: [*Azwāj* (أَزْوَاج, pairs)] is the plural of *zawj* meaning a pair, and refers to the male and female. The two complement and complete each other, allowing both of them to progress more successfully towards God.

---

[22] Ṭabāṭabāʾī, al-*Mīzān*, 20/161.

[23] Rāghib, *al-Mufradāt*.

[24] Ṭabrasī, *al-Bayān*, 10/639.

[25] *Nahj al-Balāghah*, sermon 1.

وَوَتَّدَ بِالصُّخُورِ مَيَدَانَ أَرْضِهِ.

Another meaning of *azwāj* is types or kinds. If this meaning is considered, the verse means, 'We have created you in different and unique forms, races, and personalities.'[26]

6-16.5 '*And We made your sleep for rest.*': [*Subāt* (سُبَات, rest)] is derived from *sabata*, which means lethargy, inactivity, and rest. From this root is also derived '*Sabt*' – which is the Sabbath (Saturday), on which the Jews were commanded to abstain from material pursuits and take rest, in order to replenish their inner selves.[27]

In the verse under review, *subāt* refers to the rest that comes from the stilling of the body and the mind, and disconnection from the surrounding environment, during sleep. This process is crucial for recovery and rejuvenation.

6-16.6 '*And We made the night a cloak.*': [*Libās* (لِبَاس, cloak)] means something that covers. Sleep is facilitated by the silence of the night that covers the land daily, bringing with it darkness, stillness, and calm. Night and darkness are essential for life on earth because constant daylight would cause vegetation and animal life to die. Indeed, the night is so important in human life that God swears by it in seven different places in the Qur'an, more than for any other earthly phenomenon.[28]

6-16.7 '*And We made the day for seeking livelihood.*': [*Ma'āsh* (مَعَاش, seeking livelihood)] is derived from *'āsha*, meaning to live and to seek the necessities of life.[29] It refers to the physical, animalistic aspect of life and not its spiritual aspect, which is called *al-ḥayāt*.[30] In this verse, it refers to the time or place to seek livelihood.

Just like the night, the day plays an important role in human life and activity. It is a time to strive to earn one's livelihood, acquire knowledge, and build on the land. All these are noble tasks when done to please God to support oneself and one's dependents, and sending forth for the Hereafter.

6-16.8 The alternating nights and days make up the duration of human life, allowing for the regulation and organization of man's activities.

---

26 Shīrāzī, *Namūneh*, 26/19.

27 Muṣṭafawī, *al-Taḥqīq*.

28 Shīrāzī, *Namūneh*, 26/18.

29 Rāghib, *al-Mufradāt*.

30 Ṭabāṭabā'ī, *al-Mīzān*, 20/163.

Both have a role to play; too much of a good thing, even the life-giving sun, can bring harm, while something like the darkness of night, which contains hidden dangers, is also beneficial. Q28:73 states:

وَمِنْ رَحْمَتِهِ جَعَلَ لَكُمُ اللَّيْلَ وَالنَّهَارَ لِتَسْكُنُوا فِيهِ
وَلِتَبْتَغُوا مِنْ فَضْلِهِ وَلَعَلَّكُمْ تَشْكُرُونَ

And out of His mercy He made for you the night and the day,
that you may rest therein, and [by day] may seek of His grace,
and [that] you may give thanks.

6-16.9 *'And We constructed above you seven strong [heavens].'*: Now the verses move from the phenomena of the earth to those in the sky. [*Sabʿa* (سَبْعَ, seven)]. Although the number seven is sometimes used to mean 'several', in this verse it may be an allusion to the seven heavens as mentioned in Q17:44:

تُسَبِّحُ لَهُ السَّمَاوَاتُ السَّبْعُ وَالْأَرْضُ وَمَنْ فِيهِنَّ

The seven heavens and the earth
and whatever is in them glorify Him...

It could also be a reference to the several dimensions of the cosmos (mystic philosophers speak of various overarching dimensions in existence), or the seven layers shielding the earth's atmosphere, or to the several constellations or worlds that exist beyond the earth.[31] Q37:6 states that the stars in the sky are the adornments of the first of these heavens:

إِنَّا زَيَّنَّا السَّمَاءَ الدُّنْيَا بِزِينَةٍ الْكَوَاكِبِ

Indeed, We have adorned the lowest heaven
with an adornment of stars.

[*Shidād* (شِدَاد, strong)] is the plural of *shadīd*, and it means strong and established. From the following verses, it is possible to conclude that the term refers to the strong atmospheric layers that protect the earth.[32]

6-16.10 *'And We made (therein) a shining lamp.'*: [(*Sirāj* (سِرَاج, lamp)] here refers to the sun. [*Wahhāj* (وَهَّاج, shining)] is the intensive

[31] Shīrāzī, *Namūneh*, 26/23.

[32] Ibid, 26/24.

form of *wahaja*, and means something that burns with intense heat or light.[33] The light and the heat of the sun, and all parts of the spectrum of its radiation, from ultraviolet to infrared, are inextricably linked to life-processes on earth. Its heat, in addition to the effect that it directly has on the lives of human beings, animals and plants, is the main cause of the existence of clouds, winds, and rainfall necessary for the irrigation of dry lands. The distance of the sun from the earth is designed to be exactly right for life to exist.

6-16.11 *'And We send down from the clouds water pouring forth abundantly,'*: [*al-Muʿṣirāt* (الْمُعْصِرَات, clouds)] is derived from *ʿaṣara* which means to squeeze and compress. Here, it refers to rain-laden clouds.[34]

Al-Muʿṣirāt may also refer to the winds that compress the rain clouds and cause rain, in which case '*min* (from)' in this verse would mean 'by', and the verse would read, 'and We send down abundant water by the means of strong winds.'[35]

[*Thajjāj* (ثَجَّاج, pouring forth)] is derived from *thajja*, which means to flow in profusion.

6-16.12 *'That We may bring forth thereby grain and vegetation, and gardens of dense growth'*: [*Ḥabb* (حَب, grain)] refers to grain or corn. [*Nabāt* (نَبَات, vegetation)] refers to vegetables and other edible plants. [*Alfāf* (أَلْفَاف, dense growth)] refers to thickets and dense forests.[36]

6-16.13 The verses point towards a marvellous and efficient system: the sun causes water vapour to rise, filling the clouds, which spill over into torrents of rain to nourish the vegetable kingdom, which in turn, feeds and sustains human and animal life.

They summarize how the earth becomes the means of provision for man and the other creatures who live on it.[37]

Furthermore, the earth absorbs this life-giving rain under its surface and thereafter, distributes it through the land in its rivers and springs.

---

33 Ṭabāṭabā'ī, *al-Mīzān*, 20/163.

34 Muṣṭafawī, *al-Taḥqīq*.

35 Ṭabāṭabā'ī, *al-Mīzān*, 20/163.

36 Muṣṭafawī, *al-Taḥqīq*.

37 Ṭabrasī, *al-Bayān*, 10/640.

6-16.14 Within these eleven verses, the divine gifts that constitute the most basic necessities of man's life are mentioned. Each of these favours expounds on the simile of the earth as a comforting cradle (*mihād*): the cradle of the earth allows living beings to flourish despite its swift rotation and movement, its mountains keep this cradle from shaking violently, living in pairs adds to the comfort of the inhabitants of this cradle, the phenomenon of sleep and night-time provide a time for rest in this cradle, and the day allows for useful work and striving.

Above this cradle are protective heavens, containing the life-giving sun and rain that nourish the vegetation which sustains life. This perfect harmony results in the marvellously designed cradle that is the earth. Q31:20 states:

أَلَمْ تَرَوْا أَنَّ اللهَ سَخَّرَ لَكُمْ مَا فِي السَّمَاوَاتِ وَمَا فِي الْأَرْضِ
وَأَسْبَغَ عَلَيْكُمْ نِعَمَهُ ظَاهِرَةً وَبَاطِنَةً

Do you not see that God has made subservient to you whatever is in the heavens and whatever is in the earth, and has amply bestowed upon you His favours, [both] apparent and hidden?...

The mention of all these phenomena is to remind man that everything around him has been created with a design and purpose so that he can live with comfort and dignity in the *dunyā* and prepare for his real and permanent life when he returns to God. And this is the theme of the next verses of the surah.

DISCUSSION: TYPES OF SLEEP MENTIONED IN THE QUR'AN[38]

The reason and true function of sleep, in which human beings spend at least one-third of their lives, is a subject of ongoing research.[39] What is certain is that it plays a vital role in their physical and mental wellbeing.

The Qur'an mentions sleep (*nawm*) frequently, and has used some other terms for it also:

---

[38] Adapted from: BaHammam, Ahmed, 'Sleep from an Islamic Perspective', *Annals of Thoracic Medicine*, 2011 (187-192).

[39] See: *Stages of Sleep* (https://www.sleepfoundation.org/how-sleep-works/stages-of-sleep).

1. *Sinah* (سِنَة): This is a momentary loss of awareness or drowsiness, from which one awakes promptly if disturbed. It is mentioned in a description of God in Q2:255:

لَا تَأْخُذُهُ سِنَةٌ وَلَا نَوْمٌ

...Neither slumber (sinah) *nor sleep overtakes Him...*

2. *Nuʿās* (نُعَاس): This is a short and light slumber that overcomes an individual despite being in a stressful situation. It is described for the pre-battle stress of the Muslims in Badr in Q8:11:

إِذْ يُغَشِّيكُمُ النُّعَاسَ أَمَنَةً مِنْهُ

[Remember] when He covered you with a slumber (nuʿās) *to give you calm...*

3. *Ruqūd* (رُقُود): This is a protracted and deep sleep which is mentioned for the 'men of the cave' (*aṣḥāb al-kahf*). Q18:18 states:

وَتَحْسَبُهُمْ أَيْقَاظًا وَهُمْ رُقُودٌ

And you would have thought them awake [because of their periodic movement], but they were [deeply] asleep (ruqūd)...

4. *Hujūʿ* (هُجُوع): This refers to the regular sleep at night. About the righteous, God states in Q51:17:

كَانُوا قَلِيلًا مِنَ اللَّيْلِ مَا يَهْجَعُونَ

They used to sleep (yahjaʿūn) *but little of the night.*

5. *Subāt* (سُبَات): This is a deep and restful sleep that comes from the stilling of the body and the mind. Q78:9 states:

وَجَعَلْنَا نَوْمَكُمْ سُبَاتًا

And We made your sleep for rest (subāt).

SUMMARY OF THE VERSES

In summary, the verses mention examples of God's wise and efficient arrangements for human life on earth. They draw attention to God's creation of the earth and the mountains, the male and female, the night and day, the firmament and the sun, and the system of rainfall that allows lush vegetation to grow.

REFLECTIVE LEARNING

God has kept all these provisions for man so that he may live in the comforting cradle of the earth. Within this environment, he has to strive and toil. However, the striving should not be for the sake of the world, but for the flourishing of the soul.

Let me reflect on my daily activities, and whether they cause my soul to grow daily or regress thereby.

VERSES 17 - 20

إِنَّ يَوْمَ الْفَصْلِ كَانَ مِيقَاتًا ﴿١٧﴾ يَوْمَ يُنْفَخُ فِي الصُّورِ فَتَأْتُونَ أَفْوَاجًا ﴿١٨﴾
وَفُتِحَتِ السَّمَاءُ فَكَانَتْ أَبْوَابًا ﴿١٩﴾ وَسُيِّرَتِ الْجِبَالُ فَكَانَتْ سَرَابًا ﴿٢٠﴾

Indeed, the Day of Separation [and final Judgement] is an appointed time. [17] *The day on which the trumpet shall be blown, and you shall come forth in multitudes.* [18] *And the heaven shall be opened so that it shall have [multiple] gateways.* [19] *And the mountains shall be set in motion so that they become [like] a mirage.* [20]

17-20.1 The verses now turn to the description of the great news (*al-naba al-ʿaẓīm*), the Day of Separation (*yawm al-faṣl*), which was alluded to in the statement in verses 4 and 5, '*Not at all! They shall soon come to know*'.

17-20.2 The previous verses highlighted examples of the perfectly engineered system of creation of this world, in which everything has a purpose and works efficiently and harmoniously. This points at a design and a Designer.

Now, the theme shifts to the Hereafter. The reader realizes that God, who has shown His ability to create the present system with truth (*ḥaqq*) and purpose, is just as capable of creating a new and elaborate system for the Hereafter as well. Q14:19 states:

أَلَمْ تَرَ أَنَّ اللهَ خَلَقَ السَّمَاوَاتِ وَالْأَرْضَ بِالْحَقِّ إِنْ يَشَأْ يُذْهِبْكُمْ وَيَأْتِ بِخَلْقٍ جَدِيدٍ

Have you not seen that God has created the heavens and earth in truth? If He wills He can do away with you and produce a new creation.

17-20.3 Using a powerful rhythmic prose, the next set of verses describe the momentous events that herald that Day, then go on to mention the fate of the transgressors and the righteous in turn, and finally issue a stern warning at the end of the chapter.

17-20.4 *'Indeed, the Day of Separation [and final Judgement] is an appointed time.'*: [*al-Faṣl* (اَلْفَصْل, separation)] means a separation of two things from one another so there is a distance between them.[40] Here, it refers to the sifting and separation of the righteous from the sinners, or the followers of the truth from the followers of falsehood. Thereafter, a final judgement, based on absolute justice, can be made about their fates. Such a judgement would not be possible in this world.

[*Mīqāt* (مِيقَات, appointed time)] is derived from *waqt* which means time. *Mīqāt* means an appointed time or term, or a deadline. In Haj, the last place that a pilgrim can cross before wearing the *iḥrām* is called the *mīqāt* because all the pilgrims gather there at an appointed time.[41]

Mīqāt has also been defined as the last moment of time before which an event is scheduled to take place[42] and here, it refers to the fact that God had always decreed an appointed time and place where the material world would cease to exist, and man would be brought forth for a decision to be made about his recompense. Indeed, the life of this world is just a prelude to the final Day, the *mīqāt*, that God had destined.

17-20.5 *'The Day on which the trumpet shall be blown, and you shall come forth in multitudes.'*: The next verses described the events of that Day.

[*Yunfakhu* (يُنفَخُ, it is blown)] is derived from *nafakha* which means to blow or inflate.

[*Ṣūr* (الصُّور, the trumpet)] refers to a bugle or trumpet. Normally trumpets are blown to signal different actions in war or on a march. However, the trumpet mentioned in this verse emits a sound that brings death and life.

---

[40] Rāghib, *al-Mufradāt*.

[41] Shīrāzī, *Namūneh*, 26/31.

[42] Ṭabāṭabā'ī, *al-Mīzān*, 20/165.

We have discussed the two blowings of the trumpet in some detail in the *tafsīr* of Surat al-Zalzalah (99). The verse we are reviewing here refers to the second blowing, the one that heralds the resurrection of every being.

[*Afwāj* (أَفْوَاج, multitudes, troops)] (sing. *fawj*) refers to groups of people who are moving hastily.[43] These multitudes will be assembled group after group, on the plain of resurrection (*maḥshar*), to account for their actions. Initially, they will be gathered with their leaders.

Q17:71 states:

يَوْمَ نَدْعُو كُلَّ أُنَاسٍ بِإِمَامِهِمْ

[On] the Day when We shall summon every person with their Imam...

Thereafter, the groups will be sorted into smaller and smaller companies, based on their beliefs and deeds. Each person will be led unerringly by an angel towards his particular destination in Paradise or Hell. Q50:21 states:

وَجَاءَتْ كُلُّ نَفْسٍ مَعَهَا سَائِقٌ وَشَهِيدٌ

And every person will come forth along with a driver and a witness.

On the way to their final abode, every human being will stand alone in front of his Lord, to give his final and defining account. Q19:95 states:

وَكُلُّهُمْ آتِيهِ يَوْمَ الْقِيَامَةِ فَرْدًا

And every one of them will come to Him alone on the Day of Resurrection.

17-20.6 A famous report attributed to the Prophet (s) mentions how he tearfully described to a group of his companions, certain groups that will be resurrected from amongst the Muslims. He (s) stated:

Ten groups from my nation will be resurrected apart. God will separate them from the ranks of the Muslims and transform their forms. Some will resemble apes and others will resemble pigs; some will be reversed so that their faces and feet will change places and

43 Rāghib, *al-Mufradāt*.

they will be dragged along in this manner; others will be blind, stumbling about in confusion; some will be deaf and dumb and will not understand anything; some will be chewing on their own bloated tongues and blood and pus will ooze from their mouths in a manner that will fill people with disgust; some will have had their arms and legs cut off, and others will be hanging from branches of fire. A group will be emitting a stench more foul than rotting corpses, and a group will be clothed in molten tar which will be stuck on their bodies.

As for those who appear as apes, they were slanderers. And those who appear as pigs used to consume from unlawful sources. Those who are dragged upside-down earned their livelihood from interest and usury and those who are blind were unjust in their judgements. Those who are deaf and dumb were self-centred and conceited. As for those who will be chewing on their own tongues, they are the scholars and judges who did not themselves act on what they told others to do. Those that have had their limbs cut off used to harass their neighbours and those who are crucified on gallows of fire used to spy for the rulers. Those who emit a foul stench are the ones who gave in to their base and unlawful sexual desires and also those who did not pay the purifying tax (*zakat*). As for those who are clothed in burning tar (*qaṭirān*), they used to be conceited and boastful [in dress and conduct]."[44]

This tradition describes clearly how man's inner inclinations and behaviour has a bearing on his appearance on the Day of Judgement.

17-20.7 *'And the heaven shall be opened so that it shall have [multiple] gateways.'*: [*Al-Samā'* (السَّمَاءُ, the heaven)] in this verse refers to the realm of the angels.[45]

---

[44] Ṭabrasī, *al-Bayān*, 10/643; Rāzī, *Mafātīḥ al-Ghayb*, 31/13.

عَنِ الرَّسُولِ (صَلَّى اللهُ عَلَيْهِ وَآلِهِ) – يُحْشَرُ عَشَرَةُ أَصْنَافٍ مِنْ أُمَّتِي أَشْتَاتًا قَدْ مَيَّزَهُمُ اللهُ تَعَالَى مِنَ الْمُسْلِمِينَ وَبَدَّلَ صُوَرَهُمْ، بَعْضُهُمْ عَلَى صُورَةِ الْقِرَدَةِ؛ وَبَعْضُهُمْ عَلَى صُورَةِ الْخَنَازِيرِ، وَبَعْضُهُمْ مُنَكَّسُونَ أَرْجُلُهُمْ مِنْ فَوْقُ، وَوُجُوهُهُمْ مِنْ تَحْتُ، ثُمَّ يُسْحَبُونَ عَلَيْهَا، وَبَعْضُهُمْ عُمْيٌ يَتَرَدَّدُونَ، وَبَعْضُهُمْ صُمٌّ وَبُكْمٌ لَا يَعْقِلُونَ، وَبَعْضُهُمْ يَمْضَغُونَ أَلْسِنَتَهُمْ تَسِيلُ الْقَيْحُ مِنْ أَفْوَاهِهِمْ لُعَابًا يَتَقَذَّرُهُمْ أَهْلُ الْجَمْعِ، وَبَعْضُهُمْ مُقَطَّعَةٌ أَيْدِيهِمْ وَأَرْجُلُهُمْ، وَبَعْضُهُمْ مُصَلَّبُونَ عَلَى جُذُوعٍ مِنْ نَارٍ، وَبَعْضُهُمْ أَشَدُّ نَتْنًا مِنَ الْجِيَفِ، وَبَعْضُهُمْ يَلْبِسُونَ جِبَابًا سَابِغَةً مِنْ قَطِرَانٍ لَازِقَةً بِجُلُودِهِمْ، فَأَمَّا الَّذِينَ بِصُورَةِ الْقِرَدَةِ فَالْقَتَّاتُ مِنَ النَّاسِ، وَأَمَّا الَّذِينَ عَلَى صُورَةِ الْخَنَازِيرِ فَأَهْلُ السُّحْتِ، وَأَمَّا الْمُنَكَّسُونَ عَلَى رُؤُوسِهِمْ فَآكِلَةُ الرِّبَا وَالْعُمْيُ الْجَائِرُونَ فِي الْحُكْمِ، وَالصُّمُّ الْبُكْمُ الْمُعْجَبُونَ بِأَعْمَالِهِمْ وَالَّذِينَ يَمْضَغُونَ بِأَلْسِنَتِهِمُ الْعُلَمَاءُ وَالْقُضَاةُ الَّذِينَ خَالَفَ أَعْمَالُهُمْ أَقْوَالَهُمْ، وَالْمُقَطَّعَةُ أَيْدِيهِمْ وَأَرْجُلُهُمُ الَّذِينَ يُؤْذُونَ الْجِيرَانَ، وَالْمُصَلَّبُونَ عَلَى جُذُوعٍ مِنْ نَارٍ فَالسُّعَاةُ بِالنَّاسِ إِلَى السُّلْطَانِ، وَالَّذِينَ أَشَدُّ نَتْنًا مِنَ الْجِيَفِ فَالَّذِينَ يَتَمَتَّعُونَ بِالشَّهَوَاتِ وَاللَّذَّاتِ، وَيَمْنَعُونَ حَقَّ اللهِ تَعَالَى فِي أَمْوَالِهِمْ، وَالَّذِينَ هُمْ يَلْبَسُونَ الْجِبَابَ فَأَهْلُ الْفَخْرِ وَالْخُيَلَاءِ.

[45] Ṭabāṭabā'ī, *al-Mīzān*, 20/166.

The gateways here may refer to the doors between the realm of the unseen (*ʿālam al-ghayb*) and the realm of witnessing (*ʿālam al-shuhūd*); in other words, the veils between the metaphysical world of the angels and the imaginal (*barzakhī*) world of the human beings will be lifted and the two worlds will be linked [with pathways].[46]

The doorways in the heaven are also metaphors for the ascent of supplication (*duʿāʾ*) and the descent of sustenance (*rizq*). For example, it is highly recommended to supplicate at the corner of the Kaʿbah known as al-Rukn al-Yamānī because a tradition from Imam al-Sadiq (a) states: Al-Rukn al-Yamānī is a door from the doorways of Paradise, which God has not closed since He opened it.[47]

Similarly, about sustenance Q51:22 states:

وَفِي السَّمَاءِ رِزْقُكُمْ وَمَا تُوعَدُونَ

And in the heaven is your provision
and whatever you are promised.

This idea of gateways in the heaven is also mentioned in Q7:40:

إِنَّ الَّذِينَ كَذَّبُوا بِآيَاتِنَا وَاسْتَكْبَرُوا عَنْهَا لَا تُفَتَّحُ لَهُمْ أَبْوَابُ السَّمَاءِ
وَلَا يَدْخُلُونَ الْجَنَّةَ حَتَّىٰ يَلِجَ الْجَمَلُ فِي سَمِّ الْخِيَاطِ

Indeed, those who deny Our signs and are arrogant toward them – the gates of heaven will not be opened for them, nor will they enter Paradise until the camel passes through the eye of the needle...

Just as a camel cannot pass through the eye of a needle, the supplications of the deniers would never be presented for consideration in God's presence; in other words, the doorways of the heaven would be shut to them. However, when the trumpet is blown, all these doorways become manifest for the entirety of creation.

Other exegetes say that the verse refers to the physical cleaving asunder of the skies and the formation of what appears to be gateways between the earth and the heavens. Q84:1 states about that Day:

---

46 Shīrāzī, *Namūneh*, 26/33.

47 Kulaynī, *al-Kāfī*, 4/409.

عَنِ الصَّادِقِ (عَلَيْهِ السَّلَامُ) – الرُّكْنُ الْيَمَانِيُّ بَابٌ مِنْ أَبْوَابِ الْجَنَّةِ لَمْ يُغْلِقْهُ اللهُ مُنْذُ فَتَحَهُ.

إِذَا السَّمَاءُ انْشَقَّتْ

When the sky is split open.

Yet others say that man, who formerly only had limited access to movement in the skies, shall now have multiple doors opened before him to ascend to the heavens. Those destined for Paradise will pass through its doors.[48] Q39:73 states:

حَتَّىٰ إِذَا جَاؤُوهَا وَفُتِحَتْ أَبْوَابُهَا وَقَالَ لَهُمْ خَزَنَتُهَا سَلَامٌ عَلَيْكُمْ

... When they reach it, its gates will be opened and its keepers will say, "Peace be upon you."...

Those destined for Hell will also pass through its doorways. Q39:71 states:

حَتَّىٰ إِذَا جَاؤُوهَا فُتِحَتْ أَبْوَابُهَا وَقَالَ لَهُمْ خَزَنَتُهَا
أَلَمْ يَأْتِكُمْ رُسُلٌ مِنْكُمْ يَتْلُونَ عَلَيْكُمْ آيَاتِ رَبِّكُمْ

... When they reach it, its gates shall be open and its keepers will say, "Did there not come to you messengers from yourselves, reciting to you the verses of your Lord?..."

17-20.8 '*And the mountains shall be set in motion so that they become [like] a mirage.*': [*Suyyirat* (سُيِّرَت, set in motion]. In the final description of the events that will occur at the advent of the Day of Judgement, the destruction of the earth's imposing mountains is mentioned. This cataclysmic event is reported in several different ways in the Qur'an: '*And the mountains will move away with a [wrenching] movement.*' (Q52:10),

'*And the mountains shall be made to crumble with a [violent] crumbling.*' (Q56:5),

'*And the earth and the mountains shall be lifted up and crushed with a single crushing.*' (Q69:14),

'*On the day when the earth and the mountains shall quake and the mountains shall become [as] heaps of sand let loose.*' (Q73:14),

'*And when the mountains are scattered.*' (Q77:10), and

'*And the mountains will be like carded wool.*' (Q101:5).

[48] Shīrāzī, *Namūneh*, 26/33.

The destruction of the mountains will happen in continuous stages. As they are uprooted and 'set in motion', they will no longer serve their true functions as pegs in the earth and will thus be no more than mirages of their former glory.

[*Sarāb* (سَرَاب, mirage)] refers to the mirage that shimmers in a desert giving the false impression that there is water in the distance.[49] The remnants of the mountains will similarly shimmer in the air, but they will no longer exist, and the earth will be a smooth plain.[50]

Q20:105,106 state:

وَيَسْأَلُونَكَ عَنِ الْجِبَالِ فَقُلْ يَنسِفُهَا رَبِّي نَسْفًا ﴿١٠٥﴾ فَيَذَرُهَا قَاعًا صَفْصَفًا

And they ask you about the mountains. Say: My Lord will crush them into scattered dust. And He will leave it (the earth) a level plain.

Sarāb can also refer to anything that is a mere shadow of its reality, and perhaps this is the meaning intended here.[51]

17-20.9 All these events will follow the second blowing of the trumpet, when man is resurrected to enter the Day of Judgement. The earth that was his cradle will have been upturned and the strong mountains that were firm pegs within it, will have crumbled.[52]

SUMMARY OF THE VERSES

The verses state that the Day on which human beings will be sorted and judgement passed on them had always been appointed.

It is the Day when the [second, reviving] trumpet shall be blown, and mankind will emerge from the graves in multitudes.

There will be multiple gateways from which mankind can ascend to the heavens for their final journey. And the imposing mountains that held the earth in place will be uprooted so that only a mirage of them shall remain.

---

49 Muṣṭafawī, *al-Taḥqīq*.

50 Shīrāzī, *Namūneh*, 26/33.

51 Ṭabāṭabā'ī, *al-Mīzān*, 20/166.

52 Shīrāzī, *Namūneh*, 26/33.

REFLECTIVE LEARNING

Yawm al-faṣl is a Day that has been appointed, and will definitely come to pass when God wills. I cannot change the timing of that Day, but I can change my fate on that Day.

Let me reflect on how I can use the knowledge I already have to grow my soul so that the gateways of Paradise are accessible to me on that Day.

PART 2: VERSES 21 - 40

TEXT AND TRANSLATION

إِنَّ جَهَنَّمَ كَانَتْ مِرْصَادًا ﴿٢١﴾ لِلطَّاغِينَ مَآبًا ﴿٢٢﴾ لَابِثِينَ فِيهَا أَحْقَابًا ﴿٢٣﴾
لَا يَذُوقُونَ فِيهَا بَرْدًا وَلَا شَرَابًا ﴿٢٤﴾ إِلَّا حَمِيمًا وَغَسَّاقًا ﴿٢٥﴾ جَزَاءً وِفَاقًا
﴿٢٦﴾ إِنَّهُمْ كَانُوا لَا يَرْجُونَ حِسَابًا ﴿٢٧﴾ وَكَذَّبُوا بِآيَاتِنَا كِذَّابًا ﴿٢٨﴾ وَكُلَّ
شَيْءٍ أَحْصَيْنَاهُ كِتَابًا ﴿٢٩﴾ فَذُوقُوا فَلَنْ نَزِيدَكُمْ إِلَّا عَذَابًا ﴿٣٠﴾ إِنَّ لِلْمُتَّقِينَ مَفَازًا
﴿٣١﴾ حَدَائِقَ وَأَعْنَابًا ﴿٣٢﴾ وَكَوَاعِبَ أَتْرَابًا ﴿٣٣﴾ وَكَأْسًا دِهَاقًا ﴿٣٤﴾ لَا
يَسْمَعُونَ فِيهَا لَغْوًا وَلَا كِذَّابًا ﴿٣٥﴾ جَزَاءً مِنْ رَبِّكَ عَطَاءً حِسَابًا ﴿٣٦﴾ رَبِّ
السَّمَاوَاتِ وَالْأَرْضِ وَمَا بَيْنَهُمَا الرَّحْمَٰنِ لَا يَمْلِكُونَ مِنْهُ خِطَابًا ﴿٣٧﴾ يَوْمَ يَقُومُ
الرُّوحُ وَالْمَلَائِكَةُ صَفًّا لَا يَتَكَلَّمُونَ إِلَّا مَنْ أَذِنَ لَهُ الرَّحْمَٰنُ وَقَالَ صَوَابًا ﴿٣٨﴾ ذَٰلِكَ
الْيَوْمُ الْحَقُّ فَمَنْ شَاءَ اتَّخَذَ إِلَىٰ رَبِّهِ مَآبًا ﴿٣٩﴾ إِنَّا أَنْذَرْنَاكُمْ عَذَابًا قَرِيبًا يَوْمَ يَنْظُرُ
الْمَرْءُ مَا قَدَّمَتْ يَدَاهُ وَيَقُولُ الْكَافِرُ يَا لَيْتَنِي كُنْتُ تُرَابًا ﴿٤٠﴾

Indeed, Hell has been lying in wait. [21] *A place of return for the transgressors.* [22] *In which they shall remain for ages.* [23] *They shall not taste therein [any] coolness or drink,* [24] *except boiling water and foul pus.* [25] *An appropriate recompense.* [26] *Indeed, they were not expecting an account,* [27] *and constantly called Our revelation a lie.* [28] *But We have recorded everything in a Book.* [29] *So, taste [the fruits of your deeds]! For We will not increase for you anything but chastisement.* [30] *Indeed, for the God-wary is achievement.* [31] *Gardens and vineyards,* [32] *and voluptuous women of equal age,* [33] *and a brim-full cup.* [34] *They shall not hear therein any vain words or falsehood.* [35] *A compensation from your Lord, a gift according to an account;* [36] *[from] the Lord of the heavens and the earth and what is between them, the All-merciful, they shall not be able to address Him.* [37] *The Day on which the Spirit and the angels shall stand in ranks; they shall not speak, except the one whom the All-merciful permits and who speaks what is correct.* [38] *That is the Day of Truth; so whoever desires [to do so] may take refuge with his Lord.* [39] *Indeed, We have warned you of a chastisement near at hand; [on] the Day when man shall see what his two hands have sent forth, and the disbeliever shall say, "O! Would that I were dust!"* [40]

VERSES 21 - 30

إِنَّ جَهَنَّمَ كَانَتْ مِرْصَادًا ﴿٢١﴾ لِلطَّاغِينَ مَآبًا ﴿٢٢﴾ لَابِثِينَ فِيهَا أَحْقَابًا ﴿٢٣﴾ لَا
يَذُوقُونَ فِيهَا بَرْدًا وَلَا شَرَابًا ﴿٢٤﴾ إِلَّا حَمِيمًا وَغَسَّاقًا ﴿٢٥﴾ جَزَاءً وِفَاقًا﴿٢٦﴾
إِنَّهُمْ كَانُوا لَا يَرْجُونَ حِسَابًا ﴿٢٧﴾ وَكَذَّبُوا بِآيَاتِنَا كِذَّابًا ﴿٢٨﴾ وَكُلَّ شَيْءٍ
أَحْصَيْنَاهُ كِتَابًا ﴿٢٩﴾ فَذُوقُوا فَلَنْ نَزِيدَكُمْ إِلَّا عَذَابًا ﴿٣٠﴾

Indeed, Hell has been lying in wait. [21] *A place of return for the transgressors.* [22] *In which they shall remain for ages.* [23] *They shall not taste therein [any] coolness or drink,* [24] *except boiling water and foul pus.* [25] *An appropriate recompense.*[26] *Indeed, they were not expecting an account,* [27] *and constantly called Our revelation a lie.* [28] *But We have recorded everything in a Book.* [29] *So, taste [the fruits of your deeds]! For We will not increase for you anything but chastisement.* [30]

21-30.1 After mentioning the events that herald the arrival of the Day of Judgement, the verses turn to the description of the fate of the transgressors.

21-30.2 *'Indeed, Hell has been lying in wait.'*: [*Mirṣād* (مِرْصَاد, lying in wait)] is derived from *raṣada* which means to keep a lookout for, or to lie in ambush.[53] So *mirṣād* refers to the place where one lies in wait, and waiting in ambush are the angels of Hell, or Hell itself.[54] The past tense is used here to show that Hell is already looming for the sinner due to his actions, but he is not aware of it.

[53] Rāghib, *al-Mufradāt.*

[54] Shīrāzī, *Namūneh,* 26/38.

It appears from this verse that every person will pass by Hell on their journey on the Day of Judgement,[55] and this is also mentioned in Q19:71:

وَإِنْ مِنْكُمْ إِلَّا وَارِدُهَا

And there is not one of you except that he will come to it (Hell)...

And as they pass by Hell, every transgressor will be dragged inside. Indeed, by trapping the sinful, Hell becomes a blessing for the righteous.

21-30.3 *'A place of return for the transgressors.'*: [*Ṭāghīn* (طَاغِينَ, transgressors)] are those who continually displayed *ṭughyān*, which means habitually transgressing bounds, always being unjust, and sinning excessively.[56]

[*Ma'āb* (مَآب, place of return)] is derived from *'awb*, meaning return, so *ma'āb* refers to a destination, an abode, or a place of return and refuge. And if Hell is mentioned as the place of their return, it is because through their attitude and continual defiance, they made their abode in this world a hell and they shall return to Hell in the Hereafter as well.[57] In other words, returning to Hell is returning to the manifestation of the evil acts that qualified them for hellfire in the first place.[58]

21-30.4 *'In which they shall remain for ages.'*: [*Aḥqāb* (أَحْقَاب, ages)] is the plural of *ḥuqub*, which means a very long and indeterminate time, whose beginning and end cannot be discerned.[59] The term is used by Musa (a) in Q18:60:

وَإِذْ قَالَ مُوسَىٰ لِفَتَاهُ لَا أَبْرَحُ حَتَّىٰ أَبْلُغَ مَجْمَعَ الْبَحْرَيْنِ أَوْ أَمْضِيَ حُقُبًا

And [recall] when Musa said to his attendant:
I will not give up until I reach the point where the two seas meet,
or I will continue for a long period (ḥuqubā).

---

55 Ṭabāṭabā'ī, *al-Mīzān*, 20/168.
56 Rāghib, al-*Mufradāt*.
57 Ṭūsī, *al-Tibyān*, 10/243.
58 Muṭahharī, (*Āshnāyī bā Qur'an*), *Āthār*, 28/287.
59 Shīrāzī, *Namūneh*, 26/39.

In the verse under review, *aḥqāb* refers to periods after periods in never-ending succession.[60]

Some reports mention that these verses refer to sinners who will stay in Hell for a long time. A tradition from the Prophet (s) states: The one who enters Hell will not be released until he has spent many ages (*aḥqāb*) in it. Each age (*ḥuqub*) will be over sixty years. Each year shall have three-hundred and sixty days, and each day will be one-thousand earth years in duration. So let not anyone imagine that he will come out of the fire [easily].[61] From this, and other traditions, it appears that inmates of Hell will be released eventually if they have any goodness in them.

21-30.5 *'They shall not taste therein [any] coolness or drink, except boiling water and foul pus.'*: This verse describes one aspect of the overall misery experienced in Hell: its inmates will not receive the coolness of shade (or sleep)[62] or any palatable drink that would provide relief, except hot water and foul secretions.

[*Ḥamīm* (حَمِيم, boiling water)] is derived from *ḥamma*, which means to make hot.

[*Ghassāq* (غَسَّاق, foul pus)] refers to bodily secretions and pus, that exudes from the prisoners of Hell, and some have said that this concoction will be intensely cold as well.[63]

Some exegetes have said the pronoun *hā* (it) returns to the *aḥqāb* (ages) during which they would only be able to quench their great thirst by choosing between scalding water and foul pus.[64] In any case, whether it refers to Hell itself, or the indeterminate period that they will spend in it, it is a terrible choice indeed.

21-30.6 *'An appropriate recompense.'*: [*Wifāq* (وِفَاق, appropriate)] means in accordance with and conforming to. These terrible punishments are exact manifestations and perfectly justified retribution of their attitude and deeds in the world.[65] Q66:7 states:

---

60 Ṭabāṭabā'ī, *al-Mīzān*, 20/168.

61 Majlisī, *Biḥār*, 8/276.

عَنِ الرَّسُولِ (صَلَّى اللهُ عَلَيْهِ وَآلِهِ) – لَا يَخْرُجُ مِنَ النَّارِ مَنْ دَخَلَهَا حَتَّى يَمْكُثَ فِيهَا أَحْقَابًا وَالْحُقْبُ بِضْعٌ وَسِتُّونَ سَنَةً وَالسَّنَةُ ثَلَاثُمِائَةٍ وَسِتُّونَ يَوْمًا، كُلُّ يَوْمٍ كَأَلْفِ سَنَةٍ مِمَّا تَعُدُّونَ فَلَا يَتَّكِلَنَّ أَحَدٌ عَلَى أَنْ يَخْرُجَ مِنَ النَّارِ.

62 Rāzī, *Mafātīḥ al-Ghayb*, 31/16.

63 Ibid.

64 Ṭabāṭabā'ī, *al-Mīzān*, 20/168.

65 Muṭahharī, (*Āshnāyī bā Qur'an*), *Āthār*, 28/288.

يَا أَيُّهَا الَّذِينَ كَفَرُوا لَا تَعْتَذِرُوا الْيَوْمَ إِنَّمَا تُجْزَوْنَ مَا كُنْتُمْ تَعْمَلُونَ

O disbelievers! Do not make excuses this Day!
You are only being recompensed for what you used to do.

21-30.7 *'Indeed, they were not expecting an account, and constantly called Our revelation a lie.'*: [*Innahum kānū* (إِنَّهُمْ كَانُوا, indeed, they were)]. This phrasing is for emphasis and to show their habitual attitude.

[*Lā yarjūna* (لَا يَرْجُونَ, they were not expecting)]. *Yarjūna* (expecting) in this verse has the meaning of *yakhshaẉna* (fearing).[66] They never thought of accountability or feared it.

[*Kidhdhābā* (كِذَّابا, lie)] means that they belied the Qur'an constantly and with no fear of consequence.

The transgressors did not imagine that they would ever be called to account and therefore were dismissive of God's revelation (or His signs) in their words and actions. Their continuous contempt will thereby earn them continuous punishment.

In fact, the only reason people behave with *ṭughyān* is that they have forgotten, or dismissed, the idea of being held to account for their behaviour.[67] They are the ones whose insolence is mentioned in Q26:136:

قَالُوا سَوَاءٌ عَلَيْنَا أَوَعَظْتَ أَمْ لَمْ تَكُنْ مِنَ الْوَاعِظِينَ

They said, "It is all the same to us whether you admonish us
or are not one of the admonishers."

21-30.8 *'But We have recorded everything in a Book.'*: Everything that transpires in the cosmos, including the actions of human beings and their intentions, is meticulously recorded in a Book. In Q36:12 this Book is called the Clear Register:

وَكُلَّ شَيْءٍ أَحْصَيْنَاهُ فِي إِمَامٍ مُبِينٍ

...and We have recorded everything in
a [single] clear register (imāmin mubīn).

The verse warns the transgressors of the stark reality of an accounting that awaits them, where nothing will be omitted.

---

[66] Rāzī, *Mafātīḥ al-Ghayb*, 31/18.

[67] Shīrāzī, *Namūneh*, 26/42.

21-30.9 *'So, taste [the fruits of your deeds]!'*: The use of *fa* (so) at the beginning of the verse indicates the final conclusion of the matters described in the previous verses.[68]

[*Fadhūqū* (فَذُوقُوا, so taste)]. The term is derived from *dhāqa* and *dhawq* and it means to sense or perceive a sample of something, pleasant or unpleasant, either with the five senses or by an inner realization.[69] Tastes vary, and therefore, the term is used in the Qur'an for events whose experience will be different for every soul, such as death, chastisement, and mercy.

The switch of address from the third to the first person is to warn the transgressors directly not to expect anything but the constant experience (tasting) of the chastisement that will be the proper recompense for their habitual transgression. And this is a confirmation of the previous verse, '*In which they shall remain for ages.*'[70]

21-30.10 '*For We will not increase for you anything but chastisement.*': Different forms of chastisement will be continually visited on these wretched souls. It may also be surmised that through this punishment the inmates of Hell will grow in realization of how far they are from God and the Truth (*al-Ḥaqq*), and the actual consequences of their transgression in the world, and thus their torment will increase.

They were neglectful of God's commandments, and so what little 'good' they did was lost in this world, with nothing left for them in the Hereafter. Q18:103-105 warn:

قُلْ هَلْ نُنَبِّئُكُمْ بِالْأَخْسَرِينَ أَعْمَالًا ﴿١٠٣﴾ الَّذِينَ ضَلَّ سَعْيُهُمْ فِي الْحَيَاةِ الدُّنْيَا وَهُمْ يَحْسَبُونَ أَنَّهُمْ يُحْسِنُونَ صُنْعًا ﴿١٠٤﴾ أُولَٰئِكَ الَّذِينَ كَفَرُوا بِآيَاتِ رَبِّهِمْ وَلِقَائِهِ فَحَبِطَتْ أَعْمَالُهُمْ فَلَا نُقِيمُ لَهُمْ يَوْمَ الْقِيَامَةِ وَزْنًا

Say [O Muḥammad], "Shall We tell you of the greatest losers in respect of [their] deeds? [They are] those whose efforts are lost in worldly life, while they thought that they were acquiring good by their works!" Those are the ones who disbelieve in the signs of their Lord, and in [their] meeting Him. So their deeds are in vain, and on the Day of Resurrection We will not assign any weight to them.

---

68 Ṭabāṭabā'ī, *al-Mīzān*, 20/169.

69 Muṣṭafawī, *al-Taḥqīq*.

70 Ṭabāṭabā'ī, *al-Mīzān*, 20/169.

21-30.11 A tradition from the Prophet (s) states about the verse under review: It is the severest address in the Qur'an to the inmates of Hell. Whenever they will seek relief from one type of chastisement, they will be visited with an even more grievous one.[71]

21-30.12 Although the disbelievers are addressed by God in this stern tone as they enter Hell, another verse suggests that God will not address the disbelievers at all. Q3:77 states:

إِنَّ الَّذِينَ يَشْتَرُونَ بِعَهْدِ اللهِ وَأَيْمَانِهِمْ ثَمَنًا قَلِيلًا أُولَٰئِكَ لَا خَلَاقَ لَهُمْ فِي
الْآخِرَةِ وَلَا يُكَلِّمُهُمُ اللهُ وَلَا يَنْظُرُ إِلَيْهِمْ يَوْمَ الْقِيَامَةِ

Indeed, those who exchange the covenant of God and their [own] oaths for a paltry price shall have no share in the Hereafter; and God will not speak to them, nor look upon them on the Day of Judgement...

There is no contradiction here; Q3:77 means that He will not speak to them any word of kindness.[72]

SUMMARY OF THE VERSES

In summary, the verses warn that Hell lies in wait for the transgressors who are inexorably heading towards it. They will remain in it age after age, without the respite of shade or drink. Their only nourishment will be scalding water and foulness, which is a fitting recompense for their attitude and deeds in this world.

These were people who never thought that they would have to account for their deeds, and impugned God's revelation. However, God had recorded their deeds in a secure Record, and so they would have to taste the never-ending chastisement that their actions deserved.

REFLECTIVE LEARNING

The transgressor is someone who believes that he alone is in charge of his affairs and that he does not need his Creator. As a result, he always acts for immediate self-interest, forgetting that all his deeds are being recorded for the promised Day of Accounting and Judgement.

---

[71] Rāzī, *Mafātīḥ al-Ghayb*, 31/20.

عَنِ الرَّسُولِ (صَلَّى اللهُ عَلَيْهِ وَآلِهِ) – هَذِهِ الْآيَةُ أَشَدُّ مَا فِي الْقُرْآنِ عَلَى أَهْلِ النَّارِ، كُلَّمَا اسْتَغَاثُوا مِنْ نَوْعٍ مِنَ الْعَذَابِ أُغِيثُوا بِأَشَدَّ مِنْهُ.

[72] Ibid.

Let me think about a specific disobedience of my Creator, and if it came about because I pursued my self-interest, or forgot that my acts were being witnessed and recorded and that I would be held to account for them.

Let me reflect on what I could do differently next time, if faced with the same situation.

VERSES 31 - 37

إِنَّ لِلْمُتَّقِينَ مَفَازًا ﴿٣١﴾ حَدَائِقَ وَأَعْنَابًا ﴿٣٢﴾ وَكَوَاعِبَ أَتْرَابًا ﴿٣٣﴾ وَكَأْسًا دِهَاقًا ﴿٣٤﴾ لَا يَسْمَعُونَ فِيهَا لَغْوًا وَلَا كِذَّابًا ﴿٣٥﴾ جَزَاءً مِنْ رَبِّكَ عَطَاءً حِسَابًا ﴿٣٦﴾ رَبِّ السَّمَاوَاتِ وَالْأَرْضِ وَمَا بَيْنَهُمَا الرَّحْمَٰنِ لَا يَمْلِكُونَ مِنْهُ خِطَابًا ﴿٣٧﴾

Indeed, for the God-wary is achievement. [31] *Gardens and vineyards,* [32] *and voluptuous women of equal age,* [33] *and a brim-full cup.* [34] *They shall not hear therein any vain words or falsehood.* [35] *A compensation from your Lord, a gift according to an account;* [36] *[from] the Lord of the heavens and the earth and what is between them, the All-merciful, they shall not be able to address Him.* [37]

31-37.1 The verses now turn to the destiny of the God-wary, the *muttaqūn*, who shielded themselves from the disobedience of God. For them awaits Paradise, whose comforts are briefly described next.

31-37.2 *'Indeed, for the God-wary is achievement.'*: [*Mafāzā*, (مَفَازًا, achievement)] is derived from *fawz*, and refers to the achievement of goodness, salvation, and ultimately, success.[73] It can also refer to the place where this bounty is found. Here, it has been mentioned in the indefinite form, signifying the greatness of this achievement.[74]

True achievement and ultimate success can only be determined in the Hereafter. In this regard, a tradition from Imam Ali (a) states: [True] wealth and poverty will only be determined after the [books of] actions have been presented in front of God, the Exalted.[75]

---

[73] Ṭabāṭabā'ī, *al-Mīzān*, 20/170.

[74] Ṭabrasī, *al-Bayān*, 10/646.

[75] Majlisī, *Biḥār*, 69/53.

عَنْ أَمِيرِ الْمُؤْمِنِينَ (عَلَيْهِ السَّلَامُ) – الْغِنَى وَالْفَقْرُ بَعْدَ الْعَرْضِ عَلَى اللهِ سُبْحَانَهُ.

31-37.3 *'Gardens and vineyards,'*: [*Ḥadā'iq* (حَدَائِق, gardens)] is the plural of *ḥadīqah* and refers to walled gardens which are shielded from all sides.[76] They are well watered, lush, and full of trees. It is with a similar meaning that *ḥadīqah* refers to the pupil of the eye, which is isolated by the surrounding iris and kept continually lubricated by the tears.

Thus it appears that individual abodes in Paradise will be private as well as irrigated without effort.

[*Aʿnābā* (أَعْنَابًا, vineyards)] refers to the abundance of grapes, which are reckoned to be the best of fruit, in terms of taste, nutrients, and refreshment. Various traditions describe the benefits of grapes: they bring happiness, and give strength and vitality.[77]

A tradition from the Prophet (s) states: ...The best of your fruits is the grape.[78]

Here, vineyards are mentioned after gardens, as a specific example of the general bounty.

31-37.4 *'And voluptuous women of equal age'*: The next mention is of the consorts of heaven, the celestial maidens also called *ḥūrīyah.*

[*Kawā'ib* (كَوَاعِبَ, voluptuous women)] is the plural of *kāʿib* and refers to young women who are physically mature.

[*Atrāba* (أَتْرَابًا, of equal age)] is the plural of *tirb* meaning people of similar age. It could mean that these consorts are all the same age, or that the residents of Paradise will be of similar age to their consorts.[79]

Like other blessings in Paradise, these maidens are manifestations of good human actions. However, they cannot be compared to the great spiritual beauty, dignified station, and cognition of God (*maʿrifah*) of the women who have been admitted to Paradise from this world due to their righteous actions.

31-37.5 *'And a brim-full cup.'*: [*Kas* (كَأْس, cup)] refers to a cup that is not empty or refers to its contents.

---

76 Ṭabāṭabā'ī, *al-Mīzān*, 20/170.

77 Shīrāzī, *Namūneh*, 26/48.

78 Nūrī, *Mustadrak al-Wasā'il*, 16/393.

عَنِ الرَّسُولِ (صَلَّى اللهُ عَلَيْهِ وَآلِهِ) –... خَيْرُ فَاكِهَتِكُمُ الْعِنَبُ.

79 Shīrāzī, *Namūneh*, 26/48.

[*Dihāqā* (دِهَاقًا, brim-full)] means that it will be filled to its brim with a nourishing drink or pure wine. *Dihāq* has also been defined as continuous, or pure.[80]

The people of Paradise are served these drinks by attendants. They are given exactly what they desire and require, not less so that their appetite persists, and not more than they want at that moment.

Q76:15,16 state:

وَيُطَافُ عَلَيْهِم بِآنِيَةٍ مِّن فِضَّةٍ وَأَكْوَابٍ كَانَتْ قَوَارِيرَا ﴿١٥﴾
قَوَارِيرَ مِن فِضَّةٍ قَدَّرُوهَا تَقْدِيرًا

And there will be circulated among them vessels of silver and cups of crystal; crystal [clear] but made of silver. Of which they have determined the measure.

And of course, although the wine of this world dulls the senses, the wine of Paradise will enhance the spiritual cognition of those who drink it. A tradition from Imam al-Sadiq (a) states: [The drink] shall purify him from everything that is other than God.[81]

31-37.6 *'They shall not hear therein any vain words or falsehood.'*: Because a setting with lush surroundings, beautiful women, and continual cups of drink in this world is associated with debauchery and immoral acts, the verse points out that in Paradise, the opposite will be true. The same things in Paradise will be blessings that only increase in dignified behaviour and spiritual cognition. Thus there will be no trace of immorality or sinful conduct as a result.

The people of Paradise will speak of higher wisdoms; precisely, meaningfully, and accurately.[82]

31-37.7 *'A compensation from your Lord, a gift according to an account.'*: (*Ḥisābā* (حِسَابًا, according to an account)] here means that which will be sufficient and appropriate. This verse means that these rewards will be granted by the Lord in proportion to what is deserved by each person according to their actions in the *dunyā*, and will be

[80] Ibn Manẓūr, *Lisān al-ʿArab.*

[81] Ṭabrasī, *al-Bayān*, 10/623.

عَنِ الصَّادِقِ (عَلَيْهِ السَّلَامُ) – يُطَهِّرُكُمْ عَنْ كُلِّ شَيْءٍ سِوَى اللهِ.

[82] Ṭabāṭabā'ī, *al-Mīzān*, 20/170.

sufficient to delight them.[83] Within their individual capacities to receive however, they will enjoy bounties eternally and without measure as stated in Q40:40:

وَمَنْ عَمِلَ صَالِحًا مِنْ ذَكَرٍ أَوْ أُنْثَىٰ وَهُوَ مُؤْمِنٌ
فَأُولَٰئِكَ يَدْخُلُونَ الْجَنَّةَ يُرْزَقُونَ فِيهَا بِغَيْرِ حِسَابٍ

And whoever does a righteous deed, whether male or female, and is a [true] believer – those will enter Paradise and be given provision therein without account.

Indeed, all goodness (in the form of rewards and gifts) comes from God. The usage of *Rabb* here shows that in the Hereafter also, God continues in His role as Sustainer. [84]

31-37.8 *'[From] The Lord of the heavens and the earth and what is between them, the all-Merciful,'*: This phrase expounds on the qualities of *Rabbika* (your Lord) mentioned in the previous verse; He sustains and guides the entire cosmos, and His mercy encompasses the entirety of His creation.[85]

The heavens are the realm of the angels and the earth is the realm of our universe. What is between them are the different worlds occupied by other creatures that God has created, many of which we do not know of. And in this way, the verse states that He is the Lord and Cherisher of everything in existence and is all-Merciful (*al-Raḥmān*) to the entire creation, whether they are deserving of it or not.

31-37.9 *'They shall not be able to address Him.'*: This phrase can have two meanings:

1. *Khiṭāb* (address) may mean 'question' if one takes the verse to be addressing everyone assembled on the plains of resurrection: angels, man, and *jinn*; indeed, everyone will be awestruck and silent. No one will have the courage, the right, the need, or even the permission, to question His just decisions. Q21:23 states:

لَا يُسْأَلُ عَمَّا يَفْعَلُ وَهُمْ يُسْأَلُونَ

---

[83] Ṭūsī, *al-Tibyān*, 10/248.

[84] Shīrāzī, *Namūneh*, 26/51.

[85] Ṭabāṭabā'ī, *al-Mīzān*, 20/170.

He is not questioned about what He does,
but they will be questioned.

2. Another meaning is that since the angels never question God's command, and they are included in the address, it does not refer to questioning His decrees, but refers to their inability to address God. They cannot evoke intercession (*shafāʿah*), mediate, or plead for others, except with God's permission.[86] Q2:255 states:

مَنْ ذَا الَّذِي يَشْفَعُ عِندَهُ إِلَّا بِإِذْنِهِ

... Who is it that can intercede with Him
except by His permission?...

31-37.10 These verses present an interesting contrast between the abodes of the transgressors (*ṭāghūn*) and the God-wary (*muttaqūn*):

The transgressors are trapped in Hell (*mirṣād*), they are given scalding water and foul pus to drink (*ḥamīm* and *ghassāq*), and a fitting retribution (*jazāʾan wifāqā*).

On the other hand, the God-wary are in a place of salvation (*mafāz*), they are given grapes (*aʿnāb*), heavenly consorts (*kawāʾib*) and cups of pure drink (*kasan dihāqā*), and a befitting gift (*ʿaṭāʾan ḥisābā*).

SUMMARY OF THE VERSES

In summary, these verses describe the treatment of the God-wary. They are the successful ones, who will live surrounded by lush gardens, accompanied by pleasing consorts and refreshing drink. All this will be given to them as they deserve by the all-Merciful Lord. And no one will be able to question His decisions on that Day.

REFLECTIVE LEARNING

From these verses it is clear that the criterion for entry into Paradise is *taqwā* (God-wariness). Q2:3,4 mention five qualities of the *muttaqūn*:

الَّذِينَ يُؤْمِنُونَ بِالْغَيْبِ وَيُقِيمُونَ الصَّلَاةَ وَمِمَّا رَزَقْنَاهُمْ يُنْفِقُونَ ﴿٣﴾
وَالَّذِينَ يُؤْمِنُونَ بِمَا أُنْزِلَ إِلَيْكَ وَمَا أُنْزِلَ مِنْ قَبْلِكَ وَبِالْآخِرَةِ هُمْ يُوقِنُونَ

[86] Ibid, 20/171.

[The God-wary are] Those who 1) believe in the unseen, and 2) keep up the prayer, and 3) spend out of what We have provided for them. And who 4) believe in that which was revealed to you and that which was revealed before you, and 5) have certainty about the Hereafter.

Let me reflect to what extent I have these qualities, and how I can strengthen them and thereby progress in my levels of *taqwā*.

VERSES 38, 39

يَوْمَ يَقُومُ الرُّوحُ وَالْمَلَائِكَةُ صَفًّا لَا يَتَكَلَّمُونَ إِلَّا مَنْ أَذِنَ لَهُ الرَّحْمَٰنُ وَقَالَ صَوَابًا ﴿٣٨﴾ ذَٰلِكَ الْيَوْمُ الْحَقُّ فَمَنْ شَاءَ اتَّخَذَ إِلَىٰ رَبِّهِ مَآبًا ﴿٣٩﴾

The Day on which the Spirit and the angels shall stand in ranks; they shall not speak, except the one whom the all-Merciful permits and who speaks what is correct. [38] *That is the Day of Truth; so whoever desires [to do so] may take refuge with his Lord.* [39]

38-39.1 *'The Day on which the Spirit and the angels shall stand in ranks;'*: [*Ṣaff* (صَفّ, ranks, rows)]. After they are resurrected, the Spirit (*al-Rūḥ*) and the angels (*al-malā'ikah*) will all be arrayed in ranks.

[*al-Rūḥ* (الرُّوح, the Spirit)] is a creation that is distinct from the angels and of a grander station than them.

The notion of the angels standing in ranks or rows is mentioned elsewhere in the Qur'an as well. For example, in Q37:1, God swears by the angels who stand in rows (to safeguard the transmission of God's revelation):

وَالصَّافَّاتِ صَفًّا

I swear by those who draw themselves out in ranks.

And the standing of the angels in rows for worship is mentioned in Q37:165:

وَإِنَّا لَنَحْنُ الصَّافُّونَ

And indeed, we are those who line up (al-ṣāffūn) *[for prayer].*

However, in the verse under review, *ṣaff* probably denotes standing in ranks of seniority, with the angels standing in rows according to their station and the Spirit standing in a rank apart from them.[87]

38-39.2 The same meaning is alluded to for the resurrection and assembling of human beings in front of God in Q18:48:

وَعُرِضُوا عَلَىٰ رَبِّكَ صَفًّا لَقَدْ جِئْتُمُونَا كَمَا خَلَقْنَاكُمْ أَوَّلَ مَرَّةٍ

And they will be presented before your Lord in ranks [of merit], [and He will say], "You have certainly come [back] to Us just as We created you the first time..."

38-39.3 *'They shall not speak, except the one whom the all-Merciful permits.'*: Everyone will be silent, except if permitted by God to speak (to intercede for the believers). Q21:27 states:

لَا يَسْبِقُونَهُ بِالْقَوْلِ وَهُمْ بِأَمْرِهِ يَعْمَلُونَ

[The angels] do not precede Him in speech, and they [only] act by His command.

38-39.4 *'And who speaks what is correct'.* [*Ṣawābā* (صَوَابًا, correct)] here means *qawlan ṣawābā* (correct and absolutely truthful speech), and means to say that the permission to speak is only given by the all-Merciful to those who would speak the absolute truth, conforming to reality.[88] These are individuals who are so connected to the truth (*ṣiddīqūn*) that it has become part of them.

About this verse, a tradition from Imam al-Sadiq (a) states: "By God! We are the ones who will be permitted [to speak] on the Day of Judgement, and we are the ones who will speak the correct word (*ṣawābā*)." When he (a) was asked, "What will you say?", he replied. "We will praise our Lord, and invoke blessings on our Prophet (s), and seek intercession for our partisans (*shīʿa*), and our Lord will not deny us."[89]

38-39.5 *'That is the Day of Truth.'*: [*Dhālika* (ذَٰلِكَ, that)] refers to the Day of Judgement, which has been called *yawm al-faṣl* earlier in this

---

87 Ṭabāṭabāʾī, *al-Mīzān*, 20/172.

88 Ibid.

89 Baḥrānī, *al-Burhān*, 5/570.

عَنِ الصَّادِقِ (عَلَيْهِ السَّلَامُ) – نَحْنُ وَاللهِ الْمَأْذُونُ لَهُمْ يَوْمَ الْقِيَامَةِ، وَالْقَائِلُونَ صَوَابًا. قُلْتُ مَا تَقُولُونَ إِذَا تَكَلَّمْتُمْ؟ قَالَ: نَحْمَدُ رَبَّنَا، وَنُصَلِّي عَلَى نَبِيِّنَا، وَنَشْفَعُ لِشِيعَتِنَا فَلَا يَرُدُّنَا رَبُّنَا.

surah. The distant demonstrative pronoun *dhālika* is used to denote importance, and here, it highlights the pivotal significance of that Day.[90]

[*Yawm al-Ḥaqq* (يَوْمُ الْحَقّ, Day of Truth)]. It is the Day of Truth because it will definitely come to pass. Everyone will see that the only Truth is God and whatever is connected to Him; everything else is illusory.

It is also the Day when the true reality of all affairs will be made manifest. Q7:53 states:

هَلْ يَنْظُرُونَ إِلَّا تَأْوِيلَهُ يَوْمَ يَأْتِي تَأْوِيلُهُ يَقُولُ الَّذِينَ نَسُوهُ مِنْ قَبْلُ قَدْ جَاءَتْ رُسُلُ رَبِّنَا بِالْحَقِّ

Do they await just for its final interpretation (ta'wīl)*? The Day its final interpretation comes, those who had ignored it before will say, "The messengers of our Lord had come with the truth..."*

Ḥaqq could also mean that on this Day everyone will receive his rights, and the oppressed will receive their rights from their oppressors.[91] Both these meanings are mentioned in Q24:25 which states:

يَوْمَئِذٍ يُوَفِّيهِمُ اللَّهُ دِينَهُمُ الْحَقَّ وَيَعْلَمُونَ أَنَّ اللَّهَ هُوَ الْحَقُّ الْمُبِينُ

That Day, God will pay them their deserved recompense, and they will know that God is the manifest Truth.

38-39.6 *'So whoever desires [to do so] may take refuge with his Lord.'*: [*Ma'āb* (مَآب, refuge, return)] is mentioned for the second time in the surah. As mentioned earlier, it is derived from *'awb*, meaning return. Human beings can choose the path and manner of their inevitable return to their Lord.

Earlier in the chapter (verse 22), *ma'āb* referred to Hell as a place of return for the transgressors. Here, it is mentioned as an invitation to mankind to use their free will and make God, the Sustainer (*Rabb*), the sole object of their return and refuge. In this way, they will attain what the God-wary (*muttaqūn*) will attain.

---

90 Ṭabāṭabā'ī, *al-Mīzān*, 20/171.

91 Shīrāzī, *Namūneh*, 26/59.

Indeed, the greatest motivation for man to turn to God is conviction about the Day of Truth, where all will be recompensed for their acts.

SUMMARY OF THE VERSES

In summary, the verses state that on that Day, the Spirit and the angels will stand silently in ranks. They will only speak when God, the Merciful, permits them to do so, and they will only utter that which conforms to reality and truth. This Day every Truth will be manifest to all, so those who are mindful should turn now in refuge to their Sustainer.

REFLECTIVE LEARNING

Yawm al-ḥaqq is about absolute truth; falsehood and pretence have no place on that Day. Everyone will come back to their Lord, along one path or another.

Let me reflect on the path that I am taking towards my Lord and see how well it conforms to the path of the infallibles (a), who were the *ṣiddīqūn*.

VERSE 40

إِنَّا أَنْذَرْنَاكُمْ عَذَابًا قَرِيبًا يَوْمَ يَنْظُرُ الْمَرْءُ مَا قَدَّمَتْ يَدَاهُ وَيَقُولُ الْكَافِرُ يَا لَيْتَنِي كُنْتُ تُرَابًا ﴿٤٠﴾

Indeed, We have warned you of a chastisement near at hand; [on] the Day when man shall see what his two hands have sent forth, and the disbeliever shall say, "O! Would that I were dust!" [40]

40.1 '*Indeed, We have warned you of a chastisement near at hand.*': In the final verse, God warns mankind of a Day of Chastisement that is near. [*ʿAdhāb* (عَذَاب, chastisement)] in this verse refers to the chastisement of the Hereafter, not of this world.[92]

On that Day, the negligent will be truly regretful. This verse is a reminder to man to be mindful of his purpose in this world, and this warning is from God's mercy.

[92] Ṭabāṭabāʾī, *al-Mīzān*, 20/175.

[*Qarīb* (قَرِيب, near)] can have several meanings:

1. Indeed, the life of this world and *barzakh* is very short compared to the Hereafter, so in relative terms, that Day is truly near.[93]
2. In addition, since its advent is a certainty, the Qur'an calls it near.[94] In this regard, a tradition from Imam Ali (a) states: Everything that will certainly come [to pass] is near.[95]
3. Man can only think in days, months, and years, so he imagines the Hereafter to be remote and distant.[96] But, God who is outside time, sees it as close. Q70:6,7 state:

   إِنَّهُمْ يَرَوْنَهُ بَعِيدًا ﴿٦﴾ وَنَرَاهُ قَرِيبًا

   Indeed, they see it [as] distant, but We see it [as] near.

4. Another meaning of 'near' is that the punishment (*ʿadhāb*) already encompasses the sinner, but he cannot see it because God has suspended it until an appointed time.[97] Q17:13 states:

   وَكُلَّ إِنْسَانٍ أَلْزَمْنَاهُ طَائِرَهُ فِي عُنُقِهِ وَنُخْرِجُ لَهُ يَوْمَ الْقِيَامَةِ كِتَابًا يَلْقَاهُ مَنْشُورًا

   And We have fastened every man's deeds to his neck, and on the Day of Judgement We shall produce for him a written account which he will encounter wide open.

40.2 '*[On] the Day when man shall see what his two hands have sent forth.*': [*Yanẓuru* (يَنظُرُ, he sees)]. A group of exegetes say that *yanẓuru* here means *yantaẓiru* (he awaits), and so the verse would mean, '[on] the Day when man shall wait to see the recompense of what his two hands have sent forth.'[98] Others say that he will not only look at his Book of deeds but study the good or evil recorded therein as well.[99]

---

[93] Shīrāzī, *Namūneh*, 26/60.

[94] Ṭabrasī, *al-Bayān*, 10/647.

[95] *Nahj al-Balāghah*, sermon 103.

كُلُّ آتٍ قَرِيبٌ دَانٍ.

[96] Qarāʾatī, *Nūr*, 10/368

[97] Shīrāzī, *Namūneh*, 26/61.

[98] Ṭabāṭabāʾī, *al-Mīzān*, 20/175.

[99] Ṭabrasī, *al-Bayān*, 10/647.

However, the presence of the manifestation of every one's acts (*tajassum al-aʿmāl*) in front of his eyes means that the verse does not require further elucidation.[100] Q10:30 states:

هُنَالِكَ تَبْلُو كُلُّ نَفْسٍ مَا أَسْلَفَتْ وَرُدُّوا إِلَى اللهِ مَوْلَاهُمُ الْحَقِّ
وَضَلَّ عَنْهُمْ مَا كَانُوا يَفْتَرُونَ

There every soul shall become acquainted with what it sent before,
and they shall be brought back to God, their true Master,
and what they devised shall escape from them.

[*Qaddamat yadāhu* (قَدَّمَتْ يَدَاهُ, his two hands sent forth)]. The phrase is not restricted to the acts that man did with his hands, rather the meaning here is of every action that he sent forth himself.[101] While he is alive and still able to act, Q59:18 warns him:

وَلْتَنْظُرْ نَفْسٌ مَا قَدَّمَتْ لِغَدٍ

...And let every soul look to what it has sent
forth for tomorrow...

40.3 '*And the disbeliever shall say, "O! Would that I were dust!"*': Confronted with the dreadful and evil embodiment of their acts, which will be apparent all around them, the disbelievers will be horrified and in utter despair. Q18:49 states:

وَوَجَدُوا مَا عَمِلُوا حَاضِرًا وَلَا يَظْلِمُ رَبُّكَ أَحَدًا

...And they will find all that they did present [before them].
And your Lord does injustice to no one.

The disbelievers will not want to continue into the Hell that they know they have earned, and will dearly wish that they had never been created in the first place, or that they had remained buried in the dust and not been resurrected. However, this could never be allowed, because the justice of God requires that they be brought to account in a manner that was not possible in the *dunyā*.

---

100 Shīrāzī, *Namūneh*, 26/62.

101 Modarresī, *Min Huda al-Qur'an*, 17/275.

Other meanings for the statement have been suggested by exegetes,[102] but the meaning we have already stated conforms best to Q4:42 which states:

يَوْمَئِذٍ يَوَدُّ الَّذِينَ كَفَرُوا وَعَصَوُا الرَّسُولَ لَوْ تُسَوَّىٰ بِهِمُ الْأَرْضُ

On that Day, those who disbelieved and disobeyed the Messenger will wish that they could be covered (hidden) by the earth...

SUMMARY OF THE VERSE

The verse warns man of a reckoning that is near at hand. On that Day, the reality of everything he has sent forth will be clearly apparent. Those who disbelieved in God will regret that Day, wishing that they did not exist to experience the consequences of their actions.

REFLECTIVE LEARNING

This verse speaks of a chastisement that is near in time and distance, and that the Hereafter is not as remote as we sometimes imagine.

Let me reflect on what I have sent forth and what else I can send forth, so that I do not utter the words of despair and regret on that Day, when it will be too late.

102 Rāzī, *Mafātīḥ al-Ghayb*, 31/27.

SURAT AL-NĀZIʿĀT
THE EXTRACTORS (79)

PART 1: VERSES 1 - 14

TEXT AND TRANSLATION

سُورَةُ النَّازِعَاتِ

بِسْمِ اللهِ الرَّحْمٰنِ الرَّحِيمِ

وَالنَّازِعَاتِ غَرْقًا ﴿١﴾ وَالنَّاشِطَاتِ نَشْطًا ﴿٢﴾ وَالسَّابِحَاتِ سَبْحًا ﴿٣﴾ فَالسَّابِقَاتِ
سَبْقًا ﴿٤﴾ فَالْمُدَبِّرَاتِ أَمْرًا ﴿٥﴾ يَوْمَ تَرْجُفُ الرَّاجِفَةُ ﴿٦﴾ تَتْبَعُهَا الرَّادِفَةُ ﴿٧﴾
قُلُوبٌ يَوْمَئِذٍ وَاجِفَةٌ ﴿٨﴾ أَبْصَارُهَا خَاشِعَةٌ ﴿٩﴾ يَقُولُونَ أَإِنَّا لَمَرْدُودُونَ فِي الْحَافِرَةِ
﴿١٠﴾ أَإِذَا كُنَّا عِظَامًا نَخِرَةً ﴿١١﴾ قَالُوا تِلْكَ إِذًا كَرَّةٌ خَاسِرَةٌ ﴿١٢﴾ فَإِنَّمَا هِيَ
زَجْرَةٌ وَاحِدَةٌ ﴿١٣﴾ فَإِذَا هُمْ بِالسَّاهِرَةِ ﴿١٤﴾

In the name of God, the Beneficent, the Merciful.

By those [angels] who extract [the souls of the wicked] with force. [1] *And [by] those who remove [the souls of the righteous] with gentleness.* [2] *And by those who glide along [on errands of mercy].* [3] *Then press forward as in a race.* [4] *Then regulate the affair [of their Lord].* [5] *On the Day when the Quaker shall quake.* [6] *Followed by the subsequent [quake].* [7] *On that Day hearts will beat fast.* [8] *Their [owner's] eyes will be humbled.* [9] *[Right now] they ask, "Will we indeed be returned to [our] former state of life?* [10] *Even after we are rotted bones?"* [11] *They say, "Then that would be a return with loss!"* [12] *Indeed, it will be but one shout.* [13] *And suddenly they will be [awake] on the surface of the earth.* [14]

INTRODUCTION

Surat al-Nāziʿāt (79) was the 81st chapter to be revealed. It has forty-six verses and was revealed in Makka, after Surat al-Nabaʾ (78).[1] It is named after the issue of the *nāziʿāt* (angels who extract) in the first verse of the surah.

Like many Makkan verses, the surah speaks of the Resurrection. It begins with a series of oaths to emphasize the Day of Judgement, followed by a description of the fate of the disbelievers on that Day.

This is followed by a brief account of the meeting of Prophet Musa (a) with Firʿawn at the start of his mission, and the reaction and fate of Firʿawn.

Thereafter, man is asked to consider several signs of God that are visible in the world around him.

Finally, there is a return to the mention of the Hereafter. This time it mentions how mankind will be divided into two groups, one destined for Hell, and the other for Paradise.

LINK TO THE PREVIOUS CHAPTER

The previous chapter, Surat al-Nabaʾ, started by mentioning the questioning of the idolaters about the Day of Judgement and ended by presenting the contrasting fates of the transgressors and the God-wary on that Day. This surah continues with the theme of the Resurrection and the Day of Judgement, but here the mockery of the idolaters is cited after the mention of the Day of Judgement.

The last verse of Surat al-Nabaʾ quotes the lament of the disbelievers, '*O! Would that I were dust!*' The first verse of this surah describes how the souls of such individuals are wrenched from their bodies, and how they are taken away from the *dunyā* to which they had dedicated all their activity.

The subject of the oaths of this surah is a continuation of the theme of the final verse of Surat al-Nabaʾ: '*Indeed, We have warned you of a chastisement near at hand...*'

---

[1] Maʿrifat, *ʿUlūm-i Qurʾānī*, p. 90.

MERITS OF RECITATION

- A tradition from the Prophet (s) states: Whoever recites Surat al-Nāziʿāt will not be detained and questioned on the Day of Judgement for any longer than it takes to pray one obligatory prayer, before being granted entry into Paradise.[2]
- Another tradition from the Prophet (s) states: Whoever recites this surah will be secure from the punishment of God, the Exalted. And on the Day of Judgement, God will quench his thirst with a cool drink.[3]
- A tradition from Imam al-Sadiq (a) states: Whoever recites this surah when he encounters an enemy, the enemy will not notice him and will turn aside from him. If one recites it in the presence of someone he is fearful of, he will be secure from his harm, with the permission of God, the Exalted.[4]

EXEGESIS

VERSES 1 - 5

وَالنَّازِعَاتِ غَرْقًا ﴿١﴾ وَالنَّاشِطَاتِ نَشْطًا ﴿٢﴾ وَالسَّابِحَاتِ سَبْحًا ﴿٣﴾ فَالسَّابِقَاتِ سَبْقًا ﴿٤﴾ فَالْمُدَبِّرَاتِ أَمْرًا ﴿٥﴾

By those [angels] who extract [the souls of the wicked] with force. [1] *And [by] those who remove [the souls of the righteous] with gentleness.* [2] *And by those who glide along [on their errands].* [3] *Then press forward as in a race.* [4] *Then regulate the affair [of their Lord].* [5]

1-5.1 The chapter begins with five brief oaths to emphasize the reality of the Day of Judgement.[5] Examples of similar equivocal oaths are

---

[2] Nūrī, *Mustadrak al-Wasāʾil*, 4/355.

عَنِ الرَّسُولِ (صَلَّى اللهُ عَلَيْهِ وَآلِهِ) – وَمَنْ قَرَأَ سُورَةَ وَالنَّازِعَاتِ لَمْ يَكُنْ حَبْسُهُ وَحِسَابُهُ يَوْمَ الْقِيَامَةِ إِلَّا كَقَدْرِ صَلَاةٍ مَكْتُوبَةٍ حَتَّى يَدْخُلَ الْجَنَّةَ.

[3] Baḥrānī, *al-Burhān*, 5/573.

عَنِ الرَّسُولِ (صَلَّى اللهُ عَلَيْهِ وَآلِهِ) – مَنْ قَرَأَ هَذِهِ السُّورَةَ أَمِنَ مِنْ عَذَابِ اللهِ تَعَالَى وَسَقَاهُ مِنْ بَرْدِ الشَّرَابِ يَوْمَ الْقِيَامَةِ.

[4] Ibid.

عَنِ الصَّادِقِ (عَلَيْهِ السَّلَامُ) – مَنْ قَرَأَهَا وَهُوَ مُوَاجِهٌ أَعْدَائَهُ لَمْ يُبْصِرُوهُ وَانْحَرَفُوا عَنْهُ وَمَنْ قَرَأَهَا وَهُوَ دَاخِلٌ عَلَى أَحَدٍ يَخَافُهُ نَجَا مِنْهُ وَأَمِنَ بِإِذْنِ اللهِ تَعَالَى.

[5] Shīrāzī, *Namūneh*, 26/74.

those found in the opening verses of other surahs such as al-Ṣāffāt (37), al-Dhāriyāt (51), al-Mursalāt (77), and al-ʿĀdiyāt (100).

We have discussed the usage of oaths in the Qurʾan in the *tafsīr* of Surat al-Shams (91)

1-5.2 Exegetes have presented several possibilities about what the oaths at the beginning of this surah may be referring to, such as: angels of God who remove the souls at the time of death, angels who specifically remove the souls of disbelievers, the event of death itself, the rising and setting of stars, the archers who shoot at the enemy in *jihād*, and wild animals who make attacks in plains.[6] Others have mentioned that they refer to the winds, or to the stations of the heart.[7]

However, the only explanation that links all five verses, and also conforms to the rest of the chapter as well as similar opening verses elsewhere in the Qurʾan,[8] is that they refer to the angels carrying out their duties as commanded by God. And this is confirmed by verse 5, which speaks of those who regulate God's affairs in the world, and these are His angels.[9] This regulation (*tadbīr*) requires intellect and cannot be ascribed to stars, animals, winds, and so on.

The feminine plurals used throughout are because the reference is to groups (*ṭāʾifah*) of angels, and not to individual angels.[10]

1-5.3 *'By those [angels] who extract [the souls of the wicked] with violence.'*: [*Nāziʿāt* (نَازِعَات, those who extract)] is derived from *nazaʿa* which means to pull away, divest, and remove something from its place.[11] It has also been used in the meaning of removal in a non-physical sense. For example, about those who will be entered into Paradise, Q15:47 states:

وَنَزَعْنَا مَا فِي صُدُورِهِمْ مِنْ غِلٍّ إِخْوَانًا عَلَىٰ سُرُرٍ مُتَقَابِلِينَ

And We shall remove (nazaʿnā) *from their hearts [any] rancour; [so they will be] brothers, on thrones facing each other.*

---

6 Ṭabāṭabāʾī, *al-Mīzān*, 20/179.
7 Rāzī, *Mafātīḥ al-Ghayb*, 31/31.
8 The opening verses of Surat al-Ṣāffāt and Surat al-Mursalāt.
9 Ṭabāṭabāʾī, *al-Mīzān*, 20/179.
10 Qarāʾatī, *Nūr*, 10/371.
11 Muṣṭafawī, *al-Taḥqīq*.

[*Gharqā* (غَرْقًا, with force)] may be derived from *ghariqa* which means to be immersed in water or immersed in difficulties, or *ighrāq*, which originally meant pulling a bowstring to its fullest extent, and later came to mean any work done with full force. From the context of the verse, it appears that this latter meaning is more appropriate.[12]

This verse probably refers to the force used by the angels to detach the soul of the evildoers from their bodies. These individuals have focussed all their attention on the material world. At the point of death, they stubbornly try to cling on to this life, but to no avail. Q8:50 states:

وَلَوْ تَرَىٰ إِذْ يَتَوَفَّى الَّذِينَ كَفَرُوا الْمَلَائِكَةُ يَضْرِبُونَ
وُجُوهَهُمْ وَأَدْبَارَهُمْ وَذُوقُوا عَذَابَ الْحَرِيقِ

But if you could only see the angels take the souls of those who disbelieved; they smite their faces and their backs (saying), "Taste the punishment of the burning fire!"

A tradition from Imam al-Baqir (a) states that the verse under review refers to the angels who forcefully separate the souls of the disbelievers from their bodies, just as a bowman pulls the bowstring to its full extent.[13]

1-5.4 '*And [by] those who remove [the souls of the righteous] with gentleness.*': [*Nāshiṭāt* (نَاشِطَات, those who remove gently)] is derived from *nashiṭa*, which refers to undoing a knot with ease, or to something that comes free without exertion.[14] A well from which water can be drawn easily is called *inshāt* and a camel who readily obeys the command to speed up is called *nashīṭah*. In general, the term refers to any task that is accomplished easily.[15]

The verse probably refers to the gentle manner in which the angels detach the souls of the righteous believers, who do not resist death in the manner of the previous group. Q16:32 states:

---

[12] Shīrāzī, *Namūneh*, 26/75.

[13] Majlisī, *Biḥār*, 56/167.

عَنِ الْبَاقِرِ (عَلَيْهِ السَّلَامُ) – «وَالنَّازِعَاتِ غَرْقًا» يَعْنِي بِالنَّازِعَاتِ الْمَلَائِكَةَ الَّذِينَ يَنْزِعُونَ أَرْوَاحَ الْكُفَّارِ عَنْ أَبْدَانِهِمْ بِالشِّدَّةِ كَمَا يُغْرِقُ فِي الْقَوْسِ فَيَبْلُغُ بِهِ غَايَةَ الْمَدِّ.

[14] Ṭabāṭabā'ī, *al-Mīzān*, 20/179.

[15] Shīrāzī, *Namūneh*, 26/75.

الَّذِينَ تَتَوَفَّاهُمُ الْمَلَائِكَةُ طَيِّبِينَ يَقُولُونَ
سَلَامٌ عَلَيْكُمُ ادْخُلُوا الْجَنَّةَ بِمَا كُنْتُمْ تَعْمَلُونَ

Those whom the angels cause to die while they led pure lives,
they say to them, "Peace be upon you.
Enter Paradise because of what you used to do."

This is the type of preparedness for death that a believer should pray for. A supplication from Imam al-Sajjad (a) states: O Allah, grant me ever-readiness to leave the world of deceit and turn towards the world of permanence, and preparedness for death before its time comes.[16]

1-5.5 '*And by those who glide along [on their errands].*': [*Sābiḥāt* (سَابِحَات, those who glide)] is derived from *sabaḥa*, which means moving swiftly in water or air. The term refers to any task that is pursued without delay.[17] *Tasbīḥ* (declaring God free of every defect) comes from the same root, perhaps because the one who does *tasbīḥ* moves swiftly in the worship of God.[18]

Since these verses are probably describing the activities of angels, *sābiḥāt* may refer to the groups of angels who move swiftly and promptly to carry out the various tasks that they have been assigned.

Another meaning could be that this verse is a continuation of the description of the activity of the angels of death, who swiftly soar away, carrying the souls that they have removed to their destination.[19]

1-5.6 '*Then press forward as in a race.*': [*Sābiqāt* (سَابِقَات, those who race)] is derived from *sabaqa* meaning to go ahead or precede. And since preceding others normally requires speed, the term denotes swiftness as well. This oath is preceded by 'so' (*fa*) which indicates that *sabq* and racing ahead is a consequence of their swiftness in carrying out the commands of God mentioned in the previous verse.[20]

---

[16] Ibn Ṭāwūs, *Iqbāl al-Aʿmāl*, 1/228.

اَللّٰهُمَّ ارْزُقْنِي التَّجَافِيَ عَنْ دَارِ الْغُرُورِ وَالْإِنَابَةَ إِلَى دَارِ الْخُلُودِ وَالْاِسْتِعْدَادَ لِلْمَوْتِ قَبْلَ حُلُولِ الْفَوْتِ.

[17] Muṣṭafawī, *al-Taḥqīq*.

[18] Shīrāzī, *Namūneh*, 26/75.

[19] Rāzī, *Mafātīḥ al-Ghayb*, 31/28.

[20] Shīrāzī, *Namūneh*, 26/75.

1-5.7 ‘*Then regulate the affair [of their Lord].*’: [*Mudabbirāt* (مُدَبِّرَات, those who regulate)] is derived from *dabbara*, and its verbal noun *tadbīr* means to regulate, organize, and consider the consequence of actions.[21] The angels of God are charged with carrying out every affair (*amr*) decreed by Him. Q21:27 states:

لَا يَسْبِقُونَهُ بِالْقَوْلِ وَهُمْ بِأَمْرِهِ يَعْمَلُونَ

[The angels] do not precede Him in speech,
and they [only] act by His command.

While the regulation (*tadbīr*) of affairs is attributed to the angels, it is clear that they are merely intermediary causes that create the effects which manifest God's will. Depending on which causes precede others and ‘take the lead’, a certain effect is manifested.

This *tadbīr* happens in a pre-ordained procedure that follows a system that God has created. As an example, let us consider the event of death. No death happens except with the leave of God. Q3:145 states:

وَمَا كَانَ لِنَفْسٍ أَنْ تَمُوتَ إِلَّا بِإِذْنِ اللهِ كِتَابًا مُؤَجَّلًا

And a soul cannot die except with the permission of God
– a term that is fixed...

However, death is mediated by angels, who work under the direction of ʿIzraʾīl, the Angel of death.[22]

These angels of death wait until other angels who have been placed as guardians of the soul depart from an individual.[23] As the time of death arrives, these guardian angels depart, and an angel of death takes the soul.

A tradition from Imam Ali (a) states: There is no person who is not accompanied by a guardian [angel]... And when the time of his death comes, they [depart and] allow him to be exposed to that which will cause his death.[24] In this regard, Q6:61 states:

---

[21] Ibid.

[22] Ṭabāṭabāʾī, *al-Mīzān*, 16/251.

[23] Ibid, 7/131.

[24] Majlisī, *Biḥār*, 75/64.

عَنْ عَلِيٍّ (عَلَيْهِ السَّلَامُ) – إِنَّهُ لَيْسَ أَحَدٌ مِنَ النَّاسِ إِلَّا وَمَعَهُ حَفَظَةٌ ... فَإِذَا جَاءَ أَجَلُهُ خَلَّوْا بَيْنَهُ وَبَيْنَ أَجَلِهِ.

وَهُوَ الْقَاهِرُ فَوْقَ عِبَادِهِ وَيُرْسِلُ عَلَيْكُمْ حَفَظَةً
حَتَّىٰ إِذَا جَاءَ أَحَدَكُمُ الْمَوْتُ تَوَفَّتْهُ رُسُلُنَا وَهُمْ لَا يُفَرِّطُونَ

And He is the Subjugator over His servants. He sends over you guardians until, when death comes to one of you, Our messengers take him, and they do not fail [in their duties].

However, above all this is the permission of God, without which no angel can act. Q53:26 states:

وَكَمْ مِنْ مَلَكٍ فِي السَّمَاوَاتِ لَا تُغْنِي شَفَاعَتُهُمْ شَيْئًا
إِلَّا مِنْ بَعْدِ أَنْ يَأْذَنَ اللَّهُ لِمَنْ يَشَاءُ وَيَرْضَىٰ

And how many angels there are in the heavens whose intercession will not avail at all except [only] after God has permitted [it] to whom He wills and approves.

1-5.8 The third supplication of the *Ṣaḥīfah* of Imam al-Sajjad (a) contains a lengthy description of various angels and their activities, showing that they are intermediaries between God and His creation, and play a role in causing every phenomenon that occurs on earth. A portion of the supplication is reproduced here:

...[Bless] Your angels who are of the Spirit, those of proximity to You, those who carry the [communications from the] unseen to Your messengers, and those entrusted with Your revelation...

The wardens of the rain, the drivers of the clouds, the one who roars so that thunder rolls, causing clouds to move swiftly, and bolts of lightning to flash. The companions of snow and hail, those who descend with the drops of rain as they fall, the controllers of the treasuries of the winds, and those who secure the mountains lest they disappear....

The devoted and honourable envoys, the guardians and noble scribes, the angel of death and his aides. And Munkar, Nakīr, and Rūmān, the tester in the graves. And those who circumambulate the Inhabited House (*Bayt al-Maʿmūr*), and *Mālik*, and the guardians [of Hell], and Riḍwān, and the gatekeepers of the gardens [of

Paradise], '*those who do not disobey God in what He commands them and do what they are commanded.* (Q66:6)...'[25]

The outward order of the material world (*mulk*) is facilitated by the tireless and unseen activity of the angels in the incorporeal world (*malakūt*), just like the graceful passage of a swan is facilitated by the energetic paddling of its feet hidden below the water.

SUMMARY OF THE VERSES

The verses contain five oaths: by those who extract human souls with force, by those who do so with gentleness, by those who are busy carrying out God's directives, by those who move swiftly in obedience, and by those who manage God's affairs.

REFLECTIVE LEARNING

When we leave this world we may either feel as if we are being released from a stifling prison and are going towards a world of freedom, or we may feel that we have been captured and are being led to a place of torture. It all depends on the kind of life we have led.[26]

Let me reflect on my attitude towards my own death. Am I eagerly waiting to be freed or constantly worried about being captured?

VERSES 6 - 14

يَوْمَ تَرْجُفُ الرَّاجِفَةُ ﴿٦﴾ تَتْبَعُهَا الرَّادِفَةُ ﴿٧﴾ قُلُوبٌ يَوْمَئِذٍ وَاجِفَةٌ ﴿٨﴾ أَبْصَارُهَا
خَاشِعَةٌ ﴿٩﴾ يَقُولُونَ أَإِنَّا لَمَرْدُودُونَ فِي الْحَافِرَةِ ﴿١٠﴾ أَإِذَا كُنَّا عِظَامًا نَّخِرَةً ﴿١١﴾
قَالُوا تِلْكَ إِذًا كَرَّةٌ خَاسِرَةٌ ﴿١٢﴾ فَإِنَّمَا هِيَ زَجْرَةٌ وَاحِدَةٌ ﴿١٣﴾ فَإِذَا هُم بِالسَّاهِرَةِ
﴿١٤﴾

---

[25] *Al-Ṣaḥīfah al-Sajjādiyyah*, supplication 3.

عَلَى الرَّوْحَانِيِّينَ مِنْ مَلَائِكَتِكَ، وَأَهْلِ الزُّلْفَةِ عِنْدَكَ، وَحُمَّالِ الْغَيْبِ إِلَى رُسُلِكَ، وَالْمُؤْتَمَنِينَ عَلَى وَحْيِكَ ...

وَخُزَّانِ الْمَطَرِ وَزَوَاجِرِ السَّحَابِ وَالَّذِي بِصَوْتِ زَجْرِهِ يُسْمَعُ زَجَلُ الرُّعُودِ، وَإِذَا سَبَحَتْ بِهِ حَفِيفَةُ السَّحَابِ الْتَمَعَتْ صَوَاعِقُ الْبُرُوقِ.

وَمُشَيِّعِي الثَّلْجِ وَالْبَرَدِ، وَالْهَابِطِينَ مَعَ قَطْرِ الْمَطَرِ إِذَا نَزَلَ، وَالْقُوَّامِ عَلَى خَزَائِنِ الرِّيَاحِ، وَالْمُوَكَّلِينَ بِالْجِبَالِ فَلَا تَزُولُ ...

وَالسَّفَرَةِ الْكِرَامِ الْبَرَرَةِ، وَالْحَفَظَةِ الْكِرَامِ الْكَاتِبِينَ، وَمَلَكِ الْمَوْتِ وَأَعْوَانِهِ، وَمُنْكَرٍ وَنَكِيرٍ، وَرُومَانَ فَتَّانِ الْقُبُورِ، وَالطَّائِفِينَ بِالْبَيْتِ الْمَعْمُورِ، وَمَالِكٍ، وَالْخَزَنَةِ، وَرِضْوَانَ، وَسَدَنَةِ الْجِنَانِ ...

[26] Bahmanpour, *Towards Eternal Life*, p. 15.

On the Day when the Quaker shall quake. [6] *Followed by the subsequent [quake].* [7] *On that Day hearts will beat fast.* [8] *Their [owner's] eyes will be cast down.* [9] *[Right now] They ask, "Will we indeed be returned to [our] former state of life?* [10] *Even after we are rotted bones?"* [11] *They say, "Then that would be a return with loss!"* [12] *Indeed, it will be but one shout.* [13] *And suddenly they will be [awake] on the surface of the earth.* [14]

6-14.1 In this surah, the subject or response (*jawāb*) to the oaths has been omitted, but the meaning here is 'I swear that the Resurrection will happen on a *Day when the Quaker shall quake*'.[27]

6-14.2 '*On the Day when the Quaker shall quake. Followed by the subsequent [quake].*': [*Tarjufu* (تَرْجُفُ, will quake)] and [*Rājifah* (رَاجِفَة, Quaker)] are both derived from *rajafa*, which means to shake severely, with a loud rumbling sound.[28] Here, it denotes a phenomenon (a quake) which causes very forceful reverberations. Its intensity is emphasized by the usage of the same word twice.[29]

This verse does not specify what quakes. Q73:14 ascribes it to the earth and the mountains:

يَوْمَ تَرْجُفُ الْأَرْضُ وَالْجِبَالُ وَكَانَتِ الْجِبَالُ كَثِيبًا مَهِيلًا

On the day when the earth and the mountains shall quake and the mountains shall become [as] heaps of sand let loose.

[*Rādifah* (رَادِفَة, subsequent)] is derived from *radifa* which denotes a person or event that follows another.[30]

Some exegetes say that the first quake (*rājifah*) refers to the earth while the subsequent quake (*rādifah*) reverberates through the universe.[31]

Others say that the two verses refer to the first and second blowings of the trumpet. The first blast brings death to the universe and the second causes its resurrection. These are events that will bring an

[27] Shīrāzī, *Namūneh*, 26/80.
[28] Rāzī, *Mafātīḥ al-Ghayb*, 31/34.
[29] Ṭabrasī, *al-Bayān*, 10/653.
[30] Shīrāzī, *Namūneh*, 26/81.
[31] Rāzī, *Mafātīḥ al-Ghayb*, 31/34.

end to this world (*dunyā*) and usher in the Hereafter (*ākhirah*).[32] In this regard, Q39:68 states:

وَنُفِخَ فِي الصُّورِ فَصَعِقَ مَنْ فِي السَّمَاوَاتِ وَمَنْ فِي الْأَرْضِ إِلَّا مَنْ شَاءَ اللَّهُ ثُمَّ نُفِخَ فِيهِ أُخْرَىٰ فَإِذَا هُمْ قِيَامٌ يَنْظُرُونَ

And the trumpet will be blown, and whoever is in the heavens and whoever is on the earth will fall dead except whom God wills [to exempt]. Then it will be blown again, and at once they will be standing, waiting.

6-14.3 ‘*On that Day hearts will beat fast.*’: [*Wājifah* (وَاجِفَة, beating fast)] is derived from *wajafa* which means to be agitated and deeply worried. Here it means that the heart of the one who is feeling *wajf* is pounding so hard out of fear that he can feel it.[33]

Hearts (*qulūb*) have been mentioned in the indefinite form, and this means that not all hearts will be agitated, only some. The hearts of the believers will be much calmer than those of the disbelievers.[34]

6-14.4 ‘*Their [owner's] eyes will be humbled.*’: The eyes (*abṣār*) have been attributed to hearts but here it refers to the eyes of the owners of those hearts, because the next verse states, ‘*They say... (yaqūlūna)*’.[35]

[*Khāshiʿah* (خَاشِعَة, humbled)] is derived from *khashaʿa* and means to be submissive, humbled, and fearful. Here, this *khushūʿ* has been attributed to the eyes, whereas it is a quality of the heart. This may be because the outward signs of submissiveness and fright are visible in the eyes more than anywhere else.[36]

The hearts of the sinners, oppressors, and transgressors will be extremely uneasy on that Day, because these individuals will be fully aware of the reality of their fate and their eyes will be cast down in defeat and submission.[37]

We have discussed *khushūʿ* further in the *tafsīr* of Surat al-Ghāshiyah (88).

---

32 Ṭabāṭabāʾī, *al-Mīzān*, 20/185.

33 Shīrāzī, *Namūneh*, 26/82.

34 Rāzī, *Mafātīḥ al-Ghayb*, 31/35.

35 Ibid.

36 Ṭabāṭabāʾī, *al-Mīzān*, 20/185.

37 Shīrāzī, *Namūneh*, 26/83.

6-14.5 '*[Right now] they ask, "Will we indeed be returned to [our] former state of life?'*: The verses briefly turn from the discussion of the Hereafter to mention the attitude of the disbelievers in this world.

[*Ḥāfirah* (حَافِرَة, former state)] is derived from *ḥafara* which originally meant to leave a mark in the earth. For example, a pit in the ground is called *ḥufrah*. Later, the word became a metaphor for returning to the former position, because a person retraces his footprints when he returns to where he started from.[38]

Here, *ḥāfirah* refers to a second life.[39] The verse means that they did not believe that they would live again after having died.

6-14.6 *'Even after we are rotted bones?"'*: [*Nakhirah* (نَخِرَة, rotted)] is the plural of *nakhr* which denotes a tree which has rotted and become hollow, so that a whistling sound comes from it when air passes through. Here it refers to bones that have decayed into the earth.[40]

In the *dunyā*, the transgressors displayed incredulity at the idea that their bodies would be resurrected on the Day of Judgement, and argued that such a thing was impossible after they had decayed in the earth. Yet they forgot that they had been created from dust before, when they did not even exist. Q19:9 states:

قَالَ كَذَٰلِكَ قَالَ رَبُّكَ هُوَ عَلَيَّ هَيِّنٌ وَقَدْ خَلَقْتُكَ مِنْ قَبْلُ وَلَمْ تَكُ شَيْئًا

He said, "Thus [it will be]"; your Lord says, "It is easy for Me, for indeed, I created you before, while you were nothing."

6-14.7 *'They say, "Then that would be a return with loss!"'*: [*Karrah* (كَرَّة, return)] is a reference to the resurrection on the Day of Judgement, and [*Khāsirah* (خَاسِرَة, loss)] refers to their loss on that Day.[41]

It is probable that the statement in this verse is made by the disbelievers at the time of their resurrection, when they see that their bodies have been restored after they had decayed in the earth. At that time, they will realize that they will have to account for their actions, and they will regret their return to life.[42]

---

[38] Ibid.

[39] Ṭabāṭabā'ī, *al-Mīzān*, 20/185.

[40] Muṣṭafawī, *al-Taḥqīq*.

[41] Ṭabāṭabā'ī, *al-Mīzān*, 20/186.

[42] Ibid.

Another possibility is that this verse is quoting their mockery. They continued to jest and feign fear by saying that if there really was going to be a Day of Judgement then their situation would be much worse![43] They would be in loss because they would have been taken from a comfortable life in the *dunyā* to the chastisement of the Hereafter.[44]

6-14.8 ‘*Indeed, it will be but one shout.*’: The pronoun ‘it’ (*hiya*) refers to either the second blast (*rādifah*) mentioned in verse 7, or to the return (*karrah*) mentioned in the previous verse.[45]

[*Zajrah* (زَجْرَة, shout)] denotes a piercing sound which captures attention. It refers here to the second blowing of the trumpet.[46] No more than a single blast of the trumpet will be required to revive creation from death, and assemble them from the depths of the earth.

6-14.9 ‘*And suddenly they will be [awake] on the surface of the earth.*’: The use of *idhā* (when) gives the meaning of suddenness.[47] They will come forth onto an earth that has been renewed and remodelled into an expansive plain called *al-Sāhirah*.[48]

[*Al-Sāhirah* (السَّاهِرَة, surface of the earth)]. This refers to a land that is flat or free of any vegetation.[49] A second meaning is from the root *sahara* meaning to stay awake.[50] Since this will be the first halting place of the momentous Day of Resurrection, no one will be able to sleep anymore.[51]

A tradition from Imam al-Baqir (a) states that *al-Ḥāfirah* means a new life and *al-Sāhirah* means the earth. They are in the graves but when they hear the shout (*al-zajrah*) they will come forth from their graves and assemble on the earth.[52]

---

[43] Shīrāzī, *Namūneh*, 26/84.

[44] Ṭabrasī, *al-Bayān*, 10/653.

[45] Ṭabāṭabā'ī, *al-Mīzān*, 20/186.

[46] Muṣṭafawī, *al-Taḥqīq*.

[47] Ṭabāṭabā'ī, *al-Mīzān*, 20/186.

[48] Ṭūsī, *al-Tibyān*, 10/255.

[49] Ṭabāṭabā'ī, *al-Mīzān*, 20/186.

[50] Shīrāzī, *Namūneh*, 26/86.

[51] Ṭabrasī, *al-Bayān*, 10/654.

[52] Majlisī, *Biḥār*, 7/46.

عَنِ الْبَاقِرِ (عَلَيْهِ السَّلَامُ) – فِي قَوْلِهِ:«أَإِنَّا لَمَرْدُودُونَ فِي الْحَافِرَةِ» يَقُولُ أَيْ فِي خَلْقٍ جَدِيدٍ وَأَمَّا قَوْلُهُ:«فَإِذَا هُمْ بِالسَّاهِرَةِ» السَّاهِرَةُ

SUMMARY OF THE VERSES

In summary, these verses begin with the mention of two blasts of the trumpet, the first that will bring death to creation, and the second that will restore life to everything. They describe how the realization of the Day of Accounting will cause the disbelievers to be terrified and to keep their eyes downcast in submission.

The verses then recount the sceptical words of the disbelievers regarding the Resurrection when they were in the *dunyā*.

Finally, they describe how easily and instantly God will revive mankind to stand once again on the earth.

REFLECTIVE LEARNING

In truth, that which is seen and perceived by the eyes is tinged by the level of purity of the heart. When there is faith in the heart, everything one sees is a reminder of God. In contrast, when the heart is corrupted, everything one perceives is likewise tainted.

Let me reflect on how often what I see reminds me of God.

PART 2: VERSES 15 - 26

TEXT AND TRANSLATION

VERSES 15 - 26

هَلْ أَتَاكَ حَدِيثُ مُوسَىٰ ﴿١٥﴾ إِذْ نَادَاهُ رَبُّهُ بِالْوَادِ الْمُقَدَّسِ طُوًى ﴿١٦﴾ اذْهَبْ
إِلَىٰ فِرْعَوْنَ إِنَّهُ طَغَىٰ ﴿١٧﴾ فَقُلْ هَلْ لَكَ إِلَىٰ أَنْ تَزَكَّىٰ ﴿١٨﴾ وَأَهْدِيَكَ إِلَىٰ رَبِّكَ
فَتَخْشَىٰ ﴿١٩﴾ فَأَرَاهُ الْآيَةَ الْكُبْرَىٰ ﴿٢٠﴾ فَكَذَّبَ وَعَصَىٰ ﴿٢١﴾ ثُمَّ أَدْبَرَ يَسْعَىٰ
﴿٢٢﴾ فَحَشَرَ فَنَادَىٰ ﴿٢٣﴾ فَقَالَ أَنَا رَبُّكُمُ الْأَعْلَىٰ ﴿٢٤﴾ فَأَخَذَهُ اللَّهُ نَكَالَ
الْآخِرَةِ وَالْأُولَىٰ ﴿٢٥﴾ إِنَّ فِي ذَٰلِكَ لَعِبْرَةً لِمَنْ يَخْشَىٰ ﴿٢٦﴾

Has there come to you the story of Musa? [15] *When his Lord called to him in the sacred valley of Ṭuwā.* [16] *Go to Firʿawn. Indeed, he has*

الْأَرْضُ كَانُوا فِي الْقُبُورِ فَلَمَّا سَمِعُوا الزَّجْرَةَ خَرَجُوا مِنْ قُبُورِهِمْ فَاسْتَوَوْا عَلَى الْأَرْضِ.

transgressed [all bounds]. [17] *And say to him, 'Would you [be willing to] purify yourself?* [18] *And [to] let me guide you to your Lord so that you would fear [Him]?"* [19] *Then he (Musa) showed him the great sign.* [20] *But he (Firʿawn) denied and disobeyed.* [21] *Then he turned his back, walking swiftly.* [22] *And he gathered and summoned [the people].* [23] *Then he said, "I am your lord, the most high!"* [24] *So God seized him in exemplary punishment in the Hereafter, and in this [former] life.* [25] *Indeed, in that is a lesson for whoever would fear [God].* [26]

15-26.1 Following the mention of how the disbelievers will be humbled on the Day of Judgement after mocking and denying it in this world, an example is given of a community that will meet such a fate, and why this will happen to them.

15-26.2 The next twelve verses describe an encounter of Prophet Musa (a) with Firʿawn, one of the most arrogant transgressors in history. He ruled over a community of idolaters that was similar to the Arabs but much stronger than them.

The verses serve to warn the polytheists and reassure the Prophet (s) and the believers that even more powerful communities than the idolaters of Makka had not been able to withstand the punishment of God when it overcame them in this world.[53]

15-26.3 *'Has there come to you the story of Musa? When his Lord called to him in the sacred valley of Ṭuwā.'*: The story begins with a question; this style is often used in the Qur'an to intrigue the listener and make him curious to hear the story.[54] It could also be a reminder and mean, 'has the story of Musa not [already] come to you..."[55]

Ṭuwā is the name of the sacred valley at the right flank of Mount Sinai.[56] It was here that Prophet Musa (a) was appointed as God's Messenger to his people when he was returning from Madyan to Egypt. Q20:12,13 state that God said to Musa (a):

إِنِّيٓ أَنَا رَبُّكَ فَاخْلَعْ نَعْلَيْكَ إِنَّكَ بِالْوَادِ الْمُقَدَّسِ طُوًى ﴿١٢﴾
وَأَنَا ٱخْتَرْتُكَ فَٱسْتَمِعْ لِمَا يُوحَىٰٓ

53 Rāzī, *Mafātīḥ al-Ghayb*, 31/38.

54 Shīrāzī, *Namūneh*, 26/88.

55 Rāzī, *Mafātīḥ al-Ghayb*, 31/38.

56 We have discussed sacred places in the *tafsīr* of Surat al-Tīn.

Indeed, I am your Lord. So remove your sandals, for indeed, you are in the sacred valley of Ṭuwā. And I have chosen you [for My message], so listen [well] to what is revealed [to you].

15-26.4 Thereafter, the initial phase of the mission entrusted to Musa (a) is summarized in three commands:

i) Go to Firʿawn, because he is a transgressor.

ii) Ask him if he is willing to change his ways by purifying himself..

iii) Ask him to allow you to guide him to his Lord.

15-26.5 *'Go to Firʿawn. Indeed, he has transgressed [all bounds].'* [*Ṭaghā* (طَغَىٰ, transgressed)] and its verbal noun *ṭughyān* means habitually transgressing bounds, always being unjust, and sinning excessively.[57]

The reason that the Qur'an gives for directing Musa (a) to Firʿawn is his rebellion and transgression (*ṭughyān*) against God and against the Banu Isra'il. This indicates the fundamental importance of tackling this kind of behaviour, especially on the part of the reformers, in order to improve societies. A tradition from Imam Ali (a) states: The populace cannot be righteous unless the rulers are righteous...[58]

In this verse, the Quraysh are being reminded indirectly that the Prophet (s) has been sent to them because they too, had transgressed and did not want any limits imposed on them.

15-26.6 *'And say to him, "Would you [be willing to] purify yourself?"'*: The verse reveals that Musa (a) was instructed to approach Firʿawn in a cordial manner. Q20:44 mentions it more explicitly:

فَقُولَا لَهُ قَوْلًا لَّيِّنًا لَّعَلَّهُ يَتَذَكَّرُ أَوْ يَخْشَىٰ

And [both of you] speak to him mildly, perhaps he may be reminded or fear [God].

This instruction is a powerful lesson on how to approach someone who is hostile. The initial encounter has to be polite and cordial, not abrasive and aggressive. This was the approach used by all God's Prophets (a).

---

[57] Rāghib, al-*Mufradāt*.

[58] *Nahj al-Balāghah*, sermon 216.

فَلَيْسَتْ تَصْلُحُ الرَّعِيَّةُ إِلاَّ بِصَلاَحِ الْوُلاَةِ.

[*Tazakkā* (تَزَكَّى, purify oneself)] is derived from *zakā* which means to be pure, and to grow and develop thereby.[59] This shows that what God has charged His prophets (a) to do is to encourage sinners to purify themselves (by repentance), and thereafter guide them to turn back towards Him.[60] Q3:164 states:

بَعَثَ فِيهِمْ رَسُولًا مِنْ أَنْفُسِهِمْ يَتْلُو عَلَيْهِمْ آيَاتِهِ
وَيُزَكِّيهِمْ وَيُعَلِّمُهُمُ الْكِتَابَ وَالْحِكْمَةَ

... He sent among them a Messenger from themselves,
reciting to them His revelations and purifying them,
and teaching them the Book and the wisdom...

The verse under review shows that a person cannot be forced to become purified, he must want to do so of his own accord.

Q2:256 states:

لَا إِكْرَاهَ فِي الدِّينِ

There is no compulsion in religion...

This means that even if one compels another to accept faith, one can never be sure whether that person has actually submitted to God or is merely pretending to do so. The only way people can change is when they decide to do so of their own free will.

Furthermore, the verse teaches that the journey to God's proximity begins with self-purification and only then can God's guidance cause the desired 'fear' of God.

15-26.7 *'And [to] let me guide you to your Lord so that you would fear [Him]?'*: 'Your Lord' is used to remind Firʿawn that Musa (a) only wanted to bring him back into the servitude of his true Sustainer and Cherisher.[61]

'*Guide you'* here refers to guiding him to the recognition (*maʿrifah*) of God, without which obedience to Him is not possible.[62]

[*Fatakhshā* (فَتَخْشَى, so you would fear)]. *Khashyah* here means to fear God. And it is the consequence of knowledge (*ʿilm*). Fearing God

---

59 Rāghib, *al-Mufradāt.*

60 Shīrāzī, *Namūneh*, 26/90.

61 Ibid.

62 Rāzī, *Mafātīḥ al-Ghayb*, 31/40.

means having fear and awe of Him and fearing the consequence of disobeying Him.

Transgressors like Firʿawn behave inordinately because they have lost that fear. It is a fear that only comes after knowing God and obeying Him. Q35:28 states:

إِنَّمَا يَخْشَى اللَّهَ مِنْ عِبَادِهِ الْعُلَمَاءُ

...Only those of His servants who possess knowledge [of Him] (ʿulamāʾ) *fear God...*

A tradition from the Prophet (s) states: God has said, "I shall not combine two instances of fear and two instances of security in My servants. If they feel secure from Me [in this world] I will make them feel fear on the Day of Judgement, and if they fear Me [in this world] I will make them feel secure on the Day of Judgement."[63]

Another tradition from the Prophet states: Whoever is fearful [of not reaching his destination in time] will travel even in the night, and the one who travels through the night will [certainly] reach his destination. What God has promised is worth striving for [day and night]. What God has promised is Paradise.[64]

15-26.8 *'Then he (Musa) showed him the great sign.'*: Musa (a) went to Firʿawn as commanded by God and tried to reason with him before displaying his miracles.

In the same manner, the Qur'an serves a dual purpose. For the unbelievers it was, and is, the miracle that proves the claim of the Prophet (s). For the believers it is additionally the source of guidance towards felicity and God's pleasure.

The two miracles that Musa (a) had been granted at the start of his mission were designed to impress the people who lived in a milieu in which magic and sorcery were practised.

The great sign (*al-ayat al-kubrā*) that he displayed before Firʿawn was a staff that changed into a large serpent when he cast it down,

---

[63] Nūrī, *Mustadrak al-Wasāʾil*, 11/228.

عَنِ الرَّسُولِ (صَلَّى اللهُ عَلَيْهِ وَآلِهِ) – يَا أَبَا ذَرٍّ يَقُولُ اللهُ تَعَالَى لَا أَجْمَعُ عَلَى عَبْدِي خَوْفَيْنِ وَلَا أَجْمَعُ لَهُ أَمْنَيْنِ فَإِذَا أَمِنَنِي أَخَفْتُهُ يَوْمَ الْقِيَامَةِ وَإِذَا خَافَنِي آمَنْتُهُ يَوْمَ الْقِيَامَةِ.

[64] Ḥillī, *Tanbīh al-Khawāṭir*, 1/279.

عَنِ الرَّسُولِ (صَلَّى اللهُ عَلَيْهِ وَآلِهِ) – مَنْ خَافَ أَدْلَجَ وَمَنْ أَدْلَجَ بَلَغَ الْمَنْزِلَ أَلَا إِنَّ سِلْعَةَ اللهِ غَالِيَةٌ، أَلَا إِنَّ سِلْعَةَ اللهِ الْجَنَّةُ.

and a dazzling light that emanated from his hand after he placed it on his chest. Q7:107,108 state:

فَأَلْقَىٰ عَصَاهُ فَإِذَا هِيَ ثُعْبَانٌ مُبِينٌ ﴿١٠٧﴾ وَنَزَعَ يَدَهُ فَإِذَا هِيَ بَيْضَاءُ لِلنَّاظِرِينَ

So Musa threw his staff, and suddenly it was a manifest serpent. And he drew out his hand, and suddenly it was white [with radiance] for the observers.

15-26.9 '*But he (Firʿawn) denied and disobeyed.*': Despite seeing the sign that proved the claim of Musa (a), Firʿawn stubbornly denied his message (*kadhdhaba*) and manifested his defiance by choosing the path of disobedience to God (*ʿaṣā*).[65]

This shows that denial (*takdhīb*) is the first step in disobeying God (*ʿisyān*) just as bringing faith (*īmān*) is the first step in obeying Him (*ṭāʿah*).[66]

Kadhdhaba is mentioned in a general sense and so it could apply to any of the following: that Firʿawn denied the offer of Musa (a), or the great sign of Musa (a), or even his conscience (*fiṭrah*) through which he instinctively knew that he was hearing the truth.

15-26.10 '*Then he turned his back, walking swiftly.*' [*Adbara* (أَدْبَرَ, turned his back)] means that he turned away mentally from the message of Musa (a), or withdrew to consider his next step.[67]

[*Yasʿā* (يَسْعَىٰ, walking swiftly)] here means that he immediately endeavoured to come up with a plan in response, and this is an indication of his fear.[68]

This verse shows that Firʿawn was perturbed by what he had seen. To mask his concern he pretended to be amused by the proceedings and his courtiers dutifully joined him in his laughter. Q43:47 states:

فَلَمَّا جَاءَهُمْ بِآيَاتِنَا إِذَا هُمْ مِنْهَا يَضْحَكُونَ

But when he brought them Our signs, at once they laughed at them.

15-26.11 '*And he gathered and summoned [the people]. Then he said, "I am your lord, the most high!"*.': [*Ḥashara* (حَشَرَ, gathered)]. In

[65] Rāzī, *Mafātīḥ al-Ghayb*, 31/41.

[66] Shīrāzī, *Namūneh*, 26/92.

[67] Muṭahharī, (*Āshnāyī bā Qur'an*), *Āthār*, 28/325.

[68] Ṭūsī, *al-Tibyān*, 10/258.

defiance, Firʿawn began to gather those whom he thought could counter the miracle of Musa (a). The manner of this gathering, which was on the advice of his select council (*mala'*), is described in Q7:111,112:

قَالُوا أَرْجِهْ وَأَخَاهُ وَأَرْسِلْ فِي الْمَدَائِنِ حَاشِرِينَ ﴿١١١﴾ يَأْتُوكَ بِكُلِّ سَاحِرٍ عَلِيمٍ

They said, "Postpone [the matter of] him and his brother and send gatherers to the cities so that they bring to you every learned magician."

[*Nādā* (نَادَى, summoned)] refers to his call to the magicians to gather, or alternatively, to selected people to assemble to witness the contest between his magicians and Musa (a).[69] Q26:39 states:

وَقِيلَ لِلنَّاسِ هَلْ أَنْتُمْ مُجْتَمِعُونَ

And it was said to the people, "Will you assemble?"

The message that Musa (a) had brought was about guidance to the Lord of the worlds. Firʿawn sought to attack this fundamental message, so when the people had assembled, he announced that it was he who was their great lord, and there was no authority higher than him.[70]

By adding the phrase *al-aʿlā* (the most high), he meant that despite there being other gods, including the God of Musa (a), he was the highest of them because he guaranteed their sustenance, well-being, and protection.[71] Ironically, he was himself an idol-worshipper.

Indeed, when transgressors are drunk on their power, there is no limit to what they will say or do. Q28:38 quotes his previous disgraceful statement to his inner circle:

وَقَالَ فِرْعَوْنُ يَا أَيُّهَا الْمَلَأُ مَا عَلِمْتُ لَكُمْ مِنْ إِلَٰهٍ غَيْرِي

Firʿawn said "O chiefs! I do not know a god for you other than me..."

A tradition from Imam al-Baqir (a) states that between Firʿawn's statement in the verse above and his boast '*I am your lord, the most high*' there was an interval of forty years.[72] God did not punish him in

---

69 Ṭabāṭabā'ī, *al-Mīzān*, 20/188.

70 Ṭūsī, *al-Tibyān*, 10/258.

71 Ṭabāṭabā'ī, *al-Mīzān*, 20/188.

72 Ṭabrasī, *al-Bayān*, 10/656.

this period despite his shameful claims; this respite was to complete the argument (*itmām al-ḥujjah*) against him.[73]

Another tradition from Imam al-Baqir (a) quoting the Prophet (s) states: Jibraʾil asked, "O Lord, do you leave Firʿawn alone while he says, 'I am your great lord'?" God replied, "Indeed, those who speak like you are the ones who are afraid that their quarry will get away."[74]

15-26.12 *'So God seized him in exemplary punishment in the Hereafter, and in this [former] life.'* [*Nakāl*, (نَكَال,)] is derived from *nakala* and its verbal noun *tankīl* denotes a punishment that discourages anyone who sees or hears it from doing a similar thing.[75]

Nakāl al-ākhirah refers to the chastisement of Firʿawn in the Hereafter and *nakāl al-ūlā* refers to the punishment in this world.[76]

Firʿawn was seized by a punishment that will serve as a lesson for all time: in the Hereafter he will lead a group into Hell, while in this world, he and his hosts were drowned in the sea.[77] And God preserved his body for people to be continually reminded of his fate.

Q10:92 states:

فَالْيَوْمَ نُنَجِّيكَ بِبَدَنِكَ لِتَكُونَ لِمَنْ خَلْفَكَ آيَةً

So today We will save you in your body
that you may be a sign for those who come after you...

Some exegetes are of the opinion that since *nakāl* is a punishment that serves as an example, it refers to punishment in this world. They say that the punishment was for his persistent claims to divinity. *Al-ākhirah* refers to his later claims and *al-ūlā* to his earlier ones. In this case, the verse would mean, 'so God seized him in exemplary punishment for what he said later, and what he said earlier.'[78]

---

73 Shīrāzī, *Namūneh*, 26/93.

74 Majlisī, *Biḥār*, 13/129.

عَنِ الْبَاقِرِ (عَلَيْهِ السَّلَامُ) – قَالَ رَسُولُ اللهِ صَلَّى اللهُ عَلَيْهِ وَآلِهِ: قَالَ جَبْرَائِيلُ قُلْتُ يَا رَبِّ تَدْعُ فِرْعَوْنَ وَقَدْ قَالَ «أَنَا رَبُّكُمُ الْأَعْلَىٰ» فَقَالَ إِنَّمَا يَقُولُ هَذَا مِثْلُكَ مَنْ يَخَافُ الْفَوْتَ.

75 Muṣṭafawī, *al-Taḥqīq*.

76 Ṭabāṭabāʾī, *al-Mīzān*, 20/189.

77 Shīrāzī, *Namūneh*, 26/94.

78 Ibid.

15-26.13 *'Indeed, in that is a lesson for whoever would fear [God].'*: [*Dhālika* (ذَٰلِكَ, that)] refers to the fate of Firᶜawn due to his defiance of God's Messenger (a).[79]

[*ᶜIbrah* (عِبْرَةً, lesson)] is derived from *ᶜabara* which means to cross from one side to another. Here it means a lesson or warning that allows one to cross from ignorance to knowledge, and thereby distinguish truth from falsehood.[80]

[*Yakhshā* (يَخْشَىٰ, he fears)]. Musa (a) had been sent to Firᶜawn to guide him so that he would fear God (verse 19). But because he rejected the guidance, he perished. His example became a lesson for later generations.

The greatest lesson from the rise and fall of Firᶜawn is how he became arrogant and rebellious while using God's bounties, rather than showing gratitude and servitude. The comment of Musa (a) and his invocation against Firᶜawn and his followers is mentioned in Q10:88:

وَقَالَ مُوسَىٰ رَبَّنَا إِنَّكَ آتَيْتَ فِرْعَوْنَ وَمَلَأَهُ زِينَةً وَأَمْوَالًا فِي الْحَيَاةِ الدُّنْيَا
رَبَّنَا لِيُضِلُّوا عَنْ سَبِيلِكَ رَبَّنَا اطْمِسْ عَلَىٰ أَمْوَالِهِمْ وَاشْدُدْ عَلَىٰ قُلُوبِهِمْ
فَلَا يُؤْمِنُوا حَتَّىٰ يَرَوُا الْعَذَابَ الْأَلِيمَ

And Musa said: Our Lord, indeed, You have given Firᶜawn and his chiefs splendour and riches in the life of this world, our Lord, so that they may lead [people] astray from Your way. Our Lord, obliterate their wealth and harden their hearts so that they will not believe until they see the painful punishment.

This lesson is for everyone to learn from. However, it would only benefit the one who fears God and is God-wary.

SUMMARY OF THE VERSES

In a few short phrases, these verses describe the early part of the mission of Prophet Musa (a). They talk of his appointment at *Ṭuwā* and the directive to go to the great transgressor Firᶜawn, and invite him to purify himself and allow Musa (a) to guide him to his Lord.

---

79 Ṭabrasī, *al-Bayān*, 10/656.

80 Ṭūsī, *al-Tibyān*, 10/259.

Thereafter, the verses describe Firʿawn's response. Despite being shown a great miracle, he turned away in defiance and plotted his response. He summoned his magicians and reminded them that he was their great lord.

As a result, he was seized by God's punishment both in this world and the next. And in this is an example for everyone who fears God.

REFLECTIVE LEARNING

Prophet Musa (a) informed Firʿawn that he would guide him to his Lord, but only if Firʿawn was willing to purify himself.

Let me reflect on how I can purify myself further so that the Qur'an and sunnah can guide me closer to my Lord.

PART 3: VERSES 27 - 46

TEXT AND TRANSLATION

أَأَنْتُمْ أَشَدُّ خَلْقًا أَمِ السَّمَاءُ بَنَاهَا ﴿٢٧﴾ رَفَعَ سَمْكَهَا فَسَوَّاهَا ﴿٢٨﴾ وَأَغْطَشَ
لَيْلَهَا وَأَخْرَجَ ضُحَاهَا ﴿٢٩﴾ وَالْأَرْضَ بَعْدَ ذَٰلِكَ دَحَاهَا ﴿٣٠﴾ أَخْرَجَ مِنْهَا
مَاءَهَا وَمَرْعَاهَا ﴿٣١﴾ وَالْجِبَالَ أَرْسَاهَا ﴿٣٢﴾ مَتَاعًا لَكُمْ وَلِأَنْعَامِكُمْ ﴿٣٣﴾
فَإِذَا جَاءَتِ الطَّامَّةُ الْكُبْرَىٰ ﴿٣٤﴾ يَوْمَ يَتَذَكَّرُ الْإِنْسَانُ مَا سَعَىٰ ﴿٣٥﴾ وَبُرِّزَتِ
الْجَحِيمُ لِمَنْ يَرَىٰ ﴿٣٦﴾ فَأَمَّا مَنْ طَغَىٰ ﴿٣٧﴾ وَآثَرَ الْحَيَاةَ الدُّنْيَا ﴿٣٨﴾ فَإِنَّ
الْجَحِيمَ هِيَ الْمَأْوَىٰ ﴿٣٩﴾ وَأَمَّا مَنْ خَافَ مَقَامَ رَبِّهِ وَنَهَى النَّفْسَ عَنِ الْهَوَىٰ
﴿٤٠﴾ فَإِنَّ الْجَنَّةَ هِيَ الْمَأْوَىٰ ﴿٤١﴾ يَسْأَلُونَكَ عَنِ السَّاعَةِ أَيَّانَ مُرْسَاهَا ﴿٤٢﴾
فِيمَ أَنْتَ مِنْ ذِكْرَاهَا ﴿٤٣﴾ إِلَىٰ رَبِّكَ مُنْتَهَاهَا ﴿٤٤﴾ إِنَّمَا أَنْتَ مُنْذِرُ مَنْ يَخْشَاهَا
﴿٤٥﴾ كَأَنَّهُمْ يَوْمَ يَرَوْنَهَا لَمْ يَلْبَثُوا إِلَّا عَشِيَّةً أَوْ ضُحَاهَا ﴿٤٦﴾

Are you harder to create or is the heaven? He (God) constructed it. [27] *He raised its ceiling and proportioned it.* [28] *And he made dark its night and brought out its radiance [in the day].* [29] *And after that He spread the earth.* [30] *He brought forth from it its water and its pasture.* [31] *And he set the mountains firmly.* [32] *A provision for you and your livestock.* [33] *But when the greatest overwhelming Calamity (the Day of Recompense) comes.* [34] *A Day when man will remember what he strove for,* [35] *And hellfire will be exposed for those who [can] see.* [36] *Then for him who transgressed,* [37] *and preferred the life of this world,* [38] *then indeed, hellfire will be his abode.* [39] *But as for he who feared the station of his Lord and restrained the soul from base desires,* [40] *then indeed, Paradise will be his abode.* [41] *They ask you [O Muhammad], about the Hour: when will it come?* [42] *In what [position] are you that you should speak of it?* [43] *To your Lord belongs [the knowledge of] its ultimate term.* [44] *You are only a warner for those who fear it.* [45] *It will be, on the Day that they see it, as though they have not remained [in their former lives] except for an afternoon or a morning thereof.* [46]

VERSES 27 - 33

أَأَنْتُمْ أَشَدُّ خَلْقًا أَمِ السَّمَاءُ بَنَاهَا ﴿٢٧﴾ رَفَعَ سَمْكَهَا فَسَوَّاهَا ﴿٢٨﴾ وَأَغْطَشَ لَيْلَهَا
وَأَخْرَجَ ضُحَاهَا ﴿٢٩﴾ وَالْأَرْضَ بَعْدَ ذَٰلِكَ دَحَاهَا ﴿٣٠﴾ أَخْرَجَ مِنْهَا مَاءَهَا
وَمَرْعَاهَا ﴿٣١﴾ وَالْجِبَالَ أَرْسَاهَا ﴿٣٢﴾ مَتَاعًا لَكُمْ وَلِأَنْعَامِكُمْ ﴿٣٣﴾

Are you harder to create or is the heaven? He (God) constructed it. [27] *He raised its ceiling and proportioned it.* [28] *And he made dark its night and brought out its radiance [in the day].* [29] *And after that He spread the earth.* [30] *He brought forth from it its water and its pasture.* [31] *And he set the mountains firmly.* [32] *A provision for you and your livestock.* [33]

27-33.1 *'Are you harder to create or is the heaven? He (God) constructed it.'*: [*Ashaddu khalqan* (أَشَدُّ خَلْقًا, harder to create)]. The question of anything being more difficult to do does not apply to God. Therefore, here the word 'harder' means grander and more complex.

After the mention of the defiance of Firʿawn and his fate as an example and a warning for those who would deny the Resurrection and Day of Judgement, a rhetorical question is asked to the idolaters:[81] Can the creation of man be compared to the complexity and vast creation of the heavens and the earth? This question has been answered in Q40:57:

[81] Ṭabāṭabā'ī, *al-Mīzān*, 20/189.

لَخَلْقُ السَّمَاوَاتِ وَالْأَرْضِ أَكْبَرُ مِنْ خَلْقِ النَّاسِ وَلَٰكِنَّ أَكْثَرَ النَّاسِ لَا يَعْلَمُونَ

The creation of the heavens and the earth is greater than the creation of mankind, but most of mankind do not know.

According to some exegetes, the creation of man here refers to their resurrection after their death.[82] It is a reply to the mocking of the idolaters mentioned in the earlier verses of this surah, when they asked, "*Will we indeed be returned to [our] former state of life? Even after we are rotted bones?*" God reminds man of the grandeur of the creation that they witness as a proof of His ability to resurrect them in a world of the Hereafter, which they have not yet seen.[83]

27-33.2 [*Al-Samā*ʾ (السَّمَاء, the heaven)]. The term is derived from *samawa*, meaning that which is towards the sky, or something raised high above other things and covering them.[84] Here, it refers to the universe created by God above and beyond the earth.

[*Banāhā* (بَنَاهَا, He constructed it)]. God reminds man that He has constructed the heaven, with its countless stars and galaxies, that they see around them. And when He has created something so much grander than man, He is quite capable of bringing them back to life.[85] Q36:81 states:

أَوَلَيْسَ الَّذِي خَلَقَ السَّمَاوَاتِ وَالْأَرْضَ بِقَادِرٍ عَلَىٰ أَنْ يَخْلُقَ مِثْلَهُمْ
بَلَىٰ وَهُوَ الْخَلَّاقُ الْعَلِيمُ

Is not He who created the heavens and the earth able to create the likes of them? Yes, indeed! And He is the supreme Creator, the all-Knowing.

27-33.3 *'He raised its ceiling and proportioned it.'*: [*Samkaha* (سَمْكَهَا, its ceiling)]. *Samk* refers to the roof or highest elevation of something, in contrast to *ʿumq* which refers to its depth. 'Raised the ceiling' of the heaven refers to the expansive reach of the universe that God has created.[86]

---

[82] Ṭabrasī, *al-Bayān*, 10/659.
[83] Shīrāzī, *Namūneh*, 26/98.
[84] Muṣṭafawī, *al-Taḥqīq*.
[85] Ṭabāṭabāʾī, *al-Mīzān*, 20/190.
[86] Rāzī, *Mafātīḥ al-Ghayb*, 31/45.

[*Sawwāhā* (سَوَّاهَا, proportioned it)]. The verb *sawwā* is derived from *sawiya* which means to be equal, and its verbal noun *taswiyah* means to organize, proportion, and perfect the make of something. Referring to the heaven, it means that every aspect of it has been created to perform its function perfectly.[87]

27-33.4 *'And he made dark its night and brought out its radiance [in the day].'*: [*Aghṭasha* (أَغْطَشَ, made dark)]. This refers to the darkening of the night making it difficult to see clearly.

[*Ḍuḥāhā* (ضُحَاهَا, its radiance)]. *Ḍuḥā* refers to the early hours of the morning when the sun begins to rise into the sky and its radiance spreads out. Here it refers to the day itself, which is contrasted to the night. And the night and day have been attributed to the heaven because they occur on earth (and throughout the universe)[88] due to the movement of the planets in respect to their respective suns.

We have discussed the vital role of darkness and light in the life of all creatures on the earth in the *tafsīr* of Surat al-Layl (92).

27-33.5 *'And after that He spread the earth.'*: [*Baʿda dhālika* (بَعْدَ ذَٰلِكَ, after that)]. Some exegetes have said that the verse does not mean that God created the earth after He created the heavens. Rather, *baʿda dhālika* here means *maʿa dhālika* (with that). In this case, the verse would mean, 'and moreover, He spread the earth.' This is similar to the usage in Q68:13 which describes a slanderer:

عُتُلٍّ بَعْدَ ذَٰلِكَ زَنِيمٍ

[He is] harsh, and besides that, an illegitimate pretender.

[*Daḥahā* (دَحَاهَا, He spread it)] is derived from *daḥw* meaning to expand and spread out.[89] Here it denotes facilitating the habitation of human beings on earth. The spreading of the land, from below the Kaʿbah, is called *daḥw al-arḍ*, and is marked on the day of 24th of Dhū al-Qaʿdah.[90]

---

[87] Ṭabāṭabā'ī, *al-Mīzān*, 20/190.

[88] Ibid.

[89] Ibn Manẓūr, *Lisān al-ʿArab*.

[90] Shīrāzī, *Namūneh*, 27/43.

27-33.6 *'He brought forth from it its water and its pasture.'*: The earth was made such that it yielded water through springs, rivers and other watercourses. A marvellous system of rain from the sky and water in the land makes up the water-cycle that provides a continual supply of life-sustaining water to the earth and its inhabitants.

[*Marʿāhā* (مَرْعَاهَا, its pasture)]. *Marʿā* is grassland where animals graze. The term is derived from *raʿā*, which means to tend animals. Pasture here may include all kind of plants that are consumed by both man and animals.[91] It has been used in this meaning in Q12:12:

أَرْسِلْهُ مَعَنَا غَدًا يَرْتَعْ وَيَلْعَبْ

Send him (Yusuf) with us tomorrow
that he may eat (yartaʿ) *and play...*

27-33.7 *'And he set the mountains firmly.'*: The firm mountains stabilize the earth, allowing it to store water in its expanses. We have discussed the role of the mountains in the *tafsīr* of Surat al-Naba' (78).

27-33.8 *'A provision for you and your livestock.'*: [*Matāʿ* (مَتَاع, provision)] means something that gives long lasting benefit.[92] Everything that has been mentioned in the previous verses – the canopy of the heaven, the darkness of night and light of day, the water and vegetation, and the stability provided by the mountains – is provision that vitally benefits human and animal life on earth.

This harmonious arrangement that facilitates his life encourages man to ponder about his Creator, to be in awe of His station (*maqām*), and to give thanks for His innumerable bounties.[93]

SUMMARY OF THE VERSES

The verses describe how the creation of the universe is much grander than the creation of man. As a provision for man and the animals that he domesticates, as well as all the other creatures, God created a harmonious system that gives a canopy to the earth, brings about night and day, makes available water and pasture, and protects the earth with strong mountains.

---

91 Rāzī, *Mafātīḥ al-Ghayb*, 31/47.

92 Rāghib, *al-Mufradāt.*

93 Ṭabāṭabā'ī, *al-Mīzān*, 20/191.

REFLECTIVE LEARNING

Let me reflect on how much simpler my creation was compared to the creation of the vast heavens.

Let me look at the many celestial signs in the night sky and be reminded of my humble position in creation.

VERSES 34 - 39

فَإِذَا جَاءَتِ الطَّامَّةُ الْكُبْرَىٰ ﴿٣٤﴾ يَوْمَ يَتَذَكَّرُ الْإِنسَانُ مَا سَعَىٰ ﴿٣٥﴾ وَبُرِّزَتِ الْجَحِيمُ لِمَن يَرَىٰ ﴿٣٦﴾ فَأَمَّا مَن طَغَىٰ ﴿٣٧﴾ وَآثَرَ الْحَيَاةَ الدُّنْيَا ﴿٣٨﴾ فَإِنَّ الْجَحِيمَ هِيَ الْمَأْوَىٰ ﴿٣٩﴾

But when the greatest overwhelming Calamity (the Day of Recompense) comes. [34] *A Day when man will remember what he strove for.* [35] *And hellfire will be exposed for those who [can] see.* [36] *Then for him who transgressed,* [37] *and preferred the life of this world,* [38] *then indeed, hellfire will be his abode.* [39]

34-39.1 *'But when the greatest overwhelming Calamity (the Day of Recompense) comes.'*: After a brief mention of the Hereafter in the earlier part of the surah, the arrangements made for man's transitory sojourn on earth were discussed. Now the subject of man's real life, which awaits him in the Hereafter, is revisited – this time contrasting the fates of the transgressors and the righteous.

[*Al-ṭāmmat al-kubrā* (الطَّامَّةُ الْكُبْرَىٰ, the greatest overwhelming Calamity)]. *Ṭāmmah* is derived from *ṭāmm* which means to fill and overwhelm, and is used for the Day of Judgement because it is full of the greatest difficulties.[94] *Ṭāmmah* also means a grievous incident that overwhelms the one who is exposed to it. The Day of Judgement will exceed any catastrophe that man has ever experienced, and that is why the adjective *kubrā* (greatest) is attached to it.[95]

34-39.2 *'A Day when man will remember what he strove for.'*: [*Yatadhakkar* (يَتَذَكَّر, he will remember)] is mentioned in the continuous tense here, and means that on this Day, as man sees the

[94] Shīrāzī, *Namūneh*, 26/104.

[95] Ṭabāṭabā'ī, *al-Mīzān*, 20/191.

manifestations of his various actions, which have been faithfully recorded, he will be continually reminded about issues that even he had long forgotten. Q58:6 states:

يَوْمَ يَبْعَثُهُمُ اللَّهُ جَمِيعًا فَيُنَبِّئُهُمْ بِمَا عَمِلُوا أَحْصَاهُ اللَّهُ وَنَسُوهُ

On the Day when God will resurrect them all and then inform them of what they did. God had enumerated it, while they forgot it...

This will be the Day when man will realize the true worth of the things that he had strived for in the *dunyā* and the pursuits that had occupied him.[96]

34-39.3 *'And hellfire will be exposed for those who [can] see.'*: [*Jaḥīm* (جَحِيم, hellfire)] refers to an intense fire, or a place of intense fire[97] and it is one of the names of Hell.

[*Burrizat* (بُرِّزَت, will be exposed)] is the past passive form of *baraza*, which means to come into view. On the Day of Judgement, the veils that obscured their sight in the *dunyā* will be torn away and Hell will become clearly visible to them.[98]

[*Liman yarā* (لِمَنْ يَرَىٰ, for those who see)]. This is a reference to the disbelievers and not the believers. Q26:91 states:

وَبُرِّزَتِ الْجَحِيمُ لِلْغَاوِينَ

And hellfire will be exposed to the misguided.

34-39.4 *'Then for him who transgressed, and preferred the life of this world, then indeed, hellfire will be his abode.'*: The fate of the first of two groups is discussed next. They were those who transgressed and exceeded God's bounds. Later verses will discuss those who feared God's station.

[*Ṭaghā* (طَغَىٰ, transgressed)] was the description of Firʿawn mentioned earlier in the surah. Men like him behaved inordinately because they ignored God's guidance and thus did not fear Him (as mentioned in verse 19). They chose to invest all their energy in acquiring the *dunyā* instead of working for the *ākhirah*, and so they will be given an abode in hellfire.

---

[96] Shīrāzī, *Namūneh*, 26/105.

[97] Muṣṭafawī, *al-Taḥqīq*.

[98] Shīrāzī, *Namūneh*, 27/105.

In fact their obsession with the world and the desire for instant gratification was the cause of their transgression.[99]

[*Āthara* (آثَرَ, preferred)] means gave preference to one thing over another, and here it refers to preferring the life of the *dunyā* over the *ākhirah*.[100] *Al-ḥayāt al-dunyā* can also refer to a lower and base form of life, in contrast to *al-ḥayāt al-ākhirah*, which is a noble and virtuous form of life.

[*Ma'wā* (مَأْوَىٰ, abode)] is derived from *awā* which means to seek shelter.[101] Here, *ma'wā* refers to the place where they will be made to live, which is Hell.

SUMMARY OF THE VERSES

The verses mention the Day of Calamity on which everyone will realize the worth of their striving in this world. Hell will become visible to those who should see it. The transgressors, who preferred the life of the *dunyā*, will be given an abode in hellfire.

REFLECTIVE LEARNING

The actual sinful actions of the inmates of Hell are not discussed here, rather the attitude that fuelled their conduct is mentioned. And this attitude is rebellion against God and the preference of the *dunyā* over the *ākhirah*, or preferring a low animal-like existence over a noble and spiritual one. This is a decision that each person makes based on their inner faith and conviction.

Let me reflect on what sort of existence I am living at the moment.

VERSES 40, 41

وَأَمَّا مَنْ خَافَ مَقَامَ رَبِّهِ وَنَهَى النَّفْسَ عَنِ الْهَوَىٰ ﴿٤٠﴾ فَإِنَّ الْجَنَّةَ هِيَ الْمَأْوَىٰ ﴿٤١﴾

But as for he who feared the station of his Lord, and restrained the soul from base desires, [40] *then indeed, Paradise will be his abode.* [41]

---

[99] Ibid.

[100] Ṭabrasī, *al-Bayān*, 10/660.

[101] Muṣṭafawī, *al-Taḥqīq*.

40-41.1 Two qualities of the wrongdoers were mentioned in the previous verses:

1. they transgress, and
2. they prefer the life of this world and follow their base desires.

And these attributes qualify them for Hell.

In contrast, two qualities of the righteous are now mentioned:

1. they fear the station of the Lord, and
2. they restrain the soul from base desires.

Indeed, the consequence of fearing God's station is the restraining of the soul from its base desires. It is this attitude that earns an individual the loftiest abodes in Paradise.

40-41.2 *'But as for he who feared the station of his Lord, and restrained the soul from base desires'*: [*Man khāfa maqām* (مَنْ خَافَ مَقَام, who feared the station]. Fearing the station of God means fearing His questioning about obedience to Him,[102] and His absolute justice when He will judge mankind.[103] And this fear comes from the recognition (*maʿrifah*) of God.[104]

The Qurʾan itself is a source of this *maʿrifah* because God has described His station in many verses. For example, Q15:49,50 state:

نَبِّئْ عِبَادِي أَنِّي أَنَا الْغَفُورُ الرَّحِيمُ ﴿٤٩﴾ وَأَنَّ عَذَابِي هُوَ الْعَذَابُ الْأَلِيمُ

[O Muhammad] inform My servants that indeed, I am the all-Forgiving, the all-Merciful. And that it is My punishment which is the [most] painful punishment.

A tradition from Imam al-Sadiq (a) states that while explaining (Q55:46), '*For the one who feared the station of his Lord...*, he (a) said: Whoever knows that God, the Exalted, sees him, hears what he says, and knows what he does of good or evil, and this forestalls him from committing base acts, then he is the one who '*feared the station of his Lord and restrained the soul from base desires.*'[105]

[102] Ṭūsī, *al-Tibyān*, 10/264.

[103] Muṭahharī, (*Āshnāyī bā Qurʾan*), *Āthār*, 28/349.

[104] Shīrāzī, *Namūneh*, 27/107.

[105] Kulaynī, *al-Kāfī*, 2/80.

عَنِ الصَّادِقِ (عَلَيْهِ السَّلَامُ) - فِي قَوْلِ اللهِ عَزَّ وَجَلَّ «وَلِمَنْ خَافَ مَقَامَ رَبِّهِ جَنَّتَانِ» قَالَ مَنْ عَلِمَ أَنَّ اللهَ عَزَّ وَجَلَّ يَرَاهُ وَيَسْمَعُ مَا يَقُولُهُ وَيَعْلَمُ مَا يَعْمَلُهُ مِنْ خَيْرٍ أَوْ شَرٍّ فَيَحْجُزُهُ ذَلِكَ عَنِ الْقَبِيحِ مِنَ الْأَعْمَالِ فَذَلِكَ الَّذِي « خَافَ مَقَامَ رَبِّهِ وَنَهَى النَّفْسَ عَنِ الْهَوَى»

[*Hawā* (هَوَىٰ, base desires] means any desire, good or bad, but in the context of this verse it refers to the base desires of the soul that pull man towards the material allure of this world, and thus keep him away from the remembrance of God and make him transgress His bounds. Q18:28 states:

وَلَا تُطِعْ مَنْ أَغْفَلْنَا قَلْبَهُ عَن ذِكْرِنَا وَٱتَّبَعَ هَوَاهُ وَكَانَ أَمْرُهُ فُرُطًا

...And do not obey one whose heart We have made heedless of Our remembrance and who follows his base desires and whose affair has exceeded bounds.

40-41.3 Man has been created weak, and even believers are unable to completely avoid the call of the base desires of the soul, even though they do not intend to defy God. For this reason, the verse talks of the reward of constant vigilance and restraint of the lower self, rather than absolute control over the lower self.[106]

In this regard, a supplication from Imam al-Sajjad (a) states: My God, even as I disobeyed You, I never denied Your Lordship, never belittled Your commands, never wished to expose myself to Your chastisement, and never disparaged Your threat.[107]

The one who strives hard to be obedient to God takes solace from God's infinite mercy and forgiveness. Q53:32 states:

الَّذِينَ يَجْتَنِبُونَ كَبَائِرَ الْإِثْمِ وَالْفَوَاحِشَ إِلَّا اللَّمَمَ إِنَّ رَبَّكَ وَاسِعُ الْمَغْفِرَةِ

Those who avoid the major sins and shameful deeds, except small faults, [then] indeed, your Lord is vast in forgiveness.

40-41.4 About restraining oneself from obeying the base desires of the soul, a tradition from the Prophet (s) states: God, the Blessed and Exalted, has sworn, "By My Honour, My Majesty, My Glory, My Light, My Greatness, My Loftiness, and My Elevated Station, no servant will prefer his desire over My command except that I will confound his affair and make his life difficult. I will make his heart engrossed in the world (*dunyā*) and he will not receive from it anything except what I have apportioned for him of it.

---

[106] Ṭabāṭabā'ī, *al-Mīzān*, 20/192.

[107] Ṭūsī, *Miṣbāh al-Mutahajjid*, pp. 582-598, *Du'ā' Abū Hamzah al-Thumālī*.

إِلٰهِي لَمْ أَعْصِكَ حِينَ عَصَيْتُكَ وَأَنَا بِرُبُوبِيَّتِكَ جَاحِدٌ وَلَا بِأَمْرِكَ مُسْتَخِفٌّ وَلَا لِعُقُوبَتِكَ مُتَعَرِّضٌ وَلَا لِوَعِيدِكَ مُتَهَاوِنٌ.

And by My Honour, My Majesty, My Glory, My Light, My Greatness, My Loftiness, and My Elevated Station, no servant will prefer My command over his desire except that I will assign My angels to protect him and make the heavens and the earth guarantors of his sustenance. I will secure his interest in the business of every trader and will humble the world (*dunyā*) before him."[108]

40-41.5 *'Then indeed, Paradise will be his abode.'*: The reward for this group shall be an abode in Paradise.

SUMMARY OF THE VERSES

These verses mention, in contrast, the recompense of those who feared the station of God, and restrained their souls from obeying lowly desires. They will be rewarded with an abode in Paradise.

REFLECTIVE LEARNING

Let me examine what fear keeps me away from sin. Is it fear of God's punishment in this world and the next, or the judgement of others if they find out my evil acts?

While these two fears may deter us from sin some of the time, the only way to remain continually free from sin is to truly fear the station of God. And that comes from cognizance (*maʿrifah*) of Him.

Let me reflect on how I can progress to fear God's station above everything else.

VERSES 42 - 46

يَسْأَلُونَكَ عَنِ السَّاعَةِ أَيَّانَ مُرْسَاهَا ﴿٤٢﴾ فِيمَ أَنْتَ مِنْ ذِكْرَاهَا ﴿٤٣﴾ إِلَىٰ رَبِّكَ
مُنْتَهَاهَا ﴿٤٤﴾ إِنَّمَا أَنْتَ مُنذِرُ مَنْ يَخْشَاهَا ﴿٤٥﴾ كَأَنَّهُمْ يَوْمَ يَرَوْنَهَا لَمْ يَلْبَثُوا إِلَّا
عَشِيَّةً أَوْ ضُحَاهَا ﴿٤٦﴾

108 Kulaynī, *al-Kāfī*, 2/335.

عَنِ الرَّسُولِ (صَلَّى اللهُ عَلَيْهِ وَآلِهِ) - يَقُولُ اللهُ عَزَّ وَجَلَّ وَعِزَّتِي وَجَلَالِي وَعَظَمَتِي وَكِبْرِيَائِي وَنُورِي وَعُلُوِّي وَارْتِفَاعِ مَكَانِي لَا يُؤْثِرُ عَبْدٌ هَوَاهُ عَلَى هَوَايَ إِلَّا شَتَّتُّ عَلَيْهِ أَمْرَهُ وَلَبَّسْتُ عَلَيْهِ دُنْيَاهُ وَشَغَّلْتُ قَلْبَهُ بِهَا وَلَمْ أُؤْتِهِ مِنْهَا إِلَّا مَا قَدَّرْتُ لَهُ وَعِزَّتِي وَجَلَالِي وَعَظَمَتِي وَنُورِي وَعُلُوِّي وَارْتِفَاعِ مَكَانِي لَا يُؤْثِرُ عَبْدٌ هَوَايَ عَلَى هَوَاهُ إِلَّا اسْتَحْفَظْتَهُ مَلَائِكَتِي وَكَفَّلْتُ السَّمَاوَاتِ وَالْأَرَضِينَ رِزْقَهُ وَكُنْتُ لَهُ مِنْ وَرَاءِ تِجَارَةِ كُلِّ تَاجِرٍ وَأَتَتْهُ الدُّنْيَا وَهِيَ رَاغِمَةٌ.

They ask you [O Muhammad], about the Hour: when will it come? [42] *In what [position] are you that you should speak of it?* [43] *To your Lord belongs [the knowledge of] its ultimate term.* [44] *You are only a warner for those who fear it.* [45] *It will be, on the Day that they see it, as though they have not remained [in their former lives] except for an afternoon or a morning thereof.* [46]

42-46.1 *'They ask you [O Muhammad], about the Hour: when will it come?'*: [*Al-Sāʿah* (السَّاعَة, the Hour)]. *Sāʿah* is defined as a short period of time or an hour. When used in the definite sense, *al-sāʿah*, it refers to the Final Hour or the Day of Judgement.[109]

[*Mursāhā* (مُرْسَاهَا, it will come)] is derived from *irsā* which means anchorage or coming to rest. Here, 'it will come' means 'it will be established'.[110]

Whenever the idolaters and disbelievers were reminded of the Day of Judgement by the Prophets (a) of God, their common response was to ask when that Day would come.[111]

The use of the continuous tense (*yasʾalūnaka*, they ask you) in the verse under review shows that the idolaters of Makka continually asked the Prophet (s) about this as well. They did not believe in a Day of Judgement, so they defiantly challenged him to ask God to bring it about. Q42:18 states:

يَسْتَعْجِلُ بِهَا الَّذِينَ لَا يُؤْمِنُونَ بِهَا وَالَّذِينَ آمَنُوا مُشْفِقُونَ مِنْهَا
وَيَعْلَمُونَ أَنَّهَا الْحَقُّ أَلَا إِنَّ الَّذِينَ يُمَارُونَ فِي السَّاعَةِ لَفِي ضَلَالٍ بَعِيدٍ

Those who do not believe in it seek to hasten it, but those who believe are fearful of it and know that it is the truth. Indeed, those who dispute concerning the Hour are in great error.

42-46.2 *'In what [position] are you that you should speak of it?'*: Amongst the characteristics of the Final Hour is the fact that no one, not even the Prophet (s), knows when it will occur. However, he (s) repeatedly warned the people that its time was nearer than they imagined.

---

109 Rāghib, *al-Mufradāt.*

110 Ṭabāṭabāʾī, *al-Mīzān*, 20/196.

111 Shīrāzī, *Namūneh*, 26/113.

A tradition from the Prophet (s) states that he said, "O nation of Muslims! The time I was commissioned to my mission and the time of the Hour are just [as close] as this", then he (s) held up two of his fingers joined together.[112]

Indeed, the arrival of that momentous Day will be sooner than people expect. Q70:6,7 state:

إِنَّهُمْ يَرَوْنَهُ بَعِيدًا ﴿٦﴾ وَنَرَاهُ قَرِيبًا

Indeed, they see it [as] distant, but We see it [as] near.

Some exegetes translate the verse as, '*What [knowledge of its time] will you gain by constantly remembering it?*',[113] indicating that the timing of the Day of the Judgement did not have a bearing on the mission of the Prophet (s).

42-46.3 *'To your Lord belongs [the knowledge of] its ultimate term.'*: The timing of the Final Hour is from the knowledge of the unseen known only to God and the affair ends with Him. Q7:187 states:

يَسْأَلُونَكَ عَنِ السَّاعَةِ أَيَّانَ مُرْسَاهَا قُلْ إِنَّمَا عِلْمُهَا عِنْدَ رَبِّي
لَا يُجَلِّيهَا لِوَقْتِهَا إِلَّا هُوَ

They ask you [O Muhammad], about the Hour: when will it come? Say, "Its knowledge is only with my Lord. None will reveal its time except Him..."

42-46.4 *'You are only a warner for those who fear it.'*: The role of the Prophet (s) was only to warn the people that the Final Hour would come, and it was not necessary for him to know when this would happen.[114] However, God states that this warning would only be an effective reminder for those who fear the accounting and judgement of that Day. Indeed, guidance will only be heeded by those who are initially prepared to receive it.

Q2:2 states

ذَٰلِكَ الْكِتَابُ لَا رَيْبَ فِيهِ هُدًى لِلْمُتَّقِينَ

[112] Nūrī, *Mustadrak al-Wasā'il*, 12/324.

عَنِ الرَّسُولِ (صَلَّى اللهُ عَلَيْهِ وَآلِهِ) – يَا مَعْشَرَ الْمُسْلِمِينَ إِنِّي إِنَّمَا بُعِثْتُ أَنَا وَالسَّاعَةُ كَهَاتَيْنِ قَالَ ثُمَّ ضَمَّ السَّبَّاحَتَيْنِ.

[113] Ṭabāṭabā'ī, *al-Mīzān*, 20/195.

[114] Rāzī, *Mafātīḥ al-Ghayb*, 31/51.

This is the Book about which there is no doubt,
a guidance for the God-wary.

42-46.5 *'It will be, on the Day that they see it, as though they have not remained [in their former lives] except for an afternoon or a morning thereof.'*: When human beings are resurrected in the Hereafter it seems that there will be much disagreement and confusion about the length of their previous lives in the world, in *barzakh*, and in the period between the two blowings of the trumpet. The Qur'an quotes some of these opinions. Some will say it was just ten days (Q20:103), others will say it was one day (Q20:104), and yet others will think it was just one hour of the day (Q46:35).

However, what is clear is that everyone will feel that the duration of their previous lives was fleeting and inconsequential. The verse under review states that it will appear as if it was just part of one day.

Perhaps this is due to the enhanced awareness and realization that comes to everyone on that Day, making everything they experienced before seem like a mere slumber. When one wakes from a long sleep, it is not possible to appreciate its duration. For example, the people of the cave were asleep for 309 years (Q18:25), while Prophet ʿUzayr (a) was dead for 100 years (Q2:259), yet in both cases they reckoned that they had only been unconscious for part of a day.

SUMMARY OF THE VERSES

In summary, the verses state that the timing of the Day of Judgement is only known to God, and not even the Prophet (s) knows when it will occur. He (s) is only instructed to warn about the impending arrival of that Day to those who fear its consequences.

When the Day comes, it will seem to everyone that the duration of their previous lives was but part of a day.

REFLECTIVE LEARNING

There are certain matters that are known only to God, and not even the Prophet (s) had knowledge of them. Despite this, he had conviction about their truth due to his knowledge of God.

Let me reflect on my own reluctance to accept things that I have no knowledge about due to my lack of knowledge of God.

SURAT ʿABASA
HE FROWNED (80)

PART 1: VERSES 1 - 16

TEXT AND TRANSLATION

سُورَةُ عَبَسَ

بِسْمِ اللهِ الرَّحْمٰنِ الرَّحِيمِ

عَبَسَ وَتَوَلَّىٰ ﴿١﴾ أَنْ جَاءَهُ الْأَعْمَىٰ ﴿٢﴾ وَمَا يُدْرِيكَ لَعَلَّهُ يَزَّكَّىٰ ﴿٣﴾ أَوْ يَذَّكَّرُ فَتَنْفَعَهُ الذِّكْرَىٰ ﴿٤﴾ أَمَّا مَنِ اسْتَغْنَىٰ ﴿٥﴾ فَأَنْتَ لَهُ تَصَدَّىٰ ﴿٦﴾ وَمَا عَلَيْكَ أَلَّا يَزَّكَّىٰ ﴿٧﴾ وَأَمَّا مَنْ جَاءَكَ يَسْعَىٰ ﴿٨﴾ وَهُوَ يَخْشَىٰ ﴿٩﴾ فَأَنْتَ عَنْهُ تَلَهَّىٰ ﴿١٠﴾ كَلَّا إِنَّهَا تَذْكِرَةٌ ﴿١١﴾ فَمَنْ شَاءَ ذَكَرَهُ ﴿١٢﴾ فِي صُحُفٍ مُكَرَّمَةٍ ﴿١٣﴾ مَرْفُوعَةٍ مُطَهَّرَةٍ ﴿١٤﴾ بِأَيْدِي سَفَرَةٍ ﴿١٥﴾ كِرَامٍ بَرَرَةٍ ﴿١٦﴾

In the name of God, the Beneficent, the Merciful.

He frowned and turned away. [1] Because there came to him the blind man. [2] But what would make you perceive that perhaps he might purify [himself]? [3] Or be reminded, and that the reminder would benefit him? [4] As for he who thinks himself without need, [5] to him you give attention, [6] though there is no blame on you if he does not purify [himself]. [7] But as for he who came to you striving [earnestly], [8] while he fears [God], [9] of him you are unmindful. [10] Not at all! Indeed, these verses are a reminder. [11] So whoever wills, will remember it. [12] [It is recorded] in honoured scrolls. [13] Exalted, purified. [14] [Carried] by the hands of messenger-angels. [15] Noble, righteous. [16]

INTRODUCTION

Surat ʿAbasa (80) was the 24th chapter to be revealed.[1] It has forty-two verses and was revealed in Makka, after Surat al-Najm (53). It is also called Surat al-Safarah (group of messenger-angels or scribes) after the mention of the term in verse 14.

This chapter, like many of the early Makkan surahs, contains a reminder of the Day of Judgement. The first ten verses of the surah are a criticism of the discourteous and impatient treatment of one believer to another believer who was poor and handicapped. Thereafter, there is a mention of the exalted station of the Qur'an, the consequence of ungratefulness for God's blessings, and the bounties of fruits and vegetation that God has provided for man to use, and for which he should give thanks.

Finally, the surah discusses the Day of Judgement and the contrasting fates of human beings on that Day.

God's rebuke of the believer is out of His love and is meant to encourage him to adopt better *akhlāq* which is why he speaks of it first. His rebuke to the disbelievers comes later in the surah, as a warning to those who would repudiate the message of the Prophet (s)

LINK TO THE PREVIOUS CHAPTER

The previous chapter, Surat al-Nāziʿāt, spoke of the role of the Prophet (s) as a warner to the people. Surat ʿAbasa begins with a description of an episode where the Prophet (s) is performing this role.

Surat al-Nāziʿāt ends by informing the Prophet (s) that he is only a warner to those who fear the Day of Judgement. Surat ʿAbasa begins with rebuking a believer for imagining that the Prophet's (s) time would be better spent with those who had no fear of the Day of Judgement, rather than with a believer.

Both Surat al-Nāziʿāt (verse 33) and Surat ʿAbasa (verse 32) have the same phrase: '*A provision for you and your livestock.*' with a more detailed description of God's provision (*matāʿ*) given in Surat ʿAbasa.

---

[1] Maʿrifat, *ʿUlūm-i Qur'ānī*, p. 90.

MERITS OF RECITATION

- A tradition from the Prophet (s) states: Whoever recites Surat ʿAbasa [continually and with mindfulness] will come on the Day of Judgement with a smiling and happy face.[2]
- A tradition from Imam al-Sadiq (a) states: Whoever recites Surat ʿAbasa and Surat al-Takwīr shall be under the protection of God in the Gardens of Paradise and shall reside under His shade and glory in His Paradise. And this is easy for God, if He wills.[3]
- A tradition from Imam al-Sadiq (a) states: Amongst the special merits of Surat ʿAbasa is that the one who recites it as rain is falling will be forgiven by God with every drop that falls until the rain stops.[4]

OCCASION OF REVELATION

There are two views about the occasion of revelation of this chapter and they will be discussed briefly in turn.

1. The opinion of most *Sunni* exegetes[5] is that the verses were revealed to rebuke the Prophet (s) for his conduct towards ʿAbdullah b. Umm Maktūm, a poor and blind companion.

   One tradition states: Ibn Umm Maktūm came to the Prophet (s) while he was sitting with the chieftains of the Quraysh. [Among them were] ʿUtbah b. Rabīʿah and his brother Shaybah, Abū Jahl b. Hishām, al-ʿAbbas b. ʿAbd al-Muṭṭalib, Umayyah b. Khalaf, and al-Walīd b. al-Mughīrah. The Prophet (s) was inviting them to Islam in the hope that others would become Muslims once these people accepted Islam. He (ʿAbdullah) said to the Prophet (s), "Recite for me, and teach me something from what God has taught you." He

---

[2] Nūrī, *Mustadrak al-Wasāʾil*, 4/356.

عَنِ الرَّسُولِ (صَلَّى اللهُ عَلَيْهِ وَآلِهِ) — مَنْ قَرَأَ سُورَةَ عَبَسَ جَاءَ يَوْمَ الْقِيَامَةِ وَوَجْهُهُ ضَاحِكٌ مُسْتَبْشِرٌ.

[3] Ṣadūq, *Thawāb al-Aʿmāl*, p. 121.

عَنِ الصَّادِقِ (عَلَيْهِ السَّلَامُ) - مَنْ قَرَأَ سُورَةَ عَبَسَ وَتَوَلَّى وَإِذَا الشَّمْسُ كُوِّرَتْ كَانَ تَحْتَ جَنَاحِ اللهِ مِنَ الْجِنَانِ وَفِي ظِلِّ اللهِ وَكَرَامَتِهِ فِي جِنَانِهِ وَلَا يَعْظُمُ ذَلِكَ عَلَى اللهِ إِنْ شَاءَ اللهُ.

[4] Nūrī, *Mustadrak al-Wasāʾil*, 6/210.

عَنِ الصَّادِقِ (عَلَيْهِ السَّلَامُ) — فِي خَوَاصِّ سُورَةِ عَبَسَ مَنْ قَرَأَهَا وَقْتَ نُزُولِ الْغَيْثِ غَفَرَ اللهُ لَهُ بِكُلِّ قَطْرَةٍ إِلَى وَقْتِ فَرَاغِهِ.

[5] For example: Ṭabarī, *Tafsīr*, 12/32; Ibn Kathīr, *Tafsīr*, 4/738; Ālūsī, *Rūḥ al-Maʿānī*, 30/39; Suyūṭī, *Durr al-Manthūr*, 6/315; Rāzī, *Mafātīḥ al-Ghayb*, 31/52. The latter claims that there is a consensus (*ijmaʿ*) on this opinion.

repeated his request several times. The Prophet (s) became annoyed at his continual interruption, and frowned and turned away from him. At this time, these verses were revealed.

[Thereafter,] the Prophet (s) would always honour him and say, "Welcome, O one about whom my Lord rebuked me." He would ask him, "Have you any need?" And twice, he appointed him as his representative in Madina in his absence.[6]

Those who hold this view have given several excuses for the uncharacteristic and unbecoming behaviour that they have attributed to the Prophet (s):

i) That the Prophet (s) was trying to convince powerful leaders of the Quraysh, in the sincere belief that if he was successful in calling them to Islam, they would in turn be able to influence many others. The arrival of Ibn Umm Maktūm was ill-timed and the Prophet (s) was concerned that these leaders would leave if they saw the kind of people who gathered around him, and thus this opportunity would be lost.[7]

   However, this assumes that the end justifies the means. Further-more, it implies that the Prophet (s) was willing to give preference to a group based on their wealth and status, while showing impatience with a believer who was disabled. Both these actions are contrary to the message that the Prophet (s) had brought.

ii) Mawdūdī writes in this regard, "When a caller to Truth embarks on his mission of conveying his message to the people, he naturally wants the most influential people of society to accept his message so that his task might become easy, for even if his invitation spreads among the poor and the weak, it cannot make much difference... But Allah made him realize that that was not the correct method of extending the invitation to Islam."[8]

---

[6] Rāzī, *Mafātīḥ al-Ghayb*, 31/52.

أَتَى رَسُولَ اللهِ صَلَّى اللهُ عَلَيْهِ وَسَلَّمَ ابْنُ أُمِّ مَكْتُومٍ وَعِنْدَهُ صَنَادِيدُ قُرَيْشٍ عُتْبَةُ وَشَيْبَةُ ابْنَا رَبِيعَةَ وَأَبُو جَهْلِ بْنُ هِشَامٍ، وَالْعَبَّاسُ بْنُ عَبْدِ الْمُطَّلِبِ، وَأُمَيَّةُ بْنُ خَلَفٍ، وَالْوَلِيدُ بْنُ الْمُغِيرَةِ يَدْعُوهُمْ إِلَى الْإِسْلَامِ، رَجَاءَ أَنْ يُسْلِمَ بِإِسْلَامِهِمْ غَيْرُهُمْ، فَقَالَ لِلنَّبِيِّ صَلَّى اللهُ عَلَيْهِ وَسَلَّمَ أَقْرِئْنِي وَعَلِّمْنِي مِمَّا عَلَّمَكَ اللهُ، وَكَرَّرَ ذَلِكَ، فَكَرِهَ رَسُولُ اللهِ صَلَّى اللهُ عَلَيْهِ وَسَلَّمَ قَطْعَهُ لِكَلَامِهِ، وَعَبَسَ وَأَعْرَضَ عَنْهُ فَنَزَلَتْ هَذِهِ الْآيَةُ، وَكَانَ رَسُولُ اللهِ صَلَّى اللهُ عَلَيْهِ وَسَلَّمَ يُكْرِمُهُ، وَيَقُولُ إِذَا رَآهُ: مَرْحَبًا بِمَنْ عَاتَبَنِي فِيهِ رَبِّي وَيَقُولُ: هَلْ لَكَ مِنْ حَاجَةٍ، وَاسْتَخْلَفَهُ عَلَى الْمَدِينَةِ مَرَّتَيْنِ.

[7] Iṣlāḥī, *Tadabbur-i Qur'an*, 9/162.

[8] Mawdūdī, *Tafhīm al-Qur'an* (Urdu), 6/253.

However, it seems unlikely that the Prophet (s) would have much expectation of the submission of most of the leaders named in this group. They were inveterate enemies of Islam and several of them later fought the Muslims at Badr and were killed there. About their attitude towards Islam, Q38:6 states:

وَٱنْطَلَقَ الْمَلَأُ مِنْهُمْ أَنِ ٱمْشُوا وَٱصْبِرُوا عَلَىٰ آلِهَتِكُمْ

And the chiefs from amongst them (the Quraysh) went about saying, "Continue and be steadfast over [the defence of] your gods."...

iii) That the conduct of Ibn Umm Maktūm himself was not correct. He may have been blind, but he could hear the Prophet (s) talking to some people. He should not have persistently called out for his attention but waited until the Prophet (s) was free to attend to him.

This reason also seems far-fetched. It implies that that the Prophet (s) was justified in showing discourtesy. As for Ibn Umm Maktūm, he appears to have been of sound mind because he was later appointed as the muezzin of the Prophet (s) and he acted as his deputy several times when he (s) left Madina, usually for battle. Such a man could not be accused of being unaware of social etiquette and continually calling for the attention of the Prophet (s) when he could hear that he was busy in a meeting.

iv) That the act was justified because Ibn Umm Maktūm was blind, so he was oblivious to both the act of frowning and turning away and therefore was unaffected by it.[9] Therefore, God's remonstration with the Prophet (s) was merely to advise him of even higher stages of moral perfection.

However, even though Ibn Umm Maktūm did not see the alleged actions of the Prophet (s), the others saw it and took note of it. In some ways, it is an even worse justification because it implies that the Prophet (s) committed a form of *ghībah* by disrespecting the blind man behind his back.

v) That this behaviour on the part of the Prophet (s) was not a sin at that time, rather it was the foregoing of the preferable

[9] Zamakhsharī, *al-Kashshāf*, 4/701.

act (*tark al-awlā*).[10] Only after this surah was revealed with its reprimanding tone, with the word '*kallā*' (desist) in verse 11, was this sort of conduct forbidden.

However, this is not an intellectually sound explanation, because from the very beginning, the conduct of the Prophet (s) was a *sunnah* for the people.

In summary, these exegetes have given all manner of apologetic explanations for their stance, determined to explain why the Prophet (s) of God would discriminate against a disabled and poor companion, while sitting with a group of wealthy and powerful disbelievers.

2. In contrast to the above, the opinion of most *Shīʿī* exegetes[11] is that the act of frowning at a blind and poor man cannot be attributed to the Prophet (s) because it was contrary to his nature as described in the Qurʾan and traditions. We will look at some of these evidences below:

   i) Reports about the impeccable manners of the Prophet (s) clearly indicate that he would never exhibit the slightest discourtesy, let alone insult a Muslim and that too, in front of non-Muslims. Even when he shook someone's hand, he would not be the first to pull his hand back.[12] In Surat al-Qalam, which was revealed earlier than Surat ʿAbasa, the manners and etiquettes of the Prophet (s) have been highly praised by God. Q68:4 declares:

   وَإِنَّكَ لَعَلَىٰ خُلُقٍ عَظِيمٍ

   And indeed you [O Muhammad] possess an exemplary character.

   ii) The alleged conduct of the Prophet (s) goes against several verses of the Qurʾan including:

   Q26:215, which is amongst the earliest revelations, which instructs the Prophet (s):

   وَٱخْفِضْ جَنَاحَكَ لِمَنِ ٱتَّبَعَكَ مِنَ الْمُؤْمِنِينَ

---

[10] A possibility discussed by Muṭahharī, (*Āshnāyī bā Qur'an*), *Āthār*, 28/361.

[11] Including: Syed Murtaḍā, *Tanzīh al-Anbiyāʾ*, p. 118; Ṭūsī, *al-Tibyān*, 10/268; Ṭabrasī, *al-Bayān*, 10/437; Ṭabāṭabāʾī, *al-Mīzān*, 20/203; Shīrāzī, *Namūneh*, 26/127, and others.

[12] Ṭūsī, *al-Tibyān*, 10/269.

And lower your wing [in kindness] to the believers who follow you.

And Q18:28, which states:

وَٱصْبِرْ نَفْسَكَ مَعَ الَّذِينَ يَدْعُونَ رَبَّهُمْ بِالْغَدَاةِ وَالْعَشِيِّ يُرِيدُونَ وَجْهَهُ
وَلَا تَعْدُ عَيْنَاكَ عَنْهُمْ تُرِيدُ زِينَةَ الْحَيَاةِ الدُّنْيَا وَلَا تُطِعْ مَنْ أَغْفَلْنَا
قَلْبَهُ عَنْ ذِكْرِنَا وَٱتَّبَعَ هَوَاهُ وَكَانَ أَمْرُهُ فُرُطًا

And keep yourself patient [by being] with those who call upon their Lord in the morning and the evening, seeking His countenance. And let not your eyes pass beyond them, desiring adornments of the worldly life. And do not obey one whose heart We have made heedless of Our remembrance and who follows his base desires and whose affair has exceeded bounds.

And Q6:52, which states:

وَلَا تَطْرُدِ الَّذِينَ يَدْعُونَ رَبَّهُمْ بِالْغَدَاةِ وَالْعَشِيِّ يُرِيدُونَ وَجْهَهُ مَا عَلَيْكَ مِنْ
حِسَابِهِمْ مِنْ شَيْءٍ وَمَا مِنْ حِسَابِكَ عَلَيْهِمْ مِنْ شَيْءٍ فَتَطْرُدَهُمْ فَتَكُونَ مِنَ
الظَّالِمِينَ

And do not send away those who call upon their Lord in the morning and evening, seeking His countenance. Not upon you is anything of their account and not upon them is anything of your account. So were you to send them away, you would [then] be of the wrongdoers.

iii) Every act of the Prophet (s) is an example for the Muslims. Whatever he said, did, and allowed, was something that Muslims are instructed to emulate. Q33:21 states:

لَقَدْ كَانَ لَكُمْ فِي رَسُولِ اللهِ أُسْوَةٌ حَسَنَةٌ لِمَنْ كَانَ يَرْجُو اللهَ
وَالْيَوْمَ الْآخِرَ وَذَكَرَ اللهَ كَثِيرًا

Indeed, you have in God's Messenger an excellent exemplar for anyone whose hope is in Allah and the Last Day and [who] remembers Allah often.

And Q59:7 states:

وَمَا آتَاكُمُ الرَّسُولُ فَخُذُوهُ وَمَا نَهَاكُمْ عَنْهُ فَٱنْتَهُوا

... And whatever the Messenger has given you, take it; and what he has forbidden you, refrain from it...

iv) The well-known mission statement of the Prophet (s) was: I have been sent to perfect the nobility of character.[13]

In summary, it follows that a Divinely ordained and protected Prophet, who had been charged to reform the social malaise in his community, and whose words and deeds were and are an example for all his followers to emulate, could not have responded in this fashion to a request for guidance by one of his companions.

This is not behaviour that befits any person of understanding, let alone the Prophet (s) of God.[14] Indeed, he was the best of God's creation.

A tradition from Imam Ali (a) states: The best of creation on the Day that God gathers them are the Messengers (a) and the foremost of the Messengers (a) is Muhammad (s).[15]

EXEGESIS

VERSES 1, 2

عَبَسَ وَتَوَلَّىٰٓ ﴿١﴾ أَن جَآءَهُ ٱلْأَعْمَىٰ ﴿٢﴾

He frowned and turned away. [1] *Because there came to him the blind man.* [2]

1-2.1 '*He frowned and turned away.*': [*ʿAbasa* (عَبَسَ, he frowned)] is derived from *ʿabs* meaning gloominess accompanied by distress, and *ʿabasa* denotes the expression of this emotion on the face.[16]

[*Tawallā* (تَوَلَّ, he turned away)] is derived from *waliya* which ordinarily means to be near or to be a friend, but *tawallā* can also mean to be averted or to turn away, especially when used with the

[13] Ṭabrasī, *al-Bayān*, 10/500.

عَنِ الرَّسُولِ (صَلَّى اللهُ عَلَيْهِ وَآلِهِ) – بُعِثْتُ لِأُتَمِّمَ مَكَارِمَ الْأَخْلَاقِ.

[14] Ṭabāṭabā'ī, *al-Mīzān*, 20/200.

[15] Kulaynī, *al-Kāfī*, 1/450.

عَنْ أَمِيرِ الْمُؤْمِنِينَ (عَلَيْهِ السَّلَامُ) – إِنَّ خَيْرَ الْخَلْقِ يَوْمَ يَجْمَعُهُمُ اللهُ الرُّسُلُ وَإِنَّ أَفْضَلَ الرُّسُلِ مُحَمَّدٌ صَلَّى اللهُ عَلَيْهِ وَآلِهِ.

[16] Muṣṭafawī, *al-Taḥqīq*.

present, or implied, prepositions *ʿan* or *min* (from).[17] And this is the case in this verse.

1-2.2 The mention of the blindness of Ibn Umm Maktūm is to emphasize the gravity of the disrespect shown to him. The fact that he was making efforts to be guided despite his disability required him to be shown even more respect, not less.[18]

1-2.3 Since the first verse is couched in the third person, the identity of the one to whom God's rebuke is directed is not immediately clear, although, as we have seen, almost all *Sunni* exegetes believe that it was the Prophet (s).

However, the actions of the Prophet (s) have not been referred to in the third person in the Qur'an, and if he was being addressed, the phrases *ʿabasta* (you frowned) and *tawallayta* (you turned away) would have been used.[19]

1-2.4 Indeed, the noble Prophet (s) never frowned at the disbelievers, let alone the believers.[20] The attitude of all the prophets (a) of God towards believers was the same. Q11:29 quotes Prophet Nuh (a):

وَمَا أَنَا بِطَارِدِ الَّذِينَ آمَنُوا

... And I am not one to drive away those who have believed...

1-2.5 '*Because there came to him the blind man.*': [*Al-Aʿmā* (الْأَعْمَى, the blind man]. Again the pronoun *hu* (him) is for an unspecified third person, who frowned. However, there is consensus that the man who came to the gathering was the blind companion of the Prophet (s), ʿAbdullāh b. Umm Maktūm. And since he was a believer, the Prophet (s) would certainly have greeted him with respect.

Q6:54 instructs him:

وَإِذَا جَاءَكَ الَّذِينَ يُؤْمِنُونَ بِآيَاتِنَا فَقُلْ سَلَامٌ عَلَيْكُمْ

And when those who believe in our revelations come to you, say, "Peace be on you (salāmun ʿalaykum)*..."*

[17] Rāghib, *al-Mufradāt.*

[18] Ṭabāṭabā'ī, *al-Mīzān*, 20/200.

[19] Muṭahharī, *(Āshnāyī bā Qur'an), Āthār*, 28/358.

[20] Ṭabāṭabā'ī, *al-Mīzān*, 20/200.

1-2.6 We have stated with evidence that the man who frowned and turned away could not have been the noble Prophet (s). According to most *Shīʿa* exegetes, the one who behaved in this manner was a man from the Banu Umayyah who was present in the gathering.

A report from Imam al-Sadiq (a) states: The verses were revealed about a man from the Banu Umayyah who was in the presence of the Prophet (s) when Ibn Umm Maktūm arrived. When he saw him, he moved away from him, frowned, and turned his face away from him. God, the Glorified, recounted this event and showed His displeasure at it.[21]

The Prophet (s) was probably accompanied by some of his companions in this meeting. From the tone of the verses that follow, it appears likely that the man who behaved in this manner was from the *ṣaḥābah*,[22] from whom such behaviour was not expected, even if he felt that the arrival of the blind man would be detrimental to the efforts of the Prophet (s) in convincing the leaders of the Quraysh.

It is also possible that this man was ʿUthmān b. al-ʿAffān, since he was the only known Umayyad who had accepted Islam in Makka.[23]

1-2.7 According to some reports, Ibn Umm Maktūm was the cousin of Lady Khadijah (a).[24] He was an early convert to Islam and migrated to Madina in the 12th year of the mission of the Prophet (s), when he accompanied Muṣʿab b. ʿUmayr to spread awareness of the teachings of Islam amongst the people of Yathrib.[25] After the Prophet (s) migrated to Madina, he served as his muezzin alongside Bilāl.[26] The Prophet (s) left him in charge of Madina in his absence several times.[27]

According to a report, he was killed in the course of the Battle of Qādisiyyah in the year 16/638 when the Muslims fought the

---

[21] Majlisī, *Biḥār*, 3/175.

عَنِ الصَّادِقِ (عَلَيْهِ السَّلامُ) – أَنَّهَا نَزَلَتْ فِي رَجُلٍ مِنْ بَنِي أُمَيَّةَ كَانَ عِنْدَ النَّبِيِّ (صَلَّى اللهُ عَلَيْهِ وَآلِهِ)، فَجَاءَ ابْنُ أُمِّ مَكْتُومٍ، فَلَمَّا رَآهُ تَقَذَّرَ مِنْهُ وَجَمَعَ نَفْسَهُ وَعَبَسَ وَأَعْرَضَ بِوَجْهِهِ عَنْهُ، فَحَكَى اللهُ سُبْحَانَهُ ذَلِكَ وَأَنْكَرَهُ عَلَيْهِ.

[22] Muṭahharī, (*Āshnāyī bā Qur'an*), *Āthār*, 28/356.

[23] Ibid.

[24] Ibn Ḥajar, *al-Iṣābah*, 4/495.

[25] Ibn Saʿd, *al-Ṭabaqāt*, 4/155.

[26] Yaʿqūbī, *Tārīkh*, 2/42.

[27] Balādhurī, *Ansāb al-Ashrāf*, 11/24.

Persians.[28] There is a grave bearing his name in the Bāb al-Ṣaghīr cemetery in Damascus.

SUMMARY OF THE VERSES

The verses speak in a disapproving tone about someone who frowned and turned away when a blind companion (ʿAbdullah b. Umm Maktūm) arrived at their gathering.

REFLECTIVE LEARNING

For many people frowning at a blind person may seem harmless. In fact, this is one of the justifications given by those who say it was the Prophet (s) who frowned. But these verses show that there is a higher code of morality required from a Muslim than what is the norm in society.

Let me reflect on my moral conduct – is it higher than the norm? Am I guilty of behaviour that implies rudeness or impatience towards those whom I feel are less important in society?

VERSES 3, 4

وَ مَا يُدْرِيكَ لَعَلَّهُ يَزَّكَّىٰ ﴿٣﴾ أَوْ يَذَّكَّرُ فَتَنْفَعَهُ الذِّكْرَىٰ ﴿٤﴾

But what would make you know that perhaps he might purify [himself]? [3] *Or be reminded, and that the reminder would benefit him?* [4]

3-4.1 The verses now move to a direct address. [*Yudrīka* (يُدْرِيكَ, make you know)] is derived from *darā* meaning to know and perceive.[29] The presence of the second person pronoun (*ka*) – which is usually used in the Qur'an to address the Prophet (s) – has been cited as evidence by those exegetes who say that it was the Prophet (s) who frowned.

However, whenever there is ambiguity and doubt, we must make recourse to what is known.[30] We have seen that the Qur'anic descriptions of the qualities of the Prophet (s) do not support the ascription of this behaviour to the Prophet (s). Therefore, the addressee has to be someone else.

---

[28] Ibn Saʿd, *al-Ṭabaqāt*, 4/159.

[29] Muṣṭafawī, *al-Taḥqīq*.

[30] Javādī-Āmolī, *Tasnīm*.(Transcript:http://javadi.esra.ir/-/09-09-1398-1-تفسير-سوره-عبس-جلسه)

3-4.2 Based on the foregoing, Shaykh Ṭūsī states that there is an ellipsis (*ḥadhf*) in the verse under review (and the following eight verses). It is an instruction to the Prophet (s) to address the Umayyad, and simply means: O Prophet, tell him, "But what would make you know..." [31]

As always, the message of the verses is directed beyond the immediate addressee, and all Muslims must learn from it. A tradition from Imam al-Sadiq (a) states: The Qur'an has been revealed in the style of 'I speak to you, but let your neighbour hear.'[32]

3-4.3 [*Yazzakkā* (يَزَّكَّىٰ, he purifies)] is truncated here from *yatazakka*. It is derived from *zakā* and its verbal noun *tazkiyah* means growth, purification, and development.[33] Here it means purification of the soul from sin, ignorance, and neglect. And it is only this that would facilitate its growth and allow for greater cognizance (*maʿrifah*) of God.

Self-purification (*tazkiyat al-nafs*) is an essential prerequisite for guidance towards God. Q79:18,19 quote the opening statement of Prophet Musa (a) to Firʿawn:

هَل لَّكَ إِلَىٰٓ أَن تَزَكَّىٰ ﴿١٨﴾ وَأَهْدِيَكَ إِلَىٰ رَبِّكَ فَتَخْشَىٰ

...Would you [be willing to] purify yourself? And [to] let me guide you to your Lord so that you would fear [Him]?

[*Yadhdhakkaru* (يَذَّكَّرُ, he is reminded)] is truncated from *yatadhakkar*. It is derived from *dhakara*, meaning to remember. Here, it means being reminded of something that we already know, the truths that have been coded by God in the human being (*fiṭrah*) and which over time, have been cloaked by the contamination of sin and neglect.[34]

Just by being in the blessed presence of the Prophet (s) and listening to his words would start this process of purification for the believers. Even if they are not purified in that one sitting, the admonition may serve as seeds that would flourish and benefit them later.

3-4.4 Those who are reminded by the Qur'an are the ones who use the innermost, purest aspect of the intellect, which draws fully from

---

[31] Ṭūsī, *al-Tibyān*, 10/269.

[32] Kulaynī, *al-Kāfī*, 2/630.

عَنِ الصَّادِقِ (عَلَيْهِ السَّلَامُ) – نَزَلَ الْقُرْآنُ بِإِيَّاكِ أَعْنِي وَاسْمَعِي يَا جَارَةُ.

[33] Rāghib, *al-Mufradāt*.

[34] Muṭahharī, (*Āshnāyī bā Qur'an*), *Āthār*, 28/361.

the knowledge of the *fiṭrah* and connects man to his Creator. This aspect is called its kernel (*lubb*).[35] Q38:29 states:

كِتَابٌ أَنْزَلْنَاهُ إِلَيْكَ مُبَارَكٌ لِيَدَّبَّرُوا آيَاتِهِ وَلِيَتَذَكَّرَ أُولُوا الْأَلْبَابِ

[This is] a Book which We have revealed to you, [O Muhammad], that they might reflect upon its verses and that those of deep understanding (uluʾl albāb) *would be reminded.*

3-4.5 This reminding and admonition (*tadhakkur*) is a basic part of the mission of the Prophets (a) of God. Q88:21 states:

فَذَكِّرْ إِنَّمَا أَنْتَ مُذَكِّرٌ

So remind, [O Muhammad]; indeed, you are only one who reminds.

Furthermore, reminding one another is a constant duty of the believers as well, because sometimes it may be that the admonition comes when the heart of the recipient is more receptive.
Q3:104 states:

وَلْتَكُنْ مِنْكُمْ أُمَّةٌ يَدْعُونَ إِلَى الْخَيْرِ وَيَأْمُرُونَ بِالْمَعْرُوفِ وَيَنْهَوْنَ عَنِ الْمُنكَرِ وَأُولَٰئِكَ هُمُ الْمُفْلِحُونَ

And let there arise from you a group of people calling to goodness; enjoining what is right and forbidding what is wrong. They are the ones who will be successful.

SUMMARY OF THE VERSES

The verses address the one who showed displeasure at the arrival of the blind man by asking: How do you know – perhaps he may purify himself by hearing the admonition of the Prophet (s)? Or at least be reminded, and this reminder will be beneficial later in his journey towards purification?[36]

REFLECTIVE LEARNING

It is purification that will allow guidance to settle in the heart, and only God is aware of the purity of an individual soul.

---

[35] Rāghib, *al-Mufradāt.*

[36] Ṭabāṭabāʾī, *al-Mīzān*, 20/200.

Let me reflect on whether I judge people based on a preconceived idea of their religiosity and assume that they will respond negatively to a word of guidance.

VERSES 5 - 10

أَمَّا مَنِ ٱسْتَغْنَىٰ ﴿٥﴾ فَأَنتَ لَهُۥ تَصَدَّىٰ ﴿٦﴾ وَمَا عَلَيْكَ أَلَّا يَزَّكَّىٰ ﴿٧﴾ وَأَمَّا مَن جَآءَكَ يَسْعَىٰ ﴿٨﴾ وَهُوَ يَخْشَىٰ ﴿٩﴾ فَأَنتَ عَنْهُ تَلَهَّىٰ ﴿١٠﴾

As for he who thinks himself without need, [5] *to him you give attention.* [6] *Though there is no blame on you if he does not purify [himself].* [7] *But as for he who came to you striving [earnestly],* [8] *while he fears [God],* [9] *of him you are unmindful.* [10]

5-10.1 '*As for he who thinks himself without need, to him you give attention.*': [*Istaghnā* (إِسْتَغْنَىٰ, considers himself needless)] is derived from *ghaniya*, which means to be free from want.[37] Such a person grows in arrogance and defiance because he considers himself needless due to his strength, wealth, and influence. Q96:6,7 state

إِنَّ ٱلْإِنسَٰنَ لَيَطْغَىٰٓ ﴿٦﴾ أَن رَّءَاهُ ٱسْتَغْنَىٰٓ

...Indeed, man is most surely inordinate.
Because he sees himself as self-sufficient.

[*Taṣaddā*, (تَصَدَّىٰ, give attention)] is derived from *ṣadiya*, meaning to be thirsty, and turning one's full attention to seeking water. Later, it became used for turning towards and giving one's full attention to anything.[38]

5-10.2 The Prophet (s) is instructed to tell this person that despite his desire to give the delegation of idolaters respect and attention, the message of Islam would not benefit them because most of them were complacent and considered themselves needless of any guidance.[39] They had only come to meet the Prophet (s) to see if any compromise or concession could be achieved that would align with their own interests.

[37] Muṣṭafawī, *al-Taḥqīq*.

[38] Ibid.

[39] Ṭabāṭabā'ī, *al-Mīzān*, 20/200.

5-10.3 *'Though there is no blame on you if he does not purify [himself].'*: This verse means that no person carries the blame for the actions of others. The role of the guide is to show a person the correct course by words and example. After that, every mature individual is responsible for his own deeds. Blaming others for one's actions is a futile exercise in the *dunyā* and will have no meaning in the *ākhirah*. Q74:38 states:

كُلُّ نَفْسٍ بِمَا كَسَبَتْ رَهِينَةٌ

Every soul will be held in pledge for what it has earned.

5-10.4 *'But as for he who came to you striving [earnestly]. While he fears [God]'*: [*Yasʿā* (يَسْعَىٰ, he strives)] can denote both moving quickly as well as to endeavour and strive hard.[40] Here, it refers to striving eagerly to be reminded and guided.[41]

In Surat al-Nāziʿāt (Q79:22) the same term was used for Firʿawn. However, he was striving for an evil purpose while Ibn Umm Maktūm was striving towards goodness.

The man who frowned is now admonished: You are mindful of those who have no regard for God, but are dismissive of someone who hurries to a gathering where the Prophet (s) is present, fearful for his future, and wanting to learn something that will guide him.[42]

5-10.5 Two qualities are given for the blind person. One is that he was eager to take the opportunity and rushed to hear the words of the Prophet (s) (*yasʿā*), and the other is that he did so while he was fearful (*yakhshā*). This is the kind of fear that causes a believer to be constantly in mindful awe of his Creator, to be reminded by the verses of the Qurʾan, and to attempt to strengthen the level of his faith at every opportunity. Q20:2,3 state:

مَا أَنزَلْنَا عَلَيْكَ الْقُرْآنَ لِتَشْقَىٰ ﴿٢﴾ إِلَّا تَذْكِرَةً لِّمَن يَخْشَىٰ

We have not sent down the Qurʾan to you [O Muhammad] that you be distressed. But only as a reminder (tadhkirah) *for those who fear [Allah]* (yakhshā).

---

[40] Muṣṭafawī, *al-Taḥqīq*.

[41] Ṭabrasī, *al-Bayān*, 10/665.

[42] Ṭabāṭabāʾī, *al-Mīzān*, 20/201.

5-10.6 '*Of him you are unmindful.*': [*Talahhā* (تَلَهَّى, unmindful)] is derived from *lahā*, meaning to be engaged in worthless pursuits and to neglect more important tasks.[43] Here it means to be distracted from the person one should be paying attention to, to someone else.[44] And the addition of the words *anta* (you) and *ʿanhu* (of him) in the verse are for emphasis of the criticism.[45]

This type of disregard and indifference towards people who are deemed of a lower class in a society is a habit of the arrogant. Q11:27 mentions the haughty words of the leaders at the time of Prophet Nuh (a):

فَقَالَ الْمَلَأُ الَّذِينَ كَفَرُوا مِنْ قَوْمِهِ مَا نَرَاكَ إِلَّا بَشَرًا مِثْلَنَا
وَمَا نَرَاكَ اتَّبَعَكَ إِلَّا الَّذِينَ هُمْ أَرَاذِلُنَا بَادِيَ الرَّأْيِ

The chiefs, who were the disbelievers among his people said, "We do not see you but as a man like ourselves, nor do we see any follow you but the lowest among us and following without thinking..."

The criteria of honour of the people of *dunyā* are not the same as that of God, and we should always beware of looking down at anyone. It is the ordinary folk who make up the strength of a nation. Imam Ali (a) states in his famous instructions to Mālik al-Ashtar when he despatched him as his governor to Egypt: Indeed, it is the common citizens of the nation who are the pillars of religion, the strength of the Muslims, and the defence against the enemy. Therefore, you should be [more] inclined towards them.[46]

SUMMARY OF THE VERSES

These verses criticize the conduct of a believer who gave attention to someone who considered himself needless of God, while their purification was not his concern. Furthermore, he did this while ignoring the one who was sincere and feared God.

---

[43] Ṭabrasī, *al-Bayān*, 10/817.

[44] Ibid, 10/665.

[45] Ṭabāṭabā'ī, *al-Mīzān*, 20/201.

[46] *Nahj al-Balāghah*, letter no. 53.
وَإِنَّمَا عِمَادُ الدِّينِ، وَجِمَاعُ الْمُسْلِمِينَ، وَالْعُدَّةُ لِلْأَعْدَاءِ - الْعَامَّةُ مِنَ الْأُمَّةِ، فَلْيَكُنْ صِغْوُكَ لَهُمْ، وَمَيْلُكَ مَعَهُمْ.

REFLECTIVE LEARNING

Let me reflect on my attitude when it comes to paying attention to some people and ignoring others.

On what criteria do I base my actions? Do I help those who are pious and sincerely striving to attain nearness to God, or do I pay attention to those who are powerful and influential in the society?

VERSES 11 - 16

كَلَّا إِنَّهَا تَذْكِرَةٌ ﴿١١﴾ فَمَنْ شَاءَ ذَكَرَهُ ﴿١٢﴾ فِي صُحُفٍ مُكَرَّمَةٍ ﴿١٣﴾
مَرْفُوعَةٍ مُطَهَّرَةٍ ﴿١٤﴾ بِأَيْدِي سَفَرَةٍ ﴿١٥﴾ كِرَامٍ بَرَرَةٍ ﴿١٦﴾

Not at all! Indeed, these verses are a reminder. [11] *So whoever wills, will remember it.* [12] *[It is recorded] in honoured scrolls.* [13] *Exalted, purified.* [14] *[Carried] by the hands of messenger-angels.* [15] *Noble, dutiful.* [16]

11-16.1 '*Not at all! Indeed, these verses are a reminder. So whoever wills, will remember it.*': 'Not at all (*kallā*)' is a rejection of every act of the Umayyad; the frowning and turning away, the attention to the disbelievers, and the disregard of the believer.[47] Here it means, 'do not ever repeat this behaviour.'[48]

[*Tadhkirah* (تَذْكِرَة, reminder)]. The term refers to the Qur'an. Its verses are a powerful reminder of something that man already instinctively knows within his *fiṭrah* – as we have discussed in the previous section. However, the task at hand is to continually remember and be mindful of this knowledge, and this can only be done by vigilance in keeping the heart pure from sin.

The verse also highlights the fact that man decides his own fate through his free will and is not compelled by God.[49] Q76:29 states:

إِنَّ هَٰذِهِ تَذْكِرَةٌ فَمَنْ شَاءَ ٱتَّخَذَ إِلَىٰ رَبِّهِ سَبِيلًا

Indeed, this [Qur'an] is a reminder,
so whoever wills may take a way to his Lord.

[47] Ṭabāṭabā'ī, *al-Mīzān*, 20/201.

[48] Shīrāzī, *Namūneh*, 26/133.

[49] Ṭūsī, *al-Tibyān*, 10/271.

11-16.2 '*[It is recorded] in honoured scrolls. Exalted, purified.*': [*Ṣuḥuf* (صُحُف, scrolls)] (sing. *ṣaḥīfah*) means 'anything spread out for writing.'[50] Here, *ṣuḥuf* may refer to the individual surahs of the Qur'an. It also indicates that it was recorded in some form before it was revealed to the Prophet (s).[51]

According to some reports, these honoured and exalted scrolls are a reference to the Preserved Tablet (*al-lawḥ al-maḥfūẓ*).[52]

[*Mukarramah* (مُكَرَّمَة, honoured)] is derived from *karuma* meaning to be noble.[53] Here, it means something valuable that deserves to be treated with honour and reverence. This Book is to be revered because it contains the highest wisdoms, and concepts that cannot be learned or discovered except if revealed by the Creator Himself.

[*Marfū'ah* (مَرْفُوعَة, exalted)] is derived from *rafa'a* meaning to raise. Here, it means that the Qur'an is exalted in status and elevated above any attempt to contaminate or distort it.[54]

[*Muṭahharah* (مُطَهَّرَة, purified)] is derived from *ṭahura*, meaning to be rendered pure and immaculate. Here, it means that the Qur'an is free from any falsehood, uncertainty, and intellectual inconsistency.[55] Q41:42 states:

لَا يَأْتِيهِ الْبَاطِلُ مِنْ بَيْنِ يَدَيْهِ وَلَا مِنْ خَلْفِهِ

Falsehood cannot approach it from before it or from behind it...

And Q4:82 states:

وَلَوْ كَانَ مِنْ عِندِ غَيْرِ اللهِ لَوَجَدُوا فِيهِ ٱخْتِلَافًا كَثِيرًا

... If it (the Qur'an) had been from [any] other than Allah,
they would have found within it much inconsistency.

Indeed, the Qur'an was exalted and purified at every stage of its descent. It was faithfully delivered by purified angels and its concepts were made free from any falsehood.[56]

---

[50] Shīrāzī, *Namūneh*, 26/134.

[51] Ibid.

[52] Ṭabrasī, *al-Bayān*, 10/665.

[53] Muṣṭafawī, *al-Taḥqīq*.

[54] Ibid.

[55] Shīrāzī, *Namūneh*, 26/134.

[56] Ṭabrasī, *al-Bayān*, 10/793.

Furthermore, access to its guidance is proportional to the purity of the individual. Q56:79 states:

لَا يَمَسُّهُ إِلَّا الْمُطَهَّرُونَ

None touch it (the Qur'an) except the purified.

And this is why its interpreters were purified by God Himself. Q33:33 states:

إِنَّمَا يُرِيدُ اللَّهُ لِيُذْهِبَ عَنكُمُ الرِّجْسَ أَهْلَ الْبَيْتِ وَيُطَهِّرَكُمْ تَطْهِيرًا

... God intends only to remove from you [every] impurity, O people of the [Prophet's] household, and to purify you with [thorough] purification.

11-16.3 '*[Carried] by the hands of messenger-angels. Noble, virtuous.*': [*Safarah* (سَفَرَة, messenger-angels)] is the plural of *sāfir*, and the term is derived from *safara* which originally meant to uncover and reveal something, or to move from one place to another.[57] In this verse, *safarah* refers to the messenger-angels who were charged with receiving and transmitting the Qur'an.[58]

These angels work under the direction of Jibra'il, just as the angels of death work under the supervision of ʿIzra'il.[59]

Safarah can also mean scribes, because those who write things reveal their meaning to others. Some exegetes have mentioned that these verses are referring to the companions of the Prophet (s) who were appointed as scribes (*kuttāb al-waḥy*) to write down the Qur'an.[60] However, this is unlikely because not all of them qualify for the adjectives *kirām* and *bararah*. Furthermore, these verses are speaking of the revelation of the Qur'an, and not the events that followed after it.[61]

[*Kirām* (كِرَام, noble)]. It is the plural of *karīm*, meaning noble and generous,[62] and is an attribute of these angels. It indicates the

---

57 Muṣṭafawī, *al-Taḥqīq*.

58 Ṭabrasī, *al-Bayān*, 10/665.

59 Muṭahharī, (*Āshnāyī bā Qur'an*), *Āthār*, 28/362.

60 Ṭūsī, *al-Tibyān*, 10/272.

61 Shīrāzī, *Namūneh*, 26/135.

62 Muṣṭafawī, *al-Taḥqīq*.

high station and noble nature of the angels who are charged with transmitting the word of God to His Prophets (a).[63] Q21:26, 27 state:

بَلْ عِبَادٌ مُكْرَمُونَ ﴿٢٦﴾ لَا يَسْبِقُونَهُ بِالْقَوْلِ وَهُمْ بِأَمْرِهِ يَعْمَلُونَ

...Rather, they (the angels) are honoured servants. They do not precede Him in speech, and they [only] act by His command.

[*Bararah* (بَرَرَة, righteous)] is the plural of *bārr*, and is derived from *barr*, which denotes land as opposed to sea. Because of the vastness of the land, the term is used for vastness in all goodness and benefit.[64] Here, it means that the angels of revelation are completely obedient to God's commands and free from every sin.[65] And indeed, they bring something of vast benefit.

11-16.4 These verses introduce the Qur'an as an exalted and pure Book that does not stand in need of the people, rather it is they who are in need of it for reminder and guidance.

SUMMARY OF THE VERSES

The verses emphasize that the Qur'an is a reminder of truths that human beings understand instinctively, if they wish to recall it. It is a Book that is honoured, exalted and purified, and its verses have been received and transmitted by angels who are noble and righteous messengers.

REFLECTIVE LEARNING

Those who memorize the Qur'an, and are thereby reminded and take heed of its guidance, have a high status. A tradition from Imam al-Sadiq (a) states: One who memorizes the Qur'an and acts on it shall be with the *safarah*, [who are] noble (*kirām*) and righteous (*bararah*).[66]

Let me reflect whether I am content to recite the Qur'an, or do I memorize its verses and act on them as well.

[63] Shīrāzī, *Namūneh*, 26/135.

[64] Muṣṭafawī, *al-Taḥqīq*.

[65] Shīrāzī, *Namūneh*, 26/136.

[66] ʿĀmilī, *Wasāʾil*, 6/176.

عَنِ الصَّادِقِ (عَلَيْهِ السَّلَامُ) – الْحَافِظُ لِلْقُرْآنِ الْعَامِلُ بِهِ مَعَ السَّفَرَةِ الْكِرَامِ الْبَرَرَةِ.

PART 2: VERSES 17 - 42

TEXT AND TRANSLATION

قُتِلَ الْإِنْسَانُ مَا أَكْفَرَهُ ﴿١٧﴾ مِنْ أَيِّ شَيْءٍ خَلَقَهُ ﴿١٨﴾ مِنْ نُطْفَةٍ خَلَقَهُ فَقَدَّرَهُ
﴿١٩﴾ ثُمَّ السَّبِيلَ يَسَّرَهُ ﴿٢٠﴾ ثُمَّ أَمَاتَهُ فَأَقْبَرَهُ ﴿٢١﴾ ثُمَّ إِذَا شَاءَ أَنْشَرَهُ ﴿٢٢﴾
كَلَّا لَمَّا يَقْضِ مَا أَمَرَهُ ﴿٢٣﴾ فَلْيَنْظُرِ الْإِنْسَانُ إِلَىٰ طَعَامِهِ ﴿٢٤﴾ أَنَّا صَبَبْنَا الْمَاءَ
صَبًّا ﴿٢٥﴾ ثُمَّ شَقَقْنَا الْأَرْضَ شَقًّا ﴿٢٦﴾ فَأَنْبَتْنَا فِيهَا حَبًّا ﴿٢٧﴾ وَعِنَبًا وَقَضْبًا
﴿٢٨﴾ وَزَيْتُونًا وَنَخْلًا ﴿٢٩﴾ وَحَدَائِقَ غُلْبًا ﴿٣٠﴾ وَفَاكِهَةً وَأَبًّا ﴿٣١﴾ مَتَاعًا
لَكُمْ وَلِأَنْعَامِكُمْ ﴿٣٢﴾ فَإِذَا جَاءَتِ الصَّاخَّةُ ﴿٣٣﴾ يَوْمَ يَفِرُّ الْمَرْءُ مِنْ أَخِيهِ
﴿٣٤﴾ وَأُمِّهِ وَأَبِيهِ ﴿٣٥﴾ وَصَاحِبَتِهِ وَبَنِيهِ ﴿٣٦﴾ لِكُلِّ امْرِئٍ مِنْهُمْ يَوْمَئِذٍ شَأْنٌ
يُغْنِيهِ ﴿٣٧﴾ وُجُوهٌ يَوْمَئِذٍ مُسْفِرَةٌ ﴿٣٨﴾ ضَاحِكَةٌ مُسْتَبْشِرَةٌ ﴿٣٩﴾ وَوُجُوهٌ
يَوْمَئِذٍ عَلَيْهَا غَبَرَةٌ ﴿٤٠﴾ تَرْهَقُهَا قَتَرَةٌ ﴿٤١﴾ أُولَٰئِكَ هُمُ الْكَفَرَةُ الْفَجَرَةُ ﴿٤٢﴾

May man perish! How ungrateful he is! [17] *From what thing did He create him?* [18] *From a small drop. He created him and then proportioned him.* [19] *Then He eased the way for him.* [20] *Then He causes him to die and assigns a grave to him.* [21] *Then when He wills, He will resurrect him.* [22] *Not at all! Man has not yet accomplished what He commanded him.* [23] *Then let man look at his food.* [24] *[For] that We poured down water in abundance.* [25] *Then We split the earth in clefts.* [26] *And We caused grain to grow therein.* [27] *And grapes and nutritious plants.* [28] *And olives and date-palms.* [29] *And gardens dense with trees.* [30] *And fruits and fodder.* [31] *A provision for you and your livestock.* [32] *But when the deafening cry comes.* [33] *The Day when a man will flee from his brother.* [34] *And his mother and his father.* [35] *And his wife and his children.* [36] *Every one of them on that Day shall have an affair [of his own] to preoccupy him.* [37] *[Some] faces that Day will be bright.* [38] *Laughing, [rejoicing] at good news.* [39] *And [some] faces that Day will be stained with dust.* [40] *Darkness will cover them.* [41] *Those are the disbelievers, the evil ones.*

VERSES 17 - 23

قُتِلَ الْإِنْسَانُ مَا أَكْفَرَهُ ﴿١٧﴾ مِنْ أَيِّ شَيْءٍ خَلَقَهُ ﴿١٨﴾ مِنْ نُطْفَةٍ خَلَقَهُ فَقَدَّرَهُ ﴿١٩﴾ ثُمَّ السَّبِيلَ يَسَّرَهُ ﴿٢٠﴾ ثُمَّ أَمَاتَهُ فَأَقْبَرَهُ ﴿٢١﴾ ثُمَّ إِذَا شَاءَ أَنْشَرَهُ ﴿٢٢﴾ كَلَّا لَمَّا يَقْضِ مَا أَمَرَهُ ﴿٢٣﴾

May man perish! How ungrateful he is! [17] *From what thing did He create him?* [18] *From a small drop. He created him and then proportioned him.* [19] *Then He eased the way for him.* [20] *Then He causes him to die and assigns a grave to him.* [21] *Then when He wills, He will resurrect him.* [22] *Not at all! Man has not yet accomplished what He commanded him.* [23]

17-23.1 '*May man perish! How ungrateful he is!*': [*Al-Insān* (الْإِنسَان, man)] refers to the entire human race in general, and specifically to each and every one within that race.[67] We have discussed the meaning of the term *insān* further in the *tafsīr* of Surat al-ʿAṣr (103). In brief, *Insān* should be more mindful because he has the tools to stop himself from being ungrateful, yet he has forgotten his purpose and potential.

Therefore, the curse and accusation in these verses are a censure for every individual who does whatever he pleases, follows his base desires, forgets his Lord, and defies His commandments.[68]

17-23.2 The two undesirable actions of the Umayyad man, who was a Muslim, were his disdain towards a poor believer, and his assumption that the presence of such a person in their gathering was not appropriate. The verses under review address him and men like him, and is further proof that the first two verses of the surah cannot be referring to the Prophet (s).

[*Mā akfarahu* (مَا أَكْفَرَهُ, how ungrateful he is!)] can either mean 'how ungrateful he is!' or 'what makes him so ungrateful?' and both carry a meaning of amazement.[69]

---

[67] Ṭabrasī, *al-Bayān* 10/815, Ṭabāṭabā'ī, *al-Mīzān*, 20/356.

[68] Ṭabāṭabā'ī, *al-Mīzān*, 20/206.

[69] Ṭabrasī, *al-Bayān*, 10/665.

Kufr is derived from *kafara* which means to cover something or to be ungrateful.[70] It is used to describe both disbelief as opposed to faith (*īmān*), and ingratitude as opposed to thanksgiving (*shukr*). The *kāfir* 'covers' God's signs, guidance, and blessings with negligence and ingratitude and that is why the word *kufr* is used here to describe his attitude.

The main cause of disbelief and ungratefulness is pride.

Q39:60 states:

أَلَيْسَ فِي جَهَنَّمَ مَثْوًى لِلْمُتَكَبِّرِينَ

...Is there not in Hell a residence for the arrogant?

It is probably for this reason that the next verse reminds man of his humble origins.

17-23.3 *'From what thing did He create him? From a small drop. He created him and then proportioned him.'*: These verses begin by asking man what he was created from. The answer is given immediately: a small drop of seminal fluid (*nuṭfah*). The usage of the term *nuṭfah* is to show the lowliness of man's beginnings and the address is to those who have transgressed and become arrogant.[71] Q77:20 states:

أَلَمْ نَخْلُقْكُمْ مِنْ مَاءٍ مَهِينٍ

Did We not create you from a liquid disdained?

A tradition from Imam Ali (a) states: What has the son of Adam to do with vanity? His beginning is a small drop and his end is a carcass. He can neither sustain himself nor ward off his death.[72]

[*Qaddarahu* (قَدَّرَهُ, proportioned him)] is derived from *qadara* which means to measure and estimate,[73] and its verbal noun *taqdīr* means to proportion and allocate according to a specific measure.[74] Here, it means that God in His wisdom has given each human being

---

[70] Rāghib, *al-Mufradāt.*

[71] Ṭabāṭabā'ī, *al-Mīzān*, 20/206.

[72] *Nahj al-Balāghah*, saying no. 454.

مَا لِابْنِ آدَمَ وَالْفَخْرِ: أَوَّلُهُ نُطْفَةٌ، وَآخِرُهُ جِيفَةٌ، وَلَا يَرْزُقُ نَفْسَهُ، وَلَا يَدْفَعُ حَتْفَهُ.

[73] Muṣṭafawī, *al-Taḥqīq.*

[74] Ṭūsī, *al-Tibyān*, 10/273.

a potential by allocating specific physical and psychological characteristics to him.[75]

All this is determined by the incredibly intricate genetic code present in the sperm (and ovum) that ensures that different organs, limbs, and systems develop in perfect harmony to create the human being.[76]

Each individual is thus allocated with a unique potential and he cannot go beyond what God has determined for him.[77] This *taqdīr* suffices him through the gradual stages of his life in the *dunyā* from infancy to old age, and in the realms to come as well.

However, this does not mean that man's course is predetermined and that his destiny is fixed by the *taqdīr* of God. The fact is that within the parameters determined by God, man still retains free will. It is by his choice that he adopts righteousness or displays defiance.[78]

By pondering on how vulnerable and helpless he was at the beginning of his life, and how utterly dependent he is on God's grace ever since, how can man ever be ungrateful?

17-23.4 *'Then He eased the way for him.'*: This verse means that God facilitated his entry into this world and thereafter provided sustenance and guidance to him to ease his path in life.[79]

A tradition from Imam al-Baqir (a) states: Easing the way for him refers to [easing] the path of guidance.[80]

At every stage of his life God makes guidance available to man to help him reach his potential, his perfection, and ultimately lead him to Paradise. When they are admitted to Paradise, the believers gratefully acknowledge this fact. Q7:43 states:

وَقَالُوا الْحَمْدُ لِلَّهِ الَّذِي هَدَانَا لِهَٰذَا وَمَا كُنَّا لِنَهْتَدِيَ لَوْلَا أَنْ هَدَانَا اللَّهُ

...And they shall say: All grateful praise is due to God Who guided us to this. And we would never have been guided [aright] if God had not [constantly] guided us...

---

[75] Muṭahharī, (*Āshnāyī bā Qur'an*), *Āthār*, 28/372.

[76] Shīrāzī, *Namūneh*, 26/138.

[77] Ṭabāṭabā'ī, *al-Mīzān*, 20/207.

[78] Ibid.

[79] Ṭabrasī, *al-Bayān*, 10/666.

[80] Baḥrānī, *al-Burhān*, 5/584.

عَنْ أَبِي جَعْفَرٍ (عَلَيْهِ السَّلَامُ) - « ثُمَّ السَّبِيلَ يَسَّرَهُ» يَعْنِي سَبِيلَ الْهُدَى.

17-23.5 *'Then He causes him to die and assigns a grave to him.'*: [*Amātahu* (أَمَاتَهُ, He causes him to die)] means that He determines the moment of his death.[81] This death is of his physical body in the *dunyā*, while his soul lives on in the next realm, which is *barzakh*.[82] Death is a continuation of God's favour to the believer, because it signifies an end to his test and the beginning of his recompense.[83] It brings an end to toil and labour, pain and infirmity, senility and sensory impairment, and grants him a new life that is richer and more expansive than anything he has experienced before.

[*Aqbarahu* (أَقْبَرَهُ, He assigns a grave to him)] means that He causes him to be buried, in the sense that He has guided mankind to that, so that the dead are shown dignity.[84] About Qabil, Q5:31 states:

فَبَعَثَ اللَّهُ غُرَابًا يَبْحَثُ فِي الْأَرْضِ لِيُرِيَهُ كَيْفَ يُوَارِي سَوْءَةَ أَخِيهِ

Then God sent a crow digging up the earth to show him how to cover the corpse of his brother...

Aqbarah can be considered as a metaphor for entry into *barzakh*, because it includes those who are not buried as well, for instance those who are drowned or cremated.

17-23.6 *'Then when He wills, He will resurrect him.'*: *'When He wills'* is a reference to the fact that only God knows when the Day of Resurrection will occur.[85] And that only He has the power to bring it about.

[*Ansharahu* (أَنشَرَهُ, He will resurrect him)] is derived from *nashara* which means to expand after constriction.[86] The life force that was brought to a close in the *dunyā* is now expanded into a more expansive world in the *ākhirah*.[87]

Anshara here means that God, who caused him to die and be buried, will then resurrect him from his grave to receive his recompense.[88] For the believers, this will be a great blessing. Q10:4 states:

---

[81] Modarresī, *Min Huda al-Qur'an*, 17/329.

[82] Ṭūsī, *al-Tibyān*, 10/273.

[83] Shīrāzī, *Namūneh*, 26/140.

[84] Ṭabāṭabā'ī, *al-Mīzān*, 20/208.

[85] Ibid.

[86] Muṣṭafawī, *al-Taḥqīq*.

[87] Shīrāzī, *Namūneh*, 26/141.

[88] Ṭabrasī, *al-Bayān*, 10/666.

إِنَّهُ يَبْدَأُ الْخَلْقَ ثُمَّ يُعِيدُهُ لِيَجْزِيَ الَّذِينَ آمَنُوا وَعَمِلُوا الصَّالِحَاتِ بِالْقِسْطِ

... Indeed, He begins the [process of] creation and then brings it back that He may reward those who have believed and done righteous deeds, in justice...

17-23.7 *'Not at all! Man has not yet accomplished what He commanded him.'*: *Kallā* here is a reply to the unasked question, "After all God's favours to him, has man fulfilled his obligations to his Creator?" Not at all![89]

The verse addresses the general nature of man. If he is not continually reminded of his duty to God in this world, he tends towards inordinacy and heedlessness.[90]

However, even many believers have not yet acted as God has instructed. They have not fulfilled all that God has commanded. They have not been sincere in their worship (and have thus fallen short of their potential) and they have not shown the requisite gratefulness for God's bounties.[91]

SUMMARY OF THE VERSES

In summary, the verses mention that man deserves to perish because of his ingratitude and heedlessness. He must ponder over how he was created from a small drop. Then God allocated to him his unique traits, facilitated his life, and finally caused him to leave the world and be buried. One Day, when He wills, He will resurrect him again. However, as yet, man has not done what God has commanded him to do.

REFLECTIVE LEARNING

Human beings have all been created from lowly beginnings. God has proportioned each of us uniquely in order to fulfil the potential He has given us.

Let me reflect on what God has allocated to me in terms of wealth, poverty, health, illness, the people in my life, and so on. Do I use all of these to get closer to God and thus reach the potential that He has given to me?

---

89 Ṭabāṭabā'ī, *al-Mīzān*, 20/208.

90 Ibid.

91 Ṭūsī, *al-Tibyān*, 10/274.

VERSES 24 - 32

فَلْيَنْظُرِ الْإِنْسَانُ إِلَىٰ طَعَامِهِ ﴿٢٤﴾ أَنَّا صَبَبْنَا الْمَاءَ صَبًّا ﴿٢٥﴾ ثُمَّ شَقَقْنَا الْأَرْضَ
شَقًّا ﴿٢٦﴾ فَأَنْبَتْنَا فِيهَا حَبًّا ﴿٢٧﴾ وَعِنَبًا وَقَضْبًا ﴿٢٨﴾ وَزَيْتُونًا وَنَخْلًا ﴿٢٩﴾
وَحَدَائِقَ غُلْبًا ﴿٣٠﴾ وَفَاكِهَةً وَأَبًّا ﴿٣١﴾ مَتَاعًا لَكُمْ وَلِأَنْعَامِكُمْ ﴿٣٢﴾

Then let man look at his food. [24] *[For] that We poured down water in abundance.* [25] *Then We split the earth in clefts.* [26] *And We caused grain to grow therein.* [27] *And grapes and nutritious plants.* [28] *And olives and date-palms.* [29] *And gardens dense with trees.* [30] *And fruits and fodder.* [31] *A provision for you and your livestock.* [32]

24-32.1 *'Then let man look at his food.'*: The word *fa* (so) indicates that this verse is a continuation and explanation of the previous verse. What follows are examples of bounties that man has not considered due to his ungratefulness.

[*Yanẓur* (يَنْظُر, look at)] here means 'consider'.[92] It means that if man ponders over even this one blessing, he would realize the great favour of God on him.[93]

In this verse, *insān* (man) has been repeated again because it refers to all of mankind, and not just the one who was cursed for his ingratitude and others like him.[94]

A marvellous system has been created to produce food on earth: clouds that bear water, winds that carry these clouds to different lands, rain that falls drop by drop, land that is fecund and receptive, seeds that open in the depths of the earth, and so on. By considering this beautiful harmony that brings about his food, the disbeliever may find the path to God, and the faith of the believer may increase.[95]

24-32.2 Man has been created to be omnivorous and a huge variety of foods, with different tastes and nutritious value, has been placed at his disposal by the all-Merciful Sustainer.

---

[92] Shīrāzī, *Namūneh*, 26/145.

[93] Ṭabāṭabāʾī, *al-Mīzān*, 20/208.

[94] Ibid.

[95] Shīrāzī, *Namūneh*, 26/145.

In order to survive and carry out his daily activity, man needs food for energy. Therefore, he has been created to feel hunger, he is able to derive pleasure from the various tastes of the foods he eats, and his body is designed to efficiently assimilate the food he consumes and transform it into energy. And for the great blessing of food man should always be grateful to God.

24-32.3 An interpretation (*ta'wīl*) of this verse is that it includes spiritual food also. A tradition from Imam al-Baqir (a) states: [Food in this verse refers to] his knowledge and from whom he acquires it.[96] This tradition means to inform man that he requires two kinds of food, one to nourish his body, and another to nourish his soul. Everything that man eats affects his body and everything that he learns, affects his soul. And care must be taken so that both these nutrients are wholesome and healthy. In fact, what goes into the soul is more important than what goes into the body.[97]

A tradition from Imam al-Hasan (a) states: I am amazed at the one who gives thought to his food, but does not give thought to his spiritual nourishment. He keeps his stomach away from that which would harm it, but allows into his heart that which would destroy it.[98]

24-32.4 *'[For] that We poured down water in abundance.'*: Man has not just been asked to reflect on his food, but also the system through which this food is produced.

The directive to ponder over it (*fal yanẓur*) in the previous verse applies to these phenomena also.

[*Ṣababnā* (صَبَبْنَا, We poured down)] is derived from *ṣabba* meaning to pour from a height and here, it refers to sending down rain to supply the earth with life-giving water.[99] The repetition of the word in the verse is for emphasis and to indicate abundance.[100]

A system of storage and distribution for this essential water exists within the watercourses and wells in the earth for the use of man

---

[96] Kulaynī, *al-Kāfī*, 1/49.

عَنْ أَبِي جَعْفَرٍ (عَلَيْهِ السَّلَامُ) – فِي قَوْلِ اللهِ عَزَّ وَجَلَّ: «فَلْيَنْظُرِ الْإِنْسَانُ إِلَىٰ طَعَامِهِ» قَالَ عِلْمُهُ الَّذِي يَأْخُذُهُ عَمَّنْ يَأْخُذُهُ.

[97] Muṭahharī, (*Āshnāyī bā Qur'an*), *Āthār*, 28/374.

[98] Majlisī, *Biḥār*, 1/218.

عَنِ الْحَسَنِ (عَلَيْهِ السَّلَامُ) – عَجَبٌ لِمَنْ يَتَفَكَّرُ فِي مَأْكُولِهِ كَيْفَ لَا يَتَفَكَّرُ فِي مَعْقُولِهِ فَيُجَنِّبُ بَطْنَهُ مَا يُؤْذِيهِ وَيُودِعُ صَدْرَهُ مَا يُرْدِيهِ.

[99] Ṭabāṭabā'ī, *al-Mīzān*, 20/209.

[100] Shīrāzī, *Namūneh*, 26/147.

and animals. Indeed, this rainfall is blessed, because it sets up a chain of events that sustains life. Q50:9 states:

وَنَزَّلْنَا مِنَ السَّمَاءِ مَاءً مُبَارَكًا فَأَنبَتْنَا بِهِ جَنَّاتٍ وَحَبَّ الْحَصِيدِ

And We have sent down blessed rain from the sky
and made grow thereby gardens and grain from the harvest.

24-32.5 *'Then We split the earth in clefts.'*: [*Shaqaqnā* (شَقَقْنَا, We split)] is derived from *shaqqa* meaning to split, and refers to the fact that after sending rain, the earth is made soft enough for plants to sprout and emerge in even the harshest conditions.

24-32.6 *'And We caused grain to grow therein. And grapes and nutritious plants. And olives and date-palms. And gardens dense with trees. And fruits and fodder.'*: After mentioning the rain and the soil that makes the earth fertile, these verses give eight examples[101] of the diverse and uniquely beneficial crops and vegetation that come from the earth, all for which gratitude is due:

1. [*Ḥabb* (حَبّ, grains)] refers to the genus of plants such as wheat and barley, corn, rice, lentils, and similar produce that are the staple food for mankind.[102]
2. [*ʿInab* (عِنَب, grapes)] means grapes as well as grapevines. However, here it refers to grapes.
3. [*Qaḍb* (قَضْب, nutritious plants)] refers to the huge variety of edible vegetables and herbs that are cut (*quḍiba*) from the earth.[103]
4. [*Zaytūn* (زَيْتُون, olives] can refer to olives as well as olive trees.
5. [*Nakhl* (نَخْل, date-palms)] are the source of dates.

   Every one of these is an example of highly nutritious foods.[104]
6. [*Ḥadāʾiq* (حَدَائِق, gardens)] is the plural of *ḥadīqah* and means walled gardens.

   [*Ghulb* (غُلْب, dense trees)] means trees which have a dense and luxuriant growth.

   The term refers to orchards with many large trees.[105]

---

[101] Rāzī, *Mafātīḥ al-Ghayb*, 31/59.
[102] Ṭabāṭabāʾī, *al-Mīzān*, 20/209.
[103] Muṣṭafawī, *al-Taḥqīq*.
[104] Shīrāzī, *Namūneh*, 26/149.
[105] Ṭabāṭabāʾī, *al-Mīzān*, 20/209.

7. [*Fākihah* (فَاكِهَة, fruit)] here refers to the abundant variety of fruits that are found in the world.[106] And the mention of grapes, olives, and dates separately earlier, may be because of their prominence amongst fruits.[107]
8. [*Abb* (أَبّ, fodder)]. These are the pastures on which animals and livestock graze.[108] In turn, some of these animals feed human beings also.

24-32.7 The meaning of *abb* eluded some senior companions, and this is an indication that not all companions were well versed in the meaning of the whole Qur'an. The following two reports have been recorded by several *Sunni* and *Shīʿa* exegetes[109] about the confusion that occurred regarding this term.

Abu Bakr was asked about the meaning of '*wa abbā*' and he replied, "Under which sky will I seek shade and on which earth will I take refuge if I say something about God's Book which I do not know?"[110] When his words reached Ali (a) he said, "Glory be to God! Does he not know that *al-abb* is pasture and grazing ground?..."[111]

Another report states: One day ʿUmar b. al-Khaṭṭāb recited the verses '*fa anbatnā fīhā ḥabban*' up to '*wa fākihatin wa abbā*' (verses 27 to 31 of the surah) from the pulpit. Then he said, "We have understood [the rest of] the verses, but what is *al-abb*?" Then he raised a cane that was in in his hand and said, "By God! This [matter] is an unwarranted burden (*al-takalluf*). What does it matter, O ʿUmar, that you do not know what *al-abb* is? Take what is clear for you from this Book and act according to it. As for what you do not know, leave it to its Lord."[112]

---

106 Ṭabrasī, *al-Bayān*, 10/668.

107 Shīrāzī, *Namūneh*, 26/153.

108 Muṣṭafawī, *al-Taḥqīq*.

109 As reported by Suyūṭī in *al-Durr al-Manthūr*, Qurṭubī in his *Tafsīr*, Ālūsī in *Rūḥ al-Maʿānī*, Ṭabāṭabāʾī in *al-Mīzān*, and many others.

110 Suyūṭī, *al-Durr al-Manthūr*, 6/317.

قَالَ أَيُّ سَمَاءٍ تُظِلُّنِي وَأَيُّ أَرْضٍ تُقِلُّنِي إِذَا قُلْتُ فِي كِتَابِ اللهِ مَا لَا أَعْلَمُ.

111 Mufīd, *al-Irshād*, 1/200.

فَبَلَغَ أَمِيرَ الْمُؤْمِنِينَ عَلَيْهِ السَّلَامُ مَقَالُهُ فِي ذَلِكَ فَقَالَ عَلَيْهِ السَّلَامُ: يَا سُبْحَانَ اللهِ أَمَا عَلِمَ أَنَّ الْأَبَّ هُوَ الْكَلَاءُ وَالْمَرْعَى.

112 Ālūsī, *Rūḥ al-Maʿānī*, 15/250.

وَرُوِيَ أَنَّ عُمَرَ بْنَ الْخَطَّابِ قَرَأَ يَوْمًا عَلَى الْمِنْبَرِ: فَأَنْبَتْنَا فِيهَا حَبًّا إِلَى وَأَبًّا فَقَالَ: كُلُّ هَذَا قَدْ عَرَفْنَاهُ فَمَا الْأَبُّ؟ ثُمَّ رَفَعَ عَصًا كَانَتْ فِي يَدِهِ، وَقَالَ: هَذَا لَعَمْرُ اللهِ هُوَ التَّكَلُّفُ فَمَا عَلَيْكَ يَا ابْنَ أُمِّ عُمَرَ أَنْ لَا تَدْرِي مَا الْأَبُّ، ابْتَغُوا مَا بُيِّنَ لَكُمْ مِنْ هَذَا الْكِتَابِ فَاعْمَلُوا بِهِ، وَمَا لَمْ تَعْرِفُوهُ فَكِلُوهُ إِلَى رَبِّهِ.

The accounts above indicate that even those who had assumed charge of the affairs of Muslims were not familiar with some aspects of the Qurʾan. Only four men were widely accepted as the most knowledgeable in this field: Ali b. Abu Talib (a), ʿAbdullāh b. Masʿūd, ʿAbdullāh b. ʿAbbās, and Ubayy b. Kaʿb.[113] However, among them Ali (a) was acknowledged as preeminent in his knowledge of the Qurʾan. Ibn Abīʾl Ḥadīd writes: If you study the books of *tafsīr* you will realize the truth of this because most of it can be traced back to Ali or to Ibn Abbas. And it is well known that Ibn Abbas was attached and dedicated to Ali, and was his student and disciple. Ibn Abbas was asked, "How does your knowledge compare to that of your cousin?" He replied, "It is like a drop of rain in a vast ocean."[114]

24-32.8 The marvellous thing about all the foods and plants that grow from the earth, with their diverse colours and tastes, is that they are all nourished by the same water. Q13:4 states:

وَفِي الْأَرْضِ قِطَعٌ مُتَجَاوِرَاتٌ وَجَنَّاتٌ مِنْ أَعْنَابٍ وَزَرْعٌ
وَنَخِيلٌ صِنْوَانٌ وَغَيْرُ صِنْوَانٍ يُسْقَىٰ بِمَاءٍ وَاحِدٍ وَنُفَضِّلُ بَعْضَهَا
عَلَىٰ بَعْضٍ فِي الْأُكُلِ إِنَّ فِي ذَٰلِكَ لَآيَاتٍ لِقَوْمٍ يَعْقِلُونَ

And within the earth are [diverse but] neighbouring tracts, gardens of grapevines, crops, and palm trees, [growing] from one root or otherwise, [but] watered with one water. And We make some of them exceed others in [quality and taste of] fruit. Indeed, in these things are signs for a people who use their intellect.

24-32.9 '*A provision for you and your livestock.*': In Surat al-Nāziʿāt the same phrase was used when discussing the creation of man, after which there was a mention of water and pasture in general. In this surah a more detailed description of God's provision (*matāʿ*) is given. *Matāʿ* refers to everything that gives enjoyment and benefit. And interestingly, every food mentioned as a provision for man is plant-based, indicating the dietary importance of grain, vegetables, and fruit.[115]

---

113 Dhahabī, *al-Tafsīr wa'l Mufassirūn*, 1/68.

114 Ibn Abīʾl Ḥadīd, *Sharḥ Nahj al-Balāghah*, 1/19.

إِذَا رَجَعْتَ إِلَى كُتُبِ التَّفْسِيرِ عَلِمْتَ صِحَّةَ ذَلِكَ لِأَنَّ أَكْثَرَهُ عَنْهُ وَعَنْ عَبْدِ اللهِ بْنِ عَبَّاس وَقَدْ عَلِمَ النَّاسُ حَالَ ابْنِ عَبَّاس فِي مُلَازَمَتِهِ لَهُ وَانْقِطَاعِهِ إِلَيْهِ وَأَنَّهُ تِلْمِيذُهُ وَخِرِّيجُهُ وَقِيلَ لَهُ: أَيْنَ عِلْمُكَ مِنْ عِلْمِ ابْنِ عَمِّكَ؟ فَقَالَ: كَنِسْبَةِ قَطْرَةٍ مِنَ الْمَطَرِ إِلَى الْبَحْرِ الْمُحِيطِ.

115 Shīrāzī, *Namūneh*, 26/153.

Some exegetes say that fruits (*fākihah*) denotes all the provision prepared for mankind and pasture (*abb*) denotes all provision for livestock.[116]

SUMMARY OF THE VERSES

In these verses, man is instructed to ponder about the food that he consumes. In order to produce it, God sends down abundant water on to the earth which allows all types of plants to sprout from it.

Examples are given of grain, grapes, nutritious plants, olives, date-palms, orchards, fruits, as well as pasture. These are all provided by God to sustain both human beings and their livestock.

REFLECTIVE LEARNING

In earlier verses, God had accused man of being ungrateful. In these verses, God gives examples of bounties for which man must give thanks, so as not to be like animals who eat what is in front of them without much thought.

Let me reflect on whether I ponder over the harmonious arrangement in creation that produces every morsel of the food that I eat daily and whether I am truly grateful for it.

VERSES 33 - 37

فَإِذَا جَاءَتِ الصَّاخَّةُ ﴿٣٣﴾ يَوْمَ يَفِرُّ الْمَرْءُ مِنْ أَخِيهِ ﴿٣٤﴾ وَأُمِّهِ وَأَبِيهِ ﴿٣٥﴾
وَصَاحِبَتِهِ وَبَنِيهِ ﴿٣٦﴾ لِكُلِّ امْرِئٍ مِنْهُمْ يَوْمَئِذٍ شَأْنٌ يُغْنِيهِ ﴿٣٧﴾

But when the deafening cry comes. [33] *The Day when a man will flee from his brother.* [34] *And his mother and his father.* [35] *And his wife and his children.* [36] *Every one of them on that Day shall have an affair [of his own] to preoccupy him.* [37]

33-37.1 After mentioning God's blessings and provisions that give energy to man to act, the verses turn to the Hereafter. This is to indicate that these worldly provisions are transient,[117] and the actions that they allowed mankind to perform will be evaluated

116 Ṭabrasī, *al-Bayān*, 10/668.

117 Shīrāzī, *Namūneh*, 26/156.

and recompensed one Day.[118] The purpose of the provisions was to test and establish the placement of individuals in the real life, which is the life of *ākhirah*.

33-37.2 *'But when the deafening cry comes.'*: [*Al-Ṣākhkhah* (الصَّاخَّةُ, the deafening cry)] is a sound whose vibrations overcome the ears and heart due to its intensity.[119] Some exegetes say that it is a sound that drowns out other sounds, and refers to the only thing that people hear.[120] It could also be a reference to the second blowing of the trumpet which will resurrect creation and herald the Day of Judgement.[121]

The term is not mentioned elsewhere in the Qur'an.

33-37.3 *'The Day when a man will flee from his brother. And his mother and his father. And his wife and his children.'*: That Day will be one on which everyone will be deeply concerned with his own fate.

[*Yafirru* (يَفِرُّ, he flees)] is derived from *farra* and means to move quickly away from something, or towards something.[122] Here, it means to run away in fright.

In the beginning of the surah, there was a rebuke to the man who paid attention to someone because of his wealth and social standing. Now the Qur'an states that on that Day man will seek to evade even his closest and dearest relatives, fleeing from his brother, parents, spouse, and even his children. According to some exegetes, these relatives have been mentioned in the order of increasing closeness that exists for most people.[123]

It is interesting that in a similar scene described in Surat al-Maʿārij (70), the criminals amongst mankind will not just flee from their relatives, but they will be prepared to sacrifice them in order to save themselves. Q70:11-14 state:

يَوَدُّ الْمُجْرِمُ لَوْ يَفْتَدِي مِنْ عَذَابِ يَوْمِئِذٍ بِبَنِيهِ ﴿١١﴾ وَصَاحِبَتِهِ وَأَخِيهِ ﴿١٢﴾ وَفَصِيلَتِهِ الَّتِي تُؤْوِيهِ ﴿١٣﴾ وَمَنْ فِي الْأَرْضِ جَمِيعًا ثُمَّ يُنْجِيهِ

118 Ṭabāṭabāʾī, *al-Mīzān*, 20/210.
119 Muṣṭafawī, al-*Taḥqīq*.
120 Zamakhsharī, *al-Kashshāf*, 4/705.
121 Ṭūsī, *al-Tibyān*, 10/277.
122 Muṣṭafawī, al-*Taḥqīq*.
123 Mughniyyah, *al-Kāshif*, 7/521.

... The criminal will desire that he could be ransomed from the punishment of that Day by [sacrificing] his children, his spouse, his brother, his nearest kindred who sheltered him, and everyone on the earth entirely – so that it might save him.

In the verses under discussion the sequence of relatives mentioned is from distant to near while in Surat al-Maʿārij it is from near to distant, showing the callous selfishness of the criminals.[124]

For the verses under review, exegetes have given several possible reasons why people will run from the very same individuals whom they used to turn to for support in the *dunyā*:

i) there will be a level of personal worry that will cause every altruistic instinct to flee from the minds,

ii) they will be afraid that their relatives may make a claim of their usurped rights or ask for help, and

iii) the believers will flee from the disbelievers, even if they were their closest relatives, so that they are not caught up in their fate.[125]

However, the first meaning is the most plausible, and also conforms best with what is mentioned in the next verse.

33-37.4 *'Every one of them on that Day shall have an affair [of his own] to preoccupy him.'*: [*Sha'n* (شَأْن, affair)] means a grave circumstance, situation, or affair.[126] In addition to the reasons for fleeing mentioned in the previous section, individuals will be so completely engrossed in their own worry about what they are going through that they will not be able to spare a thought for anyone else.[127] Everyone will realize that they are living through the most important day of their life, and that their eternal fate depends on its outcome.

33-37.5 A tradition states that when the Prophet (s) was asked whether people will remember their close friends on the Day of Judgement, he said, "There are three stations at which no one will remember anyone else: i) At the scales (*mīzān*), to see whether his scales are heavy or light, ii) on the path (*ṣirāṭ*) to see whether he is allowed to cross or not, iii) and when the scrolls (*ṣuḥuf*) are given out, to

124 Ṭabrasī, *al-Bayān*, 10/534.
125 Shīrāzī, *Namūneh*, 26/157.
126 Muṣṭafawī, al-*Taḥqīq*.
127 Ṭabāṭabā'ī, *al-Mīzān*, 20/210.

see whether he will be handed them in his right hand or his left. At these three places, no one will remember his closest friend, his beloved, his relative, his comrade, his children, or his parents. This is the meaning of the words of God, the Exalted, *'Every one of them on that Day shall have an affair [of his own] to preoccupy him.'* They will be engrossed in their own plight due to the intense terror that they will experience. We ask Allah, the Exalted to make that [Day] easy for us out of His mercy, and to assist us out of His Compassion and Grace."[128]

33-37.6 In a beautiful whispered-supplication (*munājah*) attributed to Imam Ali (a) he said: [O Allah!] I ask you for protection on *'the Day when a man will flee from his brother, and his mother and his father, and his wife and his children. Every one of them on that Day shall have an affair [of his own] to preoccupy him.'*[129]

SUMMARY OF THE VERSES

A deafening cry will herald the Day of Judgement. The verses describe how that event will drive concerns of kinship away from the mind.

People will run from their brother, mother, father, spouse and children. Every single person will have his own unique worries that will completely preoccupy him.

REFLECTIVE LEARNING

Can I imagine a time when I would ever flee from the people who form my closest and dearest support structure – my brother, my parents, my spouse, and my children?

The brother is the support that a person relies on, the parents are those to whom man is obliged for their care and upbringing, the spouse is the relative that one has selected to be their partner in life, and the children are the fruit of one's life.

---

[128] Baḥrānī, *al-Burhān*, 5/586.

عَنِ الرَّسُولِ (صَلَّى اللهُ عَلَيْهِ وَآلِهِ) – ثَلَاثَةُ مَوَاطِنَ لَا يَذْكُرُ أَحَدٌ أَحَدًا: عِنْدَ الْمِيزَانِ حَتَّى يَنْظُرَ أَيَثْقُلُ مِيزَانُهُ أَمْ يَخِفُّ، وَعِنْدَ الصِّرَاطِ حَتَّى يَنْظُرَ أَيَجُوزُهُ أَمْ لَا، وَعِنْدَ الصُّحُفِ حَتَّى يَنْظُرَ بِيَمِينِهِ يَأْخُذُ الصُّحُفَ أَمْ بِشِمَالِهِ، فَهَذِهِ ثَلَاثَةُ مَوَاطِنَ لَا يَذْكُرُ فِيهَا أَحَدٌ حَمِيمَهُ وَلَا حَبِيبَهُ وَلَا قَرِيبَهُ وَلَا صَدِيقَهُ وَلَا بَنِيهِ وَلَا وَالِدَيْهِ، وَذَلِكَ قَوْلُ اللهِ تَعَالَى:«لِكُلِّ امْرِئٍ مِنْهُمْ يَوْمَئِذٍ شَأْنٌ يُغْنِيه»، مَشْغُولٌ بِنَفْسِهِ عَنْ غَيْرِهِ مِنْ شِدَّةِ مَا يَرَى مِنَ الْأَهْوَالِ الْعِظَامِ، نَسْأَلُ اللهَ تَعَالَى أَنْ يُسَهِّلَهَا لَنَا بِرَحْمَتِهِ، وَيُهَوِّنَهَا عَلَيْنَا بِرَأْفَتِهِ وَلُطْفِهِ.

[129] Qummī, *Mafātīḥ al-Jinān*, 1/495.

وَأَسْأَلُكَ الْأَمَانَ «يَوْمَ يَفِرُّ الْمَرْءُ مِنْ أَخِيهِ وَأُمِّهِ وَأَبِيهِ وَصَاحِبَتِهِ وَبَنِيهِ لِكُلِّ امْرِئٍ مِنْهُمْ يَوْمَئِذٍ شَأْنٌ يُغْنِيهِ»

Let me reflect on whether my love for each of them is actually an extension of my love for God. In that case, perhaps I will not run away from them on that Day.

VERSES 38, 39

وُجُوهٌ يَوْمَئِذٍ مُسْفِرَةٌ ﴿٣٨﴾ ضَاحِكَةٌ مُسْتَبْشِرَةٌ ﴿٣٩﴾

[Some] faces that Day will be bright. [38] *Laughing, [rejoicing] at good news.* [39]

38-39.1 *'[Some] faces that Day will be bright.'*: On that Day, people will be divided into two groups: the people of felicity (*sa'ādah*) and the people of wretchedness (*shaqāwah*). Both groups will be recognizable by the state of their faces (*wujūh*).[130] The reference to faces is because the face is the first part of the body that reflects an individual's physical and emotional state.[131]

[*Musfirah* (مُسْفِرَة, bright)] is derived from *asfara* meaning to become apparent and radiate, just as the dawn dispels the dark of the night. On the Day of Judgement their faces will be radiant with the light of the purity of their faith and actions.[132]

38-39.2 *'Laughing, [rejoicing] at good news.'*: [*Ḍāḥikah* (ضَاحِكَة, laughing)] is derived from *ḍaḥika* which means to laugh in delight.[133]

[*Mustabshirah* (مُسْتَبْشِرَة, received good news)] is derived from *bashara* meaning to be happy, and here it means someone who has received exceedingly good news. The faces of those who have been given the good news of Paradise will reflect their intense joy.

SUMMARY OF THE VERSES

The verses state that the faces of those who have been given the good news of Paradise will be bright as their inner faith becomes evident. And they will be laughing in delight at their success.

---

130 Ṭabāṭabā'ī, *al-Mīzān*, 20/210.

131 Shīrāzī, *Namūneh*, 26/161.

132 Ibid.

133 Muṣṭafawī, *al-Taḥqīq*.

REFLECTIVE LEARNING

In this world there have been times when I have rejoiced at the good news of the short-lived successes of life.

Let me reflect on how I could make these short term events into an everlasting happiness in the Hereafter.

VERSES 40 - 42

وَوُجُوهٌ يَوْمَئِذٍ عَلَيْهَا غَبَرَةٌ ﴿٤٠﴾ تَرْهَقُهَا قَتَرَةٌ ﴿٤١﴾ أُولَٰئِكَ هُمُ الْكَفَرَةُ الْفَجَرَةُ ﴿٤٢﴾

And [some] faces that Day will be stained with dust. [40] *Darkness will cover them.* [41] *Those are the disbelievers, the evil ones.* [42]

40-42.1 *'And [some] faces that Day will be stained with dust.'*: By contrast, the faces of those who have been given the bad news of Hell will reflect their despair.

[*Ghabarah* (غَبَرَة, stained with dust)] is the plural of *ghubār* and is derived from *ghabara* meaning to be covered in dust, or become dark in colour. It refers to the manifestation of the dirt of *dunyā* that persists in the soul.

40-42.2 *'Darkness will cover them.'*: [*Tarhaqu* (تَرْهَق, it covers)] is derived from *rahaqa* which means to rise and envelop.[134]

[*Qatarah* (قَتَرَة, darkness)] is derived from *qatara* meaning dark smoke from a wood fire.[135]

Here, it means that darkness and gloominess will cover their faces. And this will be a reflection of their inner state. Their condition is explained further in Q10:26, 27 which state:

لِّلَّذِينَ أَحْسَنُوا الْحُسْنَىٰ وَزِيَادَةٌ وَلَا يَرْهَقُ وُجُوهَهُمْ قَتَرٌ وَلَا ذِلَّةٌ أُولَٰئِكَ أَصْحَابُ الْجَنَّةِ هُمْ فِيهَا خَالِدُونَ ﴿٢٦﴾ وَالَّذِينَ كَسَبُوا السَّيِّئَاتِ جَزَاءُ سَيِّئَةٍ بِمِثْلِهَا وَتَرْهَقُهُمْ ذِلَّةٌ مَا لَهُم مِّنَ اللَّهِ مِنْ عَاصِمٍ كَأَنَّمَا أُغْشِيَتْ وُجُوهُهُمْ قِطَعًا مِّنَ اللَّيْلِ مُظْلِمًا أُولَٰئِكَ أَصْحَابُ النَّارِ هُمْ فِيهَا خَالِدُونَ

---

[134] Ṭabrasī, *al-Bayān*, 10/669.

[135] Muṣṭafawī, *al-Taḥqīq*.

For those who have done good is the best [reward] and even more. No darkness nor humiliation will cover their faces. Those are companions of Paradise; they will abide therein eternally. But those who have earned [blame for] evil deeds - the recompense of an evil deed is its equivalent, and humiliation will cover them. They will have from Allah no protector. It will be as if their faces are covered with patches of the darkness of night. Those are companions of the Fire; they will abide therein eternally.

40-42.3 '*Those are the disbelievers, the evil ones.*': The first group that was mentioned in the previous verse was not identified, because it is clear who they are.[136] However the second group is referred to as *kafarah*, the plural of *kāfir* (disbeliever), referring to their faithless hearts, and *fajarah*, the plural of *fājir*, (evil doer), referring to their evil actions.[137]

They will be in this state because in the world they were persistently ungrateful to God and remained arrogant and disobedient to Him. May Allah protect us from such a fate.

SUMMARY OF THE VERSES

The verses state that the faces of those who have been given the dreadful news of Hell will be clouded with dust and darkness as their inner state becomes evident. These are those who had no faith and committed sinful and evil acts.

REFLECTIVE LEARNING

Every disobedience to God is an evil that creates a stain in the heart that is not evident in this world, but will be clearly manifest on faces on the Day of Judgement.

Let me reflect on what would be evident on my face if I was standing on the Day of Judgement right now.

136 Muṭahharī, (*Āshnāyī bā Qur'an*), *Āthār*, 28/384.

137 Ṭabrasī, *al-Bayān*, 10/669.

SURAT AL-TAKWĪR
THE ENFOLDING (81)

TEXT AND TRANSLATION

سُورَةُ التَّكْوِيرِ

بِسْمِ اللَّهِ الرَّحْمَٰنِ الرَّحِيمِ

إِذَا الشَّمْسُ كُوِّرَتْ ﴿١﴾ وَإِذَا النُّجُومُ انْكَدَرَتْ ﴿٢﴾ وَإِذَا الْجِبَالُ سُيِّرَتْ ﴿٣﴾
وَإِذَا الْعِشَارُ عُطِّلَتْ ﴿٤﴾ وَإِذَا الْوُحُوشُ حُشِرَتْ ﴿٥﴾ وَإِذَا الْبِحَارُ سُجِّرَتْ
﴿٦﴾ وَإِذَا النُّفُوسُ زُوِّجَتْ ﴿٧﴾ وَإِذَا الْمَوْءُودَةُ سُئِلَتْ ﴿٨﴾ بِأَيِّ ذَنْبٍ قُتِلَتْ
﴿٩﴾ وَإِذَا الصُّحُفُ نُشِرَتْ ﴿١٠﴾ وَإِذَا السَّمَاءُ كُشِطَتْ ﴿١١﴾ وَإِذَا الْجَحِيمُ
سُعِّرَتْ ﴿١٢﴾ وَإِذَا الْجَنَّةُ أُزْلِفَتْ ﴿١٣﴾ عَلِمَتْ نَفْسٌ مَا أَحْضَرَتْ ﴿١٤﴾ فَلَا
أُقْسِمُ بِالْخُنَّسِ ﴿١٥﴾ الْجَوَارِ الْكُنَّسِ ﴿١٦﴾ وَاللَّيْلِ إِذَا عَسْعَسَ ﴿١٧﴾ وَالصُّبْحِ
إِذَا تَنَفَّسَ ﴿١٨﴾ إِنَّهُ لَقَوْلُ رَسُولٍ كَرِيمٍ ﴿١٩﴾ ذِي قُوَّةٍ عِنْدَ ذِي الْعَرْشِ مَكِينٍ
﴿٢٠﴾ مُطَاعٍ ثَمَّ أَمِينٍ ﴿٢١﴾ وَمَا صَاحِبُكُمْ بِمَجْنُونٍ ﴿٢٢﴾ وَلَقَدْ رَآهُ بِالْأُفُقِ
الْمُبِينِ ﴿٢٣﴾ وَمَا هُوَ عَلَى الْغَيْبِ بِضَنِينٍ ﴿٢٤﴾ وَمَا هُوَ بِقَوْلِ شَيْطَانٍ رَجِيمٍ
﴿٢٥﴾ فَأَيْنَ تَذْهَبُونَ ﴿٢٦﴾ إِنْ هُوَ إِلَّا ذِكْرٌ لِلْعَالَمِينَ ﴿٢٧﴾ لِمَنْ شَاءَ مِنْكُمْ أَنْ
يَسْتَقِيمَ ﴿٢٨﴾ وَمَا تَشَاؤُونَ إِلَّا أَنْ يَشَاءَ اللَّهُ رَبُّ الْعَالَمِينَ ﴿٢٩﴾

In the name of God, the Beneficent, the Merciful.

When the sun is folded up, [1] *and when the stars fade away,* [2] *and when the mountains are set in motion,* [3] *and when the full-term she-camels are left untended,* [4] *and when the wild beasts are gathered,* [5] *and when the seas are made to boil over,* [6] *and when the souls are united,* [7] *and when the female infant [who was] buried alive is asked* [8] *for what sin she was killed,* [9] *and when the scrolls [of actions] are laid open,* [10] *and when the sky is stripped away,* [11] *and when hellfire is set ablaze,* [12] *and when Paradise is brought near.* [13] *[Then] every soul will know what it has brought [with it].* [14] *So, I swear by those [planets] that recede,* [15] *those that run [their course] and disappear.* [16] *And by the night as it dissipates,* [17] *and by the dawn when it breathes [light].* [18] *Indeed, it (the Qurʾan) is a Word of a noble messenger,* [19] *possessor of strength, established before the Possessor of the Throne.* [20] *[One] obeyed there, trustworthy.* [21] *Your companion is not a madman.* [22] *Without doubt he saw him (Jibraʾil) in the clear horizon.* [23] *And he does not withhold [knowledge of] the unseen.* [24] *Nor is it (the Qurʾan) the word of Shaytan, the outcast.* [25] *So where are you going?* [26] *Indeed, it is nothing except a reminder to all of creation.* [27] *For whoever wills among you to take a right course.* [28] *And you cannot will except as Allah, the Lord of the worlds, wills.* [29]

INTRODUCTION

Surat al-Takwīr (81) was the 7th chapter to be revealed.[1] It has twenty-nine verses and is one of the early Makkan surahs, revealed after Surat al-Masad (111). It is named after one of the signs of the Day of Judgement mentioned in the first verse, the folding of the sun (*takwīr*).

The first thirteen verses of this surah consist of brief descriptions of a series of momentous events, both terrifying and wondrous, that will occur as the *dunyā* comes to an end. Of these, the first six verses speak of events that will happen after the first blowing of the trumpet, and the next seven speak of events that will happen at resurrection, after the second blowing.

It is at this time that man will begin to attain a realization of the net worth of his life.

The second section of the surah mentions four oaths to emphasize that the Qurʾan is the Word of God, revealed to the Prophet (s) through the noble, powerful, and trustworthy messenger-angel Jibraʾil.

Finally, the surah declares that the Qurʾan is a reminder for anyone who wants to take the right course in his journey towards God. And in every case, man's will is subservient to the will of God.

---

[1] Maʿrifat, *ʿUlūm-i Qurʾānī*, p. 90.

LINK TO THE PREVIOUS CHAPTER

The previous chapter, Surat ʿAbasa, ended by contrasting the fates of the believers and the disbelievers on the Day of Judgement. Surat al-Takwīr begins by describing a series of different cataclysmic events that will herald the advent of that tremendous Day.

Both surahs give descriptions of how extreme fear and individual concern will cause men and other creatures to behave contrary to their natural behaviour as the *ākhirah* begins. Surat ʿAbasa describes people who are closely attached to each other in this world running away from each other, while Surat al-Takwīr states that wild beasts who normally attack one another, will herd together instead.

MERITS OF RECITATION

- A tradition from the Prophet (s) states: Whoever recites Surat *Idhā al-shamsu kuwwirat* will be protected from disgrace by God, the Exalted, when his scroll of deeds is opened.[2]
- Another tradition from the Prophet (s) states: Whoever wishes to perceive the Day of Judgement [and the way it unfolds] should recite *Idhā al-shamsu kuwwirat.*[3]
- A tradition from Imam al-Sadiq (a) states: Whoever recites Surat ʿAbasa and al-Takwīr shall be under the protective wing of God in Paradise. He will be in the shade of God's mercy and generosity in His gardens. And this is not difficult for God if He wills.[4]

EXEGESIS

VERSES 1 - 14

إِذَا الشَّمْسُ كُوِّرَتْ ﴿١﴾ وَإِذَا النُّجُومُ ٱنْكَدَرَتْ ﴿٢﴾ وَإِذَا الْجِبَالُ سُيِّرَتْ ﴿٣﴾
وَإِذَا الْعِشَارُ عُطِّلَتْ ﴿٤﴾ وَإِذَا الْوُحُوشُ حُشِرَتْ ﴿٥﴾ وَإِذَا الْبِحَارُ سُجِّرَتْ ﴿٦﴾

---

[2] Nūrī, *Mustadrak al-Wasāʾil*, 4/356.

عَنِ الرَّسُولِ (صَلَّى اللهُ عَلَيْهِ وَآلِهِ) – وَمَنْ قَرَأَ سُورَةَ «إِذَا الشَّمْسُ كُوِّرَتْ» أَعَاذَهُ اللهُ تَعَالَى أَنْ يَفْضَحَهُ حِينَ تُنْشَرُ صَحِيفَتُهُ.

[3] Ibid.

عَنِ الرَّسُولِ (صَلَّى اللهُ عَلَيْهِ وَآلِهِ) – مَنْ أَحَبَّ أَنْ يَنْظُرَ إِلَى يَوْمِ الْقِيَامَةِ فَلْيَقْرَأْ إِذَا الشَّمْسُ كُوِّرَتْ.

[4] Ḥuwayzī, *Nūr al-Thaqalayn*. 5/512.

عَنِ الصَّادِقِ (عَلَيْهِ السَّلَامُ) – مَنْ قَرَأَ سُورَةَ «عَبَسَ وَ تَوَلَّى» وَ«إِذَا الشَّمْسُ كُوِّرَتْ» كَانَ تَحْتَ جَنَاحِ اللهِ مِنَ الْجِنَانِ وَفِي ظِلِّ اللهِ وَكَرَامَتِهِ فِي جِنَانِهِ وَلَا يَعْظُمُ ذَلِكَ عَلَى اللهِ إِنْ شَاءَ اللهُ.

وَإِذَا النُّفُوسُ زُوِّجَتْ ﴿٧﴾ وَإِذَا الْمَوْءُودَةُ سُئِلَتْ ﴿٨﴾ بِأَيِّ ذَنْبٍ قُتِلَتْ ﴿٩﴾
وَإِذَا الصُّحُفُ نُشِرَتْ ﴿١٠﴾ وَإِذَا السَّمَاءُ كُشِطَتْ ﴿١١﴾ وَإِذَا الْجَحِيمُ سُعِّرَتْ
﴿١٢﴾ وَإِذَا الْجَنَّةُ أُزْلِفَتْ ﴿١٣﴾ عَلِمَتْ نَفْسٌ مَا أَحْضَرَتْ ﴿١٤﴾

When the sun is folded up, [1] *and when the stars fade away,* [2] *and when the mountains are set in motion,* [3] *and when the full-term she-camels are left untended,* [4] *and when the wild beasts are gathered,* [5] *and when the seas are made to boil over,* [6] *and when the souls are united,* [7] *and when the female infant [who was] buried alive is asked* [8] *for what sin she was killed,* [9] *and when the scrolls [of actions] are laid open,* [10] *and when the sky is stripped away,* [11] *and when hellfire is set ablaze,* [12] *and when Paradise is brought near.* [13] *[Then] every soul will know what it has brought [with it].* [14]

1-14.1 The first thirteen verses illustrate flashes of the tumultuous events of the last Hour, (*ashrāṭ al-sāʿah*) which will bring the *dunyā* to its end and herald the *ākhirah*. The different phenomena that support this earthly life will be removed in turn, beginning a universal cascade that will cause the collapse of the systems that sustain the *dunyā*.

These supports are necessary for man to be able to undergo his test in the *dunyā*. However, when that phase of his existence comes to an end, they will no longer be required, and so God will remove them.[5]

With these events, man will finally realize his true worth, when he surveys the result of his labours in the *dunyā*, and the provisions that he has accumulated for his eternal life.[6]

1-14.2 The fourteen verses under review exhibit a powerful cadence that is achieved by the use of *idhā* and *wa* at the beginning of the verses, employing nouns that have a lengthier pronunciation followed by terse verbs in the passive tense, and switching the verb and noun order so that every verse ends with the letter ta (ت). This rhythmic style adds great eloquence to the expressions, attracting the attention of the listener.

---

[5] Javādī-Āmolī, *Tasnīm*, (Transcript: http://javadi.esra.ir/-/23-09-1398-1--تفسیر-سوره-تکویر-جلسه)

[6] Muṭahharī, (*Āshnāyī bā Qur'an*), *Āthār*, 28/387.

1-14.3 '*When the sun is folded up,*': [*Idhā* (إِذَا when)] gives the meaning of suddenness and certainty, meaning that there is no doubt that these events will happen, and they will come about without warning. A sentence beginning with *idhā* is conditional and requires a main clause (*jazā'*) after the conditional clause. In this case, the *jazā'* comes after thirteen verses, indicating the great significance of the reply.

[*Kuwwirat* (كُوِّرَتْ, folded up)] is derived from *kawwara* meaning to fold or wrap into a circular shape and gather up. The term is used to describe the wrapping of a turban around the head.[7] In Q39:5, *kawwara* elegantly describes how night and day fold into each other as the earth rotates on its own axis:

يُكَوِّرُ اللَّيْلَ عَلَى النَّهَارِ وَيُكَوِّرُ النَّهَارَ عَلَى اللَّيْلِ

... He wraps the night over the day
and wraps the day over the night.

In the verse under review, *kuwwirat* is a reference to the extinguishing of the sun.[8] Its brilliant illumination will be wrapped up as it collapses on itself and loses its ability to generate light and energy. Modern science has advanced several theories about how the sun will be extinguished and has predicted that it will not happen for billions of years. However, it is likely that this momentous occurrence is from the matters related to the command (*amr*) of God, which He brings about instantly whenever He decides. Q2:117 states:

بَدِيعُ السَّمَاوَاتِ وَالْأَرْضِ وَإِذَا قَضَىٰ أَمْرًا فَإِنَّمَا يَقُولُ لَهُ كُن فَيَكُونُ

[God is the] Originator of the heavens and the earth.
When He decrees a matter, He only says to it, "Be," and it is.

1-14.4 '*And when the stars fade away,*': [*Inkadarat* (انكَدَرَتْ, fade away] is derived from *kadira* meaning both to fall and disperse, or to lose lustre and fade.[9] Here it means that just as the sun, the other stars and celestial bodies will darken, fall from their ordained courses, and be destroyed.[10] Q77:8 describes the same event:

---

[7] Muṣṭafawī, *al-Taḥqīq*.

[8] Shīrāzī, *Namūneh*, 26/171.

[9] Muṣṭafawī, *al-Taḥqīq*.

[10] Ṭabāṭabā'ī, *al-Mīzān*, 20/213.

فَإِذَا النُّجُومُ طُمِسَتْ

So when the stars are obliterated.

The fading of the sun, stars, and galaxies indicate huge upheavals in the systems that govern the cosmic world and will inevitably result in a chain of events that will destroy the earth.

In fact, some exegetes are of the opinion that *nujūm* here refers to those planets that receive their energy from the sun, which will begin to fall out of their orbits as soon as the sun is extinguished.[11]

1-14.5 '*And when the mountains are set in motion*': [*Suyyirat* (سُيِّرَت, set in motion)] is the passive from *sayyara*, which means to move something physically.[12] As soon as the celestial system is in disarray, the earth will begin to destabilize. The huge mountains that secure the earth will start to collapse in continuous stages. We have mentioned the verses that describe the disintegration of the mountains in the *tafsīr* of Surat al-Naba' (78).

As they are uprooted and set in motion, they will no longer be able to stabilize the earth, and there will be convulsions and earthquakes throughout the land as a result.

At the end, they will remain like mere mirages. Q78:20 states:

وَسُيِّرَتِ الْجِبَالُ فَكَانَتْ سَرَابًا

And the mountains shall be set in motion
so that they become [like] a mirage.

1-14.6 '*And when the full-term she-camels are left untended,*': [*'Ishār* (عِشَار, full-term)] is derived from *'ashara* meaning ten, and refers to a she-camel approaching the full term of its pregnancy, which is normally one year.[13]

[*'Uṭṭilat* (عُطِّلَتْ, abandoned)] is derived from *'aṭila*, which means to be idle or unoccupied. Here it means to be abandoned and left without supervision.[14]

In Arab lands, the pregnant camel which is about to give birth is attended to with much care because of its great value to the owner.

---

[11] Ṭāliqānī, *Partovī az Qur'an*, 3/172.

[12] Muṣṭafawī, *al-Taḥqīq*.

[13] Ṭūsī, *al-Tibyān*, 10/281.

[14] Shīrāzī, *Namūneh*, 26/172.

The phrase is used as a metaphor to indicate that the terror of the darkness of the sun coupled with the shaking of the earth will cause people to abandon their dearest possessions without hesitation.[15] A similar description is found in Q22:2:

يَوْمَ تَرَوْنَهَا تَذْهَلُ كُلُّ مُرْضِعَةٍ عَمَّا أَرْضَعَتْ وَتَضَعُ كُلُّ ذَاتِ حَمْلٍ حَمْلَهَا
وَتَرَى النَّاسَ سُكَارَىٰ وَمَا هُم بِسُكَارَىٰ

On the Day when you see it, every nursing mother will be distracted from that [child] she was nursing, and every pregnant woman will abort her pregnancy. You will see the people [appearing] intoxicated but they are not intoxicated...

Another meaning given for *ʿishār* is anything that yields something, such as the clouds. In this case, *ʿishāru ʿuṭṭilat* would be a reference to barren clouds of debris.[16]

1-14.7 ‘*And when the wild beasts are gathered,*’: [*Wuḥūsh* (وُحُوش, wild beasts)] (sing. *waḥsh*), refers to animals that live in the wild.

[*Ḥushirat* (حُشِرَتْ, gathered)] is derived from *ḥashara*, meaning to gather and assemble. It may be that the intense upheaval causes all wild animals to rush forward from their habitats,[17] and gather together in confused herds, as is sometimes seen during forest fires and other natural disasters. Due to their terror, they will not attack each other.

1-14.8 ‘*And when the seas are made to boil over,*’: [*Sujjirat* (سُجِّرَتْ, boil over)] is the passive of *sajjara* which means to boil due to heat, or be set on fire. This could mean that the seas will become vapour, or be full of fire[18] due to volcanic disruptions in their depths or fiery debris falling from the skies.[19]

These cosmic upheavals will result in the disintegration of the earth, bringing an end to the realm of the *dunyā* and ushering in the *ākhirah*.[20]

---

[15] Ibid, 26/173.

[16] Ṭabrasī, *al-Bayān*, 10/673.

[17] Ṭabāṭabāʾī, *al-Mīzān*, 20/214.

[18] Ibid.

[19] Shīrāzī, *Namūneh*, 26/175.

[20] Ṭāliqānī, *Partovī az Qurʾan*, 3/174.

1-14.9 The previous verses described six events that precede the Day of Judgement. Now the verses turn to the events that will occur after the second blowing of the trumpet, and describe the movement of human beings when they will have all been resurrected.[21]

1-14.10 *'And when the souls are united,'*: [*Zuwwijat* (زُوِّجَتْ, coupled)] here refers to being united within groups with those who share similar qualities, the righteous with the righteous and the sinners with the sinners.[22]

In this world people gather around those with whom they share interests, kinship, language, and so on. In the next world, they will be inexorably drawn to those whose spiritual stations and attitudes are similar to their own.[23] About these groupings, Q56:7-10 state:

وَكُنتُمْ أَزْوَاجًا ثَلَاثَةً ﴿٧﴾ فَأَصْحَابُ الْمَيْمَنَةِ مَا أَصْحَابُ الْمَيْمَنَةِ ﴿٨﴾
وَأَصْحَابُ الْمَشْأَمَةِ مَا أَصْحَابُ الْمَشْأَمَةِ ﴿٩﴾ وَالسَّابِقُونَ السَّابِقُونَ

And you will be in three groups: So the companions of the bliss – what are the companions of the bliss? And the companions of the misery – what are the companions of the misery? And the foremost, the foremost...

Some exegetes have said that the phrase in question could refer to the souls of mankind being reunited with their bodies,[24] or with their deeds.[25] Others have said that it could refer to the marriage of righteous souls with the consorts of Paradise, but this is unlikely because the verses are describing earlier events.

1-14.11 *'And when the female infant [who was] buried alive is asked for what sin she was killed.'*: [*Maw'ūdah* (مَوْءُودَة, female infant)] is derived from *wad* meaning a heavy weight, and here it refers to a newly born female child buried alive under the weight of earth.[26]

On this Day, the father who committed this despicable act will be called to account for his crime, or the child herself will be asked

---

21 Muṭahharī, (*Āshnāyī bā Qur'an*), *Āthār*, 28/389.
22 Shīrāzī, *Namūneh*, 26/175.
23 Muṭahharī, (*Āshnāyī bā Qur'an*), *Āthār*, 28/390.
24 Ṭabrasī, *al-Bayān*, 10/674.
25 Shīrāzī, *Namūneh*, 26/175.
26 Muṣṭafawī, *al-Taḥqīq*.

this question, giving a voice to the victim of this great injustice. The latter interpretation indicates God's wrath upon the killer of this innocent child.[27]

1-14.12 A tradition reported from Imam al-Sadiq (a) offers an interpretation (*ta'wīl*) of this verse. He stated: The killer of one who was killed because of his love for us will be questioned about his killing.[28]

1-14.13 *'And when the scrolls [of actions] are laid open,'*: [*Ṣuḥuf* (صُحُف, scrolls)] here refer to the books of deeds of every human being. [*Nushirat* (نُشِرَتْ, laid open)] is derived from *nashara* meaning to spread out, and here it refers to the station called *taṭāyur al-kutub*[29] on the Day of Judgement when the books of deeds will be opened for their owners to read. Q17:13, 14 states:

وَكُلَّ إِنْسَانٍ أَلْزَمْنَاهُ طَائِرَهُ فِي عُنُقِهِ وَنُخْرِجُ لَهُ يَوْمَ الْقِيَامَةِ كِتَابًا
يَلْقَاهُ مَنْشُورًا ﴿١٣﴾ اقْرَأْ كِتَابَكَ كَفَىٰ بِنَفْسِكَ الْيَوْمَ عَلَيْكَ حَسِيبًا

And We have fastened every man's deeds to his neck, and on the Day of Judgement We shall produce for him a written account which he will encounter wide open. [He will be told], "Read your book! You [yourself] are sufficient on this Day as a reckoner against you."

1-14.14 *'And when the sky is stripped away,'*: [*Samā'* (سَمَاء, sky)] is derived from *samawa*, meaning that which is raised high above other things and covers them.[30] In this verse it may refer to the metaphysical realm that lies beyond our physical world.[31] Q51:22 refers to this realm as the source of divine provision and recompense:

وَفِي السَّمَاءِ رِزْقُكُمْ وَمَا تُوعَدُونَ

And in the heaven is your provision, and that which you are promised.

---

[27] Muṭahharī, (*Āshnāyī bā Qur'an*), *Āthār*, 28/390.

[28] Majlisī, *Biḥār*, 23/254.

عَنِ الصَّادِقِ (عَلَيْهِ السَّلَامُ) - عَنْ قَوْلِ اللهِ عَزَّ وَجَلَّ «وَإِذَا الْمَوْءُودَةُ سُئِلَتْ *بِأَيِّ ذَنْبٍ قُتِلَتْ» قَالَ: مَنْ قُتِلَ فِي مَوَدَّتِنَا سُئِلَ قَاتِلُهُ عَنْ قَتْلِهِ.

[29] The phrase refers to one of the stations on the Day of Judgement mention in the traditions, where everyone will receive their most detailed record of deeds.

[30] Muṣṭafawī, *al-Taḥqīq*.

[31] Shīrāzī, *Namūneh*, 26/181.

[*Kushiṭat* (كُشِطَتْ, stripped away)] is derived from *kashaṭa* meaning to rip a cover away to expose what is underneath.[32]

Here it means tearing the veils that obscure the material world from the higher world of the angels, Hell and Paradise, allowing these realities to be seen clearly by all.[33]

1-14.15 *'And when hellfire is set ablaze,'*: [*Su''irat* (سُعِّرَتْ, set ablaze)] is derived from *sa''ara* meaning to ignite or kindle. Hell already surrounds the disbelievers, while they are unaware. Q9:49 states:

وَإِنَّ جَهَنَّمَ لَمُحِيطَةٌ بِالْكَافِرِينَ

...And indeed, Hell encompasses the disbelievers.

However, on that Day, it will be kindled ready to receive its wretched inmates.[34] As they enter it, they themselves will become the fuel for its blazing flames. Q2:24 states:

فَٱتَّقُوا النَّارَ الَّتِي وَقُودُهَا النَّاسُ وَالْحِجَارَةُ أُعِدَّتْ لِلْكَافِرِينَ

...So fear the fire whose fuel is men and stones;
[it is] prepared for the disbelievers.

1-14.16 *'And when Paradise is brought near.'*: [*Uzlifat* (أُزْلِفَتْ, brought near)] is derived from *azlafa* meaning to go near and approach. Just as Hell already surrounds the disbelievers, Paradise too already exists. On that Day, it will become visible to the God-wary, ready to receive them.[35] Q26:90 states:

وَأُزْلِفَتِ الْجَنَّةُ لِلْمُتَّقِينَ

And Paradise will be brought near to the God-wary (muttaqīn).

1-14.17 *'[Then] every soul will know what it has brought [with it].'*: *Nafs* here refers to the genus of mankind and refers to every single individual.[36]

[*Aḥḍarat* (أَحْضَرَتْ, brought)] is derived from *aḥḍara* meaning to present, or bring along with oneself.

---

[32] Ṭabrasī, *al-Bayān*, 10/674.

[33] Shīrāzī, *Namūneh*, 26/181.

[34] Javādī-Āmolī, *Tasnīm*,(Transcript:http://javadi.esra.ir/-/23-09-1398-1-جلسه-تكوير-سوره-تفسير).

[35] Ibid.

[36] Ṭabāṭabā'ī, *al-Mīzān*, 20/215.

This verse is the conclusion of the previous thirteen verses that began with *idhā* (when) and describe the moment when man sees his scroll of deeds exposed and the actualization of every deed that he has ever done arrayed before him. Q3:30 states:

يَوْمَ تَجِدُ كُلُّ نَفْسٍ مَا عَمِلَتْ مِنْ خَيْرٍ مُحْضَرًا وَمَا عَمِلَتْ مِنْ سُوءٍ

On the Day when every soul shall be confronted with all the good it has done and all the evil it has done...

DISCUSSION 1: INFANTICIDE IN PRE-ISLAMIC TIMES AND ABORTION IN MODERN TIMES

During the Days of Ignorance (*jāhiliyyah*) Arabs considered sons to be a source of honour and pride but daughters to be a source of shame and dishonour. When they received the news of the birth of a daughter, many of them would become angry and despondent. Q16:58 states:

وَإِذَا بُشِّرَ أَحَدُهُمْ بِالْأُنْثَىٰ ظَلَّ وَجْهُهُ مُسْوَدًّا وَهُوَ كَظِيمٌ

And when news is brought to one of them of [the birth of] a female, his face darkens, and he is filled with suppressed anguish.

However, in addition to being distraught at the news, some fathers actually deliberated over whether they should bear the perceived disgrace of raising a daughter or murder the baby by burying her alive! There were those who would dig a hole in the earth when their wives were about to give birth. If the new-born was female she would be buried alive then and there.[37] Q16:59 states:

أَيُمْسِكُهُ عَلَىٰ هُونٍ أَمْ يَدُسُّهُ فِي التُّرَابِ أَلَا سَاءَ مَا يَحْكُمُونَ

Should he keep it (the female infant) in humiliation or bury it (yadussuhu) *into the earth? Undoubtedly, evil is what they decide.*

In our day and age, such practices would be deemed barbaric. However, abortion, which is gradually gaining acceptance as the right of the pregnant woman in many countries, is no less evil. Just as in pre-Islamic Arabia, even today a female child is still undesirable in many cultures. They consider a daughter to be a poor alternative to a son, a

[37] Ibid, 12/277.

financial burden, unable to carry on the family name, and so on. As a result, some of them resort to aborting the foetus if it is female.

Yet both daughters and sons are gifts of God, in fact He mentions daughters first in Q42:49 which states:

لِلَّهِ مُلْكُ السَّمَاوَاتِ وَالْأَرْضِ يَخْلُقُ مَا يَشَاءُ
يَهَبُ لِمَنْ يَشَاءُ إِنَاثًا وَيَهَبُ لِمَنْ يَشَاءُ الذُّكُورَ

To God belongs the dominion of the heavens and the earth;
He creates what he wills. He bestows to whom He wills daughters,
and He gives to whom He wills sons.

In pre-Islamic Arabia, the killing of new-born daughters was practised by only a few tribes. It appears that this custom began after a battle between the Banu Tamīm and the Kisrā of Persia, in which a number of Tamīmī women were captured and taken to the Persian court where they were kept as slaves. Later when a peace accord was signed between the two sides, the Banu Tamīm asked for the captives to be returned. The Persians gave the women the choice to stay or return to their own people. Several women who were already married to their captors chose to stay, and this enraged the men of Banu Tamīm, who vowed to henceforth bury alive any female born in their tribe.

Some other tribes followed their example, and gradually the practice of female infanticide spread.[38]

The reasons for female infanticide can be summarized as the following:

1. That females did not play a role in bringing wealth to the family and were considered a financial burden. But Q17:31 states:

   وَلَا تَقْتُلُوا أَوْلَادَكُمْ خَشْيَةَ إِمْلَاقٍ نَّحْنُ نَرْزُقُهُمْ
   وَإِيَّاكُمْ إِنَّ قَتْلَهُمْ كَانَ خِطْئًا كَبِيرًا

   And do not kill your children for fear of poverty. We provide for them and for you. Indeed, their killing is a great sin.

2. There were constant battles and skirmishes between various tribes. The tribes needed strong warriors, and women were of no use in

[38] Ibid.

battle. Furthermore, women were taken as prisoners, and violated or held for ransom, and this brought dishonour to their tribes.[39]

Abortion is even worse, because it justifies the killing of unborn children for various reasons: unintended pregnancy, financial constraints, because they have been informed the child may be disabled and so they feel they are doing the child a favour, and so on.

SUMMARY OF THE VERSES

The verses in the first section of the surah describe twelve events that will accompany the advent of the last Hour: the extinguishing of the sun, the fading of the stars, the destruction of the mountains, the neglect of precious possessions, the assembly of wild beasts, the boiling of the seas, the uniting of souls, the accusation of the female infant who was buried alive, the display of the scrolls of actions, the removal of the sky, the kindling of hellfire, and the manifestation of Paradise. And at that time, every single individual will realize the result of their actions.

REFLECTIVE LEARNING

The entire world as we know it will dramatically come to an end and those who had formed deep relationships with it will find themselves alone. The only constant and reliable relationship is the one man forms with God. Q2:256 states:

فَمَنْ يَكْفُرْ بِالطَّاغُوتِ وَيُؤْمِنْ بِاللهِ فَقَدِ ٱسْتَمْسَكَ بِالْعُرْوَةِ الْوُثْقَىٰ لَا ٱنْفِصَامَ لَهَا

...So, whoever disbelieves in (rejects) false deities and believes in God has indeed grasped the firmest handle [of true faith], one that will never break...

Let me reflect on what I can do to keep this most important relationship strong and constant.

VERSES 15 - 21

فَلَا أُقْسِمُ بِالْخُنَّسِ ﴿١٥﴾ الْجَوَارِ الْكُنَّسِ ﴿١٦﴾ وَاللَّيْلِ إِذَا عَسْعَسَ ﴿١٧﴾ وَالصُّبْحِ
إِذَا تَنَفَّسَ ﴿١٨﴾ إِنَّهُ لَقَوْلُ رَسُولٍ كَرِيمٍ ﴿١٩﴾ ذِي قُوَّةٍ عِنْدَ ذِي الْعَرْشِ مَكِينٍ
﴿٢٠﴾ مُطَاعٍ ثَمَّ أَمِينٍ ﴿٢١﴾

---

[39] Shīrāzī, *Namūneh*, 11/270.

So, I swear by those [planets] that recede, [15] *those that run [their course] and disappear.* [16] *And by the night as it dissipates,* [17] *and by the dawn when it breathes [light].* [18] *Indeed, it (the Qur'an) is a Word of a noble messenger,* [19] *possessor of strength, established before the Possessor of the Throne.* [20] *[One] obeyed there, trustworthy.* [21]

15-21.1 Three oaths are made to emphasize the importance of the Qur'an, God's final revelation. This Word was sent down to the Prophet (s) through Jibra'il, God's powerful and trusted angel.

15-21.2 'So, I swear by those [planets] that recede, those that run [their course] and disappear.': The conjunction *fa* (so) means that the upcoming verses are connected to the previous verse.

[*Lā Uqsimu* (لَا أُقْسِمُ, I swear)] is a type of oath that the Qur'an has used several times. We have discussed its usage further in the *tafsīr* of Surat al-Balad (90), which is one of two surahs that start with this type of oath (the other being Surat al-Qiyāmah (75)).

[*Khunnas* (خُنَّس, those that recede)] (sing. *khānis*) is derived from *khanasa* which means to disappear after being visible, or to shrink from sight, only to return later.[40] It is used in Q114:4 for Shaytan, who is called *al-khannās*, because he disappears when God's name is mentioned.[41] In the verse under review, it refers to the celestial bodies that appear in the night sky before gradually receding from view as day breaks.[42]

[*Jawār* (جَوَار, those that run)] (sing. *jāriyah*) is derived from *jarā* which means to flow swiftly. It refers to objects that float like ships. Here it refers to the planets.

[*Kunnas* (كُنَّس, disappear)] (sing. *kānis*) is derived from *kanasa* which means to set and disappear.[43] *Kinās* is also used to refer to the nests and lairs of wild animals.

15-21.3 Since the next two oaths are by the night and the day, it is probable that here, the phrase *al-jawār al-kunnas* refers to the

---

[40] Muṣṭafawī, *al-Taḥqīq*.

[41] Shīrāzī, *Namūneh*, 26/189.

[42] Ṭāliqānī, *Partovī az Qur'an*, 3/183.

[43] Muṣṭafawī, *al-Taḥqīq*.

planets that run in their prescribed orbits around the sun and are seen in certain nights before they disappear in the day.[44]

Some exegetes say that these oaths refer to the five planets that can be seen with the naked eye: Mercury, Venus, Mars, Jupiter, and Saturn, which were worshipped by some in former times.[45]

A tradition from Imam Ali (a) states: *Al-Khunnas* refers to the planets that disappear in the day and become visible at night. *Al-jawār* is an adjective for them because they float in their orbits. *Al-kunnas* is also an adjective for them because they set, that is they are concealed in their constellations the way deer hide in their lairs. They are five: *Zuḥal* (Saturn), *al-Mushtarī* (Jupiter), *al-Mirrīkh* (Mars), *al-Zuharah* (Venus), and *ʿUṭārid* (Mercury).[46]

15-21.4 *'And by the night as it dissipates, and by the dawn when it breathes [light].'*: [*ʿAsʿas* (عَسْعَس, dissipate)] means to become slightly dark and can refer to both the beginning and end of the night.[47]

[*Tanaffas* (تَنَفَّس, takes breath)] means to breathe or sigh, and is a beautiful allusion to the manner in which the day breaks and its light spreads like exhaled breath.

Here, the oaths probably refer to the last part of the night and the beginning of the day, which are the best times for the worship of God.[48]

These two oaths are similar to the oaths in Q74:33,34:

وَاللَّيْلِ إِذْ أَدْبَرَ ﴿٣٣﴾ وَالصُّبْحِ إِذَا أَسْفَرَ

And by the night when it departs,
and by the morning when it brightens.

As the night departs, morning comes. This could be a metaphor for the darkness of ignorance leaving and the light of guidance entering, hence the reference to the Qurʾan in next verse.

---

[44] Ṭabāṭabāʾī, *al-Mīzān*, 20/217.

[45] Shīrāzī, *Namūneh*, 26/189.

[46] Ḥuwayzī, *Nūr al-Thaqalayn*, 5/517.

عَنْ أَمِيرَ الْمُؤْمِنِينَ (عَلَيْهِ السَّلَامُ) -«بِالْخُنَّسِ» وَهِيَ النُّجُومُ تَخْنِسُ بِالنَّهَارِ وَتَبْدُو بِاللَّيْلِ وَالْجَوَارُ صِفَةٌ لَهَا، لِأَنَّهَا تَجْرِي فِي أَفْلَاكِهَا. «الْكُنَّسُ» مِنْ صِفَتِهَا أَيْضاً لِأَنَّهَا تَكْنِسُ أَيْ تَتَوَارَى فِي بُرُوجِهَا كَمَا تَتَوَارَى الظِّبَاءُ فِي كِنَاسِهَا. وَهِيَ خَمْسَةُ أَنْجُمٍ: زُحَلُ وَالْمُشْتَرِي وَالْمَرِّيخُ وَالزُّهْرَةُ وَعُطَارِدُ.

[47] Muṣṭafawī, *al-Taḥqīq*.

[48] Shīrāzī, *Namūneh*, 26/182.

15-21.5 *'Indeed, it (the Qur'an) is a Word of a noble messenger, possessor of strength, established before the Possessor of the Throne. [One] obeyed there, trustworthy.'*: These verses are the subject (*jawāb*) of the three oaths in the previous verses. *Innahu* (indeed, it) here refers to the Qur'an and *rasūl* (messenger) refers to Jibra'il.[49]

God appoints messengers from both the angels and mankind, who have the qualities required for the task to which they have been commissioned. Q22:75 states:

اللَّهُ يَصْطَفِي مِنَ الْمَلَائِكَةِ رُسُلًا وَمِنَ النَّاسِ إِنَّ اللَّهَ سَمِيعٌ بَصِيرٌ

Allah chooses messengers from among the angels and from among the men; indeed, Allah is all-Hearing, all-Seeing.

The verse emphasizes that the matters which have been discussed in the surah and the rest of the Qur'an are not the paraphrased words of the Prophet (s), but the exact words brought to him by a noble and trusted messenger of God. That messenger is Jibra'il, the angel who transmits God's revelation.[50] To show his qualification for the mission of bringing down the Qur'an, five attributes of this great angel of God are listed:

1. He is a noble messenger (*rasūlin karīm*). This indicates his importance and honour in God's estimation. He is also *karīm* because he brings the best of gifts – knowledge and guidance from God.[51]
2. He is powerful (*dhī quwwah*). This indicates his enhanced ability to receive and transmit God's word, which requires great power.
3. He has a distinguished rank (*makīn*). This is a reference to his established position and proximity to God.
4. He is obeyed in the heaven (*muṭāʿ*). He is in charge of the other angels who assist him, and he is unquestioningly obeyed by them.
5. He is trustworthy (*amīn*). This refers to his absolute faithfulness in delivering the word of God.[52]

---

[49] Ṭabāṭabā'ī, *al-Mīzān*, 20/218.

[50] Rāzī, *Mafātīḥ al-Ghayb*, 31/69.

[51] Ibid.

[52] Ṭabāṭabā'ī, *al-Mīzān*, 20/218.

DISCUSSION 2: THE THRONE (*ʿARSH*) OF GOD

ʿArsh is defined as an elevated seat that has a canopy over it.[53] It normally signifies the throne on which a ruler sits. It has been used in this meaning for the throne of Bilqīs, the Queen of Sabaʾ. Q27:38 quotes Prophet Sulayman (a):

قَالَ يَا أَيُّهَا الْمَلَأُ أَيُّكُمْ يَأْتِينِي بِعَرْشِهَا قَبْلَ أَنْ يَأْتُونِي مُسْلِمِينَ

O assembly, which of you will bring me her throne (ʿarsh) *before they come to me in submission?*

The term is also used for the throne of Prophet Yusuf (a) in Q12:100:

وَرَفَعَ أَبَوَيْهِ عَلَى الْعَرْشِ

And he raised his parents upon the throne...

The seats that have been mentioned for the dwellers of Paradise are not called *ʿarsh* in the Qurʾan. They are referred to as *surur* (for example Q56:15) and *al-arāʾik* (for example, Q76:13).

ʿArsh of God

Over twenty verses speak of the throne (*ʿarsh*) of God, which is described as great (*ʿaẓīm,* Q23:86) and noble (*karīm*, Q23:116). The scholars have presented several views about the term.

1. The view of some *Ashʿarites* and the *Ahl al-Hadith* (*Sunni* traditionists) is that the *ʿarsh* is a concept that should be believed in without delving into what it could mean. God is established on the *ʿarsh*, but its manner (*kayfiyyah*), is unknown. Belief in it is obligatory, but questioning it is innovation and heresy (*bidʿah*).[54]
2. The view of some *Muʿtazalites* and many *Shīʿa* exegetes is that *ʿarsh* is a metaphor for the entirety of God's creation, or for the higher realm of creation, and the chair (*kursiyy*) is a metaphor for the material world.[55] Or that *ʿarsh* is a metaphorical term for God's knowledge, power, authority, and administration over His creation.[56] And this dominion of God is what is meant in verses such as Q20:5 which states:

---

53 Muṣṭafawī, *al-Taḥqīq*.

54 Shahristānī, *al-Milal wa al-Niḥal*, 1/84.

55 Shīrāzī, *Namūneh*, 20/37,38.

56 Maʿrifat, *al-Tamhīd*, 3/125.

الرَّحْمَٰنُ عَلَى الْعَرْشِ اسْتَوَىٰ

The all-Merciful (al-Raḥmān) *who is established on the Throne.*

While *ʿarsh* is a metaphor for God's power, authority, and control, it has a reality and grand existence of its own.[57] It is the locus from which the commandments of God are issued and through which He administers creation.[58] There are many verses that speak of the throne as a real entity, for example, Q40:7 states:

الَّذِينَ يَحْمِلُونَ الْعَرْشَ وَمَنْ حَوْلَهُ يُسَبِّحُونَ بِحَمْدِ رَبِّهِمْ
وَيُؤْمِنُونَ بِهِ وَيَسْتَغْفِرُونَ لِلَّذِينَ آمَنُوا

Those [angels] who carry the Throne and those around it glorify the praise of their Lord and believe in Him and ask forgiveness for those who have believed,

And Q69:17 states:

وَالْمَلَكُ عَلَىٰ أَرْجَائِهَا وَيَحْمِلُ عَرْشَ رَبِّكَ فَوْقَهُمْ يَوْمَئِذٍ ثَمَانِيَةٌ

And the angels will be on its sides, and that Day, eight (angels) will bear the Throne of your Lord above them.

In conclusion, we quote part of a lengthy tradition from Imam al-Sadiq (a) which states: "The *ʿarsh* has many different qualities which differ in description in the Qur'an according to context. When God says, '*the Lord of the mighty Throne,*' He means '[the Lord of] the mighty kingdom'. And when He says, '*the all-Merciful who is established on the Throne,*' He means that 'He encompasses the kingdom', and this grants the [unique] characteristics to everything in creation.

...The *ʿarsh* is distinct from the *kursiyy* despite being linked to it. They are two of the greatest thresholds of the unseen (*ghayb*), and both are hidden. In their concealment they are intimately connected in that the *kursiyy* is the outer doorway of the *ghayb* from where all things that come forth appear, and *ʿarsh* is the inner doorway [of the *ghayb*] wherein lies the knowledge of 'how-ness' (*kayf*), of existence (*kawn*), of measure (*qadr*), of limit (*ḥadd*), of location (*ayn*), of Divine volition (*mashiyyah*), of the attribute of Divine will (*ṣifat al-irādah*), of knowledge of words (*ʿilm al-alfāẓ*), of movements (*ḥarakāt*), of

57 Miṣbāh-Yazdī, *Maʿārif-i Qur'an*, p. 249.
58 Ṭabāṭabā'ī, *al-Mīzān*, 17/299.

abandonment (*tark*), and of the knowledge of the return and the origin (*ʿilm al-ʿawd wa al-badʾ*).

Thus they are two closely connected doorways of knowledge; the realm of the *ʿarsh* is distinct from the realm of the *kursiyy*, and its knowledge is more hidden than the knowledge of the *kursiyy*..."[59]

SUMMARY OF THE VERSE

The verses begin with three oaths: by planets that are visible in the night sky, by the night as it dissipates, and by the early part of the day as it starts to brighten.

The subject of the oaths is that the Qurʾan is the Word of God brought by the noble angel Jibraʾil, an angel of strength and lofty rank in the eyes of God, the Possessor of the Throne. This angel is obeyed and trustworthy.

REFLECTIVE LEARNING

The revelation of the Qurʾan was entrusted to God's greatest angel and sent down to His greatest Prophet (s). God swears by this process, indicating the enormous importance of the Qurʾan.

This great Book is in my possession. Let me reflect on how much importance I give it on a daily basis.

VERSES 22 - 25

وَمَا صَاحِبُكُمْ بِمَجْنُونٍ ﴿٢٢﴾ وَلَقَدْ رَآهُ بِالْأُفُقِ الْمُبِينِ ﴿٢٣﴾ وَمَا هُوَ عَلَى الْغَيْبِ بِضَنِينٍ ﴿٢٤﴾ وَمَا هُوَ بِقَوْلِ شَيْطَانٍ رَجِيمٍ ﴿٢٥﴾

Your companion is not a madman. [22] *Without doubt he saw him (Jibraʾil) in the clear horizon.* [23] *And he does not withhold [knowledge*

---

[59] Ṣadūq, *al-Tawḥīd*, 1/321.

عَنِ الصَّادِقِ (عَلَيْهِ السَّلَامُ) - إِنَّ لِلْعَرْشِ صِفَاتٌ كَثِيرَةٌ مُخْتَلِفَةٌ، لَهُ فِي كُلِّ سَبَبٍ وَضْعٌ، فِي الْقُرْآنِ صِفَةٌ عَلَى حِدَة، فَقَوْلُهُ «رَبُّ الْعَرْشِ الْعَظِيمِ» يَقُولُ الْمُلْكُ الْعَظِيمُ، وَقَوْلُهُ «الرَّحْمٰنُ عَلَى الْعَرْشِ ٱسْتَوَىٰ» يَقُولُ عَلَى الْمُلْكِ ٱحْتَوَى، وَهَذَا مُلْكُ الْكَيْفُوفِيَّةِ فِي الْأَشْيَاءِ، ثُمَّ الْعَرْشُ فِي الْوَصْلِ مُتَفَرِّدٌ مِنَ الْكُرْسِيِّ؛ لِأَنَّهُمَا بَابَانِ مِنْ أَكْبَرِ أَبْوَابِ الْغُيُوبِ، وَهُمَا جَمِيعًا غَيْبَانِ، وَهُمَا فِي الْغَيْبِ مَقْرُونَانِ؛ لِأَنَّ الْكُرْسِيَّ هُوَ الْبَابُ الظَّاهِرُ مِنَ الْغَيْبِ الَّذِي مِنْهُ مَطْلَعُ الْبِدَعِ وَمِنْهُ الْأَشْيَاءُ كُلُّهَا، وَالْعَرْشُ هُوَ الْبَابُ الْبَاطِنُ الَّذِي يُوجَدُ فِيهِ عِلْمُ الْكَيْفِ وَالْكَوْنِ وَالْقَدْرِ وَالْحَدِّ وَالْأَيْنِ وَالْمَشِيَّةِ وَصِفَةِ الْإِرَادَةِ وَعِلْمُ الْأَلْفَاظِ وَالْحَرَكَاتِ وَالتَّرْكِ، وَعِلْمُ الْعَوْدِ وَالْبَدْءِ، فَهُمَا فِي الْعِلْمِ بَابَانِ مَقْرُونَانِ؛ لِأَنَّ مُلْكَ الْعَرْشِ سِوَى مُلْكِ الْكُرْسِيِّ وَعِلْمِهِ.

of] the unseen. [24] *Nor is it (the Qur'an) the word of Shaytan, the outcast.* [25]

22-25.1 *'Your companion is not a madman.'*: This is a continuation of the subject (*jawāb*) of the previous oaths.[60] The use of the word *ṣāḥibukum* (your companion) shows the humble nature of the Prophet (s) amongst his people despite his great station.[61]

History records how the loyal companion ʿAdī b. Ḥātim al-Ṭā'ī was attracted to Islam just by observing how simply the Prophet (s) lived and how patiently and respectfully he dealt with the common people.[62]

Furthermore, *ṣāḥibukum* was used to remind the polytheists that he (s) was well known to them and had lived amongst them all his life, and they knew he was of sound mind. He was popular and respected in the community for his righteousness, and the idolaters themselves had given him the titles *al-Ṣādiq* (the truthful) and *al-Amīn* (the trustworthy). Therefore, there was no basis[63] for their name-calling except malice and resentment.

[*Majnūn* (مَجْنُون, madman)] derived from *janna* meaning to conceal. Many common words are derived from this root: the *jinn* received their name because they are concealed from our vision, *jannah* refers to a garden whose trees hide its plants, *janīn* is a foetus hidden in the womb, *junnah* is a shield that obscures the warrior, and so on.

Similarly, *majnūn* is someone whose intellect has been covered, or is possessed by *jinn* or has lost his mind.[64] It was a disgraceful name that the polytheists had given to the Prophet (s) to try to defame him, because the truth that he had brought did not sit well with them. Q23:70 quotes them:

أَمْ يَقُولُونَ بِهِ جِنَّةٌ بَلْ جَاءَهُمْ بِالْحَقِّ وَأَكْثَرُهُمْ لِلْحَقِّ كَارِهُونَ

Or do they say, "There is a madness in him"? Rather, he has brought them the truth, but most of them are averse to the truth.

---

[60] Ṭabrasī, *al-Bayān*, 10/677.

[61] Shīrāzī, *Namūneh*, 26/195.

[62] Subḥānī, *Furūgh-i Abadiyyat*, 1/851.

[63] Ṭabāṭabā'ī, *al-Mīzān*, 20/218.

[64] Muṣṭafawī, *al-Taḥqīq*.

This tactic was also used against other Prophets (a) in order to discourage people from listening to them. Q51:52 states:

كَذَٰلِكَ مَا أَتَى الَّذِينَ مِنْ قَبْلِهِمْ مِنْ رَسُولٍ إِلَّا قَالُوا سَاحِرٌ أَوْ مَجْنُونٌ

Thus, no messenger came to the people before them, except that they said, "A sorcerer, or a madman!"

22-25.2 *'Without doubt he saw him (Jibra'il) in the clear horizon.'*: [*Ra'āhu* (رَآهُ, he saw him)] means that the Prophet (s) saw Jibra'il.

[*Ufuq* (أُفُق, horizon)] refers to the extreme aspect of the skyline.[65]

The verse confirms that the Prophet (s) had clearly and unmistakably seen the messenger-angel Jibra'il in his manifest form.[66] Other verses confirm that he (s) had also seen him in the highest horizon (Q53:7) and also, based on one interpretation, at the farthest Lote-tree. (Q53:13-14). According to some traditions, the angel extended from the skies to the earth and from the east to the west.[67]

22-25.3 *'And he does not withhold [knowledge of] the unseen.'*: [*Ḍanīn* (ضَنِين, withholder)] is derived from *ḍanna* meaning to keep back and be miserly.[68]

[*al-Ghayb* (الْغَيْب, the unseen)] here refers to the news of the unseen that the people received from the Prophet (s) and which he received from God.

The verse means that the Prophet (s) was never reluctant to share the knowledge that he received from God.[69]

22-25.4 *'Nor is it (the Qur'an) the word of Shaytan, the outcast'*: *Mā* (not) used in the beginning of this verse emphasizes the negation and means to say that the Qur'an bears no resemblance whatsoever to the words of Shaytan, which inspire the soothsayers.

[*Rajīm* (رَجِيم, outcast)] is derived from *rajm* which means pelting with stones. Later, it came to denote one who is cursed or expelled. Here it is a reference to the expulsion of Shaytan from God's proximity due to his arrogant disobedience of God's command.

---

[65] Ibid.

[66] Ṭūsī, *al-Tibyān*, 10/287.

[67] Modarresī, *Min Huda al-Qur'an*, 17/370.

[68] Muṣṭafawī, *al-Taḥqīq*.

[69] Ṭabrasī, *al-Bayān*, 10/678.

22-25.5 In verse 19, the phrase, *'qawlu rasūlin karīm'* (Word of a noble messenger) was used for the Qur'an. In verse 25, the Qur'an is made distinct from *'qawlu Shayṭānin rajīm'* (the word of an outcast Shaytan). The Prophet (s) was reciting words that had been revealed to him from God through a trusted messenger. The Qur'an was distinct from the utterances of someone possessed by madness or overcome by the insinuations of Shaytan.

22-25.6 In pre-Islamic times, soothsayers and seers, known as *kāhin*, would make claims about knowing the unseen, ostensibly by associating and learning some of these secrets from the *jinn*. They would then make predictions and prophecies in the form of garbled poetry.

These insinuations from Shaytan and the *jinn* who served him were always full of lies. Q26:221-223 state:

هَلْ أُنَبِّئُكُمْ عَلَىٰ مَنْ تَنَزَّلُ الشَّيَاطِينُ ﴿٢٢١﴾ تَنَزَّلُ عَلَىٰ كُلِّ أَفَّاكٍ أَثِيمٍ ﴿٢٢٢﴾ يُلْقُونَ السَّمْعَ وَأَكْثَرُهُمْ كَاذِبُونَ

Shall I inform you upon whom the devils (shayāṭīn) *descend?*
They descend upon every sinful liar. They eavesdrop,
but most of them are liars.

The polytheists had spitefully accused the Prophet (s) of being one of these soothsayers, as another way of rejecting his message. They alleged that while he was honest and was experiencing revelation, the source of these revelations was the inspirations of the *jinn* and devils (*shayāṭīn*). Their allegation is emphatically rejected in this verse.

SUMMARY OF THE VERSES

The verses state that the Prophet (s), who has lived amongst the idolaters all his life, is not possessed or mad. He has clearly seen the messenger-angel and does not withhold from the people what he hears of the unseen.

It is beyond doubt that the Qur'an is distinct from the insinuations of Shaytan.

REFLECTIVE LEARNING

The polytheists resorted to defaming the Prophet (s), and alleging that he was being inspired by Shaytan, when they realized the truth of his message but were unwilling to make the changes that it called for.

Let me reflect on my reaction when things do not sit well with me about the religion of God. Do I make the necessary changes, or do I find justifications to continue with what I am comfortable with?

VERSES 26 - 28

فَأَيْنَ تَذْهَبُونَ ﴿٢٦﴾ إِنْ هُوَ إِلَّا ذِكْرٌ لِلْعَالَمِينَ ﴿٢٧﴾ لِمَنْ شَاءَ مِنكُمْ أَنْ يَسْتَقِيمَ ﴿٢٨﴾

So where are you going? [26] *Indeed, it is nothing except a reminder to all of creation.* [27] *For whoever wills among you to take a right course.* [28]

26-28.1 *'So where are you going?'*: The last seven verses comprehensively summarized the station of the Qur'an, the impeccable qualities of the angel charged with its revelation, the familiarity of the people with the character of God's Messenger (s) and his readiness to share the knowledge of the unseen.[70] Now God asks a rhetorical question to those who were still determined to ignore the message, by asking them why they would wish to avoid the path of the truth?[71] This is an expression of amazement at the obstinacy of the disbelievers.

Another meaning of this phrase may be, 'where can you go? – because We are always with you.'[72]

26-28.2 *'Indeed, it is nothing except a reminder to all of creation.'*: The Qur'an serves as a reminder of the truths that are already coded in the *fiṭrah* of human beings. Everyone can potentially benefit from it. However, it would only serve as a reminder to those amongst the creation who wish to take the right path in the first place.

26-28.3 *'For whoever wills among you to take a right course.'*: [*Yastaqīm* (يَسْتَقِيم, take a right course)] is derived from *istiqāmah* which means

---

70 Ṭabāṭabā'ī, *al-Mīzān*, 20/220.

71 Ibid.

72 Javādī-Āmolī, *Tasnīm*, (Transcript: http://javadi.esra.ir/-/27-09-1398-5-جلسه-تکویر-سوره-تفسیر)

to remain steady, upright, and not to deviate from a straight path.[73] Here it means that the Qur'an will serve as a reminder for the one who is prepared to be steadfast in obeying God's commandments.[74] Q36:11 states:

إِنَّمَا تُنذِرُ مَنِ ٱتَّبَعَ الذِّكْرَ وَخَشِيَ الرَّحْمَٰنَ بِالْغَيْبِ فَبَشِّرْهُ بِمَغْفِرَةٍ وَأَجْرٍ كَرِيمٍ

You can only warn one who follows the reminder (Qur'an) and fears the all-Merciful [especially] in secret. So give him good tidings of forgiveness and a generous reward.

SUMMARY OF THE VERSES

God asks where the people intend to go, if they turn away from guidance. The Qur'an is no more than a reminder for those amongst creation who want to walk the right course.

REFLECTIVE LEARNING

The Qur'an and sunnah show the true and secure path to God's proximity – *al-ṣirāṭ al-mustaqīm*. Every other path ultimately leads to deviation. Q10:32 states:

فَمَاذَا بَعْدَ الْحَقِّ إِلَّا الضَّلَالُ فَأَنَّىٰ تُصْرَفُونَ

...And what can be beyond truth except error? So how are you averted?

Our free will and choice allows us to choose which path to take in our journey back to God.

Let me reflect on whether I diligently follow the internal and external guidance I possess, so that I remain steadfast in the obedience of God, or do I give more importance to other paths?

VERSE 29

وَمَا تَشَاءُونَ إِلَّا أَنْ يَشَاءَ اللَّهُ رَبُّ الْعَالَمِينَ ﴿٢٩﴾

And you cannot will except as Allah, the Lord of the worlds, wills. [29]

---

[73] Muṣṭafawī, *al-Taḥqīq*.

[74] Ṭabrasī, *al-Bayān*, 10/679.

29.1 The will of man is dependent on the will (*mashiyyah*) of God. In the case of God, *mashiyyah* means creating an effect, and in the case of the human being it denotes wanting to do something.[75]

29.2 *And you cannot will except as Allah, the Lord of the worlds, wills.* [*Wa mā tashā'ūna* (وَمَا تَشَاءُونَ, you will not will)] may mean that:

i) you cannot will to be steadfast in God's obedience, unless God wills so, and His command (through the *sharī'ah*) and encouragement (through *thawāb*) towards His obedience indicates His will;

ii) you cannot will to be steadfast in God's obedience, unless God bestows you this ability as a blessing (*luṭf*);

iii) you cannot will anything, unless God empowers you (gives you the *tawfīq*) to do so.[76]

29.3 The previous verse spoke of the will of mankind in deciding whether they want to follow the right course. However, this verse informs them that they cannot do so unless God enables them to want to do so.

In other words, God's will plays a role in the will and action of an individual. Only once God allows an action can man will it and carry it out; however, when he does the act, he does it out of his own free will.[77]

Therefore, there is no compulsion (*jabr*), nor is their complete delegation (*tafwīḍ*), rather it is a matter between these two (*al-amr bayn al-amrayn*). As a result, man is constantly in need of God's grace, and at the same time, responsible for his deeds.[78]

29.4 The mention of God as the Lord (Sustainer) of the worlds (*Rabb al-'ālamīn*) indicates that the *mashiyyah* of God is part of His role in sustaining and nurturing mankind towards their perfection.[79] We have discussed the phrase *Rabb al-'ālamīn* further in the *tafsīr* of Surat al-Fātiḥah (1).

---

75 Muṣṭafawī, *al-Taḥqīq*.

76 Ṭūsī, *al-Tibyān*, 10/289.

77 Ṭabāṭabā'ī, *al-Mīzān*, 20/143.

78 Shīrāzī, *Namūneh*, 26/203.

79 Ibid.

SUMMARY OF THE VERSE

The verse states that man cannot will to do anything unless God, who sustains the universe, also wills it.

REFLECTIVE LEARNING

God, the Sustainer of the worlds, desires for each of us to reach our potential and perfection and thereby, Paradise. Thereafter, out of His grace (*luṭf*), He guided us by the *sharīʿah*, encouraged us through the promise of divine reward and granted us the *tawfīq* to obey Him.

Let me reflect on whether I use my free will to follow the *sharīʿah*, gain *thawāb*, and take advantage of His *tawfīq* to obey Him, or am I ungrateful for this gift and turn away from Him.

SURAT AL-INFIṬĀR
THE CLEAVING (82)

TEXT AND TRANSLATION

سُورَةُ الانفِطَارِ

بِسْمِ اللهِ الرَّحْمٰنِ الرَّحِيمِ

إِذَا السَّمَاءُ انْفَطَرَتْ ﴿١﴾ وَإِذَا الْكَوَاكِبُ انْتَثَرَتْ ﴿٢﴾ وَإِذَا الْبِحَارُ فُجِّرَتْ ﴿٣﴾
وَإِذَا الْقُبُورُ بُعْثِرَتْ ﴿٤﴾ عَلِمَتْ نَفْسٌ مَا قَدَّمَتْ وَأَخَّرَتْ ﴿٥﴾ يَا أَيُّهَا الْإِنْسَانُ
مَا غَرَّكَ بِرَبِّكَ الْكَرِيمِ ﴿٦﴾ الَّذِي خَلَقَكَ فَسَوَّاكَ فَعَدَلَكَ ﴿٧﴾ فِي أَيِّ صُورَةٍ مَا
شَاءَ رَكَّبَكَ ﴿٨﴾ كَلَّا بَلْ تُكَذِّبُونَ بِالدِّينِ ﴿٩﴾ وَإِنَّ عَلَيْكُمْ لَحَافِظِينَ ﴿١٠﴾
كِرَامًا كَاتِبِينَ ﴿١١﴾ يَعْلَمُونَ مَا تَفْعَلُونَ ﴿١٢﴾ إِنَّ الْأَبْرَارَ لَفِي نَعِيمٍ ﴿١٣﴾
وَإِنَّ الْفُجَّارَ لَفِي جَحِيمٍ ﴿١٤﴾ يَصْلَوْنَهَا يَوْمَ الدِّينِ ﴿١٥﴾ وَمَا هُمْ عَنْهَا بِغَائِبِينَ
﴿١٦﴾ وَمَا أَدْرَاكَ مَا يَوْمُ الدِّينِ ﴿١٧﴾ ثُمَّ مَا أَدْرَاكَ مَا يَوْمُ الدِّينِ ﴿١٨﴾ يَوْمَ لَا
تَمْلِكُ نَفْسٌ لِنَفْسٍ شَيْئًا وَالْأَمْرُ يَوْمَئِذٍ لِلَّهِ ﴿١٩﴾

In the name of God, the Beneficent, the Merciful.

When the sky is cleft asunder, [1] *and when the planets are dispersed,* [2]
and when the seas are burst forth, [3] *and when the graves are overturned,*
[4] *[then] every soul will know what it has sent forth and what it has left*
behind. [5] *O man! What has deceived you about your Lord, the Generous?*
[6] *Who created you, then proportioned you, and then balanced you?* [7]
He assembled you in whatever form He willed. [8] *Not at all! But you deny*
the [Day of] Recompense. [9] *And indeed, there are protectors [appointed]*
over you, [10] *noble recorders.* [11] *They know whatever you do.* [12]
Indeed, the righteous will be in bliss. [13] *And indeed, the evildoers will*
be in hellfire. [14] *They will burn therein on the Day of Recompense.* [15]
And they will never be absent from it. [16] *And what will make you*
know what the Day of Recompense is? [17] *Again, what will make you*
know what the Day of Recompense is? [18] *[It is] a Day when no soul will*

possess [the power to do] anything for another soul; and the command, that Day, will be [entirely] with God. [19]

INTRODUCTION

Surat al-Infiṭār (82) was the 82nd chapter to be revealed.[1] It has nineteen verses and is a Makkan surah, revealed after Surat al-Nāziʿāt (79).

Like many Makkan surahs, it discusses the Day of Judgement. It is named after a cataclysmic sign of that Day mentioned in the first verse – the cleaving apart of the sky (*infiṭār*). Four events are mentioned. The first three will critically disrupt the system of the world and bring the *dunyā* to an end. The last event heralds the beginning of Resurrection and the *ākhirah*.

At this time, man will realize what actions he has brought with him to the *ākhirah* and what he has left behind in the *dunyā*.

The verses ask man why he had been careless enough to be deceived about his generous Sustainer, after He created him, proportioned him, and balanced his constitution in the best manner.

Thereafter, man is reminded that his every deed is being meticulously recorded by dutiful angels who are aware of everything he does. Their records will decide everyone's fate on a Day when the righteous will be entered into Paradise and the evildoers will be sent to Hell.

The surah ends with a warning of the tremendousness of the Day of Recompense that awaits everyone. On that Day no one will avail anyone else, and the command will belong to God alone.

LINK TO THE PREVIOUS CHAPTER

The previous chapter, Surat al-Takwīr, began with a description of twelve events that would occur at the end of the *dunyā*. Surat al-Infiṭār continues with the description of these events, listing another four cataclysmic occurrences that will occur before the Day of Recompense.

There is a close symmetry between the two surahs in the descriptions of the events of the last hour. Surat al-Takwīr mentions that the sky will be stripped away (*kushiṭat*), the celestial bodies will fade away (*inkadarat*), and the seas will be set on fire (*sujjirat*). Surat al-Infiṭār mentions that the sky will be cleft asunder (*infaṭarat*), the celestial

---

[1] Maʿrifat, *ʿUlūm-i Qurʾānī*, p. 90.

bodies will be dispersed (*intatharat*), and the seas will burst through their banks (*fujjirat*).

Both surahs mention the realization that is gained by everyone when these momentous events occur. In Surat al-Takwīr, Q81:14, God states, '*every soul will know what it has brought [with it].*' Surat al-Infiṭār mentions a deeper realization that comes when '*each soul will know what it has sent forth and what it has left behind.*'

Both surahs finish by reminding man of God's ultimate and eternal authority, although in the *dunyā* man often denies it. Surat al-Takwīr ends by informing man that he cannot will to do anything, unless God also wills it, '*but you cannot will except as Allah, the Lord of the worlds, wills.*' Surat al-Infiṭār ends by stating that in the *ākhirah*, on the Day of Recompense, God's dominant authority would be clearly evident, and no one would be able to deny that '*the command, that Day, will be [entirely] with God.*'

MERITS OF RECITATION

- A tradition from the Prophet (s) states: Whoever recites this surah regularly will be protected from humiliation on the Day of Judgement and his shameful deeds will be concealed. His situation will [also] be improved on the Day of Judgement.[2]
- A tradition from Imam al-Sadiq (a) states: Who ever recites these two surahs, *Idhā al-samā'u infaṭarat* (Surat al-Infiṭār, 82) and *Idhā al-samā'u inshaqqat* (Surat al-Inshiqāq, 84), with attentiveness in his obligatory and supererogatory prayers, will not be denied any wish by God. There will be no obstruction between him and God, and God will continually look over him until he completes his accounting (*ḥisāb*).[3]

---

[2] Baḥrānī, *al-Burhān*, 5/599.

عَنِ الرَّسُولِ (صَلَّى اللهُ عَلَيْهِ وَآلِهِ) – مَنْ أَدْمَنَ قِرَاءَتَهَا أَمِنَ فَضِيحَةَ يَوْمِ الْقِيَامَةِ وَسُتِرَتْ عَلَيْهِ عُيُوبُهُ وَأُصْلِحَ لَهُ شَأْنُهُ يَوْمَ الْقِيَامَةِ.

[3] Majlisī, *Biḥār*, 82/38.

عَنِ الصَّادِقِ (عَلَيْهِ السَّلَامُ) – مَنْ قَرَأَ هَاتَيْنِ السُّورَتَيْنِ وَجَعَلَهُمَا نُصْبَ عَيْنَيْهِ فِي صَلَاةِ الْفَرِيضَةِ وَالنَّافِلَةِ «إِذَا السَّمَاءُ ٱنْفَطَرَتْ» وَ«إِذَا السَّمَاءُ ٱنْشَقَّتْ» لَمْ يَحْجُبْهُ اللهُ مِنْ حَاجَةٍ وَلَمْ يَحْجُزْهُ مِنَ اللهِ حَاجِزٌ وَلَمْ يَزَلْ يَنْظُرُ اللهُ إِلَيْهِ حَتَّى يَفْرُغَ مِنَ الْحِسَابِ.

EXEGESIS

VERSES 1 - 5

إِذَا السَّمَاءُ ٱنفَطَرَتْ ﴿١﴾ وَإِذَا الْكَوَاكِبُ ٱنتَثَرَتْ ﴿٢﴾ وَإِذَا الْبِحَارُ فُجِّرَتْ ﴿٣﴾
وَإِذَا الْقُبُورُ بُعْثِرَتْ ﴿٤﴾ عَلِمَتْ نَفْسٌ مَا قَدَّمَتْ وَأَخَّرَتْ ﴿٥﴾

When the sky is cleft asunder, [1] *and when the planets are dispersed,* [2] *and when the seas are burst forth,* [3] *and when the graves are overturned;* [4] *[then] each soul will know what it has sent forth and what it has left behind.* [5]

1-5.1 Like the previous chapter, Surat al-Takwīr, this surah begins by providing brief glimpses of the events of the last Hour (*ashrāṭ al-sāʿah*) which will bring the *dunyā* to its end. The descriptions begin with *idhā* (when), which has the meaning of suddenness and certainty. Four events are mentioned, two of them to do with the heavens and two to do with the earth.[4]

1-5.2 '*When the sky is cleft asunder,*': This verse describes the unimaginable upheaval that will occur in the universe when the first trumpet is blown.

[*Samā'* (سَمَاء, sky)] is derived from *samawa*, meaning that which is raised high above other things and covers them.[5] In this verse it refers to the galaxy that surrounds us.[6]

[*Infaṭarat* (انفطَرَتْ, cleft asunder)] is derived from *faṭara* meaning to split, and here *infiṭār* refers to the canopy of the sky being torn open. The event is described with a similar term, *inshiqāq* (splitting apart), in several verses, including Q69:16:

وَٱنشَقَّتِ السَّمَاءُ فَهِيَ يَوْمَئِذٍ وَاهِيَةٌ

And the sky will split apart, for on that Day it will be weakened.

In Q77:9 the term *furijat* (torn apart) is used:

وَإِذَا السَّمَاءُ فُرِجَتْ

And when the sky is torn apart.

---

4 Rāzī, *Mafātīḥ al-Ghayb*, 31/72.

5 Muṣṭafawī, *al-Taḥqīq*.

6 Ṭāliqānī, *Partovī az Qur'an*, 3/213.

Essentially, the realm of the *dunyā* will be destroyed and discarded as creation enters the realm of the *ākhirah*. Q21:104 states:

يَوْمَ نَطْوِي السَّمَاءَ كَطَيِّ السِّجِلِّ لِلْكُتُبِ كَمَا بَدَأْنَا أَوَّلَ خَلْقٍ نُعِيدُهُ

The Day when We will roll up the skies like the rolling up of the scroll for records. As We began the first creation, We will repeat it...

1-5.3 '*And when the planets are dispersed,*': [*Kawākib* (كَوَاكِب, planets)] (sing. *kawkab*) denotes celestial bodies – either stars or planets.[7] [*Intatharat* (انتَثَرَت, dispersed)] is derived from *nathara* meaning to scatter,[8] and its verbal noun *intithār* means that once the sky is cleaved asunder, the forces that regulate the solar system will be in disarray. As a result, the stars and planets will scatter and fall out of their orbits.

1-5.4 '*And when the seas are burst forth,*': [*Fujjirat* (فُجِّرَت, burst forth)] is derived from *fajjara* meaning to burst through a boundary. The tumult in the heavens will next cause widespread destruction on the earth. The seas and other watercourses on the earth will begin to merge with one another[9] as their natural boundaries are removed by violent quakes on land and sea.[10] The barriers between sweet and salty waters mentioned in Q55:20 will be swept away: [11]

بَيْنَهُمَا بَرْزَخٌ لَا يَبْغِيَانِ

Between them is a barrier [so] neither of them transgresses.

1-5.5 '*And when the graves are overturned;*': The term 'graves' is used in a general sense, denoting the place where the remains of the dead lie. Those who are alive at the first blowing of the trumpet will fall where they stand. In any case, the verse is describing the moment when the dead will all be resurrected[12] at the second blowing of the trumpet.

1-5.6 The scattered particles of the bodies of human beings will come together and grow in the earth of *ākhirah* like seeds. A tradition from Imam al-Sadiq (a) states: When God, the Exalted, wills to resurrect

---

7 Rāzī, *Mafātīḥ al-Ghayb*, 13/38.

8 Muṣṭafawī, *al-Taḥqīq*.

9 Ṭūsī, *al-Tibyān*, 10/290.

10 Shīrāzī, *Namūneh*, 26/211.

11 Ṭabrasī, *al-Bayān*, 10/681.

12 Ṭūsī, *al-Tibyān*, 10/290.

the creation, He makes it rain from the sky for forty days and as a result, bones knit together, and flesh grows.[13] Q50:9-11 state:

وَنَزَّلْنَا مِنَ السَّمَاءِ مَاءً مُبَارَكًا... وَأَحْيَيْنَا بِهِ بَلْدَةً مَيْتًا كَذَٰلِكَ الْخُرُوجُ

And We send down blessed rain from the sky... and We give life thereby to a dead land. Thus shall be the Resurrection [also].

We have discussed the resurrection of human beings further in the *tafsīr* of Surat al-Ṭāriq (86).

[*Buʿthirat* (بُعْثِرَتْ, overturned)] is derived from *baʿthara* meaning to overturn something and pour the contents out.[14] The verb is a composite of *baʿatha* (to resurrect) and *thawara* (to overturn)[15] and here it refers to the physical resurrection of the dead, who will be expelled from their graves and assembled for the Day of Recompense.[16]

1-5.7 '*[Then] every soul will know what it has sent forth and what it has left behind.*': This is the conclusion to the four events mentioned in the previous verses.[17]

Nafs (soul) here refers to the genus of man and denotes every single human being.[18] The verse tells us that veils that clouded people's understanding of the reality of the world and their own station before God will be removed.[19]

In the previous surah, the description of the events of the death and revival of the world were followed by the statement, '*[Then] every soul will know what it has brought [with it].*' (Q81:14). The verse under review mentions a deeper realization that will come to everyone at a later stage, '*every soul will know what it has sent forth and what it has left behind.*' This may be due to information that they receive as mentioned in Q75:13, which states:

يُنَبَّأُ الْإِنْسَانُ يَوْمَئِذٍ بِمَا قَدَّمَ وَأَخَّرَ

[13] Majlisī, *Biḥār*, 7/33.

عَنِ الصَّادِقِ (عَلَيْهِ السَّلَامُ) - إِذَا أَرَادَ اللهُ عَزَّ وَجَلَّ أَنْ يَبْعَثَ الْخَلْقَ أَمْطَرَ السَّمَاءَ أَرْبَعِينَ صَبَاحًا فَاجْتَمَعَتِ الْأَوْصَالُ وَنَبَتَتِ اللُّحُومُ.

[14] Muṣṭafawī, *al-Taḥqīq*.

[15] Rāghib, *al-Mufradāt*.

[16] Ṭabāṭabā'ī, *al-Mīzān*, 20/223.

[17] Ṭūsī, *al-Tibyān*, 10/290.

[18] Ṭabāṭabā'ī, *al-Mīzān*, 20/223.

[19] Shīrāzī, *Namūneh*, 26/212.

On that Day, man will be informed of what he sent forth and left behind.

1-5.8 [*Qaddamat* (قَدَّمَتْ, sent forth)]. *Qaddama* means forwarded or advanced.

[*Akhkharat* (أَخَّرَتْ, left behind)]. *Akhkhara* meaning delayed or left behind.[20] The exegetes have given several meanings to these two terms:

i) *Qaddamat* refers to those deeds, good or bad, that were performed in the *dunyā* and sent forth for account in the *ākhirah. Akhkharat* refers to those deeds, good or bad, that were avoided in the *dunyā* and so were not forwarded to the *ākhirah.*

If man has sent forth goodness and left behind evil, then Paradise awaits him. But if he sent forth the fruit of sinful conduct and left behind the opportunities to do good, then Hell awaits him.[21]

ii) *Qaddamat* has the same meaning as previously stated but *akhkharat* refers to what others practised because of the example he left behind, good or bad. After his death, whenever people took advantage of the good that he had left behind in terms of charity, teachings, children, and so on, the reward of it was also added to his scroll of deeds, without reducing from the reward of those who followed him. Similarly, if he left behind something evil and people were misled because of him, its sin would be added to his scroll of deeds without reducing the burden of those who followed him.[22] Q36:12 states in this regard:

إِنَّا نَحْنُ نُحْيِي الْمَوْتَىٰ وَنَكْتُبُ مَا قَدَّمُوا وَآثَارَهُمْ

Indeed, it is We who bring the dead to life and record what they have sent forth and what they left behind...

A tradition states: At the time of the Prophet (s), a beggar stood up and asked for some assistance. The people ignored him but then a man gave him something. At this, the people also gave him. Then the Prophet (s) said, "Whoever institutes a good practice shall gain the reward of those who followed him without their reward being lessened. And whoever institutes an

---

20 Muṣṭafawī, *al-Taḥqīq.*

21 Rāzī, *Mafātīḥ al-Ghayb,* 31/73.

22 Ṭabrasī, *al-Bayān,* 10/682.

evil practice which is emulated, shall bear the burden [of sin] of those who follow him without their burden being lessened."[23]

iii) *Qaddamat* refers to the deeds that he performed in the earlier part of his lifetime and *akhkharat* refers to what he did towards the end, and the meaning is that he will remember clearly even those things he did in his childhood and youth.[24]

Indeed, the *tawfīq* to reform oneself and turn repentant towards God before death is a great blessing. In one of his supplications, Imam al-Sajjad (a) states: And inspire me to do good deeds that would wash away the stain of my sins, and let me die [while I am] on Your religion and the religion of Your Prophet (s)...[25]

iv) *Qaddamat* refers to the charity that he sent forth and *akhkharat* refers to the money he left behind for his heirs. Indeed, the station of charity and the charitable is quickly obvious to the deceased. Q63:10 states:

وَأَنفِقُوا مِنْ مَا رَزَقْنَاكُمْ مِنْ قَبْلِ أَنْ يَأْتِيَ أَحَدَكُمُ الْمَوْتُ فَيَقُولَ رَبِّ
لَوْلَا أَخَّرْتَنِي إِلَىٰ أَجَلٍ قَرِيبٍ فَأَصَّدَّقَ وَأَكُنْ مِنَ الصَّالِحِينَ

And spend from what We have provided you before death comes to one of you and he says: My Lord, if only You would reprieve me for a little while so I would give charity and [thereby] be among the righteous.

1-5.9 At the moment of resurrection, individuals will gain a general realization of their fate. The obedient believer will see signs of felicity (*sa'ādah*), while the disobedient sinner will see the signs of wretchedness (*shaqāwah*). And when people reach the stage where the scrolls of deeds are handed out, their realization of their station will be complete.[26]

---

23 Ḥuwayzī, *Nur al-Thaqalayn*, 5/520.

أَنَّ سَائِلًا قَامَ عَلَى عَهْدِ النَّبِيِّ صَلَّى اللهُ عَلَيْهِ وَآلِهِ فَسَأَلَ، فَسَكَتَ الْقَوْمُ ثُمَّ إِنَّ رَجُلًا أَعْطَاهُ فَأَعْطَاهُ الْقَوْمُ. فَقَالَ النَّبِيُّ صَلَّى اللهُ عَلَيْهِ وَآلِهِ: مَنِ اسْتَنَّ خَيْرًا فَلَهُ أَجْرُهُ وَمِثْلُ أُجُورِ مَنِ اتَّبَعَهُ غَيْرَ مُنْتَقِصٍ مِنْ أُجُورِهِمْ وَمَنِ اسْتَنَّ شَرًّا فَاسْتُنَّ فَعَلَيْهِ وِزْرُهُ وَمِثْلُ أَوْزَارِ مَنِ اتَّبَعَهُ غَيْرَ مُنْتَقِصٍ مِنْ أَوْزَارِهِمْ.

24 Ṭabāṭabā'ī, *al-Mīzān*, 20/223.

25 *Ṣaḥīfah al-Sajjādiyyah*, supplication no. 31.

وَوَفِّقْنِي مِنَ الْأَعْمَالِ لِمَا تَغْسِلُ بِهِ دَنَسَ الْخَطَايَا عَنِّي، وَتَوَفَّنِي عَلَى مِلَّتِكَ وَمِلَّةِ نَبِيِّكَ.

26 Rāzī, *Mafātīḥ al-Ghayb*, 31/73.

SUMMARY OF THE VERSES

The verses in the first section of the surah describe four events that will accompany the advent of the last Hour: The cleaving asunder of the sky, the dispersal of the celestial bodies, the bursting forth of the seas, and the emptying of graves.

At that time, every single individual will realize what he had sent forth to the *ākhirah* and what he had left behind in the *dunyā*.

REFLECTIVE LEARNING

Looking at the four meanings exegetes have given to the terms *qaddamat* and *akhkharat*, let me reflect on:

i) The deeds that I want to send forth and those that I want to refrain from.

ii) The good practice that I want to leave as an example for others to follow.

iii) Those deeds that I have done in my early life, for which I should thank God or seek His forgiveness.

iv) Whether I give some charity on a regular basis.

VERSES 6 - 8

يَا أَيُّهَا الْإِنْسَانُ مَا غَرَّكَ بِرَبِّكَ الْكَرِيمِ ﴿٦﴾ الَّذِي خَلَقَكَ فَسَوَّاكَ فَعَدَلَكَ ﴿٧﴾ فِي أَيِّ صُورَةٍ مَا شَاءَ رَكَّبَكَ ﴿٨﴾

O man! What has deceived you about your Lord, the Generous? [6] *Who created you, then proportioned you, and then balanced you?* [7] *He assembled you in whatever form He willed.* [8]

6-8.1 '*O man! What has deceived you about your Lord, the Generous?*': [*Al-Insān* (الْإِنْسَان, man)] here refers to either the disbelievers or more probably, the one who denies the Day of Recompense (*Yawm al-Dīn*) mentioned later in the surah.[27] Man has been addressed as *insān* because he should know better due to the (intellectual and spiritual) qualities that he has been uniquely endowed with, which made him preeminent in creation.[28]

[27] Ṭabāṭabā'ī, *al-Mīzān*, 20/224.

[28] Shīrāzī, *Namūneh*, 26/217.

[*Gharraka* (غَرَّكَ, deceived you)]. *Gharra* here means deceived and distracted. *Mā gharraka* (what has deceived you) is a rhetorical question showing surprise and wonder. The verse means to ask: What has deceived you by luring you away from the obedience of God into His disobedience, made you deny the Resurrection and Recompense, and made you feel secure from God's requital?[29]

This situation may be due to ignorance, deception, temptation, arrogance, or negligence.[30] A tradition from the Prophet (s) states that when he (s) recited this verse, he commented: His ignorance deceived him.[31] This may be referring to man's ignorance of the station of God, or of all that He has given him, or of the real purpose of his life, and so on. Indeed, one of the manifestations of this ignorance is the mindless pursuit of the *dunyā* fuelled by the urging of Shaytan. Q31:33 warns:

فَلَا تَغُرَّنَّكُمُ الْحَيَاةُ الدُّنْيَا وَلَا يَغُرَّنَّكُمْ بِاللَّهِ الْغَرُورُ

...So do not let the life of this [low] world delude you and do not be deceived about God by the Deceiver (Shaytan).

In contrast, those who have cognizance (*maʿrifah*) of God are more grateful to Him, more mindful of His commandments and prohibitions, and always feel indebted to Him. Indeed, even the greatest *awliyā'* of God wept because they could not thank Him enough. In one of his whispered prayers, Imam al-Sajjad (a) admits: My God, tongues fall short of attaining Your praise as befits Your Majesty, and intellects are defeated in understanding the core of Your Beauty...[32]

6-8.2 [*Al-Karīm* (الْكَرِيمِ, the Generous)] means that God is the all-Generous whose every act is based on unrestricted goodness (*iḥsān*) and bestowal (*inʿām*). He grants without wanting any benefit, or to repel any harm, for Himself. He bestows more than He has to, and is ready to accept a little and give a lot.[33]

---

29 Rāzī, *Mafātīḥ al-Ghayb*, 31/74.

30 Muṣṭafawī, *al-Taḥqīq*.

31 Ṭabrasī, *al-Bayān*, 10/682.

أَنَّ النَّبِيَّ صَلَّى اللهُ عَلَيْهِ وَآلِهِ لَمَّا تَلَا هَذِهِ الْآيَةَ قَالَ غَرَّهُ جَهْلُهُ.

32 Qummī, *Mafātīḥ al-Jinān, Munājāt al-ʿĀrifīn* (The whispered prayer of the knowers).

إِلٰهِي قَصُرَتِ الْأَلْسُنُ عَنْ بُلُوغِ ثَنَائِكَ كَمَا يَلِيقُ بِجَلَالِكَ، وَعَجَزَتِ الْعُقُولُ عَنْ إِدْرَاكِ كُنْهِ جَمَالِكَ...

33 Ṭabrasī, *al-Bayān*, 10/682.

In this verse, *Karīm* is used as an adjective for *Rabb* to emphasize that His generosity is a feature of His role as Sustainer. It also highlights the gravity of the crime of any individual who allows himself to be deceived about God, when He generously provided for him without asking for anything in return, generously withheld His punishment for his disobedience, and generously kept the door of repentance open for him.[34]

A tradition from Imam Ali (a) states: How many are gradually drawn away due to [God's] good blessings, His concealment of their faults, and the good words they hear about themselves.[35]

6-8.3 '*Who created you, proportioned you, and balanced you.*': These three favours of God to every human being serve as a reminder to the neglectful. They are examples of His favours as the Generous Sustainer (*al-Rabb al-Karīm*) and are a continuation of the question asked in the previous verse.[36]

1. [*Khalaqa* (خَلَقَ, created)] means brought together man's constituent elements.[37] God created him from a lowly substance when he was nothing.[38] Q23:12-14 describe the process of man's creation:

وَلَقَدْ خَلَقْنَا الْإِنْسَانَ مِنْ سُلَالَةٍ مِنْ طِينٍ ﴿١٢﴾ ثُمَّ جَعَلْنَاهُ نُطْفَةً فِي قَرَارٍ
مَكِينٍ ﴿١٣﴾ ثُمَّ خَلَقْنَا النُّطْفَةَ عَلَقَةً فَخَلَقْنَا الْعَلَقَةَ مُضْغَةً فَخَلَقْنَا الْمُضْغَةَ
عِظَامًا فَكَسَوْنَا الْعِظَامَ لَحْمًا ثُمَّ أَنْشَأْنَاهُ خَلْقًا آخَرَ فَتَبَارَكَ اللَّهُ أَحْسَنُ الْخَالِقِينَ

And indeed We created man from an extract of clay. Then We placed him as a drop in a firm lodging. Then We made the drop into a clinging clot, and We made the clot into a lump, and We made [from] the lump, bones, and We covered the bones with flesh; then We developed him into another creation. So blessed be Allah, the Best of creators.

2. [*Sawwā* (سَوَّىٰ, proportioned)] is derived from *sawiya* which means to be proportional, and here it means to fashion every

---

[34] Rāzī, *Mafātīḥ al-Ghayb*, 31/75.

[35] *Nahj al-Balāghah*, saying 116.

كَمْ مِنْ مُسْتَدْرَجٍ بِالْإِحْسَانِ إِلَيْهِ وَمَغْرُورٍ بِالسَّتْرِ عَلَيْهِ وَمَفْتُونٍ بِحُسْنِ الْقَوْلِ فِيهِ.

[36] Ṭabāṭabā'ī, *al-Mīzān*, 20/225.

[37] Ibid, 20/265.

[38] Ṭabrasī, *al-Bayān*, 10/682.

limb and organ in proportion to create a perfect constitution for man.[39] Q95:4 states:

لَقَدْ خَلَقْنَا الْإِنْسَانَ فِي أَحْسَنِ تَقْوِيمٍ

Verily, We created man in the best constitution.

3. [*ʿAdala* (عَدَلَ, balanced)]. This may be a reference to the perfect balance of the human form by the provision of paired limbs and organs that complement each other and coordinate together to work in harmony. In addition, all the physiological processes and chemicals that sustain human life are kept in balance to maintain his health and wellbeing.[40]

   According to some exegetes, it could also be a reference to the fact that man was created to walk upright, balanced on two limbs, unlike the lower animals.[41]

6-8.4 '*He assembled you in whatever form He willed.*': [*Ṣūrah* (صُورَة, form)] refers to what is seen by the eyes in a manner that distinguishes things as distinct from each other.[42]

[*Rakkaba* (رَكَّبَ, assembled)] means to build or assemble something by placing one thing over another. Here *rakkaba* refers to the intricate interconnection of all internal and external organs in the assembly of the human form.[43]

The verse states that God created every man and woman uniquely, with individual physical, mental, and emotional characteristics based on His wisdom and will.[44]

'*Whatever form He willed*' may also mean making the person resemble his relatives and ancestors in features and character. A tradition from the Prophet (s) states: Once the embryo is implanted in the womb, God makes available the form of every ancestor between him and Adam (a).[45] Q3:6 states:

---

[39] Muṣṭafawī, *al-Taḥqīq*.

[40] Shīrāzī, *Namūneh*, 26/221.

[41] Rāzī, *Mafātīḥ al-Ghayb*, 31/76.

[42] Muṣṭafawī, *al-Taḥqīq*.

[43] Ibid.

[44] Shīrāzī, *Namūneh*, 26/222.

[45] Majlisī, *Biḥār*, 7/94.

عَنِ الرَّسُولِ (صَلَّى اللهُ عَلَيْهِ وَآلِهِ) – إِنَّ النُّطْفَةَ إِذَا اسْتَقَرَّتْ فِي الرَّحِمِ أَحْضَرَهَا اللهُ كُلَّ نَسَبٍ بَيْنَهَا وَبَيْنَ آدَمَ.

هُوَ الَّذِي يُصَوِّرُكُمْ فِي الْأَرْحَامِ كَيْفَ يَشَاءُ

It is He who forms you in the wombs however He wills.

On the day of Ashura, a report states that when his son Ali al-Akbar departed for the battlefield, Imam al-Husayn (a) said, "O God, be witness that a youth has advanced towards them who most closely resembles Your Messenger (s) in his features, manner, and speech. Whenever we desired to look again at the face of Your Prophet (s), we would look at his face."[46]

SUMMARY OF THE VERSES

God asks man what deceived him about his Generous Lord, the Lord who created, proportioned and balanced every human being, and assembled him as He wished in the best form.

REFLECTIVE LEARNING

A sermon from Imam Ali (a) states in part: O man! What has made you so bold regarding your sins, what has deceived you about your Lord, and what has made you feel at ease with your ruin? Is there no cure for your sickness and is there no awakening from your sleep? Do you not take pity on yourself the way you feel pity for others?...

So, be obedient to God, and be constant in His remembrance. Picture yourself turning away from Him while He approaches you. He calls you to His forgiveness and conceals your faults by His kindness, yet all the while, you turn away from Him toward others...[47]

Let me reflect on this important advice from Amīr al-Mu'minīn (a) and see how I can implement it in my life.

---

[46] Ibn Ṭāwūs, *al-Malhūf*, p. 166.

ثُمَّ قَالَ الْحُسَيْنُ عَلَيْهِ السَّلَامُ: اَللّٰهُمَّ اشْهَدْ، فَقَدْ بَرَزَ إِلَيْهِمْ غُلَامٌ أَشْبَهُ النَّاسِ خَلْقًا وَخُلُقًا وَمَنْطِقًا بِرَسُولِكَ صَلَّى اللهُ عَلَيْهِ وَآلِهِ، وَكُنَّا إِذَا اشْتَقْنَا إِلَى نَبِيِّكَ نَظَرْنَا إِلَيْهِ.

[47] *Nahj al-Balāghah*, sermon 222.

يَا أَيُّهَا الْإِنْسَانُ، مَا جَرَّأَكَ عَلَى ذَنْبِكَ، وَمَا غَرَّكَ بِرَبِّكَ، وَمَا آنَسَكَ بِهَلَكَةِ نَفْسِكَ؟ أَمَا مِنْ دَائِكَ بُلُولٌ، أَمْ لَيْسَ مِنْ نَوْمَتِكَ يَقَظَةٌ؟ أَمَا تَرْحَمُ مِنْ نَفْسِكَ مَا تَرْحَمُ مِنْ غَيْرِكَ؟ ... وَكُنْ لِلّٰهِ مُطِيعًا، وَبِذِكْرِهِ آنِسًا، وَتَمَثَّلْ فِي حَالِ تَوَلِّيكَ عَنْهُ إِقْبَالَهُ عَلَيْكَ، يَدْعُوكَ إِلَى عَفْوِهِ، وَيَتَغَمَّدُكَ بِفَضْلِهِ، وَأَنْتَ مُتَوَلٍّ عَنْهُ إِلَى غَيْرِهِ...

VERSES 9 - 12

كَلَّا بَلْ تُكَذِّبُونَ بِالدِّينِ ﴿٩﴾ وَإِنَّ عَلَيْكُمْ لَحَافِظِينَ ﴿١٠﴾ كِرَامًا كَاتِبِينَ ﴿١١﴾ يَعْلَمُونَ مَا تَفْعَلُونَ ﴿١٢﴾

Not at all! But you deny the [Day of] Recompense. [9] *And indeed, there are protectors [appointed] over you,* [10] *noble recorders.* [11] *They know whatever you do.* [12]

9-12.1 '*Not at all! But you deny the [Day of] Recompense.*': [*Kallā* (كَلَّا, Not at all!)]. This phrase is commonly used in the Qur'an to negate an idea and implies a command to desist and reconsider. Here, it is used to emphasize the absolute error of those who allow the generous favours of God to justify their disbelief and sinful conduct.[48] In fact, it is their disbelief and denial of the Recompense that has deceived them.

[*Tukadhdhibūn* (تُكَذِّبُونَ, you deny)] is derived from *kadhdhaba*, which means denying something out of defiance despite instinctively knowing that it is the truth.[49]

We have discussed this verse in the *tafsīr* of Surat al-Māʿūn [107].

9-12.2 God created the human being, then proportioned, balanced, and assembled him in the best form based on His mercy and wisdom. He then guided him to the purpose of his creation and showed him the difference between right and wrong. How could man then be deceived about his Generous Lord, and deny the Day when he would be recompensed for the type of life that he lived in this world?[50] Q95:4...7 state:

لَقَدْ خَلَقْنَا الْإِنسَانَ فِي أَحْسَنِ تَقْوِيمٍ ﴿٤﴾... فَمَا يُكَذِّبُكَ بَعْدُ بِالدِّينِ

Verily, We created man in the best constitution... Then what causes you to deny [after this] the [Day of] Recompense?

However, while man denies a Day of recompense, God warns him in the next verse that He has appointed watchers to record every act of the human being.

---

48 Ṭabāṭabā'ī, *al-Mīzān*, 20/225.

49 Rāghib, *al-Mufradāt*.

50 Rāzī, *Mafātīḥ al-Ghayb*, 31/77.

9-12.3 '*And indeed, there are protectors [appointed] over you, noble recorders.*' [*Ḥāfiẓīn* (حَافِظِين, protectors)] is derived from *ḥafiẓa* which means to guard, preserve, and protect. Although angels protect man from various evils and hazards, this verse highlights their role in recording the deeds of human beings.

[*Kirām* (كِرَام, noble)] is the plural of *karīm*, here meaning possessing an honoured and high station before God.[51]

These angels are His servants who are always faithful in carrying out their assignments.[52] Q21:26, 27 state:

بَلْ عِبَادٌ مُكْرَمُونَ ﴿٢٦﴾ لَا يَسْبِقُونَهُ بِالْقَوْلِ وَهُمْ بِأَمْرِهِ يَعْمَلُونَ

...Rather, they (the angels) are honoured servants. They do not precede Him in speech, and they [only] act by His command.

[*Kātibīn* (كَاتِبِين, recorders)]. The duty that these angels have been assigned with is to record all the deeds of an individual meticulously and continually. This is clear evidence that man acts out of his free will, for otherwise their recording would have no meaning.[53]

The recording angels thereby produce a 'book' that would be a witness for or against each human being on the Day of Recompense. Q45:29 states:

هَٰذَا كِتَابُنَا يَنْطِقُ عَلَيْكُمْ بِالْحَقِّ إِنَّا كُنَّا نَسْتَنْسِخُ مَا كُنْتُمْ تَعْمَلُونَ

This is Our record; it speaks about you [all] with truth. Indeed, We have had transcribed whatever you used to do.

9-12.4 '*They know whatever you do*': [*Mā taf ʿalūn* (مَا تَفْعَلُون, what you do)]. *Tafʿalūn* is used here instead of the similar term *taʿmalūn*, because *fiʿl* refers to any act that is initiated with free will as well as intention, while *ʿamal* refers to the act when it has reached completion.[54]

According to the traditions, these angels are connected with the individual in a manner that allows them an intimate awareness of their inclinations, even before their actions are visible. They unerringly record the deeds in precise detail, preserving not just the

---

51 Kāshānī, *al-Ṣāfī*, 5/296.

52 Muṣṭafawī, *al-Taḥqīq*.

53 Shīrāzī, *Namūneh*, 26/227.

54 Muṣṭafawī, *al-Taḥqīq*.

deed, but the intention behind it, and the manner in which it was performed as well.[55]

9-12.5 In one of his sermons, Imam Ali (a) stated: You should know, O servants of God, that over you... are truthful recorders, who record your deeds and [even] the number of your breaths. The gloom of the night cannot conceal you from them, nor can closed doors hide you from them.[56]

DISCUSSION: THE NOBLE RECORDERS IN THE TRADITIONS

The first five chapters in the last *juz'* of the Qur'an, al-Nabaʾ, al-Nāziʿāt, ʿAbasa, al-Takwīr, and al-Infiṭār all mention God's angels. In this section we will mention some of the many traditions that give details about one class of these angels: the recording angels appointed by God over every human being.

1. A tradition from the Prophet (s) states: There is an angel on your right who records your good deeds, and another on your left. When you perform a good deed, he writes ten [rewards]. But when you commit an evil deed, the angel on the left asks the one on the right, "Shall I write?" He replies, "He may seek God's forgiveness and repent." When he asks a third time, he says, "Yes, write. May God relieve us of him, what an evil companion! How little is his observance [of the commands] of God, the Exalted, and how little is his shame before Him. God states: '*Man does not utter any word except that with him is an observer* (raqīb) *prepared* (ʿatīd).' (Q50:18)."[57]
2. A tradition from Imam al-Kazim (a) states: His son ʿAbdullāh asked the Imam (a), "Do the two recording angels know when a person intends to commit a sin or perform a good act?" The Imam (a) replied, "Is an odious stench the same as a fragrant perfume?" He replied, "No." [Then the Imam (a) said,] "When an individual desires to perform a good act, his soul emits a beautiful fragrance. [At

---

[55] Ṭabāṭabāʾī, *al-Mīzān*, 20/226.

[56] *Nahj al-Balāghah*, sermon 157.

إِعْلَمُوا، عِبَادَ اللهِ، أَنَّ عَلَيْكُمْ ... حُفَّاظَ صِدْقٍ يَحْفَظُونَ أَعْمَالَكُمْ، وَعَدَدَ أَنْفَاسِكُمْ، لَا تَسْتُرُكُمْ مِنْهُمْ ظُلْمَةُ لَيْلٍ دَاجٍ، وَلَا يُكِنُّكُمْ مِنْهُمْ بَابٌ ذُو رِتَاجٍ.

[57] Majlisī, *Biḥār*, 5/324.

عَنِ الرَّسُولِ (صَلَّى اللهُ عَلَيْهِ وَآلِهِ) – قَالَ: مَلَكٌ على يَمِينِكَ على حَسَناتِكَ وَوَاحِدٌ عَلَى الشِّمَالِ فإذا عَمِلْتَ حسنةً كَتَبَ عَشْرًا وَإِذَا عَمِلْتَ سَيِّئَةً قَالَ الَّذِي عَلَى الشِّمَالِ لِلَّذِي عَلَى الْيَمِينِ أَكْتُبُ؟ قَالَ لَعَلَّهُ يَسْتَغْفِرُ وَيَتُوبُ فَإِذَا قَالَ ثَلَاثًا قَالَ نَعَمْ أُكْتُبْ أَرَاحَنَا اللهُ مِنْهُ فَبِئْسَ الْقَرِينُ مَا أَقَلَّ مُرَاقَبَتَهُ لِلهِ عَزَّ وَجَلَّ وَمَا أَقَلَّ اسْتِحْيَاءَهُ مِنْهُ. يَقُولُ اللهُ «مَا يَلْفِظُ مِنْ قَوْلٍ إِلَّا لَدَيْهِ رَقِيبٌ عَتِيدٌ».

this,] the angel on the right says to the one on the left, 'Depart, for he has desired to do a good act.'... And when an individual desires to commit a sin, his soul emits a foul smell. [At this,] the angel on the left says to the one on the right, 'Depart, for he has desired to commit a sinful act.'"[58]

3. A tradition from Imam al-Sadiq (a) states: There is no individual except that he is accompanied by two angels who write down whatever he says. Then they pass that on to two angels who are higher than them, who preserve whatever of it is related to good or evil and discard the rest.[59]
4. Another tradition from Imam al-Sadiq (a) states: They are called *kirām* because when they record a good act, they ascend bearing it to the heavens and present it before God, the Exalted, and bear witness to it. They say, "This one of Your servants has performed the following good deed!" But when they record a person's evil act, they ascend to the heavens with grief and sorrow. God, the Exalted asks, "What did My servant do?" They remain silent, until God asks them a second, and third time. (Then) they say, "O God, You are the Concealer, and have instructed Your servants to conceal their faults. [So] Conceal their faults, for You are the Knower of the unseen." And this is why they are called 'noble recorders' (*kirāman kātibīn*).[60]
5. Imam al-Sadiq (a) was asked by a heretic (*zindīq*), "Why has God appointed two angels over His servants to record for and against them, while He [already] knows all secrets as well as what is hidden even deeper?" The Imam (a) replied, "He wants them to submit to Him through this and has made them witnesses over His servants

---

[58] Kulaynī, *al-Kāfī*, 2/429.

عَنِ الْكَاظِمِ (عَلَيْهِ السَّلَامُ) - عَنْ عَبْدِ اللهِ بْنِ مُوسَى بْنِ جَعْفَرٍ عَنْ أَبِيهِ قَالَ: سَأَلْتُهُ عَنِ الْمَلَكَيْنِ هَلْ يَعْلَمَانِ بِالذَّنْبِ إِذَا أَرَادَ الْعَبْدُ أَنْ يَفْعَلَهُ أَوِ الْحَسَنَةِ؟ فَقَالَ رِيحُ الْكَنِيفِ وَرِيحُ الطِّيبِ سَوَاءٌ؟ قُلْتُ لَا. قَالَ إِنَّ الْعَبْدَ إِذَا هَمَّ بِالْحَسَنَةِ خَرَجَ نَفَسُهُ طَيِّبَ الرِّيحِ فَقَالَ صَاحِبُ الْيَمِينِ لِصَاحِبِ الشِّمَالِ قُمْ فَإِنَّهُ قَدْ هَمَّ بِالْحَسَنَةِ... وَإِذَا هَمَّ بِالسَّيِّئَةِ خَرَجَ نَفَسُهُ مُنْتِنَ الرِّيحِ فَيَقُولُ صَاحِبُ الشِّمَالِ لِصَاحِبِ الْيَمِينِ قِفْ فَإِنَّهُ قَدْ هَمَّ بِالسَّيِّئَةِ.

[59] Majlisī, *Biḥār*, 3/846.

عَنِ الصَّادِقِ (عَلَيْهِ السَّلَامُ) - مَا مِنْ أَحَدٍ إِلَّا وَمَعَهُ مَلَكَانِ يَكْتُبَانِ مَا يَلْفِظُهُ ثُمَّ يَرْفَعَانِ ذَلِكَ إِلَى مَلَكَيْنِ فَوْقَهُمَا فَيُثْبِتَانِ مَا كَانَ مِنْ خَيْرٍ وَشَرٍّ وَيُلْقِيَانِ مَا سِوَى ذَلِكَ.

[60] Ibid.

إِنَّمَا سُمُّوا كِرَامًا لِأَنَّهُمْ إِذَا كَتَبُوا حَسَنَةً يَصْعَدُونَ بِهِ إِلَى السَّمَاءِ وَيَعْرِضُونَ عَلَى اللهِ تَعَالَى وَيَشْهَدُونَ عَلَى ذَلِكَ فَيَقُولُونَ إِنَّ عَبْدَكَ فُلَانٌ عَمِلَ حَسَنَةً كَذَا وَكَذَا وَإِذَا كَتَبُوا مِنَ الْعَبْدِ سَيِّئَةً يَصْعَدُونَ بِهِ إِلَى السَّمَاءِ مَعَ الْغَمِّ وَالْحُزْنِ فَيَقُولُ اللهُ تَعَالَى مَا فَعَلَ عَبْدِي فَيَسْكُتُونَ حَتَّى يَسْأَلَ اللهُ ثَانِيًا وَثَالِثًا فَيَقُولُونَ إِلٰهِي أَنْتَ سَتَّارٌ وَأَمَرْتَ عِبَادَكَ أَنْ يَسْتُرُوا عُيُوبَهُمْ، اُسْتُرْ عُيُوبَهُمْ وَأَنْتَ عَلَّامُ الْغُيُوبِ وَلِهَذَا يُسَمَّوْنَ.

so that their continual presence would make them more mindful about obeying God and more restrained in disobeying Him.

There are many who intend to sin, but remember their presence and refrain [from sin] and desist, saying, 'My Lord sees me, and my guardians will bear witness to my deed.'

Out of His clemency and grace, God has also appointed them over His servants to defend them against the rebellious satans, the pests of the earth, and many calamities that the people do not perceive, with God's permission, until the command of God, the Exalted, comes [for them]."[61]

6. A tradition from the Imam (a) speaks of the daily alternation of two pairs of recording angels uniquely assigned to a human being: The two angels come to the believer at the time of the *fajr* prayer. When they descend, the two angels who were appointed over him at night ascend. And when the sun sets, the angels appointed over him at night descend, and the two angels who were recording his deeds ascend with his record to God, the Mighty and Exalted. And this process continues until the time of his death.

   At that time, to a righteous person they say, "May God recompense you for being an excellent companion! How many righteous deeds you showed us, how many pleasant words you made us hear, and how many assemblies of goodness you took us to! So today we will be pleasing to you, and we will be intercessors before your Lord. And to a sinful person they say, "May God recompense you for being a distasteful companion! You tormented us. How many ugly deeds you showed us, how many unpleasant words you made us hear, and how many evil assemblies you took us to! So today we will be displeasing to you, and we will be witnesses before your Lord.[62]

---

[61] Majlisī, *Biḥār*, 56/179.
سَأَلَ الزِّنْدِيقُ الصَّادِقَ عَلَيْهِ السَّلَامُ مَا عِلَّةُ الْمَلَائِكَةِ الْمُوَكَّلِينَ بِعِبَادِهِ يَكْتُبُونَ عَلَيْهِمْ وَلَهُمْ وَاللهُ عَالِمُ السِّرِّ وَمَا هُوَ أَخْفَى؟ قَالَ: اسْتَعْبَدَهُمْ بِذَلِكَ وَجَعَلَهُمْ شُهُودًا عَلَى خَلْقِهِ لِيَكُونَ الْعِبَادُ لِمُلَازَمَتِهِمْ إِيَّاهُمْ أَشَدَّ عَلَى طَاعَةِ اللهِ مُوَاظَبَةً وَعَنْ مَعْصِيَتِهِ أَشَدَّ انْقِبَاضًا، وَكَمْ مِنْ عَبْدٍ يَهُمُّ بِمَعْصِيَةٍ فَذَكَرَ مَكَانَهَا فَارْعَوَى وَكَفَّ، فَيَقُولُ رَبِّي يَرَانِي وَحَفَظَتِي بِذَلِكَ تَشْهَدُ. وَإِنَّ اللهَ بِرَأْفَتِهِ وَلُطْفِهِ أَيْضًا وَكَّلَهُمْ بِعِبَادِهِ يَذُبُّونَ عَنْهُمْ مَرَدَةَ الشَّيَاطِينِ وَهَوَامَّ الْأَرْضِ وَآفَاتٍ كَثِيرَةٍ مِنْ حَيْثُ لَا يَرَوْنَ بِإِذْنِ اللهِ إِلَى أَنْ يَجِيءَ أَمْرُ اللهِ عَزَّ وَجَلَّ.

[62] Ḥuwayzī, *Nūr al-Thaqalayn*, 5/523.
إِنَّهُمَا يَأْتِيَانِ الْمُؤْمِنَ عِنْدَ حُضُورِ صَلَاةِ الْفَجْرِ، فَإِذَا هَبَطَا صَعَدَ الْمَلَكَانِ الْمُوَكَّلَانِ بِاللَّيْلِ، فَإِذَا غَرَبَتِ الشَّمْسُ نَزَلَ إِلَيْهِ الْمُوَكَّلَانِ بِكِتَابَةِ اللَّيْلِ، وَيَصْعَدُ الْمَلَكَانِ الْكَاتِبَانِ بِالنَّهَارِ بِدِيوَانِهِ إِلَى اللهِ عَزَّ وَجَلَّ، فَلَا يَزَالُ ذَلِكَ دَأْبُهُمْ إِلَى وَقْتِ حُضُورِ أَجَلِهِ، فَإِذَا حَضَرَ أَجَلُهُ قَالَا لِلرَّجُلِ الصَّالِحِ: جَزَاكَ اللهُ مِنْ صَاحِبٍ عَنَّا خَيْرًا فَكَمْ مِنْ عَمَلٍ صَالِحٍ أَرَيْتَنَاهُ، وَكَمْ مِنْ قَوْلٍ حَسَنٍ أَسْمَعْتَنَاهُ، وَكَمْ مِنْ مَجْلِسِ خَيْرٍ أَحْضَرْتَنَاهُ، فَنَحْنُ الْيَوْمَ عَلَى مَا تُحِبُّهُ وَشُفَعَاءُ إِلَى رَبِّكَ، وَإِنْ كَانَ عَاصِيًا قَالَا لَهُ: جَزَاكَ اللهُ مِنْ صَاحِبٍ عَنَّا شَرًّا فَلَقَدْ كُنْتَ تُؤْذِينَا، فَكَمْ مِنْ عَمَلٍ

7. A tradition from Imam al-Sadiq (a) states: When a believing servant commits a sin, God gives him respite for seven hours, and if he seeks God's forgiveness [in this time], then nothing is recorded against him. And if this time elapses and he does not seek forgiveness, then one sin is recorded against him. A believer may remember his sin after twenty years; if he seeks his Lord's forgiveness, He will forgive him. But a disbeliever will forget his sin the moment he has committed it.[63]

SUMMARY OF THE VERSES

The verses state that people have judged wrongly when they deny the Recompense. God has appointed angels as protectors over all human beings. These angels have been described with four attributes: they are protectors, noble, recorders, and know all the deeds of the people to whom they are assigned.

REFLECTIVE LEARNING

Let me reflect on what sort of companion I have been to the angels assigned to me – an excellent companion or a distasteful one?

- Do I show them righteous deeds or ugly ones?
- Do I make them hear pleasant words or unpleasant ones?
- Do I take them to assemblies of goodness or of evil?

At the time of my death will they be intercessors before my Lord or witnesses against me?

VERSES 13 - 16

إِنَّ الْأَبْرَارَ لَفِي نَعِيمٍ ﴿١٣﴾ وَإِنَّ الْفُجَّارَ لَفِي جَحِيمٍ ﴿١٤﴾ يَصْلَوْنَهَا يَوْمَ الدِّينِ ﴿١٥﴾ وَمَا هُمْ عَنْهَا بِغَائِبِينَ ﴿١٦﴾

Indeed, the righteous will be in bliss. [13] *And indeed, the evildoers will be in hellfire.* [14] *They will burn therein on the Day of Recompense.* [15] *And they will never be absent from it.* [16]

سَيِّئٍ أَرَيْتَنَاهُ، وَكَمْ مِنْ قَوْلٍ سَيِّئٍ أَسْمَعْتَنَاهُ، وَمِنْ مَجْلِسِ سُوءٍ أَحْضَرْتَنَاهُ، وَنَحْنُ الْيَوْمَ لَكَ عَلَى مَا تَكْرَهُ وَشَهِيدَانِ عِنْدَ رَبِّكَ.

[63] Kulaynī, *al-Kāfī*, 2/437.

عَنِ الصَّادِقِ (عَلَيْهِ السَّلَامُ) – الْعَبْدُ الْمُؤْمِنُ إِذَا أَذْنَبَ ذَنْبًا أَجَّلَهُ اللهُ سَبْعَ سَاعَاتٍ فَإِنِ اسْتَغْفَرَ اللهَ لَمْ يُكْتَبْ عَلَيْهِ شَيْءٌ، وَإِنْ مَضَتِ السَّاعَاتُ وَلَمْ يَسْتَغْفِرْ كُتِبَتْ عَلَيْهِ سَيِّئَةٌ. وَإِنَّ الْمُؤْمِنَ لَيُذَكَّرُ ذَنْبَهُ بَعْدَ عِشْرِينَ سَنَةٍ حَتَّى يَسْتَغْفِرَ رَبَّهُ فَيَغْفِرَ لَهُ، وَإِنَّ الْكَافِرَ لَيُنْسَاهُ مِنْ سَاعَتِهِ.

13-16.1 The scrolls of deeds produced by the recording angels who have faithfully recorded what man has earned in his life will be distributed on the Day of Recompense. Thereafter, the people will be divided in two broad groups, the righteous (*abrār*) who will be admitted to Paradise, and the evildoers (*fujjār*) who will be sent to Hell. Q39:70 states:

وَوُفِّيَتْ كُلُّ نَفْسٍ مَا عَمِلَتْ وَهُوَ أَعْلَمُ بِمَا يَفْعَلُونَ

And every soul will be fully compensated [for] what it did; and He is most knowing of what they do.

13-16.2 ‘*Indeed, the righteous will be in bliss.*’: The use of *inna* (indeed) and *la* (surely) in this verse and the next are for emphasis and indicate that there is no doubt that this will happen.

[*Abrār* (أَبْرَار, righteous)] is the plural of *bārr* and refers to virtuous people who perform righteous deeds (*birr*) based on a sound belief and sincere intention.[64] They have fulfilled their duty to God, to His creation, and to themselves.[65]

A tradition from the Prophet (s) states: As for the signs of the righteous one (*bārr*), they are ten: He loves for the sake of God and hates for the sake of God, he accompanies for the sake of God and parts company for the sake of God, he gets angry for the sake of God and becomes pleased for the sake of God, he does good acts for the sake of God and seeks His pleasure, he displays humbleness before God, fearfully, sincerely, contritely, and diligently, and he behaves with goodness for the sake of God.[66]

[*Na'īm* (نَعِيم, bliss)] means continuous happiness and comfort, and here it refers to the blessing of an eternal abode in Paradise.[67] The continuity of this bliss is because of the constant gratefulness (*shukr*) of the recipient of God's blessings in Paradise.

13-16.3 Due to their righteous deeds, sound belief, and sincere intention, the *abrār* have earned eternal bliss and we are therefore instructed to pray to be in their company. Q3:193 states:

---

64 Shīrāzī, *Namūneh*, 26/232.

65 Ṭabāṭabā'ī, *al-Mīzān*, 1/428 (*Tafsīr* of Q2:177).

66 Majlisī, *Biḥār*, 1/117.

عَنِ الرَّسُولِ (صَلَّى اللهُ عَلَيْهِ وَآلِهِ) – وَأَمَّا عَلَامَةُ الْبَارِّ فَعَشَرَةٌ يُحِبُّ فِي اللهِ وَيُبْغِضُ فِي اللهِ وَيُصَاحِبُ فِي اللهِ وَيُفَارِقُ فِي اللهِ وَيَغْضَبُ فِي اللهِ وَيَرْضَى فِي اللهِ وَيَعْمَلُ لِلهِ وَيَطْلُبُ إِلَيْهِ وَيَخْشَعُ لِلهِ خَائِفًا مَخُوفًا طَاهِرًا مُخْلِصًا مُسْتَحْيِيًا مُرَاقِبًا وَيُحْسِنُ فِي اللهِ.

67 Shīrāzī, *Namūneh*, 26/232.

رَبَّنَا فَاغْفِرْ لَنَا ذُنُوبَنَا وَكَفِّرْ عَنَّا سَيِّئَاتِنَا وَتَوَفَّنَا مَعَ الْأَبْرَارِ

Our Lord! So forgive us our sins, and remove from us our evil deeds and make us die with the righteous.

13-16.4 '*And indeed, the evildoers will be in hellfire.*': The use of the present tense in this verse and the previous one could indicate that the *abrār* are already surrounded by bliss and the *fujjār* are already surrounded by hellfire.[68] Q29:54 states:

يَسْتَعْجِلُونَكَ بِالْعَذَابِ وَإِنَّ جَهَنَّمَ لَمُحِيطَةٌ بِالْكَافِرِينَ

They ask you to hasten the punishment. And indeed, Hell encompasses the disbelievers.

[*Fujjār* (فُجَّار, evildoers)] (sing. *fājir*) is derived from *fajara* which means to cleave. Earlier in the surah, a word from the same root (*fujjirat*) was used to describe the seas that burst forth and overcome their natural barrier. Here, the *fujjār* who have broken through all barriers of sin, are presented as the opposite of *abrār*. They are those immoral people whose sinful conduct has made them uncaringly transgress the boundary of righteousness and religiosity.[69]

[*Jaḥīm* (جَحِيم, hellfire)] is derived from *jaḥama* which means to kindle fire. *Jaḥīm* denotes an intense fire, or a place where such fire exists, and it is one of the names of Hell.

13-16.5 '*They will burn therein on the Day of Recompense.*': [*Yaṣlawnahā* (يَصْلَوْنَهَا, they will burn therein)] is derived from *ṣalā* meaning to enter the fire to roast and burn therein.[70]

[*Yawm al-Dīn* (يَوْمَ الدِّين, Day of Recompense)]. The original meaning of *dīn* is recompense, whether reward or punishment. On this Day, recompense will be allocated according to one's obedience or disobedience of God's laws, and therefore religion is also called *dīn*.[71]

13-16.6 These verses indicate the terrible fate of the *fujjār*, whose graves in the *dunyā* were pits of hell,[72] and who will now be recompensed by being cast into the much more intense Hell of the *ākhirah*.

---

[68] Ibid, 26/233.

[69] Muṣṭafawī, *al-Taḥqīq*.

[70] Ibid.

[71] Ṭabrasī, *al-Bayān*, 10/844.

[72] Shīrāzī, *Namūneh*, 26/234.

13-16.7 *'And they will never be absent from it.'*: [*Ghā'ibīn* (غَائِبِين, absent)] is derived from *ghāba* meaning to become absent or unseen. The use of *mā* (*not*) and *bi* (of) in this verse is a dual emphasis to indicate that the *fujjār*, whose foul personalities cannot be cleansed even by the fire, will never leave Hell.[73]

Fujjār is the description of the most wretched sinners; they will never be absent from chastisement of Hell, and they will have no respite. Q5:37 states:

يُرِيدُونَ أَنْ يَخْرُجُوا مِنَ النَّارِ وَمَا هُمْ بِخَارِجِينَ مِنْهَا وَلَهُمْ عَذَابٌ مُقِيمٌ

They will wish to get out of the Fire, but they will never emerge therefrom; and for them is an enduring punishment.

SUMMARY OF THE VERSES

The verses contrast the fates of two groups: the righteous (*abrār*) who will be admitted to the bliss of Paradise, and the evildoers (*fujjār*) who will be cast into Hell, to burn therein. This will be their abiding recompense on that Day.

REFLECTIVE LEARNING

The *abrār* and the *fujjār* represent the two extremities of human submission to God. Most people fall in a category between these two positions.

Let me reflect where I am on this spectrum of submission and how I can move towards the elevated station of the *abrār*.

VERSES 17 - 19

وَمَا أَدْرَاكَ مَا يَوْمُ الدِّينِ ﴿١٧﴾ ثُمَّ مَا أَدْرَاكَ مَا يَوْمُ الدِّينِ ﴿١٨﴾ يَوْمَ لَا تَمْلِكُ نَفْسٌ لِنَفْسٍ شَيْئًا وَالْأَمْرُ يَوْمَئِذٍ لِلَّهِ ﴿١٩﴾

And what will make you know what the Day of Recompense is? [17] *Again, what will make you know what the Day of Recompense is?* [18] *[It is] the Day when no soul will possess [the power to do] anything for another soul; and the command, that Day, will be [entirely] with God.* [19]

---

73 Kāshānī, *al-Ṣāfī*, 5/297.

17-19.1 ‘*And what will make you know what the Day of Recompense is? Again, what will make you know what the Day of Recompense is?*’: *Mā adrāka* is a rhetorical question asked in the Qur’an to indicate the greatness of a phenomenon,[74] and also to mean, ‘you cannot know unless God informs you,’[75] or ‘you will never truly understand its full significance.’

Here, the question is repeated to emphasize the seminal importance and gravity of that Day. Indeed, the nature of its joys and horrors are beyond human comprehension in the *dunyā*.[76]

The realization of human beings increases as they traverse the various realms of their existence. A baby in the womb cannot comprehend the realities of this world, the living cannot understand the realities of *barzakh*, and those in the *dunyā* cannot realize the realities of the *ākhirah*, until they reach that world. Q84:19 states:

لَتَرْكَبُنَّ طَبَقًا عَنْ طَبَقٍ

You will certainly travel (experience) stage after stage.

17-19.2 ‘*[It is] the Day when no soul will possess [the power to do] anything for another soul; and the command, that Day, will be [entirely] with God.*’: In this verse, God gives us an idea of one aspect of that Day.

[*Tamliku* (تَمْلِكُ, possess)] means to have power or control over something. Here, *lā tamliku* refers to the inability of anyone to protect anyone else from the recompense that they deserve, whereas they may have possessed such ability in the *dunyā*.[77]

[*Amr* (أَمْر, command)] here refers to the command and decree of God which is always dominant. In the *dunyā* people feel that they are controlled by the rulers and their institutions, or that they themselves retain control of their lives. On that Day however, God’s eternal control will be acutely felt by all.[78]

A tradition from Imam al-Baqir (a) states: The command on that Day and every day belongs to God. When the Day of Judgement

---

[74] Ṭabāṭabā’ī, *al-Mīzān*, 20/258.

[75] Ṭūsī, *al-Tibyān*, 10/323.

[76] Shīrāzī, *Namūneh*, 26/235.

[77] Ṭūsī, *al-Tibyān*, 10/294.

[78] Shīrāzī, *Namūneh*, 26/235.

arrives, every sovereign will perish, and no sovereign will remain except God.[79]

Q40:16 quotes God's irrefutable declaration:

لِمَنِ الْمُلْكُ الْيَوْمَ لِلَّهِ الْوَاحِدِ الْقَهَّارِ

... To Whom belongs the kingdom this Day?
To Allah, the One, the Vanquisher!

17-19.3 It should be noted that this verse does not contradict the concept of intercession (*shafāʿah*), because intercession happens only with the permission of God. The command belongs to God, and not to the intercessor himself.[80]

Q21:28 states

وَلَا يَشْفَعُونَ إِلَّا لِمَنِ ٱرْتَضَىٰ

...And they cannot intercede except for him whom He approves...

SUMMARY OF THE VERSES

The verses state, with repetition, that man can never fully understand what the Day of Recompense is. It is a Day on which every soul will be powerless to help anyone else. The command will belong entirely to God alone.

REFLECTIVE LEARNING

We all know that God is in control, but this fact is forgotten by many in this world.

Let me reflect how many times in my life I have sat in the passenger side pressing the imaginary 'brakes' and getting stressed because I forgot that God was driving me to what was best for me.

[79] Majlisī, *Biḥār*, 7/95.

عَنِ الْبَاقِرِ (عَلَيْهِ السَّلَامُ) – إِنَّ الْأَمْرَ يَوْمَئِذٍ وَالْيَوْمَ كُلَّهُ لِلَّهِ يَا جَابِرُ، إِذَا كَانَ يَوْمُ الْقِيَامَةِ بَادَتِ الْحُكَّامُ فَلَمْ يَبْقَ حَاكِمٌ إِلَّا اللهُ.

[80] Ṭabāṭabā'ī, *al-Mīzān*, 20/228.

SURAT AL-MUṬAFFIFĪN

THE DEFRAUDERS (83)

TEXT AND TRANSLATION

سُورَةُ الْمُطَفِّفِينَ

بِسْمِ اللهِ الرَّحْمٰنِ الرَّحِيمِ

وَيْلٌ لِلْمُطَفِّفِينَ ﴿١﴾ الَّذِينَ إِذَا اكْتَالُوا عَلَى النَّاسِ يَسْتَوْفُونَ ﴿٢﴾ وَإِذَا كَالُوهُمْ أَوْ
وَزَنُوهُمْ يُخْسِرُونَ ﴿٣﴾ أَلَا يَظُنُّ أُولَٰئِكَ أَنَّهُمْ مَبْعُوثُونَ ﴿٤﴾ لِيَوْمٍ عَظِيمٍ ﴿٥﴾ يَوْمَ
يَقُومُ النَّاسُ لِرَبِّ الْعَالَمِينَ ﴿٦﴾ كَلَّا إِنَّ كِتَابَ الْفُجَّارِ لَفِي سِجِّينٍ ﴿٧﴾ وَمَا أَدْرَاكَ
مَا سِجِّينٌ ﴿٨﴾ كِتَابٌ مَرْقُومٌ ﴿٩﴾ وَيْلٌ يَوْمَئِذٍ لِلْمُكَذِّبِينَ ﴿١٠﴾ الَّذِينَ يُكَذِّبُونَ
بِيَوْمِ الدِّينِ ﴿١١﴾ وَمَا يُكَذِّبُ بِهِ إِلَّا كُلُّ مُعْتَدٍ أَثِيمٍ ﴿١٢﴾ إِذَا تُتْلَىٰ عَلَيْهِ آيَاتُنَا قَالَ
أَسَاطِيرُ الْأَوَّلِينَ ﴿١٣﴾ كَلَّا بَلْ رَانَ عَلَىٰ قُلُوبِهِمْ مَا كَانُوا يَكْسِبُونَ ﴿١٤﴾ كَلَّا إِنَّهُمْ
عَنْ رَبِّهِمْ يَوْمَئِذٍ لَمَحْجُوبُونَ ﴿١٥﴾ ثُمَّ إِنَّهُمْ لَصَالُوا الْجَحِيمِ ﴿١٦﴾ ثُمَّ يُقَالُ هَٰذَا
الَّذِي كُنْتُمْ بِهِ تُكَذِّبُونَ ﴿١٧﴾ كَلَّا إِنَّ كِتَابَ الْأَبْرَارِ لَفِي عِلِّيِّينَ ﴿١٨﴾ وَمَا أَدْرَاكَ
مَا عِلِّيُّونَ ﴿١٩﴾ كِتَابٌ مَرْقُومٌ ﴿٢٠﴾ يَشْهَدُهُ الْمُقَرَّبُونَ ﴿٢١﴾ إِنَّ الْأَبْرَارَ لَفِي
نَعِيمٍ ﴿٢٢﴾ عَلَى الْأَرَائِكِ يَنْظُرُونَ ﴿٢٣﴾ تَعْرِفُ فِي وُجُوهِهِمْ نَضْرَةَ النَّعِيمِ ﴿٢٤﴾
يُسْقَوْنَ مِنْ رَحِيقٍ مَخْتُومٍ ﴿٢٥﴾ خِتَامُهُ مِسْكٌ وَفِي ذَٰلِكَ فَلْيَتَنَافَسِ الْمُتَنَافِسُونَ
﴿٢٦﴾ وَمِزَاجُهُ مِنْ تَسْنِيمٍ ﴿٢٧﴾ عَيْنًا يَشْرَبُ بِهَا الْمُقَرَّبُونَ ﴿٢٨﴾ إِنَّ الَّذِينَ
أَجْرَمُوا كَانُوا مِنَ الَّذِينَ آمَنُوا يَضْحَكُونَ ﴿٢٩﴾ وَإِذَا مَرُّوا بِهِمْ يَتَغَامَزُونَ ﴿٣٠﴾
وَإِذَا انْقَلَبُوا إِلَىٰ أَهْلِهِمُ انْقَلَبُوا فَكِهِينَ ﴿٣١﴾ وَإِذَا رَأَوْهُمْ قَالُوا إِنَّ هَٰؤُلَاءِ لَضَالُّونَ
﴿٣٢﴾ وَمَا أُرْسِلُوا عَلَيْهِمْ حَافِظِينَ ﴿٣٣﴾ فَالْيَوْمَ الَّذِينَ آمَنُوا مِنَ الْكُفَّارِ يَضْحَكُونَ
﴿٣٤﴾ عَلَى الْأَرَائِكِ يَنْظُرُونَ ﴿٣٥﴾ هَلْ ثُوِّبَ الْكُفَّارُ مَا كَانُوا يَفْعَلُونَ ﴿٣٦﴾

In the name of God, the Beneficent, the Merciful.

Woe to those who defraud. [1] *Who, when they take a measure from people, demand it in full.* [2] *But when they give by measure or by weight to them, they cause them loss.* [3] *Do they not think that they will be raised again,* [4] *on a tremendous Day -* [5] *a Day when mankind will stand before the Lord of the worlds?* [6] *Not at all! Indeed, the record of the wicked is in Sijjīn.* [7] *And what will make you know what Sijjīn is?* [8] *[It is] a Record inscribed.* [9] *Woe, that Day, to the deniers.* [10] *Who deny the Day of Recompense.* [11] *And none deny it except every sinful transgressor.* [12] *When Our signs are recited to him, he says, "Myths of the ancients!"* [13] *Not at all! Rather the stain of what they used to do has covered their hearts.* [14] *Not at all! Indeed, on that Day they will certainly be veiled from their Lord.* [15] *Then indeed, they will burn in the hellfire.* [16] *Then it will be said [to them], "This is what you used to deny."* [17] *Not at all! Indeed, the record of the righteous is in 'Illiyyīn.* [18] *And what will make you know what 'Illiyūn is?* [19] *[It is] a Record inscribed.* [20] *Which is witnessed by those brought near [to God].* [21] *Indeed, the righteous will be in bliss,* [22] *on thrones, observing.* [23] *You will recognize on their faces the radiance of bliss.* [24] *They will be given to drink [pure] wine, sealed.* [25] *The sealing of it is with musk. So let all those who strive, strive for this.* [26] *And it will be mixed with Tasnīm,* [27] *a spring from which those near [to God] drink.* [28] *Indeed, those who committed crimes used to laugh at those who believed.* [29] *And when they passed by them, they would wink at one another.* [30] *And when they returned to their people, they would return jesting.* [31] *And when they saw them, they would say, "Indeed, those are truly astray."* [32] *But they had not been sent as guardians over them.* [33] *So on this Day, the believers shall laugh at the disbelievers,* [34] *on thrones, observing.* [35] *Have the disbelievers [not] been rewarded [fully] for what they used to do?* [36].

INTRODUCTION

Surat al-Muṭaffifīn (83), or Surat al-Taṭfīf,[1] was the 86th chapter to be revealed.[2] It has thirty-six verses and according to many reports, it was the last Makkan surah.[3] It was revealed after Surat al-Sajdah (32), just before the migration of the Prophet (s) to Madina. The contents of the

1 Ṭabrasī, *al-Bayān*, 10/685.

2 Maʿrifat, *'Ulūm-i Qur'ānī*, p. 90.

3 Ibn ʿĀshūr, *al-Taḥrīr*, 30/166.

surah and its address to the disbelievers and polytheists add weight to the opinion that it is a Makkan surah because Makka was a centre of trade. The surah takes its name from the first verse, where the term *muṭaffifīn* is uniquely used in the Qur'an.

Like many Makkan chapters, its theme is the Day of Resurrection. The surah contrasts the behaviour of those who believe in that Day and those who deny it.

However, some reports say that it was one of the early chapters to be revealed in Madina. It is reported that when the Prophet (s) arrived in Madina, the tradesmen there were the most fraudulent of traders, but after this surah was revealed, they became scrupulous in their dealings. In particular, there is mention of a trader by the name of Abu Juhaynah, who used two separate weights for trading. He would use the heavier one to get full measure when buying but the lighter one for cheating his customers when selling.[4]

The surah begins with a stern reprimand of those who cheat others in transactions; they take full measure when they buy but when they sell, they give less than what was agreed. The Qur'an warns them that they will be called to account in front of God on a tremendous Day.

Thereafter, the verses mention the locations where the records of all the deeds of mankind are preserved. The records of the evildoers are in *Sijjīn*. They denied the Day of Recompense and ridiculed God's signs. The stain of their sins will veil them from God on that Day and their abode shall be the fire of Hell.

In contrast, the records of the righteous will be preserved in *ʿIlliyūn*. They will be in bliss, enjoying the bounties of Paradise.

The surah ends by informing the disbelievers who used to mock the believers and call them misguided, that on that Day, the believers will laugh at them. They will watch as the evildoers receive their just recompense from God.

LINK TO THE PREVIOUS CHAPTER

Surat al-Muṭaffifīn continues and expands on the theme of the previous chapter, Surat al-Infiṭār, which discussed the contrasting fates of the righteous (*abrār*) and the evildoers (*fujjār*) on the Day of Judgement.

---

[4] Ṭabrasī, *al-Bayān*, 10/687.

About the *abrār*, both surahs have the same verse, *'Indeed, the righteous will be in bliss.'* (Q82:13, Q83:22), but Surat al-Muṭaffifīn gives more information about the nature of this bliss.

Surat al-Infiṭār talked about angels whose meticulous recording results in the creation of the human book of deeds. Surat al-Muṭaffifīn mentions where these books will be stored: the books of the righteous will be in *'Illiyūn* while the books of the evildoers will be in *Sijjīn*. We will discuss these terms later in the *tafsīr* of this chapter.

MERITS OF RECITATION

- A tradition from the Prophet (s) states: Whoever recites this surah, God will quench his thirst with pure sealed wine (*al-raḥīq al-makhtūm*) on the Day of Judgement. And if it is recited over a storehouse, God will protect it from every calamity.[5]
- A tradition from Imam al-Sadiq (a) states: God will grant security from the Fire on the Day of Judgement to whoever recites Surat al-Muṭaffifīn in his obligatory prayers. The Fire will not detect him and he will not see it [either].
  On the Day of Judgement he will not have to cross the bridge over Hell and he will not be asked to account for his deeds.[6]

EXEGESIS

VERSES 1 - 3

وَيْلٌ لِلْمُطَفِّفِينَ ﴿١﴾ الَّذِينَ إِذَا ٱكْتَالُوا عَلَى النَّاسِ يَسْتَوْفُونَ ﴿٢﴾ وَإِذَا كَالُوهُمْ أَو
وَزَنُوهُمْ يُخْسِرُونَ ﴿٣﴾

Woe to those who defraud. [1] *Who, when they take a measure from people, demand it in full.* [2] *But when they give by measure or by weight to them, they cause them loss.* [3]

---

[5] Baḥrānī, *al-Burhān*, 5/603.

عَنِ الرَّسُولِ (صَلَّى اللهُ عَلَيْهِ وَآلِهِ) - مَنْ قَرَأَ هَذِهِ السُّورَةَ سَقَاهُ اللهُ تَعَالَى مِنَ الرَّحِيقِ الْمَخْتُومِ يَوْمَ الْقِيَامَةِ. وَإِنْ قُرِئَتْ عَلَى مَخْزَنٍ حَفِظَهُ اللهُ مِنْ كُلِّ آفَةٍ.

[6] Ibid.

عَنِ الصَّادِقِ (عَلَيْهِ السَّلَامُ) - مَنْ قَرَأَ فِي الْفَرِيضَةِ «وَيْلٌ لِلْمُطَفِّفِينَ» أَعْطَاهُ اللهُ الْأَمْنَ يَوْمَ الْقِيَامَةِ مِنَ النَّارِ وَلَمْ تَرَهُ وَلَا يَرَاهَا وَلَا يَمُرُّ عَلَى جِسْرِ جَهَنَّمَ وَلَا يُحَاسَبُ يَوْمَ الْقِيَامَةِ.

1-3.1 *'Woe to those who defraud.'*: [*Waylun* (وَيْلٌ, woe)] is a word that denotes God's condemnation for disbelief or wrongful conduct. This is one of two surahs (the other being Surat al-Humazah) that begins with this stern rebuke. The term includes a sense of imprecation (*laʿnah*) against the doer, meaning, 'may they be deprived of God's mercy'.[7] It also refers to a place in Hell where the person condemned in this manner will be cast.[8]

In this verse, the divine condemnation is not for idolatry or disbelief but for defrauding people, showing the great importance that Islam places on fairness and honesty when transacting business.

1-3.2 A tradition from Imam al-Baqir (a) states: God has not condemned anyone with the term *wayl* except by calling him a disbeliever. God, the Exalted, has stated, '*So woe to the disbelievers - from the scene of a tremendous Day*' (Q19:37).[9] From this tradition it can be deduced that defrauding is actually a manifestation of disbelief (*kufr*).[10]

1-3.3 [*Muṭaffifīn* (مُطَفِّفِين, defrauders)] (sing. *muṭaffif*) is derived from *ṭaffafa*, meaning to make deficient, to diminish, or to lower. In practice, *ṭaff* denotes something whose content is nearly, but not quite, full.[11] Here *muṭaffifīn* refers to those who cheat others out of petty amounts by dishonestly manipulating weights and measures.[12]

The term may also extend to other forms of cheating such as giving less time to an employer than what he is due,[13] adulteration of goods with similar-looking impurities, any form of fraudulent behaviour that is not realized by the customer, and so on.

Any society where this becomes the prevalent practice will ultimately become corrupted. The Qur'an describes defrauders as spreaders of mischief and corruption in the land (*mufsidūn*). Q11:85 quotes Prophet Shuʿayb (a):

وَيَا قَوْمِ أَوْفُوا الْمِكْيَالَ وَالْمِيزَانَ بِالْقِسْطِ

---

[7] Muṣṭafawī, *al-Taḥqīq*.

[8] Rāghib, *al-Mufradāt*.

[9] Kulaynī, *al-Kāfī*, 2/28.

عَنْ أَبِي جَعْفَرٍ (عَلَيْهِ السَّلَامُ) – وَلَمْ يَجْعَلِ الْوَيْلَ لِأَحَدٍ حَتَّى يُسَمِّيَهُ كَافِرًا. قَالَ اللهُ عَزَّ وَجَلَّ «فَوَيْلٌ لِلَّذِينَ كَفَرُوا مِنْ مَشْهَدِ يَوْمٍ عَظِيمٍ».

[10] Shīrāzī, *Namūneh*, 26/245.

[11] Ibid.

[12] Muṣṭafawī, *al-Taḥqīq*.

[13] Muṭahharī, (*Āshnāyī bā Qur'an*), *Āthār*, 28/437.

وَلَا تَبْخَسُوا النَّاسَ أَشْيَاءَهُمْ وَلَا تَعْثَوْا فِي الْأَرْضِ مُفْسِدِينَ

And O my people, give full measure and weight in fairness; and do not deprive the people of their due and do not commit abuse on the earth, spreading corruption.

However, the people of Aykah, to whom he had been sent, denied him and were destroyed as a result.

1-3.4 A tradition from Imam al-Baqir (a) states: The Commander of the Faithful (a) would walk in the markets of Kufa, one by one... He would stop before the people at every market, and call out, "O traders, be wary of God, the Almighty!" When the people heard his (a) voice, they would put down what they were holding, turn their hearts to him, and listen attentively. He would say, "Seek goodness (*istikhāra*) from God, gain blessing by dealing leniently, be friendly to the buyers, adorn yourself with forbearance, avoid making oaths, do not lie, beware of being unjust, be fair to the oppressed, do not approach usury, and fulfil '*the measure and weight and do not deprive people of their due.*'"[14]

1-3.5 *'Who, when they take a measure from people, demand it in full.'*: This verse and the next describe the business conduct of the defrauders further. [*Iktālū* (اكْتَالُوا, take measure)] is derived from *kalā* meaning to measure and weigh out. Here it means to receive a commodity by measure. Q12:63 quotes the brothers of Yusuf (a):

فَلَمَّا رَجَعُوا إِلَىٰ أَبِيهِمْ قَالُوا يَا أَبَانَا مُنِعَ مِنَّا الْكَيْلُ فَأَرْسِلْ مَعَنَا أَخَانَا نَكْتَلْ

So when they returned to their father, they said, "O our father, [further] measure (kayl) *has been denied to us, so send with us our brother that we may obtain the measure* (naktal)...

[*Yastawfūn* (يَسْتَوْفُونَ, demand in full)] is derived from *wafā*, meaning to fulfil. Here it means to take or receive completely and in full.

---

14 Kulaynī, *al-Kāfī*, 5/151.

عَنْ أَبِي جَعْفَرٍ (عَلَيْهِ السَّلَامُ) – فَيَطُوفُ فِي أَسْوَاقِ الْكُوفَةِ سُوقًا سُوقًا ... فَيَقِفُ عَلَى أَهْلِ كُلِّ سُوقٍ فَيُنَادِي: يَا مَعْشَرَ التُّجَّارِ، اِتَّقُوا اللهَ عَزَّ وَجَلَّ. فَإِذَا سَمِعُوا صَوْتَهُ (عَلَيْهِ السَّلَامُ)، أَلْقَوْا مَا بِأَيْدِيهِمْ، وَأَرْعَوْا إِلَيْهِ بِقُلُوبِهِمْ، وَسَمِعُوا بِآذَانِهِمْ، فَيَقُولُ (عَلَيْهِ السَّلَامُ): قَدِّمُوا الْإِسْتِخَارَةَ، وَتَبَرَّكُوا بِالسُّهُولَةِ وَاقْتَرِبُوا مِنَ الْمُبْتَاعِينَ وَتَزَيَّنُوا بِالْحِلْمِ وَتَنَاهَوْا عَنِ الْيَمِينِ وَجَانِبُوا الْكَذِبَ وَتَجَافَوْا عَنِ الظُّلْمِ وَأَنْصِفُوا الْمَظْلُومِينَ وَلَا تَقْرَبُوا الرِّبَا وَأَوْفُوا «الْكَيْلَ وَالْمِيزَانَ وَلَا تَبْخَسُوا النَّاسَ أَشْيَاءَهُمْ.»

Therefore, when it came to buying, these traders made sure they got full measure.

1-3.6 Some exegetes have said that the phrase *iktālū ʿalā al-nās* (as opposed to *iktālū min al-nās*) signifies that they unfairly forced their poor suppliers to get even more from them than they deserved, to the point where they caused them a loss. In any case, it appears that the attitude of being overly insistent on your own rights while readily ignoring the rights of others is criticized in this verse.[15]

1-3.7 Other exegetes say that the word *yastawfūn* indicates that when they take their full measure it is their right, and they have not been censured for this. What is condemned here is keeping double standards – insisting on full measure for oneself but denying the same right to others. It is somewhat similar to seeking one's own payment exactly when due, but delaying payments that is due to debtors.[16]

1-3.8 *'But when they give by measure or by weight to them, they cause them loss.'*: [*Kālūhum* (كَالُوهُمْ, measured them)] and [*wazanūhum* (وَزَنُوهُمْ, weighed them)] means *kālū lahum* (measured for them) and *wazanū lahum* (weighed for them) and is truncated in the manner of the speech of the people of Ḥijāz.[17]

Here, it refers to the process of selling to the people. In the previous verse, only measure was mentioned because merchants would buy or barter in bulk from their suppliers, and these transactions were by measure, not weight. In this verse, measures as well as weights have been mentioned because it refers to both wholesale and retail selling to the public.[18]

[*Yukhsirūn* (يُخْسِرُونَ, they cause loss)] is derived from *akhsara*, meaning to make deficient or cause loss. Here it means to deliberately short-change the buyer whether in measuring or weighing. Nowadays, it would extend to other financial systems of transaction as well.[19]

---

[15] Rafsanjānī, *Rahnamā*, 20/171.

[16] Shīrāzī, *Namūneh*, 26/245.

[17] Rāzī, *Mafātīḥ al-Ghayb*, 31/83.

[18] Ālūsī, *Rūḥ al-Maʿānī*, 30/70.

[19] Modarresī, *Min Hudā al-Qurʾan*, 17/404.

These two verses highlight the fact that the *muṭaffif* seeks his own rights but usurps the rights of others. This creates corruption in human society, whose wellbeing lies in the mutual respect of the rights of all its citizens.[20] Q55:9 states:

وَأَقِيمُوا الْوَزْنَ بِالْقِسْطِ وَلَا تُخْسِرُوا الْمِيزَانَ

And establish weight with justice and do not make the balance deficient.

SUMMARY OF THE VERSES

The verses rebuke those who defraud. These are the people who demand their own rights in full when they receive, but cheat people when they measure out and weigh what they give to them.

REFLECTIVE LEARNING

Muṭaffifīn are people who take satisfaction from cheating others out of small amounts. In truth, these insignificant amounts are the value that they have placed on their own faith and integrity! They behave with others in a manner that they would hate to be treated themselves.

A tradition from Imam al-Sadiq (a) states: Amongst the most difficult duties that God has imposed on mankind are three: that a person should be so fair that he does not like to do anything for his brother except that which he would like his brother to do for him...[21]

Let me reflect to what extent I desire for others what I would desire for myself. Or do I also maintain a double standard?

VERSES 4 - 6

أَلَا يَظُنُّ أُولَٰئِكَ أَنَّهُم مَّبْعُوثُونَ ﴿٤﴾ لِيَوْمٍ عَظِيمٍ ﴿٥﴾ يَوْمَ يَقُومُ النَّاسُ لِرَبِّ الْعَالَمِينَ ﴿٦﴾

Do they not think that they will be raised again, [4] *on a tremendous Day* [5] *a Day when mankind will stand before the Lord of the worlds?* [6]

---

[20] Ṭabāṭabā'ī, *al-Mīzān*, 20/230.

[21] Kulaynī, *al-Kāfī*, 2/170.

عَنِ الصَّادِقِ (عَلَيْهِ السَّلَامُ) – إِنَّ مِنْ أَشَدِّ مَا افْتَرَضَ اللهُ عَلَى خَلْقِهِ ثَلَاثًا؛ إِنْصَافُ الْمَرْءِ مِنْ نَفْسِهِ حَتَّى لَا يَرْضَى لِأَخِيهِ مِنْ نَفْسِهِ إِلَّا بِمَا يَرْضَى لِنَفْسِهِ مِنْهُ...

4-6.1 *'Do they not think that they will be raised again?'*: A rhetorical question is asked to evoke surprise at the thinking of the defrauders,[22] and serve as a warning to them.[23] They want the best for themselves but deny others the same right, forgetting that they will be resurrected to account for their actions.

4-6.2 [*Yaẓunnū* (يَظُنُّ, they think)] is derived from *ẓanna* meaning to believe or suppose.[24]

Ẓann can have a meaning of certainty[25] as in Q18:53:

وَرَأَى الْمُجْرِمُونَ النَّارَ فَظَنُّوا أَنَّهُمْ مُوَاقِعُوهَا

And the criminals will see the Fire and will be certain (ẓannū) *that they are to fall therein...*

It can also have a meaning of supposition and assumption as in Q53:28:

وَمَا لَهُمْ بِهِ مِنْ عِلْمٍ إِنْ يَتَّبِعُونَ إِلَّا الظَّنَّ وَإِنَّ الظَّنَّ لَا يُغْنِي مِنَ الْحَقِّ شَيْئًا

And they have no knowledge thereof. They follow only assumption (ẓann), *and indeed, assumption does not avail against the truth at all.*

If the defrauders are from the believers and have faith in the resurrection, then they have committed a grave injustice and sin; and even those who acknowledge the possibility that they may be resurrected to account for their deeds should be cautious to refrain from such practices.[26]

[*Mabʿūthūn* (مَبْعُوثُونَ, raised)] is derived from *baʿatha* which means to dispatch or send forward. Here it refers to the resurrection when mankind will be sent forth from their graves.[27]

4-6.3 *'On a tremendous Day.'*: The tremendous Day here refers to the Day of Judgement when the defrauders will be punished for their actions.[28] It is called tremendous (*ʿaẓīm*) because on that Day, momentous things will occur: the resurrection, the gathering of

22 Ṭabāṭabā'ī, *al-Mīzān*, 20/231.
23 Shīrāzī, *Namūneh*, 26/247.
24 Muṣṭafawī, *al-Taḥqīq*.
25 Ṭūsī, *al-Tibyān*, 10/296.
26 Rāzī, *Mafātīḥ al-Ghayb*, 31/84.
27 Muṣṭafawī, *al-Taḥqīq*.
28 Ṭabāṭabā'ī, *al-Mīzān*, 20/231.

humanity, the manifestation of actions, the presentation of the scroll of deeds, and so on. But much more tremendous than all of that will be the moment when man will stand before God.

4-6.4 *'A Day when mankind will stand before the Lord of the worlds'*: On this Day every human being will rise from his grave to face God's judgement and recompense.[29] We will all stand before Him, to give account for every deed, including our attitude towards the rights of the people.

4-6.5 Truly, this verse befits pondering over in trepidation and humility. We will stand before He who is the Creator and Sustainer of every single creation (*Rabb al-ʿālamīn*). Through our entire life He cherished us.

Even at this stage, God reminds us that He is the Sustainer. Every part of His judgement is designed to recompense in order to elevate the virtuous, or purify the sinner, thereby.

SUMMARY OF THE VERSES

The verses begin by asking the defrauders whether or not they have thought of the time when they will be resurrected. That will be a tremendous Day, when they will be raised to stand before the Lord of the Worlds.

REFLECTIVE LEARNING

Let me reflect whether I keep in mind the accountability of each of my actions before I perform them.

Let me remember that on that great Day, I will stand before God to give account directly.

VERSES 7 - 9

كَلَّا إِنَّ كِتَابَ الْفُجَّارِ لَفِي سِجِّينٍ ﴿٧﴾ وَمَا أَدْرَاكَ مَا سِجِّينٌ ﴿٨﴾ كِتَابٌ مَرْقُومٌ ﴿٩﴾

Not at all! Indeed, the record of the evildoers is in Sijjīn. [7] *And what will make you know what Sijjīn is?* [8] *[It is] a Record inscribed.* [9]

[29] Ṭabrasī, *al-Bayān*, 10/687.

7-9.1 *'Not at all! Indeed, the record of the evildoers is in Sijjīn'*: *Kallā* here is used to negate the false notion of the defrauders that their behaviour will have no consequences,[30] and is a warning to them to desist from their behaviour.[31]

[*Kitāb* (كِتَاب, record)] normally refers to something that is written, but here it could have two meanings:

i) That *kitāb* refers to God's binding decree (*al-qaḍā' al-maḥtūm*); in other words, the fate written for them lies in *Sijjīn*.[32]

ii) That *kitāb* refers to their actual book of deeds, which was prepared by the recording angels who accompanied them in their life in the *dunyā*, and *Sijjīn* is a repository or a comprehensive Register of the records of all evildoers,[33] and the *fujjār* will be together with their book of deeds in *Sijjīn*.[34] This interpretation is supported by the fact that the Qur'an uses *kitāb* in the meaning of 'book of deeds' in many instances.

It is possible to consider both interpretations as valid, because the manifestation of the records of the evildoers would indeed turn *Sijjīn* into Hell.[35]

7-9.2 [*Fujjār* (فُجَّار, evildoers)] is the plural of *fājir* and is derived from *fajara* which means to cleave and break through. It refers to those who transgress the boundaries of God's law without remorse.[36]

It is the defining characteristic of those who have no fear of a Day of Judgement. Q75:5,6 state:

بَلْ يُرِيدُ الْإِنْسَانُ لِيَفْجُرَ أَمَامَهُ ﴿٥﴾ يَسْأَلُ أَيَّانَ يَوْمُ الْقِيَامَةِ

But man desires to continue to sin (yafjur).
He asks [mockingly], "When is the Day of Resurrection?"

The *fājir* will sacrifice his faith and morals to secure the *dunyā* while the righteous (*abrār*) will sacrifice their *dunyā* to protect their faith. A tradition from Imam Ali (a) states: The believer (*mu'min*) is

30 Ṭabāṭabā'ī, *al-Mīzān*, 20/231.
31 Ṭabrasī, *al-Bayān*, 10/688.
32 Ṭabāṭabā'ī, *al-Mīzān*, 20/232.
33 Shīrāzī, *Namūneh*, 26/254.
34 Muṭahharī, (*Āshnāyī bā Qur'an*), *Āthār*, 28/439.
35 Shīrāzī, *Namūneh*, 26/255.
36 Muṣṭafawī, *al-Taḥqīq*.

one who protects his religion at the expense of his *dunyā* while the evildoer (*fājir*) is one who protects his *dunyā* at the expense of his religion.[37]

The verse includes the defrauders among the worst of evildoers, the *fujjār*.[38] A tradition from Imam Ali (a) states: Be truthful in your oaths. The businessman is a *fājir*, and the *fājir* shall be in the Fire, except for the one who takes what is due and gives what is due.[39]

7-9.3 [*Sijjīn* (سِجِّين)] is the hyperbolic form of *sijn*, which means a narrow and deep prison.[40] Here it refers to a bleak abode of eternal imprisonment. It is the name of a deep level of Hell.[41] Its harshness is unimaginable, unlike anything that is in human experience, and that is the reason for the question asked in the next verse.[42]

7-9.4 *And what will make you know what Sijjīn is?'* *Wa mā adrāka* (and what will make you know) is a phrase mostly used in the Qur'an for metaphysical matters and features of the Hereafter. It is a rhetorical question to indicate that the reality of the phenomenon is far greater than human comprehension.

Since *Sijjīn* has been contrasted against *'Illiyūn*, which denotes the highest of high elevations, *Sijjīn* can be considered as the level which is the lowest of the low.[43]

A tradition from the Prophet (s) states: The soul of the *fājir* will be taken up to the heavens but the heavens will refuse to accept it. So it will be brought down to the earth but the earth will [also] refuse to accept it. Then it will be taken [progressively] down the seven earths until it will be finally entered into *Sijjīn* where the hordes of Iblīs are stationed."[44]

---

[37] Āmudī, *Ghurar al-Ḥikam*, p. 90.

عَنْ أَمِيرِ الْمُؤْمِنِينَ (عَلَيْهِ السَّلَامُ) - الْمُؤْمِنُ مَنْ وَقَى دِينَهُ بِدُنْيَاهُ، وَالْفَاجِرُ مَنْ وَقَى دُنْيَاهُ بِدِينِهِ.

[38] Muṭahharī, (*Āshnāyī bā Qur'an*), *Āthār*, 28/439.

[39] Kulaynī *al-Kāfī*, 5/150.

عَنْ أَمِيرِ الْمُؤْمِنِينَ (عَلَيْهِ السَّلَامُ) - شُوبُوا أَيْمَانَكُمْ بِالصِّدْقِ، التَّاجِرُ فَاجِرٌ، وَالْفَاجِرُ فِي النَّارِ، إِلَّا مَنْ أَخَذَ الْحَقَّ وَأَعْطَى الْحَقَّ.

[40] Muṣṭafawī, *al-Taḥqīq*.

[41] Shīrāzī, *Namūneh*, 26/254.

[42] Ṭabāṭabā'ī, *al-Mīzān*, 20/231.

[43] Ibid.

[44] Majlisī, *Biḥār*, 55/52.

عَنِ الرَّسُولِ (صَلَّى اللهُ عَلَيْهِ وَآلِهِ) - إِنَّ رُوحَ الْفَاجِرِ يُصْعَدُ بِهَا إِلَى السَّمَاءِ فَتَأْبَى السَّمَاءُ أَنْ تَقْبَلَهَا، فَيُهْبَطُ بِهَا إِلَى الْأَرْضِ فَتَأْبَى

7-9.5 *'[It is] a record inscribed'*: This it is a description of *Sijjīn* itself, and the pronoun 'it is' (*huwa*) has been omitted (*maḥdhūf*).[45]

[*Marqūm* (مَرْقُوم, inscribed)] is derived from *raqama* which means to imprint or write boldly, and here it means something that is evident and cannot be doubted.[46] Therefore the verse would mean that *Sijjīn* is their decreed destination,[47] or that whoever enters it recognizes his deeds clearly.[48]

SUMMARY OF THE VERSES

The verses reject the complacency of the defrauders and warn that the record (or destiny) of the evildoers shall be in *Sijjīn*, whose reality cannot be imagined. It is the record of the deeds of all the *fujjār*.

REFLECTIVE LEARNING

Let me reflect which of my deeds would be in *'the record of the evildoers'* and do a complete *tawba* for it before it moves me into *Sijjīn*.

VERSES 10 - 13

وَيْلٌ يَوْمَئِذٍ لِلْمُكَذِّبِينَ ﴿١٠﴾ الَّذِينَ يُكَذِّبُونَ بِيَوْمِ الدِّينِ ﴿١١﴾ وَمَا يُكَذِّبُ بِهِ إِلَّا كُلُّ مُعْتَدٍ أَثِيمٍ ﴿١٢﴾ إِذَا تُتْلَىٰ عَلَيْهِ آيَاتُنَا قَالَ أَسَاطِيرُ الْأَوَّلِينَ ﴿١٣﴾

Woe, that Day, to the deniers. [10] *Who deny the Day of Recompense.* [11] *And none deny it except every sinful transgressor.* [12] *When Our signs are recited to him, he says, "Myths of the ancients!"* [13]

10-13.1 *'Woe, that Day, to the deniers.'*: The damnation of the defrauders (*wayl*) mentioned in the first verse is repeated here. The surah has identified them with both evildoers (*fujjār*) and deniers (*mukadhdhibūn*), showing the severe magnitude of their misconduct in God's estimation.

الْأَرْضُ أَنْ تَقْبَلَهَا، فَيُدْخَلُ بِهَا تَحْتَ سَبْعِ أَرَضِينَ حَتَّى يُنْتَهَى بِهَا إِلَى سِجِّينٍ، وَهُوَ مَوْضِعُ جُنْدِ إِبْلِيسَ.

[45] Ṭabāṭabā'ī, *al-Mīzān*, 20/232.

[46] Muṣṭafawī, *al-Taḥqīq*.

[47] Ṭabāṭabā'ī, *al-Mīzān*, 20/232.

[48] Muṭahharī, *(Āshnāyī bā Qur'an), Āthār*, 28/440.

[*Mukadhdhibīn* (مُكَذِّبِين, deniers)] is derived from *kadhdhaba*, which means denying something out of defiance.[49]

10-13.2 *'Who deny the Day of Recompense.'*: The denial mentioned in the previous verse is the denial of a Day of Recompense, on which every deed will be accounted. Some exegetes say that since believers do not verbally deny the Day of Recompense, this verse addresses those defrauders who are disbelievers. However, if *takdhīb* here is by action, then believers would be included as well, especially when we consider verse 4 to be a reminder for everyone, *'do they not think that they will be raised again?'*[50]

10-13.3 *'And none deny it except every sinful transgressor.'*: The verb *kadhdhaba* is used here for the third time in three consecutive verses, indicating the grave consequences of denial.

[*Mu'tad* (مُعْتَد, transgressor)] is derived from *i'tadā'* meaning to cross the limit. Here it means transgressing God's boundaries and violating the rights of others.

[*Athīm* (أَثِيم, sinful)] is derived from *athima* meaning to sin, but in this form it indicates a habitual sinner, who has amassed many sins.[51]

10-13.4 Faith and belief in a Day of Resurrection and Recompense is the main deterrent from sin. However, those who habitually transgress God's boundaries and get used to sinful conduct ultimately end up denying that Day. Q30:10 states:

ثُمَّ كَانَ عَاقِبَةَ الَّذِينَ أَسَاؤُوا السُّوأَىٰ أَنْ كَذَّبُوا بِآيَاتِ اللَّهِ وَكَانُوا بِهَا يَسْتَهْزِئُونَ

Then evil is the end of those who [continually] did evil
since they denied the signs of God and used to ridicule them.

This was also the verse recited by Lady Zaynab (a) in her address to Yazid to rebuke him.[52]

10-13.5 A tradition from Imam al-Sadiq (a) states: Nothing damages the heart more than sinfulness. Indeed, the heart combats sin but

---

[49] Rāghib, *al-Mufradāt*.

[50] Ṭabāṭabā'ī, *al-Mīzān*, 20/233.

[51] Ibid.

[52] Ibn Ṭāwūs, *al-Malhūf*, p. 215.

over time, [perpetual] sin overcomes it and turns it upside down [making it unreceptive].[53]

10-13.6 *'When Our signs are recited to him, he says, "Myths of the ancients!"'*: [*Āyātunā* (آيَاتُنَا, Our signs)] here refers to the verses of the Qur'an, because of the word *tutlā* (recited).[54]

[*Aṣāṭīr* (أَسَاطِير, myths)] (sing *usṭūrah*) is derived from *saṭara* which means to write line by line, but the term is mostly used for false and baseless tales and fables.[55]

[*Al-Awwalīn* (الْأَوَّلِين, the ancients)] refers to the former nations, many of which had their own mythological folklore. This was another characteristic of those who denied the Day of Recompense. By alleging that the Qur'anic accounts were mere fables, they sought to excuse themselves from paying heed to its verses.[56] This excuse has been mentioned several times in the Qur'an.

Some disbelievers likened the Qur'anic verses to the distorted stories and fables that they had heard from their ancestors. Q23:83 quotes their dismissive words:

لَقَدْ وُعِدْنَا نَحْنُ وَآبَاؤُنَا هَٰذَا مِنْ قَبْلُ إِنْ هَٰذَا إِلَّا أَسَاطِيرُ الْأَوَّلِينَ

We have been promised this before, we and our forefathers;
this is not but myths of the ancients.

Others alleged that the Prophet (s) was learning these stories from those who knew the mythology of previous nations. Q25:5 states:

وَقَالُوا أَسَاطِيرُ الْأَوَّلِينَ اكْتَتَبَهَا فَهِيَ تُمْلَىٰ عَلَيْهِ بُكْرَةً وَأَصِيلًا

And they say, "Myths of the ancients which he has written down,
and they are dictated to him morning and evening."

Others boasted that they too could narrate similar accounts. Q8:31 states:

وَإِذَا تُتْلَىٰ عَلَيْهِمْ آيَاتُنَا قَالُوا قَدْ سَمِعْنَا لَوْ نَشَاءُ لَقُلْنَا مِثْلَ هَٰذَا

---

[53] Kulaynī, *al-Kāfī*, 2/268.

عَنِ الصَّادِقِ (عَلَيْهِ السَّلَامُ) – مَا مِنْ شَيْءٍ أَفْسَدُ لِلْقَلْبِ مِنْ خَطِيئَةٍ، إِنَّ الْقَلْبَ لَيُوَاقِعُ الْخَطِيئَةَ، فَمَا تَزَالُ بِهِ حَتَّى تَغْلِبَ عَلَيْهِ، فَيَصِيرَ أَعْلَاهُ أَسْفَلَهُ.

[54] Ṭabāṭabā'ī, *al-Mīzān*, 20/233.

[55] Muṣṭafawī, *al-Taḥqīq*.

[56] Shīrāzī, *Namūneh*, 26/261.

إِنْ هَٰذَا إِلَّا أَسَاطِيرُ الْأَوَّلِينَ

And when Our verses are recited to them, they say, "We have heard. If we wished, we could say [something] like this. This is nothing but myths of the ancients."

Some exegetes have said that the verse under review was revealed about al-Naḍr b. al-Ḥārith, the maternal cousin of the Prophet (s).[57] Al-Naḍr was a hardened enemy of the Prophet (s) and his mission. He was an educated and well-travelled man, familiar with the culture and lore of the Zoroastrians, Christians and Jews.[58] He claimed that the Persian tales of Rustam and Isfandiyār were similar to the stories of the Qur'an.[59] About him, Q31:6,7 state:

وَمِنَ النَّاسِ مَنْ يَشْتَرِي لَهْوَ الْحَدِيثِ لِيُضِلَّ عَنْ سَبِيلِ اللَّهِ بِغَيْرِ عِلْمٍ وَيَتَّخِذَهَا هُزُوًا أُولَٰئِكَ لَهُمْ عَذَابٌ مُهِينٌ ﴿٦﴾ وَإِذَا تُتْلَىٰ عَلَيْهِ آيَاتُنَا وَلَّىٰ مُسْتَكْبِرًا كَأَنْ لَمْ يَسْمَعْهَا كَأَنَّ فِي أُذُنَيْهِ وَقْرًا فَبَشِّرْهُ بِعَذَابٍ أَلِيمٍ

And from the people is he who trades in frivolous discourse, without knowledge, to mislead [others] from the way of God and to take it for a mockery. For such there will be a humiliating punishment. And when Our signs are recited to him, he turns away arrogantly as if he had not heard them, as if there was deafness in his ears. So give him tidings of a painful punishment.

SUMMARY OF THE VERSES

The verses condemn those who deny the Day of Recompense, which is only belied by those who habitually transgress God's law and commit sin. When they hear the verses of the Qur'an they dismiss them as legends of the former nations.

REFLECTIVE LEARNING

Although I believe in the day of Recompense, let me reflect on which of my actions bear witness to the contrary.

---

57 Ibid, 26/262.

58 Ibn Athīr, *al-Kāmil fī al-Tārīkh*, 2/73.

59 Ibn *Kathīr, Tafsīr*, 4/41.

VERSES 14 - 17

كَلَّا بَلْ رَانَ عَلَىٰ قُلُوبِهِم مَّا كَانُوا يَكْسِبُونَ ﴿١٤﴾ كَلَّا إِنَّهُمْ عَن رَّبِّهِمْ يَوْمَئِذٍ لَّمَحْجُوبُونَ ﴿١٥﴾ ثُمَّ إِنَّهُمْ لَصَالُوا الْجَحِيمِ ﴿١٦﴾ ثُمَّ يُقَالُ هَٰذَا الَّذِي كُنتُم بِهِ تُكَذِّبُونَ ﴿١٧﴾

Not at all! Rather the stain of what they used to do has covered their hearts. [14] *Not at all! Indeed, on that Day they will certainly be veiled from their Lord.* [15] *Then indeed, they will burn in the hellfire.* [16] *Then it will be said [to them], "This is what you used to deny."* [17]

14-17.1 *'Not at all! Rather the stain of what they used to do has covered their hearts.'*: *Kallā* is used here to reject the reason that the disbelievers gave for denying the Qur'an. It was not because they thought that it contained myths, but because their hearts had been sullied by their deeds.

[*Rāna* (رَانَ, stain)] is derived from *rayn* which refers to dust or rust which coats something valuable.[60]

[*Yaksibūn* (يَكْسِبُونَ, what they did)] here refers to what they earned from their own actions.

The verse means that they themselves have damaged their hearts through their sins, in a manner that they cannot discern good from evil.[61] And that is the reason why they deny the Qur'an.

14-17.2 People's acceptance or denial of facts is not always based on thought and belief. It is not that a person inclines towards an act after pondering at length and comes up with a solution, like with a maths problem. Or if he rejects something, it is not after objectively thinking about it and deciding that he cannot accept it. The truth is that in most cases, an individual desires to act in a particular way and then works out a justification for it. In other words, many human actions and words may seem to be based on beliefs and principles, but in truth, they are merely pretexts for what they want to do anyway.[62]

However, man should never forget that his actions have an effect on his soul; when he commits evil acts, a stain appears on his heart

60 Rāghib, *al-Mufradāt.*

61 Ṭabāṭabā'ī, *al-Mīzān*, 20/234.

62 Muṭahharī, (*Āshnāyī bā Qur'an*), *Āthār*, 28/440.

that blocks his cognition of right and wrong. The soul is originally created clear and unblemished, and able to readily recognize its Creator and the path to Him. Q91:7,8 states:

وَنَفْسٍ وَمَا سَوَّاهَا ﴿٧﴾ فَأَلْهَمَهَا فُجُورَهَا وَتَقْوَاهَا

And by [the] soul and He who fashioned it. Then inspired it [to understand] what is wrong for it and what is right for it.

14-17.3 A tradition from Imam al-Baqir (a) states: There is no servant except that he has a white spot in his heart. But when he sins, a black spot appears within the white one. Then, if he repents, the blackness disappears. But if he persists in sin, the blackness extends until it overwhelms the whiteness. And when the whiteness is [completely] covered, the individual will never return to goodness ever, and this is the word of God, the Mighty and Exalted, *'Not at all! Rather the stain of what they used to do has covered their hearts.'*[63]

14-17.4 *'Not at all! Indeed, on that Day they will certainly be veiled from their Lord.'*: *Kallā* here may be an emphasis on the same phrase in the previous verse, or it could mean that the stain of sin would never leave their hearts; just as they have deprived themselves from seeing the glory of God in the *dunyā*, they will be veiled from Him in the *ākhirah* as well.[64]

[*Maḥjūbūn* (مَحْجُوبُونَ, veiled)] is derived from *ḥajaba* meaning to veil and seclude. Here it means that the damage the evildoers caused to their heart due to their sins will create a barrier between them and God. Due to this, they will be denied His proximity and mercy.[65] Q3:77 states about such people:

وَلَا يُكَلِّمُهُمُ اللَّهُ وَلَا يَنْظُرُ إِلَيْهِمْ يَوْمَ الْقِيَامَةِ وَلَا يُزَكِّيهِمْ وَلَهُمْ عَذَابٌ أَلِيمٌ

...And God will not speak to them, nor look upon them on the Day of Judgement nor will He purify them; and they will have a painful punishment.

---

[63] Kulaynī, *al-Kāfī*, 2/273.

عَنِ الْبَاقِرِ (عَلَيْهِ السَّلَامُ) – مَا مِنْ عَبْدٍ إِلَّا وَفِي قَلْبِهِ نُكْتَةٌ بَيْضَاءُ فَإِذَا أَذْنَبَ ذَنْبًا خَرَجَ فِي النُّكْتَةِ نُكْتَةٌ سَوْدَاءُ، فَإِنْ تَابَ ذَهَبَ ذَلِكَ السَّوَادُ، وَإِنْ تَمَادَى فِي الذُّنُوبِ زَادَ ذَلِكَ السَّوَادُ حَتَّى يُغَطِّيَ الْبَيَاضَ، فَإِذَا غَطَّى الْبَيَاضَ لَمْ يَرْجِعْ صَاحِبُهُ إِلَى خَيْرٍ أَبَدًا وَهُوَ قَوْلُ اللهِ عَزَّ وَجَلَّ «كَلَّا بَلْ رَانَ عَلَىٰ قُلُوبِهِمْ مَا كَانُوا يَكْسِبُونَ».

[64] Shīrāzī, *Namūneh*, 26/263.

[65] Ṭabāṭabā'ī, *al-Mīzān*, 20/234.

14-17.5 On the Day of Judgement, the most delightful experience will be the vision of God. This vision is not in the physical sense at all, but a vision that is perceived by purified hearts.

A supplication from Imam Ali (a) states: My God, grant me absolute devotion to You and illuminate the vision of our hearts with the light of their gaze towards You, so that the vision of the hearts can penetrate the curtains of light [that veil You] and arrive at the Source of Magnificence.[66]

By contrast, the most painful experience on the Day of Judgement will be deprivation of the vision of God and being veiled from Him.[67]

In another supplication, Imam Ali (a) states: My God, my Master, my Protector, and my Sustainer, even if I am able to endure Your chastisement, how will I endure separation from You?[68]

14-17.6 A tradition from Imam Ali (a) states: His words, *'Not at all! Indeed, on that Day they will certainly be veiled from their Lord,'* means that they will certainly be veiled from the reward of their Lord.[69]

14-17.7 *'Then indeed, they will burn in the hellfire.'*: [*Ṣālū* (صَالُوا, they will burn)] is derived from *ṣalā* meaning to become part of the fire and to roast and burn therein.[70] The fire of *Jaḥīm* will be the abode of the defrauders, those who denied a Day of recompense by transgressing God's bounds and sinning habitually, and those whose hearts were stained by their defiant conduct.[71] On that Day, their fate is the inescapable consequence of being veiled from their Lord.[72]

14-17.8 *'Then it will be said [to them], "This is what you used to deny."'* Then they will be reminded that this hellfire was the very thing that they use to deny (*tukadhdhibūn*). This statement is a

66 Qummī, *Mafātīḥ al-Jinān*, *Munājāt al-Shaʿbāniyah.*

إِلٰهِي هَبْ لِي كَمَالَ الْاِنْقِطَاعِ إِلَيْكَ وَأَنِرْ أَبْصَارَ قُلوبِنَا بِضِيَاءِ نَظَرِهَا إِلَيْكَ حَتَّى تَخْرِقَ أَبْصَارُ الْقُلوبِ حُجُبَ النُّورِ فَتَصِلَ إِلَى مَعْدِنِ الْعَظَمَةِ.

67 Shīrāzī, *Namūneh*, 26/263.

68 Qummī, *Mafātīḥ al-Jinān*, *Duʿāʾ al-Kumayl.*

فَهَبْنِي يَا إِلٰهِي وَسَيِّدِي وَمَوْلَايَ وَرَبِّي صَبَرْتُ عَلَى عَذَابِكَ، فَكَيْفَ أَصْبِرُ عَلَى فِرَاقِكَ؟

69 Ṣadūq, *al-Tawḥīd*, p. 257.

عَنْ أَمِيرِ الْمُؤْمِنِينَ (عَلَيْهِ السَّلَامُ) – وَأَمَّا قَوْلُهُ «كَلَّا إِنَّهُمْ عَنْ رَبِّهِمْ يَوْمَئِذٍ لَمَحْجُوبُونَ» فَإِنَّمَا يَعْنِي بِهِ يَوْمَ الْقِيَامَةِ عَنْ ثَوَابِ رَبِّهِمْ لَمَحْجُوبُونَ.

70 Muṣṭafawī, *al-Taḥqīq.*

71 Muṭahharī, (*Āshnāyī bā Qurʾan*), *Āthār*, 28/444.

72 Shīrāzī, *Namūneh*, 26/264.

reproach (*taqrīʿ*) of the attitude that will lead people to this terrible chastisement and a warning to them.[73]

DISCUSSION: THE PROGRESSIVE STAGES OF DISEASE IN THE SPIRITUAL HEART (*QALB*) MENTIONED IN THE QUR'AN

The original meaning of *qalb* is something that constantly changes from one state to another. For the human being, *qalb* denotes the faculty of spiritual intelligence through which he deliberates on, and then carries out the activities of his life.[74]

Qalb is a common term used in the Qur'an to signify the spiritual (as opposed to the physical) heart and several verses talk of the malaises which can strike it. We will mention some of them in this discussion.[75]

1. Hardening of the heart (*Qaswat al-qalb*): The hardening of the heart results from forsaking the remembrance of God and giving way to the insinuations of Shaytan. As a result, admonition has little effect on the individual and he actually begins to see his evil conduct as justified and good, and even takes pride in it. Q35:8 states:

   أَفَمَنْ زُيِّنَ لَهُ سُوءُ عَمَلِهِ فَرَآهُ حَسَنًا

   Then, is one to whom the evil of his deed has been made fair-seeming so he considers it good [like one rightly guided]?...

   And Q6:43 states:

   وَلَٰكِنْ قَسَتْ قُلُوبُهُمْ وَزَيَّنَ لَهُمُ الشَّيْطَانُ مَا كَانُوا يَعْمَلُونَ

   But their hearts became hardened (qasat qulūbuhum), *and Shaytan made attractive to them that which they were doing.*

2. Deviation (*Zaygh*): This is the beginning of the digression of the heart. Deviation and perversity manifests itself when the individual tries to seek justification for his wrongful conduct within the allegorical (*mutashābih*) verses of the Qur'an. This is the practice of the hypocrites and innovators in religion, whose deviant thinking makes them force deviant interpretations on the Qur'an. Q3:7 states:

---

[73] Ṭūsī, *al-Tibyān*, 10/300.

[74] Ṭabāṭabā'ī, *al-Mīzān*, 9/46.

[75] This discussion is based on Shīrāzī, *Payām-i Qur'an*, 1/294-303.

فَأَمَّا الَّذِينَ فِي قُلُوبِهِمْ زَيْغٌ فَيَتَّبِعُونَ مَا تَشَابَهَ مِنْهُ ٱبْتِغَاءَ الْفِتْنَةِ وَٱبْتِغَاءَ تَأْوِيلِهِ

As for those in whose hearts is deviation (zaygh),
they will follow that of it which is allegorical, seeking
discord and seeking an interpretation [suitable to them].

3. Stain (*Rayn*): The effect of continual sinning gradually creates a barrier between man and God, and the Qur'an likens it to a rust stain. Just as rust damages an implement, the heart is damaged and can no longer discern good and evil clearly. Q83:14 states:

كَلَّا بَلْ رَانَ عَلَىٰ قلُوبِهِمْ مَا كَانُوا يَكْسِبُونَ

Not at all! Rather the stain of what they used to do
has covered their hearts.

4. Sickness (*Maraḍ*): Hypocrisy causes the heart to deteriorate further and it develops a spiritual sickness. Rather than turning to God readily, it becomes more receptive to the suggestions of Shaytan. Q22:53 states:

لِيَجْعَلَ مَا يُلْقِي الشَّيْطَانُ فِتْنَةً لِلَّذِينَ فِي قُلُوبِهِمْ مَرَضٌ وَالْقَاسِيَةِ قُلُوبُهُمْ

[That is] so He may make what Shaytan proposes a trial for
those in whose hearts is a disease and those hard of heart.

5. Coverings (*Akinnah*): When a person becomes increasingly obstinate and rebellious, his heart develops several covers as a result. These covers block his ability to receive guidance. Q17:46 states:

وَجَعَلْنَا عَلَىٰ قُلُوبِهِمْ أَكِنَّةً أَنْ يَفْقَهُوهُ وَفِي آذَانِهِمْ وَقْرًا

And We have placed over their hearts coverings, lest they
understand it (the Qur'an), and in their [heart's] ears deafness.

6. Seal (*Ṭabʿ*): When a person is completely absorbed in the *dunyā* and sacrifices his religion for it, a seal is imprinted on his heart so that he no longer has any inclination towards the *ākhirah*. Q9:87 states:

وَطُبِعَ عَلَىٰ قُلُوبِهِمْ فَهُمْ لَا يَفْقَهُونَ

...And a seal is set on their hearts so they do not understand.

7. Seal (*Khatm*): Here, 'sealed' refers to something that has been closed and can no longer be changed. Those who have become completely self-centred and do just about anything that their low desires dictate, have their hearts sealed in this manner.

   Q45:23 states:

   أَفَرَأَيْتَ مَنِ ٱتَّخَذَ إِلَٰهَهُ هَوَاهُ وَأَضَلَّهُ اللهُ عَلَىٰ عِلْمٍ
   وَخَتَمَ عَلَىٰ سَمْعِهِ وَقَلْبِهِ وَجَعَلَ عَلَىٰ بَصَرِهِ غِشَاوَةً

   Have you seen he who has taken as his god his [own] desire, and God has sent him astray in spite of knowledge and has set a seal upon his hearing and his heart and put over his vision a veil?

8. Locks (*Aqfāl*): Locks are stronger than seals. These locks block even the Divine rays of guidance that are contained in the Qur'an, and so there is no hope of return. Q47:24 states:

   أَفَلَا يَتَدَبَّرُونَ الْقُرْآنَ أَمْ عَلَىٰ قُلُوبٍ أَقْفَالُهَا

   Do they not reflect on the Qur'an, or are there locks on the hearts?

9. Blindness (*ʿAmā*): At this stage, the person's spiritual eyes are now blind. He has no perception of reality. He stumbles through life in the *dunyā* and nothing he experiences reminds him of God.
   Q22:46 states:

   فَإِنَّهَا لَا تَعْمَى الْأَبْصَارُ وَلَٰكِنْ تَعْمَى الْقُلُوبُ الَّتِي فِي الصُّدُورِ

   ... For indeed, it is not the eyes that are blind, rather blind are the hearts (qulūb) *which are in the breasts* (ṣudūr).

10. Dead heart: In the last stage, the heart dies. This individual has lost every vestige of his humanity. His life is no different from that of cattle, rather, it is even worse. Q7:179 states:

    لَهُمْ قُلُوبٌ لَا يَفْقَهُونَ بِهَا وَلَهُمْ أَعْيُنٌ لَا يُبْصِرُونَ بِهَا
    وَلَهُمْ آذَانٌ لَا يَسْمَعُونَ بِهَا أُولَٰئِكَ كَالْأَنْعَامِ بَلْ هُمْ أَضَلُّ

    ...They have hearts with which they do not understand, and they have eyes with which they do not see, and they have ears with which they do not hear. They are like cattle; rather, they are even more astray.

The treatment of these spiritual sicknesses can only come from pondering on and applying the teachings of the Qur'an and the traditions of the Prophet (s) and his rightful successors (a). Q10:57 states:

يَا أَيُّهَا النَّاسُ قَدْ جَاءَتْكُمْ مَوْعِظَةٌ مِنْ رَبِّكُمْ
وَشِفَاءٌ لِمَا فِي الصُّدُورِ وَهُدًى وَرَحْمَةٌ لِلْمُؤْمِنِينَ

O mankind! There has to come to you instruction from your Lord and a cure for that which is in the [diseased] hearts, and guidance and mercy for the believers.

SUMMARY OF THE VERSES

The verses start by rejecting the assertion of the disbelievers and state that the real reason for their behaviour is that the stain of their sins has covered their hearts. As a result, on the Day of Judgement they will be veiled from God.

They will be sent to Hell, and reminded that this was what they used to deny in the *dunyā*.

REFLECTIVE LEARNING

Once the stain of sin damages the heart, man starts on a path away from God, unless he repents and reforms.

Let me reflect on the state of my heart and polish each black stain caused by a specific sin with a sincere repentance.

VERSES 18 - 21

كَلَّا إِنَّ كِتَابَ الْأَبْرَارِ لَفِي عِلِّيِّينَ ﴿١٨﴾ وَمَا أَدْرَاكَ مَا عِلِّيُّونَ ﴿١٩﴾ كِتَابٌ مَرْقُومٌ ﴿٢٠﴾ يَشْهَدُهُ الْمُقَرَّبُونَ ﴿٢١﴾

Not at all! Indeed, the record of the righteous is in 'Illiyyīn. [18] *And what will make you know what 'Illiyūn is?* [19] *[It is] a Record inscribed.* [20] *Which is witnessed by those brought near [to God].* [21]

18-21.1 These three verses (18-20) mirror the earlier three verses (9-11) about the *fujjār*, and contrast their fate with that of the *abrār* – those who do not defraud.

18-21.2 *'Not at all! Indeed, the record of the righteous is in 'Illiyyīn.'*: *Kallā* is used here again, this time to reject the false notions of the *fujjār* about the Qur'an, the Day of Judgement, and the station of the believers in the Hereafter.[76]

[*Kitāb* (كِتَاب, record)]. In the previous discussion about the possible meanings of *kitāb* we had mentioned that the term here may refer to the record of deeds, or to the decree and destiny written for these individuals.[77]

[*Abrār* (أَبْرَار, righteous)] is the plural of *bārr* referring to those who continually perform acts of righteousness (*birr*), and fulfil their duty to God, to His creation, and to themselves.[78] We have discussed the term further in the *tafsīr* of Surat al-Infiṭār (82).

[*'Illiyyūn* (عِلِّيُّون)] is the plural *'iliyy* which is derived from *'uluww* denoting the highest of high elevations in the close proximity to God. In this station there is no barrier or veil between them and Him.[79]

18-21.3 A tradition from Imam al-Baqir (a) states: *Sijjīn* is the seventh earth and *'Illiyūn* is the seventh heaven.[80] These seven realms surround the world that we know in elevation and depth.

Q65:12 states:

اللهُ الَّذِي خَلَقَ سَبْعَ سَمَاوَاتٍ وَمِنَ الْأَرْضِ مِثْلَهُنَّ

Allah is He who created seven heavens
and of the earth, the like thereof...

18-21.4 *'And what will make you know what 'Illiyūn is?'*: This rhetorical question emphasizes the greatness of *'Illiyyūn* and although addressed to the Prophet (s), it is directed to every reciter of the Qur'an. It means to say that man does not have the ability to grasp the realities of the *ākhirah* while he is still in the *dunyā*.[81]

A tradition from the Prophet (s) states: Indeed, the inhabitants of heaven see the inhabitants of *'Illiyūn* just as the bright celestial

---

[76] Rāzī, *Mafātīḥ al-Ghayb*, 31/90.

[77] Ṭabāṭabā'ī, *al-Mīzān*, 20/235.

[78] Ṭabāṭabā'ī, *al-Mīzān*, 1/428 (*Tafsīr* of Q2:177).

[79] Muṭahharī, (*Āshnāyī bā Qur'an*), *Āthār*, 28/448.

[80] Kāshānī, *al-Ṣāfī*, 5/299.

عَنْ أَبِي جَعْفَرٍ (عَلَيْهِ السَّلَامُ) – السِّجِّينُ الْأَرْضُ السَّابِعَةُ وَعِلِّيُّونَ السَّمَاءُ السَّابِعَةُ.

[81] Muṭahharī, (*Āshnāyī bā Qur'an*), *Āthār*, 28/451.

bodies are seen in the canopy of the sky.[82] When an inhabitant of *ʿIlliyūn* visits Paradise, it becomes radiant, and its residents say, "Someone from *ʿIlliyūn* has come down to us."[83]

18-21.5 *'[It is] a Record inscribed'*: This is a description of *ʿIlliyyūn*, and again, the pronoun 'it is' (*huwa*) has been omitted (*maḥdhūf*). Just like in the case of *Sijjīn*, this verse may refer to:

i) the destination decreed for the *abrār*, or

ii) a repository or a comprehensive Register of the records of all of them.

In the latter case *kitābun marqūm* would be a reference to the book of the righteous (*kitāb al-abrār*) and not to *ʿIlliyūn* itself. And it is possible to consider both interpretations as valid, because the manifestation of the records of the righteous would make its location the highest level of Paradise.[84]

18-21.6 *'Which is witnessed by those brought close [to God].'*: [*Muqarrabūn* (مُقَرَّبُون, those brought near)] is derived from *qarraba* meaning to bring near. Here it refers to those who have been brought near to God. Some exegetes have defined *muqarrabūn* as the angels who witness and oversee the lives of the *abrār*. However, the verses about them later in the surah, which speak of them eating and drinking, suggest that the term refers to an elite group of God's close servants from amongst mankind.[85]

18-21.7 In this surah, three groups of people have been mentioned: the *fujjār*, the *abrār*, and the *muqarrabūn*. In Surat al-Wāqiʿah, the three groups are described in different words. Q56:7-11 states:

وَكُنْتُمْ أَزْوَاجًا ثَلَاثَةً ﴿٧﴾ فَأَصْحَابُ الْمَيْمَنَةِ مَا أَصْحَابُ الْمَيْمَنَةِ ﴿٨﴾
وَأَصْحَابُ الْمَشْأَمَةِ مَا أَصْحَابُ الْمَشْأَمَةِ ﴿٩﴾
وَالسَّابِقُونَ السَّابِقُونَ ﴿١٠﴾ أُولَٰئِكَ الْمُقَرَّبُونَ

---

[82] Modarresī, *Min Hudā al-Qur'an*, 17/421.

عَنِ الرَّسُولِ (صَلَّى اللهُ عَلَيْهِ وَآلِهِ) - إِنَّ أَهْلَ الْجَنَّةِ يَرَوْنَ أَهْلَ عِلِّيِينَ كَمَا يُرَى الْكَوْكَبُ الدُّرِّيُّ فِي أُفُقِ السَّمَاءِ.

[83] Ṭabrasī, *al-Bayān*, 10/692.

فَإِذَا أَشْرَفَ رَجُلٌ مِنْهُمْ أَشْرَقَتِ الْجَنَّةُ، وَقَالُوا: قَدِ اطَّلَعَ عَلَيْنَا رَجُلٌ مِنْ أَهْلِ عِلِّيِينَ.

[84] Shīrāzī, *Namūneh*, 26/255.

[85] Ibid, 26/273.

And you will be in three groups: So the companions of the bliss – what are the companions of the bliss? And the companions of the misery – what are the companions of the misery? And the foremost, the foremost, they are those brought close (muqarrabūn) *[to God].*

Therefore, the *fujjār* have been defined as *aṣḥāb al-mash'amah* (the companions of the misery), the *abrār* as *aṣḥāb al-maymanah* (the companions of bliss), and the *muqarrabūn* as *al-sābiqūn* (the foremost).

18-21.8 The *muqarrabūn* are derived from the *abrār* but are a higher level than them.[86] A tradition from the Prophet (s) states: [What would be considered as] good deeds for the *abrār* would be unacceptable (insufficient) from the *muqarrabūn*.[87]

18-21.9 The quality of the *muqarrabūn* mentioned here is that they are able to witness the deeds of the *abrār*. Q16:89 states:

وَيَوْمَ نَبْعَثُ فِي كُلِّ أُمَّةٍ شَهِيدًا عَلَيْهِم مِّنْ أَنفُسِهِمْ وَجِئْنَا بِكَ شَهِيدًا عَلَىٰ هَٰؤُلَاءِ

And [mention] the Day when We will raise among every nation a witness over them from themselves. And We will bring you, [O Muhammad], as a witness over these [people]...

In fact, this ability is not just specific to the *ākhirah*. The close servants (*awliyā*) of God – the Prophets (a) and the Imams (a) – who are His proofs (*ḥujaj*) over the people in their own time, have access to the deeds of the people. Q9:105 states:

وَقُلِ ٱعْمَلُوا فَسَيَرَى اللَّهُ عَمَلَكُمْ وَرَسُولُهُ وَالْمُؤْمِنُونَ

And say: Act! For God will see your deeds, as will His Messenger and the believers...

About this verse, Imam al-Sadiq (a) has explained that *'mu'minūn'* here refers to the Imams (a), stating: The verse is referring to God's Messenger (s) and the Imams (a), to whom the actions of the people are presented every Thursday evening.[88]

---

86 Muṭahharī, (*Āshnāyī bā Qur'an*), *Āthār*, 28/447.

87 Majlisī, *Biḥār*, 25/205.

عَنِ الرَّسُولِ (صَلَّى اللهُ عَلَيْهِ وَآلِهِ) – حَسَنَاتُ الْأَبْرَارِ سَيِّئَاتُ الْمُقَرَّبِينَ..

88 Ibid, 23/345.

عَنِ الصَّادِقِ (عَلَيْهِ السَّلَامُ) – قَالَ: رَسُولُ اللهِ صَلَّى اللهُ عَلَيْهِ وَآلِهِ وَالْأَئِمَّةُ عَلَيْهِمُ السَّلَامُ تُعْرَضُ عَلَيْهِمْ أَعْمَالُ الْعِبَادِ كُلَّ خَمِيسٍ.

18-21.10 A tradition from Imam al-Baqir (a) states: Indeed, God created us from the highest *'Illiyūn*. And He created the hearts of our partisans (*shī'a*) from that which we were created from, and created their bodies from something else. So their hearts incline towards us because they were created from that which we were created from. Then he (a) recited the verses, *'Not at all! Indeed, the record of the righteous is in 'Illiyyīn. And what will make you know what 'Illiyūn is? [It is] a Record inscribed.'*[89]

SUMMARY OF THE VERSES

The verses begin with a rejection of the allegation of the disbelievers. Then they mention that the record (or destiny) of the righteous shall be in *'Illiyyūn*, whose reality is too grand to be imagined. It is a record of the deeds of the righteous that can be witnessed by the *muqarrabūn* – those who have been brought close to God.

REFLECTIVE LEARNING

Let me reflect which of my deeds would be in '*the record of the righteous*' so that I can do more of these specific deeds in order that it moves me into *'Illiyyūn*.

VERSES 22 - 28

إِنَّ الْأَبْرَارَ لَفِي نَعِيمٍ ﴿٢٢﴾ عَلَى الْأَرَائِكِ يَنْظُرُونَ ﴿٢٣﴾ تَعْرِفُ فِي وُجُوهِهِمْ
نَضْرَةَ النَّعِيمِ ﴿٢٤﴾ يُسْقَوْنَ مِنْ رَحِيقٍ مَخْتُومٍ ﴿٢٥﴾ خِتَامُهُ مِسْكٌ وَفِي ذَٰلِكَ
فَلْيَتَنَافَسِ الْمُتَنَافِسُونَ ﴿٢٦﴾ وَمِزَاجُهُ مِنْ تَسْنِيمٍ ﴿٢٧﴾ عَيْنًا يَشْرَبُ بِهَا الْمُقَرَّبُونَ
﴿٢٨﴾

Indeed, the righteous will be in bliss, [22] *on thrones, observing.* [23] *You will recognize on their faces the radiance of bliss.* [24] *They will be given to drink [pure] wine, sealed.* [25] *The sealing of it is with musk. So let all those who strive, strive for this.* [26] *And it will be mixed with Tasnīm,* [27] *a spring from which those near [to God] drink.* [28]

---

[89] Kulaynī, *al-Kāfī*, 1/390.

عَنِ الْبَاقِرِ (عَلَيْهِ السَّلَامُ) – إِنَّ اللهَ خَلَقَنَا مِنْ أَعْلَى عِلِّيِّينَ وَخَلَقَ قُلُوبَ شِيعَتِنَا مِمَّا خَلَقَنَا وَخَلَقَ أَبْدَانَهُمْ مِنْ دُونِ ذَلِكَ فَقُلُوبُهُمْ تَهْوِي إِلَيْنَا لِأَنَّهَا خُلِقَتْ مِمَّا خُلِقْنَا. ثُمَّ تَلَا هَذِهِ الْآيَةَ «كَلَّا إِنَّ كِتَابَ الْأَبْرَارِ لَفِي عِلِّيِّينَ* وَمَا أَدْرَاكَ مَا عِلِّيُّونَ* كِتَابٌ مَرْقُومٌ* يَشْهَدُهُ الْمُقَرَّبُونَ.»

22-28.1 *'Indeed, the righteous will be in bliss,'*: The next verses describe the delightful station of the *abrār*, who are the inhabitants of *ʿIlliyūn*.

[*Naʿīm* (نَعِيم, bliss)] signifies numerous and continual blessings. It is used here in the indefinite form to denote the indescribable nature of these blessings,[90] the greatest of which is that the *abrār* reside in God's vicinity. We have discussed this verse further in the *tafsīr* of the previous chapter, Surat al-Infiṭār, where it occurs also (Q82:13).

22-28.2 *'On thrones, observing.'*: [*Arāʾik* (أَرَائِك, thrones)] (sing. *arīkah*) here refers to decorated and lofty thrones in Paradise on which the *abrār* sit or recline.[91]

[*Yanẓurūn* (يَنظُرُون, observing)] has been used in a general sense without specifying what they are looking at. Indeed, from their high thrones the *abrār* will observe and survey the numerous blessings that have been granted to them.[92]

Some reports state that they observe their enemies who are being punished.[93]

However, another explanation is that they gaze at the countenance of God. This opinion is emphasized by the next verse, which talks of the radiance (*naḍrah*) of their faces, because this term has been used to describe the effect of looking towards God.[94] Q75:22,23 state:

وُجُوهٌ يَوْمَئِذٍ نَاضِرَةٌ ﴿٢٢﴾ إِلَىٰ رَبِّهَا نَاظِرَةٌ

[Some] faces, that Day, will be radiant. Looking towards their Lord.

22-28.3 *'You will recognize on their faces the radiance of bliss.'*: [*Naḍrah* (نَضْرَة, radiance)] means radiance and splendour.[95] They will be easily recognised as noble people of high station by their luminous faces, which will also reflect their joy at seeing the *naʿīm* of Paradise. God will have added indescribable beauty and brightness to their features.[96]

---

[90] Ṭabāṭabāʾī, *al-Mīzān*, 20/237.

[91] Muṣṭafawī, *al-Taḥqīq*.

[92] Ṭūsī, *al-Tibyān*, 10/302.

[93] Ṭabrasī, *al-Bayān*, 10/692.

[94] Rāzī, *Mafātīḥ al-Ghayb*, 31/91.

[95] Muṣṭafawī, *al-Taḥqīq*.

[96] Ṭabrasī, *al-Bayān*, 10/692.

22-28.4 *'They will be given to drink [pure] wine, sealed.'*: [*Yusqawna* (يُسْقَوْنَ, they will be given to drink)] is derived from *saqā* meaning to serve a drink. Here it means that they will have attendants who serve them drinks as they desire. Amongst the blessings that they will receive is wine that is sealed and kept for the *abrār* alone.

[*Raḥīq* (رَحِيق, wine)] refers to a nectar or pure wine that is delicious and has no disagreeable side-effects. It is called wine because it enhances the senses, but unlike the wine of the *dunyā*, it adds to the awareness, purity and cognizance of the drinker.[97] Q37:47 states:

لَا فِيهَا غَوْلٌ وَلَا هُمْ عَنْهَا يُنْزَفُونَ

No bad effect is there in it, nor from it will they be intoxicated.

[*Makhtūm* (مَخْتُوم, sealed)] is derived from *khatama* meaning to close with a seal. Here it means that the wine is sealed and untouched, and thereby protected from adulteration with anything that would adversely affect it.[98]

22-28.5 *'The sealing of it is with musk. So let all those who strive, strive for this.'*: [*Khitām* (خِتَام, seal)] refers to that which closes off the contents of something. When used for drinks it also means the last part of it.[99]

[*Misk* (مِسْك, musk)] here refers to the wondrous scent of the musk of Paradise.

The verse means that the seal of the vessel will be made of musk, and when it is broken, the fragrance of musk will fill the air. It can also mean that when they finish drinking, the lingering fragrance and taste will be that of musk.[100]

[*Yatanāfas* (يَتَنَافَس, he strives)] is derived from *tanāfasa* meaning to compete and race with one another to get something desirable, in this case to compete in the obedience of God.[101]

The verse means that if there is anything worth competing for in this *dunyā*, it is striving to be one of the *abrār*, to drink from the blessed *al-raḥīq al-makhtūm*,[102] and to receive what they will receive.

---

97 Shīrāzī, *Namūneh*, 26/275.

98 Ṭabāṭabā'ī, *al-Mīzān*, 20/238.

99 Muṣṭafawī, *al-Taḥqīq*.

100 Shīrāzī, *Namūneh*, 26/276.

101 Ṭabrasī, *al-Bayān*, 10/693.

102 Ṭabāṭabā'ī, *al-Mīzān*, 20/238.

Q57:21 states:

سَابِقُوا إِلَىٰ مَغْفِرَةٍ مِنْ رَبِّكُمْ وَجَنَّةٍ عَرْضُهَا كَعَرْضِ السَّمَاءِ وَالْأَرْضِ أُعِدَّتْ لِلَّذِينَ آمَنُوا بِاللَّهِ وَرُسُلِهِ

Race toward forgiveness from your Lord and a Garden whose width is like the width of the heavens and earth, prepared for those who believed in God and His Messengers...

22-28.6 *'And it will be mixed with Tasnīm, a spring from which those near [to God] drink.'*: [*Mizāj* (مِزَاجُ, mixture)] refers to a substance which is added to flavour something else.

[*Tasnīm* (تَسْنِيم)] is derived from *sannama* meaning to raise or elevate.[103] It is the name of a spring that flows from the highest stations of Paradise and it is the finest drink therein.[104] The addition of *Tasnīm* to *al-raḥīq al-makhtūm* greatly enhances its effect.[105]

22-28.7 The *muqarrabūn*, who witness the deeds of the *abrār* in *'Illiyūn* are mentioned again here. They are the only ones who may drink from *Tasnīm* it in its pure state, while the *abrār* will be allowed only an admixture of it.[106]

The verse reveals that *Tasnīm* is a more refined drink than *al-raḥīq al-makhtūm* and once again shows that the *muqarrabūn* are at a higher station of proximity to God than the *abrār*.[107]

22-28.8 A tradition from Imam al-Sajjad (a) states: Whoever feeds a hungry believer will be fed from the fruits of Paradise by God and whoever quenches the thirst of a believer will be given a drink of sealed pure wine (*al-raḥīq al-makhtūm*) by God.[108]

SUMMARY OF THE VERSES

The verses state that the righteous will be surrounded by God's blessings, which they will observe while sitting on high thrones, and

---

103 Ibn Manẓūr, *Lisān al-'Arab*.

104 Shīrāzī, *Namūneh*, 26/278.

105 Ṭabāṭabā'ī, *al-Mīzān*, 20/239.

106 Ṭabrasī, *al-Bayān*, 10/693.

107 Ṭabāṭabā'ī, *al-Mīzān*, 20/239.

108 Kulaynī, *al-Kāfī*, 2/201.

عَنِ السَّجَّادِ (عَلَيْهِ السَّلَامُ) – مَنْ أَطْعَمَ مُؤْمِنًا مِنْ جُوعٍ أَطْعَمَهُ اللهُ مِنْ ثِمَارِ الْجَنَّةِ، وَمَنْ سَقَى مُؤْمِنًا مِنْ ظَمَأٍ سَقَاهُ اللهُ مِنَ الرَّحِيقِ الْمَخْتُومِ.

radiance will be visible on their faces. In Paradise they will be given a pure wine to drink. It will be sealed with musk. Indeed, this is the station to strive for.

Their drink will be enhanced with a part of *Tasnīm*, a spring that is reserved for the *muqarrabūn* – those who have been drawn near to God.

REFLECTIVE LEARNING

Let me reflect on how what I consume has an effect on my soul, in the *dunyā* as well as the *ākhirah*.

If I always maintain a careful watch that what I eat and drink is *ḥalāl* and from legal earnings, I will also qualify to drink from the blessed *al-raḥīq al-makhtūm*.

VERSES 29 - 33

إِنَّ الَّذِينَ أَجْرَمُوا كَانُوا مِنَ الَّذِينَ آمَنُوا يَضْحَكُونَ ﴿٢٩﴾ وَإِذَا مَرُّوا بِهِمْ يَتَغَامَزُونَ
﴿٣٠﴾ وَإِذَا انْقَلَبُوا إِلَىٰ أَهْلِهِمُ انْقَلَبُوا فَكِهِينَ ﴿٣١﴾ وَإِذَا رَأَوْهُمْ قَالُوا إِنَّ هَٰؤُلَاءِ
لَضَالُّونَ ﴿٣٢﴾ وَمَا أُرْسِلُوا عَلَيْهِمْ حَافِظِينَ ﴿٣٣﴾

Indeed, those who committed crimes used to laugh at those who believed. [29] *And when they passed by them, they would wink at one another.* [30] *And when they returned to their people, they would return jesting.* [31] *And when they saw them, they would say, "Indeed, those are truly astray."* [32] *But they had not been sent as guardians over them.* [33]

29-33.1 The last section of the surah describes the mockery that the believers faced at the hands of the disbelievers and then mentions the fate of their tormentors. It is meant as a warning to the disbelievers and a consolation and encouragement to the believers.[109]

29-33.2 *'Indeed, those who committed crimes used to laugh at those who believed.'*: [*Ajramū* (أَجْرَمُوا, committed crimes)] is derived from *jarama* meaning to commit a sin or offence. The disbelievers have been called criminals here because the reason for their continual mockery of the believers was due to their faith.

[109] Rāzī, *Mafātīḥ al-Ghayb*, 31/94.

[*Alladhīna āmanū* (الَّذِينَ آمَنُوا, those who believed)] here refers to the *abrār* according to the context of the verses.[110]

The use of *kānū* (used to) in this verse indicates that this was their habitual behaviour.[111] Those who were guilty of this crime were reported to be the heads of the Quraysh like Abu Jahl, al-Walīd b. al-Mughīrah, and al-ʿĀṣ b. Wā'il who used to laugh mockingly at ʿAmmār, Ṣuhayb, Bilāl, and other Muslims.[112] They would make fun of their beliefs and acts of worship.[113]

29-33.3 *'And when they passed by them, they would wink at one another.'*: [*Yataghāmazūn* (يَتَغَامَزُونَ, wink at one another)] is derived from *ghamaza* which means to signal or make a sign with the eyes to indicate disdain.[114] Here it refers to the winking, rolling of the eyes, and other mocking gestures that the disbelievers continually made whenever they passed by the Muslims.

It appears that when a believer passed by a group of disbelievers they would laugh at him openly because of their greater number, but when the disbelievers passed by a large group of believers they would be hesitant to mock them verbally and instead would resort to facial expressions of scorn.[115]

29-33.4 If *ghamz* was by the use of eyes in those days, today it has taken the shape of pens, films, and other social mediums for defamation used by the enemies of humanity and the enemies of God and religion.[116]

29-33.5 *'And when they returned to their people, they would return jesting.'*: Their scorn of the Muslims would continue when they were sitting amongst themselves, comfortable in their echo chambers.

[*Ahlihim* (أَهْلِهِم, their people)] refers to other disbelievers who behaved like them.

[*Fakihīn* (فَكِهِين, jesting] is derived from *fakaha* meaning to be cheerful and laugh, and refers to the delight that the disbelievers took in recounting their mockery of the believers.

---

110 Ṭabāṭabā'ī, *al-Mīzān*, 20/239.

111 Muṭahharī, *(Āshnāyī bā Qur'an), Āthār*, 28/460.

112 Rāzī, *Mafātīḥ al-Ghayb*, 31/94.

113 Ṭabrasī, *al-Bayān*, 10/693.

114 Muṣṭafawī, *al-Taḥqīq*.

115 Shīrāzī, *Namūneh*, 26/284.

116 Modarresī, *Min Hudā al-Qur'an*, 17/429.

29-33.6 When faced with a truth they do not want to accept, some people deny it while others decide to oppose it, which is worse. This opposition can take many forms, but a common and effective way is to resort to mockery and ridicule.

29-33.7 *'And when they saw them, they would say, "Indeed, those are truly astray."'*: Perhaps this stage was after they saw that their mockery and laughter had no effect on the determination of the Muslims. They began to take the arrival of Islam in their land more seriously, and now whenever they saw any of the believers they declared them to be misguided and astray.[117]

29-33.8 *'But they had not been sent as guardians over them.'*: However, the Qur'an points out that it is not for these criminals to worry about the believers. They were never placed as guardians over them. In other words, their behaviour was actually based on their meanness. They were angry at what they saw as an attack on their own beliefs, and they did not really care whether the Muslims were misguided or not.[118]

SUMMARY OF THE VERSES

Four further examples of social misconduct of the disbelievers are described. They used to laugh at the believers, they would make derisive gestures when they passed by them, when they returned to their own people they would describe their mockery of the Muslims with amusement, and they would allege that the believers were misguided. However, God reminds them that they have not been appointed as guardians over the believers.

REFLECTIVE LEARNING

People hurt others through their jokes and facial expressions, and often do not consider the damage that they cause to the person and to themselves.

Let me reflect on whether I am guilty of this social misconduct, by asking those who know me.

---

[117] Shīrāzī, *Namūneh*, 26/286.

[118] Muṭahharī, (*Āshnāyī bā Qur'an*), *Āthār*, 28/460.

VERSES 34 - 36

فَالْيَوْمَ الَّذِينَ آمَنُوا مِنَ الْكُفَّارِ يَضْحَكُونَ ﴿٣٤﴾ عَلَى الْأَرَائِكِ يَنْظُرُونَ ﴿٣٥﴾
هَلْ ثُوِّبَ الْكُفَّارُ مَا كَانُوا يَفْعَلُونَ ﴿٣٦﴾

So on this Day, the believers shall laugh at the disbelievers, [34] *on thrones, observing.* [35] *Have the disbelievers [not] been rewarded [fully] for what they used to do?* [36]

34-36.1 *'So on this Day, the believers shall laugh at the disbelievers,'*: This Day refers to the Day of Judgement. In this verse the term criminals (*mujrimūn*) has been changed back to disbelievers (*kuffār*) to identify their real character,[119] which was the reason for their criminal activities.

34-36.2 Every act in the *dunyā* will be reflected with a similar punishment or reward in the *ākhirah*. Just as the disbelievers used to laugh at the believers, on this Day, the believers will laugh at them.[120] Ironically, in both *dunyā* and *ākhirah*, the laughter is because one group thinks that the other is foolish. The only difference is that the laughter of the disbelievers was undeserved while that of the *abrār* will be justified.

34-36.3 *'On thrones, observing.'*: This verse is repeated in the surah. This time, the *abrār* are sitting on their dignified thrones looking at the disbelievers receiving the recompense for their misdeeds in the *dunyā*, which included ridiculing the believers.[121] Q2:212 states:

زُيِّنَ لِلَّذِينَ كَفَرُوا الْحَيَاةُ الدُّنْيَا وَيَسْخَرُونَ مِنَ الَّذِينَ آمَنُوا
وَالَّذِينَ اتَّقَوْا فَوْقَهُمْ يَوْمَ الْقِيَامَةِ

The life of this world is beautified for the disbelievers,
and they mock at the believers. But those who are wary of God
shall be above them on the Day of Resurrection.

34-36.4 *'Have the disbelievers [not] been rewarded [fully] for what they used to do?'*: [*Thuwwiba* (ثُوِّبَ, was rewarded)] is derived from

---

119 Ṭabāṭabā'ī, *al-Mīzān*, 20/239.

120 Muṭahharī, (*Āshnāyī bā Qur'an*), *Āthār*, 28/461.

121 Ṭabāṭabā'ī, *al-Mīzān*, 20/240.

thawwaba meaning to be recompensed or paid.[122] *Thawāb* originally means recompense, whether punishment or reward, but later came to be used mainly for reward.[123]

This statement may be from God, or the angels, or the believers sitting on their thrones.[124] There is a sense of irony as the verse asks: Have the disbelievers not been subjected to the same ridicule that they used to display towards the believers?

SUMMARY OF THE VERSES

The verses state that on the Day of Judgement, it is the believers who will laugh at the disbelievers. They will be seated on elevated thrones watching their fate.

The surah ends by asking (rhetorically) whether the disbelievers have been fully requited for what they used to do in the *dunyā*.

REFLECTIVE LEARNING

Let me reflect whether I truly believe that God will recompense each and every one for their deeds, or do I feel the need to take revenge into my own hands in this world.

---

122 Muṣṭafawī, *al-Taḥqīq*.

123 Ṭabāṭabā'ī, *al-Mīzān*, 20/240.

124 Shīrāzī, *Namūneh*, 26/289.

SURAT AL-INSHIQĀQ
THE SPLITTING OPEN (84)

TEXT AND TRANSLATION

سُورَةُ الِانْشِقَاقِ

بِسْمِ اللَّهِ الرَّحْمَٰنِ الرَّحِيمِ

إِذَا السَّمَاءُ انْشَقَّتْ ﴿١﴾ وَأَذِنَتْ لِرَبِّهَا وَحُقَّتْ ﴿٢﴾ وَإِذَا الْأَرْضُ مُدَّتْ ﴿٣﴾
وَأَلْقَتْ مَا فِيهَا وَتَخَلَّتْ ﴿٤﴾ وَأَذِنَتْ لِرَبِّهَا وَحُقَّتْ ﴿٥﴾ يَا أَيُّهَا الْإِنْسَانُ إِنَّكَ كَادِحٌ
إِلَىٰ رَبِّكَ كَدْحًا فَمُلَاقِيهِ ﴿٦﴾ فَأَمَّا مَنْ أُوتِيَ كِتَابَهُ بِيَمِينِهِ ﴿٧﴾ فَسَوْفَ يُحَاسَبُ
حِسَابًا يَسِيرًا ﴿٨﴾ وَيَنْقَلِبُ إِلَىٰ أَهْلِهِ مَسْرُورًا ﴿٩﴾ وَأَمَّا مَنْ أُوتِيَ كِتَابَهُ وَرَاءَ
ظَهْرِهِ ﴿١٠﴾ فَسَوْفَ يَدْعُو ثُبُورًا ﴿١١﴾ وَيَصْلَىٰ سَعِيرًا ﴿١٢﴾ إِنَّهُ كَانَ فِي أَهْلِهِ
مَسْرُورًا ﴿١٣﴾ إِنَّهُ ظَنَّ أَنْ لَنْ يَحُورَ ﴿١٤﴾ بَلَىٰ إِنَّ رَبَّهُ كَانَ بِهِ بَصِيرًا ﴿١٥﴾
فَلَا أُقْسِمُ بِالشَّفَقِ ﴿١٦﴾ وَاللَّيْلِ وَمَا وَسَقَ ﴿١٧﴾ وَالْقَمَرِ إِذَا اتَّسَقَ ﴿١٨﴾
لَتَرْكَبُنَّ طَبَقًا عَنْ طَبَقٍ ﴿١٩﴾ فَمَا لَهُمْ لَا يُؤْمِنُونَ ﴿٢٠﴾ وَإِذَا قُرِئَ عَلَيْهِمُ الْقُرْآنُ
لَا يَسْجُدُونَ ۩ ﴿٢١﴾ بَلِ الَّذِينَ كَفَرُوا يُكَذِّبُونَ ﴿٢٢﴾ وَاللَّهُ أَعْلَمُ بِمَا يُوعُونَ
﴿٢٣﴾ فَبَشِّرْهُمْ بِعَذَابٍ أَلِيمٍ ﴿٢٤﴾ إِلَّا الَّذِينَ آمَنُوا وَعَمِلُوا الصَّالِحَاتِ لَهُمْ أَجْرٌ
غَيْرُ مَمْنُونٍ ﴿٢٥﴾

In the name of God, the Beneficent, the Merciful.

When the sky is split open, [1] *and obeys its Lord and it must,* [2] *and when the earth is stretched forth,* [3] *and has cast out all that was in it and become empty,* [4] *and obeys its Lord and it must.* [5] *O man! Indeed, you are constantly labouring towards your Lord with [great] exertion until you shall meet Him.* [6] *Then as for he who is given his record in his right hand,* [7] *he will soon be judged with an easy accounting.* [8] *And will return to his people in happiness.* [9] *But as for he who is given his record behind his back,* [10] *he will soon cry out for destruction,* [11] *and [enter to] burn in a blazing fire.* [12] *Indeed, he used to be joyful amongst his folk.* [13] *Indeed, he had thought he would never return [to God].* [14] *But yes! Indeed, his Lord was ever seeing him!* [15] *So I swear by the twilight glow.* [16] *And [by] the night and what it envelops.* [17] *And [by] the moon when it becomes full.* [18] *[That] you will certainly travel stage after stage.* [19] *So what is the matter with them [that] they do not believe?* [20] *And when the Qur'an is recited to them, they do not prostrate themselves?* [21] *But those who disbelieve will deny.* [22] *And God knows best what they hide.* [23] *So give them tidings of a painful punishment.* [24] *Except for those who believe and do righteous deeds. For them is a reward uninterrupted.* [25]

INTRODUCTION

Surat al-Inshiqāq (84) was the 83rd chapter to be revealed.[1] It has twenty-five verses and is a Makkan surah, revealed after Surat al-Infiṭār (82).

Like other Makkan surahs that are found in the last *juz'*, it discusses the events that will accompany the end of the *dunyā* and the beginning of the all-important Day of Judgement.

The surah is named after one of the great signs of that Day mentioned in the first verse: the splitting of the sky (*inshiqāq*). It begins by describing the universal submission of everything in creation to God, and how the sky and earth will undergo tumultuous changes as the *dunyā* comes to an end.

Next, man is informed that he is on an arduous journey to meet His Lord.

The surah then describes how the records of deeds will be distributed to two groups. One will receive their record joyfully in their right hand, while the other will be humiliatingly given their record from behind their back, before being entered into Hell.

The surah warns man of the danger of being carefree in the *dunyā*, unmindful of the Day of Reckoning.

Thereafter, two oaths are made before the surah states that man has already moved stage after stage in his life and asks why he does not

[1] Maʿrifat, *ʿUlūm-i Qur'ānī*, p. 90.

believe and become subservient when he hears the verses of the Qur'an?

The truth is denied by the disbelievers and God knows their true motivation.

The last verses warn that the disbelievers have been promised a painful chastisement and only the righteous believers shall receive an eternal reward.

LINK TO THE PREVIOUS CHAPTER

This surah employs a very similar style to Surat al-Takwīr (81) and Surat al-Infiṭār (82), which also begin with descriptions of the events of the last Hour.

The previous chapter, Surat al-Muṭaffifīn, speaks of the division of people on the Day of Judgement according to their faith and deeds. Surat al-Inshiqāq gives details of how two of these groups will be informed of their fate; the righteous will receive their record of deeds in their right hand and be admitted to Paradise, while the wretched will receive their records from behind their backs and will be sent to Hell.

Both surahs discuss the books of records of human beings. Surat al-Muṭaffifīn states where the books will be located and Surat al-Inshiqāq tells us how they will be later handed to the individual.

Both surahs describe people returning to their family and friends in delight. However, Surat al-Muṭaffifīn talks of the mocking laughter of the disbelievers in this world, while Surat al-Inshiqāq speaks of the deserved happiness of the believers in the Hereafter.

MERITS OF RECITATION

- A tradition from the Prophet (s) states: Whoever recites Surat *Inshaqqat* will be spared from receiving his book [of deeds] from behind his back [on the Day of Judgement].[2]
- A tradition from Imam al-Sadiq (a) states: Whoever recites these two surahs, *Idhā al-samā'u infaṭarat* (Surat al-Infiṭār, 82) and *Idhā al-samā'u inshaqqat* (Surat al-Inshiqāq, 84), and does so attentively

---

[2] Nūrī, *Mustadrak al-Wasā'il*, 4/357.

عَنِ الرَّسُولِ (صَلَّى اللهُ عَلَيْهِ وَآلِهِ) – مَنْ قَرَأَ سُورَةَ «آنْشَقَّتْ» أَعَاذَهُ اللهُ أَنْ يُعْطِيَهُ كِتَابَهُ وَرَاءَ ظَهْرِهِ.

in his obligatory and supererogatory prayers, will not be denied any wish by God. There will be no obstruction between him and God, and God will continually look over him until he completes his accounting (*ḥisāb*).[3]

EXEGESIS

VERSES 1 - 5

إِذَا السَّمَاءُ ٱنْشَقَّتْ ﴿١﴾ وَأَذِنَتْ لِرَبِّهَا وَحُقَّتْ ﴿٢﴾ وَإِذَا الْأَرْضُ مُدَّتْ ﴿٣﴾
وَأَلْقَتْ مَا فِيهَا وَتَخَلَّتْ ﴿٤﴾ وَأَذِنَتْ لِرَبِّهَا وَحُقَّتْ ﴿٥﴾

When the sky is split open, [1] *and obeys its Lord and it must,* [2] *and when the earth is stretched forth,* [3] *and has cast out all that was in it and become empty,* [4] *and obeys its Lord and it must.* [5]

1-5.1 The first five verses of the surah describe two incredible and terrifying events of the last Hour, the splitting open of the sky (*inshiqāq*) and the levelling of the earth (*madd*).

1-5.2 '*When the sky is split open,*': [*Idhā* (إِذَا, when)] gives a meaning of suddenness and certainty. Here it makes the verse a conditional sentence (*sharṭ*) and its main clause or outcome (*jazāʾ*) is postponed until the sixth verse. What is meant here is that 'when the sky is split open...then man will meet his Lord for account and judgement.'[4]

[*Inshaqqat* (اِنشَقَّتْ, split open)] is derived from *shaqqa* meaning to irreparably tear or cleave. Here it refers to the sky above the world being split open and the celestial system that protects life on earth being destroyed. In other verses of the Qurʾan the terms *furijat* (torn apart, Q77:9) and *infaṭarat* (cleft asunder, Q82:1) have been used to describe the same calamitous event. All these terms describe the sundering of the sky as the universe begins to disintegrate.[5]

---

[3] Majlisī, *Biḥār*, 82/38.

عَنِ الصَّادِقِ (عَلَيْهِ السَّلَامُ) – مَنْ قَرَأَ هَاتَيْنِ السُّورَتَيْنِ وَجَعَلَهُمَا نُصْبَ عَيْنَيْهِ فِي صَلَاةِ الْفَرِيضَةِ وَالنَّافِلَةِ «إِذَا السَّمَاءُ ٱنْفَطَرَتْ» وَ«إِذَا السَّمَاءُ ٱنْشَقَّتْ» لَمْ يَحْجُبْهُ اللهُ مِنْ حَاجَةٍ وَلَمْ يَحْجُزْهُ مِنَ اللهِ حَاجِزٌ وَلَمْ يَزَلْ يَنْظُرُ اللهُ إِلَيْهِ حَتَّى يَفْرُغَ مِنَ الْحِسَابِ.

[4] Ṭabāṭabāʾī, *al-Mīzān*, 20/242.

[5] Shīrāzī, *Namūneh*, 26/296.

1-5.3 A tradition from Imam Ali (a) states: The sky will split within its galaxy.[6] Since space is a vacuum, the splitting in this tradition refers to the brocade of stars and other celestial bodies in the Milky Way being ripped apart. The invisible forces that hold the universe together at God's command will collapse. Q13:2 refers to these invisible forces:

اللهُ الَّذِي رَفَعَ السَّمَاوَاتِ بِغَيْرِ عَمَدٍ تَرَوْنَهَا

God is He who raised the heavens without any pillars that you can see...

1-5.4 '*And obeys its Lord and it must,*' [*Adhinat* (أَذِنَتْ, obey)] is derived from *adhina* which means both to permit and allow as well as to listen and give ear to[7] Here it is used metaphorically to signify obedience to the command of God[8]

[*Ḥuqqat* (حُقَّتْ, it must)] is derived from *ḥaqqa* meaning to be true and necessary. It also denotes to deserve. Here it means God has made it incumbent on the sky to behave this way or it behoves it to do so. Indeed, when the command of God (*amr*) comes, every creation obeys instantly. Just as the sky and earth obeyed God willingly when they were created, they will also obey willingly when they are destroyed. Q41:11 states:

ثُمَّ ٱسْتَوَىٰٓ إِلَى ٱلسَّمَآءِ وَهِيَ دُخَانٌ فَقَالَ لَهَا
وَلِلْأَرْضِ ٱئْتِيَا طَوْعًا أَوْ كَرْهًا قَالَتَآ أَتَيْنَا طَآئِعِينَ

Then He directed Himself to the heaven while it was smoke and said to it and to the earth, "Come [into being], willingly or by compulsion." They said, "We come in willing obedience."

1-5.5 '*And when the earth is stretched forth,*': In the same way, the earth will undergo an amazing physical transformation as well. This shows that *ākhirah* is not just a spiritual experience. The world of matter continues to be conserved; it is transformed but does not disappear. Q14:48 states:

يَوْمَ تُبَدَّلُ الْأَرْضُ غَيْرَ الْأَرْضِ وَالسَّمَاوَاتُ وَبَرَزُوا لِلَّهِ الْوَاحِدِ الْقَهَّارِ

---

[6] Kāshānī, *al-Ṣāfī*, 5/304.

عَنْ عَلِيٍّ (عَلَيْهِ السَّلَامُ) – إِنَّهَا تَنْشَقُّ مِنَ الْمَجَرَّةِ.

[7] Muṣṭafawī, *al-Taḥqīq*.

[8] Ṭabāṭabā'ī, *al-Mīzān*, 20/242.

On the day when the earth shall be changed into a different earth, and the heavens [as well], and they shall come forth before Allah, the One, the Supreme.

[*Muddat* (مُدَّتْ, stretched forth)] is derived from *madda* meaning to flatten and elongate.[9] It means that the earth will be extended and levelled, without any hill, valley, or ocean, creating a flat and featureless arena for the gathering of creation from the beginning of time.[10] Q20:106,107 state:

فَيَذَرُهَا قَاعًا صَفْصَفًا ﴿١٠٦﴾ لَا تَرَىٰ فِيهَا عِوَجًا وَلَا أَمْتًا

And He will leave it [the earth] a level plain. You will not see therein a depression or an elevation.

Some exegetes have said that 'stretched' here means 'increased in size', to accommodate the gathering of all creatures from the earliest times.[11]

1-5.6 '*And has cast out all that was in it and become empty,*' [*Alqat* (أَلْقَتْ, cast out)] is derived from *ilqāʾ* meaning to throw.

[*Takhallat* (تَخَلَّتْ, become empty)] is derived from *khalā* meaning to be empty and vacant. This term is also used for a mother who empties her womb when she gives birth to her child.[12]

Here, the verse refers to the earth which readily casts out its entire burden, expelling its treasures, its inner core, and the dead from its depths, until it is empty.[13] Q99:2 states in this regard:

وَأَخْرَجَتِ الْأَرْضُ أَثْقَالَهَا

And the earth discharges its burdens.

'*And obeys its Lord and it must.*' Just like the skies, on this Day God has made it incumbent on the earth to behave in this manner as well. These tumultuous events bring the *dunyā* to an end, and usher in the realm of the *ākhirah*.

---

[9] Muṣṭafawī, *al-Taḥqīq*.

[10] Shīrāzī, *Namūneh*, 26/298.

[11] Rāzī, *Mafātīḥ al-Ghayb*, 31/97.

[12] Muṣṭafawī, *al-Taḥqīq*.

[13] Modarresī, *Min Hudā al-Qurʾan*, 17/443.

SUMMARY OF THE VERSES

The verses describe two events of the last Hour. The sky will split open in obedience to the command of its Lord, as it must. Similarly, the earth will be stretched forth after it has cast out everything within its depths and become empty. It too, obeys the command of its Lord, as it must.

REFLECTIVE LEARNING

The sky and the earth obey God instantly when commanded, in submission to His will. I too, must obey God instantly but sometimes choose not to.

Let me reflect on a time when I have chosen not to obey instantly and what I gained and lost from this delay.

VERSE 6

يَا أَيُّهَا الْإِنْسَانُ إِنَّكَ كَادِحٌ إِلَىٰ رَبِّكَ كَدْحًا فَمُلَاقِيهِ ﴿٦﴾

O man! Indeed, you are constantly labouring towards your Lord with [great] exertion until you shall meet Him. [6]

6.1 This verse is the main clause or outcome (*jazā'*) of the two conditional phrases that began with *idhā* (when) in the previous verses.

6.2 *Insān* here addresses all human beings who have ever lived.[14] Every one of them is on a path towards the meeting with his Lord and has been granted the potential and ability to undertake the journey.[15] We have discussed the term *insān* in the *tafsīr* of Surat al-ʿAṣr (103).

6.3 [*Kādiḥ* (كَادِحٌ, labouring)] is derived from *kadaḥa* meaning to toil and tire oneself through exertion.[16] It has a meaning of someone striving (*saʿī*) on a journey, in this case towards God.[17] This verse is a proof of the return to God (*maʿād*) after which man will be recompensed for his deeds.

---

[14] Ṭabrasī, *al-Bayān*, 10/699.

[15] Shīrāzī, *Namūneh*, 26/300.

[16] Rāghib, *al-Mufradāt*.

[17] Ṭabāṭabā'ī, *al-Mīzān*, 20/242.

For both the one who aims to acquire the *dunyā* as well as the one who wishes to acquire the *ākhirah*, this life is fraught with many struggles and setbacks, both physical and emotional.[18]

6.4 A tradition from Imam al-Sajjad (a) states: Comfort (*al-rāḥah*) does not exist in the world or for the inhabitants of this world, rather it exists in Paradise and for the inhabitants of Paradise.[19]

6.5 [*Mulāqīhi* (مُلَاقِيهِ, meet Him)]. This meeting with God may signify a number of things, all of which should fill man with great trepidation and awe. Some exegetes have said that it may mean arriving at His court on the Day of Judgement, or receiving His reward or punishment, or witnessing His glory through the inner eyes.[20]

However, the word *liqā'* suggests that there will be a real encounter with God Himself, and the use of the word *insān* in this verse implies that every single human being will experience this. Probably this means that wherever the disbelievers look, they shall perceive the presence and hand of God clearly. As for the righteous, they will be able to see Him with the vision of the heart. Q75:22,23 state:

وُجُوهٌ يَوْمَئِذٍ نَاضِرَةٌ ﴿٢٢﴾ إِلَىٰ رَبِّهَا نَاظِرَةٌ

[Some] faces, that Day, will be radiant. Looking towards their Lord.

This meeting with God, known as *liqā' Allah*, is only truly possible in the Hereafter, where every creation of God evolves and matures exponentially, and the veils of the *dunyā* are removed.

6.6 The use of the term *Rabb* (Lord and Sustainer) is an indication that this wearisome striving is part of God's plan for man's development and progress towards his perfection. The journey will end when one comes before his Lord on the Day of Judgement and it is only at this point that the labouring of mankind will come to an end.[21] Q35:18 states:

وَأَنَّ إِلَىٰ رَبِّكَ الْمُنْتَهَىٰ

...And that to your Lord is the end.

---

[18] Ṭūsī, *al-Tibyān*, 10/309.

[19] Ṣadūq, *al-Khiṣāl*, 1/64.

عَنْ عَلِيِّ بْنِ الْحُسَيْنِ (عَلَيْهِ السَّلَامُ) - الرَّاحَةُ لَمْ تُخْلَقْ فِي الدُّنْيَا وَلَا لِأَهْلِ الدُّنْيَا، إِنَّمَا خُلِقَتِ الرَّاحَةُ فِي الْجَنَّةِ وَلِأَهْلِ الْجَنَّةِ.

[20] Shīrāzī, *Namūneh*, 26/300.

[21] Ibid.

DISCUSSION 1: THE REALM OF THE *DUNYĀ* AND THE REALM OF THE *ĀKHIRAH*

Surat al-Inshiqāq speaks almost exclusively about the Day of Judgement. We are aware of the matters of the *dunyā* through experience and learning, and we even have some idea of *barzakh* from reports, dreams, etc. However, there is no way we can attain any understanding of the next world, about resurrection, accounting, judgement, and so on, except through revelation.

It is the belief in the Hereafter that completes our belief in an all-Wise and all-Just Creator, and gives purpose to our lives and our striving. Those who do not believe in the *ākhirah* are blinded into thinking that the ultimate purpose of their existence lies is the *dunyā*. Q27:4,5 state:

إِنَّ الَّذِينَ لَا يُؤْمِنُونَ بِالْآخِرَةِ زَيَّنَّا لَهُمْ أَعْمَالَهُمْ فَهُمْ يَعْمَهُونَ ﴿٤﴾
أُولَٰئِكَ الَّذِينَ لَهُمْ سُوءُ الْعَذَابِ وَهُمْ فِي الْآخِرَةِ هُمُ الْأَخْسَرُونَ

Indeed, for those who do not believe in the Hereafter, We have made their deeds fair-seeming to them, so they wander about blindly. Those are the ones for whom there will be the worst torment, and in the Hereafter they shall be the greatest losers.

God has kept two realms of existence for mankind: this world which is also called *al-nash'at al ūlā* (the first creation), and the Hereafter, which is also called *al-nash'at al ākhirah* or *ukhrā* (the last creation).

About the *dunyā* Q56:62 states:

وَلَقَدْ عَلِمْتُمُ النَّشْأَةَ الْأُولَىٰ فَلَوْلَا تَذَكَّرُونَ

And you have already known the first creation (al-nash'at al-ūlā), *so will you not take heed?*

God invites man to explore this first realm and realize how He has made it perfectly suitable to sustain his earthly life. This should leave him in no doubt that God is able to prepare for him the vast realm of the Hereafter as He has promised. Q29:20 states:

قُلْ سِيرُوا فِي الْأَرْضِ فَانْظُرُوا كَيْفَ بَدَأَ الْخَلْقَ ثُمَّ اللَّهُ يُنْشِئُ النَّشْأَةَ الْآخِرَةَ
إِنَّ اللَّهَ عَلَىٰ كُلِّ شَيْءٍ قَدِيرٌ

Say: Travel through the land and observe how He began creation. Then God will produce the creation of the Hereafter (al-nashʾat al-ākhirah). *Indeed, God has power over all things.*

There are some fundamental differences between these two realms:

i) The *dunyā* was not meant to be experienced for its own sake; rather, its pleasant bounties (*matāʿ*) are a means through which to acquire felicity and comfort in the *ākhirah.*

In the *ākhirah* however, everything is experienced for itself, because it is the permanent abode. Q40:39 states:

إِنَّمَا هَٰذِهِ الْحَيَاةُ الدُّنْيَا مَتَاعٌ وَإِنَّ الْآخِرَةَ هِيَ دَارُ الْقَرَارِ

... Truly this worldly life is only [fleeting] enjoyment, and indeed, the Hereafter – that is the home of [permanent] settlement.

ii) In the realm of the *dunyā*, the entirety of creation is still at a relatively rudimentary phase of existence. In the *ākhirah*, everything will evolve into a much more enhanced level of existence. Awareness and ability will increase in a way that we cannot comprehend at the moment. Just like an acorn becomes an oak tree, man too, will reach his full potential in that world. And thereby, he will be able to see his Lord by the vision of the heart, as long as his sins do not veil him from God. However, this was something which was not possible in the *dunyā*, even for God's greatest servants.

iii) In the *ākhirah*, every part and dimension of creation will be raised to the same level of sentience and intellect, allowing the entirety of creation in the cosmos, men, angels, *jinn*, animals, and even lifeless objects, to communicate with one another freely.[22]

Q10:28,29 state:

وَيَوْمَ نَحْشُرُهُمْ جَمِيعًا ثُمَّ نَقُولُ لِلَّذِينَ أَشْرَكُوا مَكَانَكُمْ أَنْتُمْ وَشُرَكَاؤُكُمْ
فَزَيَّلْنَا بَيْنَهُمْ وَقَالَ شُرَكَاؤُهُمْ مَا كُنْتُمْ إِيَّانَا تَعْبُدُونَ ﴿٢٨﴾
فَكَفَىٰ بِاللَّهِ شَهِيدًا بَيْنَنَا وَبَيْنَكُمْ إِنْ كُنَّا عَنْ عِبَادَتِكُمْ لَغَافِلِينَ

On the Day when We will gather them all together - then We will say to those who associated [others with Allah], "Stop in your place, you and your partners [which you worshipped]."

[22] Shīrāzī, *Namūneh*, 8/273.

Then We will remove the barrier between them, and their partners will say, "It was not us that you worshipped. Allah is sufficient as a witness between us and you, that we certainly knew nothing of your worship of us!"

In these verses, the inanimate idols have been called the partners of the idolaters and not the partners of God, as their worshippers claimed. On that Day the idols will speak and, in clear speech, reject the worship of the polytheists.[23]

iv) In the *dunyā* the hand of God is hidden for most people although He is the Cause of every effect. In the *ākhirah* however, His presence is acutely felt by everyone before every cause and effect. No one will be able to deny it. Q40:16 states:

لِمَنِ الْمُلْكُ الْيَوْمَ لِلَّهِ الْوَاحِدِ الْقَهَّارِ

... To Whom belongs the kingdom this Day? To Allah, the One, the Vanquisher!

v) In the *dunyā* people arrive in a certain timeframe, one by one, and then leave. However, everything in existence will enter the *ākhirah* at the same time.

Although the realities of that realm are outside our conception, the Qur'an has provided us with some glimpses of it. What is certain though is that within the realm of the *ākhirah* lies the real life man was created for. Those who had neglected it will realize that fact on that Day. Q89:24 quotes their words:

يَقُولُ يَا لَيْتَنِي قَدَّمْتُ لِحَيَاتِي

He shall say, "How I wish I had sent forth [some provisions] for my [real] life!"

SUMMARY OF THE VERSE

The verse reminds every human being that he is on an arduous journey, full of difficulties, heading for the meeting with his Lord.

---

23 Ṭabāṭabā'ī, *al-Mīzān*, 10/44.

REFLECTIVE LEARNING

Each day brings me a step closer to the meeting with God. Let me reflect on whether this meeting will be full of honour or filled with shame.

VERSES 7 - 9

فَأَمَّا مَنْ أُوتِيَ كِتَابَهُ بِيَمِينِهِ ﴿٧﴾ فَسَوْفَ يُحَاسَبُ حِسَابًا يَسِيرًا ﴿٨﴾ وَيَنْقَلِبُ إِلَىٰ أَهْلِهِ مَسْرُورًا ﴿٩﴾

Then as for he who is given his record in his right hand, [7] *he will soon be judged with an easy accounting.* [8] *And will return to his people in happiness.* [9]

7-9.1 '*Then as for he who is given his record in his right hand,*': [*Kitāb* (كِتَاب, record)] here refers to the record of deeds of human beings that is being meticulously recorded at every moment of their life. Nothing escapes the attention of the two recording angels assigned to every person. Q43:80 states:

أَمْ يَحْسَبُونَ أَنَّا لَا نَسْمَعُ سِرَّهُمْ وَنَجْوَاهُمْ بَلَىٰ وَرُسُلُنَا لَدَيْهِمْ يَكْتُبُونَ

Or do they think that We do not hear their secrets and their private conversations? Yes, [We do], and Our messengers are with them recording.

We will discuss these books later in the *tafsīr* of the surah.

7-9.2 After the stage of the meeting with God, everyone will be given the record of their deeds in preparation for their accounting (*ḥisāb*). Two groups are mentioned here. The first group, the people of felicity (*saʿādah*), will receive their book of deeds in their right hand. They are the people who lived their lives true to the path that God had directed for mankind. This was a noble path leading them from the dishonour of their lowly beginnings to the great honour of meeting with God. In the *dunyā* they lived a God-centred life, constantly laboured for Him, and strove to get close to Him.[24]

[24] Shīrāzī, *Namūneh*, 26/302.

They will read their record in delight and eagerly show it to off to others. Q69:19 states:

فَأَمَّا مَنْ أُوتِيَ كِتَابَهُ بِيَمِينِهِ فَيَقُولُ هَاؤُمُ اقْرَءُوا كِتَابِيَهْ

So as for he who is given his record in his right hand, he will say, "Here, read my record!"

7-9.3 [*Yamīnihi* (يَمِينِه, his right hand)]. The phrase 'right hand' for the righteous, and later, 'left hand' for the disbelievers, literally refers to the hand in which individuals will receive their record.[25] Some exegetes have said that the further significance of this is that 'right' is a metaphor for acceptance and enlightenment, while 'left' signifies rejection and abasement.[26]

Although both right and left hands are valuable creations of God, in many traditions the right hand and foot have been given precedence over the left. For example, a tradition from the Imams (a) states: It is better to enter the mosque with the right foot and leave with your left.[27]

7-9.4 Some exegetes say that those who receive their book in the right hand are the same as the 'companions of the right, or bliss' (*aṣḥāb al-maymanah*) described in the Qur'an (for example in Q90:18). They are given this title because they have been described as having a light to their right side as they traverse the path to Paradise[28] as mentioned in Q57:12:

يَوْمَ تَرَى الْمُؤْمِنِينَ وَالْمُؤْمِنَاتِ يَسْعَىٰ نُورُهُمْ بَيْنَ أَيْدِيهِمْ وَبِأَيْمَانِهِمْ بُشْرَاكُمُ الْيَوْمَ

On the Day you see the believing men and believing women, their light proceeding before them and on their right, [it will be said], "Good tidings for you this Day!..."

7-9.5 Although only two groups are mentioned in this surah, there may be more. For example, in Surat al-Wāqiʿah, three groups are mentioned: the companions of the bliss (*aṣḥāb al-maymanah*), the companions of the misery (*aṣḥāb al-mash'amah*), and the foremost,

---

25 Shīrāzī, *Payām-i Qur'ānī*, 6/75.

26 Māwardī, *Tafsīr al-Nukat wa al-ʿUyūn*, 6/84.

27 Kulaynī, *al-Kāfī*, 3/308.

عَنْهُمْ (عَلَيْهِمُ السَّلَامُ) قَالَ: الْفَضْلُ فِي دُخُولِ الْمَسْجِدِ أَنْ تَبْدَأَ بِرِجْلِكَ الْيُمْنَى إِذَا دَخَلْتَ وَبِالْيُسْرَى إِذَا خَرَجْتَ.

28 Rāzī, *Mafātīḥ al-Ghayb*, 29/455.

the foremost (*al-sābiqūn al-sābiqūn*). In Surat al-Muṭaffifīn three groups are mentioned also: the righteous (*abrār*), the evildoers (*fujjār*), and those brought near (*muqarrabūn*). It may be said that the 'foremost' are the elite from amongst the 'companions of the bliss' just as 'those brought near' are the best from the 'righteous' and they will be present together to receive their books in their right hand. However, some exegetes say that *al-sābiqūn and muqarrabūn* are of an elevated station and are not summoned to the accounting at all.[29] Q39:10 states:

قُلْ يَا عِبَادِ الَّذِينَ آمَنُوا اتَّقُوا رَبَّكُمْ لِلَّذِينَ أَحْسَنُوا فِي هَٰذِهِ الدُّنْيَا حَسَنَةٌ وَأَرْضُ اللَّهِ وَاسِعَةٌ إِنَّمَا يُوَفَّى الصَّابِرُونَ أَجْرَهُمْ بِغَيْرِ حِسَابٍ

Say, "O My servants who are believers, be wary of your Lord (have taqwā). *For those who do good in this world [the reward] is good, and the earth of God is spacious. Indeed, the steadfast will be given their reward without account."*

A tradition from Imam Ali (a) states: On that Day people will have different levels and stations. Some of them will be given an easy accounting and they will return to their people in happiness. And some will be entered into Paradise without accounting because they did not get involved much in the matters of the *dunyā*.[30]

7-9.6 '*He will soon be judged with an easy accounting.*': [*Ḥisāb* (حِساب, accounting)] is a well-known stage on the Day of Judgement.

It follows the distribution of the records of deeds. However, it does not start immediately. *Sawfa* (soon) in the verse means after a while.

It seems that people are left on their own for some time to become better acquainted with their records. They gain a realization of their true station thereby, because these records are actually the full revelation of their personalities. It is only then that they are summoned for accounting. And this accounting will be according to the level of their understanding. A tradition from Imam al-Baqir (a) states: On the Day of Accounting, God will take the servants to

[29] Muṭahharī, (*Āshnāyī bā Qur'an*), *Āthār*, 28/466.

[30] Ṭabrasī, *al-Iḥtijāj*, 1/572.

عَنْ عَلِيٍّ (عَلَيْهِ السَّلَامُ) – وَالنَّاسُ يَوْمَئِذٍ عَلَى طَبَقَاتٍ وَمَنَازِلَ، فَمِنْهُمْ مَنْ يُحَاسَبُ حِسَابًا يَسِيرًا وَيَنْقَلِبُ إِلَى أَهْلِهِ مَسْرُورًا، وَمِنْهُمُ الَّذِينَ يَدْخُلُونَ الْجَنَّةَ بِغَيْرِ حِسَابٍ؛ لِأَنَّهُمْ لَمْ يَتَلَبَّسُوا مِنْ أَمْرِ الدُّنْيَا بِشَيْءٍ.

task according to the intellect that He had granted to them in the *dunyā*.[31]

7-9.7 On the Day of Judgement great multitudes will stand to account in front of God, yet each will receive individual attention, just as in this world where every human being is able to enjoy an uninterrupted personal connection to God whenever he calls out to Him.[32] Indeed, no one act of God stops Him from other acts; listening to one petitioner does not preclude Him from hearing another. This is also mentioned in a supplication from the Prophet (s): O He who is not diverted from listening to one by listening to another, O He who is not prevented from one act by doing another, O He who does not ignore the speech of one at the speech of another...[33]

7-9.8 The verse under review states that this first group of people will be judged with an easy accounting (*ḥisāban yasīrā*). God shall overlook their lapses, and because of their faith and righteous deeds, He will even replace their evil acts with good ones.[34] Q25:70 states:

إِلَّا مَنْ تَابَ وَآمَنَ وَعَمِلَ عَمَلًا صَالِحًا فَأُولَٰئِكَ يُبَدِّلُ اللَّهُ سَيِّئَاتِهِمْ حَسَنَاتٍ
وَكَانَ اللَّهُ غَفُورًا رَحِيمًا

Except for those who repent, believe and do righteous work.
For them God will replace their evil deeds with good.
And God is all-Forgiving, all-Merciful.

This is because their souls have formed a virtuous disposition by continually doing good and avoiding evil. If these people sinned, it was out of some weakness or forgetfulness, but not defiance. They were also quick to repent. As a consequence, the small blemishes of sin will be washed away from their soul, because good and evil cannot subsist together in that realm.[35] Q4:31 states:

إِنْ تَجْتَنِبُوا كَبَائِرَ مَا تُنْهَوْنَ عَنْهُ نُكَفِّرْ عَنْكُمْ سَيِّئَاتِكُمْ وَنُدْخِلْكُمْ مُدْخَلًا كَرِيمًا

---

31 ʿĀmilī, *Wasāʾil*, 1/40.

عَنِ الْبَاقِرِ (عَلَيْهِ السَّلَامُ) – إِنَّمَا يُدَاقُّ اللهُ الْعِبَادَ فِي الْحِسَابِ يَوْمَ الْقِيَامَةِ عَلَى قَدْرِ مَا آتَاهُمْ مِنَ الْعُقُولِ فِي الدُّنْيَا.

32 Bahmanpour, *Towards Eternal Life*, p. 107.

33 Qummī, *Mafātīḥ al-Jinān, Duʿāʾ Jawshan al-Kabīr.*

يَا مَنْ لَا يَشْغَلُهُ سَمْعٌ عَنْ سَمْعٍ، يَا مَنْ لَا يَمْنَعُهُ فِعْلٌ عَنْ فِعْلٍ، يَا مَنْ لَا يُلْهِيهِ قَوْلٌ عَنْ قَوْلٍ...

34 Shīrāzī, *Namūneh*, 26/302.

35 Bahmanpour, *Towards Eternal Life*, p. 109.

If you avoid the major sins (kabā'ir) *from which you are forbidden, We will do away with your lesser sins and admit you to an honourable place.*

7-9.9 A tradition from the Prophet (s) states: If a person possesses three qualities, God will judge him with an easy accounting and enter him into Paradise by His mercy... Give to the one who deprives you, mend relations with one who cuts you off, and forgive the one who has wronged you.[36]

7-9.10 A tradition from Imam al-Baqir (a) states: The Prophet (s) said, "Everyone who undergoes accounting is punished." Someone asked him, "O Messenger of God, what then of the words of God, the Exalted, '*he will soon be judged with an easy accounting*'?" He (s) replied, "That refers to the presentation [of the book]" - meaning [merely] turning through its pages.[37]

7-9.11 Those who undergo a lenient accounting in the presence of God are soon done with this station and they return to their people, delighted with their experience.

7-9.12 '*And will return to his people in happiness.*': [*Ahlihi* (أَهْلِهِ, his people)] here could refer to other believers who are at the same station as him,[38] or it could mean his spouse, children, and relatives from amongst the believers.[39] And this is a great blessing.[40]

Q52:21 states:

وَالَّذِينَ آمَنُوا وَاتَّبَعَتْهُمْ ذُرِّيَّتُهُمْ بِإِيمَانٍ أَلْحَقْنَا بِهِمْ ذُرِّيَّتَهُمْ
وَمَا أَلَتْنَاهُمْ مِنْ عَمَلِهِمْ مِنْ شَيْءٍ

And those who believed and whose descendants followed them in faith – We will join with them their descendants and We will not deprive them of anything of their deeds...

---

36 Majlisī, *Biḥār*, 7/96.

عَنِ الرَّسُولِ (صَلَّى اللهُ عَلَيْهِ وَآلِهِ) – ثَلَاثٌ مَنْ كُنَّ فِيهِ حَاسَبَهُ اللهُ حِسَابًا يَسِيرًا وَأَدْخَلَهُ الْجَنَّةَ بِرَحْمَتِهِ ... تُعْطِي مَنْ حَرَمَكَ وَتَصِلُ مَنْ قَطَعَكَ وَتَعْفُو عَمَّنْ ظَلَمَكَ.

37 Baḥrānī, *al-Burhān*, 5/617.

عَنِ الْبَاقِرِ (عَلَيْهِ السَّلَامُ) – قَالَ رَسُولُ اللهِ (صَلَّى اللهُ عَلَيْهِ وَآلِهِ): كُلُّ مُحَاسَبٍ مُعَذَّبٌ، فَقَالَ لَهُ قَائِلٌ: يَا رَسُولَ اللهِ، فَأَيْنَ قَوْلُ اللهِ عَزَّ وَجَلَّ: «فَسَوْفَ يُحَاسَبُ حِسَابًا يَسِيرًا»؟ قَالَ: ذَاكَ الْعَرْضُ– يَعْنِي التَّصَفُّحَ.

38 Mughniyyah, *al-Kāshif*, 7/540.

39 Ṭūsī, *al-Tibyān*, 10/310.

40 Shīrāzī, *Namūneh*, 26/303.

God will unite these people with the believers from among their families by raising the status of those members who are not of the same station. They had not spent their lives with their family in the *dunyā* while remaining indifferent to their fate in the Hereafter; they were always more concerned about their family achieving success in the *ākhirah* rather than in the *dunyā*.[41] Q52:26, 27 state:

قَالُوا إِنَّا كُنَّا قَبْلُ فِي أَهْلِنَا مُشْفِقِينَ ﴿٢٦﴾ فَمَنَّ اللَّهُ عَلَيْنَا وَوَقَانَا عَذَابَ السَّمُومِ

They will say, "Indeed, previously we were fearful [and cautious] among our families So God has been gracious to us and preserved us from the punishment of the Scorching Fire."

7-9.13 [*Masrūrā* (مَسْرُورا, in happiness)] is derived from *sarra* meaning to be happy and delighted. Naturally, these people will return with great relief and delight from the momentous occasion of accounting because their Lord has been merciful and lenient with them.

A tradition from Imam al-Sadiq (a) states: If someone is satisfied with the little sustenance that God has granted him [in this world], God will be satisfied with the few good deeds [that he has performed].[42]

SUMMARY OF THE VERSES

The individual who is awarded his record of deeds in his right hand will be subject to an easy accounting. Thereafter, he will return to his kinsfolk in delight.

REFLECTIVE LEARNING

A tradition from Imam al-Sadiq (a) states: Maintaining ties with blood relatives (*ṣilat al-raḥim*) will ease the accounting on the Day of Judgement. Then he (a) recited the verse, '*And those who join that which God has ordered to be joined (blood ties) and fear their Lord and fear an evil reckoning.*' (Q13:21).[43]

---

[41] Iṣlāḥī, *Tadabbur-i Qur'an*, 9/226.

[42] Kulaynī, *al-Kāfī*, 2/138.

عَنِ الصَّادِقِ (عَلَيْهِ السَّلَامُ) – مَنْ رَضِيَ مِنَ اللهِ بِالْيَسِيرِ مِنَ الْمَعَاشِ رَضِيَ اللهُ مِنْهُ بِالْيَسِيرِ مِنَ الْعَمَلِ.

[43] Baḥrānī, *al-Burhān*, 3/247.

عَنِ الصَّادِقِ (عَلَيْهِ السَّلَامُ) – إِنَّ صِلَةَ الرَّحِمِ تُهَوِّنُ الْحِسَابَ يَوْمَ الْقِيَامَةِ. ثُمَّ قَرَأَ: «يَصِلُونَ مَا أَمَرَ اللهُ بِهِ أَنْ يُوصَلَ وَيَخْشَوْنَ رَبَّهُمْ وَيَخَافُونَ سُوءَ الْحِسَابِ.»

Let me reflect on the nature of my ties with my near kin. Can I strengthen or mend certain relationships?

Conversely, do I disobey God in order to maintain *ṣilat al-raḥim* (due to a negative influence from my family)? If so, this is not a correct application of the hadith of the Imam (a).

VERSES 10 - 15

وَأَمَّا مَنْ أُوتِيَ كِتَابَهُ وَرَاءَ ظَهْرِهِ ﴿١٠﴾ فَسَوْفَ يَدْعُو ثُبُورًا ﴿١١﴾ وَيَصْلَىٰ سَعِيرًا ﴿١٢﴾ إِنَّهُ كَانَ فِي أَهْلِهِ مَسْرُورًا ﴿١٣﴾ إِنَّهُ ظَنَّ أَنْ لَنْ يَحُورَ ﴿١٤﴾ بَلَىٰ إِنَّ رَبَّهُ كَانَ بِهِ بَصِيرًا ﴿١٥﴾

But as for he who is given his record behind his back, [10] *he will soon cry out for destruction,* [11] *and [enter to] burn in a blazing fire.* [12] *Indeed, he used to be joyful amongst his folk.* [13] *Indeed, he had thought he would never return [to God].* [14] *But yes! Indeed, his Lord was ever seeing him!* [15]

10-15.1 *'But as for he who is given his record behind his back'*: The second group, the group of wretchedness (*shaqāwah*), will be given their record of deeds from behind their backs – *min warā'i ẓahrihi*, is truncated here to *warā'a ẓahrihi*.[44]

10-15.2 For these people the *ḥisāb* will not be easy. A tradition from the Prophet (s) states: Easy reckoning (*al-ḥisāb al-yasīr*) means rewarding the good deeds (*ḥasanāt*) and overlooking the evil ones (*sayyi'āt*). But the one who is scrutinized will be chastised severely.[45] May God protect us from such a fate.

10-15.3 This is the only verse that mentions receiving the records from behind the back. In other verses it has been mentioned that the evildoers shall receive their record in their left hand. Q69:25,26 state:

وَأَمَّا مَنْ أُوتِيَ كِتَابَهُ بِشِمَالِهِ فَيَقُولُ يَا لَيْتَنِي لَمْ أُوتَ كِتَابِيَهْ ﴿٢٥﴾ وَلَمْ أَدْرِ مَا حِسَابِيَهْ

[44] Ṭabāṭabā'ī, *al-Mīzān*, 20/243.

[45] Kāshānī, *al-Ṣāfī*, 5/305.

عَنِ الرَّسُولِ (صَلَّى اللهُ عَلَيْهِ وَآلِهِ) – الْحِسَابُ الْيَسِيرُ هُوَ الْإِثَابَةُ عَلَى الْحَسَنَاتِ وَالتَّجَاوُزُ عَنِ السَّيِّئَاتِ وَمَنْ نُوقِشَ الْحِسَابَ عُذِّبَ.

But as for he who is given his record in his left hand, he will say, "How I wish I had not been given my record. And that I had not known what my account was!"

Exegetes have given several possible reasons why the wretched are given their records from behind their backs:[46]

i) Because their right hands will be chained to their neck and their left hand chained to their backs.

ii) That their faces will be inverted to face their backs. In this regard Q4:47 states:

مِنْ قَبْلِ أَنْ نَطْمِسَ وُجُوهًا فَنَرُدَّهَا عَلَىٰ أَدْبَارِهَا

...Before We alter faces then turn them backwards...

iii) It may also mean that when the record of deeds are given out, the righteous will walk with pride and dignity, while the criminal will put his record behind his back to hide it in shame and humiliation from others.

10-15.4 *'He will soon cry out for destruction,'*: [*Thubūrā* (ثُبُورا, destruction)] is derived from *thabara* meaning to perish and suffer great loss.[47] He will begin to cry out that he is destroyed (*wā thubūrā* was a cry of dismay used when faced with an ominous incident).[48]

Q78:40 states:

يَوْمَ يَنْظُرُ الْمَرْءُ مَا قَدَّمَتْ يَدَاهُ وَيَقُولُ الْكَافِرُ يَا لَيْتَنِي كُنْتُ تُرَابًا

...[On] the Day when man shall see what his two hands have sent forth, and the disbeliever shall say, "O! Would that I were dust!"

10-15.5 After the sinner is awarded his book behind his back, he too will be left for some time to digest its contents. The word *sawfa* (soon) indicates that after a short while, when his *ḥisāb* comes, he will reach the awful realization that his fate in Hell is assured. His soul has formed an evil disposition by his continuous sinning, and he cannot be purified at the stage of *ḥisāb*. Q2:81 states:

بَلَىٰ مَنْ كَسَبَ سَيِّئَةً وَأَحَاطَتْ بِهِ خَطِيئَتُهُ فَأُولَٰئِكَ

---

[46] Shīrāzī, *Namūneh*, 26/308.

[47] Muṣṭafawī, *al-Taḥqīq*.

[48] Shīrāzī, *Namūneh*, 26/308.

أَصْحَابُ النَّارِ هُمْ فِيهَا خَالِدُونَ

Yes, whoever earns evil, and his sin has encompassed him - those are the companions of the Fire; therein they shall abide.

10-15.6 *'And [enter to] burn in a blazing fire.'*: [*Yaṣlā* (يَصْلَا, burns)] is derived from *ṣalā*, meaning to be subject to fire and roast and burn therein.[49]

[*Saʿīr* (سَعِير, blazing fire)] is a fire which is extraordinarily hot and whose punishment is more severe than can be imagined.[50]

He will be made one with the Fire and his futile pleas for death will continue as he burns within its depths.[51] Q25:13 states:

وَإِذَا أُلْقُوا مِنْهَا مَكَانًا ضَيِّقًا مُقَرَّنِينَ دَعَوْا هُنَالِكَ ثُبُورًا

And when they are thrown into a narrow place therein, chained together, they will cry out therein for destruction (thubūrā).

10-15.7 *'Indeed, he used to be joyful amongst his folk.'*: Living a life of happiness surrounded by family and kinsfolk is not wrong, of course. However, even at these times, the believer maintains a balance and always has concern about his future in the next realm. He realizes that life in this world is like a game, and this prevents him from becoming overly joyful or overly despondent at what it offers. Q29:64 states:

وَمَا هَٰذِهِ الْحَيَاةُ الدُّنْيَا إِلَّا لَهْوٌ وَلَعِبٌ وَإِنَّ الدَّارَ الْآخِرَةَ
لَهِيَ الْحَيَوَانُ لَوْ كَانُوا يَعْلَمُونَ

And the life of this world is nothing but diversion and amusement. And indeed, the abode of the Hereafter – that is [true] life, if only they knew.

On the other hand, the disbeliever has no such concern at all. In the verse under review, the reason given for his miserable fate is that he had led a carefree and happy life with his family. He did whatever he liked, he did not care for God and His commandments, and he had no other purpose beyond the *dunyā*. This kind of unrestricted

---

[49] Rāghib, *al-Mufradāt*.

[50] Ṭabāṭabā'ī, *al-Mīzān*, 20/243.

[51] Rāzī, *Mafātīḥ al-Ghayb*, 31/99.

happiness is called *faraḥ* (exultation), and it is condemned in the Qur'an. Q40:75 states that those sent to Hell will be told:

ذَٰلِكُم بِمَا كُنتُمْ تَفْرَحُونَ فِي الْأَرْضِ بِغَيْرِ الْحَقِّ وَبِمَا كُنتُمْ تَمْرَحُونَ

That was because you used to exult (tafraḥūn) *in the earth without right and you used to behave insolently.*

This happiness that has been condemned in the verse under review denotes the feeling that comes to man when he thinks he has achieved his objectives. They have no fear of God or the Hereafter. For such people, the world is everything, and that is why they can only feel happiness when they receive something of the *dunyā*.[52]

10-15.8 '*Indeed, he had thought he would never return [to God].*': [*Ẓanna* (ظَنَّ, he thought)]. *Ẓann* can have two meanings: conjecture and certainty. Here it means that he was certain that there would be no resurrection.[53]

[*Yaḥūr* (يَحُور, return)] is derived from *ḥawr* meaning to return or to come and go. Words such as *miḥwar* (a point around which something returns), *muḥāwarah* (exchange of ideas), and *ḥawāriyyūn* (disciples of Isa (a) who came and went with him) are derived from this root. Here, it is referring to the return to God (*maʿād*) on the Day of Judgement for accounting and recompense.[54]

10-15.9 Such a person believed that his short life of the *dunyā* was all there was for him, and he had to make the most of it for its own sake. He felt that if he missed out in this world, there would be no other chance to experience anything.[55] He did not believe that he would be returned to God to give account for his excesses.

A tradition from Lady Fatimah (a) states: I seek refuge in God from a return [to destitution] (*ḥawr*) after plenty [of blessings] (*kawr*).[56]

10-15.10 '*But yes! Indeed, his Lord was ever seeing him!*': The verse begins by rejecting the false notion that he would not return

---

[52] Modarresī, *Min Hudā al-Qur'an*, 17/447.

[53] Ṭabrasī, *al-Bayān*, 10/700.

[54] Ṭabāṭabā'ī, *al-Mīzān*, 20/243.

[55] Muṭahharī, (*Āshnāyī bā Qur'an*), *Āthār*, 28/467.

[56] Majlisī, *Biḥār*, 36/352.

عَنْ فَاطِمَةَ الزَّهْرَاءِ (عَلَيْهَا السَّلَامُ) – وَنَعُوذُ بِاللهِ مِنَ الْحَوْرِ بَعْدَ الْكَوْرِ أَيْ مِنَ النَّقْصِ بَعْدَ الزِّيَادَةِ.

to answer to God and then states that he should know that his Sustainer was constantly watchful over his conduct.[57]

[*Baṣīrā* (بَصِيرًا, seeing)] derived from *baṣara* meaning to see, and to have insight.[58] Here it means that his Lord is ever-Present to witness every act and intention for a Day of Accounting.[59] Q96:14 asks man a rhetorical question:

أَلَمْ يَعْلَمْ بِأَنَّ اللَّهَ يَرَىٰ

Does he not know that God sees?

DISCUSSION 2: THE RECORDS OF DEEDS

The records of deeds of human beings have been mentioned in many verses of the Qur'an. In some verses the term *kitāb* (book, record) has been used which has a much wider range of meanings, including the record of deeds. These records have also been called *ṭā'ir* (fate, omen, Q17:13), *ṣuḥuf* (scrolls, Q81:10), and *zubur* (transcripts, Q54:52).

These records had remained forgotten by man for a long time, but on the Day of Judgement they are finally opened. Now every individual is able to clearly see the real form of his deeds, fully revealed.

Q17:13 states

وَكُلَّ إِنْسَانٍ أَلْزَمْنَاهُ طَائِرَهُ فِي عُنُقِهِ وَنُخْرِجُ لَهُ يَوْمَ الْقِيَامَةِ كِتَابًا يَلْقَاهُ مَنْشُورًا

And We have fastened every man's deeds to his neck,
and on the Day of Judgement We shall produce for him
a written account which he will encounter wide open.

The meaning of the record being wide open is that the spiritual forms which were confined to *Sijjīn* or *'Illiyyūn* are now attached to the individual. Or alternatively, the records of deeds that are stored in *Sijjīn* or *'Illiyyūn* are transported and 'fly back' to attach themselves to their owners, and give deeper layers of meaning to the memory of deeds that is already embedded in their souls. And this is what is referred to as the distribution of records or "*tatāyur al-kutub*".[60]

---

[57] Ṭabāṭabā'ī, *al-Mīzān*, 20/244.

[58] Muṣṭafawī, *al-Taḥqīq*.

[59] Shīrāzī, *Namūneh*, 26/310.

[60] Bahmanpour, *Towards Eternal Life*, p. 105.

The guilty will already have a growing realization of their fate. As the records arrive, they will be filled with a sense of foreboding.

Q18:49 states:

وَوُضِعَ الْكِتَابُ فَتَرَى الْمُجْرِمِينَ مُشْفِقِينَ مِمَّا فِيهِ

And the book [of deeds] will be placed [open], and you will see the criminals fearful of that [which is recorded] within it...

A tradition from Imam al-Sadiq (a) states: The servant will recall every deed that he performed and was written against him as if he was doing the act at that very moment. This is the meaning of their words, '*Oh, woe to us! What is this book that leaves nothing small or great except that it has enumerated it?*' (Q18:49).[61]

Only those who receive their records in the right hand are able to appreciate its status and understand (or read) its contents, which are the true forms of their deeds. As for those whose records are received in the left hand, they will be bewildered and unable to make proper sense of its contents. The Qur'an calls them blind. Q17:71,72 state:

يَوْمَ نَدْعُو كُلَّ أُنَاسٍ بِإِمَامِهِمْ فَمَنْ أُوتِيَ كِتَابَهُ بِيَمِينِهِ فَأُولَٰئِكَ يَقْرَؤُونَ كِتَابَهُمْ وَلَا يُظْلَمُونَ فَتِيلًا ﴿٧١﴾ وَمَنْ كَانَ فِي هَٰذِهِ أَعْمَىٰ فَهُوَ فِي الْآخِرَةِ أَعْمَىٰ وَأَضَلُّ سَبِيلًا

[On] the Day when We shall summon every person with their Imam [record [of deeds]. Then those who are given their book in the right hand will read their records, and the least injustice will not be done to them. But whoever was blind in this world, shall be blind in the Hereafter and most astray from the Path."

Different types of Books

The Qur'an speaks of three books for mankind.[62]

1. The individual book or record of the deeds for each human being. This book is produced by the recording angels who accompany him in his life in the *dunyā* and contain a comprehensive account

---

[61] 'Ayyāshī, *Tafsīr*, 2/284.

عَنِ الصَّادِقِ (عَلَيْهِ السَّلَامُ) - قَالَ يَذَّكَّرُ الْعَبْدُ جَمِيعَ مَا عَمِلَ وَمَا كُتِبَ عَلَيْهِ حَتَّى كَأَنَّهُ فَعَلَهُ تِلْكَ السَّاعَةَ فَلِذَلِكَ قَوْلُهُ: «يَا وَيْلَتَنَا مَا لِهَٰذَا الْكِتَابِ لَا يُغَادِرُ صَغِيرَةً وَلَا كَبِيرَةً إِلَّا أَحْصَاهَا».

[62] Shīrāzī, *Payām-i Qur'an*, 6/87.

of all his deeds. This is the record that will be given to some in their right hand and to others in their left hand or behind their back.

2. The books of nations, which contain the deeds of nations of God's Prophets (a). Q45:28 states:

وَتَرَىٰ كُلَّ أُمَّةٍ جَاثِيَةً كُلُّ أُمَّةٍ تُدْعَىٰ إِلَىٰ كِتَابِهَا الْيَوْمَ تُجْزَوْنَ مَا كُنْتُمْ تَعْمَلُونَ

And you will see every nation kneeling [in humbleness].
Every nation will be called to its record [and told],
"Today you will be recompensed for what you used to do."

3. A Master Book, which contains the records of all nations from the first to the last. Q36:12 states:

إِنَّا نَحْنُ نُحْيِي الْمَوْتَىٰ وَنَكْتُبُ مَا قَدَّمُوا وَآثَارَهُمْ
وَكُلَّ شَيْءٍ أَحْصَيْنَاهُ فِي إِمَامٍ مُبِينٍ

Indeed, it is We who bring the dead to life and record what
they have sent forth and We have recorded everything
in a [single] clear register (imāmin mubīn).

SUMMARY OF THE VERSES

The verses state that the one who will receive his record of deeds from behind his back will call for his destruction as he is made to enter the blazing fire. His fate is due to his carefree life amongst his relatives, thinking that he would never have to return to face God. However, God was always witnessing his acts.

REFLECTIVE LEARNING

When we are given our books, we will judge ourselves before God judges us. The manner in which we judge others in this life reveals our true nature. If we are quick to find fault in others, then on that Day we may find our own reckoning to be strict.

Let me reflect on how I judge others in this life. Would I want to be judged in the same manner myself on that Day?

VERSES 16 - 19

فَلَا أُقْسِمُ بِالشَّفَقِ ﴿١٦﴾ وَاللَّيْلِ وَمَا وَسَقَ ﴿١٧﴾ وَالْقَمَرِ إِذَا اتَّسَقَ ﴿١٨﴾
لَتَرْكَبُنَّ طَبَقًا عَنْ طَبَقٍ ﴿١٩﴾

So I swear by the twilight glow. [16] *And [by] the night and what it envelops.* [17] *And [by] the moon when it becomes full.* [18] *[That] you will certainly travel (experience) stage after stage.* [19]

16-19.1 Three oaths are made at this point as evidence to substantiate the premise mentioned earlier in verse 6, *'O man! Indeed, you are constantly labouring towards your Lord with [great] exertion until you shall meet Him'*, and to present the subject (*jawāb*) of these oaths: *'You shall certainly travel stage after stage.'* In other words, while everyone will meet his Lord, this process will unfold gradually, stage by stage. The reason for this is that the unalterable practice of God is that everything reaches its culmination in a gradual manner.[63]

16-19.2 *'So I swear by the twilight glow.'*: The conjunction *fa* (so) means that the upcoming verses are connected to the previous verses.

[*Lā Uqsimu* (لَا أُقْسِمُ, I swear)] is a type of oath that the Qur'an has used several times. We have discussed its usage further in the *tafsīr* of Surat al-Balad (90).

[*Shafaq* (شَفَق, twilight)] refers to the beautiful pale red glow in the sky that persists for a while at sunset.[64] It is defined as a blend of the light of the day with the darkness of the night.[65]

16-19.3 *'And [by] the night and what it envelops.'*: [*Wasaqa* (وَسَقَ, envelops)] means to engulf and gather up. The *mā* in the verse is *mā al-mawṣūlah* (conjunctive *mā*) and here means 'what'. The verse refers to the darkness of night which gradually covers everything that was visible in the day, causing birds, animals, and human beings to return to their homes for rest.[66] Q40:61 states:

اللهُ الَّذِي جَعَلَ لَكُمُ اللَّيْلَ لِتَسْكُنُوا فِيهِ

---

63 Iṣlāḥī, *Tadabbur-i Qur'an*, 9/227.
64 Ṭabrasī, *al-Bayān*, 10/700.
65 Rāghib, *al-Mufradāt*.
66 Shīrāzī, *Namūneh*, 26/314.

God is He who made for you the night so that you may rest therein...

16-19.4 *'And [by] the moon when it becomes full.'*: [*Ittasaq* (اتَّسَق, becomes full)] is derived from *wasaqa* as well and here it means to attain fullness. It refers to the moon which has grown stage by stage until it reaches its full size in the middle of the lunar month.

16-19.5 These three oaths, that follow the verses that spoke of man's gradual journey towards God, each describe a successive stage in the transformation of the day: twilight heralds the end of the day, the night covers the earth in darkness, and the bright moon restores light again. Similarly, the subject of the oath reminds man of his own stage-by-stage journey.[67]

16-19.6 *'[That] you will certainly travel (experience) stage after stage.'*: This is the subject (*jawāb*) of the oaths, and is addressed to all mankind.

[*Latarkabunna* (لَتَرْكَبُنَّ, you will certainly travel)] is derived from *rakiba* meaning to ride and embark. Here it is used in the emphatic form meaning 'you will certainly go or traverse through.'

[*Ṭabaq* (طَبَق, stage)] means one layer which is placed over another and gives a sense of progression. The *ṭabaqāt* refer to the different stages that man successively experiences in his journey and progress towards God.[68] He is conceived, then grows in the womb of his mother, then he is born into the world and matures from a child into an adult. In the process, he experiences difficulty after ease and ease after difficulty, poverty after wealth and wealth after poverty, sickness after health and health after sickness, and indeed, death after life and life after death.[69]

A tradition from Imam al-Sadiq (a) states: '*You will certainly travel stage after stage*' means that you will experience [the challenges of life] that generations before you also underwent.[70]

16-19.7 Man is reminded that he has already experienced many changes and there are many more yet to come. His current position

---

67 Ibid, 26/317.

68 Ṭabāṭabā'ī, *al-Mīzān*, 20/246.

69 Ṭabrasī, *al-Bayān*, 10/701.

70 *Tafsīr al-Ṣāfī*, 5/305.

عَنِ الصَّادِقِ (عَلَيْهِ السَّلَامُ) - «لَتَرْكَبُنَّ طَبَقاً عَنْ طَبَقٍ»أيْ سَيْرُ مَنْ كَانَ قَبْلَكُمْ.

is not one where he will stay long. And after he leaves the *dunyā*, *barzakh*, resurrection, accounting and many other stages await him.[71] And each stage will build on the previous one.

16-19.8 A tradition from Imam Ali (a) states: Alas at the sparseness of the provision, the length of the road, the distance of this journey, and the tremendousness of the objective![72]

SUMMARY OF THE VERSES

After making oaths by the twilight, the night whose darkness covers everything, and the moon when it reaches fullness, God states that man will travel on a journey of constant change, stage by stage.

REFLECTIVE LEARNING

The use of the phrase '*ṭabaqan ʿan ṭabaq* (stage after stage)' means that each layer of an individual's life is linked to the one before it. Everything man will experience in his future is predicated on how he lived his past. His Hereafter is similarly built on his life of the *dunyā*.[73]

Let me reflect on my past and add a layer of sincere *tawbā* immediately from which I can continue to build my future.

VERSES 20, 21

فَمَا لَهُمْ لَا يُؤْمِنُونَ ﴿٢٠﴾ وَإِذَا قُرِئَ عَلَيْهِمُ الْقُرْآنُ لَا يَسْجُدُونَ ۩ ﴿٢١﴾

So what is the matter with them [that] they do not believe? [20] *And when the Qur'an is recited to them, they do not prostrate themselves?* [21]

20-21.1 '*So what is the matter with them [that] they do not believe?*': The shift to the third person in address is to invoke wonder and disapproval at the defiant attitude of the disbelievers.[74] The verse asks that man has clearly seen that he, along with everything around him, is on a journey of change; why then does he not reflect

---

71 Muṭahharī, (*Āshnāyī bā Qur'an*), *Āthār*, 28/469.

72 *Nahj al-Balāghah*, saying 77.

آهٍ مِنْ قِلَّةِ الزَّادِ وَطُولِ الطَّرِيقِ وَبُعْدِ السَّفَرِ وَعَظِيمِ الْمَوْرِدِ.

73 Muṭahharī, (*Āshnāyī bā Qur'an*), *Āthār*, 28/470.

74 Ṭabāṭabā'ī, *al-Mīzān*, 20/243.

on this and realize that the journey will continue until a Day of Resurrection, Judgement, and Recompense?[75]

[*Lā yu'minūn* (لَا يُؤْمِنُونَ, they do not believe)] is derived from *īmān* which means belief and faith. It is a quality of the heart which starts in the mind before it becomes a conviction in the heart. Q49:14 states:

قَالَتِ الْأَعْرَابُ آمَنَّا قُلْ لَمْ تُؤْمِنُوا وَلَٰكِنْ قُولُوا
أَسْلَمْنَا وَلَمَّا يَدْخُلِ الْإِيمَانُ فِي قُلُوبِكُمْ

The Bedouins say, "We have believed." Say, "You have not [yet] believed; but say [instead], 'We have submitted,' for faith has not yet entered your hearts."

And faith would not enter hearts steeped in sin, as pointed out in Q83:14 which states:

كَلَّا بَلْ رَانَ عَلَىٰ قُلُوبِهِمْ مَا كَانُوا يَكْسِبُونَ

Not at all! Rather the stain of what they used to do has covered their hearts.

20-21.2 Despite clear signs within themselves and around them, the polytheists just took these signs for granted and refused to believe. They had forgotten or suppressed what was present in their *fiṭrah* and intellect.

A tradition from Imam al-Kazim (a) states: God has created two evidences (resources for guidance) for mankind: an external evidence and an internal evidence. The external [evidences] are the Messengers and the Imams, peace be upon them, and the internal [evidences] are the intellects.[76]

20-21.3 *'And when the Qur'an is recited to them, they do not prostrate themselves?'*: It was through the Qur'an that the disbelievers were invited to faith. The Arabs understood and valued eloquence in speech and the idolaters and disbelievers were forced to admit that the Qur'an was unmatched in its excellence. Many accepted that

[75] Shīrāzī, *Namūneh*, 26/317.

[76] Kulaynī, *al-Kāfī*, 1/13.

عَنِ الْكَاظِمِ (عَلَيْهِ السَّلَامُ) – إِنَّ لِلَّهِ عَلَى النَّاسِ حُجَّتَيْنِ حُجَّةً ظَاهِرَةً وَحُجَّةً بَاطِنَةً فَأَمَّا الظَّاهِرَةُ فَالرُّسُلُ وَالْأَئِمَّةُ عَلَيْهِمُ السَّلَامُ وَأَمَّا الْبَاطِنَةُ فَالْعُقُولُ.

this was a miracle and came to Islam. The verse asks the rest of them what was stopping them from acknowledging this truth and humbling themselves before God.[77]

[*Yasjudūn* (يَسْجُدُونَ, prostrate themselves)]. *Sajdah* here does not mean prostrating on the earth but denotes humbleness, prayer, submission, and obedience – because otherwise it would be necessary to prostrate on the ground after hearing any verse. Of course, the *sajdah* upon the earth is the greatest manifestation of these qualities.[78]

20-21.4 In this surah, God has made oaths by the deep night that gathers everything in the folds of its darkness and then by the full moon that illuminates the night. The Qur'an is the light that dispels the gloom of ignorance with the light of its guidance. Q69:38-40 state:

فَلَا أُقْسِمُ بِمَا تُبْصِرُونَ ﴿٣٨﴾ وَمَا لَا تُبْصِرُونَ ﴿٣٩﴾ إِنَّهُ لَقَوْلُ رَسُولٍ كَرِيمٍ

So I swear by what you see and what you do not see,
[that] indeed, the Qur'an is the word of a noble Messenger.

20-21.5 The message of the Qur'an resonates with the *fiṭrah* that is coded into every human being and it brings about humbleness and submission in the heart of any freethinking person who wants to be guided. However, those whose minds are closed and hearts are blocked from receiving knowledge and guidance would deny its message. Q17:107 states:

قُلْ آمِنُوا بِهِ أَوْ لَا تُؤْمِنُوا إِنَّ الَّذِينَ أُوتُوا الْعِلْمَ مِنْ قَبْلِهِ
إِذَا يُتْلَىٰ عَلَيْهِمْ يَخِرُّونَ لِلْأَذْقَانِ سُجَّدًا

Say: Believe in it or do not believe. Indeed, those who were
given knowledge before it – when it is recited to them,
they fall upon their faces in prostration.

20-21.6 The verse under review, as well as Q17:107 above, are from the recommended verses of prostration. We have discussed the verses of prostration in the *tafsīr* of Surat al-ʿAlaq (96).

---

[77] Rāzī, *Mafātīḥ al-Ghayb*, 31/104.
[78] Shīrāzī, *Namūneh*, 26/318.

SUMMARY OF THE VERSES

The verses ask two questions: what prevents the disbelievers from accepting faith? And why do they not humble themselves before God when the verses of the Qur'an are recited to them?

REFLECTIVE LEARNING

Let me reflect on what factors prevent me from humbling myself before the teachings of the Qur'an and completely submitting to God's will.

VERSES 22 - 25

بَلِ الَّذِينَ كَفَرُوا يُكَذِّبُونَ ﴿٢٢﴾ وَاللَّهُ أَعْلَمُ بِمَا يُوعُونَ ﴿٢٣﴾ فَبَشِّرْهُمْ بِعَذَابٍ أَلِيمٍ
﴿٢٤﴾ إِلَّا الَّذِينَ آمَنُوا وَعَمِلُوا الصَّالِحَاتِ لَهُمْ أَجْرٌ غَيْرُ مَمْنُونٍ ﴿٢٥﴾

But those who disbelieve will deny. [22] *And God knows best what they hide.* [23] *So give them tidings of a painful punishment.* [24] *Except for those who believe and do righteous deeds. For them is a reward uninterrupted.* [25]

22-25.1 *'But those who disbelieve will deny.'*: [*Yukaddhibūn* (يُكَذِّبُونَ, they deny)] is derived from *kadhdhaba*, which means to deny something out of defiance.[79] The verse is in the continuous (*muḍāriʿ*) tense indicating that disbelievers continued to deny the truth, especially the Resurrection. Q16:38 states:

وَأَقْسَمُوا بِاللَّهِ جَهْدَ أَيْمَانِهِمْ لَا يَبْعَثُ اللَّهُ مَنْ يَمُوتُ

And they swear by Allah their most binding oaths [that] Allah will not resurrect one who dies...

In the verse under review, the reason for their denial is given as their wilful covering (*kufr*) of what they knew instinctively to be true. They called the Prophet (s) a liar and refused to show humility. This could have been due to their stubborn adherence to the beliefs of their predecessors, or due to their prejudice and jealousy, or due to the fact that accepting Islam would force them to give up the lifestyle that they were accustomed to.[80]

---

[79] Rāghib, *al-Mufradāt.*

[80] Shīrāzī, *Namūneh*, 26/318.

22-25.2 The knowledge of the Creator is coded deep in the soul of every single human being. No one will be able to truthfully deny this on the Day of Judgement. Q7:172 states:

وَإِذْ أَخَذَ رَبُّكَ مِنْ بَنِي آدَمَ مِنْ ظُهُورِهِمْ ذُرِّيَّتَهُمْ وَأَشْهَدَهُمْ عَلَىٰ أَنْفُسِهِمْ أَلَسْتُ بِرَبِّكُمْ قَالُوا بَلَىٰ شَهِدْنَا أَنْ تَقُولُوا يَوْمَ الْقِيَامَةِ إِنَّا كُنَّا عَنْ هَٰذَا غَافِلِينَ

And [mention] when your Lord drew forth their descendants from the loins of the children of Adam and made them testify about themselves, [saying], "Am I not your Lord?" They said, "Yes, we do testify." [This] - lest you say on the Day of Judgement, "Indeed, we were unaware of this."

22-25.3 *'And God knows best what they hide.'*: [*Yūʿūn* (يوعون, they hide)] is derived from *waʿy* meaning to retain in memory or hoard in a container.[81] The term is used in Q70:18 for those who hoard. In the verse under review, it refers to what the disbelievers hoarded in their breasts of polytheism, defiance, and malevolence,[82] which is the output of hearts hardened with sin and rancour. They either hide, or are oblivious to, the reason and reality of the evil that they do. Only God is completely aware of what is hidden within them, and the various reasons for their behaviour. Q11:5 states:

أَلَا إِنَّهُمْ يَثْنُونَ صُدُورَهُمْ لِيَسْتَخْفُوا مِنْهُ أَلَا حِينَ يَسْتَغْشُونَ ثِيَابَهُمْ يَعْلَمُ مَا يُسِرُّونَ وَمَا يُعْلِنُونَ إِنَّهُ عَلِيمٌ بِذَاتِ الصُّدُورِ

Behold! They (the disbelievers) fold up their breasts to hide [their thoughts] from Him! Indeed [even] when they cover themselves in their garments, He knows what they conceal and what they declare. Indeed, He knows well what is in the hearts.

We have discussed the diseases of the spiritual heart in the *tafsīr* of Surat al-Muṭaffifīn (83).

22-25.4 The prostration that would have brought them close to God will be denied to them forever, because of the latent arrogance they harbour in their hearts. Q68:42,43 state:

يَوْمَ يُكْشَفُ عَنْ سَاقٍ وَيُدْعَوْنَ إِلَى السُّجُودِ فَلَا يَسْتَطِيعُونَ ﴿٤٢﴾ خَاشِعَةً أَبْصَارُهُمْ تَرْهَقُهُمْ ذِلَّةٌ وَقَدْ كَانُوا يُدْعَوْنَ إِلَى السُّجُودِ وَهُمْ سَالِمُونَ

81 Muṣṭafawī, *al-Taḥqīq*.

82 Ṭabāṭabā'ī, *al-Mīzān*, 20/246.

On the Day when dreadful events will unfold, and they shall be called upon to prostrate, but they (the disbelievers) shall not be able. Their eyes humbled, humiliation will cover them. And they used to be invited to prostration while they were sound [but they did not].

22-25.5 *'So give them tidings of a painful punishment.'*: The usage of the conjunction *fa* (so) indicates that the verse is a consequence of the rancour harboured by the deniers mentioned in the previous verses.

[*Bashshirhum* (بَشِّرْهُم, give them tidings)] is derived from *bashara* meaning to rejoice and be happy. *Bashārah* normally refers to good news. However, here it is used in irony to severely warn the disbelievers. That is, if they are not ready to hear the good news of salvation, then the Prophet (s) should announce to them the good news of torment.[83] They are compiling for themselves a record of deeds that will be given to them from behind their backs. And thereafter, their abode will be the fire of Hell.

22-25.6 *'Except for those who believe and do righteous deeds. For them is a reward uninterrupted.'*: [*Illā* (إِلَّا, except)] can be of two types. One is an exception (*istithnā'*) that excludes a group taken from a larger group (*al-muttaṣil*, attached) and the other excludes a group from another which they are not part of (*al-munfaṣil*, separate).

If it is taken in the former meaning,[84] the verse is speaking of the chance to change one's fate through repentance, bringing faith, and acting righteously.

If we take the latter meaning,[85] the verse would not be referring to the disbelievers, but rather those who believed and thereafter, performed righteous actions. They will receive their record of deeds in their right hands and will be admitted to Paradise.

There, unlike in the *dunyā*, they will receive God's bounties perpetually, without obligation, and without reduction, and these are all meanings of *ghayru mamnūn*.[86]

---

[83] Iṣlāḥī, *Tadabbur-i Qur'an*, 9/228.

[84] Muṭahharī, (*Āshnāyī bā Qur'an*), *Āthār*, 28/473.

[85] Ṭabāṭabā'ī, *al-Mīzān*, 20/246.

[86] Rāzī, *Mafātīḥ al-Ghayb*, 31/105.

SUMMARY OF THE VERSES

There are people who deny the truth of the Qur'an because of their defiant disbelief. And God knows what rancour they harbour. So these should be warned about a painful punishment. However, if they were to [repent and] accept the faith and perform righteous deeds, then they would be eternally rewarded [in Paradise].

REFLECTIVE LEARNING

Let me reflect on the justifications and excuses that I make for denying God's guidance, knowing that He sees the truth that I conceal in my heart.

SURAT AL-BURUJ
THE CONSTELLATIONS (85)

TEXT AND TRANSLATION

سُورَةُ الْبُرُوجِ

بِسْمِ اللَّهِ الرَّحْمَٰنِ الرَّحِيمِ

وَالسَّمَاءِ ذَاتِ الْبُرُوجِ ﴿١﴾ وَالْيَوْمِ الْمَوْعُودِ ﴿٢﴾ وَشَاهِدٍ وَمَشْهُودٍ ﴿٣﴾ قُتِلَ
أَصْحَابُ الْأُخْدُودِ ﴿٤﴾ النَّارِ ذَاتِ الْوَقُودِ ﴿٥﴾ إِذْ هُمْ عَلَيْهَا قُعُودٌ ﴿٦﴾ وَهُمْ
عَلَىٰ مَا يَفْعَلُونَ بِالْمُؤْمِنِينَ شُهُودٌ ﴿٧﴾ وَمَا نَقَمُوا مِنْهُمْ إِلَّا أَنْ يُؤْمِنُوا بِاللَّهِ الْعَزِيزِ
الْحَمِيدِ ﴿٨﴾ الَّذِي لَهُ مُلْكُ السَّمَاوَاتِ وَالْأَرْضِ وَاللَّهُ عَلَىٰ كُلِّ شَيْءٍ شَهِيدٌ ﴿٩﴾
إِنَّ الَّذِينَ فَتَنُوا الْمُؤْمِنِينَ وَالْمُؤْمِنَاتِ ثُمَّ لَمْ يَتُوبُوا فَلَهُمْ عَذَابُ جَهَنَّمَ وَلَهُمْ عَذَابُ الْحَرِيقِ
﴿١٠﴾ إِنَّ الَّذِينَ آمَنُوا وَعَمِلُوا الصَّالِحَاتِ لَهُمْ جَنَّاتٌ تَجْرِي مِنْ تَحْتِهَا الْأَنْهَارُ ذَٰلِكَ
الْفَوْزُ الْكَبِيرُ ﴿١١﴾ إِنَّ بَطْشَ رَبِّكَ لَشَدِيدٌ ﴿١٢﴾ إِنَّهُ هُوَ يُبْدِئُ وَيُعِيدُ ﴿١٣﴾
وَهُوَ الْغَفُورُ الْوَدُودُ ﴿١٤﴾ ذُو الْعَرْشِ الْمَجِيدُ ﴿١٥﴾ فَعَّالٌ لِمَا يُرِيدُ ﴿١٦﴾
هَلْ أَتَاكَ حَدِيثُ الْجُنُودِ ﴿١٧﴾ فِرْعَوْنَ وَثَمُودَ ﴿١٨﴾ بَلِ الَّذِينَ كَفَرُوا فِي تَكْذِيبٍ
﴿١٩﴾ وَاللَّهُ مِنْ وَرَائِهِمْ مُحِيطٌ ﴿٢٠﴾ بَلْ هُوَ قُرْآنٌ مَجِيدٌ ﴿٢١﴾ فِي لَوْحٍ مَحْفُوظٍ
﴿٢٢﴾

In the name of God, the Beneficent, the Merciful.

By the sky of constellations, [1] *and by the promised Day,* [2] *and by the witness and what is witnessed.* [3] *Cursed be the companions of the trench,* [4] *of the fire [well supplied] with fuel.* [5] *As they sat by it.* [6] *And they were witnesses to what they were doing against the believers.* [7] *And they did not resent them except because they believed in Allah, the Mighty, the Praiseworthy,* [8] *to Whom belongs the dominion of the heavens and the earth. And Allah is a Witness over all things.* [9] *Indeed, those who persecute the believing men and believing women and then do not repent will have the punishment of Hell, and they will have the punishment of the burning Fire.* [10] *Indeed, those who believe and do righteous deeds will have gardens beneath which rivers flow. That is the great attainment.* [11] *Indeed, the strike of your Lord is severe.* [12] *Indeed, it is He who originates [creation] and brings it back.* [13] *And He is the all-Forgiving, the all-Affectionate,* [14] *Owner of the throne, the all-Glorious,* [15] *the all-Accomplishing of whatever He wills.* [16] *Has the story of the soldiers reached you,* [17] *[those of] Firʿawn and Thamud?* [18] *But they who disbelieve are in [persistent] denial,* [19] *while God encompasses them from behind.* [20] *But it is a glorious Qur'an,* [21] *[inscribed] on a preserved Tablet.* [22]

INTRODUCTION

Surat al-Burūj (85) was the 27th chapter to be revealed.[1] It has twenty-two verses and is a Makkan surah, revealed after Surat al-Shams (91). It is named after the mention of the constellations of stars (*burūj*) in the oath contained in its first verse.

At the time of the revelation of the surah, the Muslims were constantly being tormented by the polytheists of Makka, purely because of their faith. The surah reassured the Prophet (s) of God's imminent help and strengthened the spirits of the believers so that they could remain steadfast in their religion.[2]

Throughout the surah, two opposing traits are contrasted: God's wrath with His mercy, the fate of the evildoers with that of the faithful, and God's punishment with His forgiveness.

The surah recounts a horrendous instance of torture well known to the Quraysh, namely the atrocities of the people of the trench (*aṣḥāb al-ukhdūd*). God presents the example of the people of Ukhdūd, a community of believers who followed Christianity which was the true religion at the time.[3] They were cruelly put to death only because they refused to abandon their faith. Two further groups who persecuted the believers are also mentioned: the hosts of Firʿawn and Thamūd.

The surah contains a severe warning of God's chastisement to those who torment the believing men and women because of their faith.

---

[1] Maʿrifat, *ʿUlūm-i Qur'ānī*, p. 90.

[2] Ṭabāṭabā'ī, *al-Mīzān*, 20/249.

[3] Muṭahharī, (*Āshnāyī bā Qur'an*), *Āthār*, 28/479.

Thereafter, it mentions the reward of those who believe and do righteous deeds.

The surah ends with a mention of the eminence of the Qur'an; it is the exalted Word of God that is inscribed in a preserved Tablet.

LINK TO THE PREVIOUS CHAPTER

The previous chapter, Surat al-Inshiqāq, began with the mention of the sky being split open. The destruction of the sky is mentioned repeatedly in preceding chapters as well, such as al-Takwīr (81) and al-Infiṭār (82). However, Surat al-Burūj speaks of the beautiful sky, as yet unmarked by the tumultuous events that it will go through at the end of the *dunyā*.

Whenever man looks at the protective canopy of the stars in the sky above, he should be reminded that a Day will arrive when the sky will be torn into shreds and the stars will be in disarray.

Both surahs state that the disbelievers deny the truth. In Surat al-Inshiqāq, it is stated as a fact: '*But those who disbelieve will deny.*' (verse 22). In Surat al-Burūj, the situation of the disbelievers is much worse – they are completely encased in a cocoon of stubborn denial: '*But they who disbelieve are in [persistent] denial*' (verse 19).

MERITS OF RECITATION

- A tradition from the Prophet (s) states: Whoever recites this surah shall have a great reward and will be secure from fears and difficulties.[4]
- A tradition from Imam al-Sadiq (a) states: Whoever recites '*wa al-samā'i dhāt al-burūj*' – which is the surah of the Prophets (a) – in his obligatory prayers, will be resurrected with the Prophets, Messengers, and the righteous, and will be in their company thereafter.[5]

[4] Baḥrānī, *al-Burhān*, 5/621.

عَنِ الرَّسُولِ (صَلَّى اللّٰهُ عَلَيْهِ وَآلِهِ) – مَنْ قَرَأَهَا كَانَ لَهُ أَجْرٌ عَظِيمٌ، وَأَمِنَ مِنَ الْمَخَاوِفِ وَالشَّدَائِدِ.

[5] ʿĀmilī, *Wasā'il*, 6/149.

عَنِ الصَّادِقِ (عَلَيْهِ السَّلَامُ) – مَنْ قَرَأَ «وَالسَّمَاءِ ذَاتِ الْبُرُوجِ» فِي فَرَائِضِهِ فَإِنَّهَا سُورَةُ النَّبِيِّينَ كَانَ مَحْشَرُهُ وَمَوْقِفُهُ مَعَ النَّبِيِّينَ وَالْمُرْسَلِينَ وَالصَّالِحِينَ.

EXEGESIS

VERSES 1 - 3

وَالسَّمَاءِ ذَاتِ الْبُرُوجِ ﴿١﴾ وَالْيَوْمِ الْمَوْعُودِ ﴿٢﴾ وَ شَاهِدٍ وَمَشْهُودٍ ﴿٣﴾

By the sky of constellations, [1] *and by the promised Day,* [2] *and by the witness and what is witnessed.* [3]

1-3.1 The surah begins with three oaths made by great phenomena, to emphasize the matter that follows.

1-3.2 '*By the sky of constellations*': [*Samā'* (سَمَاء, sky)] refers to the layer beyond the earth that surrounds and protects it.

[*Burūj* (بُرُوج, constellations)] (sing. *burj*) is derived from *baraja* meaning to be high and visible. It refers to lofty objects that are clearly seen and attract attention from a distance. It thereafter acquired a meaning of something that protects and guards, and the term is normally used to describe high towers and forts.[6] It is used in this meaning in Q4:78 which states:

أَيْنَمَا تَكُونُوا يُدْرِكْكُمُ الْمَوْتُ وَلَوْ كُنْتُمْ فِي بُرُوجٍ مُشَيَّدَةٍ

Wherever you may be, death will overtake you, even if you should be within towers (burūj) *of lofty construction.*

1-3.3 In astronomy, *burūj* has acquired a technical meaning, and denotes the large stars and constellations in the sky.

Some exegetes have said that *burūj* refers to the 12 constellations or mansions of the zodiac.[7] The zodiac is an imaginary belt containing 12 constellations that lie along the annual path of the sun across the sky. Each constellation occupies 30 degrees of celestial longitude.

The moon passes through each of these mansions every two and one-third days and completes its journey every twenty-seven and one-third days (the sidereal month), and it is hidden for two nights. The sun passes through each mansion in one month.[8]

Indeed, the *burūj* are from God's great signs. Q25:61 states:

---

[6] Muṣṭafawī, *al-Taḥqīq*.

[7] Rāzī, *Mafātīḥ al-Ghayb*, 31/106.

[8] Ṭusī, *al-Tibyān*, 10/316.

تَبَارَكَ الَّذِي جَعَلَ فِي السَّمَاءِ بُرُوجًا وَجَعَلَ فِيهَا سِرَاجًا وَقَمَرًا مُنِيرًا

Blessed is He who has placed in the sky great stars (burūj) *and placed therein a [burning] lamp and luminous moon.*

1-3.4 In the verse under review, the sky has been defined as *dhāt al-burūj* referring to:[9]

i) its vital role in protecting the earth from harmful radiation, space debris, and other dangers,

ii) its population of beautiful and awe-inspiring constellations of great stars that decorate its black expanse with colour.

Both these roles have been mentioned in Q15:16,17 which state:

وَلَقَدْ جَعَلْنَا فِي السَّمَاءِ بُرُوجًا وَزَيَّنَّاهَا لِلنَّاظِرِينَ ﴿١٦﴾

وَحَفِظْنَاهَا مِنْ كُلِّ شَيْطَانٍ رَجِيمٍ

And certainly We have placed great stars (constellations) in the heaven and have beautified it for the beholders. And We have guarded it from every outcast satan.

1-3.5 '*And by the promised Day,*': [*al-yawm al-mawʿūd* (الْيَوْمِ الْمَوْعُودِ, the promised Day)] is the Day of Judgement on which God has promised to gather mankind for accounting, after which He will pass His judgement over them.[10]

1-3.6 '*And by the witness and what is witnessed.*': [*Shāhidin wa mashhūd* (شَاهِدٍ وَمَشْهُودٍ, the witness and the witnessed)]. *Shāhid* can mean both one who gives witness by testifying, and one who witnesses (sees) by being present.[11]

Some exegetes have said that that *shahādah* in this verse means 'seeing' because if it meant 'testifying', the verse would have added the preposition (*al-ṣilah*) by stating *mashhūd ʿalayhi* (witnessed against) or *mashhūdin lahu* (witnessing for).[12] However, others say that the meaning is apparent and *mashhūd* can be used to mean *mashhūd ʿalayhi*, just as God has used *mas'ūlan* instead of *mas'ūlan ʿanhu* in Q17:34.[13]

---

9 Shīrāzī, *Namūneh*, 26/328.

10 Ṭabrasī, *al-Bayān*, 10/708.

11 Rāzī, *Mafātīḥ al-Ghayb*, 31/106.

12 Ṭabāṭabā'ī, *al-Mīzān*, 20/249.

13 Rāzī, *Mafātīḥ al-Ghayb*, 31/106.

1-3.7 Because the terms have been mentioned in the indefinite form in the verse, and the witness and the witnessed are not identified, the exegetes have made many suggestions about who or what they are referring to. Some possibilities about *shāhid* in the meaning of being present are:

i) That *Shāhid* refers to God who is ever-Present, and *mashhūd* are the creation, over whom He is ever-Watchful.[14] Q41:53 states:

أَوَلَمْ يَكْفِ بِرَبِّكَ أَنَّهُ عَلَىٰ كُلِّ شَيْءٍ شَهِيدٌ

...Is it not sufficient concerning your Lord that He is a Witness over all things?

ii) That *mashhūd* refers to the Day of Judgement and *shāhid* refers to everyone who will be present on that Day to witness its events. Q11:103 states:

ذَٰلِكَ يَوْمٌ مَّجْمُوعٌ لَّهُ النَّاسُ وَذَٰلِكَ يَوْمٌ مَّشْهُودٌ

...That is a Day for which the people will be gathered, and that is a Day [which will be] witnessed.

iii) That *shāhid* is the day of Jumuʿah which witnesses the worship of the *ummah* on that day, and *mashhūd* is the day of ʿArafah on which pilgrims from every remote place come to witness their blessings.[15] Q22:27,28 state:

وَأَذِّن فِي النَّاسِ بِالْحَجِّ يَأْتُوكَ رِجَالًا وَعَلَىٰ كُلِّ ضَامِرٍ
يَأْتِينَ مِن كُلِّ فَجٍّ عَمِيقٍ ﴿٢٧﴾ لِّيَشْهَدُوا مَنَافِعَ لَهُمْ

And proclaim to the people the Hajj [pilgrimage]; they will come to you on foot and on every lean camel; they will come from every distant pass – that they may witness benefits for themselves...

A tradition from the Imams al-Baqir (a) and al-Sadiq (a) states: The witness is the day of Jumuʿah, the witnessed is the day of ʿArafah, and the promised [Day] is the Day of Judgement.[16]

---

[14] Ibid, 31/108.

[15] Ṭabrasī, *al-Bayān*, 10/708.

[16] ʿĀmilī, *Wasā'il*, 13/549.

عَنِ الصَّادِقَيْنِ (عَلَيْهِمَا السَّلَامُ) – الشَّاهِدُ يَوْمُ الْجُمُعَةِ وَالْمَشْهُودُ يَوْمُ عَرَفَةَ وَالْمَوْعُودُ يَوْمُ الْقِيَامَةِ.

Some possibilities about *shāhid* meaning those who will give witness and testify are:

i) That *shāhid* refers to the Prophet (s) who will bear witness over his own nation and *mashhūd* refers to the Day of Judgement on which this witnessing will take place. Q16:89 states:

وَجِئْنَا بِكَ شَهِيدًا عَلَىٰ هَٰؤُلَاءِ

...And We will bring you, [O Muhammad], as a witness over these [people]...

ii) That *shāhid* refers to the limbs of human beings which will testify against or for them on the Day of Judgement and *mashhūd* refers to the people and their deeds. Q36:65 states:

الْيَوْمَ نَخْتِمُ عَلَىٰ أَفْوَاهِهِمْ وَتُكَلِّمُنَا أَيْدِيهِمْ وَتَشْهَدُ أَرْجُلُهُمْ بِمَا كَانُوا يَكْسِبُونَ

That Day, We will set a seal over their mouths; and their hands will speak to Us and their feet will testify about what they used to do.

iii) That *shāhid* refers to the angels who will testify about their recor-ding of the deeds of the people and *mashhūd* are the individuals whom they will testify for or against.[17]

Q50:21 states:

وَجَاءَتْ كُلُّ نَفْسٍ مَعَهَا سَائِقٌ وَشَهِيدٌ

And every person will come forth along with a driver and a witness.

1-3.8 *Shāhid* refers to every witness and *mashhūd* refers to anything that is witnessed. However, the relationship of this verse with the previous one suggests that this witnessing is referring to the Day of Judgement on which several witnesses will be brought forth, including the Prophets (a), the angels, and even the limbs of individuals, to bear witness against them or their actions.[18]

1-3.9 These three oaths are made to emphasize God's stern warning to those who torment and oppress the believing men and women because of their faith, and also to emphasize His reassuring promise to those who believe and perform acts of goodness. It is like saying: I swear by the sky of constellations through which God disperses the

[17] Ṭabrasī, *al-Bayān*, 10/708.

[18] Shīrāzī, *Namūneh*, 26/332.

satans, that God will protect the faith of the believers from the plots of Shaytan and his accomplices from amongst the disbelievers. And I swear by the promised Day on which mankind will be recompensed for their deeds. And I swear by the witness who witnesses the actions of those disbelievers against the faithful believers.[19]

SUMMARY OF THE VERSES

God begins the surah with oaths by three phenomena: by the sky containing constellations, by the promised Day of Judgement, and by the witness and what is witnessed.

REFLECTIVE LEARNING

As we discussed, *shāhid* also refers to those who will give witness and testify to my actions.

Let me reflect on what the testimony of the Prophet (s), the angels, and even my limbs, will be like on that Day.

VERSES 4 - 7

قُتِلَ أَصْحَابُ الْأُخْدُودِ ﴿٤﴾ النَّارِ ذَاتِ الْوَقُودِ ﴿٥﴾ إِذْ هُمْ عَلَيْهَا قُعُودٌ ﴿٦﴾ وَهُمْ
عَلَىٰ مَا يَفْعَلُونَ بِالْمُؤْمِنِينَ شُهُودٌ ﴿٧﴾

Cursed be the companions of the trench, [4] *of the fire [well supplied] with fuel.* [5] *As they sat by it.* [6] *And they were witnesses to what they were doing against the believers.* [7]

4-7.1 There is a discussion amongst the exegetes about the subject (*jawāb*) of the three oaths. The *jawāb* is the premise on which evidence is presented through an oath, and here it appears to be missing.

Some exegetes have said that the *jawāb* is actually verse 4, but there is an omission (ellipsis, *ḥadhf*) of the particle '*la*' (surely) at the beginning of the verse – *qutila* instead of *laqutila*. Others have said that the *jawāb* is verse 12, '*Indeed, the strike of your Lord is severe.*'[20]

It may also be that the *jawāb* has been omitted because it is so obvious that a person's mind comprehends it even if it is not

---

[19] Ṭabāṭabā'ī, *al-Mīzān*, 20/249.

[20] Rāzī, *Mafātīḥ al-Ghayb*, 31/109.

mentioned. The Day of Judgement will certainly come and on that Day, everyone will witness the outcome of their deeds.[21]

4-7.2 '*Cursed be the companions of the trench,*': [*Qutila* (قُتِلَ, killed, or cursed)]. There are different opinions about the usage of *qutila* in the verse:

i) Some exegetes have taken the word *qutila* in its literal meaning and as a statement of fact. In this case the verse would say, 'the companions of the trench were killed.' This itself may mean that *aṣḥāb al-ukhdūd* refers to the believers and they were killed, or that it refers to the killers themselves, and they were later killed by the fire that spilled over them.[22]

ii) However, most exegetes believe that *qutila* here is a curse and imprecation, and the verse means 'cursed be the companions of the trench.'[23] This is similar to the usage of the term in Q51:10:

قُتِلَ الْخَرَّاصُونَ

Cursed be the liars!

God's curse, '*may they be killed,*' was emphasized by three oaths. The consequence of the curse is that their hearts hardened so that the faith – which connects man to God – could never enter it.

Q5:13 states:

لَعَنَّاهُمْ وَجَعَلْنَا قُلُوبَهُمْ قَاسِيَةً

...We cursed them and made their hearts hard...

4-7.3 [*Ukhdūd* (أُخْدُود, trench)] refers to a ditch or trench dug in the ground.[24] As for *aṣḥāb al-ukhdūd*, some exegetes say it refers to the faithful Christians in that community who were burned to death. However, most exegetes are of the opinion that the context of the verses suggest that it refers to the perpetrators of this dreadful crime, especially verse 7, '*And they were witnesses to what they were doing against the believers.*'[25]

---

21 Iṣlāḥī, *Tadabbur-i Qur'an*, 9/237.

22 See: Rāzī, *Mafātīḥ al-Ghayb*, 31/110.

23 Ṭabāṭabā'ī, *al-Mīzān*, 20/251.

24 Rāghib, *al-Mufradāt*.

25 Ṭabāṭabā'ī, *al-Mīzān*, 20/251.

There are several reports found in the traditions about *aṣḥāb al-ukhdūd* and we have briefly discussed them later in the *tafsīr* of this surah.

4-7.4 The *aṣḥāb al-ukhdūd* were cursed for the terrible crime of burning people in the *dunyā* and God mentions their victims in the Qur'an to honour their sacrifice and because of their steadfastness in faith.[26] But the Qur'an only focuses on the actions of these people and does not mention anything about their identity. The scope of the verse includes every believer who stood fast on his faith against tyrants, even at the cost of his life.[27]

4-7.5 '*Of the fire [well supplied] with fuel.*': In linguistic terms, this verse is a substitute (*badal*) for the trench, giving further detail of its nature. It means, '*cursed be the companions of the fire [well supplied] with fuel.*'[28]

[*Waqūd* (وقود, fuel)] refers to the material that fuels a fire.[29]

Q2:24 states:

فَٱتَّقُوا النَّارَ الَّتِي وَقُودُهَا النَّاسُ وَالْحِجَارَةُ

...*So fear the Fire, whose fuel* (waqūd) *is men and stones, [it is] prepared for the disbelievers.*

The phrase *dhāt al-waqūd* (supplied with fuel) signifies that there was plentiful fuel in that fire.[30]

4-7.6 '*As they sat by it.*': *'Alayhā* (over it) in this verse means *'indahā* (by it) and refers to the men sitting around the fiery trench to watch as people were burning alive. This shows the depth of their cruelty and hard-heartedness.[31]

Although it is difficult to imagine how a group of people could sit around and watch people burn to death, there are many instances in history of ordinary people being inured to the suffering of others. For example, in ancient Rome, people would eagerly gather to

---

[26] Ṭūsī, *al-Tibyān*, 10/317.

[27] Ṭāliqānī, *Partovī az Qur'an*, 3/311.

[28] Ṭabāṭabā'ī, *al-Mīzān*, 20/251.

[29] Muṣṭafawī, *al-Taḥqīq*.

[30] Rāzī, *Mafātīḥ al-Ghayb*, 31/111.

[31] Shīrāzī, *Namūneh*, 26/334.

witness gladiatorial combat in arenas, where men fought and killed each other for public entertainment.

This hardening of the heart at the sight of brutal killing is an extreme case of what the psychologists called *Schadenfreude*. It is a word from German which means 'joy at seeing harm.' The causes of this behaviour are listed as:

i) feeling that the aggression is justified based on the group's shared belief,

ii) intense rivalry with another group that has hardened into jealousy and hatred, and

iii) a sense of deserved justice because the victims are perceived as evil or immoral.[32]

4-7.7 '*And they were witnesses to what they were doing against the believers*': [*Shuhūd* (شُهُود, witnesses)] (sing. *shāhid*) is the active participle of the verb *shahida* which means to be in attendance, as well as to testify. The believers were brought before the fire and asked to renounce their beliefs. Those who refused were cruelly pushed into the fire to burn to death therein.[33]

Some exegetes have said that the observers were comprised of those who were doing the interrogating and killing as well as others who were summoned to watch the cruel proceedings as a warning not to oppose the king.[34]

Others have said that those who were sitting around the pit wanted witnesses to testify to their leaders that they had not been remiss in carrying out their orders.[35]

Perhaps they committed these atrocities in the hope of gaining favour or wealth! It was for this reason that on the Day of Ashura, ʿUmar b. Saʿd made a show of firing the first arrow at the army of Imam al-Husayn (a), shouting, "Be my witnesses before the governor that I was the first to shoot."[36]

---

[32] Wang et al., "*Schadenfreude deconstructed and reconstructed: A tripartite motivational model*", *New Ideas in Psychology*, 52:1-11.

[33] Mughniyyah, *al-Kāshif*, 7/546.

[34] Modarresī, *Min Hudā al-Qur'an*, 17/471.

[35] Shīrāzī, *Namūneh*, 26/335.

[36] Ibn Ṭāwūs, *al-Malhūf*, p. 158.

فَتَقَدَّمَ عُمَرُ بْنُ سَعْدٍ، وَرَمَى نَحْوَ عَسْكَرِ الْحُسَيْنِ عَلَيْهِ السَّلَامُ بِسَهْمٍ، وَقَالَ: اِشْهَدُوا لِي عِنْدَ الْأَمِيرِ أَنِّي أَوَّلُ مَنْ رَمَى.

4-7.8 Some exegetes have said that *shahāda* here means testifying on the Day of Judgement. The criminals themselves would bear witness to their murder of the believers.[37]

4-7.9 The use of the verb *yafʿalūn* (what they were doing) in the continuous (*muḍāriʿ*) tense indicates that this despicable massacre continued for a lengthy time.[38]

4-7.10 The message to the believers in Makka was that their persecution was not a new thing. For the religion of Islam to prevail, they would have to bear with these hardships. And it would not be long before God's chastisement would overcome the evildoers.

The recompense of those who burned others in the fire in the *dunyā* will be the fire of Hell in the *ākhirah*. After mentioning a Fire whose fuel is men and stones, Q66:7 states:

يَا أَيُّهَا الَّذِينَ كَفَرُوا لَا تَعْتَذِرُوا الْيَوْمَ إِنَّمَا تُجْزَوْنَ مَا كُنْتُمْ تَعْمَلُونَ

O disbelievers! Do not make excuses this Day!
You are only being recompensed for what you used to do.

DISCUSSION: THE COMPANIONS OF THE TRENCH (*AṢḤĀB AL-UKHDŪD*)

This surah gives the example of the tragic episode of the *aṣḥāb al-ukhdūd*, who were either the perpetrators, or victims, of the brutal burning alive of believers in trenches filled with fire. Their identity and time-frame have been the subject of discussion amongst scholars of all Abrahamic faiths.

There are several possibilities about which group, or groups,[39] in history the Qur'an is referring to:

i) That they were a group of Banu Isrāil who followed Prophet Dānyāl (Daniel) (a) who were killed by being thrown into pits of fire.[40]

ii) That they were a group of Zoroastrians who followed a divine scripture. When one of their kings wanted to marry his own sister,

---

[37] Zamakhsharī, *al-Kashshāf*, 4/731.

[38] Shīrāzī, *Namūneh*, 26/335.

[39] Rāzī, *Mafātīḥ al-Ghayb*, 31/110.

[40] Qurṭubī, *Tafsīr*, 19/290.

the believers in the community protested, and he had them burnt in a fiery pit.[41]

iii) That they were a monk, a young man, and their followers. A young man, who was training to become the king's magician, met a monk whose words affected him greatly. He became a believer in God and was gifted with healing powers. He came to the attention of the king when he cured his minister of blindness. The king demanded to know who had healed him and tortured the minister into giving up the monk and the young man. The king arrested the two and some of their followers and demanded that they turn away from their religion. When they refused, he had his men prepare a trench full of fire and cast them and their followers into it to burn to their deaths.[42]

iv) However, the popular account is that they were the people of Dhū Nawās, the Jewish king of the Himyarite kingdom of Yemen, who attacked Najrān in the year 523CE, killing many of its Christian citizens. He ordered the survivors to renounce their faith, but they refused. So he prepared a large trench of fire and threw them in the blazing fire to be burnt alive. In this terrible manner, thousands of believers were martyred.

The news reached Rome, and the Kaiser was greatly affected by it. He instructed his vassal, the Christian king of Abyssinia, to avenge the death of the martyrs. The Abyssinian army came to Yemen and comprehensively defeated the forces of Dhū Nawās in a fierce battle, and Dhū Nawās committed suicide.[43]

The Roman Catholic Church commemorates the martyrdom of the monk ʿAbdullah b. al-Ḥārith (who is known as Saint Aretas in Catholic martyrology) and the other martyrs of Najran on 1st October every year.

SUMMARY OF THE VERSES

The verses send God's curse on the companions of the trench filled with fire. They sat by the fire and witnessed the believers being thrown into its flames.

---

[41] Shīrāzī, *Namūneh*, 26/340.

[42] Ṭabrasī, *al-Bayān*, 10/707-9.

[43] Yaʿqūbī, *Tārīkh*, 1/199.

REFLECTIVE LEARNING

The people of Ukhdūd were so committed to their faith in God that they were ready to be sacrificed in the burning fire rather than turn away from Him.

Let me reflect on my own dedication to my faith and whether I would go through hardship, be it physical, emotional, or financial, and yet stay committed to it.

VERSES 8, 9

وَمَا نَقَمُوا مِنْهُمْ إِلَّا أَنْ يُؤْمِنُوا بِاللَّهِ الْعَزِيزِ الْحَمِيدِ ﴿٨﴾ الَّذِي لَهُ مُلْكُ السَّمَاوَاتِ وَالْأَرْضِ وَاللَّهُ عَلَىٰ كُلِّ شَيْءٍ شَهِيدٌ ﴿٩﴾

And they did not resent them except because they believed in Allah, the Mighty, the Praiseworthy, [8] *to Whom belongs the dominion of the heavens and the earth. And Allah is a Witness over all things.* [9]

8-9.1 '*And they did not resent them except because they believed in Allah, the Mighty, the Praiseworthy.*': [*Naqamū* (نَقَمُوا, resent)] is derived from *naqama* meaning to dislike and reject, and thereafter to retaliate or take revenge.[44] The brutal killing of the faithful Christians was for no other reason except that they believed in God, a belief that is coded in the *fiṭrah* of all human beings.

Q40:28 states:

أَتَقْتُلُونَ رَجُلًا أَنْ يَقُولَ رَبِّيَ اللَّهُ

...Would you kill a man [merely] because he says, "My Lord is Allah?"

History is replete with examples of believers who were cruelly persecuted because of their faith in God. Q7:126 quotes the magicians who believed in Musa (a) telling Firʿawn:

وَمَا تَنْقِمُ مِنَّا إِلَّا أَنْ آمَنَّا بِآيَاتِ رَبِّنَا لَمَّا جَاءَتْنَا
رَبَّنَا أَفْرِغْ عَلَيْنَا صَبْرًا وَتَوَفَّنَا مُسْلِمِينَ

---

[44] Muṣṭafawī, *al-Taḥqīq*.

And you do not resent (tanqimu) *us except because we believed in the signs of our Lord when they came to us. Our Lord! Pour upon us patience and let us die as Muslims [in submission to You].*

8-9.2 The verse under review then goes on to list four qualities of God to endorse the rightful conduct of the believers and the futility of the defiance of the oppressors.[45] First, two names of God are mentioned:

i) [*al-ʿAzīz* (الْعَزِيز, the all-Mighty)] refers to God's authority, His majesty, and His invincible power before which everything else is helpless. His remembrance will never be removed from the hearts of the believers despite the determined efforts of the disbelievers.

ii) [*al-Ḥamīd* (الْحَمِيد, the all-Praiseworthy)] refers to God's worthiness of praise and gratitude. All fair-minded people would feel indebted to Him for His gracious favours.

The two qualities juxtapose God's attributes of glory (*jalāl*) and beauty (*jamāl*) which are the basis of all His acts.[46]

8-9.3 '*To Whom belongs the dominion of the heavens and the earth. And Allah is a Witness over all things.*' [*Lahu* (لَهُ, to Whom)] is placed at the beginning of the phrase to denote exclusivity (*inḥiṣār*), and gives the meaning of 'to Him alone, and no other.'

Two further qualities of God are mentioned here:

i) [*Lahu mulk al-samāwāti wa al-arḍ* (لَهُ مُلْكُ السَّمَاوَاتِ وَالْأَرْضِ, to Whom belongs the dominion of the heavens and the earth)] means that the command and sovereignty over creation belongs to God alone. This quality emphasizes the fact that God is all-Mighty and deserving of all praise and gratitude.

ii) [*ʿAlā kulli shayʾin Shahīd* (عَلَىٰ كُلِّ شَيْءٍ شَهِيد, Witness over all things)] means that nothing is hidden from Him in His kingdom. He sees the goodness of the righteous and the evil of the sinner.

Only a Being who has all these qualities is worthy of worship and servitude.[47]

45 Ṭabāṭabāʾī, *al-Mīzān*, 20/251.

46 Ibid.

47 Shīrāzī, *Namūneh*, 26/336.

SUMMARY OF THE VERSES

The resentment of the tormentors was for no other reason but the faith of the believers in Allah, who is the Mighty, the Praiseworthy, the Sovereign of the heavens and the earth, and a Witness over everything.

REFLECTIVE LEARNING

Remaining steadfast on my religion is not without its challenges. Sometimes, I will have to face insults, discrimination, and even suffer loss because of my faith.

Let me reflect on the connection with God that allowed believers to sacrifice and remain steadfast even when facing the most difficult of trials.

VERSES 10, 11

إِنَّ الَّذِينَ فَتَنُوا الْمُؤْمِنِينَ وَالْمُؤْمِنَاتِ ثُمَّ لَمْ يَتُوبُوا فَلَهُمْ عَذَابُ جَهَنَّمَ وَلَهُمْ عَذَابُ الْحَرِيقِ ﴿١٠﴾ إِنَّ الَّذِينَ آمَنُوا وَعَمِلُوا الصَّالِحَاتِ لَهُمْ جَنَّاتٌ تَجْرِي مِنْ تَحْتِهَا الْأَنْهَارُ ذَٰلِكَ الْفَوْزُ الْكَبِيرُ ﴿١١﴾

Indeed, those who persecute the believing men and believing women and then do not repent will have the punishment of Hell, and they will have the punishment of the burning Fire. [10] *Indeed, those who believe and do righteous deeds will have gardens beneath which rivers flow. That is the great attainment.* [11]

10-11.1 '*Indeed, those who persecute the believing men and believing women and then do not repent*': [*Fatanū* (فَتَنُوا, persecute)] is derived from *fatana* meaning to test and put on trial. *Fitnah* here means subjecting the people to suffering and punishment. The term has been used in a general sense to include the *aṣḥāb al-ukhdūd* and the polytheists of the Quraysh, who continually persecuted the men and women who believed in the Prophet (s) in an attempt to make them abandon their religion.[48]

[*Yatūbū* (يَتُوبُوا, they repent)] is derived from *tāba* meaning to turn and *tawbā* is turning to God in repentance. The verse states that

[48] Ṭabāṭabā'ī, *al-Mīzān*, 20/252.

even for these people, the door to God's mercy and forgiveness is open, if they were to be remorseful for their misdeeds and repent.

10-11.2 Although the verse is a threat to the persecutors of believers, within it lies hope for redemption as well. Many Makkans regretted their mistreatment of the believers when they became Muslims themselves. The generous gift of God of giving a sinner respite and allowing a fresh start to the repentant gives great hope to every human being.[49] Q39:53 states:

قُلْ يَا عِبَادِيَ الَّذِينَ أَسْرَفُوا عَلَىٰ أَنْفُسِهِمْ لَا تَقْنَطُوا مِنْ رَحْمَةِ اللَّهِ
إِنَّ اللَّهَ يَغْفِرُ الذُّنُوبَ جَمِيعًا إِنَّهُ هُوَ الْغَفُورُ الرَّحِيمُ

Say, "O My servants who have transgressed against themselves [by sinning], do not despair of the mercy of God. Indeed, God forgives all sins. Indeed, it is He who is the all-Forgiving, the all-Merciful."

10-11.3 In a supplication from Imam al-Sajjad (a), we read: My Lord, You have stated in the clear verses of Your Book that You accept repentance from Your servants, and You pardon evil deeds, and You love the repentant. So accept my repentance as You have promised, and pardon my evil deeds as You have guaranteed...[50]

10-11.4 '*Will have the punishment of Hell, and they will have the punishment of the burning Fire.*': [*Jahannam* (جَهَنَّم, Hell)] is the generic name of the place where obstinate disbelievers and evildoers will be sent for redemptive punishment. We have discussed its function in greater detail in the *tafsīr* of Surat al-Ghāshiyah (88).

10-11.5 The verse states that if sinners do not care to repent, then Hell awaits for them. *Fa lahum* (then for them) indicates that their consignment to Hell is a consequence of their refusal to repent.

10-11.6 [*Ḥarīq* (الحَرِيق, burning)] is the active participle of *ḥaraqa* which means to burn and set on fire. Here it refers to a blazing fire in Hell. The mention of *ḥarīq* as an additional punishment is because not all levels of Hell contain fire. For those who live there, there are other

49 Shīrāzī, *Namūneh*, 26/344.

50 *Al-Ṣaḥīfah al-Sajjādiyyah, Du'ā' al-Tawbā*, supplication 31.

وَقَدْ قُلْتَ يَا إِلٰهِي فِي مُحْكَمِ كِتَابِكَ إِنَّكَ تَقْبَلُ التَّوْبَةَ عَنْ عِبَادِكَ وَتَعْفُو عَنِ السَّيِّئَاتِ وَتُحِبُّ التَّوَّابِينَ. فَاقْبَلْ تَوْبَتِي كَمَا وَعَدْتَ وَاعْفُ عَنْ سَيِّئَاتِي كَمَا ضَمِنْتَ.

punishments as well, such as the bitter fruits of *ḍarīʿ* and *zaqqūm* and the unpleasant waters of *ḥamīm* and *ṣadīd.* However, those who unrepentantly persecute believing men and women will be cast into a fiery part of Hell to burn therein. They themselves will serve as its fuel. Q72:15 states:

وَأَمَّا الْقَاسِطُونَ فَكَانُوا لِجَهَنَّمَ حَطَبًا

And as for the deviant, they will be firewood (fuel) for Hell.

Some exegetes say that they are sent to Hell due to their disbelief, and subject to the burning fire due to their burning of the believers.[51]

10-11.7 '*Indeed, those who believe and do righteous deeds will have gardens beneath which rivers flow.*': This verse is a beautiful promise to the believers to gladden their hearts, both at the time of revelation and forever afterwards, just as the previous verse was a stern warning to the disbelievers and evildoers.[52]

10-11.8 Those who believe are the ones who are true to their commitment to *tawḥīd*; they worship God sincerely, perform righteous deeds, and avoid sins.[53] These righteous deeds are a natural consequence of sincere belief and in fact, only worthy because of it.[54] We have discussed the term 'righteous deeds' further in the *tafsīr* of Surat al-ʿAṣr (103).

10-11.9 [*Jannāt* (جَنَّات, gardens)] (sing. *jannah*) refers to the gardens of Paradise.

[*Min taḥtihā al-anhār* (مِنْ تَحْتِهَا الْأَنْهَارُ, beneath which rivers flow)]. This description of *jannah* occurs more than 40 times in the Qur'an. There are several rivers in Paradise. Q47:15 states:

مَثَلُ الْجَنَّةِ الَّتِي وُعِدَ الْمُتَّقُونَ فِيهَا أَنْهَارٌ مِنْ مَاءٍ غَيْرِ آسِنٍ وَأَنْهَارٌ مِنْ لَبَنٍ
لَمْ يَتَغَيَّرْ طَعْمُهُ وَأَنْهَارٌ مِنْ خَمْرٍ لَذَّةٍ لِلشَّارِبِينَ وَأَنْهَارٌ مِنْ عَسَلٍ مُصَفًّى

The description of Paradise, which the righteous are promised: therein are rivers of water incorruptible, rivers of milk the taste of

[51] Ṭabrasī, *al-Bayān*, 10/710.
[52] Ṭabāṭabā'ī, *al-Mīzān*, 20/252.
[53] Ṭūsī, *al-Tibyān*, 10/319.
[54] Muṭahharī, *(Āshnāyī bā Qur'an), Āthār*, 28/753.

which never changes, rivers of wine delicious to the drinkers, and rivers of clarified honey...

10-11.10 In most cases, the phrase *tajrī min taḥtihā* (flows beneath it) is used for the location of these rivers, but sometimes *tajrī min taḥtihim* (flows beneath them, for example in Q7:43) is used, and unusually, in Q9:100, *tajrī taḥtaha* (flows under it) is used and the word '*min*' is absent.[55] The phrase therefore refers to the various rivers that flow around the trees and below the high residences within these gardens.[56]

10-11.11 '*That is the great attainment.*' [*Dhālika* (ذَٰلِكَ, that is)] is used here to denote importance and significance.[57]

[*Fawz* (فَوْز, attainment)] is derived from *fāza* meaning to succeed and triumph. Just entering Paradise is a great attainment, however, here the word *kabīr* may have been added to indicate that those who stood firm in the face of persecution for their beliefs will have a higher station in Paradise than those who did not undergo these trials. They will enter Paradise full of respect, honour, splendour, and dignity.[58]

10-11.12 Indeed, all the suffering experienced in the *dunyā* is ultimately of little consequence if one attains God's pleasure and admission into Paradise. Q3:185 states:

فَمَنْ زُحْزِحَ عَنِ النَّارِ وَأُدْخِلَ الْجَنَّةَ فَقَدْ فَازَ

... And whoever is moved away from the Fire and admitted into Paradise, he indeed has attained success (faqad fāz).

SUMMARY OF THE VERSES

The verses state that those who are unrepentant after tormenting the believing men and women shall enter Hell, and moreover, be subject to a blazing fire.

In contrast, those who believe and do righteous acts shall be admitted into gardens beneath which rivers flow. And that indeed, is a great attainment.

---

55 We will discuss the meaning of this exception in the *tafsīr* of the verse, God-willing.

56 Ṭūsī, *al-Tibyān*, 5/288.

57 Shīrāzī, *Namūneh*, 26/346.

58 Ṭabrasī, *al-Bayān*, 10/710.

REFLECTIVE LEARNING

The greatest attainment is to be admitted to Paradise. Nothing else will matter.

Let me reflect on whether I keep this single criterion foremost in all the decisions I make in my life.

VERSE 12 - 16

إِنَّ بَطْشَ رَبِّكَ لَشَدِيدٌ ﴿١٢﴾ إِنَّهُ هُوَ يُبْدِئُ وَيُعِيدُ ﴿١٣﴾ وَهُوَ الْغَفُورُ الْوَدُودُ
﴿١٤﴾ ذُو الْعَرْشِ الْمَجِيدُ ﴿١٥﴾ فَعَّالٌ لِمَا يُرِيدُ ﴿١٦﴾

Indeed, the strike of your Lord is severe. [12] *Indeed, it is He who originates [creation] and brings it back.* [13] *And He is the all-Forgiving, the all-Affectionate,* [14] *Owner of the throne, the all-Glorious,* [15] *the all-Accomplishing of whatever He wills.* [16]

12-16.1 *'Indeed, the strike of your Lord is severe.'*: Now the verses warn the disbelievers and reassure the believers about the Day of Resurrection and Recompense.

[*Baṭsh* (بَطْش, strike)] is derived from *baṭasha* which means to do something with strength or forcefulness.[59] Here, it refers to God's chastisement and means that when God will seize them, they will not be able to save themselves by any means.

[*Shadīd* (شَدِيد, severe)] is derived from *shadda* meaning strong and rigorous. The strict tone of the verse is highlighted by employing stern terms such as *baṭsh* and *shadīd*, and the use of emphasis through *inna* and *la*,[60] and it is a strong warning to evildoers that the respite that they enjoy will not be long-lived. Q11:102 states:

وَكَذَٰلِكَ أَخْذُ رَبِّكَ إِذَا أَخَذَ الْقُرَىٰ وَهِيَ ظَالِمَةٌ إِنَّ أَخْذَهُ أَلِيمٌ شَدِيدٌ

And thus is the seizure of your Lord when He seizes
the people of the cities while they are committing wrong.
Indeed, His seizure is painful and severe.

[59] Muṣṭafawī, *al-Taḥqīq*.

[60] Shīrāzī, *Namūneh*, 26/346.

12-16.2 The *dunyā* is a realm where man has been allowed to exercise his free will. As a result of that freedom, some act righteously and others cause great mischief. However, when their conduct reaches a certain point, God's severe punishment comes to them.

Q43:55 states about the people of Firʿawn:

فَلَمَّا آسَفُونَا انتَقَمْنَا مِنْهُمْ فَأَغْرَقْنَاهُمْ أَجْمَعِينَ

And when they angered Us, We took retribution from them and drowned them all.

It should be noted that when matters such as anger, love, gratitude, and so on are attributed to God, it is in the context of Divine recompense and retribution.[61]

12-16.3 The warning in the verse under review was directed at the chiefs of the Quraysh who imagined themselves to be secure from God's wrath because of their strength and numbers.

In Q54:43-45 God cautions them:

أَكُفَّارُكُمْ خَيْرٌ مِنْ أُولَٰئِكُمْ أَمْ لَكُمْ بَرَاءَةٌ فِي الزُّبُرِ ﴿٤٣﴾
أَمْ يَقُولُونَ نَحْنُ جَمِيعٌ مُنْتَصِرٌ ﴿٤٤﴾ سَيُهْزَمُ الْجَمْعُ وَيُوَلُّونَ الدُّبُرَ

Are your disbelievers better than those [former ones], or is there immunity for you in the scripture? Or do they say: "We are a great multitude, working together?" [Their] multitude will be defeated, and they will turn their backs [in retreat].

God's warning to the defiant polytheists was partially realized in the ignominious defeats they suffered in their battles against the Muslims. However, what awaits them in the *ākhirah* is much greater in severity. Q44:16 states:

يَوْمَ نَبْطِشُ الْبَطْشَةَ الْكُبْرَىٰ إِنَّا مُنْتَقِمُونَ

The Day when We will strike with the greatest striking, then indeed, We will inflict retribution.

12-16.4 The use of *Rabbika* (your Lord) in the verse under review is to comfort the Prophet (s) and to emphasize God's support.[62]

---

[61] Ibid, 18/284.

[62] Ibid, 26/346.

Furthermore, it is a reminder of His role as the Sustainer for all. Even in the chastisement of God there is a favour of the possibility of purification for some of its inmates. Q55:43-45 state:

هَٰذِهِ جَهَنَّمُ الَّتِي يُكَذِّبُ بِهَا الْمُجْرِمُونَ ﴿٤٣﴾
يَطُوفُونَ بَيْنَهَا وَبَيْنَ حَمِيمٍ آنٍ ﴿٤٤﴾ فَبِأَيِّ آلَاءِ رَبِّكُمَا تُكَذِّبَانِ

This is Hell, which the criminals denied. They shall wander between it and scalding hot water. So which of the favours of your Lord will you two (men and jinn*) deny?*

12-16.5 *'Indeed, it is He who originates [creation] and brings it back.'*: [*Yubdi'u* (يُبْدِئُ, originates)] is derived from *bada'a* which means to start and initiate. Here, it refers to God as the Originator of all creation.

[*Yu'īd* (يُعِيد, brings it back)] is derived from *'āda* meaning to return, and refers to God as the One who will resurrect and bring back the entire creation in the Hereafter.

The verse reminds mankind of the invincible power of God. Just as He originally created them in the *dunyā* without any assistance,[63] He shall resurrect them again after their death for accounting and recompense in the *ākhirah*.[64] This verse gives evidence for the previous one, '*Indeed, the strike of your Lord is severe*'. His strike would be great indeed, so that absolute justice is observed.

12-16.6 *'And He is the all-Forgiving, the all-Affectionate,'*: [*al-Ghafūr* (الْغَفُور, the all-Forgiving)] is derived from *ghafara* meaning to cover and conceal. Its technical meaning is to forgive and remove the effects of sin.[65] *Ghafūr* is the hyperbolic form and refers to God's continual practice of forgiving sins, no matter how large or grave they are.[66] Q4:48 states:

إِنَّ اللَّهَ لَا يَغْفِرُ أَنْ يُشْرَكَ بِهِ وَيَغْفِرُ مَا دُونَ ذَٰلِكَ لِمَنْ يَشَاءُ

Indeed, God does not forgive that anything should be associated with Him, and forgives what is besides that to whomsoever He pleases...

63 Ṭabāṭabā'ī, *al-Mīzān*, 20/253.
64 Ṭabrasī, *al-Bayān*, 10/710.
65 Muṣṭafawī, *al-Taḥqīq*.
66 Ṭabrasī, *al-Bayān*, 10/710.

[*al-Wadūd* (ٱلْوَدُود, the all-Affectionate)] is derived from *wudd* meaning to love. *Wadūd* is the hyperbolic form and refers to God's great love for His servants. *Wadūd* denotes love that is manifested, and one of the expressions of this love is His attribute *al-Ghafūr*.

Some exegetes have said that *wadūd* may be taken as the object (*maf'ūl*) of love as well, meaning that the believers whose hearts are pure love God due to His grace and blessings.[67] Q2:165 states:

وَالَّذِينَ آمَنُوا أَشَدُّ حُبًّا لِلَّهِ

...But those who believe are intense in their love for God.

12-16.7 The verse under review adds a beautiful qualifying statement to the previous verses. It gives great comfort to the believers, and is also an invitation to the sinners to avail themselves of God's forgiveness and enter into the fold of His beloved servants.[68] At the same time that God is strict in retribution, He is quick to forgive as well.

12-16.8 *'Owner of the throne, the all-Glorious,'*: [*Dhū al-'Arsh* (ذُو الْعَرْشِ, Owner of the throne)] is a metaphor for God's complete sovereignty over creation. He does whatever He wills.[69]

Only this kind of absolute power would give meaning and significance to the attributes of *Ghafūr* and *Wadūd*.[70]

[*al-Majīd* (ٱلْمَجِيد, all-Glorious)] is derived from *majada* meaning to be illustrious and exalted. It refers to God's Perfection in His Essence and Attributes.[71]

According to most exegetes, *al-Majīd* here is mentioned as the name of God and not an attribute of the *'arsh*.[72]

12-16.9 *'The all-Accomplishing of whatever He wills.'*: [*Fa''āl* (فَعَّال, all-Accomplishing)]. The verse makes clear that the will (*irādah*) of God cannot be opposed. Whatever He wills will happen and there is no interval between His will and His action. Q2:117 states:

---

67 Ibid.

68 Mughniyyah, *al-Kāshif*, 7/547.

69 Ṭabāṭabā'ī, *al-Mīzān*, 20/253.

70 Shīrāzī, *Namūneh*, 26/347.

71 Ṭabāṭabā'ī, *al-Mīzān*, 20/254.

72 Ṭabrasī, *al-Bayān*, 10/710.

بَدِيعُ السَّمَاوَاتِ وَالْأَرْضِ وَإِذَا قَضَىٰ أَمْرًا فَإِنَّمَا يَقُولُ لَهُ كُن فَيَكُونُ

[God is the] Originator of the heavens and the earth.
When He decrees a matter, He only says to it, "Be," and it is.

God is *faʿʿāl* in both His strike (*baṭsh*) as well as in His forgiveness (*ghufrān*) and affection (*wudd*).

SUMMARY OF THE VERSES

The verses warn that God's strike will be severe. He has originated the creation and He will return it again after its death. At the same time, He is all-Forgiving and all-Affectionate. His dominion over creation is absolute and He always accomplishes what He wishes to do.

REFLECTIVE LEARNING

In a supplication attributed to Imam al-Mahdi (af), he states: I have conviction that You are the most Merciful of the merciful in situations of pardon and mercy, and the strictest of Punishers in situations that deserve chastisement and retribution.[73]

Let me reflect on my current situation due to the choices I have made. If I was to die today, would I be deserving of God's mercy or His punishment?

VERSES 17 - 20

هَلْ أَتَاكَ حَدِيثُ الْجُنُودِ ﴿١٧﴾ فِرْعَوْنَ وَثَمُودَ ﴿١٨﴾ بَلِ الَّذِينَ كَفَرُوا فِي تَكْذِيبٍ ﴿١٩﴾ وَاللَّهُ مِن وَرَائِهِم مُّحِيطٌ ﴿٢٠﴾

Has the story of the soldiers reached you, [17] *[those of] Firʿawn and Thamud?* [18] *But they who disbelieve are in [persistent] denial,* [19] *while God encompasses them from behind.* [20]

17-20.1 As evidence that God's strike is severe, and His dominion over creation is absolute, and that He always accomplishes whatever He wills, two groups from history who were destroyed are mentioned.[74]

---

[73] Ṭūsī, *Miṣbāḥ al-Mutahajjid*, pp. 402-4, *Duʿāʾ al-Iftitāḥ*.

وَأَيْقَنْتُ أَنَّكَ أَنْتَ أَرْحَمُ الرَّاحِمِينَ فِي مَوْضِعِ الْعَفْوِ وَالرَّحْمَةِ وَأَشَدُّ الْمُعَاقِبِينَ فِي مَوْضِعِ النَّكَالِ وَالنَّقِمَةِ.

[74] Ṭabāṭabāʾī, *al-Mīzān*, 20/254.

17-20.2 *'Has the story of the soldiers reached you, [those of] Fir'awn and Thamud?'*: After the mention of *aṣḥāb al-ukhdūd*, God mentions two examples of similar brutal tyranny from an older time, to inform the Muslims of Makka that there would always be people who act in this way.[75]

The fate of Fir'awn and Thamud was well-known to the people of Makka and so the verse may imply, '*the news has certainly reached you.*'[76]

17-20.3 [*Junūd* (جُنُود, soldiers)] (sing. *jund*) refers to troops in any army. Both Fir'awn and Thamud built huge monuments and maintained strong armies to protect themselves and to attack their enemies. They behaved arrogantly in the land due to their advanced civilizations and perceived military might. They belied and dismissed the Prophets (a) that God sent to them. They were ultimately destroyed, and their armies could not save them.

We have discussed Fir'awn in the *tafsīr* of Surat al-Fajr (89) and Surat al-Nāzi'āt (79), and the people of Thamud in the *tafsīr* of Surat al-Shams (91).

The verse means to reassure the Prophet (s) by saying: O Muhammad (s), recall how they belied the Prophets (a) of God, how His punishment descended on them, how the Prophets (a) remained patient, and how God helped them. So, exercise patience just as they did, until God's help also comes to you.[77]

17-20.4 *'But they who disbelieve are in [persistent] denial,'*: [*Fī takdhīb* (فِي تَكْذِيبٍ, in denial)]. *Takdhīb* is the verbal noun of *kadhdhaba*, which means denying something out of defiance despite instinctively knowing that it may be the truth.[78]

The context of the verse suggests that it is referring to the disbelievers at the time of the Prophet (s). It means that despite the clear evidence presented to them, they would dismiss these accounts as irrelevant to them, without pausing to ponder on their significance. They habitually continued to deny the truth.[79]

---

[75] Rāzī, *Mafātīḥ al-Ghayb*, 31/115.

[76] Ṭabrasī, *al-Bayān*, 10/711.

[77] Ibid.

[78] Rāghib, *al-Mufradāt*.

[79] Ṭabāṭabā'ī, *al-Mīzān*, 20/254.

17-20.5 *'While God encompasses them from behind.'*: [*Min warā'ihim* (مِن وَرَائِهِم, from behind them)]. *Warā'* denotes a direction that is beyond and apart from anything.[80] [*Muḥīṭ* (مُحِيط, encompass)] is derived from *aḥāṭa* meaning to encircle or enclose.[81]

The verse means that although they had left God behind, their turning away and denial would not negate the reality that God's power encompassed them completely.[82]

SUMMARY OF THE VERSE

The verses ask the listeners to consider accounts of the armies of Firʿawn and Thamud. But those who disbelieved continued to deny these instructive events. However, they would not be able to escape God's encompassing control over them.

REFLECTIVE LEARNING

Let me reflect on whether I learn from the lessons of the instructive events mentioned in the Qur'an, or do I read them as stories and consider them of benefit only to others?

VERSES 21, 22

بَلْ هُوَ قُرْآنٌ مَّجِيدٌ ﴿٢١﴾ فِي لَوْحٍ مَّحْفُوظٍ ﴿٢٢﴾

But it is a glorious Qur'an, [21] *[inscribed] on a preserved Tablet.* [22]

21-22.1 *'But it is a glorious Qur'an,'*: [*Majīd* (مَجِيد, glorious)]. The term has come again in this surah. Earlier it was referring to God and this time it is referring to the Qur'an. Rather than what the disbelievers think, the Qur'an is *majīd*, its promises and threats are true and undeniable.[83] It is also *majīd* in the sense of giving benefit (*karīm*), because it is an exalted discourse, it distinguishes truth from falsehood, gives admonition that softens the hearts, and provides the guidance that is vital for the success of man.[84]

---

80 Ibid.

81 Muṣṭafawī, *al-Taḥqīq*.

82 Ṭabrasī, *al-Bayān*, 10/711.

83 Rāzī, *Mafātīḥ al-Ghayb*, 31/116.

84 Ṭabrasī, *al-Bayān*, 10/711.

21-22.2 *'[Inscribed] on a preserved Tablet.'*: [*Lawḥ* (لَوْح, Tablet)] refers to something which is written on.

[*Maḥfūẓ* (مَحْفُوظ, preserved)] here means protected and preserved from change. Or it may be preserved from the knowledge of the creation and accessible only to the highest angels.[85]

21-22.3 Amongst the signs of the glory of the Qur'an is that it is found in the highest location of knowledge, *al-lawḥ al-maḥfūẓ*,[86] and cannot be altered or distorted.[87]

In two other verses, the location of the Qur'an in a distinct and honoured place has been mentioned. Q56:77,78 state:

إِنَّهُ لَقُرْآنٌ كَرِيمٌ ﴿٧٧﴾ فِي كِتَابٍ مَكْنُونٍ

Indeed, it is a noble Qur'an, in a Book well-protected.

And Q43:4 states:

وَإِنَّهُ فِي أُمِّ الْكِتَابِ لَدَيْنَا لَعَلِيٌّ حَكِيمٌ

And indeed it (the Qur'an) is in the Mother of the Book with Us, exalted and full of wisdom.

One meaning that the exegetes have given to the verse above in Surat al-Zukhruf is that the original location of the Qur'an is within the Mother of the Book (*umm al-kitāb*) which is with God. And this Book is the same as *al-lawḥ al-maḥfūẓ*, from which every Divine revelation, including all Scripture, emanates. And in that location, the Qur'an is beyond the comprehension of intellects (*'aliyy*). It is decisive (*ḥakīm*) but has not yet been differentiated into chapters and verses.[88] In this regard, Q11:1 states:

كِتَابٌ أُحْكِمَتْ آيَاتُهُ ثُمَّ فُصِّلَتْ مِنْ لَدُنْ حَكِيمٍ خَبِيرٍ

...[This is] a Book whose verses are made decisive and then expounded in detail from One who is all-Wise and all-Aware.

21-22.4 A tradition from Imam al-Sadiq (a) states: The preserved Tablet *(al-lawḥ al-maḥfūẓ)* has two aspects; one aspect is on the

---

85 Rāzī, *Mafātīḥ al-Ghayb*, 31/116.

86 Modarresī, *Min Hudā al-Qur'an*, 17/481.

87 Shīrāzī, *Namūneh*, 26/354.

88 Ṭabāṭabā'ī, *al-Mīzān*, 18/84.

right side of the *ʿarsh* [of God] and the other aspect is towards the forehead [the highest reach] of Israfil. Whenever God, the Exalted, communicates something about revelation, the Tablet knocks the forehead of Israfil. He looks into the Tablet and conveys what is in it to Jibraʾil.[89]

Of course, this tradition is using a highly metaphorical language and the true reality of the process of revelation is beyond our comprehension.

21-22.5 Another tradition from Imam al-Sadiq (a) describes the process of revelation in this manner: ... *Nūn* is an angel who conveys to the Pen (*qalam*) which is [also] an angel. The Pen conveys to the Tablet (*lawḥ*) which is [also] an angel. Then the Tablet conveys to Israfil who conveys to Mikaʾil, and Mikaʾil conveys to Jibraʾil, and Jibraʾil conveys to the Prophets (a) and Messengers (a).[90]

21-22.6 The Tablet and Pen are concepts from the metaphysical world and their descriptions are figurative in order to give us some idea of these realities. Although *lawḥ* has a metaphysical reality like the *ʿarsh* and *kursiyy*, it appears that it is used as a metaphor for God's knowledge which is eternal and cannot be changed. Every detail of the entirety of creation from its beginning is recorded in it. It is from here that the Qur'an originates.[91] Q10:61 states:

وَمَا يَعْزُبُ عَنْ رَبِّكَ مِنْ مِثْقَالِ ذَرَّةٍ فِي الْأَرْضِ وَلَا فِي السَّمَاءِ
وَلَا أَصْغَرَ مِنْ ذَٰلِكَ وَلَا أَكْبَرَ إِلَّا فِي كِتَابٍ مُبِينٍ

And not even an atom's weight is hidden from your Lord in the earth or in the heaven. Nor anything smaller than that or greater, except that it is [recorded] in a Clear Book.

---

[89] Majlisī, *Biḥār*, 54/366.

عَنِ الصَّادِقِ (عَلَيْهِ السَّلَامُ) - اللَّوْحُ الْمَحْفُوظُ لَهُ طَرَفَانِ طَرَفٌ عَلَى يَمِينِ الْعَرْشِ وَطَرَفٌ عَلَى جَبْهَةِ إِسْرَافِيلَ فَإِذَا تَكَلَّمَ الرَّبُّ جَلَّ ذِكْرُهُ بِالْوَحْيِ ضَرَبَ اللَّوْحُ جَبِينَ إِسْرَافِيلَ فَنَظَرَ فِي اللَّوْحِ فَيُوحِي بِمَا فِي اللَّوْحِ إِلَى جَبْرَائِيلَ.

[90] Ṣadūq, *Maʿānī al-Akhbār*, 1/22.

عَنِ الصَّادِقِ (عَلَيْهِ السَّلَامُ) - فَنُونٌ مَلَكٌ يُؤَدِّي إِلَى الْقَلَمِ وَهُوَ مَلَكٌ وَالْقَلَمُ يُؤَدِّي إِلَى اللَّوْحِ وَهُوَ مَلَكٌ وَاللَّوْحُ يُؤَدِّي إِلَى إِسْرَافِيلَ وَإِسْرَافِيلُ يُؤَدِّي إِلَى مِيكَائِيلَ وَمِيكَائِيلُ يُؤَدِّي إِلَى جَبْرَائِيلَ وَجَبْرَائِيلُ يُؤَدِّي إِلَى الْأَنْبِيَاءِ وَالرُّسُلِ.

[91] Maʿrifat, *al-Tamhīd*, 3/33; Shīrāzī, *Namūneh*, 26/354.

SUMMARY OF THE VERSE

The verses state the Qur'an is a glorious book, preserved in a special Tablet, *al-lawḥ al-maḥfūẓ*.

REFLECTIVE LEARNING

The glorious Qur'an is the Word of God that has come from the most perfect and complete source of knowledge.

Let me reflect on my attitude towards its contents. Do I let it suffice for my guidance or do I first seek guidance elsewhere?

SURAT AL-ṬĀRIQ
THE NIGHT COMER (86)

TEXT AND TRANSLATION

سُورَةُ الطَّارِقِ

بِسْمِ اللهِ الرَّحْمٰنِ الرَّحِيمِ

وَالسَّمَاءِ وَالطَّارِقِ ﴿١﴾ وَمَا أَدْرَاكَ مَا الطَّارِقُ ﴿٢﴾ النَّجْمُ الثَّاقِبُ ﴿٣﴾ إِنْ كُلُّ
نَفْسٍ لَمَّا عَلَيْهَا حَافِظٌ ﴿٤﴾ فَلْيَنْظُرِ الْإِنْسَانُ مِمَّ خُلِقَ ﴿٥﴾ خُلِقَ مِنْ مَاءٍ دَافِقٍ
﴿٦﴾ يَخْرُجُ مِنْ بَيْنِ الصُّلْبِ وَالتَّرَائِبِ ﴿٧﴾ إِنَّهُ عَلَىٰ رَجْعِهِ لَقَادِرٌ ﴿٨﴾ يَوْمَ تُبْلَى
السَّرَائِرُ ﴿٩﴾ فَمَا لَهُ مِنْ قُوَّةٍ وَلَا نَاصِرٍ ﴿١٠﴾ وَالسَّمَاءِ ذَاتِ الرَّجْعِ ﴿١١﴾
وَالْأَرْضِ ذَاتِ الصَّدْعِ ﴿١٢﴾ إِنَّهُ لَقَوْلٌ فَصْلٌ ﴿١٣﴾ وَمَا هُوَ بِالْهَزْلِ ﴿١٤﴾ إِنَّهُمْ
يَكِيدُونَ كَيْدًا ﴿١٥﴾ وَأَكِيدُ كَيْدًا ﴿١٦﴾ فَمَهِّلِ الْكَافِرِينَ أَمْهِلْهُمْ رُوَيْدًا ﴿١٧﴾

In the name of God, the Beneficent, the Merciful.

By the skies and the Night Comer [1] *And what makes you know what the Night Comer is?* [2] *[It is] the piercing star!* [3] *There is no soul except that it has over it a protector.* [4] *So let man consider from what he was created.* [5] *He was created from a gushing fluid,* [6] *emerging from between the backbone and the ribs.* [7] *Indeed, He is able to return him [to life].* [8] *The Day when secrets will be examined.* [9] *Then man will have no power, and no helper.* [10] *By the sky which returns [rain].* [11] *And by the earth which splits open.* [12] *Indeed, it is a decisive word,* [13] *and it is not amusement.* [14] *Indeed, they are plotting a plot.* [15] *And I am plotting a plot.* [16] *So allow respite to the disbelievers. Respite them for a while.* [17]

INTRODUCTION

Surat al-Ṭāriq (86) was the 36th chapter to be revealed.[1] It has seventeen verses and was revealed in Makka, after Surat al-Balad (90). It is named after the mention of *al-Ṭāriq* (the Night Comer) in the first verse of the surah.

Like other early Makkan chapters, Surat al-Ṭāriq warns about the Hereafter, and specifically addresses the issue of the return and resurrection of man.

The surah begins by swearing oaths by the skies and by a phenomenon called *al-Ṭāriq*. Thereafter, man is reminded that there is a guardian who watches over him constantly and protects him. There is a beautiful similarity between the starlight that travels through long expanses of space and the human soul that travels through the various realms of existence on its journey back to God.

As a proof that he will be resurrected after his death, man is asked to reflect on his simple beginning. God, who bought about a complex being from a simple drop, is able to restore him just as easily on the Day of Resurrection.

Two further oaths, by the skies that continually bring blessings and the earth that is receptive to these blessings, emphasize that the matter of the Hereafter and the truths that are contained in the Qurʾan are decisive facts, and not to be taken as idle words. Just as the piercing star brightens the dark night, the Qurʾan illuminates the path towards God.

At the end of the chapter, God reassures the Prophet (s) that the constant plotting of the disbelievers will not go unnoticed. God, too, has a plan, so the Prophet (s) should let the disbelievers enjoy a brief respite.

LINK TO THE PREVIOUS CHAPTER

The previous chapter, Surat al-Burūj, began with an oath by the skies and the heavenly constellations, and Surat al-Ṭāriq also begins with an oath by the skies and a celestial body, a piercing star.

---

[1] Maʿrifat, *ʿUlūm-i Qurʾānī*, p. 90.

Both surahs talk of the resurrection of human beings on the Day of Judgement, and God's ability to effortlessly '*bring man back again*' (Surat al-Burūj in verse 13, and Surat al-Ṭāriq in verse 8).

Surat al-Burūj ends with the mention of the Qur'an being preserved in a guarded Tablet (*al-lawḥ al-maḥfūẓ*) that exists in the highest heavens and Surat al-Ṭāriq begins with a reference to the heavens above our world.

MERITS OF RECITATION

- A tradition from the Prophet (s) states: God will grant whoever recites Surat al-Ṭāriq ten rewards for every star in the sky.[2]
- A tradition from Imam al-Sadiq (a) states: Whoever [regularly] recites Surat al-Ṭāriq in his obligatory prayers shall have a [special] station and position before God on the Day of Judgement, and will be amongst the friends of the Prophets (a) and their companions in Paradise.[3]

EXEGESIS

VERSES 1 - 3

وَالسَّمَاءِ وَالطَّارِقِ ﴿١﴾ وَمَا أَدْرَاكَ مَا الطَّارِقُ ﴿٢﴾ النَّجْمُ الثَّاقِبُ ﴿٣﴾

By the skies and the Night Comer [1] *And what will make you know what the Night Comer is?* [2] *[It is] the piercing star!* [3]

1-3.1 The chapter begins with oaths by two great phenomena in God's creation. The night sky adorned with a carpet of stars has always fascinated and intrigued mankind. Looking up at the stars and their constellations makes us immediately aware of our own insignificance within the expansiveness of creation and evokes humility in the heart of the mindful. The oaths are made in order to emphasize the importance of the message that follows.

---

[2] Nūrī, *Mustadrak al-Wasā'il*, 4/357.

عَنِ الرَّسُولِ (صَلَّى اللهُ عَلَيْهِ وَآلِهِ) – مَنْ قَرَأَ سُورَةَ الطَّارِقِ أَعْطَاهُ اللهُ بِعَدَدِ كُلِّ نَجْمٍ فِي السَّمَاءِ عَشْرَ حَسَنَاتٍ.

[3] 'Āmilī, *Wasā'il*, 6/149.

عَنِ الصَّادِقِ (عَلَيْهِ السَّلَامُ) – مَنْ كَانَتْ قِرَاءَتُهُ فِي فَرَائِضِهِ بِالسَّمَاءِ وَالطَّارِقِ كَانَ لَهُ عِنْدَ اللهِ يَوْمَ الْقِيَامَةِ جَاهٌ وَمَنْزِلَةٌ وَكَانَ مِنْ رُفَقَاءِ النَّبِيِّينَ وَأَصْحَابِهِمْ فِي الْجَنَّةِ.

1-3.2 '*By the skies and the Night Comer*': [*Samā'* (سَمَاء, sky)] is derived from *samawa*, meaning that which is towards the sky, or something that is raised high above other things and covers them.[4] When used in the unrestricted sense, it denotes what we see when we look above us. In this verse it refers to space above the earth, and in fact may mean the entire space within which God has placed His creation.[5]

The plural term *samāwāt* is also used in the Qur'an to mean skies or heavens, usually in conjunction with *al-arḍ* (the earth). It has a restricted meaning compared to *al-samā'*, and refers to the layers of the existence (*ṭabaqāt*) above and beyond the earth.[6]

Some exegetes have suggested that the first oath is by the God, the Lord of the sky (*Rabb al-samā'*).[7]

1-3.3 [*Al-Ṭāriq* (طَارِق, the Night Comer)]. The word *ṭāriq* is derived from *ṭaraqa*, which means to knock loudly so that a sound can be heard. A road is called *ṭarīq* because it is a pathway that is made level and distinct by the constantly pounding of footsteps.[8] Similarly, the term is also used metaphorically for paths that people follow. For example, spiritual paths, traditions, and customs are all called *ṭarīqah*.[9] Q20:63 quotes the words of Firʿawn's advisers:

قَالُوا إِنْ هَٰذَانِ لَسَاحِرَانِ يُرِيدَانِ أَنْ يُخْرِجَاكُمْ مِنْ أَرْضِكُمْ بِسِحْرِهِمَا
وَيَذْهَبَا بِطَرِيقَتِكُمُ الْمُثْلَىٰ

They said: These two (Musa and Harun) are most surely magicians who wish to turn you out from your land by their magic and to take away your best traditions (ṭarīqatiqum al-muthlā).

The word *ṭāriq* later came to denote a night visitor because it is at night that the footsteps of a traveller can be heard, and the door knock of a guest is more audible, unexpected, and startling.[10] Imam

4 Muṣṭafawī, *al-Taḥqīq*.
5 Javādī-Āmolī, *Tasnīm*, https://www.eshia.ir/feqh/archive/text/javadi/tafsir/98/981101/
6 Ṭabāṭabā'ī, *al-Mīzān*, 10/149.
7 Ṭabrasī, *al-Bayān*, 10/714.
8 Muṣṭafawī, *al-Taḥqīq*.
9 Rāzī, *Mafātīḥ al-Ghayb*, 31/117.
10 Muṣṭafawī, *al-Taḥqīq*.

Ali (a) used the word to refer to al-Ashʿath b. Qays who came to see him in the night, trying to bribe him. The Imam (a) is reported to have said, "A stranger incident was the night visitor (*ṭāriq*) who knocked at our door carrying a sealed vessel containing a sweet delicacy..."[11]

Finally, the term is also used for things that become visible at night such as the stars, and this is the meaning in this verse.[12]

1-3.4 '*And what makes you know what the Night Comer is?*': Since the Qurʾan has not used the word *al-Ṭāriq* in this meaning elsewhere, a rhetorical question is asked, '*And what makes you know...?*'.[13] This kind of question has been used in the Qurʾan to indicate the greatness of a phenomenon,[14] and also to mean, 'you cannot know unless God informs you,'[15] or 'you will never truly understand its full significance.'

Indeed, our understanding of the vastness of God's creation in the sky above us is very limited. The celestial bodies that we have some knowledge of are just the adornment of the first heaven and they are many layers to the *samāʾ* beyond that. Q67:4,5 state:

ثُمَّ ٱرْجِعِ ٱلْبَصَرَ كَرَّتَيْنِ يَنقَلِبْ إِلَيْكَ ٱلْبَصَرُ خَاسِئًا وَهُوَ حَسِيرٌ ﴿٤﴾

وَلَقَدْ زَيَّنَّا ٱلسَّمَاءَ ٱلدُّنْيَا بِمَصَابِيحَ

Then return [your] gaze again and yet again. [Your] gaze will return to you humbled while it is fatigued. And indeed, We have beautified the lowest heaven with lamps...

1-3.5 '*[It is] the piercing star!*': [*Najm* (نَجْم, star)] is derived from *najama* which means to emerge and become visible.[16] For this reason, in Q55:6 the term is interpreted by some exegetes as referring to stalkless plants:[17]

وَٱلنَّجْمُ وَٱلشَّجَرُ يَسْجُدَانِ

---

11 *Nahj al-Balāghah*, sermon 223.

وَأَعْجَبُ مِنْ ذَلِكَ طَارِقٌ طَرَقَنَا بِمَلْفُوفَةٍ فِي وِعَائِهَا...

12 Ṭabāṭabāʾī, *al-Mīzān*, 20/258.

13 Muṭahharī, (*Āshnāyī bā Qurʾan*), *Āthār*, 28/482.

14 Ṭabāṭabāʾī, *al-Mīzān*, 20/258.

15 Ṭūsī, *al-Tibyān*, 10/323.

16 Muṣṭafawī, *al-Taḥqīq*.

17 Ṭabāṭabāʾī, *al-Mīzān*, 19/96.

And the herbs and the trees both prostrate [to Him].

However, the more common meaning is that *najm* refers to any celestial body or constellation of stars.[18]

[*Thāqib* (ثَاقِب, piercing)] is derived from *thaqaba* meaning to make a hole and penetrate. Here, it refers to something bright enough to pierce darkness.[19] It is also used to refer to something that is at a great height, for example a soaring bird is called *al-ṭayr al-thāqib* because it pierces and cuts through the air as it ascends.[20]

Therefore, the terms *al-Ṭāriq* and *al-najm al-thāqib* here refer to a great phenomenon: a star whose light pierces the darkness of vast tracts of space to become visible on earth.

1-3.6 Several possibilities about which star *al-Ṭāriq* is referring to have been suggested by the exegetes, such as: it denotes all the stars visible at night and not any particular one, it refers to Saturn (Zuḥal), or the seven-star cluster Pleiades (Thurayā), or the moon.[21]

1-3.7 An interesting interpretation of *al-Ṭāriq*, *al-najm*, and *al-thāqib* is that these three terms refer to the stages of evolution in the life of stars.[22] In brief, all stars are formed when clouds of dust and gas (nebulae) collapse on themselves due to powerful gravitational forces, which cause the interstellar material to repeatedly 'knock together' (*ṭaraqa*).

These collisions create a huge build-up of internal temperature. This sequence results in the birth of a star (*najm*) which gradually begins to glow. It is called *najm* because its light just begins to pierce the darkness of space, just as a plant emerges by piercing through the earth.

As the temperature rises, nuclear fusion occurs and the star begins to release energy in the form of light that is bright enough to pierce the darkness of huge expanses of space, and be perceived in the night sky on earth. Now *al-Ṭāriq* is a star that has evolved into *al-najm al-thāqib*. Later in the surah, man is also asked to consider how he has evolved into his present state, from an insignificant drop.

---

18 Ṭabrasī, *al-Bayān*, 10/714.

19 Muṣṭafawī, *al-Taḥqīq*.

20 Ṭabāṭabā'ī, *al-Mīzān*, 20/258.

21 Ṭūsī, *al-Tibyān*, 10/323.

22 Ṭāliqānī, *Partovī az Qur'an*, 3/325.

Indeed, the stars are amongst the most extraordinary signs in the cosmos, and that is why God swears by them. They show man the enormous scale of God's creation, and remind him of his own insignificance. Q56:75,76 state:

فَلَا أُقْسِمُ بِمَوَاقِعِ النُّجُومِ ﴿٧٥﴾ وَإِنَّهُ لَقَسَمٌ لَوْ تَعْلَمُونَ عَظِيمٌ

So I swear (lā uqsimu) *by the setting of the stars.*
And indeed, if you only knew, that is a very great oath.

After mentioning the genesis of the mighty stars, the surah turns to the mention of the stages of human development.

SUMMARY OF THE VERSES

The verses begin by swearing an oath by the Night Comer (*al-Ṭāriq*). After asking man what would make him know what *al-Ṭāriq* is, the third verse states that it is a piercing star.

REFLECTIVE LEARNING

Just as we are not able to fully comprehend God's creation, we are unable to fully appreciate our own potential, except as He guides us. God has given us the example of His Prophet (s) and Imams (a) to emulate.

Let me reflect on how closely I model my life on their example, so as to attempt to reach my potential.

VERSE 4

إِنْ كُلُّ نَفْسٍ لَمَّا عَلَيْهَا حَافِظٌ ﴿٤﴾

There is no soul except that it has over it a protector. [4]

4.1 This verse is the response to the two oaths (*jawāb li'l qasam*). *Lammā* here is used in the meaning of *illā* (except) and the verse means that there is no soul except that it has a protector and guardian.[23]

[*Nafs* (نَفْس, soul)] when used in the unrestricted form refers to every living thing, in particular to man.[24]

[23] Ṭabāṭabā'ī, *al-Mīzān*, 20/258.

[24] Ṭāliqānī, *Partovī az Qur'an*, 3/329.

[*Ḥāfiẓ* (حَافِظ, protector)] is derived from *ḥafiẓa* which means to guard, preserve, and protect.[25] The verse does not state who this protector is, or what is being preserved and protected. It can be considered in several ways:

i) That *Ḥāfiẓ* refers to God, who guards and protects His creation at every moment.

   Indeed, He is the best of protectors. Q34:21 states:

   وَرَبُّكَ عَلَىٰ كُلِّ شَيْءٍ حَفِيظٌ

   ...And your Lord is the Protector of all things

   God sustains every soul and transfers it from one realm to another in its journey back to Him. When humans die in the *dunyā*, God's instructs His angels to decouple their souls from their material bodies and transfer their true essence completely into the imaginal body of *barzakh*. This process is called *wafāt*. Q32:11 states:

   قُلْ يَتَوَفَّاكُمْ مَلَكُ الْمَوْتِ الَّذِي وُكِّلَ بِكُمْ ثُمَّ إِلَىٰ رَبِّكُمْ تُرْجَعُونَ

   Say: The angel of death who is given charge over you will take your souls (yatawaffākum). *Then you shall be brought back to your Lord.*

   In this way, the soul, which is the essential reality of a person, is continually preserved.[26]

ii) That *ḥāfiẓ* refers to the angels assigned to protect the life and well-being of individuals during their life in the *dunyā*. The term has been used in the singular form because it refers to the genus of angels. Indeed, many angels have been assigned to protect every single individual. Q13:11 states:

   لَهُ مُعَقِّبَاتٌ مِنْ بَيْنِ يَدَيْهِ وَمِنْ خَلْفِهِ يَحْفَظُونَهُ مِنْ أَمْرِ اللهِ

   For each one are successive [angels] before and behind him who protect him by the decree of God.

   These protectors perform their duty until the angel of death is instructed to take charge of the soul.

---

25 Muṣṭafawī, *al-Taḥqīq*.

26 Muṭahharī, (*Āshnāyī bā Qur'an*), *Āthār*, 28/483.

These first two possibilities are summarized in Q6:61 which states:

وَهُوَ الْقَاهِرُ فَوْقَ عِبَادِهِ وَيُرْسِلُ عَلَيْكُمْ حَفَظَةً
حَتَّىٰ إِذَا جَاءَ أَحَدَكُمُ الْمَوْتُ تَوَفَّتْهُ رُسُلُنَا وَهُمْ لَا يُفَرِّطُونَ

And He is the Subjugator over His servants. He sends over you guardians until, when death comes to one of you, Our messengers take him, and they do not fail [in their duties].

iii) That *ḥāfiẓ* refers to angels who record and preserve the deeds of every human being.[27] This meaning is alluded to in Q82:10-12 which state:

وَإِنَّ عَلَيْكُمْ لَحَافِظِينَ ﴿١٠﴾ كِرَامًا كَاتِبِينَ ﴿١١﴾ يَعْلَمُونَ مَا تَفْعَلُونَ

And indeed, there are protectors [appointed] over you, noble recorders [of your deeds]. They know whatever you do.

And Q50:17,18 state:

إِذْ يَتَلَقَّى الْمُتَلَقِّيَانِ عَنِ الْيَمِينِ وَعَنِ الشِّمَالِ قَعِيدٌ ﴿١٧﴾
مَا يَلْفِظُ مِنْ قَوْلٍ إِلَّا لَدَيْهِ رَقِيبٌ عَتِيدٌ

When the two receivers (recording angels) receive, seated on the right and on the left. Man does not utter any word except that with him is an observer prepared [to record].

These deeds are recorded in precise detail; the angels preserve not just the deed, but the intention and manner in which they are performed as well.[28]

When his book of deeds is presented to the sinner, his astonishment is quoted in Q18:49:

وَوُضِعَ الْكِتَابُ فَتَرَى الْمُجْرِمِينَ مُشْفِقِينَ مِمَّا فِيهِ وَيَقُولُونَ
يَا وَيْلَتَنَا مَالِ هَٰذَا الْكِتَابِ لَا يُغَادِرُ صَغِيرَةً وَلَا كَبِيرَةً إِلَّا أَحْصَاهَا

And the book [of deeds] will be placed [open], and you will see the criminals fearful of that [which is recorded] within it. They will say, "Oh, woe to us! What is this book that leaves nothing small or great except that it has enumerated it?"...

---

27 Shīrāzī, *Namūneh*, 26/363.

28 Ṭabāṭabā'ī, *al-Mīzān*, 20/259.

4.2 A tradition from Imam al-Sadiq (a) states: There is no individual except that he is accompanied by two angels who write down whatever he says. Then they pass that on to two angels who are higher than them, who preserve whatever of it is related to good or evil and discard the rest.[29]

4.3 The connection between the oath in the first verse and its subject is that man must not imagine that when he dies, he disappears from the world of existence. Rather, death is like the setting of a star, which is always followed by its reappearance in another horizon.[30]

SUMMARY OF THE VERSE

In summary, the verse says no human being is ever alone; there is a constant witness and protector over him.

REFLECTIVE LEARNING

Let me give thanks for the constant preservation of my identity by God and His angels.

Let me reflect on the process of my *wafāt* and what is my true identity that will be transferred into my imaginal body of *barzakh*.

VERSES 5 - 7

فَلْيَنْظُرِ الْإِنْسَانُ مِمَّ خُلِقَ ﴿٥﴾ خُلِقَ مِنْ مَاءٍ دَافِقٍ ﴿٦﴾ يَخْرُجُ مِنْ بَيْنِ الصُّلْبِ وَالتَّرَائِبِ ﴿٧﴾

So let man consider from what he was created. [5] *He was created from a gushing fluid,* [6] *emerging from between the backbone and the ribs.* [7]

5-7.1 '*So let man consider from what he was created.*': This verse and the following two verses instruct man to ponder over his lowly beginnings.[31] The verse begins with *fa* (so), which means that it is the concluding part of the previous verse. It aims to remind man

---

[29] Majlisī, *Biḥār*, 3/846.

عَنِ الصَّادِقِ (عَلَيْهِ السَّلَامُ) - مَا مِنْ أَحَدٍ إِلَّا وَمَعَهُ مَلَكَانِ يَكْتُبَانِ مَا يَلْفُظُهُ ثُمَّ يَرْفَعَانِ ذَلِكَ إِلَى مَلَكَيْنِ فَوْقَهُمَا فَيُثْبِتَانِ مَا كَانَ مِنْ خَيْرٍ وَشَرٍّ وَيُلْقِيَانِ مَا سِوَى ذَلِكَ.

[30] Muṭahharī, (*Āshnāyī bā Qur'an*), *Āthār*, 28/484.

[31] Ṭūsī, *al-Tibyān*, 10/324.

that he is on a journey towards his Lord, and all his deeds are being preserved and transported along with him. The proof that he is on a journey will become evident to him when he compares his current elaborate constitution and considers how far he has come from his low and insignificant beginning as a single drop.[32]

[*Yanẓur* (يَنظُر, consider)] is derived from *naẓara* which means to look, consider, or ponder over. Man needs to consider his origin so as to gain a perspective on his life. His creation begins from a simple sperm cell that flows within the seminal fluid. Q80:18,19 states:

مِنْ أَيِّ شَيْءٍ خَلَقَهُ ﴿١٨﴾ مِن نُّطْفَةٍ

From what thing did He create him? From a small drop...

5-7.2 '*He was created from a gushing fluid*,': [*Dāfiq* (دَافِق, gushing)] is derived from *dafaqa* and refers to fluid that flows quickly and with force.[33] *Dāfiq* (gushing) is the active participle which is used here in the meaning of the passive participle *madfūq* (made to gush),[34] possibly because the fluid has constituents that allow it to move itself once it is within the female reproductive system.

Here, the liquid refers to the seminal fluid, which contains the sperm (*nuṭfah*) that is transferred from the male to the female.[35] If fertilization occurs as a result, a new life is conceived.

5-7.3 '*Emerging from between the backbone and the ribs.*': This phrase has been the subject of much discussion and we will consider it briefly below.

[*Ṣulb* (صُلْب, backbone)]. *Ṣulb* means something that is hard and strong. Here, it may refer to the spinal column or backbone, and later came to refer to the loins.[36]

[*Tarā'ib* (تَرَائِب, ribs)] is the plural of *tarībah*, meaning softness as opposed to *ṣulb*, and in this verse it means the front bones of the ribcage.[37] It commonly refers to the breastbone of ladies where a necklace would sit.[38]

---

32 Ṭabāṭabā'ī, *al-Mīzān*, 20/259.
33 Muṣṭafawī, *al-Taḥqīq*.
34 Ālūsī, *Rūḥ al-Ma'ānī*, 15/308.
35 Ṭabāṭabā'ī, *al-Mīzān*, 20/260.
36 Muṣṭafawī, *al-Taḥqīq*.
37 Ibid.
38 Ṭabrasī, *al-Bayān*, 10/710.

[*Yakhruju* (يَخْرُجُ, emerges)] is derived from *kharaja*, which means to go out. One meaning given by the exegetes is that emerging (*ikhrāj*) in this verse refers to the birth of the human being. At birth, the baby emerges from the womb of its mother, which lies between her backbone and ribs. In this case the verse means, 'the human being emerges from between the backbone and ribs.'[39]

However, most exegetes say that *ikhrāj* in these verses goes back to the 'gushing fluid', and here, the Qur'an is mentioning the role of the male in the creation of the human being. Therefore, interpretations relating the terms *ṣulb* and *tarā'ib* to females are implausible.[40]

5-7.4 It appears biologically incorrect to infer that seminal fluid comes from between the backbone and the ribs, because the position and function of the reproductive organs of human beings are known. However, a study of the mechanism of the emission of seminal fluid reveals that the nerve impulses that cause seminal discharge originate from the portion of the spinal cord that lies below the twelfth rib and above the remaining lumbar and sacral vertebrae (the backbone).' And this is briefly summarized by the Qur'an as '*between the backbone and the ribs.*'[41]

SUMMARY OF THE VERSES

In summary, the verses ask man to ponder over his humble origins from a gushing fluid whose emission was initiated from between his backbone and ribs.

REFLECTIVE LEARNING

Although every human being has the same lowly beginnings, each is given a specific life situation to achieve the unique potential that God has allocated to him or her.

Let me reflect on my reactions to situations in my life, and whether this enables me to move closer or further from God and my potential as a result.

---

39 Muṭahharī, (*Āshnāyī bā Qur'an*), *Āthār*, 28/484.

40 Shīrāzī, *Namūneh*, 26/367.

41 Adapted from Mohamed, Kader, *Islamic Perspective, Between the Backbone and the Ribs: A Medical Phenomenon Revealed in the Qur'an*, JIMA 42/56 (https://jima.imana.org/article/view/4956).

VERSES 8 - 10

إِنَّهُ عَلَىٰ رَجْعِهِ لَقَادِرٌ ﴿٨﴾ يَوْمَ تُبْلَى السَّرَائِرُ ﴿٩﴾ فَمَا لَهُ مِنْ قُوَّةٍ وَلَا نَاصِرٍ ﴿١٠﴾

Indeed, He is able to return him [to life]. [8] *The Day when secrets will be examined.* [9] *Then man will have no power, and no helper.* [10]

8-10.1 '*Indeed, He is able to return him [to life].*': [*Rajᶜ* (رَجْع, return)] means to restore something to its former state.[42] Here, *rajᶜihi* (his return) refers to the Resurrection, when God will bring man back to life. We have discussed whether this return of human beings on the Day of Judgement will be in bodies that are physical (*jismānī*), spiritual (*rūḥānī*), or both, later in the *tafsīr* of this surah.

The verse means that God, who created man from a simple drop, is also capable of resurrecting him after death.[43] Q22:5 states:

يَا أَيُّهَا النَّاسُ إِنْ كُنْتُمْ فِي رَيْبٍ مِنَ الْبَعْثِ فَإِنَّا خَلَقْنَاكُمْ مِنْ تُرَابٍ
ثُمَّ مِنْ نُطْفَةٍ ثُمَّ مِنْ عَلَقَةٍ ثُمَّ مِنْ مُضْغَةٍ مُخَلَّقَةٍ وَغَيْرِ مُخَلَّقَةٍ لِنُبَيِّنَ لَكُمْ

O People, if you should be in doubt about the Resurrection, then [consider that] indeed, We created you from dust, then from a sperm-drop, then from a clinging clot, and then from a lump of flesh, formed and unformed – that We may make evident [Our power] for you...

8-10.2 '*The Day when secrets will be examined.*': The Day here refers to the Day of Return (*rajᶜ*) and Resurrection.

[*Sarā'ir*(سَرَائِر, secrets)] (sing. *sarīrah*) refers to the beliefs, motivations, and the true intentions that a person keeps deeply hidden in his heart,[44] and which remains a secret between him and God.[45]

A similar word, *sirr* (plural *asrār*) also means secret, but *sarīrah* refers not just to a hidden act, but also the concealed intention behind individual behaviour. It is these deep secrets that will be exposed on that Day. Q100:10 states

وَحُصِّلَ مَا فِي الصُّدُورِ

And what is in the hearts is made manifest.

---

[42] Ṭabrasī, *al-Bayān*, 10/715.
[43] Ṭūsī, *al-Tibyān*, 10/325.
[44] Rāzī, *Mafātīḥ al-Ghayb*, 31/121.
[45] Ṭabrasī, *al-Bayān*, 10/715.

[*Tublā* (تُبْلَى, will be examined)] is derived from *balā'* which means to test. Here, it means examination and deep scrutiny.[46]

Indeed, the fullest and most just recompense can only be one that takes into account the intentions that an individual held in his breast. Q2:281 states:

وَٱتَّقُوا يَوْمًا تُرْجَعُونَ فِيهِ إِلَى اللهِ ثُمَّ تُوَفَّىٰ كُلُّ نَفْسٍ مَا كَسَبَتْ وَهُمْ لَا يُظْلَمُونَ

And beware a Day when you will be returned to God.
Then, every soul shall be paid what it has earned,
and they shall not be dealt with unjustly.

8-10.3 On the Day of Resurrection, every secret that human beings had concealed from everyone else will be exposed before God. In this way, it will be revealed which of them was virtuous and sincere and which of them was a transgressor and a hypocrite. Thereafter, they will be recompensed accordingly.[47] Q2:284 states:

وَإِنْ تُبْدُوا مَا فِي أَنْفُسِكُمْ أَوْ تُخْفُوهُ يُحَاسِبْكُمْ بِهِ اللهُ

...Whether you disclose what is within yourselves or conceal it,
God will call you to account for it...

Of course, the exposure of secrets will not be the same for every individual on the Day of Judgement. Accounting and questioning (*ḥisāb*) is to manifest God's justice and judgement, because He is already intimately aware of the actions of His creation. The righteous believers will be spared rigorous questioning and humiliation on that Day. Q84:7,8 state:

فَأَمَّا مَنْ أُوتِيَ كِتَابَهُ بِيَمِينِهِ ﴿٧﴾ فَسَوْفَ يُحَاسَبُ حِسَابًا يَسِيرًا

Then as for he who is given his record in his right hand,
he will soon be judged with an easy accounting.

8-10.4 '*Then man will have no power, and no helper.*': [*Nāṣir* (نَاصِر, helper)] is derived from *naṣara* meaning to assist and help. On that Day, neither will man possess the ability to defend himself or anyone else against chastisement, nor will he be able to call on anyone to defend him.[48] The only Helper on that Day is God.

[46] Shīrāzī, *Namūneh*, 26/369.

[47] Ṭabāṭabā'ī, *al-Mīzān*, 20/260.

[48] Ṭūsī, *al-Tibyān*, 10/325.

Q3:160 states:

إِنْ يَنْصُرْكُمُ اللَّهُ فَلَا غَالِبَ لَكُمْ وَإِنْ يَخْذُلْكُمْ فَمَنْ ذَا الَّذِي يَنْصُرُكُمْ مِنْ بَعْدِهِ
وَعَلَى اللَّهِ فَلْيَتَوَكَّلِ الْمُؤْمِنُونَ

If God should aid you, no one can overcome you;
but if He should forsake you, who is there that can aid you after
Him? And upon God let the believers rely.

DISCUSSION 1: HUMAN BODIES AT RESURRECTION

There is a difference of opinion about whether the return (*maʿād*) of human beings on the Day of Judgement will be in bodies that are physical (*jismānī*), spiritual (*rūḥānī*), or both.[49]

The overwhelming opinion of the scholars is that there will be a type of bodily resurrection. The Qur'an speaks of the resurrection of the physical body in many verses. For example:

1. Q75:3,4 state:

أَيَحْسَبُ الْإِنْسَانُ أَلَّنْ نَجْمَعَ عِظَامَهُ ﴿٣﴾ بَلَىٰ قَادِرِينَ عَلَىٰ أَنْ نُسَوِّيَ بَنَانَهُ

Does man think that We shall not assemble his bones?
Yes indeed! We are able to complete [even] his finger-tips.

2. Q36:78,79 state:

وَضَرَبَ لَنَا مَثَلًا وَنَسِيَ خَلْقَهُ قَالَ مَنْ يُحْيِي الْعِظَامَ وَهِيَ رَمِيمٌ ﴿٧٨﴾
قُلْ يُحْيِيهَا الَّذِي أَنْشَأَهَا أَوَّلَ مَرَّةٍ وَهُوَ بِكُلِّ خَلْقٍ عَلِيمٌ

And he presents for Us a comparison and forgets his own creation.
He says, "Who will give life to bones after they are disintegrated?"
Say [O Muhammad], "He will give them life who produced them
the first time; and He is Knowing of all creation."

3. Q36:51 states:

وَنُفِخَ فِي الصُّورِ فَإِذَا هُمْ مِنَ الْأَجْدَاثِ إِلَىٰ رَبِّهِمْ يَنْسِلُونَ

And the [second] trumpet will be blown; and at once
they will hasten from the graves to their Lord.

---

[49] For a longer discussion, see: Shaʿrānī, *Sharḥ Tajrīd al-Iʿtiqād*, pp. 567-70.

The nature of the physical body in the Hereafter.

Several theories have been put forward about the nature of the human body in the Hereafter.

In life, our bodies undergo constant change as cells are replaced and ultimately lost as we age. After death, these cells are assimilated back into the earth and in time, they form nutrients for other creatures and become part of them. Therefore, bringing every original cell back has two immediate problems: which cells, and whose cells? However, modern science has revealed that no more than a few cells are required to recreate a human being, and so this problem can be overcome.

A tradition from the Prophet (s) states: The earth consumes every part of the human body except the deepest part of his spinal column. When asked what that was, he (s) replied that it is like a mustard seed, and from this they will be revived.[50]

Furthermore, it is unlikely that man will return in the exact same physical body that he possessed in the life of the *dunyā* because the *ākhirah* is a different realm from the material world of *dunyā*.

Theologians have surmised that the soul will be reunited with a physical body similar to the earthly body, while philosophers have described different types of imaginal (*mithālī*) or enhanced bodies.[51]

In summary, when compared to their bodies in *dunyā*, the bodies of human beings in *ākhirah* will be similitudes of their former bodies, and not identical to them. However, the human being himself will be identical to his formal self, and not a similitude of it. This is because his real identity, which is his soul, shall remain unchanged. And for this reason, his body too can be considered to be the same as his former body.[52]

SUMMARY OF THE VERSES

The verses state that just as God created man in the first instance, He is easily able to resurrect him as well. Every soul will be brought back

---

[50] Ḥākim, *al-Mustadrak*, 4/609.

عَنِ الرَّسُولِ (صَلَّى اللهُ عَلَيْهِ وَآلِهِ) – يَأْكُلُ التُّرَابُ كُلَّ شَيْءٍ مِنَ الْإِنْسَانِ إِلَّا عَجْبُ [عَجْزُ] ذَنْبِهِ. قِيلَ: وَمَا هُوَ يَا رَسُولَ اللهِ؟ قَالَ: مِثْلُ حَبَّةِ خَرْدَلٍ مِنْهُ يُنْشَؤُونَ.

[51] Discussed by Subḥānī, *Shubuhāt wa Rudūd*, pp. 51-53.

[52] Ṭabāṭabāʾī, *al-Mīzān*, 17/113.

so that its secrets can be examined. Man will be powerless to stop this process and will not have anyone he could call for help.

REFLECTIVE LEARNING

Although man is powerless and unable to defend himself on that Day, he may qualify for intercession by those whom God has granted the right to intercede.

Let me reflect on what qualities are required to receive intercession, and whether I possess them.

VERSES 11 - 14

وَالسَّمَاءِ ذَاتِ الرَّجْعِ ﴿١١﴾ وَالْأَرْضِ ذَاتِ الصَّدْعِ ﴿١٢﴾ إِنَّهُ لَقَوْلٌ فَصْلٌ ﴿١٣﴾
وَمَا هُوَ بِالْهَزْلِ ﴿١٤﴾

By the sky which returns [rain]. [11] *And by the earth which splits open.* [12] *Indeed, it is a decisive word,* [13] *and it is not amusement.* [14]

11-14.1 '*By the sky which returns [rain]. And by the earth which splits open.*': A further two oaths are sworn by in these verses, to further emphasize the issue of the Day of Judgement and the return towards God.[53] Once again the first oath is by the sky, just as at the beginning of the surah, this time with a qualifying phrase, 'which returns'.

[*Dhāt al-raj*ᶜ (ذَاتِ الرَّجْعِ, which returns)] here could denote the celestial bodies (like *al-Ṭāriq*) that continually rise and set in the sky, or a reference to the skies as a storehouse for God's bounties.[54] Q51:22 states in this regard:

وَفِي السَّمَاءِ رِزْقُكُمْ وَمَا تُوعَدُونَ

And in the heaven is your provision and whatever you are promised.

However, many exegetes believe that the phrase is principally a reference to rain.[55] The water cycle is designed to constantly bring

[53] Ibid, 20/260.

[54] Ṭūsī, *al-Tibyān*, 10/326.

[55] Ibid.

water down and take it up again, so the sky constantly 'returns' the blessing of rain to the earth.

[*Ṣad*ᶜ (صَدْع, split open)] refers to fissures and cracks, and *dhāt al-ṣad*ᶜ here is a reference to the ability of the earth to split open to allow the rain to seep in, and for plants to sprout forth. And on the Day of Judgement, it will allow human beings to emerge from its depths also.[56]

The previously mentioned gushing fluid (*mā'in dāfiq*) gave life to the human being and now there is mention of another liquid, rain-water, which brings life to vegetation in the earth.

11-14.2 *'Indeed, it is a decisive word, and it is not amusement.'*: These verses are the reply to the two oaths in the previous verses. [*Faṣl* (فَصْل, decisive)] is derived from *faṣala* meaning to partition or separate two things so that they can be differentiated from one another.[57]

The verses may mean that the matters discussed in the previous verses about the origin and return of mankind are the decisive truth, and not idle words.[58]

However, many exegetes believe that the pronoun in *innahu* (indeed, it) refers to the Qur'an, which is a decisive word (*qawlun faṣl*) because God's revelation is a final arbiter between right and wrong, clearly distinguishing truth from falsehood.

11-14.3 Just as the rain mentioned in the previous verses impacts the earth that is prepared to receive it, the guidance of the Qur'an benefits hearts that are receptive. A tradition from the Prophet (s) states: Indeed, the similitude of the guidance and knowledge with which God appointed me is that of rain that pours down to the earth. There is a good tract of land that accepts the water and produces abundant vegetation... and that is the example of the one who [is receptive and] learns about God's religion. He benefits from what God has sent me with...[59]

---

[56] Muṭahharī, (*Āshnāyī bā Qur'an*), *Āthār*, 28/488.

[57] Muṣṭafawī, *al-Taḥqīq*.

[58] Ṭūsī, *al-Tibyān*, 10/326.

[59] Majlisi, *Biḥār*, 1/184.

عَنِ الرَّسُولِ (صَلَّى اللهُ عَلَيْهِ وَآلِهِ) – إِنَّ مَثَلَ مَا بعَثني اللهُ بِهِ مِنَ الْهُدَى وَالْعِلْمِ كَمَثَلِ غَيْثٍ أَصَابَ أَرْضًا وَكَانَ مِنْهَا طَائِفَةٌ طَيِّبَةٌ فَقَبِلَتِ الْمَاءَ فَأَنْبَتَتِ الْكَلَأَ وَالْعُشْبَ الْكَثِيرَ ... فَذَلِكَ مَثَلُ مَنْ فَقُهَ فِي دِينِ اللهِ وَنَفَعَه مَا بعَثَني اللهُ بِهِ...

11-14.4 [*Hazl* (هَزْل, amusement)] originally means something which is weak and skinny,[60] and in speech, it refers to something that is said in jest and has little value. The verses of the Qur'an are not like this, they establish the truth, and its descriptions of the Day of Judgement and Resurrection must not be taken lightly.[61]

SUMMARY OF THE VERSES

Two further oaths are made in these verses: by the sky which returns blessings to man, and by the earth which receives it.

Thereafter, God declares that the Qur'an is the decisive word on every matter and was not sent down as amusement.

REFLECTIVE LEARNING

The Qur'an is the only source of guidance that is absolutely reliable and a decisive word on every matter.

Let me reflect on whether I use it as the criterion for every matter in my life.

VERSE 15

إِنَّهُمْ يَكِيدُونَ كَيْدًا ﴿١٥﴾

Indeed, they are plotting a plot. [15]

15.1 [*Kayd* (كَيْد, plot)] is derived from *kāda* meaning to secretly conspire or hatch a plot in order to deceive.[62]

15.2 The phrase '*innahum yakīdūna*' (indeed, they are plotting) has been used to assert the fact that the polytheists and disbelievers were continually plotting the downfall of the Prophet (s) and his message. They contrived many such plots, some of which are mentioned in the discussion below:

---

60 Muṣṭafawī, *al-Taḥqīq*.

61 Ṭabāṭabā'ī, *al-Mīzān*, 20/261.

62 Muṣṭafawī, *al-Taḥqīq*.

DISCUSSION 2: THE PLOTTING OF THE POLYTHEISTS

1. Ridicule: Initially, polytheists did not perceive a great threat from the message and resorted to ridiculing the Prophet (s).
   Q21:36 states:

   وَإِذَا رَآكَ الَّذِينَ كَفَرُوا إِنْ يَتَّخِذُونَكَ إِلَّا هُزُوًا
   أَهَٰذَا الَّذِي يَذْكُرُ آلِهَتَكُمْ وَهُمْ بِذِكْرِ الرَّحْمَٰنِ هُمْ كَافِرُونَ

   And when the disbelievers see you [O Muhammad], they take you not except in ridicule, [saying], "Is this the one who speaks [badly] about your gods?" While they [themselves] are deniers at the mention of the all-Merciful.

2. Bribery: As the mission became established, the Quraysh came to Abu Talib urging him to restrain the Prophet (s) from preaching his message. In return, they offered several inducements, including great wealth and authority. However, he (s) flatly refused their overtures by famously saying, "Even if they placed the sun in my right hand and the moon in my left, I would turn it down. Rather, let them give me one word [that there is no deity but Allah], through which they will rule over the Arabs and lead the non-Arabs, and become kings in the Hereafter![63] A response of the polytheists is mentioned in Q38:5,6:

   أَجَعَلَ الْآلِهَةَ إِلَٰهًا وَاحِدًا إِنَّ هَٰذَا لَشَيْءٌ عُجَابٌ ﴿٥﴾
   وَانْطَلَقَ الْمَلَأُ مِنْهُمْ أَنِ امْشُوا وَاصْبِرُوا عَلَىٰ آلِهَتِكُمْ إِنَّ هَٰذَا لَشَيْءٌ يُرَادُ

   Does he make all the gods [into] one God? Indeed, this is a strange thing! And the chiefs from amongst them went about saying, "Continue and be steadfast over [the defence of] your gods. Indeed, this is a thing contrived [against you]."

3. Intimidation: Thereafter, in order to weaken the Prophet (s), the polytheists turned to his followers. They began to torment and mistreat the early Muslims, many of whom were slaves. Amongst them was Bilal, who was tortured at every opportunity by his

---

[63] Majlisī, *Biḥār*, 18/182.

فَأَخْبَرَ أَبُو طَالِبٍ رَسُولَ اللهِ (صَلَّى اللهُ عَلَيْهِ وَآلِهِ) بِذَلِكَ، فَقَالَ: لَوْ وَضَعُوا الشَّمْسَ فِي يَمِينِي، وَالْقَمَرَ فِي شِمَالِي مَا أَرَدْتُهُ، وَلَكِنْ يُعْطُونَنِي كَلِمَةً يَمْلِكُونَ بِهَا الْعَرَبَ، وَيَدِينُ لَهُمْ بِهَا الْعَجَمُ، وَيَكُونُونَ مُلُوكًا فِي الْآخِرَةِ.

master, Umayyah b. Khalaf. Also, Sumayyah bt. Khabbāb and her husband Yāsir were tortured to death by Abu Jahl.[64]

4. Insult: The polytheists began to abuse the Prophet (a) openly in an attempt to demoralize him. The Qur'an has mentioned some of the insulting names that they called the Noble Prophet (s). They referred to him as *majnūn* [(مَجْنُون, a madman) as in Q15:6], *shāʿir* [(شَاعِر, a poet) in Q37:36)], *sāḥir* [(سَاحِر, a magician) in Q38:4], *kāhin* [(كَاهِن, a soothsayer) in Q52:29], and *kadhdhāb* [(كَذَّاب, a liar) in Q38:4)].

5. Boycott: In time, several prominent members of the Quraysh embraced Islam. Furthermore, the two groups of Muslims who had migrated to Abyssinia were also flourishing there. To counter this, the polytheists decided to institute a social boycott against the Muslims in Makka. In the seventh year of the Prophetic mission, the leaders of all the tribes signed an agreement that they would not trade with the Muslims, or enter into marital alliances with them, or support anyone who was a Muslim. This boycott lasted three years and put unprecedented pressure on the Muslims, who were forced to leave their homes and live in a valley in the mountains of Makka belonging to Abu Talib.[65]

6. Assassination: After the end of the boycott, the two great supports of the Prophet (s), Lady Khadijah (a) and Abu Talib (a) passed away in a short space of time. The polytheists now decided that the only way to stop the spread of Islam was to kill the Prophet (s). They sent assassins from several tribes to surround his house, intending to jointly kill him so that the Banu Hashim would not be able to avenge his murder. However, this plot was frustrated also, because the Prophet (s) migrated to Madina on the same night that the killers had gathered.[66] Ali b. Abu Talib slept in his bed in his stead.[67]

7. War: Even when the Prophet (s) had migrated from Makka, the polytheists were determined to destabilize his mission and stop the spread of Islam in Arabia. They engaged the Muslims in several battles, the major ones of which were Badr, Uḥud, Khandaq,

---

64 Subḥānī, *Furūgh-i Abadiyyat*, 1/270.

65 Ibid, 1/342.

66 Ibn Hishām, *Sīrah*, 1/481.

67 Ṭūsī, *al-Amālī*, p. 447.

Khaybar, and Ḥunayn. However, they did not win any of these battles, and in the end, Islam prevailed in the land. Q17:81 states:

وَقُلْ جَاءَ الْحَقُّ وَزَهَقَ الْبَاطِلُ إِنَّ الْبَاطِلَ كَانَ زَهُوقًا

And say, "Truth has come, and falsehood has perished. Indeed, falsehood is ever bound to perish."

SUMMARY OF THE VERSE

The verse states that the disbelievers were constantly conspiring to undermine the Prophet (s) and his message.

REFLECTIVE LEARNING

Plotting against God is no different than trying to deceive a doctor.[68] God's system is such that those who plot against God will only harm themselves.

Let me reflect whether my plans are aligned with God's mission or am I plotting against Him.

VERSE 16

وَأَكِيدُ كَيْدًا ﴿١٦﴾

And I am plotting a plot. [16]

16.1 The verse refers to God's plot and reassures the Prophet (s) that the plotting of the disbelievers would not go unnoticed or unpunished. An appropriate response from God would soon follow.[69]

God has allocated free will to man, allowing him to plot and plan as he wills. However, when he plots against God and the believers, God's system leads the plotter unwittingly to his own destruction. And this is the meaning of God's plot.[70] Q52:42 warns:

أَمْ يُرِيدُونَ كَيْدًا فَالَّذِينَ كَفَرُوا هُمُ الْمَكِيدُونَ

Or do they intend a plot? But those who disbelieve are themselves ensnared in a plot!

---

[68] Muṭahharī, (*Āshnāyī bā Qur'an*), *Āthār*, 28/690.

[69] Rafsanjānī, *Rahnamā*, 20/266.

[70] Muṭahharī, (*Āshnāyī bā Qur'an*), *Āthār*, 28/489.

16.2 When referred to God, 'plot' (*kayd*) takes shape in the form of a process called *istidrāj*, which means to get close to something gradually.[71] It is the process by which God draws those who sin without care towards punishment by degrees, through respite (*imhāl*), continuance of health, and increase of favour.[72]

Q7:182,183 state:

وَالَّذِينَ كَذَّبُوا بِآيَاتِنَا سَنَسْتَدْرِجُهُمْ مِنْ حَيْثُ لَا يَعْلَمُونَ

And [as for] those who deny Our signs - We will progressively lead them (sanastadrijuhum) *[to destruction] from where they do not know.*

Of course, receiving blessings from God does not mean that one is necessarily undergoing *istidrāj*. If we give thanks for these bounties and use them for the pleasure of God, then that is not *istidrāj*. It only becomes so when one becomes arrogant and extravagant, and transgresses God's bounds as a result.[73] This is explained further by the following account. A report states that a companion asked Imam al-Sadiq (a), "I asked God, the Exalted, to grant me wealth and He granted it to me. I asked God to grant me a son, and He granted me a son. I asked Him to grant me a house and He granted it to me. Now I am afraid that this may be an instance of *istidrāj*." The Imam (a) replied, "By God, if it is accompanied by [your] grateful praise, then it is not."[74]

DISCUSSION 3: THE MEANING OF THE 'PLOTTING' OF GOD

There are several words used in the meaning of planning or plotting in the Qur'an. Some of them are: *makr*, *khudʿa*, and *kayd*, and they have very similar meanings.

1. *Makr* is derived from *makara* which means to scheme or plot. It refers to a plan devised to avert someone from their objective in a

---

71 Ṭabāṭabā'ī, *al-Mīzān*, 8/346.

72 Shīrāzī, *Namūneh*, 7/34.

73 Muṭahharī, (*Āshnāyī bā Qur'an*), *Āthār*, 27/626.

74 Kulaynī, *al-Kāfī*, 2/97.

عَنْ عُمَرَ بْنِ يَزِيدَ، قَالَ: قُلْتُ لِأَبِي عَبْدِ اللهِ (عَلَيْهِ السَّلَامُ): إِنِّي سَأَلْتُ اللهَ عَزَّ وَجَلَّ أَنْ يَرْزُقَنِي مَالًا فَرَزَقَنِي، وَإِنِّي سَأَلْتُ اللهَ أَنْ يَرْزُقَنِي وَلَدًا فَرَزَقَنِي وَلَدًا، وَسَأَلْتُهُ أَنْ يَرْزُقَنِي دَارًا فَرَزَقَنِي، وَقَدْ خِفْتُ أَنْ يَكُونَ ذَلِكَ اسْتِدْرَاجًا. فَقَالَ: أَمَا وَاللهِ مَعَ الْحَمْدِ فَلَا.

manner that they do not realize it.[75]. *Makr* can be either praiseworthy or blameworthy. For instance in Q35:43 it has been used with the adjective 'evil', because the intention of the plotters was malicious:

اِسْتِكْبَارًا فِي الْأَرْضِ وَمَكْرَ السَّيِّئِ وَلَا يَحِيقُ الْمَكْرُ السَّيِّئُ إِلَّا بِأَهْلِهِ

[On account of their] arrogance in the land and their plotting (makr) of evil, but the evil plot does not encompass except those who make it...

When it is done to divert the attention of an evildoer, then it is an act of merit. And this is the *makr* that God attributes to Himself. For example, Q8:30 states:

وَإِذْ يَمْكُرُ بِكَ الَّذِينَ كَفَرُوا لِيُثْبِتُوكَ أَوْ يَقْتُلُوكَ أَوْ يُخْرِجُوكَ
وَيَمْكُرُونَ وَيَمْكُرُ اللَّهُ وَاللَّهُ خَيْرُ الْمَاكِرِينَ

And [remember] when those who disbelieved were devising plans against you to restrain you or kill you or drive you out [from Makka]. They devised plans and Allah [also] devised plans. And Allah is the best of planners.

2. *Khudʿa* is derived from *khadaʿa* meaning a stratagem intended to mislead or deceive. A famous tradition from the Prophet (s) states: War is deception.[76]

The Qurʾan uses this term to describe the attempts of the hypocrites to deceive God by their pretence of worship. Q4:142 states:

إِنَّ الْمُنَافِقِينَ يُخَادِعُونَ اللَّهَ وَهُوَ خَادِعُهُمْ وَإِذَا قَامُوا إِلَى الصَّلَاةِ
قَامُوا كُسَالَىٰ يُرَاؤُونَ النَّاسَ وَلَا يَذْكُرُونَ اللَّهَ إِلَّا قَلِيلًا

Indeed, the hypocrites seek to deceive God, but it is He who deceives (requites their deceit to) them. And when they stand for prayer, they stand with laziness to be seen by the people, and do not remember God except a little.

In the verse above, '*He deceives them*' means that God seals their hearts, veils His signs from them, and closes the pathways to

[75] Rāghib, *al-Mufradāt*.
[76] ʿĀmilī, *Wasāʾil*, 15/133.

عَنِ الرَّسُولِ (صَلَّى اللهُ عَلَيْهِ وَآلِهِ) – الْحَرْبُ خُدْعَةٌ.

guidance for them. And in this way, *khudʿa* always comes back to damage the one who does it in the first place.[77]

3. *Kayd* is a similar word to the previous two terms. It refers to planning or plotting for a good purpose, or scheming for an evil one. In the Qur'an, God always mentions His planning after He mentions the planning of the people.[78]

   The *kayd* of God takes place in a subtle way. He does not immediately chastise those who transgress and sin. In fact, He gives them more blessings and improves their situation.

SUMMARY OF THE VERSE

The verse states that God, too, has a plot of His own.

REFLECTIVE LEARNING

Let me reflect on the bounties that I receive from God. Is there any possibility that I could be undergoing *istidrāj*? The only way to be sure that I am not doing so is by giving thanks for these bounties and using them for the pleasure of God.

VERSE 17

فَمَهِّلِ الْكَافِرِينَ أَمْهِلْهُمْ رُوَيْدًا ﴿١٧﴾

So allow respite to the disbelievers. Respite them for a while. [17]

17.1 The verse begins with *fa* (so) and means, 'now that you know that God also has plan...'[79] [*Mahhil* (مَهِّل, allow respite)] is derived from *mahala* which means to delay and proceed slowly and deliberately. Here, the commands *mahhil* and *amhil* are instructions to give respite.[80] The phrase is repeated for emphasis on acting moderately with the disbelievers.[81]

---

[77] Muṣṭafawī, *al-Taḥqīq*.

[78] Ibid.

[79] Rafsanjānī, *Rahnamā*, 20/266.

[80] Muṣṭafawī, *al-Taḥqīq*.

[81] Shīrāzī, *Namūneh*, 26/377.

[*Ruwaydā* (رُوَيْدًا, for a while)] comes from *rawd* means to do something gently or at leisure. The *yā* (ى) in the word gives the meaning of 'brief' and here, it means give them a gentle and brief respite.[82]

17.2 The verse instructs the Prophet (s) not to be hasty in acting or praying against the disbelievers. Instead, he is asked to leave them to their plotting, because it was only a matter of time before God's own promise and chastisement would overcome them.[83]

Q3:178 states:

وَلَا يَحْسَبَنَّ الَّذِينَ كَفَرُوا أَنَّمَا نُمْلِي لَهُمْ خَيْرٌ لِأَنْفُسِهِمْ

إِنَّمَا نُمْلِي لَهُمْ لِيَزْدَادُوا إِثْمًا وَلَهُمْ عَذَابٌ مُهِينٌ

And let disbelievers never think that the respite that We give them is good for them. We only give them respite so that they may increase in sin, and for them is a humiliating punishment.

SUMMARY OF THE VERSE

In summary, the verse instructs the Prophet (s) to give the disbelievers respite and leave them for a while so that God's plan unfolds for them.

REFLECTIVE LEARNING

Sometimes God gives respite and that emboldens those who defy Him. Let me reflect on whether I am one of those sinners who has been given respite to continue in the disobedience of God. Let me seek His forgiveness without delay at every lapse.

82 Ṭūsī, *al-Tibyān*, 10/327.

83 Ṭabāṭabā'ī, *al-Mīzān*, 20/261.

SURAT AL-AʿLĀ
THE MOST HIGH (87)

TEXT AND TRANSLATION

سُورَةُ الأَعْلَى

بِسْمِ اللَّهِ الرَّحْمَٰنِ الرَّحِيمِ

سَبِّحِ ٱسْمَ رَبِّكَ ٱلْأَعْلَى ﴿١﴾ ٱلَّذِي خَلَقَ فَسَوَّىٰ ﴿٢﴾ وَٱلَّذِي قَدَّرَ فَهَدَىٰ ﴿٣﴾
وَٱلَّذِي أَخْرَجَ ٱلْمَرْعَىٰ ﴿٤﴾ فَجَعَلَهُ غُثَاءً أَحْوَىٰ ﴿٥﴾ سَنُقْرِئُكَ فَلَا تَنسَىٰ ﴿٦﴾
إِلَّا مَا شَاءَ ٱللَّهُ إِنَّهُ يَعْلَمُ ٱلْجَهْرَ وَمَا يَخْفَىٰ ﴿٧﴾ وَنُيَسِّرُكَ لِلْيُسْرَىٰ ﴿٨﴾ فَذَكِّرْ إِن
نَفَعَتِ ٱلذِّكْرَىٰ ﴿٩﴾ سَيَذَّكَّرُ مَن يَخْشَىٰ ﴿١٠﴾ وَيَتَجَنَّبُهَا ٱلْأَشْقَى ﴿١١﴾ ٱلَّذِي
يَصْلَى ٱلنَّارَ ٱلْكُبْرَىٰ ﴿١٢﴾ ثُمَّ لَا يَمُوتُ فِيهَا وَلَا يَحْيَىٰ ﴿١٣﴾ قَدْ أَفْلَحَ مَن تَزَكَّىٰ
﴿١٤﴾ وَذَكَرَ اسْمَ رَبِّهِ فَصَلَّىٰ ﴿١٥﴾ بَلْ تُؤْثِرُونَ الْحَيَاةَ الدُّنْيَا ﴿١٦﴾ وَالْآخِرَةُ
خَيْرٌ وَأَبْقَىٰ ﴿١٧﴾ إِنَّ هَٰذَا لَفِي الصُّحُفِ الْأُولَىٰ ﴿١٨﴾ صُحُفِ إِبْرَاهِيمَ وَمُوسَىٰ
﴿١٩﴾

In the name of God, the Beneficent, the Merciful.

Glorify the name of your Lord, the most High. [1] *Who created and then proportioned.* [2] *And who measured and then guided.* [3] *And who brings forth the pasture.* [4] *And then turns it into dark stubble.* [5] *We will make you recite [O Muhammad] and you will not forget.* [6] *Except what Allah wills. Indeed, He knows the manifest and what is hidden.* [7] *And We will ease you towards ease.* [8] *Therefore [do] remind, in case reminding is of benefit.* [9] *He who fears [Allah] will be reminded.* [10] *But the wretched one will avoid it,* [11] *[the one] who will [enter and] burn in the greatest Fire,* [12] *neither dying therein nor living.* [13] *He has certainly succeeded who purifies himself,* [14] *and remembers the name of his Lord, and prays.* [15] *But you prefer the life of this world,* [16] *while the Hereafter is better and more enduring.* [17] *Indeed, this is [found] in the early scrolls,* [18] *the scrolls of Ibrahim and Musa.* [19]

INTRODUCTION

Surat al-Aʿlā (87) was the 8th chapter to be revealed. It has nineteen verses and was revealed in Makka, after Surat al-Takwīr (81).[1] The surah is named after the name of God (*al-Aʿlā*, the most High) mentioned in the first verse.

Some exegetes believe that the latter part (verse 15 onwards) of the surah may have been revealed in Madina. They base their opinion on the verses, '*He has certainly succeeded who purifies himself, and mentions the name of his Lord, and prays,*' which according to several reports, refers to the payment of *zakāt al-fiṭrah* and offering the Eid prayer, which only became obligatory after the legislation of fasting in Madina.[2] However it is possible that these reports are an interpretation (*ta'wīl*) of the verses or an instance of their application (*miṣdāq*).[3]

The surah begins with a mention of seven attributes of God. Thereafter, it mentions the duties of the Prophet (s), which include reminding those who would take heed.

Next, it mentions the difference in the people's response to this reminder. Those who fear God will take heed but those who are wretched will ignore it and earn the chastisement of Hell thereby.

The surah ends by stating that the truths mentioned in the last verses have been mentioned in the previous scriptures as well, specifically the books given to Prophets Ibrahim (a) and Musa (a).

Surat al-Aʿlā is one of the seven chapters of the Qur'an entitled *al-Musabbiḥāt* that begin with the glorification of God. The other six are al-Isrā' (17), al-Ḥadīd (57), al-Ḥashr (59), al-Ṣaff (61), al-Jumuʿah (62) and al-Taghābun (64).

In five of these surahs (al-Ḥadīd, al-Ḥashr, al-Ṣaff, al-Jumuʿah and al-Taghābun) it is mentioned that every creation in the heavens and the earth existentially glorifies and exalts God (*sabbaḥa lillāhi* or *yusabbiḥu lillāhi*). In Sura al-Isrā', the transcendence of God is declared in the unrestricted form (*subḥān*), and in Surat al-Aʿlā, the believer is commanded to glorify God (*sabbiḥ*).

---

1 Maʿrifat, *'Ulūm-i Qur'ānī*, p. 90.

2 Ṭabāṭabā'ī, *al-Mīzān*, 20/264.

3 Shīrāzī, *Namūneh*, 26/403.

LINK TO THE PREVIOUS CHAPTER

The previous chapter, Surat al-Ṭāriq, ended with the mention of God's respite to the disbelievers for a time, as is His established practice. Surat al-Aʿlā continues with the mention of God's attributes and power over creation.

In Surat al-Ṭāriq, God talks specifically about the lowly origin of mankind and in Surat al-Aʿlā, He compares man's life to the flourishing and decline of vegetation.

MERITS OF RECITATION

- It is reported that the Prophet (s) would not sleep before he recited the seven chapters that begin with glorification (*musabbiḥāt*). He used to say, "In these surahs there is a verse that is better than one-thousand verses." The narrator says that he was referring to the last verse of Surat al-Ḥashr.[4]
- A tradition from the Prophet (s) states: God will reward whoever recites Surat al-Aʿlā ten times for every word that He revealed to Ibrahim (a), Musa (a), and Muhammad (s).[5]
- A tradition from Imam al-Sadiq (a) states: Whoever recites this surah in his obligatory or supererogatory prayers will be told on the Day of Judgement, "Enter Paradise from any one of its doors," God-willing.[6]

EXEGESIS

VERSE 1

سَبِّحِ ٱسْمَ رَبِّكَ الْأَعْلَى ﴿١﴾

Glorify the name of your Lord, the most High.

---

[4] Majlisī, *Biḥār*, 89/312.

كَانَ رَسُولُ اللهِ صَلَّى اللهُ عَلَيْهِ وَآلِهِ لَا يَنَامُ حَتَّى يَقْرَأَ الْمُسَبِّحَاتِ وَكَانَ يَقُولُ إِنَّ فِيهِنَّ آيَةً هِيَ أَفْضَلُ مِنْ أَلْفِ آيَةٍ. قَالَ يَحْيَى: فَنَرَاهَا الْآيَةَ الَّتِي فِي آخِرِ الْحَشْرِ.

[5] Nūrī, *Mustadrak al-Wasā’il*, 4/358.

عَنِ الرَّسُولِ (صَلَّى اللهُ عَلَيْهِ وَآلِهِ) – مَنْ قَرَأَ سُورَةَ الْأَعْلَى أَعْطَاهُ اللهُ مِنَ الْأَجْرِ عَشْرَ حَسَنَاتٍ بِعَدَدِ كُلِّ حَرْفٍ أَنْزَلَهُ اللهُ عَلَى إِبْرَاهِيمَ وَمُوسَى وَمُحَمَّدٍ صَلَّى اللهُ عَلَيْهِ وَآلِهِ.

[6] ʿĀmilī, *Wasā’il*, 6/143.

عَنِ الصَّادِقِ (عَلَيْهِ السَّلَامُ) – مَنْ قَرَأَ «سَبِّحِ ٱسْمَ رَبِّكَ الْأَعْلَى» فِي فَرِيضَةٍ أَوْ نَافِلَةٍ قِيلَ لَهُ يَوْمَ الْقِيَامَةِ ادْخُلِ الْجَنَّةَ مِنْ أَيِّ أَبْوَابِ الْجَنَّةِ شِئْتَ إِنْ شَاءَ اللهُ.

1.1 The chapter begins by instructing the Prophet to glorify the name of his Lord, the most High. This command is likewise directed to the believers as well.[7]

1.2 [*Sabbiḥ* (سَبِّح, glorify)] is originally derived from *sabbaḥa* which means to praise and glorify. However, its verbal noun *tasbīḥ* has acquired a technical meaning denoting both sanctifying God (*taqdīs*) and declaring Him free from every defect (*tanzīh*).[8]

In practice, it means not ascribing to Him things that He is far above, such as other deities, partners, lords, intercessors, and sustainers, and not attributing to Him any defect such as inability, ignorance, oppression, and heedlessness.[9]

When we say *Subḥānallāh*, we acknowledge the transcendence of God above every description we can apply to Him. Q37:180 states:

سُبْحَانَ رَبِّكَ رَبِّ الْعِزَّةِ عَمَّا يَصِفُونَ

Glory be to your Lord, the Lord of Honour, above what they describe.

1.3 *Tasbīḥ* in its practical sense means glorifying God through the mention of *Subḥānallāh* which means 'Glory be to God', or more correctly, 'God is free of any defect.' It should also be accompanied by the praise (*ḥamd*) of God. Q25:58 states:

وَتَوَكَّلْ عَلَى الْحَيِّ الَّذِي لَا يَمُوتُ وَسَبِّحْ بِحَمْدِهِ

And place your trust in the ever-Living who does not die,
and glorify [Allah] with His praise...

And this is the manner of the *tasbīḥ* that is recommended in the *rukūʿ* and *sujūd* of the daily prayers.

Tasbīḥ also includes other phrases that glorify and praise God, such as *taḥmīd* (*Alḥamdu lillāh*, grateful praise be to God), *takbīr* (*Allāhu akbar*, God is greater), and *tahlīl* (*Lā ilāha illallāh,* there is no deity besides God).[10]

One can recite '*Subḥāna Rabbī al-ʿAẓīmi wa bi Ḥamdihi*' (Glory be to my Sustainer, the all-Mighty, and I gratefully praise Him) in *rukūʿ* once, and '*Subḥāna Rabbī al-Aʿlāʾ wa bi Ḥamdihi*' (Glory be to my

---

[7] Ṭusī, *al-Tibyān*, 10/328.

[8] Muṣṭafawī, *al-Taḥqīq*.

[9] Ṭabāṭabāʾī, *al-Mīzān*, 20/264.

[10] Majlisī, *Biḥār*, 82/337.

Sustainer, the most High, and I gratefully praise Him) in *sajdah* once, or any phrase such as the *taḥmīd*, *takbīr*, and *tahlīl* three times.[11]

1.4 In the traditions, the recitation of the *tasbīḥ* attributed to Lady Fatimah (a) has been emphasized greatly, especially after the daily obligatory prayers. This *tasbīḥ* includes the recitation of *Allāhu Akbar* 34 times, *Alḥamdu lillāh* 33 times and *Subḥānallāh* 33 times.

A tradition from Imam al-Sadiq (a) states: Whoever recites the *tasbīḥ* of Fatimah (a) before he moves from his place after his obligatory prayer will be forgiven his sins by God. And he should start [the *tasbīḥ*] with the *takbīr*.[12]

1.5 [*Ism* (اِسْم, name)]. Names are of two kinds: For people and objects, their name is a means to identify them, and has no particular additional relationship to them. Muslims have been encouraged to give their children good names that they may aspire to but ultimately, these names are primarily used for identifying the individual.

However, the names of God are quite different from this concept. Each name of God points to one of His attributes and is not separate from His essence. For example, when we say God's name is *al-Raḥmān*, we mean He is Mercy itself and that all Mercy emanates from Him.[13]

1.6 When man turns towards God, the Exalted, in all matters of his life and livelihood, he is instructed to do so through His beautiful Names (*al-Asmā' al-Ḥusnā*). Q7:180 states:

وَلِلَّهِ الْأَسْمَاءُ الْحُسْنَىٰ فَادْعُوهُ بِهَا

And to Allah belong the most beautiful Names,
so invoke Him by them...

A supplication attributed to Imam al-Sadiq (a) states: O Allah! I beseech You by Your greatest Name, that is most mighty, most majestic, most magnificent, and most noble. [The Name] by which if You are asked to open the closed doors of the sky with mercy, they will be opened. And by which if You are asked to widen the

---

11 Sīstānī, *Minhāj al-Ṣāliḥīn*, 1/241.

12 Kulaynī, *al-Kāfī*, 3/342.

عَنِ الصَّادِقِ (عَلَيْهِ السَّلَامُ) – مَنْ سَبَّحَ تَسْبِيحَ فَاطِمَةَ الزَّهْرَاءِ عَلَيْهَا السَّلَامُ قَبْلَ أَنْ يَثْنِيَ رِجْلَيْهِ مِنْ صَلَاةِ الْفَرِيضَةِ غَفَرَ اللهُ لَهُ وَلْيَبْدَأْ بِالتَّكْبِيرِ.

13 Muṭahharī, (*Āshnāyī bā Qur'an*), *Āthār*, 28/497.

constricted doors of the earth for relief, they would be opened wide. And by which if You were asked to ease hardships, they would be eased...[14]

1.7 '*Sabbiḥ isma*' may mean to purify His name from the meanings we consider when we apply His attributes to other than Him, or it could simply mean 'glorify the Named', that is, 'glorify Allah.'[15]

1.8 [*Rabbika* (رَبِّكَ, your Lord)]. The term *rabb* can be used for anyone who has authority and ownership of something.[16] When used for mankind it refers to a symbiotic relationship where man needs the thing he owns, just as it needs him. However, when used for God, *Rabb* denotes the Sustainer, Owner, and Cherisher of mankind, who guides them towards their perfection, without any need for Himself.[17] This is why glory belongs only to Him.

1.9 '*Your Lord*' in this verse means that the Lord to whom the Prophet (s) was guiding the people was distinct from the lords of the idolaters.[18]

The idolaters did not like to hear about the Lord that the Prophet (s) guided to. Q39:45 states:

وَإِذَا ذُكِرَ اللّٰهُ وَحْدَهُ ٱشْمَأَزَّتْ قُلُوبُ الَّذِينَ لَا يُؤْمِنُونَ بِالْآخِرَةِ
وَإِذَا ذُكِرَ الَّذِينَ مِنْ دُونِهِ إِذَا هُمْ يَسْتَبْشِرُونَ

And when Allah alone is mentioned, the hearts of those who do not believe in the Hereafter shrink with aversion, but when those [worshipped] other than Him are mentioned, then they rejoice!

1.10 [*Al-Aʿlā* (الأَعْلَى, most High)] here refers to God. The term is derived from *ʿuluww* denoting ultimate and limitless elevation. *Al-Aʿlā* essentially means the One who is superior and above anything

---

[14] Ṭūsī, *Miṣbāḥ al-Mutahajjid, Duʿāʾ al-Simāt (al-Shabbūr)*, 1/417-420.

عَنِ الصَّادِقِ (عَلَيْهِ السَّلَامُ) – اَللّٰهُمَّ إِنِّي أَسْأَلُكَ بِٱسْمِكَ الْعَظِيمِ الْأَعْظَمِ الْأَعَزِّ الْأَجَلِّ الْأَكْرَمِ الَّذِي إِذَا دُعِيتَ بِهِ عَلَى مَغَالِقِ أَبْوَابِ السَّمَاءِ لِلْفَتْحِ بِالرَّحْمَةِ ٱنْفَتَحَتْ وَإِذَا دُعِيتَ بِهِ عَلَى مَضَائِقِ أَبْوَابِ الْأَرْضِ لِلْفَرَجِ ٱنْفَرَجَتْ وَإِذَا دُعِيتَ بِهِ عَلَى الْعُسْرِ لِلْيُسْرِ تَيَسَّرَتْ...

[15] Rāzī, *Mafātīḥ al-Ghayb*, 31/125.

[16] Ṭabāṭabāʾī, *al-Mīzān*, 1/21.

[17] Muṭahharī, (*Āshnāyī bā Qurʾan*), *Āthār*, 28/495.

[18] Shīrāzī, *Namūneh*, 26/384.

else that can be considered,[19] and denotes the One whose power and capability (*qudrah*) cannot be superseded or resisted.[20]

Here, *al-Aʿlā* can also be taken as an adjective for *Rabb*, in which case the verse would mean, 'glorify His name because He is the most High Lord.'[21]

1.11 A report states that when this verse was revealed, the Prophet (s) instructed the believers to recite it in the prostrations (*sujūd*) in their prayer, just as he had instructed them to recite Q56:96, '*So Glorify the name of your Lord, the all-Mighty* (al-*ʿAẓīm*), in their bowing (*rukūʿ*).[22]

1.12 A tradition from Imam Ali (a) states: When you complete the recitation of the last of the *musabbiḥāt* surahs (al-Aʿlā), then say, "Glory be to Allah, the most High."[23]

SUMMARY OF THE VERSES

The verse instructs the Prophet (s), and the believers by extension, to glorify and sanctify the name of God, the most High.

REFLECTIVE LEARNING

The attribute *Rabb* brings to mind the closeness of God as our Cherisher and Sustainer. At the same time, the attribute *Aʿlā* denotes how He is beyond our comprehension. This verse juxtaposes these two attributes in the command to glorify Him.

This makes us realize how we can appreciate God's role in our lives, while also accept that His true essence is beyond our comprehension. This is the concept of God being Immanent and Transcendent at the same time.

Let me reflect on the beautiful names of God with this attitude. Do I use these Names to invoke Him in different circumstances?

---

[19] Rāghib, *al-Mufradāt*.

[20] Ṭabrasī, *al-Bayān*, 10/719.

[21] Ṭabāṭabā'ī, *al-Mīzān*, 20/264.

[22] Rāwandī, *Fiqh al-Qur'an*, 1/102.

أَنَّهُ لَمَّا نَزَلَ قَوْلُهُ تَعَالَى «فَسَبِّحْ بِٱسْمِ رَبِّكَ الْعَظِيمِ» قَالَ النَّبِيُّ صَلَّى اللهُ عَلَيْهِ وَآلِهِ: اِجْعَلُوهَا فِي رُكُوعِكُمْ وَلَمَّا نَزَلَ قَوْلُهُ «سَبِّحِ ٱسْمَ رَبِّكَ ٱلْأَعْلَى» قَالَ عَلَيْهِ السَّلَامُ: ضَعُوا هَذَا فِي سُجُودِكُمْ.

[23] ʿĀmilī, *Wasā'il*, 6/72.

عَنْ عَلِيٍّ (عَلَيْهِ السَّلَامُ) – إِذَا فَرَغْتُمْ مِنَ الْمُسَبِّحَاتِ ٱلْأَخِيرَةِ فَقُولُوا سُبْحَانَ اللهِ الْأَعْلَى.

VERSES 2, 3

ٱلَّذِي خَلَقَ فَسَوَّىٰ ﴿٢﴾ وَٱلَّذِي قَدَّرَ فَهَدَىٰ ﴿٣﴾

Who created and then proportioned. [2] *And who measured and then guided.* [3]

2-3.1 After the mention of two attributes, *Rabb* and *al-Aʿlā*, four further qualities of God are discussed in these two verses to expound on the two attributes.[24]

2-3.2 '*Who created and then proportioned.*': God created the universe and its inhabitants and then proportioned each and every creation according to its designated function. [*Khalaqa* (خَلَقَ, created)] means brought together its constituent elements.[25]

[*Sawwā* (سَوَّىٰ, proportioned)] is derived from *sawiya* which means to be equal, and its verbal noun *taswiyah* means to regulate, put everything in its correct place, and perfect the make of something.[26]

2-3.3 '*And who measured and then guided.*': [*Qaddara* (قَدَّرَ, measured)] is derived from *qadara* which means to measure and estimate,[27] and its verbal noun *taqdīr* means to calculate according to a specific measure. And the specific measure is what is decreed by God's wisdom.[28] Every part of the creature is created in the correct measure in terms of its size, position, function, length of life, and so on.[29]

[*Hadā* (هَدَىٰ, guided)] refers to the intrinsic and existential guidance (*al-hidāyat al-takwīniyyah*) that has been granted to every single creation to direct it towards its purpose and perfection. Q20:50 states:

قَالَ رَبُّنَا ٱلَّذِي أَعْطَىٰ كُلَّ شَيْءٍ خَلْقَهُۥ ثُمَّ هَدَىٰ

He [Musa] said, "Our Lord is He who gave each thing its form and then guided [it]."

---

[24] Shīrāzī, *Namūneh*, 26/385.

[25] Ṭabāṭabā'ī, *al-Mīzān*, 20/265.

[26] Muṣṭafawī, *al-Taḥqīq*.

[27] Ibid.

[28] Ṭūsī, *al-Tibyān*, 10/329.

[29] Muṭahharī, (*Āshnāyī bā Qur'an*), *Āthār*, 28/501.

2-3.4 Therefore, after God created and proportioned creation, He ordained its potential and guided it towards achieving the goal of its creation. This can be readily appreciated every time we discover more details about any creation of God, and points towards His role as the Sustainer (*Rabb*).

However, man, who is a creature that has superior potential and possesses free will, is also given further guidance which is legislative (*tashrīʿī*), through scriptures and the example of the Prophets (a). And interestingly, all aspects of this external guidance are designed to complete and perfect his internal (*takwīnī*) guidance.[30]

SUMMARY OF THE VERSES

The verses state that God created the entire cosmos and He proportioned each creation, allocated it a potential according to a measure based on His wisdom, and then guided it to achieve the objective of its creation.

REFLECTIVE LEARNING

Let me reflect on the blessings and guidance that God has endowed me with specifically.

Am I using these blessings to be the best version of myself that I can be?

VERSES 4, 5

وَالَّذِي أَخْرَجَ الْمَرْعَىٰ ﴿٤﴾ فَجَعَلَهُ غُثَاءً أَحْوَىٰ ﴿٥﴾

And who brings forth the pasture. [4] *And then turns it into dark stubble.*

4-5.1 Another quality of God, who is *al-Rabb*, and *al-ʿAlā*, is mentioned in these two verses. This quality refers to His provision for the quadrupeds who serve man.

4-5.2 '*And who brings forth the pasture*': [*Akhraja* (أَخْرَجَ, brings forth)] is derived from *ikhrāj* meaning to bring something out. It is as if these things were already present in the earth and God caused them to be expelled.[31]

---

[30] Shīrāzī, *Namūneh*, 26/386.

[31] Ibid, 26/387.

[*Marʿā* (مَرْعَىٰ, pasture)] is derived from *raʿā*, which means to tend animals. Here it refers to both the vegetation that animals consume as well as the place where they are taken to graze.[32]

4-5.3 '*And then turns it into dark stubble.*': After its freshness in spring and summer, the greenery gradually dies back and decomposes.

[*Ghuthāʾ* (غُثَاءً, stubble)] originally means dried vegetation that floats in floodwater like froth. Thereafter, it came to refer to anything that decays and decomposes. In this verse, it refers to dried up fodder.[33]

[*Aḥwā* (أَحْوَىٰ, dark)] here refers to the change in form and colour of fresh pasture as it dries and acquires a blackish and motley hue.[34] The decaying vegetation is absorbed naturally into the earth to rejuvenate the soil and produce new growth which is how God sustains life on earth. Some of it is fossilized in time to form coal, which is a common source of energy.[35]

4-5.4 The change of fresh greenery into dull stubble reminds man of the transience and degeneration of the life of this world. Q18:45 states:

وَٱضْرِبْ لَهُم مَّثَلَ ٱلْحَيَاةِ ٱلدُّنْيَا كَمَاءٍ أَنزَلْنَاهُ مِنَ ٱلسَّمَاءِ فَٱخْتَلَطَ بِهِ نَبَاتُ ٱلْأَرْضِ
فَأَصْبَحَ هَشِيمًا تَذْرُوهُ ٱلرِّيَاحُ وَكَانَ ٱللَّهُ عَلَىٰ كُلِّ شَيْءٍ مُّقْتَدِرًا

And present to them the example of the life of this world. [It is] like rain which We send down from the sky, and the vegetation of the earth mingles with it and [later] it becomes dry remnants, scattered by the winds. And Allah is able to do all things.

4-5.5 Everything mentioned in the last four verses: creating, proportioning, measuring out, guiding, bringing forth the vegetation that feeds man and animals, and finally making it decompose back into the earth, are all instances and proofs of God's sovereignty and administration (*rubūbiyyah*), and the wise system that He has designed to sustain life.[36]

32 Muṣṭafawī, *al-Taḥqīq*.

33 Shīrāzī, *Namūneh*, 26/387.

34 Muṣṭafawī, *al-Taḥqīq*.

35 Shīrāzī, *Namūneh*, 26/388.

36 Ṭabāṭabāʾī, *al-Mīzān*, 20/266.

Furthermore, all these aspects of God's *rubūbiyyah* make man understand that God Himself is far above any need, and that is why we have to always glorify Him.

SUMMARY OF THE VERSES

The verses mention another sign of God, the Sustainer of creation. He brings forth pasture in some seasons and then causes it to decompose and become stubble in others.

REFLECTIVE LEARNING

Let me look at how plants bloom in the spring, mature in the summer, begin to die in the autumn, and then become stubble in the winter.

Now let me look at the changes that I see in myself as I get older, and reflect on whether I am making the most of each stage of my life – for myself and others around me.

Let me not forget that death is also a stage of my life. Even when herbage decays it becomes food for other plants; let me reflect on whether I will leave behind something that will help others to grow after I leave this world.

VERSES 6 - 8

سَنُقْرِئُكَ فَلَا تَنسَىٰ ﴿٦﴾ إِلَّا مَا شَاءَ اللَّهُ إِنَّهُ يَعْلَمُ الْجَهْرَ وَمَا يَخْفَىٰ ﴿٧﴾ وَنُيَسِّرُكَ لِلْيُسْرَىٰ ﴿٨﴾

We will make you recite [O Muhammad] and you will not forget. [6] *Except what Allah wills. Indeed, He knows the manifest and what is hidden.* [7] *And We will ease you towards ease.* [8]

6-8.1 After mentioning aspects of *tawḥīd* and citing several examples of how God maintains, sustains, and guides creation (His *rubūbiyyah*), the discussion turns to the subject of *nubuwwah* and the specific groups who accept or reject the message of the Prophet (s).[37]

6-8.2 '*We will make you recite [O Muhammad] and you will not forget.*': [*Sanuqri'uka* (سَنُقْرِئُكَ, We will make you recite)] is derived from *qara'a* which means to put letters and words together and pronounce

[37] Shīrāzī, *Namūneh*, 26/393.

them.[38] However, *aqraʾa* denotes making someone else recite correctly and therefore, the verse means, 'We will inspire you to recite the Qur'an.'[39]

Furthermore, the Prophet (s) is informed that whenever Jibraʾil would recite verses to him, he (s) had been granted the ability to repeat and disseminate the verses accurately. The issue of forgetfulness of any part of the revelation would never arise for him.[40]

Revelation was inscribed into his heart so the Prophet (s) would remember every word afterwards.[41] And indeed, this is from the gifts granted to him (s).[42] Q26:193,194 state:

نَزَلَ بِهِ الرُّوحُ الْأَمِينُ ﴿١٩٣﴾ عَلَىٰ قَلْبِكَ لِتَكُونَ مِنَ الْمُنْذِرِينَ

The trustworthy Spirit has brought it down upon your heart [O Muḥammad], that you may be of those who warn.

6-8.3 '*Except as Allah wills.*': This qualifying statement may indicate that if God wills He will delay the revelation.[43] Or it could mean that granting this ability to the Prophet (s) is a gift from God but does not detract from God's omnipotence in all affairs.[44]

Without doubt, in the verse under review, '*except as Allah wills*' cannot mean, 'you will only forget what God wills from the Qur'an', because in that case, the Prophet (s) would be no different from other people and there would be no merit for him in this statement.[45]

6-8.4 The Prophet (s) was acutely aware that revelation was an important trust (*amānah*) that he was receiving from God. A report states that whenever Jibraʾil would bring down revelation to the Prophet (s), he would begin to repeat it fearing that he may forget [part of] it. Before Jibraʾil would complete the revelation, he (s) would start reciting it from the beginning. After this verse was

---

[38] Rāghib, *al-Mufradāt.*

[39] Rāzī, *Mafātīḥ al-Ghayb*, 31/130.

[40] Ṭabāṭabāʾī, *al-Mīzān*, 20/266.

[41] Muṭahharī, (*Āshnāyī bā Qur'an*), *Āthār*, 28/504.

[42] Shīrāzī, *Namūneh*, 26/394.

[43] Ṭūsī, *al-Tibyān*, 10/330.

[44] Ṭabāṭabāʾī, *al-Mīzān*, 20/266.

[45] Ibid.

revealed [he knew that] he would never forget anything.[46] Q75:16-18 state in this regard:

لَا تُحَرِّكْ بِهِ لِسَانَكَ لِتَعْجَلَ بِهِ ﴿١٦﴾ إِنَّ عَلَيْنَا جَمْعَهُ وَقُرْآنَهُ ﴿١٧﴾
فَإِذَا قَرَأْنَاهُ فَاتَّبِعْ قُرْآنَهُ

Do not move your tongue with it, [O Muhammad], to make haste with it (the Qur'an). Indeed, upon Us is its collection [in your heart] and its recitation. So when We have recited it [through Jibra'il], then follow its recitation.

6-8.5 '*Indeed, He knows the manifest and what is hidden.*': [*Jahr* (جَهْر, manifest)] is something that is clearly visible or audible, and its opposite is [*mā yakhfā* (مَا يَخْفَى, what is hidden)], which means something that cannot be seen or heard.[47]

This part of the verse is a general reminder of the fact that God is aware of whatever is said and done openly, as well as that which is concealed in the hearts. It may also be a reassurance to the Prophet (s), that God knew his unspoken concern not to make any error in receiving and transmitting His message.[48]

The phrase also gives the reason for the previous verse, '*We will make you recite...*' God is aware of everything that is manifest and hidden, and has informed the Prophet (s) through revelation of everything that man needs for guidance.[49]

6-8.6 '*And We will ease you towards ease.*': [*Nuyassiru* (نُيَسِّرُ, We will ease] is derived from *yassara*, and its verbal noun *taysīr* means to make easy and facilitate, and [*yusrā* (يُسْرَى, ease)] means easiness and without restriction.[50] The verse reassures the Prophet (s) that God will facilitate for him the path to ease (*ṭarīqat al-yusrā*), and make easy the difficult tasks that lay ahead.[51]

---

[46] Kāshānī, *al-Ṣāfī*, 5/317.

كَانَ النَّبِيُّ صَلَّى اللهُ عَلَيْهِ وَآلِهِ إِذَا نَزَلَ عَلَيْهِ جَبْرَائِيلُ بِالْوَحْيِ يَقْرَأُ مَخَافَةَ أَنْ يَنْسَاهُ. فَكَانَ لَا يَفْرَغُ جَبْرَائِيلُ مِنْ آخِرِ الْوَحْيِ حَتَّى يَتَكَلَّمَ هُوَ بِأَوَّلِهِ فَلَمَّا نَزَلَتْ هَذِهِ الْآيَةُ لَمْ يَنْسَ بَعْدَ ذَلِكَ شَيْئًا.

[47] Ṭabāṭabā'ī, *al-Mīzān*, 20/267.

[48] Muṭahharī, (*Āshnāyī bā Qur'an*), *Āthār*, 28/507, 508.

[49] Shīrāzī, *Namūneh*, 26/395.

[50] Muṣṭafawī, *al-Taḥqīq*.

[51] Shīrāzī, *Namūneh*, 26/396.

Some exegetes say that the phrase, '*We will ease you*' is not the same as '*We will ease for you*' and so the verse means to say that God would strengthen the soul of the Prophet (s) so that he was completely connected to his *fiṭrah*. In this way, his mission would become easier for him to accomplish.[52]

This ease was a great favour of God to His Prophets (a) because when they were appointed to their missions, they underwent great mental strain due to their sense of responsibility to their people, their love for them, and their desire to ensure their salvation.

SUMMARY OF THE VERSES

The verses state that God will make the Prophet (s) recite the Qurʾan and memorize it, so he would never forget a word of it. However, in all cases, God's will always persists. He is aware of what people do openly and what they conceal.

Thereafter, the Prophet (s) is reassured that God will facilitate his mission and ease his task in spreading His word.

REFLECTIVE LEARNING

God is aware of whatever is said and done openly, as well as that which is concealed in the hearts.

Let me reflect on whether my outward actions are in harmony with my inner feelings, because unlike my fellow human beings, God is a witness to both.

VERSES 9 - 13

فَذَكِّرْ إِنْ نَّفَعَتِ الذِّكْرَىٰ ﴿٩﴾ سَيَذَّكَّرُ مَنْ يَخْشَىٰ ﴿١٠﴾ وَيَتَجَنَّبُهَا الْأَشْقَى
﴿١١﴾ الَّذِي يَصْلَى النَّارَ الْكُبْرَىٰ ﴿١٢﴾ ثُمَّ لَا يَمُوتُ فِيهَا وَلَا يَحْيَىٰ ﴿١٣﴾

Therefore [do] remind, in case reminding is of benefit. [9] *He who fears [Allah] will be reminded.* [10] *But the wretched one will avoid it,* [11] *[the one] who will [enter and] burn in the greatest Fire,* [12] *neither dying therein nor living.* [13]

[52] Ṭabāṭabāʾī, *al-Mīzān*, 20/267.

9-13.1 '*Therefore [do] remind,*': The verse begins with *fa* (so, therefore) indicating that reminder is now necessary and possible since the Prophet (s) has glorified the name of his Lord, has been taught the Qur'an in a manner that he would never forget, and his path to disseminating God's message has been made easier.[53]

[*Dhakkir* (ذَكِّرْ, remind)] is derived from *dhakkara* which means to remind and call to attention.[54] Here it is a command to the Prophet (s) to remind and counsel the people.[55] The use of the word 'reminder' is a reference to the fact that every human being already carries the knowledge of right and wrong in his heart. However, he often does not act according to this knowledge due to neglect and distraction, and needs to be reminded.[56] Indeed, the main role of the Prophet (s) was to keep reminding the people. Q88:21 states:

فَذَكِّرْ إِنَّمَا أَنْتَ مُذَكِّرٌ

So remind, [O Muhammad]; indeed, you are only one who reminds.

9-13.2 '*In case reminding is of benefit.*': Exegetes have suggested two different meanings for this part of the verse. The first is, 'remind them, whether they listen or do not listen, because that is the mission you have been appointed to.'[57] Another meaning is based on the alternative significance of the particle '*in* (إِنْ)', which can mean 'if', but can also mean 'because', '(*qad* (قَدْ)'. In this case, the verse will mean, 'remind them, for reminder has benefit.'[58] It is certainly of benefit to everyone who is prepared to accept it; those who fear God will take heed and be reminded, and those who are wretched in character and conduct will not want to know anything about it, but will have no excuse later.

Thereafter, the Prophet (s) is forewarned that people will fall into two groups when confronted with the reminder.

9-13.3 '*He who fears [Allah] will be reminded.*': [*Yakhshā* (يَخْشَىٰ, he fears)]. Fearfulness could be an allusion to the deep concern that some people have about the purpose of life and the Hereafter.

[53] Ibid.

[54] Muṣṭafawī, *al-Taḥqīq*.

[55] Ṭūsī, *al-Tibyān*, 10/331.

[56] Muṭahharī, (*Āshnāyī bā Qur'an*), *Āthār*, 28/510.

[57] Ṭabrasī, *al-Bayān*, 10/721.

[58] Muṭahharī, (*Āshnāyī bā Qur'an*), *Āthār*, 28/512.

However, some exegetes believe that fear here refers to the fear of God and His chastisement.[59]

Fear of God should evoke awe and reverence, not panic and fright. This state comes from knowledge (*maʿrifah*) of God and is proportional to an individual's connection to the innermost aspect of the intellect (*lubb*), which draws fully from the knowledge of the *fiṭrah* and connects man to his Creator. It is such people who become aware when they hear the message of God and His Prophet (s) and thus, they benefit from the reminder.[60] Q13:19 states:

أَفَمَنْ يَعْلَمُ أَنَّمَا أُنْزِلَ إِلَيْكَ مِنْ رَبِّكَ الْحَقُّ كَمَنْ هُوَ أَعْمَىٰ
إِنَّمَا يَتَذَكَّرُ أُولُوا الْأَلْبَابِ

Then is he who knows that what has been revealed to you from your Lord is the truth like one who is blind? Only those who possess deep understanding (ulu'l albāb) *will be reminded.*

We have discussed this concept further in the *tafsīr* of Surat al-Nāziʿāt (79).

9-13.4 '*But the wretched one will avoid it.*': [*Al-Ashqā* (الْأَشْقَى, wretched)] is derived from *shaqiya* which means to be unhappy and miserable.[61] Here, it is used in contrast to *man yakhshā* (one who fears), and so it means that such people have no fear of God or His chastisement.[62] Q53:29 instructs the Prophet (s) to give up on them, stating:

فَأَعْرِضْ عَنْ مَنْ تَوَلَّىٰ عَنْ ذِكْرِنَا وَلَمْ يُرِدْ إِلَّا الْحَيَاةَ الدُّنْيَا

So turn aside from whoever turns his back on Our message and desires nothing but the life of this world.

[*Yatajannabuhā* (يَتَجَنَّبُهَا, will avoid it)] is derived from *janaba* meaning to avert, and here the reflexive form of the verb, *tajannaba*, means to shun and move aside from.[63] The *hā* (it) refers to the reminder.

---

59 Ṭabāṭabāʾī, *al-Mīzān*, 20/269.
60 Muṭahharī, (*Āshnāyī bā Qurʾan*), *Āthār*, 28/512.
61 Muṣṭafawī, *al-Taḥqīq*.
62 Ṭabāṭabāʾī, *al-Mīzān*, 20/269.
63 Muṣṭafawī, *al-Taḥqīq*.

These wretched people would not become mindful of the higher purpose of their existence no matter what they experience in life. They would not benefit from the reminder, and in fact, they seek to avoid it.

9-13.5 '*[The one] who will [enter and] burn in the greatest Fire,*': [*Yaṣlā* (يَصْلَى, burns)] is derived from *ṣalā*, meaning to roast and to burn.[64] Here, it means that these wretched individuals will enter into the most fiery level of Hell.

The fires of this world should serve as a reminder of the fire of Hell, which is many times hotter.

9-13.6 '*Neither dying therein nor living.*': Just like Paradise, Hell is a place of eternal life. This phrase describes the dreadful life of the wretched: he can neither die in the fire so that he is relieved of its torment, nor can he live a life in it wherein he would experience any joy.[65] Q14:17 states:

وَيَأْتِيهِ الْمَوْتُ مِنْ كُلِّ مَكَانٍ وَمَا هُوَ بِمَيِّتٍ

...And death will come to him from every quarter, but he cannot die...

SUMMARY OF THE VERSES

The verses instruct the Prophet (s) to remind the people of their duty in case it would benefit someone.

Those who have fear and awe of God will heed the reminder, but the wretched, who have no such fear, will avoid it. They shall be entered into the most fiery level of Hell, wherein they would nether die, nor live.

REFLECTIVE LEARNING

Let me reflect on the reminder of the Prophet (s) that is before me in the form of the Qur'an and sunnah.

Have I made this reminder a blueprint for my life, or can I do more in this regard?

---

[64] Rāghib, *al-Mufradāt.*

[65] Ṭūsī, *al-Tibyān*, 10/332.

VERSES 14, 15

قَدْ أَفْلَحَ مَنْ تَزَكَّىٰ ﴿١٤﴾ وَذَكَرَ اسْمَ رَبِّهِ فَصَلَّىٰ ﴿١٥﴾

He has certainly succeeded who purifies himself, [14] *and remembers the name of his Lord, and prays.* [15]

14-15.1 *'He has certainly succeeded who purifies himself,'*: [*Aflaḥa* (أَفْلَحَ, he succeeded)] is derived from *falāḥ*, meaning success, and achieving one's objective.[66]

[*Tazakkā* (تَزَكَّىٰ, purify oneself) is derived from *zakā* which means to be pure, and to grow and develop thereby.[67] We have discussed this concept further in the *tafsīr* of the Surat al-Shams (91).

The first factor that determines man's success in God's estimation is self-purification by eliminating undesirable traits from the heart.[68] Becoming pure includes purging the heart of any trace of polytheism (*shirk*), removal of the stain of sin from it through repentance, purifying it from corrupt thoughts and inclinations,[69] and weakening its attachment to this world.[70]

This process is not possible without the help of God, which should be constantly sought. Q24:21 states:

وَلَوْلَا فَضْلُ اللهِ عَلَيْكُمْ وَرَحْمَتُهُ مَا زَكَىٰ مِنْكُمْ مِنْ أَحَدٍ أَبَدًا
وَلَٰكِنَّ اللهَ يُزَكِّي مَنْ يَشَاءُ وَاللهُ سَمِيعٌ عَلِيمٌ

... And had it not been for Allah's grace and mercy upon you, not one of you would have ever been pure. But Allah purifies whom He wills, and Allah is all-Hearing, all-Knowing.

14-15.2 *'And remembers the name of his Lord,'*: Once the purification has been done, the second factor that causes success is the addition of honourable traits to the heart.[71]

---

66 Ṭabāṭabā'ī, *al-Mīzān*, 20/399.

67 Rāghib, *al-Mufradāt.*

68 Muṭahharī, (*Āshnāyī bā Qur'an*), *Āthār*, 28/514.

69 Shīrāzī, *Namūneh*, 26/403.

70 Ṭabāṭabā'ī, *al-Mīzān*, 20/269.

71 Muṭahharī, (*Āshnāyī bā Qur'an*), *Āthār*, 28/514.

Remembering the name of God is more than reciting His names. It is the remembrance of the meaning of those names.[72]

The name *Rabb* has been used here so that we can ponder over the grandeur of God, the loving care with which He sustains us, and the vast bounties that He has blessed us with. This would bring gratefulness and humility to the heart, which then gives meaning to worship. Indeed, worship is much more fruitful once we have purified ourselves.

14-15.3 *'And prays.'*: Once the stages of purification and thereafter *maʿrifah* in the heart are complete, then worship will have significance and value. This is the third, and crowning, factor that leads to man's success (*falāḥ*).[73] *Salat* has been mentioned here as an example because it is the greatest means of spiritual progress and reform.[74]

14-15.4 An interpretation (*ta'wīl*) has been given for *ṣallā* in this verse, outlining one instance of its meaning. A tradition states that Imam al-Ridha (a) asked a companion about the meaning of the verse, *'and mentions the name of his Lord...'*. The companion said, "Whenever he mentions the name of his Lord, he should stand to pray." The Imam (a) told him that this would mean that God, the Almighty, had imposed a difficult duty. Rather, it meant that whenever he mentions the name of his Lord, he should seek blessings (*ṣalawāt*) for Muḥammad (s) and his household (a).[75] Indeed, it is through their teachings and example that we can gain the greatest *maʿrifah* of God.

14-15.5 Another instance of *ta'wīl* is a tradition which states that when Imam al-Sadiq (a) was asked about the verses he said, "[It refers to] the one who pays the *zakāt al-fiṭrah* and goes out to an open space to pray the Eid prayer."[76]

---

[72] Shīrāzī, *Namūneh*, 26/404.

[73] Rāzī, *Mafātīḥ al-Ghayb*, 31/135.

[74] Muṭahharī, (*Āshnāyī bā Qur'an*), *Āthār*, 28/515.

[75] Kulaynī, *al-Kāfī*, 2/494.

عَنِ الرِّضَا (عَلَيْهِ السَّلَامُ) - عَنْ عُبَيْدِ اللهِ الدِّهْقَانِ قَالَ دَخَلْتُ عَلَى أَبِي الْحَسَنِ الرِّضَا (عَلَيْهِ السَّلَامُ) فَقَالَ لِي مَا مَعْنَى قَوْلِهِ «وَذَكَرَ ٱسْمَ رَبِّهِ فَصَلَّىٰ» فَقُلْتُ كُلَّمَا ذَكَرَ اسْمَ رَبِّهِ قَامَ فَصَلَّى. فَقَالَ لِي لَقَدْ كَلَّفَ اللهُ عَزَّ وَجَلَّ هَذَا شَطَطًا. فَقُلْتُ جُعِلْتُ فِدَاكَ وَكَيْفَ هُوَ. فَقَالَ كُلَّمَا ذَكَرَ اسْمَ رَبِّهِ صَلَّى عَلَى مُحَمَّدٍ وَآلِهِ

[76] Ṣadūq, *al-Faqih*, 1/510.

سُئِلَ الصَّادِقُ عَلَيْهِ السَّلَامُ عَنْ قَوْلِ اللهِ عَزَّ وَجَلَّ: «قَدْ أَفْلَحَ مَنْ تَزَكَّىٰ» قَالَ مَنْ أَخْرَجَ الْفِطْرَةَ فَقِيلَ لَهُ «وَذَكَرَ ٱسْمَ رَبِّهِ فَصَلَّىٰ» قَالَ

The argument made against this interpretation is that Surat al-Aʿlā is one of the early Makkī suras, and *zakāt al-fiṭrah* only became obligatory in Madina after fasting was legislated. However, the same argument can be made about the injunction to pray *salat* which is mentioned in this surah as well.

Therefore this tradition is either an example of an application (*miṣdāq*) of the verse, or it implies that the latter half of the surah was revealed in Madina.[77]

SUMMARY OF THE VERSES

The verses state the one who will succeed is the individual who purifies himself, then remembers [the meanings of] the names of His Lord, and then prays to Him.

REFLECTIVE LEARNING

Let me compare the criteria for worldly success with the criteria of success that is outlined in these verses.

Let me reflect on whether I would be successful in God's estimation.

VERSES 16, 17

بَلْ تُؤْثِرُونَ الْحَيَاةَ الدُّنْيَا ﴿١٦﴾ وَالْآخِرَةُ خَيْرٌ وَأَبْقَىٰ ﴿١٧﴾

But you prefer the life of this world, [16] *while the Hereafter is better and more enduring.* [17]

16-17.1 *'But you prefer the life of this world.'*: The verses now move from the third to the second person, perhaps to urge the reader to reflect on whether he is one of those who prefers the life of this world to the Hereafter.

[*Tu'thirūna* (تُؤْثِرُونَ, you prefer)] is derived from *athara*, and its verbal noun *īthār* means to give preference to one thing over another, considering it to be better.[78] Here, it refers to choosing the life of the *dunyā* over the *ākhirah* and devoting oneself to it without

خَرَجَ إِلَى الْجَبَّانَةِ فَصَلَّى.

[77] Shīrāzī, *Namūneh*, 26/403.

[78] Muṣṭafawī, *al-Taḥqīq*.

considering the Hereafter.[79] *Al-ḥayāt al-dunyā* can also refer to a lower and base form of life, in contrast to *al-ḥayāt al-ākhirah,* which is a noble and virtuous form of life.

16-17.2 The preference of the life of this world has been cited in contrast to the purification of the soul, the remembrance of God, and the prayer, that were mentioned in the previous verse.

16-17.3 The verse addresses both believers and disbelievers.[80] The disbeliever prefers this world and thus turns away from God. The believer, when he prefers this world, is in danger of losing his Hereafter.

Indeed, those who immerse themselves in the pleasures of the *dunyā* are gradually dragged towards the disobedience of God. A tradition from Imam al-Sadiq (a) states: The main cause of every sin is the love of this world.[81]

Another tradition states that Imam al-Sajjad (a) was asked, "What is the best of actions before God, the Almighty?" He replied, "There is no act after the recognition (*maʿrifah*) of God, the Almighty, and the recognition of His Messenger (s), that is better than despising the *dunyā*."[82]

16-17.4 *'While the Hereafter is better and more enduring.'*: Both words (better, and more enduring) are used in the comparative sense – in reply to the comparison and decision made by mankind in the previous verse.

The verse makes the point that it is irrational to prefer the *dunyā*, whose pleasures are insubstantial and fleeting, to the *ākhirah*, whose blessings are much greater and perpetual.

A tradition from Imam Ali (a) states: Everything of this *dunyā* sounds better than it looks, while everything of the *ākhirah* looks better than it sounds. So content yourself with what you have heard

---

79 Ṭabrasī, *al-Bayān*, 10/722.

80 Ṭūsī, *al-Tibyān*, 10/332.

81 Kulaynī, *al-Kāfī*, 2/315.

عَنِ الصَّادِقِ (عَلَيْهِ السَّلَامُ) – رَأْسُ كُلِّ خَطِيئَةٍ حُبُّ الدُّنْيَا.

82 Ibid, 2/130.

سُئِلَ عَلِيُّ ابْنُ الْحُسَيْنِ عَلَيْهِمَا السَّلَامُ أَيُّ الْأَعْمَالِ أَفْضَلُ عِنْدَ اللهِ عَزَّ وَجَلَّ؟ فَقَالَ: مَا مِنْ عَمَلٍ بَعْدَ مَعْرِفَةِ اللهِ جَلَّ وَعَزَّ وَمَعْرِفَةِ رَسُولِهِ صَلَّى اللهُ عَلَيْهِ وَآلِهِ أَفْضَلَ مِنْ بُغْضِ الدُّنْيَا.

and not [yet] seen [of the *ākhirah*] and by the information [you have received] of the unknown.[83]

SUMMARY OF THE VERSES

The verses state that man prefers the transient life of this world, while the Hereafter is not only better, but eternal.

REFLECTIVE LEARNING

Let me reflect on whether I am generally inclined to the *ākhirah* rather than the *dunyā* in my decisions and actions.

What is the proof of my claim?

VERSES 18, 19

إِنَّ هَٰذَا لَفِي الصُّحُفِ الْأُولَىٰ ﴿١٨﴾ صُحُفِ إِبْرَاهِيمَ وَمُوسَىٰ ﴿١٩﴾

Indeed, this is [found] in the early scrolls, [18] *the scrolls of Ibrahim and Musa.* [19]

18-19.1 [*Inna hādhā* (إِنَّ هَٰذَا, indeed, this)]. There are several opinions about what the demonstrative pronoun 'this' refers to. Some exegetes say that it refers to the whole surah, while others say that it is only the last four verses, beginning from '*He has certainly succeeded who purifies himself.*'[84] The issue of self-purification and prayer, as well as the declaration that the life of the Hereafter is better and more abiding, are basic tenets found in all Divine books.

[*Ṣuḥuf* (صُحُف, scrolls] here refers to pages on which something is written, or in the case of Musa (a) the tablets (*alwāḥ*) that he was given. Q7:145 states:

وَكَتَبْنَا لَهُ فِي الْأَلْوَاحِ مِنْ كُلِّ شَيْءٍ مَوْعِظَةً وَتَفْصِيلًا لِكُلِّ شَيْءٍ

And We wrote for him (Musa) on the tablets admonition of every kind and a clear explanation of all things...

---

[83] *Nahj al-Balāghah*, sermon 114.

عَنْ عَلِيٍّ (عَلَيْهِ السَّلَامُ) – كُلُّ شَيْءٍ مِنَ الدُّنْيَا سَمَاعُهُ أَعْظَمُ مِنْ عِيَانِهِ، وَكُلُّ شَيْءٍ مِنَ الْآخِرَةِ عِيَانُهُ أَعْظَمُ مِنْ سَمَاعِهِ، فَلْيَكْفِكُمْ مِنَ الْعِيَانِ السَّمَاعُ، وَمِنَ الْغَيْبِ الْخَبَرُ.

[84] Ṭabrasī, *al-Bayān*, 10/722.

18-19.2 Although the message of the last four verses was also contained in other scriptures, the scriptures given to the great Messengers of God, Prophets Ibrahim (a) and Musa (a) have been singled out to honour their particular books.[85]

These two Prophets (a) were highly regarded by the inhabitants of Arabia. Ibrahim (a) was the progenitor of the Arabs, and Musa (a) was the Prophet to the Jews.

18-19.3 A report states that when Abu Dharr asked the Prophet (s) if anything from the scrolls of Ibrahim (a) had been preserved in the Qur'an, he (s) told him to recite the last six verses of Surat al-Aʿlā.[86]

Another report states that Abu Dharr asked the Prophet (s) how many Books God had revealed. The Prophet (s) replied, "One hundred and four books. God revealed fifty scrolls to Shīth (a), thirty scrolls to Idrīs (a), twenty scrolls to Ibrāhīm (a), and He revealed the Tawrāt, Injīl, Zabūr, and Furqān."[87]

SUMMARY OF THE VERSES

The truths contained in this surah, or at least in its last few verses, have been part of the previous scripture also, notably those given to the Prophets Ibrahim (a) and Musa (a).

REFLECTIVE LEARNING

A successful life requires purification of the soul before turning to God in devotion and worship. However, it also requires giving priority in all affairs to the Hereafter over this world.

Let me reflect on my own life and whether I have given thought to leaving this world after living a successful life based on these criteria.

---

[85] Ṭabāṭabā'ī, *al-Mīzān*, 20/270.

[86] Ṭūsī, *al-Amālī*, 1/539.

قُلْتُ: يَا رَسُولَ اللهِ، فَهَلْ فِي الدُّنْيَا شَيْءٌ مِمَّا كَانَ فِي صُحُفِ إِبْرَاهِيمَ وَمُوسَى (عَلَيْهِمَا السَّلَامُ) مِمَّا أَنْزَلَ اللهُ عَلَيْكَ؟ قَالَ: اِقْرَأْ يَا أَبَا ذَرٍّ «قَدْ أَفْلَحَ مَنْ تَزَكَّىٰ * وَذَكَرَ ٱسْمَ رَبِّهِ فَصَلَّىٰ * بَلْ تُؤْثِرُونَ الْحَيَاةَ الدُّنْيَا * وَالْآخِرَةُ خَيْرٌ وَأَبْقَىٰ * إِنَّ هَٰذَا لَفِي الصُّحُفِ الْأُولَىٰ * صُحُفِ إِبْرَاهِيمَ وَمُوسَىٰ»

[87] Baḥrānī, *al-Burhān*, 5/638.

قُلْتُ: يَا رَسُولَ اللهِ، كَمْ أَنْزَلَ اللهُ مِنَ الْكِتَابِ؟ قَالَ مِائَةَ كِتَابٍ وَأَرْبَعَةَ كُتُبٍ، أَنْزَلَ اللهُ عَلَى شِيثٍ خَمْسِينَ صَحِيفَةً، وَعَلَى إِدْرِيسَ ثَلَاثِينَ صَحِيفَةً، وَعَلَى إِبْرَاهِيمَ عِشْرِينَ صَحِيفَةً، وَأَنْزَلَ التَّوْرَاةَ وَالْإِنْجِيلَ وَالزَّبُورَ وَالْفُرْقَانَ.

SURAT AL-GHĀSHIYAH
THE OVERWHELMING (88)

TEXT AND TRANSLATION

سُورَةُ الْغَاشِيَةِ

بِسْمِ اللَّهِ الرَّحْمَٰنِ الرَّحِيمِ

هَلْ أَتَاكَ حَدِيثُ الْغَاشِيَةِ ﴿١﴾ وُجُوهٌ يَوْمَئِذٍ خَاشِعَةٌ ﴿٢﴾ عَامِلَةٌ نَاصِبَةٌ ﴿٣﴾
تَصْلَىٰ نَارًا حَامِيَةً ﴿٤﴾ تُسْقَىٰ مِنْ عَيْنٍ آنِيَةٍ ﴿٥﴾ لَيْسَ لَهُمْ طَعَامٌ إِلَّا مِنْ ضَرِيعٍ
﴿٦﴾ لَا يُسْمِنُ وَلَا يُغْنِي مِنْ جُوعٍ ﴿٧﴾ وُجُوهٌ يَوْمَئِذٍ نَاعِمَةٌ ﴿٨﴾ لِسَعْيِهَا رَاضِيَةٌ
﴿٩﴾ فِي جَنَّةٍ عَالِيَةٍ ﴿١٠﴾ لَا تَسْمَعُ فِيهَا لَاغِيَةً ﴿١١﴾ فِيهَا عَيْنٌ جَارِيَةٌ ﴿١٢﴾
فِيهَا سُرُرٌ مَرْفُوعَةٌ ﴿١٣﴾ وَأَكْوَابٌ مَوْضُوعَةٌ ﴿١٤﴾ وَنَمَارِقُ مَصْفُوفَةٌ ﴿١٥﴾
وَزَرَابِيُّ مَبْثُوثَةٌ ﴿١٦﴾ أَفَلَا يَنْظُرُونَ إِلَى الْإِبِلِ كَيْفَ خُلِقَتْ ﴿١٧﴾ وَإِلَى السَّمَاءِ
كَيْفَ رُفِعَتْ ﴿١٨﴾ وَإِلَى الْجِبَالِ كَيْفَ نُصِبَتْ ﴿١٩﴾ وَإِلَى الْأَرْضِ كَيْفَ سُطِحَتْ
﴿٢٠﴾ فَذَكِّرْ إِنَّمَا أَنْتَ مُذَكِّرٌ ﴿٢١﴾ لَسْتَ عَلَيْهِمْ بِمُصَيْطِرٍ ﴿٢٢﴾ إِلَّا مَنْ تَوَلَّىٰ
وَكَفَرَ ﴿٢٣﴾ فَيُعَذِّبُهُ اللَّهُ الْعَذَابَ الْأَكْبَرَ ﴿٢٤﴾ إِنَّ إِلَيْنَا إِيَابَهُمْ ﴿٢٥﴾ ثُمَّ إِنَّ
عَلَيْنَا حِسَابَهُمْ ﴿٢٦﴾

In the name of God, the Beneficent, the Merciful.

Has the report of the overwhelming [event] reached you? [1] *Faces on that Day will be humbled.* [2] *Labouring [hard], exhausted.* [3] *They will burn in a blazing fire.* [4] *They will [be given] drink from a boiling spring.* [5] *For them will be no food except bitter, thorny fruit.* [6] *Which neither nourishes nor alleviates hunger.* [7] *[Other] faces, that Day, will be joyful.* [8] *Well-pleased with their striving.* [9] *In a lofty garden.* [10] *Wherein they will hear no vain speech.* [11] *Within it is a flowing spring.* [12] *Within it are thrones raised high.* [13] *And cups at hand.* [14] *And cushions set in rows.* [15] *And carpets spread out.* [16] *Do they not look at the camels – how they are created?* [17] *And at the sky – how it is raised?* [18] *And at the mountains – how they are firmly fixed?* [19] *And at the earth – how it is spread out?* [20] *So remind, [O Muhammad]; indeed, you are only one who reminds.* [21] *You are not a controller over them.* [22] *Except he who turns away and disbelieves,* [23] *then God will punish him with the greatest punishment.* [24] *Indeed, to Us is their return.* [25] *Then indeed, upon Us is their reckoning.* [26]

INTRODUCTION

Surat al-Ghāshiyah (88) was the 68th chapter to be revealed.[88] It has twenty-six verses and was revealed in Makka, after Surat al-Dhāriyāt (51). Its name comes from the first verse, which mentions the overwhelming event, *al-Ghāshiyah.*

This chapter both warns and gives good tidings of what is in store for mankind on the Day of Judgement. It depicts the dreadful situation of the sinful and the blessed station of the righteous on that Day, and describes the consequences that await each group.

The surah begins and ends with the mention of the Hereafter. In between, there is a discussion about aspects of *tawḥīd* and *nubuwwah,* which are the two foundations of belief in the resurrection (*maʿād*).

Thereafter, man is invited to look at the marvels that exist around him in order to understand that God can create whatever He wills in the *ākhirah,* just as He has done in the *dunyā.*

The surah instructs the Prophet (s) to remind the people, and informs him that this is all he has been charged to do. Those who do not heed his reminder will be punished with the greatest punishment when they return to God in the Hereafter.

LINK TO THE PREVIOUS CHAPTER

The previous chapter, Surat al-Aʿlā, ended by warning those who prefer the life of the *dunyā,* that the Hereafter is better and more enduring. Surat al-Ghāshiyah begins with a mention of the Hereafter, describing the fate of those who preferred the *dunyā* before elaborating on the dignified status of those who sent forth [good deeds] to the *ākhirah.*

---

[88] Maʿrifat, *ʿUlūm-i Qur'ānī,* p. 90.

In both surahs the Prophet (s) is told to remind, '*fadhakkir*'. In Surat al-Aʿlā (verse 9) the Prophet (s) is told to remind the people of their duty in case it would be of benefit, and in Surat al-Ghāshiyah (verse 21) the Prophet (s) is told to remind the people as that is the extent of his role. He was not sent to compel them.

Then both surahs mention the fate in *ākhirah* of those who turn away from this reminder.

MERITS OF RECITATION

- A tradition from the Prophet (s) states: Whoever recites this surah often, God will make his accounting easy on the Day of Judgement.[89] Such traditions refer to recitation that is accompanied by mindfulness, pondering, and internalizing the message of the surah.
- A tradition from Imam al-Sadiq (a) states: Whoever recites this surah often in his obligatory and supererogatory prayers, God will cover him with His mercy in this world and in the Hereafter. And on the Day of Judgement He will give him security from the punishment of the Fire.[90]

EXEGESIS

VERSE 1

هَلْ أَتَاكَ حَدِيثُ الْغَاشِيَةِ ﴿١﴾

Has the report of the overwhelming [event] reached you?

1.1 The surah begins with a rhetorical question to the Prophet (s) and subsequently, to every listener. Here it may mean, 'Has the amazing news of al-Ghāshiyah not come to you?'[91] Alternately, this type of

---

89 Baḥrānī, *al-Burhān*, 5/641.

عَنِ الرَّسُولِ (صَلَّى اللهُ عَلَيْهِ وَآلِهِ) – مَنْ أَدْمَنَ قِرَاءَتَهَا حَاسَبَهُ اللهُ حِسَابًا يَسِيرًا.

90 ʿĀmilī, *Wasāʾil*, 6/144.

عَنِ الصَّادِقِ (عَلَيْهِ السَّلَامُ) – مَنْ أَدْمَنَ قِرَاءَةَ « هَلْ أَتَاكَ حَدِيثُ الْغَاشِيَةِ» فِي فَرِيضَةٍ أَوْ نَافِلَةٍ غَشَّاهُ اللهُ بِرَحْمَتِهِ فِي الدُّنْيَا وَالْآخِرَةِ، وَأَتَاهُ الْأَمْنَ يَوْمَ الْقِيَامَةِ مِنْ عَذَابِ النَّارِ.

91 Muṭahharī, (*Āshnāyī bā Qurʾan*), *Āthār*, 28/518.

question is also asked when the aim is to highlight the greatness of an event.[92]

1.2 [*Al-Ghāshiyah* (الْغَاشِيَة, the overwhelming)] is derived from *ghashiya* which means to overwhelm, to envelop, or to cover.[93] *Al-Ghāshiyah* is one of the names used in the Qur'an for the Day of Judgement, because that Day and its events will overwhelm and include the entirety of creation.[94] The world of humans, *jinn*, angels, and everything in the physical and metaphysical world will be instantly enveloped by this occurrence.

In the *dunyā*, human beings live and die in succession, but in the *ākhirah*, every human being will be brought forth together at the same time. For this reason, it is a great event indeed.[95]
Q18:47 states:

وَحَشَرْنَاهُمْ فَلَمْ نُغَادِرْ مِنْهُمْ أَحَدًا

...We will gather them and not leave behind any one of them.

1.3 The Day of Judgement and the fate of people in the Hereafter are not concepts that the mind could grasp from experience or intuition, and only revelation can provide some idea about it. For this reason, the surah goes on to furnish some details by contrasting the experience of two groups.[96]

SUMMARY OF THE VERSE

The verse asks the Prophet (s) and the believers whether they are aware of the overwhelming event, *al-Ghāshiyah*, that is to come.

REFLECTIVE LEARNING

Al-Ghāshiyah is an event that will overwhelm everything suddenly. Let me reflect on whether I am prepared for this inescapable event that will come suddenly and without warning.

---

[92] Ṭabāṭabā'ī, *al-Mīzān*, 20/272.

[93] Muṣṭafawī, *al-Taḥqīq*.

[94] Shīrāzī, *Namūneh*, 26/414.

[95] Muṭahharī, (*Āshnāyī bā Qur'an*), *Āthār*, 28/518.

[96] Rāzī, *Mafātīḥ al-Ghayb*, 31/138.

VERSES 2 - 7

وُجُوهٌ يَوْمَئِذٍ خَاشِعَةٌ ﴿٢﴾ عَامِلَةٌ نَاصِبَةٌ ﴿٣﴾ تَصْلَىٰ نَارًا حَامِيَةً ﴿٤﴾ تُسْقَىٰ مِنْ
عَيْنٍ آنِيَةٍ ﴿٥﴾ لَيْسَ لَهُمْ طَعَامٌ إِلَّا مِنْ ضَرِيعٍ ﴿٦﴾ لَا يُسْمِنُ وَلَا يُغْنِي مِنْ جُوعٍ ﴿٧﴾

Faces on that Day will be humbled. [2] *Labouring [hard], exhausted.* [3] *They will burn in a blazing fire.* [4] *They will [be given] drink from a boiling spring.* [5] *For them will be no food except bitter, thorny fruit.* [6] *Which neither nourishes nor alleviates hunger.* [7]

2-7.1 '*Faces on that Day will be humbled.*': [*Wujūh* (وُجُوه, faces)] has been mentioned in the indefinite form, meaning that only some faces will be like this, not all.[97] These are the faces of the people of sin, defiance, and oppression. Q20:111 states:

وَعَنَتِ الْوُجُوهُ لِلْحَيِّ الْقَيُّومِ وَقَدْ خَابَ مَنْ حَمَلَ ظُلْمًا

And [on that Day] the faces will be humbled before the ever-Living, the Sustainer of existence. And the one who carries [the burden of] oppression (ẓulm) *will have failed indeed.*

[*Khāshiʿah* (خَاشِعَة, humbled)] is derived from *khashaʿa* and its verbal noun *khushūʿ* denotes visible submission, humbleness, and respectful fear.[98] For the disbelievers on that Day, the term is used to describe their humiliation which would come from being forcibly humbled before God.

This humiliation will be manifested in their bodies as described in various verses:

i) In their eyes. Q70:44 states:

خَاشِعَةً أَبْصَارُهُمْ تَرْهَقُهُمْ ذِلَّةٌ ذَٰلِكَ الْيَوْمُ الَّذِي كَانُوا يُوعَدُونَ

Their eyes humbled, humiliation will cover them. That is the Day which they had been promised.

ii) In their speech. Q20:108 states:

وَخَشَعَتِ الْأَصْوَاتُ لِلرَّحْمَٰنِ فَلَا تَسْمَعُ إِلَّا هَمْسًا

---

97 Ṭāliqānī, *Partovī az Qur'an*, 4/29.

98 Muṣṭafawī, *al-Taḥqīq*.

...Voices will be humbled before the most-Merciful,
so you will not hear except a soft sound.

iii) On their faces. As mentioned in this surah in the second verse. Q88:2 states:

وُجُوهٌ يَوْمَئِذٍ خَاشِعَةٌ

Faces on that Day will be humbled.

However, when *khushū'* is achieved voluntarily in the *dunyā*, then it denotes an inner humility that is a praiseworthy state. Q23:1, 2 state:

قَدْ أَفْلَحَ الْمُؤْمِنُونَ ﴿١﴾ الَّذِينَ هُمْ فِي صَلَاتِهِمْ خَاشِعُونَ

Successful indeed are the believers.
Who are humbly submissive in their prayers.

A supplication for the bowing (*rukū'*) in prayers from Imam al-Baqir (a) states: O Allah! ... my heart, my hearing, my sight, my hair, my skin, my flesh, my blood, my brain, my bones, my nerves and whatever my feet carry are [all] humbled before You (*khasha'a laka*), without the least defiance, pride, or regret.[99]

2-7.2 '*Labouring [hard], exhausted.*': ['*Āmilah* (عَامِلَة, labouring)] is the active participle of '*amila* which means to work and [*nāṣibah* (نَاصِبَة, exhausted)] is the active participle of *naṣaba* meaning to exhaust and wear out.[100]

Some exegetes have said that '*āmilatun nāṣibah* refers to the exhaustion and weariness of those who disbelieved in the Day of Judgement. Their constant pursuit of the *dunyā* engrossed them in labour that ultimately proved to be futile. They actually though that that they were doing good works, but these acts were not for God. Q18:104 states:

الَّذِينَ ضَلَّ سَعْيُهُمْ فِي الْحَيَاةِ الدُّنْيَا وَهُمْ يَحْسَبُونَ أَنَّهُمْ يُحْسِنُونَ صُنْعًا

[99] Kulaynī, *al-Kāfī*, 3/319.

عَنِ الْبَاقِرِ (عَلَيْهِ السَّلَامُ) - خَشَعَ لَكَ قَلْبِي وَسَمْعِي وَبَصَرِي وَشَعْرِي وَبَشَرِي وَلَحْمِي وَدَمِي وَمُخِّي وَعِظَامِي وَعَصَبِي وَمَا أَقَلَّتْهُ قَدَمَايَ غَيْرَ مُسْتَنْكِفٍ وَلَا مُسْتَكْبِرٍ وَلَا مُسْتَحْسِرٍ.

[100] Muṣṭafawī, *al-Taḥqīq*.

[They are] those whose efforts are lost in worldly life, while they thought that they were acquiring good by their works!

On the Day of Judgement, these people will feel the exhaustion of their labour in the *dunyā*.[101] They will have nothing to present in the *ākhirah* that could give them salvation from the fire of Hell.

Others are of the opinion that *ʿāmilatun nāṣibah* refers to the exhausting labour that the inmates of Hell will undergo in order to sustain themselves and survive in that dreadful environment, where they will live out their lives shackled in chains.[102]

The three adjectives – humiliated, labouring, and exhausted – describe the state of the guilty on the Day of Judgement. The realization of their grievous position on that Day will be clearly manifest on their faces. They will be broken, ashamed, and terrified. They will exhibit deep fear, and will still feel the exhaustion of their labour in the *dunyā* which has left them empty handed.[103]

Q25:23 states:

وَقَدِمْنَا إِلَىٰ مَا عَمِلُوا مِنْ عَمَلٍ فَجَعَلْنَاهُ هَبَاءً مَنْثُورًا

And We will turn to the deeds that they performed and render them as dispersed dust.

2-7.3 '*They will burn in a blazing fire.*': [*Taṣlā* (تَصْلَىٰ, they will burn)] is derived from *ṣalā*, meaning to roast and to burn and [*ḥāmiyah* (حَامِيَة, blazing fire)] is derived from *ḥamiya* meaning to be intensely hot.[104] They will enter or be made to enter (by their actions),[105] into a fire that is extraordinarily hot.

2-7.4 '*They will [be given] drink from a boiling spring.*': [*ʾĀniyah* (آنِيَة, boiling)] is derived from *ʾanā* meaning fully mature, and here it refers to the hottest that the water can be.[106]

The punishment of Hell will cause its inmates to suffer intense thirst, but only boiling water will be available for them to drink. Q18:29 states:

---

101 Ṭūsī, *al-Tibyān*, 10/334.

102 Ṭabrasī, *al-Bayān*, 10/726.

103 Ṭabāṭabāʾī, *al-Mīzān*, 20/273.

104 Rāghib, *al-Mufradāt*.

105 Muṭahharī, (*Āshnāyī bā Qurʾan*), *Āthār*, 28/520.

106 Muṣṭafawī, *al-Taḥqīq*.

وَإِنْ يَسْتَغِيثُوا يُغَاثُوا بِمَاءٍ كَالْمُهْلِ يَشْوِي الْوُجُوهَ بِئْسَ الشَّرَابُ وَسَاءَتْ مُرْتَفَقًا

...And if they call for relief, they will be relieved with water like molten lead, which will burn their faces. Wretched is the drink and evil is the resting place!

2-7.5 A tradition from Imam al-Sadiq (a) states: Every enemy who hates us is described by the verses, '*Faces on that Day will be humbled. Labouring [hard], exhausted. They will burn in a blazing fire. They will be given drink from a boiling spring.*'[107] 'Enemies' here are those who disrespected and harboured animosity towards the Prophet (s) and his Divinely appointed successors (a).

2-7.6 '*For them will be no food except bitter, thorny fruit.*': [*Ḍarīʿ* (ضَرِيع, bitter, thorny fruit)] refers to a foul-tasting and thorny plant which grows in Hell. Due to their intense hunger, the people of Hell will have no recourse but to eat it. It is called *ḍarīʿ* because the one who eats it is forced to do so with pain and wailing (*taḍarruʿ*) due to its bitterness and thorniness.[108]

The Arabs knew *ḍarīʿ* as a thorny plant in the desert which they called *al-shibriq*. When it was moist their camels grazed on it. In its dry form it was known as *ḍarīʿ* and was extremely poisonous.[109]

2-7.7 A tradition from the Prophet (s) states: *Ḍarīʿ* is something that grows in hellfire which resembles thorns. It is more bitter than aloe, more foul-smelling than a corpse, and hotter than fire – God has named it *al-ḍarīʿ*.[110]

2-7.8 Aside from *ḍarīʿ*, other foods have also been mentioned for the people of Hell, such as *ghislīn* (pus and refuse, Q69:36) and *zaqqūm* (bitter fruit, Q37:62). In the same way in some places their drink will be *ḥamīm* (scalding water Q37:67), in others it will be *ṣadīd* (festering water, Q14:16), and yet others, *ghassāq* (intensely cold water, Q38:57), and so on. This is because there are different levels

---

107 Furāt al-Kūfī, *Tafsīr*, 1/549.

عَنِ الصَّادِقِ (عَلَيْهِ السَّلَامُ) – كُلُّ عَدُوٍّ لَنَا نَاصِبٍ مَنْسُوبٌ إِلَى هَذِهِ الْآيَةِ:«وُجُوهٌ يَوْمَئِذٍ خَاشِعَةٌ عَامِلَةٌ نَاصِبَةٌ تَصْلَىٰ نَارًا حَامِيَةً تُسْقَىٰ مِنْ عَيْنٍ آنِيَةٍ».

108 Ṭabrasī, *al-Bayān*, 10/727.

109 Rāzī, *Mafātīḥ al-Ghayb*, 31/140.

110 Majlisī, *Biḥār*, 7/169.

عَنِ الرَّسُولِ (صَلَّى اللهُ عَلَيْهِ وَآلِهِ) – الضَّرِيعُ شَيْءٌ يَكُونُ فِي النَّارِ يُشْبِهُ الشَّوْكَ، أَمَرُّ مِنَ الصَّبْرِ، وَأَنْتَنُ مِنَ الْجِيفَةِ، وَأَشَدُّ حَرًّا مِنَ النَّارِ، سَمَّاهُ اللهُ الضَّرِيعَ.

of Hell, and the food and drink available in each will vary. Q15:44 states:

لَهَا سَبْعَةُ أَبْوَابٍ لِكُلِّ بَابٍ مِنْهُمْ جُزْءٌ مَقْسُومٌ

It has seven gates; for every gate there shall be a designated group [of sinners].

2-7.9 '*Which neither nourishes nor alleviates hunger.*': [*Yusminu* (يُسْمِنُ, it nourishes)] is derived from *samina* which means to fatten or to put on weight, and [*yughnī* (يُغْنِي, it alleviates)] means to suffice or make free from want.[111] The function of food is to nourish and satiate. However, both these qualities will be absent in the drink and food of Hell. Rather, the food will only cause pain. Q73:13 states:

وَطَعَامًا ذَا غُصَّةٍ وَعَذَابًا أَلِيمًا

And food that chokes and a painful punishment.

Despite this, people will drink and eat to their fill, in a vain attempt to assuage their thirst and hunger. Q56:51-55 state:

ثُمَّ إِنَّكُمْ أَيُّهَا الضَّالُّونَ الْمُكَذِّبُونَ ﴿٥١﴾ لَآكِلُونَ مِنْ شَجَرٍ مِنْ زَقُّومٍ ﴿٥٢﴾
فَمَالِئُونَ مِنْهَا الْبُطُونَ ﴿٥٣﴾ فَشَارِبُونَ عَلَيْهِ مِنَ الْحَمِيمِ ﴿٥٤﴾
فَشَارِبُونَ شُرْبَ الْهِيمِ

Then indeed you, O those astray, [and O] beliers! You will indeed be eating from the tree of zaqqūm. *And filling your bellies with it. And drinking scalding water* (ḥamīm) *over it. And drinking as thirsty camels drink!*

The people of Hell will eat and drink as much as they can of the nauseating food and water because of their intense hunger and thirst, and perhaps because they do not know when they will be allowed to go out again. Thereafter, they will be returned to the hellfire.[112] Q37:68 states that afterwards:

ثُمَّ إِنَّ مَرْجِعَهُمْ لَإِلَى الْجَحِيمِ

Then indeed, their return will be to the hellfire.

---

111 Muṣṭafawī, *al-Taḥqīq*.

112 Bahmanpour, *Towards Eternal Life*, p. 146.

DISCUSSION: THE FUNCTION OF HELL

The purpose of creating Hell, and how it fits in with the concept of God's infinite mercy, is discussed briefly below.

God is all-Merciful as well as all-Just and all-Wise. He does not create anything without purpose, and Hell is no exception. In the first instance, it serves as a warning to mankind and *jinn* to avoid sin and disobedience. And in the Hereafter, its existence serves primarily as a place of purification for the sinners.

There, a sinful soul needs to go through a more arduous, painful, and lengthy cleansing, proportional to its state of corruption, in order to become pure again. It has to live in Hell.[113] The very fact that such a procedure for purification exists is itself from God's great mercy.

In Q55:43-45 God states that Hell is from amongst His favours to mankind and *jinn*:

هَٰذِهِ جَهَنَّمُ الَّتِي يُكَذِّبُ بِهَا الْمُجْرِمُونَ ﴿٤٣﴾ يَطُوفُونَ بَيْنَهَا وَبَيْنَ حَمِيمٍ آنٍ
﴿٤٤﴾ فَبِأَيِّ آلَاءِ رَبِّكُمَا تُكَذِّبَانِ

This is Hell, which the criminals denied. They shall wander between it and scalding hot water. So which of the favours of your Lord will you two (men and jinn*) deny?*

The inmates of Hell are surrounded by fire. They live out their miserable lives in the harshest of environments. Many are finally cleansed and released, but some will abide in it for eternity, except if God wills otherwise. Q6:128 states:

قَالَ النَّارُ مَثْوَاكُمْ خَالِدِينَ فِيهَا إِلَّا مَا شَاءَ اللَّهُ إِنَّ رَبَّكَ حَكِيمٌ عَلِيمٌ

He will say, "The Fire is your dwelling-place, wherein you will abide eternally, except for as Allah wills. Indeed, your Lord is all-Wise, all-Knowing."

SUMMARY OF THE VERSES

The verses begin by describing the fate of the sinners on that Day. Their faces will reveal their humiliation, fear, and despair. They will still feel the exhaustion of their futile activities in the *dunyā*.

---

[113] For a brief description of life in Hell, see: Bahmanpour, *Towards Eternal Life*, p. 132-145.

They will be entered to burn in hellfire, where their only drink and food will be boiling water and bitter fruit. They will consume this due to their hunger, but it will only increase their torment because they will not be satiated or nourished thereby.

REFLECTIVE LEARNING

The food and drink of Hell and Paradise can only be somewhat understood by us in this world through the simple concepts that we have experienced. Their realities are far beyond anything we know.[114] However, they are manifestations and consequences of our actions in this world.

Let me reflect on the type of food and drink that my sinful conduct in this *dunyā* will earn me, even if I cannot understand their fullest reality.

VERSES 8 - 16

وُجُوهٌ يَوْمَئِذٍ نَاعِمَةٌ ﴿٨﴾ لِسَعْيِهَا رَاضِيَةٌ ﴿٩﴾ فِي جَنَّةٍ عَالِيَةٍ ﴿١٠﴾ لَا تَسْمَعُ
فِيهَا لَاغِيَةً ﴿١١﴾ فِيهَا عَيْنٌ جَارِيَةٌ ﴿١٢﴾ فِيهَا سُرُرٌ مَرْفُوعَةٌ ﴿١٣﴾ وَأَكْوَابٌ
مَوْضُوعَةٌ ﴿١٤﴾ وَنَمَارِقُ مَصْفُوفَةٌ ﴿١٥﴾ وَزَرَابِيُّ مَبْثُوثَةٌ ﴿١٦﴾

[Other] faces, that Day, will be joyful. [8] *Well-pleased with their striving.* [9] *In a lofty garden.* [10] *Wherein they will hear no vain speech.* [11] *Within it is a flowing spring.* [12] *Within it are thrones raised high.* [13] *And cups at hand.* [14] *And cushions set in rows.* [15] *And carpets spread out.* [16]

8-16.1 *'[Other] faces, that Day, will be joyful.'*: In contrast to the faces of the guilty, some faces will be full of joy. The next few verses describe the experience of the righteous believers.

The description is lengthier and richer in detail, as expected for the recompense of the virtuous. Indeed, God has created man for His mercy, and Paradise. Q11:119 states:

إِلَّا مَنْ رَحِمَ رَبُّكَ وَلِذَٰلِكَ خَلَقَهُمْ

114 Shīrāzī, *Namūneh*, 26/418.

Except those whom your Lord has given mercy [through guidance], and for that did He create them...

The righteous will be filled with relief and joy, and this will be clearly visible on their faces. The exhaustion of their labouring in the *dunyā* to gain God's pleasure and proximity will have departed from their bodies.

[*Nāʿimah* (نَاعِمَة, joyous)] is derived from *naʿima* which means to be cheerful and delighted.[115] Here it means *mutanaʿʿimah*, meaning that the radiant faces of these believers will reflect their inner happiness and satisfaction.[116] Q83:24 states:

تَعْرِفُ فِي وُجُوهِهِمْ نَضْرَةَ النَّعِيمِ

You will recognize on their faces the radiance of bliss.

8-16.2 *'Well-pleased with their striving.'*: The people of Hell had exhausted themselves in the *dunyā*, constantly engrossed in activity that proved to be ultimately useless. In contrast, when the believers will recall the sacrifices that they made and the discipline that they maintained in their lives in obeying God and serving Him, they will be delighted with the outcome of their efforts.[117]

8-16.3 Some actions that are performed are lengthy and laborious, but they do not yield much result in the *dunyā*. Other times, a small act brings about a big result. These outcomes are in the hand of God. What has more value is sincere striving, and that is what the people destined for Paradise will be pleased with on that Day. Their determined efforts and sacrifices to please God will be rewarded. Q17:19 states:

وَمَنْ أَرَادَ الْآخِرَةَ وَسَعَىٰ لَهَا سَعْيَهَا وَهُوَ مُؤْمِنٌ فَأُولَٰئِكَ كَانَ سَعْيُهُمْ مَشْكُورًا

But whoever desires the Hereafter, and strives for it with due effort, while he is a believer, then they are the ones whose striving will be appreciated [with Paradise].

8-16.4 *'In a lofty garden.'*: [*ʿĀliyah* (عَالِيَة, lofty)] is a reference to a high station and honourable place in Paradise. It may also refer to the

---

115 Muṣṭafawī, *al-Taḥqīq*.

116 Ṭabāṭabā'ī, *al-Mīzān*, 20/274.

117 Ibid.

elevated heights from which its inhabitants can survey all that they have been granted,[118] and that is why the Qur'an constantly mentions that the rivers of Paradise flow beneath its dwellers.

In this garden, they will have life that is not followed by death, delight that is not mixed with pain, and happiness that is not marred by sorrow. Whatever they desire will be easily within reach, and in fact, they will experience delights that they had not imagined.[119]

8-16.5 *'Wherein they will hear no vain speech. Within it is a flowing spring. Within it are thrones raised high. And cups at hand. And cushions set in rows. And carpets spread out.'*: Six features of Paradise, which will be enjoyed by its inhabitants, are mentioned in these verses:

1. They will not hear any vain speech. [*Lā tasmaʿū* (لَا تَسْمَعُ, they will not hear)] may mean 'you will not hear' if we take the Prophet (s) as the addressee. However, it probably is a reference to the faces (*wujūh*)[120] and means, 'the dwellers of Paradise will not hear...'

   [*Lāghiyah* (لَاغِيَة, vain speech)] is derived from *laghw* which refers to any vain or thoughtless utterance.[121] Not only will there be no falsehood, slander, disputation, or hurtful talk, there will be no *laghw* heard in Paradise. The conversations that take place will be of higher wisdoms; precise, meaningful, and conforming to reality.[122]

   This environment is possible because before people are admitted to Paradise, they are divested of the last vestiges of any rancour that they may possess, and they have no malice left in them whatsoever. Q7:43 states:

   وَنَزَعْنَا مَا فِي صُدُورِهِمْ مِنْ غِلٍّ تَجْرِي مِنْ تَحْتِهِمُ الْأَنْهَارُ

   And We shall remove from their hearts [any] rancour; beneath them rivers flow...

2. They will have access to springs that flow continually. The mention of *ʿayn* (spring) here is in the singular, perhaps to keep with the metre of the other verses in this section. However, it

---

118 Ṭūsī, *al-Tibyān*,

119 Ṭabāṭabā'ī, *al-Mīzān*, 20/274.

120 Ibid.

121 Muṣṭafawī, *al-Taḥqīq*.

122 Ṭabāṭabā'ī, *al-Mīzān*, 20/170.

refers to the type (*jins*) of the blessing and does not mean that there is only one spring in Paradise.[123] Just as in Hell, there are other noxious springs besides *Āniyah.*

Everyone dwelling in Paradise will have various flowing springs to drink from, depending on their station.[124] Several springs exist in Paradise, some of which are: Kāfūr (Q76:5), Salsabīl (Q76:18), and Tasnīm (Q83:27). Q15:45 states:

إِنَّ الْمُتَّقِينَ فِي جَنَّاتٍ وَعُيُونٍ

Indeed, the God-wary will be in gardens and springs.

3. They will be seated on thrones. [*Surur* (سُرُر, thrones)] (sing. *sarīr*) means thrones or couches. The adjective 'raised' refers to the honour of the people who sit on them.[125] Alternatively, it may refer to the thrones themselves, which are elevated so that when the believer sits on it, he is able to look out at everything he possesses.[126]

   These thrones are also used when the inhabitants of Paradise sit in gatherings with one another. Q37:44 states:

   عَلَىٰ سُرُرٍ مُتَقَابِلِينَ

   [They will be seated] on thrones facing one another.

4. They will have cups of drink at hand. [*Akwāb* (أَكْوَاب, cups)]. The Qur'an describes several drinking vessels which will be available to the people of Paradise: jugs and glasses (*abārīqa wa kas*, Q56:18), vessels of silver (*āniyatin min fiḍḍah*, Q76:15), and crystal-clear cups made of silver (*qawārīra min fiḍḍah*, Q76:16). A tradition from Imam al-Sadiq (a) states: Eyes will see through the silver of Paradise the way they can see through glass.[127]

   These vessels will be filled with a variety of nourishing drinks that the people of Paradise will have ready access to.

---

[123] Shīrāzī, *Namūneh*, 26/422.

[124] Ṭabrasī, *al-Bayān*, 10/727.

[125] Ṭabāṭabā'ī, *al-Mīzān*, 20/274.

[126] Ṭūsī, *al-Tibyān*, 10/336.

[127] Ṭabrasī, *al-Bayān*, 10/410.

عَنِ الصَّادِقِ (عَلَيْهِ السَّلَامُ) – يَنْفُذُ الْبَصَرُ فِي فِضَّةٍ كَمَا يَنْفُذُ فِي الزُّجَاجِ.

[*Mawḍūʿah* (مَوْضُوعَة, placed at hand)] indicates that depending on their capacity, these drinks will be served to them by attendants whenever they desire them. We have discussed this further in the *tafsīr* of Surat al-Naba᾿ (78).

5. They will have cushions set in rows. [*Namāriq* (نَمَارِق, cushions)] (sing. *numruqah*) means a small cushion or pillow to lean on, and [*maṣfūfah* (مَصْفُوفَة, in rows)] means that they have been placed for the use in assemblies.[128]
6. They will have carpets spread out. [*Zarābiyy* (زَرَابِيّ, carpets)] (sing. *zarbiyyah*) means a decorated lush carpet, and [*mabthūthah* (مَبْثُوثَة, spread out)] means that these carpets are laid out.[129]

8-16.6 Although the Qur᾿an uses familiar similitudes to describe Hell and Paradise, the reality of these places is very different from anything we have experienced or even imagined. About the bounties of Paradise, Q2:25 states:

كُلَّمَا رُزِقُوا مِنْهَا مِنْ ثَمَرَةٍ رِزْقًا قَالُوا هَٰذَا الَّذِي رُزِقْنَا مِنْ قَبْلُ وَأُتُوا بِهِ مُتَشَابِهًا

...Whenever they are provided with a provision of fruit therefrom, they will say, "This is what we were provided before." And they shall be given something resembling it...

The bounties mentioned in the verses under review give an idea of the luxury and comfort that awaits the dwellers of Paradise.

8-16.7 Even as the inhabitants of Paradise enjoy the blessings they are given, they still yearn for further closeness and proximity to God.

In a lengthy tradition from Imam al-Sadiq (a) we read: ...They live in this way until they hear a call from below the Throne of God saying, "O inhabitants of Paradise! How do you find the place you have returned to?" They reply, "We have returned to the best of places and our reward is the most generous of rewards. However, now that we have heard this voice we have a keen desire to gaze at Your Magnificence, and that would be the best reward for us and one that You have promised us Yourself, and You never go back on

128 Ṭabāṭabā᾿ī, *al-Mīzān*, 20/274.

129 Muṣṭafawī, *al-Taḥqīq*.

Your word." So God issues a command and seventy thousand veils are lifted away...[130] In this regard, Q9:72 states:

وَعَدَ اللَّهُ الْمُؤْمِنِينَ وَالْمُؤْمِنَاتِ جَنَّاتٍ تَجْرِي مِنْ تَحْتِهَا الْأَنْهَارُ خَالِدِينَ فِيهَا
وَمَسَاكِنَ طَيِّبَةً فِي جَنَّاتِ عَدْنٍ وَرِضْوَانٌ مِنَ اللَّهِ أَكْبَرُ ذَٰلِكَ هُوَ الْفَوْزُ الْعَظِيمُ

Allah has promised the believing men and believing women gardens beneath which rivers flow, wherein they abide eternally, and pleasant dwellings in gardens of perpetual residence; but approval from Allah is greater. It is that which is the great attainment.

SUMMARY OF THE VERSES

In summary, the verses describe the happiness of the believers on that Day. They will be visibly delighted at the result of their endeavours.

Thereafter, a description of their abode in the lofty reaches of Paradise is mentioned, focussing on blessings that they will enjoy in each other's company: pleasant speech, flowing springs, elevated seats, drinks at hand, all in a lush setting of cushions and carpets.

REFLECTIVE LEARNING

The life-long struggle in the *dunyā* of those who strived to please God will be rewarded by delight and satisfaction on the Day of al-Ghāshiyah.

The key factor in determining the fate of individuals on that Day is the nature of their striving in the *dunyā*. Q53:39 states:

وَأَنْ لَيْسَ لِلْإِنْسَانِ إِلَّا مَا سَعَىٰ

And that man shall have nothing except what he strives for.

Let me reflect on whether I strive hard in the *dunyā* and whether I sacrifice and go the extra distance to attain God's pleasure.

---

130 Majlisī, *Biḥār*, 8/207.

عَنِ الصَّادِقِ (عَلَيْهِ السَّلَامُ) - ... فَبَيْنَا هُمْ كَذَلِكَ إِذْ يَسْمَعُونَ صَوْتًا مِنْ تَحْتِ الْعَرْشِ: يَا أَهْلَ الْجَنَّةِ كَيْفَ تَرَوْنَ مُنْقَلَبَكُمْ؟ فَيَقُولُونَ: خَيْرُ الْمُنْقَلَبِ مُنْقَلَبُنَا وَخَيْرُ الثَّوَابِ ثَوَابُنَا قَدْ سَمِعْنَا الصَّوْتَ وَٱشْتَهَيْنَا النَّظَرَ إِلَى أَنْوَارِ جَلَالِكَ وَهُوَ أَعْظَمُ ثَوَابِنَا وَقَدْ وَعَدْتَهُ وَلَا تُخْلِفُ الْمِيعَادَ. فَيَأْمُرُ اللَّهُ الْحُجُبَ فَيَقُومُ سَبْعُونَ أَلْفَ حِجَابٍ...

VERSES 17 - 20

أَفَلَا يَنظُرُونَ إِلَى الْإِبِلِ كَيْفَ خُلِقَتْ ﴿١٧﴾ وَإِلَى السَّمَاءِ كَيْفَ رُفِعَتْ ﴿١٨﴾
وَإِلَى الْجِبَالِ كَيْفَ نُصِبَتْ ﴿١٩﴾ وَإِلَى الْأَرْضِ كَيْفَ سُطِحَتْ ﴿٢٠﴾

Do they not look at the camels – how they are created? [17] *And at the sky – how it is raised?* [18] *And at the mountains – how they are firmly fixed?* [19] *And at the earth – how it is spread out?* [20]

17-20.1 The surah now switches from the description of Hell and Paradise to elements in the world of creation in the *dunyā*. This is to show that the signs of God that are all around us are proof of His ability to create whatever He has described previously in the Hereafter also.[131]

17-20.2 The question, *'do they not look?'* indicates the importance of using the eyes to look thoughtfully and study the marvels of creation in order to gain cognition (*maʿrifah*) of the Creator. *Maʿrifah* of God is the key factor that dictates the fate of an individual in the Hereafter.[132] It is through this *maʿrifah* that man will truly submit to God.

Within this rhetorical question, four signs that manifest God's power are mentioned: the camel, the sky, the mountains, and the earth.

17-20.3 *'Do they not look at the camels – how they are created?'*: [*Ibil* (إبل, camels] is a term for a group of camels and has no singular.[133] The camel is mentioned as an example of the many species of animals that God has created, because the Arabs (the first audience of the Qur'an) knew this animal well.[134] Now, they were told not to merely make use of the animal, but ponder over its wondrous constitution as well.

The camel is a remarkable creature, superbly adapted for endurance in the harsh desert climate. It is indeed the 'ship of the desert'. It can go for a week without water, and much longer without food. Its feet are designed so that it can walk efficiently in loose sand.

---

131 Muṭahharī, (*Āshnāyī bā Qur'an*), *Āthār*, 28/524.

132 Shīrāzī, *Namūneh*, 26/427.

133 Rāghib, *al-Mufradāt*.

134 Ṭabāṭabā'ī, *al-Mīzān*, 20/275.

The hair around its eyes and ears create an effective barrier in a sandstorm. Its nostrils can close, and it possesses a third eyelid (a nictitating eyelid which is a transparent membrane that moves horizontally) to keep these two vital organs free of sand. It is an efficient means of transport for man and goods, and moreover, it provides wholesome meat and milk.

17-20.4 *'And at the sky – how it is raised?'*: Next, man is invited to ponder over the world above, the celestial bodies that adorn the heavens, give light and heat, and show direction; the clouds that bring rain, and the atmosphere that protects the earth and its inhabitants. The vast expanse of the universe compared to the tiny planet we inhabit makes us realize the grandness of the Creator's design.

17-20.5 *'And at the mountains – how they are firmly fixed?'*: Then man is invited to bring his gaze down and ponder over the firm mountains, which are lower than the sky but higher than the earth. Their lofty heights protect inhabitations from storms, they extend deep below the ground to anchor the earth's crust and give it stability, and their depths bring forth springs and precious minerals.

17-20.6 *'And at the earth – how it is spread out?'*: Finally, man is invited to consider the nature of the earth, which has been created to efficiently sustain life. Its outspread lands allow man to build on them. Its fields, its watercourses, its forests, and all its resources provide ample provision for its inhabitants.

When one ponders on these examples, created by an all-Capable Creator to facilitate life in this world, one has no doubt in His ability to create the phenomena that facilitate life in the next world.

17-20.7 A tradition from Imam Ali (a) states: God has placed a responsibility on every organ of the human being that is distinct from the responsibility of other organs... Amongst the responsibilities that he has placed on the eyes is to look at God's signs [and ponder over them], and lower the gaze from what God, the Exalted, has forbidden. [In this regard,] God, the most High, has said, *'Do they not look at the camels – how they are created? And at the sky – how it is raised? And at the mountains – how they are firmly fixed? And at the earth – how it is spread out?'*[135]

SUMMARY OF THE VERSES

The verses invite man to ponder over the creation of phenomena around them: the camel, the sky, the mountains, and the earth. Each has been designed perfectly to facilitate human life in the *dunyā*, and proves that the Creator can make another world in the Hereafter.

REFLECTIVE LEARNING

Let me reflect on how I strive to use the earth's resources to provide a comfortable life for myself and my family.

Do I realize that I must strive at the same time to prepare a life of comfort in the Hereafter?

Do I try to fulfil the responsibility of the eyes as mentioned by Imam Ali (a) in the tradition above?

VERSES 21 - 24

فَذَكِّرْ إِنَّمَا أَنْتَ مُذَكِّرٌ ﴿٢١﴾ لَسْتَ عَلَيْهِمْ بِمُصَيْطِرٍ ﴿٢٢﴾ إِلَّا مَنْ تَوَلَّىٰ وَكَفَرَ ﴿٢٣﴾ فَيُعَذِّبُهُ اللَّهُ الْعَذَابَ الْأَكْبَرَ ﴿٢٤﴾

So remind, [O Muhammad]; indeed, you are only one who reminds. [21] *You are not a controller over them.* [22] *Except he who turns away and disbelieves,* [23] *then God will punish him with the greatest punishment.* [24]

21-24.1 '*So remind, [O Muhammad]; indeed, you are only one who reminds.*': After mentioning the signs of God in the *dunyā* and that everything has been created with a purpose and goal, the Prophet (s) is informed that his responsibility is to keep reminding the people about their duty to God and how to attain His pleasure and proximity. Q50:45 states:

---

[135] Nūrī, *Mustadrak al-Wasā'il*, 11/146.

عَنْ أَمِيرِ الْمُؤْمِنِينَ (عَلَيْهِ السَّلَامُ) – إِنَّ اللهَ تَعَالَى مَا فَرَضَ الْإِيمَانَ عَلَى جَارِحَةٍ وَاحِدَةٍ وَمَا مِنْ جَارِحَةٍ مِنْ جَوَارِحِ الْإِنْسَانِ إِلَّا وَقَدْ وُكِلَتْ بِغَيْرِ مَا وُكِلَتْ بِهِ الْأُخْرَى... أَمَّا مَا فَرَضَهُ عَلَى الْعَيْنَيْنِ فَهُوَ النَّظَرُ إِلَى آيَاتِ اللهِ وَغَضُّ النَّظَرِ عَنْ مَحَارِمِ اللهِ عَزَّ وَجَلَّ، قَالَ اللهُ تَعَالَى: «أَفَلَا يَنْظُرُونَ إِلَى الْإِبِلِ كَيْفَ خُلِقَتْ * وَإِلَى السَّمَاءِ كَيْفَ رُفِعَتْ * وَإِلَى الْجِبَالِ كَيْفَ نُصِبَتْ * وَإِلَى الْأَرْضِ كَيْفَ سُطِحَتْ».

نَّحْنُ أَعْلَمُ بِمَا يَقُولُونَ وَمَا أَنْتَ عَلَيْهِمْ بِجَبَّارٍ فَذَكِّرْ بِالْقُرْآنِ مَنْ يَخَافُ وَعِيدِ

We are most knowing of what they say, and you are not a tyrant over them. But remind by [means of] the Qur'an whoever fears My threat.

Indeed the Prophet (s) was appointed as a *mudhakkir* (one who reminds). After bringing knowledge to the people and showing them the purpose of their creation, God's Prophets (a) are tasked with continually reminding them of their inner inclination towards God.[136]

Q87:9 states:

فَذَكِّرْ إِنْ نَفَعَتِ الذِّكْرَىٰ

Therefore [do] remind, in case reminding is of benefit.

21-24.2 A sermon from Imam Ali (a) states: God appointed His Messengers and sent a succession of His Prophets to them (the nations) to make them fulfil the covenant [to God which is coded] in their *fiṭrah*, to remind them of His forgotten blessings, to show them proofs by exhortation, to unveil for them the latent strength of the intellect, and to point out to them the signs of [God's] Omnipotence: the sky which is raised over them, the cradling earth that is placed beneath them, the livelihood that sustains them, the fullness of time that bring them to death, the infirmities that turn them old, and the events that continually betake them.[137]

21-24.3 '*You are not a controller over them.*': [*Muṣayṭir* (مُصَيْطِر, controller)] is also spelt *musayṭir* (with a س). It is derived from *ṣayṭara* which means to dominate or control by force.[138] The Prophet (s) is informed that he cannot compel the people to bring faith. Q10:99 states:

وَلَوْ شَاءَ رَبُّكَ لَآمَنَ مَنْ فِي الْأَرْضِ كُلُّهُمْ جَمِيعًا
أَفَأَنْتَ تُكْرِهُ النَّاسَ حَتَّىٰ يَكُونُوا مُؤْمِنِينَ

---

136 Muṭahharī, (*Āshnāyī bā Qur'an*), *Āthār*, 28/525.

137 *Nahj al-Balāghah*, sermon 1.

فَبَعَثَ فِيهِمْ رُسُلَهُ، وَوَاتَرَ إِلَيْهِمْ أَنْبِيَاءَهُ، لِيَسْتَأْدُوهُمْ مِيثَاقَ فِطْرَتِهِ، وَيُذَكِّرُوهُمْ مَنْسِيَّ نِعْمَتِهِ، وَيَحْتَجُّوا عَلَيْهِمْ بِالتَّبْلِيغِ، وَيُثِيرُوا لَهُمْ دَفَائِنَ الْعُقُولِ، وَيُرُوهُمْ آيَاتِ الْمَقْدِرَةِ: مِنْ سَقْفٍ فَوْقَهُمْ مَرْفُوعٍ، وَمِهَادٍ تَحْتَهُمْ مَوْضُوعٍ، وَمَعَايِشَ تُحْيِيهِمْ، وَآجَالٍ تُفْنِيهِمْ، وَأَوْصَابٍ تُهْرِمُهُمْ، وَأَحْدَاثٍ تَتَابَعُ عَلَيْهِمْ.

138 Muṣṭafawī, *al-Taḥqīq*.

And had your Lord willed, those on earth would have believed - all of them entirely. So, [O Muhammad], will you [then] compel the people in order that they become believers?

Every individual must traverse the path towards faith (*īmān*) through choice and free will. If he is forced to do so, then no useful result will be achieved.[139]

However, once a person believes and accepts the faith, then he is obliged to follow the commandments of God. Q33:36 states:

وَمَا كَانَ لِمُؤْمِنٍ وَلَا مُؤْمِنَةٍ إِذَا قَضَى اللَّهُ
وَرَسُولُهُ أَمْرًا أَنْ يَكُونَ لَهُمُ الْخِيَرَةُ مِنْ أَمْرِهِمْ

And it is not for a believing man or a believing woman, when God and His Messenger have decreed a matter, that they should [thereafter] have any choice in their affair...

21-24.4 '*Except he who turns away and disbelieves.*': The exception here refers to the command to the Prophet (s), 'so, remind (*fadhakkir*)' and the verse means to say, 'so remind... except the one who turns away and disbelieves', because reminder to such individuals is futile.[140]

About such people Q43:83 states:

فَذَرْهُمْ يَخُوضُوا وَيَلْعَبُوا حَتَّىٰ يُلَاقُوا يَوْمَهُمُ الَّذِي يُوعَدُونَ

So leave them to converse vainly and amuse themselves until they meet their Day which they have been promised.

Those who turn away (*tawallā*) and disbelieve (*kafara*), do so with defiance despite knowledge. They did not accept the reminder of the Prophet (s) and therefore qualify for severe punishment.[141]

21-24.5 '*Then God will punish him with the greatest punishment.*': [*Al-ʿadhāb al-akbar* (الْعَذَابَ الْأَكْبَرَ, greatest punishment)] here refers to the punishment of the Hereafter compared to the punishment of this world.[142] Q39:26 states:

139 Shīrāzī, *Namūneh*, 26/433.

140 Ṭabāṭabā'ī, *al-Mīzān*, 20/275.

141 Rāzī, *Mafātīḥ al-Ghayb*, 31/147.

142 Shīrāzī, *Namūneh*, 26/434.

فَأَذَاقَهُمُ اللَّهُ الْخِزْيَ فِي الْحَيَاةِ الدُّنْيَا وَلَعَذَابُ الْآخِرَةِ أَكْبَرُ لَوْ كَانُوا يَعْلَمُونَ

So God made them taste disgrace in the life of the world. But the punishment of the Hereafter is greater, if they only knew.

A tradition from Imam al-Baqir (a) states: '*Then God will punish him with the greatest punishment*' denotes chastisement that is intense and perpetual.[143]

SUMMARY OF THE VERSES

The verses instruct the Prophet (s) to remind the people and inform him that this is the extent of his role. He was not sent to compel them. His reminder is for all except those who turn away in defiance and disbelief, and they will receive God's great punishment.

REFLECTIVE LEARNING

The famous reminder of the Prophet (s) in his last days was the tradition that states: Indeed, I leave two weighty things (*thaqalayn*) among you. If you hold fast to both of them, you will never go astray: the Book of God, and my household (*Ahl al-Bayt*).[144] These are the two reminders that the Prophet (s) has left for us.

Let me reflect on whether the way I live my life is reflective of the Qur'an and the *sunnah*, or I am neglectful about the reminder of the Prophet (s).

VERSES 25, 26

إِنَّ إِلَيْنَا إِيَابَهُمْ ﴿٢٥﴾ ثُمَّ إِنَّ عَلَيْنَا حِسَابَهُمْ ﴿٢٦﴾

Indeed, to Us is their return. [25] *Then indeed, upon Us is their reckoning.* [26]

25-26.1 The verses are a consolation to the Prophet (s),[145] just as Q13:40 states:

---

143 Majlisī, *Biḥār*, 8/356.

عَنِ الْبَاقِرِ (عَلَيْهِ السَّلَامُ) – «فَيُعَذِّبُهُ اللهُ الْعَذَابَ الْأَكْبَرَ» يُرِيدُ الْغَلِيظَ الشَّدِيدَ الدَّائِمَ.

144 Kulaynī, *al-Kāfī*, 1/294.

عَنِ الرَّسُولِ (صَلَّى اللهُ عَلَيْهِ وَآلِهِ) – إِنِّي تَارِكٌ فِيكُمُ الثَّقَلَيْنِ مَا إِنْ تَمَسَّكْتُمْ بِهِمَا لَنْ تَضِلُّوا: كِتَابَ اللهِ وَعِتْرَتِي أَهْلَ بَيْتِي.

145 Shīrāzī, *Namūneh*, 26/435.

فَإِنَّمَا عَلَيْكَ الْبَلَاغُ وَعَلَيْنَا الْحِسَابُ

...Indeed, upon you is only the [duty of] conveying [the message], and upon Us is the accounting.

[*Iyābahum* (إِيَابَهُمْ, their return)]. *Iyāb* means to return back to where one came from.[146]

The entire creation is returning to God.

Q2:156 states:

إِنَّا لِلَّهِ وَإِنَّا إِلَيْهِ رَاجِعُونَ

...Indeed we belong to Allah, and indeed to Him we will return.

25-26.2 The last two verses of the surah serve as a reminder and warning to those who turn away and disbelieve. On the Day of al-Ghāshiyah they will have to stand in front of God, who will take account of their actions and pass judgement over them.

SUMMARY OF THE VERSES

The verses serve as a reminder that there will be a return back to God and thereafter, He will make everyone account for their deeds.

REFLECTIVE LEARNING

Let me reflect on the fact that one Day I will certainly stand in the presence of God to account for all my deeds in this world.

Will I be able to answer for all my actions or do I need to turn to Him now in repentance for my neglect and misdeeds, and thereafter change my ways?

---

[146] Muṣṭafawī, al-*Taḥqīq*.

SURAT AL-FAJR
THE DAWN (89)

PART 1: VERSES 1 - 14

TEXT AND TRANSLATION

سُورَةُ الْفَجْرِ

بِسْمِ اللهِ الرَّحْمَٰنِ الرَّحِيمِ

وَالْفَجْرِ ﴿١﴾ وَلَيَالٍ عَشْرٍ ﴿٢﴾ وَالشَّفْعِ وَالْوَتْرِ ﴿٣﴾ وَاللَّيْلِ إِذَا يَسْرِ ﴿٤﴾ هَلْ
فِي ذَٰلِكَ قَسَمٌ لِذِي حِجْرٍ ﴿٥﴾ أَلَمْ تَرَ كَيْفَ فَعَلَ رَبُّكَ بِعَادٍ ﴿٦﴾ إِرَمَ ذَاتِ الْعِمَادِ
﴿٧﴾ الَّتِي لَمْ يُخْلَقْ مِثْلُهَا فِي الْبِلَادِ ﴿٨﴾ وَثَمُودَ الَّذِينَ جَابُوا الصَّخْرَ بِالْوَادِ ﴿٩﴾
وَفِرْعَوْنَ ذِي الْأَوْتَادِ ﴿١٠﴾ الَّذِينَ طَغَوْا فِي الْبِلَادِ ﴿١١﴾ فَأَكْثَرُوا فِيهَا الْفَسَادَ
﴿١٢﴾ فَصَبَّ عَلَيْهِمْ رَبُّكَ سَوْطَ عَذَابٍ ﴿١٣﴾ إِنَّ رَبَّكَ لَبِالْمِرْصَادِ ﴿١٤﴾

In the name of God, the Beneficent, the Merciful.

By the dawn. [1] *And by ten nights.* [2] *And by the even and the odd.*
[3] *And by the night when it departs.* [4] *Is there not in these an oath*
for people of understanding? [5] *Have you not considered how your Lord*
dealt with [the people of] ʿAd? [6] *Of Iram, [the city] of lofty pillars,* [7]
The likes of which had not been built in the [other] lands? [8] *And [with*
the people of] Thamud, who hewed out the rocks in the valley. [9] *And*
[with] Firʿawn, the man of stakes. [10] *Who transgressed in the lands,*
[11] *and increased mischief therein.* [12] *So your Lord poured upon them*
a scourge of punishment. [13] *Indeed, your Lord is ever-Watchful.* [14]

INTRODUCTION

Surat al-Fajr (89) was the 10th chapter to be revealed.[1] It has thirty verses and was revealed in Makka, after Surat al-Layl (92). It is named after the oath made by the dawn (*al-fajr*) in the first verse.

The theme of the surah is a criticism of the manner in which the transgressors and disbelievers view the life of this world. Those who have invested their entire efforts in pursuit of the *dunyā* have been sternly warned of punishment in this world and the Hereafter.

The surah cautions that whoever believes that God is pleased with those whom He grants wealth and displeased with those whom He deprives of wealth in this world is mistaken and short-sighted in his understanding of the reality. Both wealth and poverty are merely different forms of the test that God wishes every human being to undergo in the *dunyā*. In whatever circumstances God has placed an individual, the task at hand is to send forth that which would be of use to him in the Hereafter.

Those who have capability and wealth should not transgress, and those who are powerless and poor should not give way to despair. Examples of the end of former nations who considered themselves invincible have been presented for mankind to take heed. God gave them respite for an appointed term, and then brought their arrogance to an end by destroying their civilizations.

LINK TO THE PREVIOUS CHAPTER

In the previous chapter, Surat al-Ghāshiyah, God tells the Prophet (s) that his duty is only to remind, and it is upon God to take account. In Surat al-Fajr, God gives examples of communities of whom He has taken account.

In Surat al-Ghāshiyah, God tells the Prophet (s) that he is not a watcher over the people, and in Surat al-Fajr, He attributes this quality to Himself, stating: '*Indeed, your Lord is ever-Watchful.*'

Surat al-Ghāshiyah talks of the Hereafter at the beginning and the fate of the two groups therein. Surat al-Fajr talks of the fate of the arrogant in this world and then mentions the Hereafter at the end.

---

[1] Maʿrifat, *ʿUlūm-i Qurʾānī*, p. 90.

MERITS OF RECITATION

- A tradition from the Prophet (s) states: God shall forgive the sins of the one who recites Surat al-Fajr in the ten nights (at the beginning of Dhū al-Ḥijjah). For the one who recites it in other days, it shall manifest as a light for him on the Day of Judgement.[2]
- A tradition from Imam al-Sadiq (a) states: Recite Surat al-Fajr in your obligatory and supererogatory prayers; it is the surah of al-Husayn b. Ali (a), and whoever recites it will be with al-Husayn (a), in his company, on the Day of Judgement – indeed, God is all-Mighty, all-Wise.[3]

  Abu Usāmah, who was present in the gathering, asked the Imam (a) how this surah came to be specified for al-Husayn (a) in particular. The Imam (a) replied, "The verses, '*O contented soul...*' are exemplified by al-Husayn (a), for he possessed a contented soul, well-pleased and pleasing [to God] ... This surah is especially for al-Husayn (a) and his *shīʿa*, and the *shīʿa* of the household of Muhammad (s)..."[4]

EXEGESIS

VERSES 1 - 5

وَالْفَجْرِ ﴿١﴾ وَلَيَالٍ عَشْرٍ ﴿٢﴾ وَالشَّفْعِ وَالْوَتْرِ ﴿٣﴾ وَاللَّيْلِ إِذَا يَسْرِ ﴿٤﴾ هَلْ فِي ذَٰلِكَ قَسَمٌ لِذِي حِجْرٍ ﴿٥﴾

By the dawn. [1] *And by ten nights.* [2] *And by the even and the odd.* [3] *And by the night when it departs.* [4] *Is there not in these an oath for people of understanding?* [5]

---

[2] Nūrī, *Mustadrak al-Wasā'il*, 4/358.

عَنِ الرَّسُولِ (صَلَّى اللهُ عَلَيْهِ وَآلِهِ) – مَنْ قَرَأَ سُورَةَ الْفَجْرِ فِي لَيَالٍ عَشْرٍ غَفَرَ [اللهُ] لَهُ وَمَنْ قَرَأَهَا سَائِرَ الْأَيَّامِ كَانَتْ لَهُ نُورًا يَوْمَ الْقِيَامَةِ.

[3] ʿĀmilī, *Wasā'il*, 6/144.

عَنِ الصَّادِقِ (عَلَيْهِ السَّلَامُ) – اِقْرَؤُوا سُورَةَ الْفَجْرِ فِي فَرَائِضِكُمْ وَنَوَافِلِكُمْ فَإِنَّهَا سُورَةٌ لِلْحُسَيْنِ بْنِ عَلِيٍّ عَلَيْهِ السَّلَامُ، مَنْ قَرَأَهَا كَانَ مَعَ الْحُسَيْنِ بْنِ عَلِيٍّ عَلَيْهِ السَّلَامُ يَوْمَ الْقِيَامَةِ فِي دَرَجَتِهِ مِنَ الْجَنَّةِ إِنَّ اللهَ عَزِيزٌ حَكِيمٌ.

[4] Majlisī, *Biḥār*, 44/218.

فَقَالَ أَبُو أُسَامَةَ وَكَانَ حَاضِرَ الْمَجْلِسِ: كَيْفَ صَارَتْ هَذِهِ السُّورَةُ لِلْحُسَيْنِ عَلَيْهِ السَّلَامُ خَاصَّةً؟ فَقَالَ أَلَا تَسْمَعُ إِلَى قَوْلِهِ تَعَالَى: «يَا أَيَّتُهَا النَّفْسُ الْمُطْمَئِنَّةُ» الْآيَةَ إِنَّمَا يَعْنِي الْحُسَيْنَ بْنَ عَلِيٍّ عَلَيْهِ السَّلَامُ فَهُوَ ذُو النَّفْسِ الْمُطْمَئِنَّةِ الرَّاضِيَةِ الْمَرْضِيَّةِ ... وَهَذِهِ السُّورَةُ فِي الْحُسَيْنِ بْنِ عَلِيٍّ عَلَيْهِ السَّلَامُ وَشِيعَتِهِ وَشِيعَةِ آلِ مُحَمَّدٍ خَاصَّةً.

1-5.1 The chapter begins with four oaths, although the application (*miṣdāq*) of these oaths is not clear from the verses. In brief, the harmony and design of some phenomena are presented here as a proof to emphasize the truth and importance of the matters that are subsequently mentioned in the surah.[5]

We have discussed the significance of oaths in the Qurʾan in the *tafsīr* of Surat al-Shams (91).

1-5.2 *'By the dawn.'*: [*Al-Fajr* (الْفَجْر, the dawn)] is derived from *fajara* which means to cleave. Dawn is called *fajr* because it occurs when daylight from the east cleaves the darkness of night. It is an important moment that brings an end to the night and heralds the beginning of the activity of human beings as well as other living creatures, which is perhaps why God swears by it.

Similar oaths are made by other important moments as well, for example Q74:33,34 state:

وَاللَّيْلِ إِذْ أَدْبَرَ ﴿٣٣﴾ وَالصُّبْحِ إِذَا أَسْفَرَ

And by the night when it departs,
and by the morning when it brightens.

1-5.3 Although the apparent meaning of *al-fajr* is the dawn that is a pivotal moment in every day, the exegetes have given several possible opinions about which particular dawn the oath refers to: the dawn of the first of Muharram, the dawn of the first of Dhū al-Ḥijjah, the dawn of the day of Eid al-Adha, the dawn of the first of the month of Ramadan, the dawn of Friday, and the dawn of every day.[6]

Others have said that it is the dawn of Islam and true knowledge over the darkness of ignorance that had cloaked the Arab peninsula.[7]

Finally, some exegetes give it the meaning of the moment of wakefulness that enters the darkened heart of a sinner and moves him to repent.[8]

1-5.4 Every new day is an opportunity to reform and progress. A tradition from Imam Ali (a) states: No day passes over man except

[5] Mughniyyah, *al-Kāshif*, 7/560.

[6] Shīrāzī, *Namūneh*, 26/442; Ṭabrasī, *al-Bayān*, 10/735.

[7] Modarresī, *Min Huda al-Qurʾan*, 18/86.

[8] Mughniyyah, *al-Kāshif*, 7/560.

that it says to him, "O son of Adam! I am a new day, and I am a witness over you. So [this day], say good things and do good things, and I will bear witness for you on the Day of Judgement, for you will never see me again.[9]

1-5.5 '*And by ten nights.*': The verse does not give further information about which ten nights these are. A famous opinion is that it is a reference to the first ten nights of Dhū al-Ḥijjah[10] which is when the ever-increasing multitudes of Muslims congregate in Makka to perform the annual Haj pilgrimage in submission to God.

According to some reports, the first ten nights of Dhū al-Ḥijjah were the nights that God added to the original thirty-day meeting that Prophet Musa (a) had with Him.[11]

Some exegetes have stated that these may refer to the last ten nights of the month of Ramadan, in which the Qur'an was revealed, and the great Night of Decree (*laylat al-qadr*) occurs,[12] while others have mentioned that they may refer to the first ten nights of Muharram.[13]

The nights have been mentioned in the indefinite case to indicate their importance and not their generality.[14]

1-5.6 '*And by the even and the odd.*': [*Al-Shafʿ* (الشَّفْع, the even)] means an even number or one of a pair of things that are attached to each other. [*Al-watr* (الْوَتْر, odd)] means a single or odd (uneven) number.[15]

Just as for the previous oaths, exegetes have mentioned several possibilities about what these two terms could be referring to. Some of these are:[16]

1. They refer to even and odd numbers, which govern all calculations and encompass the world of creation.

---

[9] Majlisī, *Biḥār*, 68/181.

عَنْ أَمِيرِ الْمُؤْمِنِينَ (عَلَيْهِ السَّلَامُ) – مَا مِنْ يَوْمٍ يَمُرُّ عَلَى ابْنِ آدَمَ إِلَّا قَالَ لَهُ ذَلِكَ الْيَوْمُ: يَابْنَ آدَمَ أَنَا يَوْمٌ جَدِيدٌ وَأَنَا عَلَيْكَ شَهِيدٌ. فَقُلْ فِيَّ خَيْرًا، وَاعْمَلْ فِيَّ خَيْرًا، أَشْهَدُ لَكَ بِهِ يَوْمَ الْقِيَامَةِ، فَإِنَّكَ لَنْ تَرَانِي بَعْدَهُ أَبَدًا.

[10] Ḥaskānī, *Nūr al-Thaqalayn*, 5/571; Ṭūsī, *al-Tibyān*, 10/341.

وَلَيَالٍ عَشْرٍ يَعْنِي الْعَشْرَ مِنْ ذِي الْحِجَّةِ [عَنِ ابْنِ عَبَّاسٍ وَالْحَسَنِ وَقُتَادَةَ وَمُجَاهِدٍ وَالضَّحَّاكِ.]

[11] Ṭabrasī, *al-Bayān*, 10/736.

[12] Shīrāzī, *Namūneh*, 26/442.

[13] Ṭūsī, *al-Tibyān*, 10/341.

[14] Ṭabāṭabā'ī, *al-Mīzān*, 20/279.

[15] Ibn Manẓūr, *Lisān al-ʿArab*.

[16] Shīrāzī, *Namūneh*. (summarized), 26/444, 445.

2. They refer to the three units of prayer (*salat al-shafᶜ* and *salat al-witr*) at the end of the night prayer (*salat al-layl*) which are highly recommended for spiritual progress. Q73:6 states:

إِنَّ نَاشِئَةَ اللَّيْلِ هِيَ أَشَدُّ وَطْئًا وَأَقْوَمُ قِيلًا

Indeed, the hours of the night are firmer in impression and more upright for speech.

3. Everything in creation has been made in pairs, and only God is One. Q51:49 states:

وَمِنْ كُلِّ شَيْءٍ خَلَقْنَا زَوْجَيْنِ لَعَلَّكُمْ تَذَكَّرُونَ

And of everything We have created pairs so that you may be mindful.

Therefore, these oaths can be considered to be by the creation and by the Creator. *Al-Shafᶜ* refers to creation and phenomena which exists in pairs: the earth and the sky, darkness and light, shade and sunshine, and the male and female of a species. Or it is the combination of existence (*wujūd*) and quiddity (*māhiyyah*), while *al-watr* refers to God who is One, and Indivisible.

4. *Al-Shafᶜ* refers to the Day of Tarwiyah and *al-watr* refers to the Day of ᶜArafah, following from the interpretation of 'ten nights' being the first ten nights of Dhū al-Ḥijjah.

1-5.7 *'And by the night when it departs.'*: This refers to the night as it leaves and gives way to the *fajr* (dawn) that is mentioned in the first oath.

[*Yasri* (يَسْرِ, departs)] is derived from *sarā*, which means to travel in the night,[17] and so this interesting phrase means, 'the night when it departs in the night,' as if the night is a sentient creature that heads under its own cover towards the illuminating dawn. Indeed, darkness leads to ultimate loss when it remains stagnant, but when it constantly moves towards light, there is value.[18]

1-5.8 If we consider the night to be a metaphor for hardship, this verse gives us the news that no hardship will persist for ever, and ease will always follow. Q94:5,6 state:

فَإِنَّ مَعَ الْعُسْرِ يُسْرًا ﴿٥﴾ إِنَّ مَعَ الْعُسْرِ يُسْرًا

[17] Rāghib, *al-Mufradāt.*

[18] Shīrāzī, *Namūneh,* 26/446.

For indeed, with hardship is ease. Indeed, with hardship is ease.

1-5.9 The night is mentioned with a definite article (*al*). If this is taken in the general sense, it would mean every night.[19] By interpreting the ten nights in the previous verse as a reference to the first ten nights of Dhū al-Ḥijjah, some exegetes say that in this verse the night refers to the particular night of Eid al-Adha, which the pilgrims spend on the plains of Muzdalifah. About the importance of connecting with God on the night spent in Muzdalifah (*al-Mashʿar al-Ḥarām*), Q2:198 states:

فَإِذَا أَفَضْتُم مِّنْ عَرَفَاتٍ فَاذْكُرُوا اللَّهَ عِندَ الْمَشْعَرِ الْحَرَامِ
وَاذْكُرُوهُ كَمَا هَدَاكُمْ وَإِن كُنتُم مِّن قَبْلِهِ لَمِنَ الضَّالِّينَ

Then when you depart from ʿArafāt, remember God at al-Mashʿar al-Ḥarām. *And remember Him as He has guided you, for indeed, before that (before Islam) you were amongst those who were astray.*

1-5.10 ‘*Is there not in these an oath for people of understanding?*’: [*Dhī ḥijr* (ذِي حِجْرٍ, those of understanding)]. *Ḥijr* is derived from *ḥajara*, which means to forestall or prevent. And because intellect (*ʿaql*) and understanding forestalls wrongful conduct, *dhī ḥijr* means ‘people of true intellect and understanding.’[20]

1-5.11 God does not ask elsewhere in the Qurʾan for mankind to consider His oaths, and here the question is rhetorical. As discussed, the oaths in this surah may have been made by phenomena that are relevant to the Haj, or phenomena through which one gains the cognition (*maʿrifah*) of God through submission to Him.[21]

What the verse means to say is that only people of understanding will be moved to ponder over the object of the oaths and realize the power and wisdom of God.[22] And their pondering accompanied by submission to God, will enhance their *maʿrifah* of Him.

Furthermore, they would realize that God would not swear these oaths except to stress the critical importance and undeniable truth of the subject that is to follow.

---

19 Ṭabāṭabāʾī, *al-Mīzān*, 20/280.

20 Ṭabrasī, *al-Bayān*, 10/737.

21 Shīrāzī, *Namūneh*, 26/447.

22 Mughniyyah, *al-Kāshif*, 7/560.

SUMMARY OF THE VERSES

The chapter begins with four oaths: by the dawn, by ten unspecified nights, by the even and the odd, and by the night when it departs. Then God states that these oaths are sufficient for people of understanding.

REFLECTIVE LEARNING

As we have seen, various meanings have been given to the each of the four oaths that came at the beginning of the chapter.

If we take these oaths to be referring to the guidance and ease that follows ignorance and hardship, then a common thread that emerges is their role in gaining the *maʿrifah* of God.

This *maʿrifah* does not come from book knowledge, rather it arises from fully submitting to God. Q31:22 states

وَمَنْ يُسْلِمْ وَجْهَهُ إِلَى اللهِ وَهُوَ مُحْسِنٌ فَقَدِ اسْتَمْسَكَ بِالْعُرْوَةِ الْوُثْقَىٰ
وَإِلَى اللهِ عَاقِبَةُ الْأُمُورِ

And whoever submits himself to Allah while he is the doer of good,
then he has taken hold of the firmest handhold;
and to Allah is the end of [all] affairs.

Let me reflect on my *maʿrifah* of God, which is dependent on my level of submission and servitude to Him. How can I increase my submission further so that I can increase my *maʿrifah*?

VERSES 6 - 14

أَلَمْ تَرَ كَيْفَ فَعَلَ رَبُّكَ بِعَادٍ ﴿٦﴾ إِرَمَ ذَاتِ الْعِمَادِ ﴿٧﴾ الَّتِي لَمْ يُخْلَقْ مِثْلُهَا فِي
الْبِلَادِ ﴿٨﴾ وَثَمُودَ الَّذِينَ جَابُوا الصَّخْرَ بِالْوَادِ ﴿٩﴾ وَفِرْعَوْنَ ذِي الْأَوْتَادِ ﴿١٠﴾
الَّذِينَ طَغَوْا فِي الْبِلَادِ ﴿١١﴾ فَأَكْثَرُوا فِيهَا الْفَسَادَ ﴿١٢﴾ فَصَبَّ عَلَيْهِمْ رَبُّكَ سَوْطَ
عَذَابٍ ﴿١٣﴾ إِنَّ رَبَّكَ لَبِالْمِرْصَادِ ﴿١٤﴾

Have you not considered how your Lord dealt with [the people of] ʿAd? [6] *Of Iram, [the city] of lofty pillars,* [7] *The likes of which had not been built in the [other] lands?* [8] *And [with the people of] Thamud, who hewed out the rocks in the valley.* [9] *And [with] Firʿawn, the man of stakes.* [10] *Who transgressed in the lands,* [11] *and increased mischief therein.* [12] *So your Lord poured upon them a scourge of punishment.* [13] *Indeed, your Lord is ever-Watchful.* [14]

6-14.1 The subject of the oaths (*jawāb*) has been omitted.[23] The oaths in the beginning of the chapter emphasize the fact that God, who has fashioned these phenomena, is now giving a very important message to mankind. And the first part of this message is to ponder over the history and fate of those who rebelled against Him.

6-14.2 Three powerful peoples (ʿAd, Thamud, and Firʿawn) are mentioned briefly, as examples of those who had been granted power and authority, but arrogantly defied God and transgressed. After a respite, God's power was manifested over them, and they were severely punished.

6-14.3 '*Have you not considered how your Lord dealt with [the people of] ʿAd?*': The verse is a warning to the disbelievers about the fate of previous communities who denied God.[24]

[*Alam tarā*? (أَلَمْ تَرَ, have you not considered?)] is a question referring to the fate of three communities which are mentioned in sequence, and God asks the reader to consider how He dealt with each of them.

In this regard, a tradition from Imam Ali (a) states: Even though I have not lived with those who came before me, I have studied their actions, pondered over the events of their lives, and walked in their traces, until it was as if I was one of them. In fact, by virtue of what has reached me of their affairs, it is as though I have lived with the first of them to the last. I have been able to discern the evil from the worthy, and beneficial acts from harmful ones.[25]

[*Kayfa* (كَيْفَ, how)]. How is used here to inspire curiosity about the treatment of the nation of ʿAd by God.

[*Rabbuka* (رَبُّكَ, your Lord)] shows the protective and sustaining role of God for the entirety of mankind. We have discussed this term further in the *tafsīr* of Surat al-Fātiḥah.

---

[23] Ṭabāṭabā'ī, *al-Mīzān*, 20/280.

[24] Ṭūsī, *al-Tibyān*, 10/342.

[25] *Nahj al-Balāghah*, letter 31.

أَيْ بُنَيَّ إِنِّي وَإِنْ لَمْ أَكُنْ عُمِّرْتُ عُمُرَ مَنْ كَانَ قَبْلِي فَقَدْ نَظَرْتُ فِي أَعْمَالِهِمْ وَفَكَّرْتُ فِي أَخْبَارِهِمْ وَسِرْتُ فِي آثَارِهِمْ حَتَّى عُدْتُ كَأَحَدِهِمْ بَلْ كَأَنِّي بِمَا انْتَهَى إِلَيَّ مِنْ أُمُورِهِمْ قَدْ عُمِّرْتُ مَعَ أَوَّلِهِمْ إِلَى آخِرِهِمْ فَعَرَفْتُ صَفْوَ ذَلِكَ مِنْ كَدَرِهِ، وَنَفْعَهُ مِنْ ضَرَرِهِ.

The people of ʿAd have been discussed briefly later in this surah. Aspects of the history and fate of this great civilization were known to the Makkans because ʿAd was an Arab tribe.

6-14.4 *'[Of] Iram, [the city] of lofty pillars, the likes of which had not been built in the [other] lands?'*: Iram was the fabled capital of ʿAd, the 'city of pillars' (*dhāt al-ʿimād*). In it they had constructed many fine and lofty dwellings. No city was like it. In their time, ʿAd was the most technologically advanced empire and commanded respect and fear among other nations. However, by the time of the revelation of these verses no traces of this city remained.[26]

In this verse, 'Iram' can also be considered as an inclusive substitute (*badal al-ishtimāl*) for ʿAd because their progenitor was named Iram. The destruction of that city was part of the punishment visited on ʿAd. Therefore, the verses would mean, 'have you not considered how your Lord dealt with [the people of] ʿAd, that is, the people of Iram, [the city] of lofty pillars?'[27]

An alternate meaning suggested is 'Have you not considered how your Lord dealt with [the people of] ʿAd, that is, the people of Iram, the men of huge stature?', in which case the next phrase would be, 'the like of whom had not been created in the [other] lands'.[28]

6-14.5 *'And [with the people of] Thamud, who hewed out the rocks in the valley.'*: Thamud was a nation that came after ʿAd and perhaps because of their inclination to construct large monuments, they are sometimes referred to as 'the second ʿAd.'[29]

The people of Thamud have been mentioned in more detail in Surat al-Shams (91), so we have discussed them in the *tafsīr* of that surah.

[*Jābū* (جَابُوا, they hewed out)] is derived from *jawb*, meaning to pierce and also to cut out. From the same root also comes *jawāb* (reply) which means to cut or finish a question with a correct answer.[30]

[*Ṣakhr* (صَخْر, rocks)] (sing. *ṣakhrah*) means large and strong boulders.

[*Wād* (وَاد, valley)] or *wādī*, means a riverbed or valley between two mountains, as also stated in Q15:82:

---

26 Ṭabāṭabāʾī, *al-Mīzān*, 20/281.

27 Rafsanjānī, *Rahnamā*, 20/398.

28 Rāzī, *Mafātīḥ al-Ghayb*, 31/153.

29 Maybudī, *Kashf al-Asrār*, 6/435.

30 Muṣṭafawī, *al-Taḥqīq*.

وَكَانُوا يَنْحِتُونَ مِنَ الْجِبَالِ بُيُوتًا آمِنِينَ

And they hewed out dwellings in the mountains, feeling secure.

Like the people of ʿAd before them, the people of Thamud also denied the messengers sent to them, the last of whom was Prophet Salih (a). Q26:141,142 state:

كَذَّبَتْ ثَمُودُ الْمُرْسَلِينَ ﴿١٤١﴾ إِذْ قَالَ لَهُمْ أَخُوهُمْ صَالِحٌ أَلَا تَتَّقُونَ

Thamud denied the messengers [of God]. When their brother Salih said to them, "Will you not be wary of God?"

6-14.6 '*And [with] Firʿawn, the man of stakes.*': The Firʿawn mentioned in the verse is Rameses II, the pharaoh at the time of Musa (a). The Egyptians knew about the civilizations of ʿAd and Thamud, which may have been even greater than their own. Q40:30,31 quote the believer of the people of Firʿawn (*mu'min Āl Firʿawn*):

وَقَالَ الَّذِي آمَنَ يَا قَوْمِ إِنِّي أَخَافُ عَلَيْكُمْ مِثْلَ يَوْمِ الْأَحْزَابِ ﴿٣٠﴾
مِثْلَ دَأْبِ قَوْمِ نُوحٍ وَعَادٍ وَثَمُودَ

And he who believed said, "O my people! Indeed, I fear for you [a fate] like the parties [of old]. Like the fate of the people of Nuh and ʿAd and Thamud...

6-14.7 [*Awtād* أَوْتَادِ, stakes, pegs,)] (sing. *watad*) has several possible meanings here:

i) Pegs or stakes: If this meaning is taken, then Firʿawn is called the 'man of stakes' (*dhī al-awtād*) because according to the narrations, his favoured method of punishment was to dismember his hapless victims, before driving stakes into their bodies and crucifying them on palm trees.[31] This was how he killed his wife Asiyah,[32] and threatened to kill the magicians who professed faith in the religion of Musa (a). Q7:124 states:

لَأُقَطِّعَنَّ أَيْدِيَكُمْ وَأَرْجُلَكُمْ مِنْ خِلَافٍ ثُمَّ لَأُصَلِّبَنَّكُمْ أَجْمَعِينَ

[Firʿawn said:] Surely, I will have your hands and feet cut off in opposite sides. Then I will crucify you all, together.

---

[31] Ṭabāṭabā'ī, *al-Mīzān*, 20/281.

[32] Shīrāzī, *Namūneh*, 24/303.

ii) Buildings or monuments: The word *awtād* also means large monuments. This is a plausible meaning here as well because Firʿawn is mentioned with two other communities who also built great structures: ʿAd who built cities with huge pillars, and Thamud whose dwellings were carved inside the mountains.

And indeed, the monuments built by Rameses II are still visible at the temples of Karnak and Abu Simbel carved into the Nubian mountains in Egypt.

iii) Some exegetes have said that stakes is used here because Firʿawn had a large standing army who would live in mobile tents, and *awtād* refers to the multitude of tent-poles visible in the army encampments. Therefore, it is a metaphor for Firʿawn's military strength.[33]

6-14.8 ʿ*Who transgressed in the lands, and increased mischief therein.*': The verses turn to the unjust behaviour of these three different peoples in their own lands. Two reprehensible qualities of ʿAd, Thamud, and Firʿawn are revealed: i) Instead of using their power to behave with justice and peace, they rebelled against God, transgressing without fear of reprisal, and ii) they encouraged depravity in their lands.

Thereafter, the terrible consequences of their transgression in this world are mentioned, as a prelude to their chastisement in the Hereafter.

[*Ṭaghaw* (طَغَوْا, transgressed)] comes from *ṭaghā* and *ṭughyān*, which means transgressing all bounds, being unjust, and sinning continually.[34]

[*Aktharū*, (أَكْثَرُوا, increased)] means made more excessive.

[*Fasād* (فَسَادَ, mischief)] includes every type of sin and vice that causes social degeneration.

They behaved arrogantly against the Prophets (a) of God who were sent to guide them, and ridiculed the believers.[35] As a result of their behaviour, corruption became widespread in their societies.

6-14.9 These three communities were known for their elaborate civilizations and strong buildings and homes. The Arabs are

[33] Ibid, 26/455.

[34] Rāghib, *al-Mufradāt*.

[35] Rāzī, *Mafātīḥ al-Ghayb*, 31/154.

reminded that these powerful, seemingly indestructible, nations were destroyed in an instant. Therefore, the idolaters should not feel secure from God's punishment.

6-14.10 '*So your Lord poured upon them a scourge of punishment.*': [*Ṣabba* (صَبَّ, poured)] is usually used for water, and means to pour. [*Sawṭ* (سَوْط, scourge)] means a whip or lash.

Here, the two terms are used as metaphors, and '*poured upon them a scourge*' means 'imposed incessant and severe punishment on them.' And the use of *ʿadhāb* in the indefinite form emphasizes its terrible nature.[36]

However, compared to the punishment of the Hereafter it was but a 'whipping'.[37]

6-14.11 The three communities were visited with different punishments but with the same devastating results. Although the manner of their punishment is not mentioned in this surah, it is mentioned elsewhere in the Qur'an:

i) Q69:6,7 state that ʿAd was destroyed by fearsome tornados:

وَأَمَّا عَادٌ فَأُهْلِكُوا بِرِيحٍ صَرْصَرٍ عَاتِيَةٍ ﴿٦﴾
سَخَّرَهَا عَلَيْهِمْ سَبْعَ لَيَالٍ وَثَمَانِيَةَ أَيَّامٍ حُسُومًا

And as for ʿAd, they were destroyed by a furious, violent wind, which He made rage against them for seven nights and eight days in succession...

ii) Q69:5 states that Thamud were destroyed by an unbearable sound blast:

فَأَمَّا ثَمُودُ فَأُهْلِكُوا بِالطَّاغِيَةِ

So as for Thamud, they were destroyed by the overpowering catastrophe.

iii) Q28:40 states that Firʿawn and his hosts were destroyed by drowning:

فَأَخَذْنَاهُ وَجُنُودَهُ فَنَبَذْنَاهُمْ فِي الْيَمِّ فَانْظُرْ كَيْفَ كَانَ عَاقِبَةُ الظَّالِمِينَ

[36] Ṭabāṭabā'ī, *al-Mīzān*, 20/281.

[37] Qarā'atī, *Nūr*, 10/475.

So We seized him (Firʿawn) and his army and flung them into the sea. Behold the end of the wrongdoers!

The imposing structures and developed civilizations of these three communities were of little consequence against the sudden and overwhelming chastisement of God.

6-14.12 *'Indeed, your Lord is ever-Watchful.'*: [*Mirṣād* (مِرْصَاد, ever-Watchful)] is derived from *raṣada* which means preparedness to keep watch on something. *Mirṣād* refers to both the action and the place of observing and looking out for an enemy or prey who has to pass by that route.[38] Since it refers here to God who is all-Knowing, it has been used figuratively to indicate that God constantly observes the deeds of all His creation and witnesses their intentions also,[39] and is capable of chastising them, while most of them are oblivious of His witnessing.[40]

6-14.13 God has not detached Himself from the affairs of the world after creating it; in fact, He is ever-Watchful. The usage of *Rabbaka* (your Sustainer) in this verse is because this watchfulness is part of God's role in sustaining and caring for the entirety of mankind. When He grants a nation or community authority, it is always with an associated responsibility to itself and others. If the people remain within the limits prescribed by God, and fulfil their responsibilities, then they will continue to enjoy this authority. Q8:53 states:

ذَٰلِكَ بِأَنَّ اللَّهَ لَمْ يَكُ مُغَيِّرًا نِعْمَةً أَنْعَمَهَا عَلَىٰ قَوْمٍ حَتَّىٰ يُغَيِّرُوا
مَا بِأَنْفُسِهِمْ وَأَنَّ اللَّهَ سَمِيعٌ عَلِيمٌ

That is because Allah will never change a favour that He had bestowed upon a people until they change what is within their hearts. And indeed, Allah is all-Hearing, all-Knowing.

When a community transgresses, it is granted respite so that it may reform, until the truth is manifested to them. Thereafter, if it persists in its corrupt ways, God destroys it because its existence is neither beneficial to itself nor to others.

---

38 Rāghib, *al-Mufradāt*.

39 Ṭabrasī, *al-Bayān*, 10/739.

40 Ṭabāṭabāʾī, *al-Mīzān*, 20/281.

6-14.14 The watchfulness of God is not just over the past nations, rather it is for all time both in the *dunyā* as well as the *ākhirah*. His monitoring in the Hereafter has been likened to a station that all must pass through. A tradition from Imam al-Sadiq (a) states: *Al-Mirṣād* is an archway on the path [over Hell] (*ṣirāṭ*) which no-one who is still guilty of oppressing someone can pass [without giving some compensation].[41]

This is a difficult station indeed. A tradition from Imam al-Sajjad (a) states: The good acts of the oppressor will be given to the one he wronged... [or] the evil acts of the wronged person will be added to the evil acts of the oppressor.[42]

DISCUSSION: THE PEOPLE OF ʿAD AND PROPHET HUD (A)

The people of ʿAd were an Arab nation[43] who lived in the dunes of al-Aḥqāf, in Southern Arabia.[44] They were named after their forefather, ʿĀd b. al-ʿAws, a grandson of Prophet Nuh (a).

It appears that they had an advanced and rich civilization. They had developed magnificent cities, the chief of which was Iram, the 'city of pillars', and 'unlike any city in the land'. Their extravagant lifestyle was funded by plundering the wealth of weaker nations.
Q26:128-130 state:

أَتَبْنُونَ بِكُلِّ رِيعٍ آيَةً تَعْبَثُونَ ﴿١٢٨﴾ وَتَتَّخِذُونَ مَصَانِعَ لَعَلَّكُمْ تَخْلُدُونَ ﴿١٢٩﴾ وَإِذَا بَطَشْتُمْ بَطَشْتُمْ جَبَّارِينَ

Do you construct on monuments on every high place to amuse yourselves? And take for yourselves palaces and fortresses as if you will live forever? And when you strike [others] you strike like tyrants.

Their lands were fertile and full of orchards and farms. They were tall in stature and had great physical strength.[45] Their pre-eminence amongst nations filled them with great arrogance. Q41:15 states:

---

41 Majlisī, *Biḥār*, 8/64.

عَنِ الصَّادِقِ (عَلَيْهِ السَّلَامُ) – الْمِرْصَادُ قَنْطَرَةٌ عَلَى الصِّرَاطِ لَا يَجُوزُهَا عَبْدٌ بِمَظْلِمَةٍ.

42 Kulaynī. *al-Kāfī*, 8/106.

عَنِ السَّجَّادِ (عَلَيْهِ السَّلَامُ) – يُؤْخَذُ لِلْمَظْلُومِ مِنَ الظَّالِمِ مِنْ حَسَنَاتِهِ ... يُؤْخَذُ مِنْ سَيِّئَاتِ الْمَظْلُومِ فَتُزَادُ عَلَى سَيِّئَاتِ الظَّالِمِ.

43 Ibn Kathīr, *al-Bidāyah wa al-Nihāyah*, 2/157.

44 Ṭabāṭabā'ī, *al-Mīzān*, 18/210.

45 Ibid, 20/280.

فَأَمَّا عَادٌ فَٱسْتَكْبَرُوا فِي الْأَرْضِ بِغَيْرِ الْحَقِّ وَقَالُوا مَنْ أَشَدُّ مِنَّا قُوَّةً
أَوَلَمْ يَرَوْا أَنَّ اللهَ الَّذِي خَلَقَهُمْ هُوَ أَشَدُّ مِنْهُمْ قُوَّةً وَكَانُوا بِآيَاتِنَا يَجْحَدُونَ

As for ʿAd, they were unjustly arrogant in the land, and said, "Who is greater than us in power?" Did they not consider that Allah, who created them, was greater than them in power? But they continued to reject Our signs.

The people of ʿAd did not possess true guidance and consequently, their society was steeped in idolatry. God sent Prophet Hud (a) to guide them. Q11:50 states:

وَإِلَىٰ عَادٍ أَخَاهُمْ هُودًا قَالَ يَا قَوْمِ ٱعْبُدُوا اللهَ مَا لَكُمْ مِنْ إِلَٰهٍ غَيْرُهُ إِنْ أَنْتُمْ إِلَّا مُفْتَرُونَ

And to ʿAd [We sent] their brother Hud. He said [to them], "O my people, worship Allah! You have no deity other than Him. You are but inventors [of false gods]."

In the Qurʾan they have been referred to as 'the first, or former, ʿAd'; Q53:50 states:

وَأَنَّهُ أَهْلَكَ عَادًا الْأُولَىٰ

And that He destroyed the first ʿAd.

Some exegetes believe Thamud to be the second, or later, ʿAd. Their Prophet was Salih (a). However, our discussion is about the earlier nation of ʿAd, to whom God sent Prophet Hud (a) as a guide and warner. Q46:21 states:

وَٱذْكُرْ أَخَا عَادٍ إِذْ أَنذَرَ قَوْمَهُ بِالْأَحْقَافِ

And mention [O Muhammad], the brother of ʿAd (Hud) when he warned his people in [the region of] al-Aḥqāf...

Prophet Hud (a) preached to them sincerely, but to no avail. Q11:52 quotes some of his words:

وَيَا قَوْمِ ٱسْتَغْفِرُوا رَبَّكُمْ ثُمَّ تُوبُوا إِلَيْهِ يُرْسِلِ السَّمَاءَ عَلَيْكُمْ مِدْرَارًا
وَيَزِدْكُمْ قُوَّةً إِلَىٰ قُوَّتِكُمْ وَلَا تَتَوَلَّوْا مُجْرِمِينَ

And O my people! Ask forgiveness of your Lord, and then turn to Him in repentance. He will send [rain from] the sky upon you in abundance and add strength to your strength. So do not turn away, sinful.

But they turned away in defiance, just as they had from the previous Prophets (a) that were sent to them. Q41:13,14 state:

فَإِنْ أَعْرَضُوا فَقُلْ أَنْذَرْتُكُمْ صَاعِقَةً مِثْلَ صَاعِقَةِ عَادٍ وَثَمُودَ ﴿١٣﴾
إِذْ جَاءَتْهُمُ الرُّسُلُ مِنْ بَيْنِ أَيْدِيهِمْ وَمِنْ خَلْفِهِمْ أَلَّا تَعْبُدُوا إِلَّا اللَّهَ

But if they (the polytheists) turn away, then say, "I have warned you of a thunderbolt like the thunderbolt [that struck] 'Ad and Thamud When the messengers had come to them before them and behind them, [saying], 'Worship none but Allah'...

And they mocked their last messenger, Prophet Hud (a), also. Q11:53,54 state:

قَالُوا يَا هُودُ مَا جِئْتَنَا بِبَيِّنَةٍ وَمَا نَحْنُ بِتَارِكِي آلِهَتِنَا عَنْ قَوْلِكَ
وَمَا نَحْنُ لَكَ بِمُؤْمِنِينَ ﴿٥٣﴾ إِنْ نَقُولُ إِلَّا اعْتَرَاكَ بَعْضُ آلِهَتِنَا بِسُوءٍ

They said, "O Hud! You have not brought us clear evidence, and we are not inclined to forsake our gods at your word. Nor shall we believe in you. All we can say is that some of our gods have possessed you with evil."...

Q11:59 summarizes their attitude:

وَتِلْكَ عَادٌ جَحَدُوا بِآيَاتِ رَبِّهِمْ وَعَصَوْا رُسُلَهُ وَاتَّبَعُوا أَمْرَ كُلِّ جَبَّارٍ عَنِيدٍ

Such were [the people of] 'Ad. They rejected the signs of their Lord, disobeyed His messengers and followed the order of every obstinate tyrant.

In the end, the powerful and arrogant people were destroyed by God. Q46:24,25 state:

فَلَمَّا رَأَوْهُ عَارِضًا مُسْتَقْبِلَ أَوْدِيَتِهِمْ قَالُوا هَٰذَا عَارِضٌ مُمْطِرُنَا بَلْ هُوَ
مَا اسْتَعْجَلْتُمْ بِهِ رِيحٌ فِيهَا عَذَابٌ أَلِيمٌ ﴿٢٤﴾ تُدَمِّرُ كُلَّ شَيْءٍ بِأَمْرِ
رَبِّهَا فَأَصْبَحُوا لَا يُرَىٰ إِلَّا مَسَاكِنُهُمْ كَذَٰلِكَ نَجْزِي الْقَوْمَ الْمُجْرِمِينَ

And when they saw it (the punishment) as a cloud approaching their valleys, they said, "This is a cloud bringing us rain [after a long drought]." Rather, it is that which you were asking to be hastened! A wind within which is a painful torment, destroying everything by the command of its Lord. And they became so that nothing was seen [of them] except their dwellings. Thus do we recompense the people of sin.

And Q69:6-8 state:

وَأَمَّا عَادٌ فَأُهْلِكُوا بِرِيحٍ صَرْصَرٍ عَاتِيَةٍ ﴿٦﴾ سَخَّرَهَا عَلَيْهِمْ سَبْعَ لَيَالٍ وَثَمَانِيَةَ أَيَّامٍ حُسُومًا فَتَرَى الْقَوْمَ فِيهَا صَرْعَىٰ كَأَنَّهُمْ أَعْجَازُ نَخْلٍ خَاوِيَةٍ ﴿٧﴾ فَهَلْ تَرَىٰ لَهُم مِّن بَاقِيَةٍ

And as for ʿAd, they were destroyed by a furious, violent wind, which He made rage against them for seven nights and eight days in succession, so you would see the people therein fallen as if they were hollow trunks of palm trees. Then do you see any remains of them?

SUMMARY OF THE VERSES

The verses ask man to consider the behaviour of three powerful groups, the people of ʿAd, Thamud, and Firʿawn. Despite being given power and bounties from God, they transgressed and behaved inordinately in the land. As a result, God sent down a variety of punishments on them in this world. Indeed, God is Witness to the acts of His servants.

REFLECTIVE LEARNING

Powerful nations whose people enjoyed many bounties from God fell into decay and corruption when they forgot God.

Let me reflect on the gifts that God has blessed me and my community (for example, opportunities, wealth, peace, security, or other bounties). Do I acknowledge that these bounties are from Him?

Do I set a good example by using these gifts in the way that God would want me to?

PART 2: VERSES 15 - 30

TEXT AND TRANSLATION

فَأَمَّا الْإِنسَانُ إِذَا مَا ابْتَلَاهُ رَبُّهُ فَأَكْرَمَهُ وَنَعَّمَهُ فَيَقُولُ رَبِّي أَكْرَمَنِ ﴿١٥﴾ وَأَمَّا إِذَا مَا
ابْتَلَاهُ فَقَدَرَ عَلَيْهِ رِزْقَهُ فَيَقُولُ رَبِّي أَهَانَنِ ﴿١٦﴾ كَلَّا بَل لَّا تُكْرِمُونَ الْيَتِيمَ ﴿١٧﴾
وَلَا تَحَاضُّونَ عَلَىٰ طَعَامِ الْمِسْكِينِ ﴿١٨﴾ وَتَأْكُلُونَ التُّرَاثَ أَكْلًا لَّمًّا ﴿١٩﴾
وَتُحِبُّونَ الْمَالَ حُبًّا جَمًّا ﴿٢٠﴾ كَلَّا إِذَا دُكَّتِ الْأَرْضُ دَكًّا دَكًّا ﴿٢١﴾ وَجَاءَ
رَبُّكَ وَالْمَلَكُ صَفًّا صَفًّا ﴿٢٢﴾ وَجِيءَ يَوْمَئِذٍ بِجَهَنَّمَ يَوْمَئِذٍ يَتَذَكَّرُ الْإِنسَانُ وَأَنَّىٰ لَهُ
الذِّكْرَىٰ ﴿٢٣﴾ يَقُولُ يَا لَيْتَنِي قَدَّمْتُ لِحَيَاتِي ﴿٢٤﴾ فَيَوْمَئِذٍ لَّا يُعَذِّبُ عَذَابَهُ أَحَدٌ
﴿٢٥﴾ وَلَا يُوثِقُ وَثَاقَهُ أَحَدٌ ﴿٢٦﴾ يَا أَيَّتُهَا النَّفْسُ الْمُطْمَئِنَّةُ ﴿٢٧﴾ ارْجِعِي إِلَىٰ
رَبِّكِ رَاضِيَةً مَّرْضِيَّةً ﴿٢٨﴾ فَادْخُلِي فِي عِبَادِي ﴿٢٩﴾ وَادْخُلِي جَنَّتِي ﴿٣٠﴾

And as for man, when his Lord tries him and gives him honour and bounties, he says, "My Lord has honoured me." [15] *But when He tries him and restricts his provision, he says, "My Lord has humiliated me."* [16] *Not at all! But you do not honour the orphan.* [17] *And you do not encourage the feeding of the food of the poor.* [18] *And you consume inheritance, devouring [it] indiscriminately.* [19] *And you love wealth with an immense love.* [20] *Not at all! When the earth is pounded, piece by piece.* [21] *And your Lord comes with the angels, rank upon rank.* [22] *And Hell will be brought near that Day. On that Day will man remember, but how will that remembrance [then] avail him?* [23] *He shall say, "How I wish I had sent forth [some provisions] for my life!"* [24] *But on that Day no one shall punish with [anything like] His punishment.* [25] *And no one will bind with [anything like] His binding.* [26] *[The righteous will be told:] O contented soul!* [27] *Return to your Lord, well-pleased and pleasing [to Him].* [28] *So, enter amongst My servants,* [29] *and enter My Paradise.* [30]

VERSES 15 - 20

فَأَمَّا الْإِنسَانُ إِذَا مَا ابْتَلَاهُ رَبُّهُ فَأَكْرَمَهُ وَنَعَّمَهُ فَيَقُولُ رَبِّي أَكْرَمَنِ ﴿١٥﴾ وَأَمَّا إِذَا مَا
ابْتَلَاهُ فَقَدَرَ عَلَيْهِ رِزْقَهُ فَيَقُولُ رَبِّي أَهَانَنِ ﴿١٦﴾ كَلَّا بَل لَّا تُكْرِمُونَ الْيَتِيمَ ﴿١٧﴾

وَلَا تَحَاضُّونَ عَلَىٰ طَعَامِ الْمِسْكِينِ ﴿١٨﴾ وَتَأْكُلُونَ التُّرَاثَ أَكْلًا لَّمًّا ﴿١٩﴾
وَتُحِبُّونَ الْمَالَ حُبًّا جَمًّا ﴿٢٠﴾

And as for man, when his Lord tries him and gives him honour and bounties, he says, "My Lord has honoured me." [15] *But when He tries him and restricts his provision, he says, "My Lord has humiliated me."* [16] *Not at all! But you do not honour the orphan.* [17] *And you do not encourage the feeding of the poor.* [18] *And you consume inheritance, devouring [it] indiscriminately.* [19] *And you love wealth with an immense love.* [20]

15-20.1 *'And as for man, when his Lord tries him and gives him honour and bounties, he says, "My Lord has honoured me." But when He tries him and restricts his provision, he says, "My Lord has humiliated me."'*: After the description of the three communities that lost their way despite being amply blessed with God's bounties, the discourse moves to a key principle in God's allocation of bounties – the fact that granting and withholding of favours are both parts of God's test and trial in this world.

The manner in which this test is confronted (in submission or with transgression) determines the nature of the recompense (reward or punishment) that mankind will receive in the Hereafter.[46]

In the first case, God wishes to see whether the person who is blessed with favours is grateful to Him and fulfils the rights of his fellow human beings, or does he become conceited and usurp the rights of others.

In the second case, God wants to see whether the one who is deprived remains content and patient with His allocation for him, or does he despair and blame God.

15-20.2 The phrase, *'And as for man'*, indicates that this is man's habitual way of thinking.[47] [*Al-Insān* (الْإِنسَان, man, human beings)] refers to the entire human race in general, and specifically to each and every individual within that race.[48]

---

[46] Muṭahharī, (*Āshnāyī bā Qur'an*), *Āthār*, 28/540.

[47] Qarā'atī, *Nūr*, 10/475.

[48] Ṭabrasī, *al-Bayān* 10/815, Ṭabāṭabā'ī, *al-Mīzān*, 20/356.

The *fa* (and) indicates that this verse is a continuation of the phrase in the previous verse that God is ever-Watchful (*b'il Mirṣād*). He 'sees' what His servants do when He tests them with ease and hardship.[49]

15-20.3 These two verses caution man not to be over exultant when he is honoured by God with blessings and not to assume that he has God's approval. At the same time, he must not give way to despair and conclude that he has been humiliated by God when he is deprived of His blessings.[50] It may well be that this deprivation preserves his faith.

[*Ibtalā*ʾ (ابْتَلَا, he tries)] is derived from *balā*ʾ which means test or affliction.

[*Na*ʿʿ*ama* (نَعَّمَ, to bless)] is derived from *na*ʿ*ama* which means to be in ease.

[*Qadara* (قَدَرَ, to restrict)] is derived from *qadr* which means to measure.[51]

Therefore, the verses indicate that God tries man by granting or restricting blessings, by ease or hardship, and sometimes with both.

15-20.4 Normally, a test is either for the examiner to find out the ability of an individual, or for an individual to realize his own capability. However, the trials of God are neither of these. God's tests for man-kind are opportunities to exercise their free will and make choices [based on guidance] to gradually grow to achieve their unique potential and thereby, perfection.[52]

15-20.5 Interestingly, God says that He honours the individual, but the end of the verse is critical of man's conclusion that he has been honoured. This is since God mentions honour because of His blessings, while man imagines the blessings that he has received to mean that he himself is honourable in God's eyes, and that the blessings are permanent, which is not necessarily the case.[53]

15-20.6 Both ease and hardship are a trial for mankind, as is clear from the usage of the term *ibtalā*ʾ twice. And in each case, man has an

---

[49] Ṭabāṭabāʾī, *al-Mīzān*, 20/282.

[50] Shīrāzī, *Namūneh*, 26/461.

[51] Muṣṭafawī, *al-Taḥqīq*.

[52] Muṭahharī, (*Āshnāyī bā Qur'an*), *Āthār*, 28/540.

[53] Shīrāzī, *Namūneh*, 26/461.

associated responsibility and duty that he must carry out to pass the test.[54] Q21:35 states:

وَنَبْلُوكُمْ بِالشَّرِّ وَالْخَيْرِ فِتْنَةً وَإِلَيْنَا تُرْجَعُونَ

And We test you with evil and with good as trial;
and to Us will you be returned.

In times of ease, man must realize that he is being tested and submit to God's will by showing gratitude and humility. Similarly, in times of hardship, he must also realize that he is being tested and submit to God's will by displaying patience and reliance on Him.[55]

However, often man does not react as he should. Q41:51 states:

وَإِذَا أَنْعَمْنَا عَلَى الْإِنْسَانِ أَعْرَضَ وَنَأَىٰ بِجَانِبِهِ وَإِذَا مَسَّهُ الشَّرُّ فَذُو دُعَاءٍ عَرِيضٍ

And when We bestow favour upon man, he turns away
and distances himself; but when evil touches him,
then he is full of extensive supplication.

15-20.7 If man makes an honest appraisal of his life, he will see that God has honoured him with days of comfort far more than days of hardship. However, Q11:9 states:

وَلَئِنْ أَذَقْنَا الْإِنْسَانَ مِنَّا رَحْمَةً ثُمَّ نَزَعْنَاهَا مِنْهُ إِنَّهُ لَيَئُوسٌ كَفُورٌ

And if We give man a taste of mercy from Us and then
We withdraw it from him, indeed, he is despairing, ungrateful.

And Q22:11 states:

فَإِنْ أَصَابَهُ خَيْرٌ اطْمَأَنَّ بِهِ وَإِنْ أَصَابَتْهُ فِتْنَةٌ انْقَلَبَ
عَلَىٰ وَجْهِهِ خَسِرَ الدُّنْيَا وَالْآخِرَةَ

...If he is touched by good, he is content, but if he is struck by a trial,
he turns on his face (reverts to mistrust of God). [In this way,]
He loses both this world and the Hereafter...

15-20.8 *'Not at all!'*: *Kallā* here means that man is mistaken when he assumes that God is dealing with him the way human beings deal with one another, where favour indicates approval and withholding favour indicates displeasure.

---

[54] Muṭahharī, (*Āshnāyī bā Qur'an*), *Āthār*, 28/541.

[55] Ṭabrasī, *al-Bayān*, 10/740.

A tradition from Imam Ali (a) states: And do not regard wealth and children to be the criterion for God's pleasure and displeasure...[56]

Furthermore, people who do not possess correct belief often consider the wealthy and powerful as honourable and those who are poor and lack means as dishonourable in society. In fact, sometimes people even accept oppression on themselves because of this mindset.

In this verse, God emphatically rejects this conclusion by stating, '*kallā* (not at all).' Honour and dishonour is not to do with wealth; rather, people bring honour to themselves by obeying God, and dishonour to themselves by disobeying Him.[57]

The criteria for honour in God's estimation is not the extent or paucity of blessings, because great tyrants in history have been wealthy beyond measure, while Prophets (a) and righteous believers have spent their lives in poverty.

15-20.9 The next verses speak of four attitudes and conducts that are the cause of dishonour. Interestingly, they are all to do with social conduct and not with man's direct worship of God. This shows that submission to God is to be manifested in all aspects of life.

15-20.10 '*But you do not honour the orphan. And you do not encourage the feeding of the poor.*': The first two are: not honouring the orphans and not encouraging each other to feed the poor.

When mentioning the orphans, the verse states that honouring them is most important, which means that God does not merely want the wealthy to spend on the orphans; the real requirement is that orphans should be given respect in society, and not deprived or ignored just because they have lost their father.

A tradition from the Prophet (s) states: I and the guardian of an orphan shall be as [close as] these two in Paradise – and he (s) held up his index and middle fingers.[58]

As for the poor, they have a right from the wealth of the people in the form of obligatory religious alms (*zakat*) and recommended

---

[56] *Nahj al-Balāghah*, sermon 192.

فَلَا تَعْتَبِرُوا الرِّضَى وَالسَّخَطَ بِالْمَالِ وَالْوَلَدِ.

[57] Ṭabrasī, *al-Bayān*, 10/739.

[58] Nūrī, *Mustadrak al-Wasā'il*, 2/474.

عَنِ الرَّسُولِ (صَلَّى اللهُ عَلَيْهِ وَآلِهِ) - أَنَا وَكَافِلُ الْيَتِيمِ كَهَاتَيْنِ فِي الْجَنَّةِ، وَأَشَارَ بِالسَّبَّابَةِ وَالْوُسْطَى.

charities (*ṣadaqāt*). In Q69:33,34, neglecting the duty of encouraging the feeding of the poor has been linked to lack of faith (*īmān*):

إِنَّهُ كَانَ لَا يُؤْمِنُ بِاللَّهِ الْعَظِيمِ ﴿٣٣﴾ وَلَا يَحُضُّ عَلَىٰ طَعَامِ الْمِسْكِينِ

Indeed, he never used to believe in God, the all-Mighty, nor did he encourage the feeding of the poor.

The verse under review does not speak of just individually feeding the poor, rather the expectation is to create an environment where believers encourage each other to feed the poor.[59]

We have discussed the duties towards these two groups in the *tafsīr* of Surat al-Māʿūn (107).

15-20.11 '*And you consume inheritance, devouring [it] indiscriminately.*': The next deplorable habit that follows from the previous two examples of transgression is usurping the inheritance of others.

[*Lammā* (لَّمًّا, indiscriminate, whole)]. *Lamm* means to gather, and its mention with 'consuming inheritance' here refers to devouring whole, both the wealth that is legitimate and that which is usurped. This was a common practice amongst the Makkans in the days of ignorance (*jāhiliyyah*) when it came to the wealth of women, orphans, and minors under their guardianship. They would mix their own inheritance with that of those who could not defend their rights.[60]

It can also mean that when you receive inheritance, you do not spare a thought to sharing it with needy relatives and the poor in society.[61]

15-20.12 '*And you love wealth with an immense love.*': [*Ḥubban jammā* (حُبًّا جَمًّا, immense love)]. The last trait mentioned is being obsessed with the wealth of this world. It is the main reason for the first three traits. Lust for wealth makes man blind to the values of humanity, decency, justice, and compassion. In other words, he is so obsessed with wealth that the higher values and ideals of life have no place in his heart.

Whoever is afflicted with an inordinate love of worldly riches will inevitably become careless in distinguishing between what

---

59 Muṭahharī, (*Āshnāyī bā Qur'an*), *Āthār*, 28/542.

60 Zamakhsharī, *al-Kashshāf*, 4/751.

61 Shīrāzī, *Namūneh*, 26/465.

is permitted (*ḥalāl*) and what is forbidden (*ḥarām*). He will be overcome with greed and show reluctance in giving God His due from his wealth.[62] He will forget that all his possessions will be left behind when he leaves the world.

Most damagingly, when the love of wealth grows immense (*ḥubban jammā*) and suffuses man's entire heart, then there is no room for the remembrance of God.

It is easy to be carried away and get attached to this world, and so one must work hard and constantly to keep it in perspective. Q3:14 reminds man:

زُيِّنَ لِلنَّاسِ حُبُّ الشَّهَوَاتِ مِنَ النِّسَاءِ وَالْبَنِينَ وَالْقَنَاطِيرِ الْمُقَنْطَرَةِ
مِنَ الذَّهَبِ وَالْفِضَّةِ وَالْخَيْلِ الْمُسَوَّمَةِ وَالْأَنْعَامِ وَالْحَرْثِ ذَٰلِكَ مَتَاعُ
الْحَيَاةِ الدُّنْيَا وَاللَّهُ عِنْدَهُ حُسْنُ الْمَآبِ

Beautified for mankind is the love of things that they desire: women and sons, heaped up sums of gold and silver, fine branded horses, cattle, and well-tilled land. That is the comfort of the life of this world, but God has with Him the best abode.

SUMMARY OF THE VERSES

The verses state that God tries man by either honouring him with blessings or restricting his provision. Both these states have no bearing on his standing in God's estimation. They are merely a test, and an encouragement to move towards one's potential, perfection, and thereby Paradise.

Then the verses question how man can claim to be honourable when he does not honour the orphan, encourage the feeding of the poor, consumes inheritance indiscriminately, and loves wealth with an inordinate love.

REFLECTIVE LEARNING

Let me reflect on:

1. The last bounty I received from God, and whether I saw it as an opportunity to grow towards my potential, and showed gratitude for it through my words and actions.

[62] Ṭabrasī, *al-Bayān*, 10/740.

2. The last restriction I felt in my life and whether or not I saw it as an opportunity to grow towards my potential, and showed forbearance in my words and actions.

VERSES 21 - 26

كَلَّا إِذَا دُكَّتِ الْأَرْضُ دَكًّا دَكًّا ﴿٢١﴾ وَجَاءَ رَبُّكَ وَالْمَلَكُ صَفًّا صَفًّا ﴿٢٢﴾
وَجِيءَ يَوْمَئِذٍ بِجَهَنَّمَ يَوْمَئِذٍ يَتَذَكَّرُ الْإِنْسَانُ وَأَنَّىٰ لَهُ الذِّكْرَىٰ ﴿٢٣﴾ يَقُولُ يَا لَيْتَنِي
قَدَّمْتُ لِحَيَاتِي ﴿٢٤﴾ فَيَوْمَئِذٍ لَا يُعَذِّبُ عَذَابَهُ أَحَدٌ ﴿٢٥﴾ وَلَا يُوثِقُ وَثَاقَهُ أَحَدٌ
﴿٢٦﴾

Not at all! When the earth is pounded, piece by piece. [21] *And your Lord comes with the angels, rank upon rank.* [22] *And Hell will be brought near that Day. On that Day will man remember, but how will that remembrance [then] avail him?* [23] *He shall say, "How I wish I had sent forth [some provisions] for my life!"* [24] *But on that Day no one shall punish with [anything like] His punishment,* [25] *and no one will bind with [anything like] His binding.* [26]

21-26.1 Now the verses turn to the events that will accompany the end of this *dunyā* and the advent of the next world, the Hereafter (*ākhirah*).

21-26.2 *'Not at all! When the earth is pounded, piece by piece.'*: [*Kallā* (كَلَّا, not at all)] informs everyone that matters are not as they may have surmised. The ease and hardships that they experienced in the world all had a purpose; they were part of a test whose results would soon become apparent. Those who lived just for the sake of the *dunyā* and did not send forth anything for the Hereafter will dearly wish that they could return; but this wish will neither bring them any goodness, nor avert the punishment that awaits them.[63]

[*Idhā* (إِذَا, when)] here refers to the advent of the Day of Judgement.[64]

[*Dukkat* (دُكَّت, pounded)] is derived from *dakka*, which means to demolish and make flat. The repetition (*dakkan dakka*) is to emphasize the tremendousness of the event. The surface of the earth will be pounded piece by piece until it is left as a flat, featureless,

[63] Ṭabāṭabā'ī, *al-Mīzān*, 20/284.

[64] Ibid.

expanse. This will be amongst a series of momentous events that herald the Final Day.

A tradition from Imam al-Baqir (a) states: *Dakkan dakkā* refers to the final earthquake (*zalzalah*).[65]

21-26.3 *'And your Lord comes with the angels, rank upon rank.'*: There is no mention of what happens between the end of *dunyā* and the Day of Resurrection, which are both marked with the blowing of the trumpet. Many aeons will pass between these two blowings. Finally, human beings will be resurrected and assembled to face their Creator.

The 'coming' of the Lord is from the equivocal (*mutashābih*) phrases of the Qur'an. Such verses are understood by referring them to the explicit (*muḥkam*) verses which explain this phrase by mentioning the lifting of veils, the visibility of the direct Cause in all affairs, and the undeniable knowledge that God is the clear Reality.[66]

The entirety of creation will be acutely aware of the presence of God. Q39:69 states:

وَأَشْرَقَتِ الْأَرْضُ بِنُورِ رَبِّهَا

And the earth will shine with the light of its Lord...

The coming of God has also been explained as the manifestation of God's command (*amr*) or His judgement (*ḥukm*).[67] In this regard, Q16:33 states:

هَلْ يَنْظُرُونَ إِلَّا أَنْ تَأْتِيَهُمُ الْمَلَائِكَةُ أَوْ يَأْتِيَ أَمْرُ رَبِّكَ

Do they await [anything] except that the angels should come to them or there should come the command (amr) *of your Lord?...*

A tradition from Imam al-Ridha (a) states: God, the Almighty, cannot be described as coming and going. He is above [the notion of] movement from one place to another. What is meant in the

65 Majlisī, *Biḥār*, 7/109.

عَنِ الْبَاقِرِ (عَلَيْهِ السَّلَامُ) - إِذَا دُكَّتِ الْأَرْضُ دَكًّا دَكًّا قَالَ هِيَ الزَّلْزَلَةُ.

66 Ṭabāṭabā'ī, *al-Mīzān*, 20/284.

67 Ṭūsī, *al-Tibyān*, 10/347.

verse is the coming of the command (*amr*) of your Lord, and the angels, rank upon rank.[68]

The angels will be arrayed before God and creation, respectfully standing in ranks in order of their seniority, or in order of the heavens that they inhabited.[69]

21-26.4 *'And Hell will be brought near that Day.'*: 'Brought near' probably means that the veils over it will be lifted so it becomes visible,[70] as stated in Q79:36:

وَبُرِّزَتِ الْجَحِيمُ لِمَن يَرَىٰ

And Hellfire will be exposed for [all] those who see.

The momentousness of the manifestation of Hell, and the deep dread that it will cause every observer is indescribable. When this verse was revealed to the Prophet (s), a tradition states that his face turned pale with fear, and no one dared to approach him. Then his brother [Ali (a)] rose up and went to him. He kissed his head and asked him what the matter was.

The Prophet (s) said, "Jibra'il has just brought down this verse."[71] His reaction showed his anxiety for the fate of his nation.

Although only Hell is mentioned here in keeping with the description of those who behaved dishonourably in the earlier verses, Paradise too will be brought forth, but only for the God-wary. Q26:90 states:

وَأُزْلِفَتِ الْجَنَّةُ لِلْمُتَّقِينَ

And Paradise will be brought near to the God-wary (muttaqīn).

21-26.5 *'On that Day will man remember, but how will that remembrance [then] avail him?'*: On that Day, true realization will dawn on everyone about the reason comfort or hardship was given to them in this world. It was all part of a test, and the task at hand was to

---

68 Ṣadūq, *'Uyūn Akhbār*, 1/125.

عَنِ الرِّضَا (عَلَيْهِ السَّلَامُ) – إِنَّ اللهَ عَزَّ وَجَلَّ لَا يُوصَفُ بِالْمَجِيءِ وَالذَّهَابِ، تَعَالَى عَنِ الْانْتِقَالِ إِنَّمَا يَعْنِي بِذَلِكَ وَجَاءَ أَمْرُ رَبِّكَ وَالْمَلَكُ صَفًّا صَفًّا.

69 Shīrāzī, *Namūneh*, 26/471.

70 Ṭabāṭabā'ī, *al-Mīzān*, 20/284.

71 Majlisī, *Biḥār*, 105/103.

إِنَّ رَسُولَ اللهِ (صَلَّى اللهُ عَلَيْهِ وَآلِهِ) لَمَّا أُنْزِلَتْ «وَجِيءَ يَوْمَئِذٍ بِجَهَنَّمَ» لَمْ يَسْتَطِعْ أَحَدٌ أَنْ يُكَلِّمَهُ لِشِدَّةِ خَشْيَتِهِ حَتَّى قَامَ إِلَيْهِ أَخُوهُ فَقَبَّلَ رَأْسَهُ وَسَأَلَهُ الْخَبَرَ وَقَالَ لَهُ قَدْ أَتَانِي جَبْرَائِيلُ بِهَذِهِ الْآيَةِ.

prepare for the life of the Hereafter during the trials of the earthly life, through submission to God, remaining steadfast, and following His guidance.

The worthlessness of their worldly pursuits will be evident for all,[72] and people will wholeheartedly wish that they had given more thought to sending forth anything useful for their next life, but now it will be too late.

21-26.6 *'He shall say, "How I wish I had sent forth [some provisions] for my life!"*: [*Qaddamtu* (قَدَّمْتُ, I sent forth)] refers to sending forth good actions, based on faith and *taqwā*, for the Hereafter.

[*Li ḥayātī*, (لِحَيَاتِي, for my life)]. It is interesting that man says, 'my life', and not 'my life in *ākhirah*.'[73] This is an allusion to the fact that he finally realizes that his only true life is in the Hereafter, and everything he passed through before that was a mere semblance of life. Q29:64 states:

وَمَا هَٰذِهِ الْحَيَاةُ الدُّنْيَا إِلَّا لَهْوٌ وَلَعِبٌ
وَإِنَّ الدَّارَ الْآخِرَةَ لَهِيَ الْحَيَوَانُ لَوْ كَانُوا يَعْلَمُونَ

And the life of this world is nothing but diversion and amusement.
And indeed, the abode of the Hereafter –
that is [true] life, if only they knew.

However, this remembrance will be of no avail; the time for action, remorse, and repentance will all have passed. His book of deeds will have been sealed.[74]

21-26.7 *'But on that Day no one shall punish with [anything like] His punishment. And no one will bind with [anything like] His binding.'*: [*Yūthiqu* (يُوثِقُ, will bind)] is derived from *wathaqa*, meaning to be firm, and here it means to be bound and held fast. *Wathāq* is the noun, meaning the 'binding'.

The verse means that on that Day, the punishment and binding of God will be unlike anything that anyone has experienced or

[72] Ṭabāṭabā'ī, *al-Mīzān*, 20/285.
[73] Shīrāzī, *Namūneh*, 26/473.
[74] Ibid.

imagined. And this is phrased to emphasize the severity of God's warning.[75]

SUMMARY OF THE VERSES

In summary, these verses remind man that when the *dunyā* comes to an end, the command of God is manifested, and Hell is arrayed before his eyes, he will finally realize the real worth and meaning of this world. However, at that time, this realization will not avail him at all.

He will dearly wish that he had sent something forth for his true life, which is the life of the Hereafter. The one who has been negligent in this regard will be caught fast in a punishment unlike anything he has experienced or imagined.

REFLECTIVE LEARNING

Let me reflect on what I sent yesterday from this world for my true life in the Hereafter and what I will send today, tomorrow, and everyday thereafter.

VERSES 27 - 30

يَا أَيَّتُهَا النَّفْسُ الْمُطْمَئِنَّةُ ﴿٢٧﴾ ارْجِعِي إِلَىٰ رَبِّكِ رَاضِيَةً مَّرْضِيَّةً ﴿٢٨﴾ فَادْخُلِي فِي عِبَادِي ﴿٢٩﴾ وَادْخُلِي جَنَّتِي ﴿٣٠﴾

[The righteous will be told:] O contented soul! [27] *Return to your Lord, well-pleased and pleasing [to Him].* [28] *So, enter amongst My servants,* [29] *and enter My Paradise.* [30]

27-30.1 '*O contented soul!*': The situation of the transgressors and those who lived for the *dunyā* – those who did not understand that all that was given or withheld was part of a test, and who got so caught up in the pursuit of worldly comfort that they forgot the true life in the Hereafter – is now contrasted to those who maintained their perspective and calm in the tumultuous days of *dunyā*.

If they were blessed with favours, they did not forget that they were being tested. They were grateful to God and showed kindness to His creatures. And if they were faced with hardships, they did

[75] Ṭabāṭabāʾī, *al-Mīzān*, 20/285.

not forget that they were being tested. They did not give way to despair or lose faith in God, but persevered in their trial. Through this total submission to God's will and complete trust in Him, they achieved a state of tranquillity and a contented soul (*al-nafs al-muṭma'innah*).

27-30.2 To acquire a contented state of the *nafs* is the goal of life. This is a *nafs* which has freed itself from the concerns of the body and risen to the servitude of God. This progression brings about contentment and tranquillity (*iṭmi'nān*) which comes from belief (*īmān*) coupled with constant remembrance (*dhikr*), reliance (*tawakkul*), and turning to God (*inābah*). Q13:28 states:

الَّذِينَ آمَنُوا وَتَطْمَئِنُّ قُلُوبُهُمْ بِذِكْرِ اللهِ أَلَا بِذِكْرِ اللهِ تَطْمَئِنُّ الْقُلُوبُ

Those who believe and whose hearts find contentment in the remembrance of Allah. Without doubt, in the remembrance of Allah do hearts find contentment.

27-30.3 *'Return to your Lord, well-pleased and pleasing [to Him].'*: All human beings will return to God. However, this verse mentions how the believers are personally invited, in a welcoming and loving manner, to return to their Lord.

[*Rāḍiyah* (رَاضِيَةً, well-pleased)] and [*Marḍiyyah* (مَرْضِيَّةً, well-pleasing)] are both derived from *raḍiya*, which means to approve and be satisfied. This direct invitation from God to return to Him is accompanied with the assurance that just as they are pleased with Him, He is also pleased with them.

They are well-pleased because they see the realization of every promise of God's reward, and even more than what they had expected or imagined. And they are well-pleasing to their Lord because they have displayed true servanthood and love to Him (and achieved the potential that God gave them.)[76]

Those who are pleased with God and obey Him through the teachings of His Prophet (s), should know with conviction that God loves them also. Q3:31 states:

قُلْ إِنْ كُنْتُمْ تُحِبُّونَ اللهَ فَاتَّبِعُونِي يُحْبِبْكُمُ اللهُ وَيَغْفِرْ لَكُمْ ذُنُوبَكُمْ

[76] Shīrāzī, *Namūneh*, 26/477.

Say, [O Prophet]: If you do love Allah, then follow me;
Allah will love you and forgive you your sins...

Another interpretation of the contented soul is presented by Imam al-Sadiq (a) in a tradition reported from him when he was asked if a believer would be reluctant to leave this *dunyā* at the time of death. The Imam (a) said: No by God! ... If he displays any hesitancy the angel of death says to him, "O friend of God, do not fear." Then he will show him the countenances of Muhammad (s) and his household (a) ... Then a caller will call out, "O contented soul with regards to Muhammad and his household! Return to your Lord, well-pleased with their guardianship (*wilāyah*) and well-pleasing to them due to their reward [because of you.]" ... Thereafter, he will desire nothing more than to give up his soul...[77]

27-30.4 Several traditions mention that the interpretation (*ta'wīl*) of this verse is that the 'contented soul' refers to Imam al-Husayn (a). The highest levels of submission, devotion, and contentment with God's decree were manifested by the Imam (a) in his sacrifice and martyrdom in Karbala.

27-30.5 *'So, enter amongst My servants, and enter My Paradise.'*: The verse begins with 'so' (*fa*) because this invitation is deserved by the soul who is content with God's decree in all affairs, as described in the previous verse.[78] The servants who are mentioned here are the best and most honourable of God's creation. Even if the soul of such an individual may not be at the same rank as other great personalities, nonetheless he is admitted to their vicinity.

Q4:69 states:

وَمَنْ يُطِعِ اللَّهَ وَالرَّسُولَ فَأُولَٰئِكَ مَعَ الَّذِينَ أَنْعَمَ اللَّهُ عَلَيْهِمْ
مِنَ النَّبِيِّينَ وَالصِّدِّيقِينَ وَالشُّهَدَاءِ وَالصَّالِحِينَ وَحَسُنَ أُولَٰئِكَ رَفِيقًا

---

[77] Kulaynī, *al-Kāfī*, 3/127.

عَنِ الصَّادِقِ (عَلَيْهِ السَّلَامُ) – لَمَّا سُئِلَ: هَلْ يَكْرَهُ الْمُؤْمِنُ عَلَى قَبْضِ رُوحِهِ؟ قَالَ: لَا وَاللهِ، إِنَّهُ إِذَا أَتَاهُ مَلَكُ الْمَوْتِ لِقَبْضِ رُوحِهِ جَزِعَ عِنْدَ ذَلِكَ، فَيَقُولُ لَهُ مَلَكُ الْمَوْتِ: يَا وَلِيَّ اللهِ لَا تَجْزَعْ... وَيُمَثَّلُ لَهُ رَسُولَ اللهِ صَلَّى اللهُ عَلَيْهِ وَآلِهِ وَأَمِيرُ الْمُؤْمِنِينَ وَفَاطِمَةُ وَالْحَسَنُ وَالْحُسَيْنُ وَالْأَئِمَّةُ مِنْ ذُرِّيَتِهِمْ عَلَيْهِمُ السَّلَامُ، فَيُنَادِي رُوحَهُ مُنَادٍ مِنْ قِبَلِ رَبِّ الْعِزَّةِ فَيَقُولُ: «يَا أَيَّتُهَا النَّفْسُ الْمُطْمَئِنَّةُ» إِلَى مُحَمَّدٍ وَأَهْلِ بَيْتِهِ «ارْجِعِي إِلَىٰ رَبِّكِ رَاضِيَةً» بِالْوِلَايَةِ «مَرْضِيَّةً» بِالثَّوَابِ ... فَمَا شَيْءٌ أَحَبُّ إِلَيْهِ مِنْ اِسْتِلَالِ رُوحِهِ.

[78] Ṭabāṭabā'ī, *al-Mīzān*, 20/285.

And whoever obeys God and the Messenger, those will be with the ones upon whom God has bestowed favours, from the Prophets (nabiyyūn), *the veracious* (ṣiddīqūn), *the martyrs* (shuhadā'), *and the righteous* (ṣāliḥūn). *And excellent are those as companions.*

27-30.6 These verses describe the highest accolade given to man by God. He has been crowned as a true servant of God. Thereafter, he is admitted to Paradise with honour - to a station which is more special than other levels of Paradise because God attributes it to Himself.[79]

SUMMARY OF THE VERSES

In contrast to the fate of the transgressors described in the previous verses, the one who has trained his soul to be content with God's decree will be addressed with honour and affection.

He will be invited to come back to his Lord, both pleased with Him and pleasing to Him. He will be admitted into the company of God's distinguished servants, and entered into a high station in Paradise.

REFLECTIVE LEARNING

In order to be placed in the company of God's closest servants in the Hereafter, I need to be completely at ease with whatever God allocates to me.

Let me reflect on how contented I truly am with my life situation. What is my evidence?

[79] Ibid.

SURAT AL-BALAD
THE CITY (90)

TEXT AND TRANSLATION

سُورَةُ الْبَلَدِ

بِسْمِ اللهِ الرَّحْمٰنِ الرَّحِيمِ

لَا أُقْسِمُ بِهَٰذَا الْبَلَدِ ﴿١﴾ وَأَنْتَ حِلٌّ بِهَٰذَا الْبَلَدِ ﴿٢﴾ وَوَالِدٍ وَمَا وَلَدَ ﴿٣﴾ لَقَدْ
خَلَقْنَا الْإِنْسَانَ فِي كَبَدٍ ﴿٤﴾ أَيَحْسَبُ أَنْ لَنْ يَقْدِرَ عَلَيْهِ أَحَدٌ ﴿٥﴾ يَقُولُ أَهْلَكْتُ
مَالًا لُبَدًا ﴿٦﴾ أَيَحْسَبُ أَنْ لَمْ يَرَهُ أَحَدٌ ﴿٧﴾ أَلَمْ نَجْعَلْ لَهُ عَيْنَيْنِ ﴿٨﴾ وَلِسَانًا
وَشَفَتَيْنِ ﴿٩﴾ وَهَدَيْنَاهُ النَّجْدَيْنِ ﴿١٠﴾ فَلَا اقْتَحَمَ الْعَقَبَةَ ﴿١١﴾ وَمَا أَدْرَاكَ مَا
الْعَقَبَةُ ﴿١٢﴾ فَكُّ رَقَبَةٍ ﴿١٣﴾ أَوْ إِطْعَامٌ فِي يَوْمٍ ذِي مَسْغَبَةٍ ﴿١٤﴾ يَتِيمًا ذَا
مَقْرَبَةٍ ﴿١٥﴾ أَوْ مِسْكِينًا ذَا مَتْرَبَةٍ ﴿١٦﴾ ثُمَّ كَانَ مِنَ الَّذِينَ آمَنُوا وَتَوَاصَوْا بِالصَّبْرِ
وَتَوَاصَوْا بِالْمَرْحَمَةِ ﴿١٧﴾ أُولَٰئِكَ أَصْحَابُ الْمَيْمَنَةِ ﴿١٨﴾ وَالَّذِينَ كَفَرُوا بِآيَاتِنَا
هُمْ أَصْحَابُ الْمَشْأَمَةِ ﴿١٩﴾ عَلَيْهِمْ نَارٌ مُؤْصَدَةٌ ﴿٢٠﴾

In the name of God, the Beneficent, the Merciful.

I swear by this city (Makka) [1] *And you [O Muhammad] are an inhabitant of this city.* [2] *And [I swear by] the father and what was born [from him].* [3] *We have certainly created man into toil and struggle.* [4] *Does he think that no one has power over him?* [5] *He says: I have squandered much wealth.* [6] *Does he think that no one sees him?* [7] *Have We not given him two eyes?* [8] *And a tongue and two lips?* [9] *And shown him two [clear] paths?* [10] *But he would not attempt the steep path* (al-ʿaqabah). [11] *And what can make you know what the steep path is?* [12] *[It is] the freeing of a slave,* [13] *or the giving of food on a day of hunger* [14] *to an orphan of near kin,* [15] *or a needy person lying in the dust.* [16] *And then being amongst those who believed and counselled one another to steadfastness, and counselled one another to compassion.* [17] *They are the companions of the right.* [18] *But those who disbelieved in Our signs, they are the companions of the left.* [19] *Fire will be closed over them.* [20]

INTRODUCTION

Surat al-Balad (90) was the 35th chapter to be revealed.[1] It has twenty verses and was revealed in Makka, after Surat Qāf (50). It is named after the oath made by the city of Makka (*al-Balad*), the birthplace of the Prophet (s), in the opening verse.

This surah makes clear the fact that man has been created to face challenges and hardship in this world. There is no one who will be spared bitter and difficult times in their life. It is only in the Hereafter that there exists the possibility of true ease and comfort, undisturbed by hardship.

Man can choose to travel one of two clear and challenging paths in his life: the path of obedience and servitude to God, that leads to felicity and Paradise, or the path of disobedience and defiance to God that leads to disappointment and Hell.

Towards the end of the chapter, two groups are mentioned, the 'people of the right (or bliss)' (*aṣḥāb al-maymanah*), and the 'people of the left (or misery)' (*aṣḥāb al-mash'amah*). In order to join the people of the bliss, the believer is advised to maintain steadfastness in the face of hardship, in obedience and avoiding sin, and in spreading mercy and showing compassion to those in need, the orphans, and the destitute. Otherwise, his Hereafter will be a reflection of his life in this world, and he will be joined to the people of the misery, who will be taken to a fire that will be closed over them.

LINK TO THE PREVIOUS CHAPTER

The last verses of the previous chapter, Surat al-Fajr, addressed the righteous, those who possessed a contented and tranquil soul (*al-nafs al-muṭmainnah*), inviting them to return to their Lord well-pleased and pleasing to Him. This chapter starts with a mention of the most tranquil and secure place in the world, the city of Makka, and speaks of the path to attaining this *nafs al-muṭmainnah*.[2]

---

1 Maʿrifat, *'Ulūm-i Qur'ānī*, p. 90.

2 Ṭabrasī, *al-Bayan*, 10/743.

Both chapters speak of the rights of the orphans and the poor. They both mention man's obsession with wealth, and caution that God is always watching.

In the previous chapter, God gives examples of different communities who spread mischief and corruption in the land. In this chapter, He mentions six traits that must exist in a community if it wishes to remain safe from such corruption.

MERITS OF RECITATION

- A tradition from the Prophet (s) states: Whoever recites Surat al-Balad will be granted security by God from His wrath on the Day of Judgement.[3]
- A tradition from Imam al-Sadiq (a) states: Whoever recites the chapter *La uqsimu bi hādha'l-Balad* in his obligatory prayers will be known in this world as one of the righteous, and in the Hereafter as one of those whom God has granted a [high] station. On the Day of Judgement he will be among the friends of the Prophets (a), the martyrs, and the righteous.[4]

EXEGESIS

VERSES 1 - 4

لَا أُقْسِمُ بِهَٰذَا الْبَلَدِ ﴿١﴾ وَأَنْتَ حِلٌّ بِهَٰذَا الْبَلَدِ ﴿٢﴾ وَوَالِدٍ وَمَا وَلَدَ ﴿٣﴾ لَقَدْ
خَلَقْنَا الْإِنْسَانَ فِي كَبَدٍ ﴿٤﴾

I swear by this city [Makka] [1] *And you [O Muhammad] are an inhabitant of this city.* [2] *And [I swear by] the father and what was born [from him].* [3] *We have certainly created man into toil and struggle.* [4]

1-4.1 '*I swear by this city [Makka].*': [*Lā Uqsimu* (لَا أُقْسِمُ, I swear)]. This is a type of oath that the Qur'an has employed eight times, includ-

[3] Nūrī, *Mustadrak al-Wasā'il*, 4/358.

عَنِ الرَّسُولِ (صَلَّى اللهُ عَلَيْهِ وَآلِهِ) - مَنْ قَرَأَ سُورَةَ الْبَلَدِ أَعْطَاهُ اللهُ الْأَمْنَ مِنْ غَضَبِهِ يَوْمَ الْقِيَامَةِ.

[4] Ṣadūq, *Thawāb al-A'māl*, p. 123.

عَنِ الصَّادِقِ (عَلَيْهِ السَّلَامُ) - مَنْ كَانَ قِرَاءَتُهُ فِي فَرِيضَةٍ «لَا أُقْسِمُ بِهَٰذَا الْبَلَدِ» كَانَ فِي الدُّنْيَا مَعْرُوفًا أَنَّهُ مِنَ الصَّالِحِينَ وَكَانَ فِي الْآخِرَةِ مَعْرُوفًا أَنَّ لَهُ مِنَ اللهِ مَكَانًا وَكَانَ يَوْمَ الْقِيَامَةِ مِنْ رُفَقَاءِ النَّبِيِّينَ وَالشُّهَدَاءِ وَالصَّالِحِينَ.

ing twice at the beginning of two chapters, Surat al-Qiyāmah (75) and Surat al-Balad (90).

Exegetes have given several opinions on the structure of the oath, specifically the purpose of *lā* (لَا) in the phrase, *lā uqsimu*, which would apparently mean '*I do not swear*', rather than, '*I swear*'. The opinions are summarized below:

i) That the *lā* is for negation, and is used to refute the words of the disbelievers. Therefore, the oath means to say, 'It is certainly not what you assert, rather I swear by...'[5]

ii) That the *lā* is for negation in the meaning that 'I do not need to swear by something as grand as Makka (or Qiyāmah), because its great station is already known to you.' For example, exegetes have translated the verse as, 'Although there is no need to make an oath, nonetheless, I swear by this city.'[6]

iii) Some have also said that the *lā* of negation is to add emphasis to the oath.[7] Or, that the *lā* is not for negation, rather it emphasizes the gravity of the oath. It is used in this manner in the phrase, *lā wallāh* (I swear by God)', for example.[8]

iv) That the *lā* is additional (*zā'id*), and the meaning is still '*I swear*'. This is the view of most exegetes.[9]

It appears that it is definitely an oath because of the mention of the residence of the Prophet (s) as a reason for the sanctity of Makka. And this only makes sense for the phrase, '*I swear*' and not '*I do not swear*'. As a further evidence that this usage signifies an oath, and not the negation of one, we read in Q56:75,76:

فَلَا أُقْسِمُ بِمَوَاقِعِ النُّجُومِ ﴿٧٥﴾ وَإِنَّهُ لَقَسَمٌ لَّوْ تَعْلَمُونَ عَظِيمٌ

So I swear (lā uqsimu) *by the setting of the stars.*
And indeed, if you only knew, that is a very great oath.

1-4.2 [*Hādhā al-Balad* (هَٰذَا الْبَلَدِ, this city)]: The surah begins with an oath by a city. Although the city is not mentioned by name, the fact that the chapter was revealed in Makka, and the phrase '*this city*'

---

[5] Ṭabrasī, *al-Bayān*, 10/596.

[6] Ṭabāṭabā'ī, *al-Mīzān*, Farsi translation, 20/482.

[7] Zamakhsharī, *al-Kashshāf*, 4/659.

[8] Ṭūsī, *al-Tibyān*, 10/189.

[9] Shīrāzī, *Namūneh*, 27/7.

is used in the verse, makes it clear that it refers to the holy city of Makka.

1-4.3 Although the city of Makka already had a special sanctity because of the presence of the Kaʿbah and the fact that the great Prophets (s) of God had come there to worship, the next verse introduces another reason why God swears by the city: the city of Makka became worthy of swearing by because the *ḥujjah* of God, His beloved Messenger (s), lived in that city.

1-4.4 *'And you (O Muhammad) are an inhabitant of this city.'*: The word city (*balad*) is mentioned again in the second verse although the pronoun 'it' could have been used. This is to further emphasize the status of the blessed city of Makka, especially because the Prophet (s) lived there.[10]

1-4.5 [*Ḥillun* (حِلٌّ, an inhabitant)]. The noun is derived either from *ḥulūl*, which means to exist in something, or from *ḥalāl* (permitted). In the first case, the verse would mean, 'And you (O Muhammad) are an inhabitant of this city.' Indeed, the sanctity of cities lies in the sanctity of those who reside there.[11] And this is the probable meaning of the verse.[12]

However, if we take it to be derived from *ḥalāl* (as opposed to *ḥarām*, forbidden) then it would mean that, in this city in which every sort of harm is forbidden, 'you are freely oppressed (O Muhammad) in this city.'[13] This possible meaning is mentioned in a report from Imam al-Sadiq (a), who has stated about this verse: Their ignorance reached a level where they considered it permissible to murder the Prophet (s).[14]

1-4.6 *'And (I swear by) the father and what was born [from him].'*: The use of *wālid* (father) in the singular is to signify honour.[15]

Mā (what) is normally used for things and animals and *man* (who) is used for human beings. However, here, *mā walad* (what was

---

[10] Ṭabāṭabā'ī, *al-Mīzān*, 20/289.

[11] Shīrāzī, *Namūneh*, 27/8.

[12] Muṭahharī, (*Āshnāyī bā Qur'an*), *Āthār*, 28/551.

[13] Ibid.

[14] ʿĀmilī, *Wasā'il*, 23/256.

عَنِ الصَّادِقِ (عَلَيْهِ السَّلَامُ) – «وَأَنْتَ حِلٌّ بِهٰذَا الْبَلَدِ» قَالَ فَبَلَغَ مِنْ جَهْلِهِمْ أَنَّهُمْ اسْتَحَلُّوا قَتْلَ النَّبِيِّ (صَلَّى اللهُ عَلَيْهِ وَآلِهِ).

[15] Ṭabāṭabā'ī, *al-Mīzān*, 20/290.

born) is used instead of the expected *man walad* (who was born), to show wonderment (*taʿajjub*). Therefore, the verse means to say, 'By the honourable father and what kind of offspring was born from him.'[16] Perhaps this is the same reason why *mā* is used in honour of Lady Maryam (a) in Q3:36:

فَلَمَّا وَضَعَتْهَا قَالَتْ رَبِّ إِنِّي وَضَعْتُهَا أُنْثَىٰ وَاللَّهُ أَعْلَمُ بِمَا وَضَعَتْ

But when she [the wife of ʿImran] delivered her, she said, "My Lord! I have delivered a female." And God knew better what (mā) *she had delivered...*[17]

And in this way the Qur'an demonstrates that both female and male children can enjoy great honour in God's sight.

1-4.7 Some exegetes say that this oath refers to Adam (a) and the Prophets (a) in his offspring. Others have mentioned that it refers to Prophet Ibrahim (a) and Prophet Muḥammad (s) who came from his progeny.[18] A tradition from Imam Ali (a) states that: [It includes] the Imams (a) born in his progeny.[19]

Due to the earlier reference to Makka, many exegetes believe that the father and son referred to here are specifically Prophet Ibrahim (a) and his son Prophet Ismaʿil (a), who raised the foundations of the Kaʿbah and were well-known amongst the Arabs.[20]

About them Q2:127 states:

وَإِذْ يَرْفَعُ إِبْرَاهِيمُ الْقَوَاعِدَ مِنَ الْبَيْتِ وَإِسْمَاعِيلُ رَبَّنَا تَقَبَّلْ مِنَّا

And [mention] when Ibrahim and Ismaʿil were raising the foundations of the House (Kaʿbah), *saying, "Our Lord! Accept this from us...*

Furthermore, Ibrahim (a) had prayed for the security of Makka. Q2:126 states:

وَإِذْ قَالَ إِبْرَاهِيمُ رَبِّ اجْعَلْ هَٰذَا بَلَدًا آمِنًا

And when Ibrahim said, "My Lord, make this a secure city..."

---

16 Muṭahharī, (*Āshnāyī bā Qur'an*), *Āthār*, 28/553.

17 Mughniyyah, *al-Kāshif*, 7/566.

18 Bayḍāwī, *Tafsīr*, 5/313.

19 Kulaynī, *al-Kāfī*, 1/414.

عَنْ أَمِيرِ الْمُؤْمِنِينَ (عَلَيْهِ السَّلَامُ) – وَمَا وَلَدَ مِنَ الْأَئِمَّةِ عَلَيْهِمُ السَّلَامُ.

20 Ṭabāṭabā'ī, *al-Mīzān*, 20/290; Shīrāzī, *Namūneh*, 27/9.

Therefore, the verses are an oath by the city of Makka, wherein the Prophet (s) lived, and by those who rebuilt the Kaʿbah and established the city of Makka thereby.[21]

1-4.8 The link of the oaths to their subject is the general hardship experienced by man in his earthly life. Specific examples given in the chapter are the trials faced by the Prophet (s) at the hands of the Quraysh, and the trials that Ibrahim (a) faced when he had to abandon his infant son Ismaʿil (a), and later take him for sacrifice.

1-4.9 '*We have certainly created man into toil and struggle.*': This verse is the subject (*jawāb*) of the oaths and the main message of the surah.

[*Kabad* (كَبَد, hardship)] refers to pain that is felt when there is disease in the liver or abdomen (*kabad*),[22] and it later came to denote every struggle and hardship, and this is what it means here.[23]

Indeed, through the process of birth, life, and death, man is beset by different hardships and challenges which he must overcome, including constant disappointments as his plans do not come to fruition. This is a feature of the life of this world, and to expect anything else is a mistake.

In this regard, a tradition from Imam Ali (a) states: The world is a place beset by calamities, and well-known for betrayal. Its affairs do not persist, and those who live in it are not [constantly] at peace. Its conditions are diverse, and its norms continually evolve.[24]

1-4.10 This hardship is not without purpose. The fate of an individual is linked to how he encounters these challenges and whether he uses them to get closer to God. Q84:6 states:

يَا أَيُّهَا الْإِنْسَانُ إِنَّكَ كَادِحٌ إِلَىٰ رَبِّكَ كَدْحًا فَمُلَاقِيهِ

O man! Indeed, you are constantly labouring to your Lord with [great] exertion until you shall meet Him.

---

21 Ibid.

22 Rāghib, *al-Mufradāt.*

23 Shīrāzī, *Namūneh*, 27/10.

24 *Nahj al-Balāghah*, sermon 225.

دَارٌ بِالْبَلَاءِ مَحْفُوفَةٌ، وَبِالْغَدْرِ مَعْرُوفَةٌ، لَا تَدُومُ أَحْوَالُهَا، وَلَا يَسْلَمُ نُزَّالُهَا، أَحْوَالٌ مُخْتَلِفَةٌ، وَتَارَاتٌ مُتَصَرِّفَةٌ.

SUMMARY OF THE VERSES

In summary, the verses mention oaths by the city of Makka, because it was the city inhabited by the Prophet (s), and by the father and son, Ibrahim (a) and Ismaʿil (a), who rebuilt the Kaʿbah. Finally, the subject of the oath is a clear message that God has created man to face a variety of hardships in this world.

REFLECTIVE LEARNING

Knowing that this world is designed to be a place of hardships and challenges, let me reflect on whether:

1. I mistakenly seek constant ease here at the expense of the Hereafter, which is the place of true life?
2. At times of hardship I exercise patience and perseverance (*ṣabr)* and move closer to God, or I get overwhelmed and engrossed in the hardship itself?

VERSES 5 - 7

أَيَحْسَبُ أَنْ لَنْ يَقْدِرَ عَلَيْهِ أَحَدٌ ﴿٥﴾ يَقُولُ أَهْلَكْتُ مَالًا لُبَدًا ﴿٦﴾ أَيَحْسَبُ أَنْ لَمْ يَرَهُ أَحَدٌ ﴿٧﴾

Does he think that no one has power over him? [5] *He says: I have squandered much wealth.* [6] *Does he think that no one sees him?* [7]

5-7.1 '*Does he think that no one has power over him?*': This is an analysis of man's situation in light of the statement made in the previous verse. At every turn, he will face hurdles and obstacles that will force him to change course. These factors are out of his control. And the One who is in charge of all his affairs is God, the Almighty. The verse asks rhetorically whether man is mindful that everything in his life is happening by God's permission and direction, and that he really has no power over it.[25]

5-7.2 '*He shall say: I have squandered much wealth.*': [*Ahlaktu* (أَهْلَكْتُ, I squandered)] describes spending in a way which does not benefit.[26] Indeed, wealth that is not spent in God's way is wasted.

[25] Ṭabāṭabā'ī, *al-Mīzān*, 20/291.

[26] Mustafawī, *al-Taḥqīq*.

[*Lubad* لُبَد, much)] refers to something that is piled up and here, it means a lot of wealth.[27] By making this statement it as if he feels that his wealth is his own to spend as he chooses and that no one has the power to compel him.

However, man should never imagine that God has no power over him. Otherwise, he will tread on the path of arrogance, turning away from the worship of his Benefactor, or only obeying Him when it suits him.[28]

5-7.3 Although the verses are general in their message, the context of this verse and the rest of the chapter refer to a specific individual who had accepted Islam, or was invited to Islam, and had spent a lot of his wealth. There are two such people who have been mentioned in the reports:

i) A wealthy man became a Muslim but continued in the sinful conduct of the days of ignorance (*jāhiliyyah*). When he was later remorseful and came to the Prophet (s) for advice, he was told to give wealth in charity (*infāq*) as a penalty (*kaffārah*). In this way, he spent a lot of wealth, and finally resentfully complained, '*I have squandered much wealth!*'[29]

ii) A tradition from Imam al-Baqir (a) states: This verse refers to ʿAmr b. ʿAbd Wudd.[30] When Ali b. Abi Talib (a) invited him to accept Islam on the Day [of the Battle] of Khandaq, [he refused] and asked, "What of the great wealth that I have spent among you?" But he had spent his wealth in attempts to obstruct the path of God. Thereafter, Ali (a) killed him.[31]

5-7.4 '*Does he think that no one sees him?*': This verse reminds man to be mindful that God not only sees what he does but also knows the intention with which he does it.

---

[27] Shīrāzī, *Namūneh*, 27/13.

[28] Ṭabāṭabāʾī, *al-Mīzān*, 20/292.

[29] Muṭahharī, (*Āshnāyī bā Qurʾan*), *Āthār*, 28/554.

[30] Since this surah is Makkan and the Battle of Khandaq happened in Madina, this report indicates that application of the verse (*taʾwīl*) includes ʿAmr and men like him.

[31] Majlisī, *Biḥār*, 9/251.

عَنِ الْبَاقِرِ (عَلَيْهِ السَّلَامُ) – فِي قَوْلِهِ «يَقُولُ أَهْلَكْتُ مَالًا لُبَدًا» قَالَ هُوَ عَمْرُو بْنُ عَبْدِ وُدٍّ حِينَ عَرَضَ عَلَيْهِ عَلِيُّ ابْنُ أَبِي طَالِبٍ (عَلَيْهِ السَّلَامُ) الْإِسْلَامَ يَوْمَ الْخَنْدَقِ وَقَالَ فَأَيْنَ مَا أَنْفَقْتُ فِيكُمْ مَالًا لُبَدًا؟ وَكَانَ قَدْ أَنْفَقَ مَالًا فِي الصَّدِّ عَنْ سَبِيلِ اللهِ فَقَتَلَهُ عَلِيٌّ (عَلَيْهِ السَّلَامُ).

Indeed, his actions are constantly witnessed by God. God knows exactly how much of his wealth he has spent, and why. In fact, he will be questioned about it.

A tradition from the Prophet (s) states: No servant will be allowed to move on the Day of Judgement until he has been asked [to respond to] four questions: his lifespan and how he finished it, his youth and how he spent it, his wealth and how he earned it and what he used it for, and about the love for us, the *Ahl al-Bayt* (a).[32]

SUMMARY OF THE VERSES

The verses remind and warn man that God has complete power over his life. When he boasts of the wealth that he has spent, he should realize that God sees all, and is fully aware of his intention, and consequently the true extent and value of his action.

REFLECTIVE LEARNING

Knowing that I am completely under the power of God and that He is a witness to all my acts, let me reflect on:

1. Whether I have squandered the blessings given to me by God, because I thought that they were mine to do with as I wished, forgetting the power of God over me.
2. Why I feel the need to tell others of my actions, when God witnesses the acts and the intentions behind them.

VERSES 8, 9

أَلَمْ نَجْعَلْ لَهُ عَيْنَيْنِ ﴿٨﴾ وَلِسَانًا وَشَفَتَيْنِ ﴿٩﴾

Have We not given him two eyes? [8] *And a tongue and two lips?* [9]

8-9.1 '*Have We not given him two eyes?*': In the previous verse, the rhetorical question was asked, '*Does he think that no one sees him?*'. Now, man is reminded about the two eyes that he has been granted. This verse encourages man to ponder about the question: how is it that man can see, but he imagines that God does not see?!

---

[32] Ṣadūq, *al-Khiṣāl*, 1/253.

عَنِ الرَّسُولِ (صَلَّى اللهُ عَلَيْهِ وَآلِهِ) - لَا تَزُولُ قَدَمَا عَبْدٍ يَوْمَ الْقِيَامَةِ حَتَّى يُسْأَلَ عَنْ أَرْبَعٍ: عَنْ عُمْرِهِ فِيمَا أَفْنَاهُ، وَعَنْ شَبَابِهِ فِيمَا أَبْلَاهُ، وَعَنْ مَالِهِ مِنْ أَيْنَ اكْتَسَبَهُ وَفِيمَا أَنْفَقَهُ، وَعَنْ حُبِّنَا أَهْلَ الْبَيْتِ.

8-9.2 The mention of God as the all-Seeing, juxtaposed with the blessing of sight, is instructive. While man may boast that he has earned his wealth himself and therefore can spend it as he wants, he could not make the same claim about his eyes, or other faculties which are clearly only created by God. This fact is a reminder for the arrogant.

8-9.3 The mention of 'two' eyes may be because it is only through the ability of binocular vision that man can judge depth and appreciate three-dimensional images. In other words, he can discern the distance between two things and distinguish between two paths.

8-9.4 '*And a tongue and two lips?*': The two eyes allow man to interact with the world around him, and his tongue and two lips allow him to interact with the people around him. What is perceived by the eyes can then be accurately transmitted by the tongue. A tradition from Imam al-Hasan (a) states: There are four fingers (the distance from the eye to the ear) between the truth and falsehood. What you see with your eyes is the truth while you hear many lies through your ears...[33]

8-9.5 In order to form words and converse, two lips are required to work alongside the tongue. Speech and language are basic tools in communicating thoughts, ideas and information. Without the use of the tongue and lips, knowledge, human relationships, and social systems could not flourish.

Additionally, the tongue and lips are vital in tasting and eating food.

8-9.6 A tradition from the Prophet (s) states that God, the Exalted, declared: O son of Adam! If your tongue drives you towards what I have forbidden for you, then I have given you two lips to forestall it, so close your lips. And if your eyes drive you towards that which I have forbidden for you, then I have given you two eyelids to forestall them, so close your eyes![34]

---

[33] Ḥarrānī, *Tuḥaf al-ʿUqūl*, 1/228.

عَنِ الْحَسَنِ (عَلَيْهِ السَّلَامُ) - بَيْنَ الْحَقِّ وَالْبَاطِلِ أَرْبَعُ أَصَابِعَ مَا رَأَيْتَ بِعَيْنَيْكَ فَهُوَ الْحَقُّ وَقَدْ تَسْمَعُ بِأُذُنَيْكَ بَاطِلًا كَثِيرًا.

[34] Ṭabrasī, *al-Bayān*, 10/748.

عَنِ الرَّسُولِ (صَلَّى اللهُ عَلَيْهِ وَآلِهِ) - إِنَّ اللهَ تَعَالَى يَقُولُ: يَا ابْنَ آدَمَ إِنْ نَازَعَكَ لِسَانُكَ فِيمَا حَرَّمْتُ عَلَيْكَ فَقَدْ أَعَنْتُكَ عَلَيْهِ بِطَبَقَتَيْنِ فَأَطْبِقْ، وَإِنْ نَازَعَكَ بَصَرُكَ إِلَى بَعْضِ مَا حَرَّمْتُ عَلَيْكَ فَقَدْ أَعَنْتُكَ عَلَيْهِ بِطَبَقَتَيْنِ فَأَطْبِقْ.

8-9.7 It is interesting that the verse mentions the two lips with the tongue, but the eyes were not mentioned with two eyelids. This may be for two reasons. Firstly, the function of the lips in forming words and eating food is a greater one than the function of the eyelids, and secondly, the control of the tongue is more important and of greater consequence than the control of the eyes.[35]

8-9.8 The eyes, tongue and lips are great bounties of God, and like all bounties, man can use them for good as well as evil. For this reason, God has pointed out two clear paths to him, as mentioned in the following verse.

SUMMARY OF THE VERSES

In summary, the verses remind man of God's great blessing of eyes, a tongue, and lips, without which he could not interact with the world and his fellow creatures.

REFLECTIVE LEARNING

Let me reflect on the physical bounties that God has bestowed to me.

Let me imagine what my life would be without these gifts, and truly give thanks through words and actions.

VERSE 10

وَهَدَيْنَاهُ النَّجْدَيْنِ ﴿١٠﴾

And shown him two [clear] paths? [10]

10.1 '*And shown him two [clear] paths?*': [*al-Najdayn* (النَّجْدَيْنِ, the two paths)]. The term *najd* refers to a path situated in a high place,[36] and here it has been used to refer to two separate paths that are clearly apparent.

About this verse, a tradition from Imam al-Sadiq (a) states: [It refers to] the paths of good and evil.[37]

---

[35] Shīrāzī, *Namūneh*, 27/18.

[36] Ṭabāṭabā'ī, *al-Mīzān*, 20/292.

[37] Kulaynī, *al-Kāfī*, 1/163.

عَنِ الصَّادِقِ (عَلَيْهِ السَّلَامُ) – قَالَ سَأَلْتُهُ عَنْ قَوْلِ اللهِ عَزَّ وَجَلَّ «وَهَدَيْنَاهُ النَّجْدَيْنِ» قَالَ نَجْدَ الْخَيْرِ وَالشَّرِّ.

These two paths were clearly shown to mankind in three ways:

i) The innate knowledge coded in the soul, about which Q91:7,8 state:

وَنَفْسٍ وَمَا سَوَّاهَا ﴿٧﴾ فَأَلْهَمَهَا فُجُورَهَا وَتَقْوَاهَا

And by [the] soul and He who fashioned it. Then inspired it [to understand] what is wrong for it and what is right for it.

ii) The guidance of Prophets (a) and Scriptures, about which Q3:3 states:

نَزَّلَ عَلَيْكَ الْكِتَابَ بِالْحَقِّ مُصَدِّقًا لِمَا بَيْنَ يَدَيْهِ وَأَنزَلَ التَّوْرَاةَ وَالْإِنجِيلَ

He has sent down upon you [O Muhammad] the Book with truth, confirming what was [revealed] before it, just as He revealed the Tawrāt and the Injīl.

iii) The gift of intellect and reason, which allows man to think rationally and discern right from wrong, and truth from falsehood. The role of the *ʿaql* as a tool to achieve guidance has been mentioned many times in the Qurʾan, for example, Q36:62 states:

وَلَقَدْ أَضَلَّ مِنكُمْ جِبِلًّا كَثِيرًا أَفَلَمْ تَكُونُوا تَعْقِلُونَ

And indeed he [Shaytan] has led astray a great multitude of you, so did you not use your intellect?

10.2 Both these paths, *al-najdayn*, are difficult to traverse, but there is a difference; the path of goodness and felicity is difficult in the beginning but becomes easier and more joyful to walk on as man crosses further on it, and it finally leads to eternal bliss.

The path of evil and damnation is the opposite. In the beginning it appears easy and attractive, but as one travels further it gets harder and more bleak and fruitless, and finally ends in misery.[38]

10.3 About these two paths, a tradition from the Prophet (s) states: [The path to] Paradise is surrounded by hardships while Hell is surrounded by base desires (*shahawāt*).[39]

[38] Muṭahharī, (*Āshnāyī bā Qurʾan*), *Āthār*, 28/554.

[39] Majlisī, *Biḥār*, 67/78.

عَنِ الرَّسُولِ (صَلَّى اللهُ عَلَيْهِ وَآلِهِ) – حُفَّتِ الْجَنَّةُ بِالْمَكَارِهِ وَحُفَّتِ النَّارُ بِالشَّهَوَاتِ.

10.4 It is also worth noting that man does not have to choose between unhappiness in this world and happiness in the Hereafter, or vice versa. The fruits of felicity and happiness will begin right in this world with determination and Godliness.[40] They require a measure of detachment from the world, and the next verses tell us how that can be achieved.

SUMMARY OF THE VERSE

In summary, the verse informs man that God has shown him two paths that he may traverse on: the path to goodness and Paradise and the path of disobedience and hellfire.

REFLECTIVE LEARNING

The two paths are known to us through our internal and external guidance and through the intellect.

Let me reflect on whether I refer back to these invaluable resources when faced with choices, or do I just do whatever society dictates and demands.

VERSES 11 - 16

فَلَا ٱقْتَحَمَ الْعَقَبَةَ ﴿١١﴾ وَمَا أَدْرَاكَ مَا الْعَقَبَةُ ﴿١٢﴾ فَكُّ رَقَبَةٍ ﴿١٣﴾ أَوْ إِطْعَامٌ
فِي يَوْمٍ ذِي مَسْغَبَةٍ ﴿١٤﴾ يَتِيمًا ذَا مَقْرَبَةٍ ﴿١٥﴾ أَوْ مِسْكِينًا ذَا مَتْرَبَةٍ ﴿١٦﴾

But he would not attempt the steep path (al-ʿaqabah). [11] *And what can make you know what the steep path is?* [12] *[It is] the freeing of a slave,* [13] *or the giving of food on a day of hunger* [14] *to an orphan of near kin,* [15] *or a needy person lying in the dust.* [16]

11-16.1 '*But he would not attempt the steep path.*': [*Iqtaḥama* (اقْتَحَمَ, he attempted)]. *Iqtiḥām* means to exert oneself with determination when performing a difficult and daunting task.[41]

[*Al-ʿAqabah* (الْعَقَبَة, steep path)]. This term refers to a narrow and uphill path that is difficult to traverse.

11-16.2 The verse states that despite the blessings that man has been endowed with, as mentioned in the previous verses, he is reluctant

[40] Muṭahharī, (*Āshnāyī bā Qur'an*), *Āthār*, 28/556.

[41] Rāghib, *al-Mufradāt.*

to take the hard path. Or it can mean, 'Will he not attempt the steep path', as an encouragement.[42]

Indeed, finding and staying true to the right path (*al-ṣirāṭ al-mustaqīm*) is the reason for man's creation, but it requires exertion and focus.

11-16.3 Another reason why people find the path difficult to traverse is due to their attachment to the world. In this regard, Imam Ali (a) has advised: Cut short your ties to this world, and return [to God] with the best of provision you can [from it]. Indeed, ahead of you is a steep path (*ʿaqabah*) and stations that are daunting and dangerous, which you must reach and at which you must stop. And know that [all the while,] death is stalking you.[43]

11-16.4 '*And what can make you know what the steep path is?*': *Wa mā adrāka* is a common Qur'anic phrase to indicate the high status of something. In this verse, since *al-ʿaqabah* is a path and not an action, the more correct meaning is, 'And what can make you know what it is to attempt the steep path *(iqtiḥām al-ʿaqabah)?*'[44]

A tradition from Imam al-Baqir (a) states: *And what can make you know...* means what [else] can teach you, when everything is in the Qur'an; it [alone] can teach you.[45]

11-16.5 To give some idea of the reply to the question, the next four verses describe some examples of *al-ʿaqabah*, the steep path.

11-16.6 '*[It is] The freeing of a slave.*': [*Raqabah* (رَقَبَة, neck)]. Freeing of the neck is more than a metaphor for freeing a person from the bondage of slavery; it is freeing him from the bondage of serving the dictates of his own soul.[46]

It is reported that a Bedouin Arab came to the Prophet and said, "Guide me to an act that will grant me entry into Paradise." He (s)

---

42 Ṭabrasī, *al-Bayān*, 10/749.

43 *Nahj al-Balāghah*, sermon 203.

وَأَقِلُّوا الْعُرْجَةَ عَلَى الدُّنْيَا، وَانْقَلِبُوا بِصَالِحِ مَا بِحَضْرَتِكُمْ مِنَ الزَّادِ، فَإِنَّ أَمَامَكُمْ عَقَبَةً كَؤُودًا، وَمَنَازِلَ مَخُوفَةً مَهُولَةً، لَا بُدَّ مِنَ الْوُرُودِ عَلَيْهَا، وَالْوُقُوفِ عِنْدَهَا. وَاعْلَمُوا أَنَّ مَلَاحِظَ الْمَنِيَّةِ نَحْوَكُمْ.

44 Rāzī, *Mafātīḥ al-Ghayb*, 31/169.

45 Majlisi, *Biḥār*, 9/251.

عَنِ الْبَاقِرِ (عَلَيْهِ السَّلَامُ) – « وَمَا أَدْرَاكَ مَا الْعَقَبَةُ » يَقُولُ مَا أَعْلَمَكَ وَكُلُّ شَيْءٍ فِي الْقُرْآنِ مَا أَدْرَاكَ فَهُوَ مَا أَعْلَمَكَ.

46 Muṭahharī, (*Āshnāyī bā Qur'an*), *Āthār*, 28/558.

replied, "You have asked a broad question even though you have spoken only a few words. Emancipate a person, and free a neck." The man asked, "Are they not the same thing?" The Prophet (s) replied, "No, emancipating a slave is setting him free yourself, but freeing a neck (*al-raqabah*) is to help in meeting the cost of his freedom."[47]

11-16.7 '*The giving of food on a day of hunger.*': [*Masghabah* (مَسْغَبَة, hunger)] is derived from *saghaba*, meaning severe hunger and starvation. The day of hunger is not one day; it has always existed, and it exists even now for many.

Hunger is generally defined as periods when people go for entire days without eating due to extreme poverty or lack of access to food and other resources. In 2021 it is estimated that 690 million people go hungry, an astounding one-tenth of the world's population.[48]

To feed the hungry is one of the most commendable acts in Islam, carrying a great reward. A tradition from Imam al-Sadiq (a) states: Amongst the most beloved acts in God's eyes is satisfying the hunger of a Muslim, or relieving him from distress, or paying off his debt.[49]

A tradition from the Prophet (s) states: Amongst the means to forgiveness is feeding the believers in days of hunger.[50]

11-16.8 '*To an orphan of near kin, or a needy person lying in the dust.*': [*Maqrabah* (مَقْرَبَة, near kin)] is derived from *qarābah*, which means close relation. The verse emphasizes the greater responsibility of looking after an orphan who is also a relative; otherwise it is a duty to care for and show kindness to every orphan.

The verse also indicates the priority of taking care of those who are near relatives.[51]

---

[47] Ḥuwayzī, *Nūr al-Thaqalayn*, 5/583.

جَاءَ أَعْرَابِيٌّ إِلَى النَّبِيِّ – صَلَّى اللهُ عَلَيْهِ وَآلِهِ – فَقَالَ: يَا رَسُولَ اللهِ، عَلِّمْنِي عَمَلًا يُدْخِلُنِي الْجَنَّةَ. قَالَ: إِنْ كُنْتَ أَقْصَرْتَ الْخِطْبَةَ لَقَدْ أَعْرَضْتَ الْمَسْأَلَةَ، أَعْتِقِ النَّسْمَةَ وَفُكَّ الرَّقَبَةَ. فَقَالَ أَوَلَيْسَا وَاحِدًا؟ قَالَ: لَا، عَتْقُ النَّسَمَةِ أَنْ تَنْفَرِدَ بِعِتْقِهَا، وَفَكُّ الرَّقَبَةِ أَنْ تُعِينَ فِي ثَمَنِهَا.

[48] https://www.actionagainsthunger.org/world-hunger-facts-statistics.

[49] Majlisī, *Biḥār*, 71/365.

عَنِ الصَّادِقِ (عَلَيْهِ السَّلَامُ) – مِنْ أَحَبِّ الْأَعْمَالِ إِلَى اللهِ إِشْبَاعُ جَوْعَةِ الْمُؤْمِنِ أَوْ تَنْفِيسُ كُرْبَتِهِ أَوْ قَضَاءُ دَيْنِهِ.

[50] Kulaynī, *al-Kāfī*, 2/201.

عَنِ الرَّسُولِ (صَلَّى اللهُ عَلَيْهِ وَآلِهِ) – مِنْ مُوجِبَاتِ الْمَغْفِرَةِ إِطْعَامُ الْمُسْلِمِ السَّغْبَانِ.

[51] Ṭabrasī, *al-Bayān*, 10/751.

[*Matrabah* (مَتْرَبَة, in the dust)]. Derived from *turāb* (dust), it refers to someone sitting on the ground due to extreme poverty.[52]

11-16.9 These verses mean that the person who is being used as an example did not do any of the tasks of *al-ʿaqabah*; he did not free a slave, or give food in days of hunger, neither to an orphan of near kin, nor to a needy person in abject poverty.[53]

It is narrated that when Imam al-Ridha (a) would sit to eat, he would take a large vessel and place it near his table. Then he would place the best of the food in the vessel and send it to be distributed among the poor. Thereafter, he would recite the verse, '*But he would not attempt the steep path*' and say, "God, the Exalted, knew that not everyone would be able to free a slave. For this reason, He showed them another path towards Paradise."[54]

11-16.10 The verses can also be interpreted in a different way. 'Freeing a neck' may mean freeing someone from the fire of Hell by guiding them. And 'giving food' could refer to giving the needy the spiritual nourishment of knowledge to keep them steadfast on God's path.[55] This meaning has been mentioned in a number of reports, some of which are quoted below:

A tradition from Imam al-Baqir states that in his explanation of the verse, '*Then let man consider his food*' (Q80:24), he said, "[It refers to] his knowledge, and from whom he acquires it."[56]

A tradition from Imam al-Sadiq (a) about the freeing of the neck (*fakku raqabah*) states: It is through us and our recognition (*maʿrifah*) that necks shall be freed.[57]

---

52 Shīrāzī, *Namūneh*, 27/31.

53 Ṭabāṭabāʾī, *al-Mīzān*, 20/293.

54 Kulaynī, *al-Kāfī*, 4/52.

كَانَ أَبُو الْحَسَنِ الرِّضَا (عَلَيْهِ السَّلَامُ) إِذَا أَكَلَ أُتِيَ بِصَحْفَةٍ فَتُوضَعُ بِقُرْبِ مَائِدَتِهِ فَيَعْمِدُ إِلَى أَطْيَبِ الطَّعَامِ مِمَّا يُؤْتَى بِهِ فَيَأْخُذُ مِنْ كُلِّ شَيْءٍ شَيْئًا فَيَضَعُ فِي تِلْكَ الصَّحْفَةِ ثُمَّ يَأْمُرُ بِهَا لِلْمَسَاكِينِ ثُمَّ يَتْلُو هَذِهِ الْآيَةَ «فَلَا اقْتَحَمَ الْعَقَبَةَ» ثُمَّ يَقُولُ عَلِمَ اللهُ عَزَّ وَجَلَّ أَنَّهُ لَيْسَ كُلُّ إِنْسَانٍ يَقْدِرُ عَلَى عِتْقِ رَقَبَةٍ فَجَعَلَ لَهُمُ السَّبِيلَ إِلَى الْجَنَّةِ.

55 Qarāʾatī, *Nūr*, 10/488.

56 Kulaynī, *al-Kāfī*, 1/50.

عَنِ الْبَاقِرِ (عَلَيْهِ السَّلَامُ) – فِي قَوْلِ اللهِ عَزَّ وَجَلَّ:« فَلْيَنْظُرِ الْإِنْسَانُ إِلَىٰ طَعَامِهِ» قَالَ عِلْمُهُ الَّذِي يَأْخُذُهُ عَمَّنْ يَأْخُذُهُ.

57 Majlisi, *Biḥār*, 24/282.

عَنِ الصَّادِقِ (عَلَيْهِ السَّلَامُ) – قَوْلُهُ تَعَالَى «فَكُّ رَقَبَةٍ» قَالَ بِنَا تُفَكُّ الرِّقَابُ وَبِمَعْرِفَتِنَا.

SUMMARY OF THE VERSES

In summary, these verses speak of man's reluctance to undertake a difficult path (*al-ʿaqabah*) in life. Walking on this path would include freeing a person from captivity, feeding the hungry from amongst the orphans, especially if they are relatives, and the destitute.

REFLECTIVE LEARNING

Let me reflect on the apparent difficulty of the path of determination and obedience and the apparent ease of the path of negligence and disobedience.

Let me begin my journey on the uphill path today by feeding the hungry – either with food or knowledge.

VERSES 17, 18

ثُمَّ كَانَ مِنَ الَّذِينَ آمَنُوا وَتَوَاصَوْا بِالصَّبْرِ وَتَوَاصَوْا بِالْمَرْحَمَةِ ﴿١٧﴾ أُولَٰئِكَ أَصْحَابُ الْمَيْمَنَةِ ﴿١٨﴾

And then being amongst those who believed and counselled one another to steadfastness, and counselled one another to compassion. [17] *They are the companions of the right.* [18]

17-18.1 '*And then being amongst those who believed.*': The usage of *thumma* (then) does not mean that the actions described in the previous verses are the prerequisites for these three qualities. In other words, *thumma* does not always denote sequential action, it can also refer to superiority, as in this case.[58]

17-18.2 The phrase '*and then being amongst*' is connected to the phrase in the previous verse, '*attempt the steep path,*' and so the meaning is 'they did not attempt the steep path and neither were they amongst those who believed and...'[59]

17-18.3 The verse mentions the merits of a further three qualities:

1. Being a believer and part of the Muslim nation (*min alladhīna āmanū*),

---

[58] Shīrāzī, *Namūneh,* 27/32.

[59] Ṭabāṭabā'ī, *al-Mīzān,* 20/293.

2. Counselling one another to steadfastness (*tawāṣaw bi'l-ṣabr*), and
3. Counselling one another to compassion (*tawāṣaw bi'l marḥamah*).

We will look at each merit in turn.

17-18.4 Belief in God (*īmān*) is necessary for charity to have value and honour in the next world. People who have no belief in God also perform great acts of charity for which they will be rewarded in this world. *Īmān* is the only key to transferring action to the Hereafter, and serving humanity is ultimately of worth only if it is an extension of serving God.[60] In this regard, Q4:124 states:

وَمَنْ يَعْمَلْ مِنَ الصَّالِحَاتِ مِنْ ذَكَرٍ أَوْ أُنْثَىٰ وَهُوَ مُؤْمِنٌ فَأُولَٰئِكَ يَدْخُلُونَ الْجَنَّةَ

And whoever does righteous deeds whether male or female and he [or she] is a believer... such shall enter Paradise...

17-18.5 '*And counselled one another to steadfastness and counselled one another to compassion.*': Being part of the *ummah* means to acknowledge the responsibility of the believers to each other. Once we have begun walking the path, then it is our duty to encourage others to do so also.

[*Tawāṣaw* (تَوَاصَوْا, exhort and counsel one another)] is derived from *tawāṣī*, meaning to encourage and advise one another.[61] The repetition of the word *tawāṣaw* in the same verse is for emphasis on the counsel-ling and to indicate that counselling to steadfastness and counselling to compassion are two different and independent responsibilities.[62]

[*Marḥamah* (مَرْحَمَة, compassion)] is the verbal noun derived from *raḥmah* meaning mercy.

17-18.6 Normally, the Qur'an adds the phrase, '*ʿamilū al-ṣāliḥāt* (do good deeds)' after '*āmanū* (believe)', so this verse should be no different. Therefore, here, the two duties of 'counselling to stead-fastness' and 'counselling to compassion', are examples of 'good deeds.'[63]

---

[60] Muṭahharī, (*Āshnāyī bā Qur'an*), *Āthār*, 28/560.

[61] Rāghib, *al-Mufradāt*.

[62] Rafsanjānī, *Rahnamā*, 20/455.

[63] Qarā'atī, *Nūr*, 10/490.

17-18.7 In addition to serving the downtrodden members of society himself, the believer is also charged with reaching out to fellow believers in an attempt to come closer to God together. This is so that progress towards righteousness is not only individual, but communal as well.

Of course, to be able to counsel others to *ṣabr* and *marḥamah* in good conscience, one should at least be trying to adopt these traits himself, in some shape or form. A way to do this is by undertaking the three actions mentioned in the previous verses.

17-18.8 As the path to traverse is an uphill and steep one, mutual encouragement will help greatly. Counselling one another to remain steadfast on the path of God and to exercise compassion for those who are undergoing difficulties increases cohesion and brotherly love in society.

17-18.9 Social cohesion is the philosophy of the *sharīʿah*. Acts that bring the hearts of people closer, like eating together, worshipping in congregation, maintaining ties with family, and so on, carry great reward. In contrast, acts that disunite society such as gossip and slander, oppression, breaking ties with blood relations, and so on, carry a great punishment.

Even when we pledge allegiance to the Imams (a), we have been instructed to do so as a group. In a salutation to Imam al-Husayn (a) taught by Imam al-Baqir (a), we have been taught to be mindful of our brethren in faith and say: I am at peace with those who are at peace with you...[64]

17-18.10 '*They are the companions of the right.*': [*Maymanah* (الْمَيْمَنَة, the right] is derived from *yumn*, meaning blessing.[65] It is also translated as bliss. Here, it refers to those who attempt to walk on *al-ʿaqabah*, encourage others to do so also, and combine faith and action. Thereby, they join the 'companions of the bliss', a company that is successful and permanently blessed in Paradise.

17-18.11 The Qur'an uses two terms, *aṣḥāb al-yamīn* and *aṣḥāb al-maymanah*, both meaning 'companions of the right', for those who

[64] Qummī, *Mafātīḥ al-Jinān, Ziyārat ʿĀshurā'*.

إِنِّي سِلْمٌ لِمَنْ سَالَمَكُمْ.

[65] Muṣṭafawī, *al-Taḥqīq*.

will ultimately receive their scroll of deeds in their right hand.[66] The terms are contrasted against the *aṣḥāb al-shimāl* and *aṣḥāb al-mash'amah*, meaning the 'companions of the left', who will receive their scroll in the left hand.[67]

SUMMARY OF THE VERSES

These verses highlight three qualities of those who traverse the steep path: being amongst those who believe (*min alladhīna āmanū*), counselling one another to steadfastness (*tawāṣaw bi'l-ṣabr*), and counselling one another to compassion (*tawāṣaw bi'l marḥamah*). They shall be part of the blessed company, the 'companions of the right and bliss.'

REFLECTIVE LEARNING

To be joined to the people of the bliss we need to have the three qualities described in this section. Let me reflect on:

1. How strong my belief is, and what I can do to strengthen it.
2. The method I use to counsel others to steadfastness and compassion, and compare that to how I would like to be counselled.

VERSES 19, 20

وَالَّذِينَ كَفَرُوا بِآيَاتِنَا هُمْ أَصْحَابُ الْمَشْأَمَةِ ﴿١٩﴾ عَلَيْهِمْ نَارٌ مُؤْصَدَةٌ ﴿٢٠﴾

But those who disbelieved in Our signs, they are the companions of the left. [19] *Fire will be closed over them.* [20]

19-20.1 *'But those who disbelieved in Our signs.'*: The signs of God that are present within the human being himself and in the world outside of him, are designed to guide him towards God, the Creator and Sustainer. These signs (*āyāt*) include the verses of the Qur'an and the teachings of the Prophet (s). Those who choose to ignore or disbelieve in these signs have in fact, disbelieved in God Himself.[68]

---

[66] Ṭabrasī, *al-Bayān*, 10/751.

[67] Shīrāzī, *Namūneh*, 27/33.

[68] Ṭabāṭabā'ī, *al-Mīzān*, 20/293.

19-20.2 *'They are the companions of the left.'*: [*al-Mash'amah* (الْمَشْأَمَة, the left)] is derived from *shu'm*, meaning miserable and it is the opposite of *al-maymanah*.[69] Through their denial, these people join the 'companions of the left', a party who are unsuccessful and eternally miserable.

19-20.3 *'Fire will be closed over them.'*: [*Mu'ṣadah* (مُؤْصَدَة, closed over)] is derived from *īṣād*, which is a term used for closing a door securely.[70] Here it refers to a fire by which they are covered from all sides, unable to flee. About them Q7:41 states:

لَهُمْ مِنْ جَهَنَّمَ مِهَادٌ وَمِنْ فَوْقِهِمْ غَوَاشٍ وَكَذَٰلِكَ نَجْزِي الظَّالِمِينَ

They will have a bed from Hell, and over them blankets [of fire]. And thus do We recompense the wrong-doers.

SUMMARY OF THE VERSES

In contrast to the previous group, these verses speak of those who deny and disbelieve in God's signs. They shall be part of a damned company, the 'companions of the left or misery.' And the fire of Hell shall be closed over them.

REFLECTIVE LEARNING

Let me reflect on the signs of God that exist within me and in the world around me.

Let me use these signs to increase my faith to make my footing firmer on the steep path so I can join the 'companions of bliss' and not the 'companions of misery'.

---

69 Muṣṭafawī, *al-Taḥqīq*.

70 Qarā'atī, *Nūr*, 10/490.

SURAT AL-SHAMS
THE SUN (91)

TEXT AND TRANSLATION

سُورَةُ الشَّمْسِ

بِسْمِ اللهِ الرَّحْمٰنِ الرَّحِيمِ

وَالشَّمْسِ وَضُحَاهَا ﴿١﴾ وَالْقَمَرِ إِذَا تَلَاهَا ﴿٢﴾ وَالنَّهَارِ إِذَا جَلَّاهَا ﴿٣﴾ وَاللَّيْلِ
إِذَا يَغْشَاهَا ﴿٤﴾ وَالسَّمَاءِ وَمَا بَنَاهَا ﴿٥﴾ وَالْأَرْضِ وَمَا طَحَاهَا ﴿٦﴾ وَنَفْسٍ وَمَا
سَوَّاهَا ﴿٧﴾ فَأَلْهَمَهَا فُجُورَهَا وَتَقْوَاهَا ﴿٨﴾ قَدْ أَفْلَحَ مَنْ زَكَّاهَا ﴿٩﴾ وَقَدْ خَابَ
مَنْ دَسَّاهَا ﴿١٠﴾ كَذَّبَتْ ثَمُودُ بِطَغْوَاهَا ﴿١١﴾ إِذِ انْبَعَثَ أَشْقَاهَا ﴿١٢﴾ فَقَالَ
لَهُمْ رَسُولُ اللهِ نَاقَةَ اللهِ وَسُقْيَاهَا ﴿١٣﴾ فَكَذَّبُوهُ فَعَقَرُوهَا فَدَمْدَمَ عَلَيْهِمْ رَبُّهُمْ بِذَنْبِهِمْ
فَسَوَّاهَا ﴿١٤﴾ وَلَا يَخَافُ عُقْبَاهَا ﴿١٥﴾

In the name of God, the Beneficent, the Merciful.

By the sun and its radiance. [1] *And by the moon when it followed it.* [2] *And by the day when it displayed it.* [3] *And by the night when it covers it.* [4] *And by the heaven and He who constructed it.* [5] *And by the earth and He who extended it.* [6] *And by [the] soul and He who fashioned it,* [7] *Then inspired it [to understand] what is wrong for it and what is right for it.* [8] *The one who purifies it has succeeded.* [9] *And the one who corrupts it has failed.* [10] *[The people of] Thamud belied [the truth] in their transgression,* [11] *when the most wretched of them was sent forth [to kill the she-camel].* [12] *And the Messenger of God (Salih) said to them, "It is the she-camel of God, so let her drink!"* [13] *But they rejected him, and they hamstrung her. So their Lord crushed them for their sin and levelled them [to the ground].* [14] *And He does not fear the consequences thereof.* [15]

INTRODUCTION

Surat al-Shams (91) was the 26th chapter to be revealed.[1] It has fifteen verses and was revealed in Makka, after Surat al-Qadr (97). It is named after the oath made by the sun (*al-shams*) in the opening verse.

It is occasionally referred to in the narrations as Surat *Wa al-shamsi wa ḍuḥāhā*, possibly so that it is not mistaken for Surat al-Takwīr, which begins with '*Idhā al-shamsu kuwwirat*.'

The theme of Surat al-Shams is the paramount importance of purifying/reforming the soul (*tazkiyat/tahdhīb al-nafs*). To show the fundamental significance of this action, God begins the chapter with a record eleven oaths.[2]

The chapter mentions powerful opposing forces of nature in the outer world that are held in balance by God's system of creation. Similarly, the soul, which is the 'inner world' of man, has powerful opposing forces that need to be controlled and made to work in harmony.

God informs man that He has inspired the soul to instinctively distinguish good from evil. If he purifies it, he will be successful, but if he neglects it, it will be to his ultimate detriment.

Thereafter, as an example of those who corrupted their souls, the verses warn the Makkans by recounting the dreadful fate of the people of Thamud. They belied Prophet Salih (a) who had been sent to them and killed the she-camel which was a sign to them from God.

LINK TO THE PREVIOUS CHAPTER

In the previous chapter, Surat al-Balad, God mentions the two paths, *al-najdayn*, that man has been guided to. Now, in Surat al-Shams, God informs man that this guidance has been coded into every human soul, which instinctively knows whether a path is beneficial or harmful for it.

In Surat al-Balad, God mentions the steeper of the two paths, *al-ʿaqabah*, and what needs to be done to traverse it. In Surat al-Shams, He gives us an example of a community who chose to ignore the steep path and the consequences of their defiance.

At the end of Surat al-Balad, God mentions the punishment in the Hereafter for those who disbelieved in His signs and transgressed. In

---

1 Maʿrifat, *ʿUlūm-i Qur'ānī*, p. 90.

2 Shīrāzī, *Namūneh*, 27/38.

Surat al-Shams, He gives the example of His punishment in this world by mentioning the fate of the people of Thamud.

MERITS OF RECITATION

- A tradition from the Prophet (s) states: Whoever recites this surah is like the one who has given in charity every single thing that the sun and moon shine upon.[3]
- A tradition from Imam al-Sadiq (a) states: It is recommended for the one who has reduced means and opportunities, and lots of loss and disappointments, to continually recite this surah. As a result, he will experience growth in means and opportunities.[4]

EXEGESIS

VERSES 1 - 4

وَالشَّمْسِ وَضُحَاهَا ﴿١﴾ وَالْقَمَرِ إِذَا تَلَاهَا ﴿٢﴾ وَالنَّهَارِ إِذَا جَلَّاهَا ﴿٣﴾ وَاللَّيْلِ إِذَا يَغْشَاهَا ﴿٤﴾

By the sun and its radiance. [1] *And by the moon when it followed it.* [2] *And by the day when it displayed it.* [3] *And by the night when it covers it.* [4]

1-4.1 By employing the *waw al-qasam*, Surat al-Shams begins with eleven oaths, which will be discussed in turn.

1-4.2 '*By the sun and its radiance.*': The first two oaths are by the sun and its radiant illumination. The sun provides the earth with heat and light, and this solar energy plays an essential role in sustaining life.

[*Ḍuḥā* (ضُحَى, radiance)]. This term refers to the radiance that spreads[5] and illuminates everything once the sun begins to rise into the sky. The midmorning is therefore also called *ḍuḥā*.

---

[3] Nūrī, *Mustadrak al-Wasā'il*, 4/358.

عَنِ الرَّسُولِ (صَلَّى اللهُ عَلَيْهِ وَآلِهِ) – مَنْ قَرَأَ سُورَةَ وَالشَّمْسِ فَكَأَنَّمَا تَصَدَّقَ بِكُلِّ شَيْءٍ طَلَعَتْ عَلَيْهِ الشَّمْسُ وَالْقَمَرُ.

[4] Baḥrānī, *al-Burhān*, 5/669.

عَنِ الصَّادِقِ (عَلَيْهِ السَّلَامُ) – يُسْتَحَبُّ لِمَنْ يَكُونُ قَلِيلَ الرِّزْقِ والتَّوْفِيقِ، كَثِيرَ الْخُسْرَانِ وَالْحَسَرَاتِ، أَنْ يُدْمِنَ فِي قِرَاءَتِهَا يُصِيبُ فِيهَا زِيَادَةً وَتَوْفِيقًا.

[5] Rāghib, *al-Mufradāt*.

1-4.3 '*And by the moon when it followed it.*': The third oath is by the moon (*al-qamar*) when it follows the sun. Unlike the previous oath, which is sworn by the sun as well as its radiance, this oath swears by the moon on its own because it reflects the light of the sun.[6]

The moon is the brightest light in the night sky and plays a critical role in life on earth by controlling the ocean tides, stabilizing the tilting spin-axis of the earth, and illuminating the night.

According to most exegetes, *qamar* here refers to the full moon, when it is at its brightest and most glorious.[7]

[*Talā* (تَلَا, follow)]. Here, 'follow' either means that the moon takes it light from the sun, or that the luminance of the moon is only visible once the sun sets.[8]

1-4.4 '*And by the day when it displayed it.*': The fourth oath is by the day. Day allows man to perceive his surroundings, and regulates both his physiological and psychological health.

[*Jallāhā* (جَلَّاهَا, displays it)] is derived from *jalā*, which means to manifest or display.[9] The pronoun (*hā*, it) attached to it either refers to the sun, which is displayed by the earth as it rotates to daytime,[10] or is a reference to the earth, which is lit up in the day.[11]

1-4.5 '*And by the night when it covers it.*': The fifth oath is by the night, which is as important as the day. For human beings, it is a time for essential rest and revitalization. Q6:96 states:

وَجَعَلَ اللَّيْلَ سَكَنًا

...And He has made the night for rest...

[*Yaghshāhā* (يَغْشَاهَا, covers it)] is derived from *ghashiya*, which means to cover or veil. Once more, the pronoun (*hā*, it) attached to it is a reference to the earth, or the brilliance of the sun, which is covered by the darkness of the night.

1-4.6 The oath by the day that illuminated the earth through the radiant sun is made in the past tense, while the oath by the moon that

[6] Shīrāzī, *Sūgandhā-yi Purbār-i Qur'an*, 1/80.

[7] Shīrāzī, *Namūneh*, 27/40.

[8] Ṭabāṭabā'ī, *al-Mīzān*, 20/296.

[9] Rāghib, *al-Mufradāt*.

[10] Muṭahharī, (*Āshnāyī bā Qur'an*), *Āthār*, 28/567.

[11] Ṭabāṭabā'ī, *al-Mīzān*, 20/296.

covers the earth is made in the present tense. This may be because the verses are describing the prevailing situation in the early days of the revelation of the Qur'an; the bright sun of guidance had risen but the darkness of immorality was still covering the land.[12]

A tradition from Imam al-Sadiq (a) states: The sun refers to God's Messenger (s); through him, God illuminated their religion for the people.[13]

The same tradition from Imam al-Sadiq (a) continues: The day refers to the Imam from the lineage of Fatimah (a). When asked about [any matter from] the religion of God's Messenger (s), he displays it [clearly] for the questioner, and God has mentioned this when He said, '*And by the day when it displayed it.*' The '*night when it covers it*' refers to the leaders of tyranny (the Banu Umayyah) who usurped the affair from the household of the Messenger (s) and occupied the office of which the household of the Messenger (s) was more deserving than them. Thus they covered the religion of God with oppression and tyranny.[14]

This tradition is not the *tafsīr* of the verse but an example of its application (*miṣdāq*) at different times and places (*ta'wīl*).

DISCUSSION 1: OATHS IN THE QUR'AN

Oaths are defined as phrases that confirm a statement through emphasis.[15] The audience of any message may be: i) prepared to listen to a compelling case or, ii) hesitant and uncertain or, iii) hostile and inclined to be sceptical. Accordingly, some sort of additional proof or emphasis is required to make them pause and listen.

Especially in Makka, where the audience was largely hostile, the Qur'an used oaths to communicate its message more effectively.

---

[12] Ibid, 20/297.

[13] Kulaynī, *al-Kāfī*, 8/50.

عَنِ الصَّادِقِ (عَلَيْهِ السَّلَامُ) – الشَّمْسُ رَسُولُ اللهِ (صَلَّى اللهُ عَلَيْهِ وَآلِهِ) بِهِ أَوْضَحَ اللهُ عَزَّ وَجَلَّ لِلنَّاسِ دِينَهُمْ.

[14] Ibid.

عَنِ الصَّادِقِ (عَلَيْهِ السَّلَامُ) – «وَالنَّهَارِ إِذَا جَلَّاهَا» قَالَ ذَلِكَ الْإِمَامُ مِنْ ذُرِّيَّةِ فَاطِمَةَ (سَلَامُ اللهِ عَلَيْهَا)، يُسْأَلُ عَنْ دِينِ رَسُولِ اللهِ (صَلَّى اللهُ عَلَيْهِ وَآلِهِ) فَيُجَلِّيهِ لِمَنْ سَأَلَهُ، فَحَكَى اللهُ عَزَّ وَجَلَّ قَوْلَهُ فَقَالَ «وَالنَّهَارِ إِذَا جَلَّاهَا».

«وَاللَّيْلِ إِذَا يَغْشَاهَا» قَالَ ذَاكَ أَئِمَّةُ الْجَوْرِ الَّذِينَ اسْتَبَدُّوا بِالْأَمْرِ دُونَ آلِ الرَّسُولِ (صَلَّى اللهُ عَلَيْهِ وَآلِهِ)، وَجَلَسُوا مَجْلِسًا كَانَ آلُ الرَّسُولِ (عَلَيْهِمُ السَّلَامُ) أَوْلَى بِهِ مِنْهُمْ، فَغَشُوا دِينَ اللهِ بِالظُّلْمِ وَالْجَوْرِ.

[15] Zarkashī, *al-Burhān fī 'Ulūm al-Qur'an*, 3/40.

Consequently, many early chapters of the Qur'an begin with a series of oaths, where God swears by a variety of phenomena in His creation. However, man is instructed to only swear by God and not anything else. A tradition from Imam al-Jawad (a) states: Indeed, Allah the Almighty, swears by His creation as He likes, but it is not appropriate for His creation to swear except by Him.[16]

23 chapters of the Qur'an begin with oaths. In total, 44 chapters of the Qur'an contain 118 instances of oaths in 104 verses. Of these, 95 oaths are taken by God Himself, while the rest quote the words of others such as the brothers of Yusuf (a) (Q12:73), the magicians of Firʿawn (Q26:44), the idolaters and other deniers of the Day of Judgement (Q58:14), and even by Shaytan (Q38:82).[17]

The oaths employed by the Qur'an are for two purposes:

i) they are mainly used to emphasize the subject (*jawāb*) of the oaths which is the theme under discussion, and to declare it to be the truth, and

ii) they are also used to highlight the important station of the object of the oath itself.

Oaths are always sworn by something that is important in the eyes of the one making the oath, and so both the objects of the Qur'anic oaths (*muqsamma bihā*) as well as their subjects (*muqsamma lahā*) deserve deliberation.[18]

It is also important to ponder about the oaths and their subjects to discover the link between the two. Q89:5 states:

هَلْ فِي ذَٰلِكَ قَسَمٌ لِذِي حِجْرٍ

Is there not in these an oath for people of understanding?

SUMMARY OF THE VERSES

In summary, the first four verses mention five oaths centred on the sun. They are: the sun, its radiance, the moon that follows the sun, the day which displays the sun and the night that covers its illumination.

---

[16] ʿĀmilī, *Wasā'il*, 23/259.

عَنْ أَبِي جَعْفَرٍ الثَّانِي (عَلَيْهِ السَّلَامُ) - إِنَّ اللهَ عَزَّ وَجَلَّ يُقْسِمُ مِنْ خَلْقِهِ بِمَا شَاءَ وَلَيْسَ لِخَلْقِهِ أَنْ يُقْسِمُوا إِلَّا بِهِ عَزَّ وَجَلَّ.

[17] Harīsī, *Shinākht Sūreh-hayi Qur'an*, p. 23.

[18] Shīrāzī, *Namūneh*, 17/111.

REFLECTIVE LEARNING

A tradition from the Prophet (s) states: My similitude before you is that of the sun, and the similitude of Ali (a) is that of the moon. So when the sun is absent, seek your way by the moon.[19] Those who follow the Prophet (s) and his *Ahl al-Bayt* (a) can themselves reflect the light of these close servants of God and thus play an important role on the earth.

Let me reflect on my interaction with people in my day – how well do I reflect the example and *sunnah* of these holy personalities?

VERSES 5 - 8

وَالسَّمَاءِ وَمَا بَنَاهَا ﴿٥﴾ وَالْأَرْضِ وَمَا طَحَاهَا ﴿٦﴾ وَنَفْسٍ وَمَا سَوَّاهَا ﴿٧﴾
فَأَلْهَمَهَا فُجُورَهَا وَتَقْوَاهَا ﴿٨﴾

And by the heaven and He who constructed it. [5] *And by the earth and He who extended it.* [6] *And by [the] soul and He who fashioned it,* [7] *Then inspired it [to understand] what is wrong for it and what is right for it* [8]

5-8.1 '*And by the heaven and He who constructed it.*': The sixth and seventh oaths in the chapter are by the heaven, and by God, who constructed it. The heavens are mentioned next because their existence extends beyond the sun, which is the central theme of the previous oaths.[20]

[*Al-Samā'* (السَّمَاء, the heaven)] is derived from *samawa*, meaning that which is towards the sky, or something that is raised high above other things and covering them.[21] *Samā'* and its plural, *samāwāt*, has been mentioned over 300 times in the Qur'an.

Here, it refers to the universe created by God above and beyond the earth.[22] The heaven above us is one of the grandest creations of God, and the sheer scale of its vastness is beyond man's

---

[19] Baḥrānī, *al-Burhān*, 5/671.

عَنِ الرَّسُولِ (صَلَّى اللهُ عَلَيْهِ وَآلِهِ) – مَثَلِي فِيكُمْ مَثَلُ الشَّمْسِ، وَمَثَلُ عَلِيٍّ مَثَلُ الْقَمَرِ، فَإِذَا غَابَتِ الشَّمْسُ فَاهْتَدُوا بِالْقَمَرِ.

[20] Rāzī, *Mafātīḥ al-Ghayb*, 31/175.

[21] Muṣṭafawī, *al-Taḥqīq*.

[22] Modarresī, *Min Huda al-Qur'an*, 18/135.

comprehension. Billions of galaxies with a myriad of stars and other celestial features have been created by God, to the extent that Q79:27 comments:

أَأَنتُمْ أَشَدُّ خَلْقًا أَمِ السَّمَاءُ بَنَاهَا

Are you harder to create or is the heaven? He (God) constructed it.

5-8.2 The pronoun '*mā*' before *banāhā* (constructed it) and later, *ṭaḥāhā* (extended it), and *sawwāhā* (fashioned it) refers to God, the Almighty. *Mā* (What) here is used instead of *man* (Who). *Mā* is normally used for insentient objects, and here the exegetes have offered different explanations for why it has been used in this and other verses.

Some exegetes say that this is not the *mā al-mawṣūlah* (conjunctive *mā*) which would make the verse mean, 'And by the heaven and that [Power] which constructed it.' Rather, it is *mā al-maṣdariyyah* (gerundival *mā*), which renders the verb that follows it into a verbal noun. The *mā al-maṣdariyyah* denotes wonderment, thus the verse would mean, 'By the sky and its [amazing] construction.'[23]

Others have said that if the oath is by God, the Exalted, it is not befitting that it should come after oaths by the sun and other aspects of creation. However, the reply to this objection is that there is no harm in pointing out the wondrous phenomenon of the sun before directing attention to its Originator.[24]

In any case, by considering verse 8, '*Then inspired it [to understand] what is wrong for it and what is right for it*', it becomes clear that *mā* has been used in these verses as a pronoun for God.[25]

The Qur'an has used *mā* for sentient beings in other instances as well, for example in Q4:3:

فَانكِحُوا مَا طَابَ لَكُم مِّنَ النِّسَاءِ مَثْنَىٰ وَثُلَاثَ وَرُبَاعَ

...Then marry those (mā) *who you choose of [other] women, two, three, or four...*

We have discussed the possible reasons for this usage further in the *tafsīr* of Surat al-Layl (92) and al-Balad (90).

---

23 Ṭabrasī, *al-Bayān*, 10/755; Zamakhsharī, *al-Kashshāf*, 7/570.

24 Rāzī, *Mafātīḥ al-Ghayb*, 31/175.

25 Ṭabāṭabā'ī, *al-Mīzān*, 20/297.

5-8.3 '*And by the earth and He who extended it.*': The eighth and ninth oaths are by the earth, and again, by God, who extended it. The earth is the cradle of human life and that of every other living creature. Its expansive mountains and valleys, forests and swamps, oceans and rivers, all sustain life on earth.

The earth is constantly spinning on its axis at 1000 miles per hour along its equator. Simultaneously, it is moving around the sun at a speed of 67,000 miles per hour. Through God's marvellous system of balance of forces in the cosmos, human beings are quite oblivious of this incredibly swift movement, and are able to live comfortably and flourish on the earth. Indeed, these are signs that point towards the Almighty Creator.

[*Ṭaḥāhā* (طَحَاهَا, extended it)]. *Ṭaḥā* is derived from *ṭaḥw*, which means to spread or extend.[26] The landmasses of the earth emerged from under the water as the seas gradually receded. The spreading of the land, from below the Kaʿbah, is called *daḥw al-arḍ*, and is marked on the day of 24th of Dhū al-Qaʿdah. This wondrous phenomenon facilitated the habitation of human beings on earth and allowed them to travel across its expanse – this is the meaning of God's extending of the earth.[27]

5-8.4 '*And by [the] soul and He who fashioned it.*': The tenth and eleventh oaths are by the human soul, and once more, by God, who proportioned and fashioned it. As mentioned before, *mā* points to the Fashioner and Inspirer, so it can only refer to God.

[*Nafs* (نَفْس, soul)] has several usages in the Qur'an: the human person, the human soul, and the combination of the body and soul. We have discussed this term further in the *tafsīr* of Surat al-Inshirāḥ (94).

In this instance, based on verse 8 which speaks of God's inspiration to it, *nafs* refers to the human soul which is worthy of an oath alongside its Creator.

[*Sawwāhā* (سَوَّاهَا, fashioned it)]. The verb *sawwā* is derived from *sawiya* which means to be equal, and its verbal noun *taswiyah* means to proportion, straighten, make balanced, and perfect the make of something.[28]

---

26 Ibid.

27 Shīrāzī, *Namūneh*, 27/43.

28 Muṣṭafawī, *al-Taḥqīq*.

Referring to the human soul, it means fashioning it (through the intellect) to function best when its faculties are in balance.[29]

5-8.5 All the previous oaths were made by objects in the definite form. However, interestingly, *nafs* is mentioned in the indefinite form. It could thus be a reference to the original soul of Adam (a), but more probably it is an oath by the unique kind of soul that human beings possess.[30]

5-8.6 '*Then inspired it [to understand] what is wrong for it and what is right for it.*': This is a further quality of the human soul, and the particle *fa* indicates that it is a consequence of the manner in which God fashioned it. Therefore, as part of its Divinely granted abilities, the soul instinctively knows what is detrimental for it and what is beneficial, what will pollute it and what will keep it pure. And this is the practical intellect (*al-ʿaql al-ʿamalī*).[31] It is also referred to as *fiṭrah* in Q30:30, which states:

فَأَقِمْ وَجْهَكَ لِلدِّينِ حَنِيفًا فِطْرَتَ اللهِ الَّتِي فَطَرَ النَّاسَ عَلَيْهَا

So, direct your face towards the religion, inclining to [instinctive] truth; the innate nature on which God has created man...

[*Alhamahā* (أَلْهَمَهَا, inspired it)] is derived from *lahima* which originally means to drink or swallow something. Its verbal noun *ilhām* means inspiration and enlightenment.[32] It is as if the human soul swallows and completely absorbs this knowledge. Thereafter, *ilhām* came to mean a determination, awareness, and knowledge that enters the heart of a human being. Here, *ilhām* denotes the ability to innately discern and distinguish good from evil, and this is a great bounty from the grace of God.[33]

[*Fujūr* (فُجُور, wrong)] is derived from *fajara* which means to cleave; that is why the time when the light of day cleaves the darkness of night is called *fajr*.[34] Similarly, it refers to the occasion when sinful conduct cleaves the curtain of righteousness and religiosity.[35]

---

[29] Shīrāzī, *Namūneh*, 27/44.

[30] Ṭabāṭabā'ī, *al-Mīzān*, 20/298.

[31] Ibid.

[32] Mustafawī, *al-Taḥqīq*.

[33] Ṭabāṭabā'ī, *al-Mīzān*, 20/299.

[34] Shīrāzī, *Namūneh*, 27/46.

[35] Ibid.

In this verse it refers to the knowledge of wrongful behaviour and how to restrain oneself from it.[36]

[*Taqwā* (تَقْوَى, righteousness, God-wariness)] is derived from *wiqāya* which means to safeguard and protect, and here it refers to the knowledge that allows one to guard himself from disobedience, sinfulness, and pollution.[37]

5-8.7 The verse does not mean that the inclination to good or evil have been coded into the human soul; rather, it refers to the ability to distinguish between the two.[38]

5-8.8 Whenever the Prophet (s) would recite these verses, he would pause, then say, "O God! Grant my soul its God-wariness (*taqwā*) and purify it, for You are best able to purify it. You are its Protector and its Guardian." It is reported that he would do this in his *salat*.[39]

SUMMARY OF THE VERSES

A further six oaths are made in these four verses: by the heavens, by the earth, by the human soul and three times by God, the Almighty, Who constructed, extended, and proportioned these phenomena, respectively.

REFLECTIVE LEARNING

If the soul knows what is wrong and right for it why do people sin? It is because the guiding voice of the soul is drowned out in the material existence that we are all immersed in.

Let me reflect on whether I have become accustomed to ignoring this voice, or do I listen to my *nafs* at every point of action.

VERSES 9, 10

قَدْ أَفْلَحَ مَنْ زَكَّاهَا ﴿٩﴾ وَقَدْ خَابَ مَنْ دَسَّاهَا ﴿١٠﴾

---

[36] Ṭabrasī, *al-Bayān*, 10/755.

[37] Shīrāzī, *Namūneh*, 27/46.

[38] Ibid.

[39] Majlisī, *Biḥār*, 89/220. (This prayer was also recited by Imam al-Husayn (a) in his supplications on the 15th night of Shaʿbān, see: Ibn Ṭāwūs, *Iqbāl al-Aʿmāl*, 2/715.)

كَانَ رَسُولُ اللهِ صَلَّى اللهُ عَلَيْهِ وَآلِهِ إِذَا تَلَا هَذِهِ الْآيَةَ «وَنَفْسٍ وَمَا سَوَّاهَا فَأَلْهَمَهَا فُجُورَهَا وَتَقْوَاهَا»، وَقَفَ ثُمَّ قَالَ: اَللّٰهُمَّ آتِ نَفْسِي تَقْوَاهَا وَزَكِّهَا، أَنْتَ خَيْرُ مَنْ زَكَّاهَا، أَنْتَ وَلِيُّهَا وَمَوْلَاهَا، قَالَ وَهُوَ فِي الصَّلَاةِ.

The one who purifies it has succeeded, [9] and the one who corrupts it has failed. [10]

9-10.1 This chapter contains eleven oaths, more than any other chapter of the Qur'an. It signifies that the subject of the oaths – the consequences of the purification or the corruption of the soul – is of unique and fundamental importance. And God wants to really emphasize its pivotal position in the fate of man, and the fact that this fate lies in man's owns hands. Q74:38 states:

كُلُّ نَفْسٍ بِمَا كَسَبَتْ رَهِينَةٌ

Every soul will be held in pledge for what it has earned.

9-10.2 The human being is a combination of both physical and spiritual bodies. Just as the physical body of man has states and signs of health and illness, cleanliness and pollution, development and decay, and life and death, so does his spiritual body. The physiological and psychological processes of the body, such as heart-rate, blood pressure, chemical balances, and so on have to be within certain limits for the body to function correctly. In the same way, the faculties of the soul also have to be maintained within certain parameters to perform their true function.[40]

9-10.3 The connection of the oaths to their subject, and the reason that God has mentioned the wonders of the outer and inner world of the human being, is to emphasise that all of this has been placed at man's disposal to help his soul to flourish and prosper, if he was to keep it pure and safeguard it from pollution.[41]

9-10.4 *'The one who purifies it has succeeded.'*: This verse is the first subject and reply to the eleven oaths that preceded it.

[*Zakkāhā* (زَكَّاهَا, purified it)] is derived from *zakā* and *tazkiyah*, meaning growth, purification, and development.[42]

[*Aflaḥa* (أَفْلَحَ, he succeeded)] is derived from *falāḥ*, meaning success, and achieving one's objective.[43]

---

[40] Muṭahharī, (*Āshnāyī bā Qur'an*), *Āthār*, 28/570.

[41] Shīrāzī, *Namūneh*, 27/47.

[42] Rāghib, *al-Mufradāt*.

[43] Muṣṭafawī, al-*Taḥqīq*.

Following the *sharīʿah* purifies the soul and allows the voice of the *fiṭrah* to be heard more clearly. And this leads to success.

Q24:51 states:

إِنَّمَا كَانَ قَوْلَ الْمُؤْمِنِينَ إِذَا دُعُوا إِلَى اللَّهِ وَرَسُولِهِ لِيَحْكُمَ بَيْنَهُمْ
أَنْ يَقُولُوا سَمِعْنَا وَأَطَعْنَا وَأُولَٰئِكَ هُمُ الْمُفْلِحُونَ

The only reply of the [true] believers when they are called to God and His Messenger to judge between them is that they say, "We hear, and we obey." And those are the successful.

By staying loyal to the knowledge it holds, the soul has the potential to rise above the angels, and closer to God, the Exalted, which no other creature possesses. However, when it chooses to ignore its true nature, the same soul can descend to a state worse than the animals.[44]

9-10.5 '*And the one who corrupts it has failed.*': This verse is the second reply to the eleven oaths.

[*Khāba* (خَابَ, failed)] is derived from *khaybah* meaning disappointment and failure to realize one's objective, and is the opposite of *aflaḥa*.[45]

[*Dassāhā* (دَسَّاهَا, corrupted it)]. *Dassā*, originally *dassasa*, is derived from *dasasa* meaning to bury or insert something foreign into an original thing, and thereby corrupt it.[46] The term has been used in the mention of the atrocious deed of the pagan Arabs who buried their baby daughters alive; Q16:59 states:

أَيُمْسِكُهُ عَلَىٰ هُونٍ أَمْ يَدُسُّهُ فِي التُّرَابِ

Should he keep it (the female infant) in humiliation or bury it (yadussuhu) *into the earth?...*

Since *dassā* in the verse under discussion has been contrasted to *tazkiyah*, it refers to when an individual inserts damaging disobedience into the soul, or nurtures it in a manner that stunts its growth.[47]

---

[44] Shīrāzī, *Namūneh*, 27/47.

[45] Ibid, 27/48.

[46] Muṭahharī, (*Āshnāyī bā Qur'an*), *Āthār*, 28/577.

[47] Ṭabāṭabā'ī, *al-Mīzān*, 20/298.

In explaining these verses, a tradition states that Imam al-Sadiq (a) said, "God has clearly defined for the soul what it should go towards and what it should avoid."[48]

SUMMARY OF THE VERSES

After the statement that the soul can discern what is wrong for it and what is right, these verses mention the main message of the chapter: success lies in purifying the soul and allowing it to flourish, while failure lies in corrupting it and letting it decay.

REFLECTIVE LEARNING

A tradition from Imam al-Sadiq (a) states: The one who obeys God shall succeed and the one who disobeys Him shall fail.[49] Therefore, the obedience of God causes purification of the soul, while His disobedience leads to its corruption.

Let me reflect on the level of purity of my soul by analysing the level of my obedience and disobedience to God.

Let me think of adopting at least one constant action that will increase its purity.

VERSES 11 - 14

كَذَّبَتْ ثَمُودُ بِطَغْوَاهَا ﴿١١﴾ إِذِ انْبَعَثَ أَشْقَاهَا ﴿١٢﴾ فَقَالَ لَهُمْ رَسُولُ اللَّهِ نَاقَةَ اللَّهِ وَسُقْيَاهَا ﴿١٣﴾ فَكَذَّبُوهُ فَعَقَرُوهَا فَدَمْدَمَ عَلَيْهِمْ رَبُّهُمْ بِذَنْبِهِمْ فَسَوَّاهَا ﴿١٤﴾

[The people of] Thamud belied [the truth] in their transgression, [11] *when the most wretched of them was sent forth [to kill the she-camel].* [12] *And the Messenger of God (Salih) said to them, "It is the she-camel of God, so let her drink!"* [13] *But they rejected him, and they hamstrung her. So their Lord crushed them for their sin and levelled them [to the ground].* [14]

---

[48] Kulaynī, *al-Kāfī*, 1/163.

عَنِ الصَّادِقِ (عَلَيْهِ السَّلَامُ) – قَالَ: «فَأَلْهَمَهَا فُجُورَهَا وَتَقْوَاهَا» بَيَّنَ لَهَا مَا تَأْتِي وَمَا تَتْرُكُ.

[49] Ṭabrasī, *al-Bayān*, 10/755.

عَنِ الصَّادِقِ (عَلَيْهِ السَّلَامُ) – قَدْ أَفْلَحَ مَنْ أَطَاعَ وَقَدْ خَابَ مَنْ عَصَى.

11-14.1 The verses now turn to the example of Thamud, a nation of people who had corrupted their souls. As a consequence, they became rebellious and defied God and His Prophet (a).

11-14.2 Thamud was an Arab community of idolaters who lived near the Red Sea in an area called Wadi al-Qurā or al-Ḥijr, between Madina and Sham.[50] They lived before Prophet Ibrahim (a), and most details of their civilization have been lost. However, through information preserved in the Qur'an and narrations, we can get some idea about this community.

11-14.3 The reason why the people of Thamud have been cited may be because their historical ruins were extant, and the people of Makka passed by them on their trade journeys to Syria. The frequency with which this tribe is mentioned in pre-Islamic poetry shows that its destruction was a common subject of discussion among the Arabs.[51]

11-14.4 The rest of the chapter gives some details of the defiance and transgression of the people of Thamud, even after they had witnessed a miracle from God. They used to carve their dwellings from the mountain out of lifeless stone. God brought out a living she-camel from the same mountain.

11-14.5 Earlier in the chapter, the address was to individuals to purify their souls and avoid corrupting them. Now the example of the collapse of a whole community is mentioned. This shows that the fate of nations depends on the attitude of its citizens, who collectively influence its destiny, towards success or failure.

11-14.6 '*Thamud belied [the truth] in their transgression.*': [*Ṭaghwāhā* (طَغْوَاهَا, their transgression)]. *Ṭaghwā* is identical to *ṭughyān*, which means transgressing bounds, being unjust, and behaving inordinately.[52] The particle *bi* is to show that the belying of the people was manifested in their transgression and defiance before Prophet Salih (a) who was sent by God to guide them.[53]

11-14.7 According to one meaning however, *ṭaghwā* is the name of a particular punishment, and so the verse means that the people of Thamud belied the punishment (*ṭaghwā*) that was promised; they

---

[50] Ṭabarī, *Tārīkh*, 1/226.

[51] Ibid, 1/232.

[52] Rāghib, *al-Mufradāt*.

[53] Ṭabāṭabā'ī, *al-Mīzān*, 20/399.

did not believe that anything could happen to them even if they continued in their defiance.[54] And this is the situation of many disbelievers in the world.

11-14.8 '*When the most wretched of them was sent forth [to kill the she-camel].*': [*Idh* (إِذْ, when)] is a reference to the evidence of their transgression that was mentioned in the previous verse, and means '*they transgressed, when the most wretched of them was sent forth [to kill the she-camel].*' The name of this wretched individual is reported to be Qaddār b. Sālif.[55]

[*Inbaʿatha* (انبَعَثَ, was sent forth)] is derived from *baʿatha*, which means to send or to resurrect. Here, it means they collectively delegated and despatched.[56] This verse gives an example of the height of their defiance and transgression. The worst among them (*ashqā*, most wretched) rose to kill the she-camel who had been sent as a wondrous miracle to convince the people of Thamud of the truth of the claim of Prophet Salih (a).

The tribal leaders incited this man to kill the she-camel. Such individuals exist in every society, ready to commit the most heinous crimes at the behest of their masters. They are men of evil, with no compunction and no fear of God.

11-14.9 The Prophet (s) asked Imam Ali (a), "Who is the most wretched of the early generation?" He replied, "The one who hamstrung the camel of Salih (a)." The Prophet (s) said, "You are right. But who shall be the most wretched in the later generations?" Ali (a) replied, "I do not know." The Prophet (s) then said, "He will be the one who strikes you here", and he pointed at the crown of his head.[57]

11-14.10 The next two verses mention the people's response to the request of Salih (a) not to disturb the she-camel, which was God's sign to them, and allow her to drink. Q11:64 states that Salih (a) said to them:

وَيَا قَوْمِ هَٰذِهِ نَاقَةُ اللهِ لَكُمْ آيَةً

---

[54] Ṭabrasī, *al-Bayān*, 10/756.

[55] Ṭabāṭabā'ī, *al-Mīzān*, 20/299.

[56] Muṭahharī, (*Āshnāyī bā Qur'an*), *Āthār*, 28/583.

[57] Majlisī, *Biḥār*, 11/376.

عَنِ الرَّسُولِ (صَلَّى اللهُ عَلَيْهِ وَآلِهِ) - قَالَ لِعَلِيِّ ابْنِ أَبِي طَالِبٍ (عَلَيْهِ السَّلَامُ)، مَنْ أَشْقَى الْأَوَّلِينَ؟ قَالَ: عَاقِرُ النَّاقَةِ، قَالَ: صَدَقْتَ فَمَنْ أَشْقَى الْآخِرِينَ؟ قَالَ: قُلْتُ لَا أَعْلَمُ يَا رَسُولَ اللهِ، قَالَ: الَّذِي يَضْرِبُكَ عَلَى هَذِهِ، وَشَارَ إِلَى يَافُوخِهِ.

And O my people! This is the she-camel of God –
[she is] a sign for you...

11-14.11 '*And the Messenger of God said to them, "It is the she-camel of God, so let her drink!*': Here, the Messenger of God refers to Prophet Salih (a), who preached God's message to the people of Thamud for over a hundred years, yet most of them remained obstinate in their disbelief.

[*Nāqatallāh* (نَاقَةَ اللَّهِ, the she-camel of God)]. The attribution of the camel to God is an indication of the miraculous nature of this animal. It is also a warning to the people of its sanctity.

[*Suqyā* (سُقْيَا, drinking water)] refers to the water of the town.

Therefore, the verse means, 'Be mindful of the she-camel of God and do not prevent it from drinking as it pleases.'[58]

11-14.12 '*But they rejected him, and they hamstrung her.*': Instead of being in awe of the animal and treating it with the respect that Salih (a) had asked for, they impugned him, and killed the she-camel.

[*ʿAqarūhā* (عَقَرُوهَا, they hamstrung her)]. The verb is derived from *ʿuqr*, meaning the root or origin of something.[59] When used for a camel, *ʿaqara* means to cut the tendons behind its knees to incapacitate it, and then slaughter it.

The verb is used in the plural, although only one man carried out the act. That is because many people from Thamud had a role to play in this shameful deed.[60]

11-14.13 '*So their Lord crushed them for their sin and levelled them [to the ground].*': As a result of their transgression, the devastating punishment of God descended on all of them. The Qur'an has used different descriptions for the punishment that was sent to Thamud: *ṣayḥah* (loud scream, Q11:67), *ṣāʿiqah* (thunderbolt, Q51:44), and *rajfah* (earthquake, Q7:78). And this is because there was a sequence of devastating events that led to their destruction.

11-14.14 In response to this defiant and callous act, God punished them so that no trace of them remained. [*Damdama* (دَمْدَمَ, crushed)] is derived from *damdamah* which can have several meanings:

58 Ṭabāṭabā'ī, *al-Mīzān*, 20/299.

59 Shīrāzī, *Namūneh*, 27/57.

60 Ibid.

destruction, fitting retribution, pulverizing, uprooting, manifesting wrath, and surrounding and overwhelming.[61] In fact, all these meanings are true for the verse, because the punishment rose from God's wrath, pulverized the people of Thamud, and wiped away every trace of them.[62]

[*Sawwāhā* (سَوَّاهَا, levelled it)]. The verb *sawwā* is used here for the second time in this surah, this time meaning to make level and equal.[63]

The pronoun *hā* in *sawwāḥā* goes back to either the people of Thamud who were destroyed irrespective of the high and low, rich or poor among them. It may also refer to their townships which were levelled to the ground.[64]

11-14.15 The idolaters of Makka persistently asked the Prophet (s) to bring a sign to convince them. However, if such a sign had come to them, they would have found some excuse to reject it, and then the fate of Thamud and other defiant nations would have swept over them as well. However, God had other plans for the nation of His last Messenger (s). Q17:59 states:

وَمَا مَنَعَنَا أَنْ نُرْسِلَ بِالْآيَاتِ إِلَّا أَنْ كَذَّبَ بِهَا الْأَوَّلُونَ

وَآتَيْنَا ثَمُودَ النَّاقَةَ مُبْصِرَةً فَظَلَمُوا بِهَا

And nothing stops Us from sending signs, except that the former nations denied them. And We gave Thamud the she-camel as a clear sign, but they treated her wrongfully...

11-14.16 When an entire community faces the consequences of the acts (good or bad) of a few amongst them, it means that most of them had a role to play in allowing those acts to happen, and overtly or covertly approved of them. In the case of Thamud, the entire community was subject to God's wrath, although the main agitators of mischief were their nine leaders, and the animal was killed by a single person only, Q54:29 states:

فَنَادَوْا صَاحِبَهُمْ فَتَعَاطَىٰ فَعَقَرَ

---

61 Muṣṭafawī, *al-Taḥqīq*.

62 Shīrāzī, *Namūneh*, 27/58.

63 Ṭabāṭabā'ī, *al-Mīzān*, 20/299.

64 Shīrāzī, *Namūneh*, 27/58.

But they called out to their companion,
so he undertook [the task] and hamstrung [her].

DISCUSSION 2: THE PEOPLE OF THAMUD AND PROPHET SALIH (A)

The community of Thamud came after the community of ʿAd – to whom God had sent Prophet Hud (a). They lived near Madina in an area called al-Ḥijr (Hegra),[65] in a place known today as Madāʾin Ṣāliḥ (the cities of Salih). They were an advanced society able to build secure dwellings carved into the mountains in their area. Q7:74 states:

وَاذْكُرُوا إِذْ جَعَلَكُمْ خُلَفَاءَ مِنْ بَعْدِ عَادٍ وَبَوَّأَكُمْ فِي الْأَرْضِ تَتَّخِذُونَ مِنْ سُهُولِهَا
قُصُورًا وَتَنْحِتُونَ الْجِبَالَ بُيُوتًا فَاذْكُرُوا آلَاءَ اللَّهِ وَلَا تَعْثَوْا فِي الْأَرْضِ مُفْسِدِينَ

And remember when He made you the successors of ʿAd and settled you in the land, and [now] you build yourselves palaces in open plains and carve out homes in the mountains. So remember the favours of God [upon you] and refrain from spreading evil and mischief on the earth.

God sent Prophet Salih (a) to guide Thamud out of their idolatry. The town where he was appointed to his mission was run by nine elders who were intent on spreading mischief in the land. Q27:48 states

وَكَانَ فِي الْمَدِينَةِ تِسْعَةُ رَهْطٍ يُفْسِدُونَ فِي الْأَرْضِ وَلَا يُصْلِحُونَ

And there were in the city nine family heads causing corruption and they would not reform.

Prophet Salih (a) came from a well-known and respectable family but the message of monotheism and social reform that he brought was rejected, and the people obstinately refused to listen to anything he had to say. Q11:62 states:

قَالُوا يَا صَالِحُ قَدْ كُنْتَ فِينَا مَرْجُوًّا قَبْلَ هَٰذَا أَتَنْهَانَا أَنْ نَعْبُدَ
مَا يَعْبُدُ آبَاؤُنَا وَإِنَّنَا لَفِي شَكٍّ مِمَّا تَدْعُونَا إِلَيْهِ مُرِيبٍ

They said: O Salih! Before this, you were one in whom we placed hope [to lead us]. Do you forbid us to worship what our fathers

[65] Ṭabarī, *Tārīkh*, 1/216.

worshipped? Indeed, we are in grave doubt about what you are calling us towards.

They insisted on witnessing a miracle before they would believe his claim. They came up with what they considered to be an impossible feat: Salih (a) had to produce a she-camel from the impenetrable wall of a mountain. With God's permission, this wondrous event transpired. Thereafter, Salih (a) instructed them to let the camel wander wherever she wanted and allow her alone to drink water every alternate day. Q26:155,156 state:

قَالَ هَٰذِهِ نَاقَةٌ لَّهَا شِرْبٌ وَلَكُمْ شِرْبُ يَوْمٍ مَّعْلُومٍ ﴿١٥٥﴾
وَلَا تَمَسُّوهَا بِسُوءٍ فَيَأْخُذَكُمْ عَذَابُ يَوْمٍ عَظِيمٍ

He said: Here is a she-camel. For her is a [time to] drink, and for you is a [time to] drink, [each] on a known day. And do not touch her with harm, lest you be seized by the punishment of a terrible day.

On the day when the camel alone was allowed access to the water, she would give the people milk. The situation persisted for a while, but then a group decided to kill the she-camel. They hamstrung her and killed her. Then they turned to Salih (a) in defiance and asked him what he would do now. The Prophet (s) told them that the punishment of God would arrive in three days. Q11:65 states:

فَعَقَرُوهَا فَقَالَ تَمَتَّعُوا فِي دَارِكُمْ ثَلَاثَةَ أَيَّامٍ ذَٰلِكَ وَعْدٌ غَيْرُ مَكْذُوبٍ

But they hamstrung her, and then he said: Enjoy yourselves in your homes for three days [then will be your ruin]! This is a promise that will not be belied.

A report from Imam al-Sadiq (a) states that at this time, God revealed to Salih (a): "Tell the people that if they repent and reform, I will accept their repentance and avert My punishment. But if they do not, then My punishment will arrive on the third day." ... They replied insolently, (as stated in Q7:77): "*O Salih! Bring about [right now] what you threaten us with, if you are indeed a Messenger.*"

Thereafter, Salih (a) informed them that their faces would take on a yellow tinge the next day, red the day after, and black on the third day. And on the third day, Jibra'il descended to their town in the middle of the night. He gave out a great shout that split their eardrums, cleaved their hearts, and tore apart their livers. In an instant every one of them, young and old, died. The scream (*ṣayḥah*) was accompanied by bolts of fire, which burned them all...[66] as Q11:67 states:

وَأَخَذَ الَّذِينَ ظَلَمُوا الصَّيْحَةُ فَأَصْبَحُوا فِي دِيَارِهِمْ جَاثِمِينَ

And the Blast overtook the wrong doers,
so they became motionless bodies in their homes.

Q41:18 states that only Salih (a) and his followers were spared this dreadful fate:

وَنَجَّيْنَا الَّذِينَ آمَنُوا وَكَانُوا يَتَّقُونَ

And We saved those who believed and were God-wary.

SUMMARY OF THE VERSES

In summary, these verses describe the transgression of the nation of Thamud. They belied the truth when it was presented to them and plotted to kill the she-camel that was God's sign to them.

Despite the pleas of their Prophet (a), who asked them to allow her to drink on alternate days, they hamstrung and killed her.

For their defiance, God destroyed them and left their civilization in ruins.

REFLECTIVE LEARNING

A tradition from Imam Ali (a) states: Indeed, people are grouped together according to their agreement or resistance [to any act]. Indeed, the she-camel of Thamud was killed by just a single person, but God, the Almighty, punished them all because they were all complicit in the act. That is why God mentions them [collectively] in Q26:157 which states, '*But they hamstrung her...*'[67]

---

[66] Kulaynī, *al-Kāfī*, 8/188.

عَنِ الصَّادِقِ (عَلَيْهِ السَّلَامُ) – فَقُلْ لَهُمْ إِنْ هُمْ تَابُوا وَرَجَعُوا قَبِلْتُ تَوْبَتَهُمْ وَصَدَدْتُ عَنْهُمْ وَإِنْ هُمْ لَمْ يَتُوبُوا وَلَمْ يَرْجِعُوا بَعَثْتُ عَلَيْهِمْ عَذَابِي فِي الْيَوْمِ الثَّالِثِ.

قَالُوا:«يَا صَالِحُ ٱئْتِنَا بِمَا تَعِدُنَا إِنْ كُنتَ مِنَ الْمُرْسَلِينَ.»

قَالَ يَا قَوْمِ إِنَّكُمْ تُصْبِحُونَ غَدًا وَوُجُوهُكُمْ مُصْفَرَّةٌ وَالْيَوْمَ الثَّانِي وُجُوهُكُمْ مُحْمَرَّةٌ وَالْيَوْمَ الثَّالِثَ وُجُوهُكُمْ مُسْوَدَّةٌ.

فَلَمَّا كَانَ نِصْفُ اللَّيْلِ أَتَاهُمْ جَبْرَائِيلُ عَلَيْهِ السَّلَامُ فَصَرَخَ بِهِمْ صَرْخَةً خَرَقَتْ تِلْكَ الصَّرْخَةُ أَسْمَاعَهُمْ وَفَلَقَتْ قُلُوبَهُمْ وَصَدَعَتْ أَكْبَادَهُمْ، فَمَاتُوا أَجْمَعُونَ فِي طَرْفَةِ عَيْنٍ صَغِيرُهُمْ وَكَبِيرُهُمْ، ثُمَّ أَرْسَلَ اللهُ عَلَيْهِمْ مَعَ الصَّيْحَةِ النَّارَ مِنَ السَّمَاءِ فَأَحْرَقَتْهُمْ أَجْمَعِينَ.

[67] *Nahj al-Balāghah*, sermon 201.

إِنَّمَا يَجْمَعُ النَّاسَ الرِّضَى وَالسَّخَطَ، وَإِنَّمَا عَقَرَ نَاقَةَ ثَمُودَ رَجُلٌ وَاحِدٌ فَعَمَّهُمُ اللهُ تَعَالَى بِالْعَذَابِ لَمَّا عَمُّوهُ بِالرِّضَى، فَقَالَ

Realizing that I will be included in God's wrath even if I do not carry out the acts of disobedience myself, let me reflect on whether I allow God to be disobeyed in my presence. Am I indifferent to it, or do I attempt to stop it?

VERSE 15

وَلَا يَخَافُ عُقْبَاهَا ﴿١٥﴾

And He does not fear the consequences thereof. [15]

15.1 [*ʿUqbāhā* (عُقْبَاهَا, its consequences)]: *ʿUqbā* means the ultimate end or outcome of something. The pronoun *ha* refers to the dreadful chastisement of pounding (*damdama*), or levelling (*sawwā*), that was visited on the people of Thamud.[68]

15.2 God does not fear the consequences or blame for the destruction of Thamud in the manner that kings would fear retribution from their enemies. And this is because God is completely aware of the consequences of His punishment. His Power cannot be resisted, His judgement is more just and wise than any judgement, and His will is absolute.[69]

15.3 Man, on the other hand, must always be mindful and concerned about the consequences of his actions. And this concern will remain strong in his mind as long as he strives to keep his soul pure and does not corrupt it. Q21:23 warns:

لَا يُسْأَلُ عَمَّا يَفْعَلُ وَهُمْ يُسْأَلُونَ

He is not questioned about what He does, but they will be questioned.

DISCUSSION 3: WHY ARE CHILDREN KILLED WHEN GOD'S PUNISHMENT DESCENDS ON A COMMUNITY?

The blanket punishments visited on nations such as Thamud did not spare anyone except the believers. However, in addition to the guilty, innocent children were also consumed in the punishment and this raises a question as to why God would allow this.

سُبْحَانَهُ: «فَعَقَرُوهَا فَأَصْبَحُوا نَادِمِينَ».

[68] Ṭabāṭabā'ī, *al-Mīzān*, 20/299.

[69] Ibid.

One reason is that the children, who were indeed innocent, would have no life once their parents were destroyed. God in His mercy, took them into His care in *barzakh*, where their souls could mature. In this way they are raised and prepared for Paradise.

A tradition narrated by Ibn ʿAbbas states: ʿUzayr (a) said [to God], "My Lord! I have studied all Your acts and their details and understood Your justice through my intellect, except for one instance. I do not understand why, when You punish a guilty community, your chastisement is so extensive that it encompasses the children amongst them?" [In response,] He was told, "O ʿUzayr! When a community become deserving of My punishment, I schedule its descent once the allotted lifespans of these children is complete. They die because they were meant to, while the people are destroyed because of My punishment."[70]

SUMMARY OF THE VERSE

The verse states plainly that God is not afraid of the consequence of His destruction of Thamud.

REFLECTIVE LEARNING

Every act of God is based on His perfect wisdom and power; therefore, He is the only entity Who can have no fear of the consequences of His actions.

Knowing that my own wisdom and power is limited, and disobeying God will be to my detriment, let me reflect on why I do not fear the consequences of my actions when I disobey God.

---

[70] Rāwandī, *Qaṣaṣ al-Anbiyā*ʾ, 1/240.

قَالَ عُزَيْرٌ يَا رَبِّ إِنِّي نَظَرْتُ فِي جَمِيعِ أُمُورِكَ وَأَحْكَامِهَا فَعَرَفْتُ عَدْلَكَ بِعَقْلِي، وَبَقِيَ بَابٌ لَمْ أَعْرِفْهُ إِنَّكَ تَسْخَطُ عَلَى أَهْلِ الْبَلِيَّةِ فَتَعُمُّهُمْ بِعَذَابِكَ وَفِيهِمُ الْأَطْفَالُ، فَأَمَرَهُ اللهُ تَعَالَى أَنْ يَخْرُجَ إِلَى الْبَرِّيَّةِ، وَكَانَ الْحَرُّ شَدِيدًا فَرَأَى شَجَرَةً فَاسْتَظَلَّ بِهَا وَنَامَ، فَجَاءَتْ نَمْلَةٌ فَقَرَصَتْهُ فَدَلَكَ الْأَرْضَ بِرِجْلِهِ فَقَتَلَ مِنَ النَّمْلِ كَثِيرًا، فَعَرَفَ أَنَّهُ مَثَلٌ ضُرِبَ. فَقِيلَ لَهُ يَا عُزَيْرُ إِنَّ الْقَوْمَ إِذَا اسْتَحَقُّوا عَذَابِي قَدَّرْتُ نُزُولَهُ عِنْدَ انْقِضَاءِ آجَالِ الْأَطْفَالِ فَمَاتَ أُولَئِكَ بِآجَالِهِمْ وَهَلَكَ هَؤُلَاءِ بِعَذَابِي.

SURAT AL-LAYL
THE NIGHT (92)

TEXT AND TRANSLATION

سُورَةُ اللَّيْلِ

بِسْمِ اللهِ الرَّحْمٰنِ الرَّحِيمِ

وَاللَّيْلِ إِذَا يَغْشَىٰ ﴿١﴾ وَالنَّهَارِ إِذَا تَجَلَّىٰ ﴿٢﴾ وَمَا خَلَقَ الذَّكَرَ وَالْأُنْثَىٰ ﴿٣﴾ إِنَّ سَعْيَكُمْ
لَشَتَّىٰ ﴿٤﴾ فَأَمَّا مَنْ أَعْطَىٰ وَاتَّقَىٰ ﴿٥﴾ وَصَدَّقَ بِالْحُسْنَىٰ ﴿٦﴾ فَسَنُيَسِّرُهُ لِلْيُسْرَىٰ
﴿٧﴾ وَأَمَّا مَنْ بَخِلَ وَاسْتَغْنَىٰ ﴿٨﴾ وَكَذَّبَ بِالْحُسْنَىٰ ﴿٩﴾ فَسَنُيَسِّرُهُ لِلْعُسْرَىٰ ﴿١٠﴾
وَمَا يُغْنِي عَنْهُ مَالُهُ إِذَا تَرَدَّىٰ ﴿١١﴾ إِنَّ عَلَيْنَا لَلْهُدَىٰ ﴿١٢﴾ وَإِنَّ لَنَا لَلْآخِرَةَ وَالْأُولَىٰ
﴿١٣﴾ فَأَنْذَرْتُكُمْ نَارًا تَلَظَّىٰ ﴿١٤﴾ لَا يَصْلَاهَا إِلَّا الْأَشْقَى ﴿١٥﴾ الَّذِي كَذَّبَ
وَتَوَلَّىٰ ﴿١٦﴾ وَسَيُجَنَّبُهَا الْأَتْقَى ﴿١٧﴾ الَّذِي يُؤْتِي مَالَهُ يَتَزَكَّىٰ ﴿١٨﴾ وَمَا لِأَحَدٍ
عِنْدَهُ مِنْ نِعْمَةٍ تُجْزَىٰ ﴿١٩﴾ إِلَّا ابْتِغَاءَ وَجْهِ رَبِّهِ الْأَعْلَىٰ ﴿٢٠﴾ وَلَسَوْفَ يَرْضَىٰ ﴿٢١﴾

In the name of God, the Beneficent, the Merciful.

By the night when it covers. [1] *And by the day when it appears.* [2] *And by He who created the male and the female.* [3] *Indeed, your efforts are diverse.* [4] *So, as for the one who gives [in charity] and is God-wary [in carrying out his duties],* [5] *and verifies the best [by his conduct],* [6] *We shall make easy for him the path to ease.* [7] *And as for the one who is miserly and seeks to be self-sufficient,* [8] *and belies the best [by his conduct],* [9] *We shall make easy for him the path to hardship.* [10] *And his wealth will not avail him when he falls.* [11] *Indeed, guidance is [incumbent] upon Us.* [12] *And indeed, to Us belongs the Hereafter and the Former (present day).* [13] *So, I have warned you [all] of a blazing fire.* [14] *Only the most wretched shall burn in it.* [15] *The one who denies [the truth] and turns away.* [16] *But the God-wary shall be far-removed from it.* [17] *The one who spends his wealth to purify [his soul].* [18] *And not [giving] for anyone who has [done him] a favour to be rewarded.* [19]

Only seeking the Face of his Lord, the most-High. [20] *And indeed, he will soon be pleased [with Paradise].* [21].

INTRODUCTION

Surat al-Layl (92) was the 9th chapter to be revealed.[1] It has twenty-one verses and was revealed in Makka, after Surat al-Aʿlā (87). It is named after the oath made by the night (*al-layl*) in the first verse.

Several exegetes have mentioned the story of the date tree purchased by a companion by the name of Abu Dahdah, as the occasion of the revelation of this surah. This is unlikely because the report is not reliable and, secondly, the episode of the date tree allegedly happened in Madina, while this is a Makkan surah. Additionally, its verses are general in nature and not specifically addressed to any individual.[2]

In any case, we will briefly mention the event of the date tree because it is famously reported in many commentaries.[3] This event occurred in the early days of the establishment of the Muslim state in Madina:

There was a man who had a date tree whose branches hung over the house of a poor neighbour who lived with his family. Sometimes when the owner of the tree would go up to gather the dates, some dates would fall into the house of his neighbour and the children would pick them up. At that time, the man would come down from the tree and snatch them back from their hands, and if he found them eating the dates, he would forcibly remove the dates from their mouths. The poor man complained to the Prophet (s) about this treatment...

The Prophet (s) called the owner and said, "Give me that tree and I will give you a tree in Paradise in exchange." The man refused, saying that out of all his trees, this one gave the most succulent fruit. Someone who heard this exchange asked the Prophet (s) if he would give him the same offer if he purchased the tree from the owner. The Prophet (s) said that he would.

In short, the man bought the tree for the exorbitant price of forty other trees, and then presented it to the Prophet (s), who gifted it to the needy neighbour. At this time Surat al-Layl was said to be revealed.

---

1 Maʿrifat, *ʿUlūm-i Qurʾānī*, p. 90.

2 Ṭayyib, *Aṭyāb al-Bayān*, 14/139.

3 Ṭabrasī, *al-Bayān*, 10/759.

Beginning with three oaths, the chapter warns man to set correct priorities in his striving in this world with an emphasis on his attitude about the blessings that have been bestowed on him by God.

It contrasts those who share their bounties in God's way based on their God-wariness (*taqwā*), and thereby manifest their belief in God's promise, with those who are miserly in a futile attempt to become needless of God, and who thereby belie God's promise.

The verses do not specify what a generous person gives, and what a miserly person withholds; this allows for a broader application encouraging a believer to personalize the message.

Thereafter, God reminds mankind that He has not been remiss in guiding them, and for those who choose to ignore this guidance and turn away, the chastisement of hellfire awaits. As for the one who is faithful and spends his wealth seeking only God's pleasure, Paradise shall be his abode.

LINK TO THE PREVIOUS CHAPTER

In the previous chapter, Surat al-Shams, God takes an oath by the day followed by an oath by the night. This chapter also has the oaths by the day and night, except that the order is reversed.

In Surat al-Shams, God narrated in the third person what happened to a previous nation (Thamud) that transgressed. In Surat al-Layl, the address is now to the reader directly, '*So, I have warned you (all) of a blazing fire.*'

Surat al-Shams mentioned the importance of purifying the soul and not corrupting it. Surat al-Layl mentions how this is done: '*So, as for the one who gives [in charity] and is God-wary*' contrasted with, '*And as for the one who is miserly and seeks to be self-sufficient*'.

In both chapters, the most wretched of individuals (*al-ashqā*) is mentioned. In Surat al-Shams, he is the one mean-spirited enough to kill the she-camel of God. In Surat al-Layl, the fate of such wretched beings is mentioned, '*...a blazing fire. Only the most wretched shall enter it.*'

MERITS OF RECITATION

- A tradition from the Prophet (s) states: Whoever recites Surat al-Layl [and acts on its message] shall be granted [bounties] by God until he is satisfied. He will rescue him from hardships and delight him with ease.[4]
- Another tradition from the Prophet (s) states: Whoever recites Surat al-Layl will be made self-sufficient by God through His bounty. Whoever recites it fifteen times before he goes to sleep will not see anything except goodness in his dreams and will not see anything unpleasant. Whoever recites this surah in the night prayer (*al-ʿishāʾ*) is like the one who has recited one-quarter of the Qurʾan and [furthermore,] his prayer is accepted.[5]

EXEGESIS

VERSES 1 - 4

وَاللَّيْلِ إِذَا يَغْشَىٰ ﴿١﴾ وَالنَّهَارِ إِذَا تَجَلَّىٰ ﴿٢﴾ وَمَا خَلَقَ الذَّكَرَ وَالْأُنْثَىٰ ﴿٣﴾ إِنَّ
سَعْيَكُمْ لَشَتَّىٰ ﴿٤﴾

By the night when it covers. [1] *And by the day when it appears.* [2] *And by He who created the male and the female.* [3] *Indeed, your efforts are diverse.* [4]

1-4.1 The chapter begins with three oaths by employing the *waw al-qasam*: the night when it blankets the day, the day when it appears again, and the Creator of the two genders, male and female. The first two oaths are similar to the oaths that were made in the previous chapter, Surat al-Shams, with the difference that here, the mention of the night precedes the mention of the day.

Perhaps the change in order of night and day in the adjoining chapters is for man to ponder on the wisdom and blessing of the

---

4 Kafʿamī, *al-Miṣbāh*, p. 451.

عَنِ الرَّسُولِ (صَلَّى اللهُ عَلَيْهِ وَآلِهِ) - مَنْ قَرَأَهَا أَعْطَاهُ اللهُ حَتَّى يَرْضَى، وَعَافَاهُ مِنَ الْعُسْرِ، وَيَسَّرَ لَهُ الْيُسْرَ.

5 Baḥrānī, *al-Burhān*, 5/675.

عَنِ الرَّسُولِ (صَلَّى اللهُ عَلَيْهِ وَآلِهِ) - مَنْ قَرَأَ هَذِهِ السُّورَةَ أَغْنَاهُ اللهُ مِنْ فَضْلِهِ، وَمَنْ قَرَأَهَا قَبْلَ أَنْ يَنَامَ خَمْسَ عَشْرَةَ مَرَّةً، لَمْ يَرَ فِي مَنَامِهِ إِلَّا مَا يُحِبُّ مِنَ الْخَيْرِ وَلَا يَرَى فِي مَنَامِهِ سُوءًا، وَمَنْ صَلَّى بِهَا فِي الْعِشَاءِ الْآخِرَةِ كَأَنَّمَا صَلَّى بِرُبْعِ الْقُرْآنِ وَقُبِلَتْ صَلَاتُهُ.

alternation of day and night, light and darkness. Both phenomena play a vital role, in their own way, in the life of mankind and every creature on earth.[6]

1-4.2 '*By the night when it covers.*': [*Yaghshā* (يَغْشَىٰ, it covers)] is derived from *ghashiya*, which means to cover or overcome. Although the object of the covering is not mentioned, the verse is referring to the night concealing the sun and drawing its cloak of darkness over the day.

1-4.3 '*And by the day when it appears.*': [*Tajallā* (تَجَلَّىٰ, appears)] is derived from *jalā*, which means to cast light, to manifest and to make clear.[7] Here it refers to the emergence of daylight, which dispels the dark-ness of night.

1-4.4 '*And by He who created the male and the female.*': *Mā* (What) here is used instead of *man* (Who), and is referring to God, the Creator. *Mā* may have been used to denote wonderment or to indicate God's Essence, which is unknowable.[8] And so God swears by Himself, who created everything in pairs, male and female.

Alternatively, it could be considered as *mā al-maṣdariyyah* (gerundival *mā*), which renders the verb that follows it into a verbal noun. In this case, the meaning would be, 'and by the [wondrous] creation of the male and female.'[9]

1-4.5 [*Al-Dhakara wa al-unthā* (الذَّكَرَ وَالْأُنثَىٰ, the male and the female)]. In the system of God's creation, almost every species has two genders, the male and the female, through which the propagation of the species occurs.

Since an oath is made here, the verse probably refers to the human species, who possess a unique soul that makes them the most noble of all creatures (*ashraf al-makhlūqāt*).[10]

Just as the night and the day are different yet complementary, so are the male and the female. God's system is designed in a manner that everything has an opposite and matching pair; each gender

---

[6] Muṭahharī, (*Āshnāyī bā Qur'an*), *Āthār*, 28/585.

[7] Muṣṭafawī, *al-Taḥqīq*.

[8] Shīrāzī, *Namūneh*, 27/72.

[9] Mughniyyah, *al-Kāshif*, 7/573.

[10] Rāzī, *Mafātīḥ al-Ghayb*, 31/182.

has its own qualities and duties, and together they can attain a balance and harmony that cannot be achieved alone.

1-4.6 Therefore, the first two oaths are made by the alternating days and nights that mark the passage of man's earthly life. They are to do with the environment in which God's creatures live, while the third oath is to do with the nature of the creatures themselves.[11]

1-4.7 *'Indeed, your efforts are diverse.'*: [*Saʿy*, (سَعْي, effort)] means to travel speedily and also to strive purposefully. Here, it refers to any action that is accomplished with effort and determined intention.[12]

[*Shattā* (شَتَّىٰ, diverse)] (sing. *shatīt*) is derived from *shatt*, meaning to be scattered.[13] Here, it refers to the fact that the motivation and intentions with which different people act, and consequently the value of the results that they achieve, are diverse and varied. Some are believers in God, and others disbelieve in Him. Some commit righteous acts, while others are sinful. Q32:18 states:

أَفَمَنْ كَانَ مُؤْمِنًا كَمَنْ كَانَ فَاسِقًا لَا يَسْتَوُونَ

Then, is the believer (mu'min) *like the one who is defiantly disobedient* (fāsiq)*? They are not equal.*

1-4.8 This verse is the subject (*jawāb*) of the three oaths, and the main message that God is directing us to. The oaths of the Qur'an and the subject of the oaths are always linked. The strivings and activities that individuals, nations, and groups are engaged in vary widely. With respect to their diversity and intent they are as different as the day is from the night, and the male from the female.[14]

SUMMARY OF THE VERSES

In summary, three oaths are taken: by the night, by the day, and by the Creator of the two genders that make up creation, specifically the human race. Thereafter, God states that in this world, people pass their days striving for various objectives for a variety of reasons.

---

[11] Shīrāzī, *Namūneh*, 27/72.

[12] Muṣṭafawī, *al-Taḥqīq*.

[13] Ibid.

[14] Mawdūdī, *Tafhīm al-Qur'an*, 6/360.

REFLECTIVE LEARNING

There is a wide variety in the motivation and intention behind individual behaviour and everyone must decide what his priorities are, and where to focus his striving.[15]

If Muslims act solely for God, their diverse endeavours would not be chaotic; rather, they would all lead to the same goal and thus bring about a unified *ummah.*

Let me reflect on what motivates me – is it wanting to get close to God? If so, does the intention behind all my actions reflect this?

VERSES 5 - 7

فَأَمَّا مَنْ أَعْطَىٰ وَٱتَّقَىٰ ﴿٥﴾ وَصَدَّقَ بِٱلْحُسْنَىٰ ﴿٦﴾ فَسَنُيَسِّرُهُۥ لِلْيُسْرَىٰ ﴿٧﴾

So, as for the one who gives [in charity] and is God-wary [in carrying out his duties], [5] *and verifies the best [by his conduct],* [6] *We shall make easy for him the path to ease.* [7]

5-7.1 In the next several verses of the surah, two broad categories of people are contrasted, and two traits of each are mentioned. The first category is that of the praiseworthy, and consists of those who manifest their faith by action. The Qurʾan describes them as those who have 'verified the best' (*ṣaddaqa biʾl ḥusnā*). Their two dominant traits are that they share their bounties with others and are constantly mindful of God's commandments.

5-7.2 '*So, as for the one who gives [in charity] and is God-wary.*': [*Aʿṭā* (أَعْطَىٰ, he gave)] is derived from *ʿaṭā*, which means to grant or to offer.[16] The object of the giving is not mentioned, allowing us to reflect on what we can give. Here it may refer in general to giving God the right that is due to Him from one's wealth.[17]

However, giving in this verse has not been restricted to wealth only. One can give and share whatever they have: wealth, time, strength,

[15] Shīrāzī, *Namūneh*, 27/72.

[16] Muṣṭafawī, *al-Taḥqīq*.

[17] Ṭabrasī, *al-Bayān*, 10/760.

skills, empathy, joy, and so on. A tradition from Imam al-Sadiq (a) states: I sought Paradise, and I found it in being generous.[18]

However, most exegetes mention that *aʿṭā* refers particularly to spending wealth (*infāq*) to gain God's pleasure, specifically by helping those in need.[19]

5-7.3 Wealth is granted to some and withheld from others by God. Those who have been granted wealth by God are duty-bound to share it with those who have been deprived. Q34:39 states:

قُلْ إِنَّ رَبِّي يَبْسُطُ الرِّزْقَ لِمَنْ يَشَاءُ مِنْ عِبَادِهِ وَيَقْدِرُ لَهُ
وَمَا أَنْفَقْتُمْ مِنْ شَيْءٍ فَهُوَ يُخْلِفُهُ وَهُوَ خَيْرُ الرَّازِقِينَ

Say: Indeed, my Lord extends provision for whom He will from His servants, and restricts it [for others]. And whatever you spend in His cause (anfaqtum), *He will replace it. And He is the best of providers.*

There are also many reports that encourage *infāq* and describe the reward of such action. For example:

A tradition from the Prophet (s) states: Everywhere on the Day of Judgement will be extremely hot, except in the shade enjoyed by the believers; and it will be [the extent of] their charity that provides shade for them.[20]

A tradition from Imam al-Sadiq (a) states: If anyone comes to God having had one of three habits, He will grant him Paradise: *Infāq* in times of hardship, always appearing in good cheer in front of people, and behaving with fairness.[21]

In fact, the enormous reward for charity will be so apparent to an individual the moment he leaves the world that he will regret not spending more: Q63:10 states:

---

[18] Nūrī, *Mustadrak al-Wasāʾil*, 12/173.

عَنْ الصَّادِقُ (عَلَيْهِ السَّلَامُ) - طَلَبْتُ اَلْجَنَّةَ فَوَجَدْتُهَا فِي السَّخَاءِ.

[19] Shīrāzī, *Namūneh*, 27/73.

[20] Kulaynī, *al-Kāfī*, 4/3.

عَنِ الرَّسُولِ (صَلَّى اللهُ عَلَيْهِ وَآلِهِ) - أَرْضُ الْقِيَامَةِ نَارٌ مَا خَلَا ظِلَّ الْمُؤْمِنِ، فَإِنَّ صَدَقَتَهُ تُظِلُّهُ.

[21] Ibid, 2/103.

عَنِ الصَّادِقِ (عَلَيْهِ السَّلَامُ) - ثَلَاثٌ مَنْ أَتَى اللهَ بِوَاحِدَةٍ مِنْهُنَّ أَوْجَبَ اللهُ لَهُ الْجَنَّةَ: الْإِنْفَاقُ مِنْ إِقْتَارٍ، وَالْبِشْرُ لِجَمِيعِ الْعَالَمِ، وَالْإِنْصَافُ مِنْ نَفْسِهِ.

وَأَنْفِقُوا مِنْ مَا رَزَقْنَاكُمْ مِنْ قَبْلِ أَنْ يَأْتِيَ أَحَدَكُمُ الْمَوْتُ فَيَقُولَ رَبِّ لَوْلَا
أَخَّرْتَنِي إِلَىٰ أَجَلٍ قَرِيبٍ فَأَصَّدَّقَ وَأَكُنْ مِنَ الصَّالِحِينَ

And spend from what We have provided you before death comes to one of you and he says: My Lord, if only You would reprieve me for a little while so I would give charity and [thereby] be among the righteous.

5-7.4 [*Ittaqā* (اتَّقَىٰ, was God-wary)]. *Ittaqā* and *taqwā* are derived from *wiqāya*, meaning 'to keep away from evil and harm.'[22] In brief, *taqwā* is faith manifested in practice. It is a term that incorporates fear and awe of God with self-restraint and vigilance regarding the commandments and prohibitions of God.

Taqwā determines the sincerity of intention and correctness with which an action is performed, and that is why it is mentioned as a necessary quality of those who spend in God's way.[23]

5-7.5 '*And verifies the best.*': [*Ṣaddaqa bi'l ḥusnā* (صَدَّقَ بِالْحُسْنَىٰ, verifies the best)]. This phrase means, 'verifies God's promise of the best', referring to the reward that He has promised to those who spend in His way.[24] In practical terms, it is to show by action one's conviction about the best usage of one's bounties. In giving, accompanied by *taqwā*, a person verifies that the best reward he can attain for what he has spent is that which lies with God. For such a person, God makes it easier for him to do further acts of goodness.[25]

A tradition from Imam al-Ridha (a) states: '*And verifies the best*', refers to verifying [by action] that which was promised by God's Messenger (s).[26]

5-7.6 '*We shall make easy for him the path to ease.*': [*Nuyassiruhu* (نُيَسِّرُهُ, *We shall make easy for him*)] is derived from *yassara*, and its verbal noun *taysīr* means to provide and facilitate.[27] The facilitation of the path towards success is what is called *tawfīq* from God.

---

[22] Ibn Manẓūr, *Lisān al-ʿArab*.

[23] Shīrāzī, *Namūneh*, 27/73.

[24] Ṭabāṭabā'ī, *al-Mīzān*, 20/303.

[25] Ṭabrasī, *al-Bayān*, 10/760.

[26] Nūrī, *Mustadrak al-Wasā'il*, 13/363.

عَنِ الرِّضَا (عَلَيْهِ السَّلَامُ) – «وَصَدَّقَ بِالْحُسْنَى» بِوَعْدِ رَسُولِ اللهِ (صَلَّى اللهُ عَلَيْهِ وَآلِهِ).

[27] Ṭabāṭabā'ī, *al-Mīzān*, 20/303.

In a beautiful supplication attributed to Imam al-Mahdi (af) he asks: O God! Grant us success (*tawfīq*) in obedience and [success] in remoteness from sin...[28]

5-7.7 Therefore, whoever possesses the three traits mentioned previously: in action he is giving, in attitude he is God-wary, and by conduct he confirms his belief in the principles of faith, then God will prepare for him ease.

As we mentioned in the *tafsīr* of Surat al-Balad (90), the path towards salvation, *al-ʿaqabah*, is initially steep, but once one begins to traverse it with determination, it gets easier with God's help. In other words, once he is willing to give to others based on *taqwā*, works that are difficult for others become easy for him.[29] Performing the religious obligations and avoiding the prohibitions become easy for such an individual also.

A tradition from Imam al-Baqir (a) states: '*We shall make easy for him the path to ease*' means that he will not seek any goodness except that God will make it easy for him to attain.[30]

SUMMARY OF THE VERSES

In summary, the verses state that the one who gives from what he has, and is mindful of God, proves thereby that he has conviction in God's promise of reward. God eases the path for such individuals.

REFLECTIVE LEARNING

Let me reflect on my attitude regarding all that I possess. Do I believe that it is mine, or do I believe I am merely its custodian?

All of us have a little extra that we can share with others. Let me share what I have with those who need it, in the way of God, to gain His pleasure and the immense reward that is attached to giving.

---

[28] Kafʿamī, *al-Miṣbāh*, p. 280.

عَنْ إِمَامِ الزَّمَانِ (عَجَّلَ اللهُ تَعَالَى فَرَجَهُ) – اَللّٰهُمَّ ارْزُقْنَا تَوْفِيقَ الطَّاعَةِ وَبُعْدَ الْمَعْصِيَةِ.

[29] Muṭahharī, (*Āshnāyī bā Qur'an*), *Āthār*, 28/591.

[30] ʿĀmilī, *Wasā'il*, 9/368.

عَنِ الْبَاقِرِ (عَلَيْهِ السَّلَامُ) – فِي قَوْلِ اللهِ عَزَّ وَجَلَّ «فَسَنُيَسِّرُهُ لِلْيُسْرَىٰ» قَالَ: لَا يُرِيدُ شَيْئًا مِنَ الْخَيْرِ إِلَّا يَسَّرَهُ اللهُ لَهُ.

VERSES 8 - 11

وَأَمَّا مَنْ بَخِلَ وَٱسْتَغْنَىٰ ﴿٨﴾ وَكَذَّبَ بِالْحُسْنَىٰ ﴿٩﴾ فَسَنُيَسِّرُهُ لِلْعُسْرَىٰ ﴿١٠﴾ وَمَا يُغْنِي عَنْهُ مَالُهُ إِذَا تَرَدَّىٰ ﴿١١﴾

And as for the one who is miserly and seeks to be self-sufficient, [8] *and belies the best [by his conduct],* [9] *We shall make easy for him the path to hardship.* [10] *And his wealth will not avail him when he falls.* [11].

8-11.1 This group of verses describe the behaviour of a second group. In contrast to the first group, their dominant traits are miserliness and the false conviction that they can become self-sufficient and needless. Through their actions, they show that they do not believe in the reward that has been promised by God like the previous group. Or they do not believe in the religion and the example of the Prophet (s) and his successors (a).[31]

8-11.2 '*And as for the one who is miserly and seeks to be self-sufficient.*': [*Bakhila* (بَخِلَ, is miserly)]. The term *bukhl* means miserliness and it is a moral malady that is condemned in the Qur'an and in many traditions. It is contrasted against the term *aʿṭā* (to give) in the previous verses, and therefore means 'to withhold'.

The miser, *bakhīl*, is defined as the one who is reluctant to spend what should be spent, and to share what should be shared. He clings to his wealth thinking it will avail him, but God assures him that it will not. Indeed, the true value of wealth is in what it can provide for the Hereafter. Q3:180 states:

وَلَا يَحْسَبَنَّ الَّذِينَ يَبْخَلُونَ بِمَا آتَاهُمُ اللَّهُ مِنْ فَضْلِهِ هُوَ خَيْرًا لَهُمْ بَلْ هُوَ شَرٌّ لَهُمْ سَيُطَوَّقُونَ مَا بَخِلُوا بِهِ يَوْمَ الْقِيَامَةِ

And let not those who are miserly with what God has given them of His bounty think that it is good for them. Rather, it is worse for them. That which they were miserly with shall encircle their necks on the Day of Judgement...

8-11.3 About the miser, a tradition from Imam Ali (a) states: The miser truly surprises me; he hastens towards the very poverty that he

[31] Shīrāzī, *Namūneh*, 27/76.

wants to escape, and misses the very comfort that he longs to have. In this world he lives like the destitute, but in the Hereafter he will be called to account with the wealthy![32]

8-11.4 [*Istaghnā* (اسْتَغْنَىٰ, seeks to become self-sufficient)] is derived from *ghaniya*, which means to be free from want. Some have translated this as, 'considers himself self-sufficient', but a more accurate meaning here would be, 'seeks to become self-sufficient'.[33] This attitude has been used in contrast to the *taqwā* of the previous group. It is the root cause of miserliness, in the same way that the root cause of generosity is *taqwā*, which encourages one to spend in God's way.

8-11.5 A tradition from Imam al-Sadiq (a) states: '*And as for the one who is miserly*' refers to the one who does not pay the one-fifth tax (*khums*), and '*considers himself self-sufficient*' refers to the one who considers himself needless of the guidance of the close servants (*awliyā'*) of God.[34]

8-11.6 '*And belies the best.*': A tradition from Imam al-Baqir (a) states: '*And belies the best*' refers to not believing that God will award between ten and one hundred thousand, or more, rewards for every good act.[35]

8-11.7 '*We shall make easy for him the path to hardship.*' By juxtaposing two apparently opposite terms, the Qur'an eloquently states that such people will be 'easily led to hardship' in this world, because they deprived themselves of the blessings which come from helping others. And then, in the Hereafter, they will be held to account for hoarding. Alternatively, their miserliness will make it difficult for them to sacrifice for God's sake.[36] This is because they have distanced themselves from God's mercy and considered themselves

---

[32] *Nahj al-Balāghah*, short saying 126.

عَنْ أَمِيرِ الْمُؤْمِنِينَ (عَلَيْهِ السَّلَامُ) – عَجِبْتُ لِلْبَخِيلِ يَسْتَعْجِلُ الْفَقْرَ الَّذِي هُوَ مِنْهُ هَرَبَ، وَيَفُوتُهُ الْغِنَى الَّذِي إِيَّاهُ طَلَبَ، فَيَعِيشُ فِي الدُّنْيَا عَيْشَ الْفُقَرَاءِ وَيُحَاسَبُ فِي الْآخِرَةِ حِسَابَ الْأَغْنِيَاءِ.

[33] Ṭabāṭabā'ī, *al-Mīzān*, 20/303; Shīrāzī, *Namūneh*, 27/75.

[34] Nūrī, *Mustadrak al-Wasā'il*, 7/280.

عَنِ الصَّادِقِ (عَلَيْهِ السَّلَامُ) – «وَأَمَّا مَنْ بَخِلَ» بِالْخُمْسِ وَاسْتَغْنَى بِرَأْيِهِ عَنْ أَوْلِيَاءِ اللهِ.

[35] Kulaynī, *al-Kāfī*, 4/46.

عَنِ الْبَاقِرِ (عَلَيْهِ السَّلَامُ) – «وَكَذَّبَ بِالْحُسْنَىٰ» بِأَنَّ اللهَ يُعْطِي بِالْوَاحِدَةِ عَشَرَةً إِلَى مِائَةِ أَلْفٍ فَمَا زَادَ.

[36] Shīrāzī, *Namūneh*, 27/76.

needless of Him. And in the Hereafter, the abiding torment of hellfire awaits them.[37]

A tradition from Imam al-Baqir (a) states: '*We shall make easy for him the path to hardship*' means that he will not seek any evil except that God will make it easy for him to attain.[38]

8-11.8 '*And his wealth will not avail him when he falls.*': This is a reminder that all the wealth in the world is left behind at death,[39] and one continues on his onward journey towards God accompanied by his actions only.

[*Mā* (مَا, will not)]. *Mā* here can either mean 'will not' as explained above, or it can denote a question (what?), in which case the verse would mean, 'And what will his wealth avail him when he falls?'[40] Thus, one should ponder about the real value of the wealth that he has accumulated in the world, which he will leave behind at death.

[*Taraddā* (تَرَدَّى, falls)]. The term is derived from *radiya*, meaning to perish after falling from a height.[41] In the verse under review, *taraddā* refers to the fate of the miser; he cannot use all his wealth to forestall death, or avert his punishment, when he will fall into the fire of Hell.

8-11.9 In this manner, the verses contrast two groups: a group who are believers, whose generosity is coupled with *taqwā*, and a group who do not have faith and cling to their wealth with miserliness, imagining that they are needless of God.

The first group benefits from the *tawfīq* of God and their path towards felicity is made easy. The second group is deprived of this *tawfīq* from God, and faces a life of hardship. They hoard and amass wealth unable to bring themselves to spend it, only to leave it behind for others to consume while they go to meet the wrath of God.

---

37 Ṭabrasī, *al-Bayān*, 10/760.

38 Kulaynī, *al-Kāfī*, 4/47.

عَنِ الْبَاقِرِ (عَلَيْهِ السَّلَامُ) – فِي قَوْلِ اللهِ عَزَّ وَجَلَّ «فَسَنُيَسِّرُهُ لِلْعُسْرَى» قَالَ: لَا يُرِيدُ شَيْئًا مِنَ الشَّرِّ إِلَّا يَسَّرَهُ لَهُ.

39 Ṭabāṭabā'ī, *al-Mīzān*, 20/303.

40 Ṭūsī, *al-Tibyān*, 10/364.

41 Shīrāzī, *Namūneh*, 27/77.

SUMMARY OF THE VERSES

The verses warn the one who withholds his wealth, in an attempt to become needless of God, that he will only face hardship as a result. And all the wealth that he kept from others would not avail him on the Day he would fall into Hell.

REFLECTIVE LEARNING

Miserliness is condemned in this verse.

Let me reflect on how I react when invited to give from what I possess to others. Can I see traces of reluctance and miserliness in myself?

Let me resolve to regularly spend from what I possess in God's way.

VERSES 12, 13

إِنَّ عَلَيْنَا لَلْهُدَىٰ ﴿١٢﴾ وَإِنَّ لَنَا لَلْآخِرَةَ وَالْأُولَىٰ ﴿١٣﴾

Indeed, guidance is [incumbent] upon Us. [12] *And indeed, to Us belongs the Hereafter and the Former (present day).* [13]

12-13.1 *'Indeed, guidance is [incumbent] upon Us.'*: Now the Qurʾan makes the fundamental assertion that guidance has come from God as a necessary consequence of His act of creation. This fact is gratefully acknowledged by the believers when they are admitted to Paradise. Q7:43 quotes their words:

وَقَالُوا الْحَمْدُ لِلَّهِ الَّذِي هَدَانَا لِهَٰذَا وَمَا كُنَّا لِنَهْتَدِيَ لَوْلَا أَنْ هَدَانَا اللَّهُ

...And they shall say: All grateful praise is due to God Who guided us to this. And we would never have been guided [aright] if God had not [constantly] guided us...

12-13.2 Every creature of God possesses existential (*takwīnī*) guidance, like the intellect and instinct. Q20:50 states that when Musa (a) was asked to introduce the Lord, he said:

قَالَ رَبُّنَا الَّذِي أَعْطَىٰ كُلَّ شَيْءٍ خَلْقَهُ ثُمَّ هَدَىٰ

He [Musa] said, "Our Lord is He who gave each thing its form and then guided [it]."

However, in addition to this, man who is a creature with superior potential and possesses free will, is also given further guidance that is legislative (*tashrīʿī*), through scripture and the example of the Prophets (a).

12-13.3 The purpose of the two forms of guidance, existential and legislative, is to lead a person to God and to attain His proximity. Q42:52,53 state:

وَإِنَّكَ لَتَهْدِي إِلَىٰ صِرَاطٍ مُّسْتَقِيمٍ ﴿٥٢﴾ صِرَاطِ اللَّهِ

...And indeed, you [O Muhammad] guide to the straight path, the path of God...

12-13.4 The guidance of God is made accessible to mankind. Q14:1 states:

الر كِتَابٌ أَنزَلْنَاهُ إِلَيْكَ لِتُخْرِجَ النَّاسَ مِنَ الظُّلُمَاتِ إِلَى النُّورِ
بِإِذْنِ رَبِّهِمْ إِلَىٰ صِرَاطِ الْعَزِيزِ الْحَمِيدِ

Alif, Lām, Rā. [This is] a Book which We have revealed to you, [O Muhammad], that you might bring mankind out of darknesses into the light by permission of their Lord to the path of the all-Mighty, the all-Praiseworthy.

However, man is not compelled to accept it. Rather, he is invited to embrace it out of his free will, having recognized the guidance for the mercy that it is.[42]

The burden of guidance is shouldered by God, but the burden of accepting and acting on it is the responsibility of every individual.

12-13.5 *'And indeed, to Us belongs the Hereafter and the Former':* This verse means to say that God is needless of the faith and worship of mankind, because everything already belongs to Him, and His kingdom will not be increased or reduced by the actions of man.[43] If man chooses to accept the guidance, he will benefit only himself.

12-13.6 The Hereafter is mentioned before this world, and the use of the *lām* (ل) in *laʾl ākhirah* is to emphasize the Hereafter. There could be several reasons for this:

---

[42] Shīrāzī, *Namūneh*, 27/79.

[43] Ibid.

i) The life of the Hereafter is more important. It is the final destination of man,[44] and the life that precedes it is only a pale shadow of it.

ii) As a reminder for man that God's dominion and absolute ownership will be truly manifest in the Hereafter.

iii) Perhaps it is also to remind us about the Hereafter,[45] as we tend to forget that which is not right in front of us.

SUMMARY OF THE VERSES

The verses declare that God has made it obligatory on Himself to guide mankind. The onus is on the individual to accept the gift of guidance for his own benefit.

God is needless of man's worship because He owns the entirety of creation, both in this world and the Hereafter.

REFLECTIVE LEARNING

Let me reflect on the internal and external guidance that God has made available for me.

Let me resolve to use both forms in order to consciously seek God's proximity.

VERSES 14 - 16

فَأَنذَرْتُكُمْ نَارًا تَلَظَّىٰ ﴿١٤﴾ لَا يَصْلَاهَا إِلَّا الْأَشْقَى ﴿١٥﴾ الَّذِي كَذَّبَ وَتَوَلَّىٰ ﴿١٦﴾

So, I have warned you [all] of a blazing fire. [14] *Only the most wretched shall burn in it.* [15] *The one who denies [the truth] and turns away.* [16]

14-16.1 These verses speak of the punishment for those who were miserly and belied the goodness promised by God and His Messenger (s). There is a special type of fire that awaits them.

14-16.2 *'So, I have warned You (all) of a blazing fire.'*: [*Talaẓẓā* (تَلَظَّى, blazing)], originally *tatalaẓẓā*, is derived from the verb *laẓā*,

[44] Ibid, 27/80.

[45] Ṭūsī, *al-Tibyān*, 10/365.

meaning to burn, to be aflame. The term *laẓā* has also been used to refer to Hell itself in Q70:15.[46]

14-16.3 The mention of fire in the indefinite sense indicates that this is but one out of many hellfires. However, it does not mean that only disbelievers will enter Hell, and that sinful believers will be spared it. There are other levels of Hell in which other types of criminals, from the believers and disbelievers, will be punished.[47]

14-16.4 *'Only the most wretched shall burn in it.'*: [*Yaṣlā* (يَصْلَاٰ, burns)] is derived from *ṣalā*, meaning to roast and to burn.

[*Ashqā* (الْأَشْقَى, most wretched)] is derived from *shaqiya* which means to be unhappy and miserable.[48] Here, the noun is used in the superlative form, meaning that those who will burn in this particular Hell shall be the most wretched of individuals.

Shaqāwah (wretchedness) is the opposite of *saʿādah* (felicity), which is reaching the ultimate goodness that a creature has the potential for, and in this manner attaining true happiness. In the case of the human being, it is achieving both physical and spiritual perfection, and *shaqāwah* therefore, would mean falling short of the potential one possesses, and being deprived of joy thereby.[49]

14-16.5 *'The one who denies (the truth) and turns away'*: [*Kadhdhabba* (كَذَّبَ, deny) is derived from *kadhaba* which means to lie.

[*Tawallā* (تَوَلَّى, turn away)] is derived from *waliya* which ordinarily means to be near or to be a friend, but *tawallā* can also mean to be averted or to turn away, especially when used with the present, or implied, prepositions *ʿan* or *min* (from).[50] And this is the case in this verse.

14-16.6 Two traits are described for the most wretched (*ashqā*) who will end up in the terrible Hell called *laẓā*: they deny, and they turn away. It is possible that denial here refers to their disbelief (*kufr*) and turning away refers to their persistence in *kufr*, or their refraining from performing righteous acts.[51]

---

[46] Shīrāzī, *Namūneh*, 27/80.

[47] Ṭabrasī, *al-Bayān*, 10/761.

[48] Rāghib, *al-Mufradāt*.

[49] Ṭabāṭabā'ī, *al-Mīzān*, 11/21.

[50] Rāghib, *al-Mufradāt*.

[51] Shīrāzī, *Namūneh*, 27/81.

SUMMARY OF THE VERSES

The verses now warn those who reject God's guidance of the dreadful punishment that awaits them. These people are described as wretched, as they knowingly reject and turn away from what they know to be true.

REFLECTIVE LEARNING

The verses have made clear the fate of those who reject and turn away from clear guidance due to defiance or apathy.

Let me reflect on instances of my own disobedience and seek forgiveness by a complete *tawbā*, consisting of remorse, rectification and resolving not to repeat the sin.

VERSES 17 - 21

وَسَيُجَنَّبُهَا الْأَتْقَى ﴿١٧﴾ الَّذِي يُؤْتِي مَالَهُ يَتَزَكَّىٰ ﴿١٨﴾ وَمَا لِأَحَدٍ عِنْدَهُ مِنْ نِعْمَةٍ
تُجْزَىٰ ﴿١٩﴾ إِلَّا ابْتِغَاءَ وَجْهِ رَبِّهِ الْأَعْلَىٰ ﴿٢٠﴾ وَلَسَوْفَ يَرْضَىٰ ﴿٢١﴾

But the God-wary shall be far-removed from it. [17] *The one who spends his wealth to purify [his soul].* [18] *And not [giving] for anyone who has [done him] a favour to be rewarded.* [19] *Only seeking the Face of his Lord, the most-High.* [20] *And indeed, he will soon be pleased [with Paradise].* [21].

17-21.1 The fate of the wretched group of misers, who imagined themselves needless of God, is now contrasted to the fate of the group that has *taqwā*, and spends generously in God's way.

17-21.2 *'But the God-wary shall be far-removed from it.'*: [*Yujannabuhā* (يُجَنَّبُهَا, shall be far-removed from it)] is derived from *jannaba*, meaning to keep to the side. Its verbal noun, *tajnīb* is hyperbolic, indicating that those who have *taqwā* will not only be spared this terrible hell, in fact, they will be pushed far away from it to complete safety.[52]

52 Ṭūsī, al-*Tibyān*, 10/366.

17-21.3 The verses mention some qualities of those who have *taqwā*:

i) '*The one who spends his wealth to purify.*': They spend in God's way to purify their wealth and their souls from the stain of the love of this world.

[*Yatazakkā* (يَتَزَكَّىٰ, he purifies)] refers to the intention to develop spiritual purity so as to get close to God.[53] This is a result of sincere charity, as mentioned in Q9:103:

خُذْ مِنْ أَمْوَالِهِمْ صَدَقَةً تُطَهِّرُهُمْ وَتُزَكِّيهِمْ بِهَا

Take [O Muhammad] charity from their wealth, in order to cleanse them and purify them thereby...

ii) '*And not [giving] for anyone who has [done him] a favour to be rewarded.*': They do not expect anything from the recipient of their charity, they do not make them feel obligated, and they do not give charity as a reward for a favour received. Such people have been promised that they will never experience fear of grief when they leave this world. Q2:262 assures them:

الَّذِينَ يُنْفِقُونَ أَمْوَالَهُمْ فِي سَبِيلِ اللَّهِ ثُمَّ لَا يُتْبِعُونَ مَا أَنْفَقُوا مَنًّا وَلَا أَذًى
لَهُمْ أَجْرُهُمْ عِنْدَ رَبِّهِمْ وَلَا خَوْفٌ عَلَيْهِمْ وَلَا هُمْ يَحْزَنُونَ

Those who spend their wealth in the way of God and then do not follow up what they have given with reminders or hurt, their reward is with their Lord, and no fear shall come upon them, nor shall they grieve.

iii) '*Only seeking the Face of his Lord, the most-High.*': Their sole concern in spending from their wealth is to attain the pleasure of God. Indeed, they dedicate their lives for this objective. It is such servants that God pleases with the reward of Paradise.

[*Wajh* (وَجْه, countenance, face)]. The *Wajh* of the Lord is used here as a metaphor for His reward and pleasure.[54]

When something is done for '*wajhullāh*' it means that it is fully directed to Him and seeks only His pleasure. This is the case in this verse; instead of saying, 'seeking the Lord', the

[53] Shīrāzī, *Namūneh*, 27/82.

[54] Ṭūsī, *al-Tibyān*, 10/366.

addition of the term *wajh* is for emphasis, meaning that the act is done solely for the pleasure of the Lord.[55]

17-21.4 *'And indeed, he will soon be pleased'*: God guarantees that each person who acts solely for Him will be pleased in this world and in Paradise, without specifying what will cause this pleasure. Indeed, the source of pleasure will be different for every individual according to their understanding (*maʿrifah*).

SUMMARY OF THE VERSES

In summary, these verses reassure the God-wary that they will be far removed from the punishment of hellfire. They are described as those who spend their wealth, not to oblige anyone, but to seek the pleasure of God. And in return, God will make them pleased.

REFLECTIVE LEARNING

Those who have *taqwā* spend their wealth to purify their soul, without obligation or expectation of reward from other than God.

Let me reflect on whether I feel that I have done a favour to those whom I have helped? Do I expect them to thank me or return the favour?

[55] Shīrāzī, *Namūneh*, 27/83.

SURAT AL-ḌUḤĀ
THE FORENOON (93)

TEXT AND TRANSLATION

سُورَةُ الضُّحَى

بِسْمِ اللَّهِ الرَّحْمَٰنِ الرَّحِيمِ

وَالضُّحَىٰ ﴿١﴾ وَاللَّيْلِ إِذَا سَجَىٰ ﴿٢﴾ مَا وَدَّعَكَ رَبُّكَ وَمَا قَلَىٰ ﴿٣﴾ وَلَلْآخِرَةُ خَيْرٌ
لَّكَ مِنَ الْأُولَىٰ ﴿٤﴾ وَلَسَوْفَ يُعْطِيكَ رَبُّكَ فَتَرْضَىٰ ﴿٥﴾ أَلَمْ يَجِدْكَ يَتِيمًا فَآوَىٰ ﴿٦﴾
وَوَجَدَكَ ضَالًّا فَهَدَىٰ ﴿٧﴾ وَوَجَدَكَ عَائِلًا فَأَغْنَىٰ ﴿٨﴾ فَأَمَّا الْيَتِيمَ فَلَا تَقْهَرْ ﴿٩﴾
وَأَمَّا السَّائِلَ فَلَا تَنْهَرْ ﴿١٠﴾ وَأَمَّا بِنِعْمَةِ رَبِّكَ فَحَدِّثْ ﴿١١﴾

In the name of God, the Beneficent, the Merciful.

By the forenoon, [1] *and by the night when it covers with darkness.* [2] *Your Lord has not forsaken you, nor has He become displeased.* [3] *And indeed, what will come after is better for you than that which has gone before.* [4] *And indeed, your Lord will soon give you that [with which] you shall be well pleased.* [5] *Did He not find you an orphan, then give [you] refuge?* [6] *And find you lost, then guide [you]?* [7] *And find you poor, then make you self-sufficient?* [8] *So, as for the orphan, do not oppress [him].* [9] *And as for the beggar, do not repulse [him].* [10] *And as for the favour of your Lord, proclaim [it].* [11].

INTRODUCTION

Surat al-Ḍuḥā (93) was the 11th chapter to be revealed. It has eleven verses and was revealed in Makka, after Surat al-Fajr (89).[1] It is named after the oath by the brightness of the early hours of the morning, the forenoon (*al-ḍuḥā*), mentioned in the first verse.

---

[1] Maʿrifat, *ʿUlūm-i Qurʾānī*, p. 90.

Many reports state that it is linked to the next chapter, Surat al-Inshirāḥ. For example, a tradition from Imam al-Sadiq (a) states: No two chapters should be recited (after Surat al-Ḥamd) in one unit of the obligatory prayers except al-Ḍuḥā and Alam Nashraḥ, and al-Fīl and Quraysh.[2]

It is narrated that after some chapters of the Qur'an were revealed, there was a period of fifteen[3] (or twelve, or forty) days in which no revelation came to the Prophet (s). This occurrence was used by the idolaters to cast doubts on the Prophet (s) and his mission. Umm Jamil, the wife of Abu Lahab, said to him, "O Muhammad! I see that your satan has abandoned you!"[4]

At this time, God revealed this surah to reassure the Prophet (s) and strengthen his heart. When the surah was revealed, the Prophet (s) greeted Jibra'il (a), saying, "I was eagerly awaiting you!" The angel replied, "I was even more eager than you, however I am but a servant, and cannot descend unless God commands it."[5]

The chapter begins with the mention of two oaths, then goes on to reassure the Prophet (s) that God had not abandoned him, and what was yet to come was better than what had transpired so far, and that God would award him something that would certainly please him. Thereafter, God's past favours to the Prophet (s) are recounted, and finally some commandments are issued.

LINK TO THE PREVIOUS CHAPTER

In the previous chapter, Surat al-Layl, the opening verse was an oath by the night followed by an oath by the day. This chapter also begins with oaths by the night and day, except that the order is reversed - as it was in Surat al-Shams as well.

In its last verse, Surat al-Layl mentions that on the Day of Judgement, the servant will be filled with delight as he is rewarded because of his sincere service to God, '*And indeed, he will soon be pleased (with*

---

[2] Majlisī, *Biḥār*, 82/45.

عَنِ الصَّادِقِ (عَلَيْهِ السَّلَامُ) - لَا تَجْمَعْ بَيْنَ سُورَتَيْنِ فِي رَكْعَةٍ وَاحِدَةٍ إِلَّا الضُّحَى وَأَلَمْ نَشْرَحْ وَسُورَةَ الْفِيلِ وَلِإِيلَافِ قُرَيْشٍ.

[3] Ṭabrasī, *al-Bayān*, 10/764.

[4] Rāzī, *Mafātīḥ al-Ghayb*, 31/192.

إِنَّ أُمَّ جَمِيلٍ امْرَأَةَ أَبِي لَهَبٍ قَالَتْ لَهُ: يَا مُحَمَّدُ، مَا أَرَى شَيْطَانَكَ إِلَّا قَدْ تَرَكَكَ.

[5] Ṭabrasī, *al-Bayān*, 10/764.

Paradise).' This chapter similarly talks of the delight of the servant due to God giving His most beloved servant a gift, seeking to delight him, '*And indeed, your Lord will soon give you so that you shall be well pleased.*'

MERITS OF RECITATION

- A tradition from the Prophet (s) states: Whoever recites this surah will be amongst those who have pleased God, and become deserving of the intercession of Muhammad (s). He shall be rewarded ten times the number of every orphan and beggar [in the world].[6]

  Of course, this enormous reward is for the one who recites the surah with understanding and applies its teachings.

- A tradition from Imam al-Sadiq (a) states: For the person who frequently recites the surahs al-Shams, al-Layl, al-Ḍuḥā, and al-Inshirāḥ, in the morning and at night, no part of him will remain except that it will testify on his behalf on the Day of Judgement; even his hair, his skin, his flesh, his blood, his veins, his nerves, his bones, and every part of his body that the earth absorbed of him.

  The Lord, most-Blessed and Exalted, will say: I have accepted your testimony on behalf of My servant and acknowledged it for him. [My angels,] Accompany him to My Paradise, and let him choose whatever abode he likes. I have granted [this to] him not as an obligation, but out of My mercy and grace on him. So congratulations to My servant![7]

EXEGESIS

VERSES 1, 2

وَالضُّحَىٰ ﴿١﴾ وَاللَّيْلِ إِذَا سَجَىٰ ﴿٢﴾

---

[6] Ṭabrasī, *al-Bayān*, 10/762.

عَنِ الرَّسُولِ (صَلَّى اللهُ عَلَيْهِ وَآلِهِ) – مَنْ قَرَأَهَا كَانَ مِمَّنْ يَرْضَاهُ اللهُ، وَلِمُحَمَّدٍ صَلَّى اللهُ عَلَيْهِ وَآلِهِ أَنْ يَشْفَعَ لَهُ وَلَهُ عَشْرُ حَسَنَاتٍ بِعَدَدِ كُلِّ يَتِيمٍ وَسَائِلٍ!

[7] 'Āmilī, *Wasā'il*, 6/258.

عَنِ الصَّادِقِ (عَلَيْهِ السَّلَامُ) – مَنْ أَكْثَرَ قِرَاءَةَ وَالشَّمْسِ، وَاللَّيْلِ إِذَا يَغْشَى، وَالضُّحَى، وَأَلَمْ نَشْرَحْ فِي يَوْمِهِ وَلَيْلَتِهِ، لَمْ يَبْقَ شَيْءٌ بِحَضْرَتِهِ إِلَّا شَهِدَ لَهُ يَوْمَ الْقِيَامَةِ، حَتَّى شَعْرُهُ وَبَشَرُهُ وَلَحْمُهُ وَدَمُهُ وَعُرُوقُهُ وَعَصَبُهُ وَعِظَامُهُ وَجَمِيعُ مَا أَقَلَّتِ الْأَرْضُ مِنْهُ، وَيَقُولُ الرَّبُّ تَبَارَكَ وَتَعَالَى قَبِلْتُ شَهَادَتَكُمْ لِعَبْدِي وَأَجَزْتُهَا لَهُ اِنْطَلِقُوا بِهِ إِلَى جِنَانِي حَتَّى يَتَخَيَّرَ مِنْهَا حَيْثُ أَحَبَّ فَأَعْطُوهُ مِنْ غَيْرِ مَنٍّ (مِنِّي) وَفَضْلًا عَلَيْهِ فَهَنِيئًا هَنِيئًا لِعَبْدِي.

By the forenoon, [1] *and by the night when it covers with darkness.* [2]

1-2.1 The chapter begins with two oaths by employing the *waw al-qasam.* These oaths are by two distinct times of the day: when the radiance of the sun spreads, and when the darkness of night extends over creation.

1-2.2 '*By the forenoon.*': [*Al-Ḍuḥā* (الضُّحَىٰ, forenoon)]. This term refers to the early hours of the morning when the sun begins to rise into the sky and its radiance spreads and illuminates everything. However, it may also refer to the whole day, because the brightness of daytime is contrasted to the darkness of night-time in the next verse.[8]

1-2.3 '*And by the night when it covers with darkness.*': [*Sajā* (سَجَىٰ, cover over)]. This term is derived from *sajawa* and has two meanings: to cover in darkness, or to become still and tranquil.[9] It refers to the deeper part of the night when everything is dark, peaceful, and quiet.[10]

1-2.4 These two oaths refer to the time when the sun's radiance illuminates everything, and the time when the darkness of the night casts its cloak and everything becomes still. They may have been employed here as a reference to the experience of the Prophet (s); he received the first rays of the sunlight of revelation, which illuminated everything, but it was followed by stillness, as revelation was temporarily halted. If this is indeed an allusion to revelation, it would also explain why *al-ḍuḥā* has been mentioned without restriction (denoting continuity) while *al-layl* has been mentioned with a qualifying phrase, '*when it covers*', (denoting transience).

And just like the darkness of night is not a sign of God's displeasure, the halting of revelation was not a sign that God had forsaken His beloved Messenger (s) or that He was displeased with him.[11]

Another possible link between these oaths and their subject is the allusion that constant exposure to light is wearying for man, and

---

[8] Ṭabrasī, *al-Bayān*, 10/764.

[9] Rāzī, *Mafātīḥ al-Ghayb*, 31/190.

[10] Ṭabrasī, *al-Bayān*, 10/764.

[11] Muṭahharī, (*Āshnāyī bā Qur'an*), *Āthār*, 28/608; al-Rāzī, *Mafātīḥ al-Ghayb*, 31/191.

night is required for rest and peace. Likewise, if the Prophet (s) was initially given periodic breaks in revelation (*fatrat al-waḥy*) it was to give him rest from the strain of revelation.[12]

1-2.5 Many reports state that receiving the revelation was very arduous for the Prophet (s). One of the first chapters, Surat al-Muzzammil, in Q73:5 states:

إِنَّا سَنُلْقِي عَلَيْكَ قَوْلًا ثَقِيلًا

Indeed, We shall soon send down upon you a weighty word.

The Prophet (s) was once asked how revelation came to him. He replied, "Sometimes it comes to me like the ringing of a bell, and that is the hardest on me."[13] The revelation took a toll on the heart of the Prophet (s), especially in the early days, and perhaps the pause in revelation was so that he could gradually gain familiarity with the process.[14]

SUMMARY OF THE VERSES

God takes oaths by two times in the day: the early morning when the radiance of the sun illuminates everything, and the late night when everything is cloaked in darkness.

REFLECTIVE LEARNING

Let me reflect on the passing of days and nights in my life. Death will follow life, just as surely as night follows day.

Let me make one decision that will benefit me more after death than in life.

VERSES 3 - 5

مَا وَدَّعَكَ رَبُّكَ وَمَا قَلَىٰ ﴿٣﴾ وَلَلْآخِرَةُ خَيْرٌ لَكَ مِنَ الْأُولَىٰ ﴿٤﴾ وَلَسَوْفَ يُعْطِيكَ رَبُّكَ فَتَرْضَىٰ ﴿٥﴾

[12] Mawdūdī, *Tafhīm al-Qur'an*, 6/370.

[13] Ṭabrasī, *al-Bayān*, 10/570.

فَقَالَ: يَا رَسُولَ اللهِ كَيْفَ يَأْتِيكَ الْوَحْيُ؟ فَقَالَ رَسُولُ اللهِ (صَلَّى اللهُ عَلَيْهِ وَآلِهِ): أَحْيَانًا يَأْتِينِي مِثْلَ صَلْصَلَةِ الْجَرَسِ – وَهُوَ أَشَدُّهُ عَلَيَّ.

[14] Muṭahharī, (*Āshnāyī bā Qur'an*), *Āthār*, 28/609.

Your Lord has not forsaken you, nor has He become displeased. [3] *And indeed, what will come after is better for you than that which has gone before.* [4] *And indeed, your Lord will soon give you that [with which] you shall be well pleased.* [5]

3-5.1 The subjects (*jawāb*) of the two oaths are the emphatic assurances that follow in the next three verses: God swears that He has not abandoned His prophet (s), that He has better things in store for him, and that He desires to grant him something that would please him.

3-5.2 '*Your Lord has not forsaken you*': [*Waddaʿa* (وَدَّعَ, forsake)] is derived from *tawdīʿ*, meaning to bid farewell and depart.[15]

[*Qalā* (قَلَى, displeased)]. The term denotes enmity and hostility.[16]

The verse informs the Prophet (s) that revelation had not ceased and would continue.[17] It assures the Prophet (s) that the temporary interruption in revelation did not mean that God has forsaken him after appointing him to his mission or that He was displeased with him.

The tone of the verses that follow is full of extraordinary love and affection. God uses the name *Rabb* to emphasis His role as the loving Sustainer and Nurturer.

3-5.3 '*And indeed, what will come after is better for you than that which has gone before.*': Even though the Prophet (s) had always enjoyed God's special care, better things were yet to come. Here, it means, 'the latter part of your life, O Messenger (s) of God, will certainly be better (underscored by the *lām* of emphasis) than the first part, in terms of God's aid in achieving success in completing your mission.'[18]

Another meaning is that the Hereafter would be better for him (s) than this world.[19] This *khayr* (better) is mentioned in a restricted sense – *laka* (for you) and not *lakum* (for you all) – because for the sinners the Hereafter will be much worse.[20]

---

[15] Ṭabrasī, *al-Bayān*, 10/765.

[16] Ibid.

[17] Muṭahharī, (*Āshnāyī bā Qur'an*), *Āthār*, 28/609.

[18] Ṭabrasī, *al-Bayān*, 10/765.

[19] Shīrāzī, *Namūneh*, 27/98.

[20] Rāzī, *Mafātīḥ al-Ghayb*, 31/194.

3-5.4 '*And indeed, your Lord will soon give you that [with which] you shall be well pleased.*': Since what shall be given by the Lord to the Prophet (s) is not specified, it refers to all the bounties that were uniquely granted to him. This included the preeminent authority of intercession that the Prophet (s) will be honoured with on the Day of Judgement. Indeed, he will be the most important and sought-after person on that Day.

Imam al-Baqir (a) was once asked: Which verse of the Qur'an gives the greatest hope? He (a) responded, "What do your people say about it?" The man replied, "They quote, '*O My servants who have transgressed against themselves [by sinning], do not despair in the mercy of God*' (Q39:53)" The Imam (a) replied, "We the *Ahl al-Bayt* do not say that." The man asked, "Then what do you say about it?" The Imam (a) replied, "We cite, '*And indeed, your Lord will soon give you that [with which] you shall be well pleased.*' Intercession, by God! Intercession, by God!"[21]

3-5.5 The fact that the Prophet (s) will be the chief intercessor for his nation is explained as follows: Intercession is based on guidance. If you have guided a person to the right path, your guidance will be the reason that you can intercede for him on the Day of Judgement. Similarly, if someone else has guided you, they will be your intercessor. And this chain extends back to reach the one who was the greatest guide, and that is the Prophet (s). In this way he will be the intercessor of millions.[22]

3-5.6 Just like every Prophet (a), the Messenger of God (s) had extraordinary love for his nation. He wanted the people to be guided with all his heart, and was genuinely grieved when they persisted in wasting their potential. Q18:6 states:

فَلَعَلَّكَ بَاخِعٌ نَفْسَكَ عَلَىٰ آثَارِهِمْ إِنْ لَمْ يُؤْمِنُوا بِهَٰذَا الْحَدِيثِ أَسَفًا

Perhaps you will die through your grief at their turning away [O Muhammad] if they do not believe in this message.

---

[21] Majlisī, *Biḥār*, 8/57.

عَنِ الْبَاقِرِ (عَلَيْهِ السَّلَامُ) - قُلْتُ لِمُحَمَّدِ ابْنِ عَلِيٍّ (عَلَيْهِ السَّلَامُ) أَيُّ آيَةٍ فِي كِتَابِ اللهِ أَرْجَى؟ قَالَ: مَا يَقُولُ فِيهَا قَوْمُكَ. قَالَ: قُلْتُ يَقُولُونَ «يَا عِبَادِيَ الَّذِينَ أَسْرَفُوا عَلَىٰ أَنْفُسِهِمْ لَا تَقْنَطُوا مِنْ رَحْمَةِ اللهِ»، قَالَ: لَكِنَّا أَهْلَ الْبَيْتِ لَا نَقُولُ ذَلِكَ، قَالَ: قُلْت فَأَيَّ شَيْءٍ تَقُولُونَ فِيهَا؟ قَالَ نَقُولُ: «وَلَسَوْفَ يُعْطِيكَ رَبُّكَ فَتَرْضَىٰ» الشَّفَاعَةُ وَاللهِ الشَّفَاعَةُ وَاللهِ.

[22] Muṭahharī, (*Āshnāyī bā Qur'an*), *Āthār*, 28/611.

That is why the prospect of being allowed to intercede for his people gave him great joy and contentment, as God mentions in the verse under discussion.

A tradition from Imam al-Sadiq (a) states: The happiness of my grandfather lies in the fact that no [true] monotheist shall remain in the hellfire.[23]

SUMMARY OF THE VERSES

In summary, the verses state that despite the interlude in revelation, God had not forsaken His Prophet (s), and was not disappointed in him. In fact, even more bounties lay in store for him, and God would grant him a gift which would give him great joy.

REFLECTIVE LEARNING

Let me reflect on the fact that just as God did not abandon His Prophet (s), He does not abandon us either. It is us who turn away from Him.

Do I feel His presence at times of hardship, and know that if I keep connected to Him at these times (not abandoning or blaming Him), He will lead me to something that is better for me?

VERSES 6 - 8

أَلَمْ يَجِدْكَ يَتِيمًا فَآوَىٰ ﴿٦﴾ وَوَجَدَكَ ضَالًّا فَهَدَىٰ ﴿٧﴾ وَوَجَدَكَ عَائِلًا فَأَغْنَىٰ ﴿٨﴾

Did He not find you an orphan, then give [you] refuge? [6] *And find you lost, then guide [you]?* [7] *And find you poor, then make you self-sufficient?* [8]

6-8.1 In these verses, God asks the Prophet (s) a series of questions, rather than listing His favours as statements. This style of address allows for reflection and realization. The Prophet (s) is asked to recall and ponder over the fact that God had always taken care of him and had provided for him when he was in a disadvantaged position is society.

---

[23] Ḥuwayzī, *Nūr al-Thaqalayn*, 5/595.

عَنِ الصَّادِقِ (عَلَيْهِ السَّلاَمُ) - رِضَا جَدِّي أَنْ لَا يَبْقَى فِي النَّارِ مُوَحِّدٌ.

6-8.2 '*Did He not find you an orphan, then give [you] refuge?*': [*Fa āwā* (فَآوَىٰ, then give [you] refuge)]. The Prophet (s) lost his dear father, Abdullah b. Abd al-Muttalib, when he was still in the womb of his mother, Aminah bt. Wahab. Then he lost his dear mother when he was only six years old. Through God's mercy and direction, the Prophet (s) was brought up under the loving care of his grandfather, ʿAbd al-Muttalib, and later his uncle, Abu Talib. In this manner, God, who is the ultimate *Rabb*, takes care of us through others.

Yatīm normally refers to an orphan. However, exegetes have mentioned that it also means a unique pearl (*durr al-yatīm*). In this case the verse would mean. 'God created you with unique and peerless qualities and kept you in His secure care; you had no one who could understand you, so He communicated with you and appointed you to His mission.'[24]

6-8.3 '*And find you lost, then guide [you]?*': [*Ḍāllan* (ضَالًّا, lost)] can mean both lost as well as not guided. '*And found you lost*' has been explained in several ways:[25]

i) That it means that the Prophet (s) was not initially at the stage where he could receive revelation and God guided him until he reached that station. The exegetes cite Q42:52 as evidence for this view:

مَا كُنْتَ تَدْرِي مَا الْكِتَابُ وَلَا الْإِيمَانُ

...You did not know what the Book was nor the faith...

ii) That God found him unsure of which way to proceed as a youth. He was in an environment of idolatry, material pursuit, and oppression. He wanted to change all this but did not know how to do so. God directed him at every stage towards his objective.

iii) That God found him to be a man who had recognized Him through contemplation and self-purification; he had realized truths that earned him the respected titles al-Sadiq (the truthful) and al-Amin (the trustworthy). Therefore, God gradually made the people aware of the extraordinary human being that lived in their midst and guided them to him. In this regard, a tradition

[24] Ṭabrasī, *al-Bayān*, 10/765.

[25] Ibid, 10/766.

from Imam al-Sadiq (a) states: '*And found you lost, then guided*' means, 'He guided people who did not know you so that they may know you [and your status].'[26]

iv) That in childhood, he had been lost in Makka and God guided him home. Or that he had been lost when under the care of his foster-mother Halimah, and God guided her to his location.

Exegetes have also mentioned another meaning that may add to the significance of the verse: The tree that stands alone in the desert is called *al-ḍāllah.* One may consider that in the desert of ignorance that existed at his time, the Prophet (s) stood like a lonely tree; he had the potential to turn the whole desert into a garden, but this only became possible once God sent down the guidance of revelation and appointed him to his mission.[27]

6-8.4 '*And found you poor, then make you self-sufficient.*': In the early part of his life, the Prophet (s) was not a man of means, despite coming from a prominent family. He earned his living as a shepherd, and later as an agent for merchants who took part in the biannual trade caravans of the Quraysh. It was after his marriage to the wealthy merchant Lady Khadijah (a) that his financial situation improved, and this is the reference of the verse.[28]

Other reports mention that this poverty refers to his community, who were poor in terms of knowledge and guidance.[29]

6-8.5 It is reported that Imam al-Ridha (a) explained a meaning of these three verses by stating: [They mean], he found you unique (*yatīman*), with no equal in creation, so he gave the people a refuge in you. And he found you lost (*ḍāllan*), meaning you were unknown amongst your people. Since they did not understand your merits, He guided them to [know] you. And he found you in poverty (*ʿāʾilan*), meaning that your community was in need of knowledge, so He enriched them through you.[30]

---

[26] Majlisī, *Biḥār*, 16/142.

عَنِ الصَّادِقَيْنِ (عَلَيْهِمَا السَّلَامُ) – « وَوَجَدَكَ ضَالًّا فَهَدَىٰ» أَيْ هَدَى إِلَيْكَ قَوْمًا لَا يَعْرِفُونَكَ حَتَّى عَرَفُوكَ.

[27] Mawdūdī, *Tafhīm al-Qurʾan*, 6/373.

[28] Shīrāzī, *Namūneh*, 27/105.

[29] Majlisī, *Biḥār*, 16/139.

[30] Kāshānī, *al-Ṣāfī*, 5/341.

عَنِ الرِّضَا (عَلَيْهِ السَّلَامُ) – فِي قَوْلِهِ: «أَلَمْ يَجِدْكَ يَتِيمًا فَآوَىٰ» قَالَ: فَرْدًا لَا مِثْلَ لَكَ فِي الْمَخْلُوقِينَ، فَآوَى النَّاسَ إِلَيْكَ. «وَوَجَدَكَ

6-8.6 These three verses do not specify the object of God's actions. That is, due to the absence of the personal pronoun 'you' (*ka*), the actions of 'giving refuge', 'guiding', and 'making self-sufficient' have not been specifically linked to the Prophet (s). For this reason, it is possible to interpret them in a more general way:

i) 'He gave shelter to you (*āwāka*)', or 'He gave shelter to others because of you (*āwā laka*)', or 'He gave shelter to others through you (*āwā bika*)'.

ii) 'He guided you' (*hadāka*), or 'He guided others to you (*hadā ilayka*)', or 'He guided others through you (*hadā bika*)'.

iii) 'He made you self-sufficient (*aghnāka*)', or 'He made others self-sufficient for your sake (*aghnā laka*)', or 'He made others self-sufficient through you (*aghnā bika*).'

All these meanings are possible, because the Prophet (s) himself received these gifts, believers received these gifts because of him, and these gifts were spread because of his teachings.[31]

6-8.7 A question that arises is: Why does God remind the Prophet (s) of His favours after having granted them to him? The answer is that remin-ding someone of an obligation to embarrass or chide them is a fault, which God is exalted above. The reason God is mentioning His favours here is out of His mercy, to reassure the Prophet (s) and encourage thanksgiving so that He could increase His favours even more.

SUMMARY OF THE VERSES

In summary, these verses remind the Prophet (s) of how God continually took care of him and removed the obstacles in his life. He removed the disadvantage of being an orphan, provided guidance, and granted him self-sufficiency.

REFLECTIVE LEARNING

God has always provided for me, and there is no reason for me to doubt that He will continue to do so in the future.

ضَالًّا»، أَيْ ضَالَّةٌ فِي قَوْمِكَ لَا يَعْرِفُونَ فَضْلَكَ، فَهَدَاهُمْ إِلَيْكَ «وَوَجَدَكَ عَائِلًا» تَعُولُ أَقْوَامًا بِالْعِلْمِ، فَأَغْنَاهُمُ اللهُ بِكَ.

[31] Muṭahharī, (*Āshnāyī bā Qur'an*), *Āthār*, 28/617.

Let me assess my own attitude and feelings, and gauge how much I trust in God to take care of me and support me in every situation.

Let me reflect on my level of anxiety and worry in times of difficulty, which will indicate how much I trust Him.

VERSES 9 - 10

فَأَمَّا الْيَتِيمَ فَلَا تَقْهَرْ ﴿٩﴾ وَأَمَّا السَّائِلَ فَلَا تَنْهَرْ ﴿١٠﴾

So, as for the orphan, do not oppress [him]. [9] *And as for the beggar, do not repulse [him].* [10]

9-10.1 After mentioning the three specific favours that God conferred on His beloved Prophet (s), three directives are now given. These directives are general, and addressed to all the believers: do not oppress the orphan, do not repulse the beggar, and proclaim the blessings of the Lord.

9-10.2 '*So, as for the orphan, do not oppress [him].*': [*Taqhar* (تَقْهَرْ, oppress)] is derived from *qahara* meaning to suppress or oppress someone, because one has the power to do so.[32] Here, this misuse of power has been forbidden specifically in the treatment of orphans, because of their vulnerability.

Since the Prophet (s) himself was an orphan, he could empathize with their plight and through his example, he showed us the need for and importance of being mindful of the welfare of the orphans in the community.

9-10.3 One of the evil actions prevalent in society is usurping the rights of orphans, who are powerless to defend their rights. Q4:10 warns:

إِنَّ الَّذِينَ يَأْكُلُونَ أَمْوَالَ الْيَتَامَىٰ ظُلْمًا
إِنَّمَا يَأْكُلُونَ فِي بُطُونِهِمْ نَارًا وَسَيَصْلَوْنَ سَعِيرًا

Indeed, those who devour the property of orphans unjustly
are only consuming fire into their bellies.
And soon, they shall burn in blazing Fire.

[32] Muṣṭafawī, *al-Taḥqīq*.

9-10.4 The oppression of orphans has been severely criticized in the Qur'an. This oppression can take the form of ignoring them, mistreating them, or not guiding them to the best path for them.

In contrast, looking after them with kindness and mercy, and trying to divert them from their great loss, is one of the highest recommended acts. We have discussed this matter further in the *tafsīr* of Surat al-Māʿūn (107).

9-10.5 '*And as for the beggar, do not repulse [him].*': [*Sā'il* (سَائِل, beggar)] is derived from *sa'ala* which means to ask or question. One can ask for monetary assistance as in the case of a beggar, or ask a question seeking guidance.

[*Tanhar* (تَنْهَر, repulse)] is derived from *nahara*, meaning to address someone with harsh words and drive them away.[33] Here, this behaviour has been condemned in the treatment of beggars or those who ask for something. Even if there is nothing one can do for them, they must be treated with dignity.

A tradition from Imam al-Baqir (a) states: Amongst the things that God, Almighty and Exalted, told Musa (a) in their private conversations was, "O Musa! Show kindness to the beggar even with something small, or turn him away with politeness, because [it may be that] those who approach you are not from mankind or *jinn*, but angels from the angels of the all-Merciful, sent to test you through what I have entrusted to you. They [only] ask you from what I have granted to you. So be careful about how you act, O son of ʿImran!"[34]

9-10.6 Whenever someone approaches us for assistance, we must help with whatever we can. In this regard, a tradition from the Prophet (s) states: If a beggar knocks on your door at night begging for something, do not turn him away.[35]

A tradition states that Imam al-Sadiq (a) was asked what to do if one was not convinced that a beggar was actually needy. The Imam

---

33 Ibid.

34 Kulaynī, *al-Kāfī*, 4/15.

عَنِ الْبَاقِرِ (عَلَيْهِ السَّلَامُ) - كَانَ فِيمَا نَاجَى اللهُ عَزَّ وَجَلَّ بِهِ مُوسَى (عَلَيْهِ السَّلَامُ)، قَالَ: يَا مُوسَى أَكْرِمِ السَّائِلَ بِبَذْلٍ يَسِيرٍ أَوْ بِرَدٍّ جَمِيلٍ لِأَنَّهُ يَأْتِيكَ مَنْ لَيْسَ بِإِنْسٍ وَلَا جَانٍّ مَلَائِكَةٌ مِنْ مَلَائِكَةِ الرَّحْمٰنِ يَبْلُونَكَ فِيمَا خَوَّلْتُكَ وَيَسْأَلُونَكَ عَمَّا نَوَّلْتُكَ فَانْظُرْ كَيْفَ أَنْتَ صَانِعٌ يَا ابْنَ عِمْرَانَ.

35 Ibid, 4/8.

عَنِ الرَّسُولِ (صَلَّى اللهُ عَلَيْهِ وَآلِهِ) - إِذَا طَرَقَكُمْ سَائِلٌ ذَكَرٌ بِلَيْلٍ فَلَا تَرُدُّوهُ.

(a) replied: Give [something] to the one whose plight invokes pity in your heart.[36]

SUMMARY OF THE VERSES

These verses instruct us how to behave with orphans, who should be treated with love and not harshness, and beggars, who should be treated with dignity and not scorn.

REFLECTIVE LEARNING

Let me recall the instances when God has sent people to help me in my time of need.

In the same way, God expects me to help others, for example, orphans and beggars.

Let me reflect on whether I acknowledge this opportunity and thank God for it through my words and actions.

VERSE 11

وَأَمَّا بِنِعْمَةِ رَبِّكَ فَحَدِّثْ ﴿١١﴾

And as for the favour of your Lord, proclaim [it]. [11].

11.1 [*Niʿmati Rabbika* (نِعْمَةِ رَبِّكَ, favour of your Lord)]. This is an important reminder that everything man possesses is a favour from God given in trust (*amānah*). Man is not the owner of what he has, he is merely its custodian, and he will be asked about it.

11.2 Some people show off God's favours in the face of those who do not possess them, to boast and to belittle them. Others like to claim that they have nothing despite God's many favours on them, to seek attention and make people feel sorry for them. Both these attitudes are contrary to the command in this verse.

11.3 The proclamation of God's favours is achieved by:

i) Acknowledging that God is the source of all favours and manifesting His blessings.

A tradition from Imam al-Sadiq (a) states: When God gives His servant a blessing, and the effect of it becomes manifest in him,

---

36 Ṣadūq, *al-Faqīh*, 2/68.

سُئِلَ الصَّادِقُ (عَلَيْهِ السَّلَامُ) عَنِ السَّائِلِ يَسْأَلُ وَلَا يُدْرَى مَا هُوَ، فَقَالَ أَعْطِ مَنْ وَقَعَتْ فِي قَلْبِكَ الرَّحْمَةُ لَهُ.

he becomes beloved to God (*ḥabībullāh*) and is [counted] amongst those who proclaim the favour of God. However, when God gives His servant a blessing, and its effect does not become manifest in him, he becomes one who is hateful to God (*baghīḍullāh*) and is [counted] amongst those who belie the favour of God.[37]

ii) Making one's blessings known to the people, not from pride, but in an attempt to encourage others through example.

A tradition from Imam al-Sadiq (a) states: It means to proclaim what God has granted you, made you excel over others, provided for you as sustenance, favoured you with, and guided you towards.[38]

iii) The transformation of an individual through the use of God's favours.

A tradition from Imam Ali (a) states: The effects of God's blessings on you should be observable.[39]

11.4 When the Imams (a) introduce themselves and mention their merits, it is an example of their application of this verse. It is reported that Imam Ali (a) once gave a sermon in which he praised and exalted God, sent God's blessings on His Messenger (s), then mentioned the favours of God on His Prophet (s) and on himself as well. Then he said, "If it was not for a verse in the Qur'an, I would not have mentioned what I mentioned about my station. God, the Almighty and exalted has stated, '*And as for the favour of your Lord, proclaim (it).*' O God! All praise and gratitude is due to You for Your countless blessings and vast favours."[40]

11.5 The greatest favour of God is guidance to His religion. For the Prophet (s), God's favours included his Prophethood, and being

---

[37] Kulaynī, *al-Kāfī*, 6/438.

عَنِ الصَّادِقِ (عَلَيْهِ السَّلَامُ) – إِذَا أَنْعَمَ اللهُ عَلَى عَبْدِهِ بِنِعْمَةٍ فَظَهَرَتْ عَلَيْهِ سُمِّيَ حَبِيبَ اللهِ مُحَدِّثًا بِنِعْمَةِ اللهِ، وَإِذَا أَنْعَمَ اللهُ عَلَى عَبْدٍ بِنِعْمَةٍ فَلَمْ تَظْهَرْ عَلَيْهِ سُمِّيَ بَغِيضَ اللهِ مُكَذِّبًا بِنِعْمَةِ اللهِ.

[38] Majlisī, *Biḥār*, 68/29.

عَنِ الصَّادِقِ (عَلَيْهِ السَّلَامُ) – مَعْنَاهُ فَحَدِّثْ بِمَا أَعْطَاكَ اللهُ وَفَضَّلَكَ وَرَزَقَكَ وَأَحْسَنَ إِلَيْكَ وَهَدَاكَ.

[39] *Nahj al-Balāghah*, letter 69.

عَنْ أَمِيرِ الْمُؤْمِنِينَ (عَلَيْهِ السَّلَامُ) – وَلْيُرَ عَلَيْكَ أَثَرُ مَا أَنْعَمَ اللهُ بِهِ عَلَيْكَ.

[40] Majlisī, *Biḥār*, 25/45.

عَنْ أَمِيرِ الْمُؤْمِنِينَ (عَلَيْهِ السَّلَامُ) – فَقَامَ خَطِيبًا فَحَمِدَ اللهَ وَأَثْنَى عَلَيْهِ، وَصَلَّى عَلَى رَسُولِ اللهِ (صَلَّى اللهُ عَلَيْهِ وَآلِهِ) وَذَكَرَ مَا أَنْعَمَ اللهُ عَلَى نَبِيِّهِ (صَلَّى اللهُ عَلَيْهِ وَآلِهِ) وَعَلَيْهِ ثُمَّ قَالَ: لَوْلَا آيَةٌ فِي كِتَابِ اللهِ مَا ذَكَرْتُ مَا أَنَا ذَاكِرُهُ فِي مَقَامِي هَذَا، يَقُولُ اللهُ عَزَّ وَجَلَّ: «وَأَمَّا بِنِعْمَةِ رَبِّكَ فَحَدِّثْ» اَللَّهُمَّ لَكَ الْحَمْدُ عَلَى نِعَمِكَ الَّتِي لَا تُحْصَى وَفَضْلِكَ الَّذِي لَا يُنْسَى.

chosen to convey His religion to the people. A tradition states that when Imam al-Husayn (a) was asked about the meaning of this verse, he said, "God commanded the Prophet (s) to proclaim the religion that He had blessed him with."[41]

SUMMARY OF THE VERSE

The verse instructs that one must proclaim and display the blessings of God.

REFLECTIVE LEARNING

God's favours should be proclaimed in both words and deeds.

Let me reflect on whether I proclaim God's bounties in this manner. Let me use one of His many bounties (time, wealth, strength, and so on) to bring about a change in my attitude and behaviour, and thereby proclaim His blessing and bring myself closer to Him.

[41] Ibid, 24/53.

عَنِ الْحُسَيْنِ (عَلَيْهِ السَّلَامُ) - أَمَرَهُ أَنْ يُحَدِّثَ بِمَا أَنْعَمَ اللهُ عَلَيْهِ مِنْ دِينِهِ.

SURAT AL-INSHIRĀḤ
THE EXPANSION (94)

TEXT AND TRANSLATION

سُورَةُ الاِنْشِرَاحِ

بِسْمِ اللهِ الرَّحْمٰنِ الرَّحِيمِ

أَلَمْ نَشْرَحْ لَكَ صَدْرَكَ ﴿١﴾ وَوَضَعْنَا عَنْكَ وِزْرَكَ ﴿٢﴾ الَّذِي أَنْقَضَ ظَهْرَكَ ﴿٣﴾
وَرَفَعْنَا لَكَ ذِكْرَكَ ﴿٤﴾ فَإِنَّ مَعَ الْعُسْرِ يُسْرًا ﴿٥﴾ إِنَّ مَعَ الْعُسْرِ يُسْرًا ﴿٦﴾ فَإِذَا
فَرَغْتَ فَانْصَبْ ﴿٧﴾ وَإِلَىٰ رَبِّكَ فَارْغَبْ ﴿٨﴾

In the name of God, the Beneficent, the Merciful.

Did We not expand for you your breast? [1] *And removed from you your burden,* [2] *which weighed down your back.* [3] *And We raised for you your reputation.* [4] *For indeed, with hardship is ease.* [5] *Indeed, with hardship is ease.* [6] *So when you are free, then [continue to] exert yourself.* [7] *And to your Lord turn your attention.* [8]

INTRODUCTION

Surat al-Inshirāḥ (94), also known as Surat al-Sharḥ, was the 12th chapter to be revealed. It has eight verses and was revealed in Makka, after Surat al-Ḍuḥā (93).[1] It is named after the mention of the expansion of the breast (*sharḥ*) of the Prophet (s) in the first verse.

In many traditions it is reported that this chapter is linked to the previous chapter, Surat al-Ḍuḥā. Although they are separate surahs, jurists have instructed that if al-Ḍuḥā is recited as the second surah in the obligatory prayers, then al-Inshirāḥ must also be recited after it. This is the same ruling for two other surahs, al-Fīl (105) and Quraysh (106).[2]

---

1 Maʿrifat, *ʿUlūm-i Qurʾānī*, p. 90.

2 Sistānī, *Minhāj*, 1/232, ruling 605.

The chapter continues the list of favours bestowed by God to His beloved Prophet (s) that were mentioned in Surat al-Ḍuḥā. In Surat al-Ḍuḥā three favours that secured the material life of the Prophet (s) were mentioned, and in this chapter a further three, spiritual, favours are mentioned: expansion of the breast (*sharḥ al-ṣadr*), relief from his pressing burden (*waḍᶜ al-wizr*), and exalting his reputation (*rafᶜ al-dhikr*).

The Prophet (s) is then consoled and reminded that just as always, every hardship that will come his way will be accompanied by ease.

This surah was a great encouragement to the Prophet (s) in his mission to propagate God's religion amongst the people. Through his example, it also reminds the believers never to give up in the face of difficulties, because there is ease with every hardship.

LINK TO THE PREVIOUS CHAPTER

As mentioned previously, Surat al-Inshirāḥ is considered to be linked to the previous chapter, Surat al-Ḍuḥā. They both address God's favours to the Prophet (s) at different stages of his life.

Surat al-Ḍuḥā recounts how God blessed the Prophet (s) during his life leading up to his appointment to his mission, while Surat al-Inshirāḥ speaks of his continual blessings after the important mission began.

Surat al-Ḍuḥā mentions three favours that secured the material life of the Prophet (s), while Surat al-Inshirāḥ mentions three spiritual favours.

Surat al-Ḍuḥā finishes with the order to proclaim God's favours and Surat al-Inshirāḥ begins with fulfilling this order.

MERITS OF RECITATION

- A tradition from the Prophet (s) states: Whoever recites this surah will be rewarded as the one who met Muhammad (s) when he was sorrowful, and dispelled his grief.[3]
- A tradition from Imam Ali (a) states: If one of you is beset by the whispering of Shaytan, then he should seek refuge in God, and say with his tongue and heart, "I profess faith in God and His

[3] Nūrī, *Mustadrak al-Wasā'il*, 4/359.

عَنِ الرَّسُولِ (صَلَّى اللهُ عَلَيْهِ وَآلِهِ) – مَنْ قَرَأَ سُورَةَ أَلَمْ نَشْرَحْ أُعْطِيَ مِنَ الْأَجْرِ كَمَنْ لَقِيَ مُحَمَّدًا (صَلَّى اللهُ عَلَيْهِ وَآلِهِ) مُغْتَمًّا فَفَرَّجَ عَنْهُ.

Messenger, in sincere devotion to Him." To relieve the constriction in his heart, he should recite Surat al-Inshirāḥ twice every day for seventeen days, once in the morning and once in the evening.[4]

EXEGESIS

VERSE 1

أَلَمْ نَشْرَحْ لَكَ صَدْرَكَ ﴿١﴾

Did We not expand for you your breast? [1]

1.1 The tone of this chapter is full of love, consolation, and encouragement to the Prophet (s) who had undertaken a difficult mission in a very challenging environment.

1.2 [*Nashraḥ* (نَشْرَحْ, We expand)] is derived from *sharaḥa* meaning to stretch open flesh or something similar.[5] When used for the heart as in *sharḥ al-ṣadr*, it means relieving the constriction in the chest and filling it with Divine enlightenment and remembrance.[6] In this regard, Q39:22 states:

أَفَمَنْ شَرَحَ اللهُ صَدْرَهُ لِلْإِسْلَامِ فَهُوَ عَلَىٰ نُورٍ مِنْ رَبِّهِ
فَوَيْلٌ لِلْقَاسِيَةِ قُلُوبُهُمْ مِنْ ذِكْرِ اللهِ أُولَٰئِكَ فِي ضَلَالٍ مُبِينٍ

Is he whose breast God has expanded to [accept] Islam, so that he has received enlightenment from his Lord [like the one who disbelieves]? So, woe to those whose hearts are hardened against the remembrance of God. They are in plain error.

1.3 In the opening verse of Surat al-Inshirāḥ, God is talking directly to His Messenger (s), showing his great station. This great station was achieved by the absolute sincerity of the Prophet (s) in his servitude to God. Because he did everything for God (*lillāh*), in return God did this great favour to him.

---

[4] Majlisī, *Biḥār*, 92/136.

عَنْ أَمِيرِ الْمُؤْمِنِينَ (عَلَيْهِ السَّلَامُ) – إِذَا وَسْوَسَ الشَّيْطَانُ لِأَحَدِكُمْ فَلْيَتَعَوَّذْ بِاللهِ وَلْيَقُلْ بِلِسَانِهِ وَقَلْبِهِ آمَنْتُ بِاللهِ وَرُسُلِهِ مُخْلِصًا لَهُ الدِّينَ لِضِيقِ الْقَلْبِ يَقْرَأُ سَبْعَةَ عَشَرَ يَوْمًا أَلَمْ نَشْرَحْ إِلَى آخِرِهِ كُلَّ يَوْمٍ مَرَّتَيْنِ، مَرَّةً بِالْغَدَاةِ وَمَرَّةً بِالْعِشَاءِ.

[5] Rāghib, *al-Mufradāt*.

[6] Ṭabāṭabā'ī, *al-Mīzān*, 20/314.

Additionally, by mentioning *laka* (for you) before *ṣadr* (breast), God informs the Prophet (s) that He had uniquely granted this to him (*laka* meaning only for you).

When Prophet Musa (a) was appointed to his mission, he had asked for this added capacity. Q20:25,26 state:

قَالَ رَبِّ ٱشْرَحْ لِي صَدْرِي ﴿٢٥﴾ وَيَسِّرْ لِي أَمْرِي

He [Musa] said, "My Lord, expand my breast for me.
And ease my mission for me."

However, Prophet Muhammad (s) was granted this favour without even asking for it.

1.4 [*Ṣadr* (صَدْر, breast)]. In terms of the physical heart, *ṣadr* denotes the chest cavity in which the heart is contained. However, when we discuss the spiritual heart (*qalb*), then *ṣadr* is a metaphor, just like *qalb*, both referring to non-material aspects of a human being.

The Qur'an refers to the *qalb* and *ṣadr* in Q22:46

أَفَلَمْ يَسِيرُوا فِي الْأَرْضِ فَتَكُونَ لَهُمْ قُلُوبٌ يَعْقِلُونَ بِهَا أَوْ آذَانٌ يَسْمَعُونَ بِهَا
فَإِنَّهَا لَا تَعْمَى الْأَبْصَارُ وَلَٰكِنْ تَعْمَى الْقُلُوبُ الَّتِي فِي الصُّدُورِ

Have they not travelled in the earth, so that they should have hearts (qulūb) *by which to reason and ears by which to hear? For indeed, it is not the eyes that are blind, rather blind are the hearts* (qulūb) *which are in the breasts* (ṣudūr).

1.5 *Inshirāḥ al-ṣadr* (expansion of the breast) is a Qur'anic metaphor for expanding the spiritual capacity of an individual.[7] It grants the recipient the correct understanding of truth and an increase in the ability to bear hardships. This in turn gives rise to a determined resolve and complete trust and reliance on God. Such a person would not waver in his covenant with God. In the specific case of the Prophets (a), this *inshirāḥ* also gives them the extra capacity to receive revelation and carry out the mission to propagate the message of God.

It should be noted that *inshirāḥ al-ṣadr* is not a bounty exclusive to the Prophets (a) only, but available to anyone who allows Islam into their heart. Q6:125 states in this regard:

---

[7] Ṭabrasī, *al-Bayān*, 10/770.

فَمَنْ يُرِدِ اللَّهُ أَنْ يَهْدِيَهُ يَشْرَحْ صَدْرَهُ لِلْإِسْلَامِ وَمَنْ يُرِدْ
أَنْ يُضِلَّهُ يَجْعَلْ صَدْرَهُ ضَيِّقًا حَرَجًا كَأَنَّمَا يَصَّعَّدُ فِي السَّمَاءِ

Therefore, whoever God wills to guide, He expands his breast to [contain] Islam; and whoever He wills to misguide, He makes his breast tight and constricted, as if he was climbing upwards to the sky...

The Prophet (s) was asked what was the sign that an individual had been granted expansion of the breast (*inshirāḥ al-ṣadr*). He replied: Detachment from the world of false allure (*dār al-ghurūr*), attentiveness towards the abode of permanence (*dār al-khulūd*), and preparedness for death before it comes.[8]

And these words were repeated by Imam al-Sajjad (a) in his supplication of the 27th night of the month of Ramadan.[9]

DISCUSSION 1: FIVE QUR'ANIC TERMS FOR THE NON-CORPOREAL ASPECT OF THE HUMAN BEING

The Qur'an uses five terms for the non-material or spiritual aspect of the human being. They are often thought to be synonymous, but depending on the context, they have different meanings. These five terms are: *rūḥ* (soul or spirit), *nafs* (self), *qalb* (heart), *fu'ād* (the aware heart), and *ṣadr* (breast), and are defined briefly below:

1. *Rūḥ*: This is the spirit that was breathed by God into man, that transformed him from a mere animal into a sublime creature deserving of the prostration of the angels. It is the origin of human life and gives man the ability to perceive realities and move through free volition.[10]

2. *Nafs*: This is the self or psyche of a human individual. In the Qur'an, the term has several usages: the human body, the human soul, and the combination of body and soul. Its various states have been mentioned as *al-nafs al-ammārah* (inciting soul, Q12:53), *al-nafs al-lawwāmah* (self-reproaching soul, Q75:2), *al-nafs al-mulhamah*

---

8 Ibid.

قَالُوا: وَمَا عَلَامَةُ ذَلِكَ يَا رَسُولَ اللهِ؟ قَالَ: التَّجَافِي عَنْ دَارِ الْغُرُورِ، وَالْإِنَابَةُ إِلَى دَارِ الْخُلُودِ، وَالِاسْتِعْدَادُ لِلْمَوْتِ قَبْلَ نُزُولِهِ.

9 Majlisī, *Zād al-Ma'ād*, p. 129.

10 Ṭabāṭabā'ī, *al-Mīzān*, 13/195; Shīrāzī, *Namūneh*, 12/250.

(inspired soul, Q91:8), *al-nafs al-muṭmainnah* (contented soul, Q89:27), *al-nafs al-rāḍiyah* (pleased soul, Q89:28), and *al-nafs al-marḍiyyah* (pleasing soul, Q89:28). In brief, it is the prevailing state of the individual's obedience or disobedience to God at any given time.

3. *Qalb*: The original meaning of *qalb* is something that changes from one state to another. It refers to the spiritual (as opposed to the physical) heart which is in a constant state of flux. In the Qurʾan, it is used when God refers to spiritual sicknesses of the heart. It is the faculty of spiritual intelligence through which the human being deliberates on, and then carries out, the activities of his life.[11]
4. *Fuʾād*: This is the faculty by which human beings perceive realities and make informed decisions and choices that reflect their true inner state. It is the same as the *qalb*, except that *qalb* can refer to a physical heart as well.[12]
5. *Ṣadr*: The meaning of *ṣadr* is the prominent part of anything, and this is why one of its usages is for the chest and breast of a human being. When used in a spiritual sense, it has a more expansive meaning than *qalb*, and refers to the potentials and capacities latent in a human being.[13] These capacities can be expanded or contracted, thereby increasing or diminishing an individual's confidence and ability to perform tasks.

SUMMARY OF THE VERSE

The verse reminds the Prophet (s) that God had given him the great bounty of expanding his capacity so that he could ably face the challenge of carrying out his Divine mission.

REFLECTIVE LEARNING

The gift of *inshirāḥ al-ṣadr* is not exclusive to the Prophet (s) but is available to anyone who truly submits to God.

Let me reflect on what rebellious elements I can change in myself to submit more fully to God, so as to receive this gift.

---

[11] Ṭabāṭabāʾī, *al-Mīzān*, 9/46.

[12] Miṣbāh Yazdī, *Maʿārif-i Qurʾan*, 1/392.

[13] Muṣṭafawī, *al-Taḥqīq*.

VERSES 2, 3

وَوَضَعْنَا عَنْكَ وِزْرَكَ ﴿٢﴾ الَّذِي أَنْقَضَ ظَهْرَكَ ﴿٣﴾

And removed from you your burden, [2] *which weighed down your back.* [3]

2-3.1 These verses mention a second bounty of God. Even before he was appointed to his mission, the Prophet (s) was constantly thinking of how he could change the mindset of his people. And when he was appointed as God's Messenger, he was concerned about how best to carry out the mission he was charged with. He knew well the entrenched attitudes and habits of his people. His message of monotheism was radically different from their idolatry, and was not going to be easily accepted. These matters weighed heavily on him.

2-3.2 '*And removed from you your burden.*': [*Wizr* (وِزْر, burden)] denotes a heavy burden. The term has also been used in the Qur'an for sin because its burden weighs heavily on the soul of the sinner. Q35:18 states:

وَلَا تَزِرُ وَازِرَةٌ وِزْرَ أُخْرَىٰ وَإِنْ تَدْعُ مُثْقَلَةٌ إِلَىٰ حِمْلِهَا
لَا يُحْمَلْ مِنْهُ شَيْءٌ وَلَوْ كَانَ ذَا قُرْبَىٰ

And no bearer of burdens shall bear the burden [of sins] of another. And if one who is heavily-laden calls [another] to carry his load, nothing of it will be carried, even if he should be a close relative...

A minister is called *wazīr* because he shoulders the heavy burden of leadership.[14]

2-3.3 The mention of the removal of the burden of the Prophet (s) (*waḍʿ al-wizr*) in this verse is a continuation of the favour of expansion of the breast mentioned in the first verse.[15] Thus God alleviated the burden by expanding the capacity of the heart of His Messenger (s).

2-3.4 '*Which weighed down your back.*': [*Anqaḍa ẓahraka* (أَنقَضَ ظَهْرَكَ, weighed down your back)]. The word *anqaḍa* derives from the

[14] Shīrāzī, *Namūneh*, 27/124.

[15] Ṭabāṭabā'ī, *al-Mīzān*, 20/315.

creaking sound (*naqīḍ*) of the back (*ẓahr*) of a camel when a heavy burden is placed on it.[16]

Here, the term *anqaḍa ẓahraka* is used metaphorically to describe the huge mental strain on the Prophet (s) in the face of the task that lay before him: preaching monotheism to long-standing polytheists, reforming a society that had decayed into oppression and misogyny, and changing the focus of his people from this world to the Hereafter.[17] In other words, a weight that could have broken his back.

SUMMARY OF THE VERSES

The verses mention the favour of God to the Prophet (s) when He removed the burden of worry that was pressing heavily on his back.

REFLECTIVE LEARNING

Just as God removed the burden of worry that was pressing heavily on the back of the Prophet (s), He removes the burdens of the believers also.

Let me reflect if I truly believe that at times of hardship, God will remove my burden or are there moments when I doubt this fact.

VERSE 4

وَرَفَعْنَا لَكَ ذِكْرَكَ ﴿٤﴾

And We raised for you your reputation. [4]

4.1 This verse reveals a third favour bestowed on the Prophet (s), namely the spread of his fame and reputation. God linked the mention of the Prophet (s) to His own mention, for example, in the fundamental testimony of faith (*shahādah*), in the call to prayer (*adhān and iqāmah*), and in the testimonies recited in every prayer (*tashahhud*).[18] On the Day of Judgement he will be the chief intercessor for his followers.

4.2 Towards the end of his life when he was blind, Abu Sufyan was sitting in a gathering where Imam Ali (a) was also present. The

---

16 Rāzī, *Mafātīḥ al-Ghayb*, 32/207.

17 Shīrāzī, *Namūneh*, 27/124.

18 Ṭabāṭabā'ī, *al-Mīzān*, 20/315.

muezzin gave the *adhān* and when he said, "I bear witness that Muhammad is the Messenger of God," Abu Sufyan asked, "Is there anyone with us that we should be careful of?" Someone assured him, "No." Then he said [sarcastically], "By God, my brother from the Banu Hashim accomplished something. Look where he managed to insert his name!" At that time, Ali (a) said, "May God make your eyes burn, O Abu Sufyan! God raised his name when He stated, '*And We raised for you your reputation*'."[19]

4.3 A tradition from Imam Ali (a) states: The meaning of, 'I testify that there is no deity except God' is the acknowledgement of *tawḥīd*, and the rejection of partners and every other object of worship besides God; and the meaning of, 'I testify that Muhammad is the Messenger of God' is the acknowledgement of his message, his prophethood, and honouring the Messenger of God (s). This is the meaning of the statement of God the Almighty, '*And We raised for you your reputation,*' that is, you will be remembered with Me whenever I am remembered.[20]

4.4 Eloquently, the relief (*waḍʿ*) of the burden that was weighing him down in the previous verse is juxtaposed and contrasted to the elevation (*rafʿ*) of his reputation in this verse.

4.5 [*Rafaʿnā* (رَفَعْنَا, We raised, exalted)] and [*Dhikrak* (ذِكْرَكَ, your mention, your repute)]. *Rafʿ al-dhikr* means to raise the reputation of someone, and here, it refers to the fact that God made the person, words, and deeds of the Prophet (s) famous in his own era and his remembrance (*dhikr*) is established forever on the lips and in the hearts of the Muslims in every generation.

4.6 [*Laka* (لَكَ, for you]. God says that We did this for you to help you against the concerted efforts of your enemies to defame you.[21]

---

[19] Majlisī, *Biḥār*, 18/108.

وَلَقَدْ كُنَّا فِي مَحْفَلٍ فِيهِ أَبُو سُفْيَانَ وَقَدْ كُفَّ بَصَرُهُ وَفِينَا عَلِيٌّ (عَلَيْهِ السَّلَامُ)، فَأَذَّنَ الْمُؤَذِّنُ، فَلَمَّا قَالَ: أَشْهَدُ أَنَّ مُحَمَّدًا رَسُولُ اللهِ، قَالَ أَبُو سُفْيَانَ: هَاهُنَا مَنْ يَحْتَشِمُ؟ قَالَ وَاحِدٌ مِنَ الْقَوْمِ: لَا، فَقَالَ: لِلهِ دَرُّ أَخِ بَنِي هَاشِمٍ انْظُرُوا أَيْنَ وَضَعَ اِسْمَهُ. فَقَالَ عَلِيٌّ (عَلَيْهِ السَّلَامُ): أَسْخَنَ اللهُ عَيْنَكَ يَا أَبَا سُفْيَانَ، اللهُ فَعَلَ ذَلِكَ بِقَوْلِهِ عَزَّ مِنْ قَائِلٍ «وَرَفَعْنَا لَكَ ذِكْرَكَ».

[20] Nūrī, *Mustadrak al-Wasā'il*, 4/74.

عَنْ أَمِيرِ الْمُؤْمِنِينَ (عَلَيْهِ السَّلَامُ) – مَعْنَى قَوْلِهِ: «أَشْهَدُ أَنْ لَا إِلَهَ إِلَّا اللهُ» إِقْرَارٌ بِالتَّوْحِيدِ وَنَفْيُ الْأَنْدَادِ وَخَلْعُهَا وَكُلُّ مَا يُعْبَدُ مِنْ دُونِ اللهِ، وَمَعْنَى «أَشْهَدُ أَنَّ مُحَمَّدًا رَسُولُ اللهِ» إِقْرَارٌ بِالرِّسَالَةِ وَالنُّبُوَّةِ وَتَعْظِيمٌ لِرَسُولِ اللهِ (صَلَّى اللهُ عَلَيْهِ وَآلِهِ) وَذَلِكَ قَوْلُ اللهِ عَزَّ وَجَلَّ «وَرَفَعْنَا لَكَ ذِكْرَكَ» أَيْ تُذْكَرُ مَعِي إِذَا ذُكِرْتَ.

[21] Shīrāzī, *Namūneh*, 27/125.

4.7 It may be asked that since the fame of the Prophet (s) spread after he migrated to Madina, how can this chapter be Makkan? The answer is that frequently in the Qur'an, matters that will definitely happen in the future (for example the verse about events of the Hereafter) are mentioned in the past tense. The Prophet (s) was comforted by these assurances because he knew that God's promise was always true.[22]

4.8 A tradition from Imam Ali (a) states: I asked the Prophet (s), "O Messenger of God, are you superior to Jibra'il?" He (s) replied, "O Ali, God, the Almighty, has made His Prophets, the Messengers, excel over his closest angels, and has made me excel over all the other Prophets and Messengers. And this excellence is for you after me, O Ali, and for the Imams after you. Indeed, the angels serve us and those who love us..."[23]

DISCUSSION 2: THE STATUS OF THE PROPHET (S) OF ISLAM

The Prophets (a) of God have similar roles: calling towards monotheism, dispelling false notions about God, fighting idolatry, removing ignorance, reforming their communities, giving good news about Paradise and warning of Hell, and so on.

They all have similar qualities as well: Divine protection against error and sin, absolute sincerity, truthfulness, steadfastness in God's way, the capacity to receive revelation, and the ability to display evidence of their claim to prophethood.

However, there is no doubt that some Prophets (a) were more senior and more exalted in station. Q17:55 states:

وَلَقَدْ فَضَّلْنَا بَعْضَ النَّبِيِّينَ عَلَىٰ بَعْضٍ

...And We have made some Prophets excel others...

And amongst them, our Prophet (s) was the last and best of God's Prophets (a) and possessed qualities and gifts that were uniquely granted to him that made him God's greatest creation. It is enough

---

[22] Ṭabrasī, *al-Bayān*, 10/771.

[23] Ṣadūq, *ʿUyūn Akhbār*, 1/262.

عَنْ أَمِيرِ الْمُؤْمِنِينَ (عَلَيْهِ السَّلَامُ) – فَقُلْتُ: يَا رَسُولَ اللهِ فَأَنْتَ أَفْضَلُ أَمْ جَبْرَائِيلُ؟ فَقَالَ صَلَّى اللهُ عَلَيْهِ وَآلِهِ: يَا عَلِيُّ إِنَّ اللهَ تَبَارَكَ وَتَعَالَى فَضَّلَ أَنْبِيَاءَهُ الْمُرْسَلِينَ عَلَى مَلَائِكَتِهِ الْمُقَرَّبِينَ وَفَضَّلَنِي عَلَى جَمِيعِ النَّبِيِّينَ وَالْمُرْسَلِينَ وَالْفَضْلُ بَعْدِي لَكَ يَا عَلِيُّ وَلِلْأَئِمَّةِ مِنْ بَعْدِكَ وَإِنَّ الْمَلَائِكَةَ لَخُدَّامُنَا وَخُدَّامُ مُحِبِّينَا.

of a distinction for him that in every act of worship that a Muslim performs, the obligatory part is from the instruction of God and the recommended part (*sunnah*) is from the practice of the Prophet (s).

The Qur'an mentions several unique merits of the Prophet (s):

1. He was the foremost of those who had submitted to God. This great accolade is mentioned in Q6:163:

   لَا شَرِيكَ لَهُ وَبِذَٰلِكَ أُمِرْتُ وَأَنَا أَوَّلُ الْمُسْلِمِينَ

   He has no partner. And this I have been commanded and I am the foremost of those who have submitted to Him (awwal al-muslimīn)

2. Obedience to the Prophet (s) is the same as obedience to God. This unique honour is mentioned in several verses. For example Q33:71 states:

   وَمَنْ يُطِعِ اللّٰهَ وَرَسُولَهُ فَقَدْ فَازَ فَوْزًا عَظِيمًا

   ...And whoever obeys God and His Messenger
   has indeed attained a mighty attainment.

3. Disobedience to the Prophet (s) is the same as disobedience to God. Q33:36 states:

   وَمَا كَانَ لِمُؤْمِنٍ وَلَا مُؤْمِنَةٍ إِذَا قَضَى اللّٰهُ وَرَسُولُهُ أَمْرًا أَنْ يَكُونَ
   لَهُمُ الْخِيَرَةُ مِنْ أَمْرِهِمْ وَمَنْ يَعْصِ اللّٰهَ وَرَسُولَهُ فَقَدْ ضَلَّ ضَلَالًا مُبِينًا

   And it is not for a believing man or a believing woman, when God and His Messenger have decreed a matter, that they should [thereafter] have any choice in their affair. And whoever disobeys God and His Messenger has certainly strayed into clear error.

4. The mention of the name of the Prophet (s) must be followed by invoking God's blessings on him. Indeed, this is the practice of God Himself, and His angels. Q33:56 states:

   إِنَّ اللّٰهَ وَمَلَائِكَتَهُ يُصَلُّونَ عَلَى النَّبِيِّ يَا أَيُّهَا الَّذِينَ آمَنُوا صَلُّوا عَلَيْهِ وَسَلِّمُوا تَسْلِيمًا

   Indeed, God and His angels send blessings on the Prophet. O Believers! Send blessings on him [also], and salute him with worthy salutation.

5. A genuine love and affection for the Prophet (s) in the hearts. Due to his superlative faith and righteous conduct, the Prophet (s) qualifies as the greatest exemplar (*miṣdāq*) of Q19:96:

إِنَّ الَّذِينَ آمَنُوا وَعَمِلُوا الصَّالِحَاتِ سَيَجْعَلُ لَهُمُ الرَّحْمَٰنُ وُدًّا

Indeed those who have believed and done righteous deeds – the most-Merciful will bring about for them love [in the hearts of the believers].

Besides these, the Prophet (s) has other unique merits as well, amongst which are: being a mercy for all mankind, having ascended to the highest heavens in *miʿrāj*, and being the seal of the Prophets (a).

SUMMARY OF THE VERSE

The verse states emphatically how God has ensured that the reputation of the Prophet (s) will be exalted for all time.

REFLECTIVE LEARNING

As a Muslim I continually exalt the Prophet (s) in my *adhān*, *ṣalāt*, and *ṣalawāt*.

Let me reflect on whether these are words on my lips, or do they come from the heart, and therefore govern my actions.

As one who claims to follow the Prophet (s), are any of my actions damaging to his reputation?

VERSES 5, 6

فَإِنَّ مَعَ الْعُسْرِ يُسْرًا ﴿٥﴾ إِنَّ مَعَ الْعُسْرِ يُسْرًا ﴿٦﴾

For indeed, with hardship is ease. [5] *Indeed, with hardship is ease.* [6]

5-6.1 [*Fa inna* (فَإِنَّ, for indeed)]. The usage of *fa inna* indicates that the matters raised in previous verses arise from a general law: hardship is always accompanied by ease. The verse means, 'what We did for you was always meant to happen, because hardship cannot come without ease.'[24]

5-6.2 These verses are an immense source of consolation and reassurance from God. In whatever hardship one finds himself, God

[24] Rafsanjānī, *Rahnamā*, 20/531.

has promised that ease is not far away, and one must never give in to despair.

5-6.3 [*Maʿa* (مَعَ, with)]. This means that along with every hardship there is ease, or within every hardship lies the means to achieve ease. Therefore, one should not be so overcome and engrossed with the hardship that one forgets to search for the many solutions to ease that are simultaneously available.

5-6.4 Some scholars believe that since hardship and ease cannot be present at the same time, *maʿa* here means that ease invariably follows hardship, and not that they exist together.[25] This is stated in Q65:7:

سَيَجْعَلُ اللّٰهُ بَعْدَ عُسْرٍ يُسْرًا

...God will bring about after hardship, ease.

5-6.5 [*al-ʿUsr* (اَلْعُسْر, hardship)] denotes lack of means and hardship.[26] [*Yusr* (يُسْر, ease)] means ease and lifting of restriction. It is the opposite of *ʿusr*. In fact, *yusr* rises from *ʿusr*; in other words, ease in life is not possible without first undergoing hardship.[27]

ʿUsr is mentioned in the definite form, *al-ʿusr*, and can refer to anything that is a hardship. On the other hand, *yusr* has come in the indefinite form, to indicate that every hardship will always be open to various solutions that will provide ease.[28] A report states: God, the Almighty said, "For every difficulty I created two solutions for ease. So one difficulty will not overcome two solutions for ease."[29]

5-6.6 The sixth verse is an emphasis and confirmation of the fifth, to show that with hardship there will certainly be ease. The repetition further stresses that hardship and ease constantly follow each other in the course of human history.

5-6.7 Hardship is part and parcel of human life. Different forms of it will touch everyone. It is for individuals to find the inner strength and conviction to remain steadfast in their covenant to God.

---

[25] Ṭabāṭabāʾī, *al-Mīzān*, 20/316.

[26] Muṣṭafawī, *al-Taḥqīq*.

[27] Muṭahharī, (*Āshnāyī bā Qurʾan*), *Āthār*, 28/632.

[28] Ṭabāṭabāʾī, *al-Mīzān*, 20/316.

[29] Ḥuwayzī, *Nūr al-Thaqalayn*, 5/604.

عَنْ اِبْنِ عَبَّاسٍ (رَحْمَةُ اللهِ عَلَيْهِ) – يَقُولُ اللهُ تَعَالَى: خَلَقْتُ عُسْرًا وَاحِدًا وَخَلَقْتُ يُسْرَيْنِ، فَلَنْ يَغْلِبَ عُسْرٌ يُسْرَيْنِ.

Q2:155 states:

وَلَنَبْلُوَنَّكُمْ بِشَيْءٍ مِنَ الْخَوْفِ وَالْجُوعِ وَنَقْصٍ
مِنَ الْأَمْوَالِ وَالْأَنْفُسِ وَالثَّمَرَاتِ وَبَشِّرِ الصَّابِرِينَ

And We will indeed test you with something of fear and hunger and loss of wealth and lives and fruits [of your hard work]; but give good tidings to the steadfast (al-ṣābirīn).

5-6.8 The hardship that the Prophet (s) went through in the beginning of his mission was great. He was ignored, called a liar and a madman, his followers were persecuted and boycotted, attempts were made on his life, and he was forced to leave the city of his birth. However after migration to Madina, a large part of these hardships were eased.

5-6.9 A tradition from the Prophet (s) states: Know that with steadfastness is victory, with affliction is relief, and with hardship is ease; indeed, with hardship is ease.[30]

SUMMARY OF THE VERSES

The verses give an assurance by God that hardship is always accompanied by ease. The verse is repeated twice to emphasize this important message.

REFLECTIVE LEARNING

'Hardship is accompanied by ease' is one of the most hopeful messages of the Qur'an.

Let me reflect on what was the ease within the last hardship that I endured.

Have I learnt to find the ease that accompanies every hardship?

[30] Ṣadūq, *al-Faqīh*, 4/413

عَنِ الرَّسُولِ (صَلَّى اللهُ عَلَيْهِ وَآلِهِ) – وَاعْلَمْ أَنَّ النَّصْرَ مَعَ الصَّبْرِ، وَأَنَّ الْفَرَجَ مَعَ الْكَرْبِ، وَأَنَّ «مَعَ الْعُسْرِ يُسْرًا إِنَّ مَعَ الْعُسْرِ يُسْرًا.»

VERSES 7, 8

فَإِذَا فَرَغْتَ فَٱنْصَبْ ﴿٧﴾ وَإِلَىٰ رَبِّكَ فَٱرْغَبْ ﴿٨﴾

So when you are free, then [continue to] exert yourself. [7] *And to your Lord turn your attention.* [8]

7-8.1 These verses are addressed to the Prophet (s) but apply to all and the use of *fa* (so) at the beginning is to indicate that this is linked to the previous verses: how God expanded the capacity of the Prophet (s), removed the heavy burden of worry that was weighing his back, made him famous, and thereby gave him ease with every hardship.[31]

What follows now are the 'action-points'.

7-8.2 '*So when you are free, then [continue to] exert yourself.*': [*Faraghta* (فَرَغْتَ, when you are free)]. *Faragha* generally means to be empty or unoccupied. Here, it means free of obligatory responsibility (*wājibāt*). The verse does not state any specific responsibility, and it could refer to *salat* or other duties to do with the needs of life and family. In short, it refers to free time that one can devote to oneself.[32]

[*Fa'nṣab* (فَٱنْصَبْ, so busy yourself)]. *Inṣab* is the imperative form of the verb *naṣaba*, which means exertion and striving.[33]

7-8.3 The important message here is that freedom from responsibility does not mean that one should while away the spare time in frivolous and worthless pastimes. The verses imply that one's free time should be devoted to turning to God, eager to attain His proximity. However, there are several reports of specific applications to the verses:

i) When you are free from worldly obligations, turn your attention to building your Hereafter,

ii) When you have completed the obligatory worship, embark on performing recommended acts of worship,

iii) When you have completed the struggle (*jihād*) against external forces, begin the struggle against your lower self (*jihād al-nafs*).[34]

---

[31] Ṭabāṭabā'ī, *al-Mīzān*, 20/317.

[32] Mustafawī, *al-Tahqīq*.

[33] Shīrāzī, *Namūneh*, 27/128.

[34] Ṭabrasī, *al-Bayān*, 10/773.

7-8.4 In several reports, verse 7 is said to refer to the appointment of Imam Ali (a) as the successor of the Prophet (s). For example, it has been reported that Imam al-Sadiq (a) has stated about this verse: It means: appoint (*inṣib*) Ali (a) for *wilāyah*.[35]

Therefore the verse would be translated, 'So when you are free [from the tasks of prophethood], then appoint [your successor].'

It has been alleged that the *Shīʿa* make this assertion by reciting the verse as *fanṣib* (so appoint) instead of *fa'nṣab* (so exert yourself), that is, with a *kasrah* instead of a *fatḥah*.[36] However, the assertion of the *Shīʿa* stands from the regular reading as well, and the translation of the verse would be, 'So when you are free [from the tasks of prophethood], then exert yourself in another task [nominate Ali].'[37]

7-8.5 '*And to your Lord turn your attention.*': [*Irghab* (ارْغَبْ, turn your attention)] is derived from *raghaba* which means to desire and turn to in hope. Here it refers to seeking God's pleasure and turning towards Him.[38] It also means seeking your desires (*ḥājāt*) from Him and no other.[39]

7-8.6 In providing an interpretation (*ta'wīl*) of this verse, a tradition from Imam al-Baqir (a) states: When you complete the prayer and recite the final *salām*, busy yourself in supplications about matters of this world and the Hereafter, while you are still sitting. And when you finish your supplication then turn [earnestly] to God, the Almighty, so that He may accept from you [your worship].[40]

---

35 Ḥaskānī, *Shawāhid al-Tanzīl*, 2/451.

عَنِ الصَّادِقِ (عَلَيْهِ السَّلَامُ) – «فَإِذَا فَرَغْتَ فَانْصَبْ»، قَالَ: يَعْنِي [انْصِبْ] عَلِيًّا لِلْوِلَايَةِ.

36 Ālūsī, *Rūḥ al-Maʿānī*, 15/392.

37 Shīrāzī, *Namūneh*, 27/129.

38 Ibid, 27/128.

39 Ṭabrasī, *al-Bayān*, 10/774.

40 ʿĀmilī, *Wasā'il*, 6/431.

عَنِ الْبَاقِرِ (عَلَيْهِ السَّلَامُ) – إِذَا قَضَيْتَ الصَّلَاةَ بَعْدَ أَنْ تُسَلِّمَ وَأَنْتَ جَالِسٌ فَانْصَبْ فِي الدُّعَاءِ مِنْ أَمْرِ الدُّنْيَا وَالْآخِرَةِ، فَإِذَا فَرَغْتَ مِنَ الدُّعَاءِ، فَارْغَبْ إِلَى اللهِ عَزَّ وَجَلَّ أَنْ يَتَقَبَّلَهَا مِنْكَ.

SUMMARY OF THE VERSES

In summary, the verses mean that now that you are relieved of one important task, embark on another important task.[41] Every time you are free of the responsibilities placed on your shoulders, turn your attention eagerly to God in worship and supplication.[42]

REFLECTIVE LEARNING

Let me reflect on how I spend my leisure and spare time.

Instead of only pursuing frivolous activity, can I add something to my practice to get closer to God?

---

[41] Shīrāzī, *Namūneh*, 27/128.

[42] Ṭabāṭabā'ī, *al-Mīzān*, 20/317.

SURAT AL-TĪN
THE FIG (95)

TEXT AND TRANSLATION

سُورَةُ التِّينِ

بِسْمِ اللهِ الرَّحْمٰنِ الرَّحِيمِ

وَالتِّينِ وَالزَّيْتُونِ ﴿١﴾ وَطُورِ سِينِينَ ﴿٢﴾ وَهٰذَا الْبَلَدِ الْأَمِينِ ﴿٣﴾ لَقَدْ خَلَقْنَا
الْإِنْسَانَ فِي أَحْسَنِ تَقْوِيمٍ ﴿٤﴾ ثُمَّ رَدَدْنَاهُ أَسْفَلَ سَافِلِينَ ﴿٥﴾ إِلَّا الَّذِينَ آمَنُوا
وَعَمِلُوا الصَّالِحَاتِ فَلَهُمْ أَجْرٌ غَيْرُ مَمْنُونٍ ﴿٦﴾ فَمَا يُكَذِّبُكَ بَعْدُ بِالدِّينِ ﴿٧﴾
أَلَيْسَ اللهُ بِأَحْكَمِ الْحَاكِمِينَ ﴿٨﴾

In the name of God, the Beneficent, the Merciful.

By the fig and the olive, [1] *and [by] Mount Sinai,* [2] *and [by] this secure city.* [3] *Verily, We created man in the best constitution.* [4] *Then We returned him to the lowest of the low.* [5] *Except those who believe and do righteous acts, for they shall have a reward never to be cut off.* [6] *Then what causes you to deny [after this] the [Day of] Recompense?* [7] *Is God not the most Just of judges?* [8]

INTRODUCTION

Surat al-Tīn (95) was the 28th chapter to be revealed. It has eight verses and was revealed in Makka, after Surat al-Burūj (85).[1] It is named after the oath made by the fig (*al-tīn*) in the opening verse.

In this surah, after God swears solemn oaths, He informs mankind that He created them with the best form and potential. Thereafter, they could use their free will to achieve their potential or waste it.

Those who believe in God and do acts of goodness based on this belief would have a perpetual reward, while those who deviate would fall lower than the lowest of creatures.

---

[1] Maʿrifat, *ʿUlūm-i Qurʾānī*, p. 90.

In the end, God, the all-Wise and all-Just, will judge them.

LINK TO THE PREVIOUS CHAPTER

The previous chapter, Surat al-Inshirāḥ, mentions the favours of God to the Prophet (s). In Surat al-Tīn, God describes the fates of those who profess belief in the message of the Prophet (s) and those who denied him.

At the end of Surat al-Inshirāḥ, the Prophet (s) is asked to make God his exclusive focus of attention. Surat al-Tīn mentions the high potential that exists in man due to his excellent creation; a potential that can only be realized by keeping his focus exclusively on God and following the authority (*wilāyah*) of those appointed by Him.

MERITS OF RECITATION

- A tradition from the Prophet (s) states: Whoever recites Surat al-Tīn will be granted two qualities by God as long as he is alive: wellbeing and conviction in faith. When he dies, he will be given the reward of one fast for all those who had recited this surah.[2]
- A tradition from Imam Ali (a) states: When you complete the recitation of Surat al-Tīn, say, "And we bear witness to this."[3]
- A tradition from Imam al-Sadiq (a) states: Whoever recites this surah in his obligatory or optional prayers shall be awarded from the blessings of Paradise, that which will please him, God willing."[4]

EXEGESIS

VERSES 1 - 3

وَالتِّينِ وَالزَّيْتُونِ ﴿١﴾ وَطُورِ سِينِينَ ﴿٢﴾ وَهَٰذَا الْبَلَدِ الْأَمِينِ ﴿٣﴾

---

[2] Ṭabrasī, *al-Bayān*, 10/774.

عَنِ الرَّسُولِ (صَلَّى اللهُ عَلَيْهِ وَآلِهِ) – مَنْ قَرَأَهَا أَعْطَاهُ اللهُ خَصْلَتَيْنِ الْعَافِيَةَ وَالْيَقِينَ مَا دَامَ حَيًّا فَإِذَا مَاتَ أَعْطَاهُ اللهُ تَعَالَى مِنَ الْأَجْرِ بِعَدَدِ مَنْ قَرَأَهَا صِيَامَ يَوْمٍ.

[3] Ṣadūq, *al-Khiṣāl*, 2/629.

عَنْ أَمِيرِ الْمُؤْمِنِينَ (عَلَيْهِ السَّلَامُ) – إِذَا قَرَأْتُمْ: وَالتِّينِ فَقُولُوا فِي آخِرِهَا وَنَحْنُ عَلَى ذَلِكَ مِنَ الشَّاهِدِينَ.

[4] Ṣadūq, *Thawāb al-Aʿmāl*, p. 123.

عَنِ الصَّادِقِ (عَلَيْهِ السَّلَامُ) – مَنْ قَرَأَ وَالتِّينِ فِي فَرَائِضِهِ وَنَوَافِلِهِ، أُعْطِيَ مِنَ الْجَنَّةِ حَيْثُ يَرْضَى إِنْ شَاءَ اللهُ.

By the fig and the olive, [1] *and [by] Mount Sinai,* [2] *and [by] this secure city.* [3]

1-3.1 The *waw* (و) at the beginning of the first three verses signifies an oath. The oaths of the Qurʾan have two purposes: to emphasize the subject matter to follow (*muqsam ʿalayhi*), and to indicate the majesty and importance of the thing by which the oath is taken (*muqsam bihi*).

These verses mention oaths by places and objects that are sanctified by God because He wants to emphasize the importance of the message that follows the oaths. We have discussed the subject of oaths further in the *tafsīr* of Surat al-Shams (91).

1-3.2 To indicate an oath, the Qurʾan uses the '*waw*' of *qasam* (oath), or the phrase, '*lā uqsimu*'. The Qurʾan also employs other terms for oaths: *qasam* (e.g. Q56:76, Q89:5), *ḥalf* (Q5:89), and *yamīn* (e.g. Q2:225, Q3:77). There are over a hundred oaths in the Qurʾan, where God swears by Himself, and a variety of objects, places, and times.

1-3.3 The chapter begins with an oath on four things as a prelude to the important message that is to follow. In its apparent meaning, the oaths are sworn upon two famous fruits and two important places.

1-3.4 '*By the fig and the olive*': [*Al-Tīn* (التِّين)] means fig, and [*al-Zaytūn* (الزَّيْتُون)] means olive. Although this is the only mention of the fig in the Qur'an, olives have been mentioned seven times (six times directly and once indirectly).[5]

1-3.5 As to the meaning implied in the mention of these two particular fruits, there are several opinions, two of which are discussed below:

i) That the reference is to these two well-known fruits themselves, in particular because they possess extraordinary physical (nutritional and healing) and spiritual benefits as mentioned in the traditions:

A tradition from the Prophet (s) states: If I were to speak of a fruit that had descended from heaven, I would say it was this very one [the fig].[6]

---

[5] Shīrāzī, *Namūneh*, 27/141.

[6] Ḥuwayzī, *Nūr al-Thaqalayn*, 5/607.

عَنِ الرَّسُولِ (صَلَّى اللهُ عَلَيْهِ وَآلِهِ) – رُوِيَ عَنْ أَبِي ذَرٍّ (رَحْمَةُ اللهِ عَلَيْهِ) أَنَّهُ قَالَ فِي التِّينِ: لَوْ قُلْتُ إِنَّ فَاكِهَةً نَزَلَتْ مِنَ الْجَنَّةِ لَقُلْتُ هَذِهِ هِيَ.

And a tradition from Imam al-Ridha (a) states: The fig eliminates bad breath, strengthens the teeth and bones, causes the hair to grow, and cures [many] ailments, taking away the need for other medicines. It is also reported that he (a) said, "The fig most closely resembles the fruits of Paradise."[7]

Similarly, there are many traditions about both the material and spiritual benefits of olives and olive oil. For example, a tradition states that the Prophet (s) said, "I advise you to consume olive oil because it empties the gall bladder, removes phlegm, and strengthens the sinews. It beautifies the manners, freshens the breath, and dispels sorrow."[8]

This interpretation would mean that these two oaths are taken by two sources of physical benefit, followed by two further oaths by sources that give spiritual benefit. And it is the combination of the physical and spiritual make-up of the human being that gives him the excellent and unique constitution that is the subject of the four oaths.

ii) The other opinion is that these two oaths refer to the mountainous lands of Sham and Palestine[9] (where figs and olives, respectively, grew in abundance). These were the homelands of many Prophets of God, and where they received His revelation. More specifically, *tīn* may refer to Sham which was the land to which Prophet Ibrahim (a) migrated, and *zaytūn* may be a reference to the Mount of Olives, which was the centre of the preaching and worship of Prophet Isa (a).[10]

1-3.6 The next two oaths refer to Mount Sinai and Makka, the two blessed and spiritually charged places where two other great Messengers of God, Prophets Musa (a) and Muhammad (s), received their scriptures.

---

[7] Kulaynī, *al-Kāfī*, 6/358.

عَنْ الرِّضَا (عَلَيْهِ السَّلَامُ) – التِّينُ يُذْهِبُ بِالْبَخْرِ وَيَشُدُّ الْفَمَ وَالْعَظْمَ وَيُنْبِتُ الشَّعْرَ وَيُذْهِبُ بِالدَّاءِ وَلَا يُحْتَاجُ مَعَهُ إِلَى دَوَاءٍ، وَقَالَ عَلَيْهِ السَّلَامُ: التِّينُ أَشْبَهُ شَيْءٍ بِنَبَاتِ الْجَنَّةِ.

[8] Nūrī, *Mustadrak al-Wasā'il*, 16/365.

عَنِ الرَّسُولِ (صَلَّى اللهُ عَلَيْهِ وَآلِهِ) – عَلَيْكُمْ بِالزَّيْتِ فَإِنَّهُ يَكْشِفُ الْمِرَّةَ وَيُذْهِبُ بِالْبَلْغَمِ وَيَشُدُّ الْعَصَبَ وَيُحَسِّنُ الْخُلُقَ وَيُطَيِّبُ النَّفَسَ وَيُذْهِبُ بِالْهَمِّ.

[9] Ḥaskānī, *Shawāhid al-Tanzīl*, 2/454.

فَقَالَ ابْنُ عَبَّاسٍ: أَمَّا قَوْلُ اللهِ تَعَالَى: وَالتِّينِ فَبِلَادُ الشَّامِ، وَالزَّيْتُونِ فَبِلَادُ فِلَسْطِينَ.

[10] Zamakhsharī, *al-Kashshāf*, 4/774.

1-3.7 *'And [by] Mount Sinai, and [by] this secure city.'*: [*Ṭūr Sinīn* (طُورِ سِينِينَ, Mount Sinai)] is the mountain in Egypt to which Prophet Musa (a) was summoned by God for forty nights.

[*Al-Balad al-amīn* (الْبَلَدِ الْأَمِينِ, the secure city)] refers to Makka because its security has been enshrined in law by God, a distinction that no other land in the world enjoys. Q29:67 states:

أَوَلَمْ يَرَوْا أَنَّا جَعَلْنَا حَرَمًا آمِنًا

Have they not seen that we have made [Makka] a safe sanctuary?

1-3.8 This security is also a response to the supplication of Prophet Ibrahim (a), which he made when he left his wife Hajar and infant son Ismaʿil (a) in Makka. Q2:126 states:

وَإِذْ قَالَ إِبْرَاهِيمُ رَبِّ ٱجْعَلْ هَٰذَا بَلَدًا آمِنًا وَٱرْزُقْ أَهْلَهُ
مِنَ الثَّمَرَاتِ مَنْ آمَنَ مِنْهُمْ بِاللَّهِ وَالْيَوْمِ الْآخِرِ

And when Ibrahim said, "My Lord, make this a secure city,
and provide its people with fruits, the ones of them
that believe in God and the last Day..."

1-3.9 The use of *hādhā* (هَٰذَا, this) for Makka may indicate that the chapter was revealed in Makka,[11] or highlight the superiority of Makka and the Kaʿbah over the other three locations.

1-3.10 Possibly these oaths refer to four places where the greatest Prophets (a) of God received revelation and guidance. In this case, in these opening verses, God swears by His guidance to mankind. The later verses speak about those who accepted this guidance and those who rejected it.

DISCUSSION 1: SACRED ENTITIES

Sacredness is a quality in something that makes it praiseworthy and deserving of deep respect and reverence. The reason why certain entities are more sacred than others is to do with their stronger connection to God, who Himself is the real Sacred and Sanctified being.

One of the Qur'anic terms for these sacred entities is *shaʿāʾir* (symbols or customs).[12] These are symbols that hold deep significance in the

---

[11] Ṭabāṭabāʾī, *al-Mīzān*, 20/319.

[12] Muṣṭafawī, *al-Taḥqīq*.

system of existence. They are signs placed by God to direct the believers towards Him.[13] As an example, the Qur'an calls the mountains of Safa and Marwah *sha'ā'ir;* Q2:158 states:

إِنَّ الصَّفَا وَالْمَرْوَةَ مِنْ شَعَائِرِ اللهِ فَمَنْ حَجَّ الْبَيْتَ
أَوِ اعْتَمَرَ فَلَا جُنَاحَ عَلَيْهِ أَنْ يَطَّوَّفَ بِهِمَا

Indeed, al-Safa and al-Marwah are from the symbols (sha'ā'ir) *of God. So, whoever makes the Haj to the House or performs the 'Umrah, there is no blame upon him for walking between them.*

About the respect of these sacred symbols Q5:2 states:

يَا أَيُّهَا الَّذِينَ آمَنُوا لَا تُحِلُّوا شَعَائِرَ اللهِ

O believers, do not violate the sanctity of the symbols of God...

And Q22:32 states:

ذَٰلِكَ وَمَنْ يُعَظِّمْ شَعَائِرَ اللهِ فَإِنَّهَا مِنْ تَقْوَى الْقُلُوبِ

That [is so]. And whoever honours the symbols of God, indeed, that is due to the piety of the hearts.

The Qur'an and narrations talk of the special significance of five things, and declare them sacred (*muqaddas*): sacred places, sacred times, sacred people, sacred deeds, and sacred objects. Once we become aware of the details of these entities, we are required to be respectful towards them, and in this way show our devotion to God.

1. Lands and places: There are certain lands that are particularly blessed. For example, when Prophet Musa (a) reached the sacred valley where God spoke to him, Q20:12 states that he was told:

   إِنِّي أَنَا رَبُّكَ فَاخْلَعْ نَعْلَيْكَ إِنَّكَ بِالْوَادِ الْمُقَدَّسِ طُوًى

   Indeed, I am your Lord, so remove your sandals, for indeed, you are in the sacred valley of Ṭuwā.

   Amongst the most sacred places are mosques; the greatest of which is Masjid al-Harām in Makka which houses the Kab'ah, and thereafter, Masjid al-Nabawi (s) in Madina, Masjid Bayt al-Maqdis in Jerusalem, and Masjid al-Kufa. A tradition from Imam

[13] Ṭabāṭabā'ī, *al-Mīzān*, 14/374, (exegesis of Q22:32).

Ali (a) states: There are four palaces of Paradise [that have representations] in this world: Masjid al-Harām, the Masjid of the Messenger (s), Masjid Bayt al-Maqdis and Masjid al-Kufa.[14]

Other places are considered sacred due to the presence of the graves of the close servants (*awliyāʾ*) of God, such as the graves of the Prophets (a), the Imams (a), and pious scholars.

2. Times and occasions: There are certain days and nights in the year that have been declared blessed by God. Examples include: Friday (*yawm al-Jumuʿah*), the days of Eid al-Fitr, Adha, and Ghadir, the month of Ramadan, the days of Haj, and the occasions of the birth and passing of the *awliyāʾ* of God, the Prophet (s) and his household (a).

   One of the greatest nights in the year is the night of Qadr. God has called this night blessed in Q44:3:

   إِنَّا أَنْزَلْنَاهُ فِي لَيْلَةٍ مُبَارَكَةٍ

   Indeed, We sent it down on a blessed night (the night of Qadr)...

   And greater in merit than an entire lifetime in Q97:3:

   لَيْلَةُ الْقَدْرِ خَيْرٌ مِنْ أَلْفِ شَهْرٍ

   The night of Qadr is better than a thousand months.

3. Individuals: Prophets (a), their righteous successors (a), the martyrs, God's close servants (*awliyāʾ*), and people who have sincerely worshipped God are all sacred through their close connection to God.

4. Actions: Deeds such as prayer, fasting, Haj, *jihad* in God's way, charity and all acts that are done to attain God's pleasure and proximity are also referred to as sacred signs (*shaʿāʾir*) in the narrations.

5. Objects and signs: Finally, certain objects that are directly connected to God are considered holy and sacred. These include the books of God (the Qurʾan and previous scriptures) and the house of God (the Kaʿbah).

---

14 ʿĀmilī, *Wasāʾil*, 5/283.

عَنْ أَمِيرِ الْمُؤْمِنِينَ (عَلَيْهِ السَّلَامُ) – أَرْبَعَةٌ مِنْ قُصُورِ الْجَنَّةِ فِي الدُّنْيَا: الْمَسْجِدُ الْحَرَامُ، وَمَسْجِدُ الرَّسُولِ صَلَّى اللهُ عَلَيْهِ وَآلِهِ، وَمَسْجِدُ بَيْتِ الْمَقْدِسِ، وَمَسْجِدُ الْكُوفَةِ.

When there is a combination of factors that are all sacred, then the blessings of that place become great indeed. For example, the land of Karbala was always sacred; therein lies one of God's greatest servants, al-Husayn b. Ali (a), and it witnessed the selfless act of his martyrdom in God's way. It is no wonder that a tradition from Imam al-Sadiq (a) states: The grave of al-Husayn b. Ali (a) is a garden from the gardens of Paradise...there is no senior angel or Prophet (a) of God who does not ask His permission to come for his visitation (*ziyārah*). Multitudes [of them] descend down [to Karbala] and ascend back.[15]

SUMMARY OF THE VERSES

Four oaths are sworn upon two famous fruits and two important places: the fig, the olive, Mount Sinai, and Makka.

REFLECTIVE LEARNING

The oaths in these verses are linked to the guidance of the Prophets (a) that God has commissioned at various times in human history.

Let me reflect on whether I know enough about my Prophet (s) to take him as the perfect role model and the guide towards God that he was sent to be.

VERSE 4

لَقَدْ خَلَقْنَا الْإِنْسَانَ فِي أَحْسَنِ تَقْوِيمٍ ﴿٤﴾

Verily, We created man in the best constitution.

4.1 This verse is the subject (*jawāb*) of the four oaths, emphasizing that man's constitution could not have been made any better.[16]

4.2 [*Taqwīm* (تَقْوِيم, constitution)] is the verbal noun of the verb *qāma*. The term is used for something that is made with a constitution that is suitable for a certain purpose.[17] In this verse, it refers to everything that has gone into the creation of the human being.

---

[15] Nūrī, *Mustadrak al-Wasā'il*, 10/319.

عَنِ الصَّادِقِ (عَلَيْهِ السَّلَامُ) – قَبْرُ الْحُسَيْنِ بْنِ عَلِيٍّ عَلَيْهِ السَّلَامُ ... رَوْضَةٌ مِنْ رِيَاضِ الْجَنَّةِ ... فَلَيْسَ مِنْ مَلَكٍ مُقَرَّبٍ وَلَا نَبِيٍّ مُرْسَلٍ إِلَّا وَهُوَ يَسْأَلُ اللهَ أَنْ يَزُورَهُ فَفَوْجٌ يَهْبِطُ وَفَوْجٌ يَصْعَدُ.

[16] Ṭabāṭabā'ī, *al-Mīzān*, 20/319.

[17] Muṣṭafawī, *al-Taḥqīq*.

God states that man's physical, mental, spiritual, and emotional attributes have been fashioned in the best design that would ensure his survival, progress, and achievement of his potential and the purpose of his creation. Every organ and limb, every inclination and emotion, and every aspect of his being has been designed to serve a noble purpose.[18]

4.3 What gives humans superiority in creation over every other being is the knowledge and potential of the soul that resides within them, and which is unique to them. This soul was of such preeminence that God commanded the angels to bow to man after He infused it into the human being and thus perfected his constitution. Q38:72 states:

فَإِذَا سَوَّيْتُهُ وَنَفَخْتُ فِيهِ مِنْ رُوحِي فَقَعُوا لَهُ سَاجِدِينَ

So, when I have fashioned him and breathed into him of My spirit, then fall down to him in prostration.

Q91:7-10 state:

وَنَفْسٍ وَمَا سَوَّاهَا ﴿٧﴾ فَأَلْهَمَهَا فُجُورَهَا وَتَقْوَاهَا ﴿٨﴾
قَدْ أَفْلَحَ مَنْ زَكَّاهَا ﴿٩﴾ وَقَدْ خَابَ مَنْ دَسَّاهَا

And by [the] soul and He who fashioned it. Then inspired it [to understand] what is wrong for it and what is right for it; the one who purifies it has succeeded, and the one who corrupts it has failed.

4.4 By believing and acting upon the knowledge that is embedded in his soul, man is able to rise towards God and perfection in a way that other creatures cannot. Furthermore, unlike the angels, he has free will, so when he observes God-wariness (*taqwā*) and avoids sin, his worship raises him higher than even the angels.

In the details of the glorious journey of Miʿraj we read: When he reached the farthest Lote-tree (*sidrat al-muntahā*) and encountered the veils (*al-ḥujub*), Jibraʾil said to the Prophet (s): Proceed [alone] O Messenger of God! It is not fitting that I cross this place. If I go any further, I will be burnt to ashes.[19]

---

[18] Shīrāzī, *Namūneh*, 27/144.

[19] Ibn Shahr Āshūb, *al-Manāqib*, 1/179.

فَلَمَّا بَلَغَ إِلَى سِدْرَةِ الْمُنْتَهَى فَانْتَهَى إِلَى الْحُجُبِ فَقَالَ جَبْرَائِيلُ تَقَدَّمْ يَا رَسُولَ اللهِ لَيْسَ لِي أَنْ أَجُوزَ هَذَا الْمَكَانَ وَلَوْ دَنَوْتُ أَنْمُلَةً لَاحْتَرَقْتُ.

SUMMARY OF THE VERSE

The verse states that man has been created in such a manner that he can achieve the highest levels of proximity to God amongst all His creatures.

REFLECTIVE LEARNING

The means to rise towards God are coded into my very being.

Let me reflect on how much information about right and wrong is already present within me in the form of instinct and conscience.

And do I act on this guidance or suppress it?

VERSE 5

ثُمَّ رَدَدْنَاهُ أَسْفَلَ سَافِلِينَ ﴿٥﴾

Then We returned him to the lowest of the low.

5.1 [*Radadnā* (رَدَدْنَا, We returned)] here refers to sending men to the lowest levels of Hell,[20] except for those individuals who have been mentioned in the next verse. It may also mean render (*ja'l*) or change (*taghyīr*),[21] thus meaning that God renders or changes the worth of the one who ignores the potential of his soul to the lowest of the low.

5.2 [*Asfala sāfilīn* (أَسْفَلَ سَافِلِينَ, lowest of the low)]. Because man possesses free will, he can ascend higher than any sentient being when he follows his inner compass and *fiṭrah*, and he can also sink to the lowest depths when he deviates and does not use the superior faculties he has been endowed with. When he does this, these faculties are rendered useless, as Q7:179 states:

وَلَقَدْ ذَرَأْنَا لِجَهَنَّمَ كَثِيرًا مِنَ الْجِنِّ وَالْإِنسِ لَهُمْ قُلُوبٌ لَا يَفْقَهُونَ بِهَا
وَلَهُمْ أَعْيُنٌ لَا يُبْصِرُونَ بِهَا وَلَهُمْ آذَانٌ لَا يَسْمَعُونَ بِهَا
أُولَٰئِكَ كَالْأَنْعَامِ بَلْ هُمْ أَضَلُّ أُولَٰئِكَ هُمُ الْغَافِلُونَ

And We have certainly created for Hell many of the jinn *and mankind. [Because] They have hearts with which they do not*

[20] Ṭūsī, *al-Tibyān*, 10/376.

[21] Ṭabāṭabā'ī, *al-Mīzān*, 20/320.

understand, and they have eyes with which they do not see, and they have ears with which they do not hear. They are like cattle; rather, they are even more astray. These are the heedless ones.

5.3 Another meaning that has been suggested[22] is that after man reaches the heights of strength and vitality, he is returned to weakness and frailty in old age, just as Q36:68 states:

وَمَنْ نُعَمِّرْهُ نُنَكِّسْهُ فِي الْخَلْقِ

And to whomever We grant long life, We reduce him in constitution...

However, this explanation would contradict the next verse, which gives the qualities of the people who do not fall to low depths, no matter what their age or disability.

DISCUSSION 2: ACTS OF GOD

The free will of human beings is established in scholastic theology (*kalām*). The Qur'an does not refute this concept, rather it confirms it in many verses, especially when it speaks of the recompense for good and evil acts.

Occasionally however, it appears that the Qur'an attributes certain acts to God which seem to suggest that man is compelled to act in a particular way. For instance, in this chapter, God attributes both creating humans in the best of forms, and reducing them to the lowest of the low, to Himself. In other verses, God attributes misguidance, increase in perversity in the hearts, and other similar human deviations to Himself.

In order to understand such statements, the verses need to be studied alongside other verses so that a more accurate picture may emerge. For example in the case of misguidance, two verses can be studied together to give a clearer understanding: Q7:186 states:

مَنْ يُضْلِلِ اللَّهُ فَلَا هَادِيَ لَهُ

...And whoever God sends astray, for him there is no guide.

Q2:26 mentions the parable of a mosquito and then states:

يُضِلُّ بِهِ كَثِيرًا وَيَهْدِي بِهِ كَثِيرًا وَمَا يُضِلُّ بِهِ إِلَّا الْفَاسِقِينَ

22 Rāzī, *Mafātīḥ al-Ghayb*, 32/212.

> *...He sends astray many thereby and guides many thereby. And He does not send astray thereby [any] except the transgressors* (fāsiqīn).

When studied together, these verses reveal that the misguidance of God is not something that is initially prompted by Him. It results from an individual's own decision to transgress from the correct path. Once he does that of his own accord, he no longer qualifies for Divine facilitation (*tawfīq*) and guidance, and is deprived of it; the net result is that he goes astray.

In brief, the attribution of all acts to God does not negate man's free will; it simply means that nothing happens without the permission of God.

Man's free will also exists by God's permission in the system of cause and effect that He has created.

SUMMARY OF THE VERSE

The verse states that man, despite his potential, can fall lower than the basest of creatures.

REFLECTIVE LEARNING

Just as I have the potential to rise above the angels, I have the potential to fall below the animals as well.

Let me reflect on whether I am leading a life that is closer to the angelic realm (God-focussed in my activities, pursuing my Hereafter on a daily basis, etc.) or the animalistic one (unfocussed, robotic in my activities, pursuing the material world on a daily basis, etc.)?

VERSE 6

إِلَّا الَّذِينَ آمَنُوا وَعَمِلُوا الصَّالِحَاتِ فَلَهُمْ أَجْرٌ غَيْرُ مَمْنُونٍ ﴿٦﴾

Except those who believe and do righteous acts, for they shall have a reward never to be cut off.

6.1 This verse gives the exception to the preceding verse, describing the two qualities (belief and righteous actions) of those who are protected by God from the disgrace of falling to the lowest depths of creation.

The twin attributes of correct faith and righteous acts based on that faith, are the two wings that allow man to remain ascendant. These two traits (faith and practice) are mentioned in over fifty instances in the Qur'an.

True faith is belief that manifests itself in action, and the strength of the faith will determine the conviction of the action.

6.2 [*Ghayru mamnūn* (غَيْرُ مَمْنُونٍ, perpetual)] describes a reward that is never cut off, never reduced, and for which there is no sense of obligation imposed on the recipient. This eternal recompense and favour does not begin only on the Day of Recompense. In fact, for the believer who does righteous acts, God's favour begins from his life in this world.

In a beautiful report from the Prophet (s) we read: Until a child reaches the age of maturity, the reward of every one of his good acts is written for his parent or parents, while every wrong act he commits is not written against him, or against his parents. When he reaches the age of maturity, the Pen [that records acts] is activated for him. Then, God orders the two angels who are with him to protect him and strengthen him. When he reaches forty years of age in Islam, God grants him protection from three ailments: insanity, leprosy, and damage to the nerves.

When he reaches fifty years of age, God lightens his account.

When he reaches sixty years of age, God inspires him to turn to Him with what He loves.

When he reaches seventy years of age, the inhabitants of the heavens [angels] love him. When he reaches eighty years of age, God records his good deeds and overlooks his sins.

When he reaches ninety years of age, God forgives his past and future sins, and allows him to intercede for his family members. He is now known as God's detainee on earth. And when he reaches the final years of his life and can no longer understand anything after having knowledge, God records for him good acts like those that he used to do when he was healthy, and when he commits a sin it is not recorded against him.[23]

---

[23] Ṭabrasī, *al-Bayān*, 10/776.

عَنِ الرَّسُولِ (صَلَّى اللهُ عَلَيْهِ وَآلِهِ) - الْمَوْلُودُ حَتَّى يَبْلُغَ الْحِنْثَ مَا عَمِلَ مِنْ حَسَنَةٍ كُتِبَ لِوَالِدِهِ أَوْ لِوَالِدَيْهِ، وَمَا عَمِلَ مِنْ سَيِّئَةٍ لَمْ تُكْتَبْ عَلَيْهِ وَلَا عَلَى وَالِدَيْهِ، فَإِذَا بَلَغَ الْحِنْثَ جَرَى عَلَيْهِ الْقَلَمُ، أُمِرَ الْمَلَكَانِ اللَّذَانِ مَعَهُ أَنْ يَحْفَظَا وَأَنْ يُشَدِّدَا، فَإِذَا بَلَغَ أَرْبَعِينَ سَنَةً فِي الْإِسْلَامِ

SUMMARY OF THE VERSE

In summary, the verse states that belief and good action are the criteria for success, and both are required to receive eternal reward from God.

REFLECTIVE LEARNING

The verse teaches that the key to success is belief coupled with righteous action. The stronger my belief, the more conviction there will be in my actions.

Let me reflect on whether there are aspects of my belief that I have not fully embraced or understood and therefore do not act upon as required by Islam. If so, how can I rectify it?

VERSES 7, 8

فَمَا يُكَذِّبُكَ بَعْدُ بِالدِّينِ ﴿٧﴾ أَلَيْسَ اللَّهُ بِأَحْكَمِ الْحَاكِمِينَ ﴿٨﴾

Then what causes you to deny [after this] the [Day of] Recompense? Is God not the most Just of judges?

7-8.1 ‘*Then what causes you to deny [after this] the [Day of Recompense?* ’: [*al-Dīn* (الدِّين, the recompense)]. As we have discussed in the *tafsīr* of Surat al-Fātiḥah (1), in this verse also, *al-Dīn* refers to recompense, whether reward or punishment. The question in verse 7 is addressed to all human beings, asking what drives them to deny the Day of Recompense by ignoring their potential to ascend above every other creature, and instead descend lower than the lowest of creation.

7-8.2 ‘*Is God not the most Just of judges?*’: The question is a rhetorical one, meant to emphasize the preceding verse. The verse means to say that the wisdom and justice of God demands that there should be a judgement about the worthiness of every individual. And since He is the most Wise and most Just of every judge, He will award

---

أَمَّنَهُ اللهُ مِنَ الْبَلَايَا الثَّلَاثَةِ: الْجُنُونِ وَالْجُذَامِ وَالْبَرَصِ، فَإِذَا بَلَغَ الْخَمْسِينَ خَفَّفَ اللهُ مِنْ حِسَابِهِ، فَإِذَا بَلَغَ السِّتِّينَ رَزَقَهُ اللهُ الْإِنَابَةَ إِلَيْهِ بِمَا يُحِبُّ، فَإِذَا بَلَغَ السَّبْعِينَ أَحَبَّهُ أَهْلُ السَّمَاءِ، فَإِذَا بَلَغَ الثَّمَانِينَ كَتَبَ اللهُ لَهُ حَسَنَاتِهِ وَتَجَاوَزَ عَنْ سَيِّئَاتِهِ، فَإِذَا بَلَغَ التِّسْعِينَ غَفَرَ اللهُ لَهُ مَا تَقَدَّمَ مِنْ ذَنْبِهِ وَمَا تَأَخَّرَ، وَشَفَّعَهُ فِي أَهْلِ بَيْتِهِ، وَكَانَ أَسِيرَ اللهِ فِي أَرْضِهِ، فَإِذَا بَلَغَ أَرْذَلَ الْعُمُرِ لِكَيْ لَا يَعْلَمَ بَعْدَ عِلْمٍ شَيْئًا كَتَبَ اللهُ لَهُ مِثْلَ مَا كَانَ يَعْمَلُ فِي صِحَّتِهِ مِنَ الْخَيْرِ، فَإِذَا عَمِلَ سَيِّئَةً لَمْ تُكْتَبْ عَلَيْهِ.

the most fitting reward or punishment, depending on whether the individual fulfils his unique potential or wastes it.

7-8.3 Whenever the Prophet (s) would finish reciting this surah with this verse, he would say, "Yes, indeed! And I am of those who testify to this."[24]

SUMMARY OF THE VERSES

These verses ask man to consider the irrationality of denying the Day of Recompense when God will be the all-Wise Judge and decide the fate of every single person.

REFLECTIVE LEARNING

If I am lethargic with regards to performing righteous deeds, or careless in avoiding sinful conduct, then the question in this verse also applies to me.

Let me reflect on whether my attitude and deeds reveal that in actual fact, I subconsciously deny the Day of Recompense.

---

[24] Ḥuwayzī, *Nūr al-Thaqalayn*, 5/608.

عَنِ الرَّسُولِ (صَلَّى اللهُ عَلَيْهِ وَآلِهِ) - كَانَ رَسُولُ اللهِ (صَلَّى اللهُ عَلَيْهِ وَآلِهِ) إِذَا خَتَمَ هَذِهِ قَالَ: بَلَى وَأَنَا عَلَى ذَلِكَ مِنَ الشَّاهِدِينَ.

SURAT AL-ʿALAQ
THE CLINGING SUBSTANCE (96)

TEXT AND TRANSLATION

سُورَةُ الْعَلَقِ

بِسْمِ اللَّهِ الرَّحْمَٰنِ الرَّحِيمِ

اقْرَأْ بِاسْمِ رَبِّكَ الَّذِي خَلَقَ ﴿١﴾ خَلَقَ الْإِنْسَانَ مِنْ عَلَقٍ ﴿٢﴾ اقْرَأْ وَرَبُّكَ الْأَكْرَمُ
﴿٣﴾ الَّذِي عَلَّمَ بِالْقَلَمِ ﴿٤﴾ عَلَّمَ الْإِنْسَانَ مَا لَمْ يَعْلَمْ ﴿٥﴾ كَلَّا إِنَّ الْإِنْسَانَ لَيَطْغَىٰ
﴿٦﴾ أَنْ رَآهُ اسْتَغْنَىٰ ﴿٧﴾ إِنَّ إِلَىٰ رَبِّكَ الرُّجْعَىٰ ﴿٨﴾ أَرَأَيْتَ الَّذِي يَنْهَىٰ ﴿٩﴾
عَبْدًا إِذَا صَلَّىٰ ﴿١٠﴾ أَرَأَيْتَ إِنْ كَانَ عَلَى الْهُدَىٰ ﴿١١﴾ أَوْ أَمَرَ بِالتَّقْوَىٰ ﴿١٢﴾
أَرَأَيْتَ إِنْ كَذَّبَ وَتَوَلَّىٰ ﴿١٣﴾ أَلَمْ يَعْلَمْ بِأَنَّ اللَّهَ يَرَىٰ ﴿١٤﴾ كَلَّا لَئِنْ لَمْ يَنْتَهِ لَنَسْفَعًا
بِالنَّاصِيَةِ ﴿١٥﴾ نَاصِيَةٍ كَاذِبَةٍ خَاطِئَةٍ ﴿١٦﴾ فَلْيَدْعُ نَادِيَهُ ﴿١٧﴾ سَنَدْعُ الزَّبَانِيَةَ
﴿١٨﴾ كَلَّا لَا تُطِعْهُ وَاسْجُدْ وَاقْتَرِبْ ۩ ﴿١٩﴾

In the name of God, the Beneficent, the Merciful.

Read in the name of your Lord, who created. [1] *Created man from a clinging substance.* [2] *Read! And your Lord is the most-Generous.* [3] *Who taught by the pen.* [4] *Taught man that which he did not know.* [5] *Not at all! But indeed, man is most surely inordinate.* [6] *Because he sees himself as self-sufficient.* [7] *Indeed, to your Lord is the return.* [8] *Have you seen the one who forbids* [9] *a servant when he prays?* [10] *Have you seen if he is upon guidance,* [11] *or enjoins God-wariness?* [12] *Have you seen if he denies and turns away?* [13] *Does he not know that God sees?* [14] *Not at all! If he does not desist, We will seize him by the forelock.* [15] *A lying, sinning forelock!* [16] *Then let him call his associates.* [17] *We will call the guardians of Hell.* [18] *No! Do not obey him. But prostrate [to God] and draw near.* [19]

INTRODUCTION

Most exegetes agree that the five opening verses of Surat al-ʿAlaq (96) were the first verses to be revealed.[1] Many exegetes also believe that the rest of the chapter was revealed some time later and that the first complete surah to be revealed was al-Fātiḥah (1).[2]

The surah has nineteen verses. It is named after the mention of the 'clinging substance' (*al-ʿalaq*) in the second verse.

The surah begins by addressing the Prophet (s), commanding him to read, or proclaim, the final revelation of God.

Then, it reminds man that his Lord and Sustainer created him out of a mere drop of fluid into a wondrous and complex being. God nurtured him and provided for his physical and spiritual needs, teaching him what he did not know.

It goes on to describe how and why man is ungrateful for all these bounties; instead of realizing how needy he is, he considers himself to be self-sufficient.

Man is thereafter informed that the world is a transient phase in his long journey back towards his Lord. He is also warned of the painful chastisement of those who cause a hindrance to the worship of God.

The chapter then ends with an exhortation to remain loyal to God and draw close to Him by prostration.

LINK TO THE PREVIOUS CHAPTER

The previous chapter, Surat al-Tīn, speaks of man's creation in the best constitution. Surat al-ʿAlaq begins by describing the humble beginnings of man's physical form and thereafter, God's nurturing of him.

Surat al-Tīn describes God as the creator in the first person: '*We created man...*'. This type of address denotes closeness and emphasizes the great station of man and his lofty creation. However, despite this, some descend to the lowest of the low.

On the other hand, Surat al-ʿAlaq starts with the mention of man as an insignificant clinging substance, and perhaps that is why the third person address is used: '*He created man...*'. From this insignificant beginning, man can rise to become the noblest of God's creatures.

---

[1] Shīrāzī, *Namūneh*, 27/154.

[2] Maʿrifat, *ʿUlūm-i Qurʾānī*, 1/125.

Surat al-Tīn describes the potential of man to regress from his high position, if he does not profess faith and act righteously. In contrast, Surat al-ʿAlaq describes the potential of man to progress to the highest position, through learning what he did not know.

OCCASION OF REVELATION

These verses were revealed when the Prophet (s) was in the cave of Hira. The cave faces the Kaʿbah and is situated at an altitude of 270m in a mountain by the same name, 10 kms north-east of Makka.[3] Later, the mountain came to be called Jabal al-Nūr (Mountain of Illumination) because of the momentous event that took place there.

The cave itself is quite small, 4 metres in length and 1.5 metres in width. The mountain of Hira was known to be a sacred place to the monotheists (*Ḥunafāʾ*), and ʿAbd al-Muttalib mentioned it during the attack of Abrahah, when he wrote to the Banu Khuzaʿah: As long as the mountains of Ḥirāʾ and Thabīr stand, we will remain united.[4]

The Prophet (s) would often spend time in seclusion and contemplation in the cave. According to many *Shīʿa* scholars, this was where the first revelation came to him on 27th Rajab when he was forty years old.[5]

In part of a long tradition, it is reported from Imam al-Hadi (a) that: When he (s) completed forty years, God examined his heart and found it to be the best of hearts, the most radiant, the most loyal, the most reverent, and the most humble. Then, He allowed the doorways of the skies to be opened up so Muhammad (s) could see into them. He allowed the angels to descend so Muhammad (s) could see them. He commanded mercy to flow down from the side of the Throne upon the head of Muhammad (s), so it enveloped him. And he could see Jibrāʾīl (a), the trusted spirit, the one shrouded with light, and the chief of the angels, who appeared before him. He held his shoulder and shook him, then said: "Read, O Muhammad (s)!" He replied, "What should I read?" He said, "O Muhammad (s)! *Read in the name of your Lord, who created. Created man from a clinging substance. Read! And your Lord is most-Generous. Who taught by the pen. Taught man that which he did not know.*"

---

[3] Jaʿfariyān, *Tārīkh-i Siyāsī-yi Islām*, 1/225.

[4] Subḥānī, *Furūgh-i Abadiyyat*, 1/330.

[5] Majlisī, *Biḥār*, 18/205.

Thereafter, he revealed to him what His Lord, Mighty and Majestic, had revealed to him, and then ascended. Muhammad (s) came down from the mountain. What he had witnessed of the Majesty of God and received from His Exalted Authority filled him with a feverish exhilaration.[6]

The alleged role of Waraqah b. Nawfal

Waraqah was a paternal cousin of Lady Khadijah (a).[7] He was a Christian and well versed with Christian and Jewish scripture.[8] His most important mention in history is his alleged reassurance to the frightened[9] Prophet (s) that he had met the same angel who had been sent to Musa (a) and that if Waraqah would live long enough, he would support the Prophet (s) staunchly.[10]

However, *Shīʿa* scholars dismiss this event as part of the fabricated stories from Jewish sources that have entered Islamic texts (*al-Isrāʾīliyyāt*).[11] They argue that it is absurd to imagine that the Prophet (s) would require validation from a Christian, who apparently recognised the truth but never accepted it. It has been shown that such reports were forged to discredit the Prophet (s) and promoted by the Umayyads due to their enmity towards the Banu Hashim.[12]

---

6 Ibid, 17/309.

فَلَمَّا اسْتَكْمَلَ أَرْبَعِينَ سَنَةٍ، وَنَظَرَ اللهُ عَزَّ وَجَلَّ إِلَى قَلْبِهِ فَوَجَدَهُ أَفْضَلَ الْقُلُوبِ وَأَجَلَّهَا وَأَطْوَعَهَا وَأَخْشَعَهَا وَأَخْضَعَهَا أَذِنَ لِأَبْوَابِ السَّمَاءِ فَفُتِحَتْ وَمُحَمَّدٌ (صَلَّى اللهُ عَلَيْهِ وَآلِهِ) يَنْظُرُ إِلَيْهَا وَأَذِنَ لِلْمَلَائِكَةِ فَنَزَلُوا وَمُحَمَّدٌ (صَلَّى اللهُ عَلَيْهِ وَآلِهِ) يَنْظُرُ إِلَيْهِمْ وَأَمَرَ بِالرَّحْمَةِ فَأُنْزِلَتْ عَلَيْهِ مِنْ لَدُنْ سَاقِ الْعَرْشِ إِلَى رَأْسِ مُحَمَّدٍ (صَلَّى اللهُ عَلَيْهِ وَآلِهِ) وَغَمَرَتْهُ وَنَظَرَ إِلَى جَبْرَائِيلَ (عَلَيْهِ السَّلَامُ) الرُّوحِ الْأَمِينِ الْمُطَوَّقِ بِالنُّورِ طَاوُوسِ الْمَلَائِكَةِ هَبَطَ إِلَيْهِ وَأَخَذَ بِضَبْعِهِ وَهَزَّهُ وَقَالَ: يَا مُحَمَّدُ (صَلَّى اللهُ عَلَيْهِ وَآلِهِ) اقْرَأْ قَالَ: وَمَا أَقْرَأُ، قَالَ يَا مُحَمَّدُ (صَلَّى اللهُ عَلَيْهِ وَآلِهِ) «اقْرَأْ بِاسْمِ رَبِّكَ الَّذِى خَلَقَ خَلَقَ الْإِنسانَ مِنْ عَلَقٍ اقْرَأْ وَرَبُّكَ الْأَكْرَمُ الَّذِى عَلَّمَ بِالْقَلَمِ عَلَّمَ الْإِنْسَانَ ما لَمْ يَعْلَمْ» ثُمَّ أَوْحَى إِلَيْهِ مَا أَوْحَى إِلَيْهِ رَبُّهُ عَزَّ وَجَلَّ ثُمَّ صَعِدَ إِلَى عُلُوٍّ وَنَزَلَ مُحَمَّدُ (صَلَّى اللهُ عَلَيْهِ وَآلِهِ) مِنَ الْجَبَلِ وَقَدْ غَشِيَهُ مِنْ تَعْظِيمِ جَلَالِ اللهِ وَوَرَدَ عَلَيْهِ مِنْ كَبِيرِ شَأْنِهِ مَا رَكِبَهُ الْحُمَّى وَالنَّافِضُ.

7 ʿAsqalānī, *al-Iṣābah fī Tamyīz al-Ṣaḥābah*, 6/474.

8 Ibn Khāldūn, *Tārīkh*, 2/406.

9 Ṭabarī, *Tafsīr*, 30/161.

10 Bukhārī, *Ṣaḥīḥ*, 4/55.

11 See: Subḥānī, *The Message*, chap. 11.

12 ʿĀmilī, *al-Ṣaḥīḥ min Sīrat al-Nabi al-Aʿẓam*, 2/288.

MERITS OF RECITATION

- A tradition from the Prophet (s) states: Whoever recites Surat al-ʿAlaq, it is as if he has recited all the short chapters (*al-mufaṣṣal*) of the Qurʾan (that is, he gets the rewards equivalent to doing so).[13]
- Another tradition from the Prophet (s) states: Whoever recites this surah when he boards a sea vessel will be protected from drowning by God.[14]
- Another tradition from him (s) states: Whoever recites this surah at the door of his storehouse will have his goods protected from damage and theft.[15]

EXEGESIS

VERSES 1, 2

اِقْرَأْ بِاسْمِ رَبِّكَ الَّذِي خَلَقَ ﴿١﴾ خَلَقَ الْإِنْسَانَ مِنْ عَلَقٍ ﴿٢﴾

Read in the name of your Lord, Who created. [1] *Created man from a clinging substance.* [2]

1-2.1 The revelation to the Prophet (s) began with this verse. Ibn ʿAbbas reports: The first verse revealed, or the first words that Jibraʾil spoke to the Prophet (s) in the matter of the Qurʾan were: "O Muhammad (s), say, 'I seek refuge in the all-Hearing, all-Seeing from Shaytan, the outcast.' Then he said, "Say, '*In the name of God, the Beneficent, the Merciful. Read in the name of your Lord, Who created.*'"[16]

As the events in the life of the Prophet (s) unfolded, verses were brought to him piecemeal by Jibraʾil. This method of revelation was

---

[13] Nūrī, *Mustadrak al-Wasāʾil*, 4/359.

عَنِ الرَّسُولِ (صَلَّى اللهُ عَلَيْهِ وَآلِهِ) – مَنْ قَرَأَ سُورَةَ الْعَلَقِ فَكَأَنَّمَا قَرَأَ الْمُفَصَّلَ كُلَّهُ.

[14] Baḥrānī, *al-Burhān*, 5/695.

عَنِ الرَّسُولِ (صَلَّى اللهُ عَلَيْهِ وَآلِهِ) – مَنْ قَرَأَهَا وَهُوَ رَاكِبُ الْبَحْرِ سَلَّمَهُ اللهُ تَعَالَى مِنَ الْغَرَقِ.

[15] Ibid, 5/700.

عَنِ الرَّسُولِ (صَلَّى اللهُ عَلَيْهِ وَآلِهِ) – مَنْ قَرَأَهَا عَلَى بَابِ مَخْزَنٍ سَلَّمَهُ اللهُ تَعَالَى مِنْ كُلِّ آفَّةٍ وَسَارِقٍ.

[16] Nūrī, *Mustadrak al-Wasāʾil*, 4/265.

قَالَ ابْنُ عَبَّاسٍ (رَحْمَةُ اللهِ عَلَيْهِ) – أَوَّلُ آيَةٍ نَزَلَتْ أَوْ أَوَّلُ مَا قَالَهُ جَبْرَائِيلُ لِرَسُولِ اللهِ (صَلَّى اللهُ عَلَيْهِ وَآلِهِ) فِي أَمْرِ الْقُرْآنِ، أَنْ قَالَ لَهُ يَا مُحَمَّدُ (صَلَّى اللهُ عَلَيْهِ وَآلِهِ) قُلْ أَسْتَعِيذُ بِالسَّمِيعِ الْعَلِيمِ مِنَ الشَّيْطَانِ الرَّجِيمِ ثُمَّ قَالَ: قُلْ «بِسْمِ اللهِ الرَّحْمٰنِ الرَّحِيمِ اِقْرَأْ بِاسْمِ رَبِّكَ الَّذِى خَلَقَ».

designed to continually strengthen his heart and build an intimate relationship with God. Q25:32 states:

وَقَالَ الَّذِينَ كَفَرُوا لَوْلَا نُزِّلَ عَلَيْهِ الْقُرْآنُ جُمْلَةً وَاحِدَةً
كَذَٰلِكَ لِنُثَبِّتَ بِهِ فُؤَادَكَ وَرَتَّلْنَاهُ تَرْتِيلًا

And the disbelievers say, "Why was the Qur'an not revealed to him all at once?" [It is revealed] thus so that We may strengthen your heart thereby. And We have revealed it in a well-measured manner.

1-2.2 '*Read in the name of your Lord, Who created.*': [*Iqra* (اقْرَأْ, read)] is the imperative form of the verb *qara'a*, which means to put letters and words together and pronounce them, loudly or silently, to make sense of them.[17] It can refer to both reading from a written text or repeating accurately from memory something that was written.[18]

The command, '*Iqra!*' was also the stimulus behind a culture of literacy and pursuit of knowledge which resulted in the preeminence of the Muslims in all fields of learning in the early history of Islam.[19]

[*Bi ismi* (بِاسْمِ, in the name)]. This is distinct from the *basmalah* that comes at the head of the chapter and not a repetition, because the *basmalah* is the manner in which God begins His speech and instructs the reciter to repeat it, while the phrase, '*Read in the name of your Lord*' is a command to His servants to recite in His name.[20] Some exegetes believe that the '*bi*' here is additional, and the meaning of the verse is, 'Read (recite) the name of your Lord...'[21], thus meaning, 'recite His name to the people.'

1-2.3 The reading and learning is in God's name. This means that Islam keeps God at the centre of all learning, both religious and secular. It teaches that science is not separate from religion, and that all knowledge flows from the correct understanding of theology. Otherwise, what is learned from science is used by the strong to oppress the weak.[22]

---

[17] Rāghib, *al-Mufradāt.*

[18] Muṭahharī, (*Āshnāyī bā Qur'an*), *Āthār*, 28/648.

[19] Ibid, 28/649.

[20] Ṭabāṭabā'ī, *al-Mīzān*, 20/323.

[21] Ṭabrasī, *al-Bayān*, 10/780.

[22] Muṭahharī, (*Āshnāyī bā Qur'an*), *Āthār*, 28/650.

After gaining their academic qualifications, many Muslims have separated science and faith, considering them to be largely incompatible. Furthermore, matters of faith are relegated to the mosques and ritual practices, while science, academia, and technology are given prominence.

However, Islam teaches that it is only when knowledge and faith are merged together that there can be true understanding and awareness. Those who possess these twin attributes are the ones who will dispel the confusion of the transgressors on the Day of Judgement.

Q30:56 states:

وَقَالَ الَّذِينَ أُوتُوا الْعِلْمَ وَالْإِيمَانَ لَقَدْ لَبِثْتُمْ فِي كِتَابِ اللهِ إِلَىٰ يَوْمِ الْبَعْثِ
فَهَٰذَا يَوْمُ الْبَعْثِ وَلَٰكِنَّكُمْ كُنْتُمْ لَا تَعْلَمُونَ

But those who have been given [both] knowledge and faith shall say, "You remained, according to God's decree, until the Day of Resurrection. So, this is the Day of Resurrection, but you were not aware."

1-2.4 [*Rabbika* (رَبِّكَ, your Lord)]. Part of the role of God as a Sustainer for humanity is to guide them, and the Qur'an is a major part of that guidance. Perhaps that is why the name *Rabb* is used at the start of its revelation. Furthermore, the use of the name or attribute, '*Rabb*' (used three times in this chapter) may have been to fill the Prophet (s) with comfort.[23]

1-2.5 It is interesting that God is mentioned first as '*Rabb*' – which has the meaning of Owner, Sustainer, and Cherisher – before the mention of God as '*Khāliq*', the Creator. This may be for two reasons:

i) God's name *al-Rabb* became manifest due to His creation, which is the best proof of his role as Sustainer.[24] Here, He reassures the creation that He has not left them to fend for themselves. Since He is the Creator, He also sustains the entire cosmos from its inception, and continually thereafter.

ii) It is a reply to the polytheists who accepted that God was the Creator of everything, but thereafter relied on their idols for sustenance. Q29:61 states:

---

[23] Rāzī, *Mafātīḥ al-Ghayb*, 32/216.

[24] Shīrāzī, *Namūneh*, 27/156.

وَلَئِنْ سَأَلْتَهُمْ مَنْ خَلَقَ السَّمَاوَاتِ وَالْأَرْضَ وَسَخَّرَ الشَّمْسَ وَالْقَمَرَ لَيَقُولُنَّ اللَّهُ

And if you asked them, "Who created the heavens and the earth and subjected the sun and the moon [to their paths]?" they would certainly say, "Allah!" ...

In fact, the two attributes of God, Creator (*Khāliq*) and Sustainer (*Rabb*) are linked in the sense that only the Creator can be the true Sustainer, because only He is completely aware of the needs of that which He has created.[25]

1-2.6 '*Created man from a clinging substance.*': [*Al-Insān* (الإِنسَان, man) here refers to the human race. We have discussed this concept further in the *tafsīr* of Surat al-ʿAṣr (103).

After mentioning that He is the Creator in general, God singles out the process of the creation of man in particular. Indeed, man is the noblest of His creatures.

[*ʿAlaq* (عَلَق, clinging substance)] (sing. *ʿalaqah*) is derived from *ʿalaqa* meaning to be attached or stuck to something.[26] This is a reference to the first stage of the foetus, when it is an embryo that is attached and clinging to the wall of the womb of its mother.

Therefore, the verse under review talks of the earliest stage of man's journey to becoming a wondrous and complex creature who is invited to know, love, worship, and serve His Creator.

Man is reminded of his simple and lowly beginnings, and how, from the earliest moment, and in every subsequent stage of his development, his creation is lovingly nurtured by God.

SUMMARY OF THE VERSES

In summary, the verses direct the Prophet (s) to recite to the people in the name of God, who transformed them from a small clinging substance into a wondrous creature.

[25] Miṣbāḥ-Yazdī, *Āmūzesh-i ʿAqāʾid*, p. 83.

[26] Muṣṭafawī, *al-Taḥqīq*.

REFLECTIVE LEARNING

Let me reflect on how God has nurtured me from my very inception, and how His loving care has been present at every stage of my development.

Whenever I feel a sense of independence and self-sufficiency, let me remember my humble beginnings and continual need of God's grace, so that I am not overcome with a false sense of pride.

VERSES 3 - 5

اقْرَأْ وَرَبُّكَ الْأَكْرَمُ ﴿٣﴾ الَّذِي عَلَّمَ بِالْقَلَمِ ﴿٤﴾ عَلَّمَ الْإِنسَانَ مَا لَمْ يَعْلَمْ ﴿٥﴾

Read! And your Lord is the most-Generous. [3] *Who taught by the pen.* [4] *Taught man that which he did not know.* [5]

3-5.1 '*Read! And your Lord is the most-Generous.*': The instruction to read is repeated again, to emphasize the importance of reading the Divine message to understand the purpose of one's existence. Some exegetes have said that the first verse was an instruction to the Prophet (s) himself, while the second command was to read to the people.[27]

Some have said that when commanded to read, the Prophet (s) responded, "I do not know how to read", and in reply this verse tells him, '*[You can] Read because your Lord is most generous*'. This shows that when God commands His servant to do something, out of His Generosity, He gives him the tools to be able to carry it out.[28]

In addition to merely reading and reciting the scripture, the Prophet (s) also received the deeper understanding of the verses.

[*Al-Akram* (الْأَكْرَمُ, the most generous)]. The adjective *karīm* is derived from *karuma*, meaning to be noble and generous. In this verse, God states that He is *al-Akram*, the most Generous Lord, since He grants to His creation whether they are deserving or not, and because every other one who grants is because of God's bestowal in the first place. In addition, He has made everything that humans need for their earthly existence available and within easy reach.[29]

---

27 Shīrāzī, *Namūneh*, 27/157.

28 Ibid.

29 Ṭabrasī, *al-Bayān*, 10/781.

Karīm also refers to someone who overlooks the faults of others.[30] And so, God is *al-Akram*, because He continually pardons the transgressions of mankind.

3-5.2 '*Who taught by the pen.*': [*Al-Qalam* (الْقَلَم, the pen)] refers to the implement used for writing, and the *bāʾ* (ب) before it is to indicate the means (*bā al-sababiyyah*).

Therefore the verse says that God taught reading, or reading and writing, by means of the pen.[31] Through the pen, man is able to communicate his ideas and experiences to people he has not met, teach others after him, and acquire knowledge and understanding himself. The pen is a means of preserving and transmitting knowledge, and that is why the Qurʾan swears by both the pen, and that which is derived from the use of the pen, in Q68:1:

ن وَالْقَلَمِ وَمَا يَسْطُرُونَ

Nūn. By the pen and that which they write.

Of course, it requires both the scholar to write with the 'pen' and the people to read these writings for knowledge to be transmitted.

3-5.3 '*Taught man that which he did not know.*': Man instinctively wants to learn and know things. This instinct is part of God's guidance to mankind. God taught man what was outside his experience and imagination. He taught him about his soul, the purpose of his existence, the experiences of previous nations, death and the Hereafter, and so on.

This verse may also explain the reason for the mention of the pen, which is that He taught mankind what he did not know through the means of writing,[32] which requires a pen.

3-5.4 In this manner, the beginning of revelation was accompanied by the encouragement of literacy and gaining knowledge. And it is through the gaining of knowledge from Divine scripture and the written works of scholars throughout the ages that the human being, whose origin was a simple clinging mass (*ʿalaq*), progresses towards his purpose, potential, and perfection.

---

[30] Ibn Fāris, *Muʿjam Maqāyīs al-Lughah.*

[31] Ṭabāṭabāʾī, *al-Mīzān*, 20/324.

[32] Shīrāzī, *Namūneh*, 27/158.

SUMMARY OF THE VERSES

The verses say that after fashioning the complex physical body of the human being from a few cells, the all-Generous Lord now teaches him what he did not know, and transmits knowledge through the means of the pen.

REFLECTIVE LEARNING

God granted me all that I possess without my deserving it. He fashioned me and taught me what I did not know. All this was so that I would begin to recognize Him, and thereby rely on Him, love Him, and serve Him.

When it comes to knowledge, let me reflect whether the knowledge I have gained has brought me closer to God or taken me further away from Him.

VERSES 6, 7

كَلَّآ إِنَّ ٱلْإِنسَٰنَ لَيَطْغَىٰٓ ﴿٦﴾ أَن رَّءَاهُ ٱسْتَغْنَىٰٓ ﴿٧﴾

Not at all! But indeed, man is most surely inordinate. [6] *Because he sees himself as self-sufficient.* [7]

6-7.1 While it is accepted that the first five verses were revealed at the beginning of the mission, some exegetes consider that the verses under review now were revealed a little later, and then placed here at the direction of the Prophet (s).[33] However, others believe that the complete chapter was revealed at one time.[34]

6-7.2 '*Not at all! But indeed, man is most surely inordinate.*': [*Kallā* (كَلَّا, not at all)] informs the reader that matters are not as they may have surmised, rather man is inordinate. Furthermore, the use of *kallā* at the beginning of the verse is an indication of continuity in the discourse and supports the view that all the verses in the chapter may have been revealed together.

[*Yatghā* (يَطْغَىٰ, is inordinate)]. Derived from *ṭaghā*, its verbal noun *ṭughyān* means transgressing bounds, being unjust, and behaving

[33] See: Muṭahharī, (*Āshnāyī bā Qur'an*), *Āthār*, 28/650.

[34] Ṭabāṭabā'ī, *al-Mīzān*, 20/322.

inordinately.[35] God fashioned man from humble beginnings and then nurtured his soul through knowledge. But instead of being grateful for these bounties, man grew in defiance and arrogance, forgetting that everything he possessed came from God's continual grace.

Ṭughyān also refers to the act of those who deny God and even put themselves in His place, claiming lordship like Namrud and Firʿawn. Q79:24 recounts the shameful claim of Firʿawn:

فَقَالَ أَنَا رَبُّكُمُ الْأَعْلَىٰ

Then he said, "I am your lord, the most high!"

6-7.3 '*Because he sees himself as self-sufficient.*': The reason why man becomes like this is because he is deluded by the very same bounties that he has been granted; his strength and knowledge make him believe that he is independent and needless of God. The blessings of God, and especially the bounty of knowledge should have brought with it humbleness and humility. As it is said, 'A tree laden with fruit always bends low.'

In fact, this defiance and lack of fear is clear evidence of ignorance. Q35:28 states:

إِنَّمَا يَخْشَى اللَّهَ مِنْ عِبَادِهِ الْعُلَمَاءُ

...Only those of His servants who possess knowledge fear God...

[*Raʾāhu* (رَآهُ, he sees himself)] is derived from *raʾy* (to have an opinion) and not *ruʾyah* (to see with the eyes). Therefore, the verse means 'he considers himself to be self-sufficient.'[36]

[*Istaghnā* (اسْتَغْنَىٰ, to be self-sufficient)]. Derived from *ghaniy*, meaning rich and needless, the term here does not restrict this attitude to the wealthy only; rather, it refers to the arrogance of man when he perceives his own strength, wealth, and possessions. He thinks himself invincible and self-sufficient and grows defiant in front of God.[37]

Yet man is constantly in need of God's grace, and self-sufficiency belongs to God alone. Q35:15 states:

---

35 Rāghib, *al-Mufradāt*.

36 Ṭabāṭabāʾī, *al-Mīzān*, 20/325.

37 Ṭūsī, *al-Tibyān*, 10/380.

يَا أَيُّهَا النَّاسُ أَنْتُمُ الْفُقَرَاءُ إِلَى اللهِ وَاللهُ هُوَ الْغَنِيُّ الْحَمِيدُ

O mankind! It is you who stand in need of God,
while God is He who is free of all needs, worthy of all praise.

SUMMARY OF THE VERSES

The verses state that instead of being grateful to God for His bounties and nurturing care, man becomes inordinate because he thinks himself needless of God.

REFLECTIVE LEARNING

Let me reflect on my perceived strength and resources. Have they caused me to have a false sense of self-sufficiency?

Do my attitude and actions show me to be God's abject and needy servant?

VERSE 8

إِنَّ إِلَىٰ رَبِّكَ الرُّجْعَىٰ ﴿٨﴾

Indeed, to your Lord is the return. [8]

8.1 [*Rabbika* (رَبِّكَ, your Lord]. The two previous verses were speaking about mankind in general, and in the third person. But now, every reader is addressed directly, bringing the realization that the previous verses may have been speaking about him! Like everyone else, he too will return to face his Lord and Sustainer.

[*Al-Rujʿā* (الرُّجْعَىٰ, the return)] is derived from *rajaʿa*, which means to return. Here, it is mentioned as a warning and a reminder of death and resurrection. Man is prompted to keep in mind that he is on a journey towards His Lord. He will complete stage after stage, until the Day when he will stand to account in front of Him.[38]

8.2 This return will include the removal of the veils from before the eyes. At that point man will clearly see the connection of everything with God. He will see his own situation as well. This will happen to everyone when they leave the world.

[38] Ṭabāṭabā'ī, *al-Mīzān*, 20/325.

SUMMARY OF THE VERSE

This verse reminds man that every day, he is returning back to his Lord.

REFLECTIVE LEARNING

Let me reflect on how much of my life has already gone by. Am I acutely aware of the diminishing window of time that remains for me in this world to gather the provisions that I will need in the Hereafter?

VERSES 9 - 14

أَرَأَيْتَ الَّذِي يَنْهَىٰ ﴿٩﴾ عَبْدًا إِذَا صَلَّىٰ ﴿١٠﴾ أَرَأَيْتَ إِنْ كَانَ عَلَى الْهُدَىٰ ﴿١١﴾
أَوْ أَمَرَ بِالتَّقْوَىٰ ﴿١٢﴾ أَرَأَيْتَ إِنْ كَذَّبَ وَتَوَلَّىٰ ﴿١٣﴾ أَلَمْ يَعْلَمْ بِأَنَّ اللَّهَ يَرَىٰ ﴿١٤﴾

Have you seen the one who forbids [9] a servant when he prays? [10] *Have you seen if he is upon guidance,* [11] *or enjoins God-wariness?* [12] *Have you seen if he denies and turns away?* [13] *Does he not know that God sees?* [14]

9-14.1 These six verses address every person who exhibits *ṭughyān*, and whose hostility reaches a point that they even harass those who are engaged in the worship of God. They behave inordinately and transgress all bounds, confident that their actions are somehow justified, or uncaring of the consequences. They have forgotten that every act is being witnessed and will be examined.

The example also sets the ground for the description of the stern chastisement that awaits such individuals, as described in later verses in the chapter.

9-14.2 '*Have you seen the one who forbids a servant when he prays?*': [*Araʾayta* (أَرَأَيْتَ, have you seen?)]. Three questions have been asked using this phrase, addressing the Prophet (s) and every listener. The questions are meant to invoke surprise at this behaviour.[39]

9-14.3 Although the verse is general, it initially refers to the prevention of the Prophet (s) when he stood to pray. *ʿAbd* (servant) is used in

[39] Ṭabāṭabāʾī, *al-Mīzān*, 20/326.

the indefinite to indicate the high station of the servant and his manner of worship.

9-14.4 In many reports, the perpetrator was Abu Jahl, the arch-enemy of the Prophet (s) and Islam. Abu Jahl asked [the Quraysh], "Does Muhammad (s) prostrate on the earth in your presence?" They replied, "Yes." He said, "I swear by al-Lat and al-ʿUzza, if I see him doing this, I will stamp on his neck!" He went towards God's Messenger (s) when he was praying, intending to put his leg on his neck, but then suddenly rushed back, his hands shaking. They asked, "What is the matter with you?" He replied, "A trench of fire opened between me and him, filled with a terrifying sound of flapping wings." God's Messenger (s) later remarked, "If he had come any closer to me, he would have been torn to pieces by the angels."[40]

The implication of the verse would thus be, 'Do you see [O Muḥammad], what would be the recompense of the one who seeks to prevent a servant when he prays? What would be his situation before God? What kind of punishment he would deserve?'[41]

9-14.5 Since this may be the first chapter to be revealed, this verse refers to the *salat* that he (s) used to pray before the revelation of the Qur'an. This is a proof that he (s) was a Prophet of God even before he was appointed to his mission.[42]

After the start of the mission (*biʿthah*) there is no doubt that *salat* was prayed by the Prophet (s) and the Muslims. Many early chapters speak of *salat*, for example, Surat al-Muzzammil (73) and Surat al-Muddaththir (74). And of course, Surat al-ʿAlaq itself commands a prostration (*sajdah*) in its last verse. The manner of that early form of prayer has not been clearly mentioned in the traditions.[43]

9-14.6 In the beginning, the *salat* was only prayed by the Prophet (s), Imam Ali (a), and Lady Khadijah (a). The following report is mentioned in both *Sunni* and *Shīʿa* sources:

---

[40] Kāshānī, *al-Ṣāfī*, 5/349.

قَالَ أَبُو جَهْلٍ: أَيُعَفِّرُ مُحَمَّدٌ وَجْهَهُ بَيْنَ أَظْهُرِكُمْ؟ قَالُوا: نَعَمْ، فقَالَ: وَاللَّاتِ وَالْعُزَّى لَئِنْ رَأَيْتُهُ يَفْعَلُ ذَلِكَ لَأَطَأَنَّ عَلَى رَقَبَتِهِ، فَأَتَى رَسُولَ اللهِ صَلَّى اللهُ عَلَيْهِ وَآلِهِ وَسَلَّمَ وَهُوَ يُصَلِّي زَعَمَ لِيَطَأَ عَلَى رَقَبَتِهِ فَمَا فَجِئَهُمْ مِنْهُ إِلَّا وَهُوَ يَنْكُصُ عَلَى عَقِبَيْهِ، وَيَتَّقِي بِيَدَيْهِ، فَقِيلَ لَهُ: مَا لَكَ؟ فَقَالَ: إِنَّ بَيْنِي وَبَيْنَهُ لَخَنْدَقًا مِنْ نَارٍ وَهَوْلًا وَأَجْنِحَةً. فَقَالَ رَسُولُ اللهِ صَلَّى اللهُ عَلَيْهِ وَآلِهِ وَسَلَّمَ: لَوْ دَنَا مِنِّي لَاخْتَطَفَتْهُ الْمَلَائِكَةُ عُضْوًا عُضْوًا.

[41] Ṭabrasī, *al-Bayān*, 10/782.

[42] Ṭabāṭabā'ī, *al-Mīzān*, 20/326.

[43] Ibid.

Yahya b. ʿAfif narrated from his father: I was sitting in Makka with al-ʿAbbas b. ʿAbd al-Muttalib, may God be pleased with him, before the mission of the Prophet (s) was known. A youth came and looked up towards the sky at noontime. Then he turned towards the Kaʿbah and stood to pray. Then a young lad came and stood at his right and a woman came and stood behind them both. The man bowed and so did the young lad and the woman. Then he raised his head and so did they. Then he prostrated and they both prostrated also.

I said, "O ʿAbbas! This is a wondrous affair!" Al-ʿAbbas replied, "It is [indeed] a wondrous affair. Do you know who that youth is? He is Muhammad b. ʿAbdallah b. ʿAbd al-Muttalib, my nephew. Do you know who the lad is? He is Ali b. Abu Talib, my nephew. Do you know who the woman is? She is Khadijah, the daughter of Khuwaylid."[44]

9-14.7 *'Have you seen if he is upon guidance, or enjoins God-wariness?'*: Two further questions are now asked to the one who wanted to stop the prayer of the Prophet (s). What if the worshipper, the Prophet (s), is truly guided (*ʿalal hudā*)? What if he is enjoining others to God-wariness (*amara biʾl-taqwā*)? Are you not even willing to consider that he may be rightly guided? And that you are mistaken in your enmity? In that case, the consequence for the perpetrator would be very grievous indeed.[45]

9-14.8 *'Have you seen if he denies and turns away?'*: [*Kadhdhaba* (كَذَّبَ, denies)] is derived from *kadhaba* which means to lie. Here, the intensive form of the verb means denying something out of defiance despite instinctively knowing that it is the truth.

[*Tawallā* (تَوَلَّى, turn away)] is derived from *waliya* which ordinarily means to be near or to be a friend, but here *tawallā* means to be averted or to turn away, because of the implied postposition *ʿan* or *min* (from).[46]

---

[44] Mufīd, *al-Irshād*, p. 30.

كُنْتُ جَالِسًا مَعَ الْعَبَّاسِ بْنِ عَبْدِ الْمُطَّلِبِ (رَضِيَ اللهُ عَنْهُ) بِمَكَّةَ قَبْلَ أَنْ يَظْهَرَ أَمْرُ النَّبِيِّ صَلَّى اللهُ عَلَيْهِ وَآلِهِ وَسَلَّمَ، فَجَاءَ شَابٌّ فَنَظَرَ إِلَى السَّمَاءِ حَتَّى تَحَلَّقَتِ الشَّمْسُ، ثُمَّ اسْتَقْبَلَ الْكَعْبَةَ فَقَامَ يُصَلِّي، ثُمَّ جَاءَ غُلَامٌ فَقَامَ عَنْ يَمِينِهِ، ثُمَّ جَاءَتِ امْرَأَةٌ فَقَامَتْ خَلْفَهُمَا فَرَكَعَ الشَّابُّ، فَرَكَعَ الْغُلَامُ وَالْمَرْأَةُ، ثُمَّ رَفَعَ الشَّابُّ رَأْسَهُ فَرَفَعَا، ثُمَّ سَجَدَ الشَّابُّ فَسَجَدَا، فَقُلْتُ: يَا عَبَّاسُ أَمْرٌ عَظِيمٌ، فَقَالَ الْعَبَّاسُ: أَمْرٌ عَظِيمٌ، أَتَدْرِي مَنْ هَذَا الشَّابُّ؟ هَذَا مُحَمَّدُ بْنُ عَبْدِ اللهِ ابْنُ عَبْدِ الْمُطَّلِبِ اِبْنُ أَخِي، أَتَدْرِي مَنْ هَذَا الْغُلَامُ؟ هَذَا عَلِيُّ ابْنُ أَبِي طَالِبٍ اِبْنَ أَخِي، أَتَدْرِي مَنْ هَذِهِ الْمَرْأَةُ؟ هَذِهِ خَدِيجَةُ بِنْتُ خُوَيْلِدٍ.

[45] Shīrāzī, *Namūneh*, 27/166.

[46] Rāghib, *al-Mufradāt*.

From some traditions it appears that Abu Jahl instinctively knew the truth of the claim of the Prophet (s), but he defiantly denied the message of Islam due to his jealousy.

A report states: Akhnas b. Shurayq came to Abu Jahl and asked for his opinion about what he had heard from the Prophet (s). He replied, "What have I heard?! We [Banu Makhzūm] and Banu ʿAbd Manāf have contested for honour. They fed [the pilgrims] so we fed [them], they transported [the pilgrims] so we transported [them], and they gave charitably so we gave [also]. We were as two horses, racing neck and neck, but then they said, 'A Prophet has come from us, and he brings revelation from heaven!' Now, how can we match that claim?! By God, we will never bring faith in him, nor accept his words."[47]

9-14.9 '*Does he not know that God sees?*': This rhetorical question is a warning that refers to all the three instances described in the preceding verses. A necessary consequence of the belief that God is the Creator of everything, which the idolaters like Abu Jahl acknowledged, is the belief that He is likewise aware of everything, even if the idolater may be unmindful of this fact.[48]

In fact, God is the constant witness to all of man's actions and thoughts. Conviction about this reality can have a powerful effect on man's life, putting his actions into perspective and forestalling him from acts of sin.[49] No person should feel that he can sin because he is alone, because Q90:7 warns:

أَيَحْسَبُ أَنْ لَمْ يَرَهُ أَحَدٌ

Does he think that no one sees him?

---

[47] Ibn Hishām, *al-Sīrah*, 1/315.

قَالَ: يَا أَبَا الْحَكَمِ، مَا رَأْيُكَ فِيمَا سَمِعْتَ مِنْ مُحَمَّدٍ؟ فَقَالَ: مَاذَا سَمِعْتُ، تَنَازَعْنَا نَحْنُ وَبَنُو عَبْدِ مَنَافٍ الشَّرَفَ، أَطْعَمُوا فَأَطْعَمْنَا، وَحَمَلُوا فَحَمَلْنَا، وَأَعْطَوْا فَأَعْطَيْنَا، حَتَّى إِذَا تَجَاذَيْنَا عَلَى الرَّكْبِ، وَكُنَّا كَفَرَسَيْ رِهَانٍ، قَالُوا: مِنَّا نَبِيٌّ يَأْتِيهِ الْوَحْيُ مِنَ السَّمَاءِ، فَمَتَى نُدْرِكُ مِثْلَ هَذِهِ، وَاللهِ لَا نُؤْمِنُ بِهِ أَبَدًا وَلَا نُصَدِّقُهُ.

[48] Ṭabāṭabā'ī, *al-Mīzān*, 20/326.

[49] Shīrāzī, *Namūneh*, 27/167.

DISCUSSION: THE HISTORY OF THE RITUAL PRAYERS (*SALAT*) IN ISLAM

1. Previous Nations

Salat is the highest form of worship of God, and was legislated for the believers throughout human history. A tradition from Imam al-Sadiq (a) states: The most beloved action to God, the Exalted, is *salat*, and it was the ultimate message of the Prophets (a).[50]

Although we do not have much information about the form of the prayers of previous nations, the Qurʾan mentions in several verses that they engaged in a type of worship by the name *salat*. Some examples are:

i) God's instruction to Ibrahim (a), '*...Purify my House for those who perform ṭawāf, and stand* [*in* salat], *and those who would bow and prostrate.*' (Q22:26),

ii) The supplication of Ibrahim (a), '*My Lord! Make me one who established* salat, *and [also] from my descendants...*' (Q14:40),

iii) God's revelation to Musa (a), '*There is no deity other than Me, so worship Me and establish* salat *for My remembrance.*' (Q20:14),

iv) The declaration of ʿIsa (a), '*...He has enjoined upon me* salat *and* zakat *as long as I live.*' (Q19:31),

v) About Zakariyya (a), '*So the angels called him while he was standing in* salat *in the prayer-niche...*' (Q3:39),

vi) The objection of the people of Shuʿayb (a), '*O Shuʿayb, does your* salat *command you that we should leave what our fathers worship...*' (Q11:87),

vii) About Ismaʿil (a), '*And he used to enjoin* salat *and* zakat *on his people...*' (Q19:55),

viii) The advice of Luqman (a), '*O my son, establish* salat*...*' (Q31:17), and several other instances as well.

---

[50] Kulaynī, *al-Kāfī*, 6/8.

عَنِ الصَّادِقِ (عَلَيْهِ السَّلَامُ) – أَحَبُّ الْأَعْمَالِ إِلَى اللهِ عَزَّ وَجَلَّ الصَّلَاةُ، وَهِيَ آخِرُ وَصَايَا الْأَنْبِيَاءِ.

2. *Salat* in the history of Islam

Several reports mention that the Prophet (s) used to pray the *salat* before or just after the beginning of his mission. For example, one report states:

When the Prophet (s) reached 37 years of age, he used to see someone come in his dream and address him, "O Messenger of God..." Then Jibra'il descended upon him bringing water from the heavens and said, "O Muhammad! Rise, and make ablutions for *salat*." Then Jibra'il taught him how to wash his face and his two arms from the elbows [down] and wipe the head and the two feet up to the ankles. He taught him the prostrations (*sujūd*) and the bowing (*rukūʿ*).

When the Prophet (s) was 40 years old, he taught him the *salat* and its details, but did not [yet] inform him of its prescribed timings. Thereafter, the Prophet (s) would pray the *salat* in two units throughout the day... Ali (a) saw him praying and asked what he was doing. The Prophet (s) replied, "This is the *salat* that God has instructed me to perform." He (s) invited him to Islam, and Ali accepted and prayed with him. Then Khadijah (a) accepted Islam. [For a time] no one performed the *salat* except the Prophet (s), with Ali (a) and Khadijah (a) behind him.[51]

It appears that initially, there was a simpler form of *salat* practised by the Prophet (s) which included some recitation of the Qur'an and bowing and prostration. Some scholars state that these prayers were obligatory for the Prophet (s) but recommended (*mustaḥab*) for the Muslims before the *miʿrāj*.[52]

After the *miʿrāj*, the five daily prayers were made obligatory, still in units of two. A tradition from Imam al-Baqir (a) states: When God's Messenger (s) was raised [to the heavens] he brought back [instructions for] ten units of [*wājib*] *salat*, to be prayed in twos. And

---

[51] Irbilī, *Kashf al-Ghummah*, 1/87.

أَنَّ النَّبِيَّ صَلَّى اللهُ عَلَيْهِ وَآلِهِ لَمَّا أَتَى لَهُ سَبْعٌ وَثَلَاثُونَ سَنَةً كَانَ يَرَى فِي نَوْمِهِ كَأَنَّ آتِيًا أَتَاهُ فَيَقُولُ يَا رَسُولَ اللهِ ... فَنَزَلَ عَلَيْهِ جَبْرَائِيلُ وَأَنْزَلَ عَلَيْهِ مَاءً مِنَ السَّمَاءِ، فَقَالَ لَهُ: يَا مُحَمَّدُ قُمْ تَوَضَّأْ لِلصَّلَاةِ فَعَلَّمَهُ جَبْرَائِيلُ عَلَيْهِ السَّلَامُ الْوُضُوءَ عَلَى الْوَجْهِ وَالْيَدَيْنِ مِنَ الْمِرْفَقِ وَمَسْحِ الرَّأْسِ وَالرِّجْلَيْنِ إِلَى الْكَعْبَيْنِ وَعَلَّمَهُ السُّجُودَ وَالرُّكُوعَ. فَلَمَّا تَمَّ لَهُ أَرْبَعُونَ سَنَةً أَمَرَهُ بِالصَّلَاةِ وَعَلَّمَهُ حُدُودَهَا وَلَمْ يُنْزِلْ عَلَيْهِ أَوْقَاتَهَا فَكَانَ رَسُولُ اللهِ صَلَّى اللهُ عَلَيْهِ وَآلِهِ يُصَلِّي رَكْعَتَيْنِ رَكْعَتَيْنِ فِي كُلِّ وَقْتٍ ... فَدَخَلَ عَلِيٌّ عَلَيْهِ السَّلَامُ إِلَى رَسُولِ اللهِ صَلَّى اللهُ عَلَيْهِ وَآلِهِ وَهُوَ يُصَلِّي ... قَالَ يَا أَبَا الْقَاسِمِ مَا هَذَا؟ قَالَ هَذِهِ الصَّلَاةُ الَّتِي أَمَرَنِي اللهُ بِهَا فَدَعَاهُ إِلَى الْإِسْلَامِ فَأَسْلَمَ وَصَلَّى مَعَهُ وَأَسْلَمَتْ خَدِيجَةُ وَكَانَ لَا يُصَلِّي إِلَّا رَسُولُ اللهِ صَلَّى اللهُ عَلَيْهِ وَآلِهِ وَعَلِيٌّ وَخَدِيجَةُ خَلْفَهُ.

[52] Ibn Shahr Āshūb, *Manāqib*, 1/40.

after al-Ḥasan (a) and al-Ḥusayn (a) were born, the Prophet (s) added seven units to the daily prayers out of gratitude to God, and God allowed him to do that.[53]

Therefore, the present form of seventeen units daily was legislated in Madina. A tradition states that Imam al-Sajjad (a) was asked when *salat* became *wājib* on the Muslims in the manner that it is prayed today. He replied: In Madina, when the call [to Islam] was made openly and Islam became stronger, God, the Exalted, ordained *jihād* for the Muslims. At that time the Prophet (s) added seven units to the daily prayers: two units to *ẓuhr*, two to *ʿaṣr*, one to *maghrib*, and two to the *ʿishāʾ salat.*[54]

SUMMARY OF THE VERSES

In summary, the meaning of the verses is: Have you seen the one who prevents a servant from praying and worshipping God, while he knows that God sees? And what will be his position, if the one who is praying is on guidance (*hudā*) and enjoins God-wariness (*taqwā*), and he prevents him, while God sees? And have you seen that his behaviour is defiance of the truth when he prevents the person from praying, while God sees? Does he deserve anything except grievous chastisement?[55]

REFLECTIVE LEARNING

Let me reflect on my thoughts and actions when:

1. It comes to the servants of God who are trying to get close to Him. Do I aid them by encouraging them, or do I become an obstacle to their efforts by discouraging and ridiculing them?

---

[53] Kulaynī, *al-Kāfī*, 3/487.

عَنِ الْبَاقِرِ (عَلَيْهِ السَّلَامُ) - لَمَّا عُرِجَ بِرَسُولِ اللهِ صَلَّى اللهُ عَلَيْهِ وَآلِهِ نَزَلَ بِالصَّلَاةِ عَشْرَ رَكَعَاتٍ رَكْعَتَيْنِ رَكْعَتَيْنِ فَلَمَّا وُلِدَ الْحَسَنُ وَالْحُسَيْنُ زَادَ رَسُولُ اللهِ صَلَّى اللهُ عَلَيْهِ وَآلِهِ سَبْعَ رَكَعَاتٍ شُكْرًا لِلهِ فَأَجَازَ اللهُ لَهُ ذَلِكَ.

[54] Ṣadūq, *al-Faqīh*, 1/455.

وَسَأَلَ سَعِيدُ بْنُ الْمُسَيَّبِ عَلِيَّ بْنَ الْحُسَيْنِ السَّجَّادِ (عَلَيْهِ السَّلَامُ) - فَقَالَ لَهُ: مَتَى فُرِضَتِ الصَّلَاةُ عَلَى الْمُسْلِمِينَ عَلَى مَا هِيَ الْيَوْمَ عَلَيْهِ؟ فَقَالَ: بِالْمَدِينَةِ حِينَ ظَهَرَتِ الدَّعْوَةُ وَقَوِيَ الْإِسْلَامُ وَكَتَبَ اللهُ عَزَّ وَجَلَّ عَلَى الْمُسْلِمِينَ الْجِهَادَ زَادَ رَسُولُ اللهِ صَلَّى اللهُ عَلَيْهِ وَآلِهِ فِي الصَّلَاةِ سَبْعَ رَكَعَاتٍ فِي الظُّهْرِ رَكْعَتَيْنِ وَفِي الْعَصْرِ رَكْعَتَيْنِ وَفِي الْمَغْرِبِ رَكْعَةً وَفِي الْعِشَاءِ الْآخِرَةِ رَكْعَتَيْنِ وَأَقَرَّ الْفَجْرَ عَلَى مَا فُرِضَتْ بِمَكَّةَ.

[55] Ṭabāṭabāʾī, *al-Mīzān*, 20/326.

2. It comes to my own journey and acts of worship, for example *salat*. Am I constantly aware that He watches me and observes my thoughts?

VERSES 15, 16

كَلَّا لَئِنْ لَّمْ يَنْتَهِ لَنَسْفَعًا بِالنَّاصِيَةِ ﴿١٥﴾ نَاصِيَةٍ كَاذِبَةٍ خَاطِئَةٍ ﴿١٦﴾

Not at all! If he does not desist, We will seize him by the forelock. [15] *A lying, sinning forelock!* [16]

15-16.1 *'Not at all! If he does not desist, We will seize him by the forelock.'*: [*Kallā* (كَلَّا, not at all)]. The usage again of this term is a rejection of any justification for the behaviour described in the previous verses and a command to desist.

[*La'in lam yantahi* (لَئِنْ لَّمْ يَنْتَهِ, if he does not desist)]. This is a warning of what will happen if he does not cease his misbehaviour.

[*Lanasfa'an* (لَنَسْفَعًا, seize)]. The term is derived from *safa'a*, meaning to pull or yank strongly.[56] The *lām* at the beginning is for emphasis indicating that the pulling will be violent.

[*Nāṣiyah* (نَاصِيَة, forelock)]. *Nāṣiyah* is the hair just above the forehead. It is a term used as a metaphor for man's pride and dignity, and for his mind and knowledge.[57]

The guilty will be identified, and then seized by their forelocks, on the Day of Judgement.

Q55:41 states:

يُعْرَفُ الْمُجْرِمُونَ بِسِيمَاهُمْ فَيُؤْخَذُ بِالنَّوَاصِي وَالْأَقْدَامِ

The sinners will be recognized by their marks
and will be seized by the forelocks and the feet.

15-16.2 *'A lying, sinning forelock!'*: [*Kādhibah* (كَاذِبَة, lying)] is derived from *kadhaba*, meaning to lie or to deceive.

[*Khāṭi'ah* (خَاطِئَة, sinful)] is derived from *khaṭi'a*, which means to be sinful or to make a mistake. These were the two main traits that qualified them for Hell.

---

[56] Muṣṭafawī, *al-Taḥqīq*.

[57] Ibid.

Here, the adjectives are used metaphorically for the forelock; in fact, they refer to the individual himself. The first adjective, *kādhibah* (lying), refers to his speech and false beliefs, while the second, *khāṭiʾah* (sinful), refers to his misdeeds and defiant behaviour.[58]

15-16.3 Interestingly, the part of the brain that lies under the forelock (the prefrontal cortex), is responsible for higher level cognitive processes such as planning, decision making, and controlling speech and language.[59] Truthfulness or lying, obedience or sinfulness, are all directed by this part of the brain.

At the end of the chapter, God commands that the forelock needs to be in a state of utter submission to Him, symbolized by prostration on the earth (*sajdah*).

SUMMARY OF THE VERSES

In a stern tone, these verses warn about the severe chastisement that awaits the one who lies and sins and does not desist from harassing or obstructing a worshipper of God; he will be dragged away in disgrace towards his punishment.

REFLECTIVE LEARNING

Let me reflect on what I need to desist from so that I am not classified amongst those who have a lying, sinful forelock.

VERSES 17, 18

فَلْيَدْعُ نَادِيَهُ ﴿١٧﴾ سَنَدْعُ الزَّبَانِيَةَ ﴿١٨﴾

Then let him call his associates. [17] *We will call the guardians of Hell.* [18]

17-18.1 *'Then let him call his associates.'*: [*Nādiyahu* (نَادِيَهُ, his associates)]. *Nādī* means a place of gathering for amusement.[60] A famous example from early Islamic history was the Dar al-Nadwah in Makka where the Quraysh would sit to deliberate their affairs.

[58] Suyūṭī, *al-Jalālayn*, p. 600.

[59] Miller, The prefrontal cortex, categories, concepts and cognition, (*Philosophical Transactions of the Royal Society*) 2002, 357/1123.

[60] Shīrāzī, *Namūneh*, 27/172.

However, in this verse *nādī* is not referring to the place, but the people who gather in these places.[61] The pronoun *hu* attached to *nādī* refers to Abu Jahl. The verse challenges the defiant to call on those who supported them for help.

17-18.2 *'We will call the guardians of Hell.'*: [*Al-Zabāniyah* (الزَّبَانِيَة, guardians of Hell)]. The plural of *zibniyah*, this term is derived from *zabn*, meaning to defend and drive away. It is a term used for security guards.[62] In this verse, it refers to the sentinel angels in charge of Hell. Q66:6 states about them:

يَا أَيُّهَا الَّذِينَ آمَنُوا قُوا أَنْفُسَكُمْ وَأَهْلِيكُمْ نَارًا
وَقُودُهَا النَّاسُ وَالْحِجَارَةُ عَلَيْهَا مَلَائِكَةٌ غِلَاظٌ شِدَادٌ

O believers! Protect yourselves and your families from a Fire whose fuel is men and stones, over which are appointed angels, stern and severe...

The verse under review makes clear that no one can stand against the command of God on that Day. The angels of Hell shall be summoned to take every defiant one to the fire of Hell.

SUMMARY OF THE VERSES

The verses state that if the likes of Abu Jahl summon their associates, God will call on the guardians of Hell to deal with them.

REFLECTIVE LEARNING

Let me reflect on whether I rely on associates in this world other than God, as they will be the ones that I may call upon on the Day of Judgement.

VERSE 19

كَلَّا لَا تُطِعْهُ وَٱسْجُدْ وَٱقْتَرِب ۩ ﴿١٩﴾

Not at all! Do not obey him. But prostrate (to God) and draw near. [19]

---

[61] Ṭabāṭabā'ī, *al-Mīzān*, 20/327.
[62] Shīrāzī, *Namūneh*, 27/173.

19.1 [*Kallā* (كَلَّا, not at all)]. Here, it means that people like Abu Jahl would never succeed in their attempts to stop God's true servants from worshipping Him.[63]

[*Lā tuṭiʿhu* (لَا تُطِعْهُ, do not obey him)]. This is a directive to the Prophet (s) and the believers not to let the efforts of those who want to see an end to God's worship sway their resolve. Instead, in the face of such efforts, God invites the believers to get even closer to Him by falling in prostration.

[*Usjud* (اسْجُدْ, prostrate)]. The honour and dignity of man is manifested by the forehead. Bowing the head is a sign of respect or servility. Here, he is directed to show his utmost humility and surrender to God by putting his forehead on the ground in prostration.

19.2 This is one of the four verses in the Qur'an where prostration (*sajdah*) must be performed by the reciter and the listener. These verses are known the *ʿazāʾim al-sujūd* ([verses of] obligatory prostrations). In this regard, a tradition from Imam al-Sadiq (a) states: The surahs that contain verses of obligatory prostration are Alif Lām Mīm Tanzīl (Q41:38), Ḥā Mīm al-Sajdah (Q32:15), al-Najm (Q53:62), and Iqraʾ Bismi Rabbik (Q96:19). As for the other verses [of prostration], they are recommended, not obligatory.[64]

Collectively, there are 15 verses of prostration; prostration is compulsory for four of them and recommended for the other eleven. These eleven are: Q7:206, Q13:15, Q16:50, Q17:109, Q19:58, Q22:18, Q22:77, Q25:60, Q27:26, Q38:24, and Q84:21.[65]

The specific rulings about these verses can be found in the books of jurisprudence.

19.3 [*Iqtarib* (اقْتَرِب, draw near)]. This the imperative form of *iqtaraba*, derived from *qaruba*, meaning to come near. This means that it is through prostration that one draws close to God.

---

[63] Ibid, 27/174.

[64] ʿĀmilī, *Wasāʾil*, 6/241.

عَنِ الصَّادِقِ (عَلَيْهِ السَّلَامُ) - الْعَزَائِمُ الم تَنْزِيلٌ وَحم السَّجْدَةُ وَالنَّجْمُ وَاقْرَأْ بِاسْمِ رَبِّكَ وَمَا عَدَاهَا فِي جَمِيعِ الْقُرْآنِ مَسْنُونٌ وَلَيْسَ بِمَفْرُوضٍ.

[65] Sistānī, *Minhāj al-Ṣāliḥīn*, *Kitāb al-Ṣalāt*, 1/222.

A tradition from Imam al-Ridha (a) states: The closest a servant can be to God, the Almighty, is when he is in prostration (*sajdah*), and that is why God has stated, '*Prostrate, and draw near*.'[66]

19.4 Verse 5 stated that God taught man that which he knew not. The human being could never have known how to get close to God except through His guidance. And God told him, "to get closer to Me, prostrate before Me."

SUMMARY OF THE VERSE

In this verse God instructs the Prophet (s) and the believers to ignore everyone who would forestall them from the worship of God. Instead, the believer is commanded to prostrate to His Lord, and draw closer to Him thereby.

REFLECTIVE LEARNING

Knowledge is of no use if it does not lead to the proximity of God, which is epitomized by prostration.

Let me elongate my prostrations gradually and thereby seek God's proximity constantly.

---

[66] Kulaynī, *al-Kāfī*, 3/264.

عَنِ الرِّضَا (عَلَيْهِ السَّلَامُ) - أَقْرَبُ مَا يَكُونُ الْعَبْدُ مِنَ اللهِ عَزَّ وَجَلَّ وَهُوَ سَاجِدٌ وَذَلِكَ قَوْلُهُ عَزَّ وَجَلَّ: «وَٱسْجُدْ وَٱقْتَرِبْ.»

SURAT AL-QADR
THE DECREE (97)

TEXT AND TRANSLATION

سُورَةُ الْقَدْرِ

بِسْمِ اللهِ الرَّحْمٰنِ الرَّحِيمِ

إِنَّا أَنْزَلْنَاهُ فِي لَيْلَةِ الْقَدْرِ ﴿١﴾ وَمَا أَدْرَاكَ مَا لَيْلَةُ الْقَدْرِ ﴿٢﴾ لَيْلَةُ الْقَدْرِ خَيْرٌ مِنْ
أَلْفِ شَهْرٍ ﴿٣﴾ تَنَزَّلُ الْمَلَائِكَةُ وَالرُّوحُ فِيهَا بِإِذْنِ رَبِّهِمْ مِنْ كُلِّ أَمْرٍ ﴿٤﴾ سَلَامٌ
هِيَ حَتَّىٰ مَطْلَعِ الْفَجْرِ ﴿٥﴾

In the name of God, the Beneficent, the Merciful. Indeed,

We sent it down on the Night of Decree. [1] *And what will make you know what the Night of Decree is?* [2] *The Night of Decree is better than a thousand months.* [3] *Therein descend the angels and the Spirit by the permission of their Lord, with every affair.* [4] *Peace it is, until the emergence of the dawn.* [5]

INTRODUCTION

Surat al-Qadr (97) was the 25th chapter to be revealed. It has five verses and was revealed in Makka, after Surat ʿAbasa (80).[1] It is named after the night of decree (*al-qadr*) mentioned in the surah.

The surah speaks of the blessed night of Qadr (decree) in which the Qurʾan was sent down. It is a night that is better than one thousand months, a night for supplication, seeking forgiveness, and asking for God's favour. It is the night in which the angels descend with the decrees of God for the coming year.

Although it has been classified as a Makkan surah, there are some reports that it could have been revealed in Madina.[2] In this regard,

---

1 Maʿrifat, *ʿUlūm-i Qurʾānī*, p. 90.

2 Ṭabāṭabāʾī, *Mīzān*, 20/330.

reports state that the chapter was revealed in Madina after the Prophet (s) was distressed when he saw in a dream that some men of the Banu Umayyah were ascending and descending from his pulpit (the Prophet (s) only used a pulpit in Madina, not Makka). And the chapter informed him that the night of Qadr was better than the one thousand months for which the Banu Umayyah would remain in power.[3]

LINK TO THE PREVIOUS CHAPTER

The previous chapter, Surat al-ʿAlaq, speaks of the revelation of the Qur'an as a great blessing of God through which He guided His creation. It contains the first five verses that were revealed in the gradual phase (*tanzīl*) of the Qur'anic revelation. Surat al-Qadr begins by mentioning the event of the Qur'an's instant phase (*inzāl*) of revelation, with a special mention of the great night in which this blessing occurred – the night of Qadr.

MERITS OF RECITATION

- A tradition from the Prophet (s) states: Whoever recites this surah will be rewarded like the one who fasted in the month of Ramadan, and if he recites it on the night of Qadr, his reward will be like the one who fought in the way of God.[4]
- Another tradition from the Prophet (s) states: Whoever recites this surah will have the best of creation (*khayr al-bariyyah*) as a friend and companion on the Day of Judgement.[5]
- A companion reports that he wrote to Imam al-Baqir (a), "I have incurred a great debt [that I cannot pay]." The Imam (a) wrote in reply, "Increase your prayers for forgiveness (*istighfār*) and constantly recite Surat *Innā anzalnāhu*."[6]

---

[3] Kulaynī, *al-Kāfī*, 8/222; Suyūṭī, *al-Durr Manthūr*, 6/371.

[4] Baḥrānī, *al-Burhān*, 5/700.

عَنِ الرَّسُولِ (صَلَّى اللهُ عَلَيْهِ وَآلِهِ) – مَنْ قَرَأَ هَذِهِ السُّورَةَ كَانَ لَهُ مِنَ الْأَجْرِ كَمَنْ صَامَ شَهْرَ رَمَضَانَ وَإِنْ وَافَقَ لَيْلَةُ الْقَدْرِ، كَانَ لَهُ ثَوَابٌ كَثَوَابِ مَنْ قَاتَلَ فِي سَبِيلِ اللهِ.

[5] Ibid.

عَنِ الرَّسُولِ (صَلَّى اللهُ عَلَيْهِ وَآلِهِ) – مَنْ قَرَأَهَا كَانَ لَهُ يَوْمَ الْقِيَامَةِ خَيْرُ الْبَرِيَّةِ رَفِيقًا وَصَاحِبًا.

[6] Kulaynī, *al-Kāfī*, 5/317.

عَنِ الْبَاقِرِ (عَلَيْهِ السَّلَامُ) – عَنْ إِسْمَاعِيلَ بْنِ سَهْلٍ قَالَ: كَتَبْتُ إِلَى أَبِي جَعْفَرٍ (عَلَيْهِ السَّلَامُ) إِنِّي قَدْ لَزِمَنِي دَيْنٌ فَادِحٌ، فَكَتَبَ: أَكْثِرْ مِنَ الاِسْتِغْفَارِ وَرَطِّبْ لِسَانَكَ بِقِرَاءَةِ «إِنَّا أَنْزَلْنَاهُ».

- A tradition from Imam al-Sadiq (a) states: When anyone recites Surat al-Qadr on the night of Qadr in one of the prayers that God has made obligatory, a caller calls out, "O servant of God! God has forgiven your past sins, so now you may start afresh."[7]
- A tradition from Imam al-Ridha (a) states: Whoever comes to the grave of his fellow believer and inserts his fingers anywhere on the grave and recites Surat al-Qadr seven times, he will remain safe from the Great Terror [of the Day of Judgement].[8] In another tradition, he (a) said that both the reciter as well as the person in the grave will be forgiven for their sins.[9]

EXEGESIS

VERSE 1

إِنَّا أَنْزَلْنَاهُ فِي لَيْلَةِ الْقَدْرِ ﴿١﴾

Indeed, We sent it down on the Night of Decree.

1.1 The important night of Qadr has always existed since the time human beings populated the earth. A tradition from Imam al-Jawad (a) states: God, Exalted be His mention, created *laylat al-qadr* when He initially created the world. He then created in it the first Prophet (a) and the first successor. He then decreed that there would be one night in every year when the angels would descend with the details of all affairs for its inhabitants for the coming year.[10]

---

[7] Majlisī, *Biḥār*, 89/327.

عَنِ الصَّادِقِ (عَلَيْهِ السَّلَامُ) - مَنْ قَرَأَ «إِنَّا أَنْزَلْنَاهُ فِي لَيْلَةِ الْقَدْرِ» فِي فَرِيضَةٍ مِنْ فَرَائِضِ اللهِ نَادَ مُنَادٍ يَا عَبْدَ اللهِ غَفَرَ اللهُ لَكَ مَا مَضَى فَاسْتَأْنِفِ الْعَمَلَ.

[8] Ṭūsī, *Tahdhīb*, 6/104.

عَنِ الرِّضَا (عَلَيْهِ السَّلَامُ) - مَنْ أَتَى قَبْرَ أَخِيهِ الْمُؤْمِنِ مِنْ أَيِّ نَاحِيَةٍ يَضَعُ يَدَهُ وَيَقْرَأُ إِنَّا أَنْزَلْنَاهُ فِي لَيْلَةِ الْقَدْرِ سَبْعَ مَرَّاتٍ آمَنَهُ اللهُ يَوْمَ الْفَزَعِ الْأَكْبَرِ.

[9] Ṣadūq, *al-Faqīh*, 1/181.

[10] Kulaynī, *al-Kāfī*, 1/250.

عَنْ أَبِي جَعْفَرٍ (عَلَيْهِ السَّلَامُ) - لَقَدْ خَلَقَ اللهُ جَلَّ ذِكْرُهُ لَيْلَةَ الْقَدْرِ أَوَّلَ مَا خَلَقَ الدُّنْيَا، وَلَقَدْ خَلَقَ فِيهَا أَوَّلَ نَبِيٍّ يَكُونُ وَأَوَّلَ وَصِيٍّ يَكُونُ وَلَقَدْ قَضَى أَنْ يَكُونَ فِي كُلِّ سَنَةٍ لَيْلَةٌ يَهْبِطُ فِيهَا بِتَفْسِيرِ الْأُمُورِ إِلَى مِثْلِهَا مِنَ السَّنَةِ الْمُقْبِلَةِ.

1.2 [*Innā* (إِنَّا, Indeed, We)]. The plural pronoun is used in the Qur'an in the sense of God's Majesty and Power and to indicate the greatness of the act, as in this verse.[11]

The different usages of the pronouns 'We' and 'I' have been discussed in more detail in the *tafsīr* of Surat al-Kawthar (108).

1.3 [*Anzalnāhu* (أَنْزَلْنَاهُ, We sent it)]. *Anzala* in this verse, derived from *nazala*, means to send down. However, the sending down of the Qur'an does not mean that it was moved from one location to another (*tajāfī*). Rather, it is an emanation (*tajallī*) of the original which remains in the higher realms.[12] Here it refers to God's instantaneous revelation of the entire Qur'an on the night of Qadr. This type of descent is different from the gradual revelation of the Qur'an over 23 years, which has been called *tanzīl*, which is derived from *nazzala*, giving the meaning of a continual and gradual descent.[13]

1.4 Therefore, the Qur'an underwent two forms of revelation, an instantaneous complete revelation (*inzāl*) on the night of Qadr, and a gradual measured revelation (*tanzīl*) that spanned the 23 years of the mission of the Prophet (s), beginning in the cave of Hira on the 27th Rajab, in the fortieth year of his (s) blessed life.[14] The two forms of revelation are mentioned in several verses: For example:

Instant revelation, Q44:3:

إِنَّا أَنْزَلْنَاهُ فِي لَيْلَةٍ مُبَارَكَةٍ

Indeed, We sent it down on a blessed night...

Gradual revelation, Q17:106:

وَقُرْآنًا فَرَقْنَاهُ لِتَقْرَأَهُ عَلَى النَّاسِ عَلَىٰ مُكْثٍ وَنَزَّلْنَاهُ تَنْزِيلًا

And it is a Qur'an that We have divided [into parts] so that you may recite it to the people at intervals. And We have sent it down gradually.

1.5 The gradual revelation is clear, however, about the manner of the instant revelation on the night of Qadr, there are several opinions:

---

[11] Shīrāzī, *Namūneh*, 27/181.

[12] Javādī-Āmolī, *Tasnīm*. (Transcript: http://javadi.esra.ir/-/40-10-9931-1-تفسیر-سوره-قدر-جلسه).

[13] Rāghib, *al-Mufradāt*.

[14] Shīrāzī, *Namūneh*, 27/182.

i) Some scholars believe that only the portion of the Qur'an that would be gradually revealed in a particular year was revealed to the Prophet (s) in the *laylat al-qadr* of that year.[15]

ii) Some believe that it was revealed in its complete form from a higher station to a location in the fourth heavens called the *Bayt al-maʿmūr* (the house frequented by the angels).

When Imam al-Sadiq (a) was asked about how the Qur'an was revealed in the month of Ramadan as mentioned in Q2:185, '*The month of Ramadan [is that] in which the Qur'an was revealed*,' while it had [actually] been revealed over a period of a complete 20 [or 23] years, he replied, "The Qur'an was revealed as one Word in the month of Ramadan to the *Bayt al-Maʿmūr* and thereafter, it was sent down from *Bayt al-maʿmūr* over a period of 20 years."[16]

iii) And some say that it was revealed to the heart of the Prophet (s) in a compressed form, without words and phrases.[17] Kāshānī is of the opinion that *Bayt al-maʿmūr* may be a reference to the heart of the Prophet (s).[18] This is evidenced by Q2:97 which states:

فَإِنَّهُ نَزَّلَهُ عَلَىٰ قَلْبِكَ بِإِذْنِ اللَّهِ

...[Jibra'il] indeed brought it (the Qur'an) to your heart by God's permission...

1.6 The pronoun *hu* (هُ) in *anzalnāhu* refers to the Qur'an, which was revealed in this blessed night, making *laylat al-qadr* even more significant. The pronoun is used here instead of mentioning the Qur'an by name to place the emphasis on the night of Qadr.[19] This night of indescribable grandeur is mentioned by name three times in the chapter to indicate its great station.

---

15 Maʿrifat, *Tārīkh-i Qur'an*, p. 41.

16 Ṣadūq, *al-Amālī*, 1/62.

أَخْبِرْنِي عَنْ قَوْلِ اللهِ عَزَّ وَجَلَّ: «شَهْرُ رَمَضَانَ الَّذِي أُنْزِلَ فِيهِ الْقُرْآنُ» كَيْفَ أُنْزِلَ الْقُرْآنُ فِي شَهْرِ رَمَضَانَ وَإِنَّمَا أُنْزِلَ الْقُرْآنُ فِي مُدَّةِ عِشْرِينَ سَنَةً أَوَّلُهُ وَآخِرُهُ فَقَالَ عَلَيْهِ السَّلَامُ: أُنْزِلَ الْقُرْآنُ جُمْلَةً وَاحِدَةً فِي شَهْرِ رَمَضَانَ إِلَى الْبَيْتِ الْمَعْمُورِ ثُمَّ أُنْزِلَ مِنَ الْبَيْتِ الْمَعْمُورِ فِي مُدَّةِ عِشْرِينَ سَنَةً.

17 Ṭabāṭabā'ī, *al-Mīzān*, 2/18.

18 Kāshānī, *al-Ṣāfī*, 1/65.

19 Rāzī, *Mafātīḥ al-Ghayb*, 32/228.

1.7 The month of Ramadan has always been the month in which God has revealed His books. A tradition from Imam al-Sadiq (a) states: The Tawrāt was revealed on the 6th night of the month of Ramadan, the Injīl on the 12th night, the Zabur on the 18th night, and the Qur'an was revealed on the night of Qadr.[20]

1.8 [*Fī laylati* (فِي لَيْلَةِ, in the night)]. The momentous occasion of the revelation of the Qur'an happened at night. Night was chosen to reveal God's final Book into the heart of His final Messenger. Q73:6 states:

إِنَّ نَاشِئَةَ اللَّيْلِ هِيَ أَشَدُّ وَطْئًا وَأَقْوَمُ قِيلًا

Indeed, the hours of the night are firmer in impression and more upright for speech.

1.9 Most of the connections between the higher realm and our world happen at night. The Qur'an mentions several such events. As examples:

i) Q2:51:

وَإِذْ وَاعَدْنَا مُوسَىٰ أَرْبَعِينَ لَيْلَةً

And [recall] when We made an appointment with Musa for forty nights...

ii) Q17:1:

سُبْحَانَ الَّذِي أَسْرَىٰ بِعَبْدِهِ لَيْلًا مِنَ الْمَسْجِدِ الْحَرَامِ إِلَى الْمَسْجِدِ الْأَقْصَى

Glorified is He who took His servant by night from Masjid al-Haram to Masjid al-Aqsa...

1.10 The night allows for spiritual progress in a manner that daytime does not; a tradition from Imam al-Askari (a) states: The journey towards God, most Mighty and Exalted, is one that cannot be made without staying awake at night.[21]

---

20 Kulaynī, *al-Kāfī*, 4/157.

عَنِ الصَّادِقِ (عَلَيْهِ السَّلَامُ) – نَزَلَتِ التَّوْرَاةُ فِي سِتٍّ مَضَتْ مِنْ شَهْرِ رَمَضَانَ، وَنَزَلَ الْإِنْجِيلُ فِي اثْنَتَيْ عَشْرَةَ لَيْلَةً مَضَتْ مِنْ شَهْرِ رَمَضَانَ، وَنَزَلَ الزَّبُورُ فِي لَيْلَةِ ثَمَانِيَ عَشْرَةَ مَضَتْ مِنْ شَهْرِ رَمَضَانَ، وَنَزَلَ الْقُرْآنُ فِي لَيْلَةِ الْقَدْرِ.

21 Majlisī, *Biḥār*, 75/830.

عَنِ الْعَسْكَرِيِّ (عَلَيْهِ السَّلَامُ) – إِنَّ الْوُصُولَ إِلَى اللهِ عَزَّ وَجَلَّ سَفَرٌ لَا يُدْرَكُ إِلَّا بِامْتِطَاءِ اللَّيْلِ.

1.11 [*Al-Qadr* (ٱلْقَدْر, the decree)] has several meanings. The root meaning is power and freedom to do, or not do, something. All derivatives and secondary meanings return to this meaning. For example, *qudrah* (ability), *taqdīr* (fate), *qadr* (constriction) and *qadara* (to decree, or to place value), all require a power to bring about their existence.[22] Examples of how all these meanings are relevant to the night of Qadr are discussed below:

i) Power and ability: Many verses mention *qudrah* (power) as an attribute of God. For example, Q2:284 states:

وَاللَّهُ عَلَىٰ كُلِّ شَيْءٍ قَدِيرٌ

...And God has power over all things.

If this meaning is taken, the verse would be translated as: 'Indeed, We sent it down on the Night of Power', emphasizing God's control and power over the fate of human beings.

ii) Value, honour, and worth: The word *qadr* is also used to denote the value of something. For example, Q39:67 states:

وَمَا قَدَرُوا اللَّهَ حَقَّ قَدْرِهِ وَالْأَرْضُ جَمِيعًا قَبْضَتُهُ يَوْمَ الْقِيَامَةِ

They have not honoured God with the honour that is due to Him,
while the whole earth will be in His grasp on the Day of Judgement...

In this case, the verse would mean, 'Indeed, We sent it down on the night of great value.' Certainly, the night of Qadr has incomparable value because God declares that it is better than a thousand months.

iii) Congestion and constriction: The Qur'an has used the term *qadr* in this meaning as well. For example, Q13:26 states:

اللَّهُ يَبْسُطُ الرِّزْقَ لِمَنْ يَشَاءُ وَيَقْدِرُ

God extends provision for whom He wills,
and straitens it [for others]...

Some exegetes have suggested that this meaning may apply here as well. In this case, the verse would mean, 'Indeed, We sent it down on the Night of Constriction.' This 'constriction'

---

22 Muṣṭafawī, *al-Taḥqīq*.

refers to the congestion caused by the huge number of angels descending to the earth on that night.[23] However, many exegetes reckon this meaning to be unlikely.[24]

iv) Measure and decree: The word *qadr* also refers to amount and measure. It has been used in this meaning in several verses of the Qur'an. For example Q15:21 states:

وَإِنْ مِنْ شَيْءٍ إِلَّا عِنْدَنَا خَزَائِنُهُ وَمَا نُنَزِّلُهُ إِلَّا بِقَدَرٍ مَعْلُومٍ

And there is not a thing except that with Us are its stores; and We do not send it down except according to a known measure.

The affairs of all individuals are measured out and then decreed on this night for the following year. Q44:4 states:

فِيهَا يُفْرَقُ كُلُّ أَمْرٍ حَكِيمٍ

Therein, every wise affair is made precise.

Therefore, this is a night in which man's destiny for the following year is decreed. Indeed, this is the preferred interpretation of *qadr* in this instance; therefore, the verse means, 'Indeed, We sent it down on the Night of Decree.'

A tradition from Imam al-Sadiq (a) states: The significance of *laylat al-qadr* is that on this night, God the Blessed and Exalted, decrees lifespans, sustenance, and matters that will transpire [for the people] in the coming year such as death or life, poverty or prosperity, hardship or ease, and blessings or tribulation.[25]

1.12 The Qur'an does not state which night *laylat al-qadr* is. In Q2:185, it informs us of two features of the night: that it was the night in which the Qur'an was revealed, and that it is one of the nights of the blessed month of Ramadan:

شَهْرُ رَمَضَانَ الَّذِي أُنْزِلَ فِيهِ الْقُرْآنُ

The month of Ramadan, in which the Qur'an was sent down...

---

[23] Qarā'atī, *Nūr*, 10/545.

[24] Ṭabāṭabā'ī, *al-Mīzān*, 20/331.

[25] Majlisī, *Biḥār*, 82/52.

عَنِ الصَّادِقِ (عَلَيْهِ السَّلَامُ) – وَمَعْنَى لَيْلَةِ الْقَدْرِ أَنَّ اللهَ تَبَارَكَ وَتَعَالَى يُقَدِّرُ فِيهَا الْآجَالَ وَالْأَرْزَاقَ وَمَا يَكُونُ فِي السَّنَةِ مِنْ مَوْتٍ أَوْ حَيَاةٍ أَوْ جَدْبٍ أَوْ خِصْبٍ أَوْ خَيْرٍ أَوْ شَرٍّ.

By comparing this verse with the first verse of Surat al-Qadr, we can only conclude that *laylat al-qadr* is one of the nights in the month of Ramadan.

1.13 *Laylat al-qadr* does not come at the beginning of the month of Ramadan, but occurs in its last days. Perhaps this is because the month of Ramadan is a month of blessedness and purification, and the spirituality it causes has to be built up until it reaches a crescendo on *laylat al-qadr*. Thereafter, the believer enjoys the elevated sense of spirituality until the end of the blessed month, and beyond.

1.14 Not knowing the exact night of Qadr is not as unusual as it may seem, because it applies to other situations as well. For example, God has kept His pleasure hidden in a variety of acts of worship, so that people practice all of them; He has hidden His displeasure in various acts of sinfulness, so that people avoid all of them; He has concealed the identity of His close servants (*awliyāʾ*), so that people respect everyone equally; He has kept hidden the particular supplications that He answers readily so that people call to Him with every supplication; He has kept His greatest Name (*al-ism al-aʿẓam*) hidden, so that people call to Him by all His Names; and He has not revealed the time of anyone's death, so that the individual remains ready at all times.[26]

1.15 In any case, to have some idea about which night it is, we need to turn to the narrations, some of which are quoted below:

i) A tradition from the Prophet (s) states: Seek this night in the last ten nights of the month [of Ramadan], and seek it in its odd nights.[27]

ii) A tradition from Imam al-Sadiq (a) states: On the 19th night [of the month of Ramadan] the two matters (those that He wants to bring forward and those that He wishes to defer) are collated (*yaltaqi al-jamʿān*); on the 21st night every wise affair is made distinct (*yufraqu kullu amrin ḥakīm*); and on the 23rd night whatever God, the Mighty and Exalted, wills from that is sealed

[26] Shīrāzī, *Namūneh*, 27/190.

[27] Ḥuwayzī, *Nūr al-Thaqalayn*, 5/629.

عَنِ الرَّسُولِ (صَلَّى اللهُ عَلَيْهِ وَآلِهِ) – فَالْتَمِسُوهَا فِي الْعَشْرِ الْأَوَاخِرِ، وَالْتَمِسُوهَا فِي كُلِّ وِتْرٍ.

and signed off (*yumḍā*). And this is the night of Qadr, which God has stated is better than a thousand months.[28]

iii) A tradition states that Imam al-Baqir (a) was asked about this night. He replied, "It is one of two nights, the 23rd or the 21st [of the month of Ramadan]." The companion asked, "Tell me which one?" The Imam (a) replied, "Why can you not perform your *aʿmāl* on both nights, because it is [certainly] one of them."[29]

iv) A tradition from Imam al-Sadiq (a) states: A man from the tribe of Banu Juhaynah asked the Prophet, "My home is far from Madina, so advise me which night I should come to the city [for worship]?" The Prophet (s) advised him to come on the 23rd night.[30]

From the foregoing reports, it seems that the night of Qadr is most likely on the 23rd, or possibly the 21st night, of the month of Ramadan.

DISCUSSION: ARE THE DECREES OF *LAYLAT AL-QADR* FIXED?

One of the questions that may arise is: after the night of Qadr is over, is there any point in supplicating to God and praying for His favour? Are all matters fixed and irreversible, or is there latitude for change?

Syed Ṭabāṭabā'ī comments: It is quite possible for a matter to be decreed in *laylat al-qadr* in one way, and then take place in another. Decree and the possibility of subsequent alteration are two separate issues, and God may decide to change matters.[31] Indeed, Q13:39 states:

يَمْحُو اللَّهُ مَا يَشَاءُ وَيُثْبِتُ وَعِنْدَهُ أُمُّ الْكِتَابِ

---

[28] Kulaynī, *al-Kāfī*, 4/158.

عَنِ الصَّادِقِ (عَلَيْهِ السَّلَامُ) – إِنَّ فِي لَيْلَةِ تِسْعَ عَشْرَةَ يَلْتَقِي الْجَمْعَانِ، وَفِي لَيْلَةِ إِحْدَى وَعِشْرِينَ يُفْرَقُ كُلُّ أَمْرٍ حَكِيمٍ، وَفِي لَيْلَةِ ثَلَاثٍ وَعِشْرِينَ يُمْضَى مَا أَرَادَ اللَّهُ عَزَّ وَجَلَّ مِنْ ذَلِكَ وَهِيَ لَيْلَةُ الْقَدْرِ الَّتِي قَالَ اللَّهُ عَزَّ وَجَلَّ «خَيْرٌ مِنْ أَلْفِ شَهْرٍ».

[29] ʿĀmilī, *Wasāʾil*, 10/360.

عَنِ الْبَاقِرِ (عَلَيْهِ السَّلَامُ) – قَالَ فِي لَيْلَتَيْنِ لَيْلَةِ ثَلَاثٍ وَعِشْرِينَ وَإِحْدَى وَعِشْرِينَ، فَقُلْتُ أَفْرِدْ لِي إِحْدَاهُمَا قَالَ وَمَا عَلَيْكَ أَنْ تَعْمَلَ فِي لَيْلَتَيْنِ هِيَ إِحْدَاهُمَا.

[30] Ṣadūq, *al-Faqih*, 2/160.

عَنِ الصَّادِقِ (عَلَيْهِ السَّلَامُ) – قَالَ لَيْلَةُ ثَلَاثٍ وَعِشْرِينَ هِيَ لَيْلَةُ الْجُهَنِيِّ، وَحَدِيثُهُ أَنَّهُ قَالَ لِرَسُولِ اللَّهِ (صَلَّى اللَّهُ عَلَيْهِ وَآلِهِ) إِنَّ مَنْزِلِي نَاءٍ عَنِ الْمَدِينَةِ فَمُرْنِي بِلَيْلَةٍ أَدْخُلُ فِيهَا فَأَمَرَهُ بِلَيْلَةِ ثَلَاثٍ وَعِشْرِينَ.

[31] Ṭabāṭabāʾī, *al-Mīzān*, 20/331.

God erases and confirms what He wills,
and with Him is the origin of the Book.

From the narrations and also the supplications taught by the Imams (a), it appears that there are two types of Divine decree: fixed and alterable. In one of the supplications of the month of Ramadan we read: O God, we ask You in what You decide and decree about those matters that are inevitable from the affairs based on wisdom, [to grant me] blessings that are not taken back or altered...[32]

However, the fact that there is so much emphasis on constant supplication (*duʿāʾ*) throughout the year shows that there are decrees that are alterable also, although we do not have the knowledge of which decrees are fixed, and which are not.[33]

Every affair that occurs goes through a series of steps, all of which have to be in place before the affair is realized. When asked about this, Imam al-Kazim (a) mentioned six stages in the process: God knows [the wisdom behind the act], He desires [for the act to be done], He intends [to carry it out], He allocates its measure [how long, how much, etc.], He decrees it [sending forth the details and instructions to those who will carry it out], and He signs it off [after which there can be no change].[34]

On *laylat al-qadr*, the affairs are decided up to the penultimate stage. However, once the decrees are finally signed off (*imḍā*) in the course of the year, then the matter is sealed, and no change is made after that. For example, Q11:74-76 speak of the futility of the pleading of Prophet Ibrahim (a) for the community of Prophet Lut (a) once God's decree had been sealed for them:

فَلَمَّا ذَهَبَ عَنْ إِبْرَاهِيمَ الرَّوْعُ وَجَاءَتْهُ الْبُشْرَىٰ يُجَادِلُنَا فِي قَوْمِ لُوطٍ ﴿٧٤﴾
إِنَّ إِبْرَاهِيمَ لَحَلِيمٌ أَوَّاهٌ مُنِيبٌ ﴿٧٥﴾ يَا إِبْرَاهِيمُ أَعْرِضْ عَنْ هَٰذَا
إِنَّهُ قَدْ جَاءَ أَمْرُ رَبِّكَ وَإِنَّهُمْ آتِيهِمْ عَذَابٌ غَيْرُ مَرْدُودٍ

And when the fright had left Ibrahim, and the glad tidings had reached him, he began to plead with Us for the people of Lut.

---

[32] Kulaynī, *al-Kāfī*, 4/161.

اَللّٰهُمَّ إِنِّي أَسْأَلُكَ فِيمَا تَقْضِي وَتُقَدِّرُ مِنَ الْأَمْرِ الْمَحْتُومِ فِي الْأَمْرِ الْحَكِيمِ مِنَ الْقَضَاءِ الَّذِي لَا يُرَدُّ وَلَا يُبَدَّلُ أَنْ...

[33] Muṭahharī, (*Āshnāyī bā Qurʾan*), *Āthār*, 28/695.

[34] Kulaynī, *al-Kāfī*, 4/157.

سُئِلَ الْعَالِمُ عَلَيْهِ السَّلَامُ كَيْفَ عِلْمُ اللهِ قَالَ عَلِمَ وَشَاءَ وَأَرَادَ وَقَدَّرَ وَقَضَى وَأَمْضَى.

Indeed, Ibrahim was without doubt, forbearing, compassionate, and oft-returning [to God]. [The angels said,] "O Ibrahim! Let this go. Indeed, the command of your Lord has gone forth. Indeed, a punishment is coming to them that cannot be turned back."

However, before this last stage and point of no return is reached, the most effective method of altering the decree is sincere supplication. A tradition from Imam al-Sadiq (a) states: Supplication (*duʿāʾ*) alters the ordained decree after it has been confirmed (*mubram*) and fixed [for the individual], so be consistent in supplication, for it is the key to Divine mercy.[35]

It is for this reason that the believer is instructed to constantly supplicate to God, to seek from Him whatever he wants. It is no coincidence that the night on which our destiny is decided is the same night on which the Qur'an was revealed. The Qur'an directs us to what is important, to the purpose of our existence, and the realities of our journey towards God. So it should also govern how and what we seek from Him.

Imam al-Sadiq (a) was asked whether *laylat al-qadr* was, and is, an annual occurrence. He replied: If *laylat al-qadr* was taken away, the Qur'an would be taken away.[36]

SUMMARY OF THE VERSE

In summary, the verse states that the Qur'an was revealed on the same night that the destiny of mankind is decided for the following year – the Night of Decree (*laylat al-qadr*).

REFLECTIVE LEARNING

A tradition from Imam al-Sadiq (a) states: The Night of Decree (*laylat al-qadr*) is the beginning of the year and the end (of the last one).[37]

---

35 ʿĀmilī, *Wasāʾil*, 7/26.

عَنِ الصَّادِقِ (عَلَيْهِ السَّلَامُ) – الدُّعَاءُ يَرُدُّ الْقَضَاءَ بَعْدَ مَا أُبْرِمَ إِبْرَامًا فَأَكْثِرْ مِنَ الدُّعَاءِ فَإِنَّهُ مِفْتَاحُ كُلِّ رَحْمَةٍ.

36 Kulaynī, *al-Kāfī*, 4/158.

عَنِ الصَّادِقِ (عَلَيْهِ السَّلَامُ) – سَمِعْتُ رَجُلًا يَسْأَلُ أَبَا عَبْدِ اللهِ (عَلَيْهِ السَّلَامُ) عَنْ لَيْلَةِ الْقَدْرِ فَقَالَ أَخْبِرْنِي عَنْ لَيْلَةِ الْقَدْرِ كَانَتْ أَوْ تَكُونُ فِي كُلِّ عَامٍ؟ فَقَالَ أَبُو عَبْدِ اللهِ (عَلَيْهِ السَّلَامُ) لَوْ رُفِعَتْ لَيْلَةُ الْقَدْرِ لَرُفِعَ الْقُرْآنُ.

37 Ibid, 4/160.

عَنِ الصَّادِقِ (عَلَيْهِ السَّلَامُ) – لَيْلَةُ الْقَدْرِ هِيَ أَوَّلُ السَّنَةِ وهِيَ آخِرُهَا.

Let me reflect on the importance of this one night for the year that follows in particular, and for my whole life in general.

Do I plan for this night throughout the year by continually reflecting on my progress so that my supplications to God are factored in the destiny decreed for me?

VERSES 2, 3

وَمَا أَدْرَاكَ مَا لَيْلَةُ الْقَدْرِ ﴿٢﴾ لَيْلَةُ الْقَدْرِ خَيْرٌ مِنْ أَلْفِ شَهْرٍ ﴿٣﴾

And what will make you know what the Night of Decree is? [2] *The Night of Decree is better than a thousand months.* [3]

2-3.1 '*And what will make you know what the Night of Decree is?*': [*Wa mā adrāka* (وَمَا أَدْرَاكَ, and what will make you know?)]. This phrase has been used several times in the Qur'an to indicate the greatness of the concept in question. However, in this instance, there is an extra emphasis since '*laylat al-qadr*' is repeated again in the answer provided in verse 3, and this indicates the unique significance and grandeur of this night in the system of God's creation.

In response to the question, '*And what will make you know what the Night of Decree is?*', the Prophet (s) replied, "[Even] I do not know [the fullness of its reality]."[38]

2-3.2 '*The Night of Decree is better than a thousand months.*': [*Khayrun min alfi shahrin* (خَيْرٌ مِنْ أَلْفِ شَهْرٍ, better than a thousand months]. This reply to the rhetorical question, *wa mā adrāka,* is an extraordinary announcement and merits reflection. Although some scholars believe that the mention of a thousand months is a hyperbolic allusion to the great station of this night, some are of the opinion that it refers to the span of a full life.[39] One thousand months is just over 83 years, a generous lifespan – and *laylat al-qadr* is better than that. Indeed, the direction of one's life can change in this one night.

2-3.3 This superiority is in terms of the value of worship and the blessing attached to each act done in this one night compared to a lifetime of [continuous] worship at other times. In this regard, a

---

[38] Kulaynī, *al-Kāfī*, 1/248.

عَنِ الرَّسُولِ (صَلَّى اللهُ عَلَيْهِ وَآلِهِ) – «وَمَا أَدْرَاكَ مَا لَيْلَةُ الْقَدْرِ» قَالَ رَسُولُ اللهِ (صَلَّى اللهُ عَلَيْهِ وَآلِهِ) لَا أَدْرِي.

[39] Shīrāzī, *Namūneh*, 27/183.

tradition from Imam al-Baqir (a) states that when asked the meaning of '*better than a thousand months,*' he said, "Performing righteous deeds in this night such as prayers, charity, and other good acts, is better than performing those deeds for a thousand months in which there is no *laylat al-qadr*. And if God, most Blessed, had not amplified the reward for the believers, they would not have achieved [much]. However, out of His love for us, he has amplified the reward for them."[40]

2-3.4 There are several reports that mention that it is a reference to the thousand-month rule of the Banu Umayyah. Although their reign was actually for over 90 years, from the year 40/661 to 132/750, if we remove the eight years and few months that the Hashemite ʿAbdullah b. Zubayr ruled over Ḥijāz from this total, we get one thousand months.[41]

SUMMARY OF THE VERSES

In summary, the verses state that the true nature of *laylat al-qadr* is beyond human comprehension. Any good act in this one night is potentially more beneficial than doing that act for one thousand months in which there is no *laylat al-qadr*.

REFLECTIVE LEARNING

A tradition from Imam al-Sadiq (a) states: If a person begins a good, recommended practice, then he should continue with it for [at least] one year before he substitutes it for another, if he wants to. This is because *laylat al-qadr* will occur during his practice, and so God may factor it in His decree.[42]

Let me reflect on my current recommended practices. Can I add something to them and maintain it for one year?

---

[40] Kulaynī, *al-Kāfī*, 4/457.

عَنِ الْبَاقِرِ (عَلَيْهِ السَّلَامُ) – قَالَ الْعَمَلُ الصَّالِحُ فِيهَا مِنَ الصَّلَاةِ وَالزَّكَاةِ وَأَنْوَاعِ الْخَيْرِ خَيْرٌ مِنَ الْعَمَلِ فِي أَلْفِ شَهْرٍ لَيْسَ فِيهَا لَيْلَةُ الْقَدْرِ وَلَوْلَا مَا يُضَاعِفُ اللهُ تَبَارَكَ وَتَعَالَى لِلْمُؤْمِنِينَ مَا بَلَغُوا وَلَكِنَّ اللهَ يُضَاعِفُ لَهُمُ الْحَسَنَاتِ بِحُبِّنَا.

[41] Sharīʿatī, *Tafsīr-i Navīn*, p. 277.

[42] Kulaynī, *al-Kāfī*, 2/82.

عَنِ الصَّادِقِ (عَلَيْهِ السَّلَامُ) – إِذَا كَانَ الرَّجُلُ عَلَى عَمَلٍ فَلْيَدُمْ عَلَيْهِ سَنَةً ثُمَّ يَتَحَوَّلُ عَنْهُ إِنْ شَاءَ إِلَى غَيْرِهِ وَذَلِكَ أَنَّ لَيْلَةَ الْقَدْرِ يَكُونُ فِيهَا فِي عَامِهِ ذَلِكَ مَا شَاءَ اللهُ أَنْ يَكُونَ.

VERSE 4

تَنَزَّلُ الْمَلَائِكَةُ وَالرُّوحُ فِيهَا بِإِذْنِ رَبِّهِمْ مِنْ كُلِّ أَمْرٍ ﴿٤﴾

Therein descend the angels and the Spirit by the permission of their Lord, with every affair.

4.1 [*Tanazzalu* (تَنَزَّلُ, descend)]. The full form of the verb is *tatanazzalu*, as used in Q41:30:

إِنَّ الَّذِينَ قَالُوا رَبُّنَا اللَّهُ ثُمَّ اسْتَقَامُوا تَتَنَزَّلُ عَلَيْهِمُ الْمَلَائِكَةُ

Indeed, those who say, "Our Lord is Allah," then are steadfast in the right way, the angels descend upon them...

The form of the verb is in the continuous tense (*muḍāriʿ*), indicating that the descent of the angels and the *Rūḥ* did not just occur on the night that the Qurʾan was revealed to the Prophet (s), rather it is something that happens every year on *laylat al-qadr* with the permission of God.[43]

4.2 The descent of the angels and the *Rūḥ* transpires in the spiritual realm, and the location of their descent on this important night is no other than the heart of the representative (*ḥujjah*) of God on earth. In our time, the *ḥujjah*, who is Imam al-Mahdi (af), receives the angels and the Spirit. The descent of the angels to the representative of God is mentioned in many *aḥādīth*, some of which include:

i) Imam al-Sadiq (a) has reported from his father (a): [Once,] Ali (a) recited Surat al-Qadr in the presence of his two sons al-Hasan (a) and al-Husayn (a). Al-Husayn (a) said to him, "O Father! It is as if its recitation brings a sweet taste to your mouth!" The Imam (a) replied, "O son of the Messenger (s) and my son, I have experienced in this night what you have not [yet] experienced. When it was first revealed, your grandfather sent for me and recited it to me. Then he gripped my right shoulder and said, 'O my brother, my successor, the custodian of my nation after me, and the one who will fight my enemies until the Day of Resurrection! This surah is for you after me, and for your children after you. Indeed, Jibraʾil, my brother amongst the angels, has informed me of the future of my

[43] Shīrāzī, *Namūneh*, 27/184.

nation, and will keep you informed just as he did with me during the days of my Prophetic mission. This surah contains a light that will radiate in your heart, and the hearts of your successors, up to the advent of the Qā'im (af).'"[44]

ii) Imam al-Baqir (a) was asked, "Do you know when it is the night of Qadr?" He replied, "How can we not know, when the angels surround us on that night!"[45]

4.3 [*Al-Malā'ikah* (الْمَلَائِكَة, the angels)]. In God's system of creation, angels are non-corporeal and unseen beings created by Him to carry out His affairs in the cosmos. The Qur'an has listed many functions of the angels: bringing God's revelations and commandments to His Prophets (a), managing the affairs of the world and mankind, taking the souls at the time of death, praying for the wellbeing of the believers and assisting them, recording the details of human activity, and so on. The angels are diverse in their creation, and their abilities and powers vary from one another. This is alluded to Q35:1 which states:

الْحَمْدُ لِلَّهِ فَاطِرِ السَّمَاوَاتِ وَالْأَرْضِ جَاعِلِ الْمَلَائِكَةِ رُسُلًا

أُولِي أَجْنِحَةٍ مَثْنَىٰ وَثُلَاثَ وَرُبَاعَ

All praise is due to God, Creator of the heavens and the earth, [who] made the angels messengers possessing two, three, or four wings...

In Surat al-Qadr, God describes how His angels are especially active in the night of Qadr, bringing down every decree for humanity.

4.4 [*Al-Rūḥ* (الرُّوح, the Spirit)]. There are at least two opinions about the identity of the Spirit:

---

[44] Majlisī, *Biḥār*, 25/71.

عَنِ الصَّادِقِ (عَلَيْهِ السَّلَامُ) - قَرَأَ عَلِيُّ ابْنُ أَبِي طَالِبٍ (عَلَيْهِ السَّلَامُ) «إِنَّا أَنْزَلْنَاهُ فِي لَيْلَةِ الْقَدْرِ» وَعِنْدَهُ الْحَسَنُ (عَلَيْهِ السَّلَامُ) وَالْحُسَيْنُ (عَلَيْهِ السَّلَامُ). فَقَالَ لَهُ الْحُسَيْنُ (عَلَيْهِ السَّلَامُ): يَا أَبَتَا كَأَنَّ بِهَا مِنْ فِيكَ حَلَاوَةً. فَقَالَ لَهُ: يَا ابْنَ رَسُولِ اللهِ (صَلَّى اللهُ عَلَيْهِ وَآلِهِ) وَابْنِي إِنِّي أَعْلَمُ فِيهَا مَا لَمْ تَعْلَمْ. إِنَّهَا لَمَّا نَزَلَتْ بَعَثَ إِلَيَّ جَدُّكَ رَسُولُ اللهِ (صَلَّى اللهُ عَلَيْهِ وَآلِهِ) فَقَرَأَهَا عَلَيَّ ثُمَّ ضَرَبَ عَلَى كَتِفِي الْأَيْمَنِ وَقَالَ يَا أَخِي وَوَصِيِّي وَوَالِيَ أُمَّتِي بَعْدِي وَحَرْبَ أَعْدَائِي إِلَى يَوْمِ يُبْعَثُونَ، هَذِهِ السُّورَةُ لَكَ مِنْ بَعْدِي وَلِوُلْدِكَ مِنْ بَعْدِكَ. إِنَّ جَبْرَائِيلَ أَخِي مِنَ الْمَلَائِكَةِ حَدَّثَ إِلَيَّ أَحْدَاثَ أُمَّتِي فِي سَنَتِهَا وَإِنَّهُ لَيُحَدِّثُ ذَلِكَ إِلَيْكَ كَأَحْدَاثِ النُّبُوَّةِ وَلَهَا نُورٌ سَاطِعٌ فِي قَلْبِكَ وَقُلُوبِ أَوْصِيَائِكَ إِلَى مَطْلَعِ فَجْرِ الْقَائِمِ (عَجَّلَ اللهُ تَعَالَى فَرَجَهُ الشَّرِيفَ).

[45] Ibid, 94/14.

عَنِ الْبَاقِرِ (عَلَيْهِ السَّلَامُ) - قِيلَ لِأَبِي جَعْفَرٍ (عَلَيْهِ السَّلَامُ) تَعْرِفُونَ لَيْلَةَ الْقَدْرِ فَقَالَ وَكَيْفَ لَا نَعْرِفُ وَالْمَلَائِكَةُ يَطُوفُونَ بِنَا بِهَا.

i) That it refers to the archangel Jibra'il, and he has been mentioned separately in this verse to show his eminence over the other angels.[46]

ii) That it is a creature distinct from the angels and much more powerful than them.[47] In this regard, a tradition from Imam al-Sadiq (a) states: *al-Rūḥ* (the Spirit) is greater than Jibra'il, because Jibra'il is from the angels while *al-Rūḥ* is a creation grander than [and distinct from] the angels. Has God not stated, '*Therein descend the angels and the Spirit.*'[48] We have discussed the *Rūḥ* in greater detail in the *tafsīr* of Surat al-Naba' (78).

In any case, the presence of the *Rūḥ* seems necessary for the task of bringing down God's decrees on the night of Qadr. Its exact function is not known except to the *ḥujjah* of God.

4.5 [*Bi idhni Rabbihim* (بِإِذْنِ رَبِّهِم, with the permission of their Lord)]. The use of God's name '*Rabb*' is because the angels are there to carry out the directives of God as the Sustainer and Nurturer of His creation.[49]

4.6 [*Min* (مِنْ, with)]. '*Min*' usually means from, but here it is in the meaning of 'with'. Others have said that it is in the meaning of 'in order to', in which case the verse would mean, 'Therein descend the angels and the Spirit by the permission of their Lord, in order to carry out every affair'.[50]

4.7 [*Kulli amr* (كُلِّ أَمْرٍ, every affair)]. The *amr* here refers to God's decree and apportionment for every single creature. The angels have been tasked to make preparations for the overseeing and execution of these various decrees. However, the information that they carry is first presented to the most spiritually refined heart on earth, and that is the heart of God's representative (*ḥujjah*) at that time. In this regard a tradition from Imam al-Kazim (a) states: There is no angel sent down by God to carry out an affair except that he first comes to

[46] Rāzī, *Mafātīḥ al-Ghayb*, 32/234.

[47] Shīrāzī, *Namūneh*, 27/185.

[48] Kulaynī, *al-Kāfī*, 1/386.

عَنِ الصَّادِقِ (عَلَيْهِ السَّلَامُ) - قَالَ الرُّوحُ أَعْظَمُ مِنْ جَبْرَائِيلَ إِنَّ جَبْرَائِيلَ مِنَ الْمَلَائِكَةِ وَإِنَّ الرُّوحَ هُوَ خَلْقٌ أَعْظَمُ مِنَ الْمَلَائِكَةِ أَلَيْسَ يَقُولُ اللهُ تَبَارَكَ وَتَعَالَى «تَنَزَّلُ الْمَلَائِكَةُ وَالرُّوحُ».

[49] Shīrāzī, *Namūneh*, 27/185.

[50] Ṭabāṭabā'ī, *al-Mīzān*, 20/332.

the Imam (a) of the time and presents the affair to him. Indeed, the angels sent by God come and go from the presence of the Master of the Affair (*Ṣāḥib al-Amr*).[51]

4.8 The role of the *ḥujjah* is not passive in the process of the affairs that are decreed for the believers. He continually prays for their wellbeing and success, but needs their participation also to be deserving of his prayers. A tradition from Imam Ali (a) states: Your Imam has contented himself in this world with two garments to wear and two loaves to eat. Of course, you cannot do the same but [at least] support me with piety, striving hard, chastity, and uprightness...[52]

SUMMARY OF THE VERSE

In summary, the verse describes the descent of the angels and the *Rūḥ*, with God's permission. They descend to the heart of God's *ḥujjah* (af) and inform him of the details of every wise affair that has been decreed for the following year.

REFLECTIVE LEARNING

Q9:105 states:

وَقُلِ ٱعْمَلُوا فَسَيَرَى اللهُ عَمَلَكُمْ وَرَسُولُهُ وَالْمُؤْمِنُونَ

And say: Act! For God will see your deeds,
as will His Messenger and the believers...

About this verse, Imam al-Sadiq (a) has explained that '*mu'minūn*' here refers to the Imams (a), stating: The verse is referring to God's Messenger (s) and the Imams (a), to whom the actions of the people are presented every Thursday evening.[53]

The Imam (af) is informed of my actions, good and bad; let me reflect on the effect that these actions have on him. Are they a source of joy or sadness for him?

---

[51] Kulaynī, *al-Kāfī*, 1/394.

عَنِ الْكَاظِمِ (عَلَيْهِ السَّلَامُ) - مَا مِنْ مَلَكٍ يُهْبِطُهُ اللهُ فِي أَمْرٍ مَا يُهْبِطُهُ إِلَّا بَدَأَ بِالْإِمَامِ فَعَرَضَ ذَلِكَ عَلَيْهِ، وَإِنَّ مُخْتَلَفَ الْمَلَائِكَةِ مِنْ عِنْدِ اللهِ تَبَارَكَ وَتَعَالَى إِلَى صَاحِبِ هَذَا الْأَمْرِ.

[52] *Nahj al-Balāghah*, letter 45.

[53] Majlisī, *Biḥār*, 23/345.

عَنِ الصَّادِقِ (عَلَيْهِ السَّلَامُ) - قَالَ هُوَ رَسُولُ اللهِ صَلَّى اللهُ عَلَيْهِ وَآلِهِ وَالْأَئِمَّةُ عَلَيْهِمُ السَّلَامُ تُعْرَضُ عَلَيْهِمْ أَعْمَالُ الْعِبَادِ كُلَّ خَمِيسٍ.

VERSE 5

سَلَامٌ هِيَ حَتَّىٰ مَطْلَعِ الْفَجْرِ ﴿٥﴾

Peace it is, until the emergence of the dawn.

5.1 [*Salām* (سَلَام, peace)] is derived from *salama* and means protection from every harm, apparent or hidden.[54] In this verse it is mentioned as a quality of *laylat al-qadr*. This peace is a special mercy from God to His servants who have turned to Him in this extraordinarily blessed night. Indeed, one of God's names is *al-Salām* (Q59:23).

It is a night on which mankind is free from Divine punishment, as well as the plotting of Shaytan. A tradition from the Prophet (s) states: Verily, Shaytan does not emerge in this night, until the coming of its dawn.[55]

5.2 A tradition states that Imam al-Sajjad (a) gave another meaning of *salām*. He (a) said, "God says, 'My angels and *Rūḥ* bring My greetings (*salām*) to you O Muhammad, from the moment they descend until the emergence of the dawn.'"[56]

SUMMARY OF THE VERSE

The verse states that this night brings peace to the entire world. The huge presence of the angels coupled with the absence of the influence of Shaytan allows those who would want to take advantage of the spiritual peacefulness of this night to progress a lifetime within its short duration.

REFLECTIVE LEARNING

Let me reflect on my preparation for this wondrous night. How do I appreciate the huge opportunity it presents and take advantage of its blessings?

---

54 Rāghib, *al-Mufradāt*.

55 Ḥuwayzī, *Nūr al-Thaqalayn*, 5/615.

عَنِ الرَّسُولِ (صَلَّى اللهُ عَلَيْهِ وَآلِهِ) – إِنَّ الشَّيْطَانَ لَا يَخْرُجُ فِي هَذِهِ اللَّيْلَةِ حَتَّى يُضِيءَ فَجْرُهَا.

56 Kulaynī, *al-Kāfī*, 1/248.

عَنِ السَّجَّادِ (عَلَيْهِ السَّلَامُ) – «سَلَامٌ هِيَ حَتَّىٰ مَطْلَعِ الْفَجْرِ» يَقُولُ تُسَلِّمُ عَلَيْكَ يَا مُحَمَّدُ (صَلَّى اللهُ عَلَيْهِ وَآلِهِ) مَلَائِكَتِي وَرُوحِي بِسَلَامِي مِنْ أَوَّلِ مَا يَهْبِطُونَ إِلَى مَطْلَعِ الْفَجْرِ.

The following tradition contains some idea of the unmatchable benefits and merits of *laylat al-qadr*, and it will require practice throughout the year to be ready to perform these actions perfectly on this peaceful night:

A tradition from the Prophet (s) states:

Musa (a) asked: "My Lord! I desire Your proximity".

He replied, "My proximity is for the one who stays awake on *laylat al-qadr*."

He asked, "My Lord! I desire Your mercy."

He replied, "My mercy is for the one who has mercy on the poor on *laylat al-qadr*."

He asked, "My Lord! I desire safe passage on *al-ṣirāṭ* (the bridge over hell)."

He replied, "That is for the one who gives charity on *laylat al-qadr*."

He asked, "My Lord! I desire the trees and fruits of Paradise."

He replied, "That is for the one who glorifies Me on *laylat al-qadr*."

He asked, "My Lord! I desire salvation from hellfire."

He replied, "That is for the one who seeks forgiveness on *laylat al-qadr*."

He asked, "My Lord! I desire Your pleasure."

He replied, "My pleasure is for the one who recites two units of prayer on *laylat al-qadr*."[57]

---

[57] ʿĀmilī, *Wasā'il*, 8/20.

عَنِ الرَّسُولِ (صَلَّى اللهُ عَلَيْهِ وَآلِهِ) – قَالَ مُوسَى إِلٰهِي أُرِيدُ قُرْبَكَ قَالَ قُرْبِي لِمَنِ اسْتَيْقَظَ لَيْلَةَ الْقَدْرِ، قَالَ إِلٰهِي أُرِيدُ رَحْمَتَكَ قَالَ رَحْمَتِي لِمَنْ رَحِمَ الْمَسَاكِينَ لَيْلَةَ الْقَدْرِ، قَالَ إِلٰهِي أُرِيدُ الْجَوَازَ عَلَى الصِّرَاطِ قَالَ ذَلِكَ لِمَنْ تَصَدَّقَ بِصَدَقَةٍ لَيْلَةَ الْقَدْرِ، قَالَ إِلٰهِي أُرِيدُ مِنْ أَشْجَارِ الْجَنَّةِ وَثِمَارِهَا قَالَ ذَلِكَ لِمَنْ سَبَّحَ تَسْبِيحَةً فِي لَيْلَةِ الْقَدْرِ، قَالَ إِلٰهِي أُرِيدُ النَّجَاةَ مِنَ النَّارِ قَالَ ذَلِكَ لِمَنِ اسْتَغْفَرَ فِي لَيْلَةِ الْقَدْرِ، قَالَ إِلٰهِي أُرِيدُ رِضَاكَ قَالَ رِضَايَ لِمَنْ صَلَّى رَكْعَتَيْنِ فِي لَيْلَةِ الْقَدْرِ.

SURAT AL-BAYYINAH
THE CLEAR EVIDENCE (98)

TEXT AND TRANSLATION

سُورَةُ الْبَيِّنَةِ

بِسْمِ اللَّهِ الرَّحْمَٰنِ الرَّحِيمِ

لَمْ يَكُنِ الَّذِينَ كَفَرُوا مِنْ أَهْلِ الْكِتَابِ وَالْمُشْرِكِينَ مُنْفَكِّينَ حَتَّىٰ تَأْتِيَهُمُ الْبَيِّنَةُ ﴿١﴾
رَسُولٌ مِنَ اللَّهِ يَتْلُو صُحُفًا مُطَهَّرَةً ﴿٢﴾ فِيهَا كُتُبٌ قَيِّمَةٌ ﴿٣﴾ وَمَا تَفَرَّقَ الَّذِينَ
أُوتُوا الْكِتَابَ إِلَّا مِنْ بَعْدِ مَا جَاءَتْهُمُ الْبَيِّنَةُ ﴿٤﴾ وَمَا أُمِرُوا إِلَّا لِيَعْبُدُوا اللَّهَ مُخْلِصِينَ
لَهُ الدِّينَ حُنَفَاءَ وَيُقِيمُوا الصَّلَاةَ وَيُؤْتُوا الزَّكَاةَ وَذَٰلِكَ دِينُ الْقَيِّمَةِ ﴿٥﴾ إِنَّ الَّذِينَ
كَفَرُوا مِنْ أَهْلِ الْكِتَابِ وَالْمُشْرِكِينَ فِي نَارِ جَهَنَّمَ خَالِدِينَ فِيهَا أُولَٰئِكَ هُمْ شَرُّ الْبَرِيَّةِ
﴿٦﴾ إِنَّ الَّذِينَ آمَنُوا وَعَمِلُوا الصَّالِحَاتِ أُولَٰئِكَ هُمْ خَيْرُ الْبَرِيَّةِ ﴿٧﴾ جَزَاؤُهُمْ عِنْدَ
رَبِّهِمْ جَنَّاتُ عَدْنٍ تَجْرِي مِنْ تَحْتِهَا الْأَنْهَارُ خَالِدِينَ فِيهَا أَبَدًا رَضِيَ اللَّهُ عَنْهُمْ وَرَضُوا
عَنْهُ ذَٰلِكَ لِمَنْ خَشِيَ رَبَّهُ ﴿٨﴾

In the name of God, the Beneficent, the Merciful.

Those who disbelieved among the People of the Book and the polytheists would not separate [from their errant ways] until there came to them clear evidence. [1] *A Messenger from God, reciting purified scriptures.* [2] *Within it are upright ordinances.* [3] *And those who received the Book did not become divided until after the clear evidence came to them.* [4] *And they were not commanded except to serve God, sincerely devoted to Him in religion, inclining to instinctive faith – and to establish prayers and pay the poor-rate. That is the upright religion.* [5] *Indeed, those who disbelieved from the People of the Book and the polytheists shall abide forever in the fire of Hell. They are the worst of creatures.* [6] *Indeed, those who believe and perform righteous acts, they are the best of creatures.* [7] *Their reward with their Lord shall be gardens of perpetuity beneath which rivers flow, wherein they will abide forever; God well pleased with them and they well pleased with Him. This is [in store] for whoever stands in awe of his Lord.* [8]

INTRODUCTION

Surat al-Bayyinah (98) is named after the mention of *al-bayyinah* (the clear evidence) at the end of the first verse. It is also known as '*al-Bariyyah'* (the creation) and '*Lam yakun*'. It has eight verses. Although some reports say it was sent down in Makka, most exegetes believe that it was revealed in Madina, being the 100th chapter to be revealed,[1] after Surat al-Ḥashr (59). Other reasons why the chapter is probably Madanī is because of its lengthier verses, and in particular because of the reference to the 'People of the Book' (the Christians, and especially the Jews), whom the Muslims were more in contact with after migrating to Madina.[2]

The chapter records the coming of the Prophet (s) as God's Messenger to the people of Arabia, both those who followed previous scriptures, and the idolaters. In this surah, the Messenger (s) and his message are termed as '*Bayyinah* (clear evidence)' to the people of all time. The chapter emphasizes that he (s) had been sent with the same basic message as previous Prophets (a) as part of God's promise to guide mankind.

LINK TO THE PREVIOUS CHAPTER

The previous chapter, Surat al-Qadr, was about the event of the revelation of the Qur'an, and this chapter highlights the reason for that revelation.[3]

MERITS OF RECITATION

- A tradition from the Prophet (s) states: Whoever recites Surat '*Lam yakun*' shall be in the company of the best of creation (*khayr al-bariyyah*) on the Day of Judgement, whether he is travelling or stationed.[4]

---

[1] Maʿrifat, *'Ulūm-i Qur'ānī*, p. 90.

[2] Shīrāzī, *Namūneh*, 27/196.

[3] Suyūṭī, *Tanāsuq al-Durar*, p. 141.

[4] Nūrī, *Mustadrak al-Wasā'il*, 4/365.

عَنِ الرَّسُولِ (صَلَّى اللهُ عَلَيْهِ وَآلِهِ) – وَمَنْ قَرَأَ سُورَةَ «لَمْ يَكُنْ» كَانَ يَوْمَ الْقِيَامَةِ مَعَ خَيْرِ الْبَرِيَّةِ مُسَافِرًا وَمُقِيمًا.

- A tradition from Imam al-Baqir (a) states: Whoever recites Surat '*Lam yakun*' will be preserved from polytheism (*shirk*), and will be a member of the religion of Muhammad (s). God will resurrect him amongst the believers, and give him an easy accounting.[5]
- A tradition from the Prophet (s) states: If people understood the merits of Surat '*Lam yakun*', they would leave the pursuit of family and wealth and study its message [carefully]. A man from the Banu Khuzaʿah asked, "What reward lies in it, O Messenger of God?"
He (s) replied, "Neither a hypocrite nor one in whose heart there is doubt about God, the Almighty, would [want to] recite it. By God, the senior angels have continually recited it since the time when God created the heavens and the earth, without tiring of its recitation. No servant recites it at night except that God sends angels to safeguard him in his religion and worldly affairs, and to pray for forgiveness and mercy for him. And if he recites it in the daytime, he is given the reward equivalent to that upon which the light of the day shines and the darkness of night covers."[6]

EXEGESIS

VERSE 1

لَمْ يَكُنِ الَّذِينَ كَفَرُوا مِنْ أَهْلِ الْكِتَابِ وَالْمُشْرِكِينَ مُنفَكِّينَ حَتَّىٰ تَأْتِيَهُمُ الْبَيِّنَةُ ﴿١﴾

Those who disbelieved among the People of the Book and the polytheists would not separate [from their errant ways] until there came to them clear evidence. [1]

1.1 [*Kafarū* (كَفَرُوا, those who disbelieved)]. The term *kafara* means to cover and conceal. For this reason, the night is referred to as *kāfir*

---

[5] ʿĀmilī, *Wasā'il*, 6/259.

عَنِ الْبَاقِرِ (عَلَيْهِ السَّلَامُ) – مَنْ قَرَأَ سُورَةَ «لَمْ يَكُنْ» كَانَ بَرِيئًا مِنَ الشِّرْكِ وَأُدْخِلَ فِي دِينِ مُحَمَّدٍ (صَلَّى اللهُ عَلَيْهِ وَآلِهِ) وَبَعَثَهُ اللهُ عَزَّ وَجَلَّ مُؤْمِنًا وَحَاسَبَهُ حِسَابًا يَسِيرًا.

[6] Nūrī, *Mustadrak al-Wasā'il*, 4/366.

عَنِ الرَّسُولِ (صَلَّى اللهُ عَلَيْهِ وَآلِهِ) – لَوْ يَعْلَمُ النَّاسُ مَا فِي «لَمْ يَكُنْ» لَعَطَّلُوا الْأَهْلَ وَالْمَالَ وَتَعَلَّمُوهَا، فَقَالَ رَجُلٌ مِنْ خُزَاعَةَ مَا فِيهَا مِنَ الْأَجْرِ يَا رَسُولَ اللهِ؟ فَقَالَ لَا يَقْرَأُهَا مُنَافِقٌ أَبَدًا وَلَا عَبْدٌ فِي قَلْبِهِ شَكٌّ فِي اللهِ عَزَّ وَجَلَّ، وَاللهِ إِنَّ الْمَلَائِكَةَ الْمُقَرَّبِينَ لَيَقْرَأُونَهَا مُنْذُ خَلَقَ اللهُ السَّمَاوَاتِ وَالْأَرْضَ لَا يَفْتُرُونَ مِنْ قِرَاءَتِهَا، وَمَا مِنْ عَبْدٍ يَقْرَأُهَا بِلَيْلٍ إِلَّا بَعَثَ اللهُ مَلَائِكَةً يَحْفَظُونَهُ فِي دِينِهِ وَدُنْيَاهُ وَيَدْعُونَ لَهُ بِالْمَغْفِرَةِ وَالرَّحْمَةِ، فَإِنْ قَرَأَهَا نَهَارًا أُعْطِيَ عَلَيْهَا مِنَ الثَّوَابِ مِثْلَ مَا أَضَاءَ عَلَيْهِ النَّهَارُ وَأَظْلَمَ عَلَيْهِ اللَّيْلُ.

because it conceals things; similarly, a farmer is also called *kāfir* because he conceals seed in the ground (Q57:20). However, the most common usage of the term is a general reference to those who knowingly reject a particular belief. The Qur'an has also used the term in a positive sense, as in Q2:256:

فَمَنْ يَكْفُرْ بِالطَّاغُوتِ وَيُؤْمِنْ بِاللَّهِ فَقَدِ اسْتَمْسَكَ بِالْعُرْوَةِ الْوُثْقَىٰ لَا انْفِصَامَ لَهَا

...So, whoever disbelieves in (rejects) false deities and believes in God has indeed grasped the firmest handle [of true faith], one that will never break...

1.2 The verse under review refers to the *Ahl al-Kitāb* who knowingly rejected the external guidance brought to them by Prophets and Divine scriptures and the *mushrikūn* who knowingly rejected the internal guidance that is coded into every human soul to seek truth and discern good from evil.

1.3 [*Ahl -al-Kitāb* (أَهْلِ الْكِتَابِ, People of the Book)] refers to the Jews and the Christians who possessed the Tawrāt and Injīl but had distorted their scriptures, or disobeyed the directives of God.

[*Mushrikūn* (الْمُشْرِكِين, polytheists)] refers to the idolaters of the Quraysh who had not received Divine scripture and worshipped idols as their lords.

[*Munfakkīn* (مُنْفَكِّين, those who separate)] comes from *infikāk*, which means to separate after having been connected to something. Here it may mean that they refused to separate from their deviant ways and *kufr* until they received clear proof to the contrary.[7]

[*Al-Bayyinah* (الْبَيِّنَة, clear evidence)] means a clear and manifest evidence that allows one to distinguish truth from falsehood. A tradition from Imam al-Baqir (a) states: *Al-Bayyinah* is Muhammad (s), the Messenger of God.[8] And this is also mentioned in the next verse.

1.4 Both the *Ahl al-Kitāb* and the idolaters were convinced that they were following the right way. The verse states that neither group was inclined to change their ways unless clear evidence was sent to them. During his mission, the Prophet (s) invited them to

---

[7] Ṭūsī, *al-Tibyān*, 10/388.

[8] Baḥrānī, *al-Burhān*, 5/723.

عَنِ الْبَاقِرِ (عَلَيْهِ السَّلَامُ) – قَالَ «الْبَيِّنَةُ» مُحَمَّدٌ رَسُولُ اللهِ (صَلَّى اللهُ عَلَيْهِ وَآلِهِ).

reconsider their beliefs by introducing them to Islam with clear arguments. Despite this, some were so attached to their previous practices that they refused to change even when evident truth was shown to them.

1.5 The disbelievers amongst the *Ahl al-Kitāb* are of particular interest because they had received Prophets (a) and Divine scripture, just as Muslims have. However, their religion had become distorted over time, and they were not inclined to leave their rituals even when faced with clear evidence. God warns the Muslims about this attitude in Q57:16:

وَلَا يَكُونُوا كَالَّذِينَ أُوتُوا الْكِتَابَ مِنْ قَبْلُ فَطَالَ عَلَيْهِمُ
الْأَمَدُ فَقَسَتْ قُلُوبُهُمْ وَكَثِيرٌ مِنْهُمْ فَاسِقُونَ

...And let them not be like those who were given the Book before, and long ages passed over them, so their hearts hardened. And many of them became transgressors.

1.6 Notably, it has always been the practice of mankind to dispute about the interpretation of Divine guidance. Q2:213 states:

كَانَ النَّاسُ أُمَّةً وَاحِدَةً فَبَعَثَ اللَّهُ النَّبِيِّينَ مُبَشِّرِينَ وَمُنْذِرِينَ وَأَنْزَلَ مَعَهُمُ
الْكِتَابَ بِالْحَقِّ لِيَحْكُمَ بَيْنَ النَّاسِ فِيمَا اخْتَلَفُوا فِيهِ وَمَا اخْتَلَفَ فِيهِ إِلَّا الَّذِينَ
أُوتُوهُ مِنْ بَعْدِ مَا جَاءَتْهُمُ الْبَيِّنَاتُ بَغْيًا بَيْنَهُمْ فَهَدَى اللَّهُ الَّذِينَ آمَنُوا لِمَا
اخْتَلَفُوا فِيهِ مِنَ الْحَقِّ بِإِذْنِهِ وَاللَّهُ يَهْدِي مَنْ يَشَاءُ إِلَى صِرَاطٍ مُسْتَقِيمٍ

Mankind was a single nation, and God sent Prophets as bearers of good news and as warners, and He revealed with them the Book with truth, that it might judge between people in that in which they differed. And none but the very people who were given it differed about it after clear arguments had come to them, because of jealous animosity among themselves. So God guided by His will those who believed to the truth about which they differed; and God guides whom He pleases to the right path.

And this is the same message repeated in this chapter also.

SUMMARY OF THE VERSE

The verse informs us that those who followed earlier scriptures would not have abandoned their religions until clear evidence came to them demonstrating the distortion that had entered into their beliefs and practices.

REFLECTIVE LEARNING

1. Let me reflect on whether I make any effort to share the teachings of Islam with the *Ahl al-Kitāb* and the polytheists whom I am in contact with, so that they may get a chance to evaluate their own beliefs.
2. Let me also reflect on the attitude of some of the *Ahl al-Kitāb* in the face of the message of the Prophet (s), which had come to correct their beliefs and practice. Is there a likelihood that I would react in the same way at the advent of Imam al-Mahdi (af)?

VERSE 2

رَسُولٌ مِنَ اللهِ يَتْلُو صُحُفًا مُطَهَّرَةً ﴿٢﴾

A Messenger from God, reciting purified scriptures. [2]

2.1 [*Rasūlun min Allāh* (رَسُولٌ مِنَ اللهِ, a Messenger from God)]. The verse begins by defining the *bayyinah* (clear evidence) mentioned at the end of the previous verse; the clear evidence was the blessed Prophet Muhammad (s), sent by God to communicate His message to the people.

2.2 [*Ṣuḥuf* (صُحُف, scrolls)] (sing. *ṣaḥīfah*) means 'anything spread out for writing.'[9] Here it means (the contents of) papers or scrolls, referring to the Qur'an itself as a Divine revelation.[10] The term has been used for the scriptures given to Prophet Ibrahim (a) and Prophet Musa (a) also. Q87:18,19 state:

إِنَّ هَٰذَا لَفِي الصُّحُفِ الْأُولَىٰ ﴿١٨﴾ صُحُفِ إِبْرَاهِيمَ وَمُوسَىٰ

Indeed, this is [found] in the early scrolls,
the scrolls (ṣuḥuf) *of Ibrahim and Musa."*

---

[9] Muṣṭafawī, *al-Taḥqīq*.
[10] Ṭabrasī, *al-Bayān*, 10/793.

2.3 [*Muṭahharah* (مُطَهَّرَة, purified)] refers here to the Qur'an itself. It was the declared miracle of the Prophet (s), free from any pollution in its contents. Q80:13,14 state:

فِي صُحُفٍ مُكَرَّمَةٍ ﴿١٣﴾ مَرْفُوعَةٍ مُطَهَّرَةٍ

[It is recorded] in honoured scrolls (ṣuḥuf),
exalted and purified (muṭahharah).

Muṭahharah could also mean that all the previous scriptures, purified of the distortion that had appeared in their transmission, are contained in the Qur'an. Q3:3 states:

نَزَّلَ عَلَيْكَ الْكِتَابَ بِالْحَقِّ مُصَدِّقًا لِمَا بَيْنَ يَدَيْهِ

He has sent down upon you [O Muhammad] the Book with truth, confirming that which was [revealed] before it...

2.4 After explaining that *bayyinah* refers to Prophet Muhammad (s) and the Qur'an that he brought, the verse declares that this Book contains teachings that are purified from every form of polytheism, error, and falsehood. It confirms and revises the previous scriptures that were in the hands of the people. Q20:133 states:

وَقَالُوا لَوْلَا يَأْتِينَا بِآيَةٍ مِنْ رَبِّهِ أَوَلَمْ تَأْتِهِمْ بَيِّنَةُ مَا فِي الصُّحُفِ الْأُولَىٰ

And they ask, 'Why does he not bring us a sign from his Lord?' Has not a clear evidence come to them, what was [mentioned] in the previous scrolls (ṣuḥuf)*?"*

2.5 The purified message of God had to be recited and taught by those appointed and purified by Him. The Prophet (s) therefore mentions his successors (a) as the authorities of the Qur'an, in the famous tradition of *Thaqalayn*: Indeed, I leave two weighty things (*thaqalayn*) among you. If you hold fast to both of them, you will never go astray: the Book of God, and my household (*Ahl al-Bayt*). The two will never separate from each other until they come to me at the pool [of Paradise].[11]

[11] Mufīd, *al-Irshād*, 1/233; with similar wordings: Muslim, *Ṣaḥīḥ*, 4/1883; Kulaynī, *al-Kāfī*, 1/294.

عَنِ الرَّسُولِ (صَلَّى اللهُ عَلَيْهِ وَآلِهِ) – إِنِّي تَارِكٌ فِيكُمُ الثَّقَلَيْنِ مَا إِنْ تَمَسَّكْتُمْ بِهِمَا لَنْ تَضِلُّوا: كِتَابَ اللهِ وَعِتْرَتِي أَهْلَ بَيْتِي وَإِنَّهُمَا لَنْ يَفْتَرِقَا حَتَّىٰ يَرِدَا عَلَيَّ الْحَوْضَ.

SUMMARY OF THE VERSE

In summary, the verse says that the clear evidence was presented by the Prophet (s), who taught the people the sacred and pure Qur'an.

REFLECTIVE LEARNING

The Prophet (s) recited and internalized the purified scripture, thereby becoming the practical embodiment of the Qur'an.

Let me reflect on whether I merely recite the Qur'an or do I attempt to internalize and live the Qur'an in my daily life?

VERSE 3

فِيهَا كُتُبٌ قَيِّمَةٌ ﴿٣﴾

Within it are upright ordinances. [3]

3.1 [*Fīhā* (فِيهَا, within it)]. This qualifying word indicates that while there are commands and prohibitions in the Qur'an, it is much more than just a Book of laws. According to the popular view, the legal rulings in the entire Qur'an make up less than one-tenth of its verses.[12] These are known as the '*āyāt al-aḥkām* (verses of religious rulings)'.

The Qur'an is primarily a book of guidance, from the Creator of mankind Himself.

3.2 [*Kutub* (كُتُبٌ, writings) here refers to writings, or the ordinance in written form.[13] The Qur'an has also used the term to mean injunctions and commands, for example, for fasting, Q2:183 states:

يَا أَيُّهَا الَّذِينَ آمَنُوا كُتِبَ عَلَيْكُمُ الصِّيَامُ كَمَا
كُتِبَ عَلَى الَّذِينَ مِنْ قَبْلِكُمْ لَعَلَّكُمْ تَتَّقُونَ

O believers, fasting has been decreed (kutiba) *upon you as it was decreed upon those before you, so that you may become God-wary."*

3.3 [*Qayyimah* (قَيِّمَةٌ, upright) means upright and sustained, and here it could mean:

[12] Shams al-Din, *Al-Ijtihād wa al-Tajdīd fī al-Fiqh*, p. 82.

[13] Ṭabrasī, *al-Bayān*, 10/794.

i) unshakeable in argument,
ii) correct and free from error or deviation,
iii) containing guidance that sustains the worldly and spiritual life of mankind.[14]

3.4 Therefore, the *bayyinah* or clear evidence that was being presented to the people was two-fold: a Messenger, and a Divine revelation.

SUMMARY OF THE VERSE

The verse states that the teachings of the Qur'an are upright – unshakeable in argument and free from error.

REFLECTIVE LEARNING

Let me research and reflect on the commandments contained in the Qur'an.

Which ones do I follow, and which ones do I neglect?

VERSE 4

وَمَا تَفَرَّقَ الَّذِينَ أُوتُوا الْكِتَابَ إِلَّا مِنْ بَعْدِ مَا جَاءَتْهُمُ الْبَيِّنَةُ ﴿٤﴾

And those who received the Book did not become divided until after the clear evidence came to them. [4]

4.1 The introduction of an updated message from a new Messenger, whose coming had been foretold in their own scriptures, caused division amongst the *Ahl al-Kitāb*. The division (*tafarruq*) mentioned in the verse refers to the fact that some accepted Islam, while others clung stubbornly to their old faith, despite seeing the clear proof of his claims.

4.2 It is noteworthy that the phrasing has changed from 'People of the Book' to 'those who received the Book', so this verse includes the polytheists as well, who were also divided in their response to the new message.[15] Amongst the reasons for this mixed response was that the polytheists were reluctant to change their ways due to a misplaced sense of loyalty to their tribal beliefs, while the People

---

[14] Shīrāzī, *Namūneh*, 27/202.

[15] Ṭabāṭabā'ī, *al-Mīzān*, 20/338.

of the Book were reluctant to follow an Arab Prophet.[16] This was despite the clear evidence (*bayyinah*) which is mentioned again for emphasis.

SUMMARY OF THE VERSE

In summary, the verse states that there was a mixed response to Islam amongst the people following earlier religions; some came to Islam, while others clung on to their distorted beliefs.

REFLECTIVE LEARNING

When the Imam (af) comes, he too will bring clear evidence and dispel distortions. My current level of loyalty to the guidance contained in the Qur'an and sunnah is an indicator of how I will respond to the Imam (af).

Let me reflect on whether I accept clear religious guidance unreservedly, or am I selective in obedience?

VERSE 5

وَمَا أُمِرُوا إِلَّا لِيَعْبُدُوا اللَّهَ مُخْلِصِينَ لَهُ الدِّينَ حُنَفَاءَ وَيُقِيمُوا الصَّلَاةَ وَيُؤْتُوا الزَّكَاةَ وَذَٰلِكَ دِينُ الْقَيِّمَةِ ﴿٥﴾

And they were not commanded except to serve God, sincerely devoted to Him in religion, inclining to instinctive faith – and to establish prayers and pay the poor-rate. That is the upright religion. [5]

5.1 God always wanted mankind to serve Him alone. True servitude (*ʿubūdiyyah*) is a state of being. It is a realization that a slave has no will except that of the Master and no possession except that it belongs to his Master.

5.2 The *Ahl al-Kitāb* and the polytheists had been invited to follow the same message that all the Prophets (a) had brought: worship one God sincerely, establish prayers, and give the poor-rate. This was the *dīn al-qayyimah*, the established, upright religion for all mankind, from the time of Prophet Adam (a).

[16] Shahīdī, *Taḥlīlī az Tārīkh-i Islām*, p. 56.

Essentially, the Prophet (s) was also calling them to the same belief and practice, yet they were divided in their response to his message.

5.3 [*Ḥunafāʾ* (حُنَفَاء, faithful)] (sing. *ḥanīf*) refers to those who are inclined or attracted towards the truth (the middle course) after being lost or deviated to the extremities.[17] The religion of God is called '*al-dīn al-ḥanīf*' because it calls mankind to live a balanced life and adopt the middle course in every affair in their lives.

5.4 The Qurʾan gives Prophet Ibrahim (a) the title *Ḥanīf* in several places. For example, Q3:67 states:

مَا كَانَ إِبْرَاهِيمُ يَهُودِيًّا وَلَا نَصْرَانِيًّا وَلَٰكِنْ
كَانَ حَنِيفًا مُسْلِمًا وَمَا كَانَ مِنَ الْمُشْرِكِينَ

Ibrahim was neither a Jew nor a Christian; rather he was inclining to the truth (Ḥanīf), *and a submitter to God* (Muslim), *and he was not of the idolaters.*

In Arab custom, the term *ḥanīf* was used for someone who had performed the Hajj, or practised the circumcision of their males, indicating that they followed the teachings of Prophet Ibrahim (a).[18]

5.5 Establishing prayer (*salat*) and paying the poor-rate (*zakat*) are mentioned here as they constitute two of the foremost acts of worship, representing man's duty to the Creator, and to the creation, for His pleasure.[19]

5.6 [*Dīn al-Qayyimah* (دِينُ الْقَيِّمَة, upright religion)]. The phrase *qayyimah* is repeated here. In verse 3 it referred to the Qurʾan itself, and here it describes the injunctions of religion which resonate perfectly with the innate nature of mankind that God has created within all of us. Q30:30 states in this regard:

فَأَقِمْ وَجْهَكَ لِلدِّينِ حَنِيفًا فِطْرَتَ اللَّهِ الَّتِي فَطَرَ النَّاسَ عَلَيْهَا
لَا تَبْدِيلَ لِخَلْقِ اللَّهِ ذَٰلِكَ الدِّينُ الْقَيِّمُ

So, direct your face towards the religion, inclining to [instinctive]truth; the innate nature on which God has created man. There is no altering of God's creation. That is the upright religion (al-dīn al-qayyim) ...

[17] Ṭabāṭabāʾī, *al-Mīzān*, 20/339.
[18] Ṭusī, *al-Tibyān*, 1/480.
[19] Ṭabāṭabāʾī, *al-Mīzān*, 20/339.

5.7 A tradition from Imam al-Sadiq (a) states: *Dīn al-Qayyimah* denotes the religion of al-Qā'im (af).[20] This is perhaps because the religion will be explained again by the Mahdi (af) in a manner that will be instinctively known by all to be the correct path.

SUMMARY OF THE VERSE

In summary, the verse lists the four injunctions that God has placed on the shoulders of the believers: to submit to Him, to be steadfast on the correct faith, to observe the *salat*, and to pay the *zakat*.

REFLECTIVE LEARNING

Let me reflect on whether I fulfil the four qualities stipulated by God of those who follow His religion: submission to God (*ʿubūdiyyah*), sincere devotion (*ikhlāṣ fī al-dīn*), establishing prayers (*iqām al-ṣalāt*), and paying the poor-rate (*ītāʾ al-zakāt*).

VERSES 6, 7

إِنَّ الَّذِينَ كَفَرُوا مِنْ أَهْلِ الْكِتَابِ وَالْمُشْرِكِينَ فِي نَارِ جَهَنَّمَ خَالِدِينَ فِيهَا أُولَٰئِكَ هُمْ شَرُّ الْبَرِيَّةِ ﴿٦﴾ إِنَّ الَّذِينَ آمَنُوا وَعَمِلُوا الصَّالِحَاتِ أُولَٰئِكَ هُمْ خَيْرُ الْبَرِيَّةِ ﴿٧﴾

Indeed, those who disbelieved from the People of the Book and the poly-theists shall abide forever in the fire of Hell. They are the worst of creatures. [6] *Indeed, those who believe and perform righteous acts, they are the best of creatures.* [7]

6-7.1 '*Indeed, those who... shall abide forever in the fire of Hell. They are the worst of creatures.*': The *kufr* (faithlessness, covering the truth) of the [*sharr al-bariyyah* (شَرُّ الْبَرِيَّةِ, worst of creatures)] mentioned here is of the unforgivable kind, and would always incur God's punishment. It is the *kufr* of defiance and disobedience, after demanding clear evidence, and then rejecting what they knew was the truth.

[*al-Bariyyah* (الْبَرِيَّةِ, the creatures)] denotes all creatures in general, but given the fact that animals do not possess the level of intellect

[20] Majlisī, *Biḥār*, 23/370.

عَنِ الصَّادِقِ (عَلَيْهِ السَّلَامُ) – «وَذَٰلِكَ دِينُ الْقَيِّمَةِ» قَالَ إِنَّمَا هُوَ وَذَٰلِكَ دِينُ الْقَائِمِ (عَجَّلَ اللهُ تَعَالَى فَرَجَهُ).

and free will that would allow them to change their progress towards God, the term here likely refers only to sentient creatures like man and *jinn*.

6-7.2 The two verses define the worst and the best of God's creatures, and inform us of the two extremities of human conduct and potential.

6-7.3 '*Indeed, those who believe and perform righteous acts, they are the best of creatures.*': [*Khayr al-bariyyah* (خَيْرُ الْبَرِيَّةِ, best of creatures)], by contrast, are those who profess faith and then act righteously. As their inner purity and conviction manifests in their outer words and conduct, they become better than even the angels.

6-7.4 According to many reports in both *Sunni* and *Shīʿa* sources, *khayr al-bariyyah* refers to Ali b. Abi Talib (a) and his followers. Two such reports are mentioned below:

i) *Shīʿa* source: It is reported that Imam Ali (a) has stated: While leaning his head on my chest, the Prophet (s) said to me, "Have you not heard the words of God, the Almighty, '*Indeed, [as for] the believers and those who perform righteous acts, they are the best of creatures.*'? It refers to you and your followers. You shall meet me at the fount (*ḥawḍ*) [of Kawthar]. When all the nations will be made to kneel for accounting; you shall be called '[O] the brightly shining ones (*al-ghurr al-muḥajjalīn*)'."[21]

ii) *Sunni* source: The famous Hanafi jurist and traditionist, al-Hakim al-Haskani al-Nishaburi has presented more than twenty traditions is his *Shawāhid al-Tanzīl* (Qur'anic Evidences) from the Prophet (s) when he commented on this term in the verse. He said, "It refers to you [O Ali], and your *shīʿa*. You and your *shīʿa* will come forth on the Day of Judgement pleased with God and He shall be pleased with you."[22] This tradition mentions the most outstanding instance of the verse, otherwise many pious people

---

[21] Amīnī, *al-Ghadīr*, 2/57.

عَنْ أَمِيرِ الْمُؤْمِنِينَ (عَلَيْهِ السَّلَامُ) – حَدَّثَنِي رَسُولُ اللهِ (صَلَّى اللهُ عَلَيْهِ وَآلِهِ) وَأَنَا مُسْنِدُهُ إِلَى صَدْرِي، فَقَالَ: أَيْ عَلِيُّ (عَلَيْهِ السَّلَامُ) أَلَمْ تَسْمَعْ قَوْلَ اللهِ عَزَّ وَجَلَّ «إِنَّ الَّذِينَ آمَنُوا وَعَمِلُوا الصَّالِحَاتِ أُولَٰئِكَ هُمْ خَيْرُ الْبَرِيَّةِ» أَنْتَ وَشِيعَتُكَ وَمَوْعِدِي وَمَوْعِدُكُمُ الْحَوْضُ إِذَا جَثَتِ الْأُمَمُ لِلْحِسَابِ تُدْعَوْنَ غُرًّا مُحَجَّلِينَ.

[22] Ḥaskānī, *Shawāhid al-Tanzīl*, 2/461.

عَنِ الرَّسُولِ (صَلَّى اللهُ عَلَيْهِ وَآلِهِ) – هُوَ أَنْتَ وَشِيعَتُكَ تَأْتِي أَنْتَ وَشِيعَتُكَ يَوْمَ الْقِيَامَةِ رَاضِينَ مَرْضِيِّينَ.

in the previous generations – who were not introduced to Imam Ali (a) – will also be received with honour.

SUMMARY OF THE VERSES

In summary, the verses contrast the fates of the disbelievers and idolaters, which is Hell, with the fate of the believers who perform righteous acts, which is Paradise.

REFLECTIVE LEARNING

Let me reflect on my life choices and where I currently stand on the spectrum between the worst and best creatures of God. Can I change certain priorities to move to a better position?

VERSE 8

جَزَاؤُهُمْ عِنْدَ رَبِّهِمْ جَنَّاتُ عَدْنٍ تَجْرِي مِنْ تَحْتِهَا الْأَنْهَارُ خَالِدِينَ فِيهَا أَبَدًا رَضِيَ اللَّهُ عَنْهُمْ وَرَضُوا عَنْهُ ذَٰلِكَ لِمَنْ خَشِيَ رَبَّهُ ﴿٨﴾

Their reward with their Lord shall be gardens of perpetuity beneath which rivers flow, wherein they will abide forever; God well pleased with them and they well pleased with Him. This is [in store] for whoever stands in awe of his Lord. [8]

8.1 [*ʿAdn* (عَدْنٍ, perpetual)] refers to a place where something is established firmly and permanently. A mine in which minerals are found deposited is therefore called *maʿdan*. The Qur'an uses this adjective for Paradise but not for Hell, from which an exit is possible. [*Jannāt ʿAdn* (جَنَّاتُ عَدْنٍ, perpetual gardens)] refers to special gardens of eternal abode, in which the sincere believers will live forever.

8.2 [*Khalidīna fīhā abadā* (خَالِدِينَ فِيهَا أَبَدًا, they will abide therein forever)]. The word *ʿadn* already has a meaning of perpetuity, and two further words of similar meaning, *khalidīn* and *abadā*, further emphasize the fact that they will live there for eternity.

8.3 [*Tajrī min taḥtihā al-anhār* (تَجْرِي مِنْ تَحْتِهَا الْأَنْهَارُ, *beneath which rivers flow*)] signifies an abundant, continual, and perpetually fresh source of bounty and Divine grace that will be available to the residents of

Paradise. These bounties will not tire or bore them because the result of their consumption will be a constant increase in their cognizance (*maʿrifah*) of God.

8.4 [*Raḍiyallāhu ʿanhum* (رَضِيَ اللّٰهُ عَنْهُمْ, God is well pleased with them)]. Phrases such as the 'pleasure of God' are to be understood as one of His attributes of action (*ṣifāt al-fiʿl*).[23] In this case, His 'pleasure' will manifest itself as the reward that people shall receive from Him. The pleasure of the people will be in their happiness and satisfaction with that which they receive.

8.5 As believers who submit ourselves to God, it is important that our Master is pleased with us. In this verse God tells us that His sincere servants are pleased with Him also.

8.6 [*Khashiya* (خَشِيَ, fear)] is a higher quality than *khawf* (fear); it is a fear that causes awe and reverence, not panic and fright.[24] This fearful awe comes from true knowledge of God's station and is the source of sincere servanthood, God-wariness (*taqwā*) and righteous action. Q35:28 states in this regard:

إِنَّمَا يَخْشَى اللّٰهَ مِنْ عِبَادِهِ الْعُلَمَاءُ

...Only those of His servants who possess knowledge [of Him] fear God...

SUMMARY OF THE VERSE

In summary, the verse states that gardens of eternal bliss await the believers. They are those whom God is well pleased with and they too, are well pleased with Him. These gardens of Paradise are reserved for those who hold God in reverent awe (*khashiya*).

REFLECTIVE LEARNING

Let me reflect on whether I fear God or the punishment that I deserve due to my actions because God sees both my outward behaviour (*ẓāhir*) and my inner thoughts (*bāṭin*).

Do I hold Him in the reverence and awe (*khashiya*) which He actually deserves?

---

[23] Ṭabāṭabāʾī, *al-Mīzān*, 9/376.

[24] Muṣṭafawī, *al-Taḥqīq*.

SURAT AL-ZALZALAH
THE EARTHQUAKE (99)

TEXT AND TRANSLATION

سُورَةُ الزَّلْزَلَةِ

بِسْمِ اللهِ الرَّحْمٰنِ الرَّحِيمِ

إِذَا زُلْزِلَتِ الْأَرْضُ زِلْزَالَهَا ﴿١﴾ وَأَخْرَجَتِ الْأَرْضُ أَثْقَالَهَا ﴿٢﴾ وَقَالَ الْإِنْسَانُ مَا لَهَا
﴿٣﴾ يَوْمَئِذٍ تُحَدِّثُ أَخْبَارَهَا ﴿٤﴾ بِأَنَّ رَبَّكَ أَوْحَىٰ لَهَا ﴿٥﴾ يَوْمَئِذٍ يَصْدُرُ النَّاسُ
أَشْتَاتًا لِيُرَوْا أَعْمَالَهُمْ ﴿٦﴾ فَمَنْ يَعْمَلْ مِثْقَالَ ذَرَّةٍ خَيْرًا يَرَهُ ﴿٧﴾ وَمَنْ يَعْمَلْ مِثْقَالَ
ذَرَّةٍ شَرًّا يَرَهُ ﴿٨﴾

In the name of God, the Beneficent, the Merciful.

When the earth is shaken with its earthquake. [1] *And the earth discharges its burdens.* [2] *And man shall ask, "What has befallen it?"* [3] *That Day it shall report its news;* [4] *because your Lord shall inspire it [to testify].* [5] *That Day men shall proceed in diverse companies to be shown their deeds.* [6] *So, whoever does an atom's weight of good shall see it,* [7] *and whoever does an atom's weight of evil shall see it.* [8]

INTRODUCTION

Surat al-Zalzalah (99), also called al-Zilzāl, is named after the violent earthquake at the end of time (*zalzalah*) mentioned in the first verse. It was the 93rd chapter to be revealed.[1] It has eight verses and was revealed in Madina, between Surat al-Nisā' (4) and Surat al-Ḥadīd (57), between the signing of the treaty of Hudaybiyyah and the battle of Tabuk.

The chapter talks of some of the events leading up to the Day of Judgement, including the violent quakes that will overtake the earth, the expulsion of its contents, the amazing testimony of the earth itself,

---

[1] Maʿrifat, *ʿUlūm-i Qur'ānī*, p. 90.

the resurrection of the dead for accounting, and the manifestation of their actions for them to see.

LINK TO THE PREVIOUS CHAPTER

The previous chapter, Surat al-Bayyinah, ends with a description of the fate of disbelievers and polytheists, and contrasts it with the fate of the righteous. Surat al-Zalzalah starts with a description of the advent of the realm of the Hereafter, where the fate of every individual will be decided.

MERITS OF RECITATION

- A tradition from the Prophet (s) states: Whoever recites it is like one who recited Surat al-Baqarah and he will be granted the reward of one who has recited one-quarter of the Qur'an.[2]
- A tradition from Imam al-Sadiq (a) states: Do not tire of reciting Surat al-Zilzāl, because whoever [constantly] recites it in his supererogatory (*nāfilah*) prayers, God Almighty will never allow him to be harmed by an earthquake; he will not be killed by it or by lightning or a natural disaster, until he dies [a normal death].
  At the time of his death, a noble angel sent by his Lord shall descend to him and sit by the side of his head. The angel will say, "O angel of death, be gentle with this close servant of God, for he remembered God often, and recited this chapter often."... So the angel of death removes his soul in the gentlest manner possible and then his soul is swiftly escorted to Paradise by 70,000 angels.[3]

[2] Kafʿamī, *al-Miṣbāh*, p. 451.

عَنِ الرَّسُولِ (صَلَّى اللهُ عَلَيْهِ وَآلِهِ) – مَنْ قَرَأَهَا فَكَأَنَّمَا قَرَأَ الْبَقَرَةَ وَأُعْطِيَ مِنَ الْأَجْرِ كَمَنْ قَرَأَ رُبُعَ الْقُرْآنِ.

[3] Kulaynī, *al-Kāfī*, 2/626.

عَنِ الصَّادِقِ (عَلَيْهِ السَّلَامُ) – لَا تَمِلُّوا مِنْ قِرَاءَةِ «إِذا زُلْزِلَتِ الْأَرْضُ زِلْزَالَهَا» فَإِنَّهُ مَنْ كَانَتْ قِرَاءَتُهُ بِهَا فِي نَوَافِلِهِ لَمْ يُصِبْهُ اللهُ عَزَّ وَجَلَّ بِزَلْزَلَةٍ أَبَدًا وَلَمْ يَمُتْ بِهَا وَلَا بِصَاعِقَةٍ وَلَا بِآفَةٍ مِنْ آفَاتِ الدُّنْيَا حَتَّى يَمُوتَ وَإِذَا مَاتَ نَزَلَ عَلَيْهِ مَلَكٌ كَرِيمٌ مِنْ عِنْدِ رَبِّهِ فَيَقْعُدُ عِنْدَ رَأْسِهِ فَيَقُولُ يَا مَلَكَ الْمَوْتِ ارْفُقْ بِوَلِيِّ اللهِ فَإِنَّهُ كَانَ كَثِيرًا مَا يَذْكُرُنِي وَيَذْكُرُ تِلَاوَةَ هَذِهِ السُّورَةِ ... فَيُخْرِجُ رُوحَهُ مِنْ أَلْيَنِ مَا يَكُونُ مِنَ الْعِلَاجِ ثُمَّ يُشَيِّعُ رُوحَهُ إِلَى الْجَنَّةِ سَبْعُونَ أَلْفِ مَلَكٍ يَبْتَدِرُونَ بِهَا إِلَى الْجَنَّةِ.

EXEGESIS

VERSE 1

إِذَا زُلْزِلَتِ الْأَرْضُ زِلْزَالَهَا ﴿١﴾

When the earth is shaken with its earthquake. [1]

1.1 [*Idhā* (إِذَا, when] is a reference to a time when an event will definitely occur. It is often used at the beginning of a verse in the Qur'an. Its usage here could be for a couple of reasons:

i) In response to the question that was frequently asked of the Prophet (s), "When is the final hour (*al-sā'ah*)?", for example in Q7:187. The response in this case would be, 'When the earth is shaken...'

ii) God wishes to inform mankind that a Day will come when the earth on which they perform all their actions will recount and give witness to all that transpired on its surface. And this will happen 'When the earth is shaken...'[4]

1.2 [*Zalzalah* (زَلْزَلَة, earthquake)] is derived from *zalla* which means to slip, and its doubling to *zalzalah* adds the meaning of violence and greatness to the shaking.[5] Therefore, *zalzalah* means a violent and continuous convulsion, in which everyone would slip and fall. When it is used as a verbal noun (*maṣdar*), *zilzāl*, it refers to the continuous and violent earthquakes that will convulse the entire earth, resulting in the discharge of its contents and the levelling of every mountain and landscape.[6] Q73:14 states:

يَوْمَ تَرْجُفُ الْأَرْضُ وَالْجِبَالُ وَكَانَتِ الْجِبَالُ كَثِيبًا مَهِيلًا

On the day when the earth and the mountains shall quake and the mountains shall become [as] heaps of sand let loose.

This momentous event will herald the imminent arrival of the Day of Judgement.[7]

---

[4] Rāzī, *Mafātīḥ al-Ghayb*, 32/253.
[5] Ṭusī, *al-Tibyān*, 10/393.
[6] Rāzī, *Mafātīḥ al-Ghayb*, 32/254.
[7] Ṭabrasī, *al-Bayān*, 10/798.

1.3 Annexing the word earthquake to the earth with a possessive noun (*hā*) at the end of the verse, (*zilzālahā*), indicates that the quakes will occur across the entire earth[8] or it could be a reference to the severe quake that it must go through at the beginning of the Day of Judgement.[9]

1.4 Surat al-Zalzalah may be describing the earthquake that brings the *dunyā* to an end when the first trumpet is blown. This is called the '*zalzalat al-sāʿah*' (the earthquake of the final hour) in the Qur'an. Q22:1 states:

يَا أَيُّهَا النَّاسُ اتَّقُوا رَبَّكُمْ إِنَّ زَلْزَلَةَ السَّاعَةِ شَيْءٌ عَظِيمٌ

O mankind, be mindful of your Lord. Indeed, the earthquake of the [final] Hour is a tremendous thing.

Or it may be describing a second earthquake – one that will herald the beginning of the Hereafter (*ākhirah*), because the rest of the surah talks about the earth discharging all its burdens and giving witness, and human beings assembling for accounting.[10]

Q39:68 states:

ثُمَّ نُفِخَ فِيهِ أُخْرَىٰ فَإِذَا هُمْ قِيَامٌ يَنْظُرُونَ

... Then it will be blown again, and at once they will be standing, waiting.

SUMMARY OF THE VERSE

In summary, this verse describes the tumultuous earthquakes that will convulse the entire earth at the advent of the Day of Judgement.

REFLECTIVE LEARNING

On that Day, the whole world I see around me will crumble to pieces and nothing will have any worth except my faith and deeds.

Let me reflect on the quality of some of my specific deeds and how much worth they may have on that Day.

---

[8] Shīrāzī, *Namūneh*, 27/222.

[9] Zamakhsharī, *al-Kashshāf*, 4/783.

[10] Rāzī, *Mafātīḥ al-Ghayb*, 32/254.

VERSE 2

وَأَخْرَجَتِ الْأَرْضُ أَثْقَالَهَا ﴿٢﴾

And the earth discharges its burdens. [2]

2.1 [*Akhraja* (أَخْرَجَ, discharge)] means to expel, extract, or remove one thing from another. Here it refers to the earth discharging its contents.

2.2 [*Athqāl* (أَثْقَال, weights)] (sing. *thiql*) refers to anything that is substantial in weight or value.[11] The earth will discharge two kinds of weighty burdens:[12]

i) The mineral treasures deep in the earth. Treasures are called *athqāl* because of their value in the eyes of mankind. According to some exegetes, these will be expelled and arrayed in front of the resurrected human beings, who will now realize that they were deceived by the allure of gold, diamonds, oil and so on, and that in truth they had no real worth.[13]

ii) The millions of bodies of the dead. The shaking will continue until the traces of every last human has been expelled from the earth. Q84:3,4 state:

وَإِذَا الْأَرْضُ مُدَّتْ ﴿٣﴾ وَأَلْقَتْ مَا فِيهَا وَتَخَلَّتْ

And when the earth is stretched forth and
has cast out all that was in it and became empty.

SUMMARY OF THE VERSE

In summary, this verse describes the discharging of the earth of all that was buried in its depths.

REFLECTIVE LEARNING

The earthquake that will bring resurrected human beings back assures us that life does not end with death, and that everyone in their graves will rise again to continue their journey towards God, in bodies that manifest their belief and actions.

---

11 Muṣṭafawī, *al-Taḥqīq*.

12 Ṭabāṭabā'ī, *al-Mīzān*, 20/342.

13 Ṭabrasī, *al-Bayān*, 10/798.

Let me reflect and imagine what my own body will look like on that Day.

VERSE 3

وَقَالَ الْإِنْسَانُ مَا لَهَا ﴿٣﴾

And man shall ask, "What has befallen it?" [3]

3.1 [*Al-Insān* (الْإِنْسَان, man)]. Here the term refers to every individual human being.

We have discussed the term *al-insān* in the *tafsīr* of Surat al-ʿAṣr (103).

Everyone, or perhaps the disbelievers,[14] will be struck by varying degrees of bewilderment and shock at the behaviour of the earth.

3.2 When people are resurrected and brought out of the earth, they will exclaim in confusion and amazement at the continual violent tremors that are convulsing the earth, "What is happening to the earth?" According to some reports this confusion and dismay will be more apparent amongst the disbelievers.[15]

SUMMARY OF THE VERSE

The verse describes how human beings will be unable to understand what is happening when they witness the convulsions that grip the earth.

REFLECTIVE LEARNING

The bewilderment, loneliness, and terror of the moment of resurrection is only for those who have not sent forth goodness to the Hereafter.

Let me reflect on what I can do today to protect myself from this fate on that Day.

VERSES 4, 5

يَوْمَئِذٍ تُحَدِّثُ أَخْبَارَهَا ﴿٤﴾ بِأَنَّ رَبَّكَ أَوْحَىٰ لَهَا ﴿٥﴾

That Day it shall report its news; [4] *because your Lord shall inspire it [to testify].* [5]

---

14 Ṭabāṭabā'ī, *al-Mīzān*, 20/343.

15 Rāzī, *Mafātīḥ al-Ghayb*, 32/255.

4-5.1 *Yawmaidhin* (يَوْمَئِذٍ, that Day)] is used to replace and explain the word *idhā* (when) which is mentioned at the start of the first verse of the chapter.[16]

4-5.2 *Tuḥaddithu* (تُحَدِّثُ, it shall report)] is derived from *ḥaddatha* which means to speak and relate to make people aware of something, or to say something new, or to remind people of what they have forgotten.[17] Here, it means that the earth will inform and remind every individual of their actions.

4-5.3 Thereafter, the earth will begin to bear witness and recount the actions man committed in their earthly lives. It will testify for, or against, everyone. This will happen in the same way as the limbs of individuals, and the recording angels,[18] as well as other witnesses of man's actions, both human and non-human, will all give witness.[19] For example, Q41:21 states:

وَقَالُوا لِجُلُودِهِمْ لِمَ شَهِدتُّمْ عَلَيْنَا قَالُوا أَنْطَقَنَا اللَّهُ الَّذِي أَنْطَقَ كُلَّ شَيْءٍ

And they will say to their skins, "Why have you testified against us?" They will reply, "God has caused us to speak. As He causes all things to speak"...

4-5.4 The verse indicates that the earth has awareness at every moment, knowing whatever is occurring on it. It registers every act in order to give witness on the Day of Judgement, when it will be permitted and commanded by God to testify.

4-5.5 [*Awḥā* (أَوْحَىٰ, revealed or inspired)]. *Waḥy* here means permission. The earth begins to speak because (*bi anna*) God has allowed it to do so.

The Qur'an talks of God's *waḥy* to celestial objects or animals as existential (*takwīnī*) instructions pertaining to the laws that govern their operation and behaviour. For example, Q41:12 states:

فَقَضَاهُنَّ سَبْعَ سَمَاوَاتٍ فِي يَوْمَيْنِ وَأَوْحَىٰ فِي كُلِّ سَمَاءٍ أَمْرَهَا

---

16 Ibid.

17 Ibn Manẓūr, *Lisān al-ʿArab*.

18 Q50:18 states: *Man does not utter a word except that with him is an observer prepared [to record].*

19 Ṭabāṭabāʾī, *al-Mīzān*, 20/342.

And He completed them as seven heavens in two periods, and assigned to each heaven its mandate...

And about the honeybee, Q16:68 states:

وَأَوْحَىٰ رَبُّكَ إِلَى النَّحْلِ أَنِ اتَّخِذِي مِنَ الْجِبَالِ بُيُوتًا وَمِنَ الشَّجَرِ وَمِمَّا يَعْرِشُونَ

And your Lord revealed to the honeybee, "Make your hives in the mountains and in the trees and in that which they (humans) construct."

But here *awḥā lahā* (inspired for it) is used instead of *awḥā ilayhā* (inspired to it), implying that the earth has now been given permission to speak for herself, to complain about the oppression that was done on it for millennia.[20]

4-5.6 A tradition states that the Prophet (s) asked his companions, "Do you know what its news will be?" They replied, "Only God and His Messenger know." He said, "Its news is that it will testify about every act performed on its surface. It will say, 'So and so did this on this day,' that is its news."[21]

SUMMARY OF THE VERSES

In summary, inspired by the Lord, the earth will give detailed accounts of the actions that mankind performed during their stay on its surface.

REFLECTIVE LEARNING

Let me imagine what it would be like to have my every action recorded for just one day, keeping in mind the fact that on that Day the entire record of my deeds will be played out.

Let me reflect on what each room of my house will testify on that Day.

VERSE 6

يَوْمَئِذٍ يَصْدُرُ النَّاسُ أَشْتَاتًا لِيُرَوْا أَعْمَالَهُمْ ﴿٦﴾

That Day men shall proceed in diverse companies to be shown their deeds. [6]

---

[20] Rāzī, *Mafātīḥ al-Ghayb*, 32/256.

[21] Majlisī, *Biḥār*, 7/97.

عَنِ الرَّسُولِ (صَلَّى اللهُ عَلَيْهِ وَآلِهِ) – أَتَدْرُونَ مَا أَخْبَارُهَا؟ قَالُوا اللهُ وَرَسُولُهُ أَعْلَمُ. قَالَ أَخْبَارُهَا أَنْ تَشْهَدَ عَلَى كُلِّ عَبْدٍ وَأَمَةٍ بِمَا عَمِلَ عَلَى ظَهْرِهَا تَقُولُ عَمِلَ كَذَا وَكَذَا يَوْمَ كَذَا وَكَذَا فَهَذَا أَخْبَارُهَا.

6.1 [*Yawmaidhin* (يَوْمَئِذٍ, that Day)] is used again, this time as a further description of the word *idhā* (when) used at the beginning of the chapter.[22]

[*Al-Nās* (النَّاسُ mankind) refers to mankind in its entirety indicating that the statement being made is not confined to believers, but is relevant to every human being.[23]

[*Yaṣduru* (يَصْدُرُ, proceed)] is derived from *ṣudūr*, which is used to describe the departure of camels after drinking at a waterhole.[24] Here, it refers to the process of mankind dispersing from their places of resurrection towards their stations in Paradise or Hell.[25]

[*Ashtātan* (أَشْتَاتًا, distinct groups)] (sing. *shatt*) means separated and diverse groups. Mankind will be located in distinct groups according to their beliefs and actions.[26] Q30:14 states:

وَيَوْمَ تَقُومُ السَّاعَةُ يَوْمَئِذٍ يَتَفَرَّقُونَ

And on the Day when the Hour will be established,
that Day they will be separated.

6.2 As groups are revived from their graves, there will be someone waiting to meet them, direct them to their predetermined positions, and guide them on the path they must take.[27] Q20:108 calls this guide, 'the caller *(al-dā'ī)*':

يَوْمَئِذٍ يَتَّبِعُونَ الدَّاعِيَ لَا عِوَجَ لَهُ

On that Day they shall follow the caller unerringly...

6.3 [*Liyuraw a'mālahum* (لِيُرَوْا أَعْمَالَهُمْ, to be shown their deeds)], means that they will be shown the consequences or manifestations of their deeds. Q10:30 states:

هُنَالِكَ تَبْلُو كُلُّ نَفْسٍ مَا أَسْلَفَتْ وَرُدُّوا إِلَى اللَّهِ مَوْلَاهُمُ الْحَقِّ

There every soul shall become acquainted with what it sent before,
and they shall be brought back to God, their true Master...

---

22 Rāzī, *Mafātīḥ al-Ghayb*, 32/256.

23 Shīrāzī, *Namūneh*, 27/227.

24 Muṣṭafawī, *al-Taḥqīq*.

25 Ṭabāṭabā'ī, *al-Mīzān*, 20/343.

26 Shīrāzī, *Namūneh*, 27/227.

27 See: Bahmanpour, *Towards Eternal Life*, p. 93.

6.4 The groups will become more and more sifted as each group is led to their particular place in Paradise or Hell. Q30:43 states:

يَوْمَئِذٍ يَصَّدَّعُونَ

...On that Day they shall be sifted.

SUMMARY OF THE VERSE

In summary, the verse means that on the Day of Judgement, people will be separated into distinct groups and will then proceed to be shown the consequence of their deeds.

REFLECTIVE LEARNING

On that Day, the matter will be out of my hands, and my actions will have determined my companions. In contrast, in this world, I am free to choose my companions, who often influence my actions.

Let me reflect on my choice of companions, and whether they inspire me to good actions or not.

VERSES 7, 8

فَمَنْ يَعْمَلْ مِثْقَالَ ذَرَّةٍ خَيْرًا يَرَهُ ﴿٧﴾ وَمَنْ يَعْمَلْ مِثْقَالَ ذَرَّةٍ شَرًّا يَرَهُ ﴿٨﴾

So, whoever does an atom's weight of good shall see it, [7] *and whoever does an atom's weight of evil shall see it.* [8]

7-8.1 [*Mithqāl* (مِثْقَال, weight)] means any unit by which the weight of a thing is measured, and [*dharrah* (ذَرَّة, atom)] denotes the smallest speck of dust or the tiniest amount of something.[28] Even though these tiny acts are not noticed in the *dunyā*, yet God mentions that they have a weight. In the Hereafter, the minutest details of every deed will be visible in particular forms to the doer of the act. These forms will be the manifestations of the actions of individuals and will determine their fate.

7-8.2 These two verses are very profound because they describe how every human action has an ultimate consequence. A person came to the Prophet (s) asking to be taught the Qurʾan. When he reached

[28] Muṣṭafawī, *al-Taḥqīq*.

these verses of Surat al-Zalzalah, he said, "These two verses suffice for me," and he departed. The Prophet (s) commented, "The man departs with a profound knowledge."[29]

7-8.3 A tradition from Imam al-Sajjad (a) states: You should know, O son of Adam, that beyond this [world] lies a stage that will be more formidable, more frightening, and more painful for the hearts: the Day of Judgement... On that Day, no mistakes will be overlooked, no substitute (*fidyah*) will be taken, no excuse will be accepted, and no repentance will be possible. There will be nothing except recompense for good deeds and recompense for sins. Whoever among the believers has done an ounce of goodness in this world shall encounter it, and whoever among them has done an ounce of evil shall encounter it.[30]

7-8.4 The surah begins by mentioning something big and vast – the earth, and ends with the mention of the smallest particle – the atom. The vast earth is ultimately the product of the infinitesimal atoms that it contains.

In the same way, the human being in the Hereafter will be the embodiment of the atoms of good and evil that he has done.

DISCUSSION 1: EMBODIMENT OR MANIFESTATION OF ACTIONS (*TAJASSUM AL-AʿMĀL*)

On the Day of Judgement, good deeds shall be present in pleasant forms in the shape of the blessings of Paradise, and evil acts shall take on hideous forms in the shape of torments of Hell. Q3:30 states:

يَوْمَ تَجِدُ كُلُّ نَفْسٍ مَا عَمِلَتْ مِنْ خَيْرٍ مُحْضَرًا وَمَا
عَمِلَتْ مِنْ سُوءٍ تَوَدُّ لَوْ أَنَّ بَيْنَهَا وَبَيْنَهُ أَمَدًا بَعِيدًا

---

[29] Majlisī, *Biḥār*, 89/107.

أَنَّ رَجُلًا جَاءَ إِلَى النَّبِيِّ (صَلَّى اللهُ عَلَيْهِ وَآلِهِ) لِيُعَلِّمَهُ الْقُرْآنَ فَانْتَهَى إِلَى قَوْلِهِ تَعَالَى «فَمَنْ يَعْمَلْ مِثْقَالَ ذَرَّةٍ خَيْراً يَرَهُ وَمَنْ يَعْمَلْ مِثْقَالَ ذَرَّةٍ شَرًّا يَرَهُ» فَقَالَ يَكْفِينِي هَذَا وَانْصَرَفَ. فَقَالَ رَسُولُ اللهِ (صَلَّى اللهُ عَلَيْهِ وَآلِهِ) اِنْصَرَفَ الرَّجُلُ وَهُوَ فَقِيهٌ.

[30] Kulaynī, *al-Kāfī*, 8/73.

عَنِ السَّجَّادِ (عَلَيْهِ السَّلَامُ) – اِعْلَمْ يَا ابْنَ آدَمَ أَنَّ مِنْ وَرَاءِ هَذَا أَعْظَمَ وَأَفْظَعَ وَأَوْجَعَ لِلْقُلُوبِ يَوْمَ الْقِيَامَةِ ... يَوْمٌ لَا تُقَالُ فِيهِ عَثْرَةٌ وَلَا يُؤْخَذُ مِنْ أَحَدٍ فِدْيَةٌ وَلَا تُقْبَلُ مِنْ أَحَدٍ مَعْذِرَةٌ وَلَا لِأَحَدٍ فِيهِ مُسْتَقْبَلُ تَوْبَةٍ لَيْسَ إِلَّا الْجَزَاءَ بِالْحَسَنَاتِ وَالْجَزَاءَ بِالسَّيِّئَاتِ فَمَنْ كَانَ مِنَ الْمُؤْمِنِينَ عَمِلَ فِي هَذِهِ الدُّنْيَا مِثْقَالَ ذَرَّةٍ مِنْ خَيْرٍ وَجَدَهُ وَمَنْ كَانَ مِنَ الْمُؤْمِنِينَ عَمِلَ فِي هَذِهِ الدُّنْيَا مِثْقَالَ ذَرَّةٍ مِنْ شَرٍّ وَجَدَهُ.

On the Day when every soul shall be confronted with all the good it has done and all the evil it has done, it will wish that there was a great distance between it and that [evil]...

The reality of actions has a relationship with their external form, which will become clearly apparent on the Day of Judgement. For example, the one who misappropriates and usurps the property of orphans, causing sorrow and burning to their hearts, has been likened to one who consumes fire, because this is the reality of the act that will be manifest in the Hereafter. Q4:10 states:

إِنَّ الَّذِينَ يَأْكُلُونَ أَمْوَالَ الْيَتَامَىٰ ظُلْمًا إِنَّمَا يَأْكُلُونَ فِي بُطُونِهِمْ نَارًا وَسَيَصْلَوْنَ سَعِيرًا

Indeed, those who devour the property of orphans unjustly are only consuming fire into their bellies. And soon, they shall burn in blazing fire.

And the same is the case for righteous acts as well. A tradition from Imam al-Sadiq (a) states: When the believer will rise from his grave, he will be accompanied by another form. He will ask, "Who are you?" The form will reply, "I am the embodiment of the happiness that you used to bring to your believing brother in the *dunyā*. God, the Almighty, has created me so that I can give you glad tidings [of Paradise]."[31]

In fact, some scholars are of the view that every act that we do assumes a form in the material (*dunyā*), imaginal (*barzakh*) and spiritual (*qiyāmah*) worlds. The material form is the one that is visible in this world, but the imaginal and spiritual forms remain behind the curtain of *barzakh* and *qiyāmah*, and only become visible when each of these curtains is drawn aside simultaneously.[32]

---

[31] Kulaynī, *al-Kāfī*, 2/190.

عَنِ الصَّادِقِ (عَلَيْهِ السَّلَامُ) – إِذَا بَعَثَ اللهُ الْمُؤْمِنَ مِنْ قَبْرِهِ خَرَجَ مَعَهُ مِثَالٌ يُقَدِّمُهُ أَمَامَهُ ... فَيَقُولُ مَنْ أَنْتَ؟ فَيَقُولُ أَنَا السُّرُورُ الَّذِي كُنْتَ أَدْخَلْتَ عَلَى أَخِيكَ الْمُؤْمِنِ فِي الدُّنْيَا، خَلَقَنِي اللهُ عَزَّ وَجَلَّ مِنْهُ لِأُبَشِّرَكَ.

[32] Bahmanpour, *Towards Eternal Life*, p. 104.

DISCUSSION 2: NULLIFICATION (*IḤBĀṬ*) AND EXPIATION (*TAKFĪR*) OF DEEDS

The Qur'an speaks of nullification of deeds (*iḥbāṭ*), resulting in the cancellation of the reward or effect of those good acts. This happens primarily due to disbelief (*kufr*), polytheism (*shirk*), or apostasy (*irtidād*), as well as certain sinful acts. Several sins result in *iḥbāṭ* of deeds in the Hereafter, leaving the benefits in *dunyā* as the only reward. For example, Q11:15,16 state:

مَنْ كَانَ يُرِيدُ الْحَيَاةَ الدُّنْيَا وَزِينَتَهَا نُوَفِّ إِلَيْهِمْ أَعْمَالَهُمْ فِيهَا وَهُمْ فِيهَا لَا يُبْخَسُونَ ﴿١٥﴾ أُولَٰئِكَ الَّذِينَ لَيْسَ لَهُمْ فِي الْآخِرَةِ إِلَّا النَّارُ وَحَبِطَ مَا صَنَعُوا فِيهَا وَبَاطِلٌ مَا كَانُوا يَعْمَلُونَ

Whoever desires this world's life and its finery, We will pay them in full their deeds therein, and they shall not be made to suffer loss in respect of them. These are they for whom there is nothing but fire in the Hereafter, and what they wrought in it shall go for nothing (ḥabiṭa), *and vain is what they do.*

On the other hand, good actions result in the compensation or expiation (*takfīr*) of evil deeds. Q11:114 states:

إِنَّ الْحَسَنَاتِ يُذْهِبْنَ السَّيِّئَاتِ ذَٰلِكَ ذِكْرَىٰ لِلذَّاكِرِينَ

...Indeed, good deeds take away evil deeds; this is a reminder for the mindful.

And Q29:7 states:

وَالَّذِينَ آمَنُوا وَعَمِلُوا الصَّالِحَاتِ لَنُكَفِّرَنَّ عَنْهُمْ سَيِّئَاتِهِمْ وَلَنَجْزِيَنَّهُمْ أَحْسَنَ الَّذِي كَانُوا يَعْمَلُونَ

And [as for] those who believe and do good, We shall most certainly do away with their evil deeds and We shall most certainly reward them according to the best of what they did.

DISCUSSION 3: WILL THE NULLIFIED GOOD ACTS OR THE FORGIVEN BAD ACTS ALSO BE 'SEEN'?

There are two views regarding this:

1. The acts that are nullified or forgiven are removed from the book of records entirely. This is based on the famous report from the Prophet (s), "The one who repents his sin (*al-tā'ib*) is like the one who never sinned."[33]
2. Others say that the verse under review is quite specific that all actions will be 'seen'. However, they are of the opinion that the good acts of the people of hellfire and the evil acts of the people of Paradise will be seen by them, but they will not be affected by them.[34]

SUMMARY OF THE VERSES

In summary, the verses say that every good or evil action, however seemingly small or trivial, has significance in the Hereafter.

REFLECTIVE LEARNING

Let me reflect whether there are actions that I have done, good or evil, which I consider of no value. Let me remind myself that in the record of God everything has significance.

---

[33] Kulaynī, *al-Kāfī*, 2/435.

عَنِ الرَّسُولِ (صَلَّى اللهُ عَلَيْهِ وَآلِهِ) - التَّائِبُ مِنَ الذَّنْبِ كَمَنْ لَا ذَنْبَ لَهُ.

[34] Ṭabāṭabā'ī, *al-Mīzān*, 20/343.

SURAT AL-ʿĀDIYĀT
THE CHARGING STEEDS (100)

TEXT AND TRANSLATION

سُورَةُ الْعَادِيَاتِ

بِسْمِ اللَّهِ الرَّحْمَٰنِ الرَّحِيمِ

وَالْعَادِيَاتِ ضَبْحًا ﴿١﴾ فَالْمُورِيَاتِ قَدْحًا ﴿٢﴾ فَالْمُغِيرَاتِ صُبْحًا ﴿٣﴾ فَأَثَرْنَ بِهِ
نَقْعًا ﴿٤﴾ فَوَسَطْنَ بِهِ جَمْعًا ﴿٥﴾ إِنَّ الْإِنْسَانَ لِرَبِّهِ لَكَنُودٌ ﴿٦﴾ وَإِنَّهُ عَلَىٰ ذَٰلِكَ
لَشَهِيدٌ ﴿٧﴾ وَإِنَّهُ لِحُبِّ الْخَيْرِ لَشَدِيدٌ ﴿٨﴾ أَفَلَا يَعْلَمُ إِذَا بُعْثِرَ مَا فِي الْقُبُورِ ﴿٩﴾
وَحُصِّلَ مَا فِي الصُّدُورِ ﴿١٠﴾ إِنَّ رَبَّهُمْ بِهِمْ يَوْمَئِذٍ لَخَبِيرٌ ﴿١١﴾

In the name of God, the Beneficent, the Merciful.

By the steeds that charge, snorting, [1] *Striking sparks [with their hooves],* [2] *Raiding in the early morning,* [3] *Raising a trail of dust,* [4] *Thereby cleaving together into the midst [of the foe].* [5] *Indeed, man is truly ungrateful to His Lord.* [6] *And indeed, he truly bears witness to that.* [7] *And indeed, he is truly intense in the love of wealth.* [8] *Does he not realize that when what is in the graves is poured forth,* [9] *And what is in the hearts is made manifest,* [10] *Indeed, on that Day their Lord shall be fully aware of them?* [11]

INTRODUCTION

According to some reports, Surat al-ʿĀdiyāt (100) was the 14th chapter to be revealed.[1] It has eleven verses. The name of this chapter comes from the mention of *ʿādiyāt* in the first verse, referring to horses that are made to charge at speed.

There is a difference of opinion about whether the chapter was revealed in Makka or Madina. The short, rhythmic style of the verses,

---

[1] Maʿrifat, *ʿUlūm-i Qurʾānī*, p. 90.

the multiple oaths in its opening verses, as well as the fact that the topics discussed in it are to do with the foundations of belief (*ʿaqāʾid*) and the Hereafter (*maʿād*), all resemble the Makkan chapters of the Qur'an.

At the same time, there are reports that the opening verses refer to a military expedition known as *Sariyyah Dhāt al-Salāsil* (The Expedition of Chains), which was carried out by the Muslims in the middle of the year 8/629.[2] This suggests that the chapter was revealed in Madina.

The chapter begins with an oath, which is detailed in the first five verses. The oath mentions matters that the Arabs, who were the first audience of the verses, were knowledgeable and passionate about: warhorses being used in ambush and battle against a treacherous enemy. The powerful imagery draws the attention of the reader and increases the impact of the main message of the surah.

The chapter then highlights man's ungrateful and heedless nature when it comes to God's bounties. It talks of his inordinate desire and drive to acquire good things, without care for the associated responsibilities and consequences. Thereafter, it reminds of a Day when mankind will stand to account before their Lord, who is all-Aware of their conduct.

OCCASION OF REVELATION

According to many reports, this chapter was revealed following the victory of the Muslims in the military expedition of *Dhāt al-Salāsil.*

Surat al-ʿĀdiyāt was recited by the Prophet (s) for the first time in the morning prayer. His companions remarked, "We do not know this surah?" The Prophet (s) replied, "Yes. Indeed, Ali has overcome the enemy of God, and Jibra'il (a) gave me the good news of that last night." A few days later, Ali (a) arrived in Madina with prisoners and war booty.[3]

---

[2] Shīrāzī, *Namūneh*, 27/239.

[3] Ṭabrasī, *al-Bayān*, 10/803.

DISCUSSION: THE EXPEDITION OF *DHĀT AL-SALĀSIL*

This military expedition was carried out by the Muslims after the Battle of Mūtah in the year 8/629. It is called a *sariyyah*, and not *ghazwah*, because the Prophet (s) was not present in the expedition himself.[4]

The name of the expedition is either derived from the name of a well called Salāsil where the event took place, or because the Muslims, under the command of Imam Ali (a), brought back some prisoners bound together in chains (*salāsil*).[5]

There are two types of reports about this expedition found in the records of Islamic history:

1. One group of reports states that the Banu Quḍāʿah and some of their affiliates were threatening to attack Madina. The Prophet (s) despatched ʿAmr b. al-ʿĀṣ with 300 soldiers to lead an expedition against them. The Muslims camped near a well called Salāsil, situated at a location ten-day walking distance from Madina. ʿAmr attacked their superior forces in the early dawn and caused the enemy to panic and disperse. The Muslims returned triumphant to Madina, bringing with them valuable spoils of war.[6]

2. The more plausible reports are those that state that the Prophet (s) received information that several tribes had gathered in the valley of Yābis, and had made a pact to attack Madina at night, with the intention to kill as many Muslims as they could.
   Faced with this serious threat, the Prophet (s) summoned the Muslims and made them aware of the situation. Then he despatched a contingent of men from the Muhajirun and Ansar, under the command of Imam Ali (a), to go out to meet the enemy.
   Imam Ali (a) travelled in the night and concealed the Muslim presence from spies in the day. He entered the valley from its mountainous side in the early dawn, taking the enemy unawares. Some were killed and the rest fled, leaving a large booty behind.[7]
   When the warriors returned victorious back to Madina, the Muslims lined up in two ranks to receive them. When Imam Ali (a) saw the Prophet (s), he dismounted from his horse to greet him,

[4] Ibn Saʿd, *al-Ṭabaqāt al-Kubrā*, 2/97.

[5] Majlisī, *Biḥār*, 21/77.

[6] Ibn Saʿd, *al-Ṭabaqāt al-Kubrā*, 2/131.

[7] Subḥānī, *Fūrūgh-i Abadiyyat*, chap. 47.

but the Prophet (s) said, "Mount your horse. God, the Almighty, and His Messenger are pleased with you." Then he said, "O Ali, if it was not for my concern that some factions will say of you what the Christians say of Isa (a), I would describe your status in such a manner that you would never pass a gathering of men except that they would take the soil from your feet [as a blessing]!"[8]

LINK TO THE PREVIOUS CHAPTER

The previous chapter, Surat al-Zalzalah, spoke of the Day when the earth will discharge its contents, and mankind will go towards their appointed places for the reckoning of their actions. Surat al-ʿĀdiyāt adds details to the same event but gives the reason why some will find themselves in a much worse situation than others.

MERITS OF RECITATION

- A tradition from the Prophet (s) states: Whoever recites this chapter will be granted ten rewards for every pilgrim who spends the night [of Eid] in Muzdalifah and is present in the gathering [of pilgrims].[9]
- A tradition from Imam al-Sadiq (a) states: Whoever recites this surah, and does so regularly, will be resurrected by God in the company of the Commander of the Faithful (a) specifically, and will be amongst his companions.[10]

EXEGESIS

VERSE 1

وَالْعَادِيَاتِ ضَبْحًا ﴿١﴾

By the steeds that charge, snorting, [1]

---

8 Mufīd, *al-Irshād*, 1/114.

9 Nūrī, *Mustadrak al-Wasāʾil*, 4/367.

عَنِ الرَّسُولِ (صَلَّى اللهُ عَلَيْهِ وَآلِهِ) – مَنْ قَرَأَهَا أُعْطِيَ مِنَ الْأَجْرِ عَشْرَ حَسَنَاتٍ، بِعَدَدِ مَنْ بَاتَ بِالْمُزْدَلِفَةِ وَشَهِدَ جَمْعًا.

10 Ṣadūq, *Thawāb al-Aʿmāl*, p. 125.

عَنِ الصَّادِقِ (عَلَيْهِ السَّلَامُ) – مَنْ قَرَأَ سُورَةَ الْعَادِيَاتِ وَأَدْمَنَ قِرَاءَتَهَا بَعَثَهُ اللهُ تَعَالَى مَعَ أَمِيرِ الْمُؤْمِنِينَ عَلَيْهِ السَّلَامُ يَوْمَ الْقِيَامَةِ خَاصَّةً، وَكَانَ مِنْ رُفَقَائِهِ.

1.1 The chapter begins with an oath using *wa* (و) initially, and then paints a continuous single scene by using *fa* (ف) to link the details of the oath over the next four verses.

Of the other chapters that begin with oaths, most contain several separate oaths, all preceded by *wa* (و). We have discussed the concept of oaths in the *tafsīr* of Surat al-Shams (91).

1.2 The Qur'an uses examples of different phenomena that were relevant to the seventh century Arabs because they were the first recipients of revelation. For this reason, there are several mentions in its verses of the two animals that had a prominent place in the desert culture of the Arabs, camels (*ibīl*) and horses (*khayl*). As an example, this chapter starts with a mention of horses.

The opening verses of the surah depict a vivid and awesome picture of a cavalry charge in the prelude to a battle, where warhorses bravely and loyally carry their riders on a sacred mission.

1.3 [*Al-ʿĀdiyāt* (ٱلْعَادِيَاتِ, charging horses)] (sing. *ʿādiyah*) is derived from *ʿadā*, meaning to cross a limit and separate. Here, it refers to animals crossing the limit of normal pace and moving at speed.[11]

There are several opinions reported about what animals *al-ʿādiyāt* denotes. For instance, one report states that it refers to the camels that were running at pace towards the battle ground of Badr.[12] Other reports say that it refers to the camels of the pilgrims as they hurried from Arafat to Mashʿar, and then onwards to Mina.[13]

However, as evidenced by the wording of the four adjectives that follow, it is most probable that *ʿādiyāt* in this verse refers to the fast-paced running of warhorses towards battle.[14]

1.4 [*Ḍabḥ* (ضَبْح, snorting)]. This is a panting sound made by horses when galloping hard. It is louder than whinnying and softer than neighing, and comes from their exertion.[15]

[11] Muṣṭafawī, *al-Taḥqīq*.

[12] Ṭabrasī, *al-Bayān*, 10/803.

[13] Shīrāzī, *Namūneh*, 27/241.

[14] Ṭabāṭabā'ī, *al-Mīzān*, 20/345.

[15] Muṣṭafawī, *al-Taḥqīq*.

1.5 The oath highlights the determined obedience and effort of the war-horses and the extent of their loyalty to the command of their master.[16]

REFLECTIVE LEARNING

God swears by horses that charge ahead towards the goal that they had been prepared and trained for, not distracted by looking right or left.

Let me reflect on the fact that I too have a goal and purpose to my earthly existence, which is to reach my potential, perfection, and Paradise. Am I focused on this or do I allow myself to be constantly distracted from this objective?

VERSE 2

فَالْمُورِيَاتِ قَدْحًا ﴿٢﴾

Striking sparks [with their hooves], [2]

2.1 [*Al-Mūriyāt* (الْمُورِيَات, ignite sparks)] (sing. *mūriyah*) is derived from *īrāʾ*, and means to produce sparks or fire by the friction of two things against each other.[17]

[*Qadḥ* (قَدْح, striking)]. It refers to an audible and powerful strike, here made by the hooves as on the rocky path producing sparks.[18]

2.2 This part of the oath refers to the sparks that were emitted from the metal shoes on the hooves of the horses when they struck the stony ground as they galloped up the mountain over their unsuspecting enemy.[19]

2.3 The verse gives a sense of struggle and determined striving, similar to man's lifelong struggle to remain on the path of God. Q84:6 states:

يَا أَيُّهَا الْإِنْسَانُ إِنَّكَ كَادِحٌ إِلَىٰ رَبِّكَ كَدْحًا فَمُلَاقِيهِ

O man! Indeed, you are constantly labouring towards your Lord with [great] exertion until you shall meet Him.

[16] Rāzī, *Mafātīḥ al-Ghayb*, 32/259.

[17] Muṣṭafawī, *al-Taḥqīq*.

[18] Ibid.

[19] Modarresī, *Min Huda al-Qurʾan*, 18/289.

REFLECTIVE LEARNING

God continues the oath by describing how the determined galloping of the horses left a trail of sparks behind them as they continued to their destination.

Let me reflect on my determination and sincerity in carrying out the ritual obligations. Does it bring about a discernible spark in me and through that, to those around me?

VERSE 3

فَالْمُغِيرَاتِ صُبْحًا ﴿٣﴾

Raiding in the early morning, [3]

3.1 [*Al-Mughīrāt* (الْمُغِيرَات, raiding)] (sing. *mughīrah*) is derived from *ghārah*, meaning raid or plunder. Here it is used to denote an ambush on the enemy.

[*Ṣubḥ* (صُبْح, morning)]. This refers to the critical timing of the raid, which was dawn. The first light of the day was the earliest moment for them to carry out their sacred mission. It would allow them to see what they were doing while their enemy was still unprepared.

3.2 This part of the oath describes the moment the horses had arrived at their target after a determined and focussed effort. They were now ready to carry out the task that they had set out for.

REFLECTIVE LEARNING

The preparation for effective action requires planning and focus.

Let me reflect on whether I plan and prepare with similar focus before performing an act of worship, for example, my daily *salat*.

VERSE 4

فَأَثَرْنَ بِهِ نَقْعًا ﴿٤﴾

Raising a trail of dust, [4]

4.1 [*Atharna* (أَثَرْنَ, leave behind a trail)] is derived from *ithārah*, and here it means causing dust or smoke to swirl.[20]

[*Bihi* (بِهِ, thereby)]. The particle *bihi* refers to the nature of the swift charge, which was the cause of the dust cloud.

[*Naqʿan* (نَقْعًا, dust)]. *Naqʿ* means a large cloud of dust, which covers an individual, just as water covers someone when they enter it.

4.2 This part of the oath describes how, when the horses entered the valley, their hooves had churned up a dust cloud that masked their numbers from the enemy, perhaps making them look even greater in number.

REFLECTIVE LEARNING

The light of the dawn is similar to the light of God's guidance; both allow us to see better. And yet the dust clouds that masked the soldiers of God from the disbelievers may be likened to the dust clouds of sin that become barriers to our vision.

Let me reflect on the barrier of sin that I have allowed to cover God's grace from reaching me and remove it with a sincere *tawbā*.

VERSE 5

فَوَسَطْنَ بِهِۦ جَمْعًا ﴿٥﴾

Thereby cleaving together into the midst [of the foe]. [5]

5.1 [*Wasaṭna* (وَسَطْنَ, entering the midst)]. This refers to the fact that the charge of the Muslims was so vigorous that they pierced the enemy camp and reached its centre.

[*Bihi* (بِهِ, thereby)]. The particle *bihi* here refers to the dust clouds, through which they appeared in the midst of the foe.[21] Alternatively, it may refer to the dawn, and in that case, *bihi* would mean *fīhi* (in).[22]

[*Jamʿan* (جَمْعًا, all together)]. The inclusion of this word highlights the importance and effectiveness of acting in unison.

---

[20] Muṣṭafawī, *al-Taḥqīq*.

[21] Ṭabrasī, *al-Bayān*, 10/804.

[22] Ṭabāṭabāʾī, *al-Mīzān*, 20/346.

5.2 The final part of the oath indicates that the warhorses achieved what they had set out to do, which was to strike collectively into the centre of the enemy. Before the enemy could react, the Muslim vanguard was upon them.

REFLECTIVE LEARNING

Muslims are most powerful when they work together for God, whether in performing an act of goodness communally, or standing united against an enemy.

Let me reflect in which instances in my life I tend to stand united with other members of the *ummah*, and when I usually stand divided from them.

SUMMARY OF THE FIRST FIVE VERSES

In these opening verses, God swears by the warhorses who respect the commands of their masters by displaying obedience and perseverance in a sacred cause: *jihād* (war) in the path of God.

The warhorses in themselves were not important. However, when they were used to strive sincerely in God's way, they qualified to be used by Him in an oath, as did everything related to their charge into battle also; their relentless exertion, the sparks raised by their hooves, their pre-dawn attack, and even the dust clouds that they raised.

REFLECTIVE LEARNING OF THE FIRST FIVE VERSES

Warhorses carrying the *mujāhidūn* to serve the cause of Islam were important enough for God to swear by them.

Let me reflect on how I too, can submit and serve the cause of Islam and thereby earn honour in God's estimation.

VERSE 6

إِنَّ الْإِنسَانَ لِرَبِّهِ لَكَنُودٌ ﴿٦﴾

Indeed, man is truly ungrateful to His Lord. [6]

6.1 The next verses of the chapter are the subject (*jawāb*) of the oath mentioned in the opening verses. The reader was picturing a scene of warhorses loyally galloping in obedience and servitude to their masters. The riders had pierced through the enemy ranks and reached the centre. What would happen next?!

But just when his attention was piqued, he is confronted with a troubling statement when God states what He wanted to say all along: *[I swear by those things that] 'Indeed, man is truly ungrateful to His Lord.'* This statement forcefully brings man back to himself.

6.2 [*Al-Insān* (الْإِنسَان, man)] refers to the human race in general, and accuses each and every one of us as having the tendency of being ungrateful to our Lord.[23] We have discussed the term *insān* in greater detail in the *tafsīr* of Surat al-ʿAṣr (103).

[*Kanūd* (كَنُود, ungrateful)]. Derived from *kanada*, it denotes a land where nothing grows, and is also used to describe a person who is ungrateful and miserly.[24] It can also refer to a person who shows ingratitude in the face of God's favours (*kafūr*), or who loudly complains about his problems but is silent about his blessings, or who is unsympathetic at the plight of his friends.[25]

6.3 A tradition states that when the Prophet (s) described the one who is *kanūd*, he said, "He is the one who eats alone, prevents anyone else from joining him, and beats his servant."[26]

6.4 The verse says that as a rule, man is ungrateful for the favours God has bestowed on him, and he habitually takes these blessings for granted.[27]

SUMMARY OF THE VERSE

The verse states that man is continually ungrateful despite God's abundant favours on him.

---

[23] Ibid.

[24] Rāghib, *al-Mufradāt*.

[25] Shīrāzī, *Namūneh*, 27/248.

[26] Kāshānī, *al-Ṣāfī*, 5/361.

عَنِ الرَّسُولِ (صَلَّى اللهُ عَلَيْهِ وَآلِهِ) – أَتَدْرُونَ مَنِ الْكَنُودُ؟ قَالُوا: اللهُ وَرَسُولُهُ أَعْلَمُ، قَالَ: الْكَنُودُ، الَّذِي يَأْكُلُ وَحْدَهُ وَيَمْنَعُ رِفْدَهُ وَيَضْرِبُ عَبْدَهُ.

[27] Mughniyyah, *al-Kāshif*, 7/601.

REFLECTIVE LEARNING

Let me reflect whether I am amongst those who are ungrateful to their Lord by complaining about my problems while overlooking my many blessings?

VERSE 7

وَإِنَّهُ عَلَىٰ ذَٰلِكَ لَشَهِيدٌ ﴿٧﴾

And indeed, he truly bears witness to that. [7]

7.1 [*Shahīd* (شَهِيد, witness)]. The use of the hyperbolic form *shahīd* instead of *shāhid*, indicates that man is a constant witness to his own ingratitude.

7.2 The verse declares that this kind of person is himself a testament to his ungratefulness through his attitude, behaviour, and words. If he was honest with himself, he would be forced to admit his heedlessness and ingratitude.[28] Q75:14,15 make a similar point:

بَلِ الْإِنْسَانُ عَلَىٰ نَفْسِهِ بَصِيرَةٌ ﴿١٤﴾ وَلَوْ أَلْقَىٰ مَعَاذِيرَهُ

But man is a witness over himself,
even though he puts forth his excuses.

7.3 In one report there is a different meaning given for the verse under review, attributing the witnessing to God. It is reported that Imam al-Baqir (a) stated: It means that God is a witness over him [that is, his ungrateful behaviour].[29] However, a number of renowned exegetes do not consider this report to be sound.[30]

7.4 Some exegetes are of the opinion that this witnessing refers to the witnessing against oneself that will occur on the Day of Judgement, as mentioned in many verses, for example, Q24:24

يَوْمَ تَشْهَدُ عَلَيْهِمْ أَلْسِنَتُهُمْ وَأَيْدِيهِمْ وَأَرْجُلُهُمْ بِمَا كَانُوا يَعْمَلُونَ

---

28 Muṭahharī, (*Āshnāyī bā Qur'an*), *Āthār*, 28/721.

29 Astarabādī, *Ta''wīl al-Āyāt al-Ẓāhirah*, p. 812.

عَنِ الْبَاقِرِ (عَلَيْهِ السَّلَامُ) – سَأَلْتُهُ عَنْ قَوْلِ اللهِ عَزَّ وَجَلَّ ... «وَإِنَّهُ عَلَىٰ ذَٰلِكَ لَشَهِيدٌ» قَالَ إِنَّ اللهَ شَهِيدٌ عَلَيْهِ.

30 Shīrāzī, *Namūneh*, 27/249.

On the Day when their tongues, their hands, and the feet will bear witness against them as to what they used to do.

However, once again, other exegetes say that there is no evidence for this and the verses have a more general meaning that includes man's admission of his miserliness and ingratitude in this world also.[31]

SUMMARY OF THE VERSE

The verse states that man himself bears witness to his own ingratitude to God.

REFLECTIVE LEARNING

Let me reflect on what I possess of God's bounties and favours. Do I take them for granted and forget that all I have is from Him?

Let me bear witness to my own ingratitude now, and turn to God in gratitude.

VERSE 8

وَإِنَّهُ لِحُبِّ الْخَيْرِ لَشَدِيدٌ ﴿٨﴾

And indeed, he is truly intense in the love of wealth. [8]

8.1 [*Ḥubb* (حُبّ, love)]. *Ḥubb* has been defined as 'love and inclination towards something in which one sees goodness and benefit.'[32] The term has been used in the Qur'an for both love that is praised and love that is disparaged (as in the verse under review).

Some have defined love as 'the desire and inclination for something that will grant pleasure and comfort.' They say that love or hatred for something must be accompanied by an understanding and experience of that thing, otherwise it cannot be said to be true love or hatred for that thing. They add that the highest degree of love is the love for God, because only He is truly deserving of love.[33]

---

[31] Ibid.

[32] Rāghib, *al-Mufradāt.*

[33] Narāqī, *Miʿrāj al-Saʿādah*, 1/720.

8.2 [*Al-Khayr* (الخَيْر, wealth)]. In this instance, *khayr*, which normally refers to goodness, denotes wealth and affluence. This meaning has also been used elsewhere in the Qur'an. For instance, Q2:180 states:

كُتِبَ عَلَيْكُمْ إِذَا حَضَرَ أَحَدَكُمُ الْمَوْتُ

إِنْ تَرَكَ خَيْرًا الْوَصِيَّةُ لِلْوَالِدَيْنِ وَالْأَقْرَبِينَ بِالْمَعْرُوفِ

It is prescribed for you when death approaches any of you, if he leaves wealth (khayr), *that he makes a bequest for the parents and near relatives in kindness...*

Wealth in itself is not bad at all; rather, it is the means and avenue to all types of good, like providing for the family, helping others, performing hajj, supporting religious causes, and so on. However, what is condemned here is *ḥubb al-khayr* (the love of wealth) – when the means to goodness becomes the objective itself.[34]

8.3 [*Shadīd* (شَدِيد, intense)], and *mutashaddid*, were terms used to describe those in Arab society who were known to be extremely stingy and miserly.[35] Contrasted against that is the conduct of the believers, who demonstrate this same quality - intensity - except that they direct it towards God. Q2:165 states:

وَالَّذِينَ آمَنُوا أَشَدُّ حُبًّا لِلَّهِ

...But those who believe are intense in their love for God...

8.4 The verse states that the one who is ungrateful (*kanūd*) is intensely passionate in his pursuit of wealth and possessions. This reaches the extent that he develops extreme miserliness and is unwilling to spend his wealth in the way of God.

8.5 Some exegetes take the *lām* (ل) before '*ḥubb*' to be causative (*'illah*), and thus the verse would mean, "Indeed, due to his love of wealth he truly is miserly."[36]

---

[34] Muṭahharī, (*Āshnāyī bā Qur'an*), *Āthār*, 28/722.

[35] Ṭabrasī, *al-Bayān*, 10/804.

[36] Ṭabāṭabā'ī, *al-Mīzān*, 20/347.

8.6 A tradition from Imam Ali (a) states: Indeed, miserliness, injustice, and greed are different traits which have one thing in common: mistrust (*sūʾ al-ẓann*) of God.[37]

SUMMARY OF THE VERSE

The verse states that this individual exhibits inordinate love for wealth.

REFLECTIVE LEARNING

Love is an emotion that God allows us to feel for people and things, so that we can experience what intense love means and realize that only God is deserving of it.

Let me reflect on how much I love God, and whether I love Him above everything else. For example, what is the first thing I think of in the morning and the last thing I think of at night?

VERSES 9 - 11

أَفَلَا يَعْلَمُ إِذَا بُعْثِرَ مَا فِي الْقُبُورِ ﴿٩﴾ وَحُصِّلَ مَا فِي الصُّدُورِ ﴿١٠﴾ إِنَّ رَبَّهُمْ بِهِمْ
يَوْمَئِذٍ لَخَبِيرٌ ﴿١١﴾

Does he not realize that when what is in the graves is poured forth, [9] *and what is in the hearts is made manifest;* [10] *indeed, on that Day their Lord shall be fully aware of them?* [11]

9-11.1 '*Does he not realize that when what is in the graves is poured forth.*': [*Buʿthira* (بُعْثِرَ, poured forth)]. The quadrilateral verb *baʿthara* means to overturn and pour forth.[38] Others have given it the meaning of upturning and expelling.[39]

[*Mā fīʾl qubūr* (مَا فِي الْقُبُورِ, what is in the graves)]. *Mā* (what) is normally used for inanimate objects and may be used here because the dead are still in the form of dust, or their constituent parts are not distinguishable from one human to the next.[40]

---

[37] Ḥarrānī, *Tuḥaf al-ʿUqūl*, p. 129.

عَنْ أَمِيرِ الْمُؤْمِنِينَ (عَلَيْهِ السَّلَامُ) - إِنَّ الْبُخْلَ وَالْجَوْرَ وَالْحِرْصَ غَرَائِزُ شَتَّى يَجْمَعُهَا سُوءُ الظَّنِّ بِاللهِ.

[38] Rāghib, *al-Mufradāt*.

[39] Shīrāzī, *Namūneh*, 27/251.

[40] Ibid.

9-11.2 The term 'graves' is used in a general sense, denoting the place where the remains of the dead lie. The common practice for mankind is burial in the ground, but many of those who die drown in the sea and the remains of others are burned to ashes. And those who are alive at the final blowing of the trumpet will fall where they stand. In any case, the verse is describing the moment when the dead will all be resurrected.

9-11.3 The upturning of graves and pouring forth does not stop until everything is exposed; not only the bodies of humankind, but their essence, the combination of their thoughts, beliefs, and actions, are revealed for all to see.[41]

9-11.4 Therefore, verse 9 means, 'has he forgotten that there will be a time when all who have died will be brought back along with all their deeds?'

9-11.5 '*And what is in the hearts is made manifest.*': [*Ḥuṣṣila* (حُصِّلَ, made manifest)]. *Ḥuṣṣila* is the passive form of the verbal noun *taḥṣīl*, and means to expose and separate the inner aspect.[42] Following on from the previous verse, it refers to the peeling away of the false façade that covered the hearts, and exposing the good and evil that is contained therein. All that was held in secret will be open for scrutiny. Q86:9 states about this Day:

يَوْمَ تُبْلَى السَّرَائِرُ

On the Day when all secrets will be examined.

9-11.6 '*Indeed, on that Day their Lord shall be fully aware of them.*': [*Khabīr* (خَبِير, aware)]. He is aware of everything they did, openly and in secret. Of course God was always all-Aware of every part of His creation, but now, His awareness will be realized by all. The consequence of this awareness is His recompense, which will be awarded without even the slightest amount of injustice.

---

[41] Ṭabāṭabā'ī, *al-Mīzān*, 20/347.

[42] Muṣṭafawī, *al-Taḥqīq*.

SUMMARY OF THE VERSES

In summary these verses ask us to consider the moment when everyone will be expelled from their graves to gather for the Day of Judgement. On that Day, all that was hidden in their hearts will be exposed. Thereafter, God will recompense everyone in full accordingly.

REFLECTIVE LEARNING

Let me reflect on the Day when all that I have done and the intention with which I did it will be exposed for all to see – what sort of recompense am I expecting to receive?

SURAT AL-QĀRIʿAH
THE STRIKING CALAMITY (101)

TEXT AND TRANSLATION

سُورَةُ الْقَارِعَةِ

بِسْمِ اللهِ الرَّحْمٰنِ الرَّحِيمِ

الْقَارِعَةُ ﴿١﴾ مَا الْقَارِعَةُ ﴿٢﴾ وَمَا أَدْرَاكَ مَا الْقَارِعَةُ ﴿٣﴾ يَوْمَ يَكُونُ النَّاسُ
كَالْفَرَاشِ الْمَبْثُوثِ ﴿٤﴾ وَتَكُونُ الْجِبَالُ كَالْعِهْنِ الْمَنْفُوشِ ﴿٥﴾ فَأَمَّا مَنْ ثَقُلَتْ
مَوَازِينُهُ ﴿٦﴾ فَهُوَ فِي عِيشَةٍ رَاضِيَةٍ ﴿٧﴾ وَأَمَّا مَنْ خَفَّتْ مَوَازِينُهُ ﴿٨﴾ فَأُمُّهُ هَاوِيَةٌ
﴿٩﴾ وَمَا أَدْرَاكَ مَا هِيَهْ ﴿١٠﴾ نَارٌ حَامِيَةٌ ﴿١١﴾

In the name of God, the Beneficent, the Merciful.

The Striking Calamity! [1] *What is the Striking Calamity?* [2] *And what will make you know what the Striking Calamity is?* [3] *The Day when mankind shall be as scattered moths.* [4] *And the mountains will be like carded wool.* [5] *Then, as for the one whose scales [of good deeds] are heavy,* [6] *He will have a pleasant life.* [7] *And as for the one whose scales [of good deeds] are light,* [8] *His abode will be the Abyss* (hāwiyah). [9] *And what will make you know what it is?* [10] *[It is] An intensely hot fire.* [11]

INTRODUCTION

Surat al-Qāriʿah (101) was the 30th chapter to be revealed.[1] It is named after the mention of the term 'The Striking Calamity (al-Qāriʿah)' in the first verse. The surah has eleven verses and was revealed in Makka, after Surat Quraysh (106). Like many Makkan chapters, it discusses the Hereafter.

The chapter speaks about the cataclysmic events that transform the earth and usher in the Day of Judgement. It then describes a station

[1] Maʿrifat, *ʿUlūm-i Qurʾānī*, p. 90.

where the real worth of all human actions is determined on the scales of deeds (*mīzān*). For those whose scales are heavy, Paradise is the reward. But for those whose scales are light, hellfire awaits.

LINK TO THE PREVIOUS CHAPTER

The previous chapter, Surat al-*ʿĀdiyāt*, ends with the statement, '*Indeed, on that Day their Lord shall be fully aware of them*', and Surat al-Qāriʿah begins with an answer to one who may ask what that Day is, by stating, '*The [Day of the] Striking Calamity!* (al-Qāriʿah).'

MERITS OF RECITATION

- A tradition from the Prophet (s) states: Whoever recites this surah, God will make heavy his scales (*mīzān*) with good deeds on the Day of Judgement.[2]
- A tradition from Imam al-Baqir (a) states: Whoever recites al-Qāriʿah frequently will be protected by God from the trial of Dajjāl, lest he believes in him, and also from the terrors of hellfire – if God wills.[3]

EXEGESIS

VERSES 1 - 3

الْقَارِعَةُ ﴿١﴾ مَا الْقَارِعَةُ ﴿٢﴾ وَمَا أَدْرَاكَ مَا الْقَارِعَةُ ﴿٣﴾

The Striking Calamity! [1] *What is the Striking Calamity?* [2] *And what will make you know what the Striking Calamity is?* [3]

1-3.1 The chapter begins with a single word without any further information, predicate, or adjective. The word is repeated again in the second verse. This serves to create awe and apprehension in the mind of the reader.

1-3.2 '*The Striking Calamity! What is the Striking Calamity?*': [*Al-Qāriʿah* (الْقَارِعَة, the Striking Calamity)] is derived from *qaraʿa*, which

[2] Baḥrānī, al-Burhān, 5/739.

عَنِ الرَّسُولِ (صَلَّى اللهُ عَلَيْهِ وَآلِهِ) - مَنْ قَرَأَ هٰذِهِ السُّورَةَ ثَقَّلَ اللهُ مِيزَانَهُ مِنَ الْحَسَنَاتِ يَوْمَ الْقِيَامَةِ.

[3] Ṣadūq, *Thawāb al-Aʿmāl*, p. 125.

عَنِ الْبَاقِرِ (عَلَيْهِ السَّلَامُ) - مَنْ قَرَأَ وَأَكْثَرَ مِنْ قِرَاءَةِ الْقَارِعَةِ آمَنَهُ اللهُ عَزَّ وَجَلَّ مِنْ فِتْنَةِ الدَّجَّالِ أَنْ يُؤْمِنَ بِهِ وَمِنْ فَيْحِ جَهَنَّمَ إِنْ شَاءَ اللهُ.

denotes the striking and pounding of objects with a force that causes a loud and disturbing sound.[4] Just like the usage in *qaraʿa al-bāb* (knocked on the door), it has a sense of unexpectedness as well. The name *al-Qāriʿah* highlights a special feature of the Day of Judgement: it will come as abruptly and as suddenly as an unexpected loud knock at the front door of a house at night, which startles the dwellers inside.

Al-Qāriʿah is also a term used for any unexpected calamitous event filled with peace-shattering noise. For example, Q13:31 states:

وَلَا يَزَالُ الَّذِينَ كَفَرُوا تُصِيبُهُمْ بِمَا صَنَعُوا قَارِعَةٌ

...And a disaster (qāriʿah) *will not cease to strike the disbelievers because of their [evil] deeds...*

In Surat al-Qāriʿah, the term is used as a reference to a tremendous event in the lead up to the Day of Judgement.[5] The feminine *tā marbūṭah* (ة) appended to the word may be for further emphasis of its greatness.[6]

1-3.3 It is not clear whether the first verse of Surat al-Qāriʿah is describing the tumultuous events that will herald the end of the world, when the seas will boil over, the mountains will crumble, and the sun and the moon will go dark. Or is it about the subsequent stage when the awe-inspiring scenes of resurrection will cause the hearts to beat aloud? The verses that follow next are related to the events at the end of the world although it is possible that just as elsewhere in the Qur'an, both scenes are being described, one after another.[7]

1-3.4 '*And what will make you know what the Striking Calamity is?*': [*Wa mā adrāka* (وَمَا أَدْرَاكَ, and what will make you know?)]. In the third verse, the question is rephrased in a manner that indicates the greatness of this event. The fact is, al-Qāriʿah is a matter whose reality is out of the realm of man's understanding.[8]

---

[4] Shīrāzī, *Namūneh*, 27/261.

[5] Ṭabāṭabā'ī, *al-Mīzān*, 20/348.

[6] Shīrāzī, *Namūneh*, 27/261.

[7] Ibid.

[8] Ṭabāṭabā'ī, *al-Mīzān*, 20/348.

SUMMARY OF THE VERSES

The first three verses talk of a momentous event, *al-Qāriʿah*, whose clamour and tumult will be part of the terrifying scenes of the Day of Judgement.

REFLECTIVE LEARNING

The Day of Judgement will come about suddenly. These verses describe the enormity and finality of the event.

Let me reflect on how prepared I am if it were to happen tomorrow. What can I change today in my actions in order to be more prepared tomorrow?

VERSE 4

يَوْمَ يَكُونُ النَّاسُ كَالْفَرَاشِ الْمَبْثُوثِ ﴿٤﴾

The Day when mankind shall be as scattered moths. [4]

4.1 [*Al-Nās*, (النَّاس, mankind)]. The term *al-Nās* is used when mankind is referred to collectively, without any distinction based on their faith or acts. It means that this momentous event will involve every single human being. We have discussed this term in greater detail in the *tafsīr* of Surat al-ʿAṣr (103).

4.2 [*Al-Farāsh* (الْفَرَاش, moths)] (sing. *farāshah*) means a moth. Some exegetes[9] have said that the simile refers to locusts, based on Q54:7, which states:

يَخْرُجُونَ مِنَ الْأَجْدَاثِ كَأَنَّهُمْ جَرَادٌ مُنْتَشِرٌ

...They will emerge from the graves as if they were locusts spreading out.

In any case, the simile has been used to demonstrate the widespread bewilderment and distress of the billions of human beings who are initially milling about, unsure of what is happening.

9 Ṭabrasī, *al-Bayān*, 10/808.

Interestingly, just like moths fascinated by the sparkle of the fire enter its flames, not caring that they will be burnt, so do those who in their love for this world, defiantly disobey God.[10]

4.3 [*Al-Mabthūth* (الْمَبْثُوث, scattered)] is derived from *baththa*, which means individually scattered about and widely dispersed.[11] Unlike flocks of birds or shoals of fish which move in one direction in unison, the metaphor of moths suggests that there will be widespread confusion with people moving in every direction.

Q22:2 describes it as:

وَتَرَى النَّاسَ سُكَارَىٰ وَمَا هُمْ بِسُكَارَىٰ وَلَٰكِنَّ عَذَابَ اللَّهِ شَدِيدٌ

...You will see the people [appearing] intoxicated, but they are not intoxicated; rather, the torment of God will be strong [upon them].

SUMMARY OF THE VERSE

In summary, the verse describes a scene from the prelude to the Day of Judgement. Human beings will be scattered across the earth, moving about in confusion like fluttering moths.

REFLECTIVE LEARNING

Those who do not truly believe in the Day of Judgement, do not prepare for it. Therefore, on that Day, they will be filled with confusion and fear, moving without direction like fluttering moths.

Let me reflect on my own level of belief and preparation for the Day of Judgement. What can I change today to strengthen my faith in order to be better prepared on that Day?

VERSE 5

وَتَكُونُ الْجِبَالُ كَالْعِهْنِ الْمَنْفُوشِ ﴿٥﴾

And the mountains will be like carded wool. [5]

5.1 [*Al-ʿIhn* (الْعِهْن, wool)] means wool of different textures and colours.[12] This has been referred to also in Q70:9 which states:

---

[10] Shīrāzī, *Namūneh*, 27/262.

[11] Ibn Manẓūr, *Lisān al-ʿArab*.

[12] Muṣṭafawī, *al-Taḥqīq*.

وَتَكُونُ الْجِبَالُ كَالْعِهْنِ

And the mountains shall be as [tufts of] wool.

5.2 [*Manfūsh* (مَنفُوش, carded)] comes from *nafasha* which means to disentangle, and organize fibres in rows.[13] So the simile describes the collision of mountains of different hues which finally come to rest in crumpled lines.

SUMMARY OF THE VERSE

The verse states that the mighty mountains that stabilize the earth will crumple and become like wool pulled part.

REFLECTIVE LEARNING

Imagine what will happen to human beings on a Day whose cataclysmic events have levelled the strong mountains of the earth. The arrogant and defiant human beings will be broken far quicker than the mighty and strong mountains.

Let me reflect on the reality of my own lowliness and weakness. What one thing can I do to lessen my arrogance and ego, before it is forcefully broken for me?

VERSES 6, 7

فَأَمَّا مَنْ ثَقُلَتْ مَوَازِينُهُ ﴿٦﴾ فَهُوَ فِي عِيشَةٍ رَاضِيَةٍ ﴿٧﴾

Then, as for the one whose scales [of good deeds] are heavy, [6] *He will have a pleasant life.* [7]

6-7.1 In the next series of verses, God describes how the fate of man is linked to his actions. The verses make the point that every single action has a weight and value, and this will be measured in a scale or balance called *al-mīzān* on the Day of Judgement.

The fate of two groups is then mentioned: those whose scales are heavy, and those whose scales are light.

6-7.2 '*Then, as for the one whose scales are heavy.*': [*Thaqulat* (ثَقُلَتْ, are heavy)]. *Thaqīl* means heavy and weighty, and it is obvious that the reference here is to the weight of something that is immaterial.

---

13 Ibid.

As we shall see in the discussion below, what gives weight to these scales is deeds of righteousness.

The weightiness of the scales (*thiql al-mīzān*) is a theme in many narrations, some of which are mentioned below:

i) A tradition from Imam Ali (a) states: We testify that there is no deity except God; He is One, with no partner. And that Muhammad (s) is his servant and messenger. These two testimonies elevate one's beliefs and raise one's actions. The scales that they will be placed in will not be light, and the scales from which they will be absent will not be heavy...[14]

ii) A tradition from Imam al-Baqir (a) states: The scales of one whose outward conduct is more prominent than the inner aspect will be light.[15]

iii) A tradition from Imam al-Baqir and Imam al-Sadiq (a) states: Nothing heavier is placed on the scales than *ṣalawāt* on the Prophet (s) and his progeny. Indeed, a person's actions will be placed on the scales and will be found to be light; then the Prophet (s) will bring forth the *ṣalawāt* that the person had recited on him and place them on the scales, by which they will become heavy.[16]

6-7.3 [*Mawāzīn* (مَوَازِين, scales)] (sing. *mīzān*) is any device that weighs something, material or immaterial.[17] In this case, it is referring to a special station on the Day of Judgement in which the 'worth' of every human being will be weighed. This station has been mentioned in several verses and many traditions, and will be discussed below separately.

---

[14] *Nahj al-Balāghah*, sermon 114.

نَشْهَدُ أَنْ لَا إِلَٰهَ إِلَّا اللهُ وَحْدَهُ لَا شَرِيكَ لَهُ، وَأَنَّ مُحَمَّدًا (صَلَّى اللهُ عَلَيْهِ وَآلِهِ وَسَلَّمَ) عَبْدُهُ وَرَسُولُهُ، شَهَادَتَيْنِ تُصْعِدَانِ الْقَوْلَ وَتَرْفَعَانِ الْعَمَلَ، لَا يَخِفُّ مِيزَانٌ تُوضَعَانِ فِيهِ، وَلَا يَثْقُلُ مِيزَانٌ تُرْفَعَانِ [مِنْهُ] عَنْهُ.

[15] Ḥarrānī, *Tuḥaf al-ʿUqūl*, p. 294.

عَنِ الْبَاقِرِ (عَلَيْهِ السَّلَامُ) – مَنْ كَانَ ظَاهِرُهُ أَرْجَحَ مِنْ بَاطِنِهِ خَفَّ مِيزَانُهُ.

[16] Kulaynī, *al-Kāfī*, 2/494.

عَنِ الصَّادِقَيْنِ (عَلَيْهِمَا السَّلَامُ) – مَا فِي الْمِيزَانِ شَيْءٌ أَثْقَلُ مِنَ الصَّلَاةِ عَلَى مُحَمَّدٍ وَآلِ مُحَمَّدٍ، إِنَّ الرَّجُلَ لَتُوضَعُ أَعْمَالُهُ فِي الْمِيزَانِ فَتَمِيلُ بِهِ فَيُخْرِجُ (صَلَّى اللهُ عَلَيْهِ وَآلِهِ) الصَّلَاةَ عَلَيْهِ فَيَضَعُهَا فِي مِيزَانِهِ فَيَرْجَحُ بِهِ.

[17] Shīrāzī, *Namūneh*, 27/264.

Mawāzīn is also a plural of *mawzūn* (the thing being weighed), and so the plural could refer to the total of the various acts being placed on the scales and not the scales themselves.[18]

6-7.4 '*He will have a pleasant life.*': [*ʿĪshah* (عيشة, life)] is derived from *ʿāsha* meaning to live, and the term *ʿīshah* is a verbal noun that denotes a type of life.[19] In this case the type of life is described as pleasant.

[*Rāḍiyah* (رَاضِيَة, pleasant)]. Here, this means pleasant in itself, or giving pleasure to the individual.[20]

Therefore, *ʿīshatin rāḍiyah* denotes a life full of blessing and abiding contentment, and that is only possible in Paradise. May God make us of those who are granted this life!

DISCUSSION: THE STATION OF *AL-MĪZĀN*

The true worth and value of an individual is ascertained at a wondrous, yet disquieting, station known as *al-Mīzān*, where deeds are weighed. Q21:47 states:

وَنَضَعُ الْمَوَازِينَ الْقِسْطَ لِيَوْمِ الْقِيَامَةِ فَلَا تُظْلَمُ نَفْسٌ شَيْئًا
وَإِنْ كَانَ مِثْقَالَ حَبَّةٍ مِنْ خَرْدَلٍ أَتَيْنَا بِهَا وَكَفَىٰ بِنَا حَاسِبِينَ

And We will set up the scales of justice (al-mawāzīn al-qisṭ) *on the Day of Judgement, so no soul shall be dealt with unjustly in the least. And if there is [even] the weight of a grain of mustard seed, We will bring it forth. And We are sufficient to take account.*

The scales (*mīzān*) are not designed to just measure the number of deeds, rather, they determine the value of the deeds in terms of goodness and righteousness.

The term '*mīzān*' denotes an instrument for measuring things. Obviously, different things require different measurement devices. For example, weights require scales and a counterweight, time requires a watch, lengths require a ruler, thoughts require logic, poems require meter and rhyme, etc. In short, everything has a criterion against which the quantity or quality of that thing is weighed and evaluated.

---

[18] Ibid, 27/265.

[19] Ṭabāṭabāʾī, *al-Mīzān*, 20/349.

[20] Ibid.

Similarly, the *mīzān* on the Day of Judgement has a criterion against which the value of the deeds (*aʿmāl*), morals (*akhlāq*), and beliefs (*ʿaqāʾid*) of an individual will be evaluated. The criterion for this scale will be units of truth (*ḥaqq*). Q7:8,9 state:

وَالْوَزْنُ يَوْمَئِذٍ الْحَقُّ فَمَنْ ثَقُلَتْ مَوَازِينُهُ فَأُولَٰئِكَ هُمُ الْمُفْلِحُونَ ﴿٨﴾

وَمَنْ خَفَّتْ مَوَازِينُهُ فَأُولَٰئِكَ الَّذِينَ خَسِرُوا أَنْفُسَهُمْ بِمَا كَانُوا بِآيَاتِنَا يَظْلِمُونَ

And the weight [of deeds] on that Day shall be the truth (ḥaqq); *then as for those whose scales are heavy, they are the successful ones. And as for those whose scales are light, they are the ones who will have damaged their souls by rejecting Our signs.*

In other words, the closer and more coincident with *ḥaqq* the deeds of an individual are, the heavier the scales of his deeds shall be; and consequently his station shall be more elevated and noble as well.

The wondrous feature of the *mīzān* is that it is able to register the exact amount of sincerity and truth contained within an individual's deeds. According to some narrations, these scales are the Prophets (a) and their successors, whose deeds, morals and teachings serve as the measure of sincerity and truth in the deeds of people. In a salutation to Imam Ali (a) we read: Peace be upon [you], the scale (*mīzān*) of actions.[21]

Others believe that since the word 'scales' (*mawāzīn*) has been used in the verse in plural, there exists a separate weight and measure for every type of deed.

The verses under review mention that the one whose scales are heavy is successful and the one whose scales are light is the loser. Therefore, it is not about weighing good deeds against evil ones, because evil deeds will register no weight on this scale. It may be that the heaviness of the scales are in proportion to one's potential. In other words, the scales compare an individual's good actions against the best he personally could have performed them.

Mawāzīn here could mean both scales as well as the weighed deeds themselves. According to the first meaning it may be that more than one *mīzān* exists, rather there is one for every type of deed. Therefore,

---

[21] Qummī, *Mafātīḥ al-Jinān, Ziyārah Muṭlaqah of the Commander of the Faithful (a)*, p. 600.

السَّلَامُ عَلَى مِيزَانِ الْأَعْمَالِ.

everyone will have several weighing scales to measure the units of *ḥaqq* contained in each action, for example the *ḥaqq* in *salat*, *ḥaqq* in *ṣawm*, *ḥaqq* in *zakat*, *ḥaqq* in chastity, and so on.[22]

From the foregoing, we also conclude that the scales will only be set up for those who have deeds that can be weighed. Those who have no good acts or whose good deeds have been nullified, have nothing that needs to be weighed. Q18:105 states:

أُولَٰئِكَ الَّذِينَ كَفَرُوا بِآيَاتِ رَبِّهِمْ وَلِقَائِهِ فَحَبِطَتْ أَعْمَالُهُمْ
فَلَا نُقِيمُ لَهُمْ يَوْمَ الْقِيَامَةِ وَزْنًا

Those are the ones who disbelieve in the signs of their Lord, and in [their] meeting Him. So their deeds are in vain, and on the Day of Resurrection We will not assign any weight to them.

SUMMARY OF THE VERSES

In summary, the verses say that for those whose actions weigh heavy on the *mīzān* of the Day of Judgement, there is the good news of a life of contentment in Paradise.

REFLECTIVE LEARNING

Let me reflect on my deeds and attempt to gauge their worth and heaviness on the scales (*mīzān*) of the Day of Judgement.

Let me increase the weight of my *salat* by attempting to improve every aspect of it.

VERSES 8 - 11

وَأَمَّا مَنْ خَفَّتْ مَوَازِينُهُ ﴿٨﴾ فَأُمُّهُ هَاوِيَةٌ ﴿٩﴾ وَمَا أَدْرَاكَ مَا هِيَهْ ﴿١٠﴾ نَارٌ حَامِيَةٌ ﴿١١﴾

And as for the one whose scales [of good deeds] are light, [8] *His abode will be the Abyss* (hāwiyah). [9] *And what will make you know what it is?* [10] *[It is] An intensely hot fire.* [11]

[22] Adapted from: Bahmanpour, *Towards Eternal Life*, p. 110.

8-11.1 Now, the terrible fate of the one whose scales are light (*khaffat mawāzīnuhu*) is discussed in contrast.

8-11.2 '*And as for the one whose scales [of good deeds] are light.*': [*Khaffat* (خَفَّتْ, was light)]. Derived from *khafīf* meaning light, the term refers to those whose scales were not heavy enough by the criterion used for judging their actions. The only thing of value on that Day is the goodness of actions, and they will not have enough to tip the scales.

8-11.3 '*His abode will be the Abyss.*': [*Ummuhu* (أُمُّهُ, his abode)]. *Umm* usually denotes a mother. Here it is translated as 'abode' so the usage of this term deserves some contemplation. When the mother carries the baby in pregnancy, the baby cannot leave. Later, the mother wraps herself around the child and does not release her child readily. The mother is the direction towards which the child turns.[23] The dreadful consequence for those whose scales are light is that their 'mother' now becomes the fire of Hell; it holds them fast and does not allow escape, and ironically, they themselves are drawn towards it.

8-11.4 [*Hāwiyah* (هَاوِيَةٌ, Abyss in Hell)]. Derived from *hawā*, which means to fall swiftly, this term refers to an abyss in Hell in which the guilty will be plunged. It is also a reference to the great depth of the pits of hellfire.[24]

8-11.5 '*And what will make you know what it is?*': [*Wa mā adrāka* (وَمَا أَدْرَاكَ, and what will make you know?)]. This phrase is repeated once again. Both *Qāriʿah* and *Hāwiyah* are realities whose enormity cannot be imagined.

[*Mā hiyah* (مَا هِيَهْ, what it is)]. The pronoun *hiyah* refers to *Hāwiyah.* The extra *hā* (ه) affixed to the feminine pronoun, (هِيَهْ) instead of the expected (هِيَ), is for *waqf,* and the phrase serves to emphasize the particular greatness of this fire.[25]

8-11.6 '*[It is] An intensely hot fire.*': [*Nārun ḥāmiyah* (نَارٌ حَامِيَةٌ, an intensely hot fire)]. Derived from *ḥamī* meaning intensely hot,[26]

---

[23] Shīrāzī, *Namūneh*, 27/266.

[24] Ibid, 27/267.

[25] Ṭabāṭabā'ī, *al-Mīzān*, 20/349.

[26] Rāghib, *al-Mufradāt.*

ḥāmiyah denotes a fire that is extraordinarily hot, much more intense than the other fires of Hell.[27]

SUMMARY OF THE VERSES

In summary, the verse mentions the dreadful fate of those whose scales will be light; they will be plunged into a fire whose intensity cannot be imagined.

REFLECTIVE LEARNING

Let me reflect on how I can improve the actions I already perform, by considering their weight in units of *ḥaqq*, so that I can make my light actions heavier.

[27] Rāzī, *Mafātīḥ al-Ghayb*, 32/268.

SURAT AL-TAKĀTHUR
RIVALRY IN ACCUMULATION (102)

TEXT AND TRANSLATION

سُورَةُ التَّكَاثُرِ

بِسْمِ اللهِ الرَّحْمٰنِ الرَّحِيمِ

أَلْهَاكُمُ التَّكَاثُرُ ﴿١﴾ حَتَّىٰ زُرْتُمُ الْمَقَابِرَ ﴿٢﴾ كَلَّا سَوْفَ تَعْلَمُونَ ﴿٣﴾ ثُمَّ كَلَّا
سَوْفَ تَعْلَمُونَ ﴿٤﴾ كَلَّا لَوْ تَعْلَمُونَ عِلْمَ الْيَقِينِ ﴿٥﴾ لَتَرَوُنَّ الْجَحِيمَ ﴿٦﴾ ثُمَّ
لَتَرَوُنَّهَا عَيْنَ الْيَقِينِ ﴿٧﴾ ثُمَّ لَتُسْأَلُنَّ يَوْمَئِذٍ عَنِ النَّعِيمِ ﴿٨﴾

In the name of God, the Beneficent, the Merciful.

Rivalry in accumulation distracts you. [1] *Until you visit the graves.* [2] *Not at all! You shall soon come to know.* [3] *Again, not at all! You shall soon come to know.* [4] *Not at all! If you only knew with the knowledge of certitude.* [5] *You would surely see the hellfire!* [6] *Then you will surely see it with the eye of certitude.* [7] *Then on that Day, you will certainly be questioned about the bounties.* [8]

INTRODUCTION

Surat al-Takāthur (102) was the 16th chapter to be revealed.[1] It has eight verses and was revealed in Makka, after Surat al-Kawthar (108). It takes its name from the first verse, where there is mention of mutual rivalry in accumulating wealth and possessions (*takāthur*).

The chapter talks of the senselessness and evil consequence of an existence where one is continually engrossed in this activity.

LINK TO THE PREVIOUS CHAPTER

The four chapters, al-Zalzalah (99), al-ʿĀdiyāt (100), al-Qāriʿah (101) and al-Takāthur (102) have a common theme that links them in a

---

[1] Maʿrifat, *ʿUlūm-i Qurʾānī*, p. 90.

cluster. They all speak about the Day of Judgement and the important association of man's actions in this world with his fate in the Hereafter. They are especially addressed to those who transgress God's limits and thereby earn a place in the hellfire.

The previous chapter, al-Qāriʿah, concluded with the dreadful fate of the people whose scales were light. Surat al-Takāthur begins with mentioning one of the main reasons why people would suffer such a fate on the Day of Judgement: their obsession with accumulating possessions and showing off to one another.

OCCASION OF REVELATION

According to some narrations, the verses of this chapter were revealed as a comment on the behaviour of two clans of the Quraysh, the Banu ʿAbd Manāf and the Banu Sahm, who were fierce rivals. They boasted to each other about their wealth and number of tribesmen. When Banu ʿAbd Manāf pointed out they had greater numbers, the Banu Sahm insisted that they should go the graveyards to count the number of their deceased forefathers, and in this way, they showed that their numbers were superior![2]

About this conduct, Imam Ali (a) has remarked: Do they take pride over their deceased forefathers? Or do they boast with one another (*yatakātharūn*) about the number of their deceased? They want to revive [the memory of] those lifeless and motionless bodies; [whereas] it would be more fitting to take a lesson from them rather than take pride in them. It would be more sensible to take the lesson of humbleness from them rather than honour.[3]

MERITS OF RECITATION

- A tradition from the Prophet (s) states: Whoever recites this surah before going to sleep will be protected from the trials of the grave.[4]

---

[2] Ṭabrasī, *al-Bayān*, 10/811.

[3] *Nahj al-Balāghah*, sermon 220.

أَفَبِمَصَارِعِ آبَائِهِمْ يَفْخَرُونَ؟ أَمْ بِعَدِيدِ الْهَلْكَى يَتَكَاثَرُونَ؟ يَرْتَجِعُونَ مِنْهُمْ أَجْسَادًا خَوَتْ وَحَرَكَاتٍ سَكَنَتْ؛ وَلَأَنْ يَكُونُوا عِبَرًا أَحَقُّ مِنْ أَنْ يَكُونُوا مُفْتَخَرًا، وَلَأَنْ يَهْبِطُوا بِهِمْ جَنَابَ ذِلَّةٍ أَحْجَى مِنْ أَنْ يَقُومُوا بِهِمْ مَقَامَ عِزَّةٍ.

[4] Kulaynī, *al-Kāfī*, 2/623.

عَنِ الرَّسُولِ (صَلَّى اللهُ عَلَيْهِ وَآلِهِ) – مَنْ قَرَأَ «أَلْهَاكُمُ التَّكَاثُرُ» عِنْدَ النَّوْمِ وُقِيَ فِتْنَةَ الْقَبْرِ.

- Another tradition from the Prophet (s) states: Whoever recites this surah will not be asked to account for the blessings that God granted him in the world.[5]
- A tradition from Imam al-Sadiq (a) states: Whoever recites it when it rains is forgiven his sins by God. And whoever recites it at the time of the *ʿaṣr* prayer will remain in God's protection until the sun sets on the next day, with the permission of God, the Almighty.[6]

EXEGESIS

VERSE 1

أَلْهَاكُمُ التَّكَاثُرُ ﴿١﴾

Rivalry in accumulation distracts you. [1]

1.1 The chapter begins by stating that the practice of rivalry and mutual showing-off has made man forget his purpose in life, which is to use God's blessings only to attain His proximity.

1.2 [*Alhākum* (أَلْهَاكُم, distracts you)]. The term *ilhā'* is derived from *lahw*, meaning frivolous and worthless pursuits, aimlessness, and neglect of more important tasks.[7] *Lahw* is defined as activity that engrosses a person and distracts him from his objective.[8]

Ilhā' here means distraction, and has been equated to forgetting the remembrance of God in Q63:9:

يَا أَيُّهَا الَّذِينَ آمَنُوا لَا تُلْهِكُمْ أَمْوَالُكُمْ وَلَا أَوْلَادُكُمْ عَنْ ذِكْرِ اللهِ

O believers! Do not let your wealth and children distract you from the remembrance of God...

---

[5] Baḥrānī, *al-Burhān*, 5/743.

عَنِ الرَّسُولِ (صَلَّى اللهُ عَلَيْهِ وَآلِهِ) – مَنْ قَرَأَ هَذِهِ السُّورَةَ لَمْ يُحَاسِبْهُ اللهُ بِالنِّعَمِ الَّتِي أَنْعَمَ بِهَا عَلَيْهِ فِي الدُّنْيَا.

[6] Ibid.

عَنِ الصَّادِقِ (عَلَيْهِ السَّلَامُ) – مَنْ قَرَأَهَا وَقْتَ نُزُولِ الْمَطَرِ غَفَرَ اللهُ لَهُ، وَمَنْ قَرَأَهَا وَقْتَ صَلَاةِ الْعَصْرِ كَانَ فِي أَمَانِ اللهِ إِلَى غُرُوبِ الشَّمْسِ مِنَ الْيَوْمِ الثَّانِي بِإِذْنِ اللهِ تَعَالَى.

[7] Muṭahharī, (*Āshnāyī bā Qur'an*), *Āthār*, 28/737.

[8] Rāghib, *al-Mufradāt*.

The verse above mentions wealth and children specifically as the factors that may distract an individual from the remembrance of God (*ʿan dhikrillāh*), but the first verse of Surat al-Takāthur does not indicate exactly what kind of distraction *al-takāthur* causes. It could be distraction from God, or from the reality of death, or the Day of Judgement, or the true purpose of life, or a combination of these matters.

1.3 [*Al-Takāthur* (التَّكَاثُر, rivalry in accumulation)] is derived from *kathrah*, which means plenty, and here denotes the desire to want more and competing with one another in amassing wealth and position.[9] As a result, the individual mistakenly equates the increase of his worth in the eyes of the people as the increase of his worth in the eyes of God.

1.4 *Al-Takāthur* is also similar to arrogant boasting (*al-tafākhur*)[10] because it leads to showing off and causes man to forget the Day of Accounting. Q18:34-36 state:

وَكَانَ لَهُ ثَمَرٌ فَقَالَ لِصَاحِبِهِ وَهُوَ يُحَاوِرُهُ أَنَا أَكْثَرُ مِنْكَ مَالًا وَأَعَزُّ نَفَرًا ﴿٣٤﴾
وَدَخَلَ جَنَّتَهُ وَهُوَ ظَالِمٌ لِنَفْسِهِ قَالَ مَا أَظُنُّ أَنْ تَبِيدَ هَٰذِهِ أَبَدًا ﴿٣٥﴾
وَمَا أَظُنُّ السَّاعَةَ قَائِمَةً

And he had [abundant] produce. So he said to his companion while he was conversing with him, "I am greater than you in wealth, and mightier in [number of] men." And he entered his orchard in a state [of arrogance] that was unjust to his soul. He said, "I do not think that all this will ever perish. I do not think the Hour will ever come..."

1.5 The deplorable habit of showing off and boasting is rooted in several factors that first need to be recognized by an individual before they can be removed. The most common reasons include insecurity, low self-esteem, and a desire to be liked and accepted by others. However, the Qurʾan reassures mankind that they have been uniquely honoured by God already, and it is in His servitude that true honour lies. Q17:70 states:

---

9 Ibid.

10 Shīrāzī, *Namūneh*, 27/276.

وَلَقَدْ كَرَّمْنَا بَنِي آدَمَ وَحَمَلْنَاهُمْ فِي الْبَرِّ وَالْبَحْرِ وَرَزَقْنَاهُمْ
مِنَ الطَّيِّبَاتِ وَفَضَّلْنَاهُمْ عَلَىٰ كَثِيرٍ مِمَّنْ خَلَقْنَا تَفْضِيلًا

And indeed, We have honoured the children of Adam. We carry them on the land and the sea, and We have given them good and pure things (al-ṭayyibāt) *as sustenance; and We have preferred them with special favours over a great part of Our creation.*

1.6 The irony is that after a lifetime spent accumulating and showing off, man leaves everything behind at death. According to a tradition, the Prophet (s) once recited Surat al-Takāthur and then asked his companions, "Which of you loves the wealth of his heirs over his own?" They replied, "There is none amongst us who loves that!" He (s) said, "In fact, every one of you loves it!" Then he stated: The son of Adam says, 'My wealth, my wealth.' Yet, did you truly possess anything more than what you ate and consumed, or what you wore and made threadbare, or what you gave in charity and moved on? Everything else is [in fact] the wealth of your heirs."[11]

SUMMARY OF THE VERSE

The verse criticises the one whose preoccupation with amassing wealth, showing off, and competing with others has distracted him completely from the true objective of life.

REFLECTIVE LEARNING

Let me reflect on my possessions and how attached I am to them. Would I be hesitant to give a loved possession to another for the pleasure of God?

If so, I must remind myself that these possessions are only a means to achieve felicity in the *ākhirah*.

---

[11] Ṭūsī, *al-Amālī*, 1/519.

عَنِ الرَّسُولِ (صَلَّى اللهُ عَلَيْهِ وَآلِهِ) – أَيُّكُمْ مَالُ وَارِثِهِ أَحَبُّ إِلَيْهِ مِنْ مَالِهِ قَالُوا: مَا فِينَا أَحَدٌ يُحِبُّ ذَلِكَ يَا نَبِيَّ اللهِ. قَالَ: بَلْ كُلُّكُمْ يُحِبُّ ذَلِكَ. ثُمَّ قَالَ: يَقُولُ ابْنُ آدَمَ: مَالِي مَالِي، وَهَلْ لَكَ مِنْ مَالِكَ إِلَّا مَا أَكَلْتَ فَأَفْنَيْتَ، أَوْ لَبِسْتَ فَأَبْلَيْتَ، أَوْ تَصَدَّقْتَ فَأَمْضَيْتَ؟ وَمَا عَدَا ذَلِكَ فَهُوَ مَالُ الْوَارِثِ.

VERSE 2

حَتَّىٰ زُرْتُمُ الْمَقَابِرَ ﴿٢﴾

Until you visit the graves. [2]

2.1 According to most exegetes, the verse means, 'until death comes to you while you are in this state.' However, there are some reports that say it means 'until you even go to the graveyards to count and take pride in the number of your deceased forefathers.'[12] This second meaning for the verse can be considered to be one instance of its application (*miṣdāq*).

A third meaning is that the only way to dispel this habit of *takāthur* is to draw a lesson by visiting the graveyard and reminding oneself of the futility of pursuing life for its own sake.[13]

2.2 [*Zurtum* (زُرْتُمْ, you visited)] is derived from *zawr*, which denotes the upper part of the chest, and later came to mean meeting someone or facing some task.[14] Its common derivative is *ziyārah*, which means a visitation.

In this verse *ziyārah* of graves is either a metaphor for death,[15] or going to the graveyard to count the dead according to a famous report.[16]

2.3 *Ziyārah* has the sense of a brief visit, after which the visitor leaves. The human being's stay in the grave will also be transient and relatively brief. After the world comes to an end, he will leave the grave and carry on his journey in the Hereafter.

2.4 [*Maqābir* (مَقَابِر, graves)] (sing. *maqbarah*) refers to the place of burial (*qabr*) or a graveyard.

SUMMARY OF THE VERSE

The verse says that the only thing that brings *al-takāthur* to an end is the realization that comes at death or from visiting the graveyard.

---

[12] Ṭabrasī, *al-Bayān*, 10/813.

[13] Muṭahharī, *(Āshnāyī bā Qur'an)*, *Āthār*, 28/740.

[14] Shīrāzī, *Namūneh*, 27/276.

[15] Ṭabāṭabā'ī, *al-Mīzān*, 20/351.

[16] Shīrāzī, *Namūneh*, 27/277.

REFLECTIVE LEARNING

Nothing that I amass in terms of wealth, possessions, position, etc. is transferrable to the grave. The only assets that I can take forth are those that I have given in charity or the actions that I have performed for the sake of God.

Let me reflect on what actions am I taking with me to my grave?

VERSES 3, 4

كَلَّا سَوْفَ تَعْلَمُونَ ﴿٣﴾ ثُمَّ كَلَّا سَوْفَ تَعْلَمُونَ ﴿٤﴾

Not at all! You shall soon come to know. [3] *Again, not at all! You shall soon come to know.* [4]

3-4.1 In these two verses a stern warning is issued to those who are occupied in *al-takāthur*. Soon the folly of their ways and the consequence of their distraction will become apparent to them.

3-4.2 [*Kallā* (كَلَّا, Not at all!)]. This word implies that the reality of things is completely different from what they had imagined.[17] It is a warning to desist from their preoccupation with amassing wealth and possessions.[18]

3-4.3 [*Sawfa* (سَوْفَ, soon)]. This term means before long, and refers to the fact that the realization of the futility of *al-takāthur*, and the consequences of this distraction, will come as soon as the person dies.

3-4.4 [*Taʿlamūn* (تَعْلَمُون, you will all know)]. The tone of these verses carry a barely-hidden threat. This is a promise that at death, every human being will know the truth that is veiled from them in this world in varying degrees, depending on how distracted they are from God. About the knowledge that comes to everyone at death, Q50:22 states:

لَقَدْ كُنْتَ فِي غَفْلَةٍ مِنْ هَٰذَا فَكَشَفْنَا عَنْكَ غِطَاءَكَ فَبَصَرُكَ الْيَوْمَ حَدِيدٌ

[It will be said:] You were certainly heedless of this [while in the world], and now We have removed from you your veil, so on this Day, your sight is piercing.

---

17 Ṭabrasī, *al-Bayān*, 10/812.

18 Ṭabāṭabāʾī, *al-Mīzān*, 20/351.

3-4.5 A famous tradition from Imam Ali (a) states: People are asleep. When they die, they come awake.[19]

3-4.6 The verse has been repeated for emphasis and this makes the warning even more stern. Some exegetes have said that the first of the two verses is a reference to the realization (of the consequences of *al-takāthur*) when one enters the grave, and the second is the realization when one comes out of the grave on the Day of Judgement.[20]

SUMMARY OF THE VERSES

The verses state, with repetition for emphasis, that those who spend their days engaged in *al-takāthur* will come to know their error soon.

REFLECTIVE LEARNING

It is pointless to accumulate possessions to compete and show off to others, as there will always be someone who has more.

Let me reflect on how I can realize the futility of *al-takāthur* here and now, rather than once I leave this world.

VERSES 5 - 7

كَلَّا لَوْ تَعْلَمُونَ عِلْمَ الْيَقِينِ ﴿٥﴾ لَتَرَوُنَّ الْجَحِيمَ ﴿٦﴾ ثُمَّ لَتَرَوُنَّهَا عَيْنَ الْيَقِينِ ﴿٧﴾

Not at all! If you only knew with the knowledge of certitude. [5] *You would surely see the hellfire!* [6] *Then you will surely see it with the eye of certitude.* [7]

5-7.1 '*Not at all! If you only knew with the knowledge of certitude.*': *Kallā* (not at all) is repeated here for further emphasis of the futility of *al-takāthur.*

[*Law* (لَوْ, if only)]. The placement of '*law*' before the conditional clause '*if you only knew with the knowledge of certitude*' gives the

---

[19] Raḍī, *Khaṣā'is al-A'immah* (A), p. 112.

عَنْ أَمِيرِ الْمُؤْمِنِينَ (عَلَيْهِ السَّلَامُ) – النَّاسُ نِيَامٌ فَإِذَا مَاتُوا انْتَبَهُوا.

[20] Shīrāzī, *Namūneh*, 27/279; Ṭabāṭabā'ī, *al-Mīzān*, 20/351.

meaning 'you do not have *ʿilm al-yaqīn*'. Therefore, the main clause, '*you would surely see the hellfire*' is likewise not a possibility.[21]

5-7.2 [*ʿIlm al-yaqīn* (عِلْمَ الْيَقِينِ, knowledge of certitude)]. *Yaqīn* is more than knowing, it is a knowledge that is absolutely free of any doubt.[22] In fact, for most people, this level of certitude only comes after death, which is why the Qur'an uses *yaqīn* as a metaphor for death in many verses. For example, Q15:99 states:

وَٱعْبُدْ رَبَّكَ حَتَّىٰ يَأْتِيَكَ الْيَقِينُ

And serve your Lord until certainty (death) comes to you.

5-7.3 *Yaqīn* is a high stage in the levels of faith. A tradition from Imam al-Baqir (a) states: Belief (*īmān*) is one level higher than submission (*islām*), and God-wariness (*taqwā*) is one level higher than *īmān*, and certitude (*yaqīn*) is one level higher than *taqwā*. Nothing has been distributed less amongst humanity than *yaqīn*.[23]

5-7.4 Therefore, verse 5 and 6 state that if you had absolute knowledge and conviction about the Hereafter, you would see Hell displayed before you. In other words, those who developed this level of conviction would certainly be able to see the consequence (hellfire) of a life devoted to rivalry in amassing wealth (*al-takāthur*). This is evinced by the double emphasis introduced by the *lām* and double *nūn* in the word *latarawunna* (you will indeed, surely see).

A tradition from Imam Ali (a) states: [Even] if the veils were lifted [for me], my conviction would not be greater.[24]

5-7.5 This 'seeing' would be with the eyes of the heart, as a result of *ʿilm al-yaqīn*, and would occur in this very world; however according to the tone of the verse, it is an insight that people of *takāthur* could not achieve.[25]

---

21 Ṭabāṭabā'ī, *al-Mīzān*, 20/352.

22 Rāghib, *al-Mufradāt*.

23 Kulaynī, *al-Kāfī*, 2/52.

عَنِ الْبَاقِرِ (عَلَيْهِ السَّلَامُ) – إِنَّمَا هُوَ الْإِسْلَامُ وَالْإِيمَانُ فَوْقَهُ بِدَرَجَةٍ، وَالتَّقْوَى فَوْقَ الْإِيمَانِ بِدَرَجَةٍ، وَالْيَقِينُ فَوْقَ التَّقْوَى بِدَرَجَةٍ، وَلَمْ يُقْسَمْ بَيْنَ النَّاسِ شَيْءٌ أَقَلُّ مِنَ الْيَقِينِ.

24 Majlisī, *Biḥār*, 66/209.

عَنْ أَمِيرِ الْمُؤْمِنِينَ (عَلَيْهِ السَّلَامُ) – لَوْ كُشِفَ الْغِطَاءُ مَا ازْدَدْتُ يَقِينًا.

25 Ṭabāṭabā'ī, *al-Mīzān*, 20/352.

5-7.6 '*Then you will surely see it with the eye of certitude.*': [*ʿAyn al-yaqīn* (عَيْنَ الْيَقِينِ, eye of certitude)] denotes seeing directly, and not just with the eyes of the heart. And this higher level of conviction will occur on the Day of Judgement. And the proof of that is the mention of that Day in the next verse.

5-7.7 Some scholars of ethics (*akhlāq*) have defined three levels of *yaqīn*:

i) *ʿIlm al-yaqīn*. This is the certitude and recognition (*maʿrifah*) that comes from deliberation using rational principles. For example, deducing that there is a fire when seeing smoke.

ii) *ʿAyn al-yaqīn*. This is the certitude that comes from direct witnessing and observation. For example, when one sees the fire with their eyes.

iii) *Ḥaqq al-yaqīn*. This is the certitude that comes when one perceives reality as it actually is. For example, the understanding of fire when one is burned by it.[26]

SUMMARY OF THE VERSES

In summary, the verses state that if one could develop knowledge of conviction (*ʿilm al-yaqīn*), one would see, in this world, the hellfire that awaits those who spent their life in *al-takāthur*. And thereafter, see it directly on the Day of Judgement, with a greater level of certainty (*ʿayn al-yaqīn*).

REFLECTIVE LEARNING

Let me reflect on my level of *yaqīn* and conviction in my faith, by answering the following questions:

1. Am I aware that God is seeing everything I do, say and think?
2. Is my *yaqīn* evident in the conviction with which I obey God and avoid sin?
3. Am I constantly aware of the beauty of obedience and the ugliness of disobedience?
4. Do I see Paradise behind every good act, and Hell behind every sin?

[26] Narāqī, *Jāmiʿ al-Saʿādāt*, 1/160.

VERSE 8

ثُمَّ لَتُسْأَلُنَّ يَوْمَئِذٍ عَنِ النَّعِيمِ ﴿٨﴾

Then on that Day, you will certainly be questioned about the bounties. [8]

8.1 [*Latus'alunna* (لَتُسْأَلُنَّ, you will certainly be questioned)]. This questioning will certainly happen, and this is once more strongly emphasized by the *lām* and double *nūn* annexed to the word.

[*al-Naʿīm* (النَّعِيم, bounties)]. *Niʿmah* means bounties and blessings. The form *naʿīm* used here gives a sense of continuity.[27] Therefore, the verse is referring to God's uninterrupted bounties in this world.

8.2 Everything that comes to us from God is a blessing if understood and used correctly. Sometimes, the nature of a situation causes us to misread it and see evil in good and good in evil. Q2:216 states:

وَعَسَىٰ أَنْ تَكْرَهُوا شَيْئًا وَهُوَ خَيْرٌ لَكُمْ وَعَسَىٰ أَنْ
تُحِبُّوا شَيْئًا وَهُوَ شَرٌّ لَكُمْ وَاللَّهُ يَعْلَمُ وَأَنْتُمْ لَا تَعْلَمُونَ

...And it may be that you hate a thing while it is good for you, and it may be that you like a thing while it is bad for you. God knows and you do not know.

8.3 The attitude that every situation is potentially an opportunity to move closer to God and thus we should be thankful at all times, is beautifully illustrated by Imam al-Kazim's (a) words in prison: "O God, You know that I used to ask You to give me free time to worship You. My God, You facilitated that for me and so unto You is my grateful praise."[28]

8.4 This realization is evident in the reply of Lady Zaynab (a) to the taunts of the accursed ʿUbaydullah b. Ziyad. He said to her, "What did you think of God's treatment of your brother and your household?" She replied, "I saw nothing but beauty! Death

---

[27] Muṣṭafawī, *al-Taḥqīq*.

[28] Irbilī, *Kashf al-Ghummah*, 2/232.

وَرُوِيَ بِأَنَّ بَعْضَ عُيُونِ عِيسَى بْنِ جَعْفَرٍ رَفَعَ إِلَيْهِ أَنَّهُ سَمِعَهُ كَثِيرًا يَقُولُ فِي دُعَائِهِ وَهُوَ مَحْبُوسٌ عِنْدَهُ اَللَّهُمَّ إِنَّكَ تَعْلَمُ أَنِّي كُنْتُ أَسْأَلُكَ أَنْ تُفَرِّغَنِي لِعِبَادَتِكَ اَللَّهُمَّ وَقَدْ فَعَلْتَ فَلَكَ الْحَمْدُ.

was written for them, so they hastened to the places of their martyrdom."[29]

8.5 Every bounty is meant to assist man to reach his potential, perfection, and thereby Paradise. It is the usage of these favours from God that will be questioned, and not the actual bounties themselves. And this is the meaning to be understood by the various reports about this verse. For example:

A tradition from Imam Ali (a) states: [The bounties about which one will be questioned are] security, health, and well-being.[30]

In another report, we have a further explanation by Imam al-Baqir (a) about what well-being in the above report means. The Imam (a) said: "[The bounties about which one will be questioned are] security, health, and the guardianship (*wilāyah*) of Ali b. Abu Talib (a)."[31]

8.6 The bounty of *wilāyah* of the *Ahl al-Bayt* (a) is the greatest gift for the guidance of the Muslim. It is through following their authority and guidance that one can best understand one's duty to God; how to know Him, how to correctly worship Him, and how to gain His proximity. In this regard, a tradition from Imam al-Sadiq (a) states: Indeed, God is more Kind and more Honourable than to question you after He has provided you with food and made it legitimate for you to consume. Rather, He will question you about [what you did with] the bounty of Muhammad (s) and his progeny (a).[32] And this is from the meaning of Q28:65:

وَيَوْمَ يُنَادِيهِمْ فَيَقُولُ مَاذَا أَجَبْتُمُ الْمُرْسَلِينَ

And on the Day He shall call them and say: What was the answer that you gave to the messengers?

---

[29] Majlisi, *Biḥār*, 45/116.

قَالَ: فَكَيفَ رَأَيتِ صُنْعَ اللهِ بِأَخِيكِ وَأَهْلِ بَيْتِكِ؟ قَالَتْ: مَا رَأَيْتُ إِلَّا جَمِيلًا. كُتِبَ عَلَيْهِمُ القَتْلُ، فَبَرَزُوا إِلَى مَضَاجِعِهِمْ.

[30] Baḥrānī, *al-Burhān*, 5/750.

عَنْ أَمِيرِ الْمُؤْمِنِينَ (عَلَيْهِ السَّلَامُ) – فِي قَولِ اللهِ تَعَالَى «لَتُسْأَلُنَّ يَوْمَئِذٍ عَنِ النَّعِيمِ» قَالَ: الْأَمْنُ وَالصِّحَّةُ وَالْعَافِيَةُ.

[31] Majlisī, *Biḥār*, 24/54.

عَنِ الْبَاقِرِ (عَلَيْهِ السَّلَامُ) – «لَتُسْأَلُنَّ يَوْمَئِذٍ عَنِ النَّعِيمِ» يَعْنِي الْأَمْنَ وَالصِّحَّةَ وَوِلَايَةَ عَلِيِّ ابْنِ أَبِي طَالِبٍ (عَلَيْهِ السَّلَامُ).

[32] Kulaynī, *al-Kāfī*, 6/280.

عَنِ الصَّادِقِ (عَلَيْهِ السَّلَامُ) – إِنَّ اللهَ أَكْرَمُ وَأَجَلُّ مِنْ أَنْ يُطْعِمَكُمْ طَعَامًا فَيُسَوِّغَكُمُوهُ ثُمَّ يَسْأَلَكُمْ عَنْهُ، وَلَكِنَّهُ أَنْعَمَ عَلَيْكُمْ بِمُحَمَّدٍ وَآلِ مُحَمَّدٍ (صَلَّى اللهُ عَلَيْهِ وَآلِهِ).

SUMMARY OF THE VERSE

The verse states that on that Day, everyone will definitely be questioned about how they used God's countless bounties.

REFLECTIVE LEARNING

Let me reflect on the bounties that God has blessed me with, recognizing that every bounty has the potential to bring me closer to God.

Do I see in each of my life situations an opportunity to move closer to God?

SURAT AL-ʿAṢR
THE TIME (103)

TEXT AND TRANSLATION

سُورَةُ الْعَصْرِ

بِسْمِ اللهِ الرَّحْمٰنِ الرَّحِيمِ

وَالْعَصْرِ ﴿١﴾ إِنَّ الْإِنْسَانَ لَفِي خُسْرٍ ﴿٢﴾ إِلَّا الَّذِينَ آمَنُوا وَعَمِلُوا الصَّالِحَاتِ
وَتَوَاصَوْا بِالْحَقِّ وَتَوَاصَوْا بِالصَّبْرِ ﴿٣﴾

In the name of God, the Beneficent, the Merciful.

[I swear] By time. [1] *Indeed, human beings are certainly in loss.* [2] *Except for those who believe, and do good, and exhort one another to the truth, and exhort one another to steadfastness.* [3]

INTRODUCTION

Surat al-ʿAṣr (103) was the 13th chapter to be revealed. It has only three verses and was revealed in Makka, after Surat al-Inshirāḥ (94).[1] It is named after the oath made by the time (*al-ʿaṣr*) in the opening verse.

The chapter begins with an oath, then declares that all of mankind is in a loss. Thereafter, it lists four traits possessed by the people who are exceptions to this general statement.

The all-encompassing nature of the chapter's contents has led some exegetes to comment that it is a condensed summary of the main messages of the Qur'an.[2]

---

1 Maʿrifat, *ʿUlūm-i Qurʾānī*, p. 90.

2 Ṭabāṭabāʾī, *al-Mīzān*, 20/355.

LINK TO THE PREVIOUS CHAPTER

The previous chapter, Surat al-Takāthur, ended with mention of God's questioning on the Day of Judgement about how His blessings (*al-naʿīm*) were used. Surat al-ʿAṣr begins with an oath by time (*al-ʿaṣr*), which is undoubtedly one of God's greatest blessings to mankind.

The previous chapter also spoke of the distraction caused by abundance, and the error of seeking a successful life by accumulating for the sake of this world. In Surat al-ʿAṣr, there is mention of the overwhelming loss that faces mankind; it presents as a solution four traits that will ensure true success in life.

MERITS OF RECITATION

- A tradition from the Prophet (s) states: Whoever recites this chapter will have steadfastness at the end of his life and will be amongst the people of truth on the Day of Judgement.[3]
- A tradition from Imam al-Sadiq (a) states: Whoever recites Surat al-ʿAṣr in his optional prayers will be resurrected on the Day of Judgement with a radiant face, a smile on his lips, and bright eyes, until he enters Paradise.[4]

EXEGESIS

VERSE 1

وَالْعَصْرِ ﴿١﴾

[I swear] By time. [1]

1.1 The verse begins with the *waw* of oath (*waw al-qasam*). God uses oaths to indicate the profound significance of a phenomenon, and also to emphasize the important connection of the oath with the verses that follow. Here, it is an invitation to the believer to reflect and ponder about both the object of the oath (the constant passage of time) and its subject (that man is at a loss and the four things that

---

[3] Ḥuwayzī, *Nūr al-Thaqalayn*, 5/666.

عَنِ الرَّسُولِ (صَلَّى اللهُ عَلَيْهِ وَآلِهِ) – مَنْ قَرَأَهَا خُتِمَ لَهُ بِالصَّبْرِ وَكَانَ مَعَ أَصْحَابِ الْحَقِّ يَوْمَ الْقِيَامَةِ.

[4] Majlisī, *Biḥār*, 82/39.

عَنِ الصَّادِقِ (عَلَيْهِ السَّلَامُ) – مَنْ قَرَأَ «وَالْعَصْرِ» فِي نَوَافِلِهِ بَعَثَهُ اللهُ يَوْمَ الْقِيَامَةِ مُشْرِقًا وَجْهُهُ ضَاحِكًا سِنُّهُ قَرِيرًا عَيْنُهُ حَتَّى يَدْخُلَ الْجَنَّةَ.

forestall that loss). We have discussed the usage of oaths further in the *tafsīr* of Surat al-Shams (91).

1.2 [*ʿAṣr* (عَصْر, time)] is derived from *ʿaṣara*, which means 'to press, squeeze or wring out'.[5] It has thereafter acquired several meanings related to its original root:

i) Late afternoon. Possibly *al-ʿaṣr* refers to the afternoon because the results of the day's activities are 'wrung out' and their worth is determined at that time. The daylight is slowly dwindling and the time for social activity draws to a close.[6]

   Those who take the oath to be referring to this time of the day, cite as proof instances where God has sworn by other times of the day, such as '*Wa al-ḍuḥā* (by the midday, Q93:1)', or '*Wa al-fajr* (by the dawn, Q89:1)'. Furthermore, these special times of the day, dawn and sunrise, dusk and sunset, are moments of indescribable beauty and grandeur that inspire one to turn to God, being mindful of His Majesty.

ii) Eras and epochs in the course of human history, or specific periods, for example, the *ʿaṣr* of the Prophet (s) or those of his righteous successors. The eras of these preeminent servants of God are full of lessons for humanity to learn from, and so important that God would swear by them.

   A tradition from Imam al-Sadiq (a) states that when he was asked about these verses, he said, "*Al-ʿAṣr* is the era of the advent of the Qāʾim (the Mahdi) (af)."[7] As we have mentioned before, these types of reports are amongst the interpretations (*taʾwīl*) of verses.

iii) Other meanings have also been given for the term: the days of the life of a human being with its highs and lows; the passage of the valuable resource of time that puts a negligent individual at a constant loss; the advent of Islam and the start of the mission of the Prophet (s), the duration of the revelation of the Qurʾan; and the Day of Judgement.[8]

---

[5] Muṣṭafawī, *al-Taḥqīq*.

[6] Muṭahharī,*(Āshnāyī bā Qurʾan)*, *Āthār*, 28/745.

[7] Ṣadūq, *Kamāl al-Dīn*, 2/656.

عَنِ الصَّادِقِ (عَلَيْهِ السَّلَامُ) - سَأَلْتُ الصَّادِقَ (عَلَيْهِ السَّلَامُ) عَنْ قَوْلِ اللهِ عَزَّ وَجَلَّ «وَالْعَصْرِ إِنَّ الْإِنْسَانَ لَفِي خُسْرٍ»، قَالَ (عَلَيْهِ السَّلَامُ): الْعَصْرُ عَصْرُ خُرُوجِ الْقَائِمِ (عَجَّلَ اللهُ تَعَالَى فَرَجَهُ الشَّرِيفَ).

[8] Ṭabāṭabāʾī, *al-Mīzān*, 20/355; Shīrāzī, *Namūneh*, 27/293; Ṭabrasī, *al-Bayān*, 10/815.

However, amongst all these possibilities, the most probable meaning is the reference to the passage of time in the history of mankind, which has witnessed all sorts of human behaviour, and is instructive for future generations.[9]

SUMMARY OF THE VERSE

God swears by time, without restricting its meaning further.

REFLECTIVE LEARNING

The blessing of time is a constantly dwindling resource for each of us. Every breath we take brings us closer to the end of our time on earth.

Am I aware of the urgency of this fact? Let me record my activity on one particular day so that I can reflect on my usage of this invaluable and limited resource.

VERSE 2

إِنَّ الْإِنْسَانَ لَفِي خُسْرٍ ﴿٢﴾

Indeed, human beings are certainly in loss. [2]

2.1 The use of both *innā* and *la* (in *la fī*) emphasizes the absolute certainty of the statement that human beings are in loss. *Inna*, meaning indeed, is used to dispel the doubts of anyone who may question the statement that follows.

2.2 [*Al-Insān* (الْإِنْسَان, man, human beings)] refers to the entire human race in general, and specifically to each and every one within that race.[10]

Insān (truncated from the original word *insiyān*) comes from two roots:

i) *Nisyān*, which means forgetfulness. Man has earned this name because he made a covenant with God, but forgot it. He periodically remembers that he should be doing more, but he soon forgets.

---

[9] Shīrāzī, *Namūneh*, 27/294.

[10] Ṭabrasī, *al-Bayān* 10/815, Ṭabāṭabā'ī, *al-Mīzān*, 20/356.

ii) *Uns,* which means friendliness and close association, because man is capable of forming close relationships and bonds with other creatures and God.[11]

2.3 In Surat al-ʿAṣr, the address is to mankind as *insān,* and not as *al-nās.* We have mentioned the difference between the two terms in the discussion later in the surah.

Insān should be more mindful because he possesses the tools to stop himself from absolute loss, yet he has forgotten his purpose and potential. When the reader reaches this verse, he is reminded to reflect on his own situation, and he is shown the steps needed to extricate himself from loss.

2.4 [*Khusr* (خُسْر, loss)] is derived from *khasira,* and can refer to the loss of an individual himself or the loss he suffers in his dealings. It usually means loss of something that was originally possessed. It is a loss from the original capital and not the profit.

Since the term is used in the indefinite sense (*tankīr*), it gives the impression of the gravity of the loss, indicating that truly, man is in profound loss. Just as the ice-seller watches his capital melt in the sunshine, man helplessly loses the valuable commodity of time with every breath he takes.

And it is possible also that it refers to a type of loss quite different from the loss of prestige and wealth.[12] The Qur'an speaks of how some individuals have lost their human identity itself, and its consequences; Q39:15 states:

فَاعْبُدُوا مَا شِئْتُمْ مِنْ دُونِهِ قُلْ إِنَّ الْخَاسِرِينَ الَّذِينَ خَسِرُوا أَنْفُسَهُمْ
وَأَهْلِيهِمْ يَوْمَ الْقِيَامَةِ أَلَا ذَٰلِكَ هُوَ الْخُسْرَانُ الْمُبِينُ

So, worship what you like besides Him. Say [O Prophet]: Indeed, the losers are those who lose themselves and their families on the Day of Judgement. Surely, that is a clear loss!

2.5 We may acquire possessions, knowledge, and influence in this world, but ultimately there is no gain unless we achieve something

---

11 Ibn Manẓūr, *Lisān al-ʿArab.*

12 Ṭabāṭabāʾī, *al-Mīzān,* 20/356.

that can be transferred with us when we die, and move to the next phases of our existence.

A tradition from Imam al-Hadi (a) states: The world is a marketplace in which some make a profit and others make a loss.[13]

2.6 Loss and failure is an allusion to the normal attitude of human beings, who get engrossed in the allure and challenge of worldly life to an extent that they forget its transient nature. Every moment and every day reduces their most valuable asset, which is their lifespan.

2.7 Furthermore, the passage of time gradually transforms youth, health, strength, and self-reliance to old age, illness, infirmity, and dependence. Finally, at the threshold of death, man's perception of loss and success changes, sometimes when it is too late.

Other faculties also deteriorate, such as memory, the ability to think, patience, and so on. This is the fate of everyone who lives to an old age. Q36:68 states:

وَمَنْ نُعَمِّرْهُ نُنَكِّسْهُ فِي الْخَلْقِ

And to whomever We grant long life,
We reduce him in constitution...

All these factors signify the importance of the oath that God makes at the beginning of the surah: *By time!*

2.8 It is reported that in a supplication that he would recite on every day of the month of Rajab, Imam al-Sadiq (a) stated: [O Allah!] Those who prepare for a journey to other than You have failed, and those who turn to anyone except You are losers.[14]

2.9 Loss here refers to the entirety of man's life, which does not end with his death in this world. The phase of his worldly existence is a test, the results of which will determine his fortunes in the next phases of his existence, in *barzakh*, and in the Hereafter. Therefore, unless he is part of the exceptions mentioned in the next verse, his life in all realms of his existence will be a failure and loss.

---

[13] Ḥarrānī, *Tuḥaf al-ʿUqūl*, p. 483.

عَنِ الْهَادِي (عَلَيْهِ السَّلَامُ) – الدُّنْيَا سُوقٌ رَبِحَ فِيهَا قَوْمٌ وَخَسِرَ آخَرُونَ.

[14] Qummī, *Mafātīḥ al-Jinān, Daily supplications for the month of Rajab.*

خَابَ الْوَافِدُونَ عَلَى غَيْرِكَ، وَخَسِرَ الْمُتَعَرِّضُونَ إِلَّا لَكَ.

DISCUSSION: THE DIFFERENT WAYS MANKIND IS ADDRESSED IN THE QUR'AN

Mankind has been addressed in various ways in the Qur'an: *Insān* (human being), *Nās* (mankind), and Banu Adam (children of Adam). He has also been called *Bashar* (man), but not addressed directly with this term. The Qur'anic style of addressing mankind directly is one of its beautiful qualities. A tradition from Imam al-Sadiq (a) states: The sweetness in the personal Divine address [to the believers] dispels the weariness and toil of worship.[15]

Although these different terms of address to mankind are sometimes considered to be synonymous, the Qur'an uses them with precise shades of meaning, as follows:[16]

i) *Insān* is used in reference to the human qualities of individuals, when intending to address their soul, conscience, and unique potential, and in short, their humanity.

ii) *Nās* is used when God wants to address mankind in its entirety, to indicate that the statement being made is not confined to believers, but is relevant to every human being.

iii) Banu Adam is a reference to the common qualities amongst human beings due to their shared ancestry. The address has come only five times in the Qur'an, four of which are in Surat al-Aʿrāf, within ten verses that are talking about the creation of Prophet Adam (a) from dust, and as an extension, about all human beings in general. These verses warn of the declared enmity of Shaytan towards them all.

iv) *Bashar* is another word used for man in the Qur'an. It is very similar to *insān*, but refers to the exterior form and features of the human being, whereas *insān* includes his inner merits and potentials.[17] So, for example, when the Prophet (s) is instructed to recite Q18:110, he is referring to his outward form and not in his inner excellence:

قُلْ إِنَّمَا أَنَا بَشَرٌ مِثْلُكُمْ

---

[15] Ṭabrasī, *al-Bayān*, 2/490.

عَنِ الصَّادِقِ (عَلَيْهِ السَّلَامُ) – لَذَّةُ مَا فِي النِّدَاءِ أَزَالَتْ تَعَبَ الْعِبَادَةِ وَالْعَنَاءِ.

[16] Summarized from: *Miṣbāh* Yazdī, *Insān Shināsī dar Qur'an*, pp. 35-50.

[17] Rāghib, *al-Mufradāt*.

Say: I am only a man like you...

SUMMARY OF THE VERSE

In summary, God warns in this verse that every human being is [potentially] in a loss.

REFLECTIVE LEARNING

A tradition from Imam Ali (a) states: The breath of a man is a footstep towards his death.[18] And if these moments are not filled with useful activity, then man is indeed in great and grievous loss.

Let me reflect on specific people whom I consider to be successful, thereby comparing my criteria for success and loss with that of God.

VERSE 3

إِلَّا الَّذِينَ آمَنُوا وَعَمِلُوا الصَّالِحَاتِ وَتَوَاصَوْا بِالْحَقِّ وَتَوَاصَوْا بِالصَّبْرِ ﴿٣﴾

Except for those who believe, and do good, and exhort one another to the truth, and exhort one another to steadfastness. [3]

3.1 Four traits are mentioned as the qualities of the individuals who are exceptions to the all-encompassing statement of loss in the previous verse. The first is sincere faith (*al-īmān*), and in fact, the other three traits all stem from it and are a consequence of it.[19] It is sincere faith that will inspire an individual to perform acts of righteousness, and encourage members of society towards mutual loyalty to the truth and to steadfastness.

3.2 [*Alladhīna āmanū* (الَّذِينَ آمَنُوا, those who believe)]: *Īmān* comes from *amana*, which has two similar meanings, faithfulness and belief, and peace and security.[20] Indeed, a person will only truly have belief in something when it settles in the heart and gives it peace.

Īmān (belief, faith) is a central theme in the Qur'an. It refers to belief that once professed, becomes established in the heart and is

---

[18] *Nahj al-Balāghah*, saying no. 74.

نَفَسُ الْمَرْءِ خُطَاهُ إِلَى أَجَلِهِ.

[19] Shīrāzī, *Namūneh*, 27/299.

[20] Ibn Manẓūr, *Lisān al-ʿArab*.

manifested in action. Amongst the features of *īmān* that have been mentioned in the Qurʾan and hadith is belief in an all-Merciful and all-Wise God, belief in a religion and philosophy of life that will allow the soul to flourish, belief in the messengers, guides, and books that have all been sent to instruct and exemplify to mankind, and belief in accountability and life in the Hereafter. Those who have this type of belief are the *muʾminūn*, a group honoured by God's special mercy in this world, and especially in the Hereafter. Q7:156 states:

وَرَحْمَتِي وَسِعَتْ كُلَّ شَيْءٍ فَسَأَكْتُبُهَا لِلَّذِينَ يَتَّقُونَ
وَيُؤْتُونَ الزَّكَاةَ وَالَّذِينَ هُمْ بِآيَاتِنَا يُؤْمِنُونَ

And My mercy embraces all things; therefore I shall ordain it [especially] for those who are God-wary, give the poor rate (zakat), *and believe in Our signs.*

3.3 *Īmān* can be of two types:

1. Faith that is firm and established (*al-īmān al-mustaqarr*). Just like a mature tree whose roots are strongly established, this kind of faith cannot be shaken easily, and
2. Faith that is transient and fleeting (*al-īmān al-mustawdaʿ*). Just like a rented house, this belief, is temporary and easily changed.

According to the narrations, this is one interpretation (*taʾwīl*) of Q6:98 where these two terms have been used:

وَهُوَ الَّذِي أَنْشَأَكُمْ مِنْ نَفْسٍ وَاحِدَةٍ فَمُسْتَقَرٌّ وَمُسْتَوْدَعٌ

And it is He Who brought you forth from one soul, then [you are] in an established state, or a transient one...

About this verse, a tradition states that Imam Ali (a) said, "The established (*mustaqarr*) refers to people who have been granted unshakeable faith which is established in their hearts, and the transient (*mustawdaʿ*) refers to those who were granted faith which was later removed from them."[21]

[21] ʿAyyāshī, *Tafsīr*, 1/372.
عَنْ أَمِيرِ الْمُؤْمِنِينَ (عَلَيْهِ السَّلَامُ) – فَالْمُسْتَقَرُّ قَوْمٌ يُعْطَوْنَ الْإِيمَانَ وَيَسْتَقِرُّ فِي قُلُوبِهِمْ وَالْمُسْتَوْدَعُ قَوْمٌ يُعْطَوْنَ الْإِيمَانَ ثُمَّ يُسْلَبُونَهُ.

3.4 [*ʿAmilū al-ṣāliḥāt*, (عَمِلُوا الصَّالِحَاتِ, do good actions)]: Good actions (*al-aʿmāl al-ṣāliḥāt*) here is a reference to those acts that have been legislated in the *sharīʿah* to facilitate the perfection of the human soul. These acts are a natural consequence of sincere belief and in fact, only worthy because of it.[22] Because of this, the two terms *īmān* and *al-aʿmāl al-ṣāliḥāt* are used together throughout the Qur'an.

3.5 Due to his free will, man is in control of his ultimate fate, and this fate is inseparably linked to his faith and actions. Coupled with faith, good actions will earn him eternal felicity and bad actions will bring damnation. And the value of good actions are not determined by their number, but by the sincerity of their intentions. A tradition from Imam Ali (a) states: A [small] act that is due to God-wariness (*taqwā*) is not insignificant. How can it be insignificant when it is accepted [by God]?[23]

3.6 *Al-ṣāliḥāt* has been mentioned here in the plural form, and the '*al*' adds the meaning of generality. Therefore the second trait that distinguishes those who are not in loss is the habit of performing every good deed, big and small, and not being content with just a few of them.[24]

3.7 Among the best of good actions is the regular performance of the five daily prayers. A tradition from Imam Ali (a) states: *Al-aʿmāl al-ṣāliḥāt* refers to the five obligatory daily prayers, because God, the Almighty has stated in Q7:170:

وَالَّذِينَ يُمَسِّكُونَ بِالْكِتَابِ وَأَقَامُوا الصَّلَاةَ إِنَّا لَا نُضِيعُ أَجْرَ الْمُصْلِحِينَ

And as for those who hold fast to the Book and establish the prayer – indeed, We will not allow the reward of those who do good (muṣlihīn) *to go to waste.*[25]

3.8 In brief, *al-aʿmāl al-ṣāliḥāt* can be defined as good actions that are:

i) accompanied by faith,

ii) done with a conscious intention to attain Gods pleasure and proximity,

---

22 Muṭahharī,*(Āshnāyī bā Qur'an), Āthār*, 28/753.

23 Kulaynī, *al-Kāfī*, 2/75.

كَانَ أَمِيرُ الْمُؤْمِنِينَ صَلَوَاتُ اللهِ عَلَيْهِ يَقُولُ: لَا يَقِلُّ عَمَلٌ مَعَ تَقْوَى وَكَيْفَ يَقِلُّ مَا يُتَقَبَّلُ؟

24 Shīrāzī, *Namūneh*, 27/300.

25 Rāzī, *Rawḍ al-Jinān*, 1/169.

iii) based on the teachings of the Qur'an, the Prophet (s), and the Imams (a).

3.9 In addition to listing good actions, there are many narrations that talk about the worth of actions in general terms. Two examples are:

A tradition from Imam Ali (a) states: Avoid every action which if the doer was asked about, he would deny doing it or would have to apologize for it.[26]

A tradition from Imam al-Sadiq (a) states: A good action does not reach perfection unless it has three features: it is done without delay, it is considered insignificant, and it is done in secret.[27]

3.10 The twin traits of *īmān* and *al-aʿmāl al-ṣāliḥāt* serve as a compensation for man's misdeeds. Furthermore, God rewards their good actions in the same measure as the instance when they performed it best. Q29:7 states:

وَالَّذِينَ آمَنُوا وَعَمِلُوا الصَّالِحَاتِ لَنُكَفِّرَنَّ عَنْهُمْ سَيِّئَاتِهِمْ
وَلَنَجْزِيَنَّهُمْ أَحْسَنَ الَّذِي كَانُوا يَعْمَلُونَ

And [as for] those who believe and do good, We shall most certainly do away with their evil deeds and We shall most certainly reward them according to the best of what they did.

3.11 Therefore, *īmān* is the catalyst for the transformation for an individual; the one who possesses it reflects the light of his faith in his attitude, conduct and words. Faith is like a bright lamp inside a room which not only illuminates the room itself, but attracts the attention of every passer-by and benefits them also.

3.12 However, *īmān* and *al-aʿmāl al-ṣāliḥāt* cannot exist in a society unless efforts are made to encourage one another to adhere to the truth and righteousness, and thereafter helping one another to have fortitude and steadfastness in maintaining that environment.

For this reason, these two additional traits are vital to secure man from loss.

---

[26] Majlisī, *Biḥār*, 33/508.

عَنْ أَمِيرِ الْمُؤْمِنِينَ (عَلَيْهِ السَّلَامُ) – اِحْذَرْ كُلَّ عَمَلٍ إِذَا سُئِلَ عَنْهُ صَاحِبُهُ أَنْكَرَهُ أَوِ اعْتَذَرَ مِنْهُ.

[27] Raḍī, *Khaṣā'is al-A'immah*, p. 100.

عَنِ الصَّادِقِ (عَلَيْهِ السَّلَامُ) – لَا يَتِمُّ الْمَعْرُوفُ إِلَّا بِثَلَاثٍ: تَعْجِيلِهِ وَتَصْغِيرِهِ وَتَسْتِيرِهِ.

3.13 [*Tawāṣaw* (تَوَاصَوْا, exhort one another)] is derived from *tawāṣī*, meaning to exhort, encourage and advise one another.[28] However this requires individuals to know the truth (*ḥaqq*), to have correct belief (*īmān*), to have steadfastness (*ṣabr*) and do good deeds (*al-aʿmāl al-ṣāliḥāt*) themselves, while encouraging others as well.

3.14 [*Al-Ḥaqq* (الْحَق, truth)] means something that is a fact which conforms to reality and is devoid of any falsehood.[29] It also means an act based on wisdom, as stated in Q15:85:

وَمَا خَلَقْنَا السَّمَاوَاتِ وَالْأَرْضَ وَمَا بَيْنَهُمَا إِلَّا بِالْحَقِّ

And We have not created the heavens and the earth and what is between them except in truth (ḥaqq)...

Al-ḥaqq also means that which is fair and just, as stated in Q38:84,85:

قَالَ فَالْحَقُّ وَالْحَقَّ أَقُولُ ﴿٨٤﴾ لَأَمْلَأَنَّ جَهَنَّمَ مِنْكَ وَمِمَّنْ تَبِعَكَ مِنْهُمْ أَجْمَعِينَ

[God] said, "The truth (al-ḥaqq) *[is my oath], and the truth* (al-ḥaqq) *I say, [that] I will surely fill hell with you (Shaytan) and those who follow you, all together.*

Of course, the ultimate Truth is God, and Q22:6 states:

ذَٰلِكَ بِأَنَّ اللَّهَ هُوَ الْحَقُّ

That is because God is the Truth (al-Ḥaqq)...

3.15 The verse under review thus means encouraging one another to seek the truth and to accept it. It means being careful of the rights of others and staying away from falsehood and injustice, and urging others to do the same.

3.16 Paying attention to the interests of society by guiding one another has been enjoined on the Muslim community as an obligatory duty (*al-amr biʾl maʿrūf* and *al-nahy ʿaniʾl munkar*). Q3:104 states:

وَلْتَكُنْ مِنْكُمْ أُمَّةٌ يَدْعُونَ إِلَى الْخَيْرِ وَيَأْمُرُونَ بِالْمَعْرُوفِ
وَيَنْهَوْنَ عَنِ الْمُنْكَرِ وَأُولَٰئِكَ هُمُ الْمُفْلِحُونَ

---

28 Rāghib, *al-Mufradāt*.

29 Ibn Manẓūr, *Lisān al-ʿArab*.

And let there arise from you a group of people calling to goodness; enjoining what is right and forbidding what is wrong. They are the ones who will be successful.

3.17 In some reports, *tawāṣaw biʾl ḥaqq* has been explained as living a Godly life, and at the time of death, encouraging one's family and heirs to do the same. And also encouraging them not to leave the world except on the path of monotheism and servanthood.[30] The Qur'an quotes this practice by Prophet Yaʿqub (a) in Q2:133:

أَمْ كُنْتُمْ شُهَدَاءَ إِذْ حَضَرَ يَعْقُوبَ الْمَوْتُ إِذْ قَالَ لِبَنِيهِ مَا تَعْبُدُونَ مِنْ بَعْدِي
قَالُوا نَعْبُدُ إِلَٰهَكَ وَإِلَٰهَ آبَائِكَ إِبْرَاهِيمَ وَإِسْمَاعِيلَ وَإِسْحَاقَ
إِلَٰهًا وَاحِدًا وَنَحْنُ لَهُ مُسْلِمُونَ

Were you witnesses when death approached Yaʿqub, when he asked his sons, "What will you worship after me?" They replied, "We will worship your God and the God of your fathers, Ibrahim, Ismaʿil, and Ishaq - one God. And we have submitted to Him."

3.18 [*Tawāṣaw biʾl ṣabr* (تَوَاصَوْا بِالصَّبْرِ, exhort one another to steadfastness)]: *Ṣabr* means steadfastness on the covenant made to God, and helping each other through the hardships and losses that invariably befall those who adhere to the truth and support it.[31]

3.19 A tradition from the Prophet (s) states: Steadfastness (*ṣabr*) is required in three instances: in the face of tribulations, in the path of obedience, and against the urge to sin.[32]

3.20 The last two traits are an integral part of righteous acts (*al-aʿmāl al-ṣāliḥāt*), and are possibly highlighted because social responsibility and care are an important duty of a human being. They may have been mentioned because the group of people who are not in loss are in the minority. Therefore, it is all the more important to work with other believers for mutual support and success.

3.21 The narrations contain some particular instances of the interpretation (*taʾwīl*) of these verses. Two are cited below:

---

[30] Ṭabrasī, *al-Bayān*, 10/815.

[31] Muṭahharī, (*Āshnāyī bā Qurʾan*), *Āthār*, 28/768.

[32] Kulaynī, *al-Kāfī*, 2/91.

عَنِ الرَّسُولِ (صَلَّى اللهُ عَلَيْهِ وَآلِهِ) – الصَّبْرُ ثَلاثَةٌ: صَبْرٌ عِنْدَ الْمُصِيبَةِ، وَصَبْرٌ عَلَى الطَّاعَةِ وَصَبْرٌ عَنِ الْمَعْصِيَةِ.

1. The *Sunni* scholar al-Ḥaskānī reports that the Prophet (s) said, "The words of God, the Almighty, '*By time. Indeed, mankind is certainly in loss*' refer to Abu Jahl b. Hisham. And His words, '*Except for those who believe, and do good, and exhort one another to the truth, and exhort one another to steadfastness*' refer to Ali (a) and his partisans (*shīʿa*)."[33]
2. A tradition from Imam al-Sadiq (a) states: God excluded the chosen ones from His creation when He said, '*Indeed mankind is in loss, except for those who believe*', because of their belief in the authority (*wilāyah*) of the Commander of the Faithful (a). As for, '*They enjoin each other to the truth*', it refers to advising their offspring and those who follow them to accept the *wilāyah*, and '*They enjoin each other to steadfastness*', means that they advise them to remain steadfast on this path.[34]

SUMMARY OF THE VERSE

In summary, the verse clearly declares that the only way to salvation from complete loss lies in basing one's life on four pillars:

1. A sound faith in God, obedience to His Messenger (s), and belief in the accounting of actions on the Day of Judgement.
2. Performing acts of virtue and goodness, for the pleasure of God in the way He tells us to.
3. Encouraging others to adopt the path towards the truth after recognizing the truth, and practising it oneself.
4. Encouraging others to remain steadfast on the path of the truth, by word and example.

[33] Ḥaskānī, *Shawāhid al-Tanzīl*, 2/482.

عَنِ الرَّسُولِ (صَلَّى اللهُ عَلَيْهِ وَآلِهِ) - فِي قَوْلِ اللهِ عَزَّ وَجَلَّ: «وَالْعَصْرِ إِنَّ الْإِنْسَانَ لَفِي خُسْرٍ» [هُوَ] أَبُو جَهْلِ ابْنُ هِشَامٍ «إِلَّا الَّذِينَ آمَنُوا وَعَمِلُوا الصَّالِحَاتِ وَتَوَاصَوْا بِالْحَقِّ وَتَوَاصَوْا بِالصَّبْرِ» [قَالَ: هُمْ] عَلِيٌّ وَشِيعَتُهُ.

[34] Furāt al-Kūfī, *Tafsīr*, p. 607.

عَنِ الصَّادِقِ (عَلَيْهِ السَّلَامُ) - فَقَالَ اسْتَثْنَى أَهْلَ صَفْوَتِهِ مِنْ خَلْقِهِ حَيْثُ قَالَ «إِنَّ الْإِنْسَانَ لَفِي خُسْرٍ إِلَّا الَّذِينَ آمَنُوا» يَقُولُ آمَنُوا بِوَلَايَةِ أَمِيرِ الْمُؤْمِنِينَ (عَلَيْهِ السَّلَامُ) «وَتَوَاصَوْا بِالْحَقِّ» ذُرِّيَاتُهُمْ وَمَنْ خَلَّفُوا بِالْوِلَايَةِ وَتَوَاصَوْا بِهَا وَصَبَرُوا عَلَيْهَا.

REFLECTIVE LEARNING

Let me reflect on whether:

1. My good actions (*al-aʿmāl al-ṣāliḥāt*) are due to my belief (*īmān*), or due to the expectation of society, family, and friends?
2. I am in regular contact with fellow believers where we encourage each other to keep to the path of truth and steadfastness?

SURAT AL-HUMAZAH
THE SLANDERER (104)

TEXT AND TRANSLATION

سُورَةُ الْهُمَزَةِ

بِسْمِ اللَّهِ الرَّحْمَٰنِ الرَّحِيمِ

وَيْلٌ لِكُلِّ هُمَزَةٍ لُمَزَةٍ ﴿١﴾ الَّذِي جَمَعَ مَالًا وَعَدَّدَهُ ﴿٢﴾ يَحْسَبُ أَنَّ مَالَهُ أَخْلَدَهُ
﴿٣﴾ كَلَّا لَيُنْبَذَنَّ فِي الْحُطَمَةِ ﴿٤﴾ وَمَا أَدْرَاكَ مَا الْحُطَمَةُ ﴿٥﴾ نَارُ اللَّهِ الْمُوقَدَةُ
﴿٦﴾ الَّتِي تَطَّلِعُ عَلَى الْأَفْئِدَةِ ﴿٧﴾ إِنَّهَا عَلَيْهِمْ مُؤْصَدَةٌ ﴿٨﴾ فِي عَمَدٍ مُمَدَّدَةٍ ﴿٩﴾

In the name of God, the Beneficent, the Merciful.

Woe to every slanderer and defamer! [1] *The one who amasses wealth and [continually] counts it.* [2] *He thinks that his wealth has made him immortal.* [3] *Not at all! He will certainly be thrown into the Crusher.* [4] *And what will make you realize what the Crusher is?* [5] *[It is] the fire of God, kindled.* [6] *Which rises above the hearts.* [7] *Indeed, it will be vaulted over them.* [8] *In extended columns.* [9]

INTRODUCTION

Surat al-Humazah (104) was the 32nd chapter to be revealed.[1] It has nine verses and was revealed in Makka, after Surat al-Qiyāmah (75). It is named after the mention of the slanderer (*humazah*) in the first verse.

The surah warns of the terrible punishment that awaits those who spread scandal and gossip. It mentions people who are self-conceited, amassing wealth and delighting in counting it, and imagining that they will live forever. However, only a dreadful place in hellfire awaits them.

---

1 Maʿrifat, *ʿUlūm-i Qurʾānī*, p. 90.

LINK TO THE PREVIOUS CHAPTER

In the previous chapter, Surat al-ʿAṣr, there was mention about the fact that human beings are heading for a loss unless they possess four qualities. In Surat al-Humazah, an example of the conduct that earns individuals loss and severe chastisement in the next world is mentioned.

OCCASION OF REVELATION

A group of exegetes are of the opinion that the verses of this chapter were revealed about al-Walīd b. al-Mughīrah, the chief of the Banu Makhzūm clan of the Quraysh. He was one of the wealthiest men of Makka, and his trading caravan numbered over one hundred camels. He was intensely hostile to the Prophet (s) and the message of Islam and has been indirectly condemned in several verses of the Qur'an. Al-Walīd would spread gossip and slander about the Prophet (s) behind his back and would speak to him in a mocking and scornful manner whenever he met him.

Other exegetes have mentioned that the verses condemn the similar conduct of other wealthy leaders of the polytheists such as, al-Akhnas b. Shurayq, Umayyah b. Khalaf, and al-ʿĀṣ b. Wā'il.[2]

However, even if these reports give the occasion of revelation, the verses are of a general nature and are relevant to all those who possess such qualities.[3]

MERITS OF RECITATION

- A tradition from the Prophet (s) states: Whoever recites this chapter will have a reward equal to the number of every person who mocked Muhammad (s) and his companions. And if it is recited over the eyes, it will benefit them.[4]
- A tradition from Imam al-Sadiq (a) states: Whoever recites Surat al-Humazah in his obligatory prayers will be kept away from poverty

[2] Ṭabrasī, *al-Bayān*, 10/818.

[3] Shīrāzī, *Namūneh*, 27/308.

[4] Baḥrānī, *al-Burhān*, 5/755.

عَنِ الرَّسُولِ (صَلَّى اللهُ عَلَيْهِ وَآلِهِ) - مَنْ قَرَأَ هَذِهِ السُّورَةَ كَانَ لَهُ مِنَ الْأَجْرِ بِعَدَدِ مَنِ اسْتَهْزَأَ بِمُحَمَّدٍ (صَلَّى اللهُ عَلَيْهِ وَآلِهِ) وَأَصْحَابِهِ، وَإِنْ قُرِئَتْ عَلَى الْعَيْنِ نَفَعَهَا.

by God. Its recitation will bring about increased sustenance and protect the reciter from an ignominious death.[5]

EXEGESIS

VERSE 1

وَيْلٌ لِكُلِّ هُمَزَةٍ لُمَزَةٍ ﴿١﴾

Woe to every slanderer and defamer! [1]

1.1 [*Waylun* (وَيْلٌ, woe)] is a word that denotes condemnation for evil or wrongful conduct. This is one of two surahs (the other being Surat al-Muṭaffifīn) that begins with this stern rebuke. It also includes a sense of imprecation (*la'nah*) against the doer, meaning, 'may they be deprived of God's mercy'. It also refers to a place in Hell where the person condemned in this manner will be cast.[6]

In this verse, the divine condemnation is for slandering and defaming.

1.2 A tradition from Imam al-Baqir (a) states: God has not condemned anyone except a disbeliever with the term *wayl*. God, the Exalted, has stated, '*So woe to the disbelievers - from the scene of a tremendous Day*' (Q19:37).[7] From this tradition it can be deduced that slandering and defaming is a manifestation of disbelief (*kufr*).

1.3 [*Likulli* (لِكُلِّ, to every)]. This makes the condemnation universal, including everyone who displays the evil habits that are described in the chapter.

1.4 [*Humazah* (هُمَزَة, slanderer)] is derived from *hamaza* which means to break, because this behaviour damages the reputation of others.[8] Here, it is used as an active participle in the intensive form '*fu'alah*' which indicates excessiveness, or habit. It refers to someone who,

---

[5] Ṣadūq, *Thawāb al-A'māl*, p. 126.

عَنِ الصَّادِقِ (عَلَيْهِ السَّلَامُ) – مَنْ قَرَأَ «وَيْلٌ لِكُلِّ هُمَزَةٍ لُمَزَةٍ» فِي فَرَائِضِهِ أَبْعَدَ اللهُ عَنْهُ الْفَقْرَ وَجَلَبَ عَلَيْهِ الرِّزْقَ وَيَدْفَعُ عَنْهُ مِيتَةَ السُّوءِ.

[6] Rāghib, *al-Mufradāt.*

[7] Kulaynī, *al-Kāfī*, 2/28.

عَنْ أَبِي جَعْفَرٍ (عَلَيْهِ السَّلَامُ) – وَلَمْ يَجْعَلِ الْوَيْلَ لِأَحَدٍ حَتَّى يُسَمِّيَهُ كَافِرًا. قَالَ اللهُ عَزَّ وَجَلَّ «فَوَيْلٌ لِلَّذِينَ كَفَرُوا مِنْ مَشْهَدِ يَوْمٍ عَظِيمٍ».

[8] Ibid, 27/309.

for no legitimate reason, backbites others, seeks out their faults, and criticises the conduct of people even when what they have done is not wrong.[9]

1.5 The practice is particularly despised because it destroys the reputation of individuals and breaks up the cohesion in society.[10] In verses Q68:10-12, God mentions the slanderer in the following words:

وَلَا تُطِعْ كُلَّ حَلَّافٍ مَهِينٍ ﴿١٠﴾ هَمَّازٍ مَشَّاءٍ بِنَمِيمٍ ﴿١١﴾
مَنَّاعٍ لِلْخَيْرِ مُعْتَدٍ أَثِيمٍ

And do not follow [the words of] every immoral, habitual oath-taker. A slanderer, going about with malicious gossip. A preventer of good, transgressing, and sinful.

1.6 [*Lumazah* (لُمَزَة, defamer)] is derived from *lamaza* meaning to defame and find fault. It is similar in meaning to *humazah*, with the difference that *humazah* refers to someone who insults people openly, while *lumazah* refers to the one who does it behind their back.[11]

1.7 The practice of defaming others (*lamz*) is forbidden in the Qur'an. Q49:11 states:

وَلَا تَلْمِزُوا أَنْفُسَكُمْ وَلَا تَنَابَزُوا بِالْأَلْقَابِ

Do not defame one another, nor call each other by [offensive] nicknames...

1.8 The person who behaves in this manner reveals his own weakness and insecurity just as the arrogance of a haughty person indicates that he has forgotten his own vulnerability. A tradition from the Prophet (s) states: Shall I inform you of the worst among you? They are the ones who move to slander others, cause division between friends, and seek out faults in decent people.[12]

---

[9] Ṭabāṭabā'ī, *al-Mīzān*, 20/358; Ṭabrasī, *al-Bayān*, 10/817.

[10] Shīrāzī, *Namūneh*, 27/309.

[11] Ibid, 27/310.

[12] Kulaynī, *al-Kāfī*, 2/369.

عَنِ الرَّسُولِ (صَلَّى اللهُ عَلَيْهِ وَآلِهِ) – أَلَا أُنَبِّئُكُمْ بِشِرَارِكُمْ؟ قَالُوا بَلَى يَا رَسُولَ اللهِ (صَلَّى اللهُ عَلَيْهِ وَآلِهِ)، قَالَ: الْمَشَّاؤُونَ بِالنَّمِيمَةِ، الْمُفَرِّقُونَ بَيْنَ الْأَحِبَّةِ، الْبَاغُونَ لِلْبُرَآءِ الْمَعَايِبَ.

SUMMARY OF THE VERSE

The verse condemns everyone who slanders and defames others. It does not allow any excuse or justification for such actions.

REFLECTIVE LEARNING

After seeing how severely God curses such people, let me cast a critical look at my own attitude.

Let me reflect whether I am scornful of others and speak ill of them, in their presence or especially behind their back? Do I participate in gatherings where this happens, without comment or guilt?

VERSE 2

الَّذِي جَمَعَ مَالًا وَعَدَّدَهُ ﴿٢﴾

The one who amasses wealth and [continually] counts it. [2]

2.1 The slander and disdain of others that is mentioned in the previous verse often stems from the arrogance that comes with continually amassing wealth, hoarding it, not spending it on the needy, and being obsessed by it.[13]

2.2 [*Jamaʿa* (جَمَعَ, amassed)]. Presented here in the past tense, it means that he spent his entire life gathering wealth. Some exegetes have said that it denotes hoarding wealth.[14]

[*Māl* (مَال, wealth)] here refers to worldly possessions and wealth. And the usage of the term in its indefinite form is an allusion to the worthlessness of this pursuit for its own sake. Despite his obsession with wealth, the individual can only ultimately use a small fraction of it that he requires for his basic needs.[15] In the end, he will depart from this world empty-handed.

[*ʿAddada* (عَدَّدَهُ, count)] is derived from *ʿadada*, and means to count or calculate. It is used here in the second, intensive, form of the verb,

---

[13] Shīrāzī, *Namūneh*, 27/311.

[14] Ṭabāṭabā'ī, *al-Mīzān*, 20/359.

[15] Ibid.

and means to count constantly.[16] For such a person, wealth ceases to be a means to a noble objective, but becomes the objective itself.[17]

2.3 Such an obsession with wealth makes one forget the real purpose of life and ultimately leads to perdition. About the wealth of the pharaoh and his people when they were drowned, Q44:25-28 state:

كَمْ تَرَكُوا مِنْ جَنَّاتٍ وَعُيُونٍ ﴿٢٥﴾ وَزُرُوعٍ وَمَقَامٍ كَرِيمٍ ﴿٢٦﴾
وَنَعْمَةٍ كَانُوا فِيهَا فَاكِهِينَ ﴿٢٧﴾ كَذَٰلِكَ وَأَوْرَثْنَاهَا قَوْمًا آخَرِينَ

How many gardens and water springs they left behind.
And fields of crops and grand places.
And pleasant things in which they used to take delight!
Thus [was their end], and We gave them as inheritance to others.

Their wealth and comforts did not avail them. It distanced them from God and the remembrance of the Hereafter. They could not send forth the fruits of their wealth, and God gave it to others. Q69:28-29 quotes the despairing cry of such rich and powerful individuals on the Day of Judgement:

مَا أَغْنَىٰ عَنِّي مَالِيَهْ ﴿٢٨﴾ هَلَكَ عَنِّي سُلْطَانِيَهْ

My wealth has not availed me! Gone from me is my authority!

2.4 About the amassing of wealth, a tradition from Imam al-Ridha (a) states: [Great] wealth does not gather in one place except because of five qualities: intense miserliness, lengthy aspirations, overwhelming greed, the breaking of family ties, and preference of this world over the Hereafter.[18]

2.5 It is reported that Imam al-Sadiq (a) was asked by a companion, "May my father and mother be ransomed for you! Give me some advice." The Imam (a) replied, "When God, the Almighty, has guaranteed sustenance, then what is the point of being concerned about it? And if sustenance has been pre-allocated, then what is the point of greed? And if the Day of Accounting is a certainty, then

---

16 Rāzī, *Mafātīḥ al-Ghayb*, 32/284.

17 Shīrāzī, *Namūneh*, 27/311.

18 Ṣadūq, *al-Khiṣāl*, 1/282.

عَنِ الرِّضَا (عَلَيْهِ السَّلَامُ) – لَا يَجْتَمِعُ الْمَالُ إِلَّا بِخِصَالٍ خَمْسٍ: بِبُخْلٍ شَدِيدٍ، وَأَمَلٍ طَوِيلٍ، وَحِرْصٍ غَالِبٍ، وَقَطِيعَةِ الرَّحِمِ، وَإِيثَارِ الدُّنْيَا عَلَى الْآخِرَةِ.

what is the point of amassing [wealth]? And if God's replacement [for contributed wealth] is assured, then what is the point of miserliness?"[19]

SUMMARY OF THE VERSE

The verse condemns those who constantly amass wealth and calculate their financial worth and look down on others based on possessions.[20]

REFLECTIVE LEARNING

Let me reflect on my own attitude towards the wealth I possess. Am I in pursuit of wealth for its own sake, or do I see it as an opportunity to gain God's pleasure by spending it in His way?

VERSE 3

يَحْسَبُ أَنَّ مَالَهُ أَخْلَدَهُ ﴿٣﴾

He thinks that his wealth has made him immortal. [3]

3.1 [*Akhladahu* (أَخْلَدَهُ, has made him immortal)] is derived from *khalada* meaning to be permanent and perpetual. Here it is used in the past tense, although it denotes the future (*yakhludu*), due to the present tense verb *yaḥsabu* (he thinks).[21] The verse means that this person imagines that due to his great wealth, his remembrance will remain forever. Or he behaves in this world as if he will live forever.[22]

3.2 It is true that man has been created to live forever, and this truth is hardwired into his soul. This is why he cannot contemplate the thought of death, and possesses an instinctive desire to live eternally. A tradition from the Prophet (s) states: You have not been

---

[19] Ṣadūq, *al-Tawḥīd*, p. 376.

عَنِ الصَّادِقِ (عَلَيْهِ السَّلَامُ) – جَاءَ إِلَيْهِ رَجُلٌ فَقَالَ لَهُ: بِأَبِي أَنْتَ وَأُمِّي عِظْنِي مَوْعِظَةً. فَقَالَ (عَلَيْهِ السَّلَامُ): إِنْ كَانَ اللهُ تَبَارَكَ وَتَعَالَى قَدْ تَكَفَّلَ بِالرِّزْقِ فَاهْتِمَامُكَ لِمَاذَا وَإِنْ كَانَ الرِّزْقُ مَقْسُومًا فَالْحِرْصُ لِمَاذَا وَإِنْ كَانَ الْحِسَابُ حَقًّا فَالْجَمْعُ لِمَاذَا وَإِنْ كَانَ الْخُلْفُ مِنَ اللهِ عَزَّ وَجَلَّ فَالْبُخْلُ لِمَاذَا.

[20] Muṭahharī, (*Āshnāyī bā Qur'an*), *Āthār*, 28/775.

[21] Ṭabāṭabā'ī, *al-Mīzān*, 20/359.

[22] Shīrāzī, *Namūneh*, 27/312.

created to perish, rather you have been created to live on. Indeed, you are only transferred from abode to abode.[23]

Man mistakenly seeks permanence in this world and its attractions. But these are transient and ultimately against his interests.[24] In fact, true and eternal life begins in the Hereafter, as stated in Q29:64

وَمَا هَٰذِهِ الْحَيَاةُ الدُّنْيَا إِلَّا لَهْوٌ وَلَعِبٌ وَإِنَّ الدَّارَ الْآخِرَةَ
لَهِيَ الْحَيَوَانُ لَوْ كَانُوا يَعْلَمُونَ

And the life of this world is nothing but diversion and amusement.
And indeed, the abode of the Hereafter –
that is [true] life, if only they knew.

3.3 History is replete with examples of wealthy men who forgot the true purpose of their wealth, which was to secure their Hereafter. They had to leave everything behind when they left this world, having lost the opportunity to benefit from this grace of God. About Qārūn, God states in Q28:78:

أَوَلَمْ يَعْلَمْ أَنَّ اللهَ قَدْ أَهْلَكَ مِنْ قَبْلِهِ مِنَ الْقُرُونِ مَنْ هُوَ أَشَدُّ
مِنْهُ قُوَّةً وَأَكْثَرُ جَمْعًا وَلَا يُسْأَلُ عَنْ ذُنُوبِهِمُ الْمُجْرِمُونَ

Did he not realize that God has destroyed before him generations, men who were stronger than him in might and had greater accumulations? [But] the criminals are not called [immediately] to account for their sins.

SUMMARY OF THE VERSE

This verse cites, and also refutes, the reason for the conduct of certain individuals which was mentioned in the previous verse. It means to say that they are mistaken in their obsession with wealth because they will certainly not live forever.[25]

---

23 Ṣadūq, *al-Iʿtiqādāt*, 1/47.

عَنِ الرَّسُولِ (صَلَّى اللهُ عَلَيْهِ وَآلِهِ) – مَا خُلِقْتُمْ لِلْفَنَاءِ بَلْ خُلِقْتُمْ لِلْبَقَاءِ، وَإِنَّمَا تُنْقَلُونَ مِنْ دَارٍ إِلَى دَارٍ.

24 Shīrāzī, *Namūneh*, 27/314.

25 Ṭabāṭabāʾī, *al-Mīzān*, 20/360.

REFLECTIVE LEARNING

Let me reflect on whether the wealth I possess will speak for me or against me in the Hereafter.

Am I constantly working to build my Hereafter with whatever wealth I can spare?

VERSE 4

كَلَّا لَيُنۢبَذَنَّ فِي ٱلْحُطَمَةِ ﴿٤﴾

Not at all! He will certainly be thrown into the Crusher. [4]

4.1 [*Kallā* (كَلَّا, not at all!) This word is used to emphatically negate the thinking of such people. Further emphasis is added to this negation by the *lām* in *layunbadhdhanna*, which is the *lām* of oath (*lām al-qasam*).[26]

[*Yunbadhdhanna* (يُنبَذَنَّ, be thrown)] is derived from *nabadha*, which means to throw away something that is worthless.[27]

[*Al-Ḥuṭamah* (الْحُطَمَة, the Crusher)] is derived from *ḥaṭama*, which means to shatter or crush into small pieces. This is a fitting recompense for the person who, through slander and fault-finding, sought to break the reputation of others. Now he is himself broken into pieces.

The word has been used in the Q27:18 to signify crushing when it quotes the queen of the ants:

يَا أَيُّهَا النَّمْلُ ادْخُلُوا مَسَاكِنَكُمْ لَا يَحْطِمَنَّكُمْ سُلَيْمَانُ وَجُنُودُهُ وَهُمْ لَا يَشْعُرُونَ

O ants! Enter your dwellings lest you are crushed by Sulayman and his army while they are not aware.

4.2 In any case, *al-Ḥuṭamah* is the name of a particularly dreadful level of Hell. A tradition from Imam al-Sadiq (a) states: God has made seven [increasingly severe] levels in Hell, the first is *al-Jaḥīm*... and the fourth is *al-Ḥuṭamah*. Its sparks rise like fortresses, resembling yellow camels. Its flames vaporise anyone caught in

---

[26] Ibid.

[27] Rāghib, *al-Mufradāt*.

their midst to powder, but their souls do not die; when their bodies are crushed, they are restored again.[28]

4.3 The one who relies on his own wealth and power and ignores the authority and commands of God, leads a life that has no ultimate worth. On the Day of Judgement, he will be tossed in humiliation into a level of Hell that will pound him into dust.

SUMMARY OF THE VERSE

In summary, the verse says that this person, who has a high opinion of his worth will be tossed aside into hellfire, discarded as an object of no worth, which is his true reality. He will be put into *al-Ḥuṭamah,* whose torment cannot be imagined.

REFLECTIVE LEARNING

Let me reflect on the doom that awaits those who look down on everyone else and who take great pride in their wealth. Am I included amongst them?

VERSES 5, 6

وَمَا أَدْرَاكَ مَا الْحُطَمَةُ ﴿٥﴾ نَارُ اللهِ الْمُوقَدَةُ ﴿٦﴾

And what will make you realize what the Crusher is? [5] *(It is) the fire of God, kindled.* [6]

5-6.1 '*And what will make you realize what the Crusher is?*': [*Wa mā adrāka?* (وَ مَا أَدْرَاكَ, what will make you realize?)]. This phrase is used in several places in the Qur'an for a variety of phenomena. Its function is to draw the attention of the addressee, emphasize the unimaginable enormity or grandeur of the subject under discussion, and to thereafter provide an explanation that gives some understanding of it. A tradition from Imam al-Baqir (a) states: *And what can make you know...* means what [else] can teach you, when

[28] Majlisī, *Biḥār*, 8/289.

عَنِ الصَّادِقِ (عَلَيْهِ السَّلَامُ) - أَنَّ اللهَ جَعَلَهَا سَبْعَ دَرَكَاتٍ أَعْلَاهَا الْجَحِيمُ ... وَالرَّابِعَةُ، الْحُطَمَةُ وَمِنْهَا يَثُورُ شَرَرٌ كَالْقَصْرِ كَأَنَّهَا جِمَالَاتٌ صُفْرٌ تُدَقُّ كُلُّ مَنْ صَارَ إِلَيْهَا مِثْلَ الْكُحْلِ فَلَا يَمُوتُ الرُّوحُ كُلَّمَا صَارُوا مِثْلَ الْكُحْلِ عَادُوا.

everything is in the Qur'an, and it [alone] can teach you [what you do not know].[29]

5-6.2 The next verses describe the Crusher, *al-Ḥuṭamah*; it is made of a fire of God that is already kindled, and one that will engulf the essence of its inmates.

5-6.3 '*(It is) the fire of God, kindled.*': [*Nārullāh* (نَارُ اللهِ, fire of God]. This term shows the great significance of this particular fire. It is unlike any fire experienced in this world. It is beyond the imagination of human beings, which is why God asked the rhetorical question first, '*wa mā adrāka?*'. The attribution of this fire to God, signifies its greatness, and indicates how much God despises the slanderer.

5-6.4 [*Mūqadah* (مُوقَدَة, kindled)] is derived from *awqada* meaning to set alight. Here it means that this fire is ignited in a manner such that it never stops burning.[30] It may be an allusion to the fact that the wealth which the individual thought would allow him to live forever will cause him to burn forever instead.

SUMMARY OF THE VERSES

The torment of this particular level of Hell is unimaginable. It is a fire kindled by God.

REFLECTIVE LEARNING

Slandering and belittling others stains the soul and will lead to a dreadful punishment in the Hereafter.

Let me reflect on whether I have any trace of these qualities in my own heart.

VERSES 7 - 9

الَّتِي تَطَّلِعُ عَلَى الْأَفْئِدَةِ ﴿٧﴾ إِنَّهَا عَلَيْهِمْ مُؤْصَدَةٌ ﴿٨﴾ فِي عَمَدٍ مُمَدَّدَةٍ ﴿٩﴾

Which rises above the hearts. [7] *Indeed, it will be closed over them.* [8] *In extended columns.* [9]

---

[29] Majlisi, *Biḥār*, 9/251.

عَنِ الْبَاقِرِ (عَلَيْهِ السَّلَامُ) – «وَمَا أَدْرَاكَ مَا الْعَقَبَةُ» يَقُولُ مَا أَعْلَمَكَ وَكُلُّ شَيْءٍ فِي الْقُرْآنِ مَا أَدْرَاكَ فَهُوَ مَا أَعْلَمَكَ.

[30] Shīrāzī, *Namūneh*, 27/315.

7-9.1 ‘*Which rises above the hearts.*’: [*Taṭaliʿu* (تَطَّلِعُ, rises above)] is derived from *iṭṭalaʿa* which means rising and climbing over deliberately, and with the usage of *ʿalā*, it indicates overwhelming.[31] The word is also used for the gradual rising of the sun in the horizon. Similarly, this fire will steadily eat away at the heart of its victim.

The punishments of Hell are a manifestation of the evil acts of the individual and so the rate and level of burning will be proportional to the meanness of the soul.[32]

7-9.2 [*Al-Afʾidah* (الْأَفْئِدَة, hearts)] (sing. *fuʾād*) is used in the Qurʾan to refer to the centre of human understanding, conscience, feelings, desires and intentions. It is the seat of motivation for all of one's actions.[33]

7-9.3 Indeed, unlike other fires that burn the skin first and then work inwards into the body, this particular fire begins from inside the individual. Then, it reaches outwards, destroying every organ and limb. Its source is the heart (*fuʾād*) of the wrongdoer, through which he deliberated over, and performed every action. The hearts that were full of arrogance, defiance, and spite, now become the fuel for this terrible fire.

7-9.4 The fires of Hell draw from various fuels. Q66:6 states:

يَا أَيُّهَا الَّذِينَ آمَنُوا قُوا أَنْفُسَكُمْ وَأَهْلِيكُمْ نَارًا وَقُودُهَا النَّاسُ
وَالْحِجَارَةُ عَلَيْهَا مَلَائِكَةٌ غِلَاظٌ شِدَادٌ

O believers! Protect yourselves and your families from a Fire whose fuel is men and stones, over which are appointed angels, stern and severe...

Why should this fire, that represents God’s wrath, not overcome the hearts of the individuals first? These were the people who burned the hearts of believers with ridicule, fault-finding, gossip, and humiliation in this world.[34]

---

[31] Muṣṭafawī, *al-Taḥqīq*.

[32] Muṭahharī, (*Āshnāyī bā Qurʾan*), *Āthār*, 28/776.

[33] *Miṣbāh* Yazdī, *Maʿārif-i Qurʾan*, 1/265; Muṣṭafawī, *al-Taḥqīq*.

[34] Shīrāzī, *Namūneh*, 27/316.

7-9.5 In one of his supplications, Imam al-Sajjad (a) enumerated the descriptions of Hell in the Qur'an, stating: O God! You created hellfire for those who sinned against You, and prepared and described various punishments for those cast into it. You have classified them as *ḥamīm* (scalding water, Q56:93), *ghassāq* (intensely cold water, Q38:57), *muhl* (molten metal, Q18:29), *ḍarīʿ* (thorny food, Q88:6), *ṣadīd* (fetid water, Q14:16), *ghislīn* (pus and refuse, Q69:36), *zaqqūm* (bitter fruit, Q37:62), *salāsil* (chains, Q76:4), *aghlāl* (shackles, Q13:5), *maqāmiʿ al-ḥadīd* (iron maces, Q22:21), *al-ʿadhāb al-ghalīẓ* (harsh punishment, Q11:58), *al-ʿadhāb al-shadīd* (severe punishment, Q14:2), *al-ʿadhāb al-muhīn* (humiliating punishment, Q4:14), *al-ʿadhāb al-muqīm* (lasting punishment, Q9:68), *ʿadhāb al-ḥarīq* (punishment of burning, Q8:50), *ʿadhāb al-samūm* (punishment of scorching, Q52:27), *ẓillin min yaḥmūm* (shadow of black smoke, Q56:43), *sarābīl al-qaṭirān* (garments of liquid pitch, Q14:50), *surādiqāt al-nār* (cages of fire, Q18:29), *nuḥās* (choking smoke, Q55:35), *ḥuṭamah* (crusher, Q104:4), *hāwiyah* (an abyss in Hell, Q101:9), *laẓā* (blazing flames, Q70:15), *nār al-ḥāmiyah* (intensely hot fire, Q101:11), and *nār al-mūqadah allatī taṭaliʿu ʿalā'l afʾidah* (a kindled fire that rises above the hearts, Q104:6,7).[35] May God protect us from all of these.

7-9.6 '*Indeed, it will be closed over them.*': [*Muʾṣadah* (مُؤْصَدَة, closed over)] is derived from *awṣada*, meaning closing over something and holding it fast. The word *īṣād* is used for cages whose doors are closed securely.[36] Just as the inmates of this Hell used to put their possessions in secure lockboxes, they too are now securely trapped in a locked cage of fire from which there is no escape.[37]

7-9.7 The word *ʿalayhim* (عَلَيْهِم, over them) is placed before *muʾṣadah*, giving the meaning that the fire will target them specifically. This is

[35] Majlisī, *Biḥār*, 91/135.

عَنِ السَّجَّادِ (عَلَيْهِ السَّلَامُ) – اَللّٰهُمَّ وَخَلَقْتَ نَارًا لِمَنْ عَصَاكَ، وَأَعْدَدْتَ لِأَهْلِهَا مِنْ أَنْوَاعِ الْعَذَابِ فِيهَا وَوَصَفْتَهُ وَصَنَّفْتَهُ مِنَ الْحَمِيمِ وَالْغَسَّاقِ وَالْمُهْلِ وَالضَّرِيعِ وَالصَّدِيدِ وَالْغِسْلِينِ وَالزَّقُّومِ وَالسَّلَاسِلِ وَالْأَغْلَالِ وَمَقَامِعِ الْحَدِيدِ وَالْعَذَابِ الْغَلِيظِ وَالْعَذَابِ الشَّدِيدِ وَالْعَذَابِ الْمُهِينِ وَالْعَذَابِ الْمُقِيمِ وَعَذَابِ الْحَرِيقِ وَعَذَابِ السَّمُومِ وَظِلٍّ مِنْ يَحْمُومٍ وَسَرَابِيلِ الْقَطِرَانِ وَسُرَادِقَاتِ النَّارِ وَالنُّحَاسِ وَالزَّقُّومِ وَالْحُطَمَةِ وَالْهَاوِيَةِ وَلَظَى وَالنَّارِ الْحَامِيَةِ وَالنَّارِ الْمُوقَدَةِ الَّتِي تَطَّلِعُ عَلَى الْأَفْئِدَةِ.

[36] Qarāʾatī, *Nūr*, 10/492.

[37] Shīrāzī, *Namūneh*, 27/317.

because it will be fuelled by the polluted soul of the inmate of Hell, so there is no question of exclusion or escape.[38]

7-9.8 *'In extended columns.'*: [*ʿAmad* (عَمَد, pillars)] (sing. *ʿamūd*) refers to pillars or columns.

[*Mumaddadah* (مُمَدَّدَة, extended)] is derived from *madda*, meaning to extend and stretch.

The verse means that these columns will be long and will bind them securely in that level of Hell.[39]

A tradition from Imam al-Baqir (a) states: As these columns close over them, the fire consumes, by God, their entire skin.[40]

SUMMARY OF THE VERSES

In summary, these verses say that the inmate of this Hell will be securely imprisoned in a terrifying cage of fire, from which there is no escape. It will extend in columns over him.

REFLECTIVE LEARNING

Once more, we must reflect on the fact that these dreadful punishments are the result of man's evil actions in this world and are proportional to them.

Let me reflect on whether there is anything in my own attitude and conduct that even remotely resembles the qualities of those condemned in this surah.

---

[38] Muṭahharī, (*Āshnāyī bā Qur'an*), *Āthār*, 28/778.

[39] Ibid.

[40] Baḥrānī, *al-Burhān*, 5/756.

عَنِ الْبَاقِرِ (عَلَيْهِ السَّلَامُ) – «فِي عَمَدٍ مُمَدَّدَةٍ» قَالَ إِذَا مُدَّتِ العَمَدُ أُكِلَتْ وَاللهِ الجُلُودَ.

SURAT AL-FĪL
THE ELEPHANT (105)

TEXT AND TRANSLATION

سُورَةُ الْفِيلِ

بِسْمِ اللهِ الرَّحْمٰنِ الرَّحِيمِ

أَلَمْ تَرَ كَيْفَ فَعَلَ رَبُّكَ بِأَصْحَابِ الْفِيلِ ﴿١﴾ أَلَمْ يَجْعَلْ كَيْدَهُمْ فِي تَضْلِيلٍ ﴿٢﴾
وَأَرْسَلَ عَلَيْهِمْ طَيْرًا أَبَابِيلَ ﴿٣﴾ تَرْمِيهِمْ بِحِجَارَةٍ مِنْ سِجِّيلٍ ﴿٤﴾ فَجَعَلَهُمْ كَعَصْفٍ
مَأْكُولٍ ﴿٥﴾

In the name of God, the Beneficent, the Merciful.

Have you [O Muhammad] not considered how your Lord dealt with the people of the elephant? [1] *Did He not cause their strategy to end in confusion?* [2] *And send down upon them flocks of [small] birds,* [3] *Pelting them with stones of baked clay.* [4] *Thus, He rendered them like devoured straw!* [5]

INTRODUCTION

Surat al-Fīl (105) was the 19th chapter to be revealed.[1] It has five verses and was revealed in Makka, after Surat al-Kāfirūn (109). It is named after the mention of the elephant in the first verse.

The surah succinctly recounts the outcome of the attack of the Abyssinian governor of Southern Arabia, Abrahah b. al-Ṣabbāḥ al-Ashram and the 'people (riders) of the elephant (*aṣḥāb al-fīl*)' on Makka. It is reported that Abrahah had brought with him just one powerful elephant called Maḥmūd. However, other reports mention that there were eight, or twelve, war elephants in the army.[2]

---

1 Maʿrifat, *ʿUlūm-i Qurʾānī*, p. 90.

2 Ṭabrasī, *al-Bayān*, 10/824.

The army was miraculously destroyed at *Wādī* Muḥassir[3] by a flock of small birds that God set upon them. The year became famously known as the 'Year of the Elephant' (*ʿĀm al-Fīl*). The blessed Prophet (s) was born in that year, shortly after the event.

After that year, all the people in the Arabian Peninsula developed a strong conviction about the eminence of the Kaʿbah. The reputation of Makka and the fortunes of the Quraysh grew as a result, as did their sense of self-importance.[4]

The event was so seminal in the history of the Arabs that they used its date as a reference point for later events.

About this chapter, a tradition from Imam al-Sadiq (a) states: Do not recite two chapters together (after al-Ḥamd) in any single unit of (obligatory) prayer, except al-Fīl (105) and Quraysh (106), and al-Ḍuḥā (93) and al-Sharḥ (94).[5] Based on this and other traditions, most *Shīʿa* jurists have ruled that if any one of these surahs is recited in the obligatory prayers, it should be recited with its pair.[6]

OCCASION OF REVELATION

A tradition from Imam al-Sajjad (a) states: The Quraysh came to Abu Talib (a) while God's Messenger (s) was with him. They said, "Ask him whether God has sent him to us in particular, or to all of mankind?" The Prophet (s) replied, "Rather, I have been sent to all of mankind, to white and black, to those on the tops of mountains and those in the depths of the seas; I shall invite the Persians and the Romans to my message this very year. '*O people, I am the Messenger of God to all of you.*'" (Q7:158) [On hearing this] the Quraysh reacted with contempt and arrogance, saying, "By God, if the Persians and Romans heard these words, they

---

[3] A valley between Muzdalifah (Mashʿar al-Ḥarām) and Minā. It is called Muḥassir (from *ḥassara,* frustration) because of the defeat of the plans of Abrahah and his soldiers at that location, where they were attacked and destroyed by flocks of birds.

In the Ḥaj rites, on the day of Eid al-Aḍḥā, the pilgrim is not allowed to cross from Muzdalifah into this valley on the way to Minā, until sunrise. It is recommended for the pilgrim to walk briskly through the area, which is approximately 100 paces. (Sistānī, *Manāsik al-Ḥaj wa Mulḥaqātuhā*, p. 328.)

[4] Mutahharī, (*Āshnāyī bā Qur'an*), *Āthār*, 28/783.

[5] ʿĀmilī, *Wasā'il*, 6/55.

عَنِ الصَّادِقِ (عَلَيْهِ السَّلَامُ) - لَا تَجْمَعْ بَيْنَ سُورَتَيْنِ فِي رَكْعَةٍ وَاحِدَةٍ إِلَّا الضُّحَى وَأَلَمْ نَشْرَحْ وَأَلَمْ تَرَ كَيْفَ وَلِإِيلَافِ قُرَيْشٍ.

[6] Yazdī, *ʿUrwah*, 1/646.

would drive us out of our land and destroy the Kaʿbah brick by brick." It was at this time that Surat al-Fīl was revealed.[7]

DISCUSSION 1: COMPARING AND CONTRASTING THE TERMS, 'OCCASION OF REVELATION (*SABAB AL-NUZŪL*)' AND BACKGROUND TO REVELATION (*SHA'N AL-NUZŪL*)'

In Qur'anic sciences, *asbāb* (sing. *sabab*) *al-nuzūl* refers to the particular circumstances, events, and places that are related to the revelation of a verse of the Qur'an. In other words, it is the study of the occasion that prompted the revelation of the verse.

Sha'n al-nuzūl is a similar term that is used to describe the background or context of the revelation of the verse. The terms are occasionally used interchangeably but there is a subtle difference in the two. *Sha'n al-nuzūl* is more general than *sabab al-nuzūl.*

Whenever a verse or verses are revealed immediately after an incident, that incident is referred to as the occasion of revelation (*sabab al-nuzūl*). In other words, the revelation took place following that incident.

Whenever a verse or verses are revealed about an incident concerning a person or an event, whether of the past, present or future, or concerning the obligation of Islamic laws, then that incident is referred to as the background of revelation (*shā'n al-nuzūl*).[8]

For this reason, the attack of Abrahah and the people of the elephant on the Kaʿbah is better described as the *shā'n al-nuzūl* of Surat al-Fīl, and not its *sabab al-nuzūl.*

It is also important to note that while the knowledge of the *sabab al-nuzūl* of a verse is helpful in understanding its meaning, many verses do not have a specific *sabab al-nuzūl* and are independent of any particular event.

---

[7] Fattāl al-Nīshābūrī, *Rawḍat al-Wāʿiẓīn*, 1/54; Majlisī, *Biḥār*, 35/88.

عَنِ السَّجَّادِ (عَلَيْهِ السَّلَامُ) – أَنَّهُ اجْتَمَعَتْ قُرَيْشٌ إِلَى أَبِي طَالِبٍ وَرَسُولُ اللهِ (صَلَّى اللهُ عَلَيْهِ وَآلِهِ) عِنْدَهُ فَقَالُوا: قُلْ لَهُ أَرْسَلَهُ اللهُ إِلَيْنَا خَاصَّةً أَمْ إِلَى النَّاسِ كَافَّةً؟ قَالَ: بَلْ إِلَى النَّاسِ أُرْسِلْتُ كَافَّةً إِلَى الْأَبْيَضِ وَالْأَسْوَدِ، وَمَنْ عَلَى رُؤُوسِ الْجِبَالِ، وَمَنْ فِي لُجَجِ الْبِحَارِ، وَلَأَدْعُوَنَّ السَّنَةَ فَارِسَ وَالرُّومَ. «يَا أَيُّهَا النَّاسُ إِنِّي رَسُولُ اللهِ إِلَيْكُمْ جَمِيعًا» فَتَجَبَّرَتْ قُرَيْشٌ وَاسْتَكْبَرَتْ وَقَالَتْ وَاللهِ لَوْ سَمِعَتْ بِهَذَا فَارِسُ وَالرُّومُ لَاخْتَطَفَتْنَا مِنْ أَرْضِنَا وَلَقَلَعَتِ الْكَعْبَةَ حَجَرًا حَجَرًا فَنَزَلَ قَوْلُهُ «أَلَمْ تَرَ كَيْفَ فَعَلَ رَبُّكَ».

[8] Maʿrifat, *'Ulūm-i Qur'ānī*, p. 100.

LINK TO THE PREVIOUS CHAPTER

The previous chapter, Surat al-Humazah, talks of how the Quraysh had grown so proud of the abundance of their wealth and numbers that they had failed to fulfil the rights of God. This wealth and influence stemmed largely from their custodianship of the Kaʿbah.[9]

In this surah (and in the next, Surat Quraysh), God reminds the Quraysh of His favour to them in protecting the Kaʿbah and fostering their solidarity. Therefore, instead of displaying vanity, they are instructed to worship the Lord of the House, in appreciation and gratitude.

MERITS OF RECITATION

- A tradition from Imam al-Sadiq (a) states: Whoever recites Surat al-Fīl in his obligatory prayers, then on the Day of Judgement, every plain, mountain, and valley will bear witness that he was of those who prayed their obligatory prayers, and a caller will call to them on the Day of Judgement [on behalf of God], "You have testified correctly for My bondsman; your testimony for him has been accepted. Enter him into Paradise without account, for he is one who is beloved to Me, as are his actions."[10]

EXEGESIS

VERSES 1, 2

أَلَمْ تَرَ كَيْفَ فَعَلَ رَبُّكَ بِأَصْحَابِ الْفِيلِ ﴿١﴾ أَلَمْ يَجْعَلْ كَيْدَهُمْ فِي تَضْلِيلٍ ﴿٢﴾

Have you [O Muhammad] not considered how your Lord dealt with the people of the elephant? [1] *Did He not cause their strategy to end in confusion?* [2]

1-2.1 '*Have you not considered how your Lord dealt with the people of the elephant?*': [*Alam tara*? (أَلَمْ تَرَ, have you not considered?)]. God asks the reader to consider how He dealt with a mighty army headed by elephants. Here, the verb [*tara* (تَرَ, you see)] denotes 'consider, or reflect', because the event was not physically witnessed by the

[9] Iṣlāḥī, *Tadabbur-i Qur'an*, 9/555.

[10] ʿĀmilī, *Wasā'il*, 6/56.

عَنِ الصَّادِقِ (عَلَيْهِ السَّلَامُ) - مَنْ قَرَأَ فِي فَرَائِضِهِ «أَلَمْ تَرَ كَيْفَ فَعَلَ رَبُّكَ» شَهِدَ لَهُ يَوْمَ الْقِيَامَةِ كُلُّ سَهْلٍ وَجَبَلٍ وَمَدَرٍ بِأَنَّهُ كَانَ مِنَ الْمُصَلِّينَ، وَيُنَادِي لَهُ يَوْمَ الْقِيَامَةِ مُنَادٍ صَدَقْتُمْ عَلَى عَبْدِي قَدْ قَبِلْتُ شَهَادَتَكُمْ لَهُ وَعَلَيْهِ أَدْخِلُوهُ الْجَنَّةَ وَلَا تُحَاسِبُوهُ فَإِنَّهُ مِمَّنْ أُحِبُّهُ وَأُحِبُّ عَمَلَهُ.

Prophet (s). We have discussed this phrase further in the *tafsīr* of Surat al-Fajr (89).

[*Kayfa* (كَيْفَ, how)]. 'How' is used here to inspire curiosity and wonder in the reader, and as a prelude to the detailed description of how the stratagem of the people of the elephant was countered by God.

[*Rabbuka* (رَبُّكَ, your Lord)] shows the protective and sustaining role of God, not just for the Kaʿbah, but for mankind also. We have discussed this term further in the *tafsīr* of Surat al-Fātiḥah (1).

[*Fīl* (فِيل, elephant)] refers to the species of elephants and does not mean a single elephant.[11] According to some accounts they were more than one.

1-2.2 '*Did He not cause their strategy to end in confusion?*': [*Kayd* (كَيْد, stratagem)] here refers to Abrahah's plot to destroy the Kaʿbah to try to make his own church in Ṣanʿāʾ (Sanaa, Yemen) the focus of pilgrimage. We have discussed the concept of *kayd* further in the *tafsīr* of Surat al-Ṭāriq (86).

[*Taḍlīl* (تَضْلِيل, rendered ineffective)] is derived from *ḍalla* meaning to go astray. Here it means that their strategy was reduced to tatters and they were completely destroyed. In fact, both verbs *tara* (تَرَ, you see)] and [*yajʿal* (يَجْعَل, He causes)] are used in the present tense, indicating that confounding the plans of powerful oppressors is a continual practice of God.

1-2.3 God did not stop Abrahah in Yemen. He allowed him to exercise his free will and come all the way to the sacred sanctuary to carry out his defiant act. God gives the disbelievers respite so that perhaps they may desist and reform, but they usually add to their sins instead. Ultimately, His punishment comes to them, whether in this world or the next or in both. Q3:178 states:

وَلَا يَحْسَبَنَّ الَّذِينَ كَفَرُوا أَنَّمَا نُمْلِي لَهُمْ خَيْرٌ لِأَنْفُسِهِمْ
إِنَّمَا نُمْلِي لَهُمْ لِيَزْدَادُوا إِثْمًا وَلَهُمْ عَذَابٌ مُهِينٌ

And let disbelievers never think that the respite that We give them is good for them. We only give them respite so that they may increase in sin, and for them is a humiliating punishment.

[11] Ṭabrasī, *al-Bayān*, 10/824.

SUMMARY OF THE VERSES

The meaning of these two verses is that man's well-laid and seemingly strong plans can be easily thwarted by God, when He wills. This is why he has been asked to consider how the mission of Abrahah ended in confusion.

REFLECTIVE LEARNING

These verses remind us that no matter how powerful an enemy is, and how great his strategy, there is none more powerful and mightier than God, and His plan will always prevail.

To gauge my conviction in this statement, let me reflect on my confidence in obedience to God in the face of any enemy.

VERSE 3

وَأَرْسَلَ عَلَيْهِمْ طَيْرًا أَبَابِيلَ ﴿٣﴾

And send down upon them flocks of [small] birds. [3]

3.1 [*Ṭayran abābīl* (طَيْرًا أَبَابِيلَ, flock of small birds)]. *Abābīl* means discrete groups[12] and, here describes the flocks of birds that attacked Abrahah's army from every direction. This verse and the next verse describe how the strategy of the invaders was destroyed.

3.2 The size of the enemy is not important if God is on your side. Abrahah brought huge elephants to show his power. God sent down flocks of small birds, similar to sparrows, with tiny stones to destroy them. When the small birds acted together, they achieved a mighty result. In the same way, when the Muslims remain united and not divided, they can bring about great results, just as they did in the battle of Badr, for example.

3.3 At Badr, the Muslims were few (as few as 313 according to the reports), and in the battle of Hunayn, they were many (over 12,000); however, at both times, they were under great strain until the assistance of God came to them:

About the Battle of Badr, Q8:9 states:

إِذْ تَسْتَغِيثُونَ رَبَّكُمْ فَٱسْتَجَابَ لَكُمْ أَنِّي مُمِدُّكُم بِأَلْفٍ مِّنَ الْمَلَائِكَةِ مُرْدِفِينَ

[12] Ṭūsī, *al-Tibyān*, 10/410.

When you sought aid from your Lord, and He answered you:
"I will assist you with a thousand angels, rank upon rank."

About the Battle of Hunayn, Q9:25 states:

لَقَدْ نَصَرَكُمُ اللَّهُ فِي مَوَاطِنَ كَثِيرَةٍ وَيَوْمَ حُنَيْنٍ إِذْ أَعْجَبَتْكُمْ كَثْرَتُكُمْ فَلَمْ
تُغْنِ عَنْكُمْ شَيْئًا وَضَاقَتْ عَلَيْكُمُ الْأَرْضُ بِمَا رَحُبَتْ ثُمَّ وَلَّيْتُمْ مُدْبِرِينَ

Indeed, God has given you victory on many battlefields; and even on the day of Hunayn when you rejoiced at your great number, but it did not avail you at all, and the earth, despite its vastness, was constrained for you, and you turned back in flight.

SUMMARY OF THE VERSE

The verse shows how God can use small and weak creatures, in this case, little birds, to defeat large and strong enemies, in this case, the army of elephants.

REFLECTIVE LEARNING

Working together reduces the individual workload, as shown by formations of birds who take advantage of each other's updraft to save energy. Similarly, as Muslims, we can take advantage of the spiritual energy of the worship of other Muslims in congregational prayer. Let me reflect on whether I take advantage of this by establishing and joining *salat al-jamāʿah* whenever possible.

VERSES 4, 5

تَرْمِيهِمْ بِحِجَارَةٍ مِنْ سِجِّيلٍ ﴿٤﴾ فَجَعَلَهُمْ كَعَصْفٍ مَأْكُولٍ ﴿٥﴾

Pelting them with stones of baked clay. [4] *Thus, He rendered them like devoured straw!* [5]

4-5.1 '*Pelting them with stones of baked clay.*': [*Sijjīl* (سِجِّيل, baked clay)] is Arabicized from the Persian *sang-i gil* (petrified clay).[13] The same punishment was sent to the people of Prophet Lut (a) also;

[13] Many terms in Arabic were assimilated from the languages of peoples that the Arabs interacted with in their travels. These terms were in common usage amongst them before they were used in the Qur'an.

Q11:82 states:

جَعَلْنَا عَالِيَهَا سَافِلَهَا وَأَمْطَرْنَا عَلَيْهَا حِجَارَةً مِنْ سِجِّيلٍ مَنْضُودٍ

We turned [their town] upside down, and rained upon it stones of baked clay, continually.

4-5.2 '*Thus, He rendered them like devoured straw!*': [*ʿAṣf* (عَصْف, straw)] means dried grass or straw, and the adjective [*ma'kūl* (مَأْكُول, eaten)] gives the meaning of chewed up and devoured grass. The verse means that after the attack of the birds, the mortally wounded bodies of Abrahah's soldiers were strewn around resembling devoured straw.[14]

4-5.3 Huge resources and great power make no difference against God. The elephants of Abrahah (which may be considered equivalent to modern-day 'tanks') and the soldiers of his mighty army were destroyed by small birds, carrying even smaller stones. Indeed, all power and might is with God.

4-5.4 This chapter is a lesson for all oppressors, to realize that there is a Power above theirs that has destroyed many powers in the past and can easily do so again.

4-5.5 This miraculous destruction of the army that threatened Makka, the Kaʿbah and the Quraysh was an undisputed event, because when the Prophet (s) read the verses, even the disbelievers and idolaters amongst his audience did not question its authenticity.

DISCUSSION 2: THE STORY OF THE PEOPLE OF THE ELEPHANT AND THEIR DESTRUCTION

All reports about this event state that the ruler of Yemen who invaded Makka with the intention of destroying the Kaʿbah was Abrahah b. al-Ṣabbāḥ al-Ashram.[15]

He is reported to be the grandfather of the Negus (Najjāshī), who gave asylum to the Muslims when they migrated from Makka to Abyssinia at the time of the Prophet (s).[16]

---

[14] Ṭabāṭabāʾī, *al-Mīzān*, 20/363.

[15] Ṭabrasī, *al-Bayān*, 10/822-3.

[16] Ṭabāṭabāʾī, *al-Mīzān*, 20/362.

Abrahah was an army general of the Christian Aksumite empire (based in Abyssinia, modern-day Eritrea), and was the viceroy of the emperor to Southern Arabia. He ruled for over 30 years, and was killed in 570CE (53 years before *hijrah*), when he came from Yemen to Makka intending to destroy the Kaʿbah.

He had built a large church, known as al-Qalīs (from the Greek, 'Ecclesia', meaning place of assembly) in Ṣanʿāʾ and had adorned it with gold and precious jewels. He instructed the people of Yemen to go to it for visitation and circumambulation, rather than going to Makka for pilgrimage to the Kaʿbah, which the Arabs called the 'house of God' (*baytullāh*). This instruction was largely ignored by the people. Abrahah decided that the only way to promote the church was to destroy the Kaʿbah. He could not do this without cause, but when the church was apparently desecrated by an Arab from the tribe of Banu Kinānah, Abrahah found a pretext. He vowed to destroy the Kaʿbah in retaliation.[17]

One of his other intentions was to bring the influence of Christianity to Ḥijāz, and to further the interests of Rome and Abyssinia in the region.

He set out towards Makka with an army that had war elephants, and he himself rode in command on the strongest elephant. After a few skirmishes along the way against some defenders, he arrived at Muzdalifah. The Quraysh abandoned Makka in fear, running to the mountains.[18]

Abrahah captured 200 camels belonging to ʿAbd al-Muttalib, who asked for their return. Abrahah said to him, "I have come to destroy the Kaʿbah, and you ask me to return your camels?!" ʿAbd al-Muttalib's reply is famous, "I am the master of these camels, the House has its own Master, who will protect it from you!"[19]

As Abrahah prepared to march out at dawn from his encampment near Makka, the lead elephant refused to move any further towards the Kaʿbah. Suddenly, flocks of birds appeared on the horizon. Each

[17] Balādhurī, *Ansāb al-Ashrāf*, 1/67.

[18] Ibid.

[19] Majlisī, *Biḥār*, 15/145.

أَنَا رَبُّ الْإِبِلِ وَإِنَّ لِلْبَيْتِ رَبًّا سَيَمْنَعُهُ عَنْكَ.

bird carried three stones of baked clay (*sijjīl*), one each in its beak and two talons. They dropped theses stones over the Abyssinian army with unerring accuracy, each one striking and ripping through its victim. Abrahah himself was struck by some of these stones, and desperately gave the order to retreat. He managed to get back to Yemen but died of his injuries. No one who had accompanied him survived.[20]

SUMMARY OF THE VERSES

The verses described how small birds carrying little pellets of clay were dispatched by God. They decimated Abrahah's army, leaving them like devoured straw.

REFLECTIVE LEARNING

Every bird carried three stones of baked clay (*sijjīl*), one each in its beak and two talons to attack God's enemy.

It is instructive to think about how these small birds used everything they could, even bearing the discomfort of carrying stones in their mouths, to achieve God's will.

Let me reflect whether I, like these birds, push myself to the limit, come out of my comfort zone, and use every resource available to me to obey God.

---

[20] Ṭabrasī, *al-Bayān*, 10/823.

SURAT QURAYSH (106)

TEXT AND TRANSLATION

سُورَةُ قُرَيْشٍ

بِسْمِ اللّٰهِ الرَّحْمٰنِ الرَّحِيمِ

لِإِيلَافِ قُرَيْشٍ ﴿١﴾ إِيلَافِهِمْ رِحْلَةَ الشِّتَاءِ وَالصَّيْفِ ﴿٢﴾ فَلْيَعْبُدُوا رَبَّ هَٰذَا الْبَيْتِ
﴿٣﴾ الَّذِي أَطْعَمَهُمْ مِنْ جُوعٍ وَآمَنَهُمْ مِنْ خَوْفٍ ﴿٤﴾

In the name of God, the Beneficent, the Merciful.

For the security of the Quraysh. [1] *Their security during trading journeys in the winter and the summer.* [2] *So, let them worship the Lord of this House (Kaʿbah),* [3] *Who has fed them against hunger and secured them from fear.* [4]

INTRODUCTION

Surat Quraysh (106) – also known as Surat *Īlāf* (security, commercial agreements) – was the 29th chapter to be revealed. It has four verses and was revealed in Makka, after Surat al-Tīn (95).[1] It is named after the mention of the tribe of Quraysh in the first verse.

Although it was revealed several surahs later, this chapter is a continuation and completion of Surat al-Fīl (105). For this reason, the two chapters are considered linked, but separate, and should be recited together in the obligatory prayer.[2]

LINK TO THE PREVIOUS CHAPTER

The previous chapter, Surat al-Fīl, mentions how God protected the Kaʿbah from the army of Abrahah who had come to destroy the ancient House with elephants. Surat Quraysh gives the reason why He destroyed Abrahah and his army; it was to foster the solidarity of those who lived in the holy sanctuary (*ḥaram*) and to safeguard their

---

1 Maʿrifat, *ʿUlūm-i Qur'ānī*, p. 90.

2 Sistānī, *Minhāj*, 1/232, ruling 605.

commercial agreements, because they were affiliated to the Kaʿbah and were recognized as its custodians.[3]

Prophet Ibrahim (a) prayed to God for Makka to remain secure, and to provide for its inhabitants. Q2:126 states:

وَإِذْ قَالَ إِبْرَاهِيمُ رَبِّ ٱجْعَلْ هَٰذَا بَلَدًا آمِنًا وَٱرْزُقْ أَهْلَهُ
مِنَ الثَّمَرَاتِ مَنْ آمَنَ مِنْهُمْ بِاللهِ وَالْيَوْمِ الْآخِرِ

And when Ibrahim said, 'My Lord, make this a secure city, and provide its people with fruits, the ones of them that believe in God and the last Day...'

Surat al-Fīl proves that God accepted the first part of the prayer, and Surat Quraysh that He accepted the second.

MERITS OF RECITATION

- A tradition from the Prophet (s) states: Whoever recites Surat Quraysh shall be given the reward of one who circumambulates the Kaʿbah and stays in the Sacred Mosque for worship (*iʿtikāf*).[4]
- Another tradition from the Prophet (s) states: Whoever recites it over food will never suffer any harm from it.[5]

EXEGESIS

VERSE 1

لِإِيلَافِ قُرَيْشٍ ﴿١﴾

For the security of the Quraysh. [1]

1.1 The *lām* (ل) in the opening phrase [*Li īlāf* (لِإِيلَافِ, for the security)] denotes cause (*lam al-taʿlīl*). The doer or subject (*Fāʿil*) is God Almighty, and the object (*mafʿul*) is the tribe of Quraysh. Therefore, the verse may mean that God destroyed the army of Abrahah, as

[3] Subḥānī, *Fūrūgh-i Abadiyyat*, 1/368.

[4] Baḥrānī, *al-Burhān*, 5/765.

عَنِ الرَّسُولِ (صَلَّى اللهُ عَلَيْهِ وَآلِهِ) – مَنْ قَرَأَ هَذِهِ السُّورَةَ أَعْطَاهُ اللهُ مِنَ الْأَجْرِ كَمَنْ طَافَ حَوْلَ الْكَعْبَةِ وَاعْتَكَفَ فِي الْمَسْجِدِ الْحَرَامِ.

[5] Ibid.

عَنِ الرَّسُولِ (صَلَّى اللهُ عَلَيْهِ وَآلِهِ) – مَنْ قَرَأَهَا عَلَى طَعَامٍ لَمْ يَرَ فِيهِ سُوءًا أَبَدًا.

mentioned in Surat al-Fīl, to foster the security of the Quraysh and allow them to coexist peacefully.[6]

1.2 [*Īlāf* (ايلاف, security)] is the verbal noun derived from *alafa,* meaning secure co-existence, familiarity, and mutual affection.

Alternatively, *īlāf* may also refer to the series of trade agreements, grants of security and passage, and standards of practice agreed amongst the Quraysh themselves and with their trading partners along their trade routes. These agreements were originally instituted by Hashim.[7] They were also safeguarded by the increased prestige of the Quraysh in the eyes of the rest of the Arabs when they heard how a powerful army was destroyed by small flocks of birds in defence of the Kaʿbah and Makka, which was the home of the Quraysh.

1.3 [Quraysh (قُرَيْش)] refers to the Arab tribe that inhabited and controlled Makka and the sacred sanctuary (*ḥaram*), and were descendants ofIsmaʿil (a). The tribe had ten clans; the Prophet (s) belonged to the clan of Hashim (Banu Hashim).

The name Quraysh is thought to be the title of one of the ancestors of the Prophet (s).[8] It may also be from *qarasha,* meaning to come together and gather,[9] because when Qusayy bin Kilāb became the ruler of Makka, he gathered the different tribes living in the area and gave them lands in Makka. When they settled in the area, he gave them the collective name Quraysh.[10]

Yet others believe that *qarasha* denoted trade and earning (*taqarrasha*); since they were not farmers but traders, they were known as Quraysh.[11]

SUMMARY OF THE VERSE

The verse speaks of the blessing of security and solidarity that was bestowed upon the Quraysh by God.

---

6 Ṭabāṭabāʾī, *al-Mīzān,* 20/366.

7 Yaʿqūbī, *Tārīkh,* 1/202.

8 Ibn al-Jawzī, *al-Muntaẓam,* 2/226.

9 Ibn Manẓūr, *Lisān al-ʿArab.*

10 Ṭabarī, *Tārīkh,* 2/22.

11 Balādhurī, *Ansāb al-Ashrāf,* 11/80.

REFLECTIVE LEARNING

In Makka, God protected the Kaʿbah in order to foster solidarity and unity amongst the Quraysh, who were its custodians.

Later, in Madina, He fostered solidarity between the ʿAws and Khazraj when they became Muslims.

Today, we the Muslims are all brethren, and the custodians of Islam.

Let me reflect on whether my words and actions increase unity or disunity amongst Muslims.

VERSE 2

إِيلَافِهِمْ رِحْلَةَ الشِّتَاءِ وَالصَّيْفِ ﴿٢﴾

Their security during trading journeys in the winter and the summer. [2]

2.1 [*Riḥlah* (رِحْلَة, journey)], here refers to the two annual trade journeys of the Quraysh: south to Yemen in the winter, and north to Syria (the Levant) in the summer. They were forced to go out of Makka for trade because their own lands were dry and arid and did not support much vegetation.

2.2 In time, they forged many links, signing agreements with the various tribes along their routes to ensure their safe passage. After the event of the 'people of the elephant' this solidarity (*īlāf*) grew very strong as the tribes came to respect the Quraysh and were afraid to challenge them.

2.3 The Prophet (s) himself travelled on these trade journeys. When he was 12, he accompanied his uncle Abu Talib to Syria, a journey on which they encountered the Syrian Christian monk *Baḥīrah*, who informed Abu Talib about the noble future of his nephew. Later, he travelled as an agent of Lady Khadijah (a), managing the sale of her goods in the annual trade caravans of the Quraysh. She was impressed with his honesty and demeanour, and their introduction led to the most blessed of marriages.[12]

[12] Subḥānī, *Fūrūgh-i Abadiyyat*, 1/141.

SUMMARY OF THE VERSE

In summary, the Quraysh could go about their winter and summer journeys in peace and security, because of God's protection.

REFLECTIVE LEARNING

Originally, the Quraysh believed in the religion of Prophet Ibrahim (a) (*dīn al-ḥanīf*), but gradually, as a result of the polytheistic influences of their trade partners in Syria, many of them turned to idol worship.

Let me reflect on the impact that the people I encounter in my life have on my attitudes and practices.

VERSES 3, 4

فَلْيَعْبُدُوا رَبَّ هَٰذَا الْبَيْتِ ﴿٣﴾ الَّذِي أَطْعَمَهُمْ مِنْ جُوعٍ وَآمَنَهُمْ مِنْ خَوْفٍ ﴿٤﴾

So, let them worship the Lord of this House (Kaʿbah), [3] *Who has fed them against hunger and secured them from fear.* [4]

3-4.1 '*So, let them worship the Lord of this House.*': [*Falyaʿbudū* (فَلْيَعْبُدُوا, so let them worship)]. The *fa* (فَ, so) indicates that God's command in return for His favours to the Quraysh was that they should worship Him as the true Lord of the House that He had saved from attack.

3-4.2 The phrase, [*Rabba hādhā al-bayt* (رَبَّ هَٰذَا الْبَيْتِ, Lord of this House)] is a reminder that the prestige and eminence of the Quraysh amongst the Arabs stemmed from their association with the sacred Kaʿbah, whose Lord was Allah.

[*Rabb* (رَبّ, Lord, Sustainer)]. Just as God was the *Rabb* of the House, he was also their Nourisher and Sustainer, securing them from hunger and fear of their enemy. We have discussed this term further in the *tafsīr* of Surat al-Fātiḥah (1).

Therefore, they were instructed to give up their idolatry and polytheism (*shirk*) and turn to One God, the source of their security, welfare, and prosperity.

3-4.3 One of the main reasons for the opposition of the leaders of the Quraysh to the monotheistic message of Islam and the Prophet (s) was their fear that Makka and the Kaʿbah would lose its attraction to the idolaters of other nations, who had all installed their main idols in the Kaʿbah.

3-4.4 ‘*Who has fed them against hunger and secured them from fear.*’: The last verse gives another reason why the Quraysh were indebted to God: the provision of ample food in the desert climate, and safety from attack, because all tribes were aware of how they had been Divinely protected at the time of the attack of Abrahah.

3-4.5 In return they were asked to worship God sincerely and with gratitude for His favours. Gratitude is what will give rise to growth and increase: Q14:7 states:

وَإِذْ تَأَذَّنَ رَبُّكُمْ لَئِن شَكَرْتُمْ لَأَزِيدَنَّكُمْ وَلَئِن كَفَرْتُمْ إِنَّ عَذَابِي لَشَدِيدٌ

And [recall] when your Lord announced: "If you are grateful, I will certainly increase you [in favour and growth]; but if you show ingratitude, then indeed, My punishment is severe."

SUMMARY OF THE VERSES

These verses informed the Quraysh that that the blessing of provision and security was a gift of God and in return, it behove them to turn away from idolatry and worship the Lord of the Kaʿbah.

REFLECTIVE LEARNING

God is the source of provision. The Quraysh forgot that when they feared that they would lose economically if they turned away from idol worship to the worship of God alone. Fear of loss of wealth and prestige is a dangerous stimulus for disobedience of God, and one must always be vigilant about it.

Let me reflect how many times have I justified the disobedience of God because of fear of loss; loss of employment, wealth, status, or friends?

SURAT AL-MĀʿŪN
ACTS OF KINDNESS (107)

TEXT AND TRANSLATION

سُورَةُ الْمَاعُونِ

بِسْمِ اللهِ الرَّحْمٰنِ الرَّحِيمِ

أَرَأَيْتَ الَّذِي يُكَذِّبُ بِالدِّينِ ﴿١﴾ فَذٰلِكَ الَّذِي يَدُعُّ الْيَتِيمَ ﴿٢﴾ وَلَا يَحُضُّ عَلَىٰ طَعَامِ
الْمِسْكِينِ ﴿٣﴾ فَوَيْلٌ لِلْمُصَلِّينَ ﴿٤﴾ الَّذِينَ هُمْ عَنْ صَلَاتِهِمْ سَاهُونَ ﴿٥﴾ الَّذِينَ
هُمْ يُرَاءُونَ ﴿٦﴾ وَيَمْنَعُونَ الْمَاعُونَ ﴿٧﴾

In the name of God, the Beneficent, the Merciful.

Have you considered the one who denies the Recompense? [1] *That is the one who [harshly] drives away the orphan.* [2] *And does not encourage the feeding of the poor.* [3] *So, woe be to those who pray.* [4] *[But] who are heedless about their prayers.* [5] *Those who do [good] only to be seen by others,* [6] *And withhold [small] acts of kindness.* [7]

INTRODUCTION

Surat al-Māʿūn (107) was the 17th chapter to be revealed.[1] It has seven verses. There are varying reports about where this chapter was revealed. Some exegetes believe that it was revealed in its complete form in Makka after Surat al-Takāthur (102). Others say that since it speaks of hypocrites and daily prayers, which are a phenomenon of Madina, it must be a Madanī surah.[2] Its name comes from the last word in the final verse of the surah.

The surah identifies those who call themselves Muslims, yet conduct themselves as hypocrites, by their traits. They reveal their lack of belief in the Day of Judgement by behaving harshly with the orphans and the poor. Furthermore, they are unmindful in their prayers, do good

[1] Maʿrifat, *ʿUlūm-i Qurʾānī*, p. 90.

[2] Javādī-Āmolī, *Tasnīm*. (Transcript: http://javadi.esra.ir/en/-/02-10-9931-تفسیر-سوره-ماعون).

only to show off, and display meanness of spirit by denying others even small acts of kindness.

OCCASION OF REVELATION

There are a variety of reports about whose conduct the opening verse is referring to: al-ʿĀṣ b. Wāʾil, al-Walīd b. al-Mughīrah, or Abu Sufyan. The latter used to slaughter two camels every week. However, if an orphan dared to ask for something from him, he would harshly drive him away with a cane.[3]

Of course these three individuals were disbelievers at the time of the revelation of this chapter, which also later speaks about the conduct of hypocrites.

The central theme of the chapter pertains to the actions that humans are capable of when they have no faith in the Day of Judgement.

LINK TO THE PREVIOUS CHAPTER

The two previous chapters, al-Fīl and Quraysh, recounted God's great favour to the Quraysh when He saved the Kaʿbah from the attack of Abrahah and gave them security in their trade journeys. In return, God instructed them to worship only Him as the true Lord of the Kaʿbah.

This surah tells us what the Quraysh and their leaders were actually doing instead. They lived for this world and revelled in their wealth and power, taking their blessings for granted. They were contemptuous of those who were less fortunate in their society and were mean-spirited with their neighbours. Their actions clearly indicated that they had no belief in the Hereafter, or the Day of Accounting and Judgement.

MERITS OF RECITATION

- A tradition from the Prophet (s) states: Whoever recites this chapter will be forgiven his sins so long as he has paid his *zakat*.[4]
- A tradition from Imam al-Baqir (a) states: Whoever recites Surat al-Māʿūn in his obligatory and supererogatory prayers [with conviction] will be amongst those whose prayers and fasts are

---

[3] Ṭabrasī, *al-Bayān*, 10/834; Rāzī, *Mafātīḥ al-Ghayb*, 32/301.

[4] Baḥrānī, *al-Burhān*, 5/767.

عَنِ الرَّسُولِ (صَلَّى اللهُ عَلَيْهِ وَآلِهِ) – مَنْ قَرَأَ هَذِهِ السُّورَةَ غَفَرَ اللهُ لَهُ مَا دَامَتِ الزَّكَاةُ مُؤَدَّاةً.

accepted by God, and He will not subject him to [a difficult] accounting over what he did in his worldly life.[5]

- A tradition from Imam al-Sadiq (a) states: Whoever recites this surah after his afternoon (*ʿaṣr*) prayers will remain in God's peace and protection until the time for that prayer on the next day.[6]

EXEGESIS

VERSE 1

أَرَأَيْتَ الَّذِي يُكَذِّبُ بِالدِّينِ ﴿١﴾

Have you considered the one who denies the Recompense? [1]

1.1 [*Ara'ayta* (أَرَأَيْتَ, did you see)]. *Ru'yah* can mean both seeing with the eyes, as well as considering and evaluating in the mind. Here, the question, *ara'ayta* means 'have you considered?' It is presented as an expression of disapproval on the part of God and a suggestion that it should cause surprise (*taʿajjub*) in the listener, that there are people who actually deny the Day of Judgement.[7] They might openly profess belief, but their conduct shows that they do not expect to be called to account for their wrong actions. Such people would ultimately have no line that they would not cross.

1.2 Although this question is directed to the Prophet (s), it is relevant to all listeners.[8] Muslims are invited to ponder over the sinful acts of some of the hypocrites, which is the consequence of their heedlessness and lack of belief that they would be held to account one day.

1.3 [*Yukadhdhibu* (يُكَذِّبُ, denies)]. *Takdhīb* is the verbal noun of *kadhdhaba*, which means denying something out of defiance despite instinctively knowing that it is the truth.[9] This is done when

---

5 Ḥuwayzī, *Nūr al-Thaqalayn*, 5/677.

عَنِ الْبَاقِرِ (عَلَيْهِ السَّلَامُ) – مَنْ قَرَأَ سُورَةَ «أَرَأَيْتَ الَّذِي يُكَذِّبُ بِالدِّينِ» فِي فَرَائِضِهِ وَنَوَافِلِهِ كَانَ فِيمَنْ قَبِلَ اللهُ عَزَّ وَجَلَّ صَلَاتَهُ وَصِيَامَهُ وَلَمْ يُحَاسِبْهُ بِمَا كَانَ مِنْهُ فِي الْحَيَاةِ الدُّنْيَا.

6 Baḥrānī, *al-Burhān*, 5/767.

عَنِ الصَّادِقِ (عَلَيْهِ السَّلَامُ) – مَنْ قَرَأَهَا بَعْدَ صَلَاةِ الْعَصْرِ كَانَ فِي أَمَانِ اللهِ وَحِفْظِهِ إِلَى وَقْتِهَا فِي الْيَوْمِ الثَّانِي.

7 *Mafātīḥ al-Ghayb*, 32/301.

8 Ṭabāṭabā'ī, *al-Mīzān*, 20/368.

9 Rāghib, *al-Mufradāt*.

a person suppresses their inner conscience, or the self-reproaching state of their soul (*nafs al-lawwāmah*).

Belying the recompense of one's actions is the most damaging attitude an individual can possess, because he denies himself the motivation to act virtuously and turn away from sin. Thereafter, he is inclined towards every vice because he does not fear its devastating consequences.[10]

1.4 The use of the present continuous tense in the word 'denies' indicates that they continually and habitually deny the fact that they will have to face the consequences of their actions.

1.5 [*Al-Dīn* (الدِّين, religion)] originally means recompense for good and evil actions. It is used to refer to the religion of God and also the Day of Judgement, which is the Day when everyone will be recompensed, as stated in Q82:9:

كَلَّا بَلْ تُكَذِّبُونَ بِالدِّينِ

Not at all! But you deny the Recompense (Day of Judgement)!

However, some exegetes say that since this chapter is not addressing the issues surrounding the Day of Judgement, '*dīn*' here refers to Islam itself, which incorporates the belief in the Day of Return (*maʿād*) in any case.[11]

1.6 The rest of the verses in the chapter give five qualities of these deniers, and are a warning to believers about how low a person, or a society, can fall, once they stop believing that there will be a Day of accounting for actions.

SUMMARY OF THE VERSE

The verse asks the believers to consider the state of those who belie the Day of Recompense.

REFLECTIVE LEARNING

Although as a Muslim I profess belief in the Day of Recompense, let me reflect if that belief is shown in my actions:

---

[10] Ṭabrasī, *al-Bayān*, 10/833.

[11] Javādī-Āmolī, *Tasnīm*. (Transcript: http://javadi.esra.ir/en/-/02-10-9931-تفسیر-سوره-ماعون).

1. When I do any good action, is it intended for other than God and His pleasure? Such an action will have no value on that Day.
2. When I commit a sinful act, is it because I do not imagine that there will be a Day of accountability in front of God, and the possibility of being sent to Hell?

In both these cases, I will have belied the Day of Recompense.

VERSE 2

فَذَٰلِكَ الَّذِي يَدُعُّ الْيَتِيمَ ﴿٢﴾

That is the one who [harshly] drives away the orphan. [2]

2.1 [*Fa* (فَ, so)], is used here to complete the previous verse, meaning, 'if you do not know the one who denies the Day of Recompense, then you should know that it is...', and thereafter, five traits of such people are listed in sequence in the rest of the verses.

2.2 [*Yaduʿʿu* (يَدُعُّ, drives away)] from *daʿʿa*, which means to repulse and drive away with force.

[*al-Yatīm* (الْيَتِيم, the orphan)] means one who has lost his father, or has no guardian. Therefore, the phrase *yaduʿʿu al-yatīm* means 'to turn away the orphan with disdain and force.'

2.3 Those who belie the Day of Judgement go on to commit many such sinful and despicable acts.

However, in contrast, the Qur'an specifically highlights kindness to the orphans and compassion to the poor (in the next verse).These are amongst the most highly recommended acts in Islam and moreover, are universally recognized as human values of great merit.

2.4 A famous report from the Prophet (s) states: I and the one who [voluntarily] takes care of an orphan are as [close as] these two in Paradise, as long as he is mindful of God, the Almighty – and he (s) held up his index and middle fingers.[12]

2.5 A tradition from Imam Ali (a) states: There is no believing man or woman who places their hand compassionately over the head of

[12] Ḥuwayzī, *Nūr al-Thaqalayn*, 5/597.

عَنِ الرَّسُولِ (صَلَّى اللهُ عَلَيْهِ وَآلِهِ) - أَنَا وَكَافِلُ الْيَتِيمِ كَهَاتَيْنِ فِي الْجَنَّةِ إِذَا اتَّقَى اللهَ عَزَّ وَجَلَّ وَأَشَارَ بِالسَّبَّابَةِ وَالْوُسْطَى.

an orphan, except that God writes for them a reward for every hair that their hand passes over.[13]

SUMMARY OF THE VERSE

The message of the verse is that treating an orphan harshly is one of the signs of lack of belief in the Day of Judgement.

REFLECTIVE LEARNING

We often encounter orphans, either in our home countries or when we travel. Sometimes, we may be guilty of dealing with them impatiently as we are busy going towards a sacred shrine for example.
All that is required to make the orphan happy is a kindly smile, some empathy, and perhaps, a small treat. In losing their parents, these children have often been deprived of these small acts of love.
Let me reflect on how I treat these orphans.

VERSE 3

وَلَا يَحُضُّ عَلَىٰ طَعَامِ الْمِسْكِينِ ﴿٣﴾

And does not encourage the feeding of the poor. [3]

3.1 [*Yaḥuḍḍu* (يَحُضُّ, encourage)] is derived from *ḥaḍḍa*, which means to urge and encourage others. The use of the present tense for the two verbs *yaduʿʿu* and *yaḥuḍḍu* indicates that these people would continually and routinely ignore the rights of the orphans and the poor.[14]
[*Miskīn* (مِسْكِين, poor)]. *Miskīn* refers to someone who is moved by his abject poverty to beg for aid, as contrasted with *faqīr*, who is a person that has difficulty in meeting his expenses, but does not beg.[15]

3.2 When we look at our own abject neediness of God, then we should realize that we too are *miskīn*, except that we do not always realize it. Q35:15 states:

---

[13] Majlisī, *Biḥār*, 72/4.

عَنْ أَمِيرِ الْمُؤْمِنِينَ (عَلَيْهِ السَّلَامُ) – مَا مِنْ مُؤْمِنٍ وَلَا مُؤْمِنَةٍ يَضَعُ يَدَهُ عَلَى رَأْسِ يَتِيمٍ تَرَحُّمًا لَهُ إِلَّا كَتَبَ اللهُ لَهُ بِكُلِّ شَعْرَةٍ مَرَّتْ يَدُهُ عَلَيْهَا حَسَنَةً.

[14] Shīrāzī, *Namūneh*, 27/359.

[15] Ibid, 8/6.

يَا أَيُّهَا النَّاسُ أَنْتُمُ الْفُقَرَاءُ إِلَى اللهِ وَاللهُ هُوَ الْغَنِيُّ الْحَمِيدُ

O mankind! It is you who stand in need of God,
while God is He Who is free of all needs, worthy of all praise.

When helping those who are financially poor, we should take stock of our own destitution as well.

3.3 [*Ṭaʿām al-miskīn* (طَعَامِ الْمِسْكِين, the feeding of the poor)]. *Ṭaʿām al-miskīn* literally means the food of the poor. This is not just a criticism of miserliness, but also reminds man of the fact that the poor have a right to food from the wealth of the people, in the form of religious alms (*zakat*) and other charities (*ṣadaqāt*). The food that one gives actually belongs to the poor as his right.[16] Q51:19 states:

وَفِي أَمْوَالِهِمْ حَقٌّ لِلسَّائِلِ وَالْمَحْرُومِ

And in their wealth is a right for the beggar and the deprived.

3.4 In this regard, a tradition from Imam Ali (a) states: Indeed God, the Glorious, has placed the provision of the poor in the wealth of the rich. Therefore, no poor person goes hungry except that a wealthy person has consumed his right; and God will interrogate them about that.[17]

3.5 Similarly, there are many reports about the merits of feeding other believers, and especially the poor, for example:

A tradition from Imam al-Hadi (a) states: When God was conversing with Prophet Musa b. ʿImran (a)... Musa (a) asked, "My Lord! What is the reward for the one who feeds the poor for Your sake?" God replied, "O Musa! [In return] I shall instruct a herald to call out on the Day of Judgement in front of the entire creation, 'Indeed, this person is one of those who has been freed by God from the fire of Hell!'"[18]

---

16 Ṭabāṭabāʾī, *al-Mīzān*, 20/368.

17 *Nahj al-Balāghah*, saying no. 328.

إِنَّ اللهَ سُبْحَانَهُ فَرَضَ فِي أَمْوَالِ الْأَغْنِيَاءِ أَقْوَاتَ الْفُقَرَاءِ، فَمَا جَاعَ فَقِيرٌ إِلَّا بِمَا مُتِّعَ بِهِ غَنِيٌّ، وَاللهُ تَعَالَى سَائِلُهُمْ عَنْ ذَلِكَ.

18 Ṣadūq, *al-Amālī*, p. 207.

عَنِ الْهَادِي (عَلَيْهِ السَّلَامُ) — لَمَّا كَلَّمَ اللهُ عَزَّ وَجَلَّ مُوسَى بْنَ عِمْرَانَ عَلَيْهِ السَّلَامُ ... قَالَ مُوسَى عَلَيْهِ السَّلَامُ: إِلٰهِي، فَمَا جَزَاءُ مَنْ أَطْعَمَ مِسْكِينًا ابْتِغَاءَ وَجْهِكَ؟

قَالَ يَا مُوسَى، آمُرُ مُنَادِيًا يُنَادِي يَوْمَ الْقِيَامَةِ عَلَى رُؤُوسِ الْخَلَائِقِ: إِنَّ فُلَانَ ابْنَ فُلَانٍ مِنْ عُتَقَاءِ اللهِ مِنَ النَّارِ.

3.6 Accordingly, those who are uncaring towards orphans and the poor have, in fact, belied the Day of Judgement.

SUMMARY OF THE VERSE

Not encouraging one another to feed those who are less fortunate is yet another sign of lack of belief in the Day of Judgement.

REFLECTIVE LEARNING

We will often encounter people who ask us for help directly or indirectly. It is important to keep in mind that they have a God-given share in our wealth. Since they are a means and an opportunity to fulfil our duty to God, we should treat them with dignity.
Let me reflect on whether I help people begrudgingly, or do I see it as an opportunity to serve the Creator through serving His creation.

VERSES 4, 5

فَوَيْلٌ لِلْمُصَلِّينَ ﴿٤﴾ الَّذِينَ هُمْ عَنْ صَلَاتِهِمْ سَاهُونَ ﴿٥﴾

So, woe be to those who pray, [4] *[but] who are heedless about their prayers.* [5]

4-5.1 The third trait of those who belie the Day of Judgement is neglect of their daily prayers and heedlessness in this regard.

4-5.2 '*So, woe be to those who pray.*': [*Fa* (فَ, so)], is used here to show the consequences that people who pray in this manner will face on the Day of Judgement.

[*Muṣallīn* (مُصَلِّين, those who pray)] could also mean the '*people of prayer*', that is, the Muslims. In this meaning, the verse may be talking of Muslims who should pray five times daily, but do not.[19]

Imam al-Kazim (a) when asked about the meaning of these verses, stated, "It is the wasting [of the potential benefits] of the prayer."[20]

[19] Ibn Kathīr, *Tafsīr*, 8/468.
[20] Kulaynī, *al-Kāfī*, 3/268.
عَنْ مُحَمَّدِ بْنِ الْفُضَيْلِ قَالَ: سَأَلْتُ عَبْدًا صَالِحًا (عَلَيْهِ السَّلَامُ) عَنْ قَوْلِ اللهِ عَزَّ وَجَلَّ «الَّذِينَ هُمْ عَنْ صَلَاتِهِمْ سَاهُونَ» قَالَ هُوَ التَّضْيِيعُ.

4-5.3 '*Who are heedless about their prayers.*': [*Sāhūn* (سَاهُون, those who forget)]. *Sahw* normally means to forget or neglect by mistake, but here it refers to forgetting due to heedlessness.[21]

The verse does not say that they are forgetful in their prayers (*fī ṣalātihim*), because *sahw* in prayers is quite possible and common; for this reason, there are rulings in *fiqh* that deal with how one should rectify his prayer in case something is forgotten.

The verse states that they are forgetful about their prayers (*ʿan ṣalātihim*), meaning that they have not understood the status of *salat*, and they do not care when they pray and even if they pray. And if they do pray, they hardly remember God. Q4:142 states:

إِنَّ الْمُنَافِقِينَ يُخَادِعُونَ اللَّهَ وَهُوَ خَادِعُهُمْ وَإِذَا قَامُوا إِلَى الصَّلَاةِ
قَامُوا كُسَالَىٰ يُرَاءُونَ النَّاسَ وَلَا يَذْكُرُونَ اللَّهَ إِلَّا قَلِيلًا

Indeed, the hypocrites seek to deceive God, but it is He who deceives (requites their deceit to) them. And when they stand for prayer, they stand with laziness to be seen by the people, and do not remember God except a little.

4-5.4 About the importance of prayer, and quoting this verse, Imam Ali (a) is reported to have said: No act is more beloved to God, the Almighty, than the daily prayers. Do not let any worldly affair prevent you from observing the prayer at its appointed time. Indeed, God, the Almighty, has censured some people by stating, "*Those who are heedless about their prayers*", meaning that they were neglectful and took the appointed times of prayer lightly.[22]

4-5.5 A tradition states that when Imam al-Sadiq (a) was asked about the meaning of this verse, he said, "It is abandoning the prayers, or delaying them [without excuse]."[23]

---

21 Shīrāzī, *Namūneh*, 27/360.

22 Nūrī, *Mustadrak al-Wasāʾil*, 3/44.

عَنْ أَمِيرِ الْمُؤْمِنِينَ (عَلَيْهِ السَّلَامُ) – لَيْسَ عَمَلٌ أَحَبَّ إِلَى اللهِ عَزَّ وَجَلَّ مِنَ الصَّلَاةِ، فَلَا يَشْغَلَنَّكُمْ عَنْ أَوْقَاتِهَا شَيْءٌ مِنْ أُمُورِ الدُّنْيَا، فَإِنَّ اللهَ عَزَّ وَجَلَّ ذَمَّ أَقْوَامًا فَقَالَ «الَّذِينَ هُمْ عَنْ صَلَاتِهِمْ سَاهُونَ» يَعْنِي أَنَّهُمْ غَافِلُونَ اسْتَهَانُوا بِأَوْقَاتِهَا.

23 ʿĀmilī, *Wasāʾil*, 4/114.

سَأَلْتُ أَبَا عَبْدِ اللهِ (عَلَيْهِ السَّلَامُ) عَنْ قَوْلِ اللهِ عَزَّ وَجَلَّ «الَّذِينَ هُمْ عَنْ صَلَاتِهِمْ سَاهُونَ» قَالَ هُوَ التَّرْكُ لَهَا وَالتَّوَانِي عَنْهَا.

4-5.6 Another tradition states that in his final words to his family, Imam al-Sadiq (a) said, "Our intercession will not reach the one who took the prayer lightly."[24]

SUMMARY OF THE VERSES

The verses disparage those who stand to pray, yet are heedless about Whom they stand in front of.

REFLECTIVE LEARNING

The Qur'an lists heedlessness and neglect of the prayer, as well as sluggishness during the prayer, as a sign of hypocrisy.

Let me reflect on the quality of my prayer, and think of ways that I can improve it, to ensure that I am not included amongst those who have been censured in these verses.

VERSE 6

﴿ الَّذِينَ هُمْ يُرَاءُونَ ﴿٦﴾ ﴾

Those who do [good] only to be seen by others, [6]

6.1 [*Yurāʾūn* (يُرَاءُونَ, show others)]. Without doubt, the person who does good acts only to show others has no desire for Divine recompense, and instead chooses to seek the praise of the people. This is a sure sign of faithlessness in the Day of Judgement.

6.2 Doing good deeds to show off to the people (*riyāʾ*) has been strongly condemned in the *aḥādīth*. Some examples are:

i) A tradition from the Prophet (s) states: The one who showed off for the people (*al-murāʾī*) shall be summoned forth on the Day of Judgement with the following address, "O transgressor (*fājir*)! O betrayer (*ghādir*)! O show-off (*murāʾī*)! Your acts are ruined, and your reward is lost. Go and take your reward from those for whom you performed your deeds!"[25]

---

[24] Ibid, 4/27.

عَنِ الصَّادِقِ (عَلَيْهِ السَّلَامُ) – إِنَّ شَفَاعَتَنَا لَا تَنَالُ مُسْتَخِفًّا بِالصَّلَاةِ.

[25] Shahīd al-Thānī, *Munyat al-Murīd*, p. 318.

عَنِ الرَّسُولِ (صَلَّى اللهُ عَلَيْهِ وَآلِهِ) – إِنَّ الْمُرَائِي يُنَادَى يَوْمَ الْقِيَامَةِ: يَا فَاجِرُ، يَا غَادِرُ، يَا مُرَائِي، ضَلَّ عَمَلُكَ، وَبَطَلَ أَجْرُكَ، اذْهَبْ فَخُذْ أَجْرَكَ مِمَّنْ كُنْتَ تَعْمَلُ لَهُ.

ii) A tradition from Imam Ali (a) states: How reprehensible it is for a human being to have a sick interior and a beautiful exterior![26]

6.3 About the verse under review, a tradition from Imam Ali (a) states: God is referring here to hypocrites. They do not hope for reward when they pray and do not fear any punishment for not praying. They are oblivious of the time of the prayer until it lapses. When they are in the company of the believers, they pray to show off but when they are alone, they do not bother with the prayer.

It is about them that God states, '*Those who do [good] only to be seen by others.*'[27]

6.4 A similar message is contained in another early chapter of the Qur'an, Surat al-Muddaththir: Q74:42-46 describes the admission of those who are sent to hellfire:

مَا سَلَكَكُمْ فِي سَقَرَ ﴿٤٢﴾ قَالُوا لَمْ نَكُ مِنَ الْمُصَلِّينَ ﴿٤٣﴾ وَلَمْ نَكُ نُطْعِمُ
الْمِسْكِينَ ﴿٤٤﴾ وَكُنَّا نَخُوضُ مَعَ الْخَائِضِينَ ﴿٤٥﴾ وَكُنَّا نُكَذِّبُ بِيَوْمِ الدِّينِ

"What has brought you to Saqar?" They shall say, "We were not amongst those who prayed (muṣallīn), *nor did we feed the poor. And we indulged [in vain discourse] with those who indulged. And we used to belie the Day of Judgement.*

SUMMARY OF THE VERSE

This verse speaks of the futility of actions done only to please and impress others and placing no importance to the witnessing of God.

REFLECTIVE LEARNING

1. This verse clearly condemns those who behave in one way in the presence of the Muslims and behave quite differently when alone, or in the presence of non-Muslims. Let me reflect whether I remain authentic to my faith at all times.

---

[26] Āmudī, *Ghurar al-Ḥikam*, trad. 9661.

عَنْ أَمِيرِ الْمُؤْمِنِينَ (عَلَيْهِ السَّلَامُ) – مَا أَقْبَحَ بِالْإِنْسَانِ بَاطِنًا عَلِيلًا وَظَاهِرًا جَمِيلًا!

[27] Majlisī, *Biḥār*, 80/6.

عَنْ أَمِيرِ الْمُؤْمِنِينَ (عَلَيْهِ السَّلَامُ) – يُرِيدُ الْمُنَافِقُونَ الَّذِينَ لَا يَرْجُونَ لَهَا ثَوَابًا إِنْ صَلُّوا وَلَا يَخَافُونَ عَلَيْهَا عِقَابًا إِنْ تَرَكُوا، فَهُمْ عَنْهَا غَافِلُونَ حَتَّى يَذْهَبَ وَقْتُهَا، فَإِذَا كَانُوا مَعَ الْمُؤْمِنِينَ صَلَّوْهَا رِيَاءً وَإِذَا لَمْ يَكُونُوا مَعَهُمْ لَمْ يُصَلُّوا، وَهُوَ قَوْلُهُ: «الَّذِينَ هُمْ يُرَاءُونَ».

2. The need to be appreciated leads one to instinctively show off to others. Wouldn't it be better to show off to God instead?! Let me reflect on whom I show off to in my acts.

VERSE 7

وَيَمْنَعُونَ الْمَاعُونَ ﴿٧﴾

And withhold [small] acts of kindness. [7]

7.1 [*Al-Māʿūn* (الْمَاعُون, small kindnesses)]. According to many exegetes its meaning here is the small articles of necessity that people, especially neighbours, occasionally borrow from one another.[28]

Islam lays great emphasis on social cohesion and harmony; praying together, sharing food, getting married, etc., are all acts that strengthen the fabric of society and carry great reward. Those who would deny others even small kindnesses are people who do not care if they damage these social relations, revealing that they have no faith in God's recompense on the Day of Judgement.

7.2 A tradition from Imam Ali (a) states: The Prophet (s) forbade anyone from refusing requests of small kindnesses from neighbours, and said that whoever denies his neighbour small kindnesses, God will deny him His bounties on the Day of Judgement and leave him to fend for himself. And whoever God leaves to fend for himself will be in the worst of predicaments.[29]

7.3 The last two verses are interlinked, in the meaning that the hypocrite denies God His right by showing off to the people, and denies the people their rights by withholding small kindnesses from them; therefore, he gives neither their due rights.

SUMMARY OF THE VERSE

The verse shows how mean-spirited people can become when they have no sense of gratitude to God, and belie the Day that they will stand in front of Him for accounting.

---

[28] Shīrāzī, *Namūneh*, 27/361.

[29] Ṣadūq, *al-Faqih*, 4/14.

عَنْ أَمِيرِ الْمُؤْمِنِينَ (عَلَيْهِ السَّلَامُ) – نَهَى رَسُولُ اللهِ (صَلَّى اللهُ عَلَيْهِ وَآلِهِ) أَنْ يَمْنَعَ أَحَدٌ الْمَاعُونَ جَارَهُ وَقَالَ مَنْ مَنَعَ الْمَاعُونَ جَارَهُ مَنَعَهُ اللهُ خَيْرَهُ يَوْمَ الْقِيَامَةِ وَوَكَلَهُ إِلَى نَفْسِهِ وَمَنْ وَكَلَهُ إِلَى نَفْسِهِ فَمَا أَسْوَأَ حَالَهُ.

REFLECTIVE LEARNING

The chapter began by discussing crimes against people, then talked of the crimes against God, and then reverted back to crimes against people. In fact, these two behaviours and attitudes are intertwined and cannot be separated, although people try to do so. For instance, they may say, "I am a good person, a charitable person, but I just don't pray." Or they may say, "There are people who pray regularly but they are not kind to their family and mean with their wealth."

Both these statements are justifications that attempt to separate the rights of God and the people. This chapter shows that in God's eyes, the two things are inseparable.

Therefore let me reflect:

1. Whether I am good to people but heedless of God. In that case, although I would have connected to my humanness and the *fiṭrah* that God has placed within every human being, I would have scorned the very Creator of my instincts to goodness, and denied myself the means to send forth my reward to the next world.
2. If I perform the acts of worship to God but ignore the rights of the creation. In that case I have not understood the fullness of my duty to God.

SURAT AL-KAWTHAR
THE ABUNDANCE (108)

TEXT AND TRANSLATION

سُورَةُ الْكَوْثَرِ

بِسْمِ اللهِ الرَّحْمٰنِ الرَّحِيمِ

إِنَّا أَعْطَيْنَاكَ الْكَوْثَرَ ﴿١﴾ فَصَلِّ لِرَبِّكَ وَانْحَرْ ﴿٢﴾ إِنَّ شَانِئَكَ هُوَ الْأَبْتَرُ ﴿٣﴾

In the name of God, the Beneficent, the Merciful.

Indeed, We have granted you abundance [1] *So [in gratitude] pray to your Lord and sacrifice.* [2] *Indeed, your enemy is the one [whose progeny is] cut off.* [3]

INTRODUCTION

Surat al-Kawthar (108) was the 15th chapter to be revealed in Makka.[1] It is the shortest surah of the Qur'an, containing only three succinct verses and ten words. Its powerful message is enhanced by the fact that the words and phrases used to impart its message: [*aʿṭaynāka* (أَعْطَيْنَاكَ, We granted you)], [*al-kawthar* (الْكَوْثَر, abundant good)], [*fa ṣallī* (فَصَلِّ, so pray)], [*inḥar* (انْحَرْ, sacrifice)], [*shāniʾaka* (شَانِئَكَ, your enemy)], and [*abtar* (أَبْتَر, progeny cut off)], are unique to this chapter and are not used anywhere else in the Qur'an.[2]

In this chapter, God mentions the great favour and abundance of goodness (*al-kawthar*) that He bestowed upon the Prophet (s). Those who had taunted him that his lineage would be cut because he did not have any surviving male children, were the ones who would have their lineage cut off (*abtar*) themselves.

---

1 Maʿrifat, *ʿUlūm-i Qurʾānī*, p. 90.

2 The Qur'an contains around 500 unique words, or *hapax legomena*, and they usually occur in clusters. (See: Toorawa, Shawkat, 'Hapaxes in the Qurʾān', *New Perspectives on the Qurʾān*, p. 239.

OCCASION OF REVELATION

According to most sources, this chapter was revealed in Makka in the early years of the mission of the Prophet (s).

About the occasion of its revelation, we read: Al-ᶜĀṣ b. Wā'il al-Sahmī (the father of ᶜAmr b. al-ᶜĀṣ), who was one of the chiefs of the polytheists in Makka, met the Prophet (s) as he was leaving the sacred mosque. They conversed for a while, while a group of the chiefs of the Quraysh, who were in the vicinity, watched them. When al-ᶜĀṣ entered, they asked him, "Who were you speaking with?" He replied [mockingly], "That 'tailless one' (*abtar*)!" They had attributed this derogatory name to the Prophet (s) after the death of his son ᶜAbdullah (also known as Tahir), implying that he would have no progeny to survive him. Surat al-Kawthar was revealed at this time, assuring the Prophet (s) of the great abundance that he had been granted by God, and declaring that it was his enemy and detractors whose lineage would not endure.[3]

For this reason, according to many exegetes, this chapter was revealed in honour of Lady Fatimah al-Zahra (a).[4] It was through this blessed lady and the Commander of the Faithful (a) that the progeny of the Prophet (s) flourished.

LINK TO THE PREVIOUS CHAPTER

The previous chapter, Surat al-Māᶜūn, gave four characteristics of the hypocrites: miserliness, heedlessness in prayer, showing off in prayer, and refusal to share their bounties with the less fortunate. In Surat al-Kawthar, God presents four counter attitudes. In reply to miserliness, He states that all bounty comes from Him, and those whom He has given abundance (*kawthar*) should likewise spend abundantly in His way. In reply to being heedless in prayer, he reminds the Prophet (s) and the Muslims to show their gratitude by performing the daily prayer (*fa ṣallī*) constantly and sincerely. In reply to showing off to others, He states that the prayer should be for the Lord alone (*li Rabbika*). In reply to the meanness in sharing their bounties, He commands the Prophet (s) and Muslims to sacrifice (*wa inḥar*) for others.[5]

---

[3] Ṭabrasī, *al-Bayān*, 10/836; Majlisī, *Biḥār*, 17/203.

[4] Shīrāzī, *Namūneh*, 27/375.

[5] Rāzī, *Mafātīḥ al-Ghayb*, 32/307.

MERITS OF RECITATION

- A tradition from the Prophet (s) states: God, the Exalted, will quench the thirst of the one who recites this chapter with the water of the river of al-Kawthar, and every other river in Paradise.[6]
- A tradition from Imam al-Sadiq (a) states: Whoever recites this chapter in his obligatory or supererogatory prayers will be allowed by God to drink water from [the pool of] al-Kawthar on the Day of Judgement, and he will meet and converse with the Prophet (s) at the tree of Ṭūbā.[7]

EXEGESIS

VERSE 1

إِنَّا أَعْطَيْنَاكَ الْكَوْثَرَ ﴿١﴾

Indeed, We have granted you abundance. [1]

1.1 [*Aʿṭā* (أَعْطَى, grant)] means to grant and bestow.[8] This bestowal fulfilled the promise of God when He had pledged in Q93:5:

وَلَسَوْفَ يُعْطِيكَ رَبُّكَ فَتَرْضَىٰ

And indeed, your Lord will soon give you
that [with which] you shall be well pleased

1.2 [*Al-Kawthar* (الْكَوْثَر, abundance)] is the intensive form (*fawʿal*) derived from *kathara* which means to be plentiful. While *kathrah*, and the stronger form *kathīr*, can mean plenty of good as well as evil, *kawthar* means abundant goodness (*al-khayr al-kathīr*), or the embodiment of all goodness.[9]

---

6 Baḥrānī, *al-Burhān*, 5/771.

عَنِ النَّبِيِّ (صَلَّى اللهُ عَلَيْهِ وَآلِهِ) – مَنْ قَرَأَ هَذِهِ السُّورَةَ سَقَاهُ اللهُ تَعَالَى مِنْ نَهْرِ الْكَوْثَرِ، وَمِنْ كُلِّ نَهْرٍ فِي الْجَنَّةِ.

7 Majlisī, *Biḥār*, 89/338.

عَنِ الصَّادِقِ (عَلَيْهِ السَّلَامُ) – مَنْ كَانَ قِرَاءَتُهُ «إِنَّا أَعْطَيْنَاكَ الْكَوْثَرَ» فِي فَرَائِضِهِ وَنَوَافِلِهِ سَقَاهُ اللهُ مِنَ الْكَوْثَرِ يَوْمَ الْقِيَامَةِ وَكَانَ مُحَدِّثُهُ عِنْدَ رَسُولِ اللهِ (صَلَّى اللهُ عَلَيْهِ وَآلِهِ) فِي أَصْلِ طُوبَى.

8 Rāghib, *al-Mufradāt*.

9 Ṭūsī, *al-Tibyān*, 10/417.

1.3 According to the narrations, *kawthar* refers to several things: a river in Paradise, a drinking fountain belonging to the Prophet (s) on the Day of Judgement, a reference to the offspring of the Prophet (s), a reference to the great status of the mission and prophethood of the Prophet (s), or to the great miracle that he was given, namely the Qur'an. In this verse, it has not been explicitly defined, and probably encompasses all the great and unmatched favours that the Prophet (s) was granted by God, such as revelation, wisdom, intercession, a global ummah, the seal of prophethood, etc.[10] It is noteworthy that the most abundant of bestowals is mentioned in the smallest of chapters.

1.4 The most apt meaning, keeping in mind the last verse of the chapter, is that *kawthar* is an allusion to the abundance in the lineage of the Prophet (s), from Lady Fatimah (a), and through her and Imam Ali (a), the rest of the Imams (a) of the *Ahl al-Bayt*, and their descendants. There is no family in the world that has spread with this abundance.[11]

1.5 The *Sunni* exegete al-Rāzī writes, "*Kawthar* is [also] a reference to the offspring of the Prophet (s), because when it was revealed, this chapter refuted those who alleged that he would not have any [surviving] children. The chapter declared that his lineage would continue through every age after him. Despite so many of them being killed, the world is full of his progeny, while no one worthy of mention remains of the Banu Umayyah in the world today. Look at how many great scholars rose from them, such as al-Baqir, al-Sadiq, al-Kazim, and al-Ridha, may peace be on all of them..."[12]

1.6 Abundance is a blessing which should constantly be sought from God with the view of utilizing His bounties to attain His proximity and pleasure. However, if one seeks abundance for its own sake only, then it merely serves to distance one from God. When abundance is pursued without God being the objective, then

---

[10] Ṭabāṭabā'ī, *al-Mīzān*, 20/371.

[11] Ibid.

[12] al-Rāzī, *Mafātīḥ al-Ghayb*, 32/313.

الْكَوْثَرُ أَوْلَادُهُ قَالُوا: لِأَنَّ هَذِهِ السُّورَةَ إِنَّمَا نَزَلَتْ رَدًّا عَلَى مَنْ عَابَهُ عَلَيْهِ السَّلَامُ بِعَدَمِ الْأَوْلَادِ، فَالْمَعْنَى أَنَّهُ يُعْطِيهِ نَسْلًا يَبْقَوْنَ عَلَى مَرِّ الزَّمَانِ، فَانْظُرْ كَمْ قُتِلَ مِنْ أَهْلِ الْبَيْتِ، ثُمَّ الْعَالَمُ مُمْتَلِئٌ مِنْهُمْ، وَلَمْ يَبْقَ مِنْ بَنِي أُمَيَّةَ فِي الدُّنْيَا أَحَدٌ يُعْبَأُ بِهِ، ثُمَّ انْظُرْ كَمْ كَانَ فِيهِمْ مِنَ الْأَكَابِرِ مِنَ الْعُلَمَاءِ كَالْبَاقِرِ وَالصَّادِقِ وَالْكَاظِمِ وَالرِّضَا عَلَيْهِمُ السَّلَامُ.

it is detrimental. In Q102:1, God uses [*al-takāthur* (التَّكَاثُرُ, rivalry in accumulation)], which has the same root as *al-kawthar*, but has a negative connotation:

أَلْهَاكُمُ التَّكَاثُرُ

Rivalry in accumulation distracts you.

DISCUSSION: THE USAGE OF 'I (إِنِّي, أنا)' AND 'WE (إِنَّا, نَحنُ)' FOR GOD IN THE QUR'AN

In the Qur'an, God uses both the singular as well as the plural pronoun when referring to Himself. [*Innā* (إِنَّا, Indeed We) and *Naḥnu* (نَحنُ, We] are used to emphasize God's majesty and limitless power. For instance, when He speaks of granting guidance to mankind through revelation, this pronoun is used. As an example of this usage, Q4:163 states:

إِنَّا أَوْحَيْنَا إِلَيْكَ كَمَا أَوْحَيْنَا إِلَىٰ نُوحٍ وَالنَّبِيِّينَ مِنْ بَعْدِهِ

Indeed, We have revealed to you,
as We revealed to Nuh and the Prophets after him...

On the other hand, He uses the singular pronoun [*Innī*, (إِنِّي, Indeed I) or *Anā'* [(أَنَا, I)], when He talks of His intimate relationship with His servants. For example, Q2:186 states:

وَإِذَا سَأَلَكَ عِبَادِي عَنِّي فَإِنِّي قَرِيبٌ أُجِيبُ دَعْوَةَ الدَّاعِ إِذَا دَعَانِ
فَلْيَسْتَجِيبُوا لِي وَلْيُؤْمِنُوا بِي لَعَلَّهُمْ يَرْشُدُونَ

And when My servants ask you about Me, [inform them that] indeed, I am near [to them]. I answer the prayer of the supplicant when He calls to Me. So, let them respond to Me [by obedience] and believe in Me, so that they may be guided aright.

The usage of 'We' and 'I' by God also encourages a balance between hope and fear in the believer. 'I' reminds one of how close He is; one feels the love, the proximity, and the personal care of the Creator, and wants to obey and serve Him, in the hope of pleasing Him. 'We' reminds one of His transcendence; one is filled with awe of His magnificence, might, and power, and wants to obey and serve Him, out of fear of disobeying Him.

Four surahs begin with *innā*, each instance indicating the grandeur of God.

i) In Surat al-Fatḥ, (Q48:1), He stated:

إِنَّا فَتَحْنَا لَكَ فَتْحًا مُبِينًا

Indeed, We have granted you a clear victory...

This was after the pivotal treaty of Hudaybiyyah, which opened the way to the conversion of most of Arabia to Islam.

ii) In Surat Nūḥ (Q71:1), God announces:

إِنَّا أَرْسَلْنَا نُوحًا إِلَىٰ قَوْمِهِ

Indeed, We sent Nuh to his people...

Nuh (a) was the great Prophet who was the first of the senior messengers of God.

iii) In Surat al-Qadr (Q97:1), God announces:

إِنَّا أَنزَلْنَاهُ فِي لَيْلَةِ الْقَدْرِ

Indeed, We sent it down (the Qur'an) on the Night of Decree.

Here, God refers to a grand night which is better than one thousand months.

iv) Finally, in Surat al-Kawthar, God states:

إِنَّا أَعْطَيْنَاكَ الْكَوْثَرَ

Indeed, We have granted you abundance.

This is to signify the abundant favour that He bestowed on Prophet Muhammad (s).

SUMMARY OF THE VERSE

The verse announces the great bestowal of abundance to the Prophet (s), and by extension, to the believers as well.

REFLECTIVE LEARNING

The greatest blessing to the Prophet (s) was the gift of the unique individuals within his progeny. Together, the 14 infallibles (a) formed a chain that is unmatched in the history of mankind. They are God's proofs (*ḥujaj*) on earth, and He made obedience to them an obligation (*farīḍah*) for the believers.

Let me reflect on how much I know about these great personalities, because it is through knowing them that I will know my own Imam, Muhammad al-Mahdi (af).

VERSE 2

فَصَلِّ لِرَبِّكَ وَٱنْحَرْ ﴿٢﴾

So [in gratitude] pray to your Lord and sacrifice. [2]

2.1 The prefix [*fa* (فَ, so)] indicates a consequent action is expected. The grant of a favour requires the immediate display of gratitude (*shukr*). Therefore, in return for God's abundant blessings, the Prophet (s) is instructed to keep up the prayer in His remembrance and to give sacrifice. Both these acts manifest gratitude.

2.2 [*Li Rabbika* (لِرَبِّكَ, to your Lord)] forestalls arrogance because it reminds us that it is He who is our Sustainer and the One who has provided everything we possess. Also, it advises us that prayer is solely for our Lord, to Whom we owe thanks.

2.3 [*Inḥar* (ٱنْحَرْ, sacrifice)] is the imperative form of the verb *naḥara*. Amongst the exegetes, three views have been presented about the meaning of *naḥr*:

i) The sacrifice of camels, in particular after the Eid prayers at the time of Eid al-Adha. *Naḥr* refers to the special method of slaughtering camels (*dhibḥ* is the word used for slaughtering other animals).[13] Some exegetes express doubt that the sacrifice mentioned here is exclusive only to the day of Eid and say that the command to sacrifice is of a general nature, and the slaughter of camels on the day of Eid is a particular instance of it. This is because the Muslims placed greater importance on it in those days, and the slaughter of a camel, which was considered very valuable, symbolized a great personal sacrifice.[14]

ii) According to some traditions, *naḥr* also refers to standing facing the *qiblah* in prayer, because the word refers to the throat, and the Arabs used the word to mean 'facing something'.

---

[13] Ṭabāṭabā'ī, *al-Mīzān*, 20/640 (Farsi translation).

[14] Shīrāzī, *Namūneh*, 27/373.

A tradition from Imam al-Baqir (a) states: *Al-naḥr* refers to standing up straight (facing *qiblah*) in the *qiyām* of prayer, so that one's back and neck are upright.[15]

iii) However, according to a number of traditions, *naḥr* means raising the hands in *takbīr* during prayer. Some of these reports are mentioned below:

A tradition from the Prophet (s) states that when this verse was revealed to him, he (s) asked Jibra'il (a), "What is this sacrifice that my Lord has commanded me to perform?" He replied, "O Muhammad (s), it is not a sacrifice; it is the raising of the hands in prayer."[16]

A tradition from Imam Ali (a) states: When this surah was revealed, God's Messenger (s) asked Jibra'il (a), "What is this sacrifice that my Lord has commanded me to perform?" He replied, "[O Muhammad (s),] it is not a sacrifice; rather, He only commands you to raise your hands when you say the *takbīr* as you begin the prayer, when you bow down [into *rukūʿ*], when you raise your head from the *rukūʿ*, and when you prostrate [in *sajdah*], because this is the manner of our prayer and the prayers of the angels in the seven heavens. Indeed, there is a beauty for everything, and the beauty of the prayer is the raising of hands at the time of saying *takbīr*."[17]

SUMMARY OF THE VERSE

The verses direct the believer to perform the *salat* when they receive God's great favours and then sacrifice in His way.

---

15 Kulaynī, *al-Kāfī*, 3/336; Ṭūsī, *Tahdhīb*, 2/84.

عَنِ الْبَاقِرِ (عَلَيْهِ السَّلَامُ) – قَالَ النَّحْرُ الْاِعْتِدَالُ فِي الْقِيَامِ أَنْ يُقِيمَ صُلْبَهُ وَنَحْرَهُ.

16 ʿĀmilī, *Wasāʾil*, 6/30.

عَنِ الرَّسُولِ (صَلَّى اللهُ عَلَيْهِ وَآلِهِ) – لَمَّا نَزَلَتْ عَلَى النَّبِيِّ (صَلَّى اللهُ عَلَيْهِ وَآلِهِ) «فَصَلِّ لِرَبِّكَ وَانْحَرْ» قَالَ: يَا جَبْرَائِيلُ (عَلَيْهِ السَّلَامُ) مَا هَذِهِ النَّحِيرَةُ الَّتِي أَمَرَ بِهَا رَبِّي؟ فَقَالَ: يَا مُحَمَّدُ (صَلَّى اللهُ عَلَيْهِ وَآلِهِ) إِنَّهَا لَيْسَتْ نَحِيرَةً وَلَكِنَّهَا رَفْعُ الْأَيْدِي فِي الصَّلَاةِ.

17 Majlisī, *Biḥār*, 81/351.

عَنْ أَمِيرِ الْمُؤْمِنِينَ (عَلَيْهِ السَّلَامُ) – لَمَّا نَزَلَتْ هَذِهِ السُّورَةُ قَالَ رَسُولُ اللهِ (صَلَّى اللهُ عَلَيْهِ وَآلِهِ) لِجَبْرَائِيلَ (عَلَيْهِ السَّلَامُ) مَا هَذِهِ النَّحِيرَةُ الَّتِي أَمَرَنِي بِهَا رَبِّي؟ قَالَ لَيْسَتْ بِنَحِيرَةٍ وَإِنَّمَا يَأْمُرُكَ إِذَا تَحَرَّمْتَ لِلصَّلَاةِ أَنْ تَرْفَعَ يَدَيْكَ إِذَا كَبَّرْتَ، وَإِذَا رَكَعْتَ، وَإِذَا رَفَعْتَ رَأْسَكَ مِنَ الرُّكُوعِ، وَإِذَا سَجَدْتَ، فَإِنَّهُ صَلَاتُنَا وَصَلَاةُ الْمَلَائِكَةِ فِي السَّمَاوَاتِ السَّبْعِ، وَإِنَّ لِكُلِّ شَيْءٍ زِينَةً وَإِنَّ زِينَةَ الصَّلَاةِ رَفْعُ الْأَيْدِي عِنْدَ كُلِّ تَكْبِيرَةٍ.

REFLECTIVE LEARNING

Every one of us has received innumerable bounties from God.

Let me reflect on whether I remember and recount these blessings daily when I prostrate to Him in gratitude.

VERSE 3

إِنَّ شَانِئَكَ هُوَ الْأَبْتَرُ ﴿٣﴾

Indeed, your enemy is the one [whose progeny is] cut off. [3]

3.1 [*Shānīʾ* (شَانِئ, enemy)] is the active participle (*ism fāʿil*) derived from *shanaʾān*, and denotes an enemy whose hostility is manifested in rancour and offensiveness.[18] Here, it refers to al-ʿĀṣ b. Wāʾil who had taunted the Prophet (s) at the loss of his son.[19]

[*Huwa* (هُوَ, he is)] here is for emphasis, to indicate that it is not you who is *abtar*, but rather it is your enemy whose progeny will be cut off. And this is news of the future from the hidden knowledge of God (*ʿilm al-ghayb*) delivered to the arrogant enemy.

[*Al-Abtar* (الأَبْتَر, the tailless one)] refers to an animal whose tail has been cut, and the Arabs used it as a derogatory term for a person whose lineage ended with him and was cut off (*al-maqtūʿ al-ʿaqab*).[20]

3.2 In reply to the insults of the enemy, God begins by reassuring and reminding the Prophet (s) of the abundance (*al-kawthar*) that He has given him, before cursing his enemy by depriving him of a lineage (*abtar*). There is a powerful lesson here to focus on the blessings that we already possess despite having lost or missed out on something.

3.3 This verse contrasts *abtar* with *kawthar*, emphasizing that the most important aspect of the abundant good that God had bestowed to the Prophet (s) was his noble offspring. His blessed lineage would be abundant, while his enemies' lineage would fade out.

3.4 The Prophet had received many insults from the polytheists and some of them are mentioned in the Qurʾan. He was called *majnūn*

---

18 Shīrāzī, *Namūneh*, 27/374.

19 Ṭabāṭabāʾī, *al-Mīzān*, 20/372.

20 Ibn Manẓūr, *Lisān al-ʿArab*.

[(مَجْنُون, a madman) as in Q15:6], *shā'ir* [(شَاعِر, a poet) in Q37:36)], *sāḥir* [(سَاحِر, a magician) in Q38:4], *kāhin* [(كَاهِن, a soothsayer) in Q52:29], and *kadhdhāb* [(كَذَّاب, a liar) in Q38:4)], amongst other insults. Each time, God reassured him with a verse in the Qur'an that these were just falsehoods. However, when he was called *abtar*, God responded with a whole chapter, awarding the Prophet (s) the best of offspring, and cutting off the lineage of his enemy.

3.5 In the age of ignorance (*jāhiliyyah*) women were treated as chattel. Fathers were disappointed at the news of the birth of a daughter, and some would actually consider burying the infant alive. Q16:58,59 state:

وَإِذَا بُشِّرَ أَحَدُهُمْ بِالْأُنْثَىٰ ظَلَّ وَجْهُهُ مُسْوَدًّا وَهُوَ كَظِيمٌ ﴿٥٨﴾ يَتَوَارَىٰ مِنَ الْقَوْمِ مِنْ سُوءِ مَا بُشِّرَ بِهِ أَيُمْسِكُهُ عَلَىٰ هُونٍ أَمْ يَدُسُّهُ فِي التُّرَابِ أَلَا سَاءَ مَا يَحْكُمُونَ

And when news is brought to one of them of [the birth of] a female, his face darkens, and he is filled with suppressed anguish. He hides himself from the people because of the bad news that he has received, [asking himself]: Should he keep it in humiliation or bury it in the earth? Undoubtedly, evil is what they decide.

The mention of the great bounty of his noble progeny in this chapter, and the honour with which the Prophet (s) himself treated his beloved daughter, Lady Fatimah al-Zahra (a) was a clear response to those who looked down on women in society. The Qur'an declared a daughter as *al-kawthar*, and the Prophet (s) showed that in his practice as well.

SUMMARY OF THE VERSE

This verse gives good news to the Prophet (s) and his *ummah* that the enemy of the Prophet (s) will never ultimately prosper.

REFLECTIVE LEARNING

Opposition and insult to the representatives of God is dealt with severe punishment in this world and the next.

Let me reflect on whether I take care not to knowingly do something that will place me in opposition to the words and practice of the Prophet (s) and his household (a).

SURAT AL-KĀFIRŪN
THE DISBELIEVERS (109)

TEXT AND TRANSLATION

سُورَةُ الْكَافِرُونَ

بِسْمِ اللهِ الرَّحْمَٰنِ الرَّحِيمِ

قُلْ يَا أَيُّهَا الْكَافِرُونَ ﴿١﴾ لَا أَعْبُدُ مَا تَعْبُدُونَ ﴿٢﴾ وَلَا أَنْتُمْ عَابِدُونَ مَا أَعْبُدُ ﴿٣﴾
وَلَا أَنَا عَابِدٌ مَا عَبَدْتُمْ ﴿٤﴾ وَلَا أَنْتُمْ عَابِدُونَ مَا أَعْبُدُ ﴿٥﴾ لَكُمْ دِينُكُمْ وَلِيَ دِينِ ﴿٦﴾

In the name of God, the Beneficent, the Merciful.

Say, "O Disbelievers! [1] *I will never worship what you worship.* [2] *Nor will you ever be worshippers of what I worship.* [3] *Nor will I ever be a worshipper of what you worshipped.* [4] *Nor will you ever be worshippers of what I worship.* [5] *To you is your religion, and to me is my religion!"* [6]

INTRODUCTION

Surat al-Kāfirūn (109) was the 18th chapter to be revealed, between Surat al-Māʿūn and al-Fīl.[1] It has six verses and is a Makkan chapter, revealed in the early years of the Prophet's (s) mission.[2] It is named after the unbelievers (*Kāfirūn*) who approached the Prophet (s) with a proposal to compromise by adopting each-others' faith in turn.

The Quraysh were reluctant to give up their idols because their whole political and economic dominance rested on allowing people of every nation to worship their own idol at the Kaʿbah. For this reason, they attempted to assimilate the message of the Prophet (s) and were willing to give room to 'his God' as well.

---

[1] Maʿrifat, *ʿUlūm-i Qurʾānī*, p. 90.

[2] Ṭabrasī, *al-Bayān*, 10/840.

OCCASION OF REVELATION

A group of [the chiefs of] the Quraysh including ʿUtbah b. Rabiʿah, Umayyah b. Khalaf, al-Walid b. al-Mughīrah [the father of Khalid b. al-Walid], and al-ʿÀṣ b. Saʿīd [the father of ʿAmr b. al-ʿÀṣ] came to the Messenger (s) and said, "Come, let us worship what you worship, and you worship what we worship, and let us collaborate in the affair. If the path we follow is the true one, then you will receive your benefit, and if your path is the true one, we too will receive our benefit from it. At this time, God the Almighty revealed: *Say, 'O Disbelievers! I will never worship what you worship. Nor will you ever be worshippers of what I worship...'* to the end of the chapter.[3]

A tradition from Imam al-Sadiq (a) states: The reason for the revelation of these verses and the repetition of the phrases is because the Quraysh proposed to God's Messenger (s) that, "Worship our gods for one year and we shall worship your God for a year. Then you worship our gods for one year and we shall worship your God for a year. So God replied to them in the same manner that they had spoken. As for their proposal that their gods should be worshipped for one year, the answer was, '*Say: O Disbelievers! I will never worship what you worship.*' As for their pledge to worship God for one year, the answer was, '*Nor will you ever be worshippers of what I worship.*' And in reply to their proposal that their gods should be worshipped the following year, the answer was, '*Nor will I ever be a worshipper of what you worshipped.*' And in reply to their pledge to worship God the following year, the answer was, '*Nor will you ever be worshippers of what I worship. To you is your religion, and to me is my religion!*'[4]

---

[3] Majlisī, *Biḥār*, 7/33.

إِنَّ نَفَرًا مِنْ قُرَيْشٍ اعْتَرَضُوا الرَّسُولَ (صَلَّى اللهُ عَلَيْهِ وَآلِهِ) مِنْهُمْ: عُتْبَةُ بْنُ رَبِيعَةَ، وَأُمَيَّةُ بْنُ خَلَفٍ، وَالْوَلِيدُ بْنُ الْمُغِيرَةِ، وَالْعَاصُ بْنُ سَعِيدٍ، فَقَالُوا: يَا مُحَمَّدُ (صَلَّى اللهُ عَلَيْهِ وَآلِهِ)، هَلُمَّ فَلْنَعْبُدْ مَا تَعْبُدُ، وَتَعْبُدْ مَا نَعْبُدُ، فَنَشْتَرِكَ نَحْنُ وَأَنْتَ فِي الْأَمْرِ، فَإِنْ يَكُنِ الَّذِي نَحْنُ عَلَيْهِ الْحَقَّ فَقَدْ أَخَذْتَ بِحَظِّكَ مِنْهُ، وَإِنْ يَكُنِ الَّذِي أَنْتَ عَلَيْهِ الْحَقَّ فَقَدْ أَخَذْنَا بِحَظِّنَا مِنْهُ، فَأَنْزَلَ اللهُ تَبارَكَ وَتَعالَى: «قُلْ يَا أَيُّهَا الْكَافِرُونَ لَا أَعْبُدُ مَا تَعْبُدُونَ وَلَا أَنْتُمْ عَابِدُونَ مَا أَعْبُدُ» إِلَى آخِرِ السُّورَةِ.

[4] Majlisī, *Biḥār*, 9/253.

فَسَأَلَ أَبَا عَبْدِ اللهِ (عَلَيْهِ السَّلَامُ) عَنْ ذَلِكَ، فَقَالَ: كَانَ سَبَبُ نُزُولِهَا وَتَكْرَارِهَا أَنَّ قُرَيْشًا قَالَتْ لِرَسُولِ اللهِ (صَلَّى اللهُ عَلَيْهِ وَآلِهِ): تَعْبُدُ إِلَهَنَا سَنَةً، وَنَعْبُدُ إِلَهَكَ سَنَةً، وَتَعْبُدُ إِلَهَنَا سَنَةً، وَنَعْبُدُ إِلَهَكَ سَنَةً، فَأَجَابَهُمُ اللهُ بِمِثْلِ مَا قَالُوا؛ فَقَالَ فِيمَا قَالُوا «تَعْبُدُ إِلَاهَنَا سَنَةً» –«قُلْ يَا أَيُّهَا الْكَافِرُونَ لَا أَعْبُدُ مَا تَعْبُدُونَ»، وَفِيمَا قَالُوا «وَنَعْبُدُ إِلَهَكَ سَنَةً» – «وَلَا أَنْتُمْ عَابِدُونَ مَا أَعْبُدُ»، وَفِيمَا قَالُوا «تَعْبُدُ إِلَهَنَا سَنَةً» – «وَلَا أَنَا عَابِدٌ مَا عَبَدْتُمْ»، وَفِيمَا قَالُوا «وَنَعْبُدُ إِلَهَكَ سَنَةً» – «وَلَا أَنْتُمْ عَابِدُونَ مَا أَعْبُدُ لَكُمْ دِينُكُمْ وَلِيَ دِينِ».

LINK TO PREVIOUS CHAPTER

In the previous chapter, Surat al-Kawthar, there is a reference to the insults of the disbelievers when they taunted the Prophet (s) that he had no surviving children. God replied to them that He would give him abundance, and his enemies would remain without lineage (*abtar*). The leaders of the disbelievers were still of the opinion that if they could somehow assimilate Islam into their practice, and offer the Prophet (s) some compromise, he would be forced to consider their proposal because he had no sons to continue his legacy. This chapter instructs the Prophet (s) to emphatically reject the proposal of the Quraysh sending a clear message to them that he would never compromise on any aspect of his mission.

Furthermore, in Surat al-Kawthar, their insults to the Prophet (s) were based on something that he had no control over, while in this chapter God labelled them as disbelievers, a trait that was based on their own actions.

MERITS OF RECITATION

- A tradition from the Prophet (s) states: God will grant the one who recites this surah the reward of reciting one-quarter of the Qurʾan and will distance him from the harassment of Shaytan. [Furthermore,] God will give him salvation from the terrors of the Day of Judgment.

  Whoever recites it before going to sleep will not be harmed while he sleeps. So, teach your children to recite it when they go to sleep.

  God shall accept the supplication of the one who recites it ten times at daybreak, and then asks for his wishes for this world and the hereafter, as long as there is no sin associated with what he asks for.[5]
- A tradition from Imam Ali (a) states: Whenever the Prophet (s) led us in prayer on a journey, he would [always] recite Surat al-Kāfirūn after Surat al-Ḥamd in the first unit and Surat al-Ikhlāṣ after Surat

---

[5] Baḥrānī, *al-Burhān*, 5/780.

عَنِ الرَّسُولِ (صَلَّى اللهُ عَلَيْهِ وَآلِهِ): مَنْ قَرَأَ هَذِهِ السُّورَةَ أَعْطَاهُ اللهُ تَعَالَى مِنَ الأَجْرِ كَأَنَّمَا قَرَأَ رُبُعَ الْقُرْآنِ، وَتَبَاعَدَتْ عَنْهُ مُؤْذِيَةُ الشَّيْطَانِ، وَنَجَّاهُ اللهُ تَعَالَى مِنْ فَزَعِ يَوْمِ الْقِيَامَةِ، وَمَنْ قَرَأَهَا عِنْدَ مَنَامِهِ، لَمْ يَتَعَرَّضْ إِلَيْهِ شَيْءٌ فِي مَنَامِهِ، فَعَلِّمُوهَا صِبْيَانَكُمْ عِنْدَ النَّوْمِ. وَمَنْ قَرَأَهَا عِنْدَ طُلُوعِ الشَّمْسِ عَشْرَ مَرَّاتٍ، وَدَعَا بِمَا أَرَادَ مِنَ الدُّنْيَا وَالآخِرَةِ، اسْتَجَابَ اللهُ لَهُ، مَا لَمْ يَكُنْ مَعْصِيَةً بِفِعْلِهَا.

al-Ḥamd in the second unit. Then he would say, "I have recited for you one-third and one-fourth of the Qur'an."[6]

- A tradition from Imam al-Sadiq (a) states: My father (a) would say that Surat al-Kāfirūn is equal to one-fourth of the Qur'an [in merit]. And when he finished reciting it, he would say, "I worship Allah alone, I worship Allah alone."[7]
- A tradition from Imam al-Sadiq (a) states: God will preserve from polytheism (*shirk*) the one who recites Surat al-Kāfirūn and Surat al-Tawḥīd when he goes to bed.[8]

EXEGESIS

VERSE 1

قُلْ يَا أَيُّهَا الْكَافِرُونَ ﴿١﴾

Say, "O Disbelievers! [1]

1.1 [*Qul* (قُلْ, say)] The verse begins with the command '*qul*', indicating a decisive response and declaration by God, and not the Prophet (s), to a question or matter raised. In this case, the Prophet (s) is commanded to reject the contentious suggestion by the unbelievers of Quraysh.

1.2 Even in their proposal they said that they would worship the God of the Prophet (s) every alternate year, not taking Him for their own Lord. This is a similar thing to the alternate sharing of land, farms, and goods![9]

1.3 Addressing them as 'disbelievers' is not meant to censure them, insult them, or express anger; it is merely an expression that their

---

[6] Ṣadūq, *'Uyūn Akhbār*, 2/37.

عَنْ عَلِيٍّ (عَلَيْهِ السَّلَامُ): كَانَ رَسُولُ اللهِ (صَلَّى اللهُ عَلَيْهِ وَآلِهِ) إِذَا صَلَّى بِنَا صَلَاةَ السَّفَرِ قَرَأَ فِي الْأُولَى الْحَمْدَ وَ«قُلْ يَا أَيُّهَا الْكَافِرُونَ»، وَفِي الْأُخْرَى الْحَمْدَ وَ«قُلْ هُوَ اللهُ أَحَدٌ»، ثُمَّ قَالَ: قَرَأْتُ لَكُمْ ثُلُثَ الْقُرْآنِ وَرُبُعَهُ.

[7] Ṭabrasī, *al-Bayān*, 10/839.

عَنِ الصَّادِقِ (عَلَيْهِ السَّلَامُ): كَانَ أَبِي يَقُولُ: «قُلْ يَا أَيُّهَا الْكَافِرُونَ» رُبُعُ الْقُرْآنِ، وَكَانَ إِذَا فَرَغَ مِنْهَا قَالَ: أَعْبُدُ اللهَ وَحْدَهُ، أَعْبُدُ اللهَ وَحْدَهُ.

[8] Kulaynī, *al-Kāfī*, 2/626.

عَنِ الصَّادِقِ (عَلَيْهِ السَّلَامُ): مَنْ قَرَأَ إِذَا أَوَى إِلَى فِرَاشِهِ «قُلْ يَا أَيُّهَا الْكَافِرُونَ» وَ«قُلْ هُوَ اللهُ أَحَدٌ» كَتَبَ اللهُ عَزَّ وَجَلَّ لَهُ بَرَاءَةً مِنَ الشِّرْكِ.

[9] Javādī-Āmolī, *Tasnīm*. (Transcript: http://javadi.esra.ir/-/22-10-9931-تفسیر-سوره-کافرون)

position was in no way compatible with Islam, and no compromise would ever be possible. It was a stark statement of truth, after which there was nothing but error, as Q10:32 states:

فَمَاذَا بَعْدَ الْحَقِّ إِلَّا الضَّلَالُ

And what can be beyond the truth [of monotheism] except the error [of polytheism]?

1.4 [*Al-Kāfirūn* (الْكَافِرُونَ, disbelievers)]. The term is used here as a noun, not limited to a time or place, indicating that this group of people were not just displaying their lack of belief, rather God considered them absolute disbelievers. Essentially, it means that the choice was between being a believer or a disbeliever, with no possibility of compromise.

1.5 The Qur'an uses the word *kufr* (كُفْر, disbelief) and its cognates in a wide range of meanings over 500 times. The original meaning of *kafara* is to cover something.[10] In general, the term *kufr* can be considered under three headings:

i) *Kufr* that is neither praiseworthy nor blameworthy. For example, in Q57:20, the farmer who sows seeds by covering them under the ground is called '*kāfir*':

كَمَثَلِ غَيْثٍ أَعْجَبَ الْكُفَّارَ نَبَاتُهُ ثُمَّ يَهِيجُ فَتَرَاهُ مُصْفَرًّا ثُمَّ يَكُونُ حُطَامًا

...Like the vegetation after rain, the growth of which pleases the farmer, but then it dries, and you see it turn yellow...

ii) *Kufr* that is praiseworthy. This refers to covering in the sense of denouncing something which should be rejected, and whose display earns God's displeasure, such as falsehoods, false beliefs, etc. An example of this usage is in Q2:256:

فَمَنْ يَكْفُرْ بِالطَّاغُوتِ وَيُؤْمِنْ بِاللَّهِ فَقَدِ اسْتَمْسَكَ
بِالْعُرْوَةِ الْوُثْقَىٰ لَا انْفِصَامَ لَهَا

So, whoever disbelieves in (rejects) false deities and believes... [in God has indeed grasped the firmest handle [of true faith ...one that will never break

---

[10] Rāghib, *al-Mufradāt*.

iii) *Kufr* that is blameworthy. This refers to covering up something which should be displayed, and whose rejection earns God's displeasure, such as the truth, gratitude, etc. In all but a handful of instances, this is the meaning of the term *kufr* used in the Qur'an. And for the people who display and persistently practice this form of *kufr*, a point is reached where it is of no use trying to bring them to faith. This is the group being referred to in the verse under review. Q2:6 states:

إِنَّ الَّذِينَ كَفَرُوا سَوَاءٌ عَلَيْهِمْ أَأَنْذَرْتَهُمْ أَمْ لَمْ تُنذِرْهُمْ لَا يُؤْمِنُونَ

Indeed, those who disbelieve, it is the same to them whether you warn them or do not warn them, they will not believe...

SUMMARY OF THE VERSE

In summary, this verse declares that God has decided to cut short the arguments and proposals of the disbelievers and give an emphatic response to them, that will follow in the rest of the verses.

REFLECTIVE LEARNING

It is important to consider the solemnity of having declared oneself as a Muslim. Thereafter, there can be no compromise in worship or submission to the commands of Allah. Compromise is a strategy of the disbelievers against the believers, as warned in Q68:9:

وَدُّوا لَوْ تُدْهِنُ فَيُدْهِنُونَ

They desire that you should compromise with them [about their faith and practice], so they [too] would compromise with you.

Whereas God reminds the believer in Q39:3:

أَلَا لِلَّهِ الدِّينُ الْخَالِصُ

Undoubtedly, the religion is for God alone...

Let me reflect whether I worship Allah sometimes and worship something else (for instance, my desires) at other times. In that case, is it not similar to what the disbelievers of Quraysh had proposed?

Do I accept that while there is certainly room to enquire and question before accepting the faith, there is no possibility of rejecting its laws afterwards? Q33:36 clearly states:

وَمَا كَانَ لِمُؤْمِنٍ وَلَا مُؤْمِنَةٍ إِذَا قَضَى اللَّهُ
وَرَسُولُهُ أَمْرًا أَنْ يَكُونَ لَهُمُ الْخِيَرَةُ مِنْ أَمْرِهِمْ

And it is not for a believing man or a believing woman,
when God and His Messenger have decreed a matter,
that they should [thereafter] have any choice in their affair...

VERSE 2

لَا أَعْبُدُ مَا تَعْبُدُونَ ﴿٢﴾

I will never worship what you worship. [2]

2.1 [*Lā aʿbudu* (لَا أَعْبُدُ, I will never worship)] indicates the rejection of any possibility of future worship. It is not present worship as some have translated, i.e. '*I do not worship what you worship*', which is of little value as a statement, because the Quraysh all knew that the Prophet (s) had nothing to do with their idolatry. In any case, if the present tense was intended, it would be better expressed as '*mā aʿbudu*'.[11]

2.2 The discussion in this chapter is about worship, and not about the belief in God as the Creator. The Quraysh, like many other idolaters, believed God to be the Creator of the world, but worshipped other gods. Q29:61 states:

وَلَئِنْ سَأَلْتَهُمْ مَنْ خَلَقَ السَّمَاوَاتِ وَالْأَرْضَ
وَسَخَّرَ الشَّمْسَ وَالْقَمَرَ لَيَقُولُنَّ اللَّهُ فَأَنَّى يُؤْفَكُونَ

And if you asked them, "Who created the heavens and the earth
and subjected the sun and the moon [to their paths],
they would certainly say, "Allah!" Why then have they
deviated [into polytheism and disbelief]?

[11] Zamakhsharī, *al-Kashshāf*, 4/808; Ṭabāṭabāʾī, *al-Mīzān*, 20/374.

2.3 To understand the emphatic declaration of the Prophet (s) that he would never worship what they worshipped (*mā taʿbudūn*, مَا تَعْبُدُونَ), we will briefly contrast the nature of worship as taught by Islam with the worship and beliefs of the Quraysh.

DISCUSSION 1: WORSHIP IN ISLAM (*ʿIBĀDAH*)

The term *ʿibādah* denotes faith in practice. In general terms, it encompasses worship and obedience, and leads to absolute servanthood. Although the Qur'an uses this term for the worship of false deities as well, in the context of Islam, the term signifies worship and veneration of God, and especially performing every act and practice to attain His pleasure and proximity. While performing the ritual acts symbolizes submission and servitude, *ʿibādah* extends to the whole life of the believer; it is a state of being, not just confined to periodic acts of worship.

Therefore, *ʿibādah* is a comprehensive attitude of worship, including matters such as: sincere intention (*ikhlāṣ*) to attain God's pleasure at every moment, mindfulness of God (*taqwā*) especially in the avoidance of sins, obedience (*iṭāʿah*) of His commandments, pondering (*tafakkur*) over God's plan for mankind, continuous gratitude (*shukr*), supplication and remembrance of God (*duʿā'* and *dhikr*), and trust and reliance in God (*tawakkul*). This leads to the pinnacle of *ʿibādah*, which is absolute servanthood (*ʿubūdiyyah*).

This was the worship of the Prophet (s) referred to in Surat al-Kāfirūn, and what he taught the Muslims.

DISCUSSION 2: THE BELIEFS AND WORSHIP OF THE QURAYSH

Originally, the religion observed in Makka was monotheistic due to the influence of Prophet Ibrahim (a) and Prophet Ismaʿil (a). However, with the passage of time, the religion was distorted, especially due to the influence of idolaters in the neighbouring lands where the Makkans went for trade.

Idolatry

The Syrian idol Hubal was brought to Makka by ʿAmr b. Luḥay, the chief of the Banu Khuzaʿah, who installed it in the Kaʿbah and invited people to worship it.

The Qur'an condemns their idolatry in many verses. Just two examples are cited here: Q10:18 states:

وَيَعْبُدُونَ مِنْ دُونِ اللهِ مَا لَا يَضُرُّهُمْ وَلَا يَنْفَعُهُمْ

And they worship other than God that which neither harms them nor benefits them...

And Q4:117 states:

إِنْ يَدْعُونَ مِنْ دُونِهِ إِلَّا إِنَاثًا وَإِنْ يَدْعُونَ إِلَّا شَيْطَانًا مَرِيدًا

Instead of Him, they call upon female deities; and they do not [actually] call upon anything but a rebellious Shaytan!

Later, many other idols were introduced, and paganism spread readily in Arabia. Q53:19, 20 mentions some of the popular idols, three of which were considered to be the figurines of angels whom they worshipped as daughters of Allah:

أَفَرَأَيْتُمُ اللَّاتَ وَالْعُزَّىٰ ﴿١٩﴾ وَمَنَاةَ الثَّالِثَةَ الْأُخْرَىٰ

Have you considered al-Lāt, and al-ʿUzzā, and Manāt, the third – the other one?

The polytheists and idolaters (*mushrikūn*) of the Quraysh believed in Allah as the Creator of the heavens and the earth, but in matters of worship they turned to their idols, asserting that they were partners with Him. They claimed that by worshipping their idols they gained proximity to God. Q39:3 states:

أَلَا لِلَّهِ الدِّينُ الْخَالِصُ وَالَّذِينَ اتَّخَذُوا مِنْ دُونِهِ أَوْلِيَاءَ
مَا نَعْبُدُهُمْ إِلَّا لِيُقَرِّبُونَا إِلَى اللهِ زُلْفَىٰ

Undoubtedly, the religion is for God alone; those who take protectors besides him [say,] "We only worship them so that they may bring us nearer to God..."

This idolatry and the baseless innovations that stemmed from it, were the fundamental difference with the message of Islam, which negated every form of polytheism (*shirk*).

Innovation

The Quraysh would give sacrificial and other votive offerings to their idols imagining that they would gain favour thereby. These practices are mentioned in a series of verses in Surat al-An'ām from verse 136 onwards. For example, Q6:136 states:

وَجَعَلُوا لِلَّهِ مِمَّا ذَرَأَ مِنَ الْحَرْثِ وَالْأَنْعَامِ نَصِيبًا فَقَالُوا هَٰذَا لِلَّهِ
بِزَعْمِهِمْ وَهَٰذَا لِشُرَكَائِنَا فَمَا كَانَ لِشُرَكَائِهِمْ فَلَا يَصِلُ إِلَى اللَّهِ
وَمَا كَانَ لِلَّهِ فَهُوَ يَصِلُ إِلَىٰ شُرَكَائِهِمْ سَاءَ مَا يَحْكُمُونَ

And the polytheists assign to God from that which He created of crops and livestock a share [spending it on poor pilgrims], and say, "This is for God", or so they assert, "and this is for our partners [for the upkeep of idols]". But the share of the [so-called] partners does not reach God, and that which they assign to God goes to their partners. Evil is what they decide!

'Amr b. Luḥay also instituted the innovations of *baḥīrah, sā'ibah, waṣīlah,* and *ḥām.*

Baḥīrah was a camel that had given birth to five calves, the last of which was a male. Such a camel would have its ear slit, and no one was allowed to slaughter it or ride on it again.

Sā'ibah was a camel that had been dedicated to the idols and was set free to roam as it pleased without being used as a mount or for milk. This was usually after a traveller made a vow that if he returned safely from his journey, he would dedicate his camel to the idols and make it a *sā'ibah.*

Male sheep were slaughtered to appease the idols unless they were born as twins with a female. *Waṣīlah* referred to sheep that gave birth to twins, one male and one female. The female would be the protector (*waṣīlah*) of the male twin, and the Quraysh would not slaughter these animals for meat, or to their idols. Their milk and wool could only be used by the men and not the women.

Ḥām was a male camel that had sired ten offspring. Thereafter, it was referred as *ḥāmī,* and was not used for transport, but allowed to graze freely instead.[12]

---

12 Ṭabrasī, *al-Bayān*, 3/390.

Q5:103 dismissed these innovations as baseless, stating:

مَا جَعَلَ اللَّهُ مِنْ بَحِيرَةٍ وَلَا سَائِبَةٍ وَلَا وَصِيلَةٍ وَلَا حَامٍ وَلَٰكِنَّ الَّذِينَ
كَفَرُوا يَفْتَرُونَ عَلَى اللَّهِ الْكَذِبَ وَأَكْثَرُهُمْ لَا يَعْقِلُونَ

Allah has not ordained [the innovations of] a slit-ear camel (baḥīrah), *or a she-camel let loose for free pasture* (sā'ibah), *or exemptions for twin-births in animals* (waṣīlah), *or stallion-camels freed from work* (ḥām). *But those who disbelieve invent falsehood about God, and most of them do not use reason.*

SUMMARY OF THE VERSE

The verse makes clear the declaration of the Prophet (s) that he, and as an extension those who believe in his message, would never worship as the disbelievers worshipped; they would never associate anyone or anything with God, the Almighty.

REFLECTIVE LEARNING

Let me reflect if my *ʿibādah* is just restricted to ritual acts of worship, or have I also extended the concept to all aspects of my life thus bringing about a continual state of submission (*taslīm*) and servanthood (*ʿubūdiyyah*) to God?

The polytheists of Makka believed in God also, yet they worshipped other entities. Let me reflect on whether I truly worship God alone, or do I also turn to abstract idols such as wealth and ego?

VERSES 3 - 5

وَلَا أَنْتُمْ عَابِدُونَ مَا أَعْبُدُ ﴿٣﴾ وَلَا أَنَا عَابِدٌ مَا عَبَدْتُمْ ﴿٤﴾ وَلَا أَنْتُمْ عَابِدُونَ مَا
أَعْبُدُ ﴿٥﴾

Nor will you ever be worshippers of what I worship. [3] *Nor will I ever be a worshipper of what you worshipped.* [4] *Nor will you ever be worshippers of what I worship.* [5]

3-5.1 Here the constant worship of One God by the Prophet (s) (as evidenced in verses 2 and 4) is contrasted to the changing practices of the idolaters mentioned in verses 3 and 5. The repetition of the words is not a repetition in meaning.[13]

3-5.2 Other exegetes have stated that the repetition of verses 3 and 5 are both for emphasis, as well as a twin rejection of the two proposals of the Quraysh to worship their gods in alternative years.[14] The emphasis above may be to highlight the fact that this group of people would never worship God, and this is a foretelling of the future from God's hidden knowledge (*ʿilm al-ghayb*).[15]

3-5.3 When describing the object of worship, God uses the relative pronoun *mā* (مَا, what, or that which), instead of *man* (مَنْ, who), throughout the chapter. As for the object of worship of the disbelievers, they were lifeless statues and idols, and the correct relative pronoun for inanimate objects is *mā* (what). However, for God, the appropriate pronoun should be *man* (Who). The exegetes have offered some possible reasons for this:

i) That '*mā* (مَا, what)' here, does denote '*man* (مَنْ, who)' or '*alladhī* (أَلَّذِي, who, or that which)'.

ii) That it could be a reference to the type and manner of worship of the Prophet (s) and the disbelievers; in this case, the pronoun *mā* is *maṣdariyyah*, meaning that it converts the verb that follows it into a verbal noun (*maṣdar*), and the verse would therefore mean, '*Nor will you ever be worshippers in the manner that I worship*', referring to the degree and manner of the worship of the Prophet (s) as dictated by God.

iii) Some exegetes are of the opinion that it is to conform with the phrasing of verse 2: *mā taʿbudūn*, '*I will never worship what you worship*' This is similar to other instances in the Qur'an; for example, Q9:67 states:

نَسُوا اللَّهَ فَنَسِيَهُمْ

They forgot God, so God forgot them...

Obviously, God does not forget, and the term in respect to God means 'ignored them', and has been used to keep the uniformity in the comparison.

---

[13] Ṭūsī, *al-Tibyān*, 10/421.

[14] Shīrāzī, *Namūneh*, 27/388.

[15] Ṭabāṭabāʾī, *al-Mīzān*, 20/374.

iv) Finally, by using *mā*, the verse may be referring to the attributes of God, and not His being. Therefore the meaning would be, '*you will never be worshippers of a deity who has the qualities of the Deity that I worship.*'[16]

3-5.4 The two attitudes to worship could never be united. The lofty cognition (*maʿrifah*) of God by the Prophet (s), and the infallibility (*ʿismah*) that it cloaked him in would not allow him to entertain any thought other than pure *tawḥīd*.[17] Furthermore, Q6:56 states:

قُلْ إِنِّي نُهِيتُ أَنْ أَعْبُدَ الَّذِينَ تَدْعُونَ مِنْ دُونِ اللهِ

Say: Indeed, I have been forbidden to worship those you invoke besides God...

3-5.5 The hostility and defiant attitude of the leaders of the disbelievers persisted to the end of their lives, just as verse 5 predicted.

SUMMARY OF THE VERSES

The verses make clear that the manner and object of worship of these disbelievers was so different from what was taught by the Prophet (s) that compromise was impossible. The only option was a complete submission to Islam, and this was something that the disbelievers who had idolatry entrenched in them would never accept.

REFLECTIVE LEARNING

In addition to contrasting the object of worship of the polytheists and the monotheists, these verses are emphasizing the manner of worship. Therefore, I need to reflect on how much my actions are a reflection of what God wants, rather than what I do due to cultural and social norms, personal desires, ego, etc.

Let us look once more Q51:56, where God states:

وَمَا خَلَقْتُ الْجِنَّ وَالْإِنْسَ إِلَّا لِيَعْبُدُونِ

I did not create the jinn *and mankind except to worship Me.*

By keeping in mind this broad meaning of *ʿibādah*, let me reflect on whether my manner of worship is dictated by God? In other words, am I doing every action in the way He would want me to?

---

16 Ṭabāṭabāʾī, *al-Mīzān*, 20/375; Shīrāzī, *Namūneh*, 27/388.

17 Javādī-Āmolī, *Tasnīm*. (Transcript: http://javadi.esra.ir/-/22-10-9931-تفسیر-سوره-کافرون).

VERSE 6

لَكُمْ دِينُكُمْ وَلِيَ دِينِ ﴿٦﴾

To you is your religion, and to me is my religion! [6]

6.1 Some have considered this verse as a sign of tolerance and religious pluralism, and an acknowledgement of the right of idolaters (or others) to their beliefs. However, this is not the case. The tone of the verse reveals that it is actually a declaration of aversion and disgust at the evil practice of polytheism. This is clear from the later injunction to banish every polytheist from Makka. Q9:28 states:

يَا أَيُّهَا الَّذِينَ آمَنُوا إِنَّمَا الْمُشْرِكُونَ نَجَسٌ
فَلَا يَقْرَبُوا الْمَسْجِدَ الْحَرَامَ بَعْدَ عَامِهِمْ هَٰذَا

O believers! Indeed, the polytheists are impure (najas), *so let them not approach the Sacred Mosque after this, their [final] year...*

6.2 *Lakum* (لَكُمْ, for you) is used at the beginning of the verse. When the direct object precedes the verb in this way, it indicates restriction. Therefore, the meaning would be, '*your religion is only for you.*' Similarly, the second phrase means, '*and my religion is only for me*'. Thus, there is no way to reconcile between monotheism and polytheism. No compromise and allowance could be made for the disbelievers, and hence the Prophet (s) informed them flatly that their religions stood apart from one another.

6.3 [*Al-Dīn* (الدِّين, religion)]. As already explained in the *tafsīr* of Surat al-Fātiḥah, in addition to 'religion', the word '*dīn*' also denotes reward and punishment. In this case, the verse would mean, '*you will receive the recompense for your beliefs, and I will receive the recompense for mine*'. A similar statement is made in Q42:15:

اللَّهُ رَبُّنَا وَرَبُّكُمْ لَنَا أَعْمَالُنَا وَلَكُمْ أَعْمَالُكُمْ
لَا حُجَّةَ بَيْنَنَا وَبَيْنَكُمُ اللَّهُ يَجْمَعُ بَيْنَنَا وَإِلَيْهِ الْمَصِيرُ

...Allah is our Lord and your Lord. For us are our deeds, and for you your deeds. There is no [need for] argument between us and you. Allah will assemble us together, and to Him is the [final] return.

6.4 This chapter was a clear signal to the disbelievers that the religion of the Prophet (s) was not open to any compromise. Additionally, it was a clear statement that they would never deviate him from his path, nor would they have the blessing of following the right religion themselves. And whether they liked it or not, Islam would prevail over all other religions. Q9:33 states:

هُوَ الَّذِي أَرْسَلَ رَسُولَهُ بِالْهُدَىٰ وَدِينِ الْحَقِّ لِيُظْهِرَهُ عَلَى الدِّينِ كُلِّهِ
وَلَوْ كَرِهَ الْمُشْرِكُونَ

It is He Who sent His Messenger with guidance and the religion of truth, that He might cause it to prevail over all religions, though the polytheists may be averse.

6.5 A tradition from Imam al-Sadiq (a) states: When you complete the recitation of Surat al-Kāfirūn, then declare, "My religion is Islam, and I am of those who have submitted (*muslimūn*). I will die on this faith and I will be raised on it, if God, the Almighty and Exalted, wills."[18]

SUMMARY OF THE VERSE

In summary, the verse makes clear the two polar positions of monotheism and polytheism. There can be no compromise between the two.

REFLECTIVE LEARNING

By instructing the Prophet (s) on how to respond to the disingenuous proposal of some of the Quraysh, this whole chapter highlights the fact that the pure teachings of *tawḥīd* are not compatible with any form of polytheism (*shirk*).

While Islam respects the right of a person to practice their own faith, it does not accept a half-way commitment to the religion, or amalgamation and compromise with other teachings, under the banner of Islam.

Let me reflect on this question: after I have professed my faith in Islam, do I compromise its values in my own beliefs and practice, and thereby create my own version of Islam?

---

[18] Nūrī, *Mustadrak al-Wasāʾil*, 4/179.

عَنِ الصَّادِقِ (عَلَيْهِ السَّلَامُ) قَالَ: فَإِذَا فَرَغْتَ مِنْ «قُلْ يَا أَيُّهَا الْكَافِرُونَ» فَقُلْ: دِينِيَ الْإِسْلَامُ، وَأَنَا مِنَ الْمُسْلِمِينَ، وَعَلَيْهِ أَمُوتُ، وَعَلَيْهِ أُبْعَثُ، إِنْ شَاءَ اللّٰهُ وَتَقَدَّسَ.

SURAT AL-NAṢR
THE ASSISTANCE (110)

TEXT AND TRANSLATION

سُورَةُ النَّصْرِ

بِسْمِ اللهِ الرَّحْمٰنِ الرَّحِيمِ

إِذَا جَاءَ نَصْرُ اللهِ وَالْفَتْحُ ﴿١﴾ وَرَأَيْتَ النَّاسَ يَدْخُلُونَ فِي دِينِ اللهِ أَفْوَاجًا ﴿٢﴾
فَسَبِّحْ بِحَمْدِ رَبِّكَ وَٱسْتَغْفِرْهُ إِنَّهُ كَانَ تَوَّابًا ﴿٣﴾

In the name of God, the Beneficent, the Merciful.

When there comes God's help and victory, [1] *And you see people enter God's religion in multitudes,* [2] *Then, glorify the praise of your Lord and ask for His forgiveness; indeed, He is always ready to accept repentance.* [3]

INTRODUCTION

Surat al-Naṣr (110) was the 102nd chapter to be revealed.[1] It was revealed in Mina during the farewell pilgrimage of the Prophet (s), after Surat al-Tawbah (9).[2] It is named after the mention of God's help (*naṣr*) in the first verse.

This short chapter of only three verses recounts how Islam became dominant over Arabia with God's help, and group after group entered into its fold.

It is reported to be the last complete chapter to be sent down. A tradition from Imam al-Sadiq (a) states: The first chapter to be revealed was [the opening verses of] Surat al-ʿAlaq, and the last was Surat al-Naṣr.[3]

---

[1] Maʿrifat, *ʿUlūm-i Qurʾānī*, p. 90.

[2] Ṭabrasī, *al-Bayān*, 10/842.

[3] Ḥuwayzī, *Nūr al-Thaqalayn*, 5/690.

عَنِ الصَّادِقِ (عَلَيْهِ السَّلَامُ) قَالَ: أَوَّلُ مَا نَزَلَ عَلَى رَسُولِ اللهِ (صَلَّى اللهُ عَلَيْهِ وَآلِهِ) «بِسْمِ اللهِ الرَّحْمٰنِ الرَّحِيمِ، اِقْرَأْ بِاسْمِ رَبِّكَ»، وَآخِرُهُ «إِذَا جَاءَ نَصْرُ اللهِ».

The chapter is also called *al-Tawdīʿ* (the farewell), because when it was revealed, a report states that the Prophet (s) said, "The news of my impending passing has arrived." Then he went to Masjid al-Khayf and gathered the pilgrims and announced, "May God bless the one who hears my speech and comprehends it, and then conveys it to those who did not hear it."[4]

LINK TO THE PREVIOUS CHAPTER

The previous chapter, Surat al-Kāfirūn, spoke of the opposition of the disbelievers (*kāfirūn*) to the message of the Prophet (s) and mentioned their long-lived hostility to Islam. This chapter gives the good news of how Islam would ultimately triumph over the idolatry that had occupied Arabia for 4 centuries. The Prophet (s) had laboured for over twenty years in spreading God's message, and now, with God's help, a turning point was reached and suddenly multitudes of disbelievers and polytheists began to enter the fold of Islam. Therefore, this chapter describes the final end of the opposition that had been described in the previous chapter, Surat al-Kāfirūn.

Surat al-Kāfirūn starts with '*Qul!*' (Say!), instructing the Prophet (s) to communicate God's emphatic rejection of the disingenuous proposal of the chiefs of the Quraysh. The Prophet (s) obeyed this instruction to the letter, and in return received God's help which brought about the victory mentioned in Surat al-Naṣr.

MERITS OF RECITATION

- A tradition from the Prophet (s) states: Whoever recites Surat al-Naṣr in his supererogatory or obligatory prayers, will be granted victory by God over every enemy. On the Day of Judgement, he will come forward with a book that will speak, which God will bring out from the side of his grave. Within it will be a guarantee of safe passage across the bridge over Hell, and immunity from the flames of hellfire. He will not pass by anything on that day except that it will congratulate him and give him good tidings, until he will enter

---

[4] Majlisī, *Biḥār*, 27/68.

نَزَلَتْ بِمِنَى فِي حِجَّةِ الْوَدَاعِ «إِذَا جَاءَ نَصْرُ اللهِ وَالْفَتْحُ» فَلَمَّا نَزَلَتْ قَالَ رَسُولُ اللهِ (صَلَّى اللهُ عَلَيْهِ وَآلِهِ): نُعِيَتْ إِلَيَّ نَفْسِي، فَجَاءَ إِلَى مَسْجِدِ الْخَيْفِ فَجَمَعَ النَّاسَ ثُمَّ قَالَ: نَضَّرَ اللهُ امْرَأً سَمِعَ مَقَالَتِي فَوَعَاهَا وَبَلَّغَهَا مَنْ لَمْ يَسْمَعْهَا.

Paradise. [Furthermore,] in this world (*dunyā*), doors of goodness will be opened for him, which he did not anticipate or imagine."[5]

- A tradition from the Prophet (s) also states: Whoever recites this surah shall be given the reward of the one who witnessed the conquest of Makka at the side of the Prophet (s). Whoever recites this chapter in his prayers after Surat al-Ḥamd, shall have his prayers accepted in the best manner.[6]

EXEGESIS

VERSE 1

إِذَا جَاءَ نَصْرُ اللهِ وَالْفَتْحُ ﴿١﴾

When there comes God's help and victory, [1]

1.1 [*Idhā* (إِذَا, when)] here shows that the event that is mentioned in the verse was yet to happen, but would certainly occur soon. The event in question is the help of God and victory over polytheism, so this verse is both a prophecy, as well as a mention of the reward to the Prophet (s) for his determined efforts and obedience. For this reason, one can surmise that this chapter was revealed after the treaty of Hudaybiyyah and the revelation of Surat al-Fatḥ, and before the conquest of Makka.[7]

1.2 [*Naṣr* (نَصْر, help)] has been mentioned in the definite case (*naṣrullāh*, God's help), and refers to the specific Divine help that allowed the Prophet (s) victory over the Quraysh without bloodshed in the conquest of Makka. This occurred in the year 8/629, and as prophesized, almost the whole of Arabia came under Islam.

---

[5] Ṣadūq, *Thawāb al-Aʿmāl*, p. 127.

عَنِ الرَّسُولِ (صَلَّى اللهُ عَلَيْهِ وَآلِهِ) – مَنْ قَرَأَ «إِذَا جَاءَ نَصْرُ اللهِ وَالْفَتْحُ» فِي نَافِلَةٍ أَوْ فَرِيضَةٍ نَصَرَهُ اللهُ عَلَى جَمِيعِ أَعْدَائِهِ، وَجَاءَ يَوْمَ الْقِيَامَةِ وَمَعَهُ كِتَابٌ يَنْطِقُ قَدْ أَخْرَجَهُ اللهُ مِنْ جَوْفِ قَبْرِهِ فِيهِ أَمَانٌ مِنْ جِسْرِ جَهَنَّمَ وَمِنَ النَّارِ وَمِنْ زَفِيرِ جَهَنَّمَ، فَلَا يَمُرُّ عَلَى شَيْءٍ يَوْمَ الْقِيَامَةِ إِلَّا بَشَّرَهُ وَأَخْبَرَهُ بِكُلِّ خَيْرٍ حَتَّى يَدْخُلَ الْجَنَّةَ وَيُفْتَحَ لَهُ فِي الدُّنْيَا مِنْ أَسْبَابِ الْخَيْرِ مَا لَمْ يَتَمَنَّ وَلَمْ يَخْطُرْ عَلَى قَلْبِهِ.

[6] Baḥrānī, *al-Burhān*, 5/783.

عَنِ الرَّسُولِ (صَلَّى اللهُ عَلَيْهِ وَآلِهِ) – مَنْ قَرَأَ هَذِهِ السُّورَةَ أُعْطِيَ مِنَ الْأَجْرِ كَمَنْ شَهِدَ مَعَ النَّبِيِّ (صَلَّى اللهُ عَلَيْهِ وَآلِهِ) يَوْمَ فَتْحِ مَكَّةَ، وَمَنْ قَرَأَهَا فِي صَلَاةٍ وَصَلَّى بِهَا بَعْدَ الْحَمْدِ قُبِلَتْ صَلَاتُهُ مِنْهُ أَحْسَنَ الْقَبُولِ.

[7] Ṭabāṭabā'ī, *al-Mīzān*, 20/376.

1.3 The help of God cannot be compared to any other kind of help. It is the measured and potent assistance that brings about both hidden as well as manifest success and triumph. For example, Q3:126 states:

وَمَا النَّصْرُ إِلَّا مِنْ عِنْدِ اللهِ الْعَزِيزِ الْحَكِيمِ

...And victory is only from God, the Mighty, the Wise.

The verse above mentions two particular attributes: might and wisdom. Often, leaders or nations possess might but no wisdom or conversely, wisdom, but no power; in each case, true help, resulting in victory remains unachievable. Here, God reminds us that He possesses both these qualities without limitation.

1.4 [*Fatḥ* (فَتْح, victory)] has been mentioned in the opening verse of Surat al-Fatḥ in reference to the treaty of Hudaybiyyah which was signed in the year 6/627. When the Prophet (s) signed this treaty, some Muslims felt he was giving in to the Quraysh. However, what looked like defeat to them was described as a clear and open victory by Allah. Q48:1 states:

إِنَّا فَتَحْنَا لَكَ فَتْحًا مُبِينًا

Indeed, We have granted you a clear victory...

It was this very treaty that prepared the ground for the conquest of Makka.

1.5 In Surat al-Naṣr, the term *al-fatḥ*, which is mentioned in the definite sense, refers to the conquest of Makka itself. And it was the conquest of this stronghold of opposition that became the tipping point for the conversion of almost all the polytheists to Islam.[8]

1.6 The victory of Islam over the idolaters was the victory of *tawḥīd* (monotheism) over *shirk* (polytheism) and the victory of truth over falsehood.

Indeed, when actions are performed with a pure intention for God, success and victory is witnessed in this *dunyā*, as well as the Hereafter.

---

[8] Ṭabāṭabā'ī, *al-Mīzān*, 20/377.

DISCUSSION 1: THE CONQUEST OF MAKKA

After failing to overcome the Muslims in battle, and after refusing to allow the Muslims to enter Makka to perform the *ʿumrah*, the Quraysh signed a ten-year peace treaty with the Muslims at Hudaybiyyah in the year 6/627. However, two years later, the Quraysh violated the terms of the treaty when they supported their allies Banu Bakr to kill members of the Banu Khuzāʿah who were allied to the Muslims. The Prophet (s) and the Muslims took this violation very seriously; the Quraysh realized the enormity of their mistake and Abu Sufyan himself came to Madina to apologize, but it was to no avail. A short time later, the Prophet (s) mobilized an army of 10,000 men and approached Makka. The leaders of the Quraysh knew that they could not withstand the Muslim force, and surrendered. Many of them accepted Islam.

On 20th of the month of Ramadan in the year 8/629, the Prophet (s) entered Makka victorious, and conquered the city without bloodshed. He stood next to the door of the Kaʿbah and declared an amnesty for all. He said, "I tell you what my brother Yusuf (a) said to his brothers." (as stated in Q12:92):

قَالَ لَا تَثْرِيبَ عَلَيْكُمُ الْيَوْمَ يَغْفِرُ اللهُ لَكُمْ وَهُوَ أَرْحَمُ الرَّاحِمِينَ

He said, "[There shall be] no reproach against you this day.
May God forgive you; and He is the most-Merciful of the merciful."

Thereafter, he instructed Imam Ali (a) to stand on his shoulders and break the idols that had been placed at the Kaʿbah.[9] At this time, Q17:81 was revealed:

وَقُلْ جَاءَ الْحَقُّ وَزَهَقَ الْبَاطِلُ إِنَّ الْبَاطِلَ كَانَ زَهُوقًا

And say, "Truth has come, and falsehood has perished.
Indeed, falsehood is ever bound to perish."

SUMMARY OF THE VERSE

The message of the verse is that help that leads to true victory ultimately comes only from God.

---

[9] An event recorded in both *Shīʿa* (for example, Ibn Shahr Āshūb, *al-Manāqib*, 2/135) and *Sunni* (for example, Nasāʾī, *Sunan*, 5/142) sources.

REFLECTIVE LEARNING

This surah reminds us that true victory can only come with God's help. Let me reflect:

Do I first turn to others to achieve success before I consider asking for God's help? Do I even defy God, so as to maintain the respect of the people in power?

VERSE 2

وَرَأَيْتَ النَّاسَ يَدْخُلُونَ فِي دِينِ اللَّهِ أَفْوَاجًا ﴿٢﴾

And you shall see people enter God's religion in multitudes, [2]

2.1 [*Ra'ayta* (رَأَيْتَ, you saw/you shall see)] is in the past tense, which is often used in the Qur'an to denote a definite occurrence in the future. Therefore, it means, '*you shall see*' because it foretells the event and informs the Prophet (s) that he will witness it in his lifetime.

2.2 [*Afwāj* (أَفْوَاج, multitudes)] (sing. *fawj*) refers to a group of people who are moving hastily.[10] In fact, delegation after delegation came to the Prophet (s) in Madina to accept Islam on behalf of their tribes. Yaʿqūbī mentions 26 tribes whose representatives came to meet the Prophet (s) in Madina to give their allegiance.[11] The ninth year of *hijrah* was thereafter referred to as *sanat al-wufūd* (the year of delegations).

Of course, these initial conversions were based on tribal affiliations to the chieftains, and while people had become Muslims, many did not possess faith (*īmān*) in their hearts.

2.3 Just as God had protected the Kaʿbah from Abrahah, He now protected it forever from idol worshippers.

2.4 [*Dīn* (دِين, religion)] The original meaning of *dīn* is recompense, whether reward or punishment, which is why the Day of Recompense is called *yawm al-dīn*. This recompense is according to one's obedience or disobedience to God's laws, and therefore religion is also called *dīn*.[12] And *dīnullāh* (دِينِ الله, God's religion) in

[10] Rāghib, *al-Mufradāt*.

[11] Yaʿqūbī, *Tārīkh*, 2/79.

[12] Ṭabrasī, *al-Bayān*, 10/844.

this verse refers to Islam,which is submission (*taslīm*) to God's law. It has always been thus, just as Q3:19 states:

إِنَّ الدِّينَ عِنْدَ اللهِ الْإِسْلَامُ

Indeed the [true] religion with God is the submission to His will (al-islām)...

2.5 The mission of the Prophet (s) from the start had been to bring people to Islam, the religion that God had continually revealed throughout human history. The Quraysh failed in their opposition to the Prophet (s) because they stood against him for worldly reasons, but he achieved victory over them because his struggle against them was only for the religion of God.

2.6 This great victory caused the polytheistic attitudes to gradually disappear. Those who had lost the right way now reverted to the truth and were reintroduced to the monotheism that had been first taught in that land by Prophet Ibrahim (a).

SUMMARY OF THE VERSE

In summary, the entry of group after group into the fold of Islam was the result of the two events mentioned in the previous verse: the assistance of God, and the victory (following the conquest of Makka and the acceptance of Islam by most tribes in the Arab peninsula).

REFLECTIVE LEARNING

Let me reflect on how I entered God's religion.

Am I a Muslim because I was born into it, or have I submitted to God after enquiry and conscious decision? Let me re-examine my belief system and reaffirm it.

VERSE 3

فَسَبِّحْ بِحَمْدِ رَبِّكَ وَٱسْتَغْفِرْهُ إِنَّهُۥ كَانَ تَوَّابًا ﴿٣﴾

Then glorify the praise of your Lord and ask for His forgiveness; indeed, He is always ready to accept repentance. [3]

3.1 [*Sabbiḥ* (سَبِّحْ, glorify)]. *Tasbīḥ* (glorification *subḥānallāh*) is to negate for God all things that are against His majesty, and glorify

Him above any attributes of deficiency (*al-ṣifāt al-salbiyyah*); and *taḥmīd* (grateful praise, *al-ḥamdu lillāh*) is the affirmation for God of all His attributes of perfection.

Tawḥīd is the result of the proper combination of *tasbīḥ* and *taḥmīd* as is mentioned in the *dhikr* of *rukūʿ* and *sujūd* in our *salat*.

3.2 [*Rabbika* (رَبِّكَ, your Lord)], is a reminder that everything we have of guidance and success is from God, the true Sustainer. The term *rabb* has been discussed in detail in the *tafsīr* of Surat al-Fātiḥah (1).

3.3 Glorifying and gratefully praising our Sustainer makes us remember that everything we possess is from Him. This is effective in removing the malaise of pride.

3.4 [*Istighfār*, (اسْتِغْفار, seeking forgiveness)] is derived from *ghafara*, and means to conceal or to cover.[13] However in its technical meaning, *istighfār* is to seek God's forgiveness, both verbally and in action, for one's sins and negligence. The stain of sin prevents a person from receiving Divine blessings, and it is only through continuous *istighfār* that man can remove the self-created obstacles that prevent him from receiving the favours of God, and rise towards Him. This is a reality in God's system, and in Q5:74, He asks why man does not realise it:

أَفَلَا يَتُوبُونَ إِلَى اللهِ وَيَسْتَغْفِرُونَهُ وَاللهُ غَفُورٌ رَحِيمٌ

Why do they not turn to God and ask for His forgiveness? For God is oft-Forgiving, all-Merciful.

3.5 [*Tawwāb* (تَوَّاب, oft-turning)] when attributed to mankind, *tawwāb* refers to turning to God often, seeking His forgiveness for trespasses. However, when attributed to God, it means that He continually turns to His creation, inspires them to be remorseful for their sins, and then accepts their repentance and forgives them. Q9:118 states:

ثُمَّ تَابَ عَلَيْهِمْ لِيَتُوبُوا إِنَّ اللهَ هُوَ التَّوَّابُ الرَّحِيمُ

...Then He turned to them [in mercy] so they could turn to him [in repentance]. Indeed, God is the oft-Returning, the all-Merciful.

3.6 Furthermore, it is possible that by mentioning His own forgiving nature, God reminds the Muslims to accept the new converts

---

[13] Ibn Manẓūr, *Lisān al-ʿArab*.

unconditionally, putting aside the past and not harbouring thoughts of revenge for former enmity.[14]

3.7 As the first verse indicates, success and victory are only due to God's help. For this reason, instead of pride, self-satisfaction, or seeking vengeance, the Muslims are instructed at their moment of triumph to glorify and praise God, and seek his forgiveness for their sins. Furthermore, God reminds them that He is ever ready to continually pardon the repentant.

DISCUSSION 2: THE ATTRIBUTES OF GOD

One way to classify the attributes of God is: affirmative, or present (*al-ṣifāt al-thubūtiyyah*) and negative, or absent (*al-ṣifāt al-salbiyyah*). *Al-ṣifāt al-thubūtiyyah* are attributes of God such as knowledge (*ʿilm*), power (*qudrah*), and life (*ḥayāt*), while *al-ṣifāt al-salbiyyah* are those attributes that do not befit Him, such as having a partner (*sharīk*), dependence (*ihtiyāj*), and location (*makān*).

Another way of classifying divine attributes is to divide them into the attributes of essence (*al-ṣifāt al-dhātiyyah*) and attributes relating to action (*al-ṣifāt al-fiʿliyyah*).

Attributes of essence are those that describe the divine essence and do not depend on any being other than God Himself, such as power and life. They are further divided into two: *ṣifāt al-jamāl* (attributes of beauty), because they describe the beauty and perfection of God, and *ṣifāt al-jalāl* (attributes of glory), because they describe the majesty of God.

Attributes relating to action are those that describe divine acts and inform us of a relationship between God and other beings.[15]

Another meaning of these two terms is that the *ṣifāt al-jamāl* describe God's attributes of mercy, love, and forgiveness, while *ṣifāt al-jalāl* describe His attributes of wrath, reprimand, and punishment.

---

[14] Shīrāzī, *Namūneh*, 27/401.

[15] Shomali, *The Image of God in the Qur'an*, p. 2.

SUMMARY OF THE VERSE

This verse guides us about what is necessary to keep this victory a lasting one. As long as the Muslims glorify and praise God constantly, and continually turn to Him and repent for their transgressions, they will always enjoy God's assistance and thereby, victory.

REFLECTIVE LEARNING

1. Let me reflect on whether I glorify the praise of God and ask for His forgiveness at moments of success in my life? For example, my achievement of being a devout Muslim is a great success. Have I glorified the praise of Allah and asked for His forgiveness in order to preserve this great blessing? By this action, I could move this victory of *islām* (submission on the tongue) to the even greater victory of *īmān* (submission in the heart).
2. Secondly, if I seek the forgiveness of the Creator, I need to forgive the creation in turn. Let me consider forgiving those who have caused me hurt and grief, and take the first step I need to accomplish this.

SURAT AL-MASAD
THE HALTER (111)

TEXT AND TRANSLATION

سُورَةُ الْمَسَدِ

بِسْمِ اللهِ الرَّحْمٰنِ الرَّحِيمِ

تَبَّتْ يَدَا أَبِي لَهَبٍ وَتَبَّ ﴿١﴾ مَا أَغْنَىٰ عَنْهُ مَالُهُ وَمَا كَسَبَ ﴿٢﴾ سَيَصْلَىٰ نَارًا ذَاتَ
لَهَبٍ ﴿٣﴾ وَامْرَأَتُهُ حَمَّالَةَ الْحَطَبِ ﴿٤﴾ فِي جِيدِهَا حَبْلٌ مِنْ مَسَدٍ ﴿٥﴾

In the name of God, the Beneficent, the Merciful.

May both hands of Abu Lahab perish, and may he perish. [1]. *His wealth and actions will not avail him.* [2] *He shall soon burn in a fire of blazing flames.* [3]. *And his wife [also]; the bearer of firewood,* [4] *Upon her neck [shall be] a rope of strongly twisted [palm] fibre.* [5]

INTRODUCTION

Surat al-Masad (111) – also known as Surat Lahab and Surat Tabbat, was the 6th chapter to be revealed.[1] It has five verses and was revealed in Makka, after Surat al-Muddaththir (74), in the early months of the mission of the Prophet (s). It is named after Abu Lahab, an archenemy of the Prophet (s) and his mission.

Abu Lahab (d. 2/624) was a paternal uncle of the Prophet (a). His name was ʿAbd al-ʿUzza, but he was given the epithet Abu Lahab because of his ruddy and fiery complexion (*lahab*, لَهَب, means a flickering flame).[2] He died a few days after the battle of Badr, in which he was not present, although he had sent a representative to fight the Muslims in his stead.

His wife, Umm Jamil, was the daughter of Harb b. Umayyah, and the sister of Abu Sufyan. Umm Jamil bore great enmity to the Prophet (s) and was part of the group of people who plotted to kill him.

---

1 Maʿrifat, *ʿUlūm-i Qurʾānī*, p. 90.

2 Shīrāzī, *Namuneh*, 27/417.

This surah is amongst the miracles of the Qur'an since Abu Lahab lived for at least ten years after this surah, which contains emphatic statements about his doom, was revealed.[3] Ironically, he may have been able to get his heart's desire to damage Islam by actually declaring himself to be a Muslim, even if it was done falsely!

OCCASION OF REVELATION

When verse Q26:214 was revealed, stating:

وَأَنْذِرْ عَشِيرَتَكَ الْأَقْرَبِينَ

And warn your near kin...

the Prophet (s) first called his closest relatives, the Banu Hashim and Banu ʿAbd al-Muttalib for a meal, and introduced them to his message and mission. This is known in history as the invitation of Dhū al-ʿAshīrah (near kin).

A report states that the Prophet (s) invited his relatives to a meal after which he said to them, "I have been sent to all men, black, white and red. Verily, God has instructed me to warn my closest kin; I do not bring any other message from God except that you profess that there is no deity besides Allah."

[On hearing this], Abu Lahab said, "You summoned us for this?!"

Then, they all left him and dispersed; at which point the surah *Tabbat yadā Abī Lahabin wa tabb...* was revealed.[4]

Another report states that the Prophet (s) ascended Mount Safa and called out, "*Yā Ṣabāḥāh*!" (يَا صَبَاحَاهْ) (This was a call that was issued by the Arabs as a warning or to signal impending danger). The Quraysh gathered around him and asked, "What has happened?" He replied, "Tell me, if I inform you of an enemy who will overwhelm you in the morning or in the evening, would you believe me?" They all replied, "Yes."

He said, "[Then, know that] I am a warner to you, warning of a severe chastisement that awaits you."

---

[3] Ṭabāṭabāʾī, *al-Mīzān*, 20/385.

[4] Ibid, 38/220.

عَنِ الرَّسُولِ (صَلَّى اللهُ عَلَيْهِ وَآلِهِ) - إِنِّي بُعِثْتُ إِلَى الْأَسْوَدِ وَالْأَبْيَضِ والْأَحْمَرِ، إِنَّ اللهَ أَمَرَنِي أَنْ أَنْذِرَ عَشِيرَتِي الْأَقْرَبِينَ وَإِنِّي لَا أَمْلِكُ لَكُمْ مِنَ اللهِ شَيْئًا إِلَّا أَنْ تَقُولُوا لَا إِلَهَ إِلَّا اللهُ. فَقَالَ أَبُو لَهَبٍ: أَلِهَذَا دَعَوْتَنَا؟ ثُمَّ تَفَرَّقُوا عَنْهُ فَنَزَلَتْ «تَبَّتْ يَدَا أَبِي لَهَبٍ وَتَبَّ».

Abu Lahab exclaimed, "May you perish! Did you summon us all for this?!"

So, God revealed: *Tabbat yadā Abī Lahabin*...until the end of the surah.[5]

LINK TO THE PREVIOUS CHAPTERS

Surat al-Kāfirūn (109) had declared that there could be no compromise between polytheism (*shirk*) and monotheism (*tawḥīd*), by announcing the incompatibility of Islam with the worship of the disbelievers. The fate of the two sides is then portrayed in the next two chapters. Surat al-Naṣr (110) describes the victory, with God's help, of Islam and monotheism over polytheism and disbelief. And Surat al-Masad describes the perdition of the disbelievers and polytheism, epitomized in the person of Abu Lahab.

MERITS OF RECITATION

- A tradition from the Prophet (s) states: Whoever recites this surah will not be placed by God in the company of Abu Lahab.[6]
- Another tradition from the Prophet (s) states: Whoever recites this surah before going to sleep will remain in the protection of God.[7]
- A tradition from Imam al-Sadiq (a) states: When you recite Surat *Tabbat yadā Abī Lahabin wa tabb*, curse Abu Lahab, for he was one of the liars who used to belie the Prophet (s) and the message that he had brought from God, the Almighty.[8]

EXEGESIS

---

[5] Majlisī, *Biḥār*, 18/164.

صَعِدَ رَسُولُ اللهِ (صَلَّى اللهُ عَلَيْهِ وَآلِهِ) عَلَى الصَّفَا فَقَالَ يَا صَبَاحَاهْ فَاجْتَمَعَتْ إِلَيْهِ قُرَيْشٌ فَقَالُوا مَا لَكَ فَقَالَ أَرَأَيْتُكُمْ إِنْ أَخْبَرْتُكُمْ أَنَّ الْعَدُوَّ مُصْبِحُكُمْ أَوْ مُمْسِيكُمْ مَا كُنْتُمْ تُصَدِّقُونَنِي قَالُوا: بَلَى، قَالَ: فَإِنِّي نَذِيرٌ لَكُمْ بَيْنَ يَدَيْ عَذَابٍ شَدِيدٍ، قَالَ أَبُولَهَبٍ: تَبًّا لَكَ أَلِهَذَا دَعَوْتَنَا جَمِيعًا؟ فَأَنْزَلَ اللهُ تَعَالَى «تَبَّتْ يَدَا أَبِي لَهَبٍ وَتَبَّ» إِلَى آخِرِ السُّورَةِ.

[6] Baḥrānī, *al-Burhān*, 5/787.

عَنِ الرَّسُولِ (صَلَّى اللهُ عَلَيْهِ وَآلِهِ) – مَنْ قَرَأَ هَذِهِ السُّورَةَ لَمْ يَجْمَعِ اللهُ بَيْنَهُ وَبَيْنَ أَبِي لَهَبٍ.

[7] Ibid.

عَنِ الرَّسُولِ (صَلَّى اللهُ عَلَيْهِ وَآلِهِ) – مَنْ قَرَأَهَا عِنْدَ نَوْمِهِ حَفِظَهُ اللهُ.

[8] Majlisī, *Biḥār*, 89/343.

عَنِ الصَّادِقِ (عَلَيْهِ السَّلَامُ) – إِذَا قَرَأْتُمْ «تَبَّتْ يَدَا أَبِي لَهَبٍ وَتَبَّ» فَادْعُوا عَلَى أَبِي لَهَبٍ، فَإِنَّهُ كَانَ مِنَ الْمُكَذِّبِينَ الَّذِينَ يُكَذِّبُونَ بِالنَّبِيِّ (صَلَّى اللهُ عَلَيْهِ وَآلِهِ) وَبِمَا جَاءَ بِهِ مِنْ عِنْدِ اللهِ عَزَّ وَجَلَّ.

VERSE 1

تَبَّتْ يَدَا أَبِي لَهَبٍ وَتَبَّ ﴿١﴾

May both hands of Abu Lahab perish, and may he perish. [1]

1.1 [*Tabb* (تَبّ), and *tabāb* (تَباب)], mean a constant and lasting loss[9] that ultimately results in destruction and ruin.[10] It has been used in this meaning in two other places in the Qur'an. In Q40:37, God states:

وَمَا كَيْدُ فِرْعَوْنَ إِلَّا فِي تَبَابٍ

... and the plot of Fir'awn led to nothing but destruction (tabāb).

And Q11:101 states:

فَمَا أَغْنَتْ عَنْهُمْ آلِهَتُهُمُ الَّتِي يَدْعُونَ مِنْ دُونِ اللهِ مِنْ شَيْءٍ
لَمَّا جَاءَ أَمْرُ رَبِّكَ وَمَا زَادُوهُمْ غَيْرَ تَتْبِيبٍ

...So, their gods whom they invoked besides Allah did not avail them at all when the decree of your Lord came to pass; and they added but to their destruction (tatbīb).

1.2 The word '*tabb*' (perish) has been used twice in the first verse of Surat al-Masad, and there are several reasons suggested for this:[11]

i) The first indicates the promised destruction of Abu Lahab's power and his schemes, and the second, the destruction of Abu Lahab himself.

ii) The first instance of '*tabb*' is a curse and predicted destruction, while the second indicates confirmation.

iii) The repetition is for emphasis of his assured fate.

1.3 The use of the past tense in the verse is to emphasize the certainty of the event in the future. For example, many of the verses that speak about the Hereafter use the past tense.

---

9 Rāghib, *al-Mufradāt*.

10 Ṭabrasī, *al-Bayān*, 10/852.

11 Rāzī, *Mafātīḥ al-Ghayb*, 32/351.

1.4 [*Yadā* (يَدَا, two hands)] is a metaphor for his power and ability to act, because an individual's deeds are usually attributed to his hands.[12]

1.5 [Abu Lahab (أَبِي لَهَبٍ)]. Normally the Arabs use the appellation (*kunyah*) of an individual as a mark of respect or importance. Here, the Qur'an has used the *kunyah* of Abu Lahab, perhaps because ironically, his end will be in the flames of fire (*lahab*).[13] Others have mentioned that it was because that was his name, and not his *kunyah*, or that it was the only name he was known by.[14]

1.6 The Qur'an has mentioned names of past Prophets (a) and some individuals in history. However, from amongst the people at the time of revelation, aside from Zayd bin Harithah, the adopted son of the Prophet (s), Abu Lahab is the only man specifically named in the Qur'an. Perhaps this is because he was not only a relative, but he symbolized the opposition to the message of Islam, due to his intense hostility to the Prophet (s) and his mission.

SUMMARY OF THE VERSE

The verse curses Abu Lahab by calling for the destruction of his power and ability.

REFLECTIVE LEARNING

The promise of destruction is not just a message for Abu Lahab, rather it is a divine promise that anyone who opposes the Truth in favour of their worldly desires is doomed to perish.

Let me reflect on whether I ever make a decision for worldly gain at the expense of the truth?

VERSE 2

مَا أَغْنَىٰ عَنْهُ مَالُهُ وَمَا كَسَبَ ﴿٢﴾

His wealth and actions will not avail him. [2]

---

[12] Ṭabāṭabā'ī, *al-Mīzān*, 20/384.

[13] Shīrāzī, *Namuneh*, 27/419.

[14] Rāzī, *Mafātīḥ al-Ghayb*, 32/350.

2.1 According to some exegetes, *māl* in this verse refers to his wealth, and *mā kasab* to his children; as a result he thought himself to be needless of God and secure against His punishment.[15]

2.2 The reference to his two hands (*yadā*) in the previous verse was a metaphor for Abu Lahab's power and ability; in this verse, he is warned that these things would be of no use to him in his hostility towards the Prophet (s) and Islam.

2.3 Since man's true worth is determined by his belief and actions, in reality, Abu Lahab destroyed himself with his own hands. Indeed, the wealth and influence of the disbelievers will be of no avail to them in the hereafter. Q3:10 states:

إِنَّ الَّذِينَ كَفَرُوا لَنْ تُغْنِيَ عَنْهُمْ أَمْوَالُهُمْ وَلَا أَوْلَادُهُمْ مِنَ اللَّهِ شَيْئًا
وَأُولَٰئِكَ هُمْ وَقُودُ النَّارِ

Indeed, [as for] those who disbelieve – neither their wealth nor their children will avail them against God at all. And it is they who will be the fuel for the Fire.

SUMMARY OF THE VERSE

The message of the verse is that all the power and means of those who are defiant to God will be of no avail to them in the end.

REFLECTIVE LEARNING

Let me reflect on whether my wealth and possessions, and words and actions will benefit me or will be against me in the Hereafter.

VERSE 3

سَيَصْلَىٰ نَارًا ذَاتَ لَهَبٍ ﴿٣﴾

He shall soon burn in a fire of blazing flames. [3]

3.1 [*Sayaṣlā* (سَيَصْلَىٰ, he shall soon burn)] is derived from *ṣalā* meaning to burn or to be exposed to fire. The prefix '*sa*' indicates the near future. Therefore, the verse means 'it is not long before he will burn.'

[15] Ṭabrasī, *al-Bayān*, 10/853.

3.2 [*Nār* (نَار, fire)] refers to the fire of Hell, and [*dhāt lahab* (ذَاتَ لَهَب, containing flames)] means full of blazing flames, and this description is significantly juxtaposed with the *kunyah* of Abu Lahab.

3.3 The previous verse was about the futility of Abu Lahab's efforts in the *dunyā*. This verse now talks of the future, and declares that in the Hereafter, only hellfire awaits him.

3.4 The Day of Judgement is a Day of the embodiment of actions; Abu Lahab's intransigence and hostility to the Prophet (s) was like a fire with which he blackened his soul, and in the Hereafter, that fire would be manifested as the blazing flames of his personal hell, a fire that will not die out.

3.5 Does this Divine condemnation of Abu Lahab mean that he was compelled to stay a disbeliever all his life? The answer is as follows: There is a difference between God's knowledge and compulsion. The timeless knowledge of God does not negate the free will of human beings.

SUMMARY OF THE VERSE

The verse foretold the chastisement of Abu Lahab in the fire of Hell even while he was alive.

REFLECTIVE LEARNING

On the Day of the embodiment of actions, let me reflect on what form my actions will be like when I encounter them?

VERSES 4, 5

وَامْرَأَتُهُ حَمَّالَةَ الْحَطَبِ ﴿٤﴾ فِي جِيدِهَا حَبْلٌ مِنْ مَسَدٍ ﴿٥﴾

And his wife [also]; the bearer of firewood, [4] *upon her neck [shall be] a rope of strongly twisted [palm] fibre.* [5]

4-5.1 '*And his wife the bearer of firewood.*': [*Imra'ah* (اِمْرَأَة, wife)]. This term means woman or wife, and refers to Umm Jamil, the wife of Abu Lahab, who was united with her husband in their hostility to the Prophet (s) and his message. The noun (وَامْرَأَتُهُ, and his wife) is in the nominative case, so the verses mean, 'he shall soon burn in fire... and his wife too.'

[*Ḥammālah*, (حَمَّالَة, bearer)] is derived from *ḥamala*, meaning to bear or carry, and *ḥammālah* refers to a woman who carries something often or as a profession.

[*al-Ḥaṭab* (الْحَطَب, firewood)] refers to firewood. The term *ḥammālat al-ḥaṭab* means a woman who constantly carries firewood, and was used for servants who were usually charged with bringing firewood from the desert.

4-5.2 Abu Lahab had two other wives, and it is for this reason that a further description is added here to make it clear who the verse was referring to.[16] The term *ḥammālat al-ḥaṭab* refers to Umm Jamil, and could have been used for several reasons:

i) Umm Jamil used to bring thorny firewood from the desert and scatter it in the path of the Prophet (s), and outside his house, to try to injure him. Therefore, she is disdainfully referred to as the 'bearer of firewood', and her actions too, shall be manifested as the fire of Hell.[17]

ii) The phrase may also refer to her practice of spreading false and inflammatory tales about the Prophet (s), thereby fanning the fire of hatred against him in the community.

She was the neighbour of the Prophet (s) in Makka,[18] spying on him, and informing the Quraysh of his movements.[19] After her marriage to Abu Lahab (an unusual marriage between the inimical houses of Banu Umayyah and Banu Hashim), she ignited the fire of hatred in her husband's heart for the Prophet (s) and ensured that it burned strongly.[20]

iii) The phrase may also indicate that, just like every inmate of Hell, she herself will bring the actions that will serve as the fuel for its fire. This meaning is alluded to in the Q6:31:

وَهُمْ يَحْمِلُونَ أَوْزَارَهُمْ عَلَىٰ ظُهُورِهِمْ أَلَا سَاءَ مَا يَزِرُونَ

...And they shall bear their burdens on their backs;
now surely evil is that which they bear.

---

[16] Rāzī, *Mafātīḥ al-Ghayb*, 32/354.

[17] Shīrāzī, *Namuneh*, 27/421.

[18] Fākihī, *Akhbār Makka*, 5/316.

[19] Ṭabrasī, *al-Bayān*, 10/854.

[20] Ibn Abī al-*Ḥadīd*, *Sharḥ Nahj al-Balāghah*, 15/195.

4-5.3 *'Upon her neck a rope of strongly twisted [palm] fibre.'*: [*Jīd*, (جِيد, neck)]. The Qur'an uses three words for the neck: *raqabah* (رَقَبَة), which refers to the neck, and also as a metaphor for slavery; *ʿunuq* (عُنُق), which refers to the nape or the whole neck; and *jīd* (جِيد), which is used for the lower part of the neck where something decorative, usually a necklace, is worn around it.[21] It is here that she would have a noose of palm fibre placed.

4-5.4 [*Ḥabl* (حَبْل, rope)] refers to something strong that is used to tie objects, and [*Masad* (مَسَد, palm-fibre)] is the fibre of a palm tree from which ropes can be woven.[22]

4-5.5 Umm Jamil used to carry her firewood with a rope of twisted palm-fibre. On the Day of Judgement that action shall be embodied as a rope around her neck, dragging her into hellfire.[23]

SUMMARY OF THE VERSES

The verses state that Umm Jamil carried thorny wood to torment the Prophet (s) and as a result she will be dragged on the Day of Judgement with a rope made of twisted fibre.

REFLECTIVE LEARNING

Let me reflect about those whom I have influence over and how I influence them. Do I bring them closer to God or move them further from Him?

In each case, I should bear in mind that I share in their action and therefore, its recompense.

---

21 Mutahharī, (*Āshnāyī bā Qur'an*), *Āthār*, 28/826.

22 Rāghib, *al-Mufradāt*.

23 Ṭabrasī, *al-Bayān*, 10/852.

SURAT AL-IKHLĀṢ
THE SINCERITY (112)

TEXT AND TRANSLATION

سُورَةُ الإِخْلَاصِ

بِسْمِ اللهِ الرَّحْمٰنِ الرَّحِيمِ

قُلْ هُوَ اللهُ أَحَدٌ ﴿١﴾ اللهُ الصَّمَدُ ﴿٢﴾ لَمْ يَلِدْ وَلَمْ يُولَدْ ﴿٣﴾ وَلَمْ يَكُنْ لَهُ كُفُوًا أَحَدٌ ﴿٤﴾

In the name of God, the Beneficent, the Merciful.

Say: "He is Allah, [the] One. [1] *Allah, [is] the Eternally Independent on Whom all depend.* [2] *He neither begets nor is He begotten,* [3] *and there is no one comparable to Him."* [4]

INTRODUCTION

Surat al-Ikhlāṣ (112) is one of the most well-known and important chapters of the Qur'an. It comprehensively summarizes the fundamental doctrine of *tawḥīd* (monotheism, unicity of God): *tawḥīd al-dhāt* (unity in essence), *tawḥīd al-ṣifāt* (unity of attributes), and *tawḥīd al-afʿāl* (unity in attributing all acts to God), which are practically manifested in *tawḥīd al-ʿibādah* (unicity of deserving worship). And all Islamic teachings on *tawḥīd* arise from the summary in this short chapter.

Surat al-Ikhlāṣ was the 22nd chapter to be revealed.[1] It has four verses, and was revealed in Makka after Surat al-Nās, in the early years of the mission of the Prophet (s).[2]

It is known as Surat al-Ikhlāṣ because it introduces God in a manner that allows the believer to understand His Being and Attributes and aids him in eliminating any trace of polytheism, and thereby become sincere (*mukhliṣ*) in his devotion to God.

---

[1] Maʿrifat, *ʿUlūm-i Qur'ānī*, p. 90.

[2] Ṭabrasī, *al-Bayān*, 10/854.

It has been referred to in the traditions by several other names, including *al-Tawḥīd* (the Unicity), *al-Asās* (the Foundation), *al-Tajrīd* (the Removal of wrongful notions about God), *al-Ṣamad* (the Independent), and *Qul Huwa Allahu Aḥad*.[3]

LINK TO THE CHAPTERS BEFORE AND AFTER IT

The seven chapters before it – Surat al-Fīl (105) to Surat al-Masad (111) – talk about the various hostilities of the polytheists and disbelievers against the Prophet (s) and Islam, arising from their disagreement about whom and how to worship. This chapter answers this question comprehensively.

The next two chapters then show how to safeguard this understanding of *tawḥīd* by seeking refuge in God from the external forces (mentioned in Surat al-Falaq) and internal forces (mentioned in Surat al-Nās) that would forestall a believer from turning to God.

MERITS OF RECITATION

- It is disliked (*makrūh*) not to recite this chapter at least once in the daily prayers. A narration from Imam al-Sadiq (a) states: One who passes a day without reciting Surat *Qul Huwa Allahu Aḥad* in any of his five daily prayers will be told, 'O servant of God! You are not amongst those who have prayed [as they ought to].'[4]
- A tradition from the Prophet (s) states: One who recites this chapter is like one who has recited one-third of the Qur'an.[5] Perhaps this is because approximately one-third of the Qur'an discusses aspects of *tawḥīd* (unicity of God), and this chapter comprehensively summarizes the concept.[6]
- A tradition from Imam al-Sadiq (a) states: Whoever recites the chapter *Qul Huwa Allahu Aḥad* once, is like one who has recited

3 Ibid.

4 Kulaynī, *al-Kāfī*, 2/622.

عَنِ الصَّادِقِ (عَلَيْهِ السَّلَامُ): مَنْ مَضَى بِهِ يَوْمٌ وَاحِدٌ فَصَلَّى فِيهِ بِخَمْسِ صَلَوَاتٍ، وَلَمْ يَقْرَأْ فِيهَا بِ «قُلْ هُوَ اللهُ أَحَدٌ»، قِيلَ لَهُ: يَا عَبْدَ اللهِ لَسْتَ مِنَ الْمُصَلِّينَ.

5 Majlisī, *Biḥār*, 89/334.

عَنِ الرَّسُولِ (صَلَّى اللهُ عَلَيْهِ وَآلِهِ): مَنْ قَرَأَ «قُلْ هُوَ اللهُ أَحَدٌ» عَدَلَتْ لَهُ بِثُلُثِ الْقُرْآنِ.

6 Shīrāzī, *Namūneh*, 27/430.

one-third of the Qur'an, one-third of the Tawrāt, one-third of the Injīl, and one-third of the Zabūr.[7]

- A tradition from Imam al-Sadiq (a) states: It is disliked (*makrūh*) to recite the whole chapter of *Qul Huwa Allahu Aḥad* in one breath [i.e. quickly and without reflection].[8]
- It is reported that when Imam al-Sajjad (a) was asked about *tawḥīd*, he said: "Indeed, God the Almighty knew that at the end of time there will be people who ponder deeply (*mutaʿmmiqūn*)[9], and so He revealed *Qul Huwa Allahu Aḥad* and the [first six] verses from Surat al-Ḥadīd up to '*wa Huwa ʿAlīmun bidhāt al-ṣudūr*'. And whoever goes beyond this will perish [in his faith]."[10]
- A tradition from Imam Ali (a) states: Whoever wishes to leave this world having been cleansed of his sins just as gold is purified from rock, leaving it without fault or blemish, and without anyone blaming him for wrongdoing, should recite the Description of the Lord,[11] Blessed and Exalted is He, (i.e. Surat al-Ikhlāṣ) twelve times after the five obligatory prayers.[12]
- A tradition from Imam Ali (a) states: Whoever performs his morning prayers and then recites this chapter eleven times will be protected from committing a sin that day, even if Shaytan tries to entice him.[13]

---

7 Ṣadūq, *al-Tawḥīd*, p. 260.

عَنِ الصَّادِقِ (عَلَيْهِ السَّلَامُ): مَنْ قَرَأَ «قُلْ هُوَ اللهُ أَحَدٌ» مَرَّةً وَاحِدَةً، فَكَأَنَّمَا قَرَأَ ثُلُثَ الْقُرْآنِ، وَثُلُثَ التَّوْرَاةِ، وَثُلُثَ الْإِنْجِيلِ، وَثُلُثَ الزَّبُورِ.

8 Kulaynī, *al-Kāfī*, 2/616.

عَنِ الصَّادِقِ (عَلَيْهِ السَّلَامُ): يُكْرَهُ أَنْ يُقْرَأَ «قُلْ هُوَ اللهُ أَحَدٌ» بِنَفَسٍ وَاحِدٍ.

9 According to many scholars, this is not a term of praise, but rather refers to people who waste their time in thinking about matters that are beyond human understanding. For further reading, see Masʿūdī, *Àsīb Shināsī-yi ḥadīth*, p. 215.

10 Kulaynī, *al-Kāfī*, 1/91.

سُئِلَ عَلِيُّ بْنُ الْحُسَيْنِ (عَلَيْهِ السَّلَامُ) عَنِ التَّوْحِيدِ، فَقَالَ: إِنَّ اللهَ تَعَالَى عَلِمَ أَنَّهُ يَكُونُ فِي آخِرِ الزَّمَانِ أَقْوَامٌ مُتَعَمِّقُونَ، فَأَنْزَلَ اللهُ تَعَالَى «قُلْ هُوَ اللهُ أَحَدٌ اللهُ الصَّمَدُ»، وَالْآيَاتِ مِنْ سُورَةِ الْحَدِيدِ إِلَى قَوْلِهِ «وَهُوَ عَلِيمٌ بِذَاتِ الصُّدُورِ»، فَمَنْ رَامَ مَا وَرَاءَ ذَلِكَ فَقَدْ هَلَكَ.

11 Surat al-Ikhlāṣ is called 'Description of the Lord' (*nisbat al-rabb*) in some traditions because the Jews came to the Prophet (s) and told him, "Describe to us your Lord," after which Surat al-Ikhlāṣ was revealed. (Ṣadūq, *al-Faqīh*, 1/324, footnote 2).

12 Ṣadūq, *al-Faqīh*, 1/324.

عَنْ أَمِيرِ الْمُؤْمِنِينَ (عَلَيْهِ السَّلَامُ): مَنْ أَحَبَّ أَنْ يَخْرُجَ مِنَ الدُّنْيَا وَقَدْ تَخَلَّصَ مِنَ الذُّنُوبِ كَمَا يَتَخَلَّصُ الذَّهَبُ الَّذِي لَا كَدَرَ فِيهِ، وَلَا يَطْلُبُهُ أَحَدٌ بِمَظْلِمَةٍ، فَلْيَقُلْ فِي دُبُرِ الصَّلَوَاتِ الْخَمْسِ نِسْبَةَ الرَّبِّ تَبَارَكَ وَتَعَالَى اثْنَتَيْ عَشْرَةَ مَرَّةً.

13 Ṣadūq, *Thawāb al-Aʿmāl*, p. 45.

عَنْ أَمِيرِ الْمُؤْمِنِينَ (عَلَيْهِ السَّلَامُ): مَنْ صَلَّى صَلَاةَ الْفَجْرِ ثُمَّ قَرَأَ «قُلْ هُوَ اللهُ أَحَدٌ» إِحْدَى عَشْرَةَ مَرَّةً، لَمْ يَتْبَعْهُ فِي ذَلِكَ الْيَوْمِ ذَنْبٌ، وَإِنْ

EXEGESIS

VERSE 1

قُلْ هُوَ اللَّهُ أَحَدٌ ﴿١﴾

Say, "He is Allah, (the) One. [1]

1.1 [*Qul* (قُلْ, say)]. This is an instruction to the Prophet (s) to announce the reality that God is One. It is a response to those who questioned the nature of God. History records some of these questioners as: 1) Polytheists in Makka, 2) ʿAbdullāh b. Ṣūriyā, a Jew of Madina, 3) ʿAbdullāh b. Ubayy, a hypocrite in Madina, and 4) the Christians of Najrān.[14]

1.2 There are five chapters that begin with the command '*qul*' (say): Surat al-Kāfirūn, al-Ikhlāṣ, al-Falaq, and al-Nās, popularly known as *al-qalāqil al-arbaʿah*, or the 'four *quls*', and Surat al-Jinn. In fact, the usage of the word '*qul*' (say) in the Qur'an is noteworthy, especially when this command is implicit in every Qur'anic verse, and the Prophet (s) was charged to convey the Divine message anyway. There are several possible reasons for this:

i) It is in response to a question, usually on a matter that has been subject to long and protracted discussions, and now requires a decisive response. In this case the argument was about the nature of God.

ii) It is due to the diligence of the Prophet (s) in quoting the words of God exactly as revealed to him.

iii) When reciting the words, it reinforces the concept of submission to the Divine will and injunction.[15]

1.3 [*Huwa Allah* (هُوَ اللَّهُ, He is Allah)] is the response to the question, "Who is He?" *Huwa* is added here as a pronoun of case (*Ãamīr al-shā'n*) for emphasis: ([the case is that] He is Allah).[16] This draws attention to the name Allah, which is the Divine name that refers

---

رَغِمَ أَنْفُ الشَّيْطَانِ.

[14] Ṭabrasī, *al-Bayān*, 10/859.

[15] Shīrāzī, *Namuneh*, 27/386.

[16] Ṭabāṭabā'ī, *al-Mīzān*, 20/387.

to His essence and encompasses all His attributes. (The name Allah has been discussed in the *tafsīr* of Surat al-Fātiḥah.)

1.4 [*Aḥad* (أَحَد, One)] is used instead of *wāḥid* as the attribute of God. While both mean 'one', *aḥad* does not denote 'one' in number (followed or preceded by another number, or divisible into smaller fractions), or 'one' in kind (i.e. capable of categorization and analysis), but rather, it denotes 'one' in uniqueness and matchlessness, both physically and in mental conception. Thus, as an attribute, '*aḥad*' can only be used for God.

Imam Ali (a) explained this uniqueness in the course of the battle of Jamal, when a Bedouin Arab asked him, "Do you say God is One, O Commander of the faithful?" The Imam (a) replied, "There are four ways to consider the Unity of God, two of which do not apply to Him, and two of which are affirmed of Him..." The Imam (a) then explained that one in number and one in kind do not apply to God. What applies to Him is One in uniqueness, in that nothing in creation resembles Him, and One in Essence, in that He is indivisible in His existence, in intellectual analysis, and in imagination.[17]

A beautiful statement attributed to Imam Ali (a) states: Everything other than Him when described as 'one', indicates its paucity and smallness.[18]

SUMMARY OF THE VERSE

The verse teaches that God is One, and nothing can be associated with Him in power, authority, or worship. God is indivisible and hence it is impossible to comprehend Him.

---

[17] Ṣadūq, *al-Tawḥīd*, p. 83.

إِنَّ أَعْرَابِيًّا قَامَ يَوْمَ الْجَمَلِ إِلَى أَمِيرِ الْمُؤْمِنِينَ عَلَيْهِ السَّلَامُ، فَقَالَ: يَا أَمِيرَ الْمُؤْمِنِينَ، أَتَقُولُ إِنَّ اللهَ وَاحِدٌ؟ قَالَ: فَحَمَلَ النَّاسُ عَلَيْهِ، وَقَالُوا: يَا أَعْرَابِيُّ، أَمَا تَرَى مَا فِيهِ أَمِيرُ الْمُؤْمِنِينَ عَلَيْهِ السَّلَامُ مِنْ تَقَسُّمِ الْقَلْبِ؟ فَقَالَ أَمِيرُ الْمُؤْمِنِينَ عَلَيْهِ السَّلَامُ: دَعُوهُ فَإِنَّ الَّذِي يُرِيدُهُ الْأَعْرَابِيُّ هُوَ الَّذِي نُرِيدُهُ مِنَ الْقَوْمِ، ثُمَّ قَالَ: يَا أَعْرَابِيُّ، إِنَّ الْقَوْلَ فِي أَنَّ اللهَ وَاحِدٌ عَلَى أَرْبَعَةِ أَقْسَامٍ فَوَجْهَانِ مِنْهَا لَا يَجُوزَانِ عَلَى اللهِ عَزَّ وَجَلَّ وَوَجْهَانِ يَثْبُتَانِ فِيهِ، فَأَمَّا اللَّذَانِ لَا يَجُوزَانِ عَلَيْهِ فَقَوْلُ الْقَائِلِ وَاحِدٌ يَقْصِدُ بِهِ بَابَ الْأَعْدَادِ فَهَذَا مَا لَا يَجُوزُ لِأَنَّ مَا لَا ثَانِيَ لَهُ لَا يَدْخُلُ فِي بَابِ الْأَعْدَادِ أَلَا تَرَى أَنَّهُ كَفَرَ مَنْ قَالَ ثَالِثُ ثَلَاثَةٍ، وَقَوْلُ الْقَائِلِ هُوَ وَاحِدٌ مِنَ النَّاسِ، يُرِيدُ النَّوْعَ مِنَ الْجِنْسِ، فَهَذَا مَا لَا يَجُوزُ لِأَنَّهُ تَشْبِيهٌ وَجَلَّ رَبُّنَا عَنْ ذَلِكَ وَتَعَالَى، وَأَمَّا الْوَجْهَانِ اللَّذَانِ يَثْبُتَانِ فِيهِ، فَقَوْلُ الْقَائِلِ هُوَ وَاحِدٌ لَيْسَ لَهُ فِي الْأَشْيَاءِ شِبْهٌ كَذَلِكَ رَبُّنَا، وَقَوْلُ الْقَائِلِ إِنَّهُ عَزَّ وَجَلَّ أَحَدِيُّ الْمَعْنَى، يَعْنِي بِهِ أَنَّهُ لَا يَنْقَسِمُ فِي وُجُودٍ وَلَا عَقْلٍ وَلَا وَهْمٍ كَذَلِكَ رَبُّنَا عَزَّ وَجَلَّ.

[18] *Nahj al-Balāghah*, Sermon 65.

كُلُّ مُسَمًّى بِالْوَحْدَةِ غَيْرُهُ قَلِيلٌ.

It is only when one sincerely professes and realizes that God is the only One worthy of worship, that he can attain the correct belief in *tawḥīd*, and thereafter abandon and distance himself from the worship and devotion to anything else.

REFLECTIVE LEARNING

Let me reflect on my understanding of *tawḥīd* and how is it shown in my actions.

Do I understand that worship is due only to Allah, and do I exclude the worship of all else from my practice?

VERSE 2

اللَّهُ الصَّمَدُ ﴿٢﴾

Allah, [is] the Eternally Independent on Whom all depend. [2]

2.1 [*Al-Ṣamad* (الصَّمَد, Eternally Independent)] is a term unique to this chapter and denotes an authority to whom people confidently turn to for everything.[19]

A tradition from Imam al-Husayn (a) states: *Al-Ṣamad* is one who has no hollowness, whose power is limitless, who does not eat or drink, who does not sleep, and whose existence is eternal.[20]

2.2 By using the definite article in the term *al-Ṣamad*, the Qur'an emphasizes that ultimately, everything in the cosmos depends only on God and turns only to Him, while He is completely independent and needless. Q35:15 states:

يَا أَيُّهَا النَّاسُ أَنْتُمُ الْفُقَرَاءُ إِلَى اللَّهِ وَاللَّهُ هُوَ الْغَنِيُّ الْحَمِيدُ

O mankind! It is you who stand in need of God,
while God is He Who is free of all needs, worthy of all praise.

Furthermore, as emphasized in several verses, everything belongs to Him alone. As an example, Q9:116 states:

---

[19] Ṭabāṭabā'ī, *al-Mīzān*, 20/388.

[20] Majlisī, *Biḥar*, 3/223.

عَنِ الْحُسَيْنِ (عَلَيْهِ السَّلَامُ): الصَّمَدُ الَّذِي لَا جَوْفَ لَهُ، وَالصَّمَدُ الَّذِي قَدِ انْتَهَى سُؤْدُدُهُ، وَالصَّمَدُ الَّذِي لَا يَأْكُلُ وَلَا يَشْرَبُ، وَالصَّمَدُ الَّذِي لَا يَنَامُ، وَالصَّمَدُ الدَّائِمُ الَّذِي لَمْ يَزَلْ وَلَا يَزَالُ.

إِنَّ اللَّهَ لَهُ مُلْكُ السَّمَاوَاتِ وَالْأَرْضِ يُحْيِي وَيُمِيتُ
وَمَا لَكُمْ مِنْ دُونِ اللَّهِ مِنْ وَلِيٍّ وَلَا نَصِيرٍ

Indeed, to God belongs the entire dominion of the heavens and the earth; He gives life and causes death. And you have no protector or helper other than God.

2.3 The name Allah is repeated here to show that each of the first two verses are independently able to define God. The first verse defines God by the attribute of His Essence and the second by the attribute of His action.[21]

SUMMARY OF THE VERSE

In summary, God is the eternally needless, while everything other than Him is constantly and utterly dependant on Him for their entire existence; for their creation, sustenance, guidance, and so on.

REFLECTIVE LEARNING

If I choose to turn to His creation for my needs instead, then I have deprived myself of what is available with the Creator, unless I accept that they are powerless to do anything without God's leave.

Furthermore, turning to God means turning to a support Who is not limited in ability, love, and wisdom. Q39:36 states:

أَلَيْسَ اللَّهُ بِكَافٍ عَبْدَهُ

Is God not sufficient for His servant?

With this in mind, let me reflect on whether I turn to Allah first and foremost before turning to anyone else?

Knowing that God is always available for all his needs fills a believer with confidence and reassurance, and forestalls depression and loss of hope. Q13:28 states:

أَلَا بِذِكْرِ اللَّهِ تَطْمَئِنُّ الْقُلُوبُ

Without doubt, in the remembrance of Allah do hearts find contentment!

---

[21] Ṭabāṭabā'ī, *al-Mīzān*, 20/388.

Let me reflect on how often I remember Allah and turn to Him for all my needs.

VERSE 3

لَمْ يَلِدْ وَلَمْ يُولَدْ ﴿٣﴾

He neither begets nor is He begotten. [3]

3.1 The essence of God has no concept of addition or subtraction. Nothing detaches from Him because He is not made of parts. He is eternally needless, so He has not been derived from anything either.

3.2 The idolaters believed the angels to be the daughters of God. Several verses mention this contention, for example, Q17:40 states:

أَفَأَصْفَاكُمْ رَبُّكُمْ بِالْبَنِينَ وَاتَّخَذَ مِنَ الْمَلَائِكَةِ
إِنَاثًا إِنَّكُمْ لَتَقُولُونَ قَوْلًا عَظِيمًا

"Has then your Lord preferred for you sons, and taken for Himself daughters from the angels? Indeed, you utter a grievous saying."

Meanwhile, the Jews believed Prophet 'Uzayr (a) to be God's son, while the Christians maintain that Prophet 'Isa (a) is the son of God. Q9:30 states:

وَقَالَتِ الْيَهُودُ عُزَيْرٌ ابْنُ اللهِ وَقَالَتِ النَّصَارَى الْمَسِيحُ ابْنُ اللهِ ذَٰلِكَ قَوْلُهُمْ
بِأَفْوَاهِهِمْ يُضَاهِئُونَ قَوْلَ الَّذِينَ كَفَرُوا مِنْ قَبْلُ قَاتَلَهُمُ اللهُ أَنَّىٰ يُؤْفَكُونَ

The Jews say, "'Uzayr is the son of God", and the Christians say, "The Messiah is the son of God." These are their statements from their [own] mouths. They are imitating the statements of the disbelievers before them. May God destroy them, how are they deluded?"

The verse under review emphasizes that His relationship to mankind is that He is their Creator, not their parent.

The verse negates the concept of dualism, pantheism, divine incarnation, or any notions that created beings contain a part of Divinity.

SUMMARY OF THE VERSE

In summary, the verse tells us that God is separate and distinct from every creature. Nothing has detached from His Essence and He was never in need of anything for His Existence.

REFLECTIVE LEARNING

God is the Creator of mankind, and ultimately we are all His servants. He is not biased or obliged to anyone. Those who are more honourable in His eyes are the ones who have *taqwā*, as stated in Q49:13:

إِنَّ أَكْرَمَكُمْ عِنْدَ اللهِ أَتْقَاكُمْ

...Indeed, the most noble of you in the sight of God
is the most God-wary amongst you...

Let me reflect on the fact that gaining honour and proximity to God is accessible to me; with my own efforts, I can gain His favour through piety and servitude. In what aspects of my life have I submitted my authority and free will to Allah?

VERSE 4

وَلَمْ يَكُنْ لَهُ كُفُوًا أَحَدٌ ﴿٤﴾

And there is no one comparable to Him. [4]

4.1 Every verse in this chapter is an explanation and expansion of the verse before it. Thus, '*Say, "He is Allah, (the) One,*' implies '*Allah, (is) the Eternally Independent*'. And in turn, this implies that, '*He neither begets nor is He begotten*, and therefore, '*there is no one comparable to Him*'.

4.2 [*Kufw* (كُفُو, comparable)] means equal, peer or match. Since everything depends on Him, while He is eternally needless, nothing in the cosmos can be even remotely comparable to Him, neither in essence, attribute, nor action. In this regard Q42:11 states:

لَيْسَ كَمِثْلِهِ شَيْءٌ

...Nothing is like Him...

4.3 The three qualities that have been negated for God in the previous verse and this one – that He does not beget, He was not born, and He has no peer, all explain His attribute, *al-Ṣamad.*

SUMMARY OF THE VERSE

Generally we understand realities, including Allah, by comparing them with what we know. However, this verse informs us that God cannot be compared to anything that we can describe or imagine.

REFLECTIVE LEARNING

Let me reflect on how often I project human-like emotions and reactions on God, when He has declared that nothing is comparable to Him.

To worship God and get closer to Him, I need to attain recognition (*maʿrifah*) of Him. The best way to do this is through the teachings of the Ahl al-Bayt (a), who possessed a great *maʿrifah* of Allah because they were His purified servants, as stated in Q37:159,160:

سُبْحَانَ اللَّهِ عَمَّا يَصِفُونَ ﴿١٥٩﴾ إِلَّا عِبَادَ اللَّهِ الْمُخْلَصِينَ

Glory be to God above what they describe,
except for the purified servants of God.

Let me reflect on how often I study the words and supplications of the Ahl al-Bayt (a) in order to increase my *maʿrifah* of God.

SURAT AL-FALAQ
THE DAYBREAK (113)

TEXT AND TRANSLATION

سُورَةُ الْفَلَقِ

بِسْمِ اللهِ الرَّحْمٰنِ الرَّحِيمِ

قُلْ أَعُوذُ بِرَبِّ الْفَلَقِ ﴿١﴾ مِنْ شَرِّ مَا خَلَقَ ﴿٢﴾ وَمِنْ شَرِّ غَاسِقٍ إِذَا وَقَبَ ﴿٣﴾
وَمِنْ شَرِّ النَّفَّاثَاتِ فِي الْعُقَدِ ﴿٤﴾ وَمِنْ شَرِّ حَاسِدٍ إِذَا حَسَدَ ﴿٥﴾

In the name of God, the Beneficent, the Merciful.

Say: "I seek refuge in the Lord of the daybreak, [1] *from the evil of that which He created,* [2] *and from the evil of the darkness of night when it settles,* [3] *and from the evil of those who blow on knots (magicians),* [4] *and from the evil of an envier when he envies."* [5]

INTRODUCTION

Surat al-Falaq (113) and Surat al-Nās are the last two chapters of the Qurʾan. They were revealed in Makka. Surat al-Falaq was the 20th chapter to be revealed.[1] It was revealed either along with, or just before Surat al-Nās. Both were revealed before Surat al-Ikhlāṣ.

In the traditions, they are often jointly referred to as *al-muʿawwidhatān* (the two refuges). One reason for this is that the Prophet (s) would often seek God's protection for his two grandsons al-Hasan (a) and al-Husayn (a) by reciting these two chapters.[2]

The chapters were revealed when the Prophet (s) fell severely ill. In a tradition from Imam al-Baqir (a) we read, "The Prophet (s) fell ill and was suffering a lot of pain. At that time, Jibrāil and Mikāil came to him and sat at his head and feet, respectively. Then Jibrāil sought refuge in

---

1 Maʿrifat, *ʿUlūm-i Qurʾānī*, p. 90.

2 Majlisī, *Biḥār*, 60/14.

أَنَّ النَّبِيَّ (صَلَّى اللهُ عَلَيْهِ وَآلِهِ) كَانَ كَثِيرًا مَا يُعَوِّذُ الْحَسَنَ وَالْحُسَيْنَ (عَلَيْهِمَا السَّلَامُ) بِهَاتَيْنِ السُّورَتَيْنِ.

God by reciting Surat al-Falaq and Mikail did the same by reciting Surat al-Nās."[3]

In this surah the Prophet (s) is instructed to seek refuge in God from a variety of external phenomena. God, in His mercy invites the believer to seek calm and peace in His care, and reassures him of His secure protection.

LINK TO THE CHAPTER BEFORE AND AFTER IT

The previous chapter, Surat al-Ikhlāṣ, is the essence of *tawḥīd* and Surat al-Falaq and the next chapter, Surat al-Nās tell us of the forces that attempt to move us away from *tawḥīd.*

Surat al-Falaq talks of the external forces, and Surat al-Nās of the internal forces.

MERITS OF RECITATION

- ʿUqbah bin ʿÀmir narrates: The Prophet (s) said to me, "O ʿUqbah, shall I inform you of two surahs which are amongst the best of the Qur'an?" I replied, "Yes indeed, O Messenger of God." Then he taught me the *muʿawwidhatayn* (Surat al-Falaq and Surat al-Nās) and said, "Recite them whenever you wake up or go to sleep."[4]
- A tradition from the Prophet (s) states: Whoever recites Surat al-Falaq when he goes to sleep will have a great reward. It is a safeguard from every evil and an effective protection against every evil eye.[5]
- A tradition from Imam al-Baqir (a) states: Whoever is disturbed by distressing dreams should recite Surat al-Falaq, Surat al-Nās and Àyat al-Kursī when he goes to sleep.[6]

---

[3] Majlisī, *Biḥār*, 18/71.

عَنِ الْبَاقِرِ (عَلَيْهِ السَّلَامُ): إِنَّ رَسُولَ اللهِ (صَلَّى اللهُ عَلَيْهِ وَآلِهِ) اشْتَكَى شَكْوَى شَدِيدًا وَوَجِعَ وَجَعًا شَدِيدًا، فَأَتَاهُ جَبْرَائِيلُ وَمِيكَائِيلُ، فَقَعَدَ جَبْرَائِيلُ عِنْدَ رَأْسِهِ وَمِيكَائِيلُ عِنْدَ رِجْلَيْهِ، فَعَوَّذَهُ جَبْرَائِيلُ بِ«قُلْ أَعُوذُ بِرَبِّ الْفَلَقِ»، وَعَوَّذَهُ مِيكَائِيلُ بِ «قُلْ أَعُوذُ بِرَبِّ النَّاسِ».

[4] Nūrī, *Mustadrak al-Wasā'il*, 4/291.

عَنِ الرَّسُولِ (صَلَّى اللهُ عَلَيْهِ وَآلِهِ): يَا عُقْبَةُ، أَلَا أُعَلِّمُكَ سُورَتَيْنِ هُمَا أَفْضَلُ الْقُرْآنِ أَوْ مِنْ أَفْضَلِ الْقُرْآنِ؟ قُلْتُ: بَلَى، يَا رَسُولَ اللهِ. فَعَلَّمَنِي الْمُعَوِّذَتَيْنِ، وَقَالَ: اِقْرَأْهُمَا كُلَّمَا قُمْتَ وَنِمْتَ.

[5] Baḥrānī, *al-Burhān*, 5/815.

عَنِ الرَّسُولِ (صَلَّى اللهُ عَلَيْهِ وَآلِهِ): مَنْ قَرَأَهَا عِنْدَ نَوْمِهِ، كَانَ لَهُ أَجْرٌ عَظِيمٌ، وَهِيَ حِرْزٌ مِنْ كُلِّ سُوءٍ، وَهِيَ رُقْيَةٌ نَافِعَةٌ وَحِرْزٌ مِنْ كُلِّ عَيْنٍ نَاظِرَةٍ.

[6] Ṣadūq, *al-Faqih*, 1/469.

عَنِ الْبَاقِرِ (عَلَيْهِ السَّلَامُ): مَنْ أَصَابَهُ فَزَعٌ عِنْدَ مَنَامِهِ، فَلْيَقْرَأْ إِذَا أَوَى إِلَى فِرَاشِهِ الْمُعَوِّذَتَيْنِ وَآيَةَ الْكُرْسِيِّ .

EXEGESIS

VERSE 1

قُلْ أَعُوذُ بِرَبِّ الْفَلَقِ ﴿١﴾

Say, "I seek refuge in the Lord of the daybreak. [1]

1.1 The first verse begins with a command [*qul* (قُلْ, say)], and by repeating the word, the individual acknowledges that seeking God's protection will first require obedience to His commands. Although the command is directed to the Prophet (s), it thereafter includes all the Muslims, instructing them to seek refuge in God alone.

1.2 [*Aʿūdhu* (أَعُوذُ, I seek refuge)]. The verb is derived from the root *ʿādha*, meaning to take refuge or seek protection. It is human nature to seek protection from an enemy with someone or something stronger than themselves. Asking His protection reminds man of his own frailty and need for God, Who is the only One who can truly protect him.

1.3 [*Rabb* (رَب, Lord, Sustainer)]. We have discussed this term in the *tafsīr* of the second verse of Surat al-Fātiḥah.

1.4 [*Falaq* (فَلَق, separation)] comes from the root *f-l-q*, meaning to cleave or separate one thing from another. Because dawn cleaves the curtain of night, *falaq* is used for daybreak. In Q6:96, the term is used in that meaning:

فَالِقُ الْإِصْبَاحِ

He causes the day to break...

1.5 Commentators are of the opinion that *falaq* may refer to all living creatures and plants because each comes from the splitting of a seed or germ cell. In Q6:95, God uses the word *falaq* in this sense in the verse:

إِنَّ اللَّهَ فَالِقُ الْحَبِّ وَالنَّوَىٰ يُخْرِجُ الْحَيَّ مِنَ الْمَيِّتِ وَمُخْرِجُ الْمَيِّتِ مِنَ الْحَيِّ

Indeed, God is the cleaver of grain-seed and the date-stone; He brings the living out of the dead and brings the dead out of the living...

1.6 Others have given a wider meaning to *falaq*, to include the creation of the cosmos, in the sense that the curtain of non-existence was split by God to create every being.[7]

1.7 All these meanings point to the grandeur of God, Who has fashioned these marvellous phenomena, and in Whom we are asked to seek refuge.

SUMMARY OF THE VERSE

In summary, God is the only Protector against any harm that can come to us from His creation, and this verse instructs us to therefore seek refuge in Him.

REFLECTIVE LEARNING

By using the quality, *al-Rabb*, God reminds us that He is the true Sustainer of the entire cosmos.

Let me reflect on whether I then trust in God, or turn to something or someone other than Him for protection?

VERSE 2

مِنْ شَرِّ مَا خَلَقَ ﴿٢﴾

From the evil of that which He created. [2]

2.1 [*Sharr* (شَرّ, evil)] here does not mean that the creation of God is essentially evil; in fact, everything has been created in its best form. Q32:7, states:

الَّذِي أَحْسَنَ كُلَّ شَيْءٍ خَلَقَهُ

[The Mighty, the Merciful] He who made perfect everything that He created...

2.2 Evil is the absence of good. It is an aberration that occurs when a creature deviates from the purpose of its creation and goes astray, or distances itself from the Creator, or when creation is used in a wrongful manner. For example, the venom, sharp teeth, or talons of animals are their natural defence against their enemy or a means to secure food; if they are used for this purpose, it is not evil.

---

7 See: Shīrāzī, *Namūneh*, 27/458.

2.3 *'From the evil of that which He created'*: This informs us that all of creation has the potential to cause harm, even for example, the sun, water, etc. The intricate and necessary connection between all entities in God's creation is bound to bring some evil. Believers are encouraged by this verse to maintain their link to the rest of creation to achieve goodness and benefit, but to be reassured by the fact that God will protect them from any evil that comes about thereby.

2.4 Unlike the creation, which has the potential to be evil, the Creator never harms. Even in the chastisement of God there is a favour of purification for the one being punished. Q55:43-45 state:

هَٰذِهِ جَهَنَّمُ الَّتِي يُكَذِّبُ بِهَا الْمُجْرِمُونَ ﴿٤٣﴾ يَطُوفُونَ بَيْنَهَا
وَبَيْنَ حَمِيمٍ آنٍ ﴿٤٤﴾ فَبِأَيِّ آلَاءِ رَبِّكُمَا تُكَذِّبَانِ

This is Hell, which the criminals denied. They shall wander between it and scalding hot water. So which of the favours of your Lord will you two (men and jinn*) deny?*

2.5 Similarly, many occurrences are not inherently evil, although they may seem so, because despite the experience being unpleasant, man is thereby guided or reminded of his purpose in this world.

2.6 After this general mention of evil, three specific instances are highlighted:

i) the evil of the darkness of night,
ii) the evil of the magicians, and
iii) the evil of the envious.

This is possibly because human beings are relatively unaware of these dangers and more vulnerable to them.[8]

SUMMARY OF THE VERSE

In summary, the verse asks us to seek refuge in God from the potential evil inherent in every created being.

REFLECTIVE LEARNING

Evil occurs when we deviate from the purpose of our creation and use what we have been given in a wrongful manner.

---

[8] Ṭabāṭabā'ī, *al-Mīzān*, 20/394.

Let me reflect on whether I have understood the purpose of my creation and use all that I have to realise that purpose.

Everyone has a potential to cause harm when they become detached and distant from God.

Let me reflect on what I have in my life which is potentially evil, which distances me from God, and thereby causes me harm.

VERSE 3

وَمِنْ شَرِّ غَاسِقٍ إِذَا وَقَبَ ﴿٣﴾

And from the evil of the darkness of night when it settles. [3]

3.1 The attribution of evil to night-time is because the darkness of night assists those with evil intent to commit malicious acts. Indeed, such acts happen much more in the night than in the day. Additionally, a person who is attacked by someone or something malevolent is much more vulnerable at night than in the day.

3.2 [*Ghasaq* (غَسَق, darkness)] refers to night when it grows dark. For example, Q17:78 uses the term when referring to the end of the time of the night (*'ishā'*) prayer:

أَقِمِ الصَّلَاةَ لِدُلُوكِ الشَّمْسِ إِلَىٰ غَسَقِ اللَّيْلِ

Establish prayer from the declining of the sun
until the darkness (ghasaq) *of night...*

Ghāsiq could also refer to every creature with an evil intent.

3.3 [*Waqab* (وَقَب, settle)] means to enter and settle. However, it also means a hole or ditch (used to trap).

3.4 If we consider these meanings for *ghāsiq* and *waqab*, then the translation would be, '*From the evil of every malevolent creature when it sets its trap.*'[9]

SUMMARY OF THE VERSE

In this verse we are instructed to seek God's refuge from those who would seek the cover of darkness, or malevolence hidden in their heart, to carry out their evil intent.

---

[9] Shīrāzī, *Namūneh,* 27/460.

REFLECTIVE LEARNING

Let me reflect on how I protect myself from the evil of those who would seek to harm me.

One of the greatest evils is the darkness of misguidance, and indeed, the term 'darknesses' is sometimes used in the Qur'an to mean lack of guidance. Q2:257 states:

اللَّهُ وَلِيُّ الَّذِينَ آمَنُوا يُخْرِجُهُمْ مِنَ الظُّلُمَاتِ إِلَى النُّورِ وَالَّذِينَ كَفَرُوا أَوْلِيَاؤُهُمُ الطَّاغُوتُ يُخْرِجُونَهُمْ مِنَ النُّورِ إِلَى الظُّلُمَاتِ أُولَٰئِكَ أَصْحَابُ النَّارِ هُمْ فِيهَا خَالِدُونَ

God is the Guardian of the believers; He takes them out of the darknesses into the light. As for the disbelievers, their guardians are satans; they take them out of the light into the darknesses. They are the inmates of the fire, and will abide therein forever.

Keeping this in mind, let me reflect on how to build my connection with God so that He becomes my Guardian, and takes me out of my darknesses, and leads me towards the light.

VERSE 4

وَمِنْ شَرِّ النَّفَّاثَاتِ فِي الْعُقَدِ ﴿٤﴾

And from the evil of those who blow on knots (magicians). [4]

4.1 *Nafatha* (نفث) means to spit or sputter, and since this is done by blowing from the mouth, the word is similar in meaning to *nafakha*, which means to blow.

4.2 [*al-Naffāthāt* (النَّفَّاثَات, magicians)] refers to the women who were witches and sorceresses, who would tie knots on strings, then recite some words and blow or spit on them to effect magic and cast spells on their victims.

4.3 However, some commentators believe that this may also refer to women who spread doubts and rumours in the minds of people by making cunning suggestions.[10]

[10] Shīrāzī, *Namūneh*, 27/461.

4.4 The Qur'an clearly mentions that people who resort to magic will never ultimately achieve their aims. Q20:69 states:

وَلَا يُفْلِحُ السَّاحِرُ حَيْثُ أَتَىٰ

No matter where he comes (attacks) from,
a magician will not be successful.

SUMMARY OF THE VERSE

In summary, we are instructed to seek God's refuge from those who would use magic or rumour mongering to harm us.

REFLECTIVE LEARNING

When we encounter something that appears paranormal, do we remind ourselves that seeking refuge in God is more powerful than any effect that such activity can have on us?

VERSE 5

وَمِنْ شَرِّ حَاسِدٍ إِذَا حَسَدَ ﴿٥﴾

And from the evil of an envier when he envies. [5]

5.1 This refers to the evil of the envier when he manifests his jealousy. By using [*idhā* (إِذَا, when)], the verse informs us that when someone harbours malicious envy, it will always manifest itself.

Indeed, the first murder in the history of man, when Qābīl killed his brother Hābīl, was due to envy and jealousy.

5.2 Jealousy is a favoured tool of Shaytan, frequently used by him to distract mankind and halt their progress towards God. There are many traditions warning against this evil, for example:

A tradition from Imam Ali (a) states: Jealousy is the prison of man's soul.[11]

[11] Āmudī, *Ghurar al-Ḥikam*, p. 372.

عَنِ الْإِمَامِ عَلِيٍّ (عَلَيْهِ السَّلَامُ): الْحَسَدُ حَبْسُ الرُّوحِ.

And also: I have not seen any oppressor resembling the oppressed more than the jealous one; his spirit is exhausted, his heart is restless, and his sorrow is perpetual.[12]

DISCUSSION: *ḤASAD* (ENVY)

Ḥasad (حَسَد, envy), is the verbal noun from the root *ḥasada*. It is a concept that has no exact equivalent in translation, but the words envy and jealousy are used to convey its meaning. Envy means coveting some-thing possessed by someone else, usually with feelings of resentment against them. Jealousy refers to the destructive negative emotion and action caused by fear of losing something that one already possesses. *Ḥasad* has been defined as follows:

i) To resent the fact that someone else possesses a certain blessing,

ii) Wanting a blessing to be removed from another individual,

iii) Wanting for oneself a blessing that someone else possesses.[13]

The first two forms of *ḥasad* described above are malicious in nature, while the third can be malicious or praiseworthy. When it is praise-worthy, it called *ghibṭah* (غِبطَة, admiring or constructive envy). *Ghibṭah* has been defined as the aspiration to acquire an admirable quality possessed by someone else, without any desire for that person to lose it.[14]

Ḥasad has been condemned in the traditions, while *ghibṭah* has been recommended. For example, a tradition from Imam al-Sadiq (a) states: Indeed, a believer admires but does not envy, while a hypocrite displays envy (*ḥasad*) but not admiration (*ghibṭah*).[15]

Ḥasad stems from misunderstanding the wisdom behind God's allocation and restriction of blessings. It is destructive in nature, keeping a person absorbed in bitterness and negativity, and making

---

[12] Majlisī, *Biḥār*, 73/256.

عَنِ الْإِمَامِ عَلِيٍّ (عَلَيْهِ السَّلَامُ): مَا رَأَيْتُ ظَالِمًا أَشْبَهَ بِمَظْلُومٍ مِنَ الْحَاسِدِ: نَفَسٌ دَائِمٌ، وَقَلْبٌ هَائِمٌ، وَحُزْنٌ لَازِمٌ.

[13] Ibn Manṣūr, *Lisān al-ʿArab*.

[14] Narāqī, *Jāmiʿ al-Saʿādāt*, 2/197.

هِيَ تَمَنِّي مِثْلَ مَا لِلْمَغْبُوطِ، مِنْ غَيْرِ أَنْ يُرِيدَ زَوَالَهُ عَنْهُ.

[15] Kulaynī, *al-Kāfī*, 2/307.

عَنِ الصَّادِقِ (عَلَيْهِ السَّلَامُ): إِنَّ الْمُؤْمِنَ يَغْبِطُ وَلَا يَحْسُدُ، وَالْمُنَافِقُ يَحْسُدُ وَلَا يَغْبِطُ.

them physically and spiritually unwell. A tradition from Imam Ali (a) states: The wellbeing of the body lies in the absence of *ḥasad*.[16]

Conversely, *ghibṭah* is a constructive and healthy emotion motivating a person to emulate an admirable trait in another person, resulting in self-improvement. In this regard, a tradition from Imam al-Sadiq (a) states: Whoever has a day better than his previous day is worthy of admiration (*maghbūṭ*).[17]

The evil of the envier (*ḥāsid*)

When the *ḥāsid* manifests his *ḥasad*, great harm can result. The Qur'an mentions several instances of this, for example:

i) Q12:5 states the warning of Prophet Yaqub (a) to his young son Yusuf (a):

قَالَ يَا بُنَيَّ لَا تَقْصُصْ رُؤْيَاكَ عَلَىٰ إِخْوَتِكَ فَيَكِيدُوا لَكَ كَيْدًا

He said: My dear son! Do not relate your vision to your brothers, or they will concoct a plot against you...

ii) Q5:27 describes the fratricide of Qābīl, which rose from his *ḥasad* of his brother Hābīl:

إِذْ قَرَّبَا قُرْبَانًا فَتُقُبِّلَ مِنْ أَحَدِهِمَا وَلَمْ يُتَقَبَّلْ مِنَ الْآخَرِ قَالَ لَأَقْتُلَنَّكَ

... When they both offered a sacrifice [to God], and it was accepted from one of them but not accepted from the other. (Qābīl) said, "I will certainly kill you."...

This is why the believer is instructed in Surat al-Falaq to seek refuge in God from the evil of the *ḥāsid* when he manifests his *ḥasad*.

SUMMARY OF THE VERSE

In summary, we are instructed to seek God's refuge from the evil that may befall us due to the jealousy and envy of others.

---

[16] *Nahj al-Balāghah*, saying no.253.

صِحَّةُ الْجَسَدِ مِنْ قِلَّةِ الْحَسَدِ.

[17] Ṣadūq, *Maʿānī al-Akhbār*, p. 342.

عَنِ الصَّادِقِ (عَلَيْهِ السَّلَامُ): مَنْ كَانَ آخِرُ يَوْمَيْهِ خَيْرَهُمَا، فَهُوَ مَغْبُوطٌ.

REFLECTIVE LEARNING

Both envy and jealousy arise when one does not have faith in God's wisdom in allocating bounties to individuals. In Q4:54, God asks:

أَمْ يَحْسُدُونَ النَّاسَ عَلَىٰ مَا آتَاهُمُ اللَّهُ مِنْ فَضْلِهِ

Do they envy other people because of what God has allocated to them out of His grace?

God allocates out of His grace in order to bring the believers closer to Him and to help them reach their potential, perfection and thereby, Paradise.

Keeping this in mind, do I fully understand, believe, and accept this wisdom?

Let me look at what I have, rather than what He has given to others. This will allow me freedom from the shackles of envy and allow me to progress on my journey towards Him.

SURAT AL-NĀS
THE PEOPLE (114)

TEXT AND TRANSLATION

سُورَةُ النَّاسِ

بِسْمِ اللهِ الرَّحْمٰنِ الرَّحِيمِ

قُلْ أَعُوذُ بِرَبِّ النَّاسِ ﴿١﴾ مَلِكِ النَّاسِ ﴿٢﴾ إِلٰهِ النَّاسِ ﴿٣﴾ مِنْ شَرِّ الْوَسْوَاسِ
الْخَنَّاسِ ﴿٤﴾ الَّذِي يُوَسْوِسُ فِي صُدُورِ النَّاسِ ﴿٥﴾ مِنَ الْجِنَّةِ وَالنَّاسِ ﴿٦﴾

In the name of God, the Beneficent, the Merciful.

Say: "I seek refuge in the Lord of mankind, [1] *the King of mankind,* [2] *the God of mankind.* [3] *From the evil of the slinking whisperer (Shaytan),* [4] *who whispers into the breasts of mankind.* [5] *From amongst the jinn and mankind."* [6]

INTRODUCTION

Surat al-Nās (114) is the last chapter in the Qur'anic codex. It was revealed in Makka, either along with, or after Surat al-Falaq and before Surat al-Ikhlāṣ. It was the 21st chapter to be revealed.[1]

In this chapter, just as in Surat al-Falaq, the Prophet (s) is instructed originally, and so are the Muslims by extension, to seek refuge in Allah, the Lord, the King and the God of mankind, this time from the insidious whisperings and malevolence of Shaytan.

Shaytan is a sworn enemy to man. Q7:16,17 quote his declaration:

قَالَ فَبِمَا أَغْوَيْتَنِي لَأَقْعُدَنَّ لَهُمْ صِرَاطَكَ الْمُسْتَقِيمَ ﴿١٦﴾ ثُمَّ لَآتِيَنَّهُمْ مِنْ بَيْنِ
أَيْدِيهِمْ وَمِنْ خَلْفِهِمْ وَعَنْ أَيْمَانِهِمْ وَعَنْ شَمَائِلِهِمْ وَلَا تَجِدُ أَكْثَرَهُمْ شَاكِرِينَ

He (Shaytan) said: Because You have sent me astray, I will surely sit in wait for them on Your straight path. Then I will come to them

[1] Maʿrifat, *ʿUlūm-i Qur'ānī*, p. 90.

from before them and from behind them and from their right and from their left. And You will not find most of them grateful [to You].

This chapter, which shows the only way to counter Shaytan's threat, is a very appropriate ending for the Book of God, which allows the believer to thwart all evil under the protection and guidance of God.

LINK TO THE CHAPTER BEFORE AND AFTER IT

Surat al-Falaq speaks of protection from a variety of external phenomena, that are outside man's control. Surat al-Nās speaks of seeking protection from the evil that is incited within man's own heart and soul.

After completing the recitation of the entire Qur'an, it is highly recommended to begin the recitation of the Qur'an again. The last chapter emphasizes the same concepts mentioned in the first chapter, that, God is the *Rabb*, *Malik* (or *Mālik*) and the only deity worthy of worship.

MERITS OF RECITATION

- A tradition from the Prophet (s) states: Whoever recites this surah over a painful area will receive relief with God's permission; it is a cure for whoever recites it.[2]
- A tradition from Imam al-Sadiq (a) states: Whoever recites this surah in his home every night will be secure from the *jinn*, and from [satanic] whisperings. Whoever writes it down and makes small children wear it as an amulet, they shall be protected from the *jinn*, with the permission of God Almighty.[3]

EXEGESIS

VERSE 1 - 3

قُلْ أَعُوذُ بِرَبِّ النَّاسِ ﴿١﴾ مَلِكِ النَّاسِ ﴿٢﴾ إِلَٰهِ النَّاسِ ﴿٣﴾

[2] Baḥrānī, *al-Burhān*, 5/817.

عَنِ الرَّسُولِ (صَلَّى اللهُ عَلَيْهِ وَآلِهِ): مَنْ قَرَأَ هَذِهِ السُّورَةَ عَلَى أَلَمٍ سَكَنَ بِإِذْنِ اللهِ تَعَالَى، وَهِيَ شِفَاءٌ لِمَنْ قَرَأَهَا.

[3] Ibid.

عَنِ الصَّادِقِ (عَلَيْهِ السَّلَامُ): مَنْ قَرَأَهَا فِي مَنْزِلِهِ كُلَّ لَيْلَةٍ أَمِنَ مِنَ الْجِنِّ وَالْوَسْوَاسِ، وَمَنْ كَتَبَهَا وَعَلَّقَهَا عَلَى الْأَطْفَالِ الصِّغَارِ حُفِظُوا مِنَ الْجَانِّ بِإِذْنِ اللهِ تَعَالَى.

Say: "I seek refuge in the Lord of mankind, [1] *the King of mankind,* [2] *the God of mankind.* [3]

1-3.1 [*Qul* (قُلْ, say)]. We have discussed the usage of this term in the *tafsīr* of Surat al-Falaq.

1-3.2 [*Aʿūdhu* (أَعُوذُ, I seek refuge)]. In addition to what was discussed about this term in the *tafsīr* of the previous chapter, usually, an individual will turn to one of three refuges: either to a person who is his nurturer and nourisher, perhaps someone who has looked after his needs all his life (*rabb*), or to a person who has power and authority (*malik*), or to God Himself (*Ilāh*).

1-3.3 Although Allah is the Lord, King, and God of the entirety of creation, these verses only specify His authority over mankind. This maybe because man is the noblest of God's creation,[4] or that he is the only creature in whose heart Shaytan whispers.[5]

1-3.4 The only way to fight this enemy, whose form and weapons cannot be easily detected, is to constantly seek refuge in the safe haven of God, so that we remain secure from him. Q7:200 instructs:

وَإِمَّا يَنزَغَنَّكَ مِنَ الشَّيْطَانِ نَزْغٌ فَاسْتَعِذْ بِاللَّهِ إِنَّهُ سَمِيعٌ عَلِيمٌ

And if an evil suggestion comes to you from Shaytan,
then seek refuge in God. Indeed, he is all-Hearing, all-Knowing.

God is the safest refuge because He is the true Sustainer (*Rabb*), and caters for all the needs of His servants. He is also the all-Powerful sovereign (*Malik*), and can easily avert the evil of others; and unlike false deities, He is the only Deity worthy of the worship of mankind (*Ilāh*).

1-3.5 Seeking the protection of God begins with words, after which actions must follow. *Rabb* reminds us that God is the One Who sustains and protects us unconditionally, *Malik* reminds us that He has authority over us, so we are obliged to obey Him and to submit to Him fully in all aspects of our lives, and *Ilāh* reminds us that He is our God, and we need to worship Him as a sign of gratitude for His blessings.

---

[4] Rāzī, *Mafātīḥ al-Ghayb*, 32/376.

[5] Zamakhsharī, *al-Kashshāf*, 4/823.

1-3.6 Asking for His protection reminds man of his own frailty and need for God, Who is the only One capable of truly protecting him.

1-3.7 These three qualities of God, lordship (*rubūbiyyah*), sovereignty (*malikiyyah*), and Godship (*ulūhiyyah*) have been chosen out of God's many qualities because they are directly linked to the nurturing of man, and are the focus of the whispers of Shaytan, who wishes to make man consider these qualities for other than God.

They are possibly listed in this order because *rubūbiyyah* is the closest quality to that of man, and is not reserved for God only. Anyone who nourishes and looks after someone else is their *rabb* (for example one's mother). *Malikiyyah* is a higher level of authority, and reserved for a few people who are in power and exercise control over many individuals. Finally, God Himself is the absolute Authority over all creation. This sequence leads man to consider authorities that are many to One, Final Authority; from multiplicity to Unity. These authorities are in a sequence of increasing power and ability, and at every stage, God emphasizes that it is He who is the ultimate refuge.

1-3.8 There may be a *rabb* one chooses who wants to love and nurture us, but has no power. There may be a *malik* who has power but no compassion or care for us. That is why only God is the true refuge Who is all-Loving, all-Caring, and all-Powerful.

1-3.9 The three phrases, '*rabb al-nās*' (رَبِّ النَّاس), '*malik al-nās*' (مَلِكِ النَّاس), and '*ilāh al-nās*' (إِلَٰهِ النَّاس), have been made distinct from each other without using the conjunction 'and' between them. This is because they signify three independent reasons why God is the best refuge to repel evil. Furthermore, any one of these qualities would suffice to repel the evil, depending on whether it pertains to nourishment, sovereignty, or ultimate authority.[6]

SUMMARY OF THE VERSES

The message in these verses is that Allah is the true Lord and Nourisher of mankind. It is He who has the ultimate power and sovereignty, and it is He who is the One, true God of creation. Q39:6 states:

ذَٰلِكُمُ اللهُ رَبُّكُمْ لَهُ الْمُلْكُ لَا إِلَٰهَ إِلَّا هُوَ

[6] Ṭabāṭabā'ī, *al-Mīzān*, 20/396.

... That is Allah, your Lord (Rabb)*; to Him belongs sovereignty* (mulk). *There is no god* (ilāh) *besides him...*

REFLECTIVE LEARNING

Seeking refuge in God is not by the tongue only; it should be a belief in the heart, and shown in one's actions as well.

A tradition from Imam al-Sadiq (a) states: When you recite, '*I seek refuge in the Lord of mankind,*' remind yourself that you are [truly and completely] seeking refuge in the Lord of mankind.[7]

Keeping this in mind, let me reflect on:

i) Who is my *rabb*? Even as I rely on others, do I keep in mind that their help is only through the permission of God and through His power? Do I rely on myself and imagine that I do not need anyone?

ii) Who is my *malik*? Which authority do I look up to? Am I the slave of God or do I consider myself free to act in whatever way I please?

iii) Who is my *Ilāh*? Whom do I worship? Do I worship my own desires?

VERSES 4, 5

مِنْ شَرِّ الْوَسْوَاسِ الْخَنَّاسِ ﴿٤﴾ الَّذِي يُوَسْوِسُ فِي صُدُورِ النَّاسِ ﴿٥﴾

From the evil of the slinking whisperer (Shaytan), [4] *who whispers into the breasts of mankind.* [5]

4-5.1 The verses do not warn of just the whispering, rather they warn of the evil of the whisperer himself, whose whispering is the cornerstone of his strategy. Q35:6 warns:

إِنَّ الشَّيْطَانَ لَكُمْ عَدُوٌّ فَاتَّخِذُوهُ عَدُوًّا
إِنَّمَا يَدْعُو حِزْبَهُ لِيَكُونُوا مِنْ أَصْحَابِ السَّعِيرِ

Indeed, Shaytan is an enemy to you, so take him as an enemy. He only calls to (invites) his party so that they may [ultimately] become inmates of the Fire."

[7] Majlisī, *Biḥār*, 60/246.

عَنِ الصَّادِقِ (عَلَيْهِ السَّلَامُ): وَإِذَا قَرَأْتَ «قُلْ أَعُوذُ بِرَبِّ النَّاسِ» فَقُلْ فِي نَفْسِكَ: أَعُوذُ بِرَبِّ النَّاسِ.

4-5.2 [*Waswasa* (وَسْوَسَ, whispering)] refers to the suggestion of a baseless or harmful idea into the mind of someone. It has come to refer primarily to the poisonous whisperings of Shaytan. One of the ways in which Shaytan attacks man is that he prepares his plots and snares secretly by continually whispering into the hearts of people, inciting thoughts of evil, until they unwittingly fall into his trap.

However, it is also worth noting that once Shaytan has affected it, man's own soul whispers to him also. Q50:16 states:

وَلَقَدْ خَلَقْنَا الْإِنْسَانَ وَنَعْلَمُ مَا تُوَسْوِسُ بِهِ نَفْسُهُ
وَنَحْنُ أَقْرَبُ إِلَيْهِ مِنْ حَبْلِ الْوَرِيدِ

Indeed We have created man, and We know what his soul whispers to him, and we are closer to him than [his] jugular vein.

4-5.3 [*Al-Khannās* (الْخَنَّاس, disappearing)] refers to something that disappears after coming into view. Therefore, the verses denote the continual visitation of Shaytan, who comes and goes into the heart of man, continually attempting to get him to commit evil. Or it could mean that he disappears when the person remembers God.

A tradition from the Prophet (s) states: Indeed, Shaytan places his snout [sniffing] over the hearts of the children of Adam (a); when they remember Allah, the Glorified, he retreats, but when they forget, he overwhelms their hearts. That is the slinking whisperer (*waswās al-khannās*).[8]

4-5.4 [*Ṣudūr* (صُدُور, chests)], (sing. *ṣadr*), means chest, within which is located the heart. The heart is used in the Qur'an as the locus of man's perception and conscience. Perhaps chest has been used here because Shaytan can come close but will only enter the heart if allowed in. And if this happens, then man is in great peril. In this regard, a tradition from Imam Ali (a) states: They (the hypocrites) relied on Shaytan in their affairs, and he made them his partners [in misguiding others]. He laid eggs [of rebellion] in their chests and hatched them. He gradually insinuated himself into their hearts.

---

[8] Majlisī, *Biḥār*, 60/94.

عَنِ الرَّسُولِ (صَلَّى اللهُ عَلَيْهِ وَآلِهِ): إِنَّ الشَّيْطَانَ وَاضِعٌ خَطْمَهُ عَلَى قَلْبِ ابْنِ آدَمَ (عَلَيْهِ السَّلَامُ)، فَإِذَا ذَكَرَ اللهَ سُبْحَانَهُ خَنَسَ، وَإِنْ نَسِيَ الْتَقَمَ قَلْبَهُ، فَذَلِكَ الْوَسْوَاسُ الْخَنَّاسُ.

He saw through their eyes, and spoke through their tongues. Thus, he led them on the path of sinfulness, and beautified for them that which was foul...[9]

4-5.5 A tradition from Imam al-Sadiq (a) states: When Q3:135 was revealed,

وَالَّذِينَ إِذَا فَعَلُوا فَاحِشَةً أَوْ ظَلَمُوا أَنْفُسَهُمْ ذَكَرُوا اللَّهَ فَاسْتَغْفَرُوا لِذُنُوبِهِمْ

"And those who, when they commit an indecent act or wrong themselves, remember God and seek forgiveness for their sins..."

Iblis went up on a mountain in Makka called Thawr, and called out to his minions at the top of his voice. They all assembled, and asked, "O Chief, why have you summoned us?" He replied, "This verse has been revealed, so which amongst you will suffice against it?" One of the satans arose and volunteered, describing his plan. Iblis replied, "You are not up to the task." Another rose up and outlined his plan, but Iblis told him the same thing. Then, a satan called Waswās al-Khannās said, "I will suffice. I will make them false promises and distract them with worldly aspirations, so that they fall into the habit of sin. Thereafter, I will make them neglectful about seeking forgiveness." Iblis declared, "You are the most suited to this task!", and appointed him to it until the Day of Judgment."[10]

SUMMARY OF THE VERSES

In summary, these verses warn that the believer is always the subject of the attack of Shaytan, who continually attempts to deviate him by whispering thoughts of evil conduct into his heart and mind. But it is the believer's choice whether to listen and follow or not.

---

[9] *Nahj al-Balāghah*, sermon 7.

اِتَّخَذُوا الشَّيْطَانَ لِأَمْرِهِمْ مَلاَكًا، وَاتَّخَذَهُمْ لَهُ أَشْرَاكًا، فَبَاضَ وَفَرَّخَ فِي صُدُورِهِمْ، وَدَبَّ وَدَرَجَ فِي حُجُورِهِمْ، فَنَظَرَ بِأَعْيُنِهِمْ، وَنَطَقَ بِأَلْسِنَتِهِمْ، فَرَكِبَ بِهِمُ الزَّلَلَ، وَزَيَّنَ لَهُمُ الْخَطَلَ.

[10] Ṣadūq, *al-Amālī*, p. 465.

عَنِ الصَّادِقِ (عَلَيْهِ السَّلَامُ): لَمَّا نَزَلَتْ هَذِهِ الْآيَةُ «وَالَّذِينَ إِذَا فَعَلُوا فَاحِشَةً أَوْ ظَلَمُوا أَنْفُسَهُمْ ذَكَرُوا اللَّهَ فَاسْتَغْفَرُوا لِذُنُوبِهِمْ» صَعِدَ إِبْلِيسُ جَبَلًا بِمَكَّةَ، يُقَالُ لَهُ ثَوْرٌ، فَصَرَخَ بِأَعْلَى صَوْتِهِ بِعَفَارِيتِهِ، فَاجْتَمَعُوا إِلَيْهِ، فَقَالُوا: يَا سَيِّدَنَا لِمَ دَعَوْتَنَا؟ قَالَ: نَزَلَتْ هَذِهِ الْآيَةُ فَمَنْ لَهَا؟ فَقَامَ عِفْرِيتٌ مِنَ الشَّيَاطِينِ فَقَالَ: أَنَا لَهَا بِكَذَا وَكَذَا، قَالَ: لَسْتَ لَهَا، فَقَامَ آخَرُ، فَقَالَ مِثْلَ ذَلِكَ فَقَالَ: لَسْتَ لَهَا، فَقَالَ الْوَسْوَاسُ الْخَنَّاسُ: أَنَا لَهَا، قَالَ: بِمَاذَا؟ قَالَ: أَعِدُهُمْ وَأُمَنِّيهِمْ حَتَّى يُوَاقِعُوا الْخَطِيئَةَ، فَإِذَا وَاقَعُوا الْخَطِيئَةَ أَنْسَيْتُهُمُ الِاسْتِغْفَارَ، فَقَالَ: أَنْتَ لَهَا، فَوَكَّلَهُ بِهَا إِلَى يَوْمِ الْقِيَامَةِ.

REFLECTIVE LEARNING

It is important to remember that while one cannot stop the interference of Shaytan and his whispering, one has the choice whether to allow it into the heart or not. One can stop him by remembering God.

Let me reflect on my last sin; was it due to allowing the whispering of Shaytan to enter my heart? Or was it from a trait that I had already established in my heart? Or was it both?

VERSE 6

مِنَ الْجِنَّةِ وَالنَّاسِ ﴿٦﴾

From amongst the jinn *and mankind.* [6]

6.1 The verse mentions *jinn* before mankind, perhaps because they form the main army of Shaytan. However, the verse clearly informs us that there are some amongst mankind who are so deviant that they themselves are satans, serving the cause of Iblis, which is to deviate man from God.

A tradition from Imam al-Sadiq (a) states: There is no heart except that it has two ears; one is open to a guiding angel, and the other to a deceptive satan. One counsels him [to goodness] while the other restrains him [from goodness]. Similarly, there are satans from mankind, who encourage people to sin, just like the satans from the *jinn.*[11]

DISCUSSION: SHAYTAN

The name Shaytan is derived from the root *sh-ṭ-n*, denoting something that is evil, lowly, and driven away. It is a general name of any creature (from *jinn* and mankind) who possesses these qualities,[12] and Iblis is the particular Shaytan who refused to bow to Prophet Adam (a).

Initially Iblis was a devout worshipper of God, to the extent that he was admitted into the high ranks of angels. However, he harboured within himself a deep-rooted arrogance which manifested itself as jealousy

---

[11] Majlisī, *Biḥār*, 60/245.

عَنِ الصَّادِقِ (عَلَيْهِ السَّلَامُ): مَا مِنْ قَلْبٍ إِلَّا وَلَهُ أُذُنَانِ، عَلَى أَحَدِهِمَا مَلَكٌ مُرشِدٌ، وَعَلَى الْآخَرِ شَيْطَانٌ مُفْتِرٍ، هَذَا يَأْمُرُهُ وَهَذَا يَزْجُرُهُ، كَذَلِكَ مِنَ النَّاسِ شَيْطَانٌ يَحْمِلُ النَّاسَ عَلَى الْمَعَاصِي كَمَا يَحْمِلُ الشَّيْطَانُ مِنَ الْجِنِّ.

[12] The term is also used in many traditions for harmful creatures not visible to the eye, such as bacteria.

when he was asked to bow to the first human being. According to his limited knowledge, he thought himself superior because he compared his external form (fire) with that of Adam (a) (clay).

After being driven away from Paradise, he swore to take revenge on the children of Adam (a) by deviating them from the path of God. Q15:39 quotes his oath:

قَالَ رَبِّ بِمَا أَغْوَيْتَنِي لَأُزَيِّنَنَّ لَهُمْ فِي الْأَرْضِ وَلَأُغْوِيَنَّهُمْ أَجْمَعِينَ

My Lord! Because You led me astray, I shall make [evil and disobedience] attractive to them on earth, and I will mislead them all."

SUMMARY OF THE VERSE

In summary, Shaytan is served in his mission of deviating the progeny of Adam (a) by both man and *jinn*.

REFLECTIVE LEARNING

One should distance oneself from the ways of Shaytan, the assemblies of satanic practices, and satanic thoughts and plans. Q24:21 states:

يَا أَيُّهَا الَّذِينَ آمَنُوا لَا تَتَّبِعُوا خُطُوَاتِ الشَّيْطَانِ
وَمَنْ يَتَّبِعْ خُطُوَاتِ الشَّيْطَانِ فَإِنَّهُ يَأْمُرُ بِالْفَحْشَاءِ وَالْمُنْكَرِ

O Believers! Do not follow the footsteps of the Shaytan. Whoever follows the footsteps of the Shaytan, he commands [him] towards indecency and wrongdoing...

Let me reflect on whether:

1. I am constantly aware of the whispering of Shaytan?
2. I associate with those amongst mankind who 'whisper' to me?
3. Most importantly, do I 'whisper' to others?

BIBLIOGRAPHY

MAIN SOURCES

1. TAFSĪR

Ālūsī, Maḥmūd b. ʿAbdullāh. *Rūḥ al-Maʿānī fī Tafsīr al-Qurʾan.* Beirut, 1994.

Ibn ʿĀshūr, Muḥammad al-Ṭāhir. *Tafsīr al-Taḥrīr wa al-Tanwīr.* Beirut, 1970.

ʿAyyāshī, Abū Naṣr Muḥammad b. Masʿūd. *Tafsīr ʿAyyāshī.* Tehran, 1960.

Baḥrānī, Hāshim b. Sulaymān. *Al-Burhān fī Tafsīr al-Qurʾan.* Qom, 1994.

Ḥaskānī, ʿUbaydullāh b. ʿAbdillāh. *Shawāhid al-Tanzīl li Qawāʿid al-Tafḍīl.* Tehran, 1990.

Ḥuwayzī, ʿAbd ʿAlī b. Jumuʿah. *Tafsīr Nūr al-Thaqalayn.* Tehran, 1994.

Ibn Kathīr, Ismāʿīl b. ʿUmar. *Tafsīr al-Qurʾan al-ʿAẓīm (Tafsīr Ibn Kathīr).* Beirut, 1998.

Javādī-Āmolī, ʿAbdullāh. *Tafsir-i Tasnīm.* (Transcripts: http://javadi.esra.ir)

Kāshānī, Fayḍ Muḥammad b. Shāh Murtaḍā. *Tafsīr al-Ṣāfī.* Tehran, 1994.

Mughniyyah, Muḥammad Jawād. *Al-Tafsīr al-Kāshif.* Qom, 2003.

Muṭahharī, Murtaḍā. *Āshnāyī bā Qurʾan.* Tehran 1971-78.

Qarāʾatī, Muḥsin. *Tafsīr-i Nūr.* Tehran, 2009.

Qurṭubī, Muḥammad b. Aḥmad. *Al-Jāmiʿ li Aḥkām al-Qurʾan, (Tafsīr al-Qurṭubī).* Beirut, 1985.

Quṭb, Syed. *Fī Ẓilāl al-Qurʾan.* Beirut, 2004.

Rafsanjānī, Akbar Hāshimī. *Tafsīr Rahnamā.* Qom, 2007.

Rāzī, Fakhr al-Dīn Muḥammad b. ʿUmar. *Mafātīḥ al-Ghayb (Al-Tafsīr al-Kabīr).* Beirut, 1999.

Shīrāzī, Nāṣir Makārim. *Tafsīr-i Namūneh.* Tehran, 1992.

Suyūṭī, Jalāl al-Dīn ʿAbd al-Raḥmān b. Abī Bakr, al-Maḥallī, Muḥammad b. Aḥmad. *Tafsīr al-Jalālayn.* Beirut, 1995.

Suyūṭī, Jalāl al-Dīn ʿAbd al-Raḥmān b. Abī Bakr, *Al-Durr al-Manthūr.* Qom, 1984.

Ṭabarī, Abū Jaʿfar Muḥammad b. Jarīr. *Jāmiʿ al-Bayān fī Tafsīr al-Qurʾan (Tafsīr al-Ṭabarī).* Beirut, 1991.

Ṭabāṭabāʾī, Muḥammad Ḥasan. *Al-Mīzān fī Tafsīr al-Qurʾan.* Beirut, 1970.

Ṭabrasī, Faḍl b. al-Ḥasan, *Majmaʿ al-Bayān fī Tafsīr al-Qurʾan.* Tehran, 1994.

Ṭayyib, ʿAbd al-Ḥusayn. *Aṭyāb al-Bayān fī Tafsīr al-Qurʾan.* Tehran, 1990.

Ṭāliqānī, Maḥmūd. *Partovī az Qurʾan.* Tehran, 1983.

Ṭūsī, Muḥammad b. al-Ḥasan. *Al-Tibyān fī Tafsīr al-Qurʾan.* Beirut, 1994.

Zamakhsharī, *Al-Kashshāf ʿan Ḥaqāʾiq al-Tanzīl.* Beirut, 1986.

2. ḤADĪTH

ʿĀmilī, Ḥurr Muḥammad b. al-Ḥasan. *Wasāʾil al-Shīʿah.* Qom, 1995.

Kulaynī, Muḥammad b. Yaʿqūb. *Al-Uṣūl min al-Kāfī.* Tehran, 1984.

Majlisī, Muḥammad Bāqir. *Biḥār al-Anwār.* Beirut, 1990.

Maʿrifat, Muḥammad Hādī. *ʿUlūm-i Qurʾānī,* Qom, 2002.

Nūrī, Ḥusayn b. Muḥammad Taqī. *Mustadrak al-Wasāʾil.* Beirut, 1987

Ṣadūq, Ibn Babawayh Muḥammad b. ʿAlī. *Man lā Yaḥḍuruhu al-Faqīh.* Qom 1984.

------. *Al-Tawḥīd,* Qom, 1995.

------. *Thawāb al-Aʿmāl wa ʿIqāb al-Aʿmāl.* Qom. 1985.

------. *ʿUyūn Akhbār al-Riḍā (a).* Tehran. 1980.

Raḍī, Muḥammad b. al-Ḥusayn. *Nahj al-Balāghah: Sermons, Letters, and Sayings of Imam ʿAlī (a).* Qom, 1981

DICTIONARIES

Ibn Manẓūr, Muḥammad b. Mukarram. *Lisān al-ʿArab.* Beirut 2009.

Muṣṭafawī, Ḥasan. *Al-Tahqīq fī Kalimāt al-Qurʾan al-Karīm,* Beirut 2013.

Rāghib Iṣfahānī, Abū al-Qāsim al-Husayn b. Muḥammad. *Al-Mufradāt fī Gharīb al-Qurʾan.* Beirut, 2000.

OCCASIONAL SOURCES

Āmudī, ʿAbd al-Wāḥid b. Muḥammad. *Ghurar al-Ḥikam wa Durar al-Kalim.* Qom, 1990.

Bukhārī, Muḥammad b. Ismāʿīl. *Al-Jāmiʿ al-Musnad al-Ṣaḥīḥ.* Beirut, 2017.

Daylamī, Ḥasan b. Abī al-Ḥasan. *Irshād al-Qulūb ilā al-Ṣawāb.* Tehran, 1970.

Hindī, ʿAlā al-Dīn al-Muttaqī. *Kanz al-ʿUmmāl fī Sunan al-Aqwāl wa al-Afʿāl.* Beirut, 1998.

Muslim Abū al-Ḥasan al-Nishābūrī. *Al-Musnad al-Ṣaḥīḥ,* Beirut, 1998.

Narāqī, Muḥammad Mahdi. *Jāmiʿ al-Saʿādāt,* Beirut, 2000.

Nawawī, Yaḥyā b. Sharaf. *Al-Majmūʿ Sharḥ al-Muhadhdhab.* Cairo, 1996.

Qummī, Abbas b. Muḥammad Riḍā. *Mafātīh al-Jinān.* Tehran, 2018.

Sistānī, ʿAlī al-Ḥusaynī. *Minhāj al-Ṣāliḥīn.* Qom, 1994.

Ṭūsī, Muḥammad b. al-Ḥasan. *Akhlāq-i Muḥtashamī.* Tehran, 1999.

----. *Tahdhīb al-Aḥkām.* Tehran, 1986

Printed in Great Britain
by Amazon

52800832R00414